P9-CBI-858

Tibet

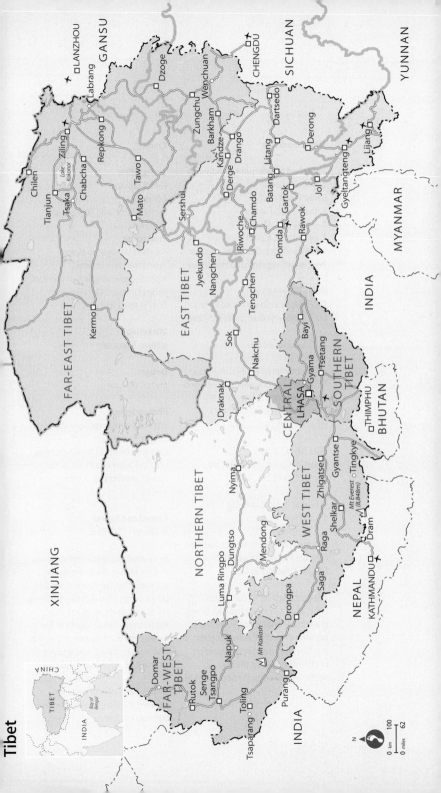

2

Tibet Handbook

Published by Footprint Handbooks
6 Riverside Court
Lower Bristol Road
Bath BA2 3DZ. England
T +44 (0)1225 469141
F +44 (0)1225 469461
Email handbooks@footprint.cix.co.uk
Web www.footprint-handbooks.co.uk

ISBN 1 900949 33 4
CIP DATA: A catalogue record for this
book is available from the British Library

In USA, published by
Passport Books, a division of
NTC/Contemporary Publishing Group
4255 West Touhy Avenue, Lincolnwood
(Chicago), Illinois 60646-1975, USA
T 847 679 5500 F 847 679 24941
Email NTCPUB2@AOL.COM

ISBN 0 8442-2190-2
Library of Congress Catalog Card
Number: 98-68298

© Footprint Handbooks Ltd 1999
Second edition

Credits

Series editor
Patrick Dawson
Editorial
Senior editor: Sarah Thorowgood
Maps: Alex Nott
Production
Pre-Press Manager: Jo Morgan
Typesetting: Ann Griffiths
Maps: Kevin Feeney, Richard Ponsford,
Robert Lunn and Claire Benison
Proof reading: Rod Gray

Marketing
MBargo, Singapore

Design
Mytton Williams

Photography
Front and back cover: Tony Stone
Images
Colour section: Eye Ubiquitous, Impact,
Life File, Paulo Netta, Pictor, Richard
Powers and Nicholas Sumner

Printed and bound
in Italy by LEGOPRINT

Every effort has been made to ensure
that the facts in this Handbook are
accurate. However, travellers should still
obtain advice from consulates, airlines
etc about current travel and visa
requirements before travelling. The
authors and publishers cannot accept
responsibility for any loss, injury or
inconvenience however caused.

Neither the black and white nor
coloured maps are intended to have any
political significance.

Tibet

Footprint

Handbook

Gyurme Dorje

Bhutan chapter researched and updated
in collaboration with Françoise Pommeret

These snow mountains are the navel of the world, a
*   place where snow lions dance.*
Their crystal-like pagodas are abodes of Supreme
*   Bliss.*
The verdant hills encircling them are fragrant
*   sources of life-restoring nectar,*
Where spiritual accomplishments are won and
*   uncorrupted meditation thrives.*
Nothing is more wondrous! Nothing more
*   amazing!*

After Milarepa (1040-1123), *Encounter with*
Rechungma

Contents

Left: prayer flags fluttering in the breeze on a bridge over the Kyi-chu river in Lhasa.

Foreword

For too long Tibet has been a far off country shrouded in mystery. Sheer geographical inaccessibility meant that few foreigners reached Tibet and those that did often told tales that were not easily believed. The resulting romantic reputation surrounding our country has not served us Tibetans well. At a time when we desperately needed support, there was insufficient understanding of the realities of the Land of Snow.

Tibet's high altitude clearly distinguishes it from its neighbours. However, as the source of many of Asia's great rivers and having a measurable effect on the regional climate, it cannot easily be ignored. The Tibetan people have a distinct identity. Our language, diet, dress and way of life are unique. Our rich and ancient culture, strongly influenced by Buddhism, has much of value to contribute to the welfare of the world. For example, living experience of meditation has given practitioners a profound understanding of the working and nature of the mind. Similarly, Tibetan physicians have valuable insights into the ways of maintaining the balance of physical health.

In an increasingly interdependent world, a world in which information has such power, it is important that we extend our appreciation of all the peoples and environments with whom we share the plant. The *Footprint Tibet Handbook* gives a thorough treatment to the whole of Tibet. It includes maps, detailed descriptions of specific locations, a general introduction and practical information for visitors. I am confident it will fulfil a longstanding need. It will be welcomed both by those who venture into Tibet and those armchair travellers who for the time being, prefer to stay at home. My congratulations to all who have contributed to this effort to make more readily available clear and reliable information about Tibet.

Dalai Lama

A foot in the door

10

Below: nomads at Namtso lake with mani stones in the foreground. *Right*: two monks at evening prayers in the Jokang temple in Lhasa.

Above: the ultimate image of Tibet - the Potala Palace in Lhasa. *Right*: prayer wheels in the Johkang temple in Lhasa.

Highlights

Roof of the world, bastion of Mahayana Buddhism and custodian of a sophisticated literary heritage which proudly rivals those of India and China, the land-locked Tibetan plateau is as vast as Western Europe yet sparsely populated. Its rivers, however, sustain billions inhabiting the neighbouring South and East Asian plains.

Modern Tibet has many attractions for visitors, despite, and perhaps on account of, its status as an occupied country. The mountainous terrain of the plateau presents the ultimate challenge for climbers, trekkers and adventurers. The power places and monasteries, sanctified by centuries of consummate meditation, inspire Buddhist pilgrims from all corners of the earth. The courage, resolve, and robust humour of the Tibetan people, determined to maintain their traditions in the face of alien cultural values imposed upon them against their will, command the respect and concern of an impotent international community who bear witness to their dilemma.

Mountain barriers

From whichever direction the plateau is approached, by land or air, the grandeur of its perennial snow-capped mountain ranges is overwhelming. The southern barrier, which isolates Tibet from the Indian subcontinent, is formed by the Great Himalaya, extending 24,500 kilometres from the Karakorums in the northwest to Mount Namchak Barwa in the southeast. Many of the world's highest summits including Jomolangma (Mount Everest, 8,848 metres), Makalu (8,463 metres), Jowo Oyuk (8,153 metres), Shishapangma (8,012 metres), Kulha Kangri (7,554 metres) and Jomolhari (7,313 metres) which border on Nepal and Bhutan, can be approached from the Tibetan side. The northern barrier, which extends through the Kunluns to the Altyn Tagh and Chole Namgyel (Qilian) ranges separates the plateau from the low-lying deserts of Central Asia, and its peaks also attract mountaineers, despite the immense distances involved in their approach.

The Tibetan plateau

Elevated between these mighty pincer ranges, the plateau covers an enormous area, 2.3 million square kilometres to be precise and is, on average, 5,000 metres above sea level. Traditionally, there are three provinces:

Utsang the arid Brahmaputra basin and, by extension, the Jangtang Plateau and Ngari region of the north and far west;

Kham the grasslands and gorges of the Salween, Mekong, Yangtze and Yalong rivers as well as their highland watersheds;

Amdo the fertile rolling grasslands around Lake Kokonor and the Yellow River basin, and, by extension, the richly forested Gyarong gorges to the south.

The tremendous diversity of the terrain, which is intersected by lateral ranges and deep river gorges, provides a wealth of unforeseen opportunities for trekking, river-rafting, mountaineering, mountain safari, and horse-riding.

Sacred mountains

Sacred peaks of snow and ice, bare rock and slate or grass-covered ranges are found throughout the plateau. Among them, the most important focal points for Buddhist and Bon pilgrimage are Mount Kailash in Ngari, Mounts Amnye Machen and Nyenpo Yurtse in Golok, Mount Kawa Karpo in Dechen, Mount Zhara Lhatse in Minyak, Mount Dakpa Shelri in Tsari, Mount Bonri in Kongpo, Mount Yarlha Shampo in Yarlung, Mount Nyenchen Tanglha near Lake Namtso Chukmo, and Lapchi Gang along with other perennial snow massifs in the Himalayan range. During the pilgrimage season, these peaks and their secret grottoes, retaining the resonance of the great hermits and

12

meditators of the past, are circumambulated by Tibetans from all parts of the plateau, as well as by devotees from India, Nepal, and the West.

Monasteries and palaces For visitors interested in the Buddhist culture of Tibet, only a few of the great monasteries and palaces of historic importance have survived the ravages of the recent past relatively unscathed, along with a small number of temples which were used as granaries. In Lhasa, there are outstanding works of art to be seen in the Potala and Norbulingka palaces of the Dalai Lamas, in the city temples of Jokhang, Ramoche, and Lukhang and in the surrounding monasteries of Drepung and Sera. Other monasteries in far-flung parts of the country, such as Tashilhunpo (the seat of the Panchen Lamas) and Labrang (the seat of the Jamyang Zhepas) still proudly display some of their original treasured artefacts. Traditional artistic skills, including painting and sculpture, are once again in great demand as local communities throughout the plateau strive to rebuild their historic shrines and temples.

Potala palace In terms of global perception, it is this relic of Tibet's past, more than any other, that uniquely symbolizes the country - like the Great Wall in China or the Vatican in Italy. Aptly named after Mount Potalaka, the sacred mountain abode of the bodhisattva of compassion, Avalokiteshvara, the Potala Palace has been identified in different ages as the residence of Tibet's two illustrious and kingly leaders: Avalokiteshvara - Songtsen Gampo during the seventh century and Dalai Lama V during the 17th century. The building, which towers 13 storeys above the city of Lhasa, rises from the slopes of Mount Marpori, for which reason it is known locally as Tse Podrang ('Summit Palace'). The outer section, or White Palace, formerly functioned as the traditional seat of government and the winter residence of the Dalai Lamas, while the inner section or Red Palace contains outstanding temples and the reliquary tombs of eight past Dalai Lamas.

People of the Tibetan Plateau There are over 4.5 million Tibetans living within the borders of present day Tibet, all easily identified by their distinctive dialects, social customs and dress, including the Topa of the highland regions (Lato and Ngari), the Tsangpa of west Tibet (Tsang), the Upa of central Tibet, the Horpa of the north (Nagchu/Jangtang), the Kongpowa of the south, the Khampa of the east, the Amdowa of the northeast, and the Gyarongwa of the extreme east. Nowadays they account for some 51 percent of the overall population of the plateau. Chinese and Muslim immigrants from the east and northeast account for 42 percent, while the remaining seven percent who inhabit remote border areas include: the tribal Monpa and Lhopa of Southern Tibet; the Qiang of Gyarong; the Jang or Naxi of southeast Kham; and the Kazakhs, Salars, Tu, and Mongols of Amdo. Beyond the confines of Tibet, the mountain peoples of Northern Nepal, Bhutan, Ladakh, and adjacent valleys of northwest India are also of Tibetan stock. Since the exile of HH Dalai Lama to India in 1959 a substantial global diaspora has emerged.

The future of Tibetan culture The people of the plateau are stout-hearted and independently minded, living in complete harmony with their environment. The upper grasslands and watersheds are the preserve of the nomads who now live their lives largely untainted by the Chinese occupation. By contrast, in the low-lying towns and cities, the palpable tension between the indigenous Tibetans and Chinese immigrant community reflects, on the one hand, the robust and courageous resolve of those who are determined to conserve their cultural heritage and, on the other, the pragmatism of those who reluctantly accommodate themselves to the ways of their colonists. Here, the central issue of conflict is not modernization, which all sides appear to espouse, but the quest for genuine autonomy and self-determination, upon which the survival of Tibet's distinctive culture depends.

Left: a doorway of Drepung monastery.
Below: A Tibetan shepherd and his family pose for a photograph in Jang district, north of Lhasa.

Left: a Tibetan boy from Labrang, Amdo province.
Above: yaks and horses meet on the trail at 14,000 feet on the Tibetan plateau in Kham province.

16

Festivals

The convergence of Tibet's spiritual and secular life can best be seen during the summer and autumnal festival season when, throughout the length and breadth of the country, finely dressed crowds assemble to spectate or participate in the diverse equestrian events, folk singing and dancing performances, contests of marksmanship and trials of strength, interspersed with the colourful pageantry of religious dance (cham). Commercial travellers vigorously ply their wares from tents, as traditional handicrafts change hands, along with modern goods, weaponry and religious artefacts.

Religious festivals
Religious festivals are important events throughout the Tibetan Buddhist world and an essential galvanising element of Tibetan culture and identity. There are monthly ceremonies, following the lunar calendar, which commemorate the deeds of Shakyamuni Buddha and Padmasambhava, and anniversaries marking the death of the great masters of the past associated with one tradition or another. Most monasteries have at least one important festival in their calendar featuring religious dance, a genre which includes morality plays, such as the *Dance of the Judgement of the Dead*; purificatory rites of exorcism, such as the famous *Black Hat Dance* re-enacting the assassination of the apostate ninth century Tibetan king Langdarma; or triumphal celebrations of Buddhism, exemplified by the elaborate Dance of Padmasambhava's Eight Manifestations.

These events provide the local populace with a wonderful opportunity to dress up, gather together, and enjoy themselves in a convivial light-hearted atmosphere. It is also an occasion for them to renew their faith and receive blessings by watching the sacred dances, or receive 'empowerment' from an officiating lama. The dances, each aspect of which has symbolic meaning, are performed by trained monks and laymen wearing ornate costumes and impressive masks.

Horse festivals
Horse festivals are also held throughout the summer and autumn months when ornate and colourful tents are pitched in large numbers along riverbanks and in the grasslands. In Gyantse, Nagchu, Damzhung, Kongpo and Amdo the festival dates generally conform to the lunar calendar, whereas in Kham, the well-known festivals of Jyekundo and Litang are now tied to the western calendar. In addition to speed-racing, there are other equestrian events, with riders stooping from their galloping steeds to pick up kataks from the ground or twirling Tibetan muskets around their shoulders before shooting at a target on the ground. Tug-of-war and weightlifting add to the spectacle - sometimes with strong-arm monks from the local monasteries participating; and there are also folk song and dance troupes representing the different regions. A brisk trade is conducted amid the copious drinking of beer, chang and hard liquor.

Nature and wildlife

Virgin wilderness
For those fascinated by nature, Tibet, like the North and South Poles, is one of the last great uncharted territories on the surface of the earth. The vibrant blue salt lakes of the Jangtang Plateau are home to migratory birds from Siberia, including the Black-necked Crane. The deep forested gorges of Kham carry all the great rivers of East and Southeast Asia, while the Yellow River meanders through the northeastern grasslands of Amdo - ancestral home of the nomadic drokpa, who live in black yak wool tents, tending their herds of yak and dri. Further west, the Brahmaputra flows along the continental suture through a landscape of high-altitude desert. Vast sand

Previous page: ceremonial procession at Mewa Gonpa, Far-east Tibet. **Left**: a stilt dancer at a festival in Repkong, Amdo. **Below**: the silver ornaments on festival costumes.

Above: Nomadic spectators witnessing a ceremonial procession at Mewa Gonpa, Far-east Tibet. Many people travel vast distances to attend rare ceremonies. **Left**: valley between Ganden to Samye.

Clockwise from top left: detail of guardian deity on the roof of the Jokhang temple in Lhasa; Tibetan medical painting at a hospital in Lhasa; monks at a shop in Tsurphu, Central Tibet; painting of offering goddess at Tashilhunpo in western Tibet. **Next page**: monks congregating outside the Potala Palace in Lhasa.

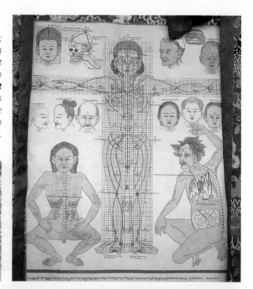

Photographs on page 23 and 24 respectively: a woman sits outside her house in Dingri, Western Tibet; detail of prayer beads.

dunes shift along its banks, concealing sheltered lateral valleys, where farming communities (rongpa) subsist on highland barley. In the far west are the deserted cave cities of the Sutlej valley and the gorge of the upper Indus.

Over 530 species of birds, 190 species of mammals, more than 40 species of reptiles, 30 species of amphibians, and 2,300 species of insects are found throughout the plateau. Wildlife reserves have been established in Amdo and in 1993, the world's second largest reserve was set up in the Jangtang region of northern Tibet. However, many species are endangered due to unrestricted hunting in earlier decades of Chinese rule.

National parks

In western and northern Tibet, there are ungulates who thrive in this open habitat, including gazelle, wild ass, wild goat, wild yak, blue sheep, urial, and ibex, as well as brown bears and wolves, and birds of prey such as the lammergeier, griffon, and golden eagle. The saline lakes of the Jangtang Plateau and northeastern Tibet are home to many different varieties of waterfowl in seasonal migration.

Natural diversity

In the Himalayan region of southern Tibet, the high snow line is the preserve of the brown bear, red panda, yak, and the rarely glimpsed snow leopard, while lower, forested slopes are the haunt of the black bear, clouded leopard, and terai langur. The deep valleys of southeastern Tibet, which are exposed to the moist humidity of the monsoon, support dense forests populated by leopards, bears, wild boar, wild goats, langur, lynx, jackals, wild dogs and spotted cats. Distinctive species such as the lesser panda and ling yang antelope are found in the Gyarong region; and in the high grasslands of Amdo and Kham there are brown bears, wild and bighorn sheep, mountain antelope, musk deer, wild ass, wild yak and mountain lizard.

Buddhist legacy

Among all the Buddhist countries of Asia, the highest developments of Indian Buddhism were preserved in Tibet. This was due partly to geographical proximity, partly to temporal consideration, and partly to the aptitude which the Tibetans themselves displayed for the diversity of Indian Buddhist traditions. The sparse population, the slow measured pace of daily life and an almost anarchical disdain for political involvement have encouraged the spiritual cultivation of Buddhism to such an extent that it came to permeate the entire culture.

Tibet: cradle of Buddhism

All schools of Buddhism in Tibet maintain the monastic discipline of the *vinaya*, the graduated spiritual practices and philosophical systems based on the sutras, and the esoteric meditative practices associated with the tantras. Different schools developed in different periods of Tibetan history, each derived from distinctive lineages or transmissions of Indian Buddhism, and among them the most influential continue to be the Nyingmapa, the Sakyapa, the Kagyupa and the Gelukpa. Throughout the country there are monasteries representative of all these diverse traditions, each of which can also claim great lamas or spiritual teachers at their head, many of them forming revered lines of incarnate or familial descent. Such are the Dalai and Panchen Lamas, the Karmapas, the Sakya Trichens and the Minling Trichens.

Academic heritage

Stereotypes and first hand impressions

So much has been written about Tibet over the years that there are few countries in the world that have had to endure more exaggerated stereotyping. The geographical remoteness and rugged terrain combined with a self-imposed isolationism and tragically misplaced conservatism during the 19th and early 20th centuries ensured that very few outsiders ever reached the plateau. This has given rise to two contrasting misconceptions: from the westerner's point of view, the plateau was seen as a tranquil Buddhist utopia, aloof from the brutality and turbulence of global conflicts; for the Chinese, Tibet was a barbarous, uneducated land of feudal serfdom.

Western misconceptions Over the centuries, Tibet undoubtedly developed a unique and highly literate Buddhist culture. Meditative insights, great artistic endeavours and acts of universal compassion were indeed sustained by successive generations of Tibetan spiritual teachers, but much of Tibet's political history is conveniently ignored by western commentators. It is a story of regional and religious factionalism that reduced a once mighty empire to civil war, abject reliance on Mongol force of arms and subsequent manipulation by the Manchu emperors of China. Tibet does have "hidden lands" (*beyul*) or remote valleys, which are deemed to be more conducive to the practice of Buddhism, but the romantic Hollywood myth of *Shangrila*, the land where time stands still, is a pretentious fantasy. Although the name Shangrila sounds Tibetan, it is actually a foreign import, transcribed in the Tibetan language from the Chinese equivalent: Xiang Ge Li La!

Eastern misconceptions Since ancient times, imperial China has viewed surrounding countries, such as Tibet, as vassal states of the Middle Kingdom and inhabited solely by unrefined barbarians. The immense contributions to Chinese culture made by the Toba Wei and other ethnic groups from the Wei and Tang dynasties onwards, is conveniently overlooked, as is the fact that successive Mongol, Chinese and Manchu emperors are known to have held the great spiritual teachers of Tibet in high esteem, and not simply for cynical political reasons. Han chauvinism is equally rampant in contemporary China, even if it meets with official disapproval. Mainland Chinese, however well educated, often find it hard to understand that Tibetan culture may credibly have rivalled and in some respects surpassed their own ancient heritage.

The price of modernization The justification frequently mooted by the Chinese for the so-called Communist 'liberation', or occupation of Tibet, is that the old, barbarous feudal social system had to be modernized in order to keep up with the social and economic demands of the 20th century. Nowadays, no one on any side of the argument seeks to justify the social inequalities and harsh penalties present in the old social order of Tibet, but before 1951, Tibetan society did naïvely reflect in many ways the traditional values of the feudal and tribal societies of its neighbours. Given this, many believe that social and economic modernization would have taken its course in Tibet just as it did elsewhere in the latter half of the 20th century, with or without the influence of Chinese Communism.

If Tibetans had been allowed to implement social reforms with genuine autonomy, the devastation of the Cultural Revolution in Tibet could have been avoided and the current trend towards the Sinicization of Tibetan culture, encouraged by successive waves of Chinese economic migrants would not have occurred. Throughout modern Tibet, draconian laws of a different order now apply, with party cadres replacing the landed gentry at the upper echelons of society, even if the same persons frequently appear to have held top positions under both the old and new régimes!

Essentials

Essentials

NB For specific information on the Kathmandu Valley and Bhutan, please see pages 720 and 867.

Planning your trip

Where to go

Since the plateau as a whole is as large as Western Europe, it is obviously impossible to go everywhere in the course of a single trip! There are four main gateway cities offering access to the plateau: Kathmandu (in Nepal), Chengdu (in Sichuan), Kunming (in Yunnan), and Lanzhou (in Gansu); or five with the addition of Kashgar (in Xinjiang, very difficult to enter through but easier as an exit point).

Tibet itself is conveniently divided into seven geographical regions: Lhasa (the capital); Central Tibet (Kyichu Valley); Southern Tibet and Western Tibet (the lower and upper reaches of the Brahmaputra River and its lateral valleys); Northern Tibet (Jangtang Plateau); Far-west Tibet (Ngari); Eastern Tibet (Kham); and Far-east Tibet (Amdo and Gyarong). Each region has at least one computer-generated map with the major rivers and lateral valleys clearly shown.

The counties forming each of these regions have many places of interest close to the motorable roads. Lesser jeep tracks and trekking routes are also described within each of the counties, usually following the contours of its river valleys and mountain passes. Each county begins with a tinted panel showing both Tibetan and Chinese names in English and script as well as population and area statistics. In most cases, a distance chart has been included, showing the accessibility of the main places of interest and towns.

NB   Good, accurate maps on Tibet are extremely rare, particularly those with topographic information. This Handbook has drawn on extensive field visits to compile these schematic county plans. The regional maps, showing topographic features, roads, towns, and all the places of interest referred to in the text, are all drawn with the most up-to-date information available. Refer to the Introduction for the key map providing an overall view of the Tibetan plateau and the adjacent countries south of the Himalayan range – Bhutan, Nepal, and peripheral parts of North India.

Having decided upon an itinerary, the next step is to determine whether you wish to go out as an individual traveller or make your travel arrangements through a tour operator. The latter option, though more expensive, is the only one which will reliably enable you to visit the so-called 'closed' areas of Eastern and Far-west Tibet. All arrangements including international flight connections to any of the five gateway cities, Chinese visas, and Tibet travel permits will be made by your tour operator. This does not imply having to take a 'package' tour as operators are quite used to organizing tours for very small groups or even single travellers.

Organized and FIT Travel

On the other hand, if you have a low budget, time to spare, great physical endurance, and are able to accept the risk of being unceremoniously ejected from the closed areas of the country, the former option is perfectly feasible. With the formal opening of Kandze prefecture in December 1998, much of the plateau, including those parts of Kham under the jurisdiction of Sichuan and Yunnan provinces, and most of Amdo have been officially designated as 'open' areas, properly accessible to the individual traveller. At the time of writing, most of the Tibet Autonomous region including Chamdo and Ngari prefectures are still closed as are the towns of Jyekundo and Golok prefectures, under the authority of Qinghai province and the Mili Autonomous county of Sichuan province. In between, there is the grey area of Lhasa and its environs, said to be 'open', but often highly restricted. Individual travellers, after obtaining a standard Chinese visa, should first consult the information on the gateway cities given in this guide – Kathmandu (page 729), Chengdu (page 453), Kunming (page 428), Lanzhou (page 554), and Kashgar (page 372). Of these, access from Lanzhou, Kunming and Chengdu currently offer the best prospects for the FIT travel.

When to go

April-June and September-November are generally the best and most popular months. The rainy season, though mild in comparison with that of India and Southeast Asia, can bring flash floods and high rivers, which break up the poor road surfaces. Be prepared to trek across landslides in the rainy season. However, the Tibetan plateau, and particularly the south is not as cold as one tends to imagine. With the exception of high passes the snow, even in winter, rarely stays on the ground for more than a few hours. The days are generally warm and it is only at night that the temperature can really drop. Rather than the cold it is the extreme dryness of the air which characterizes Tibetan weather. Nearly all of the rain falls in July and August, and there is practically no snow below 5,000 metres.

The winters are tough, especially in the north. There can be icy winds, and passes are often blocked with snow. Nevertheless, the sun shines continuously and the light is superb. Long distance travel in this period is much more rigorous. However, in the sheltered valleys of Lhasa, Tsetang, Zhigatse and Southern Kham the winter days are mild and beautiful. From December to March the streets of Lhasa are full of weird and wonderful peoples from the four corners of Tibet. In many respects, this is one of the best times of the year to visit not only Tibet, but also Hong Kong and Nepal. West Tibet tends to be drier, while the east is more subject to the weather patterns of Southeast Asia. During August, especially, Tibet can be very wet, but this is also a very good time of year to visit festival sites.

Recommended Tours

The following tours, representative of the diverse region, will assist you make your choice of destination; but they are by no means exclusive. A number of them overlap and it is obviously possible to swop between them. In each of the regional sections, the recommended route is highlighted at the beginning. The right hand column cross-references their stages to specific pages of the guide, and you will be able to read around these in more detail before planning your route.

NB   All except the third entail long overland journeys exceeding 1,000 kilometres.

1 Cultural Tour of Central, Southern, & Western Tibet

Length: 15 days
Best time to visit: April-June, late September-November

This itinerary is usually the one preferred by first-time visitors to Tibet, in that it combines the main historic palaces and monasteries of Tibet's heartland, with a close Himalayan encounter, and relatively comfortable travel and accommodation en route. Starting from the gateway city of Kathmandu in Nepal, you fly to Lhasa and then to the former capitals of Tsetang and Zhigatse, before cutting through the highland region, overland to Nepal. Travel by four-wheel drive or minibus (if you do not visit Everest Base Camp).

Alternatively, you can extend the trip by organizing an extension from the Chongye Tombs to Lhodrak and reach Nakartse on the road to Gyantse from the south (see pages 201-214).

Day 1	Kathmandu		Day 8	Chongye Tombs	201
	Gongkar Airport	729		Tradruk Temple	191
	Overnight: Lhasa	66		Yumbu Lagang Palace	194
Day 2-6	Lhasa	66		Overnight: Tsetang	
Day 7	Lhasa		Day 9	Mindroling	169
	Samye Monastery	172		Overnight: Gyantse	254
	Overnight: Tsetang	182			

Day 10	Zhalu Monastery		Day 13	Everest Base Camp	299
	Overnight: Zhigatse	263		Overnight: Shelkar	
Day 11	Zhigatse		Day 14	Dingri	
Day 12	Sakya Monastery	280		Overnight: Dram	305
	Overnight: Shelkar	296	Day 15	Return to Kathmandu	

This is an itinerary for the hardy adventurer or gritty pilgrim, combining the regions of Western, Northern, and Far-west Tibet, and culminating in the circuit of the sacred Mount Kailash and the cave cities of Toling and Tsaparang. Travel by four-wheel drive vehicle.

2 Mount Kailash & Guge Kingdom
Length: 25 days.
Best time to visit: May-July, September-October.

Essentials

Day 1	Kathmandu	729	Day 11	Tsaparang	360
	Overnight: Dram	305	Day 12	Toling	356
Day 2	Dingri		Day 13	Tirthapuri	334
	Overnight: Shelkar	296	Day 14	Darchen	336
Day 3	Dzarongpu Monastery	299	Day 15-18	Mount Kailash trek	336
	Overnight: Everest			Manasarovar Lake	346
	Base Camp	299	Day 19-20	Manasarovar Lake	
Day 4	Overnight: Shelkar			Chiu Monastery	348
Day 5	Lhartse	287		Overnight: Purang	335
	Overnight: Tingkye	294	Day 21	Mayum La Pass	314
Day 6	Tsochen	319	Day 22	Baryang	313
Day 7	Gertse	321	Day 23	Saga	311
Day 8	Gegye	330	Day 24	Nyalam	305
Day 9	Senge Tsangpo	332	Day 25	Dram	
Day 10	Tsamda	353		Return to Kathmandu	

Around Lhasa, it is possible to explore the Kyi-chu valley of Central Tibet, with relatively short travel stages. For those disinclined to undertake a long expedition, this itinerary highlights rural life and the historic monasteries of the Upper Kyi-chu, in close proximity to the capital. Enjoy bathing in the hot springs at Zhoto Tidro. Travel by a four-wheel drive vehicle.

3 Kyi-chu Valley
Length: 15 days
Best time to visit: April-October

Day 1	Kathmandu	729	Day 10	Zhoto Tidro Hermitage	
	Gongkar Airport	160	Day 11	Drigung Monastery	150
	Overnight: Lhasa	66	Day 12	Uruzhva Temple	
Day 2-5	Lhasa			Katsel	148
Day 6	Yerpa Caves	141		Overnight: Gyama	148
Day 7	Taklung Monastery	145	Day 13	Ganden Monastery	142
Day 8	Reting Monastery	146	Day 14	Lhasa	
Day 9	Zhoto Tidro Hermitage	151	Day 15	Return to Kathmandu	

This combines a tour of the beautifully forested Kongpo region of Southern Tibet with the Northern and Southern overland routes to and from Chamdo in Kham. **NB** The route is easily reversed. The stretch from Nyangtri to Pasho is often impassable in the rainy season or when the road is cut up by glacial snow-melt. Travel by a four-wheel drive vehicle.

4 Brahmaputra Gorges & the Salween-Mekong Traverse
Length: 19 days
Best time to visit: April-June, late September-October

Day 1	Kathmandu	729	Day 4	Draksum Lake	240
	Gongkar Airport	160	Day 5	Buchu Temple	233
	Overnight: Lhasa	66	Day 6	Timpei Caves	230
Day 2-3	Lhasa		Day 7	Nyangtri	232

Essentials

Day 8	Po-me	405	Day 14	Tengchen	388
Day 9	Pasho	410	Day 15	Tengchen Monastery	
Day 10	Chamdo	395	Day 16	Sok Dzong	384
Day 11	Chamdo		Day 17	Nakchu	382
Day 12	Riwoche	390	Day 18	Lhasa	
Day 13	Riwoche Temple	391	Day 19	Return to Kathmandu	
	Overnight: Riwoche				

5 Lhasa to Chengdu Overland
Length:
21 days
Best time to visit:
April-June, late September-October

This increasingly popular itinerary enables visitors to travel through the 'closed' areas of East Tibet from Lhasa via Chamdo and Derge to Chengdu in Sichuan. There are a number of important monasteries en route, such as those at Chamdo, Derge, Kandze, and Lhagang. **NB** The journey can be rugged and facilities are poor en route. It is easily reversed; and the northern route from Lhasa to Chamdo (pages 66 and 395) can be substituted for the southern one shown here. Also, the southern route from Chamdo via Batang and Litang to Dardo (pages 395-451) can be followed instead of that via Derge which is included here. Travel by a four-wheel drive vehicle.

Day 1	Kathmandu-Lhasa	66	Day 12	Chamdo	
Day 2-4	Lhasa		Day 13	Derge	467
Day 5	Samye Monastery	172	Day 14	Derge	
	Overnight: Tsetang	182	Day 15	Kandze	496
Day 6	Gyatsa	220	Day 16	Kandze	
Day 7	Menling	227	Day 17	Tawu	501
Day 8	Nyangtri	232	Day 18	Lhagang Monastery	445
Day 9	Po-me	405	Day 19	Dartsedo	447
Day 10	Pasho	410	Day 20	Wolong Panda Reserve	452
Day 11	Chamdo	395	Day 21	Chengdu	453

6 Lhasa to Lanzhou Overland
Length:
16 days
Best time to visit:
May-October

This route traverses the desolate West Kokonor plateau of the Far-east Tibet region, to reach the fabled Kokonor – one of Inner Asia's largest lakes, before travelling through Kumbum, Repkong and Labrang, which are at the cultural heart of Amdo. The Repkong style of painting is particularly renowned. **NB** This itinerary is reversible. Travel by a four-wheel drive vehicle or minibus (but take care on the stretch from Repkong to Labrang).

Day 1	Kathmandu-Lhasa	66	Day 11	Ziling	537
Day 2-4	Lhasa		Day 12	Kumbum Monastery	542
Day 5	Nakchu	382		Overnight: Ziling	
Day 6	Amdo	383	Day 13	Repkong	570
Day 7	Toma	510	Day 14	Labrang	627
Day 8	Kermo	512	Day 15	Labrang	
Day 9	Lake Kokonor	521	Day 16	Lanzhou	554
Day 10	Lake Kokonor				

This truly memorable journey combines the route from Lhasa to Chamdo in Kham with a descent of the Mekong River, bypassing the plunging glaciers of the sacred Mount Kawa Karpo into the rich flowering landscapes of Dechen county and Yunnan. **NB** This itinerary is reversible; and the northern route from Lhasa to Chamdo (pages 66 and 262) could be substituted for the southern one shown here. Also it is possible to go from Markham across the Yangtze to Batang and thence southwards into Yunnan via Chaktreng (page 440).

7 Lhasa to Kunming Overland

Length:
18 days
Best time to visit:
April-June, late September-November

Day 1	Kathmandu	729	Day 10	Chamdo	
	Gongkar Airport	160	Day 11	Dzogang	414
	Overnight:Lhasa	66	Day 12	Markham	416
Day 2-4	Lhasa		Day 13	Tsakhalho	416
Day 5	Draksum Lake	240	Day 14	Dechen	417
Day 6	Nyangtri	232	Day 15	Gyeltang	420
Day 7	Po-me	405	Day 16	Lijiang	423
Day 8	Pasho	410	Day 17	Dali	427
Day 9	Chamdo	395	Day 18	Kunming	428

Starting in the gateway city of Chengdu and ending in Lanzhou, this is a detailed itinerary combining the grasslands of Kham and Amdo with the Amdo cultural heartland around Kumbum, Repkong, and Labrang. There are many monasteries en route such as those at Lhagang, Kandze, Dzokchen, Zhechen, Jyekundo, Zhiwu, and so on. **NB** This itinerary is reversible. Travel by a four-wheel drive vehicle or minibus (but take care on the stretch from Repkong to Labrang).

8 Kham and Amdo Overland

Length:
22 days
Best time to visit:
May-October

Day 1	Hong Kong/Beijing		Day 13	Jyekundo	
	Overnight:Chengdu	453	Day 14	Mato	597
Day 2	Chengdu		Day 15	Mount Amnye Machen	508
Day 3	Wolong Panda Reserve	452		Overnight:Wenchuan	595
Day 4	Dartsedo	447	Day 16	Chabcha	589
Day 5	Lhagang Monastery	445		Overnight:Lake Kokonor	521
Day 6	Tawu	501	Day 17	Ziling	537
Day 7	Kandze	496	Day 18	Kumbum Monastery	542
Day 8	Dzogchen Monastery	471		Overnight:Ziling	
Day 9	Dzogchen Monastery		Day 19	Repkong	570
Day 10	Zhechen Monastery	473	Day 20	Labrang	627
	Overnight:Sershul	475	Day 21	Labrang	
Day 11	Zhiwu	477	Day 22	Overnight:Lanzhou	554
Day 12	Jyekundo	481			

This exciting itinerary combines the Labrang, Repkong and Kumbum heartland of Amdo with the nomadic region of Golok and the Jonangpa and Nyingmapa monasteries of the upper Gyarong in Far-east Tibet. **NB** It can easily be reversed. Travel by a four-wheel drive vehicle.

9 Golok and Gyarong Overland

Length:
21 days
Best time to visit:
April-June, September-October

Day 1	Hong Kong/Beijing		Day 7	Tarthang Monastery	605
	Overnight:Lanzhou	554	Day 8	Jigdril	605
Day 2	Labrang Monastery	627	Day 9	Ngawa	613
Day 3	Repkong	570	Day 10	Ngawa	
Day 4	Ziling	537	Day 11	Barkham	618
Day 5	Kumbum Monastery	542	Day 12	Dzamtang	612
	Overnight:Chabcha	589	Day 13	Dzamtang	
Day 6	Darlag	603	Day 14	Sertal	609

Essentials

Day 15	Sertal		Day 19	Tsenlha	622
Day 16	Drango	499	Day 20	Wolong Panda Reserve	452
Day 17	Lhagang Monastery	445	Day 21	Chengdu	453
Day 18	Dartsedo	447			

10 Eastern Kham Overland

Length: 26 days

Best time to visit: May-June, late September-October

This focusses on the gorges and grasslands of eastern Kham (currently in Sichuan). It combines the Chinese Buddhist pilgrimage site of Mount Emei with a number of renowned Nyingmapa, Sakyapa and Gelukpa monasteries. **NB** This can be reversed. Travel by four-wheel drive vehicle.

Day 1	Hong Kong/Beijing		Day 13	Pelyul Monastery	
	Overnight:Chengdu	453	Day 14	Katok Monastery	460
Day 2	Chengdu		Day 15	Katok Monastery	
Day 3	Emei Shan	452	Day 16	Dzongsar Monastery	465
Day 4	Emei Shan		Day 17	Derge	467
Day 5	Haiyan	527	Day 18	Derge	
Day 6	Dartsedo	447	Day 19	Dzogchen Monastery	471
Day 7	Nyachuka	442	Day 20	Dzogchen Monastery	
Day 8	Litang	432	Day 21	Kandze	496
Day 9	Batang	430	Day 22	Kandze	
Day 10	Litang		Day 23	Lhagang Monastery	445
	Overnight:Nyachuka		Day 24	Dartsedo	
Day 11	Nyarong	498	Day 25	Wolong Panda Reserve	452
Day 12	Pelyul Monastery	462	Day 26	Chengdu	

11 Nature Parks of Amdo

Length: 23 days

Best time to visit: April-October

The last of these recommended itineraries runs from Chengdu to Lanzhou, passing through the beautiful nature parks of the Minjiang valley and those of the Amnye Machen range, Drakar Tredzong, and Lake Kokonor. The scenery is spectacular and rewarding. **NB** This itinerary can be reversed. Travel by a four-wheel drive vehicle or minibus; and by horse around the north side of Mount Amnye Machen.

Day 1	Hong Kong/Beijing		Day 12-14	Amnye Machen	599
	Overnight:Chengdu	453	Day 15	Machen	
Day 2	Chengdu		Day 16	Tsogyenrawa	598
Day 3	Zungchu	655	Day 17	Drakar Tredzong	593
Day 4	Sertso Park	653	Day 18	Drakar Tredzong	
Day 5	Dzitsa Degu Park	658	Day 19	Chabcha	589
Day 6	Dzitsa Degu Park		Day 20	Lake Kokonor	521
Day 7	Dzoge	648	Day 21	Ziling	537
Day 8	Labrang Monastery	627	Day 22	Kumbum Monastery	542
Day 9	Repkong	570		Ziling	
Day 10	Machen	599	Day 23	Lanzhou	554
Day 11	Xueshan	600			

Finding out more

There is no unified tourist organization as such for the Tibetan plateau, since each province under which Tibet is administered has its own Tourism Bureau. For practical information, you will have to rely on international tour operators or the domestic travel agencies. These are listed under the relevant towns but you will also find a list of the more reliable operators under useful addresses on page 61. A number of overseas operators run tours in the Tibetan area. They vary greatly in price, depending upon the number of days, the number of persons in a group, the remoteness and distance

covered by the itinerary, and the package arrangement (ie full board or half-board). Prices are slightly lower than comparable tours of Bhutan, ranging from US$100 per day to over US$200 per day. For further details see under usefull addresses on page 61. **Tibetan Cultural Organizations** There are lots of these scattered around the world. For a comprehensive listing of such organizations, see *A Handbook of Tibetan Culture*, edited by Graham Coleman and published by Rider (1992). We give a number of them on page 63 of useful addresses.

Before you travel

Essentials

Getting in **Visas and permits** A valid passport including a standard Chinese **entry visa** is essential. Such visas are generally obtainable from most Chinese embassies and consulates, sometimes on sight of flight tickets and Travellers' Cheques. In the high season (August/September) confirmation of booking through a domestic Chinese travel agency is required, and this is all that one needs to travel to those parts of the Tibetan plateau which are officially designated as 'open' to individual travellers. The cost of a standard Chinese tourist visa varies from US$12-120 according to the nationality of the applicant and the type of visa required. Individual visas may be issued for single or double entry, with a validity of one, two, or three months. Group visas may be issued for parties of five and over, for the specific duration of a fixed itinerary (single or double entry). Multiple entry visas are normally issued for business or educational purposes only, ranging in validity from six to 12 months, and are more expensive (US$120-250). Normally three working days are required to process an application from the date of its submission, but express services are also available at a premium.

 Tibetan embassies and consulates

Australia, 15 Coronation Dr, Yarralumla, ACT 2600, T062-2734780, 2734781. Consulate: 77 Irving Rd, Toorak, Melbourne, Victoria, T03-8220604.
Austria, Meternichgasse 4, 1030 Vienna, T06-753149/7136706.
Belgium, 443-5, Avenue de Tervureen, 1150 Brussels, T02-7713309/7712681.
Canada, 515 St Patrick's St, Ottawa, Ontario KIN 5H3, T0613-2342706/2342682.
France, 11 Ave George V, 75008, Paris, T1-47233677/43367790.
Germany, Karfurtsenallee 12, Bonn 2 (Bad Godesberg), T0228-361095/362350.
Hong Kong, Visa Office, Ministry of Foreign Affairs of the PRC, 5/F Low Block, China Resources Building, 26 Harbour Rd, Wanchai, T5851794/5851700.
Italy, 56 via Bruxelles, 56-00198 Rome, T06-8413458/8413467.
Japan, 3-4-33, Moto-Azabu, Minato-ku, Tokyo, T03-34033380/34033065.
Nepal, Baluwatar, Kathmandu, T412332/415383.
Netherlands, Adriaan Goekooplaan 7,

2517 JX The Hague, T070-3551515/9209.
New Zealand, 2-6 Glenmore St, Wellington, T064-4721383/4721384.
Spain, C/Arturo Soria 113, 28043 Madrid, T01-5194242/3651.
Sweden, Lodovagen 8 115 25, Stockholm, T08-7836739/7830179.
Switzerland, Kalecheggweg 10, 3006 Bern, T031-447333/434593.
UK, 49-51 Portland Pl, London W1N 3AH, T0171-6311430. Consulate: 43 Station Rd, Edinburgh EH12 7AF, T0131-3164789.
USA, 2300 Connecticut Ave NW, Washington DC 20008, T3282500/3282517, F202-3282582. Consulates: 3417 Montrose Boulevard, Houston, Texas 77006; 104 South Michigan Ave, Suite 1200, Chicago, Illinois 60603; 1450 Laguna St, San Francisco, CA 94115; 520 12th Ave, New York, NY 10036. The only foreign embassy on the Tibetan plateau is the **Royal Nepalese Consulate**: Gyatso To Lam, Lhasa, T0891-6322881. In Chengdu there is a US Consulate General, 4 Lingshiguan Rd, Zhongbei, T028-5583992.

Internal travel: the need for permits

In order to understand these restrictions on internal travel, it is important to keep in mind the political situation in China and Tibet. It took a backward turn in 1989 with martial law being declared in Lhasa for over a year. Although martial law ostensibly has been lifted, tourists are still closely watched. It is important to be aware that Tibet is an occupied country, so one must take care not to jeopardize the position of anyone who may help while you are there. The current attitude of the Chinese authorities to foreign tourists in Tibet is ambivalent. They want their money yet know that many tourists sympathize with the Tibetans and their wish for self-determination.

For this reason and because it is more financially lucrative they have forbidden the `backpacking lone traveller' and insist on supervised group tours at fixed rates. This they justify by saying that you are travelling on the "roof of the world" and thus, the more remote your journey the more you should pay for the privilege, despite little or no facilities! This means that your enjoyment of a journey through remote areas of Tibet will, to a large extent, depend upon your own ability not to be disturbed by repeated requests for fees, permits and even for photography, as well as some exorbitant rates for hotel accommodation. However, with the recent opening of much of Kham and Amdo, it is hoped that the internal travel permit will gradually be phased out.

Aliens' Travel Permit and Military Permit   In January 1999, there are fewer parts of Tibet which are completely closed to the individual traveller who has simply obtained a standard Chinese visa. Such areas are confined to the Tibetan Autonomous Region, the Golok and Jyekundo prefectures of Qinghai province, and the Mili Autonomous county of Sichuan province. To visit such parts of Tibet a standard Chinese visa is not sufficient. Individual travel is not permitted within these areas (although there are inevitably individuals who can reach Lhasa or Chamdo from Kermo or Chengdu overland with some degree of risk). In order to visit these so-called 'closed areas', a special **Aliens' Travel Permit** (ATP) must be issued by the police in either Lhasa, Chengdu, Kunming, Lanzhou, or Ziling (sometimes reinforced by a **military permit** also).

To obtain such permits, it is necessary to make your travel arrangements through a bona fide agency, providing details of age, sex, nationality, passport number, occupation, and address, preferably two months before departure. The visa authorization will then be faxed or telexed to the Chinese embassy of your choice, and on that basis a standard Chinese visa will be issued. Alternatively, those who enter China with a standard Chinese tourist visa can also make ad hoc arrangements with a local agency in any of the above cities to obtain an ATP and (if required) a military permit before entering the closed areas of the Tibetan plateau. To be safe it is better to make prior arrangements through a tour operator or travel agent before leaving home.

The permits themselves specify every destination and town that you wish to visit and cannot be changed once you have arrived in the closed area of your choice. Therefore be certain to detail all possible destinations in your request as well as the route(s) you wish to follow.

Until 1993 it was essential for all foreign visitors to complete a customs declaration   Customs
form on arrival and countersign its duplicate on exiting the country, thereby keeping a close monitor on the import of luxury electronic goods in particular. Such controls have recently been relaxed for travellers arriving by air, and it is also permissable to import four bottles of liquor, two cartons of cigarettes, and 72 rolls of still film or 1,000 metres of video film. **NB** No 16 millimetre cameras are permitted, except when special

licenses have been arranged for filming.

Foreigners are generally not subject to more than perfunctory baggage checks on entering and leaving Tibet, but in periods of political tension (which are commonplace) controls may be tightened. Certain items such as Dalai Lama pictures, critical literature and Tibetan national flags are sensitive; and the export of antique objects, including religious statues and jewellery, which were made before 1959 is officially prohibited. Old carpets and household items are more easily taken out, and it is best if some receipt or proof of purchase can be shown. There are shopkeepers in Lhasa who can arrange such receipts for a variety of purchases, regardless of their source!

What to take It is always best to keep luggage to a minimum. A sturdy rucksack or a hybrid backpack/suitcase, rather than a rigid suitcase, covers most eventualities and survives bus boot, roof rack and plane/ship hold with ease. Serious trekkers will need a framed backpack. A complete checklist of items required for long treks or overland journeys is given below under Trekking, pages 45-47.

Everybody has their own list. Obviously what you take depends on where are intending to go and also what your budget is. Over the years, a selection of those most often mentioned include by travellers follows - pick and choose as you wish:

air cushions for slatted seats; an inflatable **travel pillow** for neck support; **strong shoes** (remember that footwear over nine and a half English size, or 42 European size, is difficult to obtain); a small **first-aid kit** and handbook; fully **waterproof top clothing**; **waterproof treatment** for leather footwear; **wax earplugs** (which are almost impossible to find outside large cities) and an airline-type **eye mask** to help you sleep in noisy and poorly curtained hotel rooms; **sandals** (rubber-thong Japanese-type or other – can be worn in showers to avoid athlete's foot); a **polyethylene sheet** two metres by one metre to cover possibly infested beds and shelter your luggage; **polyethylene bags** of varying sizes (up to heavy duty rubbish bag size) with ties; a **toilet bag** you can tie round your waist (if you use an **electric shaver**, take a rechargeable type); a **sheet sleeping-bag** and pillow-case or separate pillow-case (they are not changed often in cheap hotels); a one and a half to two metre piece of **100% cotton** that can be used as a towel, a bedsheet, beach towel, makeshift curtain and wrap; a **mosquito net** (or a hammock with a fitted net); a **straw hat** which can be rolled or flattened and reconstituted after 15 minutes soaking in water, a **clothes line**; a **nailbrush** (useful for scrubbing dirt off clothes as well as off yourself); a **vacuum flask**; a **water bottle**; a **small dual-voltage immersion heater**; a small dual-voltage (or battery-driven); **electric fan**; a light nylon waterproof **shopping bag**; a universal bath- and basin-**plug** of the flanged type that will fit any waste-pipe (or improvise one from a sheet of thick rubber); **string**; **velcro, electrical insulating tape**; large **penknife** preferably with tin and bottle openers, scissors and corkscrew (the famous Swiss Army range has been repeatedly recommended - for knife sharpening, go to a butcher's shop); **alarm clock** or watch; **candle**; **torch** (flashlight) – especially one that will clip on to a pocket or belt; **pocket mirror**; **pocket calculator**; an **adaptor and flex** to enable you to take power from an electric-light socket (the Edison screw type is the most commonly used). Remember not to throw away spent batteries containing mercury or cadmium; take them home to be disposed of, or recycled properly.

Useful medicaments are given in the Health section (page 51); to these might be added some lip salve with sun protection, and pre-moistened wipes (such as 'Wet Ones'). Always carry toilet paper. Natural fabric sticking plasters, as well as being long-lasting, are much appreciated as gifts. Dental floss can be used for backpack repairs, in addition to its original purpose. **Contact lens solution** can be difficult to find, especially outside major cities. Ask for it in a chemist/pharmacy, rather than an optician's. **Never** carry firearms. Their possession could land you in serious trouble.

Have a check-up with your doctor, if necessary and arrange your immunizations well in advance. Try ringing a specialist travel clinic if your own doctor is unfamiliar with health in Tibet. You should be protected by immunization against typhoid, polio, tetanus and hepatitis A. Vaccinations

Malaria prophylaxis are strongly advised for visitors to affected countries such as Nepal and Bhutan but since a particular course of treatment is recommended to a specific part of the world (which can change in time) seek up-to-date advice from the Malaria Reference Laboratory, T0891-600350 (recorded message, premium rate) or the Liverpool School of Tropical Medicine, T0151-7089393. In the USA, try Centre for Disease Control, Atlanta, T404-3324555.

Yellow fever vaccination with a certificate is only required if you are coming from infected areas of the world . Vaccination against cholera or smallpox is not necessary, but occasionally immigration officials might ask to see a certificate.

Before you travel make sure the medical insurance you take out is adequate.

Money

The national currency is the Yuan (¥) or Renminbi (RMB), popularly called 'kwai'. 10 Jiao (pronounced 'mao') = 1 Yuan and 10 Fen = 1 Jiao. The exchange rate is approximately US$1 = ¥8. Currency

In China TCs are accepted and major currency denominations are easily changed in the larger cities. However, with the exception of *Lhasa Hotel* and the *Bank of China*, Lhasa Branch, credit cards are not yet used in Tibet. In general, it is more efficient to exchange money in the hotels than in the banks – particularly in Chengdu, Kunming, Ziling, and Lanzhou. Travellers' cheques & credit cards

China has at long last abandoned its cumbersome dual currency system, which formerly obliged the banks and hotels to convert foreign currency into Foreign Exchange Certificates (FEC) for use in the hotels or tourist shops. The 'people's currency' (Renmimbi) is now fully convertible, leaving only the US dollar with a higher street value than the official rate of exchange.

The *Bank of China* has branches in Lhasa, Dram (Zhangmu), Zhigatse, Tsetang, Ziling (Xining), Lanzhou, Kermo (Golmud), Chengdu, and Kunming, which will change travellers' cheques and hard currency. Unofficial money changers prefer US$ cash. Remember to carry a sufficient amount of RMB for long overland drives or treks. Even if your tour is pre-arranged, when travelling in remote areas, it is always wise to carry extra cash to cover unforeseen contingencies (such as payment of entrance and photographic fees). Exchange

Getting there

The only civilian airports on the Tibetan plateau are at Gongkar, near Lhasa, at Pomda (*Ch* Bangda) near Chamdo, and at Kermo. Air

Transport to Lhasa from Gongkar Airport   1¾ hours' drive by bus, minibus, or land cruiser.

Flights to Lhasa   China South-west Airlines have connections to Lhasa from Chengdu (two hours) daily at ¥1,320; Kathmandu (55 minutes) on Tuesday and Saturday at US$200, Chongqing (two hours five minutes) on Wednesday and Sunday at US$238, Ziling (two hours 25 minutes) on Monday and Friday at US$161 and Beijing (four hours) on Sunday at US$385. Tickets to Lhasa can be obtained from CAAC or China South-west offices in Kathmandu (T411302), Hong Kong (T8610322), Chengdu (T6239991), or Beijing (T4014441/6013336), but it is easiest to liaise with your travel agent.

Flights to Chamdo China South-west Airlines have connections to Pomda Airport near Chamdo from Chengdu on Tuesday and Friday (one hour five minutes) at US$85.

Flights to Kermo China North-west Airlines have Sunday flights from Ziling (one hour 10 minutes) and Xian (two hours 45 minutes) at US$84 and US$153 respectively.

There are also scheduled flights to Chengdu, Lanzhou, Kunming, and Lijiang: all important starting points for overland journeys through East Tibet. Specifically for Chengdu, there are daily flights from Beijing, flights from Bangkok (China South-west on Monday, Thursday and Saturday), and daily flights from Hong Kong (China South-west daily; Dragon Air on Tuesday/Sunday). China South-west Airlines have their own office in Bangkok at Shingpa Buli 38/1, Supola, T2585765/2585771, F00662-2599389. For Lanzhou, there are daily flights from Beijing, Guangzhou, and Urumqi. For Ziling, there are flights from Beijing (China North-west on Wednesday, Friday and Sunday), Chengdu (on Monday and Thursday), Guangzhou (on Wednesday and Saturday) and Urumqi (on Saturday). For Kunming there are daily connections from Bangkok, Hong Kong, Beijing, Guangzhou, and Chengdu, as well as from Rangoon (Wednesday), and Vientiane (Thursday). For Lijiang and Dali there are daily flights from Kunming. In all cases, please recheck your flight time prior to departure.

For ticketing services out of Lhasa, contact China South-west Airlines, Nyangdren lam, Lhasa, T0891-6333331, F0891-633330.

Train   The only railway within the Tibetan plateau is that running from Ziling to Kermo in Amdo (US$14 per soft-seat, US$16 per hard-sleeper, and US$25 per soft-sleeper). There are daily express and local services. Plans to extend the railway from Kermo to Lhasa have so far floundered on account of the difficulty of laying tracks on a permafrost surface and boring ice tunnels through the Kunluns. However this project is shortly to be reviewed and studies have also been undertaken to explore the possibility of extending the Yunnan railway via Gyeltang into Tibet.

Road   The main motorable roads into Tibet commence at Kalpa in the Kinnaur region of India (presently closed), Kathmandu in Nepal, Gangtok in Sikkim (presently closed), Kunming via Lijiang in Yunnan, Chengdu via Ya'an, Han Yuan, Wolong, or Guan Xian in Sichuan, and Lanzhou via Ziling or Labrang. On some of these overland routes public transport is available but you may not be permitted to use it. See the bus schedule information given in the sections on Lhasa, Dartsedo, Chengdu, Ziling, Kunming, Ganlho Dzong and Lanzhou.

All those points of land access feature long itineraries exceeding 2,000 kilometres, and traverse the toughest watersheds in the world – those of the Indus, Sutlej, Brahmaputra, Salween, Mekong, Yangtze, Yalung, Gyarong, Yellow River, or Minjiang. It is therefore important that the correct choice of vehicle is made. Organized groups will normally travel in Japanese air-conditioned buses where the roads are good, or a four-wheel drive Toyota land-cruisers on the tougher routes, with a Dong Feng support truck to carry the baggage and camping equipment. In the case of those itineraries which emphasize trekking, horse-riding or mountaineering, baggage will be transported by yak caravans or pack-animals.

Touching down

Airport information

At Gongkar airport, transportation to Lhasa or Tsetang is normally provided by the local travel services. Public buses are also available to Lhasa (¥50). Airport taxes are payable at departure time: ¥50 for domestic flights to Chengdu and ¥90 for the international flights to Kathmandu.

Baggage An experienced traveller carries as little luggage as possible. Remember that you are allowed no more than the normal weight and that you may be liable to pay for excess baggage. You should also carry essentials, medication, reading material, cameras, flashlights, and other necessities (eg toilet paper) at all times in your flight bag or, as many prefer, in a lightweight backpack. If you are trekking or undertaking a long overland drive, you may have to supply your own tent and sleeping bag. Bring your own water-bottle, a screw-top cup or jar (for thirst-quenching jasmine tea), and a pocket-knife with bottle opener/corkscrew attachments, as well as a can opener, scissors, sewing kit, and pocket-size screwdriver. A complete checklist of items required for long treks or overland journeys is given below under **Trekking**, pages 45-47.

Tourist information

The various provinces into which the Tibetan plateau is divided have their own respective tourist authorities. Tourism within the Tibetan Autonomous Region is administered by the *Tibet Tourism Bureau (TTB)*, Yuanlin Rd, T34315, F0891-6334632. For information on travel to East Tibet, contact: *Sichuan Provincial Tourism Bureau*, 180 Renmin Nan Rd, T028-5527478. *Yunnan Provincial Tourism Bureau*, Huancheng Nanlou St, Kunming, T0871-3132895. *Qinghai Provincial Tourism Bureau*, 21 Huanghe Rd, T6143711, F0086-9718238721. *Gansu Provincial Tourism Bureau*, 209 Tianshui Ave, Lanzhou, T0931-8426847.

Rules, customs and etiquette

Clothing   The air temperature in Tibet can change very quickly with a passing cloud and the coming of the night. A flexible system of 'layered' clothing is recommended: thermal underwear, cotton shirts, a warm pullover and windproof jacket, and some light rain-gear, as well as a sun-hat and a scarf or face-mask to ward off the dust. For overland travel or trekking, strong but lightweight walking boots are useful, and gloves, woollen hats and thick socks all have their place. For the hot springs, people may want to bring swimwear. A rucksack is indispensable for trekking and many people will find their own down jacket and sleeping bag a great asset.

    Apart from the larger tourist hotels, no laundry or dry-cleaning service is available. If you wish to avoid the do-it-yourself option, it is sometimes possible to come to a private arrangement for laundry services with local guesthouse attendants.

Conduct   The challenge in Tibet is to remain polite and curteous in social relationships regardless of the difficulties which arise! Remember that loss of self-control is less likely to bring about your desired response. When visiting a monastery or temple, **do not** smoke, wear a hat, or interrupt prayers and on-going ceremonies. External photography is generally allowed, whereas internal photography of the images and murals within a temple may be prohibited, or acceptable for a fee (normally imposed

Touching down

Essentials

Official time *Tibetan time is absurdly the same as time in Beijing since a single time zone prevails throughout the regions controlled by China, ie GMT + 8 hours. This accounts for the long daylight evenings and dark early mornings. Consequently, the border crossings between Tibet and Nepal or between Xinjiang and Pakistan may be the only places on the ground where travellers experience a sense of jet-lag!*

Hours of business *Government buildings, banks and offices are open from Monday-Friday (0930-1230, 1530-1800). Saturday (only recently) and Sunday are public holidays, as are the main festivals of the Chinese calendar: New Year's Day (1 January), Tibetan New Year, Chinese New Year (Spring Festival), International*

Working Women's Day (8 March), International Labour Day (1 May), Youth Day (4 May), Children's Day (1 June), Founding of the Chinese Communist Party (1 July), Army Day (1 August), and National Day (1 October).

Weights and measures *Metric – the same as in China. Traditional measurements are also in use. 1 kilo equals 2 gyama (Ch jin), 1 hectare equals 15 mu, 1 km equals 2 litres, 1 metre equals 3 chi.*

Voltage *220 volts, 50 cycles AC. The current is variable and the hours of operation unpredictable. Carry a range of plug conversion adapters. Rely on battery-operated equipment. A strong flashlight is also essential.*

---

by the authorities). Always ask before photographing. Bribes are officially frowned upon, but often accepted when discreetly offered. Small gifts, however, are widely appreciated. Photographs of important lamas from the various Buddhist or Bon traditions are revered throughout the monasteries, villages, and towns of Tibet, but photographs of the Dalai Lama, which cannot presently be sold in public, should be avoided unless they can be given discreetly in confidence. At the time of arrival or departure, it is customary to exchange gifts. See also the sections on **Trekking**, page 45, and **Media**, page 43.

Visiting monasteries   When visiting monasteries, you will not usually have to remove shoes, as in India, but do remember to be modestly dressed, to remove your hat, to abstain from smoking, and to proceed around or through sacred shrines in a clockwise manner. Never sit down pointing your feet towards the images of a temple or its inner sanctum! You may feel privileged to bear witness to the revival of this ancient culture, even if distressed by the obvious signs of wanton destruction, mostly dating from the 1960s, and by the apparent lack of activity in some monasteries. This can be balanced at the end of your trip by a visit to neighbouring Kathmandu or Bhutan, where many of Tibet's greatest lamas have actively resurrected their communities in exile. Independent Bhutan also preserves the ancient spiritual heritage of Tibet intact, having avoided the depredations of the Chinese Cultural Revolution. Nonetheless, in many remote monasteries of East and Far-east Tibet you will be heartened by the genuine non-sectarian approach and commitment to the meditative and scholarly life shown by elderly and young monks or nuns alike, with scant material resources.

More difficult is the reintroduction of systematic Buddhist learning and meditation practice. Many of the great Tibetan masters who reside in exile have returned home for visits to encourage a Buddhist renaissance; but the authorities often continue to react with suspicion and misunderstanding. This is particularly noticeable in and around Lhasa, where the political indoctrination of monks and nuns is widespread and a renewed hardline campaign futilely seeks to marginalize the influence of the Dalai Lama, oblivious to the abject failure of past repression. It is clear for all to see that the hearts and minds of the Tibetan people are with the Dalai Lama in his quest for genuine autonomy and self-determination.

Tipping is officially frowned upon, but widespread in hotels and travel agencies. Tipping
Remember to tip your driver in Tibet as well as your guide. In view of the road
conditions, the driver will often receive more than the guide.

Safety

In urban areas pickpockets are commonplace, and venues of entertainment, such as
karaoke bars and discotheques, can sometimes erupt into flashpoints of violence,
reminiscent of the Wild West. Foreign visitors should be aware of the risks facing the
indigenous population who engage in acts of political dissent; and seek not to leave
friends or acquaintances in a compromised position. Do not distribute photographs of
the Dalai Lama in public places or even upon random request! In general it is best if
unwitting visitors make little contact with Tibetans in urban areas, but, as always, what
one can or cannot do will depend upon who one knows. Some secret policemen are
themselves among the most affable and gracious hosts when introduced socially by
those with the right connections! In general the crime rate in Tibet is low, and you will
be received courteously throughout the length and breadth of the country. Some
remote village communities may be suspicious of passing strangers, but you are more
at risk from the dangerous road conditions than from the country's inhabitants.
Overland travel in Tibet remains a pastime for the adventurous!

The various branches of the police force, known as the Public Security Bureau (*Tib* Police
Chide Lekhung, *Ch* Gonganju), monitor traffic, crime, political dissent, and visa
extensions. Offices are found in all cities, towns, and lesser townships, but visa
extensions are only possible in Lhasa, Zhigatse, Tsetang, Kermo, and Ziling. These
offices are also responsible for issuing Alien Travel Permits (ATP) for the 'closed' areas of
the Tibetan plateau.

Where to stay

A wide choice is only available in Lhasa, Ziling and the gateway cities. Kathmandu,
Lanzhou, Chengdu and Kunming offer the full range of luxury to budget
accommodation. On the plateau itself, three-star hotels, such as *Lhasa Grand Hotel*,
Lhasa Hotel and the *Qinghai Hotel* in Ziling, are at the top of the range. Outside of the
main towns, be prepared to sleep in government guesthouses and truck stops which
are highly variable and often decidedly unclean, sometimes lacking even basic
facilities. Camping is often much preferable.
  Hotel categories are determined by the price of the average double room, exclusive
of local taxes.

The hotels in Tibet range from three-star downwards. Throughout the plateau there Hotels
are no four-star or five-star hotels (although departure points in Kathmandu,
Chengdu, Lanzhou, Kunming and Lijiang do have better facilities). Within Lhasa, the
better hotels, such as *Lhasa Grand Hotel, Lhasa Hotel, Tibet Hotel, Himalaya Hotel, Kyichu
Hotel, Sernye Hotel, Post and Telecommunication Hotel*, and *Sunlight Hotel*, vary in price
from US$88 to 25, and provide a full meal plan in the range US$51 to 20. Outside Lhasa,
there are large modern hotels in Ziling, Tsetang, Zhigatse, Gyantse, Bayi, Shelkar, Dram
(*Ch* Zhangmu), Senge Tsangpo (*Ch* Shiquanhe), Purang, Nakchu, Chamdo, Jol, Derge,
Batang, Litang, Dartsedo, Jyekundo, Repkong, Machen, Barkham, Machen, Dzitsa Degu,
and Zungchu. Although these establishments like to present themselves as being
luxury hotels, most are in fact rather bland and basic. About half of them do at least
provide hot running water and attached bathrooms, and their prices range from
US$40 to 20, with full meal plan at US$30 to 15. Special mention should be made of

the *Gyaltang Dzong Hotel* in Gyeltangteng (*Ch* Zhongdian) which is constructed in an elegant traditional Tibetan dzong style, run under an experienced international management, offering an international cuisine and cultural study programme.

Guesthouses   Some of the older, more traditional hotels offer a very good service. The *Lapulen Hotel* at Labrang (a converted summer palace) is an outstanding example, but there are also some reasonably clean and friendly **guesthouses** in places like Sok Dzong, Tengchen, Dzogang, Markham, Dabpa, Derong, Manigango, Drango, Kandze, Zhiwu, Tawu, Chabcha, Mato, Darlag, Jikdril, Ngawa, and Hong Yuan. The traveller should be aware that such guesthouses have shared toilet and bathroom facilities. Bring your own disinfectant and toilet paper!

Camping   In smaller places, you can stay in simple **transport stations** or head out of town to set up a **camp** (in which case you will also need a stove and cooking utensils). All rooms are on a twin-share or triple basis, although single supplements are generally available. For further details of the hotels in each city or town, see the relevant **Essentials** sections.

Getting around

There are only a few paved roads in Tibet. Most roads are therefore subject to clouds of dust and delays occur in summer due to landslides. Public transport in remote areas is largely reserved for Tibetans and hitchhiking is illegal. Some truck drivers though may be prepared to give lifts to independent travellers. Make sure that you obtain adequate transport for your chosen destination (often four-wheel drive landcruisers with support trucks). For this reason alone, truly independent travel over long distances is not easy.

Air & train   Once inside Tibet, there are no internal air connections for foreign travellers, although this may soon change if flights are introduced between Gongkar and Pomda or Kermo airports. The only rail link runs from Lanzhou through the Tsongkha valley to Ziling and on past Lake Kokonor to Kermo.

Road   In the absence of other forms of domestic transportation, people are totally dependent on the roads. The road network is extensive but extremely precarious. The only paved roads on the Tibetan plateau are those from Lanzhou to Ziling via Tsongkha, Ziling to Repkong and adjacent counties, Ziling to Lhasa via Kermo, Ziling to Wenchuan, Domda to Jyekundo, Lhasa to Tsetang via Gongkar Airport, Lhasa to Zhigatse and Dingri, Lhasa to Bayi (currently being paved), and Dartsedo to Drango via Lhagang. The others are all unpaved dirt roads, plagued by palls of dust and landslides in the rainy season. Roads crossing high passes are periodically snowbound from late October through to March. The principal means of road transport for local people is by public bus, and for visitors, four-wheel drive land-cruisers or Japanese buses. Vehicles are always hired along with their driver. Owing to the rugged nature of the terrain, many routes in Tibet are for the adventure traveller only, but this does not preclude children. No special facilities are provided for children, but many youngsters adapt easily to the magnificent outdoor environment. Tour operators will normally offer a reduced price for children under 16 years of age.

Hitchhiking is officially prohibited in the Tibetan area, but some drivers will take risks to offer a ride to foreign visitors in order to make a little money. It is useful for potential hitchhikers to know the districts to which Tibetan number plates refer: 01: Lhasa; 02: Nyangtri; 03: Chamdo; 04: Lhokha; 05: Zhigatse; 06: Ngari; 07: Nakchu; and 08: Kermo (Golmud).

Words and phrases

Pronunciation and spelling   *The spelling adopted for the representation of both Tibetan and Sanskrit names in this work is designed with the general reader in mind, rather than the specialist. Exact transliterations have therefore been avoided.*

Tibetan   *Tibetan spellings have been chosen which broadly reflect a modern Central Tibetan pronunciation (not necessarily that of Lhasa). Please note that a final e is never silent, but pronounced in the manner of the French é. Ph is never pronounced like an English f, but like a p with strong aspiration. Among the important regional variants, the general reader should be aware that in some parts of the country, ky or khy may be*

pronounced as ch, gy as j, b as w, dr as b, and ny as hmy. Also suffixes may be elided, and the basic vowel sounds may change, such that u becomes i, and so forth.

Sanskrit   *In the absence of diacritics to represent Sanskrit letters, the following simplified conventions have been observed throughout: palatal c is rendered as c (but to be pronounced as in* Italian *ch); palatal s is rendered sh, and retroflex s as a simple s. The names of all deities are given, wherever possible, in their Sanskrit rather than Tibetan forms. For a correspondence between the Sanskrit and Tibetan names see the glossary page 919 and the iconographic guide, page 883.*

Keeping in touch

English is spoken by very few people in Tibet, and French or German by even fewer!   Language The best language for communication is Tibetan, and for a brief outline of the dialects of the Tibetan language (To-ke, Tsang-ke, U-ke, Kham-ke, Amdo-ke etc), see the **Background**, page 695. In recent decades Chinese has become something of a lingua franca, preferred even by Tibetans from different parts of the plateau when communicating with one another. There have been conscious attempts to reverse this trend by moving towards a universally standard form of Tibetan, but the obstacles are formidable. One should not forget the minority languages spoken within Tibet: the Qiangic dialects of East Tibet, the Monpa and Lhopa dialects of South Tibet, the Mongol, Tu, and Salar languages of the northeast, and so forth.

Some simple Tibetan phrases The basic word order of the Tibetan language is Subject- Object- Verb. For a list of useful works on the Tibetan language see the bibliography below. Some basic phrases include: **greetings** (Central Tibet: *tashidelek* or *chapenang*; Kham: *ka-a-te*; Amdo: *ke-demo*); **thank you** (Central Tibet: *tu-je-che* or *tu-je-nang'*; Kham and Amdo: *katro*); and **goodbye** (Central Tibet: *kalepeb* (if staying) or *kaleshuk* (if leaving); Kham: *yakpo songa* or *yamo*; Amdo: *demo che-a*).

Postage stamps for letters and postcards are available in most towns and large hotels   Postal services on the plateau, but you are advised to stock up in Chengdu, Lhasa, Lanzhou, or Kunming at the beginning of your trip. Larger packages should be mailed from Chengdu, Ziling, Lanzhou, Kunming, or Lhasa. Postcards cost ¥1.60 (airmail), and aerogrammes ¥1.90. Parcels sent by surface mail begin at ¥52 to UK and ¥30.60 to USA for a one kilo parcel; and ¥82 to UK or ¥77 to USA for a one kilo airmail parcel. When sending mail it is best to have the country of destination written in Chinese. For collecting mail, there is a post restante facility in the Lhasa GPO, but it is better to use such facilities at the larger hotels: *Lhasa Grand Hotel, Lhasa Hotel,* and so forth.

Telephone services

Area codes are listed on the inside front cover

The major hotels in Lhasa and Ziling have international IDD telephone connections, and in these cities, as well as the departure points (Kathmandu, Chengdu, Kunming or Lanzhou) you can send and receive international telefax messages. In many smaller towns, DDD calls can be made and received locally, or to the provincial capital, but be prepared for long delays. Such remote places may be contactable by telegram.

Tibet international dialling code is, of course, the same as that of China 86.

Media

Newspapers and books are available throughout the country. In Lhasa, try the *Xinhua Bookstore* near the Jokhang Temple, or the better stocked branch next to the *Tibet Hotel*. Other towns and cities have similar outlets. Few publications are in English, but there is prolific publishing in Tibetan of both classical and modern texts. The newspapers are of limited value, even for those who read Tibetan (*Mimang Tsakpar*) or Chinese (*Renmin Ribao*). The only English newspaper is the *China Daily*. There are local television and radio broadcasting services in each of the provinces or prefectures into which Tibet is now divided. Lhasa, Qinghai, and Kandze television services are all active in programme making. Some productions are voiced over or subtitled in Tibetan.

Private entertainment includes both traditional festivals (on which see the next section), sporting contests, gambling (especially Mahjong), and the new wave of cinemas, video parlours, pool tables, discotheques, clubs, bars and karaoke establishments which thrive in all urban areas.

Food and drink

Food

Organized tours in Tibet may include a full package with three meals daily, or a half package with breakfast and dinner only. In Lhasa a minimum package (hotel only) is also available. International cuisine (Western, Nepalese, Indian) is only available in the *Lhasa Hotel* and a small number of outside restaurants. A few specialist restaurants will offer Tibetan dishes, Guangdong, or Peking dishes. Otherwise the standard cuisine offered in restaurants throughout the Tibetan plateau is Sichuan or Muslim style.

Tibetan cuisine, for the most part, is pretty basic, the staple consisting of large amounts of **tsampa** (roasted barley flour) and endless bowls of **butter tea**. Naturally you will have a chance to taste this delicacy during your stay, but it is highly unlikely that you will want to repeat the experience every day! On the other hand, there are some very good dishes to be had. The famous **momo**: a steamed meat dumpling which resembles the Chinese *jiaoze*, or Tibetan country-style **noodles** (*then-thuk*), and whilst you are in Lhasa you can arrange to have traditional Tibetan banquet (18 dishes), including *lasha* (lamb with radish), *gyuma* (black pudding), *thu* (cheesecake), and *dresi* (sweet rice), topped up with copious cups of 'chang', the local wine.

In nomadic areas, the staple diet consists of yak meat and mutton (fresh or dried), supplemented by delicious yoghurt. Cheese also comes in many varieties: hardened cubes which must be carefully sucked to avoid damaging the teeth, moderately soft whisps which are easy to digest, and, in East Tibet, an assortment of cheeses similar to cottage cheese and to cheddar (*Tib* Jo-she). Desserts are not generally served but delicious apples, apricots, peaches, and walnuts are available in season.

During day trips and long overland journeys, it is sometimes necessary to take a picnic lunch – either supplied by the hotels or the local travel agency. Organized tours, which entail camping, will have a cook who can prepare a full campsite meal, or take over the kitchen of a roadside restaurant. In drier regions of West and Far-west Tibet, you must carry more tinned provisions, while in the more fertile eastern regions, fresh vegetables are plentiful. To supplement this diet, you may wish to carry instant soups, cheeses, pâtés, biscuits, chocolates, coffee, and so forth, which can be very welcome if the weather suddenly turns nasty, or if you have stomach trouble.

Drink

Beer and soft drinks are generally served with all meals in Tibet, but imported alcohol is available only in the larger tourist hotels. Bottled mineral water can be bought easily in the towns. Tea and thermos bottles of hot water are provided in hotel and guesthouse rooms, and this is probably the most refreshing remedy for the dry and dusty atmosphere prevalent on the Tibetan plateau. Boiled water is essential for drinking and indeed for brushing the teeth. Some restaurants will also provide Indian style sweet milk tea or Nescafé. However, butter tea (*soja/poja*) or salted black tea (*ja-dang*) are generally drunk at home. The national alcoholic drinks are *chang* (*chang*), a fortified barley ale, and *arak* (*arak*), a type of distilled liquor. Dried fermented millet (*tomba*) is brewed in areas bordering Sikkim and Bhutan, while 'Lhasa Beer' (*Lhasa Pijiu*) and other brands of beer, as well as Chinese spirits, can be purchased throughout the plateau.

Essentials

Shopping

The Tibetans invariably bargain for their purchases and expect foreign visitors to do the same. In the markets, feel free to talk with your hands and pocket calculator! Avoid buying artifacts which have in fact been imported from Nepal! Among the most interesting objects available nowadays are traditional jewellery, metalwork, carpets, woodwork, painted scrolls, and textiles. According to government regulations you are not to export antiques unless you have obtained a receipt or red seal.

Photography Simple print film is commonly available in the larger towns and cities in Tibet, but slide film is hard to obtain even in the tourist shops of the *Lhasa Hotel*. You are therefore advised to stock up before leaving home. Outside photography is free of charge, but be careful not to film sensitive and strategic industrial or military installations. Internal photography in temples and monasteries may be permitted for a fee. Always ask first! Recommended films: for colour prints, Fuji HR100 or equivalent, and Fuji HR1600 for interiors; for colour slides, Kodak chrome 3 ASA 25 and 64, and Kodak Tungsten ASA 160 for interiors; for black and white, Kodak T-max ASA 100, and Kodak Tri-X for interiors. A UV filter or polarizer can help reduce the exposure problem caused by high altitude solar glare in Central and West Tibet. Mornings and late afternoons usually offer the best conditions for filming, and at other times try under-exposure by half a stop. There is some spectacular scenery, but if you go during the wet season make sure to protect film against humidity, and at all times try to protect your equipment from dust. Use a lens hood.

Specialist interest travel

Trekking The sheer vastness of the Tibetan plateau offers great scope for trekking. Some remote areas are even now only accessible on foot or horseback. Trekking conditions are very different from those in Bhutan and Nepal, where the travel agencies have had many years' experience at organizing treks. The best months are April-June and September-November, although even in the rainy season trekking is not always problematic.

On organized treks, tour operators will provide cooking equipment, food, and sometimes tents. In general on such expeditions you will want to travel with the bare minimum of equipment. You don't want to carry anything more than what is essential. Nonetheless, away from Lhasa the travelling is hard, so self-sufficiency is important, and there are a number of required items.

Dietary supplements for trekking First, although organized tours will have a cook to prepare main meals, the dishes will often be basic, especially if you are trekking in West or Far-west Tibet, where fresh vegetables are non-existent. Therefore it is strongly recommended that you bring a small camping stove of your own with a fuel bottle, as well as some freeze dried meals for the sake of variation in diet. You can also prepare your own hot drinks (coffee, cocoa, etc) whenever you want to. You may also like to bring some high protein fruit and nut, or muesli bars as well as chocolate, beef jerky, cheese, pâté, and so forth.

Clothing for trekking Second, because the temperatures on the Tibetan plateau are subject to extreme fluctuations you need to think in terms of 'layered clothes' that you can peel off and put on with ease. The weather will be warm to hot during the day and can be cool to freezing at night, and is often wet and windy depending on the location and season. At high altitude, the dry atmosphere stops perspiration so you won't become as dirty as usual and need not wash completely nor change clothes every couple of days. So you do not need to bring more than two or three items of any clothing. Also, if you intend to take an address book, do leave a duplicate at home in case of loss or water damage.

The following items of clothing are recommended for long treks: good comfortable walking shoes or boots (be sure to wear them in first); Band-Aid/elastoplast for blisters; thick wool socks (at least three pairs); light sandals or canvas shoes; long underwear (silk is good as winds can be icy); sufficient changes of underwear and T-shirts; cotton or woollen shirts (with pockets); wool sweaters (at least two, one to be worn over the other); trousers or jeans (possibly one heavy, one light-weight); a rain coat; a down-filled jacket; a sun hat, dark glasses, scarf or cravat (essential); and gloves. In general, Gortex is recommended for both walking boots and trekking clothes.

Trekking equipment Third, some of the following items will be supplied by the tour agency responsible for organizing your trek, but you should ensure that you obtain the others prior to your departure from Lhasa or wherever. Various camping items can be purchased or hired cheaply in Kathmandu. Carry your luggage in a backpack or heavy duty travel bag (with strong straps/handles), and keep your immediate necessities in a small knapsack, or shoulder bag (camera bag).

You should bring your own sleeping bag (suitable for all-weather outdoor conditions), an insulation mat, an umbrella, a flashlight (headlamp recommended) and extra alkaline batteries, a water flask and/or thermos bottle, a small stove (multifuel if possible) and fuel bottle, cooking and eating utensils, a Swiss-type army knife (with bottle and can openers etc), matches (waterproof preferable), a waterproof pouch or belt for money and passport, a medical kit (as outlined above under **Health**),

Himalayan Environment Trust Code of Practice

Campsite *Leave it cleaner than you found it.*

Deforestation *Make no open fires and discourage others making one for you. Limit use of water heated by firewood (use of dead wood is permitted – available in Sikkim but scarce elsewhere). Choose accommodation where kerosene or fuel-efficient wood burning stoves are used.*

Litter *Remove it. Burn or bury paper and carry away non-degradable litter. If you find other people's litter, remove their's too! Pack food in biodegradable containers. Carry away all batteries/cells.*

Water *Keep local water clean. Do not use detergents and pollutants in streams and springs. Where there are no toilets be sure you are at least 30 metres away from water source and bury or cover waste. Do not allow cooks or porters to throw*

rubbish in nearby streams and rivers.

Plants *Do not take cuttings, seeds and roots – it is illegal in all parts of the Himalayas.*

Giving to children encourages begging.

Donations *to a project, health centre or school is more constructive.*

*Respect **local traditions and cultures**. Respect **privacy** and ask permission before taking photographs.*

*Respect **holy places**. Never touch or remove religious objects. Remove shoes before entering temples.*

*Respect local **etiquette**. Dress modestly, particularly when visiting temples and shrines and while walking through villages; loose, lightweight clothes are preferable to shorts, skimpy tops and tight-fitting outfits. Avoid holding hands and kissing in public.*

suntan lotion, and (if possible) your own lightweight tent.

Some remote trekking trails are not well-defined, so it is easy to lose the way; and high-altitude rescue is non-existent. It is therefore essential to trek with a reliable local guide. Pack animals can be hired locally for certain treks, as in the Everest region, the Kailash region, the Kongpo region, and the upper Kyichu region.

NB When trekking in Tibet, please observe the Himalayan Code of Practice (see box), and be serious about the conservation of the ecology and the environment, even if locals or guides set a bad example. They only do so because of the general apathy or depression experienced by dispossessed persons the world over!

Some travel agencies will offer cycling trips on the plateau, especially between Lhasa and Kathmandu. Contact Tibet International Sports Travel in Lhasa. **Cycling**

For details of climbing fees and organization in the Himalayas and in the Tibetan Autonomous Region as a whole, refer to an international tour operator, or directly to the **Tibet Mountaineering Association** (F0891-6336366), or to **Tibet International Sports Travel** (F0891-6334855), both in Lhasa. For the Minyak Gangkar, Kawalungring, and Minshan ranges, refer to the **Sichuan Mountaineering Association** based in Chengdu (T028-5588047, F00-86-28-5588042). For the Amnye Machen range refer to the **Qinghai Mountaineering Association** in Ziling (T0971-8238877, F00-86-971-8238933). and for the Kawa Karpo range, refer to the **Yunnan Mountaineering Association**. The local travel agencies listed in this guide can also provide relevant information, as can the head office of the **China Mountaineering Association** in Beijing. **Mountaineering**

For a listing of the most popular routes on the Tibetan plateau, see above, pages 28-32. Special interest itineraries can also be arranged for Buddhist groups, botanists, mountaineers, or trekkers. **Suggested routes on the Tibetan Plateau**

Essentials

Festival dates, 1999-2000

Lunar Date	Western Date	Event
1st of 1st Month	17 February (2000: 6 February)	Losar, Tibetan New Year
8th of 1st Month	23 February	Monlam, the Great Prayer Festival
15th of 1st Month	2 March	Day of Offerings
10th of 4th month	24-26 May (2000: 11-13 June)	Tsurphu Tsechu Festival
15th of 4th Month	30 May (2000: 16 June)	Enlightenment of Buddha
18th of 4th Month	2-10 June (2000: 16-25 June)	Gyantse Horse Festival
15th of 5th Month	28 June (2000: 16 July)	Samye Doldhe Festival
15th of 5th Month	28 June (2000: 16 July)	Local Deities' Day
15th of 5th Month	28 June	Tashilhunpo Festival
4th of 6th Month	16 July	Dharmacakra Day
10th of 6th Month	23 July	Birth of Padmasambhava
15th of 6th Month	28 July (2000: 15 August)	Ganden Serthang Festival
13-16th of 6th Month	26-29 July (2000: 14-17 July)	Tashilhunpo Monlam
29th of 6th Month	10 August	Drepung Zhoton (Yoghurt Festival)
1st of 7th Month	12-18 August (2000: 29 August-4 September)	Zhoton (Yoghurt Festival)
27th of 7th Month	6 September	Bathing Festival
30th of 7th Month	9 September	End of Rain Retreat
30th of 7th Month	9 September	Damzhung Horse Festival
1st of 8th Month	10 September	Ongkor (Harvest Festival)
22nd of 9th Month	31 October	Descent from the God Realms
15th of 10th Month	23 November	Palden Lhamo Procession in Barkhor
25th of 10th Month	2 December	Anniversary of Tsongkhapa
6th of 11th Month	14 December	Nine Bad Omens
7th of 11th Month	15 December	Ten Auspicious Omens

Holidays and festivals

National holidays   The dates of traditional festivals vary according to the lunar calendar, whereas most modern Chinese holidays are tied to the solar calendar.

Public Holidays: 1999

1 January	New Year's Day	4 May	Youth Day
17 February	Tibetan New Year	1 June	Children's Day
	Chinese New Year/ Spring Festival	1 July	Founding of the Chinese Communist Party
8 March	International Working Women's Day	1 August	National Army Day
		1 October	National Day
1 May	International Labour Day		

Festivals   The Tibetan lunar calendar is calculated each year by astrologers from the *Mentsikhang* in Lhasa and Dharamsala. It is based on a cycle of 60 years, each of which is named after one of 12 animals and one of five elements in combination. For example, 1999 is called the earth hare year. A calendrical year normally contains 12 months, but the addition of an extra intercalary month for astrological reasons is not uncommon. In general, the Tibetan lunar month is about two months behind the western calendar. Many festivals are traditionally held throughout the Tibetan calendar – some are nationwide and others applicable to a certain area only. They may also be religious or secular in character. The main horse festival season falls between the fifth and the seventh months of the year (usually July-September), and some are now fixed in relation to the solar calendar, eg **Jyekundo Horse Festival**, which begins on 25 July, and the **Litang Horse Festival**, commencing in recent years on 10 July.

Major events in the Tibetan calendar are shown opposite. The next year's calendar is prepared in the late autumn or winter and only then can the dates be matched to the western calendar. In addition, the **10th** day of every month is dedicated to Padmasambhava who introduced the highest Buddhist teachings from India in the eighth century. The **25th day** of each month is a Dakini Day, associated with the female deities who are the agents of Buddha-activity. The **29th day** of each month is dedicated to the wrathful doctrinal protector deities, while the **15th** and **30th** are associated with the Buddha, and the **8th** with the Medicine Buddha.

Health

No vaccinations are required for China, although anti-malaria medication is **General advice** recommended for low-lying subtropical areas of Southeast Tibet during the rainy season. Immunization against polio, tetanus, rabies (fairly commonplace), hepatitis, meningitis, and typhoid should also be considered. Avoid unboiled water and ice-cubes, as well as uncooked vegetables and unpeeled fruit since dysentery is commonplace. It is strongly recommended that everyone has a check-up by their doctor before embarking on a prolonged overland journey in remote parts of Tibet, and that you prepare by undertaking some physical exercise each day (walking, swimming or jogging).

Generally, the dry and sunny atmosphere in Tibet means that bacteria are not as plentiful and as virulent as at lower altitudes in Nepal, India, and China. Thus, one remains fairly healthy while travelling in Tibet. Altitude sickness is the commonest ailment and you are advised to take plenty of fluids throughout your stay. You should have a daily intake of four litres at high altitude, and keep your water-bottle handy and filled up, or be sure to drink sufficient soft drinks, mineral water, or soup in the course of the day. Otherwise the effects of the high altitude are much more likely to cause you to feel headaches, light-headedness, nausea, or sleeplessness. Always remember to replenish your water-bottle when stopping near a stream, spring or lake in the course of a long overland journey (see box on page 57 for hints on sterilization). It is important to pace yourself well when walking in Tibet. Move slowly and in a relaxed manner to minimize discomfort. Apart from paracetamol, aspirin and mild sleeping tablets which can help, the following remedies have sometimes been recommended by experienced travellers and mountaineers: Coca 30 and Phosphorum 30 (homeopathic); and acetazolomide (eg the diuretic Diamox). In view of the demanding nature of travel on the plateau, most agencies require a medical certificate signed by your doctor if you are over the age of 65.

Apart from altitude sickness, the major irritant to health in Tibet is the dryness of the atmosphere which often causes respiratory problems or cracking of the lips. You are advised to carry throat lozenges and an expectorant for dry coughs such as Actifed, as well as an effective lip-salve such as Blistease or Carmex.

Don't forget to consult your doctor before departure and ensure that you bring adequate supplies of any necessary prescribed drug (to be carried in hand luggage). Oxygen pillows or bottles are sometimes available on standard Central Tibetan routes, and on certain trekking routes, the first-aid kit will be carried by an 'ambulance' horse.

Essentials

The following information has been compiled for us by Dr David Snashall, Senior Lecturer in Occupational Health, United Medical Schools of Guy's and St Thomas' Hospitals and Chief Medical Adviser, Foreign and Commonwealth Office, London.

Health risks & medical facilities
The traveller to the Tibetan Plateau is inevitably exposed to health risks not encountered in North America or Western Europe. Despite the fact that most of the area lies geographically within the Temperate Zone, the climate is occasionally tropical in, for example, the Himalayan foothills. In general tropical diseases are not a major problem for visitors. Because much of the area is economically underdeveloped, infectious diseases still predominate in a way in which they used to predominate in the West some decades ago. There is an obvious difference in health risks between the business traveller who tends to stay in international class hotels in large cities, and the backpacker trekking through the rural areas. There are no hard and fast rules to follow; you will often have to make your own judgements on the healthiness or otherwise of your surroundings.

There are some well qualified doctors in the area, hardly any of whom speak English but the quality and range of medical care diminishes very rapidly as you move away from big cities. There are systems and traditions of medicine wholly different from the western model and you may be confronted with unusual modes of treatment such as herbal medicine and acupuncture. At least you can be sure that local practitioners have a lot of experience with the particular diseases of their region. If you are in one of the five gateway cities, it may be worthwhile calling on your Embassy to provide a list of recommended doctors.

If you are a long way away from medical help, a certain amount of self medication may be necessary and you will find many of the drugs available have familiar names. However, always check the date stamping and buy from reputable pharmacies because the shelf life of some items, especially vaccines and antibiotics, is markedly reduced in hot conditions. Unfortunately in the sub-Himalayan areas of Nepal and Bhutan, many locally produced drugs are not subjected to quality control procedures and so can be unreliable. There have, in addition, been cases of substitution of inert materials for active drugs.

With the following precautions and advice, you should keep as healthy as usual. Make local enquiries about health risks if you are apprehensive and take the general advice of European and North American families who have lived or are living in the area.

Before travelling

Take out medical insurance. Make sure it covers all eventualities, especially evacuation to your home country by a medically equipped plane if necessary. You should have a dental check up, obtain a spare glasses prescription, a spare oral contraceptive prescription (or enought pills to last) and, if you suffer from a chronic illness (such as diabetes, high blood pressure, ear or sinus troubles, cardio-pulmonary disease or nervous disorder), arrange for a check up with your doctor, who can at the same time provide you with a letter explaining the details of your disability in English and if possible Tibetan and/or Chinese. Check the current practice in countries you are visiting for malaria prophylaxis (prevention). If you are on regular medication, make sure you have enough to cover the period of your travel.

Children & babies
Younger travellers seem to be more prone to illness abroad, but that should not put you off taking them. More preparation is necessary than for an adult and perhaps a little more care should be taken when travelling to remote areas where health services are primitive. This is because children can become more rapidly ill than adults, although they often recover more quickly.

Diarrhoea and vomiting are the most common problems so take the usual

Medical supplies

You may like to take some of the following items with you from home:

Sunglasses
ones designed for intense sunlight

Earplugs
for sleeping on aeroplanes and in noisy hotels

Suntan cream
with a high protection factor

Insect repellent
containing DET for preference and antihistamine cream

Mosquito net
lightweight, permethrin-impregnated for choice

Tablets
for travel sickness

Tampons
can be expensive in some countries in Latin America

Condoms

Contraceptives

Water sterilizing tablets

Antimalarial tablets

Anti-infective ointment eg Cetrimide

Dusting powder for feet etc
containing fungicide

Antacid tablets
for indigestion

Sachets of rehydration salts
plus anti-diarrhoea preparations

Painkillers
such as Paracetamol or Aspirin

Antibiotics
for diarrhoea etc (immodium or 'Arsenicum Album 6', a homeopathic medication for diarrhoea). Streptomagma tablets, tetracycline or metronidazole are available on prescription for dysentery, infections and bronchitis

Antiseptic cream
for cuts and burns

Disinfectants
(or wipes) for wounds and latrines

Vitamin supplements

Floradix iron supplement
to be taken two weeks prior to departure since it increases the red blood cells which absorb oxygen

First Aid kit
Small pack containing a few sterile syringes and needles and disposable gloves. The risk of catching hepatitis etc from a dirty needle used for injection is now negligible, but some may be reassured by carrying their own supplies – available from camping shops and airport shops but see further note on page 55.

Essentials

precautions, but more intensively. Make sure all basic childhood **vaccinations** are up to date, as well as the more exotic ones. Children should be properly protected against diphtheria, mumps and measles. Consult your doctor for advice on BCG innoculation against tuberculosis. Protection against mosquitoes and drug prophylaxis against malaria are essential. Many children take to `foreign' food quite happily. Milk in Nepal and Tibet is generally unpasteurized and should be well boiled. Powdered milk may be the answer, although you should be certain that the water source is safe. Breast feeding where appropriate is the best option.

The treatment of **diarrhoea** is the same as for adults except that it should be started earlier and be continued with more persistence. Children get dehydrated very quickly in the tropics and can become drowsy and uncooperative unless cajoled to drink water or juice plus salts. Oral rehydration has been a lifesaving technique for children.

Upper respiratory infections such as colds, catarrh and middle ear infection are common – antibiotics should be carried against the possibility. **Outer ear infections** after swimming are also common – antibiotic ear drops will help.

Protect children against the sun with a hat and high factor sun lotion. Severe sunburn at this age may well lead to serious skin cancer in the future.

Smallpox vaccination is no longer required anywhere in the world. Neither is cholera vaccination recognized as necessary for international travel by the World Health Organisation – it is not very effective either. There is no requirement for Yellow Fever. It

Vaccination & immunization

is a live vaccination not to be given to children under nine months of age or persons allergic to eggs. Immunity lasts for 10 years, an International Certificate of Yellow Fever Vaccination will be given and should be kept because it is sometimes asked for. The vaccination is practically without side effects and almost totally protective.

Vaccination against the following diseases are recommended:

Typhoid A disease spread by the insanitary preparation of food. A number of new vaccines against this condition are now available; the older TAB and monovalent typhoid vaccines are being phased out. The newer, eg Typhim Vi, causes less side effects, but are more expensive. For those who do not like injections, there are now oral vaccines.

Poliomyelitis Despite its decline in the world this remains a serious disease if caught and is easy to protect against. There are live oral vaccines and in some countries injected vaccines. Whichever one you choose it is a good idea to a have booster every three to five years if visiting developing countries regularly.

Tetanus One dose should be given with a booster at six weeks and another at six months, and 10 yearly boosters thereafter are recommended. Children should already be properly protected against diphtheria, poliomyelitis and pertussis (whooping cough), measles and HIB, all of which can be more serious infections than at home. Measles, mumps and rubella vaccine is also given to children throughout the world, but those teenage girls who have not had rubella (german measles) should be tested and vaccinated. Hepatitis B vaccination for babies is now routine in some countries. Consult your doctor for advice on tuberculosis inoculation.

Infectious Hepatitis is less of a problem for travellers than it used to be because of the development of two extremely effective vaccines against the A and B form of the disease. A combined hepatitis A & B vaccine is now available – one jab covers both diseases.

Other vaccinations might be considered in the case of epidemics, eg meningitis. There is an effective vaccination against rabies which should be considered by all travellers, especially those going through remote areas or if there is a particular occupational risk, eg for zoologists or veterinarians.

Further information Further information on health risks abroad, vaccinations etc may be available from a local travel clinic. If you wish to take specific drugs with you such as antibiotics these are best prescribed by your own doctor. Beware, however, that not all doctors can be experts on the health problems of remote countries. More detailed or more up-to-date information than local doctors can provide are available from various sources.

In the UK there are hospital departments specializing in tropical diseases in London, Liverpool, Birmingham and Glasgow, and the Malaria Reference Laboratory at the London School of Hygiene and Tropical Medicine provides free advice about malaria, T(0891)600350. In the USA the local Public Health Services can give such information and information is available centrally from the Centre for Disease Control (CDC) in Atlanta, T(404)3324559.

There are additional computerized databases which can be assessed for destination-specific up-to-the-minute information. In the UK there is MASTA (Medical Advisory Service to Travellers Abroad), T(0171)6314408, F(0171)4365389, Tx8953473 and Travax (Glasgow, T(0141)9467120, ext 247). Other information on medical problems overseas can be obtained from the book by Dawood, Richard (Editor) (1992) *Travellers' Health: How to stay healthy abroad*, Oxford University Press 1992, £7.99. We strongly recommend this revised and updated edition, especially to the intrepid traveller heading for the more out of the way places. General advice is also available in the UK in *Health Information for Overseas Travel* published by the Department of

Health and available from HMSO, and *International Travel and Health* published by WHO, Geneva.

Staying healthy

Generally, the dry and sunny atmosphere means that bacteria are not as plentiful and as virulent as at lower altitudes in Nepal, India and China. However, practically nobody escapes this one, so be prepared for it.

Intestinal upsets

Foods to avoid Most of the time, intestinal upsets are due to the insanitary preparation of food. Do not eat uncooked fish or vegetables or meat (especially pork), fruit with the skin on (always peel your fruit yourself) or food that is exposed to flies (especially salads).

Unpasteurized milk products, including cheese, are sources of tuberculosis, brucellosis, listeria and food poisoning germs. You can render fresh milk safe by heating it to 62°C for 30 minutes, followed by rapid cooling or by boiling it. Matured or processed cheeses are safer than fresh varieties.

Tap water may be unsafe, especially after heavy rain and the same goes for stream water or well water. Filtered or bottled water is usually available and safe. Ice for drinks should be made from boiled water but rarely is, so stand your glass on the ice cubes, instead of putting them in the drink. Dirty water should first be strained through a filter bag (available from camping shops) and then boiled or treated. Bringing the water to a rolling boil at sea level is sufficient but at high altitude you have to boil the water for longer to ensure that all the microbes are killed. Various sterilizing methods can be used and there are proprietary preparations containing chlorine or iodine compounds.

This is usually caused by eating food which has been contaminated by food poisoning germs. Drinking water is rarely the culprit. River water is more likely to be contaminated by sewage and so swimming in such dilute effluent can also be a cause.

Travellers' diarrhoea

Infection with various organisms can give rise to travellers' diarrhoea. They may be viruses, bacteria, eg Escherichia coli (probably the most common cause worldwide), protozoal (such as amoebas and giardia), salmonella and cholera. The diarrhoea may come on suddenly or rather slowly. It may or may not be accompanied by vomiting or by severe abdominal pain and the passage of blood or mucus, when it is called dysentery.

How do you know which type you have caught and how to treat it?

If you can time the onset of the diarrhoea to the minute ('acute') then it is probably due to a virus or a bacterium and/or the onset of dysentery. The treatment in addition to rehydration is Ciprofloxacin 500 mg every 12 hours; the drug is now widely available and there are many similar ones.

If the diarrhoea comes on slowly or intermittently ('sub-acute') then it is more likely to be protozoal, ie caused by an amoeba or giardia. Antibiotics such as Ciprofloxacin will have little effect. These cases are best treated by a doctor as is any outbreak of diarrhoea continuing for more than three days. Sometimes blood is passed in amoebic dysentery and for this you should certainly seek medical help. If this is not available then the best treatment is probably Tinidazole (Fasigyn), one tablet four times a day for three days. If there are severe stomach cramps, the following drugs may help but are not very useful in the management of acute diarrhoea: Loperamide (Imodium) and Diphenoxylate with Atropine (Lomotil). They should not be given to children.

Essentials

Any kind of diarrhoea, whether or not accompanied by vomiting, responds well to the replacement of water and salts, taken as frequent small sips of some kind of rehydration solution. There are proprietary preparations consisting of sachets of powder which you dissolve in boiled water or you can make your own by adding half a teaspoonful of salt (3.5 grammes) and four tablespoonsfuls of sugar (40 grammes) to a litre of boiled water.

Thus the lynch pins of treatment for diarrhoea are rest, fluid and salt replacement, antibiotics such as Ciprofloxacin for the bacterial types and special diagnostic tests and medical treatment for the amoeba and giardia infections. Salmonella infections and cholera, although rare, can be devastating diseases and it would be wise to get to a hospital as soon as possible if these were suspected.

Fasting, peculiar diets and the consumption of large quantities of yoghurt have not been found useful in calming travellers' diarrhoea or in rehabilitating inflamed bowels. Oral rehydration has on the other hand, especially in children, been a life saving technique and should always be practised, whatever other treatment you use. As there is some evidence that alcohol and milk might prolong diarrhoea they should be avoided during and immediately after an attack.

Diarrhoea occurring day after day for long periods of time (chronic diarrhoea) is notoriously resistent to amateur attempts at treatment and again warrants proper diagnostic tests (most towns with reasonable sized hospitals have laboratories for stool samples). There are ways of preventing travellers' diarrhoea for short periods of time by taking antibiotics, but this is not a foolproof technique and should not be used other than in exceptional circumstances. Doxycycline is possibly the best drug. Some preventatives such as Enterovioform can have serious side effects if taken for long periods.

Paradoxically **constipation** is also common, probably induced by dietary change, inadequate fluid intake in hot places and long bus journeys. Simple laxatives are useful in the short-term and bulky foods such as maize, beans and plenty of fruit are also useful.

High altitude Acute mountain sickness can strike from about 3,000 metres upwards. It is more likely to affect those who ascend rapidly (eg by plane) and those who over-exert themselves. Teenagers seem to be particularly prone. Past experience is not always a good guide: the Author, having spent years in Peru travelling constantly between sea level and very high altitude never suffered the slightest symptoms, then was severely affected climbing Kilimanjaro in Tanzania.

On reaching heights above 3,000 metres, heart pounding and shortness of breath, especially on exertion are almost universal and a normal response to the lack of oxygen in the air. Acute mountain sickness takes a few hours or days to come on and presents with headache, lassitude, dizziness, loss of appetite, nausea and vomiting. Insomnia is common and often associated with a suffocating feeling when lying down in bed. Keen observers may note that their breathing tends to wax and wane at night and their face tends to be puffy in the mornings – this is all part of the syndrome. If the symptoms are mild, the treatment is rest, painkillers (preferably not Aspirin based) for the headache and anti-sickness pills for vomiting. Oxygen may help at very high altitudes but is unlikely to be available unless on an organized tour in Tibet.

The best way of preventing acute mountain sickness is a relatively slow ascent and, when trekking through the Himalayas to high altitude, some time spent in the foothills getting fit and adapting to moderate altitude is beneficial. On arrival at places over 3,000 metres, a few hours rest in a chair and the avoidance of alcohol, cigarettes and heavy food will go a long way towards preventing acute mountain sickness. Should the symptoms be severe and prolonged, it is best to descend to a lower

First Aid kits

Although pre-packaged first aid kits for travellers are available from many camping and outdoor pursuit shops, it is unlikely that you will ever need to use at least half of their contents. If you are visiting very remote areas, for example if you are trekking, it becomes more important to ensure that you have all the necessary items. You may want to bring with you a supply of sticky plasters and corn plasters (Band Aid etc), intestinal treatments such as Imodium, and antihistamine tablets. Flagyl can be bought across the chemist's counter in Nepal, whereas in UK at least, a doctor's prescription is required. Paracetamol is readily available. Tibet's larger hospitals and medical centres do not seem to have any shortage of sterile, single-use needles, but to be safe you should bring your own supply, the standard `green' size are the most versatile. If you have any specialized requirements, it is recommended that you bring them with you.

altitude and to reascend slowly or in stages. The symptoms disappear very quickly with even a few 100 metres of descent. If a slow staged attempt is impossible because of shortage of time, then the drug Acetazolamide (Diamox) can be used as a preventative and continued during the ascent. There is good evidence of the value of this drug in the prevention of acute mountain sickness but some people do experience funny side effects. The usual dose is 500 milligrammes of the slow release preparation each night, starting the night before ascending above 3,000 metres.

Other problems experienced at high altitude are sunburn, excessively dry air causing skin cracking, sore eyes (it may be wise to leave your contact lenses out) and stuffy noses. It is unwise to ascend to high altitude if you are pregnant, especially in the first three months, or if you have any history of heart, lung or blood disease, including sickle cell.

There is a further, albeit rare, hazard due to rapid ascent to high altitude – a kind of complicated mountain sickness presenting as acute pulmonary oedema or acute cerebral oedema. Both conditions are more common the higher you go. Pulmonary oedema comes on quite rapidly with breathlessness, noisy breathing, cough, blueness of the lips and frothing at the mouth. Cerebral oedema usually presents with confusion, going on to unconsciousness. Anybody developing these serious conditions must be brought down to low altitude as soon as possible and taken to hospital.

Rapid descent from high places will aggravate sinus and middle ear infections and make bad teeth ache. The same problems are sometimes experienced during descent at the end of an aeroplane flight. Do not ascend to high altitude in the 24 hours following scuba-diving. Remember that the Himalayas and other mountain ranges are very high, very cold, very remote and potentially very dangerous. Do not travel in them alone, when you are ill or if you are poorly equipped. As telephone communication can be non-existent, mountain rescue is extremely difficult and medical services may not be up to much.

Despite these various hazards (mostly preventable) of high altitude travel, many people find the environment healthier and more invigorating than at sea level.

Heat & cold Remember that, especially in the mountains, there can be a large and sudden drop in temperature between sun and shade and between night and day, so dress accordingly. Loose fitting cotton clothes are still the best for hot weather. Warm jackets and woollens are essential after dark at high altitude.

Insects These can be a great nuisance although more so in the subtropical areas of Nepal and Bhutan than in the high altitude plateau of Tibet. Some of course are carriers of serious diseases such as malaria, dengue fever or filariasis and various worm infections. The best way of keeping mosquitoes away at night is to sleep off the ground with a mosquito net and to burn mosquito coils containing Pyrethrum. Aerosol sprays or a 'flit' gun may be effective as are insecticidal tablets which are heated on a mat which is plugged into the wall socket (if taking your own, check the voltage of the area you are visiting so that you can take an appliance that will work. Similarly, check that your electrical adaptor is suitable for the repellent plug.)

Or you can use personal insect repellent of which the best contain a high concentration of Diethyltoluamide. Liquid is best for arms and face (take care around eyes and make sure you do not dissolve the plastic of your spectacles). Aerosol spray on clothes and ankles can deter mites, ticks and leeches. Liquid DET suspended in water can be used to impregnate cotton clothes and mosquito nets. If you are bitten, itching may be relieved by cool baths and antihistamine tablets (care with alcohol or driving), corticosteroid creams (great care – never use if any hint of sepsis) or by judicious scratching. Calamine lotion and cream have limited effectiveness and antihistamine creams have a tendency to cause skin allergies and are, therefore, not generally recommended. Bites which become infected (commonly in the tropics) should be treated with a local antiseptic or antibiotic cream such as Cetrimide as should infected scratches. Skin infestations with body lice, crabs and scabies are unfortunately easy to pick up. Use Gamma benzene hexachloride for lice and Benzyl benzoate for scabies. Crotamiton cream alleviates itching and also kills a number of skin parasites. Malathion lotion five percent is good for lice but avoid the highly toxic full strength Malathion used as an agricultural insecticide.

Sunburn & heat stroke

The burning power of the sun is phenomenal, especially at high altitude. Always wear a wide brimmed hat and use some form of sun cream or lotion on untanned skin. Normal temperate zone suntan lotions (protection factor up to seven) are not much good. You need to use the types designed specifically for the tropics or for mountaineers or skiers with a protection factor between seven and 15. Glare from the sun can cause conjunctivitis so wear sunglasses, especially near the snowline.

There are several varieties of 'heat stroke'. The most common cause is severe dehydration. Avoid dehydration by drinking lots of non-alcoholic fluid.

Athlete's foot

This and other fungal infections are best treated by sunshine and a proprietary preparation such as Tolnaftate.

Itchy rashes

A very common itchy rash is avoided by frequent washing and by wearing loose clothing. It is helped by the use of talcum powder to allow the skin to dry thoroughly after washing. It may be caused by bed bugs, lice etc which are commonly found in the bedding in truck stops.

Other risks and more serious diseases

Rabies

This is present in Tibet though less endemic than in other countries in the region such as India. If you are bitten by a domestic or wild animal, don't leave things to chance. Scrub the wound with soap and water/or disinfectant, try to have the animal captured (within limits) or at least determine its ownership where possible and seek medical assistance at once. The course of treatment depends on whether you have already been vaccinated against rabies. If you have (and this is worthwhile if you are spending lengths of time in developing countries) then some further doses of vaccine are all that is required. Human diploid cell vaccine is the best, but expensive: other, older kinds of vaccine such as that derived from duck embryos may be the only types available. These are effective, much cheaper and interchangeable generally with the human derived types. If not already vaccinated then anti-rabies serum

Water purification

There are a number of methods for purifying water in order to make it safe to drink. Dirty water should first be strained through a filter bag, and then boiled or treated. Bringing water to a rolling **boil** at sea level is sufficient to make water safe for drinking, but at higher altitudes you have to boil the water for longer to ensure that all the microbes are killed.

Various sterilizing methods can be used, and there are propriety preparations containing **chlorine** (eg `Puritabs') or **iodine** (eg `Pota Aqua') compounds. Chlorine compounds generally do not kill protozoa (eg giardia). Prolonged usage of iodine compounds may lead to thyroid problems, although this is rare if used for less than a year.

There are a number of **water filters** now on the market, available both in personal and expedition size. There are broadly two types of water filter, **mechanical** and **chemical**. Mechanical filters are usually a combination of carbon, ceramic and paper, although they can be difficult to use. Ceramic filters tend to last longer in terms of volume of water purified. The best brand is possibly the Swiss-made Katadyn. Although cheaper, the disadvantage of mechanical filters is that they do not always kill viruses or protozoa. Thus, if you are in an area where the presence of these is suspected, the water will have to be treated with iodine before being passed through the filter. When new, the filter will remove the taste, although this may not continue for long. However, ceramic filters will remove bacteria, and their manufacturers claim that since most viruses live on bacteria, the chances are that the viruses will be removed as well. This claim should be treated with scepticism.

Chemical filters usually use a combination of an iodine resin filter and a mechanical filter. The advantage of this system is that, according to the manufacturers' claims, everything in the water will be killed. The disadvantage is that the filters need replacing, adding a third to the price. Probably the best chemical filter is manufactured by Pur.

(immunoglobulin) may be required in addition. It is wise to finish the course of treatment whether the animal survives or not.

AIDS is not the huge problem that it is in India where it is increasing in its prevalence **AIDS** probably faster than in most countries with a pattern typical of developing societies. Generally in Asia it is not wholly confined to the well known high risk sections of the population, ie homosexual men, intravenous drug abusers, prostitutes and the children of infected mothers. Heterosexual transmission is now the dominant mode and so the main risk to travellers is from casual sex. The same precautions should be taken as when encountering any sexually transmitted disease. The AIDS virus (HIV) can be passed via unsterile needles which have been previously used to inject a HIV positive patient but the risk of this is very small indeed. It would, however, be sensible to check that needles have been properly sterilized or disposable needles used. The chance of picking up hepatitis B in this way is much more of a danger. Be wary of carrying disposable needles yourself; Customs officials may find them suspicious. The risk of receiving a blood transfusion with blood infected with the HIV virus is greater than from dirty needles because of the amount of fluid exchanged. Supplies of blood for transfusion are now largely screened for HIV in all reputable hospitals, so the risk must be very small indeed. Catching the AIDS virus does not necessarily produce an illness in itself; the only way to be sure if you feel you have been put at risk is to have a blood test for HIV antibodies on your return to a place where there are reliable laboratory facilities. The test does not become positive for many weeks.

Malaria is not prevalent in Tibet with the exception of subtropical border zones such **Malaria**

Essentials

as Pemako. Take advice from a Travel Clinic if you are likely to travel through India, Nepal, South Bhutan, Pakistan or China where you may be subject to some risk. It remains a serious disease and you are advised to protect yourself against mosquito bites as above and to take prophylactic (preventive) drugs.

Start taking the tablets a few days before exposure and continue to take them for six weeks after leaving the malarial zone. Remember to give the drugs to babies and children also. Opinion varies on the precise drugs and dosage to be used for protection. All the drugs may have some side effects and it is important to balance the risk of catching the disease against the albeit rare side effects.

The increasing complexity of the subject is such that as the malarial parasite becomes immune to the new generation of drugs it has made concentration on the physical prevention from being bitten by mosquitos more important. This involves the use of long sleeved shirts or blouses and long trousers, repellants and nets. Clothes are now available impregnated with the insecticide Permethrin or Deltamethrin, or it is possible to impregnate the clothes yourself. Wide meshed nets impregnated with Permethrin are also available, are lighter to carry and less claustrophobic to sleep in.

Prophylaxis and treatment

If your itinerary takes you into a malarial area, seek expert advice before you go on a suitable prophylactic regime. This is especially true for pregnant women who are particularly prone to catch malaria. You can still catch the disease even when sticking to a proper regime, although it is unlikely. If you do develop symptoms (high fever, shivering, headache, sometimes diarrhoea), seek medical advice immediately. If this is not possible and there is a great likelihood of malaria, the treatment is:

Chloroquine, a single dose of four tablets (600 mg) followed by two tablets (300 mg) in six hours and 300 mg each day following.

Falciparum type of malaria or type in doubt: take local advice. Various combinations of drugs are being used such as Quinine, Tetracycline or Halofantrine. If falciparum type of malaria is definitely diagnosed, it is wise to get to a good hospital as treatment can be complex and the illness very serious.

Infectious hepatitis (jaundice)

The main symptoms are pains in the stomach, lack of appetite, lassitude and yellowness of the eyes and skin. Medically speaking there are two main types. The less serious, but more common is Hepatitis A for which the best protection is the careful preparation of food, the avoidance of contaminated drinking water and scrupulous attention to toilet hygiene. The other, more serious, version is Hepatitis B which is acquired usually as a sexually transmitted disease or by blood transfusions. It can less commonly be transmitted by injections with unclean needles and possibly by insect bites. The symptoms are the same as for Hepatitis A. The incubation period is much longer (up to six months compared with six weeks) and there are more likely to be complications.

Hepatitis A can be protected against with gamma globulin. It should be obtained from a reputable source and is certainly useful for travellers who intend to live rough. You should have a shot before leaving and have it repeated every six months. The dose of gamma globulin depends on the concentration of the particular preparation used, so the manufacturer's advice should be taken. The injection should be given as close as possible to your departure and as the dose depends on the likely time you are to spend in potentially affected areas, the manufacturer's instructions should be followed.

Gamma globulin has really been superceded now by a proper vaccination against Hepatitis A (Havrix) which gives immunity lasting up to 10 years. After that boosters are required. Havrix monodose is now widely available as is Junior Havrix. The vaccination has negligible side effects and is extremely effective. Gamma globulin injections can be a bit painful, but it is much cheaper than Havrix and may be more available in some places.

Hepatitis B can be effectively prevented by a specific vaccine (Engerix) – three shots over six months before travelling. If you have had jaundice in the past it would be worthwhile having a blood test to see if you are immune to either of these two types, because this might avoid the necessity and costs of vaccination or gamma globulin. There are other kinds of viral hepatitis (C, E etc) which are fairly similar to A and B, but vaccines are not available as yet.

Snake bite If you are unlucky enough to be bitten by a venomous snake, spider, scorpion, or centipede attempt (within limits) to catch the animal for identification. The reactions to be expected are fright, swelling, pain and bruising around the bite, soreness of the regional lymph glands, nausea, vomiting and fever. If, in addition, any of the following symptoms supervene get the victim to a doctor without delay: numbness, tingling of the face, muscular spasm, convulsions, shortness of breath or haemorrhage. Commercial snake bite or scorpion sting kits may be available but are only useful for the specific type of snake or scorpion for which they are designed. The serum has to be given intravenously, so is not much good unless you have had some practice in making injections into veins. If the bite is on a limb, immobilize the limb and apply a tight bandage between the bite and the body, releasing it for 90 seconds every 15 minutes. Reassurance of the bitten person is very important because death from snake bite is, in fact, very rare. Do not slash the bite area and try to suck out the poison because this sort of heroism does more harm than good. Hospitals usually hold stocks of snake bite serum. Best precaution: do not walk in snake territory with bare feet, sandals or shorts.

Influenza This and respiratory diseases are common, perhaps made worse by polluted cities and rapid temperature, climatic changes and the proximity of the Tibetan plateau to China.

Returning home

Remember to take your anti-malaria tablets for six weeks if you have been travelling in endemic areas such as Nepal or South Bhutan. If you have had attacks of diarrhoea, it is worth having a stool specimen tested in case you have picked up amoebic dysentery. If you have been living rough, a blood test may be worthwhile to detect worms and other parasites.

Further reading

Guidebooks The present guidebook is the only comprehensive treatment of the Tibetan plateau, which includes Kham and Amdo, in addition to the Kathmandu Valley and Bhutan. For information on the Buddhist sites of Central and West Tibet, you might also refer to Stephen Batchelor's *The Tibet Guide* (Wisdom, 1987, updated 1997), and to Keith Dowman's *The Power Places of Central Tibet* (RKP, 1988) and The Sacred Life of Tibet (Thorsons, 1997). For trekking, the best sources are Victor Chen's *Tibet Handbook* (Moon Publications, 1994), and Gary McCue's *Trekking in Tibet (Cordee,* 1991).

History For a broad appraisal of Tibetan culture, refer to the classic works, RA Stein's *Tibetan Civilization* (Faber, 1972), Tsepon Shakabpa's *Tibet: A Political History* (Potala, 1984), Christopher Beckwith's *The Tibetan Empire in Central Asia* (Princeton, 1987), and Snellgrove & Richardson's *Cultural History of Tibet* (Weidenfeld and Nicholson, 1968). For recent history and the current Tibetan situation, see the present Dalai Lama's two biographies, *My Land and My People*, and *Freedom In Exile*; also Hugh Richardson's *Tibet and its History* (Shambhala, 1984), Melvyn Goldstein's *History of Modern Tibet*

1939-1959 (University of California Press, 1989), John Avedon's *In Exile from the Land of Snows* (Wisdom 1986), and Mary Craig's *Tears of Blood* (Harper Collins 1992).

Central, Western & Far-western Tibet
In addition to the aforementioned guidebooks, the following works provide useful background reading: G Tucci's *To Lhasa and Beyond* (Instituto Poligrafico dello Stato, 1956), Charles Bell's *Portrait of The Dalai Lama* (Collins, 1946), Heinrich Harrer's *Seven Years in Tibet* (Rupert Hart-Davis, 1953), Goldstein & Bell's *Nomads of Western Tibet*, John Snelling's *The Sacred Mountain* and Roberto Vitali's *The Kingdoms of Gu-ge Pu-hrang.*

Eastern & Far-eastern Tibet
There are fewer useful sources on East and Far-east Tibet. The best are Eric Teichman's *Travels of a Consular Official in Eastern Tibet* (Cambridge University Press, 1922), Andre Migot's *Tibetan Marches* (Penguin, 1957), Chogyam Trungpa's *Born in Tibet* (Unwin, 1979), Gallen Rowell's *Mountains of the Middle Kingdom*, Joseph Rock's *The Amnye Machen and Adjacent Regions* (SOR, 1956), Frank Kingdon Ward's *Mystery Rivers of Tibet* (Cadogan, 1986), Jacques Bacot's *Le Tibet Revolte* (Hachette, 1912), Warren Smith's *A History of Tibetan Nationalism and Sino-Tibetan Relatations*, Steven Marshall and Susette Cooke *Tibet outside the TAR* (CD Rom) and for light relief Marie de Poncheville's *Sept Femmes au Tibet* (Albin Michel, 1990).

Religion
For a general understanding of Mahayana Buddhism and its Tibetan context, see Tucci's *The Religions of Tibet* (Berkeley, 1980), Paul Williams' *Mahayana Buddhism* (RKP, 1989), Tulku Thondup's *Buddhist Civilization in Tibet* (RKP, 1987), Paltrul Rinpoche's (transl) *The Words of My Perfect Teacher* (Harper Collins, 1994), David Snellgrove's *Indo-Tibetan Buddhism* (Serindia, 1987), and John Powers' *Introduction to Tibetan Buddhism* (Snowlion, 1995). For detailed information on the different schools of Tibetan Buddhism, see Dudjom Rinpoche (Trans Dorje and Kapstein), *The Nyingma School of Tibetan Buddhism*, and M Ricard (trans), *The Life of Shabkar* (Suny, 1994). On the Kagyupa tradition, see Lobzang Lhalungpa's translation of *The Life of Milarepa* (Dutton, 1977), Karma Thinley's *The Sixteen Karmapas* (Shambhala, 1978), and Douglas and White's *Karmapa: the Black Hat Lama of Tibet* (Luzac, 1976); and on the Sakyapa school, *The History of the Sakya School* (Ganesha, 1983). For a detailed study of the Gelukpa school, see J Willis, *Enlightened Beings: Life Stories from the Ganden Tradition* (Wisdom, 1995), and Pabongka Rinpoche (transl), *Liberation in the Palm of Your Hand* (Wisdom, 1991). Lastly, on the pre-Buddhist Bon tradition, see Samten Karmay's *The Treasury of Good Sayings: a Tibetan History of Bon* (OUP, 1972), and Per Kvaerne's *The Bon Religion of Tibet* (Serindia, 1995).

Tibetan language & medicine
For the modern Tibetan language, the best works are Kalzang Gyurme's *Le Clair Miroir* (translated into French from Tibetan by Nicholas Tournade and Heather Stoddard), and Stephan Beyer's *The Classical Tibetan Language*, while on the medical tradition, see Parfianivitch, Dorje and Mayer (eds), *Tibetan Medical Paintings* (Serindia, 1993).

Maps
The best English language maps available in Tibet are the *China Tibet Tour Map*, published by the Mapping Bureau of the TAR in 1993; the *Map of Mountain Peaks on the Qinghai-Xizang Plateau*, published by the China Cartographic Publishing House in 1989; and the *Lhasa City Map*, published by Amnye Machen Institute in 1995. The *Tibetan Language Map of the Ngawa Autonomous Prefecture*, published in Sichuan, is detailed, but accessible only to Tibetan readers as is the large series of Tibetan language maps of TAR. Some Chinese maps are also useful, especially the detailed *China Road Atlas*, which provides distances between points on all motorable roads.

Among maps of Tibet published in the West, those prepared by Michael Farmer, and published in *The Nyingma School of Tibetan Buddhism* (Wisdom, 1991) have extremely accurate topographical features, and clearly contrast the river systems with a subtle use of contour shading. The maps published in Switzerland by Peter Kessler are important for their contribution to traditional Tibetan toponymics. Other maps published in the United States include the *Operational Navigational Charts* (ONC) and the *Joint Operations Graphic Series* (JOG), the latter being reproduced in Victor Chen's *Tibet Handbook*. These and others are available at Stanford's Map Centre, 12-14 Long Acre, London WC2E 9LP (T0171-8361321).

Useful addresses

Domestic tours & tour operators

The main domestic travel agencies are listed under their respective cities, especially Lhasa, Kunming, Chengdu, Ziling, and Lanzhou. Among these the best are:

Lhasa:
Windhorse Adventure Travel (WHAT), *Lhasa Hotel*, Room 1120, T6836793, 6832432, 6832221 x 1120, F0086-8916836793, Tx68012 TTB CN. *Tibet International Sports Travel* (TIST), *Himalaya Hotel*, 6 E Lingkor lam, T6331421, F0086-8916334855. *Tibet Tourist Corporation* (TTC) – also known as China International Travel Service, Lhasa Branch (CITS), West Dekyi lam, T6836626/6835046, F00-86-8916836315/6835277; and *China Workers' Travel Service* (CWTS): Tibet Branch, Holiday Inn Lhasa, Room 1104, T6824250, 6832221 ext 1104, F0086-8916334472, Tx69025 WTBL CN.

Chengdu:
Trans Himalaya, Chengdu (CTH), 97 Xida Jie, Chengdu, T/F00-8628-6248977. *Golden Bridge Travel Service* (CGBTS), 38 Jia Hua Yuan Rd, Chengdu, T7730708, F0086-28-7730728. *China International Travel Service, Chengdu* (CCITS), 65 Renminnan Lu (Section 2), Chengdu 610021, T6672602, F00-8628-6672970; and *Tibet Foreign Trade Travel Service, Chengdu Office*, Room 307, 72 Shuanglin Rd, Chengdu, T4337891, F0086-284313632.

Kunming:
Yunnan Overseas Travel Corporation, 154 E Dongfeng Rd, Kunming, T3188905, F0086-8713132508. *Yunnan Exploration and Amusement Travel*, 1/F Building B (North Section), 73 Renmin West Rd, Kunming, T5312283, F0086-8715312324.

Lanzhou:
CITS, Lanzhou Branch, 361 Tianshui Ave, Lanzhou, T8826181, 8861333, F0086-9318418556; Gangu Silk Road Travel, 361 Tianshui Ave, Lanzhou, T8414498, F0086-931-8418457.

Ziling:
CITS, Xiling Branch, 156 Huanghe Rd, Ziling, T6131081, F0086-9716131080.

International tour operators

Summit Trekking   Nepal
Kopundol Height, Lalitpur, PO Box 1406, Kathmandu, T977-1521894, F977-1523737.

Arniko Travel
PO Box 4695, Naxal, Nagpokhari, Kathmandu, T977-1412667, F977-1521880.

Himalayan Journeys
PO Box 969, Kantipat, Kathmandu, T977-1226138, F977-1227068.

Essentials

Essentials

Kailash Himalaya Trek
PO Box 4781, Bagbazar, Kathmandu,
T977-1229249, F977-1223171.

Adventure Travel Nepal Ltd
PO Box 272, Lazimpath, Kathmandu,
T977-1415995/223328, F977-1414075/
419126.

Tibet Travels and Tours Pvt Ltd
PO Box 1397, Thamel, Kathmandu, T977-
1410303, F977-1415126.

*Kathmandu-Lhasa Tours and
Travels Pvt Ltd*
PO Box 9179, Jyatha, Thamel,
Kathmandu, T977-1231060,
F977-1240220.

*China Tibet Qomolangma
Travelways Ltd*
PO Box 1147, Lal Durbar Marg,
Kathmandu, T977-1410411,
F977-1419778.

Hong Kong *China Tibet Qomolangma
Travelways Ltd*
37/F Times Tower, 393 Jaffe Rd,
T852-28383391, F852-28341535.

Abercrombie & Kent
27/F Tai Sang Commercial Building,
24-34 Hennessy Rd, Wanchai,
T852-28657818, F852-28660556.

Mera Travel
Room 1308 Argyll Centre Phase I, 688
Nathan Rd, T852-23916892, F852-
27891649.

China Travel Service
Kowloon Branch, 1/F Alpha House, 27-33
Nathan Rd, T852-7214481, F7216251.

UK *Trans Himalaya*
54 Croscombe Gardens, Frome, Somerset,
BA11 2YF, T44-1373-455518, F44-1371-
455594, E gd@trans-himalaya.demon.co.
uk, www.trans-himalaya.ndirect.co.uk,
have the most specialized itineraries in
East Tibet and Central Tibet, as well as
short budget tours.

Bales Tours
Bales House, Barrington Rd, Dorking RH4 3EJ, T44-1306885991.

Encounter Overland
267 Old Brompton Rd, London SW5 9JA, T44-1713731433, F44-1713706951.

Occidor Adventure Tours
10 Broomcroft Rd, Bognor Regis, West Sussex PO22 7NB, T01243-582178, F44-1243587239.

Himalayan Kingdoms
20 The Mall, Clifton, Bristol, BS8 4DR, T44-1179237163.

Himalayan Kingdoms Expeditions
45 Mowbray St, Sheffield S3 8CN, T44-114276 3322, F44-1142763344.

Snow Lion Expeditions   USA
Oquirrh Place, 350 South 400 East, Suite G2, Salt Lake City, UT 84111, USA, Reservations: T1-800-525-TREK.

EastQuest
1 Union Square West, New York, NY 10003, T (212) 741-1688, (800) 638-3449, F (212) 741-1786.

Geographic Expeditions
2627 Lombard St, San Francisco, CA 94123, T415-9220448, F415-3465535.

Wilderness Travel
801 Allston Way, Berkeley, Ca 94710, T415-5480420.

Mountain Travel
6420 Fairmount Ave, El Cerrito, CA 94530, T415-5278100.

Distant Horizons
619 Tremont St, Boston, MA 02118, T617-2675343, F617-2670323.

Tibetan Cultural Organizations

Tibet Information Service, PO Box 87, Ivanhoe, Victoria, 3079, T03-6634484   Australia

Canada   *Canada-Tibet Friendship Society*, PO Box 6588, Postal Section A, Toronto, Ontario, M5W 1X4, T0416-5313810

France   *Shalu Association for Tibetan Cultural Heritage*, 127 rue de Sevres, Paris 75006, T331-45679503

India   The most important offices are the *Library of Tibetan Works and Archives*, Gangchen Kyishong, Dharamsala, HP 176215, T01892-2467

  Information Office of the Tibetan Government in Exile, Gangchen Kyishong, Dharamsala, HP, 176215, T01892-2457/2598

  Tibet House, 1 Institutional Area, Lodhi Rd, New Delhi 110003, T611515

Japan   *Tibetan Cultural Centre of Japan*, 2-31-22, Nerima, Nerima-ku, Tokyo, T03-39915411

Nepal   *Office of Tibet*, PO Box 310 Lazimpat, Kathmandu, T11660

UK   *Tibet House*, 1 Culworth St, London NW8 7AF, T0171-7225378

  Tibet Foundation, 10 Bloomsbury Way, London WC1A 2SH, T0171-4042889, E getza@gn.apc.org

  Tibet Information Network, 7 Beck Rd, London E8 4RE, T0181-5335458

  The Orient Foundation, Queene Anne House, 11 Charlotte St, Bath, BA1 2NE (T01225-336010).

  Appropriate Technology for Tibetans, 117 Cricklewood Broadway, London, NW2 3JG (T0181 450-8090, F0181 450-9705).

USA   *Tibet House*, 3/F 241 E 32nd St, New York, NY 10016, T0212-2135392

  Tibetan Cultural Centre, 3655 South Snoddy Rd, Bloomington, Indiana 47401, T0812-8558222

  Monasteries in Tibet Fund, 256 S Robertson Blvd, Suite 9379, Beverley Hills, CA 98211

  Kham Aid Project, 619 South Olive St, Suite 204, Los Angeles, CA 90014, T0213 489-7688, F 0213 489-7686

  Trace Foundation, 31 Perry Street, New York City, NY 10014, T0212 367-7380, F 0212 367-7383.

Lhasa ལྷ་ས་

3

Lhasa

ལྷ་ས

*The holy city of Lhasa (Ch Lasa Shiqu) is the historic
capital of Tibet, situated on the north bank of the
Kyi-chu River, where the valley opens out to its fullest
extent. To the north of the city lies an impenetrable
5,200 metres range, extending from Mount Gephel Utse
(above Drepung in the west) to Mount Dukri Tse
(above Pawangka) and Mount Sera Utse (above Sera in
the east). To the south, on the far bank of the river, is the
Chakyak Karpo range. Smaller hills are located within
the valley: the most prominent being Marpori ('Red
Mountain') on which the Potala Palace is constructed,
Chakpori (where Tibet's medical college and temples
once stood, now dominated by a radio mast), and
Bonpori (surmounted by a Chinese temple dedicated to
Ling Gesar). The Kyi-chu River at Lhasa meanders past
several island sandbanks, among which Kumalingka
('Thieves' Island'), the best known and an adjacent
island are now the site of an extensive housing
development scheme in neo Sino-Tibetan architectural
style. The principal tributaries of the valley, ie those of
Dongkar, Lhalu, Nyangdren and Dokde, have all been
integrated into the Chera irrigation system.*
Recommended itineraries: 1, 3 (also 4-7).

Ins and outs

Getting there   The Lhasa valley extends from the Dongkar intersection, near the confluence of the Tolung River with the Kyi-chu at its western extremity, as far as Ngachen and the hill top ruins of Dechen Dzong, which overlooks the roads to Yerpa and Ganden in the extreme east. Access is by road from the southwest (Gongkar Airport, Zhigatse, Gyantse, Tsetang), from the north (Ziling, Damzhung, Yangpachen), and from the east (Chamdo, Kongpo and Meldro Gangkar). Gongkar Airport is 96 km southeast from Lhasa.

Getting around   Most visitors to Lhasa, whether arriving by air or land, will have their transportation organized by the travel services. Public buses running throughout the city charge only ¥2 for daytime travel and ¥3 for night-time travel. For bus routes, see transport page 129. Taxis (minimum fare ¥10) and cycle rickshaws (average fare ¥5) also widely available, and it is always possible to hire a bicycle. For longer drives, private vehicle hire with a driver is possible. Contact any of the local travel agencies, or the **Taxi Stand**, adjacent to the Moonlight Disco on Do Senge lam; or the **District Car Rental Company**, on West Lingkhor lam.

History of Lhasa

Population: 160,000
Altitude: 3,490m
Phone code: (86)-891
Area: 664 sq km
Temperature:
January: maximum 10°,
minimum -8°,
July: maximum 25°,
minimum 10°.
Oxygen 68%.
Annual precipitation
1,462 mm, of which
90% falls in summer
and early autumn
(July/September)
Colour map 3, grid B3

Most buildings of Lhasa may conveniently be assigned to one of three distinct phases of construction (although older sites have undergone extensive renovations in subsequent centuries). The earliest phase coincides with the construction of the Jokhang and Ramoche temples along with the first Potala Palace during the seventh century; the middle phase with the building of the great Gelukpa monasteries, the new Potala Palace and Norbulingka Palace during the 15th-18th centuries; and the third phase with the recent expansion of the city under Chinese rule.

Neolithic potsherds and implements of bone and stone which were excavated at Chogong near Sera in 1984 suggest that the Lhasa valley was a place of human habitation thousands of years before Songtsen Gampo unified Tibet and established his capital there. However, it was in the sixth century that Songtsen Gampo's grandfather, Takri Nyenzik, gained control over most of

Early history   the 12 petty kingdoms into which Tibet had been divided. He did so by overthrowing his own brother-in-law, Tri Pangsum of Phenyul, who had usurped power from Takyawo of Nyenkar (Meldro) and tyrannized the clans of the Upper Kyi-chu valley (those of Wa, Nyang, Non and Tsepong). Takri's son, Namri Songtsen, later succeeded to the throne and gained complete control over the Kyi-chu valley, thereby establishing the framework of the Tibetan Empire; and it was the latter's son, Songtsen Gampo, who became the first king of unified Tibet. He subjugated the ancient kingdom of Zhangzhung in the west, and then moved his capital from Chingwa Taktse in Chongye to Rasa, founding the first **Potala Palace** on Mount Marpori in 637, and the Rasa Trulnang (ie Jokhang) temple in 641. Following the construction of the Jokhang temple, the original name of the city, Rasa, was altered to Lhasa or Lhaden (see below, page 78).

King Songtsen Gampo's building activities were influenced by his Buddhist consorts: in his early years, the Newar queen Bhrkuti had the **Jokhang** temple constructed at the centre of a geomantically important network of temples around the country (see below, page 78). In his later years, the Chinese queen Wencheng constructed the **Ramoche** temple; and his Tibetan queen Monza Tricham founded the temple at **Dra Yerpa**, north of the city. Other significant constructions from that period included the nine storey **Pawangka tower/hermitage**; and the temples of **Meru Nyingba**, **Tsamkhung**, and **Drak Lhaluphuk**. Lhasa flourished as the capital of the Tibetan Empire until the assassination of King Relpachen by Langdarma in the ninth century resulted in the fragmentation of the country, and the desecration of the sacred sites.

The next major period of development began in 1409 when Tsongkhapa instituted the Great Prayer Festival at the Jokhang temple, and the three great monasteries of the Lhasa region were founded: **Ganden** in 1409, **Drepung** in 1416, and **Sera** in 1419. The Jokhang temple was also renovated and augmented during this period through the patronage of the kings of the Phakmodru Dynasty. Eventually, in 1642, Lhasa was restored as the capital of Tibet, following the defeat of the armies of the king of Tsang by the Mongol forces of Gushi Qan. With the latter's assistance, Dalai Lama V established a theocratic form of government (*chosi nyiden*) which endured until the occupation of Tibet by Communist forces in 1951. The four regency temples of Lhasa developed during this period; but above all, to symbolize the enhanced status of Lhasa, Dalai Lama V rebuilt the 13-storey **Potala Palace**. Later, in the 18th century Dalai Lama VII began the construction of the summer palace complex at **Norbulingka**.

15-18th century

Until recent decades, there were only three principal routes around Lhasa, followed by pilgrims and traders alike: the **Nangkhor** (inner circuit) around the Jokhang temple, the **Barkhor** (intermediate circuit) with its prolific market stalls, and the **Lingkhor** (outer circuit) which skirted the entire city including the Potala Palace. Pilgrims and traders alike would move around the holy city on these circuits, invariably in a clockwise direction. The great religious sites of the city were thus the focal points of attraction: Jokhang temple surrounded by its Barkhor shrines, Ramoche and Chakpori, the Potala and Norbulingka palaces, and the outlying monasteries of Drepung, Nechung, Sera and Pawang-ka. Residential parts of the city and its suburbs also had their distinct names: Rabsel, Hawaling and Telpung-gang to the south and southwest of the Barkhor; Tromzigang, Kyire and Banak Zhol to the north of the Barkhor; Zhol village, nestling below the Potala, Denpak to the northwest of the city, Lhalu, Pelding, and Nyangdreng to the north, Dokde and Tsangrel to the northeast, Ngachen and Changdrong to the east, and so forth. A number of the modern roads have been named after these places, which by-and-large survive, although the village of Zhol has now been relocated in apartment blocks behind the Potala at Lhalu.

The third and most recent phase of construction in Lhasa has been carried out under the Chinese occupation, during which the city has been subjected to grotesque expansion and transformation, its noble buildings obscured by the nondescript concrete tower blocks characteristic of many present day Chinese cities. Lhasa currently functions as the capital not of the whole of Tibet, but of the Tibetan Autonomous Region (*Ch* Xizang Zizhiqu). As such it is responsible for the administration of seven districts: Lhasa, which has seven counties under its jurisdiction; Lhokha, which has 12 counties; Nyangtri, which has seven counties, Zhigatse, which has 18 counties; Ngari, which has seven counties; Nakchu, which has 12 counties; and Chamdo, which has 14 counties (taking recent administrative changes into account).

Modern Lhasa

Most of the new buildings constructed in Lhasa reflect a cumbersome two tier or three tier bureaucracy, in that government departments of the TAR, Lhasa District, and Lhasa Municipality have their separate offices dispersed throughout the city. However unwelcome this development may be, it cannot be ignored, and, indeed, it is with reference to the plan of contemporary Lhasa, rather than the traditional pilgrimage circuits, that the visitor will make his or her way to the ancient and medieval sites of historic importance, described in the following pages.

Finding your way around

Most visitors will approach Lhasa from the southwest or north, whether driving the short distance from Gongkar Airport, or the longer overland routes from Nepal via Zhigatse and from Ziling via Kermo and Nakchu. These approach roads converge to the west of the city at Dongkar. Just to the west of Dongkar, the valley begins to open out into a wide plain and the Potala Palace is visible from afar. A large military HQ has recently been constructed near the intersection, where an important petrol station complex and the *Dongkar Restaurant* are also located. From Dongkar two roads lead into town: the main paved route, Chingdrol lam (*Ch* Jiefang lu; also known as Tsang-gyu lam) follows the river bank upstream all the way to the east end of the city, and a dirt road extension of Dekyi lam (*Ch* Beijing lu) skirts the Lhasa Cement Factory (*Ch* Sunyitrang) to enter the city through the defile between Chakpori and Marpori hills, which formerly marked the true gateway to the city.

Chingdrol lam Chingdrol lam, which also functions as a provisional ring road, passes through one of the most rapidly developing parts of the city, favoured by the influx of Chinese immigrants who have established their small businesses (shops,

Lhasa Surroundings

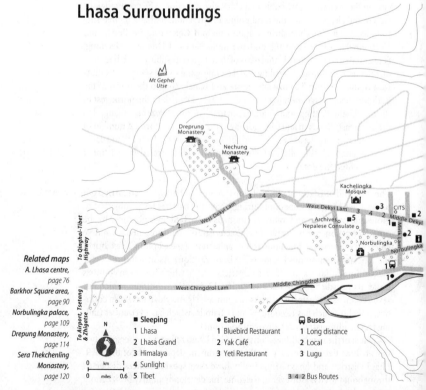

- **Sleeping**
  1 Lhasa
  2 Lhasa Grand
  3 Himalaya
  4 Sunlight
  5 Tibet

- **Eating**
  1 Bluebird Restaurant
  2 Yak Café
  3 Yeti Restaurant

- **Buses**
  1 Long distance
  2 Local
  3 Lugu

  3 4 2 Bus Routes

restaurants, and karaoke bars) to service the army, which occupies much of the land in this sector of the city. The road is divided into West Chingdrol lam (Chingdrol Nub lam), Middle Chingdrol lam (Chingdrol Bar lam), and East Chingdrol lam (Chingdrol Shar lam).

Starting from **Dongkar**, you pass to the north side of **West Chingdrol lam**, an engineering and machinery institute, and a large military complex including within it warehouses, carpentry workshops, small farms, the Chinese Martyrs' Cemetery, Middle School Number Nine, the College of Agriculture and Animal Husbandry, and the Military Publications Office. Looking further north you will see the palls of smoke rising above the yellow buildings of the Lhasa Cement Factory, and behind them, like a cluster of brilliant white grains of rice on the hillside of Gephel Utse, the buildings of **Drepung Monastery**. On the south side of West Chingdrol lam, towards the river, you will pass in succession the leather factory, the local police station, the post office warehouse, the freight depot, the Kawachen Carpet Factory, the Gang-gyen Development Company, and the Hospital for Skin Diseases.

Continuing on to **Middle Chingdrol lam**, you pass on the north side the TAR Agricultural Machinery Company, the TAR schools of banking, hygene, and finance, and the Long Distance Bus Station. A memorial dedicated to the workers who died in the construction of the Ziling-Lhasa highway stands opposite the junction with Mirik lam (*Ch* Minzu lu), on which the Norbulingka Palace and *Lhasa Hotel* are located (see below, page 108). Just to the west of this monument is the *Bluebird Restaurant*, serving the best Sichuan hot-pot in Lhasa. Ahead at this point you will observe the radio and television mast on the summit of Mount Chakpori, where Lhasa's medical colleges and temples once stood. Continuing eastwards on Middle Chingdrol lam, you will pass to the north the Armed Police HQ and the TAR Government Offices, while to the south new motorable concrete bridges now replace the ancient colourful prayer-flag strewn bridge to **Kumalingka** ('Thieves' Island') and the adjacent islands which have been transformed from their status as derelict sandbanks into neat rows of Sino-Tibetan prefabs, reputedly designated for private housing.

After the intersection with Kharngadong lam, which leads towards the Potala Palace and has a number of fashionable restaurants and nightclubs, you continue on to **East Chingdrol lam**, passing in succession to the south: the *Gesar Hotel*, the PLA Tibet Area Military Command, the Women and Childrens' Hospital, the Bank of China Lhasa Branch, the Sports Stadium, and the *Minorities Hotel*. To the north you pass the *Shangrila Tibetan*

Restaurant, the *Shambhala Guesthouse*, the Tibetan Medical School and Middle School Number Eight; and (after the Do Senge lam turn-off leading to the Hospital of Traditional Medicine and the Jokhang temple), you pass the Lugu Bus Station, the Peoples' Art Museum, the *Kadak Hotel*, and the Boot Factory. At this point East Lingkhor lam bisects the road. If, at this crossroads, you continue on East Chingdrol lam, you will pass on the north side the Lhasa Municipality Government Buildings, and on the south side a cinema. Then, continuing on East Chindrol lam after the Lingyu lam intersection, which leads north to the *Sunlight Hotel*, and south to an upmarket red-light district and the Lhasa District Communist Party Headquarters, you will pass on the south the Tibet University campus and the Carpet Factory. From this point the road forms a T-junction with East Zamchen lam, leading northwest into town or southeast across the **Lhasa Zamchen Bridge** towards the Upper Kyi-chu valley and Kongpo.

Dekyi lam   Taking the unpaved road into Lhasa from Dongkar, you follow a more traditional route, along Dekyi lam (*Ch* Beijing lu) which also stretches the entire length of the city and is divided into West, Middle and East sections. On **West Dekyi lam** (*Tib* Dekyi nub lam), you pass to the south the factories and residential compounds of the Lhasa Cement Factory (*Ch* Sunyitrang), and the Mineral Research Laboratory. Thereafter, passing through Denpak village, you will observe, on the hillside immediately above, **Drepung Monastery** and **Nechung Monastery** (see below, page 118). Then, to the north of the road you will pass the Lhasa City Engineering and Construction Unit and the TAR Road Transport Maintenance Head Office; while to the south is the TAR Customs Office, a green painted building with a clock-tower, marking the place where Dekyi lam is intersected by lanes leading north (to Pari Zimkhang, the TAR Communist Party School and the erstwhile *TAR Tourism Bureau and guesthouse*) and south (to the Import-Export Control Bureau, the Historical Archives of TAR, the Animal and Plant Inspection Department, and Chingdrol lam).

Continuing east on **Middle Dekyi lam** (Dekyi Bar lam) you pass to the north: the TAR Hygene Head Office, the TAR Opera Troupe, the TAR Finance Head Office, the Muslim Cemetery Kache Lingka, behind which the new Northern Ring-road is under construction, the China Building Bank, the School of Performing Arts, the TAR Civil Administration Buildings, the TAR Scientific Association, the Tibet Tourism Corporation Offices, the Windhorse Adventure Travel Company Office, the TAR Road Planning Office, and the TAR Petroleum Company. To the south you will pass: the TAR Statistics Department, the TAR Insurance Offices, the *Tibet Hotel*, the Xinhua Bookshop, the Workers' Convalescent Home, the Lhokha District Office, and *Lhasa Hotel*. In this section of the road, there are also many small Tibetan and Chinese restaurants geared to the tourist market and Tibetan state employees (in contrast to those on Chingdrol lam which largely service the army).

Turning right on to **Mirik lam** (*Ch* Minzu lu) which connects Dekyi lam with Chingdrol lam, you will pass on the east the TAR Peoples' Conference Hall and Theatre, the Golden Bridge Travel Office, and the TAR Motor Parts Fitting Company; while to the west is the main entrance to the *Lhasa Hotel*, a side road leading to the Royal Nepalese Consulate and the Yarlung Travel Service, the entrance to **Norbulingka Palace**, the TAR Cultural Relics Association, the TAR Workers' No 2 Hospital, and the Long Distance Bus Station.

A road known as **Norbulingka lam** or **West Lingkhor lam** leads from the entrance of Norbulingka Palace towards Chakpori Hill and intersects with Middle Dekyi lam at a large roundabout dominated by two grotesquely sculpted golden yaks, before continuing into Lhalu and North Lhasa. On the north side of this road, you will pass **Kundeling Monastery**, and the *Transport Office Guesthouse*, while to the south you pass the old Television and Radio Broadcasting Offices, the Ling Gesar temple on Bonpori Hill, and the **Trak Lhaluphuk** temple complex on Chakpori Hill. The extension of West Lingkhor lam into Lhalu and North Lhasa is described below (see page 75).

Continuing east on **Middle Dekyi lam** from the Mirik lam intersection, you pass on the north side the *Lhasa Grand Hotel*, the local Dekyi lam police station, the Electrical Studies Centre, the new TAR Telecommunication Tower Building, a fashionable seafood restaurant, and the Foreign Trade Company, adjacent to the Golden Yak Roundabout. On the south side, you will pass the TAR High Court, the TAR Mapping and Survey Department, several restaurants, and the Lhasa Petrol Station.

After the roundabout, **East Dekyi lam** (Dekyi Shar lam) begins, passing through the defile between Chakpori and Marpori Hills, where a reconstructed stupa gateway (Drago Kani) once more dominates the approach to the city. The road here opens out on to the vast and newly constructed **Zhol Square**. On the north side of the square you will see in succession the newly constructed TAR Television and Radio Station, the lingkhor circuit around the Potala Palace, a Mobil Oil gas station, behind which is an upmarket Tibetan restaurant, and the entrance to the renowned **Potala Palace** itself, with the 15th century Zhamarpa Palace in the foreground. To the south, is the enclosed **Zhol Doring** (see below, page 89), and the open expanse of Zhol Square (formerly the Cultural Palace Park).

At this point, crossing **Kharngadong lam** (which leads northwards to the *Airline Hotel* and the vegetable market and southwards to the TAR government offices, Kodak and Fuji photographic stores, and the Lhasa Fire Brigade), you pass on the north side, the Lhasa Post Office. Then (after the Nyangdren lam T-junction which leads to the CAAC Airline Office), you will pass the TAR Seismology Head Office, a children's play centre, and the Do-senge lam intersection, which leads north to the TAR newspaper offices and south to Primary School No 1, a large supermarket, the city taxi stand, discotheque, and local bus station. Continuing on East Dekyi lam, to the north you will pass the *Yak Hotel*, the Ramoche lam turn-off leading to **Ramoche Temple** (see below, page 92), and the Peoples' Court. On the south side, you will pass the Residential Unit for Tibetan Overseas Compatriots, the *Kyichu Hotel* and the Mentsikhang lam turn-off, which leads to the *Pentoc Guesthouse*, the *Tashi Dagye Hotel*, the *Snowlands Hotel* and the Hospital of Traditional Medicine (Mentsikhang). Continuing along East Dekyi lam, you will pass on the south side the Tromzikhang Market, the *Kyire Hotel*, the *Gang-gyen Hotel*, and the *Banak Zhol Hotel*. After the East Lingkhor lam intersection, which leads south to the Public Security Bureau and East Chingdrol lam, the road then passes to the north the Peoples' City Hospital, and then forms a T-junction with Lingyu lam, before connecting with East Zamchen lam, and heading northwest into town or southeast towards the bridge.

Named after the traditional pilgrimage circuit around the city of Lhasa, this **Lingkhor lam** motor route is still frequented by devotees who come from all parts of Tibet to circumambulate the holy city. There are three sections: West Lingkhor lam, extending northeast from the Golden Yak Roundabout towards Lhalu; North Lingkhor lam, extending due east behind the Potala Palace and Lukhang Temple, as far as the Mongolian Horseman Roundabout and the *Plateau Hotel* intersection; and East Lingkhor lam, extending due south from the latter to the riverside. On **West Lingkhor**, after passing the Foreign Trade Office on the left, you pass the main Lhasa branch of the Bank of China, the Lhalu Middle School, China Agricultural Bank, and the District Car Rental Company; and on the right, overshadowed by the Potala Palace, the side entrance to the TAR Television and Broadcasting Head Office.

Turning onto **North Lingkhor lam** (also known as Dzuktrun lam), you then pass on the left side of the road, the TAR Political Affairs Head Office, the TAR United Front Work Division, the Peoples' Publishing House Bookstore, and (after the Nyangdren lam intersection) the TAR Architectural Survey and Design Institute, the TAR Geology and Mineral Head Office, the TAR Office of Foreign Affairs, Lhasa City Police Head Office, the Gang-gyen Store, the *Ying Qiao Hotel*, the Silver Bridge Travel Company, and the *Plateau Hotel* (Gao Yuan). On the south side, you will pass the north face of the Potala Palace, the **Lukhang Temple** and its surrounding park, and (after the Nyangdren lam intersection) the Peoples' Hospital (Mimang Menkhang), the Ramoche lam turn-off which leads to Ramoche Temple (see below, page 92), and the TAR Meteorological Bureau, and the Telecommunications Building.

Lastly, **East Langkhor lam** passes the Lhasa City Communist Party Headquarters, lawcourts, and public security buildings, and (after the Dekyi lam intersection), the *Banak Zhol Gonkhang*, the TAR Public Security Bureau, the approach to the mosque Gyel Lhakhang, and the Boot Factory. After the Chingdrol lam intersection, it passes to the west a large supermarket, Middle School Number One, and the lane leading to the *Post and Telecommunication Hotel*, while to the east are the TAR Mountaineering Institute, the *Himalaya Hotel* and the *Xue Lian Hotel*.

Yutok lam & the Barkhor radial roads of Central Lhasa

From the entrance to the Cultural Palace and the TAR Government Buildings, **Yutok lam** (also called Mimang lam) leads eastwards to the gates of the Jo-khang, Tibet's holiest shrine and the true centre of Lhasa. On the south side of this approach road, are the *Xinhua Bookstore*, the public baths, a large department store, and the restored 18th century Yutok bridge. On the corresponding north side are the *TAR Guesthouse Number One* and the *Sernye (Gold Grain) Hotel*. After the Do Senge lam intersection, the *Lhasa City Cinema* is located on the south side along with the *Friendship Store*, while the *Moonlight Discotheque*, the taxi stand, the local bus station, and the **Hospital of Traditional Medicine** (Mentsikhang) are all on the north side. It is from this point onwards, as the Jokhang is approached from the west, that the radial road network of ancient Lhasa begins. Although the replacement of traditional buildings has greatly diminished the appeal and warmth of the narrow lanes and gulleys around which Lhasa citizens lived their lives for centuries, the structure of the road network remains unchanged, except on the west side where the Jokhang plaza was constructed in the 1960-70 period. Four large prayer-flags are situated within the Barkhor ('intermediate circuit') market which surrounds the Jokhang, known respectively as **Ganden Darchen** in the northeast, **Juyag Darchen** in the west, **Kelzang Darchen** in the southwest, and **Sharkyaring Darchen** in the southeast. Working clockwise from the west side, there is a northern lane, called **Mentsikhang lam**, due east of the Hospital of Traditional Medicine, which leads to East Dekyi lam and is known for its hotels (*Snowlands, Pentoc* and *Tashi Dagye*), its restaurants (*Snowlands, Tashi, Barkhor,* and others), and its tea houses. The regency temple **Tengye Ling** is approached via an alley behind the hospital. A second road runs northeast from the plaza towards the **Tromzikhang** market via the butter and meat markets, also giving access to East Dekyi lam. Having entered upon the Barkhor circuit, the third road extends southeast from the northeast corner. The fourth road, known as **Waling lam** (or Dunsisung lam), leads southeast from the

Prayer Flags

In Tibet, any prominent place exposed to the wind may be adorned with multicoloured prayer flags (darchok), permitting the natural power of the wind to distribute the blessings of their inscribed prayers as they flap to and fro, for which reason they are known also as `horses of the wind' (lungta). Domestic rooftops and monastery compounds often have large poles to which these flags are attached, and renewed annually on the 3rd day after the Tibetan New Year. Similarly, most mountain passes (la-tse) are marked by cairns of stones (some inscribed with mantras), to which sets of prayer-flags are attached. Wherever public buses or private jeeps cross over a major pass, the passengers will invariably disembark to add a stone to the cairn, or tie a newly prepared set of prayer flags and burn incense as an offering to the spirit of the mountain, who would have been tamed and appointed protector of

Buddhism by Padmasambhava back in the 8th century. Some will cast paper prayer-flags into the air from the bus window, rejoicing loudly in the ancient paean: "Kyi-kyi so-so! May the gods be victorious!" (lha-gyel-lo).

A single set of cotton prayer-flags is ordered in the sequence: blue, white, red, green and yellow, respectively symbolizing the five elements: space, water, fire, air and earth. In each corner of the flag there may be a protective animal: garuda (top-left), dragon (top-right), tiger (bottom-left), and lion (bottom-right), while the mantra-syllables forming the main part of the inscription may vary according to the preferred meditational deity of the devotee. Those of the three bodhisattvas: Avalokiteshvara, Manjughosa, and Vajrapani are commonplace, as are the mantras of the female bodhisattva Tara, who protects travellers from the diverse dangers of the road.

southeast corner towards the nunnery of **Ani Tshamkhung**, the mosque of Gyel Lhakhang and East Chingdrol lam. The fifth, known as **Rabsel lam**, leads southwest from the southeast corner, and the last **Gyedu lam** (or Lugu lam), leads southwest from the southwest (*Barkhor Café*) corner to the Lugu Bus Station and Chingdrol lam.

There are a number of north-south roads intersecting with Chingdrol lam and Dekyi lam, the two main east-west arteries of the city. Among these, the most important are: Mirik lam, Kharngadong lam, Do Senge lam and Lingyu lam (all of which have been described above), and those roads which penetrate further into North Lhasa, namely: Lhalu lam, extending due north from West Lingkhor lam via Lhalu to Pelding commune; Nyangdren lam, extending due north from the Post Office on Dekyi lam to Pawangka and Sera Monastery (see below, page 119); Sera lam, extending due north from the TAR Foreign Affairs Office on Dekyi lam towards Drapchi and Sera Monastery; and Dokde lam, extending northeast from the *Plateau Hotel* intersection out of town.

North Lhasa

On the west side of **Lhalu lam**, you pass on the New Zhol village, Lhalu village, and Pelding, where there is a quarry and an oxygen production plant. On the east side you pass the TAR Women's Affairs Office, the Lhasa district Welfare Office, the TAR Procurator's Office, and the Chamdo District Office.

On **Nyangdren lam**, you pass on the west side the CAAC Airline Office, the TAR Government Personnel Department, Lukhang Park side entrance, and (after the Lingkhor lam intersection), the TAR Religious Affairs Office, Lhasa City Maintenance Department, the TAR Transport Company, the local police station, the Compounding Factory of the Hospital of Traditional Medicine, the TAR Gymnastics Association, the Gymnasium, the Zhigatse District Office, the Ngari District Office, Middle School Number Five, Lhasa Teacher

Training College and the School of Hygene. On the east side, you will pass several Chinese restaurants including one which specializes in Peking Duck, and (after the Lingkhor lam intersection) the Tuberculosis Control Centre, the Fine Art Company, the Nakchu District Office, a computer store, several Chinese restaurants, the Inpatients Hospital of Traditional Medicine, the University of Traditional Medicine (Sorik Lobdra Chenmo), the Sports and Physical Education School, the Ngari Branch of the Lhasa City Bank, Xinhua Press, and a number of workers' schools. Thereafter, the road leads due north to the Military Hospital and Pawangka, while a detour leads due east to **Sera Monastery** and the nearby Sky Burial Site.

On **Sera lam**, you will pass on the west side the TAR Foreign Affairs Office, the Ground Satellite Receiving Station, the Armed Police Hospital, the Race Course, a fertilizer factory, a hydro-electric power plant, and the TAR Construction and Engineering Corporation. On the east side, the road passes the Lhasa District Public Security Bureau, the TAR Academy of Social

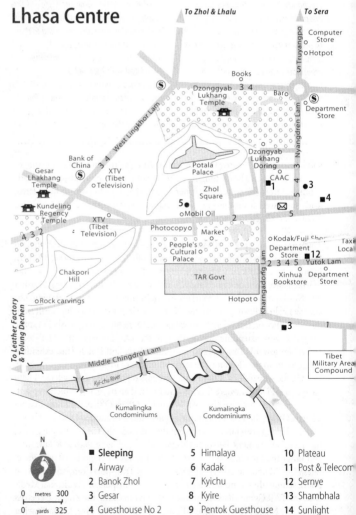

Lhasa Centre

Related maps			
A. Barkhor Square area, page 90			
Jokhang, page 83			
Ramoche Temple, page 92			
Potala, page 98			

■ **Sleeping**	5 Himalaya	10 Plateau
1 Airway	6 Kadak	11 Post & Telecom
2 Banok Zhol	7 Kyichu	12 Sernye
3 Gesar	8 Kyire	13 Shambhala
4 Guesthouse No 2	9 Pentok Guesthouse	14 Sunlight

Sciences, the Drapchi suburbs and prison, and the Lhasa Beer brewery.

On **Dokde lam**, you pass on the west side the *Ying Qiao Hotel*, the *Silver Bridge Travel Company*, the Lhasa Television and Broadcasting Head Office, the Power Station Construction Company, the Epidemic Prevention Department, the North Fire Station, an armed police unit, and various electrical or engineering companies within the Drapchi suburbs. On the east side, you pass the *Plateau Hotel*, the Ganlho Amdo Office, the armed police reserve units and TAR security offices, Middle School Number Four, the Commercial School, pharmaceutical companies, motor repair units and agricultural machine suppliers.

Among the outlying easterly parts of the city, **Ngachen lam**, the extension of North Lingkhor lam, leads out of town towards a power station of the same name and the hilltop ruins of **Dechen Dzong**. En route, you pass on the north side the Domestic Satellite Earth Station and an armed police auxiliary unit, while to the south side are yet another armed police auxiliary unit, the entrance

East Lhasa

Lhasa

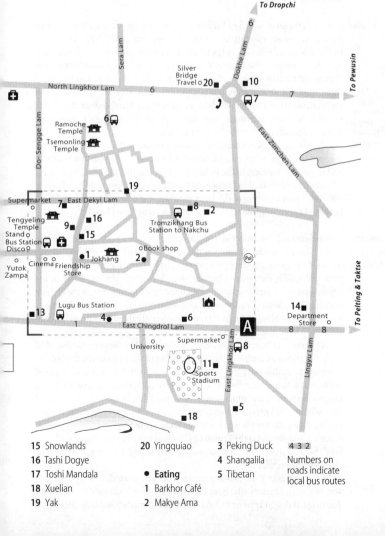

15	Snowlands	20	Yingquiao	3	Peking Duck	4 3 2
16	Tashi Dogye			4	Shangalila	Numbers on
17	Toshi Mandala		• **Eating**	5	Tibetan	roads indicate
18	Xuelian		1 Barkhor Café			local bus routes
19	Yak		2 Makye Ama			

to the affluent suburb of Karma Kunzang, Middle School Number Three, and a flour mill.

On East Zamchen lam,which extends southeast from the *Plateau Hotel* round about across the Kyi-chu River, intersecting en route with Lingyu lam and Chingdrol lam, the most important building is the Radio and Television Bureau of Lhasa District.

South Lhasa   The south bank of the Kyi-chu River is relatively undeveloped. Most buildings belong to the military, but there are a number of outlying farming villages: Dekyi Khangsar, Zhapa, Nupa, Gepho and so forth. At Drib, the regency temple of **Tsekchokling** has been rebuilt.

Sights in Central Lhasa

Jokhang Temple ཇོ་ཁང

Location:
To the east of Barkhor
Square in the Old City
Maps:
Barkhor Square,
page 90
Jokhang (ground floor),
page 83
Jokhang (upper floors),
page 87
■ *Admission:*
¥25 per person

During the reign of Songtsen Gampo's father, the king of the Kathmandu valley was one Amshuvarman, who instated his own era in 576 (he was preceded by Shivadeva and followed by the latter's son Udayadeva in 621, and thereafter by the usurper Jisnugupta/Visnugupta in 624). Udayadeva's son Narendradeva fled to Lhasa when his father was overthrown, and remained there until his return from exile, probably with Tibetan assistance, and enthronement in 641, after which he introduced the Matsyendranath cult. He is said to have vanished into the foot of Kathmandu's celebrated Matsyendranath image at the time of his death.

It was during Narendradeva's sojourn in Lhasa that Songtsen Gampo married the Nepalese princess Bhrikuti, who arrived in Lhasa in 632 or 634 and began construction of the Potala. Later, he married the Chinese princess Wencheng who arrived in Lhasa in 641 and remained there until her death in 680/681. In consequence of this latter marriage, the Tang emperor Kao Tsung bestowed upon Songtsen Gampo the title Baowang, 'jewel king'.

Geomantic
importance of
the Jokhang

The Jokhang is Tibet's most sacred shrine, the focal point of pilgrims from the entire Tibetan plateau. Situated at the heart of the old town of Lhasa, it was founded by Queen Bhrikuti on a site deemed by Queen Wencheng to be the principal geomantic power-place in Tibet, identified with the heart of the supine ogress. To facilitate the construction of the Jokhang, in 638 the Othang Lake had been filled in with earth, transported by goats. The original name of the town Rasa ('place of the goat') was subsequently altered to Lhasa ('place of the deity') following the temple's consecration.

However, further obstacles had to be eliminated by the construction of 12 outlying geomantic temples before the building of this central temple could be completed. In this way, the Jokhang came to form the centre of a grand geomantic scheme whereby temples were erected in three successive rings of four on the body of the 'supine ogress' which is Tibet (ie on her shoulders and hips, elbows and knees, and hands and feet). On the Jokhang's eventual completion (647), the temple was known as **Rasa Trulnang** ('magical apparition of Rasa'); and also as **Gazhi Trulnang** ('magical apparition endowed with four joys') because its construction was said to have brought happiness to the four classes of the populace.

The main gate of the Jokhang temple faces west towards Nepal in recognition of Queen Bhrikuti who bore the expense of the Jokhang's construction. The original design appears to have had a Newar model, and only later was it

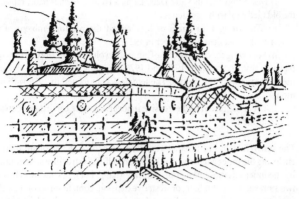

Jokhang rooftops
in Lhasa

said to have been modelled on Vikramashila Monastery in Northwest India. The earliest phase of building, traces of which indicate distinctive Newar influence, are to be seen in the original door-frames of the four ground-floor inner chapels dedicated to Mahakarunika, Amitabha, Shakyamuni, and Maitreya; and those of the second storey at the centre of the destroyed north wing, and the Zhalre Lhakhang of the east wing, as well as the Songtsen Chapel of the west wing. The fact that the Newar queen wished to make the third storey but never did may indicate her premature death. Later, when the third storey was added, the temple was said to represent the three buddha-bodies (Trikaya) or three world-systems (Tridhatu).

Bhrikuti installed the primary images in a pentoid arrangement (five main chapels flanked by vihara-like cells) within a square hall: the deity Aksobhya in the centre flanked by Amitabha and Maitreya; with Mahakarunika and Shakyamuni Acalavajra on the north and south wings respectively. There were four gates: one in each of the four walls, and 37 columns represented the 37 sections of the Vinaya.

Songtsen Gampo erected the protector shrines, with images of naga kings, Ravana and Kubera to safeguard the temple from the elements. He also concealed his treasures (*terma*) in important pillars of the Jokhang; a custom perhaps linked to the age-old Tibetan tradition of concealing wealth at the foundation of buildings or pillars.

The Jokhang has undergone continuous renovation since its original estab-**Renovations** lishment. The main phases of renovation may be attributed to the following:

a) Queen Jincheng refurbished the temple, King Senalek Jinyon cleared the outer courtyard, and King Relpachen built the Meru and Karu temples to the rear; while adding certain minor images.

b) Atisha discovered Songtsen Gampo's testament, the *Kachem Kha-kolma*, in the Jokhang; while Zangkar Lotsawa Phakpa Sherab enlarged the central chapel and altered the Zhelre Lhakhang.

c) Dakpo Gompa Tsultrim Nyingpo (1116-69) renovated the other chapels, including the Zhalre Lhakhang murals of the second storey and built the inner circuit (*nangkhor*).

d) Gade Zangpo and Monlam Dorje of Tsel Gungtang (14th century) renovated the first two storeys of the present great hall (area 25,084 square metres).

e) Phakdru Drakpa Gyeltsen built the front extension or Outer Jokhang in 1409.

f) Desi Sangye Gyatso and Dalai Lama VI added further halls, replacing the old tiled roof with a golden roof.

g) The Mongol Ta Lama of Sera added the rooftop emblem of the dharma-wheel flanked by two deer in 1927.

h) Following the damage of the Cultural Revolution, one third of the complex was restored between 1972 and 1975. Presently the site is 2,600 square metes in area with 121 statues. The temple was reopened in 1979 with nine monks.

i) The most recent and extensive renovations were carried out between 1992 and 1994.

Layout The Inner Jokhang in three storeys forms a square (82.5 square metres), enclosing the inner hall known as Kyilkhor Thil. This structure is surrounded by the inner circum-ambulation pathway (nangkhor), beyond which is the two storeyed Outer Jokhang or western extension, containing secondary chapels, storerooms, kitchens, toilets and residential quarters. The Meru Nyingba temple adjoins the Jokhang on the east side, while the south and west sides are adjoined by other buildings. This whole structure is surrounded by the intermediate circumambulation pathway (*barkhor*); which in turn is surrounded by the old city of Lhasa, with the Potala beyond. The outer walkway (*lingkhor*) on which pilgrims even now circumambulate the entire holy city of Lhasa forms an outer ring-road, and much of it has been encorporated into the modern road infrastructure of the city.

Outer Jokhang

In the square in front of the entrance, the Jokhang plaza, formerly known after its flagpole, the Juya Darchen, there is the stump of a willow reputedly planted by Princess Wencheng. It is flanked by two more recent willows and enclosed within a new stone wall. In front of the stump is the pock-marked obelisk of 1794 admonishing against smallpox, and another inscriptionless stele. In an adjacent enclosure to the north is the six metres obelisk of 823 with an inscription commemorating the Sino-Tibetan peace treaty of 821/822.

The **entrance portico** (Khyamra Gochor) with six fluted columns is fronted by a courtyard (*dochal*) where pilgrims prostrate and have worn the flagstones smooth. Side-murals depict the Four Guardian Kings and the Four Harmonious Brethren. The structure is surmounted by a balcony hidden by a yak-hair curtain, from which dignitaries would observe ceremonies conducted below. The upper north wing of the Outer Jokhang contains the **Labrangteng**; from which successive Dalai Lamas would observe important ceremonies. It has a grand reception hall; while below are storerooms, and the **Sitar Courtyard**, where living animals would be ransomed from the slaughterhouse as an act of merit. The south wing of the Outer Jokhang contains the offices of the Panchen Lamas (formerly those of the Tibetan cabinet).

Gyalchen Zhi Lhakhang (Zimgo Chinang Nyiwar) Entering from the left and after passing two large prayer wheels, the pilgrim first sees statues of the Four Guardian Kings backed by 17th and 19th century frescoes of gandharvas and nagas, and flanked by those of Samantabhadra's paradise. This ante-chamber leads through the inner door.

Kyamra Chenmo (Main Courtyard) Within the main assembly hall, the 19th century murals on the west wall depict Gushri Qan, Dalai Lama V and Pancen Lama IV; and the Thousand Buddhas of the Aeon. The murals of the south wall depict the founding of the three large monasteries around Lhasa, and the life of the Buddha. The west murals above the entrance depict the nine aspects of Amitayus, and the meditational deities Guhyasamaja, Cakrasamvara, and Bhairava, as well as Kalacakra.

The hall (32 metres by 39 metres) was constructed by Tsongkhapa for the Great Prayer Festival in 1409. It is in the form of an open atrium, with large murals along its cloistered walls (dating from 1648). On the north side is the two storeyed residence of the Dalai Lama, with its gilded roof and window overlooking the courtyard. The rooftop view from this outer hall overlooks the elaborate western façade.

Along the north wall are, in succession:

1) The **Namthar Gosum Lhakhang**, with images of the Buddhas of the Three Times, the Eight Bodhisattvas, and the two gatekeepers. A staircase leads down from the Dalai Lama's private quarters;

2) **Shugtri Chenmo**, the Dalai Lama's stone throne, backed by paintings of Shakyamuni, Avalokiteshvara and Manjushri, with the Thousand Buddhas;

3) **Dolma Lhakhang**, containing an image of Cintamani Tara flanked by White and Green Tara, and backed on the left and right respectively by images of Nyaknyon Sewa Rinchen (who sculpted the original Cintamani image) and Atisha. Its rear (west) wall has images of the Twenty-one Taras in two tiers, originally commissioned by Dalai Lama VII, with Shantaraksita, Padmasambhava and Trisong Detsen forming a trio on the north side, along with Tsongkhapa and his foremost students. A long stone altar stands in front of the inner gateway. Outside the door is a stone bearing a handprint of Longdol Lama.

4) Embedded within the northwest column at the entrance to the inner circumambulation pathway are two stones, said to have been thrown there by Tsangnyon Heruka Sangye Gyeltsen and Unyon Kunga Zangpo.

5) The **Inner Circumambulation** (*nangkhor*) is lined with prayer-wheels and murals outlined in gold on red background, which depict the Thousand Buddhas and scenes from the *Avadanakalpalata*, interspersed with stupas and relief-images. On the north side are four successive chapels entered from the westernmost one, namely: **Tamdrin Sangdrubling** (with images of Hayagriva and Kurukulla), **Mahakarunika**, **Sarvavidvairocana**, and the innermost dedicated to the **Eight Medicine Buddhas**. On the east side are: **Neten Chudruk Lhakhang**, which contains images commissioned by Desi Sangye Gyatso; the **Gurubum Lhakhang** (containing 100,000 images of Padmasambhava surrounding three central images), and the **Sera Dago**, which is a gate connecting the Jokhang with Meru Nyingba temple and the **Dago Rung-khang** kitchen (used during the Great Prayer Festival by the monks of Sera). On the south side, outside the wall, is the **Sung Chora** debating courtyard, renovated in 1986, and containing a yellow stone platform where thrones (*shugtri*) for Tsongkhapa, the Dalai Lama, and the Ganden Tripa were set up during the Great Prayer Festival, and where the annual Geshe examinations were held. Also, outside the wall on this south side are the temples dedicated to the Eight Medicine Buddhas, the Sixteen Elders, the Graduated Path (*lamrim*), and the Eight Sugatas; and a three-storey Ngakhang, or tantric college, offering an excellent rooftop view of the Jokhang.

During the Great Prayer Festival, the monks of the three main monasteries would be seated in the assembly hall – those from Sera in the north, Drepung in the centre, and Ganden in the south. The Dalai Lama would be flanked by Shartse Choje and Jangtse Choje, the hierarchs of the two colleges of Ganden monastery, and the entire ceremony would be supervised by the Ganden Tripon (head of the Gelukpa school), and the Tsokchen Umdze from Drepung.

Inner Jokhang

Ground Floor **Main Gate (Zhung-go)**: embedded in the flagstones in front of the gate is a fossil known as Amolongkha, and a footprint of Dalai Lama XIII. The gate is ornamented with Derge crafted metalwork and surrounded by murals depicting Maitreya (left), Je Yabsesum (above), and Dipamkara (right).

Entrance Hall The outermost rooms of the portico including the Driza Zurphu Ngapa are empty, while the innermost chambers depict the wrathful pretector deities: yaksas (**Nojinkhang**), Shridevi and Mahakala on the north side; and benign naga kings (**Lukhang**) as well as the Othang Lake seal on the south side. These protectors are said to have appeared to Songtsen Gampo in a vision during the original construction of the Jokhang, and were charged with its protection.

Kyilkhor Thil The two-storey inner hall is divided into three sections – two with short col-
(Inner Hall) umns (*kawa thungthung*) and one with long columns (*kawa ringbo*). Immediately beyond the entrance, there are two rows of short columns running north-south, the southernmost ones bearing tangkas of the Sixteen Elders. Then, in the centre of the hall, are six large statues: a six metres west-facing image of Padmasambhava (erected by Khyentse Rinpoche and consecrated by Minling Chung Rinpoche), a four metres north-facing image of Barzhi Jampa (commissioned by the Barzhi family), a 10 metres west-facing image of Thuwang Zangthama, a eight metres north-facing image of Miwang Jampa (cast in 1736, its auras and jewels have been replaced), and at their centre a four metres Mahakarunika with a small Padmasambhava to its rear. The tallest columns (nine in four groups) which support the skylight are painted and date from the period of Gade Zangpo's restoration.

An inner row of 12 short columns (*kawa thung-thung*) with six to each side of the Jowo Lhakhang, running south-north in front of the inner sanctum, probably dates from the seventh century. These are characterized by short bases and round shafts, suggesting an authentic Nepalese design. Five of them (three at the north end and two at the south end) were plastered probably in the 14th century for protection or reinforcement – by Gade Zangpo and his son. A cornice comprising 144 lion-faced figures also dates from the earliest phase, as do some of the interior door-frames.

Within the hall, there are various chapels which the pilgrim will pass through in a clockwise manner, as follows:

West Wing **Je Rinpoche Dakpa Namgye Lhakhang** This chapel contains a central image of Tsongkhapa, surrounded by his eight pure retainers, including Khedrubje and Gyeltsabje, who accompanied the master on his meditative retreats at Chokhorgyel and elsewhere. Outside the entrance, a monk occasionally inscribes with gold ink on red paper the names of deceased persons or petitioners, which are then burned as offerings.

Amitabha Lhakhang Outside this chapel is the Tagpa Chorten, a stupa originally fashioned by Sakya Pandita in the 13th century, and containing certain relics of King Songtsen Gampo.

North Wing **Menlha Desheg Gye Lhakhang**: this chapel is dedicated to the Eight Medicine Buddhas.

Mahakarunika Lhakhang Within the chain metal curtain of this chapel, the door of which appears to have an original frame, there is a restored image of the deity Mahakarunika. The original image, known as Thuje Chenpo Rangjung Ngaden, is said to have been imbued with the life-force of five beings (*ngaden*), namely: King Songtsen Gampo, his two foreign queens, and the gatekeeping deities Amritakundalin and Hayagriva. It also contained buddha relics from Bodh Gaya in India which had been brought to Tibet by Lodro Jungne an emanation of King Songtsen Gampo. That original image was severely damaged during the Cultural Revolution, and part of it smuggled to Dharamsala. One portion, however, is contained within the new replica. The image is one of the four in the Jokhang with a gilded roof. The chapel also contains secondary images of: Khasarpani, Tara, Marici, Hayagriva, Lokeshvara, Bhrikuti, Prajnaparamita, and Amritakundalin. Outside the entrance to this chamber are a series of new images depicting (L-R): Phakmodrupa, Tangtong Gyelpo, a laughing Milarepa, Lama Zhang, and Zhikpo Dudtsi who devoted much of his energy to repairing the dykes which protected the Jokhang from the flooding Kyi-chu waters.

Jampa Truze Lhakhang The principal image is a seated Maitreya with an impressive aureole, and fronted by an old restored image of Manjughosa. On its left are images of Amitabha, White Tara, Vajrapani, Avalokiteshvara and Manjughosa. On its right is Tsongkhapa flanked by the reliquaries of Ngaripa Tsondu Nyingpo (who sculpted the chapel's original images) and Ngok Lekpei Sherab. In the centre of the chapel is a stone butter bowl, made by Tsongkhapa. Over the door is a replica of an original Mani Stone engraving (which was one of the Jokhang's most precious artefacts). The stone platform outside the door was once used by King Songtsen Gampo and his queens while bathing, and it is said that the actual clay of the Maitreya image within was mixed with bath water prior to its construction.

Othang Gyatso Lhakhang This chapel contains a stone slab, which is

Jokhang (Ground floor)

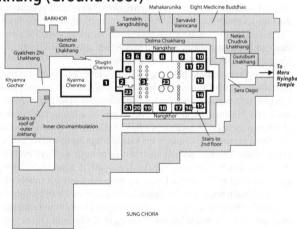

N
Not to Scale

1 Main gate
2 Driza Zurphu Ngapa Nojinkang (N) Lukhang (S)
3 Kyilkhor Thil
4 Je Rinpoche Namgye Lhakhang
5 Amitabha Lhakhang
6 Tagpa Chorten
7 Menlha Desheg Gye Lhakhang
8 Mahakarunika
9 Jampa Truze Lhakhang
10 Othang Gyatso Lhakhang
11 Tsongkhapa Lhakhang
12 Amitabha Lhakhang
13 Jowo Shakyamuni Lhakhang
14 Jestun Jampa Gonpo Lhakhang
15 Chenrezi Sengedradrok Lhakhang
16 Yungdrung Phuk
17 Janzik Lhakhang
18 Jampa Chezhi Lhakhang
19 Menlha Deshek Gye'i Lhakhang
20 Sangye Rabdun
21 Tsepak Lhagu Lhakhang
22 Chogyel Tonmi Lhakhang
23 Nine tall columns

said to give access to a subterranean lake below the Jokhang's foundation. Annual offerings were formerly made in this chapel by the Tibetan Government. Now it is mostly blocked-off by the Tsongkhapa Lhakhang.

Tsongkhapa Lhakhang A covered elevated platform supports a small image of Tsongkhapa called Nangyen Ngadrama, which is flanked on the left by Sakya Choje Kunga Tashi and Buton Rinchendrub, and on the right by Asanga, Sonam Gyeltsen, Dorje Gyel-tsen, and Karmapa III. The original central image is said to have been made in Tsongkhapa's lifetime, but there are other traditions attributing its miraculous construction to the protector deity Dharmaraja, or alternatively to a later Mongol emperor.

East Wing **Amitabha Lhakhang (Room where final obstacles are dispelled)** The entrance to this chapel is guarded by Vajrapani and Ucchusmakrodha – the former could not be budged by Langdarma's henchmen, and the latter reputedly repelled a Chinese invasion following the death of Songtsen. Note the original sloping Newar door-frame with its unpainted patina. Inside is an image of Amitabha flanked on the left by Vajrapani and on the right by Hayagriva, while the Eight Bodhisattvas are on the side-walls. Outside the chamber to the south is a stone platform with images of Songtsen Gampo, his two foreign queens, and Guru Saroruhavajra (commissioned by Dalai Lama XIII). The platform originally supported images of the Four Guardian Kings, as sculpted by Tripa Monalm Dorje, using clay from Samye. The fourth 'light-emanating' image of the Jokhang, Dolma Darlenma, was also once positioned in this chapel. The statue had received its name after reputedly requesting Sakya Pandita for an offering scarf.

Jowo Lhakhang Foyer The highly polished wooden floor of the foyer is flanked by two pairs of guardian kings (with wrathful demeanour on the south side and smiling demeanour on the north side). The original guardians, now destroyed, were attributed either to Princess Wencheng or Princess Jincheng. The elaborately decorated high ceilings display a marked Newar influence. An image of Padmasambhava, sculpted in the 18th century by Orgyan Drodul Lingpa, admonishes the naga spirits to stay away.

Jowo Shakyamuni Lhakhang The inner sanctum, which is the largest and loftiest chapel of the Jokhang and one of four with a gilded roof, contains Tibet's most revered image – the 1.5 metres image of **Jowo Rinpoche**, representing the Buddha at the age of 12. This image was reputedly made of an alloy of precious metals mixed with jewels by Visvakarman in Kapalavastu, and in later times presented to China by the king of Magadha to commemorate the defeat of the Yavanas. Subsequently it was brought to Tibet by Princess Wencheng. One tradition recorded by Tucci states that the original was partially destroyed in 1717 by the Dzungars, the present image being stylistically later. Originally housed in the Ramoche temple, it was later brought to the Jokhang by Wencheng on the death of Songtsen Gampo and interred in a chamber on the south side behind a painting of Manjughosa. Queen Jincheng subsequently recovered it and installed it as the central image of the Jokhang. Later it was buried in sand after Trisong's disloyal Bon ministers chose to return it to China and 300 men could not move it. During that period, the temple was converted to a slaughterhouse. Subsequently the image was once again buried in sand by Langdarma who had the gates of the Jokhang plastered with the picture of a monk drinking wine. The head-dress and ear-ornaments (*na-gyen*) originally date from time of Tsongkhapa (but have been replaced in recent times), and the pearl-studded robe from that of the Da Ming emperor. The image was conserved without damage during the Cultural Revolution, during which period the temple was utilized as a military barracks and its outer courtyard as a slaughterhouse.

Entering the inner sanctum, the pilgrim finds the main image seated upon a three-tiered stone platform; flanked by smaller images of Maitreya and Manjughosa. There are ornate silver-plated pillars with dragon motifs supporting an overhead canopy; and a silver sphere above the crown, which was donated by a Mongol Qan. Side-steps at the south and north sides grant access to the pilgrim, who can then make offerings directly to the image. Behind the Jowo Rinpoche image, there is a copper plaque with an inscription commemorating Anige's 13th century restoration of the throne-back and the aureole. In front of the plaque is an east-facing image of Dipamkara Buddha called Acala, which stands back-to-back with Jowo Rinpoche, and is claimed to have once been the central image. Facing the latter, at the back of the chapel is a six metres image of Thubpa Gangchentso, flanked by the Twelve Bodhisattvas, along with the gatekeepers Vajrapani and Hayagriva – all of which were sculpted by Zangkar Lotsawa. Other statues of the inner sanctum depict Dalai Lama VII, Dalai Lama XIII and Tsongkhapa.

Outside the chapel to the south is a raised platform with images of Atisha flanked by Dromtonpa and Ngok Lekpei Sherab. Behind Dromtonpa is a mural depicting a 'speaking' form of Tara (Dolma Sungjonma).

Jestun Jampa Gonpo Lhakhang This chapel, which has an original seventh century Newar door-frame, contains as its main image Jampa Chokhor. This image is held to have been an emanation of King Krikin, which was brought to Tibet from Nepal as part of Princess Bhrikuti's dowry. The present statue is a replica but the finely carved aureole may be original. Flanking the main image are the Eight Taras Who Protect from Fear; with Avalokiteshvara in the form Chenrezi Semnyi Ngalso in front, and a replica of Princess Wencheng's stove in the northwest corner. The original Maitreya image formerly was the centrepiece of the second storey.

Outside on a platform are images of Amitayus, Dolpopa Sherab Gyeltsen, and Four-armed Avalokiteshvara.

Chenrezi Sengedradrok Lhakhang The main image here is of Amitabha, flanked by six emanations of Avalokiteshvara, of which the first left gives the chapel its name. Outside is a 1.5 metres stone column with a hole at the top, to which pilgrims press their ears in order to hear the sound of the mythical anga bird at the bottom of Othang Lake.

Yungdrung Phuk In the southeast corner beyond the stairs are two images of   **South Wing** Padmasambhava and one of King Trisong Detsen, along with a painting of the Medicine Buddha, which is said to have been fashioned out of light rays emanating from Avalokiteshvara's heart.

Janzik Lhakhang This chapel contains a series of recently reconstructed meditational deities in yab-yum posture. Outside are new murals depicting Songtsen Gampo and his two foreign queens with the ministers Gar and Tonmi. The original paintings had been commissioned by Monlam Dorje of Tsel Gungtang.

Jampa Chezhi Lhakhang This chapel, which is one of the four with a gilded roof, contains an image of Maitreya, which was brought from Drepung to replace the (now destroyed) silver Maitreya, which was traditionally escorted around the Barkhor on the 25th day of the first lunar month during the Jampa Dendren ceremony. Other statues contained within this chapel include: Manjughosa, Khasarpani, Mahakarunika, Vajrasattva, and Jambhala, as well as Lharje Gewabum, who is said to have built one of the Kyichu dykes. Behind the image of the protector Gek Tarje at the northeast corner of the chapel, and alongside a Padmasambhava image, is a 0.5 metres gilded goat's head, replacing a reputedly self-arising original. This depicts the legendary Queen of Goats (Dungtse Ra'i Gyelmo) who presided over the filling-in of the Othang Lake.

Menlha Deshek Gye'i Lhakhang (Jowo Besai Lhakhang) This is the chapel in which the Jowo Rinpoche image was hidden by Princess Wencheng within a cavity behind the buddha-image of the east wall. The main images depict Amitabha and the Eight Medicine Buddhas. The image of Manju-ghosa, known as Jampeyang Koyolma, which is depicted on the outer wall, is said to have spoken to Princess Jincheng, agreeing to move aside so that the statue could be extracted. West of the entrance are images of the Five Founders (Gongma Nga) of Sakya.

Sangye Rabdun Lhakhang This chapel depicts the Seven Generations of Past Buddhas, one of which supposedly flew there from India.

Tsepak Lhagu Lhakhang This chapel depicts the Nine Aspects of Amitayus, deity of longevity. Outside on the southwest wall is a mural depicting Prajnaparamita, with a reputedly self-arising eye, which appeared when an old lady miraculously had her sight restored on praying to the image. Other murals in this alcove depict the Three Deities of Longevity (Tselha Namsum).

West Wing **Chogyel Tonmi Lhakhang** In this royal chapel, King Songtsen Gampo is flanked (on the left) by: Gar, Bhrikuti, Nyatri Tsenpo, and Trisong Detsen; and (on the right) by: Relpachen, Lhatotori, Wencheng, and Tonmi Sambhota. Formerly it also contained images of Mongza Tricham, Gungru Gungtsen, and Zhang Lonnyi. The room has original offering bowls and lamps. Outside are important murals depicting the foundation of the Jokhang and the events of Songtsen Gampo's reign, including the construction of the first Potala Palace.

Second Floor **Zhalre Lhakhang** The chapel immediately above the Jowo Rinpoche
(access from Lhakhang was remodelled by Zangkar Lotsawa when the lower chamber was
south-east enlarged. Only the westernmost part of the original chamber remains, offering
corner) a view of the chapel below, and this is approached by a recently constructed catwalk – the original approach being walled-off to prevent pilgrims walking above the Jowo Lhakhang. The remaining east inner wall contains original frescoes. Unfortunately, the seventh century frescoes of the north wall were removed in the 1980s. The southern frescoes and the well-preserved three-panelled mural of the east wall suggest a synthesis of Tibetan and Pala styles, predating the integrated Tibeto-Newar style of the 15th century.

Guru Lhakhang (Barkhang Lopon) A seventh century tapering door-frame with metal lattices leads into this chapel, where the central image depicts Padmasambhava in the awesome form known as Nangsi Zilnon, flanked by his two foreign consorts and eight manifestations. The original Pala-style paintings of the outside walls (probably by Zangkar Lotsawa) were restored in 1991.

Demchok Lhakhang Here the principal image depicts the meditational deity Cakrasamvara in union with the female consort Vajravarahi.

Thuwang Tsokhor Bypassing three empty chapels, the pilgrim arrives at this shrine, which has images of Shakyamuni surrounded by the Eight Bodhi-sattvas; and also Jowo Shakyamuni, flanked by Shariputra and Maudgalyayana.

Ku-nga Gonkhang (Gonkhangphuk) This chapel contains nine 1.5 metres images of the protector deities, including the five forms of Pehar known as Gyelpo Ku-nga, as well as Hayagriva, Shridevi, and Nechung, and the gate-keepers Du-tsen and Lu-tsen.

Chogyel Songtsen Lhakhang The main shrine of the west wing, surmounted by a gilded roof, is dedicated to King Songtsen Gampo. Note the seventh century door-frames. The king's ale pot, known as Chogyel Trungben, or Chang-no Tamgochen, which may perhaps be of Scythian or Kushan origin, is kept in a cabinet on a wooden stand between the two gates. The central image of the king, flanked by his two foreign wives, is said to have been originally commissioned by Bhrikuti (the middle finger of the main image is said to be that of Songtsen himself and the image an exact likeness). Behind are images of the Seven Generations of Past Buddhas and wall-painted mandalas. The south wall has further images of Songtsen Gampo with Wencheng and his Tibetan consort.

Jokhang (Upper Floors)

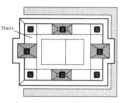

Roof
1 Jowo Gyaphib
2 Jampa Gyaphib
3 Chogyel Gyaphib
4 Tuje Gyaphib
5 Pelhayum Drakmo Lhakhang

6 Tsering Chenga Lhakhang
7 Lhachak Shokhang
8 Neten Chudruk Lhakhang

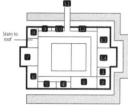

Third Floor
1 Pelachok Dukhang
2 Palen Lhamo Lhakhang
3 Pelha Bedongma Lhakang
4 Lama Lhakhang
5 Tsephak Lhakhang
6 Sangdejiksum Lhakhang
7 Neten Chudruk Lhakhang

8 Menlha Deshegye Lhakhang
9 Menlha Tsokhor Lhakhang
10 Tonpa Tsokhor Lhakhang
11 Drelzam
12 Deshegye Lhakhang
13 Thuwang Tsokhor Lhakhang
14 Jowo Utho Lhakhang

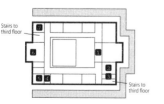

Second Floor
1 Zhalre Lhakhang
2 Guru Lhakhang

N

Not to scale

3 Demchok Lhakhang
4 Thuwang Tsokhor
5 Ku-nga Gonkhang
6 Chogyel Songtsen Lhakhang
7 Thupa Rigdruk Lhakhang

Thupa Rigdruk Lhakhang The chapel of the northwest corner is dedicated to Four-armed Avalokiteshvara, flanked by the Six Sages of the Six Realms. Note the multiplicity of murals depicting Amitayus in red on a cream background.

The chapels of the north wing and those beyond the Zhalre Lhakhang on the east-wing have been destroyed and are presently unrestored.

The frescoes of the third floor depict the protectors, especially Shridevi. Many murals however have four or five layers of paint, of which the lower layers have yet to be inspected. Only three chapels are open:

Third Floor
(access from the southeast & northwest corners)

Pelhachok Lhakhang (Meru Tsho-khang) This chapel is dedicated to the protectress Shridevi, and it is cared for by the monks of Meru Sarpa Tratsang. There are new murals in white, red and gold on black background, which depict Shridevi, Mahakala, and Bhairava. The murals outside this chapel depict Six-armed Mahakala, Dalai Lama V, the regent Desi Sangye Gyatso, and Gushri Qan, with Magzorma, Shridevi, and the Twelve Tenma.

Palden Lhamo Lhakhang This chapel contains a peaceful image of Shridevi.

Pelha Bedongma Lhakhang Here, the wrathful image of frog-faced Shridevi is separate d from the previous chapel by a partition wall. On the 13th day of the 10th lunar month, this image would be displayed for three days, and on the full-moon day it would be carried around the Barkhor during the festival known as Pelhe Rida.

Closed chapels on this floor include: (west) Lama Lhakhang, Tsephak Lhakhang, Sangdejiksum Lhakhang, Neten Chudruk Lhakhang; (north) Menlha Deshegye Lhakhang, Menlha Tsokhor Lhakhang, Tonpa Tsokhor Lhakhang, Drelzam, Deshegye Lhakhang, Thuwang Tsokhor; and (east) Jowo Utho Lhakhang.

The Roof There are four gilded roofs (*gyaphib*) and four corner chapels on the roof of the Jokhang. The former comprise: the **Jowo Gyaphib** in the Centre-East, the largest gilded roof, which was donated by Tew Mul, the ruler of Yartse Kingdom of west Tibet in the 14th century; the **Jampa Gyaphib** in the Centre-South; the **Chogyel Gyaphib** in the Centre-West, which was commissioned by Dalai Lama V; and the **Tuje Gyaphib** in the Centre-North, which was donated by the kings Punimul and Pratimul of Yartse in the late 14th century.

As to the four corner chapels: the **Pelhayum Drakmo Lhakhang** in the southeast (now closed) is dedicated to Magzorma, the **Tsering Chenga Lhakhang** in the southwest (now closed) is cared for by the monks of Tsurphu; the **Neten Chudruk Lhakhang** in the northeast (now closed) was formerly utilized by the Tibetan Government during the Great Prayer Festival; and the **Lhachak Sho-khang** in the northwest (now closed) once functioned as a government stationery supplier. Also on the Jokhang roof are the **Lhabum Lubum** charm vases; and the **Tamnyen Darchen** flag, which was erected by Desi Sonam Chopel following the defeat of Beri Kingdom during the 17th century. The bright sunlit roofs present a great contrast to the dark smoke-filled chapels of the Jokhang's interior.

Barkhor Buildings and Temples

Nangtseshak Jail This 720 square metres two-storey prison adjoining the north wall of the Jokhang was of great notoriety in the past, but is now disused. In front there is a square, which nowadays functions as a carpet bazaar. The lane entrance to Meru Nyingba temple is located here.

Meru Nyingba Temple This temple is situated on the northeast side of the Jokhang, and approached from the north arc of the Barkhor. It was one of six temples built by King Relpachen – this one on the site of an earlier temple where Tonmi Sambhota had finalized the Tibetan alphabet. It was destroyed by Langdarma and subsequently rebuilt by Atisha to become Gelukpa under Dalai Lama III Sonam Gyatso (1543-89). The oldest existing structure is the **Jambhala Lhakhang**, the main building being of recent 20th century construction. The temple is dedicated to doctrinal protectors, especially the diverse forms of Pehar.

Gongkar Chode Branch Temple This Sakya protector shrine is located up a staircase on the right of the lane entrance to Meru Nyingba temple. The central image is of the protector Gonpo Pelgon Dramtso, and was formerly flanked by images of Panjara, Shridevi, and Six-armed Mahakala.

Jambhala Lhakhang This ancient temple lies below the Gongkar Chode branch temple. Originally it was part of King Relpachen's construction. It is only 7.5 metres by 7.2 metres with a low ceiling, and is said to be where Tonmi Sambhota devised the Tibetan alphabet. Later it became affiliated to Nechung Gonpa.

The Dukhang (Assembly Hall) This south-facing three-storey complex

Lhasa Obelisks

*The obelisk or stele is a significant historical monument, constructed to symbolize royal dominion or important political and spiritual events, and often surrounded in its four directions by stupas. The obelisks of Lhasa include those in front of the **Jokhang**, namely the legible 3.5m stele constructed in 823 by King Relpachen to commemorate the peace treaty signed with Tang China, the illegible smallpox stele of 1794, and the inscriptionless stele of the Ming period with animal carvings on its plinth.*

*In front of the **Potala**, there are four other obelisks: the 3.5m quadrilingual Kangxi stele of 1721 commemorating the*

*defeat of the Dzungars, and the 4m quadrilingual Qianlong stele of 1791 commemorating the two defeats of the Gorkhas in 1788 and 1791 respectively, have recently been repositioned in the foreground of the building. Considerably older than these, however, are the **Outer Zhol Obelisk** (Zhol Chima) and the **Inner Zhol Obelisk** (Zhol Nangma). The former is an 8m stele constructed by Trisong Detsen in 763 to commemorate the exploits of his General Takdra Lugong whose forces occupied the Chinese capital at Xi'an; and the latter is located below the Potala stairway.*

is approached through a courtyard flanked by a monastic cloister. The main building, constructed by Nechung Khenpo Sakya Ngape in the 19th century, is an extremely active temple. It was renovated in 1986. Mani prayer wheels flank either side of the entrance; the left frescoes depict the protector deity Dorje Drakden; skylight frescoes depict Tsongkhapa and his foremost students; Atisha with his foremost students, and Padmasambhava flanked by Shantara-ksita and King Trisong Detsen. The central image on the altar is a new Avalokiteshvara; with a large copper Padmasambhava to the right, and a sand mandala on the left.

Behind this altar is the **inner sanctum**, containing an image of Padmasambhava in the form Nangsi Zilnon in the centre flanked by the five aspects of Pehar known as Gyelpo Ku-nga; and the gatekeepers Hayagriva and Thoktsen. Frescoes above depict Tsongkhapa, Samantabhadra, and Dalai Lama XIII. The side chapels have images of Dorje Drakden (left) and Shridevi (right).

Upstairs is the **Tsepame Lhakhang** containing 1,000 small images of Amitayus.

Meru Nyingba Monastery

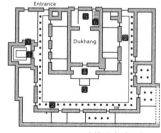

4 Mani wheels and entrance
5 Inner sanctum
6 Stairs to Tsepame Lhakhang
7 Stairs to Gongkar Chode Branch Temple

1 Jambhala Lhakhang
2 Monastic cloisters
3 Courtyard

This three-storey residence of the Pawangka Rinpoche, a powerful Gelukpa master who rose to prominence in the early 20th century, is located on the east side of the Barkhor.

The Pawangka Labrang

This temple is located on the east side of the Barkhor. One of Lhasa's three oracles was based here, the others being at Nechung and Gadong in the Tolung valley. The Karmashar Choje oracle would make one annual prophecy concerning affairs of state on the 30th day of the sixth lunar month after travelling in procession from **Karmashar** to **Sera** monastery accompanied by Cham dancers

Karmashar Lhakhang

drawn from the corpse-cutter (*ragyabpa*) and police (*korchagpa*) professions. The prophecy would then be written down and pinned on the door of Karmashar for public inspection.

Ani Tshamkhung Nunnery

This is one of Lhasa's three nunneries, the others being Drubtob Lhakhang on Chakpori and Chubzang Gonpa at Pawangka. It is located on the left side of Waling Street, which leads southeast from the Barkhor to the Mosque (Gyel Lhakhang). Admission fee: ¥5 per person. Passing through the perimeter wall, to which the kitchen and living quarters are attached, the yellow two storey building is located at the rear of the courtyard. The **Tshamkhung** (meditation hollow) of Songtsen Gampo located downstairs and approached from a small passage on the right side of the building, contains the chamber where the king meditated in order to prevent flooding of the Kyi-chu River. Inside is the meditation hollow – a 1.5 square metres whitewashed earthen well 1.5 metres deep and below floor level, which is approached by four steps and surmounted by a glass-framed shrine.

A reconstructed black-stone Nga-drama image of Songtsen Gampo overlooks the opening and the king's stone seat is positioned in front. During the first Great Prayer Festival (Monlam Chenmo) in 1419 the site was occupied by Drubtob Chenpo Kuchora and his successor Ngari Drubtob Chenpo. The first temple was erected by Tsong Khapa's student Tongten (1389-1445); and the second storey added by Pawangka Rinpoche in the early 20th century.

The nuns of Tshamkhung held regular fasting or *nyun-ne* ceremonies and were responsible for lighting butter lamps in the Jokhang. Restored between

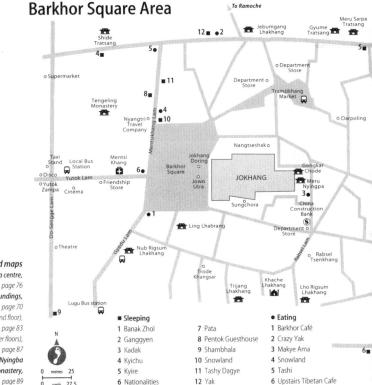

Barkhor Square Area

To Ramoche

Meru Sarpa Tratsang

Shide Tratsang

Jebumgang Lhakhang

Gyume Tratsang

12 ■ ● 2

5 ●

4 ■

○ Supermarket

○ Department Store

■ 11

Department ○ Store

Tengeling Monastery

8 ■

Tramzikhang Market

● 4

Nyangtri ○ Travel Company

■ 10

○ Darpoling

Nangtseshak ○

Taxi Stand

Local Bus Station

Mentsi Khang

Jokhang Doring ○

Gongkar Chode

○ Disco

Yutok Lam

Barkhor Square

JOKHANG

Meru Nyingpa

○ Yutok Zampa

○ Cinema

○ Friendship Store

Jowo Utra ○

3 ●

China Construction Bank

Sungchora ○

Department ○ Store

● 1

Ling Lhabrang

○ Theatre

Nub Rigsum Lhakhang

Rabsel Tsenkhang ○

Trode Khangsar ○

Khache Lhakhang

Lho Rigsum Lhakhang

Trijang Lhakhang

Lugu Bus station

■ 9

Related maps
Lhasa centre,
page 76
Lhasa surroundings,
page 70
Jokhang (ground floor),
page 83
Jokhang (upper floors),
page 87
Meru Nyingba
Monastery,
page 89

N

0 metres 25
0 yards 27.5

■ Sleeping		● Eating	
1 Banak Zhol	7 Pata	1 Barkhor Café	
2 Ganggyen	8 Pentok Guesthouse	2 Crazy Yak	
3 Kadak	9 Shambhala	3 Makye Ama	
4 Kyichu	10 Snowland	4 Snowland	
5 Kyire	11 Tashy Dagye	5 Tashi	
6 Nationalities	12 Yak	6 Upstairs Tibetan Cafe	

Lhasa

1982-84, there are now more than 80 nuns at Tshamkhung. The present **assembly hall**, on the second floor, has a Thousand-armed Avalokiteshvara as its main image – with (right side) Tsongkhapa and his students, Vajrayogini, Aksobhya, Shakyamuni and White Tara; and (left side) Amoghasiddhi, Cakrasamvara, Ling Rinpoche, Pawangka Rinpoche and Green Tara. A large centrally suspended tangka depicts Tsongkhapa with his foremost students.

Gyel Lhakhang Lhasa has some 2,000 Muslims, some descendents of 17th century immigrants from Ladakh and Kashmir, the remainder newly arrived immigrants from the Ziling and Linxia regions. At 2,600 square metres, the Gyel Lhakhang is the largest mosque in Lhasa, located at the end of Waling Street, running from the Sharkyaring flagpole via Ani Tshamkhung. It was constructed in 1716, and subsequently rebuilt twice – in 1793 and 1960. Friday prayers attract over 600 worshippers. The adjacent streets have many Muslim restaurants.

The Small Mosque Situated due south of the Jokhang and west of Gyel Lhakhang, this mosque of 20th century construction has a ground floor bath-house and an upstairs Koranic schoolroom.

Lingtsang Labrang A two-storey building on the south side of Barkhor Square, with Chinese-style murals and an excellent rooftop view of the Jokhang, this was previously a residence of the late Ling Rinpoche, senior tutor to HH Dalai Lama XIV.

Trijang Labrang This three-storey building directly south of the Jokhang was once the seat of the late Trijang Rinpoche, the Junior Tutor of HH Dalai Lama XIV. It is now the headquarters of the Lhasa Cinema Company.

Tonpa This now dilapidated three-storey building on the south stretch of the Barkhor is said to have once been a residence of Tonmi Sambhota, inventor of the Tibetan script. At present, the building functions as the headquarters of the Barkhor Residents' Committee.

The Mentsikhang (Institute of Tibetan Medicine and Astrology) The original two-storey Mentsikhang, founded by Dr Khyenrab Norbu in 1916, is opposite the new Lhasa cinema on Mimang lam. The present multi-storeyed building slightly to its east functions as the outpatients department and the offices of the Tibetan Medical and Astrological Research Institute. The penultimate floor has an exhibition of Tibetan medical artefacts; and the top floor has a shrine dedicated to Yutok Yonten Gonpo, flanked by Desi Sangye Gyatso and Khyenrab Norbu; as well as a medical tangka exhibition hall.

Lhasa

Yutok Zampa This is a renovated ancient bridge 300 metres west of the Jokhang, now contained within the Lhasa Customs Office. Formerly it linked the old city of Lhasa with the suburbs. Named after its 18th century turquoise-tiled Chinese roof, the bridge is 6.8 metres wide and 28.3 metres in span; with thick two metres stone walls which probably date from the seventh century. The bridge has five openings at each end.

The Four Rigsum Lhakhang These four temples surround the Jo-khang in the cardinal directions, each of them containing images of the Lords of the Three Enlightened Families. Among them, the eastern temple, **Shar Rigsum Lhakhang**, was formerly located across from the Mosque, the southern one, **Lho Rigsum Lhakhang**, was originally a royal residence and the first building of the Barkhor. Its single-storey chapel is now a private residence. The northern one, the **Jang Rigsum Lhakhang**, was formerly located opposite the Banak Zhol behind Meru Tratsang, and the western one, the **Nub Rigsum Lhakhang**, was located on a site west of the present Mentsikhang and north of the Yutok Zampa. Of these, only the southern temple survives intact.

Ramoche temple ར་མོ་ཆེ and adjacent tratsangs

Ramoche Temple

Location:
About 1 km north from Barkhor Square, the temple is on Ramoche lam across East Dekyi lam

Maps:
Lhasa centre, page 76
Ramoche Temple, page 92

■ *Admission:*
¥15 per person

Founded by Princess Wencheng at the same time as the Jokhang, Ramoche is reputed to be the princess' burial site, divined by her to be connected directly with the hells or with the subterranean crystal palace of the nagas. It originally was built to contain Tibet's holiest image – **Jowo Rinpoche**, which had been transported to Lhasa via Lhagang in a wooden cart. The construction of the temple was completed around the same time as the Jokhang. Later, when Tang China threatened to invade Tibet during the reign of Mangsong Mangtsen (649-76), the Jowo Rinpoche image was hidden by Wencheng in a secret chamber within the Jokhang; later to be unearthed by Princess Jincheng (post 710) who then placed it within the central chapel of the Jokhang.

As a substitute the image of **Jowo Mikyo Dorje**, representing the Buddha as an eight year old, which had been made by Vishvakarman and brought to Tibet by the Nepali queen Bhrikuti, was taken from the south chamber of the Jokhang to Ramoche, and installed there as the main image.

Originally, Ramoche was built in Chinese-style but, after being destroyed by fires, the present three-storeyed building was constructed in Tibetan style. In 1474 it was placed under the authority of Kunga Dondrub, a second generation

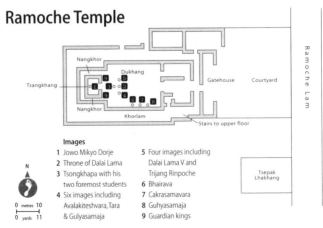

Ramoche Temple

Nangkhor
Dukhang
Tsangkhang
Nangkhor
Khorlam
Gatehouse   Courtyard
Ramoche Lam
Stairs to upper floor
Tsepak Lhakhang

Images
1 Jowo Mikyo Dorje
2 Throne of Dalai Lama
3 Tsongkhapa with his two foremost students
4 Six images including Avalakiteshvara, Tara & Gulyasamaja
5 Four images including Dalai Lama V and Trijang Rinpoche
6 Bhairava
7 Cakrasamavara
8 Guhyasamaja
9 Guardian kings

N

0 metres 10
0 yards 11

student of Tsongkhapa. It then became the assembly hall of the **Gyuto Tratsang**, the Upper Tantric College of Lhasa, located further east, and housed 500 monks. During the period 1959-66, Ramoche housed a communist labour training committee. The temple has, however, been restored since 1985, and the central Jowo Mikyo Dorje image, which had been severed in two parts during the Cultural Revolution, was repaired when its torso was returned to Tibet, having been found in Beijing by the late Panchen Lama X, that same year. According to some, this image may not be the original, in that Ramoche was also damaged by Mongol incursions in earlier centuries. Presently, the temple is once again occupied by the Upper Tantric College monks and undergoing repairs.

Entrance Ramoche is located on Ramoche lam, a lane near East Dekyi lam, close by the Tromzikhang market. The temple is entered via a large courtyard, leading up to an east-facing three-storey gatehouse, bedecked by 10 large fluted columns and two rows of eight mani wheels. The upper chambers of the gatehouse comprise later chapels and cells for monks.

Khorlam The circumambulatory path around the temple has new rows of mani wheels on the south, west, and north sides. Outer murals depict the Three Deities of Longevity (Tselha Namsum).

Dukhang (Assembly Hall) The assembly hall is approached with the hermitage (*drubkhang*) on the left. The corridor has archaic bas-relief images and beams painted with the Six Syllabled Mantra, while the right wall has a painting of Dorje Yudronma, protectress of the Upper Tantric College. By the entrance at the end of the right wall is an image of Vajrapani.

The **assembly hall** has 27 lion sculptures below the skylight. The central images flank and back the throne of Dalai Lama. Behind in a glass cabinet are Tsongkhapa with his foremost students; to the left are Gyuto Khenpo I Kunga Dondrub, Jowo Shakyamuni, Avalokiteshvara, Tara, and then, further left, Guhyasamaja. To the right of the throne are: Tsongkhapa, Trijang Rinpoche Dalai Lama V, and Shakyamuni. Against the left wall are images of the three meditational deities Guhya-samaja, Cakrasamvara, and Bhairava.

Tsangkhang (Inner Sanctum) Surrounded by an inner circumambulation path (*nangkhor*), the **inner sanctum** is 5.4 by 4.4 metres. Here, **Jowo Mikyo Dorje** is seated on a large stone platform, facing west. The entrance is flanked by the Four Guardian Kings. Above the central image are the Seven Generations of Past Buddhas, with the Eight Bodhisattvas to the right and left. The rear wall has images of Tsongkhapa and Maitreya; while the gatekeepers Vajrapani and Hayagriva flank the entrance.

Upper Floors The second floor of Ramoche is largely residential; but there is one main chapel containing images of Buddha as King of the Nagas, surrounded by the Sixteen Elders. An inner sanctum contains images of the Eight Medicine Buddhas and a copy of the *Kangyur*. On the third floor, the front chambers are the Dalai Lama's private apartments, and the rear chamber a private chapel, with a gyaphib-style roof, enclosed by a wooden balustrade.

Tsepak Lhakhang Located south of Ramoche,. it has new large images of Amitayus, flanked by Shakyamuni and Maitreya. The inner walls have murals depicting the Thirty-five Confession Buddhas and lineage-holders from all the four major schools of Tibetan Buddhism. In the outer circumambulation (*korlam*), there are 1,127 wall-painted images of Amitayus, in gold outlined on a red background.

Jebumgang
Lhakhang

This temple, located at the junction of Ramoche lam and East Dekyi lam, behind the public toilets, is dedicated to Tsongkhapa and it contains 100,000 small images of this master. The building was used as a granary during the Cultural Revolution.

Gyume
Tratsang

Gyume Tratsang, the Lower Tantric College of Lhasa, is located on East Dekyi lam across the street from the Tibet-Gansu trade centre and the *Kirey Hotel*. A number of tantric colleges were established by Tsongkhapa's student Je Sherab Senge (1382-1445), including Se Gyupa (in Tsang), Chumelung (west of Lhasa), and Gyume Tsatsang, and those affiliated directly with Tsel Gungtang, Sera, Dechen and Meldro. Among these, the present Gyume complex dates from its reconstruction by Kalon Techen Phagto in the 18th century.

The **ground floor**, approached from the debating courtyard, houses the press for the Lhasa *Kangyur*, and a large assembly hall with an **inner sanctum** (*tsangkhang*) containing new six-metre images of Tsongkhapa and his students. An adjacent protector shrine contains murals of the meditational deities Guhya-samaja, Cakrasamvara and Bhairava, along with the protectors Mahakala, Shridevi, Dharmaraja and Vaishravana.

On the **second floor** of the main temple is the **Dolma Lhakhang**, the images of which include (left to right): Manjughosa, Vajrapani, Tara, Amitayus, Shakyamuni, Tsongkhapa with students, Maitreya in the form Jampa Chokhorma, Cakrasamvara (with a 'speaking' Tara to the rear), Guhyasamaja, Dalai Lama XIII, Tsongkhapa, Je Sherab Senge (the founder of Gyume), and Maitreya. New murals on the west wall depict the Eight Aspects of Tara and Vijaya. A balcony attached to the Dolma Lhakhang overlooks the aforementioned north inner chapel of the ground floor.

On the third floor is the **Kangyur Lhakhang** with an old bronze Shakyamuni as its centrepiece, flanked by a set of the *Kangyur* volumes. Its west wall has images of Tsongkhapa and his foremost students. An adjacent **Zhalre Lhakhang** overlooks the aforementioned six-metre images.

The fourth level contains the private apartments (*zimchung*) of the Dalai Lamas. The Gelukpa tantric study programme at such colleges was known for its austere strictness, and, at Gyume, was accessible only to superior monks from Ganden, Sera and Drepung. Currently there are 40 monks.

Shide Tratsang

Shide Tratsang is located on the north side of East Dekyi lam, west of its intersection with the Mentsikhang lam, and down a side lane. It is said to have been founded by King Relpachen and is included among the six lhakhang surrounding the Jokhang. Fom the 14th century onwards, it has been a dependency of Reting Monastery. The extant building is entered from roof level near the **Reting Labrang** – an attractive garden-enclosed building towards Tsomonling, which is still active as the residence of the present Reting Rinpoche.

Meru Sarpa
Tratsang

Meru Sarpa Tratsang is located opposite the *Kirey Hotel* on East Dekyi lam, but is now occupied by the TAR Theatre Troupe. There is an assembly hall with three small chapels. Formerly affiliated with Shide Tratsang, this college separated after 1684 and its preceptor later (post 1912) became a candidate for the regency. Its monks became affiliated with **Gyume Tratsang**. The present buildings date from the 19th century and were constructed by Sakya Nga-pe, the abbot of Nechung.

Regency Temples of Tengyeling and Tsomonling

The regency temples of Kundeling, Tengyeling, Tsomonling and Tsechokling were constructed during the 17th century after Dalai Lama V had assumed both spiritual and temporal power. Among these, Tengyeling and Tsomonling are located within Inner Lhasa; Kundeling lies to the south of Parmari, in the western area of the city, and Tsechokling lies south of the Kyi-chu River.

Tengyeling is located behind the Mentsikhang and on a lane, the entrance of which directly faces the *Snowland Hotel*. The main assembly hall once contained three eastern chapels, approached by a triple entrance, and an interior western hall; but the compound of the monastery is presently occupied by Tibetan homes and the Lhasa No 1 Middle School. Only the **Protector Chapel (Gonkhang)**, at roof level, is now active. Affiliated with Samye Monastery. it contains reconstructed images of Cimara flanked on the left by Pehar and Padmasambhava, and on the right by Hayagriva and Vajrakumara. Formerly the most important of the regency temples, Tengyeling was the seat of the successive Demo Qutuqtus, who provided three regents of Tibet – the first during the period of Dalai Lama VIII from 1757-77, the second during the period of Dalai Lamas IX and X from 1810 to 1819, and the third during the period of Dalai Lama XIII from 1886-95 when the incumbent qutuqtu was deposed by the Dalai Lama XIII on his assumption of temporal power. When Chao Erh-feng invaded Lhasa in 1910, Tengyeling offered support – for which reason the monastery was later damaged by the Tibetans in 1912, and converted temporarily into a post office. In its place, Meru Sarpa (opposite the *Kirey Hotel*) was classed as a regency temple.

Tengyeling

བསྟན་རྒྱས་གླིང་

The residence of the Demo Qutuqtu (**Demo Labrang**) to the north has now been transformed into the *Kyichu Hotel* on East Dekyi lam. Slightly west of this building is a new Government Reception Centre, built to receive Tibetans returning from abroad.

Tsomonling (properly pronounced Tsemonling) is located south of Ramoche. The large courtyard is surrounded on three sides by two-storey monastic cells, which are now occupied by the laity. The building on the north side of the courtyard has two wings: the **Karpo Podrang** in the east and the **Marpo Podrang** in the west. The former is a three-storey building, dating from 1777, which contains: the assembly hall, the reliquary chamber of Numun Qan I and II, and six chapels (ground level), the protector chapel (second level), and the residence of the monastic preceptors (third level). The latter, dating from the 19th century, contains: the assembly hall with reliquaries of Nomun Qan III and IV, two protector chapels, and a chapel dedicated to the Eight Medicine Buddhas. Tsomonling is the residence of the successive Nomun Qan Qutuqtus, two of whom served as regents: during the period of Dalai Lama VIII from 1777-84, and during the period of Dalai Lamas X and XI from 1819 until 1844, when the incumbent was exiled to China.

Tsomonling

ཚོ་སྨོན་གླིང་

Potala Palace རྩེ་པོ་ཏ་ལའི་ཕོ་བྲང

Lhasa

Location:
About 2 km northwest
from Barkhor Square,
the palace lies outside of
the Old City on East
Dekyi lam
Maps:
Lhasa centre,
page 76
Red Palace, Potala,
page 101
■ *Admission:*
¥45 per person
Open: 0900-1600 except
Sunday, longer on
Wednesday & Saturday.
Some rooms closed
1230-1430

*Aptly named after Mount Potalaka, the sacred mountain abode of the bodhisattva of compassion, Avalokiteshvara, the Potala Palace has been identified in different ages as the residence of Tibet's two illustrious and kingly emanations of Avalokiteshvara – Songtsen Gampo during the seventh century and Dalai Lama V during the 17th century. The building which towers above the city of Lhasa rises from the slopes of Mount Marpori, for which reason it is known locally as **Tse Podrang** ('Summit Palace'). The outer section, known as the **White Palace** has functioned as the traditional seat of government and the winter residence of the Dalai Lamas, while the inner section known as the **Red Palace** contains outstanding temples and the reliquary tombs of eight past Dalai Lamas. In terms of global perception, it is this relic of Tibet's past, present, and future national aspirations, more than any other, which uniquely symbolizes the country, like the Great Wall in China or the Vatican in Italy. This 13-storeyed edifice was among the world's tallest buildings prior to the advent of the 20th century skyscraper, and undoubtedly the grandest building in Tibet. It has many external vantage points – from the outer circumambulatory path (lingkhor), from Kumalingka Island, from the adjacent Chakpori Hill, from the Jokhang roofs, and so forth. Wherever one goes in downtown Lhasa, the resplendent golden roofs of the Potala are visible on the skyline.*

Getting there   While tourists normally approach from the rear drive-in entrance on the north side of Mount Marpori to avoid the steep climb, the main entrance is from the Eastern Gatehouse above Zhol Square on West Dekyi lam. The outer walls of the Potala form a quadrangle, with fortified gates to the south, east and west, and Mount Marpori to the north. There are watch-towers on the southeast and southwest corners. The auxiliary buildings in the foreground include the Zhamarpa Palace, the Printing Press (Parkhang), the Kashag offices, and the prison.

The two printing presses are particularly significant: the **Ganden Phuntsoling Parkhang** (southeast corner) is a two-storey 600 square metres structure, contemporaneous with the White Palace. Its woodblocks which dated from 17th-18th century have been destroyed except for a few which were transferred to the Mentsikhang. The **Gang-gyen Potidengtsunkhang** was constructed during the reign of Dalai Lama XIII and funded by Genden Tripa XCI, whose reliquary is within its grounds. It is a vast six-storey building at the western perimeter wall, containing the Zhol edition of the *Kangyur* and *Tangyur* (second floor). The actual printing room is on the third floor in the **Jampa Lhakhang**, where precious images of Maitreya flanked by Atisha and Tsongkhapa, Amitayus, King Trisong Detsen, Padmasambhava, and White Tara have all been destroyed. The **protector chapel** (*gonkhang*) on the third floor was built only in 1949 but its enormous Bhairava image has been destroyed. In addition to the aforementioned woodblocks, the building now houses the religious archives of the Tibetan Autonomous Region.

Traditionally the chapels of the Potala were only open to the public on set days such as the fourth day of the sixth lunar month, and in the fourth lunar month. Now, in the absence of the Dalai Lama, it has the air of a museum, and is accessible six days a week. **NB** pilgrims may enter throughout the day on Wednesday and Saturday so queues will be longer.

Entrance

The Potala Palace has four approaches: the **Eastern Staircase** (Shar-gyi Do-ke) which leads to the Sharchen Chok jail tower; the **Western Staircase**

History of the Potala Palace

Little remains of the original 11-storeyed Potala Palace which King Songtsen Gampo built on Mount Marpori in 637. An illustration of this earlier structure, which was destroyed by lightning in the reign of King Trisong Detsen, is found on the outer wall of the Lamrim Lhakhang within the Red Palace. It appears, however, that the foundations of the present palace do date from the earlier period, as do two of the chapels contained within the Red Palace, namely the **Songtsen Nyipuk** and the **Phakpa Lhakhang** (see below, page 102).

When Lhasa was reinstated as the capital of Tibet in the 17th century, after an interim period of 900 years, during which time the seat of government had been located successively at Sakya, Tsetang, Rinpung, and Zhigatse, one of the first acts to be carried out by Dalai Lama V was the reconstruction of this national symbol. Prior to its completion, he himself lived at the Ganden Palace in Drepung Monastery, and the largest building below Mount Marpori had been the palace of the Zhamarpas, who had dominated the political life of Lhasa until the defeat of their powerful patrons at Zhigatse in 1641. Nonetheless, the fortress (dzong) of the Kings of Zhigatse is said to have been taken as the prototype or model for the construction of the new Potala Palace.

Dalai Lama V preserved the original foundations of the 7th century edifice and had the **White Palace** built between 1645 and 1653. 7,000 workers and 1,500 artisans were employed on this construction, along with Manchu and Newar artists. The murals of the east Wing and the **Kangyur Lhakhang** were completed in 1648, and the following year he moved from Drepung. The **Inner Zhol**

Obelisk (Doring Nangma) was constructed to commemorate this event.

The central upper part, known as the **Red Palace**, is mostly attributed to the regent Desi Sangye Gyatso (r 1679-1703) and dated 1690-93. Its interior was finished in 1697. However, Dalai Lama V died in 1682 and his death was concealed by the regent until 1694, enabling him to complete the task without the distraction of political upheavals. There is also an extant Jesuit drawing, dated 1661, which interestingly suggests that 2 storeys of the Red Palace were actually constructed before his demise. Work on the funerary chapel was carried out between 1692-4, costing 2.1 million taels of silver.

Renovations

Enlargement was carried out through the 18th century. Then, in 1922, the renovation of the chapels and halls adjacent to the Phakpa Lhakhang was undertaken, along with that of the East Wing of the White Palace; and the Zhol printing press was enlarged. In 1959 the south façade was shelled during the suppression of the Lhasa Uprising, but the damaged porch of the Red Palace and the Potala School (Tse Lobdra) were subsequently restored by the late Panchen Lama X. The most recent renovations have taken place since 1991: the inner walls have been strengthened, the electrical supply stabilized, and extraneous buildings in the foreground of the palace removed to create a large square.

Altogether, the interior area of the 13-storeyed Potala Palace is 130,000 sq m. The building is 118m high, 366m from east to west, and 335m from north to south. There are 1,000 rooms, housing approximately 200,000 images.

(Nub-kyi Do-ke) which leads into the Western Courtyard (Deyang Nub) and the Namgyel Monastery; the **Northern Staircase** (Jang-gi Do-ke) or drive-in entrance at a higher level which was formerly used only by the Dalai Lamas; and the **Central Staircase** (U-kyi Do-ke) which bifurcates – one branch leading to the Western Gatehouse and the other to the Eastern Gatehouse. The latter is the principal entrance into the Potala, passing the Taktsang Gormo tower and the Tse Lobdra (senior seminary), before reaching the spacious Eastern Courtyard (Deyang Shar).

The White Palace

Deyang Shar
(Eastern
Courtyard)
This 1,500 square metres courtyard has the Tse Lobdra (senior seminary) on its northeast corner and a two-storey residential and office complex on the north and south wings. The **Tse Lobdra** was an eclectic school, founded by Dalai Lama VII (1708-57), which drew teachers from Mindroling and elsewhere.

The four-storeyed eastern façade of the White Palace overlooks this courtyard, the Dalai Lama's private apartments being in the uppermost gallery. A triple wooden ladder (Sum-ke Go) leads from the courtyard to the entrance foyer and the main gate. The south wall of the foyer depicts the gold handprints (*chak-je*) of Dalai Lama XIII and an edict of Dalai Lama V, proclaiming Desi Sangye Gyatso as his regent. The murals here depict the Four Guardian Kings, the construction of the Mentsikhang on Mount Chakpori, the arrival of Princess Wencheng, and the Jokhang construction.

Ascend the four flights of stairs to the roof of the White Palace, where the private apartments of the Dalai Lamas are located.

Eastern Private
Apartments
(Nyiwo Shar
Ganden Nangsel)
The gate leading into the living quarters of Dalai Lama XIV is marked by tiger-skin maces. The **outer reception room** has an elaborately decorated throne, flanked by portraits of Dalai Lama XIII and Dalai Lama XIV. On the northwest wall adjacent to the entrance there is a fine mural depicting the legendary land of Shambhala; and on the southeast wall there is a cracked mural depicting the Mahabodhi Temple at Vajrasana in India. A balcony overlooks the Eastern Courtyard, and there are antechambers on the southeast and southwest corners, which lead into the Dalai Lama's private quarters. These rooms include an **audience chamber** for informal receptions, foreign visitors, and the sealing of official documents. Its altars contain images depicting Simhavaktra, the Three Deities of Longevity (Tselha Namsum), and so forth,

The Potala

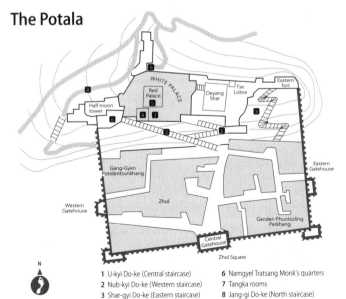

1 U-kyi Do-ke (Central staircase)
2 Nub-kyi Do-ke (Western staircase)
3 Shar-gyi Do-ke (Eastern staircase)
4 Deyang Nub
5 Tsokchen Nub
6 Namgyel Tratsang Monk's quarters
7 Tangka rooms
8 Jang-gi Do-ke (North staircase)
9 Exit to north car park

0 metres 50
0 yards   55

Lhasa

*The Potala Palace in
Lhasa*

and there is an interesting mural illustrating Dhanyakataka, the sacred abode in South India where the *Kalacakra Tantra* was first revealed. A small **Protector Chapel (Gonkhang)** has statues of Six-armed Mahakala, Shridevi, Dorje Drakden, and a table replete with the Dalai Lama's personal ritual implements. The **bedroom/dining room** with its images of the Three Deities of Longevity and Tsongkhapa mural is preserved as it was at the time of the Dalai Lama's departure in 1959. An inner door leads to the bathroom.

The living quarters of the previous Dalai Lamas comprise: an ornate **reception hall** where audience would be given to the Tibetan cabinet and Manchu ambans; a **bedroom** with murals hand-painted by Dalai Lama XIII; and an **audience chamber** where government council meetings would be held. This last room contains images of Thubwang Tazurma, Je Tashi Dokarma, Padmasambhava and Dalai Lama V.

Western Private Apartments
(Nyiwo Nub Sonam Lekhyil)

Within the White Palace, the East Main Hall is the largest chamber (25.8 metres by 27.8 metres), with 64 pillars, extending three-storeys in height. It was in this hall that each successive Dalai Lama was enthroned, the New Year commemorated, and credentials received from Manchu envoys. The murals depict events from early Tibetan history and the background of the different Dalai Lamas. An inscription in Chinese above the throne reads "May the emancipating service of the Dharma be spread throughout the Universe". The **Golden Urn** from which the names of certain Dalai Lamas were latterly drawn is now kept in the Norbulingka Summer Palace (see below, page 108).

East Main Hall
(Tsomchen Shar)

Between the White Palace and the Red Palace, there is a yellow building in which the two extant giant applique tangkas (*go-ku*) are kept. These were traditionally unfurled from the walls of the Potala at the beginning of the Yoghurt Festival; but in recent years have only been displayed on one occasion (1994). The third tangka was offered to **Batang Monastery** in the early decades of the present century.

Tangka Rooms

The Western Courtyard (Deyang Nub) serves as a focal point for the **Namgyel Monastery**, which was originally founded at Drepung by Dalai Lama III. At the southern perimeter of the courtyard are the monk's cells from which the aforementioned giant applique tangkas were unfurled. The walls of the Namgyel Monastery depict the protector deities and lamas of all the four major lineages.

Namgyel Monastery & Western Courtyard

The Red Palace

Unlike the White Palace which was used for administrative purposes and as a residence, the Red Palace which looms from the centre of the White Palace has a spiritual function. Its many temples are interspersed with the eight golden reliquary stupas (*serdung*) containing the embalmed remains of Dalai Lama V and Dalai Lamas VII-XIII. Four floors extend below the south façade of the Red Palace, but this space is demarcated only for aesthetic reasons. The north façade is constructed on solid rock. The functional part of the Red Palace has four floors, which are aligned with all but the highest of the storeys of the White Palace.

The **West Main Hall** (Tsokchen Nub) is the central structure of the Red Palace. It is flanked on all four sides by chapels two storeys high, entered from the ground level of the atrium; while the upper three floors have running galleries, reached in succession by a series of ladders and trap-doors. The galleries of the upper two storeys outwardly adjoin a further series of chapels, and inwardly they connect via footbridges with a central pavilion, the construction of which leaves sufficient space for light to filter into the West Main Hall below.

Access to the Red Palace is from the roof of the Potala via an entrance to the fourth floor facing the West Private Apartments (Nyiwo Nub Sonam Lekhyil).

Fourth Floor   **Jamkhang Phuntsok Khyil (east)** This chapel contains a large gilded-copper Maitreya image, which was commissioned by Dalai Lama VIII in honour of his relative – the deceased mother of Panchen VI Palden Yeshe. Facing the image is the throne of Dalai Lama VIII. The library is positioned on the far wall – containing the *Kangyur, Tangyur*, and the *Collected Works of Dalai Lama V*. Images adjacent to Maitreya include Dalai Lama V (containing clippings from his own hair), the Three Deities of Longevity (Tselha Namsum), the Lords of the Three Enlightened Families (Riksum Gonpo), Acala, Samayatara, Padmasambhava, and Kalacakra. A wooden three-dimensional palace (*vimana*) of the meditational deity Kalacakra is kept in the corner. Many old tangkas were destroyed in this chapel by an electrical fire in 1984.

Lolang Lhakhang Phuntsok Kopa (southeast) Originally constructed by Desi Sangye Gyatso, this chapel contains the celebrated three-dimensional mandalas of the meditational deities Guhyasamaja, Cakrasamvara, and Bhairava, which were commissioned by Dalai Lama VII in 1749. An image of that Dalai Lama is adjacent to the throne; and the murals depict his own life, as well as the ordination of Tibet's first seven trial monks in the eighth century. There are also many small images representative of all four major schools of Tibetan Buddhism.

Sasum Namgyel Lhakhang (south) This former residential chamber was converted into a chapel by Dalai Lama VII whose throne it contains. The west wall has a large silver image of Eleven-faced Avalokiteshvara (285 kilos) which was commissioned by Dalai Lama XIII. A portrait of Emperor Qianlong on the north wall was an enthronement gift to Dalai Lama VIII, dated 1762. Beneath it is the quadrilingual inscription "May Emperor Kangxi live for many thousands of years!", which was commissioned in 1722, and presented as a gift to the young Dalai Lama VII. In a glass cabinet are images of Tsongkhapa and his foremost students, Atisha, Dalai Lama VII, Panchen Lama IV, Panchen Lama VI, and so forth; and on the wall to the left is a 120 volume edition of the

Manchu Kangyur, with trilingual covers, some samples of which have been placed in a glass cabinet in front.

Chi-me Deden Zimchung Kadam Khyil (southwest) This, the largest room on the fourth floor, functioned as a residence of Dalai Lama VI from 1697-1706. It was converted into a chapel by Dalai Lama VIII in 1797. The central image depicts Amitayus, with a thousand small images of the same deity in surrounding niches. Other images include: a standing Avalokiteshvara, the masters of the graduated (*lam-rim*) lineage, the Sixteen Elders, the Four Guardian Kings, Tsongkhapa (from China) and the Nyingmapa protectress Ekajati. The murals depict the early Kadampa lineage-holders and Indian kings.

Serdung Gelek Dojo (west) A gateway leads via an enclosed passageway to a staircase, through which one descends four storeys to enter the well-lit **reliquary chamber of Dalai Lama XIII**. A viewing gallery is constructed on the

Lhasa

Red Palace (Potala)

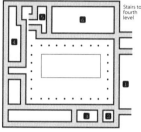

Third level
1 Dukhor Lhakhang
2 Shakyamuni Lhakhang
3 Tsepak Lhakhang
4 Tuwang Lhakhang
5 Chogyel Drupuk
6 Kunzang Jedro Khang

Fourth level
1 Jamkhang Phuntsok Khyil
2 Lolang Lhakhang Phuntsok Kopa
3 Sasum Namgyel Lhakhang
4 Chi-me Deden Zimchung Kadam Khyil
5 Lama Lhakhang
6 Gelek Zibak Serdung
7 Phakpa Lhakhang
8 Tashi Obar Serdung
9 Sasum Ngon-ga Serdung
10 Stairs to Serdung Gelek Dojo

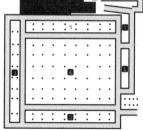

N

0 metres 15
0 yards 16

Ground level
1 Lamrim Lhakhang
2 Rigdzin Lhakhang
3 Serdung Dzamling Gyenchik
4 Tsomchen Nub Sizhi Phuntsok
5 Trungrab Lhakhang
6 Exit to north gate
7 Stairs to second level

Second level
1 Running galleries
2 Skylight
3 Stairs to third level

fourth floor. The ornate reliquary stupa, built between 1934-36, is 13 metres in height, weighing over 10,000 taels, with a central image of Eleven-faced Avalokiteshvara. In front is a newer image of Dalai Lama XIII; and on the altar is an offering mandala made of over 200,000 pearls. Murals depict events in the life of Dalai Lama XIII, including his 1910 pilgrimage to India. Ornate brocade ceiling hangings are suspended from the galleries above.

Lama Lhakhang (west) This chapel contains an image of Tsongkhapa, flanked by Dalai Lamas VI-XII.

Gelek Zibar Serdung (northwest) This chamber contains the **reliquary stupa of Dalai Lama VIII**, which was constructed in 1805. The stupa has an inset image of Eleven-faced Avalokiteshvara. Other images include: Dalai Lama VIII, Buddha in the form Tuwang Dudul (commissioned by Dalai Lama IX), and an applique tangka depicting Tibet's first king, Nyatri Tsenpo.

Phakpa Lhakhang (northwest) This is the most revered chapel within the Potala Palace, dating from the original seventh century construction. It houses a **'self-arising' gilt sandalwood image of Avalokiteshvara** which was one of four discovered in Nepal by Akaramatishila in the seventh century, when a sandalwood trunk split open. The triple staircase entrance is surmounted above the door with a trilingual inscription: "Wondrous Fruit of the Field of Merit", which was presented by the Manchu Emperor Tongzhi in the 19th century. The central image is flanked by two other standing images representing Tara and Avalokiteshvara. To the left are Dalai Lama X and Tsongkhapa, while to the right are Dalai Lamas VIII and IX. Other statues include: Kharsapani from Tanak, red sandalwood images of the Eight Bodhisattvas (commissioned by Dalai Lama V), silver images of the Lords of the Three Enlightened Families, Eleven-faced Avalokiteshvara, and Shakyamuni with the Sixteen Elders.

Inside the cabinet on the left are: stone footprints of Padmasambhava (from Gungtang Pass), Tsongkhapa, and Nagarjuna; an image of Jetsun Drakpa Gyeltsen called Dzetoma, an image of Panchen Shakyashri (in Tibet from 1204-14), a jade image of Drogon Chogyel Phakpa Lodro Gyeltsen, and an image of Tangtong Gyelpo. To the right of the door, adjacent to a large Vajrapani image, is an old image of Atisha.

Outside, note the bell and the image of Panchen Lama VI overlooking the approach to this chapel.

Tashi Obar Serdung (north) The **reliquary chapel of Dalai Lama VII** has a multi-doored entrance. The stupa itself is nine metres in height, with 100,000 precious stones, and surrounded by four large images. In front is a three-dimensional depiction of the Tushita Buddhafield, and on the south wall an image of Maitreya.

Sasum Ngon-ga Serdung (northeast) This chapel contains the golden **reliquary stupa of Dalai Lama IX**, along with a silver image of this Dalai Lama; and 114 volumes of the *Kangyur* inscribed in gold, a silver image of Tsongkhapa, and further images of the Sixteen Elders, which were commissioned by Dalai Lama VIII. The chapel is flanked on the west by the **Protector Chapel** (Gonkhang) and on the east by the narrow **Neten Lhakhang**.

Third Floor **Dukhor Lhakhang (east)** The gilded copper three-dimensional palace of the meditational deity Kalacakra, contained in this chapel, was constructed by

Desi Sangye Gyatso, 6.2 metres in diameter. There is also a life-size image of Kalacakra, surrounded by the 172 Kalacakra lineage-holders. On the right are seven religious kings of Tibet and the 25 kings (*khalki*) of Shambhala; as well as a gilt Enlightenment Stupa (Jangchub Chorten), eight silver stupas symbolizing the major events of the Buddha's life, and images of Manjughosa, Shridevi, Padmasambhava, and 38 deities in the retinue of Kalacakra. The murals depict Shambhala and the Kalacakra lineages.

Shakyamuni Lhakhang (southeast) This chapel contains the throne of Dalai Lama VII, and images depicting Shakyamuni, flanked by the eight standing bodhisattvas, and a manuscript edition of the *Kangyur*.

Tsepak Lhakhang (south) This chapel contains images of the nine aspects of Amitayus; flanked by White Tara and Green Tara. The murals depict the Potala Palace during the late 18th century, as well as the charismatic master Tangtong Gyelpo and the iron bridge constructed by him across the Brahmaputra at Chuwori Chakzam.

Tuwang Lhakhang (west) Here the central image is Shakyamuni Buddha, flanked by the Eight Bodhisattvas. There is also a throne of Dalai Lama VII, a manuscript *Kangyur*, and decorations commissioned by Dalai Lama VIII.

Chogyel Drupuk (northwest) This, along with the aforementioned Phakpa Lhakhang, is the oldest chamber of the Potala Palace, approached by a ramp which leads into a recessed cavern, supported by one large column which penetrates to the floor above and seven smaller columns. There are 28 images in the room. In a niche in the south face of the tall column is an image of Dalai Lama V, and at its base the stove of King Songtsen Gampo. Of the 28 images, the main deities depicted are Maitreya (1.5 metres), Avalokiteshvara (twice), Shaykamuni, Vaishravana, and White Tara. Most depict historical personages, such as the following: the youthful clean-shaven Dalai Lama V along with archaic images of Songtsen Gampo, his two foreign queens and Minister Gar Tongtsen (north); King Gungri Gungtsen and Minister Tonmi Sambhota (west); Tsongkhapa, Songtsen Gampo with Queen Mongza Tricham and other members of the royal family (east); and, lastly, Songtsen Gampo with Gungtang Lama Zhang (south).

Kunzang Jedro Khang (northeast) Here there are outer and inner chambers, the former comprising a Shakyamuni temple, and the latter, also known as the Natsok Lhakhang, containing small images in Chinese bronze, as well as larger images of Tsongkhapa, Amitayus, Six-armed Mahakala, and Shridevi.

Second Floor The chapels are closed on the second floor. However, there are **extraordinary murals** depicting the construction of the Potala Palace and various renowned monasteries, the Great Prayer Festival of Lhasa, and the funeral procession of Dalai Lama V. The gates overlooking the reliquary stupa of Dalai Lama V are particularly revered by pilgrims.

First Floor **West Main Hall (Tsomchen Nub Sizhi Phuntsok)** At 725 square metres, the West Main Hall is the largest room in the Potala Palace. It has eight tall and 36 short pillars, wrapped in raw silk material. The central throne of Dalai Lama VI is surmounted by a plaque, presented by Emperor Qianlong, which carries the legend: 'originally pure lotus place'. The 280 square metres murals, dating from the 17th century, depict Dalai Lama V, the Buddha-field of Mount

Potalaka, and the Tibetan kings. There are two large embroidered tapestries depicting the Three Ancestral Religious Kings and the Dalai Lamas, which were presented by Emperor Kangxi. Applique tangkas depict Amitabha and the Seven Generations of Past Buddhas, surrounded by the Thirty-five Confession Buddhas (north); the four main Kadampa deities flanked by the Eight Bodhisattvas and Tara who Protects from the Eight Fears (east); the Buddhas of the Three Times surrounded by the Sixteen Elders (south); and the Medicine Buddhas, the Lords of the Three Enlightened Families, and the Seven Generations of Past Buddhas (west). The four side-chapels were originally constructed by Desi Sangye Gyatso:

Lamrim Lhakhang (east)   This chapel is dedicated to the ancient Indian and Tibetan masters of the 'extensive lineage of conduct' and the 'profound lineage of view', as represented by the Kadampa and Gelukpa schools. In the centre is a gilded silver image of Tsongkhapa, with Asanga (progenitor of the former lineage) to the right, and Nagarjuna (progenitor of the latter lineage) to the left. Near the right wall are two Enlightenment Stupas.

Rigdzin Lhakhang (south)   This chapel, dedicated to the ancient Indian lineage-holders of the Nyingma school, has 20 columns. The central image depicts Padmakara (40 kilos), flanked by the consorts Mandarava and Yeshe Tshogyel. To the left are gilded silver images of the Eight Awareness-Holders (Vidyadhara), who were the teachers of Padmasambhava; and to the right are similar images representing the Eight Manifestations of Padmasambhava. Behind on the east, west, and south walls are the volumes of a *Kangyur* manuscript, written in gold and black ink.

Serdung Dzamling Gyenchik (west)   This chapel contains three reliquary stupas, the largest being that of Dalai Lama V, named **Unique Ornament of the World (Dzamling Gyenchik)**. It extends over 14 metres in height, almost to the roof terrace of the fourth storey. Its gold embellishments weigh approximately 3,700 kilos, and its jewels are 10 times more valuable. It has in its lattice window a gold image of Eleven-faced Avalokiteshvara. At the western end of the chapel are the reliquaries of Dalai Lama X (**Khamsum Serdung Gyen-chok**) and Dalai Lama XII (**Serdung Serjin Obar**), who both died as minors. Behind these lesser reliquaries is a gold manuscript version of the Kangyur and Tangyur and the Collected Works of Tsongkhapa and his students. The central stupa is flanked by eight stupas symbolizing the eight major events in the life of the Buddha; and on the east wall there are murals depicting Dalai Lama V.

Trungrab Lhakhang (north)   The images of this chapel depict the illustrious past emanations of India and Tibet. At the centre is a solid gold Shakyamuni and a solid silver Dalai Lama V. To the right are King Songtsen Gampo, Dromtonpa, and Tsharchen Losel Gyatso. To the left are the first four Dalai Lamas. In front are the Eight Medicine Buddhas, the Buddhas of the Three Times, the Lords of the Three Enlightened Families and the aspects of Padmasambhava portrayed in the teaching-cycle known as *Spontaneously Present Wishes* (*Sampa Lhundrub*). Behind is a Tangyur manuscript presented to Dalai Lama VII by the Manchus, and a *Kangyur* offered by Desi Sangye Gyatso. On the far-left is the **reliquary stupa of Dalai Lama XI (Serdung Pende Obar)** with a silver image of King Songtsen Gampo in its lattice window.

From here, the pilgrim exits via the rear (north) gate of the Potala.

Sights around the Potala

Southeast of the Potala Palace on Karngadong Road is the Kharngadong Lhakhang, which contains ancient carved stone tablets, said to have been removed from the Jokhang.

Kharngadong Lhakhang

The excavation of mortar for the construction of the Potala Palace in the 17th century left behind a crater which became Lake Lukhang (270 metres by 112 metres). The small island (40 metres wide) on this lake was once frequented as a retreat by Dalai Lama V, and a three-storeyed temple dedicated to the naga spirits (Lukhang) was constructed by Desi Sangye Gyatso and Dalai Lama VI in the Zangdok Pelri style. There, annual offerings were traditionally made by the Tibetan Cabinet (Kashag) to appease the nagas. Renovations were carried out subsequently by Dalai Lama VIII in 1791, by Dalai Lama XIII in the early decades of this century, and in 1984. In recent years the temple once housed a small Tibetan language primary school, but this has unfortunately closed following the death of the resident teacher.

Dzong-gyab Lukhang Temple

Ground Floor The chapel of the ground floor, known as **Meldro Sechen Lhakhang**, has a raised platform supporting images of Nagaraja, riding an elephant and with five snakes above the head, and White Tara. The murals of the vestibule depict the buddha-fields of Zangdok Pelri and Abhirati.

Second Floor Here the principal image depicts Shakyamuni Buddha in the form Nagendraraja, with nine snakes above the head, symbolizing the nine naga kings. Eleven-faced Avalokiteshvara is to the left and the Twenty-one Taras to the right. A 'self-arising' stone image of Padmasambhava sits in front. The murals of the south and east walls depict the life of Pema Obar – one of the immortal themes of Tibetan opera; while those of the west and north depict the legend of the Indian king Gyelpo Lek-kye.

Third Floor The murals of this floor are outstanding, those of the east wall depicting the Eighty-four Mahasiddhas of ancient India, Padmasambhava's Twenty-five Tibetan disciples (Jewang Nyer-nga) and a number of sacred sites, such as Mindroling Monastery, Samye Monastery, Gangri Tokar hermitage, Sakya Monastery, and Mount Kailash. On the south side is the private apartment of the Dalai Lamas, who would traditionally visit the temple during the fourth month of the lunar calendar. The west wall uniquely depicts the yogic postures of the Anuyoga and Atiyoga meditations – each vignette captioned with the appropriate instructions. Lastly, the north wall depicts the Hundred Peaceful and Wrathful Deities and after-death scenes.

Drak Lhalupuk and other Chakpori Shrines

Chakpori

Opposite the Potala to the southeast is the 3,725 metres Chakpori, an south-shaped hill, considered sacred to Vajrapani. The slopes of Chakpori contain more than 5,000 rock-carvings, some of which were reputedly carved by Newar sculptors so as to correspond to the visions of King Songtsen Gampo, who saw images emerge from the hillside during his retreat on the adjacent Mount Marpori.

The east ridge of Chakpori is separated from Mount Marpori by the newly

Lhasa

constructed stupas on West Dekyi lam. Traditionally, this marked the entrance to the city of Lhasa (**Dago Kani**). Beneath the cliffs on the east side are the caves and temple complex of **Drak Lhalupuk**. On the summit a nunnery was constructed in the 15th century by Tangtong Gyelpo, but this was relocated further downhill in 1695 by Desi Sangye Gyatso and Nyingto Yonten Gonpo, who built in its place the **Medical College** (Menpa Tra-tsang). A celebrated hilltop temple affiliated with the Medical College, which contained an outstanding coral image of Amitayus made by Tangtong Gyelpo, a pearl image of Mahakarunika and a turquoise image of Tara, was destroyed in 1959, and subsequently replaced by a radio mast. Lhasa Television and Lhasa Radio have their offices below the west slopes of the hill; while the TAR Television and Radio stations are now relocated on the north side of West Dekyi lam, next to the Potala.

Drak Lhalupuk

བྲག་ཀླུ་ཀླུ་ཕུག

Location:
About 500 metres from
the Potala behind
Chakpori Hill
Maps:
Lhasa centre,
page 76
■ **Admission:**
¥5 per person

Follow a dirt road hugging the base of Mount Chakpori's southeast ridge to the **Drak Lhalupuk Cave**, also called Chogyel Zimpuk. Beyond the gateway to the site is the monastic residential building and the **Karzhung Cave**, containing new religious posters. A flight of stone steps then leads up to the two-storey grotto chapel. On the first floor is the **Tungshak Lhakhang**, containing images of Shakyamuni Buddha, Manjughosa, Tangtong Gyelpo, and the Three Deities of Longevity. The murals here depict the Thirty-five Confession Buddhas.

On the second floor is the **Zhalye Lhakhang**, containing the throne of the Dalai Lamas, and the actual **grotto entrance** on its right wall. An inscribed history of the site and images of Padmasambhava and Amitayus, along with large stone butter lamps, mark the entrance to the grotto. This original habitation was founded circa 645 by Songtsen Gampo's Tibetan queen Ruyong Gyelmo Tsun, reputedly at a site where the subterranean nagas had been detained during the draining of the marsh for the Jokhang's construction. The grotto later came to be associated with Padmasambhava, Nyang Tingzin Zangpo and Phakpa Chegom.

The **oblong cave** measures 27 square metres, its width varying between 4.5 metres and 5.5 metres. A central column of rock supports the ceiling, which forms a narrow circumambulatory passage with the walls. There are 71 sculptures within the grotto, the earliest of which were sculpted by Newars. Of these, 69 are carved directly into the granite, 47 of them dating from the earliest period, 19 from the 12th/13th century, and three from the 14th/15th century.

Fourteen of those sculptures are on the surfaces of the central column. Its east face has sculpted images of Shakyamuni (1.3 metres), with Shariputra and Maudgalyayana, flanked by Maitreya and Avalokiteshvara. The south face depicts Aksobhya Buddha flanked by the bodhisattvas Samantabhadra and Akashagarbha. The west face depicts three medicine buddhas; and the north face Shakyamuni with his two students.

The **south wall of the grotto** has 32 statues in three rows (17, 1, 14). Of these the **top row** has an image of Drubtob Nyima Ze – the yogin who opened and decorated the grotto; along with Yeshe Tsogyel, Dipamkara Buddha and Manjughosa; followed by Longchenpa; Avalokiteshvara with Vajrapani and Amitabha; Ksitigarbha; Shakyamuni with Samantabhadra and Nivaranaviskambhi; Maitreya with Namkei Nyingpo and Yeshe Tsogyel; and Shakyamuni with Yeshe Tsogyel and Tara. The **middle row** has a small Shakyamuni image; and the **lower row** has fine Newar style images of Ksitigarbha, Avalokiteshvara, Maitreya, Samantabhadra, crouching Maitreya, Akashagarbha, Ksitigarbha, Acala, Nivaranaviskambhi, peaceful Vajrapani, Tara, Dolma Rechikma, and Tara. Next to the Ksitigarbha image of the lower row is a **clacking stone**, said to have been used by King Songtsen Gampo when communicating with his Chinese consort Wencheng, who was in retreat in the adjacent cave.

The **west wall of the grotto** has six images: Kharsapani, the Buddhas of the Three Times, Mahakala, and Padmasambhava. The northwest corner has a free-standing Shridevi, flanked by Padmasambhava and Vajrapani.

Lastly, the **north wall** has 17 images in two rows, including Amitabha and Shakyamuni (**top row**), and Maitreya (thrice), Avalokiteshvara (thrice), Nivaranaviskambhi, Tonmi Sambhota, King Songtsen Gampo with his two foreign queens, Minister Gar Tongtsen, and Shakyamuni Buddha with his two students (**lower row**).

Adjacent to the grotto is the Neten Lhakhang, a new three-storey yellow build- **Neten** ing, constructed in 1987 by adolescents and consequently nicknamed the Youth **Lhakhang** Monastery. The ground floor has monastic quarters. The **main chapel on the second floor** has an entrance passage with (on the left) Tsongkhapa and his two foremost students, and (on the right) 11 statues, including two arhats, Shakyamuni, Khedrupje, and Shakyamuni on the upper row; and Huashang, Dharmatala, and the Four Guardian Kings on the lower row.

The central shrine has a new image of Shakyamuni Buddha with his two main disciples (donated by Dharamsala) and the Sixteen Elders in two rows on either side. There is also a private apartment set aside for the Dalai Lama. The balcony overlooks the Potala Palace and the city. This second floor chapel also has a landing which opens onto the **Gyaza Drubpuk** – the meditation cave of Princess Wencheng. The latter contains a bas-relief one metre image of Avalokiteshvara, and on the right wall Wencheng's clacking stone cavity. On the left of the landing is another rock face, with a 'self-arising' relief image of Vajrapani.

The nunnery of Drubtob Lhakhang, named after Tangtong Gyelpo **Drubtob** (1385-1464), stands above and to the right of the Drak Lhalupuk Cave. It is **Lhakhang** considered a branch of Shugseb Nunnery (see below, page 155). The original site was consecrated by the meditations of Tangtong Gyelpo, and earlier by those of Nyang Tingzin Zangpo. The central image is Tangtong Gyelpo, while the right wall has an image of Yutok Yonten Gonpo and the reliquary stupa of Dr Khyenrab Norbu, founder of the Lhasa Mentsikhang. The back wall has paintings of the Three Ancestral Religious Kings and the Medicine Buddha in gold line on a red background.

Sights in West Lhasa

South of Mount Chakpori, on the summit of Parmari, a mountain sacred to the **Bonpori Gesar** bodhisattva Manjughosa, is the **Gesar Lhakhang**, a Chinese style temple, which **Lhakhang** was built in 1792 by the Manchu ambans on behalf of the Qianlong emperor to commemorate the defeat of the Gorkhas. The temple was dedicated to the Chinese god of war and justice Guan Di, who for political reasons was identified with Gesar. A Chinese inscribed obelisk on the western side is dated 1793.

The temple, under the jurisdiction of Kundeling which lies at its base, comprises a lower **southern courtyard** containing the obelisk and leading to the main temple, and a higher northern chapel known as the **Jamyang Lhakhang**. The **main temple** has a new image of Gesar, backed by a thousand images of Tara, while the side walls have a thousand images of Padmasambhava.

Kundeling Regency Temple Kundeling, one of the four regency temples, is located to the west of the Potala Palace and south of Parmari, at the end of a side-road which branches off West Dekyi lam at the petrol station. The original complex was large and several chapels stood within a pleasant wooded garden. Kundeling's main four-storey temple housed an assembly hall with a ceiling nearly the height of the building. The **main chapel**, dedicated to Tsongkhapa, once contained the reliquary stupas of the successive Tasak Qutuqtus, two of whom served as regents of Tibet – one during the period of Dalai Lama VIII and Dalai Lama IX between 1791 and 1819, and the other during the period of Dalai Lama XIII from 1875 to 1886. Presently, there is a small rebuilt chapel on the site.

Norbulingka Palace ནོར་བུ་གླིང་ཁ

This 40 hectare park is entered from a main gate on Mirik lam, south of the *Lhasa Hotel* and the Nepalese Consulate. Admission fee: ¥25 per person. The site was developed as the Summer Palace of the Dalai Lamas, from the mid-18th century, when Dalai Lama VII selected it on account of a medicinal spring where he would bathe owing to his frail disposition. Thus the initial **Uyab Podrang** was built, and its site subsequently augmented in 1755 by the construction of the **Kelzang Podrang**. Later, the complex became known as the Summer Palace because the Tibetan government would move here from the Potala on the 18th day of the third lunar month. Dalai Lama VIII (1758-1804) expanded the complex, building the debating courtyard (chos-rva), the **Tsokyil Podrang** (marking the location of the original medicinal spring), the **Lu-khang Lho Pavilion**, the **Druzing Podrang**, and the adjacent southeast perimeter wall. Dalai Lama XIII (1876-1933) later upgraded the gardens of the Kelzang and Chensel palaces, developed the Tsokyil Podrang area, and finally in 1930 oversaw the construction of the **Chensel Lingka** in the northwest area of the park. This new complex itself contains three palaces: **Chensel Podrang**, **Kelzang Dekyil Podrang**, and **Chime Tsokyil Podrang**. Finally, Dalai Lama XIV constructed the new palace or **Takten Migyur Podrang** between 1954-56.

Norbulingka is divided into three areas: the palaces, the opera grounds, and the government buildings, among which the opera grounds comprise the open air stage and gardens to the east of the complex, adjacent to the entrance, where operatic performances are held during the Yoghurt Festival. Further north and to the west of the Takten Migyur Podrang are the government offices and Lonyenkhang (the former cinema), now occupied by the park attendants and the Cultural Office of Tibet.

The actual palace section comprises four integral complexes which are visited by the pilgrim in the following sequence: Kelzang Podrang (southeast), Takten Migyur Podrang (north), Tsokyil Podrang (C), and Chensel Podrang (northwest).

Kelzang Podrang Complex This three-storey palace is named after Dalai Lama VII, Kelzang Gyatso, who commissioned its construction in 1755. The central feature of the complex is the north-facing reception hall known as **Tshomchen Nyiwo**, entered via a south-facing cloister, which permits bright sunlight to enter the chamber through its large skylight. The centrepiece is the Dalai Lama's throne, backed by images of Shakyamuni, the Eight Medicine Buddhas, and the Sixteen Elders. Murals depict the Lords of the Three Enlightened Families, the Three Ancestral Religious Kings, and there are also 100 applique tangkas depicting the Three Deities of Longevity.

On the second floor (approached by stairs at the southwest of the portico) are the following chapels: **Nechu Lhakhang** (north) has images of the Buddha and the Sixteen Elders, the complete works of Tsongkhapa, and murals depicting the Yarlung kings; **Tashi Namrol Lhakhang** (east) is a protector chapel containing images of Six-armed Mahakala, Shridevi, Dharmaraja, Yamantaka, and the meditational deities Guhyasamaja, Cakrasamvara and Bhairava. There are two libraries (northwest and northeast); and the private apartments of the Dalai Lamas. The latter include: the study room known as **Tosam Gokyil** (southeast), which has murals depicting Shakyamuni, Tsongkhapa's five visions, and Manjushri riding a snowlion; the **Reception Hall** with its life-size images of Buddha and Kalacakra, and murals depicting the life of Dalai Lama XIII and his retinue; and the **Cultural Hall** (Rik-ne Khang), which functions as a library and has murals depicting Avalokiteshvara, Tsongkhapa's five visions, and the symbol of elemental power and buddha attributes (*namchu wangden*).

The single-storey east-facing **Uyab Lhakhang** is the oldest building in Norbulingka. It is located west of the Kelzang Podrang and was used as a meditation chamber by the Dalai Lamas. Note the simpler construction. The central room contains a golden throne and image of Shakyamuni Buddha, with murals depicting the Three Ancestral Religious Kings, the Sixteen Elders, the Potala Palace, the Jokhang Temple, Reting Monastery, and Norbulingka Palace. There is also a small study library (**Chakpe Khang**) and a meditation room (**Nyendzok Khang**).

The two-storey **Khamsum Zilnon** Pavilion is located 70 metres northeast of the Kelzang Podrang, and built into the grounds of the palace. It was formerly used as a observation point for the Dalai Lamas and their entourage during the Yoghurt Festival. Originally constructed by Dalai Lama XIII, it was replaced with a more elaborate structure by the Reting regent during the present century. The chambers of the Dalai Lamas, their tutors and officials are on the second floor.

The south-facing **Chakpekhang**, located north of the Uyab Phodrang, houses metaphysical texts and its murals depict Shakyamuni Buddha, the great Buddhist commentators of ancient India known as the 'six ornaments and two supreme ones', Kalacakra, the Sixteen Elders, the Eight Medicine Buddhas, and so forth. The south-facing **Debating Courtyard** (Chora), located north of the Chakpekhang, was once reserved for metaphysical discussions between the Dalai Lamas and their tutors.

Norbulingka Palace

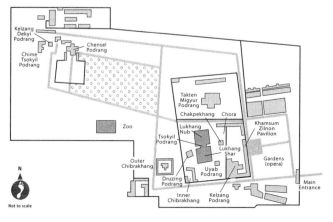

Takten Migyur Podrang Complex Also known as the New Palace (Podrang Sarpa) on account of its recent construction (1954-56), the Takten Migyur Podrang is an elaborate two-storey building, located north of the Tsokyil Podrang. The roof is surmounted by the wheel and deer emblem, and the south-facing façade has large glass windows.

Ground Floor Tiger-skin maces symbolizing royal dominion flank the entrance. The **Tshomchen Nelenkhang** in the southeast is a European-style reception room distinguished by a gold image of Manjushri flanked by gilded copper images of the Eight Medicine Buddhas.

Second Floor The **South Assembly Hall** (Tshomchen Lhoma Sizhi Dogukyil) has two entrances on the west side, while the south wall is composed of floor-to-ceiling windows. The north wall has images of Shakyamuni Buddha flanked by Manjushri and Maitreya, surmounted by a wall-length embroidered frieze depicting the great Indian Buddhist commentators. On the east wall there is an applique tangka of Yamantaka, suspended above the splendid throne of the Dalai Lama. The **celebrated murals** of the west, north, and east walls depict 301 scenes from Tibetan civilization – commencing with its legendary origins and continuing down to the period of Dalai Lama XIV.

The **Zimchung Drodren Semchok-khang** is the name given to the Dalai Lama's private quarters, comprising an **anteroom** and an inner chamber. The former has an embroidered sofa, above which is an ornate silk applique depicting Atisha, Ngok Lekpei Sherab and Dromtonpa, surmounted by the Kadampa protector deities. There is an altar on the north wall with silver images of the Lords of the Three Enlightened Families, and an old Philips gramophone, complete with 78 revolutions per minute records. The **inner chamber** to the east is the bedroom, bedecked with an Indian-style silver altarpiece dedicated to images of Avalokiteshvara, the Three Deities of Longevity, and Green Tara. A tangka depicts Tsongkhapa and various Gelukpa masters. Other items of interest include an art-deco bed, British plumbing and a Russian radio.

North of the anteroom is another west-facing chamber with a sofa of Indian sandalwood and a shrine containing an image of Shakyamuni Buddha flanked by a silver Vajrayogini and a gilded copper Tsongkhapa. The **Library** (Zimchung Chakpekhang), located in the northwest corner, has a principal image of Manjushri, a throne of the Dalai Lamas, and the murals of its west wall depict the great pilgrimage sites of Indian Buddhism. The **Zimchung Evam Gakyil**, located within this library, is the meditation room of the Dalai Lama, surmounted by paintings of the three meditational deities Guhyasamaja, Cakrasamvara and Bhairava; as well as Padmasambhava flanked by Shantaraksita and King Trisong Detsen. A silver shrine contains images of Guhyasamaja, Mahakala, and Manjushri; while a low table supports the three-dimensional celestial palace (*vimana*) of Mahakarunika.

The **North Assembly Hall** (Ogmin Goden Choling) is the principal reception room of the New Palace, dominated by its elevated gold throne, backed by gilded copper images of Maitreya flanked by Atisha and Tsongkhapa. The outer murals of the west and east walls depict the 56 episodes of the Buddha's life (above) and the 202 deeds of Tsongkhapa (below). The inner murals of the west wall depict the court of the present Dalai Lama, including the foreign envoys present in Lhasa during the 1940s, while those of the inner east wall depict the entire series of Dalai Lamas. Notice that the first four lack the wheel emblem, indicating that they lacked the unique fusion of spiritual and temporal power held by their successors. The murals of the south wall depict the legendary abode of Shambhala, the Sixteen Elders, and the Four Guardian Kings.

The **Zimchung Dogu Phuntsok**, entered from the east wall of the North

Assembly Hall, functioned as an office and the daytime quarters of the Dalai Lama's mother. It has a white sandalwood shrine replete with sandalwood images of Shakyamuni, the Six Ornaments and Two Supreme Ones of ancient India, Milarepa, and Atisha. On the north wall are gold images of Atisha with Ngok Lekpei Sherab and Dromtonpa; while its murals depict Tsongkhapa and his eight main students, with the founders of the major Gelukpa monasteries.

The **Zimchung Jeltrekhang** (southeast corner) where the Dalai Lama would relax with his family members has French furniture, and its white sandalwood shrine, holding images of Shakyamuni Buddha and the Sixteen Elders, was presented in 1956 by the Mahabodhi Society of India.

Outside this room on a landing, there are murals depicting the omni-directional wheel-shaped geometric poems (*kunzang khorlo*), which cleverly illustrate the names of the Tibetan Kings and the Dalai Lamas. Other murals depict Padmasambhava, flanked by Shantaraksita and King Trisong Detsen, the symbol of elemental power and buddha attributes (*namchu wangden*), the Four Harmonious Brethren (*tunpa punzhi*), the Twenty-five Kulika Kings of Shambhala and the Three Deities of Longevity. Lastly, there is an enigmatic drawing known as Domtson Dampa, which was used to refer obliquely to the great masters of the early phase of Buddhist propagation in Tibet during the persecution of Langdarma. It incorporates a lotus motif, symbolizing Padmasambhava, a book symbolizing Shantaraksita, a sword symbolizing King Trisong Detsen (who are also identified respectively with the Lords of the Three Enlightened Families), a two-headed duck indicative of Shantaraksita and Kamalashila, and a two-headed parrot representing the translators Kawa Peltsek and Chogrolui Gyeltsen.

The 18th century recreational complex of Tsokyil Podrang comprises three islands on an artificial lake. Among these, the central island accommodates the **Lhundrub Gyatsel Tsokyil Podrang**, the site of the original medicinal spring used by Dalai Lama VII. The palace was built in Chinese style with a pagoda roof in 1784 by the regent Demo Qutuqtu Delek Gyatso. A boating lake was subsequently added in 1887 by the young Dalai Lama XIII, and, at the same time, animals were first introduced to Norbulingka Zoo. **Tsokyil Podrang Complex**

The **Lukhang Nub** pavilion was constructed on the north island, also in 1784. Its pagoda roof is supported by several Tibetan-style architectural features including an architrave of *pema* twigs. The shrine is dedicated to Nagaraja, its murals depicting Ling Gesar and the legendary competition of magical prowess held between Milarepa and the Bonpos at Mount Kailash (see page 346). The **Lukhang Shar** pavilion, east of the lake, houses ritual implements.

West of the lake is the two-storey **Druzing Podrang**, also known as Dekyi Kunga Kyilwei Podrang, which was built by Dalai Lama XIII as a library and retreat. Pebbles deposited as a cairn by him are still visible outside the entrance. The building was renovated in 1982.

On the ground floor, the **assembly hall** (Tsomchen Chime Gatsel) contains a wooden image of Avalokiteshvara, which replaces an original Thousand-armed Mahakarunika image now in the White Palace of the Potala. Flanking it are images of Amitayus and a Shakyamuni (in stone from Bodh Gaya), along with the Eight Bodhisattvas. There are also 1,000 small images of Amitayus, and a library with a good collection of medical, historical, and Buddhist works, some in Chinese and Mongolian. On the **second floor**, the bedroom (northwest) has murals depicting Yamantaka, the Eight Manifestations of Padmasambhava, and the Eight Taras who Protect from the Eight Fears.

An **inner meditation cell** used by Dalai Lama XIII for Yamantaka meditation has images of Shakyamuni and Tsongkhapa. Further east is an **official chapel** containing images of Padmasambhava, Tsongkhapa with his foremost students, Avalokiteshvara, Manjushri, Amitayus and Shakyamuni, along with a throne surmounted by murals depicting the Five Buddhas of the Enlightened Families.

Chibrakhang The stables (Chibrakhang) occupy two buildings to the rear of the Tsokyil Podrang and Kelzang Podrang complexes. Of these, the **Inner Chibrakhang** has murals depicting the rearing of horses. It contains a two-storey building, the upper one being where the Dalai Lamas prepared for outings. The **Outer Chibrakhang** with its stables contains three rusting motor cars, which were the property of the present Dalai Lama – a 1931 Dodge and two 1927 Austins; and to its east is an outdoor stage platform, utilized during the Yoghurt Festival.

Chensel Podrang Complex A pathway leads through the zoo behind the three aforementioned palace complexes, to the **Chensel Podrang**, at the northwest extremity of Norbulingka. The main three-storeyed building was commissioned by the minister Chensel during the early years of Dalai Lama XIII, and rebuilt by the latter in 1926-28. A second floor balcony overlooks the courtyard where monks from Drepung would once perform religious dances.

Ground Floor The **Main Audience Hall** (Tsomchen Nyiwo) is where monastic ceremonies and *geshe* examinations were once held. The throne is on a raised platform at the north side, with an image of Dalai Lama XIII to its rear and a cabinet containing a silver image of Dalai Lama I in front. The side cabinets contain 36 silver statues of the Three Deities of Longevity. Murals depict the 108 deeds of Shakyamuni Buddha and the 80 aspects of Tsongkhapa's career.

Second Floor The study room, known as **Rabsel Paksam Dokyil**, is entered from the west side, its walls decorated by black and white photos taken in 1910 during the Dalai Lama's flight to Calcutta. Also on this floor are the rooms of the Dalai Lama's attendants; and the **Dingjakhang** – a well-lit south-sided balcony.

Third Floor On the third-storey is the **Sizhi Pelbar Assembly Hall**, where the Dalai Lama would give empowerments and private teachings. It contains images of Thousand-armed Mahakarunika (lifesize) and Thousand-armed Sitatapatra, along with the protector Dorje Drakden. The murals depict the successive Dalai Lamas, from I to XIII, and the main Gelukpa monasteries. There is also an inner meditation chamber called **Tsungdrel Teksum Juggo**.

There are also two smaller palaces within the complex. Some 160 metres west of the main Chensel Podrang is the two-storey **Kelzang Dekyi Podrang**, which was constructed between 1926-28, as an audience hall and later as a residence. On its ground floor, the **Zimchung Tashi Onang** contains the personal treasury of Dalai Lama XIII, while on the second floor (entered from the east staircase) there is a **Reception Room** with smaller partitioned chambers to the west. Images include Shakyamuni, Avalokiteshvara, and Khedrupje; while the murals include the sacred abodes of Mount Potalaka, Vajrasana, Wutaishan, Tushita and Dhanyakataka.

Further west of this building is the simply constructed **Chime Tsokyil Podrang**, in which Dalai Lama XIII passed away in 1933, and south of that is the **Usilkhang**, a dilapidated pavilion where the Dalai Lamas would wash their head.

The original Muslim quarter of Lhasa is the Khache Lingka, three kilometres **Khache Lingka**
west of the Potala Palace towards Drepung, and entered via a lane opposite the
Tibet Hotel. It contains two mosques and a cemetery, the site of which was
bequeathed to the Muslim community by Dalai Lama V and his regent Sangye
Gyatso. Part of the land has recently been leased by a Delhi-based Tibetan
businessman who intends to construct a garden hotel. The new Northern Ring
Road is also being constructed immediately to the east of Khache Lingka.

Drepung Monastery འབྲས་སྤུངས་དགོན་པ

Drepung Monastery (admission ¥10) is located eight kilometres northwest of   *Location:*
Lhasa on the Gephel Utse ridge above West Dekyi lam. It was founded in 1416   *Eight kilometres*
by Jamyang Choje Tashi Palden (1397-1449), and named after the sacred   *northwest of Lhasa on*
abode of Shridhanyakataka in South India. Jamyang Choje was one of   *the Gephel Utse ridge*
Tsongkhapa's foremost disciples, and it is known that Tsongkhapa himself   *above West Dekyi lam*
taught at the site of the new monastery. The complex developed rapidly with   *Maps:*
the assistance of the Phakmodru kings, especially Nedong Namka Zangpo, so   *Lhasa surroundings,*
that there were 2,000 monks in its second year of existence. In the early years of *page 70*
the 16th century, Dalai Lama II took possession of the **Ganden Podrang** at   ■ *Admission:*
Drepung, which was later to become an important centre of political power in   *¥10 per person*
Tibet. At the time when Dalai Lama V assumed spiritual and temporal power
in 1641, Drepung had over 10,000 monks, who hailed from 321 different
branch monasteries and lived according to nationality in 50-60 different
houses, making it the largest monastery in the world. Drepung's influence
within the Gelukpa world extended far to the east and northeast through
Amdo and Mongolia. The abbot-preceptor of Drepung, known as the **Tripa**
Khenpo, was formerly an influential figure within the Tibetan government.

Much of the 20,000 square metres complex at Drepung has survived
unscathed, despite repeated plunder inflicted upon it – by King Tsangpa Desi
of Zhigatse during the civil war in 1618, by the Mongols in 1635, by Lhazang
Qan in 1706, and by the Chinese during the recent Cultural Revolution. Many
of the surviving buildings date from the 17th-18th century. The monastery
reopened in 1980, with a population of approximately 500, most of them
young novices, but in recent years the numbers have been considerably
reduced in consequence of the active programme of political indoctrination
initiated here by communist party cadres.

The complex comprises the **Central Assembly Hall** (Tsokchen
Lhakhang), the **Ganden Palace** (Ganden Podrang), and a series of seven col-
leges (Tratsang), each originally under the control of one or other of Jamyang
Choje's students, and each containing its own residential units (Khangtsang).
Four of these colleges survive to the present, namely: **Ngakpa**, **Loseling**,
Deyang, and **Tashi Gomang**. The other three, Dulwa, Sha-khor, and
Tosamling, unfortunately declined during the 18th century. The pilgrim's
circumambulatory route around Drepung follows the sequence described
here, viz: Ganden Podrang, Assembly Hall, Ngakpa Tratsang, Jamyang
Lhakhang, Loseling Tratsang, Tashi Gomang Tratsang, and Deyang Tratsang.

In 1518 the magnificent residence of **Dokhang Ngonmo** in the southwest cor- **Ganden**
ner of Drepung was offered by Miwang Tashi Drakpa of Phakmodru to Dalai   **Podrang**
Lama II, and its name was thereafter changed to **Ganden Podrang**. It continued to function as the residence of the successive Dalai Lamas until Dalai Lama
V moved into the newly reconstructed Potala Palace in the late 17th century.
Nonetheless, the government established by him continued to refer to itself by
the name Ganden Podrang until 1959.

Left of the entrance gateway is the **Sangak Podrang**, which serves as a protector shrine. The outer chamber contains an image of Dalai Lama V, the throne of the Dalai Lamas, above which exquisite applique tangkas are suspended, and backed by glass-cased images of the meditational deities Guhyasamaja, Cakrasamvara, and Bhairava; as well as Tsongkhapa and his foremost students. Attached to the side walls are elevated bookcases containing manuscript volumes of the *Kangyur* and *Tangyur*. The **inner sanctum** with its distinctive gold on black murals contains images of Dharmaraja, Bhairava, Six-armed Mahakala, and Shridevi.

At the northern perimeter of the terrace, is a steep flight of stairs leading to the **main courtyard**, where religious dances were once performed and where the Drepung Yoghurt Festival even now begins in summertime. This courtyard is flanked by two-storey residential quarters, which were once occupied by the monks of Namgyel Monastery (before their move to the Potala Palace).

Beyond the courtyard, the lower storey of the palace contains an **Assembly Hall**, which houses Atisha's personal image of 'speaking' Tara (Dolma Sungjonma), and other images of Mahakarunika, and the protector deities. The **upper storey** contains the Private Apartments of the Dalai Lamas, which have images of Tsongkhapa with his main students, and an elaborate throne.

Central Assembly Hall (Tsokchen Lhakhang) The 4,500 square metres three-storey central assembly hall is the largest and grandest building in Drepung, rebuilt by Miwang Sonam Topgyel in 1735. Its wide terrace, approached by a flight of 17 steps, overlooks the city of Lhasa and the Kyi-chu valley. The entrance actually in use is a gateway on the left side of the building.

Ground Floor The main hall on the ground floor (50 metres by 36 metres) has 182 columns and the two-storeyed central atrium is well lit from above. On the left side of the hall are the **Lubum Lhakhang**, containing two sunken stupas blessed by the nagas, and the silver-plated **reliquary stupas of Dalai Lama III and Dalai Lama IV**, which are accessible to the public only on the eighth day of the seventh lunar month during the Yoghurt Festival. Beyond the Lubum Lhakhang is the **Lhamo Lhakhang**, containing a painting of the protectress Shridevi, made from the nose-blood of Dalai Lama V, as well as her three-dimensional celestial palace (*vimana*).

The **main altar** of the Assembly Hall has images of the Sixteen Elders to the far left and right in symmetrical groups of eight. The central group of images and sacred objects comprises: the reliquary of the 95th Ganden Tripa, a silver image of Sitatapatra (built in 1951), a gilded copper two-storey high image of Manjughosa in the form Chokhorma Sungjonma, and other statues of Shakyamuni Buddha, Tsongkhapa Khamsum Zilnon (donated by Longchen Shatra), Thuba Tsultrima, Dalai Lama XIII, Jamyang Choje Tashi Palden, and Dalai Lamas VII, III, IV, V, IX, and VIII. The 18th century murals depict scenes from the *Avandanakalpalata*.

Behind this wall is the **western inner sanctum** known as the **Temple of the Buddhas of the Three Times** (Dusum Sangye Lhakhang), which

Drepung Monastery

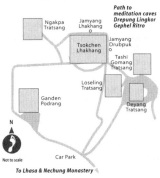

Path to meditation caves
Drepung Lingkor
Gephel Ritro

Ngakpa Tratsang
Jamyang Lhakhang
Jamyang Drubpuk
Tsokchen Lhakhang
Tashi Gomang Tratsang
Loseling Tratsang
Ganden Podrang
Deyang Tratsang

N

Not to scale   Car Park

To Lhasa & Nechung Monastery

retains original 15th century features. Its west wall has images of Hayagriva, the gatekeeper, and four standing bodhisattvas, the north wall has silver-plated images of the Buddhas of the Three Times, with smaller gilded copper images of Shakyamuni and his two foremost disciples in front, and the Nine Stupas of Dhanyakataka to the rear. The east wall has images of Tsongkhapa, four standing bodhisattvas, and the gatekeeper Vajrapani. Small images of King Songtsen Gampo, his queens and entourage are additionally attached to the columns. Formerly, a Kalacakra ceremony was held in this temple on the 15th day of the third lunar month. East of this chapel is the second or **eastern inner sanctum**, known as the **Miwang Lhakhang**, which contains an 18th century two-storey high image of Miwang Jampa.

Second Floor The northwest corner of the second storey contains the most venerated chapel in Drepung, known as the **Jampa Tongdrol Lhakhang**. The central 15 metres image depicting Maitreya Buddha at the age of eight was constructed by the Phakmodru kings according to the instructions of Tsongkhapa. Its forehead contains buddha relics and a hair from Tsongkhapa's own head, while its throat has a conch shell and its heart contains relics of Kanthaka, the steed of Shakyamuni Buddha. The entrance to this chapel is closed, and access is only gained from the floor above. The Chinese plaque above the chapel entrance was donated by one of the Manchu ambans in 1846.

Also on the second floor is the **Kangyur Lhakhang** which contains three of the 17 *Kangyur* manuscripts and blockprints kept in Drepung, viz: the Litang edition donated by Muji, the king of Jang; the Qing edition donated by the Kangxi Emperor; and a gold inscribed edition donated by Depa Lobzang Todol as a birthday gift to Dalai Lama V.

Third Floor The **Zhelre Lhakhang**, which permits a view of the head and torso of the Maitreya image below, has a portico where pilgrims prostrate. The chapel also contains over 400 original bronze images, and, until 1994, the image was also graced by the presence of a celebrated white conch with a counter-clockwise spiral, which is said to have been buried by Shakyamuni Buddha, rediscovered by Tsongkhapa, and then presented to Jamyang Choje following the construction of Drepung. This has sadly been stolen by art thieves. Two reliquaries contain the remains of Dalai Lama II and Jamyang Zhepa, while the smaller images in front of Maitreya are (left to right): Tog-me Zangpo, Tsongkhapa, Seu Rinchen, Tsongkhapa (again) and Jamyang Choje. Eleven other images, including various Dalai and Panchen Lamas, grace the side-walls.

The **Dolma Lhakhang** contains three 'self-arising' and 'speaking' 17th century images of Tara, namely: the Nedong Chime Dolma who protects the water source at Drepung; the Yamdrok Dolma who protects the monastery's wealth; and the Gyantse Tsechen Dolma who confers authority on Drepung. The chapel also contains the edition of the Dzamling Yashak *Kangyur*, its 114 volumes inscribed in gold ink with ornately carved sandalwood covers. Other images include: Six-armed Mahakala, and Prajnaparamita whose heart contains an amulet box with a Tsongkhapa tooth relic. At the exit of this chapel is a tangka depicting the Hundred Peaceful and Wrathful Deities.

An adjacent **Printery** contains the *Collected Works of Tsongkhapa*, the *Collected Works of Dalai Lamas I & II*, various editions of the Kangyur, the *Biography of Atisha*, and the *History of Ganden*, as well as treatises on vinaya, grammar and a catalogue of publications.

Roof The Assembly Hall has two golden roofs, one covering the temple dedicated to the Buddhas of the Three Times, and the other covering the Jampa Tongdrol temple. Other rooftop chapels include the **Gyelpo Lhakhang** which has images of the early kings and the Dalai Lamas flanking the central enthroned image of Dalai Lama V; the **Tsokchen Jowo Khang** which contains a silver Jowo Shakyamuni image flanked by 13 silver stupas; and the **Jampakhang** dedicated to Maitreya. Southwest of the Assembly Hall is the residence of Drepung's most senior incumbent lama, Lamrim Rinpoche, who until his recent demise commanded wide respect and devotion.

Jamyang Drubpuk A small meditation cave at the eastern base of the Assembly Hall contains bas-relief images of Tsongkhapa and Jamyang Choje, and an old painting of Tsongkhapa. The rear cave wall backs onto the Assembly Hall.

Jamyang Lhakhang Located behind the Assembly Hall, this shrine supported by a single pillar has a 'self-arising' image of Manjushri and murals depicting Jamyang Choje, his first disciple, and the Twelve Tenma protectresses. An iron staff substitutes for Jamyang Choje's lost walking stick which pilgrims once rubbed on their backs to cure rheumatic pains. Adjacent reliquary stupas contain the remains of Lama Umapa of Gadong and Bumdrak Dunpa.

Ngakpa Tratsang This college dedicated to tantric studies is located west of the Central Assembly Hall. It was founded in 1419, originally to admit into tantric studies graduates of the other exoteric colleges. Adepts of the Ngakpa Tratsang would subsequently be admitted to the Upper Tantric College (Gyuto) or the Lower Tantric College (Gyume) in Lhasa. The **assembly hall** (Dukhang) which is the later of the two main buildings has images of the Indo-Tibetan *lamrim* lineage-holders, with Tsongkhapa and various Dalai Lamas at the centre. The **Jikje Lhakhang** behind the assembly hall was constructed by Tsongkhapa himself, and houses the sacred image of Bhairava known as 'Chogyel Caktakma', Dharmaraja holding an iron chain. The embalmed remains of Ra Lotsawa are contained within this image. Other statues here depict: Dorje Drakden, Mahakala, Shridevi, Dalai Lama V and Tsongkhapa.

Loseling Tratsang The college of dialectics, known as Loseling (1,860 square metres), is located southeast of the Central Assembly Hall. The abbot-preceptor of Loseling was highly influential, presiding over 23 residential units (*khangtsang*). The **assembly hall** has 102 columns, and it contains numerous volumes of scripture. From left to right the main images and sacred objects are: the reliquary stupa of Loseling Tripa I Legden Rinpoche; the reliquary stupa of the late Kangyur Rinpoche; images of Dalai Lamas V, VIII, and VII; a Bhairava mandala and image of Jamyang Choje; an image of Ganden Tripa XV Sonam Drakpa alias Dorje Shukden; images of Tsongkhapa and Dalai Lama XIII; the throne of Sonam Drakpa; the reliquary stupa of Loseling Dedrub Rinpoche; and images of Tsongkhapa with his foremost students, and Sitatapatra. The niches of the side walls hold 1,000 small images of Amitayus.

There are three inner sanctums. In succession, these are: **Neten Lhakhang** which has images of the Sixteen Elders in three tiers flanking an Enlightenment Stupa; the **Jampa Lhakhang** which has a large Maitreya with Shakyamuni Buddha (left), Tsongkhapa (right), and Dalai Lama XIII (centre), as well as Atisha flanked by Dromtonpa and Ngok Lekpei Sherab; and the **Tubpa Lhakhang** which has a small Shakyamuni image flanked by stupas. The upper level has a **Protector Chapel** accessible only to males. Here, Bhairava is flanked by the meditational deities Guhyasamaja, Cakrasamvara, and the protector Mahakala.

Located east of Loseling, this is the second largest college at Drepung, with 16 **Tashi Gomang** residential units (*khangtsang*). Traditionally it housed monks from Amdo, **Tratsang** Mongolia and Nakchuka. The **assembly hall** has 102 columns, and images (left to right) of: Six-armed Mahakala (twice), Dalai Lama VI, Tsongkhapa (four), Dipamkara Buddha, Avalokiteshvara (twice), Dalai Lama VII, Maitreya, Amitayus, and Jamyang Choje. Distinctive murals depict the 108 episodes in the life of Shakyamuni Buddha.

There are three inner sanctums, in succession: **Tsepak Lhakhang** which has images of the Three Deities of Longevity; the **Mikyopa Lhakhang** which has three tiers of images, with Aksobhya at the centre of the top tier, flanked by Shakyamuni and a smaller Aksobhya. The middle tier has Shakyamuni, Avalokiteshvara, Maitreya, and a small Tsongkhapa in front; and on the lowest tier, there are five images of the celebrated Gomang lama Jamyang Zhepa. Lastly the **Dolma Lhakhang** has tiered images of the Twenty-one Taras and the Sixteen Elders. In its second storey is a protector shrine dedicated to Dorje Drakden. Here, the central image is Mahakala, flanked by Bhairava and various local deities.

This, the smallest of the four Tratsang, is dedicated to the Medicine Buddhas. **Deyang** The **assembly hall** has images of Tsongkhapa with his foremost students, **Tratsang** Sitatapatra, White and Green Tara, and Dalai Lama V; while its gatekeepers are the protector deities Dorje Drakden and Shridevi. The **Jowokhang** at the rear of the assembly hall contains an image of Maitreya flanked on the left by Deyang Jangchub Palden and Dalai Lama VII, and on the right by Tsongkhapa, Shakyamuni, Dalai Lama III, Rato Tripa I Yonten Gyatso, and Deyang Tripa II. The monastic kitchen lies east of the assembly hall.

Around Drepung there are five cave hermitages once associated with the mon- **Five Meditation** astery's founder. These are: the destroyed **Nyare Barti Chikhang** (near **Caves of** Ganden Podrang); the enclosed **Warti Shobokhang** (at the western perimeter **Jamyang Choje** where water is drawn for the monastery); the aforementioned **Jamyang Druphuk**; **Wartsokhang** (in the willow garden of Deyang Tratsang); and **Gozhima Shamma** (south of Loseling near Tewu Khangtsang).

There is a one and a half hour pilgrim's circumambulation of Drepung Monas- **Drepung** tery, which leads west of the perimeter wall and uphill in the direction of **Lingkor** Gephel Ritro, before descending in the direction of Nechung. En route the following features of sacred geography are observed: four 'self-arising' golden fish at Ganden Podrang, Tashi Kangsar, Ngakpa Tratsang and Gungru Kham-tsang respectively; a 'self-arising' Green Tara called Dolma Kangchakma; other paintings of Tara at Chiri Rizur, a 'self-arising' Jambhala, a stone throne associated with Dalai Lama V; and a 'self-arising' stone engraved with the Six Syllable Mantra of Avalokiteshvara.

The hermitage known as Gephel Ritro is located three to four hours walk above **Gephel Ritro** Drepung Monastery on the Lingkhor. It was founded by Tsepa Drungchen Kunga Dorje in the 14th century. Here, monk herders produce excellent curd, which was formerly reserved for the Dalai Lamas. The ascent from the hermitage to the summit of Gephelri takes another two hours. Juniper offerings are regularly made at the summit, especially on the full moon of the fourth month of the lunar calendar.

Nechung Monastery གནས་ཆུང་དགོན་པ

Located one kilometre southeast of Drepung, Nechung Monastery is the abode of the protector deity Pehar and the seat of the State Oracle of Tibet. Pehar is said to have had legendary associations with Zahor and later, under the name Shingjachen, with the Bhatahor Kingdom of Central Asia. Following the subjugation of that kingdom by the Tibetan army under Prince Murub Tsepo, Padmasambhava converted Pehar's five forms to Buddhism, renaming them Gyelpo Ku-nga. The first Tibetan abode of Pehar was at Peharling in Samye. Later a second abode was established at Tsel Gungtang but the image of Pehar in that locale caused havoc, prompting Lama Shang to expel it in a casket into the Kyi-chu River. Retrieved from the river at Drepung, the Pehar image escaped from the casket in the form of a dove which flew into the tree at Nechung. This tree is nowadays in the rear left-side chapel, along with an image of Pehar and photo of the Nechung Oracle.

The first temple at Nechung was constructed in the 12th century; and Pehar since then is said to have periodically left the tree to foretell the future through his medium Dorje Drakden who would possess the Nechung Oracle, making pronouncements on natural disasters, political appointments and so forth. Originally a Nyingmapa establishment, Nechung later developed a close relation with nearby Drepung; and from the time of Dalai Lama V its oracles have held highly influential positions within the political life of Tibet, acting frequently as an intermediary between Pehar and the Dalai Lama.

Each Great Prayer Festival at Lhasa, the oracle would leave Nechung for Meru Monastery via the Barkhor and appear publicly on the 24th day of the first month of the lunar year to ward off obstacles. Above all, the oracle was required to undertake a rigorous training in tantric liturgies. When possessed by Dorje Drakden, the oracle would whisper his pronouncements, which would then be interpreted and written down by monk attendants on long blackboards dusted with limestone powder.

The oracle was also generally accessible to the nobility who paid generously for private divinations. In 1904, the medium was obliged to abdicate by Dalai Lama XIII owing to false prognostications concerning the Younghusband Expedition. In 1930 a new medium emerged to confirm the recognition of the new Dalai Lama XIV in 1937. He gave advice during the 1950s concerning the movement of the Dalai Lama and his *geshe* examinations of 1958. The following year, he fled to India with his entourage of six monks. The present incumbent, Lobzang Jikme, was not discovered as a tulku but appointed in Dharamsala where he presently resides with 20 monks. In 1976 the Drepung monks of Mungod were alarmed by his predictions concerning the well-being of the Dalai Lama.

The buildings of Nechung mostly survived the Cultural Revolution apart from its guilded roofs and embellishments. The complex, nestling within a grove of juniper and fruit trees, is approached via a lane marked by a water tower, southeast of Drepung. The **residence of the Nechung Oracle** is located behind the main buildings, while the **School of Buddhist Dialectics** (Nangten Lobdra) is located down a lane to the left of the main entrance.

The courtyard is entered by three gates, of which the southern one is always closed, reputedly because Dorje Shugden is said to be waiting constantly outside this gate to usurp power on the departure of Pehar. Murals here depict Pehar and retinue; and there is an inscriptionless obelisk dedicated to Pehar. The three-storeyed temple at the north end of the courtyard is approached by steps flanked by stone lions. The portico is flanked by murals depicting Pehar and Dorje Drakden.

Ground Floor The assembly hall with its dark murals depicting the Deities of the Eight Transmitted Precepts (Kabgye) is adjoined by three chapels: among these, the **Jordungkhang** (west) contains the sacred tree stump abode of Pehar's dove emanation, flanked by two Pehar images in peaceful and wrathful guises, along with further images of Padmasambhava and Tsongkhapa; the **Tsenkhang Uma** (centre) has a central image of Shakyamuni flanked by the pedestals of the now destroyed Eight Bodhisattvas. Formerly it also housed the throne of the Nechung Oracle backed by the Kutshab Rinpoche image of Padmasambhava through which Pehar was controlled. Lastly, the **Gon-khang** (east) is dedicated to Magzorma, and has images of Nyima Zhonu and (formerly) of Pehar in the form Kundu Gyelpo. **NB** This last image was regarded as the regent of Nechung in times when no oracle was recognized.

Second Floor There are two chapels on the second floor, the larger of which is the audience room of the Dalai Lamas, containing a throne and images of Tsongkhapa, Dalai Lama V, Shakyamuni Buddha, Maitreya, and Avalokiteshvara. The smaller chapel has images of Tsongkhapa and his foremost students, Shakyamuni Buddha, Avalokiteshvara, and Tara.

Third Floor Here there is a single chapel with an image of Padmasambhava in the charismatic form Nangsi Zilnon, which was constructed in 1981. Formerly, the temple also housed the national treasures known as the **Pehar Kordzo**.

Sights in North and East Lhasa

Sera Thekchenling Monastery སེ་ར་ཐེག་ཆེན་གླིང་

Located at the base of Mount Purbuchok, which forms part of the watershed between the Kyi-chu and the Penpo-chu rivers, Sera Thekchenling was founded in 1419 by Tsongkhapa's disciple Jamchen Choje Sakya Yeshe of Tsel Gungtang (1355-1435). Prior to this foundation, Tsongkhapa and his foremost students had established hermitages in the ridge above (Sera Utse). In time, the monastic community at Sera came to number between 5,000 and 6,000 monks. The complex comprises the Great Assembly Hall (Tsokchen), three colleges (previously there were four or five, including Sera To to which were gradually amalgamated), and 30 residential units (*khangtsang*). A long driveway divides the complex into eastern and western sectors – the former containing the Great Assembly Hall and the Homdong Kangtsang, and the latter containing the three colleges. The pilgrimage route follows a clockwise circuit in the sequence: Sera Me Tratsang, Ngakpa Tratsang, Sera Je Tratsang, Hamdong Khangtsang, Tsokchen Assembly Hall, and Tsongkhapa's hermitage on Mount Phurbuchok. Admission fee: ¥25 per person.

The Sera Me college, constructed in 1419, covers a large area (1,600 square metres) and has 13 residential units (*khangtsang*). It is the college promoting elementary studies at Sera. Its **assembly hall** was destroyed by lightning and rebuilt in 1761 by Kunkhyen Jangchub Penpa. It now has eight tall and 62 short columns, with main images of Shakyamuni (in copper) flanked by Maitreya, Manjushri and Amitayus, as well as by Bhaisajyaguru, Tsongkhapa and his students, Dalai Lama VII, Pawangka Rinpoche, and various former monastic preceptors of Sera Me.

There are five inner chapels attached to the assembly hall, here described

Sera Me
Tratsang

from west to east (ie left to right): **Tawok Lhakhang** contains an image of Tawok, protector of the east; **Je Rinpoche Lhakhang**, contains a stupa with an inset image of Tsongkhapa flanked by images of Tsongkhapa and Shakyamuni; **Neten Lhakhang** contains images of the Buddhas of the Three Times flanked by the Sixteen Elders in their mountain grottoes, and volumes of the *Prajnaparamita*; **Jowokhang** once contained the celebrated image of Miwang Jowo Shakyamuni, which has now been replaced with a large new Buddha image, flanked by the Eight Bodhisattvas, and guarded at the gates by Hayagriva and Acala; and lastly, **Tsongkha Lhakhang** contains an image of Je Rinpoche flanked by Atisha, Dromtonpa, Dalai Lamas I-III, Dalai Lama V, Jamchen Shakya Yeshe, Gyeltsen Zangpo, who was the first preceptor of Sera, and Kunkhyen Jangchub Penpa, the founder of the college, and so forth.

The second storey contains the **Nyima Lhakhang** which has a central image of Shakyamuni Buddha in the form Tuwang Tsultrim; and the **Kangyur Lhakhang**, now containing 1,000 small images of Tara since its volumes were destroyed during the Cultural Revolution. The third storey has the Dalai Lamas' private apartments.

Ngakpa Tratsang

This three-storeyed college building was built in 1419 by Jamchen Choje Shakya Yeshe and refurbished by Lhazang Qan in the early 18th century. It is the smallest of the current three colleges at Sera, focussing, as its name suggests, on tantric studies. The ground floor contains the assembly hall and two inner chapels.

The **assembly hall** has 42 short and four tall columns with elaborately carved capitals. The central image is an original Jamchen Choje Shakya Yeshe wearing a black hat, which was probably presented to Sera by Emperor Yongle (1360-1424) of the Ming Dynasty. Flanking this image are: Maitreya, Gyeltsen Zangpo, who was the first preceptor of Sera, Pawangka Rinpoche, Tsongkhapa with his foremost students, Dalai Lama XIII, Chokyi Gyeltsen, and Sera Je's founder Lodro Rinchen.

As for the two chapels: **Neten Lhakhang** contains images of Shakyamuni Buddha flanked by two sets of the Sixteen Elders, the upper series in Tibetan style and the lower series in Chinese lacquer, which was presented by Emperor Yongle to Jamchen Choje Shakya Yeshe. **Jigje Lhakhang** contains an original 15th century image of Bhairava, flanked by Mahakala, Dharmaraja, Shridevi, and so forth.

The second storey of the building has the **Tsepame Lhakhang** where the central image of Amitayus is flanked by the reliquary stupas of Gyeltsen Zangpo and Jetsun Chokyi Gyeltsen, as well as by images of the Eight Medicine Buddhas. The third storey has the Dalai Lamas' private apartments.

Sera Je Tratsang

Sera Je is the largest of the three colleges at Sera, covering an area of 1,700 square metres, with 17 residential units (*khangtsang*) which housed mostly immigrant monks from east Tibet and Mongolia. It was founded by Gungyel Lodro Rinchen Senge, a student of Tsongkhapa and Jamchen Choje Shakya Yeshe. The building originally had three-storeys, the fourth being added during a period of expansion in the 18th century when the number of columns in the

Sera Thekchenling Monastery

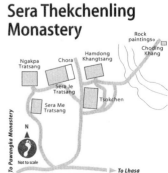

assembly hall was increased to 100. The finely decorated **assembly hall** has murals depicting the deeds of the Buddha, the thrones of the Dalai Lamas and Panchen Lamas, and, on its north wall, a series of reliquary stupas, and images of Dalai Lamas VIII and XIII, Reting Tulkus II and IX, and Sera Je's founder, Lodro Rinchen.

The following chapels are visited sequentially on the west and north sides of the assembly hall: **Dusum Sangye Lhakhang** contains images of the Buddhas of the Three Times and the Eight Bodhisattvas. **Tamdrin Lhakhang** contains the most sacred image of Sera Monastery, **Hayagriva**, sculpted by Lodro Rinchen himself, and enclosed within a gilded copper embossed shrine. The upper left compartment of the shrine contains the **Sera Phur Zhal** dagger, which is traditionally placed on public view only on the 17th day of the 12th lunar month once the Dalai Lama has touched it. The dagger reportedly flew from India to Mount Phurbuchok near Sera and was hidden as a treasure (*terma*) at Yerpa before being unearthed by the treasure-finder (*terton*) Darcharuba. The chapel is also bedecked with military regalia befitting a protector shrine room. **Jampa Lhakhang** contains images of Maitreya, Eleven-faced Mahakarunika, and Tsongkhapa with his foremost students, all surrounded by an impressive library. The **Tsongkhapa Lhakhang** contains images of Tsongkhapa with his foremost students, and important lamas of Sera Je as well as Nagarjuna and the other great Buddhist commentators of ancient India, and the gatekeepers Hayagriva and Acala. **Jampeyang Lhakhang** (northeast) contains two Manjushri images and one Maitreya image, the central Manjushri in the teaching gesture (*dharmacakramudra*) looking out onto the debating courtyard.

On the second floor, the **Zhelre Lhakhang** (west) permits a view of the sacred Hayagriva image on the floor below, but also contains a small image of Nine-headed Hayagriva, flanked by Padmasambhava, Dalai Lama V, and the protector deities. On the third floor, there is the **Namgyel Lhakhang**; and on the fourth, the private apartments of the Dalai Lamas and the preceptors of Sera Je.

The famous **Debating Courtyard** (Chora) contains a stone into which 13 syllables A are said to have dissolved once Tsongkhapa had completed his commentary on Madhyamaka philosophy, written in the hermitage above Sera.

Hamdong Khangtsang This is one of the principal residential units (*khangtsang*) attached to Sera Je college. Its **assembly hall** has minor images of Tsongkhapa, Chokyi Gyeltsen, Shakyamuni Buddha, and the Three Deities of Longevity. It has two inner chapels: The **Jampakhang** contains a 'speaking' image of Tara, which is said to guard the spring water of Sera, and an image of the late lama Tubten Kunga who renovated Sera before the Cultural Revolution. The **protector chapel** (Gonkhang) contains an image of the protector deity Gyelchen Karma Trinle.

Great Assembly Hall (Tsokchen) The four storeyed south-facing **Great Assembly Hall** is the largest building in Sera Monastery (2,000 square metres), with 89 tall and 36 short columns. It was constructed in 1710 by Lhazang Qan. It is entered via a 10 columned portico. Large applique tangkas are suspended from the ceiling along the side walls and there is a central skylight. The main image is that of Jamchen Choje Shakya Yeshe, the founder of Sera, flanked by Dalai Lamas V, VII, and XII, as well as by a five metres gilded Maitreya supported by two lions, Tsongkhapa and his foremost students, Chokyi Gyeltsen, Desi Sangye Gyatso, and others.

There are three inner chapels, described here in succession: **Jampa Lhakhang** contains a six metres two-storey high image of Maitreya, which is the centrepiece of the building, flanked by the Eight Bodhisattvas and the gatekeepers Hayagriva and Acala. On the south wall is a Yongle eighth year edition of the *Kangyur* (dated 1410), originally in 108 volumes although three have been lost. This is the oldest extant *Kangyur* printed from woodblocks, and each volume has a cover carved in gold on red lacquer. The **Neten Lhakhang** contains clay images of the Sixteen Elders, each of which encloses an authentic wooden image – the original wooden series having been presented to Sera by the Ming emperor Xuan Zong. Lastly, the **Jigje Lhakhang** contains images of Bhairava and consort flanked by Shridevi and other protectors.

The second floor contains the **Zhelre Lhakhang** (centre), affording a view of the large Maitreya below, with a small Tsongkhapa at its heart. The **Tu-je Chenpo Lhakhang** contains a large image of Eleven-faced Avalokiteshvara, which was originally discovered at Pawangka, and which is said to have a blessing transmitted via a staff from its heart directly to the pilgrim's head. Other images here include Tara and Six-armed Mahakala. The **Shakyamuni Lhakhang** has an image of Shakyamuni, flanked by images of various Gelukpa lamas.

The third and fourth floors contain the private apartments of the Dalai Lamas and those of the monastic preceptors of the Great Assembly Hall.

Choding Khang The hermitage of Je Tsongkhapa, known as **Choding Khang**, is located behind the Great Assembly Hall, on the slopes of Sera Utse Hill. It is entered at roof level via a path adjacent to the painted rock carvings of Tsongkhapa, Jamchen Choje Shakya Yeshe, and the protector Dharmaraja. The building replaces the original hermitage, which was destroyed during the Cultural Revolution. Further up the slope is the meditation cave associated with the master, while the hermitages of the Upper Tantric College (Gyuto) and Lower Tantric Colleges (Gyu-me) of Lhasa are located in front.

Sera Utse Continuing up the trail from Choding Hermitage for one and a half hours, the pilgrim will reach the **Sera Utse**, a hermitage predating the construction of Sera itself. It comprises a two-storeyed chapel, with monks' quarters which afford a wondrous view of the city of Lhasa, and a protector shrine dedicated to Pehar and Shridevi. An eastward trail leads around the mountain to Ragachok and Phurbuchok in the upper Dode valley; while a westward trail leads to the Tashi Choling hermitage in the Pawangka valley, two hours and a quarter distant.

Pawangka Monastery པ་འབངས་ཁ and adjacent sites

Pawangka is located some eight kilometres northeast of Lhasa, in a defile on the lower slopes of Mount Dukri to the west of Sera Monastery, and it is approached from behind the Lhasa Military Hospital. The original temple was constructed as a tower on the 300 square metres plinth which surmounts an enormous 20 metres high granite rock, itself said to represent an obelisk upon a turtle. The building is said to have been modelled on Devikoti, a temple in Guwahati, Assam, which in turn had associations with Kusinagara, the sacred place where the Buddha himself passed away. (Other Tibetan sites linked to Devikota include Ragya near Lhasa, Sheldrak near Tsetang and Phurmoche near Tashilhunpo.)

Below, at the entrance to the Pawangka defile, is a boulder, painted white with a red border along the top, where the local protector Gonpo Drashe Marpo is said to reside. Above, is a smaller whitewashed monolith – the two respectively being known as the female and male turtles (Rubal Pomo).

The original structures at Pawangka may well predate the Jokhang and Ramoche because King Songtsen Gampo and his queens seem to have gone there on the advice of Shridevi in order to suppress the supine ogress. They constructed a nine-storey palace, known as **Nyangdren Pawangka Podrang**, and there they went into retreat in order to determine the best sites for the construction of their geomantic temples. The Lords of the Three Enlightened Families affirmed their support for this endeavour by leaving 'self-arising' impressions of themselves in stone, which were later placed within the **Rigsum Gonpo Lhakhang**, which the king constructed along with 108 stupas. This temple also contains an original stone inscription of the Six-syllabled Mantra, prepared by Tonmi Sambhota who created the Tibetan alphabet here during a three year sojourn, following his return from India.

Above the main chapel is the **Gyaza Gonchu Podrang**, the residence of Princess Wencheng. At the eastern extremity of the site is the **Pawang Durtro**, Lhasa's most important charnel ground, symbolizing the skull of Cakrasamvara; while there is also the **Tashi Choling** mountain hermitage, the newly reconstructed **Chubzang nunnery**, and the ridge-top **Tokden Drubpuk cave retreat** dedicated to Cakrasamvara.

Subsequently, during the eighth century, King Trisong Detsen and Padmasambhava stayed seven days in the **Tsechu Lhakhang cave** at the base of the site. Tibet's original seven trial monks lived here for some time, but the buildings and stupas were destroyed by Langdarma in 841, in consequence of which the protectress Shridevi advised Lhalung Peldor to kill the apostate king. A two-storey monastery was reconstructed in the 11th century by Potowa's student Drakar, and it housed 200 monks, who gradually rebuilt the 108 stupas. Chogyel Phakpa later carried out further renovations; and the monastery was eventually completed by Khonton Peljor Lhundrub in 1619. A block of stone was brought from Devikota in Kamakhya, Assam, giving Pawangka the name Devikota. Dalai Lama V added an extra floor in the course of his renovations; so that subsequently the site was visited by all Dalai Lamas when they had obtained their geshe degree. The preceptors of Pawangka were later appointed directly by the Tibetan Cabinet (Kashag). In the 19th century, the hierarch of Pawangka was the teacher of the late Trijang Rinpoche, senior tutor to the present Dalai Lama.

The entire pilgrim's circuit of Pawangka takes approximately one day in summertime, following the sequence: Pawangka, Tashi Choling, Tokden Drubpuk, and Chubzang Nunnery.

Pawangka Circumambulation

A shorter circuit around the base of **Pawangka Rock** begins at the main steps, and runs clockwise. The **east face of the rock** contains: a cave shrine containing one metre images of the Lord of the Three Enlightened Families, Shakyamuni and Acala. The **south face** contains: rocks representing the buttocks and sexual organs of the female tortoise; and King Songtsen Gampo's cave retreat (eight metres by 12 metres) with its original 'self-arising' bas relief image of Shridevi, and other images including the king with his two foreign queens, and Padmasambhava, flanked by Shantaraksita and King Trisong Detsen. The **west face** has a shrine dedicated to Ganden Tripa Tenpa Rabgyel who passed away here.

The present complex is a three-storey circular building, the remains of King Songtsen Gampo's original tower, which is approached from the north by a series of steps. The other three sides are sheer rock faces. The interior floor plan is semi-circular, except for the northern section which is square. Repairs were made to this surviving structure in the 1980s; and 18 of the 108 stupas

Nyangdren Pawangka Podrang

have now been rebuilt. The ground floor contains the storerooms but no chapels; while the second floor contains the assembly hall (*tsokhang*), the protector chapel (*gon-khang*), and the Four-pillared Temple (Kabzhima Lhakhang).

Among these, the **assembly hall** contains a central reliquary stupa, with an original Shakyamuni in its inner sanctum, flanked by (left side) a 'self-arising' statue of Jowo Lokeshvara, transported from Gyama, the birthplace of King Songtsen Gampo; and (right side) a 'self-arising' image called Chubzang Doku Chenrezi which was brought from Chubzang; and (below in front) another Shakyamuni image, returned recently from Beijing. On the north wall of the assembly hall (adjacent to the protector chapel entrance) are in succession images of: Shantaraksita, Dalai Lama V, King Songtsen Gampo with his foreign queens, and Dalai Lama XIII. On the west wall are Padmasambhava flanked by Shantaraksita and King Trisong Detsen, while on the east (next to the window) are old tangkas with the throne of the late Panchen Lama X below.

The **protector chapel**, entered from the East side of the assembly hall, contains the following newly constructed images: Dorje Yudronma, Vaishravana, Dharmaraja, Guhyasamaja, Cakrasamvara, Bhairava, Magzorma, Gonpo Taksha Marpo (the local protector), and Lhamo Duzorma.

The **Four-pillared Temple**, entered from the left of the assembly hall, has new images of: Tonmi Sambhota, the kings Lhatotori Nyentsen, Trisong Detsen, Songtsen Gampo and Relpachen, Minister Gar Tongtsen, Khonton Peljor Lhundrub, Reting Trichen, Tenpa Rabgyel, and Lhatsun Rinpoche. On the roof is the private apartment of the Dalai lamas, containing images of: Cakrasamvara, Tara, Atisha, Tsongkhapa with his foremost students, and Avalokiteshvara.

Rigsum Gonpo Lhakhang   The **Rigsum Gonpo Lhakhang**, located southeast of the main building, was founded by King Songtsen Gampo. Beyond its entrance courtyard and within the portico to the left is the stone slab carved by Tonmi in person with the Six-syllabled Mantra of Avalokiteshvara, contained within a glass case. The left wall contains: new images of Tsongkhapa with his foremost students, Shakyamuni, and Eleven-faced Avalokiteshvara. Beyond is an **inner sanctum** containing murals of Thousand-armed Avalokiteshvara and Cakrasamvara, with the throne of the Dalai Lamas and the aforementioned highly venerated 'self-arising' images of the Lords of the Three Enlightened Families, which are of archaic design and were reputedly embellished by Newar craftsmen in the seventh century.

Adjacent to the entrance is a small shrine containing one of Cakrasamvara's three stone eyes (the others are at Tokden above and at Gari nunnery west of Pawangka). Northwest of this chapel is a newly constructed white reliquary; while north of the main building is a shrine containing 'self-arising' images of Tara (left) and Bhaisajyaguru (right). Below this shrine is a single-storey hermitage where Tsongkhapa stayed for one year in retreat.

Gyaza Gonchu Podrang   Uphill from Rigsum Gonpo Lhakhang is the yellow chapel of the **Gyaza Gonchu Podrang**. The ground floor contains the **Zikpa Lhakhang**, which commemorates Tsongkhapa's five visions (Zikpa Ngaden), and contains new two metres images of Tsongkhapa with his foremost students, murals of Vajrapani and Manjushri, and images of Tiger-riding Mahakala and Hayagriva. A side chamber to the left has new images of the Eight Medicine Buddhas, and some old tangkas.

Upstairs is the main chapel, dedicated to Princess Wencheng, with images of Tara, Shakyamuni Buddha, Tsongkhapa with his students, and King Songtsen Gampo with his foreign queens.

To the right (east) of the Gyaza Gonchu Podrang is the ruined Lhatsun Labrang; along with the ruined Tsongkha Lhakhang and the Karthog Lhakhang Khapa. The **Lhatsun Labrang** is entered through a south-facing courtyard, and at its rear, approached through a one metre high passage is a meditation cave of King Songtsen Gampo. To the west of the complex is a white washed rock carving of the Arapacana mantra (ie that of the bodhisattva Manjushri).

Lhatsun Labrang

To the north of the Lhatsun Labrang is the rocky abode of the protector of Pawangka – a 15 metres high boulder, symbolizing the male turtle, which was formerly separated from its lower counterpart by King Songtsen Gampo's 108 stupas in order to prevent their meeting which was predicted to presage various national disasters. The rock was formerly linked to Pawangka by a heavy iron chain, which was destroyed by Langdarma along with the upper six-storeys of the original tower. Left of the upper monolith and halfway up Mount Dukri are the **Sepuk meditation caves**, which contain 'self-arising' images of the Twenty-one Taras.

Upper White Rock

The Tashi Choling hermitage is located on the slopes above the charnel ground, and is accessible by a pathway leading uphill from the Lhatsun Labrang. A two-storey building stands at the north side of the courtyard and below a backdrop of ruins. On the right is a shrine containing original images of the Three Deities of Longevity, and smaller images of Shakyamuni, Bhaisajyaguru, the previous Pawangka Rinpoche, and so forth. The central pillar has a finely carved head of Hayagriva.

Tashi Choling Hermitage

Located 45 minutes walk above Pawangka, this hermitage comprises three caves, the main one containing one of Cakrasamvara's three eyes carved in stone, and a 'self-arising' spring, dedicated to Vajravarahi. It was a former retreat of the previous Pawangka Rinpoche, while one of the lesser caves was that of his disciple Tokden Gyaluk.

Tokden Drubpuk

Chubzang Nunnery is located at the floor of a ravine, 30 minutes walk south-east of Tashi Choling. The complex comprises an enclosed debating courtyard and an assembly hall, with an entrance courtyard and kitchen. The **inner sanctum** of the assembly hall contains two sets of Tsongkhapa with his foremost students. There are over 80 Gelukpa nuns presently at Chubzang.

Chubzang Nunnery

Sights in South Lhasa

Tsechokling Regency Temple བཙེ་མཆོག་གླིང་

Tsechokling, classed as one of the four regency temples, is located on the south bank of the Kyi-chu in Drib village. Constructed in 1782 by Yeshe Gyeltsen, tutor of Dalai Lama VIII, the main building (700 square metres) formerly contained a set of the Nartang *Kangyur* and a copper image of Tsongkhapa. It never actually provided a regent, but has survived the Cultural Revolution and is now under the guidance of Tsechok Rinpoche.

Ramagang སྐར་ཆུང་ར་མ་སྒང་

The temple of Ramagang, in the extreme southwest of the Lhasa valley, was constructed during the reign of King Relpachen, in traditional design, with a central temple and obelisk surrounded by four stupas in the cardinal directions. Nothing survives of this structure at the present day, although the stupas were photographed by Hugh Richardson in the 1940s.

Essentials

Sleeping
■ *on maps, pages 70, 76 and 90*
Price codes: see inside front cover

A *Lhasa Grand Hotel (Xizang Da Sha)*, 196 Middle Dekyi lam, T6826096, F6832195. A 3-star hotel, has 531 rooms, including 22 deluxe suites (US$93 per room), 184 deluxe standard rooms (US$52 per room), 52 triples (US$19 per room), and 52 economy rooms (US$15 per room), with oxygen, beauty salon, hairdresser, shops, business centre, and a dining hall with a seating capacity of 1200. **A** *Lhasa Hotel (Lhasa Fandian)*, 1 Minzu Road, T6822221, F6835796. A 3-star hotel, has 450 rooms, superior category in S and C blocks with piped oxygen in rooms (US$108 per room), and the inferior category in north block without piped oxygen (US$71), all rooms have attached bath, 5 restaurants (*Himalayan* for Tibetan and Nepalese dishes, *Sichuan* for Chinese dishes, *Everest* and *Gallery* for western buffet, and the *Hard Yak Café* for à la carte western meals), a full meal plan costs US$54, and breakfast US$16, also has swimming pool, *Tin Tin Bar*, coffee shop, karaoke bar, business centre, tour agency, gift shop, hairdressing and massage service, beauty salon, medical consultations (including Tibetan traditional medicine), and in-house movies.

B *Kyichu Hotel*, Dekyi lam, T6331541/ 6333147, F6320234. Has pleasant rooms with attached hot showers, business centre, shop, Nepalese restaurant and good location. **B** *Tibet Hotel*, 221 West Dekyi Rd, Lhasa, T6833738/6834966, F6836787. Has 200 beds (US$60 per double room), with attached bathrooms, restaurant (full meal plan US$32, breakfast US$8.50), travel agency, and discotheque. **B** *Tibet Post and Telecommunications Hotel (Xizang Youdian Binguan)*, 5 First Lane, East Lingkhor lam, T6329874/6321445, F6321723. Has 50 rooms include delux, standard, and triples, all with a/c and private telephone, and 5 restaurants. **B** *Sernye Hotel (Gold Grain Hotel/Jingu Fandian)*, 14 Yutok lam, T6830550/6336446, F6330367. Has 139 rooms with attached bathroom (range US$20-60), well sunlit on south side, with elevators, restaurant, dining room, disco, OK, and IDD payphones in lobby.

C *Himalaya Hotel*, 6 East Lingkhor Rd, Lhasa, T6322293, F6334855. Located near the river and within easy walking distance of the Barkhor, it has 116 bedrooms with attached bath (US$36 per double), Chinese and Tibetan restaurants (full meal plan at US$21, breakfast US$6.50), shop, sauna, business centre facilities, and travel agency. **C** *Sunlight Hotel*, 27 Linyu lam, Lhasa, T6322227, F6335675. Has 133 beds (US$42 per double room), some with attached bathrooms, and restaurant (full meal plan US$32, breakfast US$8.50). **C** *Airline Hotel*, Kharngadong lam, T6833444, F6833438. Centrally located, with large standard rooms (US$24 per room) and smaller standard rooms (US$20 per room). **C** *Kadak Hotel*, East Chingdrol lam, T6337771. Has fine

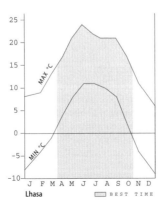

Lhasa   ☐ BEST TIME

rooms with attached bath on 4/F (¥300 per room), dining room, disco and OK. **C** *Xuelian Hotel*, East Lingkhor lam, T6323824. Has 80 beds. **C** *Number One Municipal Guesthouse*, Yutok lam. Has both expensive and basic accommodation, and good but plain Chinese meals.

D *Pentoc Guesthouse*, 2/F Zong He Fu Wu Bldg, East Mentsikhang lam, T/F(6330700/86326686). Has single rooms (US$10), doubles (US$15), twin rooms (US$17.50), and dorm beds (US$4.50), with hot showers, IDD service, in house travel agency, and mountain bike rental. **D** *Yak Hotel*, 36 East Dekyi lam, T6323496. Has 170 beds (range ¥200-90), some with attached bathroom, and others with shared bathing facilities, also Crazy Yak Restaurant. **D** *Snowlands Hotel*, Mentsikhang Rd/Tuanji lu, T6323687. Has 30 rooms, some of new construction with attached bathroom, and most of inferior standard with basic washing facilities, but arguably one of the best restaurants in Lhasa, serving Indian and Nepalese food.

E *Kyire Hotel*, East Dekyi lam, T6323462. Has 266 beds, big rooms (range ¥80-25), shared showers, and friendly restaurant. **E** *Banak Zhol Hotel*, East Dekyi lam, T6323829. Has 246 beds, thin walls, and shared shower facilities. Also in this category are **E** *Gang-gyen Hotel*, East Dekyi lam, T6339700/6337666. **E** *Tashi Mandal Hotel*, T6325804. Has double room (¥32 per room). **E** *Tashi Dagye Hotel*, Mentsikhang lam. **E** *Plateau (Gaoyuan) Hotel*, North Lingkhor lam, T6324916. Has 180 beds, good rooms and showers. Lastly **E** *Ying Qiao Hotel*, North Lingkhor lam. Which is a grandiose building boasting an in-house travel agency but no running water.

Among the major hotels, only *Lhasa Hotel* offers a wide range of Himalayan, Chinese, and Continental dishes. Good Chinese cuisine is available at the *Lhasa Grand Hotel*, the *Himalaya Hotel*, the *Tibet Hotel*, and the *Sernye Hotel*, while the *Kyichu* and *Snowlands* offer Nepalese and Indian fare. Lhasa city has many restaurants of varying cuisine and standard. For Tibetan food, including *momo*, and *thukpa* try the **Sonam Dokhang**, West Dekyi lam, T6832985, where the food is excellent but expensive. **Yeti Restaurant**, West Dekyi lam, T6833168, which is good and reasonably priced. **Friend's Corner**, Tsomoling. **Jamdrol Restaurant**, Karma Kunzang, T6336093, which caters exclusively to TTC tour groups; **Yak Café**, Mirik lam, T6834967. **Snowlands Restaurant**, near *Snowlands Hotel*, Mentsikhang lam, T6337323. **Dakini Restaurant**, West Dekyi lam. **Crazy Yak**, near *Yak Hotel*, East Dekyi lam, T6336845, which is good and reasonably priced, with Tibetan operatic and folk dance performances in the evenings. **Barkhor Café**, overlooking Lugu lam and the Jokhang Temple, T6326892. **Yutok Restaurant**, Yutok Zampa, T6330931. **Tibetan Corner Restaurant**, T6325915. **Tashi Restaurant**, Tsomoling. **Tashi Restaurant Number Two**, *Kyire Hotel*, T6323462. **Tibet Unute Restaurant**, Tsomoling; and **Lost Horizons Café**, Tsomo-ling.

For Amdo food, try the **Amdo Zakhang**, Beautiful World Entertainment Centre, Tsomoling. For Sichuan food, the **Thanduohua** is excellent and cheap. For Hotpot dishes, try **Bluebird Restaurant** (Qing Niao), West Chingdrol lam; and **Yangyang Restaurant**, Tsomoling. For Cantonese dishes and seafood, in addition to Sichuan cuisine, try the **Crystal Palace** (*Ch* Shuijing Gong), 180 Dekyi lam, T6333885. For Peking duck, try the **Gau Ya Restaurant**, on Kharngadong lam and on Nyangdren lam, opposite CAAC.

For the best and most expensive Nepalese and Indian dishes (also continental cuisine) try the **Snowlands Restaurant**, near *Snowlands Hotel*, Mentsikhang lam, T6337323. **Barkhor Café**, overlooking Lugu lam and the Jokhang Temple, T6326892. The recently opened **Makye Ama**, to the rear of the Jokhang, overlooking the Barkhor. Highly recommended.. **Kyichu Hotel**, Dekyi lam. **Grand Highland Palace**, 3/F Luga Market, near CAAC, T6339391. **Mountain Restaurant**, Kyire, T6338307. For Western dishes, in addition to these, try **Friend's Corner**, Tsomoling, where the food is good, clean and cheap.

Eating
● *on maps, pages 70, 76 and 90*

Yak Café, near *Lhasa Hotel* on Mirik Lam, T6334967, which serves clean but expensive food, and is popular with tour groups. *Tashi Restaurant*, Tsomoling, which caters mostly to individual tourists; and *Lost Horizons Café*, Tsomoling.

Entertainment Lhasa has many varied forms of entertainment. The local people devote much time to picnics, parties, and board games, especially Majong. The drinking songs of Lhasa are particularly renowned. Tibetan operas are performed at the *TAR Kyormolung Operatic Company*, the *TAR Academy of Performing Arts*, the *Lhasa City Academy of Performing Arts*, and in Norbulingka Park during the Yoghurt Festival in summer (see below, Festivals). Traditional Tibetan music may also be heard at the *Himalayan* restaurant in *Lhasa Hotel*, and the *Crazy Yak Restaurant*. There are a number of nightclubs, fashion shows, discotheques (including the Moonlight or New York Disco), and a profusion of karaoke bars and video parlours. The main *Lhasa City Cinema* is located on Yutok lam. However, the museums such as the *Potala Museum and Exhibition Hall* on Middle Dekyi lam, and the *Peoples' Art Museum* on the corner of East Chingdrol lam and Do Senge lam have little to offer in contrast to the magnificence of the city's temples, monasteries, and palaces. The *TAR Historical Archives*, located behind the Customs Office on West Dekyi lam, T6824184/6824823, has a fascinating collection of documents, some of which date from the era of Chogyel Phakpa.

Festivals For the dates of traditional Tibetan festivals, including those of Lhasa, see above, **Essentials**, page 48.

Shopping **Books, maps, cards and newspapers** *The Xinhua Bookshop*, West Dekyi lam, next to *Tibet Hotel*. Has a wide range of Tibetan cultural publications. Try also the *Xinhua Bookstore*, on Yutok lam, and the *Peoples' Publishing House Bookstore*, on North Lingkhor lam.

Handicrafts The traditional market of Lhasa is located around the Jokhang temple in the Barkhor and its radial road system. Tibetan handicrafts may be found here, including textiles, carpets, jewellery, metalwork, leather goods, photographs, and religious artefacts, including paintings, incense, and books. Antiques are available, but can only be exported with discretion. Bargaining here is the norm and, as a visitor, you should strive to reduce the proposed price by as much as 50 percent. Handicrafts are also available from the *Friendship Store* and other antique shops on Yutok lam or at the *Kyichu Hotel*, and from more expensive shops in the *Lhasa Hotel* and the *Himalaya Hotel*. For Tibetan tents and tent fabrics, contact *Tent Factory*, off East Dekyi lam. For new carpets, contact the *Carpet Factory*, off East Chingdrol lam. The *Boot Factory*, on East Chingdrol lam is also worth visiting. The Barkhor nowadays also has a number of department stores, including a new two-storeyed shopping complex with escalator access, opened in 1994. Chinese textiles, clothing, household utensils, and electrical goods are available here. Most shops will accept only RMB currency, and a few will be happy to receive payment in US dollars. Unofficial currency exchange facilities are instantly available; and the Bank of China is not too far distant on West Lingkhor lam. There are interesting open air markets around Tromzikhang, north of Barkhor and on Kharngadong Road, near the Potala.

Photography Print film and processing are available at photographic shops on Middle and East Dekyi lam, and on Kharngadong lam; both slide and print film may be available at *Lhasa Hotel*, though you are advised to carry all your film supplies from home.

Stamps Stamps are available at GPO, on corner of East Dekyi lam and Kharngadong lam; and also at the reception counters or shops in the major hotels.

Norbulingka Bus Station Fares

There are daily departures to all major destinations within TAR and Kermo.

Destination	Distance	Local Fares	Foreign Fares
Gongkar	104 km	¥18 (S)	¥27.40 (S)
Dranang	144 km	¥19 (S); 21 (D)	¥38 (S); 38 (D)
Tsetang	191 km		¥50.40
Zhigatse (direct)	280 km	¥38 (S); 41 (D)	¥61.60 (S); 65.80 (D)
Gyantse	264 km	¥36 (S); 38 (D)	same as local fare
Phari	427 km	¥57 (S); 62 (D)	from Zhigatse only
Dromo	473 km	¥67 (S); 70 (D)	from Zhigatse only
Dingri	642 km	¥86 (S); 93 (D)	¥145.20 (S); 171.40 (D)
Nyalam	794 km	¥107 (S); 115 (D)	¥208.60 (S); 215.20 (D)
Dram	824 km	¥111 (S); 119 (D)	¥217.20 (S); 223.80 (D)
Damzhung	162 km	¥24 (S)	¥35.60 (S); 38.80 (D)
Nakchu	326 km	¥44 (S); 47 (D)	¥71.80 (S); 78.20(D)
Draknak	464 km	¥63 (S); 67 (D)	¥102 (S); 111.40(D)
Yanshiping	653 km	¥88 (S); 95 (D)	¥143.60 (S); 156.60 (D)
Marchudram Babtsuk	745 km	¥101 (S); 109 (D)	¥164 (S); 178.80 (D)
Kermo	1,165 km	¥158 (S); 170 (D)	¥256.40 (S); 279.60 (D)
Ziling	1,947 km	¥263 (S); 283 (D)	¥340
Lhartse	567 km	¥68 (S); 74 (D)	Same as local fare
Gyamda	279 km	¥82 (D)	¥138
Bayi	371 km		¥153
Nyangtri	406 km	¥153 (S)	¥153
Tramog	639 km		N/A
Chamdo	1,121 km	¥151 (S); 163 (D)	N/A
Pomda Airport	950 km	from Chamdo only	from Chamdo only
Jomda	1,348 km	from Chamdo only	from Chamdo only
Drichu Zampa	1,436 km	from Chamdo only	from Chamdo only
Chengdu	2,415 km	¥443 (S); 477.30 (D)	¥520

NB *S = standard bus, D = deluxe bus.*
There is also a small service charge, transportation surcharge and standard or delux bus

Textiles Friendship Store Yutok lam, and the shops around the Barkhor offer traditional fabrics including brocade silk, and traditional ready-to-wear Tibetan clothing.

Sport

Gymnasium On Nyangdren lam. **Health clubs** At massage and beauty parlour in *Lhasa Hotel*, on Mirik lam. Suana at *Himalaya Hotel*. **Race course** On Nyangdren lam. **Sports Stadium** On East Lingkhor lam.

Transport

Local buses There are seven routes around Lhasa: **1**. Lugu-Leather Factory (via Chingdrol lam); **2**. Disco Bus Station-Tolung Dechen (via Norbulingka and the Peoples' Hospital); **3**. Disco Bus Station-Cement Factory (via Lukhang, Golden Yak, and *Tibet Hotel*); **4**. Disco Bus Station-Drepung (via Lukhang and *Tibet Hotel*); **5**. Disco Bus Station-Sera (via Yutok lam and Nyangdren lam); **6**. Ramoche-Drapchi (via North Lingkhor lam and Dokde lam); **7**. *Plateau Hotel*-Ngachen Power Station (via Ngachen lam); **8**. East Lingkhor lam-Taktse (via East Zamchen lam and Pelting).

Air Lhasa is connected via Gongkar Airport (96 kilometres southeast) to Chengdu

Lhasa

(daily flights), Kathmandu (Tuesday/Thursday/Saturday), Beijing (Sunday), Chongqing (Wednesday/Sunday) and Ziling (Monday/Friday).

Long distance buses   Long distance travel by public bus is uncomfortable, irregular, and slow. There are three long distance bus stations: the main Norbulingka Bus Station on West Chingdrol lam (see block), the Lugu Bus Station (for Nyemo, Lhundrub and Tsetang), and the Tromzikhang Bus Station (for Nakchu and Kermo). Hitchhiking is officially discouraged, but not impossible for the adventurous and well seasoned traveller.

Directory   **Airline offices**   *CAAC*, Nyangdren lam, near Potala Palace.

Banks   *Bank of China*, West Lingkhor lam. Limited exchange facilities are also available at *Lhasa Hotel* and *Himalaya Hotel*. Larger hotels will accept credit card payments. Money changers in Barkhor will accept and change US dollars into RMB at a rate slightly above that of the banks.

Communications   Fax: *Lhasa Grand Hotel*, *Lhasa Hotel*, *Post and Telecommunications Hotel*, *Himalaya Hotel*, *Tibet Hotel*, *Sernye Hotel* and *Kyichu Hotel*. Also new Telecommunications Tower on West Dekyi lam. **General Post Office:** East Dekyi lam. Postal facilities also available in major hotels. **IDD and DDD calls:** many outlets throughout the city in addition to the above hotels and the General Post Office.

Embassies & consulates   *Royal Nepalese Consulate*, Gyatso To Rd, near Norbulingka, T6822881, issues 15-day or 30-day tourist visas for Nepal within 24 hrs.

Hospitals & medical services   *Peoples' Hospital*, North Lingkhor lam, T6322200 (emergency department). *TAR No 2 Hospital*, Gyatso To lam, T6822115 (emergency department). The Italian-run *CISP Emergency Medicine Centre* in TAR, 7 North Lingkhor lam, T6321059, F(86891)6321049; and the *Swiss Red Cross*, 4 Nyangre Road, T6320175.

Tour companies & travel agents   *Windhorse Adventure Travel(WHAT)*, Lhasa Hotel Rm 1120, 6832221 x 1120/6832432, F(86891)6836793, Tx68012 TTB CN. *Tibet International Sports Travel (TIST)*, Himalaya Hotel, 6 East Lingkhor lam, T6331421/6334082, F(86891)6334855. *Tibet Tourist Corporation (TTC)* also known as *China International Travel Service* – Lhasa Branch (CITS), West Dekyi lam, T6836626/6835046, F(86891)6836315/6835277. *China Workers' Travel Service (CWTS)*: Tibet Branch, Lhasa Hotel, Lhasa, Rm 1104, T6824250, 6832221 ext 1104, F(86891)6834472, Tx69025 WTBL CN. *Lhasa Hotel Tour Department*, 1 Mirik lam, T6824509, F(86891)6834117. *Tibet Mountaineering Association (TMA)*, 8 East Lingkhor lam, T6322981, F(86891)6336366, Tx68029 TMA CN. *Lhasa Travel Service*, Sunlight Hotel, 27 Linyu lam, T6335196, 6333944, F(86891)6335675, Tx68016 TRCLS CN. *China Youth Travel Service (CYTS)*, Rm 1103, Lhasa Hotel, 1 Mirik lam, T6824173, F(86 891) 6823329, Tx68017 CYTS CN. *Golden Bridge Travel Service (GBT)*, Lhasa Branch, 13 Mirik lam, T6823828/6824063, F(86891)6825832, Tx68002 GBTCL CN. *China Tibet Qomolungma Travel (CTQT)*, Rm 1112, Lhasa Hotel, 1 Mirik lam, T6836863, F(86891)6836861. *Tibet Friendship Travel Service*, North Nyangdren lam, T6334534, F(86891)6334533. *Asia Dragon Tour Corporation (Yarlung Travel Service)*, 3 Mirik lam, T6835181, F(86891)6835182. *Tibet Air International Travel Service*, 14 Kharngadong lam, T6333331, F(86891)6333330. *Tibet Kailash Travel*, Lhasa Office, Yuanlin lam, T/F(86891)6832598. *Tibet Foreign Trade International Travel Service*, 182 M Dekyi lam, T6329222, F(86891)6336322. *Nyangtri Travel Service*, Pentoc Guesthouse, Mentsikhang lam, T/F(86891)6330700/6326686. **NB** Other hotels including *Tibet*, *Ying Qiao*, and *Sernye* also have established their own travel companies.

Tourist offices   *Tibet Tourism Bureau (TTB)*, Yuanlin lam, T6834315/6333635, F(86891)6834632.

Useful addresses   Police & public security: *Foreigners' Registration Office*, East Lingkhor lam, near *Banak Zhol Hotel*. *TAR Foreign Affairs Office*, on West Lingkhor lam, T6824992. *Lhasa City Police*, near Academy of Social Sciences.

Central Tibet
Kyi-chu Valley

4

Central Tibet

Kyi-chu Valley

The fertile Kyi-chu Valley in which the city of Lhasa is located is one of the more densely populated parts of Tibet. The valley extends from the river's glacial sources in the northern snow ranges of Nyenchen Tanglha, which form a watershed between the Salween and Brahmaputra, as far as its southern confluence with the Brahmaputra (Tib Yarlung Tsangpo) at Chushul. Upper Kyi-chu includes the districts of Tolung, Phenyul, Lungsho, Dri and Meldro, which lie to the NW and NE of Lhasa, while the valley downstream from Lhasa is known as Lower Kyi-chu. Currently, the entire Kyi-chu area is divided into six counties administered from Lhasa, namely: Tolung Dechen, Damzhung, Taktse, Lhundrub, Meldro, and Chushul.

Recommended itineraries: 3 (also 4, 6).

Central Tibet

Tolung Dechen County སྟོད་ལུང་བདེ་ཆེན

Tolung Dechen
County (1)
堆龙德庆县
Doilungdeqen
Population: 41,210
Area: 2,926 sq km
Colour map 3, grid B2

The paved Lhasa-Ziling Highway leads northwest from the Dongkar intersection, west of Lhasa, and follows the east bank of the Tolung-chu upstream via Tolung Dechen to Yangpachen (77 kilometres). Here, the northern route to Zhigatse branches off to the southwest, following the Lhorong-chu tributary upstream and across Zhugu La pass into Tsang (see below, page 246), while the highway turns northeast for Damzhung (85 kilometres from Yangpachen).

The Tolung valley has for centuries been the stronghold of the Karma Kagyu school in Central Tibet owing to the presence there of three great monasteries: **Tsurphu**, **Nenang**, and **Yangpachen**. The present county capital of **Tolung Dechen** is located at **Namka Ngozhi**, a rapidly developing town one kilometre beyond the Dongkar intersection.

Lower Tolung

Gadong
Monastery

དགའ་གདོང་
དགོན་པ

Located on the slopes above Namka Ngozhi, this Kadampa monastery was founded by Zingpo Sherapa in the 11th century. It subsequently became the seat of an important oracle, and there is a meditation cave where Tsongkhapa had visions of Manjughosa. A trail leads from the monastery to the summit of Gephel Utse, above Drepung, from where there is also a trekking route into Phenyul.

Kyormolung
Monastery

སྐྱོར་མོ་ལུང་
དགོན་པ

If you continue on the Chushul road from Dongkar (rather than taking the Ziling highway), you will immediately cross the Dongkar Bridge. An unpaved track to the right leads up the west bank of the Tolung-chu for seven kilometres to Kyormolung. Founded by the Kadampa Vinaya master Balti Wangchuk Tsultrim (1129-1215), it was later associated with Tsongkhapa and three Gelukpa colleges were established. The fine masonry and murals of the main temple have survived the ravages of recent decades. From Kyormolung there are also trekking routes to Nam and Chushul.

Zhongwa
Lhachu

ཞོང་བ་ལྷ་ཆུ

Near Kyormolung is the sacred site of Zhongwa Lhachu, where there is a natural spring, said to have been brought forth by Padmasambhava's magical prowess. The staff of Padmasambhava was formerly kept in the chapel constructed by Balti Rinpoche, and the spring itself is said to offer visions of the Eight Manifestations of Padmasambhava.

Upper Tolung

Nenang
Monastery

གནས་ནང་
དགོན་པ

Following the Ziling highway from Tolung Dechen on the east bank of the Tolung-chu for 26 kilometres (to kilometre road marker 3,853), you cross the river via the **Lungpa Zampa** bridge (ignoring an earlier bridge of similar iron construction), and enter the Drowolung valley where both Tsurphu (28 kilometres) and Nenang (19 kilometres) monasteries are located. The valley begins at Gurum

Tolung Dechen

To Damzhung
(85 km)

To Zhugu La
Pass (56 km)

Yangpachen

50

Lungpa
Zampa

Nenang 5 14 Nakar

LHASA

14

26

Namka
Ngoshi 11

Tsurphu

Dongkar

Zhongwa
Lhachu

N

To Nyetang
(17 km)

Not to Scale

township, and divides after eight kilometres, the southern trail leading via Nampa village and Nampa La pass to Chushul, and the western road to **Nakar** from where the Tsurphu and Nenang paths diverge. A signpost by the roadside marks the way to **Nenang**, on the far side of the ridge above Nakar. The monastery was founded by Zhamarpa I Tokden Drakpa Senge in 1333, and it later became the seat of the successive incarnations of Pawo I Chowang Lhundrub (1440-1503), the most renowned of whom was the historian Pawo II Tsuklak Trengwa (1504-66). The previous Pawo Rinpoche XVII (b 1912) recently passed away in India, where he had lived for a number of years. His reincarnation, a small child from Nangchen in Kham was recognized by the present Karmapa. He presides over a community of 50 monks. The principal temples at Nenang are the **Lhakhang Chenmo**, which is currently under reconstruction, and the **Jampa Lhakhang**. At present, the latter functions as the assembly hall. The lower storey houses the throne of Pawo Rinpoche and the library, along with an inner sanctum dedicated to Maitreya, which contains gilded clay images of the Buddhas of the Three Times, Padmasambhava, Pawo Rinpoche XII, Tsongkhapa, Trisong Detsen, Milarepa, Marpa, Pawo Rinpoche XVII, and Karmapa XVI. Murals to the rear depict Vajradhara, Karmapa, Marpa, and Tsdongkhapa, while those of the side walls depict the lineages of the Karmapas and the Pawo Rinpoches. There is a large gilded stupa reliquary containing the ashes of Pawo Rinpoche XVII, flanked by two smaller ones containing relics of Karmapa XVI and Pawo XII. On the second floor, there is a gallery and a series of tangkas depicting protector deities such as Shridevi, and murals of Nenang Monastery itself. The residence of the incumbent is on the third floor.

Central Tibet

Continuing along the main pathway from Nakar, which follows the Tsurphu Phu-chu upstream, after 14 kilometres, you reach Tsurphu Monastery, the seat of the Karmapa, and one of the two main strongholds of the Karma Kagyu school in Tibet (the other being at Karma Gon in Lhato, see below, page 400). As you approach the monastery you will pass the ruins of the Karmapa's summer palace, surmounted by a satellite dish, to the left.

Tsurphu Monastery
ཕོད་ལུང་མཚུར་ཕུ

Altitude: 4,300 metres
■ *Admission : ¥15*
Colour map 3, grid B2

The Site The temples, palaces, and monastic colleges of Tsurphu were severely damaged during the 1960s, following the flight of Karmapa XVI to India, but rebuilding has progressed steadily since 1983-4, largely through the efforts of Drupon Dechen Rinpoche and the good auspices of the Hawaian based Tsurphu Foundation. Presently there are 300 affiliated monks. As you drive into the courtyard, to the left you will observe the terraced slope on which the applique scrolls of Tsurphu were once hung during religious festivals. An obelisk stands within the courtyard, reputedly erected by King Relpachen to commemorate the building of the 9th century Changbu Lhakhang at Tsurphu. Turning to face the main buildings, on the left is the Zhipa Tratsang, in the middle is the Karmapa Labrang and Assembly Hall (Karmapa Tsokhang), also known as the 'lower citadel of Dharma' (Chogar Ogma), and to the right is the Zuri Tratsang. The ruins of the Jamyang Lhakhang Chenmo with its massive four metres thick walls are located behind the Assembly Hall, while higher up the slope stands the reconstructed palace of the regent of Tsurphu, known as Gyeltsab Podrang Chokhang or 'upper citadel of Dharma' (Chogar Gongma). The regent, Gyeltsab Rinpoche, would preside over Tsurphu during the interregnum following the death of one Karmapa and the investiture of the next. The first to assume this role was Gyel-tsab I Goshi Peljor Dondrub (1427-89) who installed Karmapa VII Chodrak Gyatso (1454-1506), and from the time of Karmapa X Choying Dorje (1604-74), who offered the site to Gyeltsab VI (1659-98), the successive Gyeltsab Rinpoches have occupied this building.

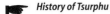

History of Tsurphu

Tsurphu was founded in 1187 by Karmapa I Dusum Khyenpa (1100-93) who hailed from the Trehor region of Kham, and was one of the principal followers of Gampopa. The construction marked the site of the 9th century ruins Changbu Lhakhang, where he had received a vision of the Cakrasamvara mandala. As the founder of the Karma Kagyu school, renowned for its ascetic discipline and yogic prowess, Dusum Khyenpa is also credited with the inception of the tulku institution, which later came to dominate Tibet's spiritual and political life during the middle ages. It was he who clearly predicted the circumstances of his subsequent rebirth, and his successor, Karma Pakshi (1204-1283) became the first formal incarnation (tulku) to be recognized in Tibet.

Karma Pakshi constructed the main temple in 1263. It housed an image of the Buddha called Dzamling-gyen, which was said to contain original relics. Since that time altogether 17 Karmapa incarnations have occupied Tsurphu Monastery, some, such as Rangjung Dorje, renowned for their profound spiritual insights, and

others such as Chodrak Gyatso and Mikyo Dorje for their vast scholarship. During the age of the Mongol Qans and Ming Emperors, the Karma Kagyu school flourished, and when Sakya's power was eclipsed, it became the most influential force in Tibetan political life under the successive dynasties of Phakmodru, Rinpung and Tsang. During this period (16th-early 17th century), when the capital of Tibet was located in Tsetang and Zhigatse, it was the Karma Kagyu school based in Tsurphu and Yangpachen which held sway throughout the Lhasa region. However, the defeat of the Tsangpa kings by the Mongol armies of Gushi Qan in 1642 at the culmination of a prolonged Civil War left the school isolated and cut off from its political power base, enabling Dalai Lama V to establish the Gelukpa theocracy at Lhasa, which persisted until the Chinese occupation of Tibet. Since 1959, when the previous Karmapa XVI established his residence at Rumtek in Sikkim, the Karma Kargyu school has developed an extensive network of Buddhist organizations and centres throughout the world.

The present incumbent, Gyeltsab XII (b 1960), resides at Rumtek in Sikkim.

Among these buildings, the **Zhipa Tratsang** was the first to be restored. The upper storey contains a series of five protector shrine rooms, dedicated respectively to Mahakala in the form of Bernakchen, to Shridevi, Vaishravana along with Tseringma, Dorje Drolo and Vajrakila. Outside on the verandah are a number of macabre stuffed animals, suspended from the ceiling.

To the east of the Zhipa Tratsang, is the reconstructed **Karmapa Labrang** and **Assembly Hall** (Tsokhang), which have been built on their original site. It now functions as the main temple for Tsurphu, standing in lieu of the ruined **Jamyang Lhakhang Chenmo** to its rear, and upstairs is the residence of the newly recognized Karmapa XVII (b 1985), who hold public audience each afternoon. The lower throne room with its fine murals in Chinese style depict the Sixteen Elders and its images include those of Marpa, Milarepa, and Gampopa, along with Karmapas I, II and XVI. There is also an interesting mural depicting the traditional plan of Tsurphu. Nowadays this chamber functions as a monastic assembly hall. Behind an adjacent general store, the ruins of the Lhakhang Chenmo are testament to the wanton destruction carried out against the culture of Tibet in the 1960s. This massive fortress once contained Tsurphu's most highly venerated image: an enormous 20 metres bronze cast statue of Shakyamuni Buddha, known as the 'Ornament of the World' (Dzamling-gyen), which had been commissioned by Karma Pakshi in the 13th century. Reconstruction is now near completion, and the destroyed

The Seventeen Karmapas

Karmapa I	Dusum Khyenpa (1110-1193)		Karmapa X	Choying Dorje (1604-1674)
Karmapa II	Karma Pakshi (1204-1283)		Karmapa XI	Yeshe Dorje (1677-1702)
Karmapa III	Rangjung Dorje (1284-1339)		Karmapa XII	Jangchub Dorje (1703-1732)
Karmapa IV	Rolpei Dorje (1340-1383)		Karmapa XIII	Dudul Dorje (1733-1797)
Karmapa V	Dezhin Shekpa (1384-1415)		Karmapa XIV	Tekchok Dorje (1798-1868)
Karmapa VI	Tongwa Donden (1416-1453)		Karmapa XV	Khakhyab Dorje (1871-1922)
Karmapa VII	Chodrak Gyatso (1454-1506)		Karmapa XVI	Rikpei Dorje (1921-1981)
Karmapa VIII	Mikyo Dorje (1507-1554)		Karmapa XVII	Orgyen Trinle Dorje (b 1985)
Karmapa IX	Wangchuk Dorje (1556-1603)			

image was finally replaced in 1997. Visitors can see a handprint left by the new incarnation in the masonry.

Further east is the partially restored **Zuri Tratsang**, an upper chamber of which contains the room used by Situ Rinpoche on his recent visit to Tsurphu from India. Here, there are documents describing the account of his recognition of the new Karmapa incarnation in 1992.

Further uphill and behind this entire complex are the reconstructed buildings of the independently functioning **Gyeltsab Podrang**, which includes a vast assembly hall, where the monks under the authority of Gyeltsab Rinpoche convene. The original five-storey structure dates from 17th century.

The precipitous cliffs above Tsurphu contain the hermitage known as **Drubdra Samtenling**, and to its left is the hermitage of **Pema Khyung Dzong**, once frequented by Karma Pakshi and Karmapa III Rangjung Dorje (1284-1339). Higher up is the cave where Karma Pakshi performed a meditative retreat in darkness (*muntsam*), and a number of smaller hermitages. There is a pilgrim's circuit around Tsurphu, which takes about three hours, commencing west of the perimeter wall and encompassing the Tsurphu charnel ground to the north and the aforementioned cliff-side hermitages.

Trekking There are also three trekking routes from Tsurphu: north via the 5,300 metres Lhasar La pass to the Lhorong-chu valley and Yangpachen (three or four days); south via Nampa La pass to Chushul (two or three days); amd southwest via the Tsurphu La pass to Nyemo in Tsang (two or three days).

From Lungpa Zampa (see above page 134), the Ziling Highway continues north, following the east bank of the Tolung-chu to Yangpachen, via the township of Mar and the old Dechen Dzong. The town of Yangpachen is the site of a geothermal power plant and hot houses which supply vegetables to the Lhasa area. There is a small hospital, a petrol station, an army compound, and a few Sichuan-style restaurants.

Yangpachen monastery is located about 14 kilometres along the turn-off for Zhugu La pass (5,300 metres) and Zhigatse. It was founded in 1490 by Mu

**Tupten
Yangpachen
Monastery**

ཐུབ་བསྟན་
ཡངས་པ་ཅན་
དགོན་པ

Rabjampa Thujepel on the advice of Zhamarpa IV Chokyi Drakpa (1453-1524), with funds provided by Donyo Dorje of Rinpung. Since that time it has been the main residence of Chokyi Drakpa's subsequent incarnations, the Zhamarpa hierarchs, who wear a red hat in contrast to the black hat worn by the Karmapa. The Zhamarpas held sway in Upper Tolung until 1792 when the status of Zhamarpa X (1742-92) was anulled by the Tibetan government, following his alliance with the Gorkha invasion force in an attempted restoration of Kagyu power. The woodblock edition of Golotsawa's *Blue Annals* were removed from the library at Yangpachen and transferred to Kundeling in Lhasa at that time.

The monastery has been under reconstruction since 1986, and in its **Pelkor Gonkhang**, there is an original image of the protector Six-armed Mahakala. The present incumbent, Zhamarpa XIII (b 1952), resides in India.

From Yangpachen, the northern route to Zhigatse follows the Lhorong-chu upstream to Zhugu La pass for 56 kilometres, and thence descends into the Upper Nyemo and Oyuk districts of Tsang (see below, page 246). To the south of the road, near Yangra, the Kagyu nunnery of **Dorjeling** is once again active.

Damzhung County འདམ་གཞུང་

Damzhung County (2)
当雄县
Damxung
Population: 34,025
Area: 8,094 sq km
Colour map 3, grid A2

*The Ziling highway leading northeast via Yangpachen opens out into Damzhung county, the capital of which is located at Damchuka. To the north, the road skirts the **Nyenchen Tanglha** range (7,088 metres), abode of the protector deity of the same name, which divides the Upper Kyi-chu region from the Jangtang Plateau and the Salween. The Dam-chu and Nyingdrong-chu rivers, which have their sources near Damzhung flow southeast to converge with the Reting Tsangpo at Phodo before flowing down through Meldro and Taktse counties to Lhasa.*

Damzhung

The town has sprung up as an important stopping point on the highway for freight trucks and buses. There are a number of roadside restaurants, serving Tibetan, Sichuan, and Muslim food, among which Chamdo Zakhang and Amdo Zakhang are both clean; and in the government compound approached via a bridge to the rear, there is a large guesthouse (¥60 per bed, ¥260 per room), a public security bureau, and cinema.

After Damzhung, the highway continues northeast for a further 27 kilometres to **Chorten Rang-go** in Umatang, which lies just beyond the county border, before cutting through the Nyenchen Tanglha range to enter the Salween River system. This point is marked by a series of eight roadside stupas, symbolizing the eight major events in the life of Shakyamuni Buddha. There is also a trekking route from here, which descends into the upper Reting Tsangpo valley.

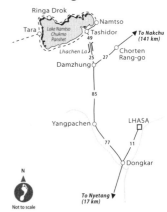

Damzhung

Ringa Drok
Namtso
Tara
Lake Namtso
Chukmo
Panshet
Tashidor
To Nakchu
(141 km)
49
Lhachen La
25   27
Chorten Rang-go
Damzhung

85

LHASA
Yangpachen
Chorten Rang-go
Dongkar

77   11

N

Not to scale

To Nyetang
(17 km)

The eight stupas at Chorten Rang-go symbolizing events in the Buddha's life

Central Tibet

An unpaved road cuts across country from a turn-off southwest of Damzhung, passes via the cliff-hanging **Jangra Monastery** of the Gelukpa school, and after 25 kilometres crosses the Lhachen La pass (5,150 metres). On the 49 kilometre descent from the pass there are spectacular views of the tidal **Namtso Chukmo lake**, which is 70 kilometres long and 30 kilometres wide, making it the second largest saltwater lake on the Tibetan plateau (after Kokonor). The average altitude is 4,718 metres, and the landscape is dominated by the snow peak of Nyenchen Thanglha to the southwest.

Namtso Chukmo Lake

གནམ་མཚོ

Colour map 3, grid A1

    Namtso township, near the east corner of the lake has a small guesthouse and pack animals, which are hired out to those taking the pilgrimage circuit around the lake. The full circuit takes about 18 days on foot, and it is possible to drive only as far as **Tashidor**, a cave hermitage near the bird sanctuary, marked by two lofty sheer rock towers. The overall distance from Damzhung to Tashido is 74 km. The hermitage caves, which are said to have particular associations with Padmasambhava and his consort Yeshe Tsogyel, were frequented by many great lamas of the past, including Karmapa III Rangjung Dorje. Nowadays, they are occupied by occasional hermits of the Nyingma

Lake Namtso Chukmo

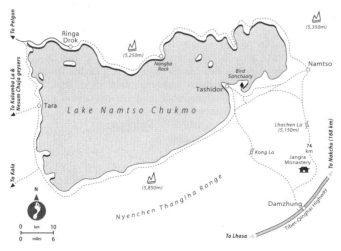

and Kagyu schools. A newly constructed cave temple is maintained by three nuns and two monks, under the supervision of Lama Donga Trinle Ozer, who resided here for 10 years, and Ngawang Tupten Lama who is in charge of the rebuilding. The temple follows the Nyingma tradition, holding *Konchok Chidu* ceremonies on the 10th day of the lunar month, and *Dudjom Troma* ceremonies on the 25th. The **bird sanctuary** itself teems with migratory flocks from April to November, and you may glimpse the rare black-necked crane.

There is a short pilgrimage circuit of the Tashidor promontory with its long mani-stone wall, passing near the shore; but the longer 18 day circuit of the lake requires careful preparation. Moving anticlockwise (in the Bon manner), on the north shore a detour leads along an 10 kilometres long headland known as Doring, where the hermitage of the ancient Bon scholar Tong-gyang Tuchen of Zhang-zhung was once located and where there are significant ruins, documented by John Belizza. At **Nyingdo**, further west, there are extensive ruins of an ancient Bon monastery. Then, the north promontory of **Nangba Rock** will be reached on the 8th day of the circuit. Here the ruins of the Bonpo Tachok Gonpa are accessible. **Ringa Drok** near the northwest corner will be reached on the 10th day, and **Tara** on the west shore on the 12th.

Moving on   From Ringa Drok, there is a motorable road to Pelgon; and from Tara, there is another 12-day wilderness trek leading southwards via Kalamba La pass (5,240 metres) and the **Nesum Chuja geysers** (which freeze in winter) to Zabulung in North Shang (see below, page 251).

Taktse County སྟག་རྩེ

Taktse County (3)
达孜县
Dagze
Population: 23,517
Area: 1,354 sq km
Colour map 3, grid B3

Taktse county extends from the north of Lhasa Zamchen bridge as far as Lamo on the south bank of the Kyi-chu, and Logon on the north bank. As such, it includes two very important sites: the caves of Drak Yerpa and Ganden Monastery, both situated northeast of Lhasa. The county capital is nowadays located at Taktse or Dechen Dzong, 21 kilometres distant from Lhasa; and from here there are trekking routes to Samye (see below, page 172).

Tsel Gungtang
ཚལ་གུང་ཐང

The residence of Lama Zhang, the 11th century founder of the Tselpa Kagyu school, was formerly situated 10 kilometres east from Lhasa and south of the present Lhasa-Kongpo highway. The complex included a Kumbum stupa, two early temples, a residential building, and a later Tsuklakhang. None of these structures have yet been restored.

Dechen Dzong
བདེ་ཆེན་རྫོང

The county capital, located near the hilltop ruins of Dechen Dzong, which once guarded the approaches to Lhasa from the north, contains a Gelukpa temple, known as **Samdrubling**, which was preserved as a granary during the 1960s, and therefore has kept some of its original frescoes undamaged. Public buses run from East Lingkhor lam in Lhasa via Pelting to Dechen Dzong.

Dromto
འབྲོམ་སྟོད

Dromto township, situated on the north side of the Taktse Zampa bridge, which spans the Kyi-chu upstream from Taktse, is surmounted by a stupa, marking the meditation hermitage of the

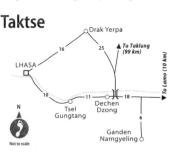

Taktse

History of Drak Yerpa

*King Songtsen Gampo and his two foreign queens are said to have meditated here in the **Peu Marsergyi Lhakhang**, where they discovered 'self-arising' symbols of buddha-body, speech and mind, and in the **Chogyel Puk**. Later, Padmasambhava concealed many terma objects around Yerpa, including the celebrated ritual dagger of Sera (**Sera Phurzhal**), which was eventually rediscovered by the treasure-finder Darcharuba at Sewalung. Padmasambhava also passed some 7 months in retreat in the **Dawa Puk**, which is regarded as one of his three foremost places of attainment (drub-ne). In the 9th*

century Lhalung Pelgyi Dorje stayed at Yerpa in solitary meditation, both prior to and after his assassination of the apostate king Langdarma.

*Then, following the later phase of Buddhist propagation in Tibet, Yerpa came to greater prominence under Kadampa influence: Lu-me founded 108 temples on the hillside, including a **Vairocana Lhakhang**. Marton Chokyi Jungne founded the **Jampa Lhakhang**, and Atisha himself passed 3 years here, constructing with the aid of his foremost disciples, the **Kyormo Lhakhang** and the **Chokhang**.*

Kadampa master Nyen Lotsawa Darmatra (11th century). Two roads diverge here on the north side of the bridge: left to Drak Yerpa and right to Phenyul and Jang (see below, page 144).

It takes about two hours to drive to the caves of Drak Yerpa, situated northeast of Lhasa, either via the Taktse Zampa bridge or via Kawa and Yerpa Da villages on the more direct route from Lhasa (16 kilometres). Following the Yerpa-chu tributary of the Kyi-chu upstream, and past a reservoir, you will arrive at this historic complex of caves and temples, some of which date from the earliest period of Buddhist activity in Tibet. The amphitheatre ridge of Yerpa and some of its larger caves are visible afar from the Lhasa-Kongpo road on the south bank of the Kyi-chu. The highest point on the ridge is the peak of **Yerpa Lhari**, abode of the local deity, at the extreme northeast end of the ridge.

Drak Yerpa: the Caves of Mystic Realization

བྲག་ཡེར་པ

The Site The caves are approached via the ruined 11th century Kadampa monastery of **Yerpa Drubde**, situated some 100 metres below the dark cavernous grottoes of the white cliffs.

Among the many caves and ruined shrines, the following (described from west to east) are most important: **Tendrel Drubpuk** associated with Atisha and his Kadampa followers; **Chakna Dorje Puk**, containing a 'self-arising' stone image of Vajrapani; **Jampa Lhakhang**, the largest cave, which once contained a celebrated 13th century image of Maitreya along with the Eight Bodhisattvas, and below which are relief images of the Lords of the Three Enlightened Families; **Drubtob Puk**, dedicated to the Eighty-four Great Accomplished Masters (*mahasiddha*) of ancient India; **Chogyel Puk**, where King Songtsen Gampo meditated in the 7th century and which once contained images of the king and the protectress Shridevi; Dawa Puk, containing a sculpted image of Padmasambhava, a 'self-arising' image of Ekajati and stone footprints of Padmasambhava and his student Lhalung Pelgyi Dorje; **Lhalung Puk**, where Lhalung Peldor hid for some years during the period of Langdarma's persecution; and **Neten Lhakhang**, which was constructed by Lu-me in 1011 and formerly contained images of Shakyamuni Buddha surrounded by the Sixteen Elders. Below this last shrine is the stone throne used by Atisha and a charnel ground. Atisha's hermitage, the ruins of which are even now visible had 300 monks as recently as the 19th century, when it served as the summer residence for the Upper Tantric College (ie Ramoche). A reconstructed temple at Drak Yerpa, containing images of Shakyamuni, Avalokiteshvara and Padmasambhava was recently demolished by the hard-line Lhasa authorities on the grounds that it has not been built on one of the historically recognised sites!

Ganden Namgyeling

དགའ་ལྡན་རྣམ་

རྒྱལ་གླིང་

■ *Admission : ¥25*
Colour map 3, grid B4

Situated 45 kilometres east of Lhasa, the monastery of Ganden Namgyeling was founded in 1409 by Tsongkhapa on the Gokpori ridge of Mount Wangkur, overlooking the south bank of the river and the Phenyul valley beyond. It is approached via a turn-off at a village 39 kilometres from Lhasa (road markers 1,529 and 4,591 kilometres) and thence by a zigzagging motorable road for a further six kilometres.

Named after the paradise of Maitreya, Ganden was the first and foremost Gelukpa monastery, constructed by Tsongkhapa himself. The site, where he himself had meditated was known to have had ancient associations with King Songtsen Gampo and his queens in that **Mount Wangkur** was named after a coronation ceremony performed at the birth of the king, and the adjacent **Mount Tsunmo Dingri** was named after the queens' favourite picnic ground. The sacred Jowo Rinpoche image of Lhasa is said to have indicated the significance of the site to Tsongkhapa, who founded the monastery in 1409 and the Chikhorkhang in 1415. The Assembly Hall (*Tsokchen*) was built in 1417, and the two colleges of Ganden known as Jangtse (North Point) and Shartse (East Point) were respectively founded by two of his closest disciples – respectively Namka Pelzangpo and Neten Rongyelwa. A tantric college (*Gyudra*) was also established by another of his students named Je Sherab Senge.

Following the death of Tsongkhapa in 1419, the succession passed first to Gyeltsabje and later to Khedrupje. In this way, the Ganden Tripa (throne-holder of Ganden) came to preside over the Gelukpa school, each generally holding office for seven years (although originally longer periods of office were observed). Formerly there were over 3,000 monks at Ganden, but following the brutal destruction of the complex during the Cultural Revolution (more severe than at any of the other five large Gelukpa establishments), the number was reduced to about 300. Then, over the last two years many of those remaining monks and novices were forced to depart for their village homes or to exile in India following an authoritarian clamp-down on their activities. The Xinhua News Agency recently reported, on the other hand, that buildings covering an area of 11,000 square metres had been renovated at Ganden, 41 kilos of gold had been utilized to regild the roofs, and murals 1,660 square metres in area had been restored over the last four years, all at a cost of US$3 million!

Ngachokhang This small temple, located to the right of the trail after the bus stop, is where Tsongkhapa instructed his students. The main chamber has images of Tsongkhapa, flanked by his two foremost students, while the extremely active protector chapel to its left (out of bounds to women) has images of Shridevi, Mahakala, Dharmaraja, and Bhairava. Upstairs are the Dalai Lamas' private apartments and throne.

Ganden Namgyeling

Serdung Lhakhang Passing the debating courtyard and the meditation hermitage (**Gomde Khang**) on the right, the pilgrim reaches the restored **Serdung Lhakhang**, a red painted building with a large white stupa. On the ground floor there is an interior courtyard and a Dharmaraja chapel. The main chamber or **Yangpachen Chapel** is on the second floor, containing the restored golden reliquary of Tsongkhapa (*serdung*), known as Tongwa Donden ('Meaningful to Behold'). Constructed in 1629, the chapel is named after a stone to the rear of the golden reliquary, which is said to have flown miraculously from Shravasti (Yangpachen) in India. The present silver stupa replaces the original, destroyed in 1959, which had been gilded by Gushi Qan's grandson and covered with a felt and sandalwood tent by Dzungarwa Tsering Dondrup in 1717. A few retrieved relics and skull fragments of Tsongkhapa have been placed within the restored stupa, and a cabinet to the left contains the master's celebrated tooth relic, within a small stupa casket, as well as his begging bowl, tea cup and vajra. The tooth relic is used in the making of barley impressions for consecrating miniature terracotta images (*tsatsa*), or for distribution to the faithful. Large images of Tsongkhapa and his foremost students stand in front of the stupa. Left of the entrance is the main Assembly Hall, the side-chapels of which contain images representing the Buddhas of the Three Times, and 1,000 small images of Tsongkhapa.

Sertrikhang Uphill and to the right of the Serdung Lhakhang is the **Sertrikhang Chapel**, containing the throne of Tsongkhapa and the successive Ganden Tripas, which is flanked by the volumes of the *Kangyur* and backed by large images of Tsongkhapa with his two foremost students. The throne is a replica of a 15th century original made by Newar craftsmen. This chapel was originally the inner sanctum of Ganden's largest assembly hall – yet to be reconstructed.

Zimchung Tritokhang Adjacent to the Sertrikhang and to the right is the Official Residence of the Ganden Tripa, known as **Zimchung Tritokhang**. The upper storey contains images of Tsongkhapa and his foremost students, with a full set on the Kangyur stacked on the wall behind. A throne used by the Ganden Tripa is located at the far end of the room. On the ground floor, there are four chapels: among them, the **Demchok Lhakhang** contains an awesome image of Cakrasamvara, flanked by others representing Gyeltsabje, Mahakala, and Vajrayogini (closed to women). The **Dzomchen Lhakhang** contains images of Tsongkhapa and students, flanked by recent lamas Pawangka Rinpoche and Trijang Rinpoche. The **Nyangde Lhakhang** is the simple chamber where Tsongkhapa passed away, and the **Gyelwa Lhakhang** is the private apartment reserved for the visiting Dalai Lamas. It contains images of Tsongkhapa, Panchen Lama X, and the Thirty-five Confession Buddhas.

Amdo and Trehor Khangtsang Following the track uphill to the left the pilgrim passes in succession the **Amdo Khangtsang** and the **Trehor Khangtsang**. The former has brocade hangings depicting the Thirty-five Confession Buddhas and Sixteen Elders, with an image of the protectress Machen Pomra and the eye of Dharmaraja (kept in a cabinet). The latter has images of Tsongkhapa with his two foremost students.

Pilgrim's Circuit of Ganden Thereafter, the pilgrim's circumambulatory route follows the one hour Lingkhor around the hilltop, starting from a prominent group of prayer-flags. There are 'self-arising' imprints of Phadampa Sangye, the Sixteen Elders, Dharmaraja, Tsongkhapa's hat, the

Central Tibet

Lords of the Three Enlightened Families, and so forth. Passing the **Vision Rock**, which induces supernatural visions when viewed through a hole made by a fist, the pilgrim reaches the highest point on the circuit, **Tsongkhapa's prostration spot**, and then descends to the charnel ground (*durtro*) and the narrow cleft called **Gauge of Negativity** (which is said to measure the extent of the pilgrim's negativity). Thereafter, the pilgrim will pass the rock impressions of Tsongkhapa and his students, said to have been made by Tsongkhapa's own fingernails, and other impressions representing Simhavaktra, Dharmaraja's tongue, and a nectar-dripping rock.

Tsongkhapa's **Ozer Puk** hermitage contains 'self-arising' and 'speaking' images of Shridevi, Shakyamuni, Amitayus, and Tsongkhapa himself, surmounted by Atisha and Dromtonpa. Further uphill is another Dharmaraja shrine. Lastly, the pilgrim visits the black cone shaped **Nesel Rock**, on which pilgrims place their stomachs while spitting or even vomiting out disease!

Lhundrub County ལྷུན་གྲུབ་

Lhundrub County (4)
林周县
Lhunzhub
Population: 47,122
Area: 6,795 sq km
Colour map M3, grid A4

The districts of Phenyul and Jang which lie to the north of Lhasa include the valley of the Lha-chu or Phenpo-chu, which rises near Yangpachen and flows southeast to converge with the Kyi-chu opposite Ganden Monastery, and the 'northern region' (Jang) of the Pa-chu and Reting Tsangpo, which converge with the Kyi-chu further upstream at Phodo Dzong, the county capital, 148 kilometres driving distance from Lhasa. These two river systems are divided by the Chak La pass (5,300 metres).

There are three points of access from the south: via the paved Lhasa-Kongpo road and Taktse Zampa bridge, via Drigung and Lhundrub/Phodo Dzong; or via the unpaved road from Sera Monastery, Dokde and Yerpa. There are also trekking routes leading into Phenyul: from Lhasa via Pempogo La pass; from Tolung via Mount Gephelri ridge; and from Damzhung into Jang. Culturally, this region of Tibet has had strong associations with both the Kadampa school (especially at Reting, Nalendra, and Langtang), and with the Kagyu school (at Taklung). The Kadampa establishments were in later centuries adopted by the Gelukpa and Sakya schools.

Phenyul འཕན་ཡུལ

Logon
ལོ་དགོན་

Located on the northwest bank of the Kyi-chu, 20 kilometres northeast of the Phenyul turn-off, Logon Monastery was founded by the Kadampa master Chengawa Tsultrim Bar (1038-1103) and maintained by his illustrious student Jayulpa. Later it was adopted by the Gelukpas and became the seat of the incarnate master Lo Sempa Chenpo.

Langtang Monastery
གླང་ཐང་དགོན་པ

Located some six kilometres southwest of Phenpo township, on a track which crosses the Phenpo-chu (and continues over Pempogo La pass to Lhasa), the Kadampa monastery of

Lhundrub

Langtang was founded in 1093 by Langritangpa Dorje Senge (1054-1123). At its high point there were over 2,000 monks, but in later centuries its status greatly diminished and it was absorbed by the Sakya school. More recently, many of its buildings were encorporated within a local farming commune, leaving only one temple and assembly hall, with Langtangpa's revered 'speaking image' of Tara intact. Below are the ruins of the Lhakhang Chenmo and a Kadam stupa containing Langtangpa's own relics.

Located 12 kilometres west of Langtang near the south bank of the Phenpo-chu, Nalanda Monastery was founded in 1435 by the renowned scholar Rongton Chenpo Mawei Senge (1367-1449), and later absorbed by the Sakyapa, who recognized him as one of the 'six jewels of Tibet'. The ruins at Nalanda are extensive, but there is a renovated assembly hall, including an image of Rongtonpa himself and a stone bearing his footprint. There are also two restored residential buildings and a large Kadam stupa. More recently, the hermitages and college have been re-established by Khenpo Tsultrim Gyeltsen of the Lhasa Mentsikhang.

Nalanda Monastery

དཔལ་ན་ལེན་ད་

The monastery of Ganden Chungkor is located at Phenpo township, the most fertile part of Phenyul. There are still original murals, well worth a visit.

Ganden Chungkor

The large Kadam stupa known as Shara Bumpa is located west of Kusha village on the road to Langma and the Chak La pass. It was constructed by Sharapa Yonten Drak (1070-1141), and is revered by pilgrims who believe that by circumambulating it blindness can be cured.

Shara Bumpa

ཤ་ར་འབུམ་པ

Jang བྱང

Driving through the valley of the old Lhundrub Dzong, past Rinchen Tang, and the village of Langma, the road leaves the Phenyul valley and crosses Chak La pass (5,300 metres) before dropping sharply to Taklung (4,084 metres) in the upper Pha-chu valley, 120 kilometres from Lhasa. Nomadic camps will be seen on the high pastures.

Taklung Monastery

སྟག་ལུང་དགོན་པ

The Kagyu monastery of Taklung was founded by Taklung Tangpa Tashipel (1142-1210) in 1180 on a location previously inhabited by the Kadampa lama Potowa. Taklung Tangpa Tashipel was one of the foremost students of Phakmodrupa Dorje Gyelpo, renowned for his austere observation of monastic discipline. Through his efforts and those of his nephew Kuyalwa and the latter's successor Sangye Yarjon, the monastic population of Taklung eventually expanded to 7,000; and it survived the Mongol incursions of General Dorta Nakpo unscathed. The main temple, the Tsuklakhang, was completed in 1228. An eastern branch of Taklung was also established by the fourth preceptor, Sangye On, at Riwoche in Kham (see below, page 391), and this eventually came to eclipse the mother monastery in its importance. Mangalaguru, the fifth preceptor, continued to develop this original seat, but from the 16th century onwards, Gelukpa influence at Taklung became pronounced, as the hierarchs of Sera and Drepung sought to control the appointment of its preceptors and the instatement of its incarnate lamas.

The monastery lies along a track to the west of the Pha-chu River, below a mountain which is said to have a rock near its summit inscribed with a 'self-arising' seed-syllable A, symbolic of the emptiness underlying all phenomena. A nectar stream, descending from that seed-syllable, flows down towards the Pha-chu. At the end of the approach road, three buildings are visible across the stream, and above the ruins on the left side: **Jampa Lhakhang**,

Central Tibet

dedicated to Maitreya; the **Reliquary Lhakhang**, containing the remains of the three enormous stupas which once held the relics of Taklung's three founders, Taklung Tangpa Tashipel, Kuyalwa, and Sangye Yarjon; and the **Dargyeling Temple**, containing a large image of Aksobhya Buddha and a side-chapel which functions as a protector shrine. The protector deities favoured here are Genyen, Nyenchen Tanglha, and Tseringma.

Looking downhill to the right of the road, the residence of Taklung Tsetrul, the incarnate lama of Taklung, has now been obscured within a cluster of village houses. Further uphill are the ruins of the great **Tsuklakhang** (the Jokhang of Taklung), the monastic kitchen, and finally, the reconstructed **Assembly Hall** (Zhelrekhang), which contains images of Taklung Tangpa Tashipel and Tangtong Gyelpo, as well as frescoes depicting the meditational deity Cakrasamvara, surrounded by the Taklung lineage-holders.

Sili Gotsang Hermitage

 སི་ལི་གོད་ཚང

Continuing downstream from Taklung, you drive past a sheer cliff on the left, where the Sili Gotsang Hermitage is located, adorned with prayer flags. This retreat was founded by Taklung Tangpa Tashipel in the 12th century and used also by the great Drukpa Kagyu master Gotsangpa (1189-1258). It has recently been renovated by the monks of Taklung, and contains in addition to the hermitages a protector shrine dedicated to Mahakala.

Also on the left side of the road, is a Tashi Gomang style stupa with multiple apertures, originally constructed by the Tibetan Government to mark the place where the Kyi-chu waters first flow southwards in the direction of Lhasa.

Lhundrub/ Phodo Dzong

ལྷུན་གྲུབ་རྫོང

Following the Pha-chu downstream to Lhundrub (Phodo), the county capital, you will pass on the right a strikingly conical mountain peak which forms the backdrop to the town. Three rivers converge at Lhundrub: the Pha-chu flowing from Taklung; the Rong-chu/Dam-chu flowing from the Damzhung area; and the Reting Tsangpo (or Miggi) flowing from the north of Reting. The swelling waters of the Kyi-chu, formed by this confluence, are crossed by two suspension bridges, one which leads up the Reting valley, and a second which spans the Kyi-chu to the east of town. Below the fort (*dzong*), there is also an extant iron-chain bridge dating from the age of Tangtong Gyelpo. This is the valley of **Lungsho**, which extends southeast as far as Drigung, and once contained important 11th century Kadampa temples, such as Tsongdu and Gyel Lhakhang.

Reting Monastery

ར་སྒྲེང་དགོན་པ

Altitude: 4,100 metres
■ *Admission : ¥15*
Colour map 3, grid A4

The road follows the Reting Tsangpo upstream for 47 kilometres through the beautiful Miggi valley to arrive at Reting, located at 4,100 metres, amidst a remarkable juniper wood on the lower slopes of **Mount Gangi Rarwa**. The monastery (admission fee: ¥15 per person) was constructed in 1056 by Dromtonpa, the foremost Tibetan student of the great Bengali Buddhist master Atisha, two years after the latter had passed away at Nyetang, south of Lhasa. Here it was that Dromtonpa established the principal seat of his **Kadampa school**, and, according to legend, 20,000 juniper trees and springs emerged from the hairs of his head.

His successors Neljorpa Chenpo and Potowa expanded the monastery following Dromtonpa's death in 1064; but the Mongol armies of Dorta pillaged the site in 1240. Later, in the 14th century, Tsongkhapa visited Reting and experienced a vision of Atisha, on the basis of which he composed his celebrated *Great Treatise on the Graduated Path to Enlightenment* (*Lamrim Chenmo*). From the time of Dalai Lama VII, the abbots of Reting became eligible to serve as regent of Tibet, and they in fact did so from 1845-55, and 1933-47.

Amid the ruins of Reting, which was badly damaged in the 1960s, it is hard to grasp the former splendour of the buildings. To the extreme west of the hill-side there once stood the five storeyed **Reting Labrang**, the palace of Reting Rinpoche, flanked by stupas. In the centre, stood the **Assembly Hall** (*du-khang*), or **Chokhang Chenmo**, containing a highly revered solid gold image of the meditational deity Guhyasamaja in the form of Manjuvajra, 45 centimetres in height, which was the principal meditative object of Atisha, said to have been naturally formed from the union of the primordial buddha Vajradhara and his consort. The hall also once contained a 'speaking image' of Tara and a stupa known as Tashi Pelbar. Only part of this magnificant building has been reconstructed in recent years, and the image of Manjuvarja is still the most venerated object of offering.

To the left of the building, is a consecrated spring; and to its right there was formerly the residence of Dromton and a chamber containing his teaching throne. Immediately above the Assembly Hall was the residence of Tsongkhapa, where the aforementioned *Lamrim Chenmo* was composed, and where a lifelike (Ngadrama) image of Atisha was formerly housed. The residence of Tsongkhapa's teacher Remdawa was situated higher still. On the upper east slopes of the hillside, there was a nunnery known as **Samtenling**. Dromtonpa's meditation cave is located in a restored chapel on the hilltop Drak Senge ridge, adjacent to a shrine dedicated to the local deity **Garwa Nagpa**. Outside the cave are a sacred spring, the life-supporting tree of Dromtonpa, and a willow tree embodying Mahakala.

Other hermitages located on the ridge contain the remains of Dromtonpa's stone seat, from which Tsongkhapa later delivered his *Foundation of All Excellence*; while adjacent stone thrones have been adorned with images of Atisha, Dromtonpa and Maitreya. A red painted rock on the same ridge indicates the residence of Chingkawa, the protective divinity of Reting, which Atisha himself has brought from Nalanda in India.

Below the monastery, in the 'plain of boulders' (**Pawang Tang**), there is a large rock, known as Khandro Bumdzong, which is revered as the abode of the female deity Sangwa Yeshe.

Located 49 kilometres northeast of Lhasa near the Taktse-Meldro road, Lamo Monastery (1109) was one of the earliest shrines constructed by Lu-me following his return to Central Tibet, when he initiated the later phase of Buddhist propagation.

Lamo Monastery

ལ་མོ་དགོན་པ

Meldro Gungkar
County མལ་གྲོ་གུང་དཀར

*Meldro county, administered from the town of Meldro Gungkar, 67 kilometres east of Lhasa, extends from the Gyamazhing Valley, due east of Lamo in the south, as far as Drigung in the north. The capital **Meldro Gungkar**, which has a small guesthouse and roadside restaurants, stands at the confluence of the Kyi-chu and Meldro Phu-chu rivers, controlling the northern approaches to Drigung and Lungsho valleys, and the eastern approaches to the forested region of Kongpo. The most important sites within the county are: Gyama, birthplace of King Songtsen Gampo; Uru Katsel, a 7th century geomantic temple; Tangkya Lhakhang on the north bank of the Kyi-chu; Uruzhva Lhakhang, an ancient 9th century Nyingma temple; Drigung Til Monastery, and Zhoto Tidro hermitage.*

Meldro Gungkar
County (5)
墨竹工卡县
Maizhokunggar
Population: 36,684
Area: 4,679 sq km
Colour map M2, grid B4

Gyama

རྒྱ་མ

The turn-off for the Gyamazhing valley is located 58 kilometres northeast of Lhasa and 10 kilometres southwest of Meldro Gungkar, at the village of **Ngonda**. Within the lower reaches of this valley is the reconstructed temple of **Gyelpo Khangkar**, containing images of Songtsen Gampo and his two foreign queens, which is said to be situated near the birthplace of the king himself.

Further up the valley, you will pass in succession the former Kadampa monasteries of Dumburi, Gyamo Trikhang, and Rinchen Gang. Among these, the monastery of **Dumburi**, founded in the 12th century by Dumburipa Dawa Gyeltsen, is still in ruins. **Gyamo Tri-khang**, founded by Sangye Onton, the monastic preceptor of neighbouring Rinchen Gang, has a renovated assembly hall and two chapels, upper and lower. One of its four earthen stupas (originally consecrated by Gyar Gomchenpo Tsultrim Senge in the 12th century) still stands. Lastly, **Rinchen Gang**, which was founded in 1181 by Gyar Gomchenpo Zhonu Drakpa and expanded by his nephew Sangye Onton, has a reconstructed roof-top shrine with new frescoes and relief images. The monastery had past connections with the Kashmiri Pandita Shakyashri and later came under the influence of the Sakyapa tradition.

Uru Katsel

དབུ་རུ་
བཀའ་ཚལ

Situated north of the confluence of the Kyi-chu and Meldro Phu-chu rivers, Katsel was originally one of the four district-controlling geomantic temples, specifically constructed by King Songtsen Gampo on the right shoulder of the supine ogress, who represented the rigour of the Tibetan terrain. The antiquity of the **Tukdam Tsuklakhang** at Katsel, with its unusually sloping walls, has been remarked upon by Hugh Richardson, who visited the site during the 1940s. Subsequent temples were added to the complex from the time of Padmasambhava onwards, and the monastery was later adopted by the Drigungpas.

The main building at Katsel has been reconstructed in three storeys, the lowest of which has three successive chapels. Of these, the **innermost chapel** contains central images of the Buddhas of the Three Times; and side images of Green Tara and Drigung Rinchen Phuntsok, as well as a stupa in which the latter's relics are preserved. The **middle chapel** contains a library, including the volumes of the *Kangyur* and *Tangyur*.

The **second storey** contains images of the Three Deities of Longevity, namely: Amitayus, White Tara and Vijaya, in the inner sanctum, and other images of Tsongkhapa, Shakyamuni, Drigungpa Jikten Gonpo, and Mahakarunika along the left wall. In the far left corner there is an applique depicting the protectress Tseringma; while adjacent to the door are the volumes of the *Collected Works of Ratna Lingpa* and the *Biography of Drigung Rinchen Phuntsok*.

The **third storey** has a large chapel with fine murals depicting the lamas of the Drigungpa lineage, flanked by tangkas of Padmasambhava, Lama Chodpa, Machik Labdron, and Shakyamuni Buddha, and surmounted by tangkas depicting Padmasambhava, Shantaraksita, and King Trisong Detsen. The inner wall has images of the Drigung protectress Apchi in her peaceful and wrathful forms, as well as Dorje

Meldro Gungkar

Uru Katsel: a 7th geomantic Temple

Central Tibet

Yudronma, Pehar in the form Tukyi Gyelpo, and Cimara, along with tangkas depicting Vajrasattva, Apchi and Mahakala.

Located in the village of Tangkya on the north bank of the Kyi-chu, and accessible via a bridge a few kilometres north of Katsel, this geomantic temple was originally constructed in the 7th century by King Songtsen Gampo, and later restored by Lu-me during the 12th century. Further shrines were later added to the complex, including the 12th century temple built to house the remains of the Nyingma lama Zhikpo Dudtsi (1149-99). Subsequently, the temple came under the influence of other traditions: the Taklung Kagyupa, the Jonangpa, and the Gelukpa, before being absorbed by the Namgyel Monastery of the Potala Palace. The present temple appears to contain three original clay images, extracted from one of the earlier (long destroyed) structures, and some bronze Kadam-style stupas.

Tangkya Lhakhang

ཐང་སྐྱ་ལྷ་ཁང

Uruzhva Lhakhang (also written as Zhayi Lhakhang) is located on the south bank of the Mangra-chu, about 1.5 kilometres upstream from Drigung township (see below, page 150). It is a small temple of considerable historic significance for two reasons. Firstly, there are original 9th century obelisks flanking the entrance gate, which have inscriptions proclaiming the royal rewards and estates granted to Nyangben Tingzin Zangpo, the childhood friend of King Trisong Detsen who helped ensure the succession of the latter's son Senalek Jinyon in 804. The obelisk on the left is in good condition, while the one on the right is fragmented. It was Nyangben who persuaded Trisong Detsen to invite Vimalamitra, the Buddhist master of the Dzogchen esoteric instructions (*mengakde*), from India, and who then became the principal recipient of these teachings in Tibet. Vimalamitra concealed the teachings at Uruzhva in the early 9th century and these were subsequently rediscovered in the 11th century by the temple caretaker Dangma Lhundrub Namgyel, from which time their transmission has continued unbroken until the present. The second reason for the importance of Uruzhva is that the temple complex was restored during the 14th century by the great Nyingmapa master Longchen Rabjampa who fully comprehended its earlier significance for the Dzogchen tradition. Later in the 18th century the site came under the influence of Sera Monastery and was reconstructed by Dalai Lama VII.

Uruzhva Lhakhang

དབུ་རུ་ཞྭའི་ལྷ་ཁང

The original chapels of the temple, including the shrine dedicated to the Eight Manifestations of Padmasambhava (**Guru Tsengye Lhakhang**) were destroyed during the Cultural Revolution. The restored building is on two levels, the lower storey containing three chapels, and the upper storey a single chamber. Downstairs, the chapel to the left is still bare, the chapel to the right contains images of Padmasambhava along with the three important protectors of the Dzogchen teachings, namely: Dorje Lekpa, Ekajati, and Rahula, and a torma offering shrine. The rear chapel, in the form of an open air gallary, contains the reconstructed **Tramen Chorten**, under which Longchen Rabjampa interred the sacraments of the Damsi demons at the time of his 14th century renovations. The upper shrine, used as an assembly hall, contains a solitary image of Longchen Rabjampa.

To the left and right of the courtyard in front of the temple are the monastic residential buildings (*tratsang*), and behind the left wing there is another newly reconstructed stupa. The **Zangyak Drak** hillside to the left contains a meditation cave associated with the temple's founder Nyangben Tingzin Zangpo, and the **Karpo Drak** peak to the right has caves associated with both Padmasambhava and Dangma Lhundrub Namgyel.

Drigung Til Monastery

འབྲི་གུང་མཐིལ་
དགོན་པ

■ *Admission* : ¥15
Colour map 3, grid A5

The Monastery of Drigung Til is located some 72 kilometres north of Meldro Gungkar, in the valley of the Zhorong Tsangpo, the principal northeast tributary of the Kyi-chu, which flows from its source above the nomad encampment of **Tantuk Sumdo** for over 60 kilometres to enter the Kyi-chu opposite the ruins of the old hilltop Drigung Dzong. There are trekking routes which lead from the upper reaches of this valley into the Nyangchu district of Kongpo and the Nyiphu district of Pome (see below, page 405). The township of **Drigung qu**, which has a small guesthouse, is located near the confluence, on a promontory between the Zhorong Tsangpo and the Mangra-chu estuaries.

The road to Drigung Til Monastery runs upstream from Drigung township through the deep Zhorong Tsangpo gorge to Yangri Gonpa (now destroyed and integrated within a military compound), and thence for 30 kilometres to the township of Menpa. The monastery is located above, on the slopes of a steep cliff overlooking the valley. The name Drigung ('back of the dri') refers to the distinctive contour of the cliff and its ridge, which resembles the back of a dri ('female of the yak').

There are more than 50 buildings scattered across the upper slopes of the ridge, but three central temples act as a focal point for the entire complex. The **Assembly Hall** (*dukhang*) contains exquisite images of Vajradhara and Shakyamuni Buddha, as well as Padmasambhava in the form of Nangsi Zilnon, Drigung Jikten Gonpo, the founder of the monastery, and Rinchen Phuntsok, who presided over its greatest development. In the centre of the hall are further images depicting Jikten Gonpo and his two immediate successors, Sherab Jungne and Drakpa Jungne, who are collectively known here as Yabsesum.

The other important temples are connected by an open air gallery. Among them, the **Serkhang** to the right of the gallery contains the reliquary stupa, stone footprint and conch of Jikten Gonpo, along with images of Manjughosa, Jikten Gonpo (twice), Ksitigarbha, the protectress Apchi in her peaceful and wrathful forms, and the thrones of the Chetsang and Chungtsang incarnations.

The **Dzamling Gyen** Temple to the left of the gallery contains the reliquaries of Drigung Rinchen Phuntsok, Dorje Rinchen, and the yogin Bachung Rinpoche, who passed away in 1989 after devoting many years to Drigung's reconstruction. Towards the northeast of the ridge, there is a **Protector Chapel** (*gonkhang*) containing images of the protectress Apchi, and a hermitage, once frequented by Jikten Gonpo, and more recently by Bachung Rinpoche. It contains another stone footprint of Jikten Gonpo, along with a clay image of Tara, and tangkas depicting Shakyamuni and Tara.

The ruins of the residence (*labrang*) of the Drigung Chetsang and

History of Drigung Til

The Drigungpa are one of the eight schools derived from the teachings of Phakmodrupa Dorje Gyelpo (1110-1170), whose seat was established at Densatil, northeast of Tsetang (see below, page 217). In 1167, a hermitage was founded at Drigung Til by Minyak Gomring, a disciple of Phakmodrupa, and in 1179, one of Phakmodrupa's most senior disciples, named Jikten Gonpo (1143-1217), inaugurated the monastery. Drigung Til acquired a high reputation for its excellence in meditation, and during the 13th century even rivalled Sakya in its political influence until its destruction by the Mongols in 1290. Following its rebuilding, the monastery once again acquired great wealth, but ceased to have a political role in the affairs of Tibet. The Drigung Kagyu tradition has several connections with that of the Nyingmapa, particularly the tradition of Longchen Rabjampa, who during the 14th century was a most influential figure in the Drigung region. The high point of its development is assigned to the 16th century, during the period of Drigung Rinchen Phuntsok, who is also considered as a Nyingmapa lineage holder. In recent centuries the Drigungpa have had two important incarnating lamas, the Chetsang and the Chungtsang; and in 1959 there were over 500 monks.

Chungtsang incarnations have not as yet been renovated, but there are active meditation hermitages (*drubkhang*) scattered across the hillside. To the north-west of the ridge is the famed **Drigung Charnel Ground** (Drigung Durtro) to which the dead will be brought from far-off districts of Central Tibet, Kongpo and Nakchuka for sky burial. The circle of stones on which the corpses are dis-membered, some 12 metres in diameter is said to represent the mandala of Cakrasamvara. Around the charnel ground are stupas and a third stone foot-print of Jikten Gonpo. Two recently constructed chapels are located to the left, one containing murals of the Hundred Peaceful and Wrathful Deities (which appear to the deceased during the intermediate state after death and before rebirth), and the other containing the shaven hair of the dead. The pilgrim's circumambulation route encompasses the main temples, hermitages and charnel ground of Drigung.

The hermitage of Zhoto Tidro (also written as Zhoto Terdrom) is located in a side-valley which branches north off the Zhorong Tsongpo valley a few kilo-metres before Mepa township at the base of Drigung Til. The approach to the hermitage (*Altitude*: 4,500 metres) follows a narrow but drivable track which ascends a precipitous cliff above the Rep-chu River and comes to a halt at a vantage point overlooking a gorge, replete with aromatic herbs and containing a medicinal hotspring (**Chutsen Chugang**) and an important nunnery. Two guesthouses have been constructed beside the hot springs, which offer relax-ing bathing facilities. One is run by the nunnery and the other by TTC, Lhasa.

Zhoto Tidro Hermitage

History In 772 when King Trisong Detsen offered his queen Yeshe Tsogyel to Padmasambhava, hostile Bonpo aristocrats forced the master and his new consort to flee the royal court for the sanctuary of the limestone caves and hot springs of Zhoto Tidro. Padmasambhava concealed a number of trea-sures (*terma*) in the **Kiri Yangdzong** cave above Tidro, which were discovered in later centuries by Dorje Lingpa, Drigung Rinchen Phuntsok and others. Yeshe Tsogyel herself remained in meditation at Tidro for many years, for which reason the original nunnery was constructed at this particular site. The earliest buildings appear to date from the Kadampa period, but reconstruction has taken place on a number of occasions, the most recent being after the

Cultural Revolution. The nunnery, presently housing more than 80 nuns, is headed by the elderly Khandro-la, a veritable emanation of Yeshe Tsogyel, and in its temple there are splendid images of Padmasambhava, his two consorts, and eight manifestations, as well as Shakyamuni Buddha, and a Drigungpa throne.

Tidro Pilgrimage

Starting from the **hot springs**, the hardy traveller may follow the pilgrim's route to the Padmasambhava caves high in the mountains above Tidro. Immediately below the springs, there is a 15 metres long subterranean channel through which the river passes. Legend says that Padmasambhava himself created the tunnel in order to drain a lake inhabited by malignant water spirits by throwing his vajra at the ridge above, and the mark of the vajra can still be observed in the rocks at the tunnel entrance. He then created the hot springs for the benefit of future practitioners. The average temperature of the springs is 40°C, and they are known to contain sulphur, limestone, bitumen, coal and other minerals which can reputedly alleviate gastric disorders, tumours, paralysis, rheumatism, dermatitis, poor blood circulation, and general debility over a one week stay, according to a publication of the Meldro Gungkar Mentsikhang.

The **inner circumambulation** (*nangkor*) leads from the hot springs and the nunnery towards a west ridge which is reached by crossing a bridge over the river. The trail then ascends the Norbu La pass and plunges into another valley before rising to a charnel ground site and the ridge from which the **Kiri Yangdzong** cave is accessible by traversing a limestone rock face with natural hand and foot holds. This 50 metres high cavern contains active hermitages and important meditation caves, the most significant being the **Tsogyel Sangpuk**, where Yeshe Tsogyel received the empowerments and teachings of the *Innermost Spirituality of the Dakinis* (*Khandro Nyingtig*) from Padmasambhava, and subsequently passed many years in retreat. The circuit is completed by descending the limestone face and the scree slopes below to enter a gorge containing the ruined hermitage of Drigung Rinchen Phuntsok (**Drang Monastery**). From here, the path leads back to the hot springs. There is also an **outer circumambulation** (*chikor*), which encircles the entire Tidro and Drigung region, by taking an east valley from the base of the limestone rock face.

Chushul County ཆུ་ཤུལ

Chushul County (6)
曲水县
Quxu
Population: 27,346
Area: 1,482 sq km
Colour map M2, grid B4

*The valley of the Lower Kyi-chu extends from Lhasa southwards, and includes important sites on both banks of the river, as far as its confluence with the Brahmaputra, which is spanned by the **Chushul Zamchen** bridge. On the south bank of the Brahmaputra opposite the Chushul confluence is the sacred Mount Chuwori (see below, page 160). Four main roads diverge at Chushul: due west to Zhigatse via Nyemo and northeast to Lhasa (both on the north bank of the Brahmaputra), and southwest to Gyantse via Gampa La and Lake Yamdrok, or due east to Gongkar Airport and Tsetang (both on the south bank of the Brahmaputra). The distance from Lhasa to Chushul is 36 kilometres on an excellent paved surface, and a further eight kilometres to the bridge at Dagar.*

The West Bank of the Lower Kyi-chu

Following the paved Lhasa-Chushul highway southwest from the Dongkar intersection for 15 kilometres, you will reach on the left the turn-off for Tashigang, a Sakya monastery under the guidance of Bero Khyentse Rinpoche. The assembly hall (*dukhang*) has an image of Sakya Pandita, flanked by images of Shakyamuni, Avalokiteshvara, and Mahakala. Skylight murals depict the Sixteen Elders, Shakyamuni, Tara, and Atisha. Above the throne of the Dalai Lama, there is a 17th century tangka depicting Bhaisajyaguru, the Buddha of Medicine. The protector shrine is located upstairs. Currently, there are about 30 monks at Tashigang.

Tashigang

བཀྲ་ཤིས་གང་

Located 17 kilometres southwest of Dongkar on the right side of the highway, a short distance after passing a large painted relief image of Shakyamuni on the rock face, this celebrated temple dates from the time of the great Bengali master Atisha, who passed away at Nyetang in 1054. The temple is said to have survived the Cultural Revolution virtually unscathed owing to the intervention of Chou En Lai at the expressed request of the Government of East Pakistan (now Bangladesh). An adjacent 15th century Gelukpa Monastery, known as Dewachen, was destroyed at that time. From the outside, the temple appears to be insignificant, but the sacred artefacts contained within it testify to the importance of the Kadampa tradition in 11th-13th century Tibet. Presently there are only nine monks at Nyetang.

Nyetang Dolma Lhakhang

སྙེ་ཐང་སྒྲོལ་མ་ ལྷ་ཁང་

■ *Admission : ¥8*
Colour map 3, grid B2

Central Tibet

A double gateway leads via a courtyard to a covered terrace, where there are 11th century images of the Four Guardian Kings, and two sunken stupas containing the robes of Atisha and his disciple Dromtonpa. In the extreme left and right corners of the terrace there are large prayer wheels, while the murals inset between the chapel doors depict Atisha with his two foremost students, Dromtonpa and Ngok Lekpei Sherab, as well as Shakyamuni, Maitreya, and Manjughosa.

There are three interconnecting chapels, entered from the door to the left and exited by the door to the right. The first, known as the **Namgyel Lhakhang**, contains a large Victory Stupa (Namgyel Chorten), flanked on the left and right by smaller Kadam-style stupas containing relics of Naropa, among which the three metres high **Naropa Dungten** holds the precious skull of Naropa, along with Atisha's books and begging bowl. In front of the stupas are small 500 centimetres images of the Eight Medicine Buddhas with a clay representation of Atisha at the centre. Images on the left wall depict Tara, Avalokiteshvara, and Amitayus.

The second chapel, known as the **Dolma Lhakhang**, contains 17th century bronze images of the Twenty-One Taras, which are stacked in two tiers, occupying three walls of the chamber. The central images in the **upper tier** represent Shakyamuni (dated 1288), White Tara (a 'speaking image'), Serlingpa Dharmkirti, who was the teacher of Atisha, and Dalai Lama XIII. Other images of the Buddhas of the Five Families (*Pancajina*), dating from 11th century, are in the upper right corner. In the **lower tier**, the central objects of offering preserved inside a glass cabinet include a conch shell from Nalanda, an image of Thousand-armed Mahakarunika, a stupa containing Serlingpa's remains, a small image of Shakyamuni brought by Atisha from India, and a tangka depicting Six-armed Mahakala, which is said to have been painted with the blood from Atisha's nose. An original 'speaking image' of Tara disappeared from the cabinet during the Cultural Revolution, but it is said to have been preserved secretly at Norbulingka by the late Panchen Lama X. Other sacred objects within this chapel include a round urn containing

Atisha's bone relics, a bronze 13th century image of Avalokiteshvara Karsapani from India, and, until its theft by international art thieves in 1992, an image of Maitreya known as Atsa Jampa, which was reputedly spared the wrath of the Mongols by uttering the exclamation atsa ('ouch!').

Lastly, the **Tsepak Lhakhang** contains large 12th century images of the Buddhas of the Three Times and the Eight Bodhisattvas. Among these, the central image is of the Buddha of the Present in the form of Amitayus, fashioned by Dromtonpa from the funerary ashes of Atisha. The stupa containing his remaining ashes has been removed to nearby Tashigang. In the centre of the chapel is the backrest of Atisha's clay throne, with an attached image of Atisha himself, said to have been made in his own lifetime. The inner gates of this last chapel are guarded by large images of the gatekeepers Vajrapani (east) and Hayagriva (west).

Rato Monastery

ར་སྟོང་དགོན་པ

Located at Rato village in a side-valley, some five kilometres behind Nyetang Dolma Lhakhang, Rato Monastery was founded in the 11th century by Taktsangpa; and it had later associations with the Kadampa master Ngok Loden Sherab and Tsongkhapa. Noted for the study of Buddhist logic and metaphysics, the monastery had about 400 monks at the height of its development. The principal incarnate lamas of Rato are all in exile, living in India, Germany, and the United States; and there are presently no more than 90 monks.

The **Assembly Hall** (*Dukhang*) at Rato has central images of Tsongkhapa with his foremost disciples, and an image of Tara, said to have been the personal property of Atisha. Behind these along the rear wall are images of Shakyamuni Buddha and Atisha, flanked by the Kadampa lamas: Luchok Dorjechang, Ngok Loden Sherab, Manga Draksang, Chokla Ozer, Ngok Lekpei Sherab, and Yonten Phuntsok.

Behind, within the **inner sanctum** (*tsangkhung*) is an image of Tsongkhapa, standing in lieu of the former magnificent images of the Buddhas of the Three Times and the Eight Bodhisattvas. The extant murals of the assembly hall appear to date from the 17th-18th century. These depict protector deities, such as Dharmaraja and Tsedrekpa; bodhisattvas such as Tara, Manjughosa, Avalokiteshvara, Vajrapani, and Sitapatatra; the lamas of the *lamrim* lineage, and the buddhas of confession and medicine.

Among the other reconstructed temples at Rato: the **Nyitri Lhakhang** contains a protector shrine and the Dalai Lama's private apartments in its upper storeys, the **Jamkhang** contains a large Maitreya, and the **Rinchen Ritro Hermitage** has associations with Longdol Lama. In the mountains to the north there are also meditation caves belonging to Rato Monastery.

Chushul

ཆུ་ཤུལ

The highway from Lhasa to Chushul continues southwest from Nyetang Dolma Lhakhang, via the village of Nam, opposite which a new bridge has been constructed across the Kyi-chu, leading to Shugseb Nunnery (see below, page 155). Inland from Nam there was the original Drukpa Kagyu

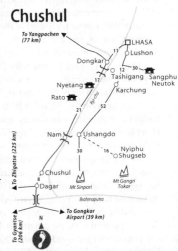

Chushul

To Yangpachen
(77 km)

LHASA

Lushon
11

Dongkar

12 30
17   Tashigang   Sangphu
Nyetang   Neutok
Karchung

Rato

21   52

Nam   Ushangdo

30   16   Nyiphu
                     Shugseb

Chushul

Dagar 8   Mt Sinpori   Mt Gangri
                              Tokar

Brahmaputra

To Zhigatse (225 km)

To Gyantse
(206 km)

To Gongkar
Airport (39 km)

N

Not to scale

Monastery of **Druk Jangchub Choling**, founded before Ralung by Tsangpa Gyare in 1189.

The town of **Chushul** has grown considerably in recent years, owing to its position near the intersection of the four main roads of Central, Western and Southern Tibet. There is a large two-storey guesthouse, and an overt military presence at **Dagar**, location of Chushul Zamchen bridge. Formerly, an iron suspension bridge made by Tangtong Gyelpo spanned the Brahmaputra slightly downstream from here, but it was damaged in the mid 20th century.

The East Bank of the Lower Kyi-chu

From the military compound at Drib near the regency temple of Tsechokling on the south bank of the Kyi-chu opposite Lhasa, there is an unpaved road which follows the river downstream in a southwest direction. Ramagang, the site of **Sangda Karchung Monastery**, is located slightly inland from Lushon village about 12 kilometres along this track. The monastery was founded by King Senalek Jinyon (r 804-814), who erected an inscribed obelisk and stupas in each of the temple's four directions, along the design of Samye Monastery. Drepung is visible across the river from the ruins of Sangda Karchung.

Karchung
Ramagang
སྔར་ཆུང་ར་མ་
སྒང་

Located about 30 kilometres south and inland from Lushon village, on the upper slopes of a side-valley which forks to the left, Sangphu Neutok Monastery was founded in 1073 by Ngok Lekpei Sherab and developed by his nephew, Ngok Loden Sherab. These scholar translators were close disciples of Atisha. Originally there were two Kadampa colleges here, known as Lingto and Lingme. Under the guidance of Chapa Chokyi Senge (1109-69) the monastery eventually gained renown for its eclectic approach to the study of Buddhist philosophy, and it became a mixed institution with seven Sakyapa and four Gelukpa colleges. The meditation caves of Yakde Panchen and Rongton Sheja Kunzi were located in the upper ranges; while lower down by the river at Sangda, some 16 kilometres distant, the reliquary of Ngok Loden Sherab was formerly preserved. In recent centuries the monastery declined but it was restored by Dalai Lama XIII prior to its more recent destruction during the Cultural Revolution.

Sangphu
Neutok
Monastery
གསང་ཕུ་ནེའུ་ཐོ
ག་གི་ཆོས་གྲ

Following the Kyi-chu downstream from Sangda for approximately 52 kilometres, via the villages of Sheldrong, Namgyel Gang, and Tshena Sha, a side-valley leads across the plain of Nyinda (sometimes called Shuntse) to the ruins of Ushangdo Temple. This area is also accessible from Nam on the west bank, via the new Kyi-chu suspension bridge.

The nine-storey temple of Ushangdo was the greatest construction project undertaken by the Tibetan king Relpachen (r 815-838). It is said to have been a pagoda-style building with a Chinese roof of blue turquoise. The three lower floors were used by the king and his ministers, the three middle floors by the Indian panditas and their Tibetan translators for the revision of the translation methodology; and the upper three storeys contained images. The building appears not to have survived Langdarma's persecution; but a small temple with a remarkable Jowo Shakyamuni image was later constructed on the site. Unfortunately, today only its ruins are visible.

Ushangdo
Peme Tashi
Gephel
ཨུ་ཤང་རྡོ
དཔེ་མེད
བཀྲ་ཤིས་དགེ
འཕེལ

Shugseb is located 16 kilometres above Ushangdo in the uplands of Nyiphu. The site was originally consecrated by the *yogini* Machik Labron (1055-1149), who meditated in the caves of Shugseb, but the first retreat centre was actually established here by Gyargom Tsultrim Senge (1144-1204), a student of Phakmodrupa, and founder of the Shugseb Kagyu order. From the 14th century

Nyiphu
Shugseb
Nunnery
ཉི་ཕུ་ཤུག་གསེབ

onwards, Shugseb has been an important centre for nuns of the Nyingma school, owing to the teaching activity of Longchen Rabjampa at nearby Gangri Tokar; and the female incarnation of Shugseb, the Shugseb Jetsunma, ranks as one the the highest female incarnations in the whole of Tibet.

There are presently 80 nuns living in huts around the restored temple of Shugseb. Downstairs, the temple has new images of Padmasambhava and Machik Labron, while the upper storey contains the residence of the Jetsunma. From Shugseb there are three to four day trekking routes east to Dorje Drak and south to Sinpori.

Gangri Tokar

གངས་རི་
ཐོད་དཀར

The ridge of Mount Gangri Tokar (5,336 metres) is located about one hour hiking distance above Shugseb Nunnery. From the perspective of pure sacred vision, the site is said to represent the left knee of the female deity Vajravarahi, whose breasts and vagina are identified with the springs arising nearby. The great Nyingma master Longchen Rabjampa (1308-63) arrived here at the invitation of his protectress Dorje Yudronma. Here, in the cave hermitage of **Orgyan Dzong** and its inner sanctum, called **Dawa Chushel Puk**, he meditated, and redacted his terma revelations (entitled *Kandro Yangtig, Zabmo Yangtig,* and *Lama Yangtig*); and composed his great treatises including the *Seven Treasuries* (*Dzodun*) and the *Three Trilogies* (*Korsum Namsum*).

The cave presently contains a new image of Longchen Rabjampa. The stumps of two juniper trees (the abodes of Longchen Rabjampa's protectors Rahula and Dorje Yudronma) are visible outside the entrance to the cave. A natural stone image of Rahula and rock abode of Dorje Yudronma are also to be seen. East of Orgyan Dzong are the other meditation caves, among them the **Melong Puk** hermitage of Melong Dorje, **Samten Puk**, **Dewa Puk**, and **Shar Zimpuk**, the last and most remote being especially favoured for the practice of the highest Dzogchen teachings, known as All-surpassing Realization (*thogal*).

Riwo Tsenga

རི་བོ་རྩེ་ལྔ

Southwest of Gangri Tokar is the five peaked ridge known as Riwotsenga, which is named after the celebrated Buddhist range of Wutaishan in China. There are a number of meditation caves here, including the Zangyak Namka Dzong, the Guru Drupuk, and Lharing Longchen Drak.

Sinpori

སྲིན་པོ་རི

Mount Sinpori lies 30 kilometres south of Ushangdo, on a promontory between the Kyi-chu and Brahmaputra rivers, east of the confluence. This barren desert-like terrain once contained an important 13th century Sakya temple which had been constructed by the Bengali scholar Vibhuticandra on the advice of Panchen Shakyashri. The temple was dedicated to the deity Cakrasamvara, and housed a 'speaking image' of Cakrasamvara.

Sinpori is also accessible by ferry from Chushul, by trekking from Shugseb via Leuchung, or walking from Dorje Drak on the north bank of the Brahmaputra.

Southern Tibet
Lhokha & Kongpo

5

Southern Tibet
Lhokha & Kongpo

Southern Tibet is the region demarcated by the lower Brahmaputra (Tib Yarlung Tsangpo) valley, extending east from its confluence with the Kyi-chu as far as Kongpo on the borders of Powo and Pemako, where it turns through narrow gorges and flows southwest into India. As such, the region includes the lateral valleys adjoining the Brahmaputra on both its north and south banks, and the valleys of its south-flowing tributaries, which enter East Bhutan and Arunachal Pradesh to converge with this great river south of the Himalayas in West Bengal or Assam. Currently, this vast region, revered as the cradle of Tibetan civilization, is divided into 16 counties, four of which are administered from Nyangtri (ie Gyamda, Nyangtri, Nang, and Menling), and the remainder from Tsetang, the capital of the Lhokha district (ie Gongkar, Dranang, Nedong, Chongye, Tso-me, Lhodrak, Nakartse, Zangri, Chusum, Lhuntse, Tsona, and Gyatsa). The distance from Lhasa to Gongkar Airport is 96 km and to Tsetang 183 km.
Recommended itineraries: 1 and 4 (also 7)

Gongkar County གོང་དཀར

Gongkar County (7)
贡嘎县
Gonggar
Population: 41,624
Area: 2,532 sq km
Colour map M3, grid C3

*Gongkar county is located on the banks of the Brahmaputra at a point where the river valley reaches its widest extent, for which reason **Gongkar Airport** (the civilian airport serving Lhasa) was constructed there in the late 1970s. A second runway and terminal facilities were completed in 1994. The airport lies to the west of **Rawa-me**, the county capital at the entrance to the Namrab valley; 96 kilometres from Lhasa and 87 kilometres from Tsetang. The borders of Gongkar county extend from the sacred Mount Chuwori opposite Chushul, southwards to Gampa La pass (4,794 metres), which is the gateway to Lake Yamdrok and West Tibet, and eastwards as far as the Dol valley on the south bank of the Brahmaputra and Dorje Drak monastery on the north bank. Thus, it includes the southern lateral valleys of Gongkar, Namrab, and Drib; as well as the northern lateral valleys of Leuchung and Trango.*

Mount Chuwori

ཆུ་བོ་རི

The sacred mountain of Chuwori which broods over the sandbanks around the confluence of the Kyi-chu and Brahmaputra rivers is considered to be one of the most auspicious places for meditation practice in Tibet. In the past, the mountain is said to have had 108 springs and 108 hermitages dating from the time of King Trisong Detsen in the eighth century. Padmasambhava had a hermitage near the summit at **Namkading**, and it is said that 108 of his yogin followers attained the body of light here at Chuwori. Later, during the 12th century, new hermitages were constructed by the Nyingmapa lama Taton Joye, Karmapa I Dusum Khyenpa, and Tsangpa Gya-re, and in the 13th century by Dorje Drak Rigzin II Lekdenje.

On the lower slopes of the mountain, the monastery of **Chakzam Chuwori** was founded by Tangtong Gyelpo, facing the celebrated iron suspension bridge which he constructed across the Brahmaputra to Yolri Gong near Chushul (damaged in the early decades of this century, and now replaced by the Chushul Zamchen bridge). At the south end of the old suspension bridge, there was also a Kumbum stupa, containing an image and relics of Tangtong Gyelpo himself.

The monastery of **Pema Wangchuk** was located on a northwest spur of Mount Chuwori, and on the east side, near the Tsechu ('water of life') Spring where pilgrims flock even now, there was once an active Nyingmapa monastery called **Tsechu Kopa** or Tsechuling, founded by Menlungpa Lochok Dorje. All these sites are in ruins at the present day; but this does not deter pilgrims who make the circuit of the mountain via Phab La (4,250 metres) in four hours.

Gampa La Pass

གམ་པ་ལ

The approach to Gampa La pass (4,794 metres), which offers spectacular views of the **Nojin Gangzang** snow ranges and the turquoise **Yamdrok Yutso Lake** is 28 kilometres from the south end of the Chushul Zamchen bridge. The switchback road winds its way up from Samar, past deep barren gorges, which are evidence of the Brahmaputra tectonic fault line. Near the pass, which is bedecked with colourful prayer flags, there is a turn-off to the right side of the road,

Gongkar County

leading to a sensitive mining installation. For the route from Gampa La to Nakartse, see below, page 214.

Driving east from the southern end of the Chushul Zamchen bridge for 26 kilometres, you will observe to the left the hilltop ruins of **Gongkar Dzong**, from which the entire Gongkar region was ruled until the 1950s. This is usually the first glimpse a visitor arriving in Tibet by air will have of the wanton destruction inflicted on Tibetan culture since the Chinese occupation.

Gongkar Valley

གོང་དཀར

Gongkar Chode Just beyond this hilltop promontory, at the entrance to the Gongkar valley, there is an important monastery called **Gongkar Chode** or Gongkar Dorjeden, which was founded in 1464 by Dorjedenpa Kunga Namgyel of the Sakya School. Here there are important extant murals typical of the free-flowing Khyenri school of painting, which were the original work of Jamyang Khyentse Wangchuk (b 1524). The 64 pillared **Assembly Hall** (*dukhang*) has new images of Dorjedenpa, Padmasambhava, Shakyamuni Buddha, and Sakya Pandita, and original Khyenri murals of the Five Founders of Sakya (Gongma Nga) flanking the entrance to the inner sanctum. The walls of the circumambulatory walkway around the inner sanctum have original murals depicting the Twelve Deeds of Shakyamuni and the Thousand Buddhas of the Aeon, although no trace remains of the original three-storey high image of Shakyamuni containing the skull of the Indian master Gayadhara, which once graced the inner sanctum.

The **Gonkhang** to the left contains gold on black painted murals of Mahakala in the form Panjaranatha (Gonpo Gur), and his retinue, the preferred protectors of the Sakya tradition.

Upstairs, there are exquisite murals depicting the plan of the original monastery, and the Sakyapa meditational deities, headed by Hevajra (in the **Kyedor Lhakhang**), as well as others depicting the Sakya *Lamdre* lineage; and also a **Kangyur Lhakhang**. On the third storey the **Lama Lhakhang** is dedicated to the monastery's founder Dorjedenpa Kunga Namgyel. Restoration work appears to be hampered because the immense weight of the upper storey has destabilized the building. Formerly, there were other buildings at Gongkar Chode, including a distinctive three-storeyed **Lamdre Lhakhang** and four colleges, which are all in a bad state of disrepair.

Following the road inland from Gongkar Chode for five kilometres, you will reach **Dechen Chokhor**, a 13th century hermitage and monastery of the Drukpa Kagyu school, located on the slopes 150 metres above the road. One small chapel has been rebuilt amid the ruins. Further inland there are one to two day trekking routes from Gongkar valley to Lake Yamdrok via the Dra La pass (5,342 metres) and Chilung.

Continuing east on the main road below Gongkar Chode, **Gongkar Airport** and the entrance to the Namrab valley will be reached after a further 10 kilometres. Accommodation is available at the *Gongkar Hotel*, T(0893)6182221, near the airport. A small and clean Tibetan restaurant outside the gate to the airport serves mo-mo and tea.

Namrab Valley

རྣམ་རབ

The Sakyapa monastery of **Tubten Rawa-me**, founded by Rawalepa (1138-1210) is situated within the town. It is in a state of disrepair, and has a prominent TV antenna on the roof. By the roadside in Rawa-me, the county town, there are a number of small Tibetan and Chinese restaurants, and tea-shops selling Indian-style sweet milk tea.

Rawa-me

Southern Tibet

Some five kilometres inland from Rawa-me in the Kyishong township area is the Sakya monastery of **Dakpo Tratsang**, founded by Tashi Namgyel (1398-1459), a disciple of the illustrious Rongton Sheja Kunzik. There is a large renovated assembly hall with some original murals and new images of Sakya Pandita, Tashi Namgyel and Gorampa Sonam Senge. The adjacent protector shrine is dedicated to the deity Pangboche.

Further inland and situated 150 metres on a remote hillside is **Zhung Trezhing**, a hermitage frequented by Ngokton Choku Dorje (1036-1102), a close disciple of Marpa Lotsawa. After he passed away at that site, his nephew Ngok Kunga Dorje (1157-1234) founded the Trezhing monastery, where a distinct Kagyu lineage (apart from those derived from Milarepa and Gampopa) was maintained. In the past Marpa's skull was preserved here in a reliquary stupa.

Drib Valley

གྲིབ་

The main road east from Gongkar Airport to Tsetang passes through the township of Chedezhol, at the entrance to the Dol or Drib valley after 17 kilometres. Here there is an active cottage industry engaged in the production of colourful striped ladies' aprons (*pangden*). The ruins of **Chedezhol Dzong** can be seen on a ridge to the east.

Dungpu Chokhor Some four kilometres inland is the monastery of Dungpu Chokhor, originally founded by Drapa Ngonshe in the 11th century; and later absorbed by the Sakyapas in the 15th century. The **Assembly Hall** has some old frescoes, depicting Mahakala in the form Panjaranatha flanked by other protectors, and the Twelve Deeds of Shakyamuni Buddha, as well as important Sakya meditational deities headed by Hevajra, the Five Founders of Sakya, and (under the skylight) the lamas of the *Lamdre* lineage. The **inner sanctum** has an original 'speaking' Tara image, adorned with coral; and there are side chambers containing a printery (left) and a Vairocana image surrounded by Taras (right). Upstairs is a chamber where HH Dalai Lama XIV stayed during his flight from Lhasa to India in 1959.

About three kilometres further inland and on a side-valley east of Khyimzhi village is the monastery of **Sungrabling**, which was originally founded as a Sakya establishment by Nyakton Sonam Zangpo in the 14th century and later absorbed by the Gelukpa.

Trekking Further up the Drib valley, via the township of Namgyel Zhol and Drib La pass, there are three to four day trekking routes to the north shores of Lake Yamdrok.

Dorje Drak Monastery

ཕུབ་བསྟན་ རྡོ་རྗེ་བྲག

Accessible by ferry from Chedezhol (50 minutes), the monastery is located at the base of a vajra-shaped rock on the north bank of the Brahmaputra.

The celebrated Nyingma monastery of Tubten Dorje Drak maintains the *terma* tradition of the Nyingma school known as the Northern Treasures (Jangter), which derives from Rigdzin I Godemchen Ngodrub Gyeltsen (1337-1409). In 1632, the monastery was relocated on its present secure site from Tsang, when the young Rigdzin III Ngagiwangpo and his guardian Jangdak Tashi Topgyel were forced to flee the wrath of the kings of Tsang. The site was greatly developed by Rigdzin IV Pema Trinle (1641-1717) before his untimely death at the hands of the Dzungar Mongols. Thus, the monastery was sacked by the Dzungars in 1717, and again obliterated during the 1960s. Nonetheless it has been gradually restored in recent years through the efforts of the present incarnation of Dordrak Rigdzin, who resides in Lhasa, and those of Kelzang Chojor and the local community.

Assembly Hall The Assembly Hall (*tshokchen*) has a large image of

Padmasambhava, replacing an original made by Rigdzin IV Pema Trinle, as well as painted scrolls depicting the Hundred Peaceful and Wrathful Deities, and murals depicting the Eight Manifestations of Padmasambhava. There are three thrones, the central one reserved for Dordrak Rikdzin himself, and the others for Taklung Tsetrul Rinpoche (who resides in exile in Simla and Ladakh), and Chubzang Rinpoche. In the **inner sanctum** there is a 'self-arising' stone image of Two-armed Avalokiteshvara, a collection of relics retrieved from images destroyed in the 1960s, and a library containing the *Kangyur* and the *Nyingma Gyudbum*.

The **oldest chapel** to the right (in which no women are allowed) once contained images of the 'three roots' (guru, meditational deity and dakini) of the Dorje Drak tradition; but now it contains a few old images, a copy of the Derge edition of the *Nyingma Gyudbum*, and a number of precious objects: the vajra and bell of Rigdzin IV Pema Trinle, a treasure chest (*terdrom*), part of Milarepa's staff, and a detailed 3-D plan of how the monastery once looked. Prior to the Dzungar army's destruction of Dorje Drak in 1717, this ancient chapel had been renowned for its enormous columns and skull-painted gates.

Upstairs Upstairs there is a newly installed **printing press**; and to the left of the complex there is a **Protector Chapel**, containing images of Vajrakila and so forth. Another recently rebuilt temple contains new images of the afore-mentioned 'three roots'; but the ruined residences of Dordrak Rigdzin and Taklung Tsetrul are currently under restoration.

Kora The pilgrims' circuit leads around the 'vajra rock' to the hermitage of **Dorje Drak Utse**, passing en route rock paintings and sacred footprints.

A hermitage of the Drukpa Kagyu master Lingje Repa is nearby at **Napu Cholung**. There is also a four day trekking route from Dorje Drak to Lhasa, via Phushar, Trango township, and Trango La pass (4,977 metres) to the north.

Trekking

Dranang County གྲ་ནང་

*Dranang county, with its administrative capital at **Dratang**, is made up of a series of lateral valleys adjoining the Brahmaputra valley, both north and south of the river. These include the Drakyul, Zurkhar and Drakmar valleys on the north bank, and those of Dranang and Drachi on the south bank. The distance from Chedezhol to Dratang along the main Gongkar-Tsetang highway is 23 kilometres.*

Dranang County (8)
扎囊县
Zhanang
Population: 33,293
Area: 1,426 sq km
Colour map M3, grid C3

Drakyul Valley གྲ་གས་ཡུལ

The cave complexes of **Drak Yangdzong** and **Dzong Kumbum**, are a maze of interconnecting limestone passages and natural caverns, replete with bizarre rock formations, stalagmites and stalactites.

Drakyul is most easily approached by ferry from **Yangkyar**, a hydro-electric station 3 kilometres west of Dranang on the Gongkar-Tsetang highway; or alternatively via the Dorje Drak ferry from Chedezhol. The pilgrimage or trek begins at **Drakda**, birthplace of Nubchen Sangye Yeshe, 4 kilometres from the north ferry station, where the Drak-chu flows into the Brahmaputra. **NB** Alternative routes are also possible: trekking via Dorje Drak monastery and Phushur (2 days); trekking from Samye via Zurkhar (1 day); or even from Lhasa via Trango La pass (4 days) and from Taktse (4 days).

Getting there

Tsogyel Latso   From the ferrry station you should first visit the Tsogyel Latso in Drakda village (four kilometres distant). This is an oracle lake revered as the life-supporting talisman of Yeshe Tsogyel, and is said to reveal the secrets of past and future events in its waters. Opposite, on the north shore, is **Kazhima Lhakhang**, an undestroyed branch of Samye Monastery, containing images of Padmasambhava, Vajrayogini, and Yeshe Tsogyel herself.

Ngadrak   Then, proceed to **Ngadrak**, a Karma Kagyu monastery on the west bank of the Drak-chu, some six kilometres further inland. This large establishment, under the authority of Nenang, comprises an assembly hall adjoined by five chapels, and a monastic residential area, where the caretakers of the Drakyul caves can be found. Two kilometres further north from Ngadrak is **Pema Dzong**, a relatively intact fortress dating originally from the 14th century.

Drak Yangdzong caves   Assisted by the caretakers of Drakyul (a strong flashlight is essential), the pilgrim will approach **Drak Yangdzong** via the **Chusi Nunnery** (approximately 20 kilometres per 5¼ hours), which is still largely in a ruinous state. The three main caves, which are all south-facing, are then reached by climbing a white limestone cliff (named Shinje Rolpei Podrang). Many carved relief images are visible near the cave entrances, depicting Padmasambhava, Shakyamuni Buddha, Milarepa, animal figures, and so forth.

    The first cave, **Shinje Drup-ne Zho**, is a vast cavern, 100 square metres in area, with walls 15 metres high and 10 metres wide. The cave is presently occupied by hermits from Dorje Drak, but the paintings of the interior chapel depict the Mindroling lineage. The main images are of Padmasambhava in the form Nangsi Zilnon, flanked by his consorts: Mandarava and Yeshe Tsogyel.

    The second cave, **Shinje Rolpei Drub-ne**, further west, is entered via a ladder and a narrow tunnel with a rope pulley, which exits into a deep cavern by way of a sandalwood ladder. Here are the Guru Drupuk, with its divinely shaped rocks representing Maitreya and other deities, and the **Guru Sangwa Drupuk** – the foremost goal of the Drakyul pilgrimage, where Padmasambhava passed three years in retreat.

    The third cave, called **Jago Rangjung Drupuk** (or Nego Sarpa), 40 metres further west, is eight metres wide, 50 metres deep, and in places over 10 metres high. The amazing limestone formations within it are held to be part of a 'hidden land' (*beyul*) replete with nectar, which was revealed for the first time in the 17th century by Rigdzin IV Pema Trinle of Dorje Drak. The **Shiwa-tsel Charnel Ground** is located higher up the hillside to the west.

Dzong Kumbum caves   The **Dzong Kumbum** cave complex (4,800 metres) lies about 10 kilometres above Nga-drak. As at Drak Yangdzong, the approach to the cave is bedecked with multiple rock carvings. The entrance is 30 metres high, and it is 35 metres deep, with five labyrinthine tunnels behind – all of them associated with Padmasambhava.

Dranang Valley གྲ་ནང

The Dranang valley is well endowed with an unusual variety of interesting sites, both prehistoric and Buddhist,

Dranang County

Not to scale

Hidden Lands

*The cave complexes are revered as Padmasambhava's foremost pilgrimage place of buddha-body in Central Tibet. From the perspective of the pilgrim's pure sacred vision the landscape assumes the atttributes of diverse deities. These caves have been renowned since the time of Padmasambhava, when 55 of his disciples are said to have attained the body of light after meditating here. Padmasambhava himself frequented these caves, along with his consort Yeshe Tsogyel, whose birthplace, **Sewalung** in Karchen, is in the lower reaches of Drakyul. Other major disciples of Padmasambhava associated with the valley and its natural hermitages were Nubchen Sangye Yeshe and Nanam Dorje Dudjom. Subsequently in the 13th century, the Dzogchen master Melong Dorje occupied the **Ngarpuk** cave in upper Drakyul; but the caves have always been remote from mundane human habitation. It is said that even now there are `hidden lands' (beyul) at Drakyul, inaccessible to all but the fortunate.*

for which reason it is renowned as the abode of the '13 saints or holymen of Dranang' (Dranang Kyebu Dampa Chuksum), who include illustrious figures such as Drapa Ngonshe, Tsangpa Gya-re, Orgyen Lingpa, Longchen Rabjampa, and Terdak Lingpa. To spend some time in this district, you can stay at the small guesthouse in Dratang, the county capital, or commute from Tsetang, 47 kilometres further east.

A short two kilometres' drive inland from Dratang town on the west fork of the track leads to Dratang Monastery, an important conservation site for the artistic heritage of Tibet.

Dratang Monastery

■ *Admission : ¥15*
Colour map 3, grid C3

History The temple complex was founded in 1081 by Drapa Ngonshe, a native of Dranang valley and one of the 13 saints associated with it, and completed in 1093 by his nephews.

The complex was later absorbed by the Sakyapas in the 14th-15th century, damaged by the Dzungar armies in the 18th, repaired in the 1920s and 1930s by the later Reting Rinpoche, regent of Tibet from 1922-41, and once again severely damaged by the Chinese in the 1960s. Nonetheless, despite these vicissitudes of time, the ground floor of the main building has preserved a series of frescoes which are unique in Tibet, in that they are said to represent an important synthesis of the Pala Indian style and Central Asian style (Tucci: 1949).

The Complex Like Samye, the main temples of Dratang are surrounded by an elliptical wall (the only surviving one of three original concentric walls around the complex). No images survive at Dratang. The 20-pillared **Assembly Hall** and protector shrine to its left are empty, but for late murals from the Sakyapa period in the former.

The **inner sanctum** to the west is entered through a triple gateway, adorned with paintings of the Four Guardian Kings and various bodhisattvas. The corridor murals depict the life of Shakyamuni and the careers of major bodhisattvas, such as Amitayus and Avalokiteshvara. The eight-pillared inner sanctum itself once contained a large 3.4 metres image of the Buddha as Thubpa Jangchub Chenpo, flanked by the Eight Bodhisattvas, but these have all been destroyed. The murals have survived – those on the south, north, and west walls dating from the 11th century, and those of the east extremities of the north and south walls (near the gates) from the later Sakyapa period. There are

Southern Tibet

Southern Tibet

Drapa Ngonshe and Tibet's Medical Tradition

Drapa Ngonshe was particularly renowned throughout Tibet as the discoverer (in 1038) of the Four Medical Tantras (Gyud-zhi), said to have been redacted from Indian sources by Vairocana and concealed at Samye in the 8th century. These texts form the basis of the entire Tibetan medical tradition. However, Drapa Ngonshe is also credited with the construction of 128 Buddhist temples and shrines throughout Central and Southern Tibet, among which the Dratang Monastery was the most significant. An eclectic spiritual teacher, who had associations with the Nyingma, Zhiche, and Kadampa schools, he established Dratang as a preeminent centre for the study of tantra among the New Translation Schools (Sarmapa).

some 10 groups of early paintings, depicting Buddha figures surrounded by large throngs of bodhisattvas; the stylistic features of physionomy, clothing, jewellery and ornamentation all being suggestive of non-Tibetan influences – both Indian Pala, and Central Asian Khotanese. The best preserved are those of the west wall, where the stylistic line and vibrant colours can be seen to their best advantage.

Restoration has been continuing slowly at Dratang, where the temple is still being used for grain storage. If the monks succeed in their application to have the temple returned to their ownership, the granary will have to be moved, as will the adjacent military HQ and workshops. However, leakage and damp which formerly threatened the 11th century murals have been halted, which is all to the credit of the Shalu Foundation, based in Paris.

Jampaling   Located on the slopes about three kilometres to the east of Dratang, and reached via the east fork on the inland track, is the Gelukpa monastery of Jampaling, founded in 1472 by Tonmi Lhundrub Tashi, a descendant of Tonmi Sambhota. There were formerly nine buildings within the complex, all of which have been partially or completely destroyed in the 1960s. The 13-storey stupa of Jampaling, known as **Kumbum Tongdrol Chenmo**, was formerly the largest of its type in Tibet, exceeding the dimensions of the great stupa at Gyantse (see below, page 253), but constructed in a similar multi-chapel style. The murals were the work of Jamyang Khyentse Wangchuk, founder of the free-flowing Khyenri style of painting, extant examples of which are still seen at Gongkar Chode (see above, page 161).

Reconstruction proceeds at a slow pace here, but the **Maitreya Temple (Jampa Lhakhang)** has been rebuilt on its original site northeast of the stupa. The rear wall of its assembly hall contains some old murals which survive from the earlier structure. Among the other buildings, the 18 metres **Tangka Wall** is in a good state of preservation, as is the **Jungden Monastery** of the Sakya school, some 200 metres east of the temple. The monastic college, the Jampaling Labrang, and the unusual series of shops formerly maintained on the site by Bhutanese and Nepalese traders have been erased.

Serkong Tombs   Located in a side-valley, some 11 kilometres west of Dratang Monastery, are the 11 trapezoid and single stupa-shaped tumuli of Serkong. The largest tumulus which is in the northeast is 20 metres high at the front and seven metres high at the rear, with sides 96 metres long, rear 87 metres, and front 92 metres. To its left there is an excavated tomb. Four chambers were dug into the bedrock of the hill below the tumulus: an entrance passage, an entrance cavity, a tomb chamber, and an extension chamber where the deceased's personal effects would be interred. The tombs here are probably contemporaneous to those of Chongye (where the Yarlung Dynasty kings were buried) and those of Nang Dzong further east (see below, page 224). The Serkong tombs appear to have been plundered after the collapse of the Yarlung Dynasty, and later in the 18th century by the Dzungar armies.

The vast ruins of **Pema Choling Nunnery** extend for some 5,000 square metres across the hillside above Serkong. Only the lowest storey of the assembly hall survives.

Driving the short 15 kilometres distance from Dratang to Dingpoche in upper Dranang valley, you will have an opportunity to visit other places of interest en route. The Gelukpa monastery of **Riwo Namgyel** is located on the east slopes of the valley (3,900 metres), about six kilometres above the village of **Gyurme** where Tsangpa Gya-re was born. The monastery was founded ca 1470 by Gonten Gyelpo, and it developed into an extensive site (11,000 square kilometres) with over 60 monks. Later it was absorbed by the Namgyel Monastery of the Potala Palace in Lhasa. The severely damaged assembly hall has recently undergone restoration. **Riwo Namgyel Monastery**

Getting there About 8 kilometres south of Dratang and beyond Gyurme village, the road passes through Gyeling township, where Gyeling Tsokpa monastery is located. **Gyeling Tsokpa Monastery**

This eclectic establishment was founded in 1224 by students of the Kashmiri Panchen Shakyashri, and was in the 15th century adopted as a residence by Go Lotsawa Zhonupel, author of the *Blue Annals*.

The three-storey temple is surrounded by a wall and moat, and the lowest storey functions as a basement. The **second storey** contains the assembly hall and three chapels forming an inner sanctum. Of these, the central **Jokhang** contains old murals depicting Shakyamuni Buddha, Avalokiteshvara, Amitayus, and the Four Guardian Kings. The side chapels are utilized as protector shrines, and the entrance to the assembly hall has murals depicting the progenitors of the Nyingma lineage in Tibet: Padmasambhava, Shantaraksita, King Trisong Detsen, and the Twenty-five Disciples (Jewang Nyernga). The main relics of the monastery, including old tangkas and a small 'self-arising' statue of Shakyashri, have been removed to the **Gatsel Puk** hermitage, four kilometres higher up the ridge, where there is also a new temple containing images associated with the *Longchen Nyingtig* tradition.

Getting there Following a westerly trail which begins some 5 kilometres south of Gyeling township, you will reach Peldrong township, where there are 10 plundered neolithic tombs, and from where the Nyingmapa monastery of Nyingdo is accessible. **Nyingdo Monastery**

This Mindroling branch monastery was originally constructed by Rinchen Lingpa in the 13th century and developed by his successor Nyingdo Tamched Khyenpa (1217-77). The most important object in this monastery (which is now being rebuilt) is a talismanic pillar from Khyungpo in the upper Salween region of East Tibet, said to offer protection from pestilences, drought and hail.

Getting there The road continues south from Nyingdo, via Rinchengang (or Raldrigang), from which there is a trekking route northeast to Mindroling in the Drachi valley (28 kilometres), as far as Kyilru township, where there is a yellow-walled temple, recently renovated. From Kyilru, there is a trail to the west, leading via Dekyiling village to the fortified Drukpa Kagyu monastery of Dingpoche. **Dingpoche Monastery**

This monastery was founded in 1567 by Rinchen Pelzang, a student of Pema Karpo (1526-92) on the summit of a secluded flat spur; and yet it has not escaped destruction over the course of its history – whether at the hands of the Dzungars in the 18th century, or at the hands of the Chinese more recently. The four-storeyed temple, said to represent the mandala of the deity Cakrasamvara, once contained large images of Shakyamuni and his two foremost disciples.

Amid the ruins, some rebuilding has taken place since 1984: there is a new assembly hall (*dukhang*), a new **Jokhang** (with images of Jowo Shakyamuni, White Tara, and Rinchen Pelzang), a new **Guru Lhakhang** (with images of Padmasambhava and his two main consorts), and a **Gonkhang** (with images of Four-armed Mahakala, Shridevi, and Dingpoche Chokyong). The **courtyard** (Chora) to the south of the complex contains a series of meditation cells (*chokhung*), dug into the ground and covered with blue and white tent canopies, which are utilized even now for solitary retreat. A rebuilt Victory Stupa (Namgyel Chorten) lies outside the perimeter wall to the southwest, and a partially destroyed Enlightenment Stupa (Jangchub Chorten) within the southeast corner.

At the hermitage of **Dra Yugang Drak** in the cliffs above Dingoche, there is a Padmasambhava cave, where Orgyen Lingpa subsequently (14th century) discovered a number of *terma*-texts that are no longer extant. Minling Trichen Terdak Lingpa stayed here in retreat and constructed an image of Padmasambhava; but the complex was badly damaged in the 1960s.

Yarje Lhakhang   Southwest of Kyilru township and Dekyiling village, the jeep road continues to Yarje Lhakhang, the birthplace of the renowned treasure-finder Orgyen Lingpa, which structurally survived the persecution of the 1960s, and contains new images of Padmasambhava and Avalokiteshvara in the form Simhanada ('Lion's Roar'). There is also a wall painting which depicts Yarje Orgyen Lingpa himself.

Derong   Continuing south from Kyilru township and southeast of Dingpoche, you will
Nunnery   reach the village of Tashiling and, on the slopes above, the nunnery of **Derong** (also written Drophu Todrong). Below the nunnery is the ruined house, reputed to be the birthplace of Longchen Rabjampa (1308-64), the most illustrious of all Nyingmapa masters in Tibet. The buildings are currently undergoing reconstruction.

Dargye Choling   The last site of interest in the upper Dranang valley is the ruined Nyingmapa
Monastery   monastery of Dargye Choling, some four kilometres southwest of Dingpoche. Founded by Natsok Rangdrol and developed by Sangdak Trinle Lhundrub during the 17th century, it was the precursor of Mindroling Monastery in the neighbouring Drachi valley. The latter's son, Minling Trichen Terdak Lingpa, was born here in 1646.

Drachi Valley   གྲ་ཕྱི་

There are two entrances to the Drachi valley from the main Gongkar-Tsetang highway, the first three kilometres due east of Dratang, on the west bank of the Drachi-chu, and the second a further five kilometres to the east on the east bank. The valley is broad but infertile, for which reason there are fewer habitations here than in neighbouring Dranang. Two sites of great importance stand out, namely: Tsongdu Tsokpa in lower Drachi, and Mindroling in upper Drachi. There are also three clusters of ancient burial sites which were recently discovered in the valley.

Located 250 metres inland on the east approach road, the large Sakyapa monastery of Tsongdu Tsokpa mostly survived the ravages of the 1960s because, like other Sakya monasteries in this part of Southern Tibet, it was utilized as a granary during the Cultural Revolution. Originally a Kadampa establishment founded by Lu-me, the later Sakya foundation is attributed to the Kashmiri pandita Shakyashri during the 13th century, who set up four Buddhist groups in Tibet, known as the Tsokpa Zhi. Other teachers have also had associations with this site, notably: Khyungpo Neljor Tsultrim Gonpo of the Shangpa Kagyu school (12th century) and Go Lotsawa Zhonupel (15th century).

Tsongdu Tsokpa Monastery

The main temple, formerly four storeys and now only three storeys high, is entered via a staircase, which leads to the middle storey. No trace remains of the clay image of Shakyashri and the heart of Khyungpo Neljor, which were once preserved here. Few old paintings remain and these appear to date from the 19th century. Among them the most interesting are the representations of Two-armed Avalokiteshvara at the entrance, the skylight murals depicting the Eight Medicine Buddhas and the Eight Manifestations of Padmasambhava, and the Thousand Buddhas and Eight Bodhisattvas depicted within the inner sanctum.

Getting there Mindroling is some 8 kilometres inland on the west approach road to upper Drachi, above the village of Mondrub.

Orgyen Mindroling Monastery

This, the largest Nyingmapa monastery in Central Tibet (100,000 square metres) was founded in 1670 by Terdak Lingpa Gyurme Dorje, on a site where, in the 11th century, Lu-me Tsultrim Sherab had built the Kadampa chapel of Tarpaling. Terdak Lingpa thus became the first Minling Trichen (throneholder of Mindroling), a position held by his familial descendants until the mid-19th century, after which the succession fell to the familial descendants of his incarnation. The present throneholder, Minling Trichen XII Kunzang Wangyel, resides at the Mindroling branch monastery in Dehra Dun, India. Mindroling's extensive buildings have been severely damaged by the Dzungar armies in the 18th century, and subsequently by the Chinese. Nonetheless, reconstruction has been continuing in recent decades through the efforts of the late Minling Chung Rinpoche Ngawang Chodrak (1908-80) and Kusho Jampal, and there is much of interest to see.

■ *Admission: ¥15*
Colour map 3, grid C3

The Courtyard There are two gates leading into the courtyard of the former monastic citadel – the main gate on the northeast side and the second gate on the southeast, where vehicles are parked. To enter via the main gate, walk around the residential compound on the southeast wing. Inside the courtyard (from left to right) are: the east-facing **Tsuklakhang** with its impressive masonry façade, the north-facing **Drubcho Sangak Podrang**, the east-facing **Namgyel Podrang**, and the south-facing **Labrang Chokhor Lhunpo Podrang**. On the east wing of the courtyard are the monastic quarters and guesthouse. Among these, the **Namgyel Podrang** (restored as recently as 1944) is in ruins, and the 13-storey stupa named **Kumbum Tongdrol Chenmo**, which had been constructed by Terdak Lingpa himself has been completely erased. The other three buildings will be described in turn.

Tsuklakhang Lowest Level The three and a half storey **Tsuklakhang** has an assembly hall on its lowest level, with adjoining chapels on three sides. To the south are the **Panchen Lhakhang** and the **Zhalyekhang**, the latter containing exquisite Kadam-style stupas, the silver reliquary of Minling Trichen IX Dechen Chodrub, a clay image of Terdak Lingpa, and images of the Eight

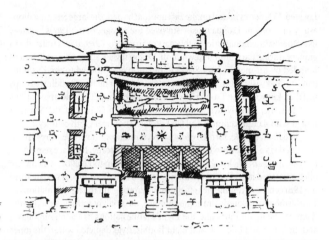

The façade of Mindroling Tsuklakhang

Throneholders of Orgyen Mindroling

Minling Trichen I	*Terdak Lingpa Gyurme Dorje (1646-1714)*
Minling Trichen II	*Pema Gyurme Gyatso (1686-1717)*
Minling Trichen III	*Gyelse Rinchen Namgyel (1694-1760)*
Minling Trichen IV	*Gyurme Pema Tendzin*
Minling Trichen V	*Trinle Namgyel*
Minling Trichen VI	*Pema Wangyel*
Minling Trichen VII	*Gyurme Sangye Kunga*
Minling Trichen VIII	*Trichen Yizhin Wangyel*
Minling Trichen IX	*Dechen Chodrub [aka Minling Chung Khenpo]*
Minling Trichen X	*Kunga Tendzin [son of Terdak Lingpa's incarnation, Rangrik Dorje]*
Minling Trichen XI	*Dondrub Wangyel [the latter's son]*
Minling Trichen XII	*Kunzang Wangyel, the latter's son (b 1931)*

Manifestations of Padmasambhava. On the north side is the protector shrine which formerly housed a central image of Mahottara Heruka (Chemchok Heruka), and now has wrathful protectors within. The large **inner sanctum** on the west has a four metres high ornate image of Shakyamuni, flanked by his two foremost disciples, and the Eight Bodhisattvas. Its gates are guarded by Vajrapani and Hayagriva.

Second Level On the second storey, the main chapel is the **Tersar Lhakhang** on the southeast side. It contains three dimensional mandalas of the cycles entitled *Wrathful Deities of the Magical Net (Mayajala)*, and the *Gathering of the Sugatas of the Eight Transmitted Precepts (Kabgye Deshek Dupa)*, as well as deities corresponding to the new terma revelations of Terdak Lingpa, the silver reliquary of Minling Trichen X Kunga Tendzin, and the Nartang *Kangyur*. There is also a collection of sacred objects: a part of Guru Chowang's wrist bone with a natural buddha image growing therefrom, an image consecrated by Terdak Lingpa in person, and precious images discovered by the treasure-finders Guru Chowang, Jigme Lingpa, Dorje Lingpa and others. There is also a set of the *Nyingma Gyudbum*, published in India by the late Dilgo Khyentse Rinpoche.

To the right of this chapel is the **Jetsun Migyur Peldron Lhakhang**, containing the silver reliquary of Terdak Lingpa's daughter, and various scriptures. Beyond it are the rooms of the monastic steward and caretaker. Facing the Tersar Lhakhang is the **Neten Lhakhang** (now empty).

On the left side, in the **Pema Wangyel Lhakhang**, there are reliquaries including that of Minling Trichen VI Pema Wangyel. Adjacent to that is the **Lhakhang Onangkyil**, with reliquaries including the silver stupa of Minling Trichen VII Gyurme Sangye Kunga. To its left are smaller chapels named **Changlochen** and **Silweitsal**.

Third level The highest chapels are those on the third storey and above. Among them, the **Lhakhang Dewachen** is the hermitage of Lochen Dharmashri, the learned brother of Terdak Lingpa, containing images of Lochen Dharmashri and a painting of Terdak Lingpa consecrated with his own handprints and footprints in gold. The **Lama Lhakhang** contains a central image of the primordial Buddha Samantabhadra in union with his consort Samantabhadri, and **outstanding murals**, which depict the entire Nyingmapa lineages, from ancient India until the 18th century.

Drubcho Sangak Podrang On the north side of the courtyard, the **Drubcho Sangak Podrang**, which has been utilized as a granary since the 1960s, contains some original murals, although its foremost image: Four-armed Avalokiteshvara, no longer exists. Its outer walls do preserve a famous fresco of Padmasambhava which is said to have spoken to Terdak Lingpa, requesting him to remain in the world to help living beings and not pass away into the light body.

Orgyen Mindroling Monastery

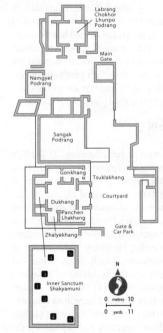

1 Shakyamuni Buddha
2 Shariputra
3 Maudgalyayana
4 Eight Standing Bodhisattvas
5 Two Gatekeepers

Labrang Chokhor Lhunpo Podrang The lowest storey of the **Labrang Chokhor Lhunpo Podrang** has been well renovated in recent years. Its central image depicts Terdak Lingpa, and the throne is that of the Minling Trichen. The floor surface of the hall is utilized for the construction of large sand-mandalas during the fourth month of the lunar calendar. Within the inner sanctum are large four metres images of Padmasambhava, Shantaraksita and King Trisong Detsen, flanked by the Eight Manifestations of Padmasambhava.

Trekking Retreat hermitages connected with Mindroling are located higher up the valley; and there are trekking routes – one day to Dargye Choling in upper Dranang and four days to Chongye in the east.

Following the Gongkar-Tsetang highway east from the entrance to Drachi valley, you reach the Samye

Namseling Manor

ferry crossing, after five kilometres. Inland from here is the little visited but elegant 14th century manor house of Namseling. This seven-storey building is a rare example of the Tibetan noble fiefs, hardly any of which survived the Cultural Revolution. Presently, the first storey has been restored, with the second to sixth to be completed in coming years. There are plans to establish a centre for weaving and pottery here.

Jing Okar Drak On the Gongkar-Tsetang highway, 22 kilometres east of Drachi valley entrance, there is a turn-off which leads to Okar Drak in Jing. The meditation caves here have associations with Padmasambhava and the Dzogchen master Dzeng Dharmabodhi (1052-1169). Later, *termas* were discovered here by Dorje Lingpa (1346-1405) and Terdak Lingpa of Mindroling.

Zurkhar Valley

Getting there
Colour map 3, grid C3
The ferry crossing to Samye is located 13 kilometres east of Dratang and 39 kilometres west of Tsetang. There are no fixed departure times and the crossing takes 1-1½ hours, zigzagging to avoid sandbanks. From the jetty on the north bank at Zurkhardo there are trucks and tractors available to transport pilgrims and tourists to the monastery, some 9 kilometres further east. Samye can also be approached by trekking from Taktse, Ganden, and Gyama to the east of Lhasa.

Zurkhardo From the village of Zurkhardo there is an inland route via Nekar and Kharu villages to **Dongakling**, a 15th century monastery founder by Tsongkhapa's disciple Jangsem Kunga Zangpo. The inner sanctum of the monastery contains the founder's mummified remains.

Taking the road to Samye from the ferry, after a short distance you will pass on the left side a series of five resplendent white stupas, which stand out at intervals against the sandy rocks. These are the **Stupas of Zurkhardo**, reputedly constructed by Shantaraksita to commemorate the place where King Trisong Detsen first met Padmasambhava. These stupas, which symbolize the Buddhas of the Five Families, are in an archaic style, their plinth and *bumpa* surmounted by a tall spire and *bindu*. They are visible from afar on the south bank of the Brahmaputra. Zurkhardo has a clean and pleasant guesthouse.

Samye Monastery བསམ་ཡས་ཆོས་གྲྭ

History
Colour map 3, grid C4
Tibet's first monastery was constructed most probably between 775 and 779, although there are other sources suggesting alternative dates, eg 763 (Tang Annals) and 787-799 (Buton). King Trisong Detsen, revered by Tibetans as an emanation of Manjushri, acceded to the throne at the age of 13, and with the assistance of Ba Trizhi he invited Shantaraksita of Zahor, who presided over Vikramashila monastery, to formally establish Buddhist monasticism in Tibet. Buddhist geomantic temples had been constructed in Tibet by King Songtsen Gampo and his queens some 130 years earlier; but owing to the hostility of Bonpo aristocratic families, the formal institutions of the Buddhist religion had not emerged. So it was that when Trisong Detsen directly confronted this arcane opposition to Buddhism, he invited Padmasambhava of Oddiyana (modern Swat) to subdue the hostile elemental forces of Tibet and make them amenable or subservient to Buddhism. Padmasambhava traversed the entire plateau, transforming negative forces into Buddhist protectors, and introducing the highest tantras and their teachings to his fortunate disciples. On the summit of Mount Hepori (see below, page 179), east of Samye, he crushed the local demons and consecrated the site for the construction of Tibet's first monastery.

The preceptors of Samye Monastery were held in high esteem, both socially and politically, throughout Tibet from the eighth until the late 10th century. But following the disintegration of the Yarlung Dynasty and the introduction of the second phase of Buddhist propagation, the site gradually came under the influence of other non-Nyingma traditions: the Kadampas, during the period of Ra Lotsawa; the Sakyapas during and after the period of Lama Dampa Sonam Gyeltshen (14th-16th century), and the Gelukpas under the rule of the Dalai Lamas. Samye thus became a symbol of Tibet's national identity, in which Nyingma, Sakya and Geluk schools have all had strong interests.

Sadly, the original buildings are no longer intact, having been damaged by civil war (11th century), fires (mid 17th century, and 1826), earthquakes (1816), and the Chinese occupation (1960s). Yet, the Tibetans have always endeavoured to rebuild and enhance the complex after each round of destruction. Notable among these were the renovations carried out by Ra Lotsawa (11th century), Sonam Gyeltsen (14th century), Dalai Lama VII (1770), the Tibetan government (1849), and the late Panchen Lama X (1986 onwards). During the Chinese occupation, the village was encouraged to encroach upon the temple, and even in the late 1980s pigs and other farm animals could be seen wandering through the sacred shrines. The current policy is to redefine the area of the monastery by pushing back the village.

Driving into Samye, you pass on the right the edifice of Khamsum Sang-khang Ling, which is the only extant temple among the three built outside the perimeter wall by King Trisong Detsen's three queens. This is a four storey building, which was reconstructed by Reting Rinpoche during the 1940s. It contains interesting murals. The high ceilinged assembly hall occupies two floors. Its

Khamsum Sangkhang Ling

Southern Tibet

Samye Monastery

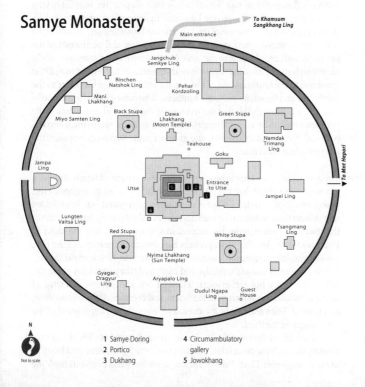

To Khamsum
Sangkhang Ling

Main entrance

Jangchub
Semkye Ling

Rinchen
Natshok Ling

Pehar
Kordzoling

Mani
Lhakhang

Miyo Samten Ling

Black Stupa

Dawa
Lhakhang
(Moon Temple)

Green Stupa

Namdak
Trimang
Ling

Teahouse

Goku

Jampa
Ling

Utse

Entrance
to Utse

Jampel Ling

To Mnt Hepori

Lungten
Vaitsa Ling

Red Stupa

White Stupa

Tsangmang
Ling

Nyima Lhakhang
(Sun Temple)

Gyagar
Dragyur
Ling

Aryapalo Ling

Dudul Ngapa
Ling

Guest
House

N

Not to scale

1 Samye Doring
2 Portico
3 Dukhang

4 Circumambulatory
   gallery
5 Jowokhang

Samye Monastery

Southern Tibet

inner sanctum has paintings of the Sixteen Elders, and, in its circumambulatory corridor, of Shakyamuni Buddha. On the third floor, there are murals depicting the 1849 reconstruction of Samye, as well as Padmasambhava, Shakyamuni Buddha, Amitabha, and so forth. An unusually well-lit chapel on the fourth floor contains the protector shrine, with finely carved beams and columns, as well as extant murals of Shakyamuni, Amitabha, Amitayus, and the protectors. One of the best camp sites at Samye is located in a meadow to the southwest of this building.

Perimeter Wall and Stupas
The road into Samye, after by-passing the Khamsum Sangkhang Ling, skirts the reconstructed perimeter wall, distinctively crowned with a succession of 1,008 small stupas. The wall, which is now oval-shaped (the original having had a zigzag design), is over one kilometre in circumference, three to four metres high, and over one metre thick. There are four gates: one in each of the intermediate sectors (northeast, southeast, southwest and northwest) of the perimeter wall, each leading to the central Utse temple via an enormous 40-50 metres high stupa. All of the four stupas have been recently reconstructed: the green one to the northeast, the red one to the southwest, the black one to the northwest, and the white one to the southeast. The main gate lies to the northeast, and it is through this that the truck from the ferry will enter. Within the perimeter wall, there are two pilgrim's circuits, an outer route which encompasses all the secondary temples, and an inner route which encompasses the Utse temple at the centre.

Samye Utse
The east-facing Utse temple has four storeys, the second of which also has a terrace at a lower level than its entrance. Each of the three lower storeys are five to six metres high. Traditionally, the three lowest storeys and their interiors are said to have been fashioned by craftsmen from neighbouring Buddhist lands: the lowest in Indian style, the second in Chinese style, and the third in Khotanese style. Another view, perhaps based on the appearance of the Utse following its later renovation, suggests that the first is in Tibetan style, the second in Chinese style, and the third in Indian style. At the present day, these stylistic features are not self-evident, although one can observe elements of Chinese Buddhist architecture in the beams and columns of the second floor, and Central Asian features in the dress and inwardly sloping posture of the new images on the third.

To the left of the entrance is a five metres high stone obelisk, the **Samye Doring**, dating from the original construction, which proclaims Buddhism as the state religion of Tibet. Pairs of ancient stone lions and elephants flank the entrance; and above, in the portico, there is a large eighth century bronze bell which the king's Tibetan queen Poyong Gyelmotsun offered at the time of the original construction. This is one of three once extant bells from the period of the Yarlung Dynasty – the others being in the Jokhang of Lhasa, and at Tradruk (see below, page 191).

Entering through the portico (admission fee: ¥25 per person), with its inscriptions documenting the history of the monastery and murals depicting the Four Guardian Kings, there is a circumambulatory gallery complete with prayer wheels. Murals here depict the Thirty-five Confession Buddhas, the land of Shambhala, and the renovation work of 1849.

First Floor The inner building has three main doors, one leading to the central assembly hall (*dukhang*), a second to the Avalokiteshvara chapel in the south wing and a third to the protector shrine in the north wing. Entering the large **Assembly Hall** (actually by a small door to the left of its main gate), there are east-west running rows of monks' seats. The images to the left depict in succession: Tangtong Gyelpo, Buton Rinchendrub, Shantaraksita, Kamalashila, Vimalamitra, and Yudra Nyingpo (south wall), and Vairocana, Shantaraksita, Padmasambhava, Trisong Detsen, and Songtsen Gampo (west wall). Among these, the Padmasambhava image replaces an outstanding original, which is said to have "resembled him in person" (Ngadrama). The Dalai Lama's throne in the centre of the hall is backed by images of Longchen Rabjampa and Jigme Lingpa (twice). The images on the right depict Atisha, flanked by his Kadampa students Dromtonpa and Ngok Lekpei Sherab, and the three celebrated emanations of Manjushri: Longchen Rabjampa, Tsongkhapa, and Sakya Pandita.

The assembly hall leads into the inner sanctum or **Jowokhang** via three tall gates, symbolizing the three approaches to liberation: emptiness, signlessness, and aspirationlessness. Here, there is an inner circumambulatory corridor, with interesting murals depicting the past and final lives of Shakyamuni Buddha. The walls of the inner sanctum are more than two metres thick, and the ceiling has wonderful painted mandalas. The principal image is a four metres Shakyamuni in the form Jowo Jangchub Chenpo, flanked by 10 standing bodhisattvas (ie the standard set of eight plus Trailokyavijaya on the left and Vimalakirti on the right), and the gatekeepers Hayagriva and Acala. On the left, next to Shakyamuni, is Padmasambhava in the wrathful form Nangsi Zilnon. Many books including the *Kangyur* and *Tangyur* fill the rear wall, and in the outer right corner is a Dalai Lama throne, backed by a tangka depicting Kalacakra.

The **Protector Chapel** (Gonkhang) is entered through a door on the right side of the assembly hall. It contains (from left to right) images of: Ekajati, Mahakala in the form Panjaranatha (Gonpo Gur), and Vajrakumara (west wall); Peldon Masung Gyelpo, Cimara, and Shridevi (north wall), and the retinue of Panjaranatha (east wall). A large stuffed snake and assorted weaponry are also kept in this room.

On the south wing of the Assembly Hall, entered by a separate east-facing gate, is the chapel dedicated to Thousand-armed Avalokiteshvara, known as **Chenrezi Chaktong Chentong Lhakhang**. Built in the 14th century by the Sakya Lama Dampa Sonam Gyeltsen in memory of his deceased mother, it contains an enormous Avalokiteshvara image. On the south wall are an incomplete series of relief images depicting the Eight Manifestations of Padmasambhava, as well as Milarepa, Atisha, and Green Tara. In the northeast corner, there is a glass case containing some mortal remains of Jangsem Kunga Zangpo (on which see above, page 172).

Southern Tibet

Second Floor The second floor is approached via a staircase to the left of the main entrance and a low terrace, where the monks quarters are located. There is an open gallery with remarkable murals, 92 metres in length, which depict the history of Tibet, from the Yarlung period and the life of Padmasambhava, through the Sakya and Phakmodru periods, to the accession of Dalai Lama V and his successors. Notice the striking depictions of the white-bearded Terdak Lingpa and the Mongol king Gushi Qan. There are also scenes depicting athletic contests and sports.

Samye Utse

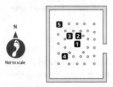

N

Not to scale

Fourth Floor
1 Central pillar
2 Kalacakra
3 Four pillars
4 Sixteen pillars
5 Twenty one pillars

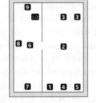

Third Floor
1 Circumambulatory
corridor
with frescoes
2 Stairs
3 Sarvavid Vairocana
4 Bodhisattvas
5 Entrance door

Second Floor
1 Stairs
2 Open gallery
3 Chapels
4 Dalai Lama rooms
5 Relic chamber
6 Main hall
7 Shantaraksita
8 Nangsi Zilnon
9 King Trisong Detsen
10 Secret passage

Ground Floor
1 Portico
2 Dukhang
3 Dalai Lama's throne
4 Jowokhang
5 Nangkhor
6 Jowo Jangchub
Chenpo
7 Gonkhang
8 Chenrezi Chaktong
Chentong Lhakhang
9 Stairs

In the northeast corner there are two chapels, the one to the left is an active protector shrine, and the other dedicated to the Nine Aspects of Amitayus.

In the southeast corner, a passageway leads into the **private apartments of the Dalai Lama**. Here, there are interesting murals depicting the former appearance of Samye. There is also a relic chamber, where the most precious objects of the monastery are now housed. These include: an image of Padmasambhava in the form Guru Saroruhavajra which had been discovered by Nyangrel, the skull of Shantaraksita, a turquoise buddha retrieved from the kingdom of Bhatahor, a turquoise amulet containing hairs of Padmasambhava, the left stone footprint left by Padmasambhava at Gungtang La (the right one being in the Phakpa Lhakhang of the Potala Palace), the staff of Vairocana, a meteorite vajra, and a vajra from the ancient perimeter wall.

The spacious **main hall**, which exhibits some Chinese architectural features at the roof, contains large gilded images of Shantaraksita (south), Padmasambhava in the form Nangsi Zilnon (west) and King Trisong Detsen (north). Flanking Padmasambhava are smaller images of Amitayus, Padmasambhava's tiger-riding form Dorje Drolo (offered by Semo Dechen of Lamaling), an old image of Jigme Lingpa, and Shakyamuni. To the right of the entrance there is a secret passage, where Vairocana is said to have hidden in order to escape the wrath of Queen Tsepong.

Third Floor The newly

The Utse Temple at Samye

reconstructed third floor is approached via a staircase on the left side of the second storey. There is a circumambulatory corridor with gates on each of its four sides. The outer walls of the corridor depict the Twenty-five Disciples of Padmasambhava (Jewang Nyernga), and above these there are lattices through which the outer satellite temples of Samye are visible. The inner walls of the corridor depict the Buddhas of the Five Families: Aksobhya (east), Ratnasambhava (south), Amitabha (west), and Amoghasiddhi (north).

Entering via the east door, the central image is that of the four faced Sarvavid Vairocana (Kunrik Nampa Nangze), flanked by Vairocana and Vimalamitra on the left and Padmasambhava, and Shantaraksita on the right. Each of the four doors is guarded by two gatekeepers (Hayagriva and Acala), and in each of the corners formed by the doors there are sets of the standing bodhisattvas, distinctively robed and sloping inward, in the Central Asian manner.

Fourth Floor The highest floor of the Utse temple is approached via a step-ladder on the west side of the third floor and a passageway which leads around to the entrance on the east. There is a central image of Kalacakra and the central pillar of juniper (formerly sandalwood) which acts as the life-axis of the building. Surrounding it are three rows of columns: the innermost with four pillars symbolizes the Four Guardian Kings, the second with 16 pillars symbolizes the Sixteen Elders, and the third with 21 pillars symbolizes the Twenty-one Taras. The splendid gilded roofs, which were fully restored in 1989, can be seen from the south bank of the Brahmaputra many miles distant.

Outer Temples Restoration has begun on the outer temples within the complex. These include the four temples of the cardinal directions: Jampel Ling (east), Aryapalo or Tamdrin Ling (south), Jampa Ling (west), and Jangchub Semkye Ling (north); along with the eight temples of the intermediate directions: Namdak Trimang Ling (northeast), and Tsangmang Ling (southeast); Gyagar Dragyur Ling (southwest) and Dudul Ngapa Ling (southeast); Lungten Vaitsa Ling (southwest) and Miyo Samten Ling (northwest); and Rinchen Natshok Ling (northwest) and Pehar Kordzoling (northeast). The Dawa Lhakhang lies to the north of the Utse while the Nyima Lhakhang (south of Utse) has yet to be restored. According to the traditional colour symbolism, the temples to the east were white, those to the south yellow, those to the west red, and those to the north black or dark green. In the case of the current phase of reconstruction, these distinctions are not always apparent.

The Eastern Temples The temple of **Jampel Ling**, dedicated to Manjughosa, is currently undergoing restoration. There are murals depicting Manjughosa and the Thousand Buddhas of the aeon; and a large *mani* wheel. During the 1980s it served as a commune office.

The satellite temple to its northeast, **Namdak Trimang Ling**, was formerly the residence of Shantaraksita and the Vinaya college. Within its inner sanctum were images of the Buddhas of the Three Times. To the southeast of Jampel Ling, **Tsangmang Ling** formerly contained the printing press of Samye monastery.

Other buildings on the east side include the remains of the stone platform to the northeast of the Utse, once used for displaying applique tangkas at festival times, a throne utilized by the late Panchen Lama X when he visited Samye in the 1980s, and on the west side a small shop and tea house.

The Southern Temples The temple of **Aryapalo**, dedicated to Hayagriva, which originally predates the Utse, has already been restored. It is a two storeyed building, entered from the south. The ground floor temple contains images of Hayagriva (east), Lokeshvara, Chenrezi Semnyi Ngalso, and Four-armed Avalokiteshvara (north), and within a west side chapel, images of the Three Ancestral Religious Kings (Chogyel Namsum), Avalokiteshvara and Manjushri.

Among its peripheral temples, **Gyagar Dragyur Ling** in the southwest is located in a beautiful courtyard, with west and east cloistered galleries depicting the Indian panditas and Tibetan translators of the eighth century. This was where the Buddhist translation programme was established by King Trisong Detsen back in the eighth century. Within the chapel are images depicting Avalokiteshvara in the form of Simhanada, and the Indian yogin Padampa Sangye. In front is an applique frieze depicting the Eight Manifestations of Padmasambhava. **Upstairs** there are images of Padmasambhava flanked by the kings Songtsen Gampo and Trisong Detsen. To the left are images of the Indian panditas, including the Six Ornaments, the Two Supreme Ones, and Jinamitra; while to the right are the Tibetan translators, including Nubchen Sangye Yeshe, Vairocana, Zhang Yeshede, Kawa Paltsek, Chokrolui Gyeltsen, Khonlui Wangpo Sungwa, Jnanendraraksita, and so forth.

The temple of **Dudul Ngapa Ling** to the southeast of Aryapalo temple was formerly a tantric chapel, as yet unrestored. There is a small occasional guesthouse in the village on the south side of the complex.

The Western Temples The temple of **Jampa Ling**, dedicated to Maitreya, was where the Chinese monks resided during the eighth century; and it was the venue of the Great Debate between Kamalashila and Hoshang Mo-ho-yen (see above, page). The inner sanctum is semi-circular, corresponding to the shape of the western continent in Indian cosmology; its murals depict Maitreya and Shakyamuni, and there is a new image of the latter.

Its peripheral temple to the southwest, **Lungten Vaitsa Ling**, dedicated to the translator Vairocana, has some extant murals depicting Shakyamuni Buddha and the translator. **Miyo Samten Ling**, which lies to the northwest, was a meditation hall utilized by Chinese monks in the eighth century.

The Northern Temples The temple of **Jangchub Semkye Ling**, dedicated to Prajnaparamita, has been used for storing timber in the recent past, but is currently undergoing renovation. To its northwest is the peripheral temple, **Rinchen Natshok Ling**, a small chapel with murals depicting Shakyamuni; and to the northeast is the renowned temple of **Pehar Kordzoling**, where Samye's ancient Sanskrit texts were stored in the care of the protector deity

The Establishment of Buddhism in Tibet

*Padmasambhava's labour in crushing the local demons on Mount Hepori paved the way for the establishment of Buddhist monasticism in Tibet. King Trisong Detsen, at Shantaraksita's suggestion, ensured that the complex was to be modelled on the plan of **Odantapuri Monastery** (modern Bihar Shariff), where the buildings themselves represented the Buddhist cosmological order (with Mount Sumeru in the centre, surrounded by four continents and eight subcontinents, sun and moon, all within a perimeter wall known as the Cakravala). This construction would therefore come to symbolize the establishment of a new Buddhist world order in Tibet. Humans were engaged in this unprecedented building project by day, and spirits by night. Hence the monastery's full name: **Glorious Inconceivable Temple of Unchanging Spontaneous Presence** (Pel Samye Migyur Lhundrub Tsuklakhang).*

King Trisong Detsen then established an integrated programme for the translation of the Buddhist classics into Tibetan, bringing together teams of Indian scholars (pandita) and Tibetan translators (lotsawa). He and a celebrated group of 24

subjects received instruction on the highest tantras from Padmasambhava in particular, but also from Vimalamitra, Buddhaguhya and others, and through their meditations they attained the supreme realizations and accomplishments of Buddhist practice. In addition, Shantaraksita was requested to preside over the ordination of Tibet's first seven trial monks, namely: Ba Trizhi (Srighosa), Ba Selnang (Jnanendra), Pagor Vairocana (Vairocanaraksita), Ngenlam Gyelwa Choyang, Khonlui Wangpo Sungwa (Nagendraraksita), Ma Rinchen Chok, and Lasum Gyelwei Jangchub.

In 792 a debate was held between Kamalashila, an Indian proponent of the graduated path to buddhahood, which emphasizes the performance of virtuous deeds, and Hoshang Mo-ho-yen, a Chinese proponent of the instantaneous path to buddhahood, with its emphasis on meditation and inaction. Kamalashila emerged as the victor, but it is clear from Nubchen's treatise Samten Migdron that both views were integrated within the overall path to buddhahood. It was in these ways that the king established the future of Buddhism in Tibet.

Pehar. A turquoise image of this deity, also known as Shingjachen, was brought to Samye from Bhatahor in Turkestan following a successful military campaign in the early ninth century. Among the temple's treasures there was also a talismanic leather mask, called Sebak Muchung, which was believed to come alive. Nowadays, there is a **small teahouse** within the village on the north side of the complex.

Sun and Moon Temples The clinic located south of the Utse was formerly the **Nyima Lhakhang** or Sun Temple. This shrine was dedicated to the Yaksa Cimara and is therefore sometimes called **Tseumar Chok**. The **Dawa Lhakhang**, north of the Utse, is a particularly archaic structure, with murals depicting the Thousand Buddhas.

Mount Hepori is approached to the east of Samye Utse, beyond the government buildings of Samye township. This hill, which offers an incredible bird's eye view of the Samye complex, is revered as one of the four sacred hills of Central Tibet (along with Chakpori at Lhasa, Chuwori at Chushul, and Zodang Gongpori at Tsetang). It was from here that Padmasambhava bound the local divinities of the region under an oath of allegiance to Buddhism. On the summit of Hepori is a rebuilt **Lhasangkang**, or Temple for the Smoke Offering to the Local Deities, and to its northeast is a Padmasambhava meditation cave.

Hepori

Southern Tibet

Southern Tibet

Cimara, The Red Protector: Judgement Night

Tseumar Chok was the abode of Cimara, the red protector of Samye who took over Pehar's role after the latter had been transferred to Nechung near Drepung (see above, page 179). In an awesome room adjacent to the protector shrine, which was opened once a year, Cimara would by night dispense the judgement of the dead

upon evil-doers, chopping them to shreds on a wooden block. The monks of Samye were often, it is said, aware of the thudding sound of the chopping block and the bloody stench which filled the air during the night. This wooden block required replacement once a year.

On its slopes there were once reliquary stupas, containing the remains of Shantaraksita (east), and those of three of the greatest eighth century translators, namely: Kawa Peltsek (north), Zhang Yeshede (south ridge), and Chokrolui Gyeltsen (south end).

Chimphu Caves མཆིམས་ཕུ

The upper valley, Chimphu, forms a natural amphitheatre, its west and east ridges divided by the waters of a sacred stream. To the southeast, there is the **Chimphu Utse nunnery**, which has a large newly constructed temple containing images of Hayagriva (left); Jowo Shakyamuni, Padmasambhava, and Four-armed Avalokiteshvara (centre); and Vajrasattva Yabsum, Ekajati, Gonpo Maning, Rahula, Dorje Lekpa and a local protector (right).

Currently there are over 100 retreatants and hermits at Chimphu – the majority from East Tibet. Most of the caves are accessible from this temple to the northwest, clustered around the 15 metres high Zangdok Pelri rock.

Getting there
Colour map 3, B4

The Chimphu hermitage is located some 16 kilometres northeast of Samye in the upper reaches of the adjacent Chimyul valley. Pilgrims begin the 5 hour walk to the caves before sunrise, but it is also possible to hire a tractor at Samye village, which would take you to a clearing some 30 minutes walking distance below the Chimphu Utse Temple.

Taking the right path from the north end of Samye, you will cross the local irrigation canal and the Samye River before turning left into the Chim valley. Passing the deserted villages of Chimda, you then climb steeply through a sylvain grove where aromatic herbs are in evidence to reach a stupa.

Caves on the ascent At the base of the Zangdok Pelri rock, is the **Sangwa Metok Cave**, where Jigme Lingpa in the 18th century received the visions of Longchen Rabjampa, which inspired him to reveal the *Longchen Nyingtig*, and compose the *Yonten Dzo*. Outside is a rock-carved image of Manjushri, said to have been executed by Padmasambhava's own hand. Nearby is the **Lower Cave of Nyangben Tingdzin Zangpo (Nyangpuk Ogma)**, where both Nyangben and King Trisong Detsen stayed in retreat, the **Meditation Cave of Yeshe Tsogyel (Tsogyel Drubpuk)**, and a rock bearing an impression of Padmasambhava's hat and Yeshe Tsogyel's foot.

The trail divides into upper and lower branches at the 12 metres long **Guruta Rock**, where there is an enormous Padmasambhava footprint. On its lower side is the **Upper Cave of Nyangben Tingdzin Zangpo (Nyangpuk Gongma)**, where the *Vima Nyingtig* was concealed by Nyangben in the ninth century and later mastered by Longchen Rabjampa in the 14th. Further west there is a small charnel ground, and above the rocks there are further hermitages – those of Ma Rinchen Chok, Shubu Pelzang, and the **Tamdrin Puk**, where Gyelwa Choyang propitiated Hayagriva.

Drakmar Keutsang cave 100 metres above the Zangdok Pelri rock is the most important of all the caves at Chimphu, the **Drakmar Keutsang**. This is revered as the primary pilgrimage place of buddha-speech in Central Tibet, where Padmasambhava first gave teachings on the eight meditational deities known as Drubpa Kabgye to his eight main disciples, including the king Trisong Detsen. A two storey temple has been constructed around the cave, which is at the rear on the ground level. On the altar in the temple there are new images of Padmasambhava, flanked by his two foremost consorts and eight manifestations. Formerly the most precious objects here were the Jema Atron image of Padmasambhava which had been fashioned by Vairocana and Tami Gontson, and the image of Prajnaparamita which belonged to King Trisong Detsen. The present cave does contain an image of Padmasambhava, a blue Vajravarahi, and a Jowo image, the vision of which is said to equal the vision of Padmasambhava in person.

The Drakmar Keutsang is renowned for another reason, in that it was here that Padmasambhava temporarily resuscitated the deceased Princess Pemasel and taught her the *Kandro Nyingtig* for the first time. The place where this resurrection occurred is a flagstone bearing the imprint of her body in front of the cave entrance, known as the **Pemasel Durtro**. Pilgrims are rubbed vigorously on the back and shoulders with a stone reputedly brought from the Shitavana charnel ground in India.

Above the ground level, there is a terrace offering spectacular views of the Brahmaputra valley below, and in the west side of the upper chamber there is a four metres tunnel leading to the **Meditation Cave of Vairocana (Bairo Drubpuk)**. This cave contains images of the translator Vairocana and Longchen Rabjampa.

Ridge-top caves There are some cave hermitages at the top of the Chimphu ridge, including the **Longchen Gurkarpuk** (associated with Padmasambhava and Trisong Detsen's chief minister), the **Tsogyel Zimpuk** (associated with Yeshe Tsogyel), the cave utilized by the latter's Nepalese consort Atsara Sale, the **Longchen Puk** (associated with Longchen Rabjampa), and on the far side of the ridge, the **Chimphu Drigugu**, where Padmasambhava stayed in retreat and Vimalamitra concealed the *Vima Nyingtig* texts. High up on the northeast ridge of Chimphu is **Rimochen**, a site associated with Longchen Rabjampa.

Caves on the descent On the descent from the Drakmar Keutsang, the trail passes a hermitage containing the reliquary of Gonjo Rinpoche from Kham, and the **Reliquary of Longchen Rabjampa** (Longchen Dung-ten), who passed away at Chimphu in 1363. The site is marked by a commemorative obelisk. There is a water-of-life spring (*tshe-chu*) by the trail, and on the descent from there, a hermitage with a stupa consecrated by Karmapa III Rangjung Dorje in the 14th century and another once frequented by Nubchen Sangye Yeshe. From here the trail leads down to the Chimphu Utse nunnery and the road back to Samye or to Lo at the mouth of the Chim River.

Following the Drakmar valley six kilometres north from Samye through Yugar and Samphu village, on the west bank of the Drakmar-chu, you will arrive at Drinzang, the birthplace of King Trisong Detsen. This was once the country residence of the latter's parents, King Tride Tsukten and Queen Jincheng. The ruins of the palace and a temple, formerly housing images of the religious

Drakmar
Drinzang

བྲག་དམར་

མགྲིན་བཟང་

Southern Tibet

kings, can be seen. The house where the king was born once had red and white sandalwood trees growing in its courtyard, but only ruins now remain.

Yemalung
Hermitage
གཡའ་འ་མ་ལུང་

About 16 kilometres further inland from Drakmar Drinzang, on an east fork in the road above Ninggong village, you will reach the remote hermitage of Yemalung. The trail leads past a charnel ground and sacred spring, to the narrow rock tunnel called **Bardo Trang** where pilgrims crawl through to test their degree of preparation for the intermediate state after death! The cliff-top cave hermitage of Padmasambhava contains a new image of the master himself; and rocks marked with his handprints and mantra inscriptions. The meditation cave of his disciple Vairocana is located in the slopes above. The terma text entitled *Innermost Spirituality of the Awareness Holder (Rikdzin Tuktik)*, which was concealed at Yemalung by Padmasambhava was subsequently unearthed here in 1663 by Terdak Lingpa of Mindroling.

Trekking From Nyinggong, below Yemalung, there are three- to four-day trekking routes across Gokhar La pass (5,357 metres) to Taktse Dzong; and across Jukar La to Ganden.

Tsetang ཚེད་ཐང་ and Nedong སྙེའུ་གདོང་ County

Tsetang &
Nedong County (9)
乃东县
Tsetang & Nedong
Population: 45,175
Area: 2,339 sq km
Colour map M2, grid B4

*Tsetang is one of Tibet's largest cities, and the capital of Lhokha district of the Tibetan Autonomous Region, exercising direct control over the affairs of 13 counties: Gongkar, Tranang, Nedong, Chongye, Tso-me, Lhodrak, Nakartse, Zangri, Chusum, Lhuntse, Tsona, Gyatsa, and Nang. The county capital is located at **Nedong**, which, as the seat of the Phakmodru Dynasty, functioned as the capital of the whole of Tibet from 1349 until its eclipse by the Rinpung fiefdom in 1435.*

Tsetang is considered to be the cradle of Tibetan civilization, in that the Zodang Gongpori caves above the town are said to be the place where the Tibetan race originated. Further south in the Yarlung valley kingship and agriculture were first introduced. The first palace is at Yumbu Lagang and the first Buddhist temple at Tradruk.

Tsetang ཚེད་ཐང་

Ins and outs

Getting there
The distance from Tsetang to Lhasa is 183 kilometres, to Gongkar Airport 87 kilometres, and to Dranang 47 kilometres. The county of Nedong extends on the north bank of the Brahmaputra from Do Valley in the west as far as On Valley in the east; and the entire length of the Yarlung Valley (72 kilometres) from Jasa and Sheldrak in the northwest as far as Mount Yarlha Shampo.

Getting around
There are two main roads which intersect at the crossroads in downtown Tsetang. A bizarre sculpture symbolizing the play of the monkey and ogress has been erected as a landmark at this road junction. The road west from the crossroads leads to Gongkar and Lhasa, while the east road leads to Gyatsa and Menling, the north road to the Brahmaputra River bank and the On Valley ferry, and the south road to Chongye and

Tsona. The Yarlung River (Yarlha Shampo-chu) flows due northwards on the west side of the intersection, and is spanned by two bridges – one on the Gongkar highway and the second (the old Namo Zampa) on the Chongye road further south.

Population: 40,000
Altitude: 3,100m
Phone code: 86-893
Oxygen: 86%
Colour map 3, grid C4

Approaching the city from the Gongkar/Lhasa direction, the triangular peak of **Mount Zodang Gongpori** is visible long before the buildings are seen nestling below it. At the entrance to the city, on the right side of the road, there is a petrol station and a bus station. A turn-off on the right bypasses the city centre, leading to the southwest and on to Sheldrak and Chongye. Continue on the main road, crossing the Yarlung bridge, with the Tsetang Hospital on the left. Both sides of the road are then occupied by truck stops and down market karaoke bars. As you approach the crossroads, there are grocery and electrical shops. Turning left at the crossroads, beside the *Himalayan Tibetan Hotel*, you will reach the vegetable, butter and meat markets, where there are small tea shops (left), and, opposite the entrance to Tsetang Commune Number Nine, a discotheque (right, upstairs).

Turning right at the crossroads into **Nedong Road**, you will pass, on the left side, a large department store, a turn-off into the open-air market, a carpet store, a book store, a souvenir store, the Public Security Bureau, the Nedong County Government Buildings, the Post Office, and a military barracks. On the right you will pass grocery and electrical stores, some of which are run by Hui Moslems from Ziling area, the Tsetang Middle School, the Lhokha District Government Offices, the *Tsetang Guesthouse*, the *Tsetang Hotel*, and (just before the Chongye turn-off) the small *Nedong Guesthouse*.

If at the crossroads, you drive due east, onto **Gyatsa Road** you will reach on the right side a turn-off leading to the monasteries and houses of the old town: **Tsetang Monastery**, **Ngachopa Tra-tsang**, **Trebuling Monastery** and **Sangak Samtenling Nunnery**. On the left, you will pass the telecommunications building, the trade department and commercial buildings, before eventually reaching the Brahmaputra River, where a new bridge from Tsetang to On has been constructed near the site of Tangtong Gyelpo's former **Nyago Chakzam** bridge.

If you take the aforementioned turn-off into the open-air market from Nedong Road, you will find rows of stalls selling cheap Chinese household articles, clothing and shoes. A few stalls have traditional Tibetan items: tangkas, books, and religious artefacts. Behind these stalls there is a square, where the Bank of China, the cinema and dance hall are located. Turning left in front of the bank and first right, you will enter the old Tibetan quarter, where the aforementioned monasteries are located.

Tsetang County

Southern Tibet

History

Mount Lhababri on the west side of the valley is regarded as the place where the first Tibetan king of the Yarlung Dynasty, Nyatri Tsenpo arrived from the heavens, or from India, to rule among men. He occupied the fortress of **Yumbu Lagang** to the south of Tsetang, and his descendants introduced agriculture into the valley at a place called **Zortang** (which some identify as a plot of land at Lharu below Yumbu

Southern Tibet

Tsetang: Playground of the Monkey and Ogress

Tsetang means 'playground' – a reference to its importance as the place where a monkey emanation of Avalokiteshvara frolicked in the company of an ogress, thereby giving birth to the six progenitors of the original Tibet clans (see below, page 669). The monkey thus symbolizes the compassion of the bodhisattvas and the ogress the destructive or violent aspect of the Tibetan character. Legend associates **Mount Zodang Gongpori** behind Tsetang with the location of the monkey's cave.

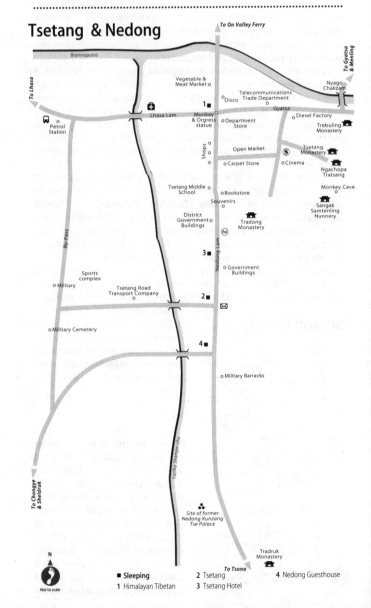

Tsetang & Nedong

To On Valley Ferry

To Gyatsa & Menling

Brahmaputra

To Lhasa

Nyago Chakzam

Vegetable & Meat Market

Telecommunications Trade Department

Disco

Gyatsa

Diesel Factory

1

Lhasa Lam

Monkey & Orgress statue

Department Store

Trebuling Monastery

Petrol Station

Tsetang Monastery

Shops

Open Market

Ngachopa Tratsang

Carpet Store

Cinema

Monkey Cave

Tsetang Middle School

Bookstore

Sangak Samtenling Nunnery

Souvenirs

District Government Buildings

Tradong Monastery

By-Pass

Nedong Lam

3

Government Buildings

Sports complex

Military

Tsetang Road Transport Company

2

Military Cemetery

4

Military Barracks

To Chongye & Sheldrak

Yarlha Shampo-chu

Site of former Nedong Kunzang Tse Palace

Tradruk Monastery

N

To Tsona

Nedong Guesthouse

Not to scale

■ **Sleeping**

1 Himalayan Tibetan

2 Tsetang

3 Tsetang Hotel

4 Nedong Guesthouse

Lagang, and others with one to the north of town (now within Commune Number Nine).

After Songtsen Gampo unified Tibet in the seventh century and moved his capital to Lhasa, the Tsetang area gradually declined in its importance. But in 1349, **Nedong**, which is now a suburb of Tsetang, became the capital of the Phakmodrupa Dynasty which ruled Tibet until the end of the 15th century. It was during this period that the important monasteries of Tsetang were originally constructed by Tai Situ Jangchub Gyel-tsen and his successors. In addition, Tsongkhapa received his ordination at **Bentsang Monastery** (Tse Tsokpa), which had been founded by Shakyashri in the early part of the 13th century.

Later, during the 18th century, Dalai Lama VII encouraged the development of the Gelukpa school in the Tsetang area, in consequence of which Tsetang Monastery was transformed into **Ganden Chokhorling**, and the **Sangak Samtenling** nunnery was established.

Sights

Located near the entrance to the old Tibetan quarter, Tsetang Monastery was originally a Kagyu site, founded in 1351 by Tai Situ Jangchub Gyeltsen of the Phakmodrupa Dynasty. As such, it held allegiance to Densatil as its mother monastery (see below, page 217). Later, in the mid-18th century, during the lifetime of Dalai Lama VII Kelzang Gyatso, the Kagyu buildings were dismantled and a Gelukpa monastery named **Ganden Chokhorling** erected to replace it. Refurbishing took place from 1900-12, but in the 1960s only the outer shell was spared. There are two main buildings, which have more recently been undergoing renovation: the assembly hall (*dukhang*) with a large skylight overlooking its Jokhang, and a residential *labrang* with attached debating courtyard.

Tsetang Monastery

Located slightly to the east of Tsetang Monastery, this Kagyu site was also constructed by Tai Situ Jangchub Gyeltsen in the 14th century. There were fine images of Shakyamuni, Amitabha, and Maitreya. Although the complex was severely damaged during the civil war of the 16th century and the Dzungar occupation of the 17th century, it is now being actively rebuilt.

Ngachopa Monastery

Trebuling Monastery is located northeast of Ngachopa within the Shannan Diesel Factory compound. Its asssembly hall (*tsokchen*) and residential building still stand. However, the sacred images of Tara and Shakyamuni in the form Thupa Ngadrama which it once housed have not survived.

Trebuling Monastery

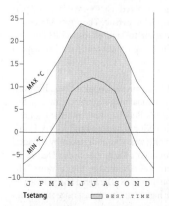

This active nunnery, located on the slopes of Mount Zodang Gongpori above Tsetang monastery, was originally a 14th century Sakyapa establishment of the Tsarpa sub-school. It was founded on a former meditation site of Lama Dampa Sonam Gyeltsen and his student Yarlung Senge Gyeltsen. From the mid-18th century, however, it came under the influence of the Gelukpas, and a new

Sangak Samtenling Nunnery

Southern Tibet

foundation was established by Kyerong Ngawang Drakpa. Some of its sacred relics were salvaged during the 1960s. The main image within the assembly hall is a reputedly seventh century Mahakarunika, flanked by Tara, Tsongkhapa, and Tangtong Gyelpo, with the Sixteen Elders and Thirty-five Confession Buddhas behind in their individual stucco grottoes. Rear chapels contain further images of Kyenrong Ngawang Drakpa flanked by Avalokiteshvara, in the form Simhanada, and Manjughosa; and of Tsongkhapa with his foremost students, along with Atisha and Tangtong Gyelpo.

Museums The **Tsetang Museum**, founded in 1994, has an impressive collection of artefacts but poor security which resulted in an unfortunate theft in February 1996.

Excursions

Zodang Gongpori Mount Zodang Gongpori is one of the four sacred hills of Central Tibet, renowned for its remote cave (4,060 metres), where the monkey emanation of Avalokiteshvara is said to have impregnated a demonic ogress, thereby giving birth to the six ancient Tibetan clans. The cave, which is located at 4,060 metres near the summit, is perched precipitously 500 metres above the Yarlung Valley. Within the cave is a naturally produced rock image of the monkey, and there are paintings of simian figures on the southeast wall. Legend holds that a 'hidden land' (beyul) is contained within Mount Zodang Gongpori, its entrance (bego) being located on the east side of the mountain. A two-day pilgrim's trek leads around the mountain, via the monkey cave, Gonpo La pass (4,750 metres), and the celebrated Tubpa Serlingpa Cave, which functioned as a retreat centre for Ngachopa Monastery.

Nyago Chakzam Bridge Five large stone bridge supports are all that remain of the 14th century iron bridge, which provided a vital link between Tsetang and the On valley until the present century. With a span of 150-250 metres this was one of the celebrated engineer's greatest construction projects. The ruins on the south bank have long been regarded as a shrine to Tangtong Gyelpo's memory, but nowadays a modern bridge has been constructed at Nyago.

Nedong Kunzang Tse Palace Once located in the extreme south of Tsetang, west of the main road, this 15th century Tibetan capital no longer exists. Behind the Dzong there was the **Tse Tsokpa Monastery**, established by Shakyashri in the 13th century. Later, it became known as **Bentsang Monastery**, and as such it survived intact until the 1960s. This was where Orgyen Lingpa's sacred relics were stored and pills compounded from them by Dala Lama XIII in person. The greatest treasures of Ben-tsang were removed for safe-keeping to Tradruk, especially the Chinese applique Buddha, dating from the Ming Dynasty, and the Padmapani made of 29,000 pearls.

Jasa Lhakhang

བྱ་ས་ལྷ་ཁང་

Some three to four kilometres west of Tsetang on the Gongkar/Lhasa highway, there is a turn-off for Jasa Lhakhang. An original ninth century temple on this site, containing a great image of Vairocana Buddha, was reputedly commissioned by Chogyel Pelkortsen, grandson of King Langdarma and ruler of Tsang. Later, in the 11th century, reconstruction work was undertaken by the local lords Yuchen and Jasa Lhachen, who founded a Kadampa temple. During the period of Sakya ascendancy, this in turn was absorbed by the Sakyapas. The present site contains a small shrine, rebuilt in 1988. The Pema Shelpuk cave of Sheldrak (see below, page 190) is visible high on the southeast ridge from Jasa.

Essentials

B *Tsetang Hotel (Zedong Hotel)*, 21 Nedong Rd, T7820219/7820570/7821802, F7821688. Has 118 comfortable rooms with attached bath and television, on 4 floors (US$55 per double room), no elevator, solar heated water supply, most effective after 2000, excellent Cantonese restaurant (full meal plan US$33, breakfast U$9), under the careful management of Mr Sonam Tendzin, souvenir and gift shop, foyer bar and games room, hairdressing service, and occasional business centre, large rooms available for special functions. **C** *Tsetang Guesthouse*, has clean superior rooms on top floor, but cold water only, there are 2 Chinese restaurants, 1 with set Chinese meals. **E** *Himalayan Tibetan Hotel*, is cheap and centrally located at the crossroads.

Sleeping
■ *on map, page 184*
Price codes:
see inside front cover

Among the hotels, the *Tsetang Hotel* offers excellent Chinese food. The *Tsetang Guesthouse* has Chinese set meals which are good value for money. There are smaller restaurants in the city centre, serving Tibetan dumplings (*momo*) and noodle soup (*thukpa*); and simple Sichuan dishes.

Eating
● *on map, page 184*

Cinemas The *Tsetang Cinema* is located on the Town Square, near the *Bank of China*.

Entertainment

Music Tibetan operas and traditional music are occasionally performed at concerts in the *Tsetang Hotel* (enquire at reception). There are discotheques, karaoke bars, and video parlour facilities, up-market near *Tsetang Hotel* and down-market, near the truck stops on Lhasa Rd and the old Town Square.

Sport The sports ground is south of *Tsetang Hotel* on Nedong Road.

Bookshops *Xinhua Bookstore*, near crossroads on east side.

Shopping

Handicrafts There are souvenir gift shops in the *Tsetang Hotel* and near the crossroads on the east side. Look out for leather goods, carpets, and religious artefacts. Imported liquor and cigarettes are available at the shop in the *Tsetang Hotel*.

Modern goods There is a new department store, near the crossroads, and several smaller shops selling mineral water, beer, tinned foods, clothing and electrical goods. Almost all the shops will accept only RMB currency, and rarely accept payment in US dollars. It is best to change currency in Lhasa before reaching Tsetang, but the *Bank of China* can reputedly assist in emergencies. The open-air market near the old city is well worth a visit, although unique products and antiques are hard to find.

Photography Print film and processing are available at *Tsetang Hotel* gift shop, and at photographic shops, especial Muslim owned electrical stores on the west side near crossroads.

Stamps Stamps are available at Post Office, southeast of *Tsetang Hotel* on opposite side of the road, or at the *Tsetang Hotel* reception counter.

Air Tsetang is connected via Gongkar Airport (87 kilometres southeast) to Chengdu (daily flights), Kathmandu (Wednesday/Saturday), Beijing (Sunday), Guangzhou (Wednesday), Shanghai (Tuesday/Friday), and Ziling (Monday/Friday).

Transport

Road Most visitors to Tsetang, whether arriving by air or land, will have their transportation organized by the travel services. Long distance car and jeep transportation is more easily available from Lhasa, but also through the Tsetang Road Transport Company, located behind the *Tsetang Hotel*, on the Chongye side-road. Long distance travel by public bus is more common. The bus station for Lhasa is located to the west of Lhasa Road, near the Petrol Station.

Southern Tibet

Directory **Banks** *Bank of China*, Town Square, near old Tibetan quarter of Tsetang, but as yet there is no foreign exchange facility at Tsetang apart from a desk at the *Tsetang Hotel*. **Communications** Post Office: opposite *Tsetang Hotel* on Nedong Rd. Another also on Gyatsa Rd. **Hospitals & medical services** *Tsetang City Hospital*, west of crossroads on north side of Lhasa Rd. *Tsetang Hospital of Traditional Medicine*, east of crossroads on Gyatsa Rd. **Tour companies & travel agents** *Tsetang Hotel Travel Company*, and *CITS*, Shannan Branch, both based at the *Tsetang Hotel*. **Useful addresses** Police & public security: *Tsetang City Police and Public Security Bureau*, south of crossroads, on east side of *Tsetang Hotel* approach road.

Do Valley ཌོ

From the village of Lo, where the Chim River enters the Brahmaputra, east of Samye, there is a track which follows the river bank eastwards to Kyerpa, and thence inland to Do Podrang in the Do valley. At Lowo Dongteng, there was formerly a stupa dedicated to Tashi Obar, a deity in the retinue of Cimara.

On Valley འོན

Colour map 3, grid B4 Until the construction of the new bridge at Nyago, the On valley had to be approached by a seven hour trek from Kyerpa at the entrance to the Do valley, or, more easily, by boat from the **Nyago Druka ferry station**, four kilometres east of Tsetang. The valley extends north from Ngari Tratsang at its entrance to the Padmasambhava cave of Onphu Taktsang in its upper reaches. In its mid-reaches, there is the hermitage of Tashi Doka, the Choding monastery, and the Khachu (Keru) Lhakhang.

Ngari Tratsang The ruins of Ngari Tratsang stand guard over the entrance to the On valley from the south. This was a Gelukpa monastery, constructed in 1541 by Dalai Lama II Gendun Gyatso, for the training of monks from Far-west Tibet. It once contained relics which the Tibetan army had plundered from Central Asia, back in the eighth century. From here, there are jeepable roads leading inland through the On-chu valley to On township and Ahor; or via the Brahmaputra River bank to Zangri and Olka.

Tashi Doka Hermitage This site resembles an oasis, endowed with mountain willows and a sacred spring. In 1415, Tsongkhapa meditated here, in a cave hermitage (*zimpuk*) higher up the slopes, and encountered his disciple Gendun Drupa, the future Dalai Lama I, for the first time. While in retreat, Tsongkhapa is also said to have been approached by a celestial sculptor named Tashi who made seven images of the master in a single day. Hence the name Tashi Doka. Tsongkhapa reputedly shaved his head seven times in the course of a single day to provide relics for the statues. Within the cave there are some extant images of Tsongkhapa, and down below, in the assembly hall (*dukhang*), there are images of Tsongkhapa, Avalokiteshvara, the Eight Medicine Buddhas, Amitayus, Tara, and the Sixteen Elders.

Getting there The hermitage of Tashi Doka is located some 8 kilometres inland, above the village of Trimon, and to the east of the On-chu River.

Choding Monastery This monastery appears to have been founded by four Nyingmapa disciples of Dampa Sedrakpa, and named by Lama Zhang Tselpa in the 12th century. Later it became the most powerful Gelukpa institution in the On valley, and its incarnate lama, Gyese Rinpoche XIV Jigme Yeshe Drakpa was appointed regent of Tibet between 1728-35.

Getting there The ruins of Choding lie further northeast in a side-valley, which is remotely visible from Kachu Lhakhang.

Some of the earliest statues in Tibet are to be seen here – the central Buddha image reputedly dating from the period of King Tride Tsukten, father of Trisong Detsen (eighth century). The buildings at Khachu (Keru) comprise: the ruined **Namla Lhakhang**, which originally may have been constructed by King Tride Song-tsen and was later rebuilt as recently as 1957; the **Jowo Lhakhang**, or inner sanctum of the assembly hall, which appears to be of early eighth century construction and contains 13 highly significant images; the **Katang Chugong**, an 11th century temple once frequented by Atisha; the **Assembly Hall** (*dukhang*) and adjacent buildings, which were developed circa 16th-17th century; and the peripheral temples and monastic residential compound, which were renovated in 1957.

Khachu (Keru) Temple

Epigraphic and documentary evidence attributes the main **Jowo Lhakhang** to the reign of King Tride Tsukten; who is believed to have founded altogether five temples to house Buddhist texts bequeathed by the Indian masters Buddhaguhya and Buddhashanti. The antiquity of this temple is also suggested by the architecture of its walls, ceiling beams, and columns, and the regal motifs of its capitals. The chamber is unusually high – 6.5 metres in contrast to its width 8.8 metres and depth 7.6 metres; suggesting that it was first built to contain the massive 3.2 metres Buddha image within it; and the originality of its sculpted clay images also suggests a Khotanese influence. The well-rounded 3.2 metres Buddha image has a compassionate but stern visage, with a massively thick chest. The Eight Bodhisattvas (three metres) are well-proportioned and elegant with fine Mongoloid features, but distinctive shoulder-drapery and bare arms and chests. By the left wall are two bodhisattva-like figures representing King Tride Tsukten and Queen Jincheng, the parents of Trisong Detsen. Lastly, the gatekeepers Hayagriva and Vajrapani are robust and muscular. The peripheral figures probably date from the second phase of building, carried out by Dro Trisumje, a chief minister of King Relpachen, in the ninth century.

Getting there This early eighth century building is located at Gyelzang village, about 2 kilometres north of On township (*Tib* Samkhar), on the west bank of the On-chu.

North of On township (Samkhar), the trail leads to Dikna township and Chabtang village, where five interconnected stupas can be seen, upon an L-shaped platform. These were constructed by Lama Zhang Tselpa during the 12th century, and are now in a state of disrepair. A branch of Lhalung Monastery (see below, page 213) was also once located on the summit of Mount Utse Teng (4,600 metres) nearby. Heading north from Chabtang, the On valley then divides into three branches, one of which leads southwest to Do Podrang in Do valley, the second slightly northwest to Onphu Taktsang, and the third north to Balo on the Meldro-Gyamda highway.

Tshezik Stupa

Among the many tiger lairs frequented by Padmasambhava in his meditations, three are pre-eminent: Onphu Taktsang in Lhokha, Paro Taktsang in Bhutan, and Rongme Karmo Taktsang in Derge. Among these, Yeshe Tsogyel twice visited Onphu Taktsang in the course of her life to flee from an unwanted suitor and to receive the Vajrakila empowerments from Padmasambhava. In addition to the Nyingmapa, the site also once had strong associations for the no longer extant Taktsangpa Kagyu school (founded 1405).

Onphu Taktsang

Southern Tibet

Gettting there Taking the northwest trail from Chabtang, follow the power lines as far as Drigang, and then **Ahor**, beyond which point no motor vehicle can travel. The cave hermitages are 4½ hours uphill trekking distance from Ahor, passing en route a destroyed nunnery.

Yarlung Valley ཡར་ལུང

The 72 kilometres long Yarlung valley, which gave its name to the ancient line of Tibetan kings and is sometimes called the cradle of Tibetan civilization, is replete with interesting temples, monasteries, castles, caves, stupas and peaks. Three power places (ne-sum): Sheldrak, Tradruk and Yumbu Lagang (or Rechung Puk); and three stupa recepticles (ten-sum): Takchen Bumpa, Gontang Bumpa, and Tsechu Bumpa are particularly important.

The Lower Yarlung Valley

Sheldrak Caves

Colour map 3, grid C4 There are three important caves in the Pema Tsekri range, which dominates the west entrance to the Yarlung valley: the east-facing **Sheldrak Drubpuk** is the first of Padmasambhava's meditation caves in Tibet, from where the indigenous hostile forces and demons were bound under on oath of allegiance to Buddhism. The northeast-facing **Tsogyel Sangpuk**, or secret meditation cave of Yeshe Tsogyel, is identified by a distant prayer flag to the south of the main cave; and the west-facing **Pema Shelpuk** is the celebrated *terma*-site where Orgyen Lingpa revealed the seminal text entitled *Life and Liberation of Padmasambhava (Pema Katang)*. It is accessible from the Sheldrak Monastery or more directly by traversing a somewhat dangerous ridge above the main cave. The last of these caves is also visible from Jasa to the west of Tsetang.

Getting there To reach Sheldrak from Tsetang, take the Chongye road and turn off on the right at a dirt track before the Tsechu Bumpa Stupa. Jeeps can negotiate this track, which follows a Yarlung tributary upstream, for 4-5 kilometres, and tractors can reach the village of Sekhang Zhika which lies at the top of the ridge. From here, it is a tough - hour trek to the cave. If you walk all the way from Tsechu Bumpa Stupa, it will take 5-6 hours.

Sheldrak Monastery Above the village of **Sekhang Zhika** is a charnel ground, marked by a stupa consecrated to Hayagriva. The pathway then follows the ridge to the right, leading up to **Sheldrak Monastery**. This restored temple has six monks (the original was apparently dedicated to the 14th century treasure-finder Sangye Lingpa). It contains images of Padmasambhava with his two foremost consorts, the Eight Manifestations of Padmasambhava, and Karmapa III Rangjung Dorje. There are photographs depicting the *Longchen Nyingtig* assemblage of deities.

Sheldrak Drubpuk Cave Continuing uphill to the right, the path crosses a sacred spring (drubchu) and climbs steeply for 100 metres via a rock-hewn stairway to the **Sheldrak Drubpuk Cave** (4,550 metres). The cave, which is itself at the base of a rock pinnacle called **Kritkita Dzong**, offers through its window a bird's eye view of the contours of the Yarlung valley below: Tradruk, Rechung Puk, Yumbu Lagang, and Mount Yarlha Shampo are all discernible at a glance.

The Sheldrak Drubpuk cave is one of the most revered pilgrimage places on the Tibetan plateau, symbolizing Padmasambhava's buddha attributes. As such, it is classed alongside Drak Yangdzong symbolizing buddha-body, Chimphu Drakmar Keutsang symbolizing buddha-speech, Lhodrak Kharchu Chakpurchen, symbolizing buddha-mind, and Monka Nering Senge Dzong in Bhutan, symbolizing buddha-activities. Thirty-five mantra adept followers of Padmasambhava were associated with Sheldrak during the eighth to ninth century, and later masters such as Orgyen Lingpa and Terdak Lingpa discovered *termas* in the nearby Pema Shelpuk cave.

The original **'speaking' image of Padmasambhava**, which once graced the cave, has been relocated at Tradruk Monastery, and the altar now has newly constructed images of the Great Master flanked by his two foremost consorts. The rock surface of the west wall has natural impressions representing Avalokiteshvara, the Twenty-five Disciples of Padmasambhava, the Boudhnath Stupa in Nepal, and a crescent moon of the third day of the month.

Northwest of the cave is the **sacred spring** which one of Padmasambhava's disciples, named Nyak Jananakumara, is said to have brought forth from dry rock. Below the cave entrance, there is a reconstructed two-storey temple, with complete images of the Eight Manifestations of Padmasambhava on each level. This is where the caretaker of Sheldrak resides.

Just south of the turn-off for Sheldrak on the main Tsetang-Chongye road, there is the reconstructed Tsechu Bumpa stupa – one of the three sacred stupas of Yarlung. Circumambulation of this stupa has long marked the beginning or end of the Sheldrak pilgrimage. This stupa is said to have at its core a rock-crystal Buddha image from India, which was presented to King Trisong Detsen by the translator Chokrolui Gyelsten. Others believe it to contain the armour of King Songtsen Gampo himself. On full moon days the stupa is said to exude the water of life (*tsechu*). The site is marked by a large collection of *mani* stones. **Tsechu Bumpa Stupa**

East of the Tsechu Bumpa Stupa, at the village of **Khartok**, are the ruins of the Tsentang Yui Lhakhang, a temple which has been attributed to Queen Jincheng, mother of Trisong Detsen, or alternatively to one of Songtsen Gampo's queens. The temple once had distinctive blue glazed turquoise roof tiles, which would corroborate the reports of its Chinese origin. During the 15th century, this temple was an important centre for the development of dialectics within the Sakya school. Nearby, at **Tsentang Gozhi**, the first king of ancient Tibet, Nyatri Tsenpo, is said to have made contact with his Bonpo subjects after descending from the heavens at **Lhababri**. And since 1984, some 233 earth and stone mound tombs have been discovered in the vicinity of Tsentang. **Tsentang Yui Lhakhang**

At the southern extremity of the Pema Tsekpa range, below Sheldrak, there are three hills, the highest of which is Lhababri. This so-called 'hill of divine descent' is where Tibet's first king Nyatri Tsenpo is said to have alighted from the heavens – although there are early historical accounts (eg that of Nelpa Pandita), which claim the king to have been a descendant of the Licchavi king Rupati (*Tib* Magyapa). The king was carried shoulder-high as if on a sedan chair (nyatri) to Yumbu Lagang, where the first palace of the Yarlung kings was constructed. **Mount Lhababri**

Tradruk Temple ཁྲ་འབྲུག་ལྷ་ཁང་

Tradruk temple is the earliest of Tibet's great geomantic temples apart from the Jokhang (some sources even claim it to predate the latter). It was reputedly constructed by King Songtsen Gampo on the left shoulder of the supine **History**
Colour map 3, grid C4

Southern Tibet

■ *Admission : ¥25*
Colour map 3, grid C4

Southern Tibet

ogress, symbolizing the rigours of the Tibetan terrain (see below, page 672). The name Tradruk is said to be derived from a 'falcon' (*Tra*) emanated by the power of Songtsen Gampo's meditations, which overwhelmed a local 'dragon' (*druk*) divinity to facilitate the temple's construction. Later, the site was venerated as one of the three royal temples of Tibet by the kings Trisong Detsen and Mune Tsepo. During that period, offering ceremonies pertaining to the Vinaya and Abhidharma were performed at Tradruk. Plundered during the persecution of Langdarma, the site was renovated and expanded in 1351, and later by Dalai Lama V, who added the golden roof, and Dalai Lama VII. By the late 18th century, Tradruk had 21 temples. The assembly hall and many of the chapels were obliterated during the Cultural Revolution, but the newly reconstructed buildings were reconsecrated in 1988.

Lower Floor Chapels

As you approach the entrance, which still has its splendid original timbers intact, there is a **Mani Lhakhang** on the right, containing a large *mani* wheel. The portico no longer has its ancient bell – one of three which dated from the Yarlung period (the others are at Samye and the Jokhang – see above, pages 172 and 78). An intermediate pilgrim's circuit (*barkor*) is accessible from the courtyard beyond the portico. Continuing into the main temple, the **Tsuklakhang**, the plan of which is reminiscent of the Jokhang, you will find the assembly hall surrounded by a series of 12 chapels. From left to right, these comprise: the Ngakpa Lhakhang (west), the Gonkhang (north) and the Tuje Lhakhang (north); the Rabten Lhakhang (north), the Sangye Lhakhang (north), the Chogyel Lhakhang (east), the Dolma Lhakhang Tashi Jamnyom (east), the Tuje Lhakhang (east), the Tsepak Lhakhang (south), the Menlha Lhakhang (south), the Orgyen Lhakhang (south), and the Tongdrol Lhakhang (west).

Tradruk Temple

Among these, the most important is the inner sanctum – the **Dolma Tashi Jamnyom Lhakhang**. This is the original Songtsen Gampo geomantic temple – once containing natural stone images of the Buddhas of the Five Families from Mount Zodang Gongpori, and a standing image of Tara, known as Dolma Shesema ('Tara who consumes her offerings'). New clay images of the Buddhas of the Five Families now replace the original stone statues, the fragments of which have been inserted within their respective replicas as a consecratory core. These are flanked by the Eight Bodhisattvas, and the gatekeepers.

To the left of the inner sanctum, the **Chogyel Lhakhang** contains new images depicting King Songtsen Gampo, his two foreign queens and chief ministers. To the right of the inner sanctum is the **Tuje Lhakhang**, containing an old image of Thousand-armed Mahakarunika flanked by Manjughosa and Vajrapani. In the

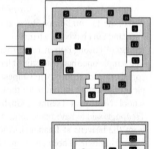

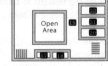

N
Not to scale

Ground Floor
1 Entrance Portico
2 Mani Lhakhang
3 Tsuklakhang
4 Ngakpa Lhakhang
5 Gonkhang
6 Tuje Lhakhang
7 Rabten Lhakhang
8 Sangye Lhakhang
9 Chogyel Lhakhang
10 Dolma Tashi Jamnyom Lhakhang
11 Tuje Lhakhang

12 Tsepak Lhakhang
13 Menlha Lhakhang
14 Orgyen Lhakhang
15 Tongdral Lhakhang
16 Stairs

Upper Floor
17 Monastic Kitchen
18 Protector Chapel
19 Drubtob Lhakhang
20 Outer Chamber
21 Middle Chamber
22 Inner Chamber

corner is a stove reputedly used by Queen Wengcheng in person.

Among the chapels of the west wing, the **Ngapa Lhakhang** contains images of Dalai Lama V flanked by other Gelukpa and Kadampa masters, the **Tongdrol Lhakhang** depicts Tsongkhapa surrounded by his major disciples, and the **Gonkhang** has images of Mahakala and his retainers. Among the chapels of the north wing, both the **Tuje Lhakhang** and the **Rabten** temples contain images of the Eleven-headed Thousand-armed Mahakarunika; while the **Sangye Lhakhang** has Shakyamuni flanked by Shariputra and Maudgalyayana. Among the chapels on the south wing, the **Tsepak Lhakhang** has images of Amitayus flanked by White Tara and Vijaya; and the **Menlha Lhakhang** has images of all the Eight Medicine Buddhas, with Bhaisajyaguru at the centre. Lastly, the **Orgyen Lhakhang** has an outer chamber with images of Amitayus and Mahakala, and an inner chamber with Padmasambhava flanked by Mandarava and Yeshe Tsogyel.

Upper Floor Chapels Ascending to the second floor, on the right side there is a monastic kitchen and a **protector chapel** with images of Mahakala and Brahma. The main chapel is the **Drubtob Lhakhang** at the rear, which has three chambers. The outermost chamber is empty. The **middle chamber** contains the remnants of a set of the Eighty-four Mahasiddhas (from whom the chapel derives its name), the 16 volumes of the *Shatasahasrikaprajnaparamita*, and a wonderful tangka depicting Padmapani, made of 29,000 pearls, which had been originally housed at Bentsang/Tse Tsokpa monastery (now destroyed, see above, page 186).

The **innermost chamber** contains on the rear wall the wonderful original Padmasambhava image which had been salvaged from Sheldrak cave, flanked by new images of his foremost consorts, and on the right, a series of extremely rare applique tangkas, which had also been retrieved from Bentsang. These include an exquisite applique tangka of White Manjushri, others of Avalokiteshvara and Naropa, and, above all, the large applique tangka of the Buddha clad in red robes against a blue background, which may perhaps date from the Ming period, but is reputedly one of three of a kind in Tibet made by Wengcheng (the others are kept in the Reliquary Stupa of Dalai Lama V in the Potala Palace and in the Maitreya Lhakhang at Zhigatse).

Outer temples There are four places of interest outside the temple proper: the **Neten Lhakhang** (west), dedicated to the Sixteen Elders, where there were formerly images of Songtsen Gampo and Padmasambhava; the **Sangak Podrang** (south) where monks from Mindroling have performed tantric rituals since the 17th century; the **Guru Lhakhang** (southeast), and the site of the now destroyed **Namgyel Lhakhang** (north), a branch of Bentsang Monastery (see above, page 186) where Tsongkhapa received monastic ordination in the 14th century.

Getting there Located on the east side of the Yarlung valley, only 7 kilometres south of Tsetang, Tradruk temple nowadays lies within Tradruk village to the south side of the Tsetang-Podrang road.

Rechung Puk This famous Kagyupa hermitage sits atop the **Mila Tse** spur which overlooks the bifurcation of the Yarlung and Chongye valleys. This is the retreat of Milarepa's illustrious disciple Rechungpa Dorje Drak (1083-1161) of Loro, who, following the example of his teacher, practised asceticism and meditation here. The site thus became known as Rechung Puk. Later, in 1488, while residing at Rechung Puk, the yogin Tsangnyon Heruka, whose actual name was Sangye Gyeltsen, composed the Life of Milarepa and the *Hundred Thousand*

Songs of Milarepa, which have since become classic texts of Tibetan Buddhism, well-known throughout the world.

Formerly there were 1,000 monks at Rechung Puk, and some rebuilding has taken place since the destruction of the 1960s. The temple contains images of Padmasambhava flanked by his foremost consorts, and Tsangnyon Heruka. Rechungpa's cave to its rear contains the stone seat of Rechungpa and new images of Marpa, Milarepa, and Rechungpa. Gotsangpa's highly esteemed sculpture of Tsangnyon Heruka, which once graced this cave, no longer exists; but there are rock footprints attributed to Milarepa, Rechungpa, Karmapa I, and also to Tsangnyon Heruka. A new assembly hall (*dukhang*) and retreat centre (*drubkhang*) have been constructed above the cave. At the top of the ridge is the ruined base of the **Mila Tse Watchtower**, dating from the Phakmodrupa period.

Getting there The hermitage of Rechung Puk is approached via a turn-off on the right, 3 kilometres south of Tradruk.

Gongtang Bumpa Stupa At the foot of the Mila Tse spur on its west side is the six metres Gongtang Bumpa Stupa, one of the three major stupas of the Yarlung valley. This stupa is said to have been built on the advice of Vairocana, the eighth century translator, who resolved a boundary dispute between the rulers of Nedong and Chongye while he was meditating in a nearby cave. The stupa therefore has come to define the entrance to the Chongye valley. A new temple to the west contains images of Hayagriva, flanked by Padmasambhava and Lhodrak Longka Geling.

Bairo Puk Slightly south of the Gongtang Bumpa Stupa at the east side of the approach to Chongye valley, there is a meditation cave associated with the great translator Vairocana, one of the foremost disciples of Padmasambhava and Dzogchen lineage-holder. Nowadays, it contains only the copper base of its former image, but there is a more enduring rock handprint of Vairocana, and some rock-inscriptions. Heading south from here, you will enter the Chongye and Tso-me counties of Southern Tibet, see below, page 201 and 206.

Riwo Choling Monastery East of Tsharu village, which lies to the south of Tradruk, are the vast ruins of the Gelukpa monastery of Riwo Choling, originally founded by Tsongkhapa's student, Panchen Lama I, Khedrup Je in the 15th century. The monks of Riwo Choling have long acted as caretakers of the Yumbu Lagang Palace.

Yumbu Lagang

ཡུམ་བུ་བླ་སྒང་

■ Admission: ¥15
Colour map 3, grid C4

History The resplendent hilltop Yumbu Lagang is reputedly a reconstruction of Tibet's oldest building. Some sources state that when Nyatri Tsenpo emerged as the first king of Tibet in 247 or 127 BC he was escorted to Mount Tashitseri, the 'talismanic hill' (**Lagang**) of 'tamarisk' (**Ombu**), by his Bonpo followers, and there the first palace, Yumbu Lagang, was established on its summit. This is also suggested by the theme of the murals depicted inside the second storey of the building. Later, the palace appears to have been refurbished by Lhatotori Nyentsen, the 28th king (b 374 CE). In 433 or 446 CE, Buddhist texts including the *Karandavyuhasutra*, are said to have miraculously fallen upon the palace roof; heralding the first appearance of Buddhism in Tibet. In Nelpa Pandita's *History*, however, it suggests that the Indian scholar Buddharaksita arrived in Tibet with these texts, and deposited them there for the sake of posterity. Known as the 'awesome secret' (*nyenpo sangwa*), the texts were not understood but venerated until Songtsen Gampo embraced Buddhism, five reigns later. According to the *Injunctions of the King* (*Gyelpo Katang*), Lhatotori Nyentsen's tomb is located within the ridge above

Yumbu Lagang. Extensions to the palace were added in subsequent centuries: the two lower chapels by Songtsen Gampo, and the gold roof by Dalai Lama V. These ancient structures were obliterated during the Cultural Revolution.

Yumbu Lagang, Palace of the early kings

The present building dates only from 1982. The three-storey tower is 11 metres high, and its sides measure 4.6 metres and 3.5 metres. Its two lower storeys are entered from behind the shrines of their adjoining chapels, and the third by a ladder from the roof terrace. At its apex, the central pillar (*tsokshing*) of the tower is bedecked by kataks and sacred threads, and on each side, there is an observation window.

The site The **ante-chamber to the lower chapel** has murals depicting the mystical visions of Tsongkhapa. Then, inside the **lower chapel** (originally constructed by King Songtsen Gampo) there is a central image of Buddha Shakyamuni in the form Jowo Norbu Sampel. This image is flanked by regal statues: Nyatri Tsenpo on the left and Songtsen Gampo on the right. Further images on the left are: Tonmi Sambhota, Trisong Detsen, and Lhatotori Nyentsen; and on the right: Relpachen, Namde Osung, and Minister Gar Tongtsen.

The **second floor chapel** is entered via an open terrace. Inside there is a gallery around which pilgrims walk to observe its fascinating murals and images, as well as those of the Buddha and the kings below. Here there is a gilded sandalwood Lokeshvara image (reminiscent of the sandalwood Lokeshvara in the Potala), as well as others depicting Amitayus, Shakyamuni, and Padmasambhava flanked by Shantaraksita and Trisong Detsen.

The murals are particularly relevant. **On the left** are depicted: Nyatri Tsenpo's descent from the heavens at Mount Lhababri and his arrival at Yumbu Lagang; the descent of the 'awesome secret' on the palace roof during the reign of Lhatotori Nyentsen; the arrival of Padmasambhava in the Sheldrak cave; and the Twenty-one Taras. **On the right** are the Eight Manifestations of Padmasambhava, and Shakyamuni with the Sixteen Elders; while beside the door are the protectors Shridevi and Yarlha Shampo.

Getting there Yumbu Lagang Palace is located 6 kilometres south of Tradruk and 3 kilometres after the turn-off for Rechung Puk (see above, page 193).

Below Yumbu Lagang to the northwest is Zortang, the first cultivated field in Tibet. Farmers even now ensure a good harvest by sprinkling soil from this field on their own fields. The temple of **Lharu Menlha**, containing images of the Eight Medicine Buddhas, was formerly built near this field.

Zortang

The Upper Yarlung Valley

Five kilometres south of Yumbu Lagang is **Podrang** township, described as the oldest inhabited village in Tibet. Here there is a turn-off on the left, leading northeast, eventually to Eyul. Along this road in Shang-yang commune, are the 119 stupas known as **Gyatsagye**, dated to the 17th century, and on a nearby slope, the six to seven metres high **Takchen Bumpa Stupa**, which is one of the

Podrang Township & Takchen Bumpa Stupa

three major stupas of Yarlung (see above, page 190). This stupa is named after Sadaprarudita (*Tib* Taktu Ngu), a bodhisattva figure who appears in the *Prajnaparamita* literature, and whose 'constantly weeping' left eye is said to be preserved within it. The construction dates from the Kadampa period and is attributed to one Geshe Korchen (12th century). Adjacent to the stupa, there is a small Drukpa Kagyu monastery named **Takchen Bumoche**.

Chode O &   **Chode O** was founded by Dalai Lama V and expanded by Dalai Lama VII. Its
Chode Gong   assembly hall has three storeys, the middle one containing the principal images of Shakyamuni with his foremost disciples, the Sixteen Elders and Eight Medicine Buddhas.

Chode Gong is an older institution, founded by Ra Lotsawa during the 11th century and developed later by the Gelukpas. Its four-storey temple has an assembly hall and inner sanctum dedicated to Tsongkhapa and his students, as well as Dalai Lama XIII, the Buddhas of the Three Times and the Eight Bodhisattvas.

Getting there   After Podrang the Yarlung valley begins to narrow. 17 kilometres further south, there is the side-valley in which Chode O (Lower Chode) monastery is located, and after a further 6 kilometres, the road passes through Chode Gong (Upper Chode) monastery in Yarto township.

Yabzang   At Yarto township, one kilometre after Chode Gong, there is a further bifurca-
Monastery   tion – one track leading southeast, and the other west for three kilometres to Yabzang monastery. **Yabzang**, founded by Gyurme Long in 1206, was the seat of the small Yabzang Kagyu school, which derives from the latter's teacher Geden Yeshe Chenye, himself a disciple of Phakmodrupa. The site is largely ruinous at the present. Its approach has a ramp reminiscent of the Potala at Lhasa.

Mount Yarlha   24 kilometres beyond Yarto township, the road crosses Yarto Drak La pass
Shampo   (4,970 metres). The main peak, abode of the protector **Yarlha Shampo** (6,636 metres) lies southwest from here. At this watershed pass, the Yarlung valley comes to an end and the road passes via Nyel valley (Lhuntse county) into Tsari (see below, page 224) and via Droshul valley (Tsona county) to the Bhutanese and Indian borders.

Lhuntse County ལྷུན་རྩེ

Lhuntse County (16)
隆子县
Lhunze
Population: 28,962
Area: 5,991 sq km
Colour map 2, grid C4

The county of Lhuntse extends from the watershed at Yarto Drak La pass, through the valleys of the Nyel-chu and Jar-chu, as far as their confluence with the Tsari-chu. Together these rivers (along with the Loro-chu in Tsona county) form the headwaters of the **Subansiri** *(Tib Shipasha-chu), a major south-flowing tributary of the Brahmaputra, which enters the Indian state of Arunachal Pradesh (Tib Monyul Tsona), immediately after the confluence. The road from Tsetang to Yarto Drak La pass is 61 kilometres and thence to* **Kyitang**, *the capital of Lhuntse county, a further 80 kilometres. Kyitang lies 21 kilometres east of the main Tsetang-Tsona frontier road.*

In the east of the county, 108 kilometres from Lhuntse by motor road, is Sangak Choling, one of the three main gateways to Tsari, the sacred mountain of Southern Tibet which attracts pilgrims from all over the country (see below, page 198).

Upper Nyel Valley (Nyelto) གཉལ་སྟོད

Following the main road south from Tsetang across Yarto Drak La pass, there is a turn-off on the left after 10 kilometres (at marker 194) for Chumdo Gyang and Eyul. Crossing Shopotak La pass (5,001 metres) after a further 23 kilometres, you will enter the upper reaches of the **Nyel** valley. The Gelukpa monastery of **Gateng** is passed on the descent from the pass after 15 kilometres, and then, at **Shobo Shar** village, another turn-off to the left leads to **Shopo** township in Upper Nyel. The routes from Shopo to Jarto (Upper Jaryul) and Sangak Choling will be described below, page 198.

Continuing on the main Tsetang-Tsona highway for a further four kilometres (Tsona lies 90 kilometres to the south), you will arrive at the **Kyitang turn-off**, again on the left. The road to the right leads on to Tsona, via Ritang township and monastery. Taking the left road, which follows the Nyel valley, after 21 kilometres you will reach Kyitang.

Kyitang

The administrative capital of the county, the town is largely comprised of government buildings and military compounds; but there are some monasteries of interest in the Kyitang area, especially **Chi-le Gonpa** of the Kagyu school, near the old Lhuntse Dzong and **Trakor Monastery**, which are both located to the west of Kyitang; as well as **Tebura Monastery** to the northwest, and **Shangtse (Yangtse) Monastery** near Lower Nyel (Nyel-me) to the northeast.

Lower Nyel Valley (Nyel-me) གཉལ་སྨད

A motorable road continues for 48 kilometres from Kyitang down the Nyel-chu valley via **Zhingpa** township as far as **Jaryul** township, which lies east of the Nyel-chu's confluence with the Loro-chu. The Loro-chu valley is nowadays administered by Tsona county (see below, page 199).

Colour map 2, grid C5

Trekking

From Nyenrong on this road, there is a three-day trekking route via Le La pass (5,240 metres), Khyimpu and Jar-me, to Sangak Choling, which is the gateway to Tsari in the northeast.

An alternative more difficult trek follows the Nyel-chu downstream from this confluence with the Loro-chu, to a second confluence with the Jar-chu at **Lung**. The rapids form a deep gorge which must be crossed and recrossed by a precarious bridge and ladder! The village of **Dron** is the last Tibetan village on the Nyel/Loro-chu, and further downstream the territory is occupied by Assamese Lopas. Many of Dron's villagers are engaged in guiding pilgrims to

Southern Tibet

Lhuntse County

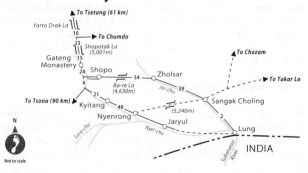

Tsari, which is still 10 trekking days to the east from this point. At Lung, the combined headwaters of the Subansiri flow south into India.

NB There is a strong military presence at Lung. The border is disputed, and travel restrictions apply. From Lung there is a jeep road leading through Jar-me (Lower Jaryul) to Sangak Choling, 33 kilometres to northwest.

Upper Jaryul Valley (Jarto) བྱར་སྟོད

From **Shopo** township in Upper Nyel (one kilometre east of the main Tsetang-Tsona highway, see above, page 197), a jeep road crosses the Ba-re La watershed (4,630 metres) between the Nyel and Jarto valleys to **Zholsar** township (34 kilometres). En route, you should stop to visit **Dzongka Chode** monastery, which has a collection of old Buddhist texts. From Zholsar, the road follows the narrow Jarto valley downstream and southeast to **Sangak Choling**, 39 kilometres distant.

Trekking There are two trekking routes which diverge from this road: a one-day trek from **Shoposang** (opposite the ruins of Tengtse monastery) which leads southwest via the Mo La pass (5,400 metres) to Lower Nyel (Nyel-me); and another five-day trek from **Pejorling**, which leads north via the Kharpo-chu valley to **Chozam**, the northern gateway to the Tsari pilgrimage in Nang county (see below, page 223). It is also possible to make a four-day trek from **Chumdo Gyang**, following the Eyul road, and then diverging from it to cross the Pu La watershed pass to Zholsar, via Drongzhu, Kyekye, Tengchung, and Phudrok in Jarto.

Sangak Choling The monastery of Sangak Choling was founded by Pema Karpo of the Drukpa Kagyu school (1527-92); and expanded by his successor Drukchen V Paksam Wangpo (1593-1641). This is one of the main gateways to the Tsari pilgrimage circuit, which lies only two-days trek to the east. The Drukpa Kagyu school had a particular affinity with Tsari, in that it was Tsangpa Gya-re, the founder of the principal Drukpa monasteries in West and Central Tibet who first opened Tsari as a place of pilgrimage.

Sangak Choling, destroyed in the 1960s, has been under reconstruction since 1986, and now stands within a township of the same name. The main temple has a central Shakyamuni image.

Tsari Pilgrimage To reach the pilgrim's circuit from Sangak Choling, it is necessary to trek via Cha La pass (5,060 metres). Begin by following the Kyu-chu gorge upstream through a glacial valley. After 12 kilometres the road divides, the northeast track leading to **Takar La** and the lesser circuit, and the north track leading to **Chozam** on the higher circuit. Traditionally, the latter, which is also known as the 'circumambulation of the ravines of Tsari' was undertaken only once every 12 years. For a description of the Tsari pilgrimage routes, see the section on Nang county below, page 223.

Lower Jaryul Valley (Jarme) བྱར་སྨད

Below Sangak Choling, the jeep road continues for 25 kilometres, following the Jar-chu downstream to its confluence with the Nyel/Loro-chu at Lung. Arunachal Pradesh (India) lies a short distance to the south. The border is sealed and it is not possible to enter into India.

Tsona County མཚོ་སྣ

Tsona county is the modern name for **Monyul***, the vast region to the east of Lhodrak and south of Lhuntse bordering on Bhutan and Arunachal Pradesh. Presently, it includes the Drushul valley and the headwaters of the Tawang-chu, as far south as the sacred terma site of Shawuk Tago, as well as the adjacent valleys of the Loro Karpo-chu and Loro Nakpo-chu, which are tributaries of the* **Subansiri** *(Tib Shipasha-chu). Traditionally, Monyul has also included Tawang and neighbouring parts of what is now the Indian state of Arunachal Pradesh, as well as Bhutan itself, which in the Tibetan language is often called Southern Monyul.*

Tsona County (17)
错那县
Cona
Population: 13,935
Area: 5,698 sq km
Colour map 2, grid C4

This region is the land of the Monpa people (see below, page 698); and although parts of it have long been culturally within the Tibetan orbit, it was not brought under direct rule from Lhasa until the 17th century, around the time when a series of unsuccessful military campaigns were also conducted against the Drukpa theocracy of Bhutan. During the 17th century the Dalai Lama VI Tsangyang Gyatso was born at **Orgyen Ling** in Monyul. From then on, Monyul was recognized as having 32 districts: four in Lekpo, six in Pangchen, eight in Dakpa, three in Lawok, six in Drangang, four in Rongnang, and one in Shawuk Hrojangdak. The present county capital is located at **Zholshar**, 198 kilometres due south of Tsetang.

Upper Tawang Valley

At **Ritang** in Upper Nyel, 28 kilometres from Kyitang, there is a reconstructed monastery containing bas-relief carvings which have been restored through the good auspices of the Shalu Association in Paris. Some 13th-14th century murals are also said to have survived here.

After leaving Ritang, the main road from Tsetang to Tsona runs due west. A turn-off on the right at **Yope** leads northwest towards Trigu Tso and Tso-me (see below, page 206), but the main road cuts southwest through the Nangme-chu valley (a tributary of the Nyel-chu). Then, after crossing Hor La pass (40 kilometres from Ritang), the road turns abruptly due south, passing on the left the large **Nara Yutso Lake**. Further south, at the small **Nyapa Tso** lake,

Tsona County

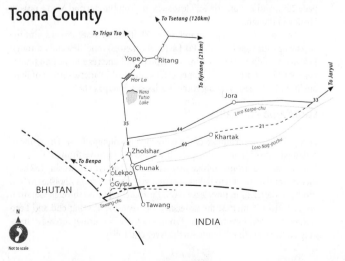

Southern Tibet

there is a turn-off northeast for the Loro valley (35 kilometres from Hor La pass). A further eight kilometres beyond this turn-off, you will reach Zholshar, the county capital, located in the upper reaches of the Tawang-chu valley.

Zholshar　**Zholshar** (Tsona) is a particularly sensitive town, since the road from here leads directly downstream to **Tawang**, a frontier town with a monastery allied to Drepung in Lhasa, but now firmly on the Indian side of the disputed border.

Shawuk Tago　The most important site on the Tibetan side of the border is undoubtedly **Shawuk Tago**, which lies on the western ridge of the valley, just north of the border. This is a sacred meditation cave associated with Padmasambhava, where the Dzogchen master Melong Dorje subsequently meditated during the 13th century, and where in 1680 Terdak Lingpa unearthed his terma text entitled *Great Compassionate One as the Universal Gathering of the Sugatas (Tuje Chenpo Deshek Kundu)*.

Drushul Valley

Drushul, situated north and west of Zholshar, is the name of the long gorge of the Nyashang-chu River, a major tributary of the Tawang-chu, which converges with the latter at the Indo-Bhutanese border, south of Tawang. On the Tashigang district of East Bhutan, which lies across that border, see below, page 864. Drushul is renowned as the birthplace and residence of the Nyingma master and treasure-finder Ratna Lingpa (1403-78). It was here at **Dokhar Lhundrub Podrang** that he compiled his celebrated edition of the *Collected Tantras of the Nyingmapa (Nyingma Gyudbum)*.

Trekking　There is a six-day trekking route from Zholshar to Me La pass, on the Northeast Bhutanese border, which follows the Nyashang-chu River downstream through Drushul valley. En route you pass through **Mishi** village and **Dokhar** township, a beautifully forested area situated deep in the gorge. Here, there are eight peaks and eight rivers symbolizing the attributes of the Eight Medicine Buddhas. The trail then cuts southwest across the Chak La pass (4,920 metres), to enter the moist **Khechu** valley, with its alpine conifer forests. This valley leads west to **Benpa** township in Lhodrak (a further three-days, see below, page 209), and a southerly trail leads via the Yombu-chu and Me La pass to **Shinbe** in Bhutan.

An alternative seven-day trek from Zholshar (Tsona) crosses into the Nyashang-chu valley via the Po La (4,540 metres), and descends through **Lekpo** township and its environs to **Gyipu** (73 kilometres and the East Bhutanese border at **Jangpu** (17 kilometres). On the Tashi Yangtse district of Bhutan into which these trekking routes lead, see below, page 865.

Loro Karpo-chu Valley

Loro valley is the birthplace of the renowned Rechungpa Dorje Drak, one of Milarepa's two foremost disciples. It is possible to drive through the Loro Karpo-chu valley from Zholshar (Tsona), northeast to **Jora** township (52 kilometres), and thence on to Jaryul. Alternatively, the trek from Zholshar to Jora can be undertaken in three easy days. En route, you pass through **Gersum**, Nyala La (5,175 metres; the watershed between the Tawang-chu and Loro Karpo-chu), and **Loroto** village. From Jora there is a further three-day trekking pathway north to Lhuntse in the Nyel-chu valley.

Loro Nakpo-chu Valley

Drive south from Zholshar to **Chunak** and thence northeast to **Khartak** (60 kilometres), following the Loro Nakpo-chu downstream. A three-day trek from Khartak to Jaryul township in Lhuntse county descends through the river's narrow gorge to its confluence with the Loro Karpo-chu, west of **Tritongmon Monastery** (21 kilometres). From this point, it is 33 kilometres to **Jaryul** township, from where transport is available to Lhuntse.

Chongye County འཕྱོངས་རྒྱས

*The valley of Chongye, southwest of Yarlung, was the ancient capital of the Tibetan kings until Songtsen Gampo consolidated his newly unified kingdom at Lhasa in the seventh century. Subsequently, it became the royal burial ground par excellence. The valley extends from its confluence with the Yarlung Shampo-chu below Rechung Puk as far as the Chongye River's source in Chugo township. The modern county capital, **Chongye**, lies at the heart of the Chongye valley, 28 kilometres from Tsetang; but the county also includes the outlying townships of Cho and Gyelmen in its lateral valleys to the west.*

Chongye County (10)
穷结县
Qonggai
Population: 15,636
Area: 827 sq km
Colour map 3, grid C4

The motor road to Chongye leaves Tsetang, south of the *Tsetang Hotel*, and cuts across the Yarlung Shampo-chu River, before following the western side of the Yarlung valley past the Chinese military cemetery. This complex was headquarters of the Chinese military operation during the Sino-Indian border war of 1962. It then cuts south to Tsechu Bumpa, where the Sheldrak pilgrimage begins (see above, page 190). Beyond **Gontang Bumpa** (see above, page 194), the road enters the Chongye valley, following the Chongye River upstream. At **Bena** there is a turn-off on the right, which leads to Cho township, the birthplace of Nyak Jananakumara, one of the foremost disciples of Padmasambhava, who attained his meditative realizations at Sheldrak cave (see above, page 190). The main road continues south through **Ju** township, where the principal site is Tangpoche monastery.

Getting there

The yellow buildings of **Tangpoche Monastery**, also known formally as Solnak Tang, are located to the east of the valley, not far from Bairo Puk (see above, page 194). This Kadampa institution was founded in 1017 by a group of Lu-me's followers known as the 'seven and a half monks' (*bande-mi che-dang-gye*), who included Drumer Tsultrim Jungne, one of the 10 men of Utsang responsible for revitalizing the monastic ordination in Central Tibet at that time. Shortly afterwards, it became the residence of the Kadampa spiritual benefactor Khuton Tsondru Yungdrung (1011-75), and he invited Atisha to visit the monastery. It subsequently became an important centre for the study of Buddhist philosophy; and formerly contained a number of precious relics, including a black Prajnaparamita image, nicknamed

Tangpoche
(Solnak Tang)
ཐང་པོ་ཆེ

Chongye County

Bonpo Tomb Culture

The funeral custom of earth-burial is rare in Central Tibet, where charnel ground dismemberment (sky burial) is the norm (for ordinary people) and cremation or embalming preferred (for important lamas). Nonetheless, during the Yarlung period, when Bonpo tomb culture was at its most influential (see below, page 670), the Tibetan kings were traditionally interred in colossal tumuli, along with their worldly wealth (and in the earliest cases with their retainers buried alive). After the collapse of the Yarlung Dynasty, the custom of burying kings in tombs came to an end. During the 1980s a number of other tomb sites have been excavated in Southern Tibet in the lateral valleys of the Brahmaputra, such as Dranang, Yarlung, and Nang, but, however large, none appear to have the grandure and historic significance of the Chongye tombs.

Zilpachen ('lustrous'), and an image of Atisha. Tangpoche was gradually absorbed by the Gelukpas, following Tsongkhapa's visit here in the 14th century. The present assembly hall has extant murals, dated 1915, commissioned by Dalai Lama XIII; and some small images and tangkas of age.

Chongye Town

འཕྱོང་རྒྱས་

Although the county capital is a town of greater antiquity than Lhasa, and even in the early 1990s was regarded as a sleepy backwater, it has within the last few years been rapidly reconstructed. From afar (Dungkhar or Pelri) Chongye now has the air of a small Chinese town, with its high rise concrete buildings. Three roads intersect at the main square – the Tsetang road from the north, the southwest track through the old village to Riwo Dechen monastery, and the southeast road to the Tombs, Dungkhar, and Tso-me.

The government buildings include guesthouse and dining facilities, although most visitors will prefer to stay at Tsetang and commute. There are small road-side shops, selling groceries and household utensils, and a stone carving factory, where local agate is turned into ornaments and bowls.

Chingwa Taktse Castle

འཕྱིང་བ་

སྟག་རྩེ་རྫོང་

Located to the southwest, on the Chingwari ridge above the town, this ruined edifice was the ancient residence of the Yarlung kings, and the centre of their power prior to the construction of Lhasa. Behind it was the fief of the Chongye Depa, the hereditary lord of Chongye, who claimed descent from the Zahor region of Northwest India and had a well-established Nyingmapa background. It was into this family, as the son of Miwang Dudul Rapten, that Dalai Lama V was born in 1617. A chapel in the old fortress (*dzong*) commemorated this event.

Riwo Dechen Monastery

རི་བོ་བདེ་ཆེན་

དགོན་པ་

On the slopes below Chingwa Taktse Castle, you will see the ruins and reconstructed buildings of Riwo Dechen monastery. The Tomb of Songtsen Gampo provides an excellent vantage point for viewing this complex and the ruined castle on the ridge above. Riwo Dechen was founded during the 15th century by the Gelukpa lama Lowo Pelzang, a student of Khedrubje Gelek Pelzangpo (1385-1438), one of Tsongkhapa's

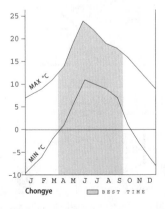

Chongye   ▮ BEST TIME

foremost disciples who was retrospectively recognized as Panchen Lama I. Although the original buildings are in a ruinous state, a new monastery has been constructed alongside the original, and there are over 100 monks. The main Maitreya temple was consecrated in 1985.

The Tombs of the Kings

A short distance to the south of Chongye town and east of the Chongye River, are the tombs of the greatest kings of the Yarlung Dynasty. Tumuli of 16 kings have been identified in the Chingwardo and Dungkhar valleys. Another two, those of the 28th king Lhatotori Nyen-tsen and the 30th Drong-nyen Deu, are also said to be situated in Chongye valley, respectively below the ruins of Chingwa Taktse Castle and at Zhangdar, further north. Admission fee: ¥15 per person.

Colour map 3, grid C4

While there are various conflicting descriptions of the tombs at Chongye, the following account is derived from the chronicle in Jigme Lingpa's *Collection of Tales (Tamtsok)*, an 18th century essay based on earlier sources, such as the *Gar Karchag* and *Tentsik Gyatso*, and composed by a native of Chongye, who happens to have been one of Tibet's greatest and most incisive writers of all time.

History

The tombs of the earliest legendary and prehistoric kings are no longer visible. The first seven kings, from Nyatri Tsenpo to Sibtri Tsenpo, are said to have ascended to the heavens at the time of their demise by means of a sky-cord (*mu*). The eighth and ninth kings (known as the 'two celestial kings of Teng') are said to have been interred at Ya and Dza; the 10th to 16th (known as the 'six earthly kings of Lek') were interred at Yapangtsam; and the 17th to 24th (known as the 'eight middle kings of De') were buried at Chuwo'i Zhung. None of these sites have been identified as yet, their tombs having 'vanished like snow falling on a lake'. Subsequent kings were buried in the plain of **Chinyul Darmotang** (at Chongye), where there are many unidentified mounds of earth, perhaps containing the tombs of the 'five linking kings of Tsen'. The last of these, the 28th king Lhatotori Nyentsen is said to be interred within Chingwa Taktse Castle.

Nowadays, there are 16 identifiable tombs – 10 in the Chingwardo valley, and six in the adjacent Dungkhar valley. Some of these are on the slopes of Mulari hill, which divides these two valleys. Songtsen Gampo's immediate ancestors and descendants are all interred here.

Chongye Tombs

Chinwardo Valley
1 Banso Marpo
2 Banso Dozher Hralpo
3 Banso Lharichen
4 Banso Lhari Tsuknam
5 Banso of Prince Jangsa Lha-on
6 Banso Lhari Dempo
7 Banso Gyelchen Trulzhi
8 Banso of King Langdarma
9 Banso of Prince Namde Osung
10 Banso Trulri Truknang

Dunghar Valley
11 Banso of Trinyen Zungtsen
12 Banso of King Takri Nyentsen
13 Banso Gungri Sokpolek
14 Banso Gungri Gungje
15 Banso Gyangri Gyangden
16 Banso of King Mutik Tsepo

Southern Tibet

Chongye/ **Banso Marpo** or **Muri Mukpo** Among the 10 tombs of the
Chingwardo Chongye/Chingwardo valley, the largest (1) is that of Tibet's unifying 33rd
Tombs king, Songtsen Gampo. This enormous tomb, is 13.4 metres high with its sides
each measuring 129 metres. Literary sources describe in detail the vast treasures and entire chapels contained within it. Yet, there are other traditions
claiming that Songtsen Gampo vanished into light at the time of his passing,
into either the Jowo Rinpoche image or the Rangjung Ngaden image of Lhasa!

On the summit of the tomb, offering a bird's eye view of the entire
Chongye valley, there is a reconstructed 13th century temple, originally attributed to the Nyingmapa lama Menlungpa Shakya-o. The temple is entered
through an outer annex with a **Mani Lhakhang** on the right (murals here
depict the primordial Buddha Samantabhadra in union with Samantabhadri).
Beyond an inner courtyard, the **chapel** contains images of Songtsen Gampo,
flanked by his two foreign queens and chief ministers. The **inner sanctum** has
images (left to right) of: Amitayus, the Buddhas of the Three Times, and
Padmasambhava in the form Nangsi Zilnon. The gatekeepers are Vajrapani
and Hayagriva. The murals depict the Thirty-five Buddhas of Confession (left)
and the Eight Manifestations of Padmasambhava (right).

The other nine tombs on the Chongye/Chingwardo side of the valley are
visible from the summit of Songtsen Gampo's tomb. As described by Jigme
Lingpa, these comprise:

Banso Dozher Hralpo (2), the mausoleum of the 35th king Mangsong
Mang-tsen (left of Songtsen Gampo tomb).

Banso Lharichen (3), the mausoleum of the 36th king Dusong
Mangpoje, aka. Trulgyi Gyelpo (right of Mangsong Mangtsen's tomb).

Banso Lhari Tsuknam (4), the mausoleum of the 37th king Tride
Tsukten Me Aktsom (on the slopes of Mulari, left of Dusong Mangpoje's
tomb).

Banso (5) of Prince Jangsa Lha-on (front of Tride Tsukten Me Aktsom's
tomb).

Banso Lhari Dempo (6), the mausoleum of the 39th king Mune Tsepo
(right of Tride Tsukten Me Aktsom's tomb).

Banso Gyelchen Trulzhi (7), the mausoleum of the 41st king Tri
Relpachen (front of Dusong Mangpoje's tomb, with an inscribed obelisk in the
foreground. The obelisk has been recently been enclosed within a small building to offer some protection from the elements. Jigme Lingpa adds that this

Temple at Chongye Banso Marpo

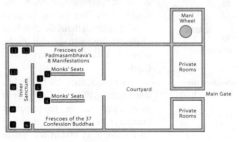

tomb has also been wrongly attributed to Dengtri, the son of Senalek Jinyon).

Banso (8) of the 42nd and last king Langdarma (between those of Dusong Mangpoje and Relpachen).

Banso (9) of prince Namde Osung (behind Dusong Mangpoje's tomb).

Banso Trulri Truknang (10), the mausoleum of the 38th king Trisong Detsen (behind and to right of Tride Tsukten Me Aktsom's tomb, on the left slopes of Mulari, adjacent to Dungkhar valley. **NB** Local reports suggest this tomb is on the far side of Mulari. The ancient obelisk marking this tomb has been missing since the 18th century. Jigme Lingpa notes that it was removed by farmers.

In the adjacent Lower Dungkhar valley, there are six further identified tombs: **Banso** (11) of the 29th king, Trinyen Zungtsen.

    Dungkhar Valley Tombs

    Banso (12) of the 31st king Takri Nyentsen (right of Trinyen Zungtsen's tomb).

    Banso Gungri Sokpolek (13), mausoleum of the 32nd king Namri Songtsen (left of Trinyen Zungtsen's tomb).

    Banso Gungri Gungje (14), mausoleum of the 34th king Gungri Gungtsen (left of Namri Songtsen's tomb).

    Banso Gyangri Gyangdem (15), mausoleum of prince Murub Tsepo (west side of valley).

    Banso (16) of the 40th king Mutik Tsepo, aka. Senalek Jinyon (nearby Murub Tsepo's tomb, although some say it is in front of Dusong Mangpoje's tomb).

The Dungkhar valley where the last six tombs are located is also the abode of Jigme Lingpa, the great Nyingmapa yogin (1729-98), who established his hermitage above Dungkhar village, 12 kilometres from Chongye. It was from this hermitage that his Longchen *Nyingtig* tradition spread throughout Tibet. Since the 19th century, Tseringjong has been an active nunnery for practitioners of the *Longchen Nyingtig*. There are now 30 nuns at Tseringjong, which has been under reconstruction since 1985. The meditative spirit which gave rise to this powerful hermitage is still apparent at the present day.

    Tseringjong Nunnery ཚེ་རིང་ལྗོངས

    Approaching the temple from the road, there is a Mani Wall to the right, with stones depicting the Thirty-five Buddhas of Confession, and a sacred spring to the left. Then, passing a tree and teaching throne of Jigme Lingpa's on the left, and another tree reputedly grown from the hair of Jigme Lingpa on the right, the building is entered via a door next to the kitchen.

    An antechamber then leads into the temple proper (door on right). The central images depict Padmasambhava flanked by Songtsen Gampo and Trisong Detsen. Behind these images against the rear wall are further images, depicting Longchen Rabjampa and Jigme Lingpa among others. In front of all these images is a throne, and on the left wall (next to the door) an image of the protectress Dorje Yudronma. A printed set of the Lhasa *Kangyur* sits against the right wall. Within the **inner sanctum**, there is the most precious silver reliquary containing the remains of Jigme Lingpa, flanked by images of Longchen Rabjampa (left) and Jigme Lingpa (right).

Located in a northeast side-valley, and approached via a turn-off to the left a few kilometres upstream from Songtsen Gampo's tomb is the monastery of Pelri Tekchokling. The original temple was founded in the 15th century by Sonam Tobgyel, lord of Chongye. It subsequently became the residence of the Nyingmapa *terton* Sheab Ozer (1517-84), but it is most renowned as the birthplace of Jigme Lingpa. The reconstructed main temple contains murals

    Pelri Tekchenling Monastery དཔལ་རི་ཐེག་ ཆེན་གླིང

depicting the Eight Manifestations of Padmasambhava, as well as the lineage of Longchen Rabjampa and Sherab Ozer. The ruined building where Jigme Lingpa was born is currently marked by a whitewashed stone.

Gyelmen Chen-ye Lhakhang ক্রুঅ'স্থুব'ক্ষুব' ঘাঅম'শ্লু'মে	Heading up the Chongye valley, before the steep ascent to Lugu La pass begins, there is a turn-off on the right (west), leading to Gyelmen township. Here, the most important site is the **Chen-ye Lhakhang**, a Kadampa centre renowned for its monastic discipline, which was initially established by Geshe Drapa, and later absorbed by the Gelukpa school. The most precious relic here was the right eye of Shariputra, foremost student of Shakyamuni Buddha, after which the temple was called 'right-eye temple' (Chen-ye Lhakhang).

The main road continues uphill through **Chugo** township, near the source of the Chongye-chu River, as far as the **Lugu La** pass (4,600 metres), which forms the watershed between the north-flowing tributaries of the Brahmaputra, and the Lhodrak region to the south. The pass offers fantastic views of the nomadic grasslands and lakelands around Trigu Lake.

Tso-me County মৰ্ক্ষু'স্থুদ্

Tso-me County (11) 措美县 Comai Population: 11,815 Area: 6,075 sq km Colour map 2, grid C4	*From Lugu La pass (4,600 metres), the road leads southwest to Trigu Lake and the Tamzhol valley of East Lhodrak. This region is nowadays called Tso-me, and administered from its county capital at **Tamzhol**. The distance from Chongye to Tamzhol is 83 kilometres. At the northwest shore of Trigu Lake, south of the pass, **Chaktse Trigu** township lies in a vast exposed lakeland plain. Almost every building has a windmill attached. The township is an important intersection, since roads lead from here northwest towards Lake Yamdrok (motorable for 34 kilometres); southeast to Ritang (76 kilometres) near Lhuntse, and southwest to Tso-me (46 kilometres).*

Trigu Lake শ্রি'শু'মৰ্ক্ষ	The bird sanctuary of Trigu Lake is located in a pristine nomadic area of internal drainage. There are hot springs near its northwest corner; and yak pastures all around. The motion and subtle colour tones of its waters are said to portend good and bad auspices; and, like neighbouring Lake Yamdrok, it is said to have a talismanic connection with the well-being of the Tibetan nation. Prosperity is considered directly proportionate to the rise in its water level. The 46 kilometres drive from Trigu to Tamzhol (Tso-me) town is one of the most memorable in Southern Tibet. The road cuts southwest away from the lake shore, and ascends the Shar Khaleb La pass (5,129 metres). Beyond, there is a remarkable canyon where the bare red hillsides are severely contorted and eroded, like those around Tsaparang in Far-west Tibet (see below, page 360). To the west, you can see the peaks of Chungkha Mori (5,220 metres), Droktri Sharma (5,837 metres) and Zholchen Chenri (6,166 metres), which partake of this landscape and its tectonic upheavals, forming a definite watershed between the north and south flowing tributaries of the Brahmaputra. The descent to Tamzhol gives access through lateral valleys to the ruined monasteries of Rimon and Tashi Choling.

Tamzhol (Tso-me) Town	The town of **Tso-me** is dramatically set within the eroded gorge of the Tamzhol-chu (sometimes known as Lhodrak Shar-chu), which rises from the watershed at Shar Khaleb, and surges southwest through the East Lhodrak region to converge with the Kuru-chu (Lhodrak Nub-chu) below Kharchu (see below, page 208).

Trekking From Tso-me, the main road leads downstream to Benpa and Khomting Lhakhang (84 kilometres); but it is also possible to undertake a four-day trek to Lhodrak (Dowa Dzong), via Zholra valley, Menzang La pass, and Shera La pass.

Revered as one of the supreme places for meditation in Tibet since the time of Padmasambhava, the distinctive Mawochok ridge known as **Drakmar Dorje Tsenga** ('five-fold indestructible peak of red rock') dominates the town of Tso-me from the northeast. The site is said to derive its power from the three mountain abodes of the three main bodhisattvas: Avalokiteshvara, Manjushri and Vajrapani, which lie immediately to the south.

Mawochok Monastery

ষ্ট'র্ন'র্ন্নিশ্ম

History The monastery was the seat of Nyangrel Nyima Ozer (1136-1204), a revered incarnation of King Trisong Detsen, who, along with Guru Chowang and Rigdzin Godemchen, is regarded as one of the three supreme treasure-finders (*terton*) of Tibet. As a child, he meditated at the base of Mawochok mountain and received the name Nyima Ozer in a vision. Thereafter, he established his residence on the ridge above, from which time the monastery developed. The original buildings were destroyed in the 1960s, along with most of Mawochok's treasures, including a famous set of images depicting the three bodhisattvas (Avalokiteshvara, Manjushri, and Vajrapani), King Trisong Detsen's own master copy of the *Gathering of the Eight Transmitted Precepts* (a text rediscovered as *terma* by Nyangrel himself), and a large bronze stupa.

Main temple Approaching the main temple from the east, there are three buildings to its left: a **protector shrine**, dedicated to Six-armed Mahakala, and two enormous stupa reliquaries, known as **Tukten Chorten** and **Tashi Obar**, which are greatly revered. They contain the relics of Nyangrel and his son Drogon Namka Pelwa. Among these, Nyangrel's own stupa is said to have been consecrated by the Kashmiri pandita Shakyashri, who was invited to Mawochok in 1204 during the funeral ceremonies.

The **main temple** is entered from the east, although the main images and inner sanctum are to the north. Inside in the northwest corner, next to a wooden prostration board, there are **amazing murals** depicting the life of Nyangrel himself. On the east wall is a copy of the Derge version of the *Kangyur*. The main images are of Padmasambhava and Nyangrel. Within the **inner sanctum**, are new images of the three bodhisattvas: Manjushri, Avalokiteshvara, and Vajrapani, interspersed with other images of Amitayus, Vajrasattva, Avalokiteshvara (again), Nyangrel, and an old image of the latter's son Ngadak Drogon Namka Pelwa. There are currently 23 monks, and the reconstruction is the work of Mawochok Chozang Tendzin Gyatso Rinpoche, an aged incarnate lama who resides at Tsetang.

Tso-me County

Pilgrimage Circuit The pilgrim's circuit around the mountain top

Southern Tibet

encompasses Nyangrel's sacred spring and meditation cave, as well as a charnel ground, and rock impressions of snowlions and Eleven-faced Avalokiteshvara. Nearby are the three scared peaks of the three bodhisattvas: Vajrapani on the left, Avalokiteshvara in the centre, and Manjushri on the right. Further to the south are the mountains of Benpa in lower Tamzhol and, beyond, the high Himalayas on the Bhutan-Tibet border.

Essentials It is possible to stay within the simple guesthouse compound, which caters mostly to truckers and government employees. The town has a general store, a cinema, and a few shops, mostly owned by its expanding Chinese population.

Nezhi Zhitro Lhakhang
གནས་གཞི་ཞི་ཁྲོ་ལྷ་ཁང་

A few kilometres below Tamzhol (Tso-me) town, following the Tamzhol-chu downstream, the road passes a ruined watchtower and Phakmodrupa's earthen stupa of **Na'okyok** on the far bank of the river. After Letang village, the road crosses the river to the west bank and descends to **Nezhi** township. Here, you can visit **Nezhi Zhitro Lhakhang**, the residence of the descendants of the Nyingmapa *terton* Guru Chowang (1212-70), where the images are dedicated to the latter's particular terma tradition. Guru Chowang, like Nyangrel, is one of the supreme *terton* of the Nyingma school and, again like Nyangrel, hailed from the Lhodrak region of Southern Tibet. As a young man, he received the *bodhicitta* vows from Sakya Pandita here in 1229. Formerly the golden reliquary of Guru Chowang was housed here.

The temple Within the reconstructed temple, which is entered from the east side, the central images are of Padmasambhava and his two foremost consorts. In the far northwest corner there is a large image of Guru Chowang, and by the central pillars tangkas depicting the assemblies of the Hundred Peaceful and Wrathful Deities. There are **two inner sanctums**: the one to the west is dedicated to the Eight Deities of the Transmitted Precepts, who are the wrathful meditational deities of the Nyingma school, in the form revealed by Guru Chowang's own terma revelation, entitled *Kabgye Sangwa Yongdzok*. The second to the north was formerly dedicated to the peaceful deities but now contains images of the Buddhas of the Three Times, flanked by Atisha and the Eight Bodhisattvas. Hayagriva and Vajrapani guard its gates.

Watchtowers The road continues southwest from Nezhi, through **Dajung** and **Lu-me**, passing en route a riverside Padmasambhava cave. Below Lu-me, clusters of 15-20 metres high **watchtowers** are frequently to be seen. The construction of such defensive towers is well known in other border areas of the Tibetan plateau, including Gyarong. The road then winds its way downstream to **Darma Dzong** (in Dengpa township), before climbing high above the river to enter Benpa township.

Lhodrak County ལྷོ་བྲག

Lhodrak County (12)
洛扎县
Lhozhag
Population: 16,805
Area: 4,027 sq km
Colour map 2, grid C3

Traditionally the Lhodrak region of Southern Tibet included both the Kuru-chu (Lhodrak Nub-chu) and the Tamzhol-chu (Lhodrak Shar-chu) river valleys, which respectively extend southwest and southeast to converge below Kharchu, north of the Bhutanese border. Currently, Lhodrak is divided between Tso-me and Lhodrak counties, the latter comprising the upper reaches of the Kuru-chu, from Monda La pass as far as Kharchu; and the lower reaches of the Tamzhol-chu, from its Benpa-chu confluence as far as Kharchu.

The entire county lies to the south of the Brahmaputra watershed, and yet north of the Himalayan massives. This geographically confined but stunningly beautiful region has long been one of great historic importance, where vital traditions of both the Nyingma and Kagyu schools have flourished, acting as a cultural bridge between Tibet and East Bhutan.

The county capital is located at **Dowa Dzong** on the Zhung-chu tributary of the Kuru-chu. The distance from Tso-me to Khomting Lhakhang is 84 kilometres, and the distance from Dowa Dzong to Khomting Lhakhang is 67 kilometres.

NB The rapid rivers of Lhodrak are best traversed in spring, early summer, and autumn. During the rainy season flash flooding can seriously disrupt itineraries.

Benpa township is located on the west-flowing Benpa-chu tributary of the Tamzhol River. The valley formed by the Benpa-chu connects with the Khechu and Drushul valleys of Tsona county (see above, page 199) via the Ngamogong La pass.

Benpa Township
འབེན་པ

Benpa Drukrel Lhakhang once contained a large gilded copper image of Padmasambhava. Also, one kilometre upstream from Benpa township, is the Kagyu monastery of **Benpa Chakdor**, named after its large image of the bodhisattva Vajrapani (*Tib* Chakdor). The assembly hall contains stone footprints of Milarepa, Karmapa I, and Gotsangpa. Within the temple to its rear there are renovated images of Vajrapani, flanked by Marpa and Padmasambhava.

The main road from Benpa to Khomting Lhakhang (34 kilometres) leads via **Drak Sinmo Barje** (also called Sengeri), where the clawmarks of the ogress of the rocks, who gave birth to the Tibetan race (see above, page 669) can be seen on the cliff face. From Pelri there is a side-valley leading to Pode La pass (4,965 metres) on the Bhutanese border. This leads to **Monka Nering Senge Dzong**, in Bhutan – the foremost hermitage of Padmasambhava symbolizing buddha-activities.

Lhakhang Township Lhakhang overlooks the confluence of the Kuru-chu and Tamzhol rivers. It was once an important trading post between East Bhutan, Lhasa and Tsetang. There is a pleasant guesthouse, general store and outside pool tables.

Khomting Lhakhang
མཁོ་མཐིང་ལྷ་ཁང

The Temple This geomantic temple, which stands in the middle of Lhakhang township, is one of the border-taming (*thadul*) series of temples constructed by Songtsen Gampo during the seventh century: specifically located on the left elbow of the supine ogress, who represents the rigours of the Tibetan terrain (see below, page 672).

It is a yellow building with a shingled roof, surrounded by four large trees,

Lhodrak County

which are said to have been planted by Guru Chowang in the 13th century. It once contained a renowned image of Four-faced Sarvavid Vairocana, who embodies all the Buddhas of the Five Families, flanked by the Eight Bodhisattvas. The face representing Amoghasiddhi is said to have been made by King Songtsen Gampo in person. It was within this image that Nyangrel Nyima Ozer (12th century) discovered his terma texts entitled *Gathering of the Sugatas of the Eight Transmitted Precepts (Kabgye Deshek Dupa)*. Nothing remains of these images apart from their plinths, but the painted columns and the murals above the door depicting the three bodhisattvas, Avalokiteshvara, Manjushri and Vajrapani, are exquisite. This temple urgently requires funds for its restoration. Upstairs, in the **Tsedak Gonkhang**, there are some small extant images and black-on-gold murals of the protectors.

South to Bhutan   Below Khomting Lhakhang, a two hour trail to the left leads below Chakpurchen towards the **Kharchu Pelgyi Pukring** cave, where in the 15th century Ratna Lingpa discovered *terma* concealed by Namkei Nyingpo. Opposite the cave is the cliff-top **Senge Zangpo Dzong**, where a temple associated with the Dzogchen lineage-holders Melong Dorje (1243-1303) and Rigdzin Kumaradza (1266-1343) can be seen. On the west bank of the river (reached by crossing the bridge over the Kuru-chu/Lhodrak Nub-chu below Khomting Lhakhang), there is the **Tselam Pelri**, where caves of both the Nyingma and Drigung Kagyu tradition are found. This road leads south to **Ngotong Zampa** bridge on the Bhutan border.

Kharchu   Situated 2¾ hours' walking distance above Khomting Lhakhang, on a spa-
Monastery   cious hilltop alpine meadow is **Kharchu Monastery**, the seat of Namkei
མཁར་ཆུ་དགོན་པ   Nyingpo Rinpoche of the Nyingma school. The monastery lies above a semi-nomadic camp, where the dwellings have yak wool tents covering adobe and stone walls, and picturesque flower gardens.

Built on a promontory overlooking the deep forested gorge of Chakpurchen, where Padmasambhava's supreme hermitage symbolizing buddha mind is located, the site has long been associated with some of the greatest figures of the Nyingma and Kagyu traditions: Namkei Nyingpo, Vairocana and Yeshe Tsogyel (among Padmasambhava's 25 disciples), Shelkar Dorje Tsodron, Gotsangpa, Nyangrel Nyima Ozer, Guru Chowang, Melong Dorje, and Drukchen Pema Karpo, the last two of whom respectively founded the main temple and the monastery. From the time of Dalai Lama V, the monastery has been the seat of the reincarnations of Namkei Nyingpo.

The rebuilt two-storeyed temple has (downstairs) an **assembly hall** containing new large images of Padmasambhava and Aksobhya Buddha, along with Marpa and Milarepa. The exquisite murals depict the lineage holders of both the Nyingma and Kagyu schools. **Upstairs**, there is a skylight offering a splendid view of the images and murals below, and the *labrang* residence containing the throne of the present Namkei Nyingpo Rinpoche, who currently resides at Bumtang in Bhutan (see below, page 861). The complex also includes a kitchen and residential area for monks, a large stupa, a sky-burial site, and a two metres high water-powered mani wheel. This monastery has one of the most idyllic settings in Tibet, and its lofty isolation can best be seen from a high point on the road to Senge township on the west bank of the Kuru-chu River (see below).

Getting there   To reach Kharchu follow the path uphill from the *Lhakhang Guesthouse* and turn right, behind the military barracks. The trail bifurcates after 15

minutes. Take the left track, and ascend to a second bifurcation after 1 hour at a rock painted image of Jambhala, god of wealth, and bear right. This will lead after a further arduous 1½ hours to the summit.

Padmasambhava's supreme cave of buddha-mind is reached via a steep forested trail below the hermitages next to the stupa at Kharchu. En route the pilgrim's circuit takes in the **Lhamo Kharchen** hermitage of Phakmodrupa, the **Khandro Dora** platform, the **Chakpurchen Cave**, and the meditation caves of Namkei Nyingpo. The three-storey hermitage of **Lhamo Kharchen**, containing rock footprints of Phakmodrupa, is reached along this trail, across the Kharchu River by means of an old wooden bridge. Back on the near side of the bridge a trail then climbs uphill to the **Khandro Dora**, where there is an inscribed stone obelisk, and then plunges abruptly to **Chakpurchen Cave**.

Chakpurchen Cave

The cave entrance is approached by means of a perilously unstable wooden bridge. Inside the cave is a multi-storey wooden hermitage of the Kagyu school, from the top of which there is a long dark passageway zigzagging toward the cave of buddha-mind, shaped like Padmasambhava's own body. (Tradition holds that he created this meditation cavern by tunnelling directly into the mountain, and remained there in dark retreat for seven years.) The cave contains a natural rock impression of Padmasambhava's iron dagger (*chakpur*), hence the name of the cave. Lastly, the meditation caves of Namkei Nyingpo are reached to the left of Chakpurchen.

This most revered site of the Kagyu school in Tibet comprises the residence of Marpa Chokyi Wangchuk (1012-96) at Drowolung and the nine-storeyed tower constructed as an ascetic penance by his foremost disciple Milarepa (1040-1123; or 1052-1135).

Sekhar Gutok

སྲས་མཁར་
དགུ་ཐོག

Getting there These places are located in the township of **Se**, 35 kilometres northwest of Khomting Lhakhang, in the valley of the Se-chu, an east-flowing tributary of the Kuru-chu (Lhodrak Nub-chu). Access by vehicle is extremely difficult during the rainy season (July-August), when the road is susceptible to severe mud avalanches.

Senge The road from Khomting Lhakhang crosses both the Tamzhol-chu and the Kuru-chu in quick succession and then climbs northeast, past a hydroelectric station and large military complex, to reach **Senge** township at the top of the ridge. The views of the Kuru-chu gorge to Bhutan in the south are fantastic from this vantage point. Nearby is the **Senge Drupuk** cave, which has associations with Padmasambhava, Yeshe Tsogyel, and Milarepa. The town has guesthouse facilities, but is there basically to service the army.

The main road then descends to recross the Kuru-chu at **Sinmo Zampa** bridge. After eight kilometres, it divides – the east fork leading to Lhodrak Dzong and the west to Se. Take the latter. At **Gosung Nangma** a trail on the right leads off to Drubtso Pemaling (see below, page 212). The main road leads southwest to Se township, passing on the left side the **Menchu hot spring** (an important health spa).

Sekhar Gutok The nine-storeyed tower of Sekhar Gutok was constructed as a great act of penance by Milarepa on behalf of Darma Dode, the son of Marpa. For adherents of the Kagyu school, and the Tibetan population as a whole, this single building and the manner of its construction encapsulate the self-sacrifice and renunciation required for success on the Buddhist spiritual path. The tower still stands, its distinctive pagoda roof now replaced with a flat roof; and three of its seven floors contain original murals. Marpa's chapel has

Southern Tibet

some excellent old tangkas. The adjacent two-storey monastery which once housed 100 monks, still contains some original images of the Karmapas, and precious relics such as the skull fragment of Dagmema (wife of Marpa).

Drowolung Monastery

 གྲོ་བོ་ལུང་

དགོན་པ

The residence of Marpa Chokyi Wangchuk at Drowolung, near Sekhar Gutok, is the original Kagyu foundation in Tibet. It was here that Marpa engaged in the translation of the texts which he had brought from India, and transmitted his teachings and realizations to the four 'great pillars' who were his foremost disciples: Ngok Choku Dorje, Tsurton Wangi Dorje, Meton Tsonpo, and Milarepa. The ruined **Podrang Marpa** residence once contained Marpa's reliquary, and images of Marpa and his son Darma Dode. Behind this building is the retreat centre (*drubkhang*) and to its left is the stone throne of Karmapa I. A hill side stupa marks the way to the cave hermitage, where the grottoes of Marpa, Milarepa and Gampopa are all discernible. Simple guesthouse facilities and groceries are available.

Trekking There is also a trekking route to Sekhar Gutok from Senge township via the Khana La and Rolpa La passes.

There is another three to four hours' trek from Sekhar Gutok to the remote cave of **Taknya Lungten Puk**, where Milarepa undertook his first one year retreat. Guides from Sekhar can show the way. Marpa's birthplace at **Zhe** lies two to three hours' walking distance north of Sekhar at the foot of Mount Tashi Denga. Trekking routes also lead south to Namgung La pass and southwest to Monla Karchung La pass, both on the Bhutanese border.

Drubtso Pemaling

སྒྲུབ་མཚོ་པད་གླིང

This glacial lake nestling in the shadows of the Kulha Kangri Himalayan massive (7,554 metres) was consecrated by Padmasambhava as one of the main places for meditation in Tibet.

Getting there There are three points of access to the lake: a relatively easy 5-6 hours' trek from Sekhar Gutok to Drubtso Pemaling, via Gosum Nangma and Chupak; a harder 7-8 hours' trek from Sekhar Gutok via Tuk and Rongpo La pass (5,050 metres); and a 9 hour trek from Lhalung via Drum La pass (5,135 metres). A trail southwest from Tuk on the second of these treks also leads to Langdo and the main trade route to the Bumtang district of Bhutan (via Mongla Karchung La pass).

Padmasambhava's meditation cave is located on the slopes of **Mount Damchen Gara Nakpo**, overlooking the magical turquoise-coloured lake. The trail to the cave follows a precipitous track, leading firstly down to the lake-shore ruins of **Pemaling Monastery**, which was founded by Pema Lingpa (1450-1521). Here, there was once a renowned image of Vajrapani, as well as smaller images of Padmasambhava, Phakmodrupa, and Karmapa I. The cave, where Padmasambhava subdued the demon Gara Nakpo through his meditative powers, lies one hour above the ruins (there is one restored building where pilgrims stay), and is surrounded by glaciers on three sides. The nearby **Lhachu** waterfall is said to be the entrance to a 'hidden land' (*beyul*) within Mount Kulha Kangri. The lake is said to emit mystical or atmospheric apparitions and sounds, notably those of the so-called 'ox of the lake' (*tsolang*). The lake also forms part of the eight- to nine-day Kulha Kangri pilgrimage circuit, which can only be undertaken by crossing into Bhutan.

Dowa Dzong

དོ་བ་རྫོང

The road from Sekhar Gutok to Dowa Dzong, the capital of Lhodrak county, follows the Kuru-chu upstream for 32 kilometres (or 67 kilometres from Khomting Lhakhang). En route it passes through **Karpo** township, where there is a small shop/restaurant next to a freight truck checkpoint. Before entering town, the valley widens and the ruined fortress of **Dowa Dzong** is visible above the road on the left. The town has an increasing number of Chinese immigrants.

Essentials There is a 3-storey guesthouse with restaurant facilities. On the main street, north of the square, there are several karaoke bars and shops. **Banks** The *Bank of China* is located to the right of the road, adjacent to the square. **Useful information** Government buildings: the PSB, Post Office and government compound are located to the left of the road, adjacent to the square.

This fascinating monastery is located to the west of Dowa Dzong, on the north bank of the Kuru-chu. Although it is the principal seat of the Lhodrak Sungtrul and Lhodrak Tuk-se incarnations, following in the *terma* tradition of Pema Lingpa (1450-1521), it has also had earlier associations with the Karma Kagyu school and later connections with the Gelukpa. The original foundation is attributed to Lhalung Pelgyi Dorje, the ninth century assassin of Langdarma who hailed from this part of Southern Tibet. Later, in 1154, Karmapa I Dusum Khyenpa developed the site into a monastery, and from the 17th century onwards the buildings were occupied by the Lhodrak incarnations of the Nyingma school, with the approval of Dalai Lama V and the Tibetan government.

| Lhalung |
| Monastery |
| ལྷ་ལུང་དགོན་པ |

The present buildings largely date from the period of Lhodrak Sungtrul III Tsultrim Dorje (1598-1669) and they were later expanded by Lhodrak Sungtrul VIII Kunzang Tenpei Nyima (1763-1817). Formerly the monastery had a grand appearance, its perimeter wall surrounded by 108 stupas and 108 willow trees (which have since been destroyed).

The Temple Beyond the entrance courtyard, the assembly hall has a Zhitro Lhakhang to its right, and to the rear a Gonkhang and the *labrang* residence of Lhodrak Tuk-se. On the hills to the northeast is a nunnery founded by Longchen Rabjampa.

The **ground floor** of the **Assembly Hall** once housed important eight metres high clay images of the Seven Generations of Past Buddhas (Sangye Rabdun), along with other images of the first seven lineage-holders of Pema Lingpa, and the Three Deities of Longevity (Tselha Namsum). These and the tangkas painted by Lhodrak Tuk-se Gyurme Dorje (b 1641) no longer exist. There is a new image of Padmasambhava against the north wall, and on the west, some damaged murals depicting his life. The decorated pillars have archaic features. In the centre of the hall are the thrones of the Lhodrak Sungtrul and Lhodrak Tuk-se incarnations, both of whom are currently in Bhutan.

The **second storey** has a central skylight overlooking the lower hall, surrounded by a gallery from which various chapels extend. On the south side, next to the staircase, there is an oblong room with an image of Pema Lingpa and extremely valuable **frescoes** of historic importance depicting in three successive panels the lives of Nyangrel Nyima Ozer, Pema Lingpa, and Guru Chowang – the three greatest figures of the Lhodrak region. Adjacent to the door are further murals depicting the deities of the *Barchad Lamsel*, and above the door is Hayagriva. On the west side, the **protector shrine room** has an image made personally by Tilopa, and on the north side there are two chapels: the first houses the foremost objects of the monastery in a glass case. These include a stupa containing the heart of Lhalung Pelgyi Dorje, the vajra of Jatson Nyingpo, stone footprints of Guru Chowang aged eight and 13, and original images of Amitayus in union with consort. The second contains the reliquary of Lhodrak Sungtrul X. On the east side, there is a chapel containing the life-supporting stone (*lado*) of Guru Chowang.

In the reconstructed **Zhitro Lhakhang** to the east of the assembly hall there are new images on the north wall representing: Garab Dorje, Srisimha, Padmasambhava, Yeshe Tsogyel, and Pema Lingpa. On the west and east walls respectively there are relief images of the Hundred Peaceful and Wrathful Deities, each in their respective grottoes. Behind the assembly hall, in the **Gonkhang**, where Lhodrak Sungtrul VIII had a meditative vision of Padmasambhava, is a 'speaking' image of Padmasambhava in the form Guru Saroruhavajra, with a teardrop trickling from its eyes. Upstairs is the residence named **Orgyen Zimpuk**.

Further east from the Gonkhang is the **Mani Ratna Labrang** or residence of the Lhodrak Tuk-se incarnations. It contains the throne and stone footprint of Lhodrak Tuk-se, aged seven, with a mat used only by the Karmapas, and a sealed meditation recess. Outside in the courtyard is a stone *udumbara* lotus.

Layak Guru West of Lhalung in Monda township is the temple of **Layak Dzara Guru**
Lhakhang **Lhakhang**, also called **Samdrub Dewachenpo**, which was constructed in the
ལ་ཡག་གུ་ར་ 13th century by Guru Chowang. Formerly this temple contained a Jowo image
ལྷ་ཁང་ discovered by Guru Chowang in person, along with relics and a painting of this master. The original temple, styled after the ramparts of Nalanda monastery in India, is illustrated in the Lhalung frescoes. It is not yet possible to determine whether the 1949 reconstruction bears any resemblance to the original, since the temple is firmly locked and still used as a granary. The rear annex is now a private residence. Southwest of Layak at **Negon** there is a reconstructed branch of this monastery.

From **Monda** the road climbs northwest to ascend Monda La pass (5,266 metres), the watershed between the lakeland plateau to the north and the south-flowing rivers of Lhodrak. The view of **Kulha Kangri** from Monda La is unrivalled. Beyond the pass is the **Monda Kangri** (6,425 metres). The distance from Monda township to Nakartse is 102 kilometres, and to Lhasa, 256 kilometres. South of the watershed, there is a trail leading west of Monda township across the Trel La pass, leading to Khangmar county of West Tibet.

Nakartse County སྣ་དཀར་རྩེ

Nakartse County (13) *The county of Nakartse is a vast high altitude depression containing the two larg-*
浪卡子县 *est lakes in Southern Tibet: Phuma Yutso and Yamdrok Yutso. Along with Trigu*
Nagarze *Lake (see above, page 206), these form a natural barrier between the*
Population: 29,512 *Brahmaputra valley to the north and the watershed passes of Lhodrak to the*
Area: 7,660 sq km *south. The county also acts as a major road link between Central Tibet (U), to the*
Colour map 2, C3 *north of Gampa La pass, and West Tibet (Tsang), to the west of Nojin Ganzang*
range and Khari La pass (5,045 metres). It has for centuries therefore been a vital
trading link between Lhasa and Bhutan, Sikkim, Nepal and West Tibet. The
county capital is located at Nakartse, 154 kilometres from Lhasa, 118 kilometres
from Gyantse, and 102 kilometres from Lhodrak.

Phuma Yutso From Monda La pass, the sound of Lhodrak's rushing rivers is left behind, and
Lake the road to Nakartse descends into the awesome tranquillity of the lakeland
ཕུ་མ་གཡུ་མཚོ plains to the north. It skirts the east shore of Phuma Yutso (5,040 metres), a superb turquoise-coloured lake with three small islands in a vast but sparsely

populated high-altitude setting. Apart from seasonal nomadic camper groups, herds of yak, and fierce mastiffs, there are only three lakeside villages: **Tu** in the east (on the main road), **Talma** in the south, and **Phuma Jangtang** in the west.

Trekking Tu, Tulma and Phuma Jangtang are linked by a trekking route that encircles the lake in eight- to nine-days. Locals undertake this pilgrimage circuit in the springtime, culminating at the Nyingma monastery of **Sengegon** near the northeast end of the lake. Strange mists and lights are often seen refracted on its surface. Perennial snow peaks grace the northwest horizon, the nearest being Gyetong Soksum (6,244 metres) and Jangzang Lhomo (6,324 metres), with **Nojin Gangzang** (7,191 metres) in the far distance. There is a trekking route from the northwest corner of the lake via Chanda La pass, to Ralung monastery in Tsang (see below, page 253).

Beyond the Ye La pass at the northeast extremity of the lake, the road enters a slightly lower tundra plain, where the rivers drain north into Lake Yamdrok Yutso. Here, large flocks of sheep and goats can be seen grazing, and large villages dot the landscape: notably **Ling** to the east and **Zhamda** on the motor road.

The township of Taklung (or Lho Taklung) lies a few kilometres north of Zhamda village, near the southeast shore of Lake Yamdrok Yutso. At 4,450 metres, this is the largest market town between Gyantse and Lhodrak, and the site of an important summer trade fair, attended by Bhutanese merchants from Bumtang, as well as native Tibetans from Tsang and Southern Tibet. From here, there are trekking routes along the southern shore of Yamdrok Yutso, to Docho township, and thence to Dramda township on the east shore.

Lho Taklung

ཕོ་རྟག་ལུང་

Southern Tibet

Sights The town has two principal monasteries and a ruined dzong. The hilltop **Taklung Monastery**, presently unrestored, is a major branch of Dorje Drak (see above, page 162), maintaining the tradition of the Northern Treasures. Its incarnate lama, Taklung Tsetrul Rinpoche now lives in Simla and Ladakh.

The Sakyapa monastery of **Tarling Chode** lies below the hill, within the township. This is the residence of Taktsang Lotsawa, a vociferous 14th century debating opponent of Tsongkhapa. There are two main buildings separated by a courtyard. The **Assembly Hall** has a large image of Padmasambhava, backing on to a protector shrine where the main image is of Panjaranatha (Gonpo Gur). Its **inner sanctum** contains the reliquary of Taktsang Lotsawa, images of the Buddhas of the Three Times, and Hevajra murals.

The second building has a **Mani Lhakhang**, and a two-storey **Guru Lhakhang**, containing a giant image of Padmasambhava in the form Nangsi Zilnon, surrounded by his eight manifestations in their respective grottoes. On the adjacent wall is an image of Ekajati, protectress of mantra. The upper floor, entered by a staircase behind the Mani Lhakhang offers a close-up view of Nangsi Zilnon's charismatic face.

Nakartse County

Sleeping Simple accommodation is available in the government guesthouse and the primary school compound.

**Yamdrok Yutso
Lake**

ཡར་འབྲོག་
གཡུ་མཚོ

The sacred lake of Yamdrok Yutso (4,408 metres) is revered as a talisman, supporting the life-spirit of the Tibetan nation. It is said that should its waters dry, Tibet will no longer be habitable. By far the largest lake in South Tibet (754 square kilometres), the pincer-shaped Yamdrok Yutso has nine islands, one of which houses a monastery and a Padmasambhava stone footprint. Within its hook-shaped western peninsula, there is another entire lake, **Dremtso** and beyond its southeast extremity yet another, named **Pagyutso**. There are good motorable roads skirting the north and west shores of the lake, and trekking routes which complete the circuit. The Yamdrok region is traditionally famous for its salty dried meat, and, more recently, for its fishing.

The main highway from Lhasa to Gyantse descends to the northern lakeshore from Gampa La pass (4,794 metres) where the visitor from Lhasa or Tsetang will enjoy the unforgettable vista of its pincer-shaped expanse of turquoise water, with the mysterious **Mount Donang Sangwari** (5,340 metres) on the peninsula beyond, and the snow peaks of **Nojin Gangzang** (7,191 metres) in the distance. Passing a new but controversial hydro-electric power station, and reaching the shore at **Tamalung**, from which there is a ferry crossing to the peninsula, the highway runs southwest to **Peldi Dzong** and around the **Yarzik** inlet. At this point, there is a trekking route leading west to **Rampa** township and Ringpung valley in Tsang (see below, page 251). The highway then runs due south as far as **Nakartse**, via Dablung, where another ferry crossing leads to the peninsula. Thereafter, it cuts away from the lake to **Lango**, and ascends towards the **Khari La** pass (5,045 metres) – a defile between the formidable roadside glaciers of Nojin Gangzang (north) and Jangzang Lhomo, which also marks the border between South Tibet and West Tibet (Tsang). Just before Lango, the Lhodrak highway turns off the Gyantse highway on the left, and leads southeast towards Lho Taklung and Zhamda (see above, page 215).

Trekking There is a seven-day trekking circuit around the Yamdrok peninsula, commencing from and ending at **Nakartse**, via Samding Monastery, Sharwa (south of Dremtso Lake), Ngardrak township (northeast of Dremtso), and Mekpa (northwest of the peninsula). En route, you can visit the sacred

Yamdrok Lake

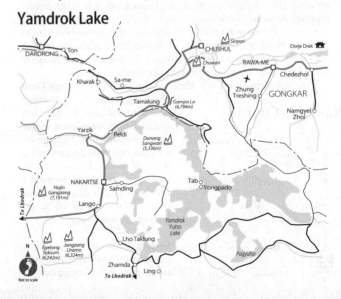

Mount Donang Sangwari, where there are Padmasambhava and Yeshe Tsogyel caves; and which offers outstanding views of the snow peaks of Southern and Central Tibet from its summit.

A second four-day trek leads eastward from the Tamalung ferry to **Dramda** on the east shore of the lake, from where there are further trekking options to Yarlung, Chongye, and Trigu Lake.

A third trekking route crosses the peninsula, via the **Tamalung** ferry on the north shore, as far as Tab, and then crosses the main body of the lake to the southern shore, via **Yongpado** island monastery. From here the townships of the nomadic pasture to the south of the lake can be reached – Ling and Docho among them.

The county town of Nakartse, situated on the Lhasa-Gyantse highway, has grown in recent years on the basis of the wool trade and its status as a transit point for freight trucks and passenger buses. A wool processing factory has been constructed here. The Chinese population influx is evident in the number of Chinese-owned shops and Sichuan-style eateries. On the ridge above the town is the rebuilt **Nakartse Monastery**; and the ruins of the old dzong, birthplace of the mother of Dalai Lama V.

Nakartse

སྣ་དཀར་རྩེ

Essentials Guesthouse facilities are available. There is one excellent little Tibetan restaurant, popular with travellers, truckers, locals and even Chinese, serving noodles, momo, Tibetan butter tea, and sweet Indian-style tea.

This celebrated monastery, eight kilometres east of Nakartse, commands the isthmus between the Yamdrok Yutso Lake pincer and Dremtso. Founded in the 12th century by Khetsun Zhonudrub, Samding has since the 14th century been a bastion of the Bodongpa school, derived from Bodongpa Chokle Namgyel (1306-86). The abbess of Samding, Samding Dorje Phagmo, has long been revered as the highest female incarnation in Tibet. In 1716 she is renowned for having transformed her nun followers into sows in order to thwart the wrath of the Dzungar armies! The present incarnation resides at Lhasa.

Samding Monastery

བསམ་སྡིང་དགོན་པ

Zangri County ཟངས་རི

The county of Zangri lies downstream from Tsetang on both banks of the Brahmaputra. On the south bank it extends for some 35 kilometres as far as Rong township, including the villages situated between the Yarlung and Eyul (Si-chu) valleys. On the north bank it extends from the village of Jang below Densatil monastery (16 kilometres east of Ngari Tratsang) as far as Mount Ode Gungyel (6,998 metres), including the valleys of Zangri, Olka and Dzingchi. The present district capital is located at **Zangri**.

Zangri County (14)
桑日县
Sangri
Population: 14,213
Area: 2,469 sq km
Colour map 3, B4

Densatil Monastery གདན་ས་མཐིལ་དགོན་པ

Rong township, some 35 kilometres from Tsetang, lies on the south bank of Brahmaputra. Here are the ruins of **Langkor Dzong** and **Chagar Monastery**, which was founded by Dalai Lama III. There is a fine but simple *Tibetan restaurant* at the crossroads in Rong, serving noodles, momo, fresh butter tea, and chang.

Rong
Colour map 3, B5

To reach Densatil, take the track leading to the river bank and the **Lukhang Druka ferry** across to the north shore. At this point the river has narrowed to some 300

Getting there

Unfortunately a hardline and doctrinaire attitude towards outsiders prevails in Zangri. Camping may be preferable to the unwelcoming guesthouse facilities here.

metres and the crossing is swift. After 1 kilometre the road forks – west to Jang and east to Zangri. Take the former road, following the Brahmaputra upstream to **Jang**, which lies at the entrance to the concave valley of Densatil. From here there is a steep 3 hour climb to the monastery. A slightly longer 4 hour climb is possible from a point further upstream, approaching the monastery from the rear side of Mount Drakri Karpo, via a zigzagging track which almost reaches the summit before cutting around to enter the valley from the west side at a point higher than the monastery itself. The first route is preferable, in that it offers the shade and refreshing streams of the woodlands, whereas the latter is dry and dusty. Either of these points of access can also be reached on foot from Ngari Tratsang north of Tsetang.

History Located amid a juniper and rhododendron woodland, within a sheltered concave ridge near the summit of **Mount Drakri Karpo**, is the Kagyu monastery of Densatil (4,750 metres). Founded in 1158 by Phakmodrupa Dorje Gyelpo (1110-70), this monastery became one of the most influential in Tibet, giving rise to eight diverse branches of the Kagyu school – the Drigungpa, Taklungpa, and Drukpa foremost among them. Between 1349 and 1435 or 1478, the Phakmodrupa family ruled Tibet from their castle at Nedong, near Tsetang (see above, page 677), and their ancestral monastery at Densatil acquired great wealth and precious religious artefacts. The main temple, **Tsuklakhang Marpo**, once contained 18 exquisitely engraved silver-plated reliquaries containing the relics of the past lineage-holders of Densatil, and six gold pendants. Little evidence of this grandure remains at the present day.

The site Approaching the monastery from the west, below the meditation hermitages, the road follows the contours of the ridge to reach what remains of the complex. Adjacent to the kitchen, there is a small temple containing a copy of the *Kangyur*, and fine old images of Vajravidarana, Cakrasamvara, and Vajravarahi. A ladder leads up to the next level, where to the left, is the chapel built on the site of Phakmodrupa's celebrated straw meditation hut (**Chilpei Khangpa**), and to the right a chapel containing an image of Vajravarahi and stone footprint of Phakmodrupa. Behind these chapels are the massive red walls of the ruined **Tsuklakhang Marpo**.

Take the pilgrim's circuit around the temple, and see the large elegantly carved **Mani Wall** on the east side. From the ridge to the west of the monastery there are stupendous views of the Brahmaputra valley – both upstream towards Tsetang and downstream towards Gyatsa.

Zangri Kharmar Temple

ཟངས་རི་མཁར་ དམར་ལྷ་ཁང་

Retracing the jeep road from Jang towards the ferry, take the left fork to **Zangri**, the county capital. This is a relatively prosperous town, with its wide streets and walled orchards. The grand mansion house of the noble lords of Zangri, named **Samdrub Podrang**, still stands within the township. About eight kilometres east of town, on a 50 metres red rock promontory above the Zangri-Olka road, there is the reconstructed temple and cave hermitage of **Zangri Kharmar**. This was once the residence of Tibet's celebrated female yogini Machik Labdron. Both the

Zangri & Chusum

temple and the cave have fine images of Machik Labdron and her Indian teacher Phadampa Samgye, as well as Karmapa Rangjung Dorje, who later (14th century) redacted the *Chodyul* cycle of practices associated with her.

From Zangri, the road continues northeast, following the north bank of the Brahmaputra, as far as the power station of Olka Lokhang. Here, it leaves the river, which, from this point onwards, flows rapidly through a narrow gorge no more than 200 metres wide. Mount Palungri/Draklho Kyizhung (5,730 metres) slopes down to the south river bank, as does the sacred **Mount Ode Gungyel** (6,998 metres) on the north bank. The latter is the abode of the mountain deity of the same name, regarded as the father of Mount Nyenchen Tanglha (see above, page 138), and revered by Buddhist and Bon pilgrims alike. Tibet's second mortal king, Pude Gungyel, a culture hero who discovered base metals and agriculture, was named after this protector deity.

Mount Ode Gungyel

ཨོད་དེ་གུང་རྒྱལ

The township of Olka, 20 kilometres inland from the power station, lies at the bifurcation of two valleys. It is dominated by the ruins of Olka Takste Dzong, which the Dzungar Mongols pillaged in the 18th century. The motor road runs north following the fertile **Dzingchi** valley, but soon comes to an end.

Olka Takste Dzong

ཨོལ་ཁ་སྟག་རྩེ

Trekking A four-day trek leads on via Dzingchi township and Magon La pass to **Rutok Gonpa** (on the Meldro-Gyamda road). The other track runs northeast into the more arid **Olka** valley, from which there is another four-day trek, via the Lung La pass, to Chokhorgyel and Lhamo Latso oracle lake (see below, page 221).

Dzingchi Monastery This ancient monastery was founded in the 10th century at the inception of the later diffusion of Buddhism in Tibet by Garmiton Yonten Yungdrung, a student of Lachen Gongpa Rabsel, who maintained the monastic ordination in Amdo during the interregnum following Langdarma's persecution. The most important image was of Maitreya. Later, in the late 14th century, Tsongkhapa renovated the temple and refurbished its Maitreya image. His student, Gyeltsabje Darma Rinchen, who became the first throne-holder of Ganden and first head of the Gelukpa school, was firmly associated with Dzingchi, and his subsequent incarnations resided there. Taranatha's silver reliquary was kept in the Maitreya temple for almost 300 years until its destruction during the Cultural Revolution. Three temples have been recently renovated – the **Assembly Hall** (*tsokhang*), the **Maitreya Temple**, and the **Labrang** residence of the Gyeltsab Rinpoches. A large stone mansion in the west of Dzingchi is the birthplace of Dalai Lama XI.

Garpuk This Padmasambhava meditation cave is situated in the hills east of Dzingchi, but may also be reached from Samtenling in Olka. In later centuries, Gampopa and Tsongkhapa both spent time meditating in the cave. No restoration appears to have been yet carried out.

Olka Cholung Monastery Cholung is an important Gelukpa hermitage, founded by Tsongkhapa on the north slopes of Mount Ode Gungyel. There are many stone prints attributed to the master himself; and the reconstructed buildings have an impressive ambience. Located one and a half hours' trekking distance from Olka Taktse, within the Olka valley, Cholung has guesthouse facilities and food is available. Further northeast at **Chuzang**, there is another Tsongkhapa hermitage with two reconstructed chapels and stone imprints of the master's feet and hands.

Southern Tibet

Olka Samtenling Monastery This ruined hermitage has been associated at different times with the Kagyupa followers of Gampopa and the Gelukpa followers of Tsongkhapa.

Chusum County རྩ་གསུམ

Chusum County (15)
曲松县
Qusum
Population: 13,954
Area: 2,332 sq km
Colour map M3, grid C6

*Chusum county is the modern name for the ancient principality of **Eyul Lhagyari**, whose inhabitants have long claimed descent from King Songtsen Gampo. This broad valley is formed by the arid gorge of the Si-chu River, which rises near the Podrang La pass (5,030 metres) and flows northwest to enter the Brahmaputra downstream from Rong. The county capital is located at **Eyul Lhagyari** (Chusum), 59 kilometres from Tsetang, and 24 kilometres from Rong, on a turn-off to the left side of the road. Notice the distinctive yellow markings on the traditional buildings of Eyul: its palace, monastery and farm houses. Iron ore mining is an important industry here.*

The ascent from Chusum to Podrang La follows a gradual gradient along an unusually straight road. At **Shakjang** township (eight kilometres from Eyul Lhagyari), there is a turn-off on the right leading to Tozik, **Eyul Chumdo Gyang** (36 kilometres) and thence to Lhuntse county (see above, page 196). Beyond Shakjang, the valley widens to two kilometres and the gorge deepens to 70 metres. There are cave habitations on the eroded upper ridges; and it was here at **Zarmolung**, in a former Padmasambhava meditation cave called Khyungchen Dingwei Drak, that the Nyingmapa yogini Jomo Menmo (1248-83) received the visionary *terma* text entitled *Gathering of All the Secrets of the Dakinis (Khandro Sangwa Kundu)*. The distance from Shakjang to the pass is 61 kilometres; and from there to Gyatsa, a further 27 kilometres.

Gyatsa County རྒྱ་ཚ

Gyatsa County (18)
加查县
Gyaca
Population: 15,883
Area: 3,727 sq km
Colour map M3, grid B6

*Gyatsa county lies at the heart of West Dakpo, a region of South Tibet renowned for its walnuts and apricots. On the south side of the Brahmaputra, it extends along the highway from Podrang La pass downhill through Lhasol township to the riverside at Dzam, and thence downstream via Drumpa and Lingda to Pamda (55 kilometres). The county capital is located at **Drumpa**, alongside the Dakpo Tratsang Monastery. A trekking route leads southeast from here, via Loklen (Darmar) township and Ke La pass, to Sangak Choling, the gateway to Tsari. On the north bank of the Brahmaputra, the county also includes the townships of Ngarab and Gyatsa, which are reached via a modern suspension bridge. A motorable track follows the Terpulung-chu valley upstream, to Chokhorgyel monastery in Metoktang (35 kilometres). From here, it is a four-hour trek to Lhamo Latso, Tibet's celebrated oracle lake, on whose waters visions portending the rebirth of Dalai Lamas can be seen. From Gyatsa township, yet another route leads southeast via Lung (20 kilometres), to Daklha Gampo monastery, in the lower reaches of the Gyabpurong-chu.*

West Dakpo

Dakpo Tratsang
Monastery

Dakpo Tratsang, also known as **Dakpo Shedrubling**, was original a Karma Kargyu monastery belonging to the Zhamarpas. In 1589, Zhamarpa VI Chokyi Wangchuk (1584-1635) was enthroned here. Later in the 17th century, this establishment, like many other Karma Kagyu monasteries in Tibet, was converted to the Gelukpa tradition by Mongol force of arms. Many of the original buildings including the main temple have survived intact, and there is a recently restored debating courtyard. Accommodation and food are available here, or at the guesthouse in **Drumpa**, the county town, which lies alongside the monastery.

Chokhorgyel Monastery

A 35 kilometres drive from Gyatsa township on the north bank of the Brahmaputra (across the suspension bridge east of Drumpa) passes through the valley of the Terpulung-chu. Half way up this valley, at **Tselgyu**, there is an attractive village of stone houses with thatched and shingled roofs. The marshland of its upper reaches, known as the **Plain of Flowers (Metoktang)**, abounds with a rich diversity of flora and vegetation: rhododendron, poplar, willow, walnut, apricot, and medicinal herbs, including the highly valued caterpillar fungus (*Cordiceps sinensis*; *Tib* yartsa gunbu).

At **Chokhorgyel**, the headwaters are hemmed in by three peaks, abodes of the protector deities Zhidag (north), Shridevi (south), and Begtse (east), and three valleys diverge: the northwest route to Olka across Gyelung La pass and Loyul (three-days trekking distance); the northeast route to Lhamo Latso Lake (four hours); and the south route to Gyatsa.

The ruins of **Chokhorgyel Monastery** are extensive, including two large temples – the Lukhang and Tsuklakhang, and two colleges. The foundation dates from 1509, when Dalai Lama II Gendun Gyatso (1476-1542) had a hermitage and meditation cave here. The Dalai Lamas subsequently constructed a residence at the base of the northern peak, and would spend time here in the course of their visionary pilgrimages from Olka to Lhamo Latso Lake.

Lhamo Latso Lake

ལྷ་མོ་བླ་མཚོ

Getting there To reach the oracle lake from Chokhorgyel, it is necessary to trek for 4 hours. The trail passes below the ruins of **Nyingsaka Monastery**, and, crossing a stream, turns north at the base of **Mount Lhamonying** (abode of the protector Begtse). A sharp ascent leads, often through snow-covered ground, to an amphitheatre-shaped ridge (5,300 metres), and an ancient stone throne of the Dalai Lamas, dramatically overlooking the visionary lake, 150 metres below.

Lhamo Latso Lake is considered sacred to Gyelmo Makzorma, a form of the protectress Shridevi, and it is revered as the life-supporting talisman (*la-ne*) of the Dalai Lamas. Visions portending the circumstances of the rebirth of future Dalai Lamas and Panchen Lamas are observed in its sacred waters. For example, in 1933, the regent Reting Rinpoche had a vision of the present Dalai Lama's birthplace and circumstances in Amdo. There is a pilgrim's circuit around the shores of the lake and at the eastern extremity prayer flags mark the spot where Shridevi's shrine once stood.

Gyatsa County

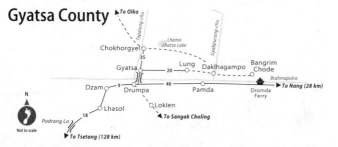

Trekking A four- to five-day trekking route from the north end of the lake also leads down into the Gyabpurong-chu valley, through the villages of Ba and Che, to reach Daklha Gampo monastery.

Daklha Gampo
Monastery

དྭགས་ལྷ་
སྒམ་པོ་དགོན་པ

The Kagyu monastery of **Daklha Gampo** lies on a ridge to the northeast of the eight-peaked Daklha Gampo mountain range, in the lower reaches of the Gyabpurong-chu valley. The distinctively contorted pinnacles of this range stand as an obvious landmark from the highway on the opposite bank of the Brahmaputra.

The complex was founded in 1121 by Gampopa Dakpo Lharje (1079-1153), on a site previously sanctified as a geomantic power place ('head of the ogress') by King Songtsen Gampo and transformed into a repository of *terma* by Padmasambhava. Gampopa came to meditate at the nearby **Namkading** after receiving the teachings and transmissions of the Kagyu lineage from Milarepa. He established three early chapels: **Jakhyil**, **Gomde Zimkhang** and **Chokhang Nyingma**; and gave instructions to his foremost students, who became the fountainheads of their great Kagyu lineages: Phakmodrupa Dorje Gyelpo, Karmapa I Dusum Khyenpa, and Seltong Shogom. They acquired their realizations in the many meditation caverns dotted across the range. Daklha Gampo is therefore revered as the primary Kagyu monastery for the teaching and practice of *Mahamudra* in Tibet, and it was carefully developed by the successive generations of Gampopa's familial lineage, such as Gampo Tsultrim Nyingpo, and those of his incarnation lineage, such as Gampopa Tashi Namgyel (1512-87). In 1718 the Dzungar armies sacked the monastery, but it was soon rebuilt, its national influence restored. A few chapels have been renovated following the more recent depradations of the 1960s, including original images of Avalokiteshvara and Cakrasamvara.

This region of Dakpo is also the birthplace of Karma Lingpa – one of Tibet's greatest treasure-finders (*terton*). During the 14th century he unearthed at Mount Gampodar within the Daklha Gampo range the *terma* of Padmasambhava, which has received most worldwide acclaim: *The Tibetan Book of the Dead (Bardo Thodol Chenmo)* and its cycle known as *Zhitro Gongpa Rangdrol*.

Getting there To reach the monastery drive east from Gyatsa township for 20 kilometres, hugging the river road as far as **Lung**. From here, there is a 6¼ hour trek to the monastery, via the villages of Rukhag Nyipa, and Ngakhang; but the trail is hard to find without the assistance of a local guide from Lung. Alternatively, there is a 2-day trek from **Bangrim Chode** monastery further east, accessible via the Dromda ferry on the Brahmaputra.

Nang County

Nang County ནང་རྫོང་

Nang county is the name given to the present administrative division of East
Dakpo, the principal gateway to the sacred mountain of Tsari, and the region
through which the Brahmaputra River cuts its way through an unnavigable 33
kilometres horse-shoe gorge as it flows towards Longpo and Kongpo. The county
extends along the main Tsetang-Menling highway for 79 kilometres, from
Dromda Druka ferry in the west (46 kilometres from Gyatsa), as far as Zhu in the
east. Both banks of the river are characterized here by windswept sandbanks
interspersed by small oases of walnut and apricot. The county capital is located at
Lang (Nang Dzong) where the gorge begins, 28 kilometres east of Dromda. The
north-flowing Kurab-chu, Lapu-chu and Kyemtong-chu tributaries all offer
trekking access to Tsari region in the south. By contrast, on the north bank of the
Brahmaputra, the only major valley is Arnaktang.

Nang County (19)
朗县
Nang Xian
Population: 12,097
Area: 6,477 sq km
Colour map M2, grid B5

Kurab-chu Valley

On the south bank of the Brahmaputra, commencing from **Dromda Druka**,
there is a trekking route to Sangak Choling, the southwest gateway to Tsari. The
route follows the Kurab-chu tributary upstream via **Ganden Rabten**
(seven kilometres), Kurab Namgyel (five kilometres), and Sinmonang, before
bifurcating. Take the east track, crossing the watershed passes of Gongmo La
pass (5,298 metres) and Kharpo La (5,001 metres). **Ganden Rabten Monastery** is a branch of Ganden Phuntsoling near Lhasa. At **Kurab Namgyel** you
can see the hilltop ruins of the dzong from which the whole Tsari was once
administered.

Back on the highway, at **Trungkhang Druka** (five kilometres east of
Dromda), there is a ferry crossing to **Lhenga** on the north bank of the
Brahmaputra. The birthplace of Dalai Lama XIII (1876-1933) lies four kilometres east of Lhenga at **Trungkhang**. The former residence of Tibet's previous spiritual and temporal leader is sealed at present.

Trungkhang

The small county town of **Lang** (Nang Dzong) is a riverside settlement, which
has grown up along the Brahmaputra's sharp bend. Guesthouse and simple
restaurant facilities are available.

Lang
Colour map 2, grid B5

Lang

From here, there are three routes: the
riverside highway to Nye and
Dungkar (33 kilometres), the
short-cut to Nye via Kongpo Nga La
pass (4,400 metres); and the inland
route, following the Lapu-chu valley
upstream to **Latok** township (18
kilometres).

Taking the last of these routes,
there is a scenic two-day trek to
Chozam, the main gateway to Tsari.
En route, you pass through the small
logging villages of Bara and Pelrab,
after which the trail bifurcates: the
east track leading alongside the beautiful forested alpine lake of **Tso**

Southern Tibet

Bunang and across Sur La pass (4,850 metres) to Chozam; and the west track crossing the Tangma La pass to **Chorten Namu** and thence to Chozam.

Dungkar Both the riverside highway and the Kongpo Nga La short-cut lead from Lang to Nye village and Dungkar township. A ferry leads across to **Dungkar monastery**, the seat of Tibet's celebrated contemporary historian, the late Dungkar Lobzang Trinle.

Dakpo Zhu Some 14 kilometres east of Dungkar, there is a turn-off, which leaves the highway at the entrance of the Kyemtong-chu valley. Following this road for a further two kilometres, you will arrive at **Dakpo Zhu**, a one time haunt of the Nyingmapa yogin Dzeng Dharmabodhi (1052-1136).

Kyemtong-chu Valley

Colour map 2, grid B5 The main motorable pilgrimage route to Tsari follows the Kyemtong-chu valley upstream, and across the Bibi La pass (4,785 metres) to Chozam and **Mikhyimdun**. North of Kyemdrong township on the east bank of the Kyemtong-chu, at **Lishan**, there is a large recently discovered archaeological site (815,000 square kilometres), including 184 tombs which have been dated to 700 CE. Above Kyemdrong township, there are trails leading up the valley through Shelrika towards Mount Dakpa Shelri. However, the road to Tsari, motorable for 34 kilometres, cuts southwest to leave the valley. It passes through a deep shrub-filled gorge to level out at an alpine riverside meadow near **Sumbatse**, and then ascends through conifer and rhododendron forest to cross the Bibi La. Lush meadows give way to stunning forests on the descent into **Mikhyimdun** (Tsari township).

Tsari ཙ་རི

Mount Dakpa Shelri (5,735 metres) and its environs in Tsari form one of Tibet's most revered pilgrimage circuits – generally ranking alongside those of Mount Kailiash and Mount Amnye Machen. For the Kagyu school in particular, Tsari is classed along with Mount Kailash and Lapchi Gang as one of the three essential power places of the meditational deity Cakrasamvara. Two of Cakrasamvara's 24 power-places mentioned in the *Root Tantra of Cakrasamvara* are said to be within Tsari, Caritra and Devikota.

This holy land of Mount Dakpa Shelri is described as having four gateways, associated with the four bodhisattvas: Manjushri (east), Vajrapani (south), Tara (west) and Avalokiteshvara (north). During the earliest phase of Buddhist propagation in Tibet, Padmasambhava and Vimalamitra (eighth to ninth century) are said to have entered through the southern gate, and made Tsari a repository of *terma*. Kambalapada and Bhusuku (10th-11th century) entered via the eastern gate. Tsangpa Gya-re Yeshe Dorje (1161-1211) entered through the western gate at the third attempt; and lastly Sonam Gyeltsen of Ralung entered via the northern gate. The four gateways may be identified respectively with Geli Shinya (south), Mikhyimdun (east), Sangak Choling/Podrang Yutso (west), and Chikchar (north).

The main impetus for the opening of the Tsari region as a sanctuary for meditation and focal point of pilgrimage came from Phakmodrupa Dorje Gyelpo (1110-70), who on the advice of Gampopa, encouraged his students to go there. The major sites have therefore come to be associated with Tsangpa Gya-re and his Drukpa Kagyu followers, and to a lesser extent with the Drigung and Karma Kagyu schools. As explained in the *Guidebook to Tsari*,

Tsari Nyingma Pilgrimage

The Tsari Nyingma pilgrimage around Mount Dakpa Shelri has three distinct routes: shortest, intermediate and longest. The longest and most arduous, known as **Tsari Rongkor**, took 10-15 days. It became an official pilgrimage at the behest of the Tibetan Government, and was held once every 12 years in a monkey year to commemorate the date of Tsangpa Gya-re's original opening of Tsari. Sometimes 100,000 people would participate. The shorter routes would be followed between April and September of any year. Dalai Lama XIII undertook the Tsari pilgrimage in person. Unfortunately, the route passed through Lhopa aboriginal territory in the south, and the government was often obliged to send an armed escort, notwithstanding oaths of fealty sworn by the natives. The route follows the Tsari-chu downstream from Chozam and Chikchar, via Mikhyimdun and on to its confluence with the Subansiri (Tib Shipasha) at Geli Shinya. It then follows the latter river upstream to its confluence with the Yulme-chu, before cutting northwest through the Yul-me valley to Yulto and Chozam. On the map the route therefore inscribes a diamond shape. At the present day it is impossible to complete the whole circuit since its southern tropical sections lie within the Indian territory of Arunachal Pradesh across a disputed frontier. The major sacred sites, which are all in the north, can still be visited, taking the lesser pilgrimage circuit via the Dolma La pass.

composed by Drukchen VIII Chokyi Nangwa (1768-1822), there are three distinct focal points in Tsari: **Mount Dakpa Shelri**, **Lake Tsokar**, and **Mount Tsari Sarma Tashijong**, which are likened to the parts of a symbolic vajra: the western prong, the central knob, and the eastern prong. Among these, the first two come within the **Old Tsari (Tsari Nyingma)** pilgrimage route, and the last within the **New Tsari (Tsari Sarpa)** pilgrimage route.

Chikchar Located on a beautifully forested mountain ridge above Chozam, Chikchar marks the beginning of all the pilgrimage circuits around Mount Dakpa Shelri. The blue and yellow mountain poppies (*Meconopsis*) which are well-known throughout the higher elevations of East Tibet are in evidence here. And it was here, in close proximity to the sacred snow peak, that in the 12th century Tsangpa Gya-re had a vision of the Cakrasamvara assemblage and consecrated the locale. In the 13th century, after the arrival of Sonam Gyeltsen of Ralung and many hermits who left the neighbouring districts of Dakpo and Kongpo to avoid an epidemic, Drukpa Kagyu monasteries were founded within the Chikchar valley at Densa Pangmo, Uripangmo, and Gopangmo. The most important building, however, was the **Dorje Phakmo Lhakhang**, founded between 1567-74 by Drukchen Pema Karpo (1527-92) at Bodo or Bokhung Zhungdo, where Tsangpa Gya-re had previously had a vision of the deity Simhavaktra becoming absorbed into the rocks. Northwest of Chikchar, at **Dotsen Tsuklakhang**, there were stones representing the sexual organs of Cakrasamvara and his consort Vajravarahi, which became a focal point of pilgrimage for childless couples. Formerly, no pilgrims were allowed to ride their horses beyond Chikchar, but a jeep road now extends down the Tsari-chu valley towards **Lo Mikhyimdun** (Tsari township) on the present Indian frontier.

Lo Mikhyimdun and Lake Tsari Tsokar Pilgrims following the longest pilgrimage in former times would trek to **Lo Mikhyimdun**, and thence continue downstream to the Subansiri confluence. Below **Chikchar**, the Tsari-chu enters a narrow gorge, and around **Poso Sumdo** the landscape abounds in

Tsari Nyingma

Southern Tibet

rhododendrons, hemlock and juniper. (A trail from here leads across Bibi La pass to Kyemtong, see above, page 224.) The border township of **Lo Mikhyimdun** is now the site of an army garrison; and the local population is more than half Lhopa. Cultivated fields of barley and potatoes are found beyond this point. From here, there is an essential two-day trek to the sacred lake of Tsari Tsokar, further east.

Tsari Tsokar is a stunningly beautiful clear milky lake, surrounded by glaciers and forested shorelines. It was opened for meditation and pilgrimage by Karmapa III Rangjung Dorje (1284-1339) and Karmapa IV Rolpei Dorje (1340-83), and the slopes around its shores harbour meditation grottoes such as the **Khyungtsang Puk**.

The Inner Pilgrimage Circuit (Kyilkhor) This seven-day trek, which is still followed at the present day, is best undertaken between July-September. In spring and autumn, the passes may be closed by snow. The route ascends the Chikchar valley to **Lapu**, location of Kambalapada's Lawapuk cave and the abode of the protectress Dorje Yudronma. Higher up there is the hermitage of Drukchen V Paksam Wangpo (1593-1641). It then crosses the **Dolma La** pass (4,910 metres) to the talismanic lake of Cakrasamvara, the **Demchok Latso**, and the **Miphak Gonpo** ravine. No female pilgrims were traditionally allowed to venture beyond the pass. Ascending the glacial Shakam La pass (4,910 metres), skirting en route a lake sacred to Avalokiteshvara, the trail then continues southwest, to Droma La (4,390 metres) and Go La passes, before reaching **Podrang**, high above the east bank of the Yulme-chu River. Here is the most sacred of Tsari's many lakes, the **Podrang Yutso**, revered as the talismanic lake of Vajravarahi, where Tsangpa Gya-re and Gotsangpa both meditated. The latter's hermitage is above the lake, at **Namkapuk**, on the slopes of Mount Khandro Doi Lhakhang.

From Podrang the route turns sharply north, following the Yulme-chu upstream. It crosses Tabgyu La pass (4,700 metres) to enter the **Taktsang** ravine (4,025 metres), and the Shadu La pass (4,725 metres). Just beyond, at **Kaladungtso Lake**, there is the hermitage of the yogin Dungtso Repa.

The trail then descends into the **Domtsang** ravine, from which point women may again participate in the pilgrimage, and passing through **Chaktang Trang**, it reaches in succession **Yul-me** (3,500 metres) and **Yulto** (4,025 metres) villages. This is the stronghold of the Drigung Kagyu school at

Tsari Nyingma

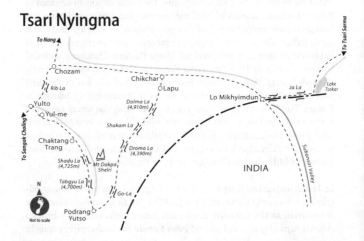

Tsari, and there is a temple dedicated to Vajravarahi.

From Yulto, there is a trek southwest across the Takar La (5,090 metres) and the Kyu valley to Sangak Choling (see above, page 198). The main trail, however, turns northeast to reach the **Chozam** plain, via either the Dorje Drak La or Rib La pass.

Chozam, a village of shingled stone houses, marks the end of the Tsari pilgrimage; and there are access points from here to the main highway in Dakpo (Kurab Namgyel, Lang, and Zhu). The lush plains of **Senguti**, which extend for some 10 kilometres below Chozam and alongside the meandering headwaters of the Tsari-chu, abound in silver firs, primulas, rhododendrons, honeysuckle, and so forth.

Tsari Sarma is the name given to the sacred wildlife sanctuary around the headwaters of the Nelung Phu-chu, which flows northeast to join the Brahmaputra in Menling county. There are three points of access: a six-day trek from Kyemtong via the Lang La pass (4,815 metres), Nepar village, and the upper reaches of the Nelung Phu-chu; a four-day trek from Nelung township on the highway in Menling county; or a shorter trek from Lake Tsari Tsokar (see above, page 225) via the Langtsang La pass and Langong. **Tsari Sarma**

The sanctuary of **Tsari Sarma** was founded by Rigdzin Kumaradza (1266-1343), a lineage-holder of the Nyingmapa school and the principal teacher of Longchen Rabjampa. Until recent times, the prohibition on hunting in this region was strictly enforced, and there was an abundance of wildlife: pheasants, deer, wild sheep, musk deer, wolves, and foxes. The three-day pilgrimage around Tsari Sarma commences from **Tashijong** village, passing the sacred lakes of **Yutso Sarma** and **Tsonyam Sarma**, abode of secret dakinis. To the south, the Lo La pass leads across the Assamese Himalayas (Pachakshiri) into the Indian state of Arunachal Pradesh. The border remains firmly closed to outsiders.

Southern Tibet

Menling County སྨན་གླིང་

*Menling county is the name currently given to the old districts of **Longpo** and **Lower Kongpo**, south of the Brahmaputra. It extends for 195 kilometres, from a small estuary 13 kilometres east of Dakpo Zhu, as far as Pe township in Lower Kongpo, where the Brahmaputra is channelled through a mighty gorge between Mounts Namchak Barwa and Gyala Pelri at the eastern extremity of the Himalayas. At this point, the river changes its eastern course irrevocably, first to the north and then abruptly to the southwest. The county capital is located at **Dungdor**; now encorporated within Nyangtri (rather than Lhokha) district. From here Tsetang lies 368 kilometres due west, and Lhasa 550 kilometres (via Bayi and Gyamda). The successive lateral valleys extending south from the Brahmaputra towards the Indian border are home to the tribal Monpa and Lhopa populations.*

Menling County (20)
米林县
Mainling
Population: 15,015
Area: 8,718 sq km
Colour map 2, grid B5

Longpo

The highway from East Dakpo enters Longpo 13 kilometres east of Dakpo Zhu and after 42 kilometres reaches Orong township in Orong valley. There are a number of sites in Longpo connected with the Nyingmapa *terton* Sangye Lingpa of Kongpo (1340-96), who, throughout his life, also maintained close connections with the Karma Kagyu tradition. At **Jagoshong**, he discovered *terma* concerning Mahakarunika and the *Extraction of Elixirs* (*chulen*). In the Orong area,

Orong & Nelung
Colour map 2, grid C2

at **Orsho Lungdrom**, he unearthed a precious gemstone called 'tiger-meat god'; and in the **Nelung** township area, 22 kilometres further east, the site at Drongsar where he first encountered Karmapa IV Rolpei Dorje is still revered. You can trek from Nelung to Tsari Sarma (see above, page 227).

Tashi Rabden   On the north bank of the Brahmaputra, the main place of interest is the Tashi Rabden Monastery, in the Tashi Rabden Phu-chu valley, which once housed 130 monks. There are also further treasure-sites associated with Sangye Lingpa – at **Longpo Kada Trang** and **Longpo Jangde Bumpa**. On the south bank, opposite the confluence of the Tashi Rabden-chu, is the Yulsum Phu-chu valley, which once marked the western extremity of Kongpo.

Dungdor   Dungdor, the county capital, is located 41 kilometres downstream from
(Menling   Nelung. The climate is warm and humid; and the countryside quite thickly for-
Dzong)   ested with conifers and junipers.

Essentials Here, there is a government guesthouse, pleasantly constructed of wood, and hot water for washing is available in an outhouse. Sichuan restaurants, Chinese shops, Tibetan market stalls and karaoke bars provide some fascination for the Lhopa tribal visitors.

Inland from Dungdor, there is a military road following the Neyul Phu-chu upstream for 21 kilometres to **Lago Zampa bridge**, and thence to the Neyul Dom La and Dungkar La passes, which lead across the closed border into India.
    Further east, at **Shoga**, there is a stone footprint of Padmasambhava and a ruined stupa, which once rotated at the sound of the Vajra Guru mantra. From here, there is another trail following the Shoga Phu-chu upstream to Shoga La pass, and the Indian border; and at Gangka, 19 kilometres east of Dungdor, the large **Gangka Zamchen** suspension bridge leads over to the north bank of the Brahmaputra. This last bridge is also rumoured to have a military underpass, ensuring that access to the frontier cannot be cut off.

Lower Kongpo

If you cross the Gangka Zamchen bridge to the north bank, you will reach the area of Middle Kongpo and Upper Kongpo (see below, page 240). Continuing, instead, on the south bank, where the road rapidly deteriorates, you will bypass the lateral valleys of **Bamdrong** and **Bhaga**, which respectively lead a short distance to Lado La and Bhaga La passes on the Indian border. The latter route has an important military installation, and an extremely well-lit and well-maintained military road.

Menling

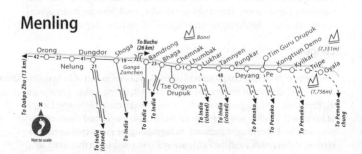

Driving along the south bank from Gangka Zamchen bridge, notice on the **Tse Orgyen** opposite bank, the large estuary of the Nyang-chu, which flows into the **Drupuk** Brahmaputra from the north, alongside the town of Nyangtri, and in the shadows of the sacred mountain, Kongpo Bonri. In the hills high above Chemnak, is the meditation cave of **Tse Orgyen Drupuk**.

At this site in the eighth century, Padmasambhava gave a longevity-empowerment to an old woman who was the only one able to reach the cave and receive the empowerment. The juniper tree next to the cave is said to have sprung from his *khatvanga*. Inside the cave is a 'self-arising' Padmasambhava image in stone and a nectar-producing rock. Older people from Chemnak claim to have seen nectar coming out of the rock. On the altar lies a new brass image of Padmasambhava.

On the ascent to the cave there are several decaying stupas and a sacred stone reputedly shaped like a dying person on all fours, prostrating before a lama with two vultures in attendance, one on either side. Once there was also a temple dedicated to Amitayus, named **Lungtok Chime Lhakhang**, where a stupa made from Padmasambhava's nasal blood (**Shangtrak Chorten**) was preserved.

Getting there After the military installations of Bhaga and before reaching the township of Chemnak (Chabnak), there is a turn-off on the right, which leads southwest and close to the Indian border.

The Gelukpa monastery of Chemnak, also called **Demo Chemnak**, is an impos- **Chemnak** ing building with a shingled roof, situated on a wooded ridge above the road. **(Chabnak)** The temple was restored in 1983. An ante-chamber has fine murals depicting the **Monastery** Four Guardian Kings and the protectors: Six-armed Mahakala, Bhairava, Dharmaraja, and Shukden. Within the main **assembly hall**, there are 21 tangkas and a series of murals depicting the Thirty-five Buddhas of Confession. The main images, behind the throne, are of Maitreya, flanked by a 'speaking' image also of Maitreya, and Tsongkhapa with his foremost students, flanked by two forms of Avalokiteshvara. Along the left wall are images of Padmasambhava with Shantaraksita and King Trisong Detsen; while the right wall has a very large image of Padmasambhava in the form Nangsi Zlinon. The **inner sanctum** contains 1,000 small images of Tsongkhapa. The imagery reflects the eclectic nature of the community at Chemnak, who include followers of the late Dudjom Rinpoche, head of the Nyingma school, among their numbers.

Getting there Chemnak township lies 23 kilometres east of the Gangka Zamchen bridge. It is also possible to reach Chemnak by coracle from Karma (Tsela Dzong) on the northern bank of the Brahmaputra below Drime Kunden.

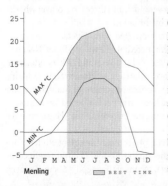

Menling

About one kilometre east of **Chemnak to Pe** Chemnak, there is a coracle ferry at **Lhumbak** village; and further east, at **Luzhar**, a dirt track leads down to a cable ferry across the Brahmaputra. Both of these crossings offer access to important sites on the north bank, such as Mount Bonri, Demo Chemkar monastery, Menri, Chu Jowo, and Nyangtri, on which see below, page 232. Inland from the ferry crossing on the south bank, a trail follows the Luzhar phu-chu

Southern Tibet

Black Flayed Hide and Mosquitoes

Padmasambhava encountered Yamsha Nakpo (Black Flayed Hide) at Chaktak Bumpu. According to the Guru's biography, when the demon blocked his passage by placing one foot firmly on Mount Dozhong La and the other on Mount Gyela Pelri, the Guru clapped his hands in astonishment, making the sound "Chaktak Bumbu". He promptly turned into a fish which swam upstream and then into a bird. Yamsha Nakpo turned into a bird of prey and went in swift pursuit, but the Guru evaded his grasp by vanishing into the cave-wall (hence the name of the cave). The demon could not follow. Padmasambhava remained in meditation in the cave for 3 years, 3 months and 3 days until he could manifest signs of accomplishment.* He then pierced the cave-wall with his ritual dagger*, stabbing the demon in the process. The stab-mark can still be seen above the altar.

Local informants further explain that Padmasambhava also tamed the wild beasts of Tim Gura Drupuk, including many man-biting birds, and instead permitted the relatively minor irritation of midges and mosquitoes which still thrive here!

---

upstream to Luzhar La pass and the Indian border.

After Luzhar, the road passes through **Tamnyen** township, where glacial streams burst forth from Tamnyen La pass (on the Indian border) to devastate the motorable surface. At **Pungkar**, there is a small general store, and rudimentary guesthouse facilities. Then, approaching **Deyang**, where flash seasonal flooding again is a serious hazard, there is a trail leading up to Deyang La on the border. Finally, at **Pe** township, 48 kilometres from Chemnak, there is a Chinese compound, with medical facilities, a small guesthouse and some supplies. Better to camp near the Tibetan village of Pe, where there are excellent campsites, offering wonderful majestic views of **Mount Namchak Barwa** (7,756 metres), until 1992 the world's highest unclimbed peak. Here, the Brahmaputra narrows to only 100 metres; and there are ferry boats crossing to Timpei on the north bank.

Tim Guru Drupuk Above the village of **Timpei** in Yulsum district on the north bank of the Brahmaputra and dominated to the southeast by Mount Namchak Barwa are the celebrated caves where Padmasambhava and his students practised meditation in the eighth century. Outside the main cave if one looks across the river one will see a group of prayer-flags marking the site called **Chaktak Bumbu**. This is where Padmasambhava reputedly encountered the demon Yamsha Nakpo (Black Flayed Hide).

The cave hermitage of **Tim Guru Drubpuk**, rebuilt under the guidance of Nakpo Zilnon Rinpoche of Buchu in Kongpo, is approached via a steep flight of steps. An **ante-chamber** contains a verandah and three large prayer wheels. Within the temple, which is cared for by the old Khampa ladies of Timpei village, the **chapel** has a single column supported by a Tibetan-style capital (*zhu*). The window on the right offers incredible views of Mount Nakchak Barwa. Tangkas, including two of the Peaceful and Wrathful Deities, adorn the walls, and on the left there is the entrance to the **cave** – an inner recess, containing three images of Padmasambhava, concealed images of Mandarava and Yeshe Tsogyel, and in the centre of the floor an as yet unopened *terma* repository. The aperture in the cave wall forming the shape of a ritual dagger is above the *terma* rock.

As well as Padmasambhava, several of his most important students are said to have occupied other caves higher up the hillside. There are eight caves altogether, those of Padmasambhava, Namkei Nyingpo, Yeshe Tsogyel,

Tamdrin Tulku, Chung Tulku, Vairotsana, Guru Drakpo and Senge Dongma, while the last is called Tsalung Jangsa (the place where yogic exercises were practised).

From Tim Guru Drubpuk, there is a three-day trekking route via Sekundo and Nyima La pass to **Dongpatral** near the Kongpo to Po-me highway. The route abounds in diverse species of flowers.

On the south bank of the Brahmaputra, the motorable road continues beyond **Kongtsun Demo**
Pe for a few kilometres as far as **Kyilkar**, passing beyond the approach to
Dozhong La pass (4,115 metres) and towards Mount Namchak Barwa. This is
the district called **Yulsum Trenadong** ('defile where three regions of Puwo,
Kongpo and Pemako converge'). It marks the beginning of the Brahmaputra
rapids. Here, Padmasambhava is said to have subdued one of the 12 subterra-
nean goddesses (*Tenma Chunyi*) of Tibet, and nearby there is a cave known as
Trekar Drupuk where Padmasambhava stayed in meditation.

The name Kongtsun Demo has also been identified as the secret name for
the deity Dorje Pokham Kyong. According to various descriptions she is either
black or cherry-brown in colour with gold and turquoise head ornaments,
holding a vessel of blood or a divination arrow and chest. She rides a horse with
a turquoise mane, or a garuda.

The site at the present time shows few signs of repair. There is a small pilgrim's resthouse consisting of a single room, beside which a large prayer flag
has been erected.

The Pepung La pass above Pungkar, the Dozhong La pass (4,115 metres) **Mount**
above Pe township, and the Nam La pass (5,225 metres) above Kyilkar all give **Namchak Barwa**
access to the hidden valley of **Pemako** in Metok county (see below, page 407).

The motorable road on the south bank of the Brahmaputra comes to an
end at Kyilkar, but a three-day trekking route continues on to **Gyala**, via Tripe,
which is the base camp for **Mount Namchak Barwa** (7,756 metres), and
Lungpe. The **Nambulung** valley before Tripe also leads to Mount Namchak
Barwa, and it is revered as an abode of the epic hero Ling Gesar. This mountain
is the highest peak of the East Himalayas; and it has a towering snow pinnacle
shaped like a ritual dagger (*phurba*), for which reason it is known as 'blazing
meteorite' (*namchak barwa*) in as much as the best ritual daggers are made of
meteorite. Sanctified as a repository of *terma* – some of which were discovered
by Sangye Lingpa (1340-96) and others by Dudul Dorje (1615-72), the mountain remained unclimbed until a Japanese expedition of 1992 astonishingly
scaled its snow pinnacle.

Gyala village is situated on a plain above the river which entails a tough climb up **Gyala Shinje**
the Tsalung cliff-face. The white sands of the river bank below Gyala offer an **Badong**
attractive camp site. Here the river is navigable, and on the far bank, at **Gyala
Shinje Badong**, there is the **Dampa Chokhang** temple, dedicated to Yama
Dharmaraja, the 'lord of death' (*Tib* Shinje Chogyel), which contains an image
of Padmasambhava. Alongside the derelict temple there are five rocks shaped
like banners with water streaming down between them. Behind the waterfalls, a
rock image of Yama in either black or white form is visible during the spring and
autumn when the river level is at its lowest. Here, the *terton* Sangye Lingpa discovered his Yamantaka texts, entitled *Yamantaka Lord of Life* (*Shinje Tsedak*).

Getting there   The cave and its adjacent temple can be reached by dug-out log
boat. From the north bank, at **Pe Nub** village, the 2-day Bonpo pilgrimage circuit of
Mount Gyala Pelri (7,151 metres) begins.

Southern Tibet

The Brahmaputra Gorges

During the winter when the Brahmaputra is at its lowest level it is possible to undertake the extremely difficult five-day trek to **Pemakochung**, following the course of the surging rapids through one of the world's deepest gorges, formed by the Namchak Barwa and Gyala Pelri massives, which are only 21 kilometres apart. Within a contorted stretch of 45 kilometres, the river plunges 3,000 metres to the Pemako foothills and the Indian plains beyond.

The trail passes the hot springs of Kenda-chu, the Gotsangpa Drupuk, the Nyuksang cliff, and the Senge Dzong cliff. Before Pemakochung, the trail hugs the river bank (winter access only), and passes the **Kinthup Falls**. At Pemakochung itself, there is a small Nyingmapa monastery. Two days further trekking downstream is the **Drakpuk Kawasum Cave**, repository of the key and gateway to the 'hidden valley' of Pemako. Beyond this point, the virtually impenetrable trail follows the river's course as it is propelled north via a series of mighty cascades, including the **Rainbow Falls**, discovered by Kingdon-Ward in 1924. On 8 November 1998, Ian Baker led an expedition sponsored by the National Geographic Society through the gorge, where it was determined that the Rainbow Falls plunged 25 metres and that further on through a virtually impenetrable 8 kilometres stretch of twisting gorge there is another 30-35 cataract which they named the Hidden Falls. Here the Brahmaputra torrent narrows to only 20 metres. The gorge contains subtropical flora, pine, spruce, hemlock, rhododendron, craggy fir and species of fauna such as the takin, which are also found in neighbouring Bhutan. The region is sparsely inhabited by Lhopa peoples. Crossing Sordem La pass and Karma La pass (2,560 metres), the trail eventually reaches **Tongdem**, where the river converges with the Po Tsangpo in Po-me county (see below, page 405).

Nyangtri County ཉང་ཁྲི

Nyangtri County (21)
林芝县
Nyingchi
Population: 30,157
Area: 9,634 sq km
Colour map 2, grid B6

*Kongpo is the name given to the Nyang-chu River valley and the area of the Brahmaputra into which it flows, extending from the high Mamzhong La pass (5,000 metres) west of Gyamda to Menling in the southwest and the massive snow peaks of Namchak Barwa and Gyala Pelri in the southeast. It may for practical purposes be divided into three areas: **Lower Kongpo** includes the sites on the south bank of the Brahmaputra, from Menling to Pemakochung, which have already been described. **Middle Kongpo** includes the sites on the north bank of the Brahmaputra and the Nyang-chu River and its estuary below Bepa; and **Upper Kongpo** includes the upper reaches of the Nyang-chu from Bepa to Mamzhong La and Kongpo Bar La passes. Middle Kongpo corresponds to present day Nyangtri county, and Upper Kongpo to Gyamda county.*

The capital of Nyangtri county (nowadays mispronounced and misspelt Nyingtri) was formerly located at **Nyangtri**, a small town on the east bank of the Nyang-chu estuary, but its role has in recent years been increasingly usurped by the city of **Bayi**, 19 kilometres to the north. As its name suggests, Bayi (1 August, ie Chinese Army Day) was originally a military base, which has undergone rapid development and is now the preferred settlement for Chinese immigrants, since it is

Nyangtri County

To Gyamda (69 km)
Bepa
58
Bayi
Serkhyim La
Tongjuk
46
To Po-me
Lamaling
Gomga Zamchen
29
19
32
Chu Jowo
Buchu
26
Luding
Mnt Bonri
To Dungdor (19 km)
To Pe (71 km)
Nyangtri
Brahmaputra
To Tim Guru Drupuk

N

Not to scale

considerably lower than Lhasa and has a pleasant climate. Bayi is now the capital of the recently formed Nyangtri District, which includes the seven counties of Menling, Nyangtri, Gyamda, Nang, Metok, Po-me and Dzayul. From Dungdor (Menling Dzong) to Bayi via the Gangka Zamchen bridge the distance is 74 kilometres.

Getting there From Lhasa to Bayi via Gyamda the distance is 476 kilometres; from Bayi to Nyangtri 19 kilometres; and from Bayi to Po-me 226 kilometres.

Middle Kongpo

Driving across Gangka Zamchen bridge from Dungdor (Menling), Buchu township, on the west side of the Nyang-chu estuary, will be reached after 26 kilometres.

The golden roof of **Buchu Sergyi Lhakhang** is visible from afar, on the east side of the three kilometres wide estuary at Nyangtri, and on the south bank of the Brahmaputra, near Chemnak. This is the most ancient Buddhist shrine in Kongpo and one of four 'border taming' temples (Tadul Lhakhang) built by King Songtsen Gampo in the seventh century. It was constructed according to geomantic theory on the right elbow of the ogress who represented the Tibetan landscape. Originally therefore the temple was associated with the Nyingma tradition. By the 17th century, however, three schools of Buddhism had developed a strong presence in Buchu valley, namely the Drukpa Kagyu at Do Chorten, the Nyingmapa at Dechenteng, and the Gelukpa at Buchu Sergyi Lhakhang itself. Later, the temple was formally adopted by the Gelukpa in the time of the regent Demo Rinpoche (r 1886-95). However, there have only been eight monks based at Buchu in recent years.

The temple has two storeys, surmounted by a golden roof. On the lower level, it formerly contained images of the Eight Manifestations of Padmasambhava and upstairs were eight images of Amitayus. These latter have not yet been restored, and of the eight manifestations, only the lower part of the large Padmasambhava survives with mantra-core (*zungjuk*) intact.

The outer structure of the building was protected in the 1960s when it was used as a granary. Around the outer walls are 50 prayer wheels. Within the gates, there is a courtyard with a small flower garden and an incense burner. An **ante-chamber** contains inscriptions on the left and right entrances, outlining the history of the temple, and murals depicting Shridevi and Dorje Lekpa (left), Damchen Karnak, Kongtsun Demo, and the Wheel of Rebirth (right), and the Four Guardian Kings (front). On the right side there is also a large prayer wheel.

Beyond the ante-chamber, there are two main halls. The two-pillared **outer hall** contains the volumes of the *Kangyur* and *Tangyur*, a magnificent but rarely seen image of Padmasambhava in the standing form called Pema Totrengtsal (right side), smaller images of Amitabha and White Tara (left side), the protectors Dorje Lekpa and Kongtsun Demo, and 1,000 small images of Shakyamuni Buddha. In a glass case to the left of these there is the 'life-supporting stone' (*lado*) of the oath-bound protector of the temple. It has a hole, reputedly pierced in former times by Padmasambhava's ritual dagger.

The **inner hall** contains images of Padmasambhava, Shantaraksita and King Trisong Detsen, and (flanking the altar), images of Songtsen Gampo and Mahakarunika. Behind the main altar on a circumambulatory path is a 'self-arising' *terma* stone (*rangjung terdo*), dating from the era of King Songtsen Gampo. It has a hole in the middle and is now used as a butter-lamp offering. The rear wall has small images of the Thousand Buddhas; and in the right corner, adjacent to the door, is a finely decorated *torma*-offering shrine.

Buchu Sergyi Lhakhang

བུ་ཆུ་གསེར་གྱི་ལྷ་ཁང་

Southern Tibet

The Zangdok Pelri Temple at Lamaling

Southern Tibet

Lamaling
(Zangdok Pelri Monastery)
Behind Buchu on the ridge of a low-lying hill called **Norburi** is Lamaling, the main seat of the late Dudjom Rinpoche (1904-87), head of the Nyingma school. The original temple was built on the hilltop in Zangdok Pelri style, but destroyed by an earthquake in 1930. The second, 20 square metres and smaller in size, was then constructed on the tableland below. When the earlier temple was destroyed, the 'life-supporting' stone (*lado*) of Buchu reputedly moved and this was seen as an omen. Then, when Dudjom Rinpoche performed certain ceremonies outside the new building, a three-horned goat is said to have appeared, wandered up and down, and vanished into a stone, which can still be seen in front of the ruined temple. The new temple was destroyed during the 60s. In 1987, its ruined walls still bore the fingerprints of Dudjom Rinpoche's son Dorje Pasang, who was killed at that time.

The only extant original image from Lamaling is of Mahottara Heruka. It is kept along with a stone footprint of Padmasambhava. A Dorje Trolo stupa was erected to the west of the ruined temple walls in 1987; and since 1989, restoration began in earnest under the supervision of Dudjom Rinpoche's daughter Semo Dechen and her husband, Lama Chonyi Rinpoche. An exquisite **Zangdok Pelri Temple** and garden complex has been newly constructed on the hillside, and a motorable road now links Lamaling with the Buchu valley below. The new images of Lamaling represent the best metal casting tradition of the artisans from Chamdo.

Dechenteng Monastery
Southwest of Lamaling in the direction of Drime Kunden, and separated from it by a small evergreen forest is a branch monastery of Mindroling, called **Dechenteng**. The site was donated by Mindroling to the late Dudjom Rinpoche, and was used by him as the venue for an important series of empowerments (*Rinchen Terdzo*) on one occasion. As in the case of Lamaling, the original structure was destroyed by the 1930 earthquake, and then replaced by a smaller building. At present the site is overgrown by incarvelia flowers and walnut trees.

Chokhorling Monastery
Southwest of Lamaling and below the abode of Drime Kunden are the ruins of two monasteries bearing the name of Chokhorling; one is Nyingma, the other known as **Ganden Chokhorling** is a branch of Sera. The latter, a 19th century temple founded by Nyiden Loyang, had 100 monks. Huge tangkas were once hung out from the temple walls during religious dance performances. Now its ruined walls have magnificent frescoes of the Buddhas of the Three Times and a Wheel of Rebirth, which survived despite their exposure to the elements.

Drime Kunden: The Compassionate Prince

Prince Vasantara (Drime Kunden), as recounted in a sutra and in a later opera bearing his name, was an emanation of Avalokiteshvara sent into exile by his father for giving a precious gemstone to an enemy. In the course of his wanderings, Drime Kunden reputedly lived for 12 years in a hermitage behind the waterfall, formed of his own tears. When Drime Kunden first arrived in Kongpo a yogin emerged from the woods and asked whence he had come. He answered, saying he had been sent there by his father. The yogin recognized him and asked him to stay.

As a bodhisattva, he tamed the wild tigers and bears which previously ate stray humans and he made them respect human life. After 12 years he gave his final teaching to the beasts, saying that as long as they were to practice loving kindness and compassion his presence or absence would make no difference.

Above Chokhorling is a beautiful waterfall concealing the Kongpo retreat of the legendary compassionate prince Vasantara (Drime Kunden).

Drime Kunden Hermitage

On the ascent to the waterfall and hermitage, you pass many important sites. The rocks and groves are identified with major events in the life of Drime Kunden. Ascending from Chokhorling one first passes his protector shrine, a bank of rhododendron flowers, and a series of his footprints, handprints and knee-prints in stone. Higher up the hillside, there is a spring, the water of which he brought forth when Ma Khandro offered him ale to drink. The water is said to benefit the eyesight, the significance lying in the legend that Drime Kunden's own sight was restored after he had offered up his own eyes. The waterfall itself is said to benefit bathers to the extent of an empowerment ceremony received by 108 monks. Above the waterfall is the hermitage of Drime Kunden's wife, Tsampo Mendrel Tsema. It comprises a dakinis' dancing platform and a cave where pregnant women go to find omens. If the cave closes behind them, remedies have to be applied to avoid stillbirth or miscarriage and perhaps the mother's death.

In the **main hermitage** is a footprint of Drime Kunden covered by a stone. It also contains a tangka of White Tara which, when regarded purely without clinging, enables one to see the deity rather than the tangka. During each fourth month a fasting ceremony is held here. Opposite this hermitage is the residence of the protector, Chokyong Jarok Dongchen, and a 'self-arising' rock shaped like the *kalantaka* bird which would bring messages from Drime Kunden's parents. Above the hermitage, the circumambulation of the Pabri mountain (4,350 metres) is said to have the same blessing as 10 million recitations of the *Vajra Guru* mantra.

In a clearing, on the descent, is a stupa below which there is a footprint and imprint of the seat where Drime Kunden would teach birds and wild beasts. The tree above the seat served as a canopy at that time. Nearby there are also the elbow-prints and handprints of his wife, who waited for him during this final teaching.

From Chokhorling and Drime Kunden, the road leads down to the village of **Karma**, near the ruins of **Tsela Dzong** (2,955 metres), and the main road to Dungdor (Menling). From Karma, there is also a coracle ferry to Chukhor on the east side of the Nyang-chu estuary, and to Chemnak on the south bank of the Brahmaputra.

Bayi

Phone code: 86-894
Colour map 2, B6

Following the road from Buchu along the west bank of the Nyang-chu for 29 kilometres, you will reach Bayi. The village of **Drakchi**, which once occupied this strategic site, has been completely absorbed by the recent urban development. The current population, largely Chinese, exceeds 25,000. Here, the **Bayi Zamchen** bridge spans the Nyang-chu River.

Ins and outs The bus station is located to the south of the roundabout on the Lhasa-Nyangtri road.

Approaching the town, before the bridge, you will pass the College of Agriculture and Animal Husbandry (Zhingdrok Lobdra) on the left. This complex contains the *Oasis Hotel*. A temple under the supervision of Tibet's great historian, Dungkar Lobzang Trinle, is nearby.

Crossing the long bridge, you then enter the main part of town on the east bank of the Nyang-chu. The main roads of Bayi form a grid pattern, with two north-south streets intersected by two east-west streets. The north-south street immediately across the bridge has a number of small general stores, several Sichuan restaurants, a cinema and several late-night karaoke establishments.

Two streets branch off this road, the first leading east towards an intersection with the main Lhasa-Nyangtri road. At that intersection there is the four-storeyed *Government Guesthouse*. The second turn-off leads east into the main commercial street. Continuing along this commercial thoroughfare, you reach the town's major crossroads, where there is a large roundabout. The Government Buildings and the Bus Station are to the south, the Post Office and Xinhua Bookstore are on the east, and a high-rise modern department store with large display windows is on the east. Electrical goods are available here. From this crossroad, the main road to Lhasa (476 kilometres) runs north, passing the *Government Guesthouse* on the left, and the main road to Nyangtri (19 kilometres) runs south, passing the Nyangtri Textile Factory on the right.

Excursions A short distance east of Bayi town is **Mount Pelri**, a sacred peak from whose summit Padmasambhava reputedly dried up a lake covering the valley below, to ensure the region's future habitation. Pilgrims circumambulate the mountain in two to three hours, paying their respects to Padmasambhava's rock handprint,

Bayi

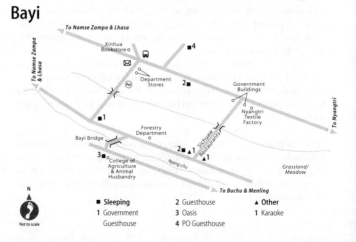

To Namse Zampa & Lhasa

To Namse Zampa & Lhasa

Xinhua Bookstore

Department Stores

Government Buildings

Nyangtri Textile Factory

Forestry Department

Bayi Bridge

College of Agriculture & Animal Husbandry

Nyang-chu

Grassland/ Meadow

To Nyangtri

To Buchu & Menling

N

Not to scale

■ **Sleeping**	2 Guesthouse	▲ **Other**
1 Government Guesthouse	3 Oasis	1 Karaoke
	4 PO Guesthouse	

Karaoke: the end of Tibetan songs?

Walking through the streets of any town or city in Tibet during the evening, look out for the neon lights flashing above a darkened doorway, and you will have found the local karaoke parlour. Often the legend **OK** boldly pulsates above the entrance. There are upmarket and downmarket sorts, but one thing is certain: the remarkable pervasiveness of this popular Asian pastime has taken hold even in the most remote places in Tibet since 1991. The large expensive establishments often have spacious dance floors, fluorescent strobe lighting, multicoloured smoke effects, and disco or live Chinese pop and dance music interspersed with the actual karaoke. The disco formation dance known as "thirty-six" (Ch sansi-liu), in which a large group of dancers pirouette in unison is always popular. The big moment comes when some budding impresario orders and pays for a requested song, and then takes the floor, microphone in hand to croon the latest number from Taipei, Hong Kong or mainland China, or perhaps a long-standing favourite. A good turn is rewarded by generous applause and the gift of a scented artificial flower. Tibetans often surpass the Chinese immigrants in their renditions of these Chinese songs, and couples take to the dance floor, accompanying the soloist. The karaoke repertoire includes a few pleasant duets; but, alas, no Tibetan music. In fact, there is a danger that traditional Tibetan singing which still has great popularity will be eclipsed by this all-powerful medium. Some speculate that the plain-clothed public security policemen intentionally run the show, and it is true that in this environment many of them become the most congenial of drinking companions. The best hope for Tibetan popular song at this juncture is that the karaoke medium can be adapted to the advantage of the Tibetans as well as for the promotion of popular Chinese culture. Sometimes in the small hours of the morning, the Tibetans will switch off the big wall screen, and take the microphone to sing impromptu Tibetan songs. Everyone will join in, including the secret policemen and their girlfriends!

The downmarket places can often be found beside truck stops or military barracks. To enter is to experience the seedy side of life in Tibet.

Drinking is an important element of this popular culture, and some groups of revellers will often carry crates of green-bottled Chinese or Tibetan beer into the karaoke bar. A bucket of cold water may be placed on the floor for refridgeration! As the evening wears on, even the most secret of policemen will loosen up and reveal all! On the other hand, drunkenness can lead to flashpoints of violence; and macho Khampa men may be quick on the draw with their long ornate knives. Brawling between rival groups has been known to close down certain establishments not long after their opening.

Apart from karaoke clubs, the small towns also have a number of exceedingly boring Chinese video parlours, and a large number of pool tables or even electronic gambling machines.

kneeprint, as well as a stupa dedicated to Phakmodrupa Dorje Gyelpo.

Sleeping *Oasis Hotel (Linzhi Binguan)*, (0894) 5821300 x 8107. Has 71 rooms at ¥338, best and most comfortable accommodation in town, hot water is available in the washrooms, and there is a student cafeteria open to hotel guests. *Government Guesthouse*, Lhasa-Nyangtri Rd. Best rooms ¥65, privately owned guesthouse and *Post Office Guesthouse* just off Commercial St.

Eating There are a number of Sichuan restaurants near the bridge fronted by waitresses who seductively and competitively flaunt their cuisine. Restaurants and coffee shops can also be found on Commercial Street.

Southern Tibet

Nyangtri

Colour map2, grid B6 The old county capital stands below Bonri, the sacred Bon mountain of Kongpo, at the east estuary of the Nyang-chu River, 19 kilometres south of Bayi. The streets of Nyangtri form a T-junction: the main road to Po-me and Chamdo, turning east to ascend the Serkhyem La pass, and the south road following the riverside to Luding, and then following the Brahmaputra downstream on the north bank. Towards the northwest of town, at **Kushuk Drong**, there is a 2,000-year-old juniper tree, sacred to the Bonpo, which is protected within a walled enclosure (■ *Admission fee: ¥15 per person*).

Essentials The government buildings, public security bureau, and larger shops are all situated close to the main intersection beyond which is the bus station and guesthouse compound, on the south road out of town. Nearby are small restaurants and teashops.

Sigyel Gonchen The Bonpo monastery of Sigyel Gonchen, approached via a turn-off on the left below Nyangtri, is a major pilgrimage attraction for the Bonpo adherents of Khyungpo Tengchen and Hor. Founded in the 14th century by Kuchok Rikpa Druk-se, it once housed 100 monks.

Taktse Yungdrungling Monastery The motor road passes through Taktse township, above which is another Bon monastery known as Yungdrungling. Originally founded by a Bonpo from Amdo named Dongom Tenpa Lhundrub, it has recently undergone limited reconstruction, and is popular with Bonpo pilgrims from Ngawa and other parts of Amdo. There are precious relics housed here, including a tooth relic of Shenrab Miwoche, founder of the Bon religion.

Mijik Tri Durtro This Bonpo burial ground, believed to contain the tumulus of Tibet's first mortal king, Drigum Tsenpo, lies a short distance north of Luding at the confluence of the Nyang-chu and Brahmaputra rivers. Bon literary sources refer to this tomb as **Gyangto Labub**, and there are many dire prophecies pertaining to its subsidence, as it appears over time to have moved closer to the river bank! From Luding there is a ferry crossing to the south bank of the river; and slightly further, at Drena (on the north bank), there is the place where King Drigum Tsenpo's funeral was conducted, in the shadows of **Mount Lhari Gyangto**. At Yungdrung Dzin village, there is a ninth century obelisk, with an inscription recounting the affinity which King Drigum Tsenpo's sons had with the local divinity of Mount Lhari Gyangto. ■ *Admission fee: ¥15 per person.*

Chu Jowo Temple Slightly east of the confluence, on the north bank of the Brahmaputra, stands the temple of Chu Jowo. This contains a relief image of Jowo Rinpoche in the guise of Four-armed Avalokiteshvara. In this form, Jowo Rinpoche, Tibet's most sacred image contained in the Lhasa Jokhang, is said to have appeared in the Brahmaputra River, honouring a pledge he had made to Kongpo Ben, a devout shoemaker from Kongpo while on a previous pilgrimage to Lhasa. Before returning to Lhasa, Jowo Rinpoche vanished into a stone, taking on the form of the relief image which is revered today. The

Nyangtri

To Bayi

Government Buildings

N

Not to scale

Bus Station Guesthouse

Tar Medical College

Department Store

Bookshop

To Menri

● Restaurants

To Pome

place where the image is said to have appeared in the river is close by the present temple. The site was restored through local patronage in 1985.

Mount Bonri is the highest of the three sacred Bonpo peaks on the north bank **Mount Bonri** of the Brahmaputra (Muri is further west and Mount Lhari Gyangto south-west). Bonpo pilgrims from all parts of Tibet circumvent the slopes of Bonri, particularly during the winter months. Starting at Menri township (41 kilo-metres from Nyangtri), where there are guesthouse facilities and shops, the three-day trek passes to the left of the Demo valley. Here are the ruins of **Demo Chemkar** monastery, a Gelukpa monastery, which was once the residence of Tibet's regent Demo Tupten Jigme (r 1810-17). The route towards Bonri La (4,540 metres) passes many sites associated with Shenrab and his epic struggle against the demon Kyapa Lagring; as well as the sacred tree, **Sembon Dungshing**, which has been revered as a cemetery for babies since its conse-cration by Kuchok Ripa Druk-se in 1330. The summit is said to have a stone footprint of Tibet's first king Nyatri Tsenpo. The descent from the pass leads via Zhabchin Dong and Darbong to Nyangtri.

From Nyangtri, the highway to East Tibet ascends for 32 kilometres and then **Rong chu Valley** cuts across the Serkhyem La pass, to enter the valley of the north-flowing **Rong-chu**. This valley, which is renowned for its poppies, giant rhubarb, and other diverse species of flora, can also be reached by trekking from Tim Guru Drupuk via the Nyima La (see above, page 230). From Serkhyem La pass to Tongjuk township the distance is 46 kilometres. En route you pass through a logging centre at **Lunang**, and **Chu Nyima**, the traditional border between Kongpo and Powo regions. For a detailed description of the route from here to Chamdo in East Tibet via Powo and Pasho, see below, page 405.

The road north from Bayi follows the Nyang-chu upstream, passing large **Bepa** well-established military camps and installations on both sides of the road. The rushing waters of the Nyang-chu, flanked by beautiful conifer forests on both banks, ranks among the most memorable sights in Tibet. Pristine streams surge down to swell the river, among them the Zha-chu and Nezhi-chu, which converge at **Nezhi**. At **Bepa** township, 58 kilometres from Bayi, you reach the border between Nyangtri and Gyamda counties, and thence enter into Upper Kongpo.

Gyamda County རྒྱ་མདའ

This is an area of stunning natural beauty: verdant alpine forests and clear run-ning streams abound, and there are incredible lakes, epitomized by the island lake of Draksum Tso. Upper Kongpo extends from the Nangsel Zampa bridge where the Nyang-chu River merges with its Drak-chu tributary, northwest of Bepa township, as far as the Mamzhong La pass (5,000 metres), which forms the watershed between the Meldro and Nyang-chu rivers. The county capital is located at Ngapo Zampa (Kongpo Gyamda), 127 kilometres north of Bayi, and 206 kilometres northeast of Lhasa. Other feeder rivers swell the river's current, notably the Banang-chu (which flows north through Drongsar township), and the Pe-chu (which flows northeast through Gyazhing township).

Gyamda County (22)
工布江达县
Gongbogyamda
Population: 20,841
Area:12,593 sq km
Colour map2, grid B5

Upper Kongpo

Driving north from Bepa township, you will notice on the right the 15 metres **Pangri Jokpo** high stone towers, which are found in many parts of Upper Kongpo. At **Hermitage**

Nangsel Zampa bridge, 21 kilometres from Bepa, the valley of the Drak-chu abuts the Nyang-chu valley from the northeast. Turn right along a dirt track before crossing the bridge, and you will shortly reach the path leading to the ridge-top Pangri Jokpo hermitage.

A steep two hours climb through barley fields, shrubbery and forested slopes brings you to a clearing below this isolated tranquil retreat, founded by the *terton* Jatson Nyingpo (1585-1656). The hermitage, which for many years has been tended by two elderly female hermits from Nangchen, comprises a **Mani Lhakhang** and the **main temple**, built against the rock walls. The temple is exceptionally well lit through its northwest facing glass windows, and the views it offers of the Nyang-chu valley below are suggestive of Swiss or Austrian landscapes. The temple has both outer and inner chapels. The former contains images of Padmasambhava, Guru Drakpo, and Simhavaktra – a trio renowned as the *Union of All Rare and Precious Things* (*Konchok Chidu*), described in *terma* texts revealed by Jatson Nyingpo himself. The liturgies of these texts are popular throughout both the Nyingma and Kagyu traditions. Alongside these images, to the right is a bass-relief image of Jatson Nyingpo, with a longevity-arrow (*dadar*), which is claimed to have been his personal possession. Prajnaparamita texts and small images of Padmasambhava are in the background. The **inner chapel** contains images of Ling Gesar (in peaceful and wrathful forms), and of Avalokiteshvara (twice), and Shakyamuni Buddha. An **inner sanctum** contains 1,000 small images of Padmasambhava.

Jatson Nyingpo passed away at Pangri Jokpo. His birthplace at **Waru Nam-tsul** is on the opposite side of the valley.

Lake Draksum Tso Returning to the Nangsel Zampa bridge, cross over, and take the right turn-off (on the north bank of the Drak-chu River). The road leads to **Zhoka** township (20 kilometres), near the ruins of the old Zhoka Dzong. En route, you will pass on the left **Len** village, noted for its 12-cornered tapering towers. According to one tradition, these are ancient fortifications, similar in function to those of Lhodrak (see above, page 208) and Gyarong (see below, page 616), and they are said to have been made by demons headed by Ling Gesar's enemy Dud Achung Gyelpo in the remote past. Others sources suggest, however, that they were used for trapping birds of prey, which would dive into the towers in pursuit of their baited quarry.

At **Zhoka**, there is a hydroelectric power station and a small market. Two roads diverge here, the north route leading to **Drukla** township, following the Drukla-chu upstream, and the east route, following the Draksum-chu upstream to the lake which is its source. Take the latter, and cross the **Zhoka Zampa** bridge. The road now passes through a disused but somewhat surreal complex of telecommunication and remote tracking systems (one motorable trail leads through a fenced perimeter directly towards a hewn-out mountainside bunker!).

Gyamda County

Continue to follow the river upstream for 18 kilometres to **Tsomjuk**, where a bridge crosses it at the point where it exits from the lake. Just beyond Tsomjuk, there is a newly constructed guesthouse in chalet-style, complete with dining room, karaoke, dance floor and other amenities favoured by Chinese holiday-makers. At **Jepa**, on the south side of the lake, the road ends at a newly constructed series of log cabins, owned by the local Tsomgo Tourist Bureau. Large applique Tibetan tents dot this idyllic campsite. Below you have a wonderful view of the jade-green lake, 16 kilometres long by three kilometres wide, girded by steep forested slopes, and with the Tsodzong Island (3,600 metres) positioned like a pearl at its centre. The flat-bottomed ferry boat is drawn across to the island by an overhead cable. Recently, motor boats and speed boats have also been introduced to the lake by the local tourist authority, which caters mainly for visitors from China.

Tsodzong Island The temple on Tsodzong Island is the birthplace of the *terton* Sangye Lingpa (1340-96), although there are earlier associations with Padmasambhava and King Trisong Detsen. In the early years of the 20th century, the complex was refurbished by the late Dudjom Rinpoche (1904-87); and is now undergoing further renovation, following its destruction during the 1960s. Konchok Tsering is sponsoring the project, under the guidance of Dudjom Rinpoche's daughter, Semo Dechen, and her husband Chonyi Rinpoche of Lamaling. The present caretakers, Neten and Atsang, are practitioners of the Dudjom lineage.

The main image of the temple depicts Guru Drakpo. Its head was originally brought to the island by Sangye Lingpa, riding a tigress which left its paw marks among the rocks to the west of the island. Other images depict Padmasambhava, Shakyamuni Buddha, Avalokiteshvara, and the protectress Kongtsun Demo. There is also a 'self-manifesting' stone letter A, as described in Jatson Nyingpo's own *terma*. The caretakers' house holds other treasures: a royal seal of King Songtsen Gampo, the bowls used by Sangye Lingpa and the late Dudjom Rinpoche, and a precious manuscript said to be in Jatson Nyingpo's own handwriting.

The pilgrim's circuit of the island begins with this temple, and then moves clockwise, passing the hermitage of Dudjom Rinpoche, a rock from the Shitavana charnel ground, the body imprint of Ling Gesar, the stone paw of the tigress, the stone prints of Sangye Lingpa (**all on west side**); the 'life-supporting' tree (*lashing*) of the demon Dud Achung Gyelpo which was cut down by Gesar's golden axe, a treasury belonging to the Karmapa, a tree associated with Ma Khandro, the consort of Drime Kunden (see above, page) which has leaves naturally inscribed with seed-syllables and animal year-signs (**all on north side**); a stone snake which has associations with Ling Gesar, and the Tashi Obar stupa, under which is a nectar stream (**all on east side**). Finally, a white stone represents the mistress of the lake, Tsomen Gyelmo (**south side**).

Beyond the far shore of the lake, there are four prominent snow peaks: Mount Ama Jomo Taktse (5,963 metres) to the northwest, Mount Namla Karpo (6,750 metres) to the north, Mount Naphu Gomri (5,663 metres) to the northeast, and Mount Darchenri to the east. These sites also have associations with Ling Gesar.

Pilgrim's circuit There is a two-day pilgrims' circuit around the lake, commencing from the bridge of **Tsomjuk** and passing by the ruined Gelukpa monastery of **Pibang**, the Vajravarahi cave, the two glacial feeder rivers on the lake's east side (Ortse-chu and Nangu-chu), the ruined Kagyupa monastery of **Darchenri**, and **Tsomgo** township, at the head of the lake. Near the **Jepa** campsite on the south side, there is another glacial feeder river, known as the Penam-chu.

Returning to Zhoka, if you take the north turn-off, you will reach **Drukla** township after 15 kilometres. Here there are more ancient defence towers and the ruins of the **Drukla Monastery**. A trekking route leads further north, for 105 kilometres to join the old Lhasa-Chamdo caravan highway near Lake Atsa (see below, page 402).

Ngapo Zampa (Gyamda Town)

Colour map 2, grid B5 Returning to Nangsel Zampa bridge, turn right, and follow the main highway west along the course of the Nyang-chu. After 40 kilometres, you will pass the **Sharlung Zampa** bridge at Sharlung township, where the Banang-chu tributary flows into the Nyang-chu from the south. There is a side-road from here leading south to **Drongsar**.

Eight kilometres further along the main highway, you will reach the county capital, known as **Ngapo Zampa** (Kongpo Gyamda. *Altitude*: 3,200 metres). This is a small town comprising one main street reached via bridges at its west and east ends.

Above the town of Gyamda is the monastery of **Neu Dechen Gon**, associated with the late Dudjom Rinpoche's teachings on Vajrakila. In a nearby mountain-hermitage are the **Tselha Namsum** meditation caves, associated with the female yogini Machik Labdron.

Essentials *Gyamda Dzong Guesthouse* (¥8 per bed) and the *Post Office Guesthouse* (Yigzam Dronkhang, ¥8 per bed) are both on the north side of the main street, west of the Bus Station. The *Grain Department Guesthouse* (Drurik Lekhung Dronkhang, ¥15 per bed) is on the south side of the main street, west of the petrol station. There are a number of good and inexpensive Sichuan restaurants.

Gyamda Township and the Chamdo Caravan Trail 23 kilometres northwest of Ngapo Zampa, the road passes through Gyamda township, formerly known as **Gyamda Dzong**. From here, there is a four-day trek following the headwaters of the Nyang-chu through **Nyangpo** district and across Tro La pass (4,890 metres) to **Artsa**, where a motorable dirt road leads northwest to Nakchu and southeast down the Yi'ong Tsangpo valley. This latter route follows the old caravan trail from Lhasa to Chamdo (see below, page 381), which commenced at Gyamda Dzong.

Nyang-chu Headwaters Beyond Gyamda township the highway continues to **Chimda** (17 kilometres), where Padmasambhava's student Nyak Jananakumara once fled from violent assailants, and where, later, in the 14th century Sangye Lingpa discovered *terma* pertaining to the cycles of wrathful mantras. The road continues from there to **Gyazhing** township (44 kilometres) and eventually, after a further 63 kilometres, to the watershed pass of **Mamzhong La** (5,000 metres). Near the pass, 13 kilometres after Gyazhing, the road diverges from the main river. (A trekking trail leads upstream to Azhang Kongla pass and thence to Dakpo.) From the watershed to Lhasa via Meldro Gungkar and Taktse counties, the distance is 149 kilometres.

Ngapo Zampa

Western Tibet

Tsang and Lato

6

Western Tibet

Tsang and Lato

*Western Tibet is the region demarcated by the Upper
Brahmaputra (Tib Yarlung Tsangpo) valley, extending
upstream from its confluence with the Kyi-chu River, as
far as the headwaters in Drongpa county (east of Mount
Kailash). Separated on the south from Nepal, Sikkim
and WestBhutan by the high Himalayan range, and
separated on the north from the Jangtang Plateau by the
Gangtise and Nyenchen Tanglha ranges, this region
includes the traditional provinces of* **Tsang** *and* **Lato**. *As
such, it embraces the lateral valleys adjoining the
Brahmaputra on both its north and south banks, the
valleys of the south-flowing Gangetic tributaries which
traverse Nepal, and those of the south-flowing
Brahmaputra tributaries which traverse Sikkim and
West Bhutan.*

*The distance from Lhasa to Zhigatse is: 281 km via
Nyemo and Chakdam; 348 km via Gampa La pass and
Gyantse; 338 km via Yangpachen and Zhugu La pass.*
Recommended Itineraries: 1,2.

Nyemo County སྙེ་མོ

Nyemo County (23)
尼木县
Nyemo
Population: 26,248
Area: 2,077 sq km
Colour map 2, grid B3

*The county of **Nyemo** extends from the upper reaches of the Lhorong-chu in the north, across the watershed formed by the snow peaks of **Jomo Gangtse** (7,048 metres) and **Kumalungpa Gangri** (5,858 metres), and through the fertile valleys of the Nyemo Ma-chu and its tributaries, the Zhu-chu and Phakpu-chu. The county capital is located at **Dardrong**, where the Nyemo Ma-chu and Zhu-chu rivers converge.*

Getting there There are two motorable routes into Dardrong: one from Markyang township (50 kilometres) on the northern Lhasa-Zhigatse highway and another from Ton township (25 kilometres) on the central Lhasa-Zhigatse highway.

Trekking Nyemo is a wonderful area for trekking in close proximity to Lhasa. There is a trail from **Dorjeling nunnery** near Yangpachen (see above, page 138), following the Lhorong-chu upstream via Gyedar and Yangyi, before crossing the Zhagong La pass into the Upper Zhu valley. Another trek from Tsurphu monastery links up with that trail at Gyedar; and a third leads from Nakar, south of Tsurphu, to Angang township in the Lower Zhu valley (see above).

Of all these the easiest point of access is via the central highway. Driving west from Chushul, you continue on the north bank of the Brahmaputra, passing the **Chushul Zamchen** bridgehead at **Dagar** (eight kilometres), and the townships of Sa-me (25 kilometres), and Ton (30 kilometres), before reaching the turn-off for **Dardrong** at the mouth of the Nyemo Ma-chu (20 kilometres). Dardrong is five kilometres inland.

Nyemo Ma-chu valley From **Dardrong**, a jeep track follows the Nyemo Ma-chu upstream for 50 kilometres to **Markyang** on the northern Lhasa-Zhigatse highway. En route, you will pass through **Lhundrubgang** in Zangri township, which was once the base of an important Tibetan opera troupe. Following its amalgamation with the Jago troupe in neighbouring Zhu valley, it became renowned throughout Tibet as the **Nyemowa Opera Troupe**. Further upstream at **Jekhar** in Dragor (Pagor) township, where the Phakpu-chu converges with the Nyemo Ma-chu, there is the birthplace of **Vairotsana**, the greatest native of Nyemo, who ranks among Tibet's finest translators of the eighth century; and a foremost student of Padmasambhava. His footprint, impressed in rock at the age of eight, is said to be kept there as an object of veneration.

At Markyang on the northern highway, you can turn southwest for **Oyuk** valley (see below, page 248) or northwest, heading across the high **Zhugu La** pass (5,454 metres) with its stupendous views of the Jomo Gangtse snows. Yangpachen in the Upper Tolung valley lies 56

Nyemo County

Western Tibet

The Brahmaputra/Yarlung Tsangpo River

*The **Brahmaputra** is one of Asia's major rivers, extending 2,900 km from its source in Far-west Tibet to its confluence with the Ganges in India. There are three head-streams: **Kabji**, **Angsi**, and **Tachok Khabab**, the last of which rises in the Jemayungdrung glacier 60 km southeast of Lake Manasarovar. From their convergence these headwaters, known initially as the **Tachok Tsangpo** and later as the **Yarlung Tsangpo**, flow east for 1,127 km along the tectonic suture line. Then, after being forcibly channeled south through the awesome gorges between Mount Namchak Barwa and Mount Gyala Pelri, the river enters the Arunachal Pradesh province of India where it is known as the **Dihang**. In Assam it is joined by several Himalayan streams: the Lohit, Dibang, Subansiri, Kameng, Bhareli, Dhansiri, Manas, Champamati, Saralbhanga, and Sankosh. Lastly, in the*

Duars, it is joined by the Tista, before finally converging with the Ganges north of Goalundo Ghat.

*In its upper reaches the river is navigable for 644 km from **Lhartse** eastwards, and there are coracles crossing the river at 3,962m.*

*The flora along the banks of the Upper Brahmaputra is confined to shrubbery, interspersed with dwarf willow and poplar trees. The true forests begin growing only in the mid-reaches, in **Dakpo** and **Kongpo**, where the climate is moister and warmer. In the southeast, around **Po-me** and **Pemako**, coniferous forests cover the mountain slopes in thick areas. Conifers with an undergrowth of rhododendron grow at 3,000-4,000m; hemlock, spruce, and larch at 2,500-3,000m; pine trees at 1,500-2,500m; and tropical monsoon forest below 1,500m.*

kilometres beyond Zhugu La pass. If you take the Oyuk road, after seven kilometres you will pass through **Senshang** township. From here there is a long and arduous trekking route to **Lake Namtso** via the Kyangu La pass (5,769 metres) and Putserteng hamlet.

From Dardrong, a trail follows the Zhu-chu upstream through a fertile valley to Angang township (19 kilometres). Here are the ruins of **Zhu Kungarawa**, an 11th century Kadampa monastery founded by Ngok Lotsawa. At **Jago**, northeast of Mount Gangri Pelkye (5,894 metres), there is the former home of Nyemo's second opera troupe, prior to its amalgamation with the troupe of Lhundrubgang (see above). From here there is a trekking route to Nakar near Tsurphu monastery (see above, page 246). Another trekking route leads from **Sagang** in the Upper Zhu valley across Zhagong La pass to Gyedar, where trails bifurcate for Yangpachen and Tsurphu.

Nyemo Zhu valley

Namling County རྣམ་གླིང་

*Namling is the current administrative name given to the valleys of **Oyuk**, **Tobgyel**, and **Shang**, which all have long and illustrious associations with both Buddhism and Bon. Through these valleys there respectively flow the Nang-gung-chu, Tobpu-chu, and Shang-chu rivers, with their various tributaries, which rise amid the southern slopes of the Nyenchen Tanglha range to the north, and flow southwards to converge with the Brahmaputra.*

Namling County (24)
南木林县
Namling
Population: 61,104
Area: 9,695 sq km
Colour map 2, grid B2

Getting there The northern and central Lhasa-Zhigatse highways meet at **Trakdruka** on the south bank of the Brahmaputra, opposite Lower Oyuk. The former winds its way from Senshang across the Do-ngu La pass (4,846 metres) to Oyuk township and thence to Trakdruka ferry (65 kilometres). The latter follows the north bank of the Brahmaputra upstream from Nyemo, via Dzongkar to the **Nub Khulung Zamchen** bridge in Lower Oyuk, after which it runs along the south bank to Tradruka (75 kilometres). The Tobgyel and Shang valleys are both accessible by ferry crossings from the south bank of the river, the former at **Drakchik** ferry (19 kilometres west of Tradruka) and the latter at Tama ferry (58 kilometres west of Tradruka) or **Dongkar** ferry (at Zhigatse, 80 kilometres west of Tradruka). The county capital is located at **Ringon** in the Shang valley.

Oyuk Valley

Dingma Monastery
Colour map 2, grid B2

Descending from the Do-ngu La pass into Upper Oyuk, the northern Lhasa-Zhigatse highway enters the Nang-gung-chu valley. Below Rinchenling, 27 kilometres after the pass, the Mang-chu tributary converges with the Nang-gung-chu at Domtang village. A trekking route to **Zabulung** in Upper Shang (see below, page 251) follows the **Mang-chu valley** northwest via Rikdzom and Mangra township, and across the Mang La pass. Near the entrance to this valley you can see on a hill the remains of the ancient 11th century Kadampa monastery of **Dingma**, founded by Ram Dingma Deshek Jungne, a student of the Geshe Potowa (1031-1105). At **Lukdong** in this vicinity there is also a meditation hermitage associated with Padmasambhava.

Oyuk Gongon Lhakhang

Oyuk township (Taktse) lies seven kilometres below the confluence of the Nang-gung-chu and Mang-chu rivers.

The principal shrine is the **Gongon Lhakhang**, which was reputedly constructed by King Songtsen Gampo as one of a series of peripheral geomantic temples. Some even classify it among the 'border-taming' temples. Later in the eighth century, the temple was frequented by Padmasambhava and his students, among them Namkei Nyingpo and King Trisong Detsen. The latter's personal weapons were once housed here.

Sleeping There are guesthouse facilities here.

Trekking From Oyuk township, there are three-day trekking routes, which lead southwest via Sogchen township into the valley of the Tobpu-chu, or into

Namling

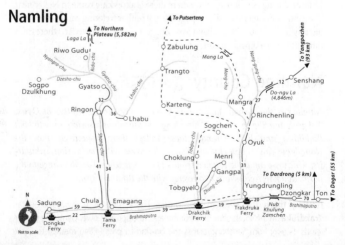

that of its eastern tributary, where **Menri Monastery** is located (see below, page 250). A jeepable dirt road also leads northwest to Karteng and the Shang Lhabu-chu valley (see below, page 250).

Oyuk Jara Gon

At **Jarasa** in Lower Oyuk, there is the abode or castle (Kukhar) of the protector deity Dorje Lekpa: guardian of the Dzogchen teachings. Here, at the hermitage called **Oyuk Chigong** or Oyuk Jara Gon, the great meditation master Chetsun Senge Wangchuk (10th-11th century) remained in retreat, and received the teachings of the *Innermost Spirituality of Vimalamitra* (*Bima Nyingthig*) in a vision from Vimalamitra. Some of these teachings he concealed and others he imparted to his foremost student, Zhangton (1097-1167). Eventually he passed into rainbow light at the age of 125! There are graphic descriptions in Tibetan literature of how Zhangton was assisted by the protector Dorje Lekpa in his efforts to rediscover the concealed teachings of the *Innermost Spirituality of Vimalamitra*. Later, in the 19th century, when Jamyang Khyentse Wangpo was on pilgrimage here from East Tibet, he recollected the teachings he had received in a past life (as Chetsun Senge Wangchuk) and redacted them into the teaching cycle now known as the *Innermost Spirituality of Chetsun (Chetsun Nyingthig)*.

Moving on Passing due south through the villages of Nubmalung and Tashigang, the road eventually reaches the Brahmaputra ferry crossing at Tradruka, 31 kilometres south of Oyuk township.

Yungdrungling Monastery

Located above the east bank of the Nang-gung-chu near its confluence with the Brahmaputra, this is one of the most influential Bonpo monasteries in recent Tibetan history. Founded during the 19th century by Nangton Dawa Gyeltsen on the ridge of the holy Bonpo mountain, **Olha Gyel**. The complex had 700 monks prior to its destruction in 1959, but now there are scarcely more than 30. Amid the ruins of its assembly hall, residential buildings, hermitages and colleges, a few shrines have been reconstructed. The **Tongrol Lhakhang** contains the reconstructed reliquary of the monastery's founder; and murals depicting the Bonpo lineage-holders and ritual mandalas.

Tobgyel Valley

Colour map 2, grid B2

Following the Tobpu-chu upstream from its confluence with the Brahmaputra opposite Drakchik Ferry, at **Tobgyel** township (Magada), the valley bifurcates: the west branch following the Tobpu-chu upstream to Tshar, Choklung, the Gelukpa monastery of **Drungzhi**, and **Sogchen**. The east branch follows the Zhung-chu upstream, via Gangpa into a Bonpo stronghold. Here are the celebrated Bonpo monasteries of Ensakha, Kharna, and Menri.

Getting there The entrance to the **Tobgyel** valley may be approached by coracle from the **Drakchik** ferry (19 kilometres west of Tradruka) on the south bank of the Brahmaputra, or by trekking – either along the north bank from Yungdrungling in Lower Oyuk, or via the Tobpu-chu headwaters from Oyuk township and Sogchen.

Ensakha & Kharna Monasteries

The Bon monastery of **Ensakha** was founded in Lower Topgyel by Druje Yungdrung Lama in 1072. Following its devastation by floods in 1386, the Bon community moved to Menri. Ensakha was eventually reconstructed and continued to function as a small monastery until recent times. Further upstream are the **Kharna-ri** caves, where Bonpo meditators and hermits have practiced for centuries; and where a new monastery was founded in 1838 by Sherab Yungdrung.

| Menri Monastery | The Bonpo monastery of **Menri**, higher up the slopes of the Zhung-chu valley, was established in 1405 by Nya-me Sherab Gyeltsen, following the destruction by floods by its precursor, Ensakha monastery. This event is said to have been predicted by Shenrab Miwoche, legendary founder of the Bon religion. For centuries Menri functioned as the most important Bon teaching centre in the country, attracting monks from Tengchen, Ngawa, and Gyarong. Prior to its destruction in 1959 there were 350 monks at Menri; but now there are about 50. The ruins are extensive: formerly there were four colleges, a school of dialectics, and a large assembly hall. The oldest building is the **Red Meditation Hermitage (Drubkhang Marpo)**, constructed by the monastery's founder. |

Shang Valley

Getting there The Shang valley may be approached from the south bank of the Brahmaputra, either via the **Tama ferry** (58 kilometres west of Tradruka), or the **Dongkar ferry** (80 kilometres west of Tradruka). The former crossing alights near **Emagang** on the west bank of the Shang-chu river estuary; and the latter at **Sadung**, from where the road leads downstream to Chula on the west bank of the Shang-chu. Both roads into Shang are motorable, the west bank as far as Gyatso township (73 kilometres) and the east bank as far as Lhabu (70 kilometres) and Trangto. (There is also a jeep trail from Oyuk township via Karteng to Trangto; and another from Lower Tobgyel to Emagang.) A bridge for motor vehicles spans the river at **Ringon**, the county capital, and above Takna the two main branches of the Shang-chu River diverge: the valley of the Gyatso-chu extending northwest and that of the Shang Lhabu-chu extending east and northeast.

| Emagang Shangda Palchen | In Lower Shang, the most important site is **Shangda Palchen**, the seat of the Zur family in Emagang township. Here, near the village of **Trampa**, the successive generations of the Zur family made their hermitages and securely established the transmission of the *Nyingmapa Oral Teachings* (*kama*) during the 10th century, in the aftermath of the interregnum following Langdarma's persecution. This family lineage originated with Zur Shakya Jungne (10th-11th century), his nephew Zurchungpa Sherab Drak (1014-74), and the latter's son Zur Drophukpa Shakya Senge (1074-1135), whose students carried the Nyingmapa teachings throughout Tibet. The detailed accounts of their lives are among the most lively biographical passages of Nyingmapa literature. When the Sakyapas became the dominant force in Tibetan political life during the 13th century, they maintained a close rapport with the Zurs, encouraging Zur Zangpopel to redact the Nyingmapa anthology of tantras. Later Zurchen Choying Rangdrol (1604-69) established a close connection with Dalai Lama V. |

| Ringon (Namling) | Four roads intersect at **Ringon**, the county capital of Namling: the two southern routes to Dojo and Emagang and the northern routes to Gyatso and Lhabu. The cliff-hanging monastery of **Ganden Chokhorling** at Ringon has, in recent centuries, been the largest monastery in Shang: shared by both the Gelukpa and Sakyapa schools. Above the monastery are the ruins of **Ringon Taktse Dzong** fortress. Another small monastery, **Dechen Rabgye Gonpa**, is associated with the Panchen Lamas. |

| Gyatso-chu Valley | The motor road continues on the west bank of the river upstream from Ringon. Below Luya, the Shang Lhabu River branches to the east. Heading northwest along the course of the Gyatso-chu tributary, you will reach Gyatso township after 32 kilometres. Here the Dzesho, Nyangra, and Ridu headwaters |

of the Gyamtso-chu converge. Of these, the Ridu-chu leads to the **Riwo Gudu** or **Drak Gyawo** hermitage of the master Zurchung Sherab Drak; and the Dzesho-chu to the limestone cave complex of **Sogpo Dzulkhung** hermitage. In the latter, there is a Padmasambhava cave containing the impression of the master's penis in rock. From **Ridu**, the Laga La pass (5,582 metres) leads through the Nyenchen Tanglha range north towards the Jangtang lakes.

Zhang Zhang Dorjeden

Located five kilometres east of Ringon, on the south bank of the Shang-chu, this is one of the best known of the 108 monasteries reputedly established by Khyungpo Neljor, founder of the Shangpa Kagyu school. It was here that this master passed away and was interred in a reliquary fashioned of gold and silver.

Zabulung

Padmasambhava is said to have consecrated five entire valleys for Buddhist practice in each of the four cardinal directions and at their centre. **Zabulung** valley lies at the centre of this grand design, and as such is the most revered pilgrimage place in the province of Tsang. Located northeast of Ratang (Lhabu), Karteng, and Trangto, in the Shang Lhabu-chu valley, this site is renowned for its spectacular **hot springs** and the **Shang Zabulung Monastery**, where there is a meditation cave associated with Padmasambhava and his consort Yeshe Tsogyel. Throughout history, important Nyingmapa *tertons* have undergone profound spiritual experiences here: Dorje Lingpa (1346-1405) and Lhatsun Namka Jigme (b 1597) among them.

Trekking A trekking route continues northeast following the Shang Lhabu-chu upstream to the nomadic areas of **Lhabupu**, **Serka**, and eventually to **Putserteng**.

Rinpung County རིན་སྤུངས་

*Rarely visited by outsiders at the present day, **Rinpung** in Rong Valley was once the citadel of the Rinpung princes who ruled Tibet from 1435 until 1565. The county is located on the south bank of the Brahmaputra; extending from the south side of the **Nub Khulung Zamchen bridge**, 20 kilometres east of Tradruka ferry, and downstream as far as **Samda** (west of Kharak). Most settlements are to be found in the lateral valley of the **Rong-chu**, which rises at **Yarzik** in Pelde township on the extreme northwest tip of Lake Yamdrok and flows into the Brahmaputra at **Shangpa** (Rinpung township); but the county also includes the valleys of the Yakde-chu and the Bartang-chu; as well as the southwest running valley of the Men-chu, the principal tributary of the Rong-chu. The county capital is located at **Jamchen Zhol** in the Rong-chu valley, 31 kilometres southeast of the Nub Khulung Zamchen bridge.*

Rinpung County (25)
仁布县
Rinpung
Population: 27,693
Area: 1,885 sq km
Colour map 2, grid B3

Rinpung Dzong

This fortress town is located on a ridge overlooking the west bank of the Rong-chu River. The ruined fortress or **Dzong** of **Ringpung** is further inland on a ridge to the west of the river. It overlooks a large village of some 100 houses.

The Rinpung princes first came to prominence during the reign of the Phakmodrupa king Drakpa Gyeltsen (1374-1440), who appointed **Namka Gyeltsen** as Lord of the Rinpung estates and Governor of Sakya and Chumik.

In 1435, his relation **Rinpung Norbu Zangpo** seized power from Phakmodru, gradually bringing to an end the influence of this aristocratic house of Nedong (see above, page 186). Finally in 1478 his son **Donyo Dorje** inflicted a decisive defeat on the kings of Phakmodru; and founded Yangpachen, the seat of the Zhamarpas of the Karma Kargyu school. The family's power was eventually eclipsed in 1565 by **Zhingzhakpa Tseten Dorje** of the Samdrubtse fiefdom at Zhigatse.

Getting there Via the road from Nub Khulung Zamchen bridge, which enters the Rong-chu valley at Shangpa.

Rong Jamchen   The road continues inland, following the Rong-chu upstream, past a hydro-electric power station, to **Jamchen Zhol**, the county capital. The most important site is the three-storeyed **Rong Jamchen Chode** – a Sakyapa monastery which later also acquired Gelukpa associations – originally founded by Zhonu Gyelchok in 1367. The Rinpungpa prince Norbu Zangpo donated an enormous 10 metres high Maitreya image. In the early decades of the present century there are said to have been 1,500 Gelukpa and Sakyapa monks based here. The present reconstructed assembly hall lies below the ruins of the original complex.

Essentials There is a government compound with shops and spartan guesthouse facilities, and a military barracks.

Dekyiling   The road continues to follow the river upstream as far as **Dekyiling**, where the Men-chu tributary flows into the Rong-chu from the southwest. A motorable road follows the Men-chu upstream and across the Yung La pass (4,720 metres) to **Gyantse** (42 kilometres). In this valley you can visit the college of **Dreyul Kyemotsel**, founded in 1449 by Rinpungpa Kunzang, who was a patron of the Sakyapa lamas Sangyepel and Gorampa Sonam Senge (1429-89).

Also, 10 kilometres up the valley near Kyi-shong is **Khambulung**, where Jangdak Tashi Topgyel of the Northern Treasures (Jangter) tradition (b 1557) discovered certain *terma* revelations. The **Ngurmik Drolma Lhakhang** once contained a celebrated image of Tara, which is now housed at Tashilhunpo in Zhigatse (see below, page 266). Seven kilometres further south is the **Gongra Lhundrubding**; also known as **Gongra Ngeden Dorje Ling**, an important Nyingmapa centre, where the Anuyoga texts were transmitted by Gongra Lochen Zhenpen Dorje (1594-1654).

Rong Chutsen   The small hot spring known as **Dumpa Chutsen** is located at Chutsen village, Hot Springs &   just before the Rong-chu valley forms a narrow gorge. Within the gorge at Rampa   **Rampa** is the hermitage of Padmasambhava's eighth century disciple, **Nanam Dorje Dujom**. The trail continues southeast to **Yarzik** on the shore of Lake Yamdrok (see above, page 216).

Rinpung

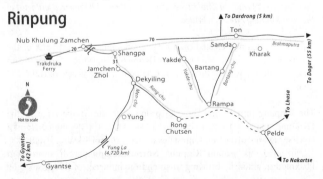

From Rampa, there are two side-valleys branching northeast which lead to the **Yakde &**
Brahmaputra via Yakde and Bartang respectively. **Yakde** is the birthplace of **Bartang valleys**
Yakde Panchen Khyenrab Gyatso (1299-1378), a foremost student of
Karmapa III, Rangjung Dorje, who also has associations with the Sakyapa
school.

Gyantse County རྒྱལ་རྩེ

*The fertile valley of the **Nyang-chu** River, which is the principal tributary of the* Gyantse County (26)
Brahmaputra in Tsang, rivals the Kyi-chu valley of Central Tibet in its impor- 江孜县
tance as a prosperous farming region and centre of population. The valley is Gyangze
*divided into upper and lower reaches; **Upper Nyang**, corresponding to present* Population: 55,865
*day Gyantse county, and **Lower Nyang** to Panam county. Upper Nyang there-* Area: 3,595 sq km
fore extends from the watershed of the Khari La pass as far as the town of Gyantse, Colour map 2, grid B3
and includes the peripheral valleys formed by the tributaries: Nyeru Tsangpo,
Lu-chu, and Narong Dung-chu.

*The county capital is located at **Gyantse**, a strategic intersection of great his-*
toric importance, 91 kilometres east of Khari La pass (262 kilometres from
Lhasa), 67 kilometres southeast of Zhigatse, and 189 kilometres northeast of
Yadong.

Ralung Monastery, the principal seat of the **Drukpa Kagyu school** in Tibet, is **Ralung**
located in a spectacularly dramatic setting below the snow peaks and glaciers རྭ་ལུང་དགོན་པ
of Nojin Gangzang (7,191 metres), Jangzang Lhamo (6,324 metres), and
Gyetong Soksum (6,244 metres).

Getting there The turn-off for Ralung is signposted above Ralung village, 16 kilometres after Khari La pass (5,045 metres) on the left (south) side of the Lhasa-Gyantse
highway (51 kilometres from Gyantse). Access is also possible by trekking from Lake
Phuma Yutso (see above, page 214) or from Yakde and Rampa (see above, page 253).
From the turn-off, the trail follows the **Zhak-chu** valley for 7 kilometres to reach the
monastery.

To the right of the massive ruined ramparts of the Central Temple, the
Tsuklakhang (which formerly contained large images of Amitayus and Lingje
Repa), more modest temples have recently been reconstructed. Beyond this
complex are the ruins of the **Ralung Kumbum** stupa and the cave hermitage
attached to the monastery, which has always been renowned for its ascetic and
meditative approach.

Founded by Tsangpa Gya-re (1126-1216) in 1180, on a site consecrated
with the name Ralung by his own master Lingje Repa (1128-88), the

Gyantse County

Hierarchs of the Drukpa Kagyu School

Drukchen I	Tsangpa Gya-re (1161-1211)	Drukchen VII	Trin-le Shingta (1718-1766)
Drukchen II	Choje Kunga Peljor (1426-76)	Drukchen VIII	Kunzik Chokyi Nangwa (1767-1822)
Drukchen III	Jamyang Chodrak (1477-1523)	Drukchen IX	Jigme Migyur Wangyel (1823-1883)
Drukchen IV	Pema Karpo (1527-92)	Drukchen X	Mipam Chokyi Wangpo (1884-1930)
Drukchen V	Paksam Wangpo (1593-1641)	Drukchen XI	Tendzin Khyenrab Gelek Wangpo (1931-1960)
Drukchen VI	Mipam Wangpo (1641-1717)	Drukchen XII	Jigme Pema Wangchen (b 1963)

monastery quickly supplanted **Druk Monastery** (see above, page 253) as the foremost seat of the Drukpa Kagyu school in Tibet. It was maintained originally by the so-called 'nine hierarchs named Senge', and subsequently by the successive incarnations of Tsangpa Gya-re, among whom the most renowned was the writer and historian Drukchen Pema Karpo (1527-92). The present incarnation, the 12th, resides in India. During the 17th century, Zhabdrung Ngawang Namgyel (1594-1651) fled from Ralung to establish a Drukpa theocracy in **Bhutan** (see below, page 842).

Some 21 kilometres below the Ralung turn-off, the highway passes through **Lungmar** township at the entrance to the **Nyerulung** valley. Here there is a large hydro-electric project under construction. The valley of the Nyeru Tsangpo leads directly upstream to the Yak La pass on the frontier of the Bhutanese district of Gasa. The main road then climbs from Lungmar to cross Simi La pass after 12 kilometres, en route for Gyantse. After Nyangto township, it is joined eight kilometres before reaching town by the road from Dekyiling on the east (see above, page 252).

Gyantse

Colour map 2, grid B3   *Gyantse was once considered to be Tibet's third largest town – after Lhasa and Zhigatse, but nowadays its status has undoubtedly diminished, in size being surpassed by Tsetang, Chamdo, Derge, Kandze, Dartsedo, Jyekundo, Chabcha and Barkham, among others. Nonetheless Gyantse has preserved much of its old-world atmosphere, and Tibetan rural life continues here, virtually unchanged, against a backdrop of magnificent 14th-15th century fortresses and temples. The hilltop fortress commands a strategic view of all approaching roads: from Zhigatse in the northwest, Simi La pass (and Lhasa) in the southeast, and Yadong on the Sikkim frontier in the southwest. For centuries it has dominated the wool and timber trade routes from Nepal, Sikkim and Bhutan.*

Orientation   Four routes intersect at a crossroads to the south of town: the southern highway to Lhasa leading southeast (262 kilometres), the Chakrigyab lam, leading to the east side of town and Kharto township (50 kilometres), the Zhigatse and Dromo road (which bifurcates on the west bank of the Nyang-chu, across the Gyantse Zamchen bridge) leading southwest, and the main road into town, Dzongdun lam which leads northwest.

On the Lhasa road, near the intersection, there is the *Transport Station Guesthouse*, the Bus Station and *Bus Station Guesthouse*, the Post Office, and a petrol station. The *Gyantse Hotel* is located to the left (southwest) of this intersection towards the bridge, opposite a pharmacy and alongside a number of small Sichuan and Tibetan restaurants which cater to truckers and bus drivers. Beside the bridge there is a PLA camp, which is also the site of Younghusband's camp site at Gyantse. Heading northwest into town on **Dzongdun lam**, the road circumverts the castle hill, and then runs due north to approach the vast enclosure of the Pelkhor Chode temple. The secondary loop known as **Chakrigyab** runs behind the hill to complete the castle's circumambulatory path. On the left side of Dzongdun lam, as you approach the temple gates, you will pass the *Furniture Factory Guesthouse*, a school, and (after the canal) the *Clothing Factory Guesthouse*, a number of small shops and the vegetable market. On the right side there is a newly constructed temple and a number of shops selling groceries, electrical goods, and traditional wares (Gyantse was once renowned for its Tibetan carpets). To the east of this main street, an older parallel lane runs between cramped village houses towards the original gates of the precinct and the Gyantse Carpet Factory.

If you follow the Chakrigyab lam east from the intersection, you will cross the canal and pass on the left the steep lane which leads uphill to Gyantse Dzong, before turning northwest into the old town to approach the Pelkhor Chode complex and the Gyantse Nunnery. If instead you continue eastwards, you will reach a T-junction and the Gyantse Middle School. Head south for Kharto township or north for the Peoples' Hospital, the Race Track and the Stadium.

The hilltop offers an unrivalled view of Gyantse town, and there is a small **Gyantse Dzong**

Western Tibet

Gyantse

museum, documenting the excesses of the British **Younghusband** expedition, which severely damaged the fortress in 1904. ■ *Admission fee: ¥15 per person.* For the history of the fortress, see box, page 257.

Pelkhor Chode Temple Complex དཔལ་འཁོར་ཆོས་སྡེ

History The great monastic complex of Gyantse is known as **Pelkhor Chode** after the name of Langdarma's son Pelkhor-tsen who is said to have resided here in the ninth century. The main temple, the **Tsuklakhang** was built by **Prince Rabten Kunzang Phak** between 1418-25. Reflecting the eclectic spiritual background of his ancestors who had long been affiliated to both the Sakyapa and Zhalupa schools, the prince sought to establish an ecumenical community, and he was aided in this task by Khedrupje Gelek Pelzangpo (1385-1438), a foremost student of Tsongkhapa, retrospectively recognized as the first Panchen Lama.

Within the high perimeter walls, other buildings were gradually established: the great **Kumbum** stupa was completed in 1427; followed by an increasing number of colleges which by the end of 17th century numbered 16: representing the Sakyapa, Zhalupa and Gelukpa schools.

At the beginning of the 19th century, there were 18 colleges: the Karma Kagyu and Drukpa Kagyu schools also being represented. However, the **Pelcho Khenpo** or preceptor who presided over the whole monastery and had administrative powers in Gyantse town, was Gelukpa. Only two of these outlying college buildings are now extant; and they contain little of interest.

The northeast corner of the enclosure wall comprises the **Goku Tramsa**, on which large applique tangkas would be displayed during the Gyantse festival (fourth month of the lunar calendar). Commissioned by the prince Rabten Kunzang Phak between 1418 and 1419, these enormous hangings depict Shakyamuni Buddha flanked by his two foremost students, as well as Maitreya, Manjushri, and so forth.

The Main Temple The **main temple (Tsuklakhang)**, which does survive intact, contains important 15th century murals and images.

Ground Floor The Ground Floor, entered via a portico with new images of the Four Guardian Kings, has a protector shrine (**Gonkhang**) on the left, between the stairs and the main assembly hall entrance. This is a strongly atmospheric chapel, in which the images depict the main Sakya protectors: Panjaranatha (Gonpo Gur), Six-armed Mahakala, Shridevi and Ekajati. The terrifying frescoes depict charnel ground scenes in bold colours. Within the 48-pillared assembly hall, there are a few original paintings and sculptures from the 15th century, which reveal a distinctive Tibetan style.

The **inner sanctum** (north), which is surrounded by a corridor painted with scenes from the *Sutra of the Auspicious Aeon (Bhadrakalpikasutra)*, contains enormous images of the Buddhas of the Three Times – the central Shakyamuni flanked additionally by standing images of Manjughosa and Maitreya.

To the left (west), there is the **Vajradhatu Chapel (Dorje Ying Lhakhang)** containing a central clay image of Sarvavid Vairocana, surrounded by the other four meditational buddhas and 20 peripheral figures of this mandala. There is also a gold inscribed manuscript version of the *Kangyur* dated 1431 – one volume of which is currently on display.

To the right (east) is the **Royal Chapel (Chogyel Lhakhang)**, containing exquisite clay images of the ancient kings: Songtsen Gampo, Trisong Detsen

Western Tibet

Gyantse Dzong, the Fortress of Gyantse

The original fortress of Gyel-khar-tse is attributed to Pelkhor-tsen, son of the anti-Buddhist king Langdarma, who vainly sought to perpetuate the Yarlung Dynasty from West Tibet following the assassination of his father.

The walls of the present structure were reputedly built in 1268, following the rise to power of the Sakyapas, and in 1365 a palatial castle was founded on the hilltop by the local prince, Phakpa Pelzangpo (1318-1370), who had acquired influence at the court in Sakya through his reputation as a brave general in the southern military campaigns conducted by his Sakyapa overlords, and at Zhalu, where in 1350 he entered into a marriage alliance with the lords of Zhalu. As a dowry he was granted the fiefdom of Changra, west of Gyantse, and he invited the great Buddhist master Buton Rinchendrub of Zhalu to reside in a temple which he had constructed there. In 1365, in addition to the Gyantse Castle, he also founded the Tsechen Chode

(Shambu Tsegu) castle and temple complex at the entrance to the Gyantse valley and adopted it as his principal seat. The incarnation of Buton, Drubchen Kunga Lodro, also resided there.

Later, in the 14th century, when Phakpa Pelzangpo's son, Kunga Phakpa, expanded the Gyantse complex, the royal residence was moved into Gyantse itself. During this period when the power of Sakya and its Mongol patrons was being eclipsed by the Phakmodrupa Dynasty at Nedong, the princes of Gyantse were able to maintain considerable independence and exerted great influence in both camps.

The first hilltop temple, known as Sampel Rinchenling, was built next to the castle by Prince Kunga Phakpa (1357-1412). Its ruined walls still contain extant 14th century murals – some executed in an authentic Newari style, and others in the Gyantse Tibetan style, which evolved therefrom.

and Tri Ralpachen. The latter also contains images of Atisha, Kamalashila, Padmasambhava, Shantarakshita, Manjushri, 11-faced Avalokiteshvara, Vajrapani, and Shakyashri of Kashmir. The large Maitreya in the centre of the chapel appears to have been added subsequently when the Gelukpa tradition became the dominant school at Gyantse (no mention of it is made in the *Nyang Chojung* inventory). A recessed chamber on the south wall of this chapel contains the Silver **Reliquary of Prince Rabten Kunzang Phak**, the temple's founder, and many volumes of canonical texts. There are also small images of Amitabha, Shakyamuni, Khedrupje, Panchen Lama IV and Dalai Lama V.

Upper Floor   The Upper Floor has five chapels which open out on to a central gallery. The staircase is located at the southwest corner of the antechamber. To the left (west) is the '**Path and its Fruition' Temple (Lamdre Lhakhang)**, containing clay images of the lineage-holders of the Sakyapa school, from Vajradhara, Nairatmya, and Virupa onwards. In the centre of the chapel is a three dimensional mandala palace of the deity Cakrasamvara. Exquisite murals depict the yogic activities of the Eighty-four Mahasiddhas of ancient India. Next, the **Maitreya Chapel** contains bronze images of Indian or Newari origin, the most sacred being a small image of Tara.

In front (north), the **Tsongkhapa Chapel** contains images of Tsongkhapa, Dalai Lama VII, Shakyamuni, Buton Rinchendrub, Sakya Pandita, Padmasambhava, and Sakyapa lamas of the *Lamdre* lineage.

To the right (east), the **Neten Lhakhang** is dedicated to the Sixteen Elders, each image in Chinese style being set within a grotto. There are also images of the Five Aspects of Manjushri and the Four Guardian Kings.

Gyantse Kumbum, The Stupa of 100,000 Deities

The principal deities of the 75 chapels are outlined as follows; for a detailed description, please consult The Great Stupa of Gyantse by F Ricca and E Lo Bue.

First Storey Here there are staircases in each of the four cardinal directions, leading to the temples of the second storey. The principal entrance is on the south side.

Second Storey 20 chapels (of which one constitutes the staircase). These depict the deities of the Kriyatantras in the following clockwise sequence: 1 (South Centre) Mahamuni with Bhaisajyaguru and Suparikirtinamasriraja; 2 (south) Marici; 3 (south) Bhutadamara Vajrapani; 4 (west) Krodha Bhurkumkuta/ Ucchusmakrodha; 5 (west) Aparajita Sitapatatra; 6 (West Central) Amitayus in Sukhavati; 7 (west) Parnasabari; 8 (west) Hayagriva; 9 (north) Acala; 10 (north) Mahavidya/ Grahamatrika Kurukulla; 11 (North Central) Dipamkara Buddha; 12 (north) Vasudhara; 13 (north) Vyaghravahana Mahakala; 14 (east) Mahabala; 15 (east) Dhvajagra; 16 (East Central) Maitreya in Tusita; 17 (east) Vaishravana; 18 (east) Four Guardian Kings (staircase to third storey); 19 (south) Panjaranatha Mahakala; and 20 (south) Usnisavijaya.

Third Storey 16 chapels, depicting the deities of the Kriyatantras and Caryatantras, in the following clockwise sequence: 1 (south) Vadisimha Manjughosa; 2 (south) Avalokiteshvara Jaganatha; 3 (south) Amitayus; 4 (south) Khadiravani Tara; 5 (west) Avalokiteshvara Simhanada; 6 (west) Avalokiteshvara Amoghapasha; 7 (west) Black Hayagriva; 8 (west) Kurukulla; 9 (north) Manjughosa; 10 (north) Vajravidarana; 11 (north) Vimalosnisa; 12 (north) White Tara; 13 (east) Samantabhadra; 14 (east) Vajrapani; 15 (east) Aksobhya Buddha; 16 (east) Five Protective Dharanis (Pancaraksa murals; ascending staircase).

Fourth Storey 20 chapels, depicting the deities of the Yogatantras, in the following clockwise sequence: 1 (south) Vajravalanalarka; 2 (south) Vajrasattva; 3 (South Central) Amitayus (with Paramadya mandalas); 4 (south) Vajrasattva; 5 (south) Jvalana; 6 (west) Prajnaparamita; 7 (west)

Vairocana; 8 (West Central) Ratnasambhava; 9 (west) Jnanasattva Manjushri; 10 (west) Vajrasattva; 11 (north) Vajrapani; 12 (north) Jvalanalarka; 13 (North Central) Amoghasiddhi; 14 (north) Sarvavid Vairocana; 15 (north) Amitayus; 16 (east) Buddhardharmaraja; 17 (east) Buddhavishvarupa; 18 (East Central) Aksobhya; 19 (east) Buddhasurya; 20 (east) ascending staircase and murals depicting the Eight Stupas.

Fifth Storey 12 chapels, depicting lineage-holders, in the following clockwise order: 1 (south) Atisha and his Kadampa followers; 2 (south) Buton Rinchendrub and his Zhalupa followers; 3 (south) Virupa and the Lamdre lineage of Sakya; 4 (west) Togme Zangpo and his Kadampa followers; 5 (west) Phadampa Sangye and his Chodyul and Zhiche followers; 6 (west) Tilopa and his Kagyupa followers; 7 (north) Dolpopa Sherab Gyeltsen and his Jonangpa followers; 8 (north) King Songtsen Gampo and the royal family; 9 (east) Shantarakshita, Padmasambhava and Kamalashila, with a select group of translators; 10 (east) Padmasambhava with his consorts Mandarava and Yeshe Tsogyel; 11 (east) Shakyashri and his followers; 12 (east) ascending staircase; murals of the Dashakrodha kings.

Sixth Storey (the 'Bowl' or Bum-pa) 4 chapels, depicting Yogatantra deities in the following clockwise order:
1 (south) Vajrasana Shakyamuni; 2 (west) Shakyasimha Buddha; 3 (north) Prajnaparamita; 4 (east) Vairocana.

Seventh Storey (Lower 'Spire' or Harmika) 1 chapel depicting the 10 mandalas of the Father Class of Unsurpassed Yogatantras.

Eighth Storey (Upper 'Spire' or Harmika) 1 chapel depicting the 11 mandalas of the Mother Class of Unsurpassed Yogatantras.

Ninth Storey (the 'Pinnacle' or Bindu) 1 chapel depicting a gilded-copper image of Vajradhara Buddha, flanked by the masters of the Kalacakra but backed by garish new murals.

Lastly, on the Upper Floor, just before the stairs there is a second **Neten Lhakhang** chapel dedicated to the Sixteen Elders (east) containing images of Shakyamuni flanked by his two foremost students and backed by the Sixteen Elders in their individual grottoes.

Top Floor The **Uppermost Floor** has a single chapel: the **Zhalyekhang**, containing 15 magnificent wall-painted mandalas, each eight metres in diameter. They are all associated with the foremost meditational deities of the Unsurpassed Yogatantras (*Anuttaryogatantras*): Kalacakra, Guhyasamaja, Cakrasamvara, Hevajra, Yamantaka and so forth. There are also images

Gyantse Kumbum

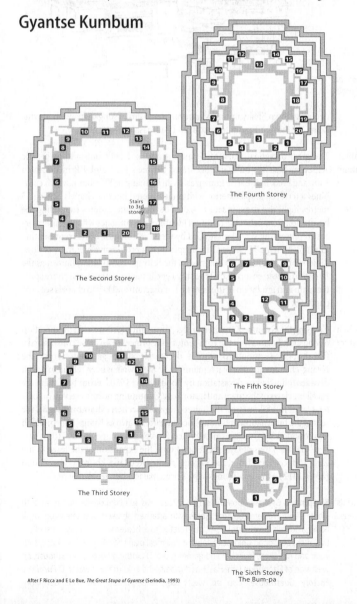

The Fourth Storey

The Second Storey

Stairs to 3rd storey

The Fifth Storey

The Third Storey

The Sixth Storey
The Bum-pa

After F Ricca and E Lo Bue, *The Great Stupa of Gyantse* (Serindia, 1993)

Western Tibet

The Kumbum and Pelkhor Chode at Gyantse

Western Tibet

depicting Jowo Shakyamuni, Maitreya, Manjushri, Tsongkhapa with his students, Amitayus, Tara, Sitatapatra, and Padmasambhava.

Gyantse Kumbum

■ *Admission: ¥15*

The great octagonal stupa of Gyantse – one of Tibet's outstanding artistic achievements, was built and decorated between 1427-39 by Prince Rabten Kunzang Phak in the style known as Tashi Gomang or Kumbum, which combines a terraced stupa exterior with multi-layered interior chapels. Rising 35 metres high, the stupa is said to have 108 gates, nine storeys (including the base) and 75 chapels. One tradition identifies the 108 gates with the nine storeys (representing space) multiplied by the 12 astrological signs (representing time). Within the 75 chapels, the images form a progressive hierarchy of three dimensional mandalas, as outlined in the Sakyapa compilation known as the *Drubtob Gyatsa*, ensuring that the stupa encapsulates within it the entire spiritual path and gradation of the tantras. For diagram and key to chapels see box, page 258.

Tsechen Monastery

Crossing the **Gyantse Zamchen** bridge, turn right (northwest) in the direction of Zhigatse. Formerly in the 15th century the princes of Gyantse constructed a fine bridge, surmounted with a decorative stupa gateway, across the Nyang-chu, but no trace of it remains. Even the town has been rebuilt in recent decades following its devastation by floods in the 1950s. From here there are excellent views of the town and its fortress. Continuing northwest, you quickly pass, after five kilometres, the hilltop ruins of **Tsechen (Shambu Tsegu)**, the seat of the incarnation of Buton Rinchendrub, known as Kunga Lodro, which was founded by Gyantse's first Prince Phakpa Pelzangpo (1318-70). It was here that the kings of Gyantse resided until the expansion of the town in the early 15th century. Later, the Sakyapa master Rendawa Zhonu Lodro Zhonu (1349-1412), who was Tsongkhapa's principal teacher, resided here.

Essentials

■ *on maps*
Price codes:
see inside front cover

Sleeping B *Gyantse Hotel*, T(08019)8172222. Has 103 comfortable rooms in both Tibetan and Western (Chinese) style, with attached showers and television, on 4 floors, a double room costs US$47, no elevator, solar heated water supply, most effective after 2000, good Chinese restaurant (full meal plan US$33, breakfast US$9), souvenir and gift shop, foyer bar and games room. **D** *Clothing Factory Guesthouse*, on west side of Dzongdun lam. Has 3-bed rooms, and cold running water. **D** *Furniture Factory Guesthouse*, also on west side of Dzongdun lam. Has dormitory accommodation, but cold water only. Other dormitory accomodation is available at the *Bus Station Guesthouse* and the *Transport Station Guesthouse* on the Lhasa road, after the bus station.

Eating *Gyantse Hotel* has reasonable but expensive Chinese food. For simpler fare, try the truck-stop restaurants opposite the *Gyantse Hotel*, the adjacent *Chinese Restaurant*, which has an English menu, or the *Mandala Tibetan Restaurant*, nearer the crossroads. Tibetan dumplings (*momo*) and noodles (*thukpa*) are also available at the *Clothing Factory Guesthouse*, ground floor.

Entertainment Outside the horse festival season, the only forms of entertainment are pool and karaoke.

Festivals The Gyantse horse-festival and archery contest is one of the oldest in this part of Tibet, having been introduced by prince Rapten Kunzang Phak in 1408. It lasts for 5 days, commencing on the 15th day of the 4th month of the lunar calendar. In 1999, this corresponds to 30 May.

Shopping **Handicrafts** There is a souvenir gift shop in the *Gyantse Hotel*, but try the *Carpet Factory*, or stores on the east side of Dzongdun lam for Tibetan textiles, carpets, handicrafts and religious artefacts. **Modern goods** There is a large department store at the intersection, and other general stores on the east side of Dzongdun lam, selling modern Chinese goods: clothing, tinned foods, and basic electrical supplies. **NB** Shops will accept only RMB currency. It is best to change currency in Lhasa before reaching Gyantse.

Transport Most visitors to Gyantse will have their transportation organized by the travel services. Long distance car and jeep transportation is more easily available from Lhasa or Zhigatse. However, long distance travel by public bus is possible from either Lhasa or Zhigatse. The bus station for Lhasa is located by the crossroads.

Directory Banks Not available. **Hospitals & medical services** *Gyantse Peoples' Hospital*, east of crossroads and north of T-junction. There is a pharmacy opposite the hospital and another opposite the *Gyantse Hotel*. **Tour companies & travel agents** *CITS*, Gyantse Branch, based at *Gyantse Hotel*. **Useful addresses** Police & public security: *Gyantse City Police and Public Security Bureau*, south of crossroads, near *Gyantse Hotel*.

Drongtse Monastery 14 kilometres north of Tsechen, overlooking the highway, is the renovated assembly hall of **Drongtse Monastery**, a Gelukpa institution founded in 1442 by the ascetic yogin Rinchen Gyatso, in accordance with a prophecy of Tsongkhapa. Later, Drongtse was adopted as a branch of Tashilhunpo. The ancient colleges for the study of the sutras and tantras have not been rebuilt, but the yellow **Assembly Hall** has been reconstructed in the 1980s. It contains a renovated image of Shakyamuni, and (in its upper storey) old images of Manjushri and Maitreya. Behind the monastery is a small chapel containing rock-carved images of Amitayus, Padmasambhava, Tara, and other deities.

Tsi Nesar In a side-valley 100 metres to the left of the highway, six kilometres north of Drongtse, are the reconstructed buildings of **Tsi Nesar**, an ancient geomantic temple (ie a peripheral temple of the 'district-controlling' or 'border-taming' class) attributed to King Songtsen Gampo. No trace remains of its precious murals and images, which reputedly dated back to the 12th century. An adjacent eighth century temple constructed by King Trisong Detsen to house an image of Prajnaparamita, which was consecrated by Padmasambhava, has also been destroyed.

Kyilkhar Caverns

The **Six Tunnels of Kyilkhar** (Kyilkhar Trangdruk) is an elaborate complex of limestone grottoes, which is associated with Padmasambhava and his consorts. It can be circumambulated by pilgrims in a single day.

A large outer cavern known as the **Assembly Hall** (Dukhang) serves as an antechamber, leading into the **Guru Lhakhang** cave (left side) where there are relief images of Padmasambhava and a stone footprint of Yeshe Tsogyel, aged eight. Adjacent to it is the **Gonkhang** cavern, where protector rituals would be performed. A long 10 metres tunnel extends from this antechamber towards an inner recess at the rear of the Dukhang. This is the **meditation cave of Yeshe Tsogyel**; and within it a tunnel leads, via a ladder and suspended rope, to the **Eighteen Tunnels of the Intermediate State** (Bardo Trangchen Chobgye) and the slippery **Elephant's Stomach Tunnel** (Langchen Tropa). Returning to the Dukhang, opposite the entrance to the cave of Yeshe Tsogyel is the **Cave of Mandarava**. Throughout the complex there are many natural rocks forming sacred images discerned by those of pure vision.

Getting there Cross the Gyantse Zamchen bridge and turn right towards Zhigatse. After 1 kilometre, a dirt road on the left leads to **Changra** township. From here, a 34 kilometres drive southwest crosses Namru La pass to reach **Gabzhi** in Kyilkhar township. An alternative 46 kilometres route is also possible from Panam, via **Dojung** (see below). The valley bifurcates at Gabzhi. The southwest branch, marked by the **Kyilkhar hot springs** and a stupa built by Tibet's eighth century physician Yutok Yonten Gonpo, leads to **Se** township (see below, page 280). Take the southeast branch to the caverns.

Panam County པ་སྣུམ

Panam County (27)
白朗县
Bainang
Population: 36,182
Area: 2,410 sq km
Colour map 2, grid B2

*The county of **Panam** is a prosperous farming belt, extending from Jangto township on the east bank of the Nyang-chu, downstream as far as Gadong township (20 kilometres), and from **Sharchok Zampa bridge**, following the Gyelkhar Zhung-chu tributary upstream to **Dojung** and **Wangden** townships (28 kilometres).*

The county capital is located at **Panam**, on the west bank of the Nyang-chu, 37 kilometres southeast of Zhigatse and 40 kilometres northwest of Gyantse (or in local terms 16 kilometres west of Jangto and four kilometres south of Norbu Khyungtse). Jangto and the Gyelkhar Zhung-chu valley are all traditionally part of **Upper Nyang**; while **Lower Nyang** is said to begin from Norbu Khyungtse and extends as far as Zhigatse.

This relatively low-lying area has been targeted in recent years for Chinese settlement; and there have been protracted negotiations with the European Union Development Fund for aid to implement a massive programme of agricultural development and irrigation, largely, it is feared, at the expense of the delicate eco-system and for the well-being of the immigrants rather than the locals.

Panam County

Located above Jangto township on the east bank of the Nyang-chu, this temple was founded in 1213 by Jangchub Pelzangpo, a student of the Kashmiri pandita Shakyashri. Formerly, it contained the robe, bowl and shoes of Shakyashri.

Pokhang Monastery

Above Pokhang, is **Nyangto-kyi Phuk**, a hermitage associated with Zhalu which was responsible for training adepts in yogic practices, such as the 'inner heat' (*tummo*) and the 'control of vital energy' (*lungom*). Accomplished masters from this hermitage would sometimes participate in the **Yuldruk Barkor cross-country run**: a seemingly impossible two-week marathon tour of Utsang and Lhokha, starting and ending in Zhalu, which was instituted on a 12-yearly basis (pig year) by Buton Rinchendrub in the 13th century and later adopted by the Tibetan government.

Nyangto-kyi Phuk

The Gyelkhar Zhung-chu valley, in which Wangden is located, contains twenty-two small villages and three monasteries. This area has long been famous for carpet weaving. The rugs of Wangden, which have highly distinctive designs and colour combinations, and a 'warp-faced' backing, were in great demand throughout the Tibetan plateau, and special carpets were commissioned for the use of Dalai Lama V and the monks who participated in the annual Great Prayer festival of Lhasa. Efforts are now being made to revive the weaving tradition of the impoverished Wangden valley.

Wangden

Zhigatse County གཞིས་ཀ་རྩེ

Zhigatse Town

Zhigatse, commanding the confluence of the Nyang-chu and Brahmaputra rivers, is still Tibet's second largest city, but it may not remain so for long in view of the recent rapid development of other cities in East Tibet, such as Chamdo, Kandze, Dartsedo and Barkham. The city is slightly higher than Lhasa, at 3,900 metres; with an oxygen content of 67 percent and average annual temperatures are 16° in mid-summer and -5° in mid-winter.

Zhigatse County (28)
日喀则县
Xigaze
Population: 79,337
Area: 2,678 sq km
Colour map 2, grid B2

Originally known as the **Samdrubtse Estate (Zhika Samdrubtse)** it was until the 16th century far less significant than the other great sites of the Nyang-chu valley and its environs: **Zur Sangakling**, **Zhalu**, **Nartang**, **Ngor**, and **Gyantse**. Further southwest lay **Sakya**, the capital of Tibet from 1268 to 1365. During the 14th-15th century the estate became a fiefdom of the Phakmodrupa kings; and after the usurption of power by the Rinpungpa princes, it was developed as a royal residence. **Tashilhunpo Monastery** was founded under their auspices in 1447 by Dalai Lama I Gendun Drupa.

History

Yet, the princes of Zhigatse became powerful patrons of the Karma Kagyu school, particularly following the foundation of the Zhamarpa's residence at Yangpachen (see above, page 137).

In 1565, the power of the Rinpungpas was itself usurped by **Karma Tseten (Zhingshakpa Tseten Dorje)** of the **Nyak** family. He made Zhigatse the **capital of Tibet**. In religious affairs, he adopted a sectarian posture, which favoured the Karma Kagyu school at the expense of others. When he persecuted the Northern Treasures (*Jangter*) community of the Nyingmapa school, he is said to have been ritually slain in 1599 by Jangdak Tashi Topgyel. Unfortunately this made little difference since the son who succeeded him, **Karma Tensung Wangpo**, maintained the same policy. He forged an alliance with the

Chogthu Mongols and captured Lhasa and Phenyul in 1605.

On his death (1611), he was succeeded by his son, **Karma Phuntsok Namgyel**, who, in 1613, established a new 15-point legal system for Tibet. His imposing **castle** at Zhigatse is said to have been a prototype for the Potala palace at Lhasa. In 1616 he forced Zhabdrung Ngawang Namgyel to flee Ralung Monastery for Bhutan, and following the latter's establishment there of a theocratic Drukpa state, the kings of Tsang engaged in a series of unsuccessful military campaigns against Bhutan. In 1618 he also established a Karma Kagyu Monastery, known as **Tashi Zilnon**, on the hill above Tashilhunpo, and once again sent Mongol armies against Lhasa.

Following his death in 1621, he was succeeded by his son, **Karma Tenkyong Wangpo** (1604-42). During this period (1626) Zhigatse was visited by Jesuit missionaries. From 1635-42 much of Tibet was plunged into civil war, the power of the Tsangpa kings of Zhigatse and their Chogthu allies being challenged by the Gelukpas of Lhasa, who were backed by the powerful Mongol armies of Gushri Qan. Mongol forces sacked Zhigatse in 1635, and eventually occupied the city in 1642, slaying Karma Tenkyong. From this point on until the present Lhasa has functioned as the capital of Tibet.

Though deprived of its primary political power, Zhigatse continued to flourish as the seat of government in **Tsang** and as the residence of the **Panchen Lamas**. It became an important trading centre. Goods imported from India included ironwares, cotton, dyes, spices and sugar; from China they included porcelain, tea and figs; from Ladakh came dried fruits and turquoise, while various grains and yak products came from within Tibet. The old hilltop castle was damaged by the Dzungar armies in 1717, and finally ruined after the communist suppression of 1959.

At present, Zhigatse is the capital of **Zhigatse** district of the Tibetan Autonomous Region, responsible for the administration of 19 counties.

The distance from Zhigatse to Lhasa is 348 kilometres via Gampa La pass and Gyantse, 281 kilometres via Nyemo, or 338 kilometres via Yangpachen and Zhugu La pass. From Zhigatse to Dram (*Ch* Zhangmu) on the Nepalese border the distance is 475 kilometres; and to Darchen at Mount Kailash in Far-west Tibet the distance is 1,018 kilometres.

Orientation   There are four approaches into town: the southern route from **Gyantse**, the eastern route from **Nyemo**, the western route from **Lhartse**, and the north-western route from the outlying areas of **Dongkar**, **Tanak**, and **Phuntsoling**. Of these, the southern approach offers the most dramatic views of Tashilhunpo's red masonry and resplendent golden roofs against the stark background of **Dolmari Hill**, and in the distance, beyond the haze of the Brahmaputra, the darker higher peaks of the **Gangtise** watershed range.

A petrol station on the left side of this approach road marks the beginning of town, after which the dirt road gives way first to cobbles and then to a paved surface. This is the **Lho** (Southern) quarter of town. A meteorological observatory, CITS Zhigatse Branch, the Bank of China, the

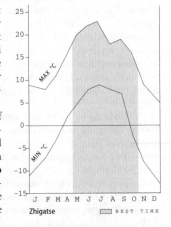

Zhigatse   BEST TIME

Zhigatse Hotel, and the Transport Building are passed on the right side, alongside a number of small restaurants and tea-shops. On the left side (after a newly constructed road which leads west to the Stadium, the Summer Palace and the Foreign Trade Bureau), there are the *Post Hotel*, the *River Hotel*, and the Bus Station. Arriving at a major intersection, turn right (east) for Nyemo and Lhasa, or left (west) along Mount Everest Road for Tashilhunpo Monastery, and Lhartse. Continuing due north on the main road, you will pass on the left the Customs Office, large glass-fronted department stores, a palatial karaoke nightclub, and the Bank of China, and on the right the *Xinhua Bookstore* and the *Peoples' Hospital*, followed by the *Hospital of Tibetan Medicine*. A second intersection leads west (left) from here towards the downtown area, or east (right) past a residential building for overseas Tibetans and a solar energy experiment station, before bifurcating: north to the Zhigatse Municipal Government and the ruins of Zhigatse Dzong, or due east for Nyemo and Lhasa. Continuing north along the main road, you reach the commercial centre of the town and residential districts (**2nd**, **3rd** and **4th Dronglhan**). Beyond, on the left, you pass into the **Jang** (Northern) quarter of town. After the People's Cinema, you reach a T-junction. Turn right for the Dongkar ferry.

Returning to the *Zhigatse Hotel*, after the Bus Station, turn left on Mount Everest Road towards Tashilhunpo. Soon you cross a road parallel to the first. This is the main street, leading to the town centre, the **1st Dronglhan**. Here are the Post Office, further department stores, Muslim tea-houses, the Shandong Finance Building, a cinema, and the Zhigatse District Government Buildings. A T-junction at the end of this street leads southwest towards the monastery (via the Public Security Bureau and Solar Energy Bath-house). Take this road, and soon, after the *Samdruptse Hotel* on the right, another turn-off leads into the commercial centre and open-air market, below the ruined fortress of the **Zhigatse Dzong**. The market is one of the best outside the Barkhor in Lhasa, and traditional artefacts of value can occasionally be found amongst the tourist trinkets. The privately run *Tendzin Hotel* overlooks the market. North of the

Western Tibet

Zhigatse

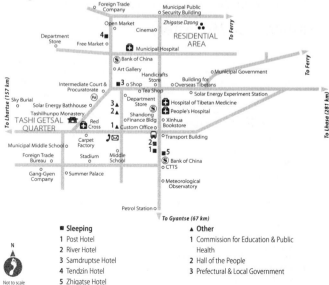

N

Not to scale

■ Sleeping
1 Post Hotel
2 River Hotel
3 Samdruptse Hotel
4 Tendzin Hotel
5 Zhigatse Hotel

▲ Other
1 Commission for Education & Public Health
2 Hall of the People
3 Prefectural & Local Government

market, and below the Zhigatse Dzong you pass into a residential area of town houses. A road leads northeast of the Dzong towards the **Dongkar ferry**.

Returning to the post office at the intersection of main street, continue west towards **Tashilhunpo Monastery**. Walled enclosures on the left and right sides lead respectively into the compounds of the Zhigatse Gang-gyen Carpet Factory and the Red Cross Medical Training Centre. Beyond these, there is another intersection, almost opposite the entrance to Tashilhunpo (which leads down to the Public Security Bureau and the market). West of the intersection, a turn-off on the left leads to the **Summer Palace of the Panchen Lamas**, while the houses of the old quarter of **Tashi Getsal** are clustered around the base of **Dolmari** on the right, beyond the monastery.

Tashilhunpo Monastery བཀྲ་ཤིས་ལྷུན་པོ་དགོན་པ

History Tashilhunpo, the seat of the Pancen Lamas, was founded in 1447 by **Dalai Lama I, Gendun Drub**, on the slopes of Drolmari, west of the fortress of Zhigatse Dzong. The original building (the assembly hall known as **Kelzang Lhakhang**) was built above a sacred sky-burial site, the stone slab of which is still to be seen on the floor within. An adjacent chamber, the **Tongwa Donden Lhakhang**, containing the silver reliquaries of Dalai Lama I Gendun Drub, Panchen Lama II and Panchen Lama III, dates from 1478.

In 1618 a Karma Kagyu monastery known as **Tashi Zilnon** ('suppressor of Tashilhunpo') was constructed on the higher slopes of Dolmari by Karma Phuntsok Namgyel, but no traces of it are now to be seen. The assembly hall of Tashilhunpo and its connecting chapels were refurbished and enlarged following the Civil War by Dalai Lama V and his teacher Panchen Lama IV.

A **Kudung Lhakhang**, containing the reliquary of Panchen Lama IV was built in 1662; and the splendid **Labrang Gyeltsen Tonpo** residence of the Panchen Lamas dates from the period of Panchen Lama VI (1738-80).

The **Namgyel Lhakhang** and the massive **Jamkhang Chenmo**, containing the world's largest gilded bronze image (26 metres high), were subsequently added to the west of the complex by Panchen Lama IX (1883-1937). Formerly, the site also contained five distinct gold-roofed mausolea enshrining the relics of

Tashilhunpo Monastery

1 Jamkhang Chemno and Ganden Lhakhang	7 South extension wing
2 Namgyel Lhakhang	8 North extension wing
3 Kundung Lhakhang	9 East wing
4 Kelzang Kyamra	10 South wing
5 Dukhang	11 Dungten Tashi Namgyel
6 Tongwa Donden Lhakhang	12 Dungsten Sisum Namgyel

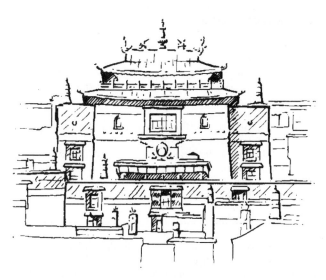

The Mausoleum of Panchen Lama IV at Tashilhunpo

Panchen Lamas V-IX, but these were erased during the 1960s.

The late Panchen Lama X (1938-89) towards the end of his life commissioned a new collossal mausoleum named **Dungten Tashi Namgyel** on the north side of the assembly hall courtyard. Within it he personally reinterred the mortal remains of his five predecessors side-by-side. The most recent construction at Tashilhunpo is the new mausoleum, the **Dungten Sisum Namgyel**, which was built to house his own relics, following his untimely death in 1989.

Around the assembly hall there were formerly four colleges: **Shartse** teaching general subjects, **Ngakpa** teaching the tantras, **Tosamling** teaching dialectics, and **Kyilkang**. Of these **Ngakpa** has now been relocated to the front of the assembly hall; while **Kyilkhang** has assumed the functions of the other defunct colleges combined, particularly dialectics.

One of Tibet's most influential monasteries, Tashilhunpo's many branches extend from **Yong He Gong** in Beijing and **Chengde** in Manchuria to **Gyantse**, and in more recent years to **Karnataka** state in South India.

Orientation

■ *Admission: ¥30*

Tashilhunpo Monastery is counted among the six largest Gelukpa monasteries in Tibet, formerly housing 4,700 monks at its peak. Like Labrang Tashikyil and Kumbum Jampaling Monastery in Amdo, it has the appearance of a monastic city. There is a three kilometres pilgrimage circuit (*lingkor*) around the complex, including the Dolmari ridge to the rear, and the buildings should ideally be visited in a clockwise sequence, from west to east. Insist on following the correct route if your local tour guide tries to lead you through in reverse! The main buildings are therefore to be visited in the following sequence:

Jamkhang Chenmo

This tall building to the west of the complex houses the world's largest gilded copper image, 26 metres in height. Constructed during the First World War, this massive **Maitreya**, embodying loving kindness, contains 6,700 teals of gold and 150 metric tons of copper, and within it an enormous juniper tree from **Reting** monastery functions as a life-supporting axis (*sok-zhing*). The body of the image is encrusted with ornaments and precious stones, and its overwhelming visage exudes an aura of calm benevolence. The surrounding murals of the chapel depict 1,000 Maitreyas, drawn in gold line on a red background.

The succession of Panchen Lamas

Panchen Lama I	Khedrub Je Gelek Pelzangpo (1385-1483)	Panchen Lama VII	Tenpei Nyima (1782-1854)
Panchen Lama II	Sonam Chokyi Langpo (1438-1504)	Panchen Lama VIII	Tenpei Wangchuk (1855-1882)
Panchen Lama III	Ensapa Lobzang Dobdrub (1505-1566)	Panchen Lama IX	Chokyi Nyima (1883-1937)
Panchen Lama IV	Lobzang Chokyi Gyeltsen (1567-1662)	Panchen Lama X	Trinle Lhundrub Chokyi Gyeltsen (1938-1989)
Panchen Lama V	Lobzang Yeshe (1663-1737)	Panchen Lama XI	Gendun Chokyi Nyima (b 1989)
Panchen Lama VI	Palden Yeshe (1738-1780)		

Other murals near the entrance depict the three Kadampa teachers: Atisha, Dromtonpa and Ngok Lekpei Sherab; as well as the triad of meditational deities: Guhyasamaja, Cakrasamvara, and Bhairava. Fifteen other small chapels extend throughout the lower and upper floors, and among these special mention should be made of the **Zhelre Lhakhang** and **Utrok Lhakhang**, from which Maitreya's face and crown are respectively seen at close quarters. The **Ganden Lhakhang**, which faces the entrance to the Jamkhang Chenmo, contains 1,000 images of Tsongkhapa.

Namgyel Lhakhang Constructed by Panchen Lama IX (1883-1937), the Namgyel Lhakhang contains large impressive images of Tsongkhapa and his two foremost students, flanked by Maitreya and Manjushri. In recent years it has been used as a school of dialectics, and is sometimes closed to the public. The impact of this chapel is understandably dwarfed by the awesome majesty of Maitreya in the previous chapel.

Labrang Gyeltsen Tonpo The residence of the Panchen Lamas, which was founded by Gendun Drubpa in 1447, and developed and refurbished by Panchen Lama VI Palden Yeshe (1738-80), is a three-storeyed white building, with a series of seven interconnecting red-painted chapels along its front façade. More recent renovations were carried out between 1976-78.

From west to east (left to right) the outer chapels are as follows: **Gyanak Lhakhang** was built by Panchen Lama VI in honour of the Qianlong Emperor, who was his disciple, and it contains images of Vajradhara, Bhaisajyaguru, Tsongkhapa and Tara. **Lhendzom Zimpuk** is the chamber where the Panchen Lamas would receive official visitors including the Manchu amban. It contains two thrones and a series of 17 applique tangkas depicting the previous lives of the Panchen Lama, which were commissioned in Hangzhou by Panchen Lama IX.

Chime Peldrub Lhakhang is dedicated to Amitayus, flanked by Shakyamuni and Manjughosa. The chapel also contains a full set of the *Kangyur* and *Tangyur*. The next chamber, **Dzegya Gonkhang**, approached via a staircase, contains an image of the protectress Chamsing.

The **Puntsok Kunkyil Lhakhang** contains images of Tsongkhapa and his foremost students. **Kuntu Lhakhang** contains an assemblage of smaller images. Lastly, **Yulo Dolma Lhakhang** contains images of the 21 forms of Tara. Upstairs in the front wing of the Labrang is the chamber where the late

Panchen Lama X's embalmed remains were placed within a glass shrine from 1989 until the construction of his mausoleum was completed in 1994.

This red gold-roofed chapel contains the silver reliquary of Panchen IV **Kudung** Lobzang Chokyi Gyeltsen (1567-1662) – teacher of Dalai Lama V and the first **Lhakhang** to be recognized by the title Panchen Erdeni, embodiment of Buddha Amitabha. His predecessors were retrospectively recognized as such. The importance of this reliquary is known by the fact that among all the mausolea of Tashilhunpo, only this one was left standing during the Cultural Revolution. The 11 metres high reliquary stupa contains an image of Panchen Lama IV in its niche, and in front are images of the deities symbolizing longevity: Amitayus, White Tara, and Vijaya. The courtyard has a fine bell.

The Courtyard The large flagstoned courtyard known as **Kelzang Khyamra** **Kelzang** is east of the Kudung Lhakhang and approached via a high-walled lane. Notice **Tsuklakhang** the tall prayer-flag pole (Dukar Khorlo Darchen) which is refurbished each New Year and is said to have talismanic properties. The courtyard is where religious dances would be performed. On its west wing is the **Kelzang Tsuklakhang** and on the north are the colossal new mausolea constructed in recent years to hold the relics of past Panchen Lamas. An additional two-storey complex of chapels flanks the east wing of the courtyard.

West Wing of the Courtyard: the Assembly Hall Turning to the west wing, the Kelzang Tsuklakhang is a three-storey complex. The outer walls have murals depicting the Thousand Buddhas of the Auspicious Aeon (Bhadrakalpa), each with its own verse inscription taken from the *Bhadrakalpika-sutra*.

The downstairs **Assembly Hall (Dukhang)** is the oldest structure at Tashilhunpo, founded in 1447 by Dalai Lama I and completed in 1459. Measuring approximately 274 metres by 46 metres, its interior is supported by 48 columns. It was constructed above a **sky-burial slab**, which is still visible on the floor between the high rows of seats. Alongside the massive throne of the Panchen Lama, there are main images of Maitreya in the form Ajita flanked by Avalokiteshvara and Manjughosa, and a series of images attached to the pillars – depicting the deities of longevity, Amitayus, White Tara, and Vijaya, as well as peaceful and wrathful forms of Avalokiteshvara. Applique tangkas made in Hangzhou depict 17 past incarnations of the Panchen Lamas.

The dark **inner sanctum** comprises two chapels: the **Dolma Lhakhang** containing a Newari sculpted image of Cintamanicakra Tara, flanked by Green Tara (twice), Amitayus, and Je Sherab Senge; and the **Jowo Lhakhang**, containing images of Shakyamuni flanked by his foremost students, the Eight Bodhisattvas, and two additional images of Manjughosa. Attached to the pillars in the latter chapel are images of Dalai Lama I and Panchen Lama IV.

South Extension Wing of the Assembly Hall Above the Assembly Hall, the two-storeyed south extension wing of the Kelzang Tsuklakhang contains seven chapels, three of which are downstairs and four upstairs. In clockwise sequence (east to west), the former comprise: the **Ngonga Lhakhang**, containing a central Kadam-style stupa; the **Gyanak Lhakhang**, containing a silver image of Jowo Shakyamuni, flanked by the Sixteen Elders and Panchen Lama IX; and the **Rinchen Lhakhang**, containing a natural Chinese bronze image of Maitreya, flanked by Vajradhara, Tara, and Avalokiteshvara.

A staircase leads from here to the upper storey, where the four chapels are as follows: the **Ngurmik Lhakhang**, containing a miraculous Tara image of

Indian origin which was brought to Tibet at the request of Ngurmikpa Darma Nyingpo in the 12th century; the **Pandrub Lhakhang**, containing a silver image of Panchen Lama IV flanked by Sitatapatra and 11-faced Mahakarunika; the **Gadong Lhakhang**, containing a large bronze image of Maitreya, which was commissioned by Panchen Lama IV; and the **Natsok Lhakhang**, containing images representative of the diverse Buddhist traditions, with Tsongkhapa and his foremost students at the centre. From here, a staircase leads down to the ground level and to the north wing of the Tsuklakhang complex via a passageway.

North Extension Wing of the Assembly Hall Above the Assembly Hall, the two-storeyed north extension wing of the Kelzang Tsuklakhang contains three chapels on its lower level and two on its higher level (each of the last two being approached via a separate staircase).

From west to east these comprise: (downstairs) the **Gonkhang**, containing images of the dharma protectors Bhairava flanked by six-armed Mahakala, Dharmaraja, and Shridevi; (downstairs) the **Zhelre Lhakhang**, which offers a view of the head and shoulders of Maitreya in the Assembly Hall below, flanked by smaller exquisite images of Manjushri and Avalokiteshvara which were sculpted personally by Panchen Lama VI; (upstairs) the **Kunzik Dukhang**, containing images of Shakyamuni, his foremost disciples and the Sixteen Elders, as well as an active shrine dedicated to the protectress Shridevi in a recess to the right; (downstairs) an oblong-shaped **Zhelrekhang**, offering an excellent view of Shakyamuni within the inner sanctum of the Assembly Hall below, and housing a mandala of the Medicine Buddha and tangkas which depict the Six Ornaments and Two Supreme Ones of ancient India; and, lastly, (upstairs) the **Tongwa Donden Lhakhang**, containing eight stupas among which are the precious reliquaries of Dalai Lama I, Panchen Lama II and Panchen Lama III, and a stone footprint of the celebrated Nyingma lama Guru Chowang (see above, page 208 and 214).

East and South Wings of the Courtyard On the east and south wings of the courtyard, there is a further series of 11 chapels connected by L-shaped galleries on two levels, those on the lower floor having been constructed by Panchen Lama IV and those on the upper floor by Panchen Lama V.

Clockwise (from northeast to southeast and southeast to southwest), the former comprise: the **Jowokhang**, containing Jowo Shakyamuni surrounded by the Thousand Buddhas of the Auspicious Aeon; the **Nguldung Lhakhang**, containing an image of Vajradhara and a central silver stupa donated by Gushri Qan; the **Parkhang** (Printery), housing the extant **Nartang** woodblocks for a complete set of the *Kangyur* and a partial set of the *Tangyur*; the **Jokhang**; the **Dolma Lhakhang**; and, finally, the **Ganden Lhakhang**, the last of which contains a central image of Tsongkhapa.

The chapels of the upper floor (again clockwise) comprise: the **Tsepak Lhakhang**, dedicated to Amitayus; the **Kangyur Lhakhang**, with images of Shakyamuni and his foremost disciples, where monks congregate each morning to recite texts from the Buddhist Canon, the *Kangyur* stored herein; the **Dechen Lhakhang**, containing images of Amitabha flanked by Maitreya and Manjushri; the **Ganden Lhakhang**, containing images of Tsongkhapa flanked by Dalai Lama V, Panchen Lama VI, Panchen Lama VIII, and the Indian and Tibetan lineage-holders of their *Lamrim* tradition; and, finally, the **Tingye Dolma Lhakhang**, containing a fire-protecting image of Tara, attributed to Shakyashri, the Pandita of Kashmir (1145-1243).

North Wing of the Courtyard On the north wing of the courtyard there are two extraordinary new mausolea, the larger of which, named **Dungten Tashi Namgyel**, was consecrated in 1988 by the late Panchen Lama X to replace the five older reliquary buildings destroyed during the Cultural Revolution. It houses an enormous reliquary stupa containing, side by side, the mortal remains of Panchen Lamas V-IX. Alongside this building is an even more recent construction: the mausoleum of the late Panchen Lama X, named **Dungsten Sisum Namgyel**, which was consecrated in 1994. The sum of US$7.75 million is said to have been spent on the construction of these mausolea. Both of these new buildings require an additional admission fee.

South of the entrance to the **Kelzang Khyamra** courtyard, a passageway leads downhill, back towards the gates of Tashilhunpo. To the right of the main path (as you exit), there is the reconstituted **Ngakpa** college. A flight of stairs leads to the assembly hall, where there are images of Tsongkhapa, flanked by his two foremost disciples and Panchen Lama IV. Next to the central throne, there is a canopied mandala of the deity Yamari. Liturgical rituals are performed here each morning. **Ngakpa Tratsang**

This college, dedicated to formal debate and the study of dialectics, has an assembly hall containing images which include Shakyamuni Buddha, Dalai Lama I, Tsongkhapa, and Panchen Lama IV. The **inner sanctum** contains images of Shakyamuni flanked by his two foremost students, the Eight Bodhisattvas and Sixteen Elders, and with a small image of Panchen Lama IX in front. Upstairs the **Gonkhang** is dedicated to the protectress Chamsing. **Kyilkhang Tratsang**

Northeast of Tashilhunpo Monastery is the nine-storeyed tangka wall known as **Goku Trampa**, where a 40 metre applique depicting the Buddhas of the Three Times is ceremonially displayed during the winter and summer prayer festivals. **Goku Trampa**

Outside the monastery grounds, and on a branch road to the southwest (see above, page 268) is the **Summer Palace of the Panchen Lamas**, which was constructed between 1956-59 to replace the former summer residence. The building is not presently open to the public. **Dechen Phodrang**

Western Tibet

Sleeping B *Zhigatse Hotel (Rikaze Hotel)*, T/F(86892)8822551/8821900. Has 123 comfortable and recently upgraded rooms with attached showers and television, on 4 floors (US$55 per double room), no elevator, solar heated water supply, sometimes effective after 2000, vastly improved Chinese restaurant (full meal plan at US$32, breakfast US$9), souvenir and gift shop, foyer bar, large rooms available for special functions. **D** *Tendzin Hotel*, 20 rooms, is cheap, friendly, Tibetan-run and centrally located, opposite the open-air market, showers available. **D** *Samdruptse Hotel*, near Zhigatse Government Buildings and cinema. Has superior accommodation and cheaper dormitory-style accommodation, good value and location. **E** *River Hotel*, and *Post Hotel*, both south of the bus station on main road into town from Gyantse, have dormitory-style accommodation, and cheap restaurants located nearby. **Essentials**
■ *on map, page 265*
Price codes:
see inside front cover

Eating Among the hotels, the *Zhigatse Hotel* offers reasonable Chinese food, and the *Tendzin* and *Samdruptse* have simple Tibetan dishes. There are many smaller cheap road-side restaurants, serving Sichuan, Tibetan, and Muslim cuisine.

Entertainment There are discotheques, upmarket karaoke cabaret and low-market karaoke bars, and video parlour facilities, mostly on the main motor road north of Bus Station. There are 2 cinemas: one adjacent to the Government Buildings and a second, the Peoples' Cinema, towards the north of town, east of the market.

Festivals For the dates of traditional Tibetan festivals, see above, Essentials, page 48. Tashilhunpo's main festival is held on the 15th day of the 5th lunar month, which in 1999 corresponds to 28 June.

Shopping Handicrafts There is a souvenir and gift shop in the *Zhigatse Hotel*. The Gang-gyen Carpet Factory, Mount Everest Road, Zhigatse, southeast of Tashilhunpo entrance, has a wide selection of carpets in various designs. Credit card payment and shipping facilities are available. For metalwork, jewellery, and traditional religious or household artefacts, try the open-air market.

Modern goods There are large glass-fronted department stores in the main commercial street, near Government Buildings, and on the main motor road from Gyantse, selling textiles, groceries, electrical goods. Smaller grocery and electrical stores are also to be found. The shops will generally accept only RMB currency, and rarely accept payment in US dollars. The receptionist at the *Zhigatse Hotel* will sometimes change US currency, but It is best to change currency in Lhasa or Dram (*Ch* Zhangmu) before reaching Zhigatse, and not depend upon the banks or money changers.

Photography Print film and processing are available at the department stores, and smaller electrical shops in town.

Stamps Stamps are available at *Post Office*, on main commercial street, or at the *Zhigatse Hotel*, reception counter.

Transport Most visitors to Zhigatse, whether arriving via Lhasa, Dram (Zhangmu) or Kailash, will have their transportation organized by the travel services, although public buses are also available from Lhasa, Gyantse and Dram. Long distance car and jeep transportation is more easily available from Lhasa, but occasionally through CITS, Zhigatse Branch. The public bus station is located to the southeast of town on the Gyantse Road, opposite the *Zhigatse Hotel*.

Air Zhigatse Airport, located in Jangdong township, 45 kilometres east of town, on the central Lhasa highway, is not open to civilian traffic. The distance from Zhigatse to Gongkar Airport is 264 kilometres due east. There are flights to Chengdu (daily), Kathmandu (Tuesday/Saturday), Beijing (Sunday), Chongqing (Wednesday/Sunday), Guangzhou (Wednesday), Shanghai (Tuesday/Friday) and Ziling (Monday/Friday).

Directory Banks *Bank of China*, at crossroads, opposite *Hospital of Tibetan Medicine*. **Hospitals & medical services** *Peoples' Hospital*, east of Gyantse lam, north of *Zhigatse Hotel*. *Zhigatse Hospital of Tibetan Medicine*, at crossroads, north of *Peoples' Hospital*, opposite *Bank of China*. **Communications** Post Office: on Mount Everest Rd at junction with main commercial street. **Tour companies & travel agents** *CITS*, Zhigatse Branch, near *Zhigatse Hotel*, T2525. **Useful addresses** Police & public security: *Zhigatse City Police and Public Security Bureau*, east of Tashilhunpo Monastery, near market.

Southern Zhigatse County

Zhalu Monastery, the Seat of Buton Rinpoche ཞ་ལུ་དགོན་པ

Gyengong Lhakhang

■ *Admission : ¥25*
Colour map 2, grid B2

Approaching Zhalu from the turn-off at Khyungram, some 18 kilometres southeast of Zhigatse (or 49 kilometres from Gyantse), you will pass on the right the smaller two-storeyed **Gyengong Lhakhang**, said to be the first temple built in Tibet at the beginning of the Later Diffusion of Buddhism in 997. Its founder was Loton Dorje Wangchuk, a disciple of Lachen Gongpa Rabsel, and teacher of Jetsun Sherab Jungne. The main image here is of Rabtenma, a form of the protectress Shridevi; and it was here that in the 13th century the Sakya Pandita received ordination as a Buddhist monk. Nowadays, pilgrims are aware of a curious mushroom growing from one of the entrance pillars, which is said to have miraculously appeared and is protected by a glass covering.

The **Serkhang Tramo** temple of Zhalu, which stands within a walled enclo- **Serkhang**
sure at Zhalu village, was built originally in 1040 by Jetsun Sherab Jungne of **Tramo Temple**
Zhangzhung, and renovated in 1290 and 1333 by Gonpopel, Drakpa Gyeltsen, and Buton Rinchendrub with funds provided by the Mongol emperor Oljadu (1265-1307). This east-facing building has a striking Chinese-style roof, made of yellow and green glazed 'turquoise' tiles with porcelain relief carvings; and its interior murals reveal an important synthesis of Pala, Newari, Tibetan, and Chinese forms, suggesting that the art of Zhalu became the precursor for the later Gyantse style.

Entering the courtyard, there is a monastic residential compound on the north wing (upstairs), where Zhalu's 23 monks now live. Formerly, there were 3,800 monks at the highpoint of the complex's development. Most belonged to the **Zhalupa** school, a minor but highly influential Buddhist tradition, founded by Buton Rinchendrub on the basis of the Sakya and Kadam teachings.

On the south (left) of the courtyard, there is a staircase leading to the former residence of the encyclopediaist **Buton Rinchendrub**, who redacted the 227 manuscript volumes of the *Tibetan Buddhist Canon* and the 26 volumes of his own *Collected Works* here in the 14th century. An inscribed stone plaque is said to date from the temple's foundation in 1040.

The **Serkhang Tramo** itself has been entered via a northeast extension area since the original east gateway was sealed by the construction of a **Protector Temple** or **Gonkhang** annex in the early 14th century.

Ground Floor The temple has three storeys, the ground floor containing an assembly hall (Tsokhang) with seven abutting chapels and a pilgrim's circuit (*khorlam*). An empty chapel is located immediately to the west (right) of the entrance, and the murals of the east wall are currently undergoing restoration.

To the east (left) of the entrance is the **Protector Temple**, the **Gonkhang**, a 14th century T-shaped chapel dedicated to Vaishravana, which incorporates within it sections of the original 11th century walls. The murals here interestingly juxtapose the **East-Indian Palasyle** paintings of the original building with the work of the celebrated Newar artist **Anige** (1245-1306), who developed his distinctive 'western style' at the Yuan capital in Dadu (modern Beijing).

Continuing past the Protector Temple, you will reach the entrance to the **pilgrim's circuit**, decorated with extraordinary vivid and detailed murals of the 100 deeds of Shakyamuni Buddha, which represent the Anige school. Each band of painting has its unique inscription, taken from texts such as the *Jatakamala* and the *Ratnakuta sutras*, which describe the deeds of the Buddha. Here the influence is predominantly Newar, interspersed with a few figures suggestive of Chinese or Central Asian styles. Three small chapels are entered from the pilgrim's circuit, on the south, west and north sides; but of these, only the last has well preserved murals, depicting Avalokiteshvara, Hayagriva, and so forth.

Zhigatse County

Western Tibet

Exiting from this passageway, the four central chapels are then approached. The **Segoma Lhakhang** (south) which once housed the renowned **Zhalu Library** contains a fragmented *Kangyur* and wall paintings of the Buddhas of the Five Families in Newari style. The **Lkakhang Lhoma** and **Lhakhang Jangma** (west) now contain only painted *tsatsa* (attributed to Atisha) and stucco halos (*torana*). Lastly, the **Gosum Lhakhang** (north) contains a number of damaged images and quite well preserved Newar-style murals.

Middle and Upper Floors Ascending to the middle floor, there is a **chapel dedicated to Prajnaparamita**, which was renovated in the 14th century. It has a circumambulatory passageway (*khorlam*) with fascinating murals, which illustrate the synthesis of Newar and Yuan styles developed by Anige and his followers, among whom the Tibetan artist Chimpa Sonambum is identified by name. The chapel itself has been used as a storage chamber for religious dance masks and costumes.

The upper floor has four chapels, dating from the restoration work undertaken by Kunga Dondrub and Buton Rinchendrub in the 14th century.

Among these, the **Deden Lhakhang** (west) contains faded four metres mandalas of the *Yogatantras* and a number of images, including the most precious relic of Zhalu Monastery: a self-originated **black stone image of Avalokiteshvara Kharsapani**, with a natural Vajrabhairava image at its rear side. There are also many fine Indian and Kashmiri bronze images, some of which are associated with the pandita Shakyashri. The gilded copper stupas contain relics of Atisha and Buton Rinchendrub. The other images are also notable: a large austere figure of Buton Rinchendrub, the Eight Medicine Buddhas, Maitreya, Amitayus, Padmasambhava, Vajrasattva, and Vajrapani. There is a sealed ritual vase of the Indian tantric Mahasiddha Virupa, known as **Bumchu Nyongdrol**, which was brought to Tibet by Gayadhara. This is opened once every 12 years, so that pilgrims can partake of its sacred waters. A leather bag contains a sandalwood mandala in 108 pieces and a glass cabinet has a self-sounding conch-shell. Formerly, there were eight imperial edicts here dating from the time of **Chogyel Phakpa**.

The **Tsepame Lhakhang** (north) contains mandalas of Sarvavid Vairocana, and more than 20 images, including fine bronzes.

The **Tangyur Lhakhang** (east) where Buton's manuscript version of the *Tangyur* was housed before its destruction, has mandalas of Maitreya, and a circumambulatory passageway with murals depicting Avalokiteshvara and the eight stupas, which suggest a later Tibetan development of the Anige style.

Lastly, the **Neten Lhakhang** (south) contains mandalas of Paramadya, Vajradhatu, Vajrashekhara, and Trailokyavijaya; an image of Kalacakra, and images of Buton Rinchendrub and his disciple Rinchen Namgyel, along with a set of the former's 26 volume *Collected Works*. The outer walls of this chapel depict the life of Buton, an allegorical chart on the taming of mental excitement and sluggishness in the course of the meditation known as calm abiding (*satipathana*), and an astronomical chart, which reflects one of Buton's own particular interests.

Ripuk Retreat This cave hermitage attached to Zhalu Monastery was developed by Buton, on a site sanctified for retreat by Atisha himself. **Ripuk** over the centuries acquired renown as a centre for meditative retreat, and developed into a complex with two assembly halls, housing over 300 monks. Formerly, it contained a precious image of Buton Rinchendrub and a stupa called **Tongdrol Chenmo**, which Buton himself dedicated on behalf of his deceased mother. South of Zhalu in the mountains is **Tarpaling**, the residence of Buton's teacher

Tarpa Lotsawa. There is also a two-day trek eastwards to Ngor Monastery via the Showa La and Cha La passes.

Getting there Some 18 kilometres southeast of Zhigatse (or 49 kilometres from Gyantse), at Khyungram in Gyatso township, there is a turn-off on the right, which leads (4 kilometres) to Zhalu Monastery, the seat of Buton Rinchendrub (1290-1364) who was the great codifier of the Tibetan translations of the Indian Buddhist canon.

Within Chakdam township to the east of Zhigatse, and opposite the estuary of **Zur Sangakling** the Shang River (see above, page 250), there is an area of great importance to the Nyingma school of Tibetan Buddhism. This is **Zur Ukpalung**, the seat of Zurpoche Sakya Jungne, who preserved and propagated the Nyingma teachings following Langdarma's persecution and the subsequent interregnum. It is located in **Phaktangma** district and, although no longer extant, the impact of the Zur family's activities in this retreat centre over five centuries should not be underestimated. At the village of **Zur Sangakling**, where a temple was restored in 1421, the ritual dagger (*phurba*) of the Zur family was formerly preserved.

Upstream, closer to Zhigatse, the road passes the derelict site of **Thubten Serdokchen**, the residence of Zilungpa Sakya Chokden, which was founded in 1469 as a school of dialectics.

Downstream from **Phaktangma** district, on the south bank of the **Phungpo** Brahmaputra is **Mount Phungpo Riwoche**, one of the 'four sacred mountains **Riwoche** of Tibet'. Padmasambhava passed time here in the **Yupuk** cave retreat, and later in the 10th-11th century it was an important site for the Dzogchen lineage since the master Nyang Jangchub Dra attained the rainbow body here. Subsequently the mountain became a favourite haunt of Yungtonpa Dorjepel (1284-1365). Also, at Yupuk, in the hermitage of Padmasambhava, the treasure-finder Dumpa Gyazhangtrom discovered Yamantaka *terma*, and Dorje Lingpa (1346-1405) discovered an image of Vajrasattva.

Turning right at the **Zamshar** bridge, on the south side of town, the **Nartang** Zhigatse-Dram highway cuts southwest towards the Tak La Nub pass, which **Monastery** forms a watershed between the Dzirak-chu and Shab-chu (Re-chu) rivers.

Nartang Monastery is located 14 kilometres from Zhigatse to the north side of this road, and is approached along an easy motorable track. This prominent Kadampa monastery was founded in 1153 by Tumton Lodro Drakpa, a disciple of Sharapa. Formerly, there was a **Kumbum (Tashi Gomang)** style stupa here, constructed during the 15th century, but it was destroyed during the Cultural Revolution. The main image was a form of Tara known as **Chumik Drolma**.

In the 17th century, Nartang came under the influence of Tashilhunpo; and it acquired particular renown for its xylograph (woodblock) compilation of the the Buddhist canon, the *Kangyur* and *Tangyur*, which was carved here between 1730-42 at the behest of Miwang Pholhane Sonam Topgyel, the then ruler of Tibet. A series of eight woodblocks depicting the Sixteen Elders were also commissioned; but only one now survives. Along with the extant fragments of the xylographs of the Nartang Canon, it is now preserved at Tashilhunpo.

The high ruined walls of Nartang are extensive, and three small temples have been rebuilt. Among them, the reconstructed **assembly hall**, approached via a portico decorated with murals of the Guardian Kings of the four directions, contains images of the Buddhas of the Three Times, and new murals

Tibetan carpets

Tibetan carpets are traditionally made on tall free-standing looms, on which pre-dyed woollen weft is threaded through a cotton warp and around a horizontal rod. The loops thus formed are then cut in half with a knife, which forms the pile and releases the rod. This so-called cut-loop method facilitates speedy production, in contrast to the slowly crafted Persian carpet (in which thousands of individual knots are tied). The density of the carpet is determined by the number of knots or loops per square inch, and the use of a wooden mallet to beat down each row. Most Tibetan carpets have had a fairly low density (40-80 knots or loops per square inch), and it was only in the early 1980s that the first 100 knot carpets were made by the Tibetan refugees Mr Topgyel and Mr Tseten Gyurme based in Nepal. After cutting, the carpets are trimmed, sculpted, and washed.

Traditionally Tibetan carpet making was a cottage industry, which developed in the Khampa Dzong area south of Gyantse, and the carpets produced even now in the Gyantse area are renowned. Many motifs are found, including dragons, flowers, medallions, birds, tiger-skins, and various natural scenes. There are 36 natural pigments in use; and these are now supplemented by a variety of chemical dyes. The size varies considerably; from the small square cushion-sized mats and single bed-sized rugs (ka-den), to the large floor-sized carpets (sa-den). There are production outlets for Tibetan carpets in Gyantse, Zhigatse and Lhasa; and in East Tibet, at Kandze, where there are local variations in design including the renowned rainbow border. Some of the best Tibetan carpets in both traditional and modern designs are now made, however, by Tibetan refugees living in Nepal and India.

which are currently being completed by artists from Tashilhunpo. There are **three inner sanctums**: The **first (left)** has images of Panchen Lama IV, flanked by two attendants, the **second (centre)** has a central glass case containing an image of Tsongkhapa behind which are images of Shakyamuni Buddha flanked by Shariputra, Maudgalyayana, and the standing bodhisattvas, while the **third (right)** has images of the protector deities Bhairava, Pehar and Shridevi. Upstairs, there is a **reliquary chamber** containing small images, mani stones, and the sacred footprint of Lama Kyoton Monlam Tsultrim of Narthang. To the left of the courtyard, another **small temple** contains an image of Shakyamuni Buddha and hundreds of precious xylographs, which are remnants of the *Nartang Canon*. Behind the assembly hall is the **Nechung Lhakhang**, which has a small courtyard with a stupa and prayer wheels, leading to a single chamber with small images of Tsongkhapa, Avalokiteshvara, Shakyamuni, and Pehar. Currently the monastery has only 26 monks. North of Nartang in the mountains is the **Jangchen Ritro** hermitage, where monks affiliated to Nartang would spend time in retreat.

Ngor Evam Chokden Monastery Southwest of the Nartang turn-off, the highway passes north of **Chumik Ringmo**, where Chogyel Phakpa held a conclave concerning the Sakya hegemony of Tibet in 1277. The local monastery was destroyed by floods in the 15th century.

Ngor Evam Chokden was founded in 1429 by Ngorchen Kunga Zangpo (1382-1444) of the Sakya school. The monastery became an important independent bastion of the *Lamdre* teachings, and developed its own branches throughout Tibet, as far as Jyekundo and Derge in Kham.

It was formerly renowned for its Sanskrit library and Newar-style murals. There were once five assembly halls, 18 colleges, and 400 monks, but presently it is restricted to only 25 monks.

The main temples are the **Lamdre Lhakhang** and the **Tartse Lhakhang**, the former (restored) containing images of Hayagriva, Mahakala, Virupa, Ngorchen Kunga Zangpo, Shakyamuni, and various hierarchs of the monastery. Below, there is a row of 60 renovated stupas, which once contained valuable mandala paintings, now preserved, documented and published in Japan.

Getting there Jeepable tracks lead southeast from Chumik Ringmo and due south from Nartang to **Norburi** hill and **Berong** village, from which Ngor Monastery is accessible on foot.

Southwest of Berong are the **cave hermitages of Ngorchen Kunga Zangpo**, one of which contains his stone footprint. **Berong** village below Ngor may also be reached by trekking from Jamchu on the Zhigatse-Gyantse road via the Dzirak-chu or Zha-chu valleys; and another trek leads up the Dzirak-chu valley from Chumik to Chushar, and thence across Dug-nga La pass, into the Shab valley (see below, page 279).

Zhetongmon County བཞེད་མཐོང་སྨོན

*The county of Zhetongmon, reached from Zhigatse via the Dongkar cable ferry to the north of town, comprises three major lateral valleys on the north bank of the Brahmaputra. These are, namely: **Tanak**, the valley of the Tanakpu-chu and its Namoche-chu tributary which supply Zhigatse with much of its electricity; **Zhe**, the valley of the Rong-chu and Zhe-chu rivers; and the upper headwaters of the Mu Tsangpo valley, comprising the Langna-chu and Gya-me-chu. The county capital is located at **Zhe Geding**, 138 kilometres northwest of Zhigatse.*

Zhetongmon
County (29)
谢通门县
Xaitongmoin
Population: 34,929
Area: 8,722 sq km
Colour map 2, grid B2

Western Tibet

Tanak

From **Dongkar** and **Zhudrong** villages on the north bank of the Brahmaputra, take the west track which follows the river upstream. The **Upper Dongkar** valley is largely inhabited by nomads, but it does contain a productive coal mine.

Colour map 2, grid B2

Zhetongmon County

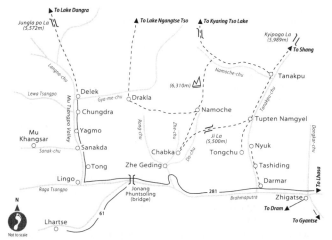

Continuing upstream, you will pass the villages of Chonyi, Tangpe, and Gede, before reaching the entrance to the **Tanak** valley at **Darmar**. Leave the Brahmaputra here and head into the valley.

Above Tashiding on the east bank of the Tanakpu-chu, there is a one hour trek to **Dolma Puk**, the cave hermitage of the Nyingmapa teacher Tanak Dolmawa Samdrup Dorje (1295-1376). It was here that this renowned master transmitted the oral teachings of the Nyingma school, including the Mahayoga and Anuyoga texts, to his own son Sangye Rinchen (1350-1431), and student Zurham Shakya Jungne. It was here, in turn (and the nearby hermitages of **Namkading** and **Lagungo**), that Sangye Rinchen passed the teachings on to Zhangton Namka Dorje and he to his own student Rikdzin Yudruk Dorje. Samdrub Dorje's birthplace lies further upstream at **Nesar**.

At **Nyuk**, a village known for its terracotta pottery, there is the hermitage and nunnery of **Orgyen Guru**, associated with Padmasambhava. The Dzogchen master Kumaradza passed one winter season in retreat here during the 13th century, and in the 15th century it was here that Rigdzin II Lekdenje of the Jangter tradition conferred the Anuyoga teachings.

Across the Tanakpu-chu River, on the west bank is the **Tongchu Power Station**, which supplies Zhigatse town. Further upstream is **Tupten Namgyel**, an illustrious Sakya monastery founded in 1478 by Gorampa Sonam Senge. At **Tanakpu** township there is the **Bur Chutsen** hot springs, known for their medicinal properties. Trails lead from the upper reaches of the Tanak valley, via the Kyipogo La pass, to **Shang** in the northeast and, via the Namoche-chu valley and Lungzang La to **Kyaring Tso Lake** on the Jangtang plateau.

Zhe Valley

Colour map 2, grid B2   **Getting there**   The broad 100 square kilometres Zhe valley, in which the county capital **Zhe Geding** is located, may be reached from **Darmar** at the entrance to Tanak by following the Brahmaputra further upstream via Orgyen, Rungma and Kharu villages; or from **Tupten Namgyel Monastery** via a side-valley and the Ji La pass (5,500 metres). The plain is drained by the Rong-chu in the west, the Zhe-chu in the centre and the Do-chu in the east.

Heading inland from **Kharu** up the **Do-chu** valley, you will reach the Bon monastery of **Ser Darding**, where a small temple has been rebuilt. The ruined assembly hall was sacked by the Dzungar armies in the 18th century and more recently by the red guards.

    Zhe Geding has guesthouse and restaurant facilities in the government compound; as well as an open air market, a post office and a tea shop. A track leads north out of town across a bridge to the renovated monastery of **Zhe Tratang Chenpo**, where there are some original murals. In the southwest of the county, there is **Zhe Ngulchu Chodzong**, the residence of Gyalse Tokme Zangpo (1295-1359) who propagated the compassionate cult of Avalokiteshvara in Tibet.

Trekking   Heading inland from Chabka township, **Namoche** village is located beyond the head of the Do-chu valley, nestling below the snows of **Mount Zhe Lapu Gangri** (6,310 metres). A trail from here follows the Namoche River downstream to its confluence with the Tanakpu-chu; and an arduous 17-day trekking route can be undertaken via Khampalho village and

Drakla township to **Lake Ngangtse Tso** in the Jangtang Northern Plateau (see below, page 315).

Upper Mu Valley

The **Mu valley**, extending through dramatic gorges towards the Nyenchen Tanglha range, has long been an important caravan route for traders. The lower reaches of the valley may be reached from **Zhe** by following the Brahmaputra upstream, or more easily via the motorable bridge at **Phuntsoling** (see below, page 288). The village of Lingo stands at the arid confluence of the Mu-chu and Raga Tsangpo rivers. Entering the gorge of the **Mu-chu**, there are many rock carvings and paintings to be seen. Above **Tong**, the river banks are terraced and cultivated.

At **Sanakda**, where the Sanak-chu converges with the Mu-chu, a trail leads west to **Mu Khangsar**. The ritual dagger discovered as *terma* by Darcharuwa was kept at **Mu-se**, before being transferred to Sera Monastery in Lhasa (see above, page 119). The main trail continues north via **Yagmo** and **Chungdra**, where the Lewa Tsangpo converges from the west, and **Delek** township where the Gya-me-chu and Langna-chu headwaters come together. En route, you can detour to visit the ruins of **Lelung Monastery**, which has both Bonpo and Buddhist associations; and, in the upper reaches, the monastery of **Takmolingka**, which was founded by Muchen Konchok Gyeltsen of the Ngorpa Sakya school in 1436.

Trekking It is possible to undertake a demanding 30-day trek through the gorges of the Mu valley, following the well travelled yak caravan route across Janglapo La pass (5,572 metres) to the Bon pilgrimage sites of **Lake Dangra** in the Jangtang Plateau (see below, page 323).

Western Tibet

Sakya County ས་སྐྱ

*The county of **Sakya** comprises the lateral valleys of the **Shab-chu** and the **Trum-chu**, which flow northwest to converge with the Brahmaputra respectively at **Rungma** and **Lhartse**. The main Zhigatse-Dram highway crosses the Shab-chu at **Shab Geding**, 60 kilometres from Zhigatse; and a motorable track extends southeast through the long Shab valley for 35 kilometres as far as **Se** township. Beyond Se, there are trekking trails which lead via the remote upper reaches of this valley to **Gampa** county on the Sikkim border. The shorter **Trum-chu** valley, extending from the **Sakya Zampa** bridge as far as **Drongu La** pass, is motorable for its entire length. The route continues beyond the pass via **Mabja** to **Tingkye** county (106 kilometres from the bridge), from where branch roads diverge: west to **Shelkar** (123 kilometres), east to **Gampa** (129 kilometres), and south to **Drentang** in the **Bum-chu** (**Arun**) valley on the East Nepal border (87 kilometres).*

*The administrative county capital is located at **Sakya** in the Trum-chu valley, 21 kilometres upstream from the Sakya Zampa bridge.*

Sakya County (30)
萨迦县
Sakya
Population: 38,705
Area: 6,661 sq km
Colour map 2, grid C2

Shab Valley

Located east of **Shab Geding**, and in a gorge north of the highway, this ruined but important monastery was founded in the mid-12th century by Rinpoche Gyeltsa, a student of Phakmodrupa, and developed by his own student Jampapel, otherwise known as Tropu Lotsawa (1173-1225). He studied

Tropu Jamchen Chode Monastery
Colour map 2, grid B2

Sanskrit in Nepal, and was instrumental in inviting many Indian panditas to Tropu, notably Shakyashri of Kashmir, Mitrayogi, and Buddhashri. He had a large 80 cubit image of Maitreya constructed there, and a large Kumbum-style stupa was added later in the 15th century. The lineage became known as the Tropu Kagyu; its most renowned adherent being Buton Rinchendrub of Zhalu (see above, page 272).

Se Township & the Upper Shab-chu Valley

Shab Geding was formerly the residence of the preceptors of Sakya. A ruined fortress is prominent on the hillside to the north of the road. Here, the highway crosses the river via the **Shab Geding Zampa bridge**; and there are side-roads leading north towards **Rungma** on the Brahmaputra and south to **Se** township in the **Shab** valley. Taking the latter route, you can drive through **Tsesum** and as far as Se. An alternative two-day trekking route leads from Ngor Monastery to Se via Duk-ngal La pass (4,550 metres) and Rabdeling.

Three hours' trekking above Se, you can visit the fortified monastery of **Se Rinchentse**, and the nearby birthplace of Remdawa Lodro Zhonu, a celebrated master of the Sakya school who was Tsongkhapa's main teacher. Little but ruins remain, though the site does contain a sacred spring (associated with Padmasambhava) and a hilltop shrine dedicated to the local deity Pen-je.

Trekking From Se township, there is a four-day trek via **Lazhung** to **Sakya**; and from **Mula**, further southeast in the **Shab** valley, there is another four-day trek via the **Gye-chu** valley, **Yago** and **Gurma** to **Gampa** county (see below, page 293). Alternatively, if you continue to trek upstream along the course of the Shab-chu, at **Netsi**, the valley bifurcates: the left branch following the Tradong-chu source, and the right following the Chusum-chu, both of which lead in the direction of South **Khangmar** county (see below, page 290).

Trom-chu Valley

Sakya Monastery ས་སྐྱ་དགོན་པ

Colour map 2, grid B1

The Sakya tradition is one of the four main Buddhist schools in Tibet. It was from here that the whole of Tibet was governed during the period of the **Sakyapa hegemony** (1268-1365), and even now there are buildings of historic importance to be seen, which were spared the destruction of the Cultural Revolution.

Getting there

After crossing the **Tso La pass**, which acts as a watershed between the Shab-chu and Trum-chu rivers, turn left (south) at the **Sakya Zampa** bridge to leave the highway, and follow the latter upstream to **Sakya** township (21 kilometres). The great monastery of Sakya is located 3 kilometres to the left (east) of the township on a side road.

The Five Patriarchs of Sakya

The **Khon** family had been influential in Tibet since the eighth century, when **Khon Luiwangpo Sungwa** ranked among the foremost translators of Buddhist Sanskrit texts. Subsequently, during the 11th century, **Khon Konchok Gyelpo** (1034-1102) moved from Southern to Western Tibet, where he

Sakya County

Western Tibet (side margin)

Sakya: the 'Pale Earth' religious complex

Before arriving at Lhartse a side road turns south off the main highway to the town and monastery of Sakya. After 21 km driving up the valley of the river Trum one reaches the monolithic structure of the Great Sakya Temple. The massive windowless walls, up to 35m high are 100m long and form a square citadel enclosing a temple and monastic complex. Its formidable presence is accentuated by its dark grey colour and its protruding rain spouts carved as mythological gargoyles. It rises above fields to the west and south, a village to the east in front of its main gate and past a slope which runs north, down to the river. Above the river on the far bank rises a jumble of houses and ruins surrounding a second complex of temples and living quarters. This array of houses is about a kilometre in length and is striking in appearance since all buildings are painted with a grey/blue wash embellished with red, white and blue stripes below the roof line and windows. The earth of the ridge behind and for some distance around is pale grey in colour, giving Sakya its name (Tib "sa" = earth; "kya" = pale).

*These two areas on either side of the river demarcate the two main monastic institutions of Sakya. The **South Monastery (Chode Lho)** within the great walled citadel is called the Great Temple (**Lhakhang Chenmo**) and it emphasized the study of the Buddhist sutras, while the **North Monastery (Chode Jang)** taught the esoteric Buddhist practices of tantra.*

studied with Drokmi Lotsawa – a foremost translator and mystic who had also taught Marpa. Drokmi himself had studied with many great Indian masters such as Gayadhara and Virupa, from whom he had received the lineage of the *Hevajra Tantra*. In 1073, Khon Konchok Gyelpo founded the temple of **Gorum Zimchi Karpo** on the north bank of the Trum-chu River, which eventually became the heart of the complex known as **North Sakya (Chode Jang)**. The foremost images of the Gorum Temple were a bronze Manjughosa in the form Jamyang Zi-o Barwa and the leather mask known as Gorum Sebakma, which was kept in the Protector Chapel (Gonkhang). This temple is now destroyed; and the whereabouts of its precious relics are unknown.

The son of Khon Konchok Gyelpo was **Sachen Kunga Nyingpo** (1092-1158), who is revered as the first patriarch of Sakya. He studied with Zhangton Chobar, a second-generation student of Drokmi's, and was able to codify the Sakya teachings known as the *Lamdre*, the 'Path and its Fruit', as well as the *Two Recensions of the Hevajra Tantra (Tak-nyi)*. Two of Sachen Kunga Nyingpo's four sons, **Sonam Tsemo** (1142-82) and **Drakpa Gyeltsen** (1147-1216) also became renowned patriarchs of Sakya; and throughout this period the vast complex of North Sakya was developed into 108 temples. Among these, the most important extant or renovated structures are: the **Tantric College (Ngakpa Tratsang)**, the **Dolma Lhakhang** (with a bronze Tara containing the relics of Bari Lotsawa), the **Victory Stupa** containing the relics of Khon Konchok Gyelpo, the **Demchok Lhakhang** (dedicated to Cakrasamvara), the **Mukchung Gonkhang**, the **Yutok Lhakhang**, the **Zhitok Labrang** (containing a number of reliquaries), the **Dolma Lhakhang**, the **West Protector Chapel (Gonkhang Nub)** which contained images of the Chamdrel protectors, and the **Zurkhang Tsuklakhang**, containing an image of Drakpa Gyeltsen named Dzetoma.

The fourth patriarch of Sakya was **Sakya Pandita Kunga Gyeltsen** (1182-1251), a grandson of Sachen Kunga Nyingpo, who was universally regarded as the greatest lama and most prolific scholar of his age. He was invited by Godan Qan to the Mongolian royal court in 1244, and remained there until

Western Tibet

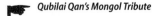

Qubilai Qan's Mongol Tribute

The Mongol armies conquered almost the whole of Asia and eventually extended their rule into Europe as far as Hungary. The Mongol qans ruled an empire which, at its greatest extent, was among the largest in the history of mankind. Their 'patron-priest' relationship with the throne-holders of Sakya reflects the unique rapport established by Sakya Pandita and his nephew at the Mongol court. It was they who foresaw that only by such a means could Tibet avoid the tragic fate of Xixia and other kingdoms which had pointlessly attempted to resist the advance of the Mongol armies by military means.

The model established by the Sakyapas was later adopted by the Tsangpa and Gelukpa rulers of Tibet, and it has in recent times been used by China as one of the main historical justifications for their occupation of Tibet. Qubilai Qan's relationship with Drogon Chogyel Phakpa, and the tributes which they mutually offered at that time are now cited as proof that Qubilai 'ruled over Tibet'. The implication that China has ruled Tibet ever since could, it has been suggested, by the same logic be made against Hungary or any other country conquered by the Mongols, who racially are quite distinct from the Chinese! At the present day, Outer Mongolia is an independent nation. Inner Mongolia has been occupied by China, and its Han Chinese immigrant population now outnumbers the original Mongol inhabitants, despite its 'autonomous' status.

his death in 1251, the same year in which the Qan himself passed away.

Drogon Chogyel Phakpa (1235-80), also known as Lodro Gyeltsen, was the last of the so-called 'five patriarchs of Sakya' (Sakya Gongma Nga). As the nephew and heir of Sakya Pandita, he accompanied his uncle to Mongolia, and later was appointed as the personal mentor and advisor to Godan's successor **Qubilai Qan** (1216-94). Drogon Chogyel Phakpa is credited with the invention of the first Mongolian script, known as Hor-yig, which is still utilized by the Tu peoples of Northeast Tibet for ceremonial purposes. With Mongol support, he became the first effective ruler of Tibet since the fragmentation of the Yarlung Dynasty during the ninth century. He established a network of Sakya temples and monasteries throughout the remote parts of East Tibet, particularly around Dzongsar, Derge, Jyekundo, Kandze and Minyak, and he received the title Rinchen Chogyel, 'precious spiritual ruler'. To set the seal on his assumption of power, he oversaw the building of the Great Temple on the south bank of the Trum-chu. This imposing **Lhakhang Chenmo**, predating the building of its outer walls, was begun in 1268 at his behest, with funds provided by Qubilai Qan, who by this time had become the Emperor of China. The construction was eventually completed in 1276 by the regent Shakya Zangpo. Its contents will be described below (see page 283).

In the first half of the 14th century, as a result of Chogyel Phakpa's system of dividing the large monastic structures into smaller units led by their own spiritual preceptors, the then throne-holder **Kunga Lodro Gyeltsen** divided the ruling Khon family into four houses (*labrang*), each of which would take turns to provide the throne-holder. However, by the 15th century two of these houses failed to produce heirs and the rivalries between two brothers of the Ducho Labrang eventually led to a reduction in their number. Power was consequently divided between the two houses of **Dolma Podrang** and **Phuntsok Podrang**, who over succeeding centuries provided the throne-holder in rotation. Two chapels in the upper storey of the **Lhakhang Chenmo** were built by the early throne-holders of these families and named after their illustrious houses.

By 1354, in the interim, the political power of the Sakyapas in Tibet had diminished, both as a result of internal feuding and in consequence of the collapse of the Mongolian Yuan Dynasty in China. The political vacuum was filled by the Phakmodrupa family, who were based at Tsetang and favoured the Kagyu tradition.

The unique familial succession of Sakya, nonetheless, continued down to the present day, and its throne-holders are even now revered as important spiritual and regal figures in the Tibetan world. The present throne-holder of the **Dolma Podrang** house, HH Sakya Trizin (b 1945), is the 42nd in line (or 44th if Khon Konchok Gyelpo and Bari Lotsawa are included) and he resides at Rajpur in North India. He has an outstanding command of English and lucidly communicates the philosophical perspective and tradition of the Sakya school throughout the world.

In the first half of the 15th century, **Ngorchen Kunga Zangpo** (1382-1457) founded the Ngor sub-school, and, later, in the first half of the 16th century, **Tsarchen Losal Gyatso** (1502-56) founded the Tsarpa sub-school. The former established a number of important branches in Jyekundo and Derge districts of Kham. **Sakya Sub-schools**

The temples on the north bank of the Trum-chu were built first. Among these the Gorum Temple to the northeast was the oldest, built in 1073 by Khon Konchok Gyelpo. The Utse Nyingba, Utse Sarpa, and Manjughosa temples were constructed successively by Sachen Kunga Nyingpo, Choje Drakpa Gyeltsen, and Sakya Pandita Kunga Gyeltsen around the meditation cave of Sachen. Most of these original temples were destroyed during the 1960s, but there are a number of lesser chapels and residential buildings which are well worth visiting. Some of these have been enumerated above. The **Four-Storey Palace (Zhitok Podrang)** and the **Blissful Abode of Secret Mantra (Sangak Dechenling)** are particularly memorable. Aware of the importance of the ancient complex of North Sakya, the monastic preceptors of the present day spend much of their time here. **The Temples of North Sakya**

Western Tibet

On the south bank of the Trum-chu, dominating the surrounding college buildings and palaces, is the impressive citadel known as the **Lhakhang Chenmo**. At present there are five rooms open to the public, four of which house images and reliquary stupas containing the mortal remains of Sakya's past throne-holders, including some of the original five patriarchs (Gongma Nga). The fifth contains manuscript fragments and images retrieved from the ruins of the older temples close to the patch of pale earth on the north bank. **The Temples of South Sakya**
■ *Admission ¥30*

The main entrance faces east and is offset from the central axis of the outer gateway. The building is over two storeys high, and has an inner courtyard which gives access to the main temples.

The Upper Chapels The upper chapels are approached via a flight of stairs accessed from the portico of the inner gateway. Among them, the **Phuntsok Podrang Lhakhang** is, as its name suggests, the chapel associated with the ruling house of Phuntsok Podrang. It contains fine murals and statues, the principal image depicting Manjughosa. There are also statues of the past lineage-holders and reliquary stupas containing the tombs of early throne-holders associated with this branch of the family line.

On the east side is the **Dolma Podrang Lhakhang**, containing five reliquary stupas of important throne-holders hailing from this branch of the family. The altar has images depicting the Three Deities of Longevity, with White

Tara first and foremost.

On the northeast corner, there is a locked chamber containing Sakya's precious collection of Sanskrit palm-leaf manuscripts.

The Lower Chapels On the south (left) side of the inner courtyard is the **Phurba Drubkhang**, a large well-lit chamber in which Vajrakila rituals are performed, and which has a number of bookcases, positioned between images of Shakyamuni Buddha and Manjushri. All these contents were retrieved from the rubble of the temples of North Sakya, following the destruction of the Cultural Revolution. On the left wall is the wrathful figure of Havajra in union with the female consort Nairatmya. This is the deity described in the main tantra practiced in the Sakya tradition. It was Drokmi Lotsawa who first translated the text into Tibetan, and it thereafter became the main meditational practice of Khon Konchok Gyelpo.

On the north (right) side of the inner courtyard, is the **Nguldung Lhakhang**, which has as its inner sanctum, the **Lhakhang Jangma**. The former houses 11 silver reliquary stupas containing the remains of past throne-holders of Sakya, with that of Ngakchang Kunga Rinchen foremost among them. The 12-pillared **Lhakhang Jangma** has six reliquary stupas containing the remains of important past abbots of Sakya who did not belong to the familial line; and in addition, a series of outstanding wall-painted mandalas, including those of Sarvavid Vairocana and Mayajala.

The Assembly Hall (Dukhang) Facing the entrance inside the courtyard is the enormous **Assembly Hall (Dukhang)**. This is nowadays the most significant of the temples at Sakya. Its walls are 3.5 metres thick and up to 16 metres high. The roof is supported by 40 huge wooden columns made from entire tree trunks. Among these, the four central columns near the entrance are about two metres in circumference. The northwest pillar, known as **Sechen Kawa**, was a gift from Qubilai Qan. It was moved by hand from Drentang. The southeast pillar, known as **Takmo Kawa** ('tigress pillar'), is said to have been transported from India by a large tigress whose skin, six metres long, was tied to the column. The one to the southwest, known as **Drongpo Kawa**, is said to have been brought by a wild yak who wept tears at a pass on the way, thus giving rise

Sakya Lhakhang Chenmo

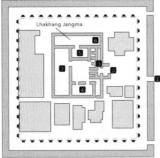

1 Outer entrance	4 Phurba Drubkhang
2 Portico	5 Nguldung Lhakhang
3 Stairs to Upper	6 Lhakhang Jangma
Chapels	7 Dukhang

to a miraculous spring. Lastly, the northeast pillar, known as **Nakpo Trakdzak Kawa** ('pillar bleeding black blood'), is named after a serpent spirit (*naga*) who reputedly wept black blood when it was cut down. The trunk is said to cure diseases when a nail is driven into it.

Around the three walls facing the entrance are a superb series of larger than life-size images, many of them refinely cast. Made at different times and showing a variety of different styles and influences, they mostly depict Shakyamuni Buddha, and contain the relics of the main masters of the Sakya tradition. This is not usually found in Tibetan temples.

Passing clockwise along the

southeast, south, west and north walls in succession from the eastern door, you will notice the following images and precious objects: **Southeast Wall**: a gold manuscript edition of the *Kangyur* commissioned by Chogyel Phakpa (1); **South Wall**: a gold manuscript edition of the *Kangyur* commissioned by Yumchok Tendzin Wangmo (2); a cast image of Shakyamuni Buddha (Tubwang Totsema) containing the relics of Shakya Zangpo (3); an image of Shakyamuni Buddha with a hair-ringlet made of white conch, containing the relics of Sharpa Rinchen Gyeltsen (4); images of Avalokiteshvara and Padmasambhava (5); **West Wall**: an image of Shakyamuni Buddha containing the relics of Sakya Pandita (6); the reliquary stupa of Trichen Ngawang Tutob, previous throneholder of Sakya (7); a cast 'speaking' image of Shakyamuni Buddha, named Tuwang Sungjon Tatsema, commissioned by Sachen Kunga Nyingpo (8); a cast image of Shakyamuni Buddha named Lhachen Pelbar, which contains the relics of Chogyel Phakpa (9); the renowned white conch-shell of Sakya, kept in a glass case (10); a cast image of standing Tara which was brought to Tibet by Atisha (11); a cast image of Tara containing the Jamyang Tsogyelma image on which Sakya Pandita meditated when he defeated a Hindu zealot in debate at Kyirong (12); the main image of the temple – a cast Shakyamuni Buddha named Tuchen Totsema, which was commissioned by Drogon Chogyel Phakpa (13); images of the 37 deities of the *Sarvavid Vairocanatantra* in the foreground (14); a large throne named Zhuktri Tarchikma which the first three patriarchs of Sakya once used, and a smaller throne in front used by the monastic preceptors of Sakya (15); three white-robed images depicting the first three patriarchs of Sakya (16); an image of Manjughosa named Jamyang Metubma, containing the relics of Tekchen Chokyi Lama (17); a cast image of Maitreya named Jamgon Totsema, containing the relics of Jetsun Pejung (18); a cast image of Vajradhara containing the relics of Dharmatala (19); a reliquary stupa named Chodong Dzamling Osel, containing the relics of Trichen Tutob Wangchuk (20); a clay image of Shakyamuni Buddha named Tuwang Totsema, containing the relics of the minister Anglen (21); a cast image of Manjughosa named Jamyang Chokhorma, containing the relics of Sharpa Dukhorwa (22); and **North Wall**: a cast image of Shakyamuni, containing the relics of Sabzang Mati Panchen (23); a cast image of Jowo Aram, containing the relics of Gangkarwa Rinchenpel (24).

Of these objects, the White Conch is revered as the most sacred object in the temple. It was given to Drogon Chogyel Phakpa by Emperor Qubilai Qan, and is regarded as the remains of the Buddha from a previous existence when born as a shellfish. It existed at the time of the present Shakyamuni Buddha, and was used by him in antiquity before

Assembly Hall (Dukhang)

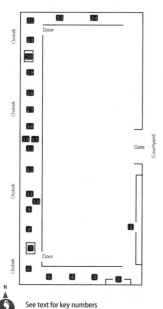

See text for key numbers

N

Not to scale

The biggest book in the world?

Near the far northwest corner of Sakya's Great Library is what could be the largest book in the world. It is a fully illuminated manuscript in gold lettering of the "Sutra of the Perfection of Discrimination Awareness in One Hundred Thousand Fascicules" (Prajnaparamitasutra). It lies in a special rack and its pages, in traditional single leaf format, are approximately 1.75m wide by 0.75m deep by 0.5m thick bound between two huge cover planks.

being transported from India to China, and thence to Tibet. You may have to persist in order to be shown it!

The **murals** of the upper gallery depict the lamas of the *Lamdre* lineage; those of the south wall the Hundred Deeds of Shakyamuni Buddha; those of the west wall the life of Drogon Chogyel Phakpa; and those of the north wall the five original patriarchs of Sakya. On the ceiling are hundreds of mandalas representing the outer and inner tantras of the New Translation Schools.

Under these statues in a series of glass cases to the right of the central shrine are objects of art from the Emperors of Mongolia and China that no doubt represent a small part of the treasures of tribute or offerings made to the Sakya masters before the ravages of the Cultural Revolution.

The Great Library It is well worth asking your guide to show you the library (Chotsek or 'Pendzokhang'). To do so you may have to pay something extra (anything from ¥1.00 to ¥5.00). However once this is done you will be led behind the line of statues to a vast collection of Buddhist texts towering to the ceiling that have been gathering dust for centuries. They are stacked two storeys or eight stacks high in racks, made up of 'pigeon holes' in more than 60 sections, the length of the whole Assembly Hall. There in the gloom are thousands of texts the extent of which are only seen with a strong torch. It brings to mind what a portion of the great library of Alexandria must have been like.

Sakya town

Colour map M2, grid B1 The town and villages of Sakya are very poor, as is much of Tibet these days, and it is not unusual to be vigorously pursued by gangs of children begging you for money. Do give whatever you can manage but do not give away large amounts randomly just because one child may be more appealing. It is always good to make a donation in the main shrines by placing it on the altar or on Offering Mandalas that usually hold some donations from prior visitors. This will benefit the whole monastery. If you give money to an individual it is normally used by that person alone.

Also the monks and guides of Sakya are obliged to collect the maximum in fees and taxes from every visitor. These are then paid to the government. If not they can be severely punished for showing any generosity to the tourists. Be warned.

Sakya Town

To North Sakya Temples (1 km)

Trum Cho

Guest House

Shop

South Sakya Temple Complex

0 metres 50

0 yards 55

Western Tibet

There is a rest house next to the Great Temple at its northeast corner. Rooms of between 5 and 10 beds are available and cooking remains one's own responsibility. Another guest house lies a few 100 metres east on the eastern side of the main street which runs north-south, located east of the Great Citadel. The rate for foreign tourists may be approximately ¥10 to ¥20 per night. **Sleeping**

The dirt track continues south from Sakya to leave the Trum-chu River valley via the **Drongu La pass**, for Mabja in the upper reaches of the **Bum-chu (Arun)** valley. **Tingkye** county lies further south (see below, page 294), some 85 kilometres from Sakya township; and there is also a four-day trekking route to **Kharda** and the east face of **Mount Everest** (see below, page 297). **Mabja & the Upper Bum-chu (Arun) River valley.**

Lhartse County ལྷ་རྩེ

*Lhartse county, traditionally known as **Nyingri** district, is located on the south bank of the Brahmaputra, east of the Shab-chu valley. It extends upstream from **Phuntsoling** at the confluence of the **Raga Tsangpo** (Dokzhung Tsangpo) and Brahmaputra, as far as **Chushar (Lhartse)**, where the **Chushar, Mangkar,** and **Trum-chu** rivers all flow into the Brahmaputra. The county capital at **Chushar** straddles three important motor roads: east to **Zhigatse** via Chutsen and Lepu (157 kilometres), south to **Dram** (Ch Zhangmu) via Shekar and Dingri (315 kilometres), and west to **Ngamring** (60 kilometres), the gateway to Mount Kailash in Far-western Tibet.*

Lhartse County (31)
拉孜县
Lhaze
Population: 39,276
Area: 41,701 sq km
Colour map 2, grid B2

16 kilometres west of **Shab Geding**, there is a turn-off on the north side of the Zhigatse-Dram highway, leading to **Tashigang** (14 kilometres) and **Jonang Phuntsoling** (20 kilometres). The **Monastery of Bodong East**, located near Tashigang, was founded by Geshe Mudrapachenpo in 1049. It subsequently became the residence of Tibet's great grammarian Pang Lotsawa Lodro Tenpa (1276-1342) and of the Bodong Panchen Cho-le Namgyel (1375-1451). The latter was the prolific writer of some 100 volumes of treatises on sutra, tantra and traditional sciences including poetics and monastic discipline. The temple at Bodong, which gave rise to an independent Buddhist lineage in Tibet, once contained a revered image made from the ashes of Bodong Panchen himself. At **Nyenyo Jagoshong**, further north, there was once a peripheral 'border-taming temple', attributed to King Songtsen Gampo, containing an image of Vaishravana.

Bodong Monastery

བོ་དོང་དགོན་པ

Jonang Phuntsoling was formerly the stronghold of the Jonangpa school, which since the 17th century has been confined to remote areas of Dzamtang and Ngawa in South Amdo (see below, page 613), following the closure of their mother monastery and its transformation into a Gelukpa establishment. The original foundation was made by **Kunpangpa Tu-je Tsondru** (1243-1313), a lineage-holder of Yumo Mikyo Dorje who received the Kalacakra teachings from the Kashmiri pandita Somanatha in the 11th century, and founded the school, renowned for its

Jonang Phuntsoling

ཇོ་ནང་ཕུན་ཚོགས་གླིང

Lhartse County

Western Tibet

philosophical exposition of 'extraneous emptiness' (*zhentong*), the view that all the attributes of Buddhahood are extraneously empty of mundane impurities and defilements, but not intrinsically empty in a nihilistic sense, their experience thereby transcending all notions of existence and non-existence.

The most important figure connected with this school was **Dolpopa Sherab Gyeltsen** (1292-1361), a prolific commentator on the combined sutra and tantra traditions including the *Kalacakra Tantra*. He refined the philosophical exposition of 'extraneous emptiness' and expanded the monastery. In particular, nearby to his own hermitage, which lies below a Padmasambhava meditation cave on **Mount Jomo Nagyel** (5,744 metres), he built the Kumbum-style stupa named **Tongdrol Chenmo** in the side-valley of **Jonang**, a two hours walk from the monastery. This 20 metres high stupa is almost of the same dimensions as the Kumbum at Gyantse. It is octagonal in shape and has seven storeys. The extant murals are said to reflect the provincial **Lato** style, which represents an early synthesis of Nepalese **Newar** and indigenous Tibetan elements, incorporating fewer Chinese inspired elements than the paintings of Zhalu or Gyantse.

The main monastery at Phuntsoling and the Kumbum were subsequently expanded by **Taranatha** (1575-1634), with funds provided by the kings of Tsang; and given the name **Takten Phuntsoling**. Following the civil war, the monastery was absorbed by the Gelukpa school and its name was altered to **Ganden Phuntsoling** during the lifetime of Taranatha's fifth incarnation.

The red buildings of the monastery presently stand within **Phuntsoling village**. The main four-storey temple has an inner sanctum containing images of Aksobhya Buddha, flanked by the Eight Bodhisattvas. The library containing gold-inscribed texts on black or indigo paper is no longer extant; though some of its woodblocks have been preserved at Derge in Kham, and elsewhere. In 1998 the monastery was closed and its monks evicted following the failure of a programme of communist indoctrination. The hilltop **residence of Taranatha** is in ruins; whereas the **Tangka Wall (goku)** and **Mani Stone Wall** have survived. A protector shrine dedicated to Bektse, named **Drakram Gonkhang**, was founded nearby by Bodong Rinchentse.

Getting there Phuntsoling township is located at the confluence of the Brahmaputra and Raga Tsangpo (Dokzhung Tsangpo) rivers, 50 kilometres from **Shab Geding** on a branch road to the northwest of the Zhigatse-Dram highway, and 61 kilometres from **Lhartse** county town via another dirt road which follows the Brahmaputra downstream to the confluence. A weak suspension bridge spans the river here, immediately above the defunct **Phuntsoling Chakzam**, which was constructed by Tibet's famous bridge-builder Tangtong Gyelpo during the 15th century. The area is dominated by an enormous shimmering white sand dune to the west.

Gyang   The district traditionally known as **Gyang** or **Drampa** lies 50 kilometres southwest of **Phuntsoling**, to the east of the Lhartse plain. Here in the seventh century, King Songtsen Gampo founded one of his primary geomantic temples, the **Drampagyang Lhakhang**, which once contained a celebrated image of Vairocana Buddha, but is now in ruins.

At neighbouring **Gyang Yonpolung**, there are the ruins of a small Nyingmapa temple below meditation caves associated with Padmasambhava, Yeshe Tsogyel, and Namkei Nyingpo. It was in this locale that, during the 14th century, the treasure-finder Zangpo Drakpa discovered the popular liturgical text known as the 'Seven Chapters' (*le'u bdun-ma*). This text included an inventory, which paved the way for Rigdzin

Godemchen's revelation of the **Northern Treasures** (*Jangter*) at **Zangzang Lhadrak** (see below, page 310) in 1366.

Further northwest, and on the other side of the Lhartse-Phuntsoling road, is the destroyed Kumbum-style stupa of **Gyang Bumpoche**, built by the Sakyapa Sonam Tashi (1352-1417) and Thangtong Gyalpo (1385-1464), and decorated in the **Lato** style of painting.

From the 17th century onwards, this area was developed by the Panchen Lamas, who had a summer palace constructed nearby, and made lavish donations to the temple and the stupa.

The Gelukpa monastery of **Lhartse Chode** is located 10 kilometres north of Chushar, the modern county town of Lhartse. Behind the monastery on a hill are the ruins of the old **Lhartse Dzong**, and to the east are the buildings of old Lhartse village. Formerly there were 1,000 monks in this institution, which dates originally to the 13th century. The assembly hall contains some 17th century murals, and restoration work is continuing.

Lhartse Chode & Gayadhara Lhakhang

Below the ruined fortress is the **Gayadhara Lhakhang**, which was built around the cave hermitage of Drokmi Lotsawa (993-1050) and his contemporary, the Kashmiri pandita Gayadhara. These figures were the teachers of Khon Konchok Gyelpo who founded the original Gorum Temple at Sakya in 1073, giving birth to the Sakyapa school.

10 kilometres south of Lhartse Chode and the old Lhartse village, is **Chushar**, the county capital of modern Lhartse. The town is an important staging post on the roads from **Zhigatse, Dram (Zhangmu)** on the Nepal border, and **Mount Kailash** in Far-west Tibet. Three river valleys extend upstream to the south: the Trum-chu, which leads via the **Zhichen Chutsen hot springs** to **Sakya** (see above, page 279); the Mangkar-chu which leads to the **Mangkar** hermitages; and the Chushar, which leads across **Gyatso La** pass (5,252 metres) on the main highway, eventually reaching **Shelkar** at the confluence of the **Bum-chu (Arun)** river and its **Lolo-chu** tributary. The distance from **Chushar** to **Shelkar** is 75 kilometres. The road for **Ngamring** and **Mount Kailash** branches off the Gyatso La road after the **Chushar Zampa bridge** and crosses the Brahmaputra via the **Drapu ferry** or the newly-built **Lhartse Chakzam bridge**. Here **Mount Yakri** (5,641 metres) dominates the road on the far bank of the river.

Chushar Town
Colour map 2, grid B1

Western Tibet

Until recently **Chushar** was a small 'one horse' Tibetan town, with one main government shop down a side street, three guesthouses, a post office, a grocery store, a cinema and one petrol pump consisting of a rubber hose protruding from the broken window of an oil-stained mud hut. The petrol station had been a popular meeting point! It lay opposite the two small Sichuan and Muslim restaurants in town. In 1993 Chushar underwent a radical transformation. It was inundated with Han Chinese who held permits for shops on the main high street. This coincided with a modern Chinese petrol station at the east edge of town and the construction of the bridge across the Brahmaputra. The main street has now begun to take on the characteristics of thousands of other

Chushar

towns across China. The rows of concrete cubicle boxes for shops that stretch down either side of the main street, selling little of practical use, are all, bar one, run by Han Chinese (who, before 1992, never were seen in any numbers in Lhartse). Perhaps for the traveller it gives a sense of security in its familiarity! Here one can pick up any last minute purchases, such as three minutes noodles or Chinese beer, for the journey across the Jangtang Northern Plateau.

Mangkar valley The track to **Mangkar** leaves Chushar via the street running due south between the post office and the cinema. Take the east track at the next inter-section, and head south to **Samdrub** and **Mangpu**, deep in the Mangkar gorge. The snow peaks of **Lhago Gangri** (6,457 metres) dominate its upper reaches. From **Mangpu**, a trekking trail leads to the right into the Mangkar valley, where there are said to be 13 great meditation caves. Among these, the cave hermitage of Tsarchen Losal Gyatso (1502-67), founder of the Tsarpa sub-school of the Sakyapa tradition, lies within the **Monastery of Tubten Gepel**, and his tomb is located at the nearby monastery of **Dar Drongmoche**. Ma Rinchen Chok, one of Padmasambhava's 25 disciples, was born in middle Mangkar.

In the upper reaches are the ruins of **Ganden Dargyeling**, a Gelukpa monastery, and various meditation caves associated with Drokmi Lotsawa, who transmitted the Sakyapa teachings here to Khon Konchok Gyelpo. These include: the **Osel Dawa Puk**, where Drokmi meditated; the **Dragyur Puk**, where he translated Sanskrit texts; and the **Sungak Lamdre Puk** where he received the transmission of the 'Path and its Fruit' (*Lamdre*). At nearby **Mugulung hermitage**, Drokmi gave teachings to Marpa Lotsawa of the Kagyu school and Zurpoche Shakya Jungne of the Nyingma school.

Trekking From Mangkar, there is a three-day trekking route to Sakya via **Drumchok**, a shorter trek southwest to the Lolo-chu valley, and yet another due south to the Bumtsopu-chu valley.

Khangmar County ཁང་དམར

Khangmar County (32)
康马县
Kangmar
Population: 17,670
Area: 5,172 sq km
Colour map 2, grid C2

*Khangmar county includes the valleys of the **Drumpayu-chu** and Nyeru-chu rivers, which flow due north from their Himalayan watersheds to converge with the **Nyang-chu**, at **Nenying** and **Lungmar** respectively. The main highway from Gyantse to **Dromo** (Ch Yadong) on the Bhutan and Sikkim borders passes through the **Drumpayu** valley; and from the **Nyeru** valley, there are mountain passes leading directly into the **Gasa** district of **North Bhutan**.*

*The county capital is located at **Khangmar** (Nyangchu), 48 kilometres south of Gyantse. At **Kala** township (44 kilometres further south), there is a security checkpost which monitors all traffic heading towards the border. **Nenying** and **Yemar** temples are sites of historic importance located in Khangmar county.*

Nenying Monastery 15 kilometres south of Gyantse, in the lower valley of the Drumpayu-chu, you can visit the monastery of **Nenying**, which was founded in the late 11th century by Jampel Sangwa of Samye. Over subsequent centuries, Nenying was devel-oped eclectically by the Bodongpa and the Gelukpa traditions, amongst others. The renovated assembly hall contains a large new image of Tsongkhapa, and further north there is an old temple, probably surviving from the original com-plex, which contains faded murals of the Pala style, reminiscent of those at Gyantse Dzong. Neying is currently administered from **Sapugang** township, 11 kilometres further south, where there are interesting coloured rock carvings.

At Sapugang, the road crosses to the east bank of the **Drumpayu-chu**, and one **Gamru** kilometre further south, at **Darmar**, there is a trail turning southwest from the main highway. This trail follows the **Gamrupu-chu** upstream, through a wide side-valley, to **Gamru** township. Above Gamru, the trail eventually crosses the **Drulung La pass**, which forms a watershed between the **Tradong** source of the **Shab-chu** and the **Drumpayu-chu** rivers.

The county capital is located 18 kilometres south of **Darmar**, in a sheltered **Khangmar** side-valley close to the highway. The government buildings have guesthouse and dining facilities; but the PSB vigilantly inspect passers-by to ensure that those heading south towards the sensitive Sikkim and Bhutanese borders have bona fide travel permits.

From **Khangmar**, a motorable side-road leads southeast to cross the Nelung **Nyerulung** La pass and enter **Nyeru** township in the Nyeru Tsangpo valley. Trekking routes from here follow the valley downstream to **Lungmar** and **Ralung Monastery** (see above, page 253), or northeast across country to **Phuma Yutso Lake** and **Lhodrak** (see above, page 212). There are also trails into the **Gasa** district of **North Bhutan** via the **Yak La pass** (east of Lake Drumpa Yutso) and via **Wakye La pass** above the source of the Nyeru-chu.

NB   These passes are only accessible to local Bhutanese traders who ply their wares in Dromo county.

Yemar Temple, located 12 kilometres south of **Khangmar** and just to the **Yemar** north of **Salu** township, on a ridge above the highway, is a deserted but extremely important temple, where life-size images survive from the 11th century. Its foundation is attributed to one Lharje Chojang, considered to be a previous emanation of the Kashmiri pandita Shakyashri, who himself visited the site in 1204. The temple has three chapels surrounded by a perimeter wall and an inner circumambulatory path. The **central chapel** (north) is dedicated to the Buddha Amoghadarshin, flanked by six forms of Maitreya; the **West chapel** (left) to Amitayus, flanked by 16 standing bodhisattvas, and the **East chapel** (right) contains a relief sculpture depicting the Buddha's **Subjugation of Mara**. The Italian Tibetologist Prof Tucci has compared the images of Yemar (Iwang) with those of **Tsi Nesar**, **Kyangpu**, and **Dratang**, which are no longer extant, and concluded that the garments and facial features suggest an early Tibetan synthesis of Indian **Pala** and **Khotanese** Central Asian styles. Restoration work at Yemar is on-going. The internal renovation of the West chapel and the East chapel has now been completed, and the old perimeter wall, surmounted by 108 stupas, has been rebuilt. Restoration of the central chapel has not yet been carried out, and no decision has been made as to whether monks will once again be permitted to reside there.

Khangmar County

Western Tibet

Kala   The highway continues south from **Yemar**, passing through **Samada** township, where the ruined **Kyangpu** temple is located, and **Mangdza**, from where a side-trail follows the Drumpayu-chu to its source and the Yak La pass to Bhutan. At **Mangdza**, the main road leaves the valley and enters the **Kala plain**. 34 kilometres south of Yemar at Kala township, the highway skirts the northeast shore of **Lake Kalatso**. Here there is an important police checkpoint, which can only be passed by unauthorized travellers prepared to undertake a cross country trek around **Lake Kalatso** to the west, or via **Lapchi Gonpa** to the east. A motorable branch road leads west from Kala to **Gampa** county (110 kilometres). From **Lapchi Gonpa**, a difficult trek leads to **Gasa** in Bhutan.

Dromo County གྲོ་མོ

Dromo County (33)
亚东县
Yadong
Population: 10,842
Area: 3,968 sq km
Colour map 2, grid C2

*Dromo county is a stunningly beautiful area, comprising the valley of the **Amo-chu** (or Dromo Machu) River, also known in neighbouring Sikkim as the **Chumbi valley**, and the parallel valleys of its more westerly tributaries: the **Tangkarpu-chu** and **Khambuma-chu**. These three rivers all converge at **Sharsingma**, the county capital of Dromo (Ch Yadong), before flowing into the **Ha** (Lhade) district of West Bhutan. The terrain varies dramatically: north of the Tang La pass (4,639 metres), which marks the Himalayan watershed, the landscape of the Tibetan plateau is barren; but offering stupendous views of the snow peaks of **Jomolhari** on the Bhutanese border, and **Longpo Gyeldong** on the Sikkimese border. Further south, the roads plunge through lush gorges, where alpine forest and flowers abound. **Sharsingma** (2,865 metres) is 160 kilometres south of **Khangmar**, 18 kilometres northwest of **Dorin** in North Bhutan, and 16 kilometres northeast of **Dzaleb La pass** (4,386 metres), on the Sikkimese frontier.*

Himalayan Watershed   From **Kala**, the highway skirts the west shore of **Lake Dochentso**, and continues south, passing through **Guru**, where Younghusband's British Expeditionary Force engaged the Tibetan army in 1904. At **Duna** township, 40 kilometres south of the Kala checkpoint, there is a trekking route northwest to the Butang-chu valley, a tributary of the **Khambuma-chu**. The main road gradually ascends **Tang La**, the Himalayan watershed pass (4,639 metres), from which the snow peaks of **Jomolhari** (7,314 metres) and **Longpo Gyeldong** (7,128 metres) are clearly visible, the former only eight kilometres distant. The pass is crossed 22 kilometres south of Duna.

Phari Dzong   Below the **Tang La pass**, the highway enters the valley of the **Amo-chu** (Chumbi), and continues gently downhill to **Phari Dzong** (4,360 metres), nine kilometres distant. Phari township is a bustling market town located on an exposed 'sow-shaped' hilltop and was often given the dubious distinction of being the dirtiest town in Asia! It strategically overlooks the trading route via **Tremo La pass** to **Paro** in West Bhutan (see below, page 844), and the various westerly trails which

Dromo County

penetrate the **Dongkya** range to enter Sikkim. From here, there are two motorable roads to **Sharsingma** (Yadong), one via the **Khambuma-chu** valley and the other via the **Dromo** valley.

22 kilometres drive northwest from Phari, you will reach **Tengkar** in the upper Khambuma-chu valley. From here, **Khambu Monastery** and its 12 medicinal hot-springs are in close proximity. The glacial waters of this alpine valley, hemmed in by the Dongkya Sikkim range and the Himalayas, are highly revered.

Khambuma Valley

Trekking Trekking routes lead from the Khambuma valley into Northeast Sikkim, ie from **Khambu-to** via the **Tso La pass**, and from **Khambu-me** via the **Chimkipu** valley. Further south, the Khambuma-chu merges with the Tangkarpu-chu, and thereafter with the Dromo Amo-chu at **Sharsingma** (Yadong).

The fertile Dromo valley, which yields an abundance of buckwheat, barley, and potatoes, is divided into three sectors: **Dromo-to** township, where the river flows through gentle alpine meadows, bypassing the Bonpo settlements of **Zhulung**, **Sharmang** and **Nubmang**; **Sharsingma** (Yadong), a relatively low-lying town (2,865 metres) where the three rivers converge; and **Dromo-me** where flowering plants and conifer forests abound.

Dromo Valley

Logging is the main industry; and the gorges still are relatively rich in wildlife, including pheasants, Tibetan snowcocks, and Himalayan black bears with their characteristic white V-shaped markings. The capital, **Sharsingma**, is 46 kilometres south of **Phari Dzong**. It is a hospitable town, despite the security concerns entailed by its proximity to the border. Indian-style sweet tea and Himalayan-style fermented millet (*tongba*) are popular beverages in this part of the country.

Sleeping The town has guesthouse and restaurant facilities, in addition to schools, a bank, a post office, and hydro-electric station.

Crossing the **Dromo Zamchen bridge** the highway leads southwest and steeply uphill from Sharsingma through rhododendron forests to the **Natho La** and **Dzaleb La passes** on the Sikkim border.

Gampa County གམ་པ

*Gampa county is the region covered by the headwaters of the **Yeru Tsangpo**, which rises north of the snow peaks of the Tibet-Sikkim Himalayas: **Mount Lonpo Gyeldong** (7,128 metres), **Mount Lhachen Zangdrak** (6,889 metres), and **Mount Tarchen Drokri** (6,830 metres) at the eastern extremity of the **Chorten Nyima La** (see below, page 295). The Yeru Tsangpo meanders west into Tingkye county, where it converges with the Bum-chu (Arun) before flowing south into East Nepal. Also included in Gampa county are the side-valley of its major tributary: the **Kholchu Tsangpo**, which flows south to its confluence west of Dargye village; and those of the latter's minor tributaries, the **Jemalung-chu** and **Gye-chu**, which converge at Gyelung.*

Gampa County (34)
岗巴县
Gamba
Population: 7,822
Area: 3,979 sq km
Colour map 2, grid C2

The county capital is located at **Gampazhol**, 110 kilometres west of Kala (on the Gyantse-Dromo road), and 95 kilometres northwest of Drakang (below Duna on the Gyantse-Dromo road). Access is also possible by undertaking a four-day trek from **Badur** in the Shab valley (see above, page 279) to **Gampa**

Western Tibet

Dzong via Yakgo La pass, Gye-chu valley, Gurma village, and Dargye township.

Gampa Dzong   This impressive old fortress, which was frequently photographed by British Everest Expeditions during the early decades of this century, overlooks the new county town, where the Chinese bureaucrats have something of a hardline reputation. The main focal point of pilgrimage in this county is the **Chorten Nyima** hermitage (see below, page 295) on the south border of **Gampa** and **Tingkye** counties. The hermitage can be approached by a motorable track from **Gampa Dzong**, via **Mende** (Gampa township), and **Dranglung** village.

Tingkye County གདིང་སྐྱེས

Tingkye County (35)
定结县
Dinggye
Population: 15,332
Area: 4,900 sq km
Colour map 2, grid C1

*Tingkye county comprises the lower valley of the **Bum-chu (Arun)** River, from the point below **Tsogo** where it flows due south to enter East Nepal via **Drentang** township, and the valleys of its major tributaries: the **Yeru Tsangpo** and **Chenlung-chu** (the latter flowing into the Yeru Tsangpo via the Bumtsopu-chu). The county capital, **Tingkye Dzong**, is located above the confluence of the **Bum-chu** and **Yeru Tsangpo**, at a strategic intersection. The distance from Tingkye Dzong to Sakya is 85 kilometres, to Shelkar: 134 kilometres, and to Gampa Dzong: 129 kilometres.*

Lower Bum-chu Valley   From **Jigkyob Zampa bridge**, located 31 kilometres north of **Tingkye Dzong**, 92 kilometres east of Shelkar, and 54 kilometres south of Sakya, there is a four-day trekking route to **Kharda** in the Lower Bum-chu valley. Passing south of the confluence of the Bum-chu and Yeru Tsangpo, the trail skirts on the east the snow peak of **Mount Nyarori** (6,724 metres) in the Ama Dribma range, which acts as a watershed between these rivers. Continuing on the east bank of the river, it then cuts through several lateral ravines, via **Kharkung**, and ascends the Chokchu La pass, offering wonderful views of **Mount Makalu** (8,470 metres).

Descending to the confluence of the Trakar-chu with the Bum-chu above **Chugo**, the trail subsequently crosses the Bum-chu by bridge to the west bank, and heads south through alpine forest for **Kharda**, the gateway to the **Khangzhung** east face of **Mount Everest**, and the Kharda glacier (see below, page 300).

Below **Kharda**, a difficult trail heads down the west bank of the Bum-chu to **Drentang** township, joining the main road from **Tingkye** and **Zar** (45 kilometres). South of Drentang, the river flows into Nepal, where it is known as the **Arun**. A major dam is to be constructed in the deep **Arun** gorges of east Nepal.

Gampa & Tingkye Counties

Lake Tsomo Dramling   Southeast of Chenlung township, there is a sacred lake known as **Tsomo Dramling**, where pilgrims undertake a circumambulation, starting from **Tashitse** on the south-west shore and passing through Dotra on the northeast shore.

In the county capital, **Tingkye Dzong**, there is an important petrol station, and various amenities geared to service the army, which has a large base in town. From here, the motor road follows the Yeru Tsangpo upstream for 42 kilometres to **Zar** bypassing Chushar across the river. At **Pukhu**, north of **Zar**, there is a small rebuilt Kagyu monastery.

Zar Monastery

    Zar township, with its ruined fortress and monastery, lies on a ridge below **Mount Gang Langchen**, which is 'shaped like the head of an elephant'. The monastery, which belongs to the Gelukpa school, has two renovated buildings, including a three-storey assembly hall. On the slopes of Mount Gang Langchen there are meditation caves and lakes associated with Padmasambhava, Yeshe Tsogyel, and Yutok Yonten Gonpo.

Getting there Above **Zar**, the road bifurcates, the southerly track leading across **Nye La pass** to **Dekyi** and **Drentang** on the Nepal border (45 kilometres); and the easterly road to **Tingkye** township. Below **Tashi Rabka** on the former, there are also trekking routes into Nepal via the **Rabka La pass** (4,972 metres) and the **Yangmagang La pass** (5,182 metres).

Chorten Nyima is regarded at the gateway to the hidden land of Sikkim (Drejong), the heart of which lies within the folds of Mount Kangchendzonga. It is an extremely active pilgrimage centre, and there is a nuns' retreat hermitage to the west. The three cliff-top stupas, which are the focal point of pilgrimage, are attributed to Namkei Nyingpo and Yeshe Tsogyel, students of Padmasambhava, who himself meditated here.

Chorten Nyima

    The largest of the stupas, known as **Rangjung Shelgyi Chorten**, contains a crystal stupa which reputedly fell from the sky. Additionally, there are three sky burial sites, consecrated originally by Padmasambhava and Namkei Nyingpo, and medicinal springs, renowned for possessing the 'eight attributes of pure water'. These are now utilized as the source of the fabled Chorten Nyima Mineral Water, which is bottled and marketed inside Tibet! The **assembly hall** in its upper storey contains images of Hayagriva and Manjughosa, as well as a small 'self-arising' ritual dagger (*phurba*) engraved with an image of Hayagriva.

    The **Tamdrin Lhakhang** contains within it the meditation cave of Padmasambhava, and relics such as the Guru's stone footprint and a bronze image of Jowo Shakyamuni. The site can also be approached from **Gampa Dzong**, via **Dranglung** (see above, page 294).

Western Tibet

Getting there Driving east from Zar, after 26 kilometres, you will reach the prosperous farming village of **Muk**. Take the left turn at the next intersection, 1 kilometre beyond Muk (the right leads to **Gye Gonpa** and **Jewo Gonpa** in the Gen-chu valley). Then, leave the main Tingkye-Gampa road at the subsequent junction, 8 kilometres further on, turning right to head due south. A river bed trail leads directly to the snow peaks of the **Chorten Nyima range**, nestling on the frontier between Sikkim and Nepal. The world's third highest peak **Mount Kangchendzonga** (8,585 metres) lies further south. The range has 13 peaks, the highest being **Mount Chorten Nyima** (6,927 metres) itself. Glacial streams rise within the range, heading south to converge with the **Tista** River in Sikkim.

Dingri County དིང་རི

Dingri County (36)
定日县
Tingri
Population: 40,199
Area: 14,156 sq km
Colour map 2, grid C1

*The westernmost parts of Tsang province are traditionally known as **Lato**, the 'highland' region of Tibet; and this vast area is divided into North Lato and South Lato. The former comprises the upper reaches of the Brahmaputra and Raga Tsangpo, corresponding to present day Ngamring, Saga, and Drongpa counties, and the latter comprises the Bum-chu (Arun), Matsang Tsangpo (Sunkosi), and Kyirong Tsangpo (Trishuli) valleys, corresponding to present day Dingri, Nyalam, and Kyirong counties.*

Among these, Dingri county occupies the upper reaches of the **Bum-chu (Arun) River**, and the lateral valleys formed by its tributaries, the foremost of which are: the Lolo-chu, Shel-chu, Rongpu-chu, Trakar-chu, Kharda-chu, Ra-chu Tsangpo, and Langkor Gya-chu. It also includes the valleys of the **Rongshar Tsangpo** and **Lapchi Gang Tsangpo** which flow southwest into Nepal to join the **Sunkosi River**. The county is bordered on the south by the formidable barrier of the high Himalayan range, including **Mount Everest** (Jomolangma/Jomo Gangkar), **Makalu**, and **Cho Oyo** (Jowo Oyuk).

Location   The county capital is located at **Shelkar**, 75 kilometres from **Lhartse**, 123 kilometres from **Tingkye**, and 240 kilometres from **Dram** (Zhangmu) on the Tibet-Nepal border.

Shelkar   The Zhigatse-Dram highway runs southwest from Lhartse, across the high **Gyatso La pass** (5,252 metres), and then descends steeply into the barren Lato plains, following the Lolo-chu downstream. On the descent, the Everest range can be seen in the distance, and the **Lolo hot springs** are visible by the roadside, 38 kilometres below the pass.

Below Pelbar, 12 kilometres further on, a turn-off on the right leads into **Shelkar**, following the **Shel-chu** tributary upstream (seven kilometres). The

Western Tibet

Dingri County

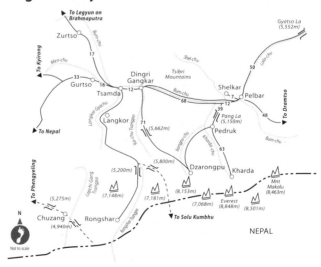

ruined fortress and monastery are prominent on the upper slopes of **Mount Shelkar Dorje Dzong**, overlooking the town. The headquarters of the **Jomolangma Nature Preserve** is located here. Since its inception in 1989 it has assumed some responsibility for the maintenance and ecology of the entire Everest region, 27,000 square kilometres.

Essentials In Pelbar The *Everest Hotel* is located at the small township of **Pelbar**, and most groups will stay here rather than at the old guesthouse in **Shelkar**. The rooms have attached bathrooms, generally without water! (double room US$32, breakfast US$7, full meal plain US$28).**In Shelkar** Simple guesthouse with an excellent Chinese restaurant, a grocery store, a bookshop.

Shelkar Chode Monastery, founded originally in 1266 by the Kagyu lama Sindeu Rinchen, has been a Gelukpa monastery since the 17th century. There were formerly some 300 monks here, and an active branch of the monastery has been established in Boudha, Nepal. The restored **assembly hall** contains images of Tsongkhapa and his foremost students, alongside Padmasambhava and Vajradhara.

A motorable road leads up the **Shel-chu valley** from Shelkar as far as **Gemar** township (50 kilometres), on the north side of the **Tsibri** range. Pilgrims can sometimes be seen approaching as they circumambulate the sacred Tsibri mountain in a clockwise direction.

The **Tsibri** mountain range, true to its name, resembles a series of protruding ribs (*tsibma*). During the 11th century, the remote crags of Tsibri were inhabited by Padampa Sangye, the Indian master who introduced the lineages of **Chod** and **Zhije** into Tibet. Subsequently, Gotsangpa Gonpopel (1189-1258) of the Drukpa Kagyu school founded his hermitage on the southeast cliff-face. His own student, Yangonpa Gyeltsenpel (1213-58) was born locally at **Lhadrong**; and his successors effectively established many Drukpa foundations around the mountain. **Tsibri**

In the present century, a series of 11 retreat hermitages was established around the mountain by Tsibri Tripon Lama who came here from Central Tibet in 1934. Among them were **Dingpoche**, **Langtso** and **Tashi Tongmon**. Some of these sites are functioning at the present time. However, the large **Nerang Printery** which he also founded to the southwest of Tsibri is no longer extant.

The nuns of **Nabtra**, the Nyingmapa monastery on the northeast side of Tsibri, under the guidance of Nabtra Rinpoche, were renowned for their meditative excellence and expertise in the traditions of Mindroling and *Longchen Nyingtig*. The previous Nabtra Rinpoche was a mantrin of great status; and his present incarnation now lives in Nepal. Pilgrims often undertake the five-day circuit of **Tsibri** mountain on foot via Khangsar, **Nakhok**, **Ngonga**, **Pangleb**, and **Tsakor**. Further north from Tsibri is the watershed range dividing South Lato from North Lato. **Mount Drakri** (5,871 metres) is the highest of these peaks.

Below Shelkar, the highway from Lhartse intersects the roads leading east to Tingkye and west to the Nepal border. Taking the Tingkye road, after some 48 kilometres you will reach **Dramtso** township on the north shore of **Lake Tingmo Tso**. **Tsogo** township lies south of the lake and on the south bank of the Bum-chu. **Lake Tingmo Tso**

Bounded on the east by the deep gorge of the **Bum-chu (Arun) River** and on the west by that of the **Matsang Tsangpo (Sunkosi)** are some of the world's **Everest Range**

Western Tibet

highest mountains of the East Himalayan range, forming a natural barrier between Tibet and Nepal. Clustered together in close proximity, these comprise: **Makalu** (8,463 metres), **Lhotse** (8,501 metres), **Everest**, known locally as Jomolangma or Jomo Gangkar (8,848 metres), **Bumo Ritse** (7,068 metres), **Jowo Oyuk** (8,153 metres), **Jowo Guru** or Menlungtse (7,181 metres), and **Jowo Tseringma** or Gauri Shangkar (7,148 metres). There are stunningly beautiful treks in the environs of each of these peaks, and among them, those around **Mount Everest** are particularly well known.

On the Tibet side, **Mount Everest** may be approached from the north face at **Dzarongpu**, or the East **Kangzhung face** at **Kharda** or Karma. A motorable dirt track leaves the Shelkar-Dram highway on the left (south) 12 kilometres after **Pelbar** and five kilometres after the police checkpoint at **Tse**. Take this turn-off and drive across **Pang La pass** (5,150 metres) to the cultivated valley of **Pedruk** (39 kilometres). From the pass there are wonderful views of the Everest range.

Pedruk facilities At Pedruk there is a run-down hotel named *Jomolangma* (camping preferable), a noodle restaurant cum tea shop, and a well-stocked general store.

Two roads diverge at **Pedruk**, the 63 kilometres east track leading to **Kharda** (see below, page 294) and the west track to **Dzarongpu**. Take the latter, and continue up the **Rongpu-chu** valley to **Paksum** and **Chodzom** (4,510 metres). Above Chodzom is the deserted Nyingmapa hermitage of **Chopuk**, which is built into the limestone cliffs to the west of the road. Here, a 71 kilometres motorable track (three days trekking) from **Dingri Gangkar** village via the **Rachu Tsangpo** valley and **Lamar La pass** (5,662 metres) connects with the route, which then continues up to **Dzarongpu Monastery** (4,980 metres).

Everest Region

Everest

For 13 years after it was found to be the highest mountain in the world, **Peak XV** had no European name. In 1865 the then Surveyor Gen of India suggested that it be named after his predecessor, Sir George Everest, the man responsible for the remarkable Great Trigonometrical Survey which ultimately determined its height. Everest himself, while honoured, was privately unhappy, as it was official policy that mountains be given their local vernacular name. However, an exception was made and the name stuck.

Everest has been climbed many times and by many routes since 1953. The route taken by Hunt's expedition is the 'Ordinary Route', disparagingly called the 'Yak' route by Sherpas. The first Chinese expeditions to reach the summit from the north side did so in 1960 and 1975. We shall never know if the British mountaineers Mallory and Irvine preceded them in 1924, when they perished on the mountain! Following his achievement on Annapurna's South Face, Chris Bonington led two expeditions to tackle Everest's Southwest Face and succeeded in 1975, with Dougal Haston reaching the summit. In 1970 Yuichiro Muira tried to ski down the Lhotse Face from the South Col, spent most of it airborne and out of control and ended unconscious on the edge of a crevasse! Rheinhold Messner and Alison Hargreaves have climbed it without oxygen. Peter Hillary followed in his father's footsteps and stood on the summit in 1990. In Apr 1988, two teams of Japanese met on top, having scaled the North and South Faces. There to record the event was a television crew!

On 29 September 1992 a 'GPS' survey using signals from satellites determined the height of Everest as 8846.1m. Although this is 2m lower than believed previously, Everest is still higher than K2, despite claims to the contrary made in the New York Times in Mar 1987. In Apr 1993 the team that first climbed Everest trekked to the Base Camp for a 40th anniversary reunion – to find 1,500 other climbers waiting their turn to go to the top of the world.

Western Tibet

Dzarongpu Monastery Communities of nuns affiliated with the Nyingmapa monastery of Mindroling have been living in the Dzarongpu area since the late 18th century. The complex was revitalized at the beginning of the 20th century by Trulzhik I Ngawang Tendzin Norbu (d 1940) who constructed a temple named **Do-ngak Choling**. Branch monasteries were also established across the **Nangpa La pass** in the **Shar Khumbu** region of East Nepal (see below, page 302). At the high point of its development, Dzarongpu had over 500 monks and nuns.

Early British mountaineering expeditions have provided invaluable documentary evidence concerning the monastery's development and Trulzhik Rinpoche's activities. The recently renovated **assembly hall** contains an image of this master, whose present incarnation lives in Nepal, alongside an image of Terdak Lingpa, founder of Mindroling. In addition to the liturgical texts of the Mindroling cycle, the *Longchen Nyingtig* is also an important spiritual practice for the small number of monks and nuns (20) who live here.

Sleeping A small guesthouse offers simple accommodation adjacent to the temple; and there is a large camping space below the stupa.

Rongpu Face Above Dzarongpu Monastery, the trail continues up to the **Everest Base Camp** (5,150 metres), located in a sheltered spot below the morraine slopes leading up to the **Central Rongpu Glacier**. Memorial plaques, including one dedicated to Mallory, stand alongside a traditional Tibetan stupa. The views of the north face of Everest from this vantage point are particularly fine. A trail skirts the east side of the glacier and crosses a creek to reach the **Advanced Base Camp** (5,760 metres), from which mountaineering ascents of the north face and the northeast ridge can be made. **Camp I** is located at 5,460 metres, **Camp II** at 6,088 metres, and **Camp III** at 6,368 metres.

NB Trekking above the Everest Base Camp should only be undertaken by those who have fully acclimatized and are properly prepared for high altitudes. Nonetheless it is possible to reach Camp III without resorting to professional mountaineering equipment.

Kangzhung Face Taking the east track from **Pedruk** village to **Kharda** (63 kilometres), the motor road first follows the **Trakar-chu** downstream to its confluence with the **Bum-chu (Arun)**, and then traces the latter downstream to **Kharda** township (see above, page 294).

An alternative route from Everest Base Camp entails six days' trekking via Doya La pass and Chongpu valley, as far as Kharda. Situated deep in the Bum-chu gorge, **Kharda** is a forested, fertile, and heavily populated area.

Kharda facilities There is a small guesthouse, a general store, and a government compound.

Follow the Kharda-chu upstream to **Yulbar**, where the four day trek to the **Kangzhung face** via Langma La pass (5,350 metres) begins. The view from the pass of Makalu's jagged peaks is particularly impressive.

Head into the **Karma** valley, where there are further stunning views of

Everest

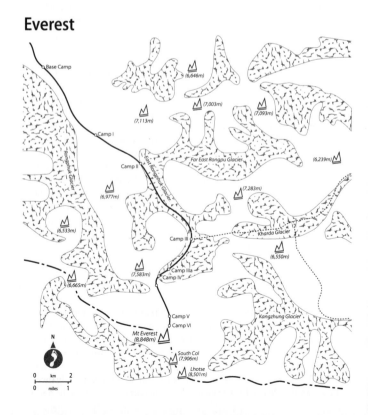

Makalu; and then climb towards the source of the Karma River, to the **Kangzhung Face Base Camp** in the Petang Ringmo meadow. Here, the campsite offers dramatic close-up views of Mount Everest and Mount Lhotse. A 5,950 metres ridge further to the west provides even closer views of all three of these 8,000 metres peaks – Everest being only five kilometres distant.

Another four-day trek follows the **Karma-chu** downstream to its confluence with the **Bum-chu**, crossing Samchung La pass (4,600 metres), and passing through a valley containing 13 glacial lakes of varied pristine hues, and the **Sakyetang plain**. The low-lying confluence (2,300 metres), close to **Drentang** on the East Nepal border, abounds in subtropical vegetation and flora. From here, you can follow the Bum-chu upstream towards Tingkye or Shelkar.

Dingri Gangkar (4,500 metres) lies on the slopes of a ridge, overlooking the Everest range, at the heart of the wide 80 kilometres plain formed by the **Bum-chu (Arun) River**. Two major tributaries converge with the Bum-chu at Dingri: the **Rachu Tsangpo**, which rises near Dzarongpu below Mount Everest and the **Langkor Gyachu**, which rises above Rongshar. — **Dingri Gangkar**

For centuries the town has dominated the trade routes linking Tibet with **Shar Khumbu** in East Nepal via the Nangpa La pass (two days' trekking), and **Kodari** via the Nyalam Tong La pass (182 kilometres). Trekking routes also lead north across the plain to Zangzang and Chung Riwoche in **North Lato**.

During the late 18th century when the Tibetan government requested the assistance of Emperor Qianlong's Chinese army to repel the Gorkha invasions of Tibet, a fortress was constructed on the hill above the town. Along with many other fortifications from that period which cover the plain as far as **Gurtso**, it now lies in ruins.

The town itself has in recent decades been rebuilt in cramped conditions to accommodate the military camp, which lies to the south of the highway. The village houses lie to the south of the army camp in close proximity (although only the camp has functional electricity). From the rooftops there are memorable views of the entire Everest range – particularly clear during full-moon nights.

The distance from **Shelkar** to **Dingri** is 68 kilometres, and from **Dingri** to **Dram** on the Nepal border 182 kilometres. Trekking routes also extend from Dingri to Dzarongpu and the Everest Base Camp, via Lamar La pass (71 kilometres), and to the Jowo Oyuk Base Camp.

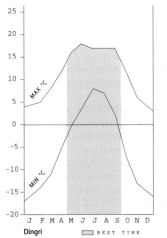

Dingri   ☐ BEST TIME

Sleeping On the north side, at the **Dingri bridge**, there is the *Sunshine Hotel*, owned by a local entrepreneur, who can organize pack animals for local treks. Another guesthouse is located within the army camp. Both have restaurant facilities: one traditionally Tibetan and the other essentially Sichuanese.

Drive west from Dingri along the highway for 12 kilometres as far as **Tsamda**, where there is a hot spring bathing facility. From here there is a motorable dirt track leading to **Langkor Monastery**. Avoid driving in the summer months when the — **Dingri Langkor**

Langkor Gyachu River bursts its banks. Otherwise hire a horse and cart from Dingri Gangkar. Langkor village and monastery are located inland from the highway on a south-facing ridge, in full view of **Mount Jowo Oyuk**.

This ranks among the most important pilgrimage places of the entire Lato region, in that it was here in 1097 that the Indian yogin Phadampa Sangye founded a hermitage and disseminated the teachings of Chod and Zhije in Tibet for the first time. His foremost Tibetan student was the yogini Machik Labdron (on whom see above, page 712). Here, Phadampa Sangye delivered a memorable teaching on ethics and conduct to the people of Dingri, entitled "*Hundred Verses of Admonition to the People of Dingri*" (*Dingri Gyatsa*).

A festival is held here each year on the 14th day of the sixth month of the lunar calendar. The **temple** is located within the village of **Langkor**. The track follows the contour of the hillside, passing a medicinal spring said to have been brought forth by Padmasambhava. The temple contains images of Phadampa Sangye and Tangtong Gyelpo, and partially faded original murals depicting Padmasambhava and Milarepa. Adjacent cave hermitages are associated with Padmasambhava, Phadampa Sangye, and Machik Labdron.

Trekking A three-day trek from **Langkor** also leads to **Nyalam** via the **Tong La pass**. This was the traditional trading route between Dingri and Central Nepal prior to the construction of the motor road.

Rongshar The beautiful **Rongshar** valley, southwest of Dingri, is the sacred abode of the 11th century yogin Milarepa, and at the same time a botanist's paradise, nestling below the high snow peak of **Mount Jowo Tseringma** (Gauri Shangkar). To reach Rongshar, head due south from Dingri in the direction of the **Nangpa La pass** (5,800 metres), which eventually leads into the **Shar Khumbu** area of East Nepal.

Passing through the villages of Penak, Shator-me, and Shator-to, the trails divide at **Kyarak** (38 kilometres). For the pass cross over to the east bank of the **Kyarak-chu** and trek due south via the glaciers of the **Jowo Oyuk** base camp. For Rongshar, remain on the west bank of the river, and head southwest towards **Puhrel La** pass (5,200 metres), one day drive or three days' trekking from Dingri. Crossing this pass, and entering into the **Rongshar** valley, the barren landscape gives way to junipers and rhododendrons (4,650 metres), and the road soon plunges down, following the course of the **Rongshar Tsangpo** via **Taktsang** (4,030 metres), where side-valleys branch off to **Salung** (northwest) and **Zhung** (southeast). The valley abounds in large fragrant white rose bushes.

On the descent to **Tsamgye** (Rongshar township), **Mount Jowo Tseringma** (7,148 metres) comes into view, dominating the valley from the south. Avoid the bureaucrats here, and continue downstream to **Chuwar Monastery** (3,300 metres), dramatically situated above the confluence of the **Rongshar Tsangpo** and **Menlung-chu**. The gorge of the latter leads east to **Mount Menlungtse** (7,181 metres).

Many sites in this region have associations with Milarepa, who lived in the remote hermitages of the Rongshar valley for many years, eventually passing away at Chuwar. The Nepalese-style temple at **Chuwar Monastery** is therefore the focal point of pilgrimage in the valley. Downstream from **Drubden**, where there are cave hermitages of both Milarepa and Gampopa, the Rongshar Tsangpo enters Nepal (2,750 metres), where it is known as the **Bhotkosi**, a major tributary of the **Sunkosi River**. Another trail climbs 400 metres from Drubden to **Drintang** and the **Drakmar caves**, where Milarepa taught his disciple Rechungpa. Here the cave hermitages directly face the snow peaks of Mount Jowo Tseringma.

From **Drintang** in lower Rongshar, a trekking route leads via Trode and north | **Lapchi Gang**
across Gangchen La pass (4,940 metres) into the forested valley of **Lapchi Gang**. The snow peaks of this revered valley are regarded as the abodes of the meditational deities Cakrasamvara, Vajrapani, Manjughosa, and Avalokiteshvara. Here, the **Lapchi Gang Tsangpo** flows in a course parallel to that of the Rongshar Tsangpo, crossing the Tibet-Nepal border.

There are a number of 11th century hermitages associated with Milarepa in the upper and lower reaches, including the **Dudul Cave**, **Bepa Gong Cave**, and **Se Cave**, which are classed among his 'four great meditation caves'. The pagoda-roofed monastery, known as **Chura Gepheling**, is situated above the confluence of the east and west tributaries of the Lapchi Gang Tsangpo. The **assembly hall** contains a venerated image of Milarepa, reputedly made by Rechungpa from his master's nose-bleed, and a stone said to be the master's life-supporting talisman (*lado*).

Ascending the valley of the west tributary, you pass through **Chuzang**, where Milarepa subdued a hostile demon who sought to obstruct the opening of the Lapchi Gang hermitages to Buddhist practitioners. **Jamgang La pass** (5,275 metres) at the head of the valley leads across the watershed to **Pengyeling Monastery** on the Dingri-Nyalam stretch of the Nepal highway.

Nyalam County གཉའ་ལམ

*Nyalam county comprises the townships of **Menpu** and **Zurtso** around the head-waters of the **Bum-chu River**, and those of **Tsangdong**, **Tsongdu**, and **Dram** in the **Matsang Tsangpo (Sunkosi)** valley. The highway from Lhasa traverses the Great Himalayan range at **Yakrushong La pass** (5,200 metres), also known nowadays as **Nyalam Tong La**, and then precariously follows the course of the **Matsang Tsangpo** downstream to the Tibetan customs barrier at **Dram (Zhangmu/Khasa)**, and the **Friendship Bridge** on the Nepal border. This is currently Tibet's most important land border with the outside world. The trading community of **Dram** are among the most prosperous people in all Tibet.*

Nyalam County (37)
聶拉木县
Nyalam
Population: 12,058
Area: 5,570 sq km
Colour map 1, grid C5

Western Tibet

The county capital is located at **Tsongdu (Nyalam)**, 30 kilometres north of the border, and 152 kilometres from **Dingri**. The **Arniko Highway** which runs from **Kodari** to **Kathmandu** (122 kilometres) via **Barabise** was constructed by the Chinese in 1960s.

Nyalam County

From **Dingri**, the highway cuts northwest to **Gurtso** (28 kilometres), where the **Men-chu River** joins the **Bum-chu**. The township of **Zurtso** is located 17 kilometres further north near the source of the Bum-chu, and a jeepable track leads via Zurtso to **Legyun** and **Taktse** on the Brahmaputra in North Lato.

Gurtso has a military camp with spartan guesthouse facilities, and a vital road maintenance depot, responsible for clearing snowfall from the high Himalayan passes to the south. The highway follows the **Men-chu** upstream (southwest)

Bum-chu
(Arun River)
Headwaters

from Gurtso, passing Menpu township and **Menkhab-to** village, where ruined 18th century fortifications can be seen.

After 33 kilometres (road marker 614), the road bifurcates: the west route leading to **Kyirong** and Far-west Tibet (see below, page 328). Striking views of **Mount Shishapangma** (8,012 metres), the highest peak entirely inside Tibetan territory, dominate the west horizon.

Mount Shishapangma There are three approaches to the spectacular snow peaks of **Shishapangma** (Goshainathan), which at 8,012 metres was the last of the world's 8,000 metres peaks to be climbed. The northern base camp is accessible from **Serlung** on the Kyirong road, the eastern side from a turn-off 42 kilometres south of the **Lalung La pass**, and the southern base camp from Nyalam by trekking upstream through the **Tsongdupu-chu valley**. The latter also offers fine views of the **Langtang Himalayan** peaks to the southwest.

Himalayan Passes The highway cuts through the Himalayan range via the Lalung La pass (5,124 metres) and the Yakrushong La pass (5,200 metres), which are crossed in quick succession. The latter is sometimes known as **Nyalam Tong La** ('pass from which Nyalam is visible'), although the original Tong La pass lies further east on the traditional Dingri-Nyalam trade route. Pilgrims stop at the second pass to raise prayer flags, burn incense, scatter 'wind-horse' paper inscriptions, and build cairns. This is the last contact with the Tibetan plateau. Below the passes, the road descends steeply into the valley of the **Matsang Tsangpo** (Sunkosi River). Trails to the east lead directly to **Langkor** and **Dingri** via the Tong-La. At **Tsangdong** township, also known as **Nesar**, 40 kilometres below the second pass, the climate changes from the dryness of the plateau to the warm moist air of the Indian subcontinent. A trail to the east leads to **Lapchi Gang** via Tashigang.

Pengyeling Monastery The temple of **Pengyeling**, 44 kilometres south of the last Himalayan pass, is built around the sacred **Namkading Cave** of Milarepa, which overlooks the approach to the hidden valley of **Lapchi Gang**. The buildings are invisible from the motor road (at road marker 683), some three kilometres below the highway, and above the west bank of the **Matsang Tsangpo**. An antechamber contains on its side-walls a detailed description of the pilgrimage sites associated with Milarepa in the environs of Pengyeling and Lapchi. The **Namkading Cave** contains rock impressions of Milarepa's seated meditation posture and handprint – the latter having appeared in the rock when Milarepa assisted his student Rechungpa prop up the low ceiling with a boulder. Images include Milarepa, Tsongkhapa, and the protectress Shridevi, whose mule also reputedly left a footprint in the stone when she appeared in a vision to Milarepa.

Nyalam

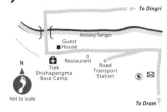

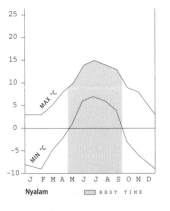

Nyalam   ▭ BEST TIME

The **main temple**, to the east of the cave entrance contains an assembly hall with a principal image of Padmasambhava. The caretaker of Pengyeling lives above and behind the temple where there are smaller caves associated with Rechungpa and the protector deities of the Gelukpa tradition. This one-time Kagyu temple complex has been affiliated to the Gelukpa monastery of Sera since the late 17th century.

The town of Nyalam (3,750 metres) traditionally known as **Tsongdu**, lies 11   **Nyalam**
kilometres south of **Pengyeling**, deep within the gorge of the **Matsang Tsangpo** at the point where both the river and the road cut through the Himalayan range. **Mount Dorje Lakpa** rises above the town to the west. For centuries this has been the main trading post between Tibet and Nepal. The valley of the **Tsongdupu-chu** tributary runs northeast towards the southern base camp of **Mount Shishipangma**. The Bod-chu tributary joins the Matsang Tsangpo from the east below the town.

Essentials There are three simple guesthouses (the best being the *Nyalam Hotel* to the east of the highway). Small roadside restaurants serve Sichuan country-style cuisine. There is also an important truck stop, a petrol station, and a small hospital.

Dram (Zhangmu)

Below Nyalam, the road plunges through the **Matsang Tsangpo** gorge, hug-   *Colour map1, grid C5*
ging a precipice above the rapids. There are spectacular waterfalls on both sides of the gorge. 12 kilometres below Nyalam, there is the 54 bed *Chusham Hotel*, which is well-located in a tranquil part of the valley near the **Chusham hot springs**, but often lacking in electricity.

The border town of **Dram** (*Ch* **Zhangmu**; *Nepali* **Khasa**) lies 31 kilometres below Nyalam at an average altitude of 2,300 metres. The sprawling town extends down the hillside for over four kilometres through a series of switchback bends. In the rainy season (July-September) motor vehicles are sometimes unable to reach the town from Nyalam (and also from the **Friendship Bridge**) owing to landslides which are a constant hazard to the local population. Nonetheless, the people of Dram tend to be among the wealthiest in Tibet. Black market trading in assorted commodities, gold, and currency is rife.

The **Gonpa Sarpa** monastery is located at the lower end, adjacent to the **China Customs Building**.

Sleeping *Zhangmu Hotel*, double rooms are available at US$32 (breakfast US$7; full meal plain US$28), lower end of town, adjacent to the China Customs Building. Curiously, this 5-storeyed hotel has its reception office on the top floor, which is at road level, and its restaurant on the lowest floor. Electricity is erratic and the rooms are often damp. *Zhangmu Guesthouse*, opposite the *Zhangmu Hotel*, has inferior accommodation. Best rooms on 6/F.

Eating There are many small roadside restaurants in town serving Sichuan, Tibetan and Nepalese cuisines.

Directory Banks Located in the upper end of town. **Communications** Post Office: located in the upper end of town.

Dram

To Nyalam
Tibet Foreign Trade Shop
Army
Foreign Registration Office
Cemetery
Nepalese Restaurant
Transport Station Guesthouse
Himalayan Lodge
PSB
New Monastery
Guesthouse
Zhangmu Hotel
China Customs & Immigration

N

To Friendship Bridge & Nepal

Not to scale
● Restaurants

Western Tibet

At the Border The customs and immigration posts open at 1000 Beijing time, and by the time you have gone through all formalities and driven or walked the 8 kilometres downhill to the actual frontier on the **Friendship Bridge** (Dzadrok Zampa), the Nepalese customs will be on the point of opening at 0930 Nepal time (some 2½ hours difference).

Kyirong County སྐྱིད་གྲོང་

Kyirong County (38)
吉隆县
Gyirong
Population: 10,158
Area: 8,8869 sq km
Colour map 1, grid C5

*Kyirong county in **South Lato** occupies the valleys of the **Kyirong Tsangpo River** (Trishuli) and its tributaries as well as the adjacent **Gungtang-chu** headwaters and the basin of **Lake Pelkhu Tso**. To the south straddling the Tibet/Nepal border lie the mighty snow peaks of the Himalayan range: Ganesh Himal (7,406 metres), Langtang (7,232 metres), and Shishapangma (8,012 metres). Further north there are trails crossing the high watershed passes into North Lato, and the Brahmaputra valley. The Kyirong gorge and valley form one of Tibet's most beautiful picturesque alpine regions; and it boasts sites of historic importance, connected with King Songtsen Gampo, Padmasambhava, Milarepa, and Sakya Pandita, among others. The county capital is located at **Dzongka**, 127 kilometres east of the turn-off on the Gurtso/Nyalam road (see below, page 307), 103 kilometres south of Saga, and 75 kilometres north of Rizur Zampa on the Nepal border.*

Lake Pelkhu Tso On the Gurtso-Nyalam road, which connects with the Arniko Highway to Kathmandu, there is a turn-off below **Lalung La pass**, north of the Himalayan range, which cuts westwards, following the **Nakdo-chu** tributary of the **Men-chu** (itself a source of the Bum-chu) upstream to Serlung. The road passes through the desolate plain of Digur Tang, with its enormous sand dunes and the snow peaks of **Shishapangma** (8,012 metres) and **Langtang** (7,232 metres) in close proximity to the south. Leaving the Bum-chu basin, it then descends into the depression of **Pelkhu Tso** (4,600 metres), a stunningly beautiful lake into which the glacial streams of the Da-chu and Lha-chu drain.

Below the cliffs on the east shore is the cave hermitage of Milarepa, known as **Laphu Pemadzong**. The road skirts the south shore of the lake and then turns abruptly north, following the west shoreline. In the afternoons this terrain is exposed to strong biting winds, reminiscent of those in the Dingri plains. Reaching the base of **Jakhyung La pass** (5,180 metres), also known as Ma la, the road forks. Take the right turn which leads north into **Saga** county (69 kilometres), via a small lake called **Tso Drolung**; or cross the pass (left) to reach the county capital at **Dzongka**.

Trekking Trekking routes also skirt the north shore of the lake to reach **Gongmo**, from where the trail crosses **Shakyel La pass**, to reach Trepa and **Drakna** township on the Brahmaputra. **Drakna Druka** is an important ferry crossing on the Brahmaputra; and trails lead downstream from here to Lhartse or upstream to Tango and Saga county.

Kyirong County

Dzongka, the county capital, lies 34 kilometres below **Jakhyung La pass**, overlooking the confluence of the **Kyirong Tsangpo** and its main tributary, the **Zarong-chu**. There is a trail following the latter upstream and across Tagya La pass to Achen and the Brahmaputra.

Owing to its mild climate and location, Dzongka thrived over the centuries as an important centre for Nepalese trade. Most of the ancient perimeter walls were destroyed by the Gorkha armies of the 18th century; but a significant portion of the southwest section survives even now. Within this enclosure is the Gelukpa monastery of **Ganden Palgyeling** which has some original murals and sculptures. Further north are the new buildings of Dzongka – the government compound and the commercial quarter. The once inhabited cave settlement of **Lhamog Gonpa** is located on a hill promontory above the town.

If you take the south road from Dzongka, following the **Kyirong Tsangpo** downstream, you will reach the township of Kyirong after 68 kilometres. At **Orma** village the river valley narrows into a spectacular 35 kilometres gorge devoid of settlements. Side-valleys occasionally extend east or west from the gorge. At Gun, a trail leads east to **Tsalung**, the birthplace of Milarepa in Gunda district (4,300 metres). Further south, at Longda, a trail leads west from the gorge to the ruined **Drakar Monastery**. Above it the important cave hermitage of Milarepa, known as **Drakar Taso** (3,600 metres), contains wood-carved images of Padmasambhava, Milarepa, and Maitreya.

The main road continues its descent of the gorge to **Drotang** (3,320 metres), from where another trail leads west to Kyangpa Monastery and Milarepa's cave hermitage at **Kyangpa Namka Dzong**. Mount Riwo Pelbar is visible to the southwest. The Kyirong gorge eventually opens out at **Ragma** (3,000 metres), where there are cultivated fields.

The **Ragma** valley, extending eastwards from the Kyirong Tsangpo, contains the **Jangchub Dzong** cave hermitage of Milarepa and **Riwo Pelbar Monastery** with its nearby Padmasambhava power place. The main Kyirong valley, forested and alpine in character, descends through Magal, Garu Monastery, and Pangzhing village, before reaching the heart of Kyirong.

Jamtrin Temple Jamtrin Gegye Lhakhang, northeast of Kyirong township, is one of the four geomantic 'further taming temples' (*yangdul lhakhang*) founded by King Songtsen Gampo during the seventh century. The four-storey temple in an unusual pagoda design is said to be located on the right foot of the supine ogress.

Phakpa Wati Lhakhang The most historically significant building in the township of Kyirong (2,774 metres) is the four-storeyed Phakpa Wati Lhakhang. This Nepalese pagoda-style temple once contained the renowned Phakpa Wati image of standing Lokeshvara, the bodhisattva of compassion. According to legend, King Songtsen Gampo during the seventh century despatched the incarnate monk Akarmatishila to Nepal, where in a forest of the Indo-Nepalese borderland, he found a sandalwood tree-trunk, which had split open in four segments to reveal the four 'self-arising' images of Lokeshvara. Known collectively as the 'four sublime brothers' (Phakpa Chezhi) these are: Phakpa Lokeshvara (the most sacred image in the Potala Palace; Phakpa Ukhang (in Khorzhak); Phakpa Jamali (in Nepal); and Phakpa Wati. This last image was originally brought to Lhasa with the others, but expelled to Kyirong by Bonpo ministers during the eighth century. There it remained, in the Phakpa Wati Lhakhang until 1656 when it was transported

Dzongka

Upper Kyirong Gorge

Lower Kyirong Valley

Western Tibet

Stabbing at shadows

In the 13th century, Sakya Pandita visited Phakpa Wati Lhakhang, and it was here that he defeated the Hindu master Haranandin in debate. In order to subdue the intruder he requested help from the Nyingmapa yogin Darcharuwa, who had discovered a renowned ritual dagger (kila) at Yerpa and acquired extraordinary yogic prowess. Legend recounts that when Haranandin flew into the sky, 'flapping his hands like wings', Dracharuwa stabbed his shadow with the ritual dagger, causing him to fall to the ground, 'like a bird struck by a stone'! Subsequently no non-Buddhist masters from India sought to propagate their views inside Tibet.

back to Lhasa for safekeeping. The temple has outer murals depicting the great monasteries of Lhasa.

Jadur Bonpo Monastery The important Bonpo site known as Jadur, near Yangchu Tangkar village outside Kyirong township, is a focal point for Bonpo pilgrims heading in the direction of Mount Kailash. A festival is held here during the fourth month of the lunar calendar.

Samtenling Monastery Accessible by a full day trek from Kyirong township via Neshar, Samtenling Gonpa is the largest monastery of the valley. Originally a Kagyu site, frequented by the yogin Repa Zhiwa, it was later converted to the Gelukpa school in the 17th century, following the defeat of the Tsangpa kings in the civil war; and thereafter regarded as a branch of Shelkar Chode. The large complex of ruined buildings at Samtenling testifies to the monastery's former grandure, and the snow peaks of Langtang and Ganesh Himal form a memorable backdrop. A flourishing branch of Kyirong Samtenling was established at Boudha in Kathmandu during the early 1960s.

Kyirong-Nepal Two roads diverge south of Kyirong township, the westerly one following the **Kyirong Tsangpo** downstream to the Nepal border (29 kilometres) – passing through **Khimbuk** village, **Rizur Zampa** bridge (spanning the Lende Khola-chu), and **Rashuwa Dzong**. On the Nepal side, the road passes through Syabunbesi and Dunche, before reaching Trishuli and Kathmandu. The easterly road is motorable only as far as **Langchu**, and thereafter it becomes a trekking route, passing through Dra, Kharbang, and Sa-le, before fording the border stream at **Chusumdo**. On the Nepalese side, it continues on to Sadang Kadu and the Langtang National Park. Without crossing the border, you can follow another trail eastwards to the Laga La glacier (west of Mount Shishapangma).

Gungtang The **Gungtang** valleys, which form part of the **Gandaki** headwaters, are more remote than that of Kyirong, located on a jeepable side-road 187 kilometres from Saga and 216 kilometres from Dzongka. This road crosses the celebrated **Gungtang La pass** (also known as Jang La), from which Padmasambhava entered Tibet during the eighth century. Stone footprints of Padmasambhava from the rocks of Gungtang La are kept in the Phakpa Lhakhang of the Potala Palace and at Samye Monastery. A trekking route also leads more directly from Dzongka to Chang and thence into the heart of Gungtang.

The southern approaches from Nepal are more rugged – traversing the passes of Gya La, Lachen La, Lachung La, and Monla Drakchen. The main settlements of Gungtang are Rud, Nying, Nyam, and **Chang** – the last of which has a medicinal hot spring. **Okla Gonpa** is the principal monastery.

Ngamring County ངམ་རིང་

Ngamring County (39)
昂仁县
Ngamring
Population: 38,433
Area: 17,804 sq km
Colour map 1, grid C6

*The region of North Lato comprises the counties of **Ngamring**, **Saga** and **Drongpa**, which occupy the upper reaches of the Brahmaputra, and those of its major tributaries, including the **Raga Tsangpo** and **Rikyu Tsangpo**. Among these, Ngamring county, sometimes referred to as the gateway to Mount Kailash and Far-western Tibet, is the barren area which divides the Raga Tsangpo and the Brahmaputra. The main road runs northwest from Lhartse, crossing the Brahmaputra via the Lhartse Chakzam bridge or the Drapu ferry, to enter the county. It then passes through Gekha and Zangzang townships to rejoin the river at Saga. The most important historical sites are located at **Chung Riwoche** and **Zangzang Lhadrak**. The county capital of **Ngamring** is located to the northeast of Gekha on a turn-off, 60 kilometres from Lhartse, and 240 kilometres from Saga.*

After crossing the Brahmaputra at **Lhartse Chakzam** bridge, the recent construction of which has put an end to the adventures of the ferry crossing, the road ascends a rocky river valley, with **Mount Yakri** (Yakpo Gangri, 5,614 metres) to the northeast and the bright blue waters of **Lake Langtso** to the south. A longer valley then leads up to **Gekha** township, 53 kilometres from Lhartse. Gekha lies at the southeast corner of **Lake Ngamring Kye-tso**, and has a road transport station, with simple accommodation and dining facilities. The county capital, **Ngamring** is located on a side-road seven kilometres northeast of Gekha, on the northeast shore of the lake. There are excellent views of the lake from the road. In town, the main site is **Ngamring Monastery**, an original 13th century Sakyapa foundation, which was partially converted to the Gelukpa school in the 17th century.

Gekha & Ngamring

From Ngamring there is a branch road which follows the **Dokzhung Tsangpo** section of the Raga Tsangpo downstream towards Lingo at its arid confluence with the Mu-chu in Zhetongmon county (see above, page 279). This jeepable trail passes through **Chowok** (Mekhang) township after 57 kilometres, and terminates at **Yagmo** township after a further 23 kilometres.

Dokzhung Tsangpo valley

Some 500 metres before reaching Gekha township on the drive from Lhartse, there is a seemingly insignificant dirt track leading left (southwest), which crosses the low ranges dividing the Raga Tsangpo from the Brahmaputra. At **Matho**, 39 kilometres from that turn-off, an iron bridge spans the Brahmaputra, carrying vehicles across to **Do-pe** township on the south bank. A further 14 kilometres drive will bring you into view of the magnificent Chung Riwoche stupa across the river on the north bank. A motorable iron bridge spans the river here, alongside an original iron-chain footbridge attributed to Tangtong Gyelpo.

Chung Riwoche Kumbum

Ngamring County

The stupa of **Chung Riwoche** overlooks the Brahmaputra, from its vantage point at the base of **Mount Pal Riwoche** and the ruins of Chung Riwoche Monastery. It was constructed during the period 1449-56, and had associations with both the Sakyapa school and Tangtong

Western Tibet

Gyelpo's own Chakzampa tradition. The design and extant murals are reminiscent of similar stupas at Jonang Phuntsoling and Gyang Bumpoche (see above, page 287 and page 289). According to the biography of Tangtong Gyelpo, it is largely the work of local artists of the so-called **Lato style**, which derives from the art of **Zhalu** but exhibits a more naive brushstroke and line technique than the cosmopolitan style of the **Gyantse Kumbum** (see above, page 258).

The stupa has eight storeys and a basement with its own interior circumambulatory walkway. The rectangular chapels on the floors from the second to the fifth are contained within the terraced steps (*bangrim*) of the stupa, while the circular chapels of the sixth and seventh are in the bulbous dome (*bumpa*). The eighth floor is in the form of an open circular roof terrace, surmounted by a recently restored bell. The extant wall-painted mandalas are representative of the Sakyapa school.

Trekking Chung Riwoche can also be approached on the north bank of the Brahmaputra on a poor road surface from **Matho** and **Nyinkhar**, or by trekking from **Zangzang** via Choka. A more ambitious seven-day trek from South Lato follows the old trade route from **Dingri Gangkar** (see above, pages 301). It crosses the **Bum-chu (Arun)** River and Khangsar village, before traversing the watershed **Me La** pass (5,224 metres), which offers distant views of **Mount Drakri** (5,871 metres) and **Mount Bulhari** (6,040 metres) to the east. A second pass, **Kure La** (5,498 metres) is then crossed, and on the descent the trail passes west of **Yulchen** township before reaching the south bank of the Brahmaputra at Chung Riwoche. Trails also follow the river banks upstream from Chung Riwoche to **Drakna** township in Kyirong county (see above page 306).

Ralung Chutsen If one continues northwest from Gekha on the main route, a hot spring known as **Ralung Chutsen** comes into view on the right side of the road a few kilometres past the northwest shore of Ngamring Kyetso lake. Here there is a hot spring bathing house with simple guest rooms; and, if you arrive in the late afternoon, is a reasonable place to stop for the night. Apart from the guest rooms there are good grass-covered campsites. The baths themselves consist of square stone pools inside private rooms with large skylights open to the stars (if you bathe in the evening). The elderly Tibetans who manage it will flush the existing water away and replace it with fresh water if you ask politely. A small fee is charged per person whether you stay in a tent or in a room. A stop here is preferable to **Raga** which is two hours or so further on. **NB** If you stay at the hot springs and intend travelling on the **northern route to Mount Kailash**, it is important to leave early the next day in order to reach **Tsochen** before nightfall.

Zangzang Lhadrak The district of Zangzang is renowned as the birthplace of **Rigdzin Godemchen** (1337-1408), the celebrated treasure-finder (terton) of the Nyingmapa school, who discovered and revealed the **Northern Treasures** (*Jangter*). On the 60 kilometres drive from Gekha to Zangzang township, **Mount Trazang** is passed to the southwest of the road. The master's birthplace is at Toyor Nakpo, northeast of this mountain, on the summit of which he unearthed the keys to his treasure-texts in April 1366. Almost two months later, in the nearby cave of **Zangzang Lhadrak**, he discovered the 500 seminal works of the Northern Treasures tradition in a blue treasure-chest with five compartments. The tradition which he founded spread throughout remote areas of Ladakh and South Tibet, as far as Dartsedo in Kham; and these original sites continue even now to be revered focal points of pilgrimage for adherents of this lineage. The new town of **Zangzang** has a somewhat drab and bleak appearance. Most traffic does not stop here, but instead continues on to **Raga**, 122 kilometres beyond Zangzang.

Jangtang routes from Zangzang

A few kilometres northwest of Zangzang township on the main road, there is a turn-off which heads due north in the direction of the **Jangtang Plateau**. Following this jeepable trail, after **Kang-lhe** village, the road leaves the Raga Tsangpo basin and crosses the watershed into the Jangtang lakeland. Some 55 kilometres from the turn-off, the trail bifurcates, one branch following the **Taklung-chu** northwest for 50 kilometres to **Tsha-tse** township, on the south-east shore of **Lake Zhuru-tso**; and the other heading north for 76 kilometres along the valley of the **Tatok Tsangpo**, to **Tso-me** township. Arduous trekking routes from these two townships skirt the east shore of the large lake **Dangra Yutso**, as far as **Ombu** on the north shore. From there, a jeep road leads 167 kilometres to join the main Amdo-Gertse road at **Nyima** (see below, page 323).

Upper Raga Tsangpo

The main road from Zangzang to Saga runs west, following the south bank of the Raga Tsangpo upstream. After 39 kilometres it crosses **Gye La pass**, and then, at **Gyedo** village, there is a turn-off on the right (north) for the lakes **Chudrang-tso** and **Amchok-tso**.

Raga township lies on the main road, 69 kilometres beyond the pass and near the source of the Raga Tsangpo. It is merely a cluster of mud-walled compounds used as rest rooms for truckers. A jeepable dirt trail leads south for 26 kilometres to **Tengkar** on the Brahmaputra, from where it is possible to trek to **Drakna** township and **Pelkhu Lake** (see above, page 306).

Raga's importance lies in the fact that it is the closest settlement to one of West Tibet's most important road junctions. Some 14 kilometres after Raga, the main road splits in two: the northern branch heading into the Jangtang Plateau for **Tsochen** (242 kilometres), and thence to **Gertse**, **Gegye** and **Senge Tsangpo**; and the southern branch rejoining the Brahmaputra at **Saga** (58 kilometres), and following it upstream to its source in Drongpa county. The former is sometimes known as the **northern route to Mount Kailash** and the latter as the **southern route to Mount Kailash**. In this text, the southern route will be described first, since it remains within the **North Lato** district of West Tibet as far as Drongpa.

Saga County ས་དགའ

*Saga county in **North Lato** is the region occupied by the upper Brahmaputra and its tributaries: the **Rukyok Tsangpo** and **Kyibuk Tsangpo**. The county capital is located at **Kyakyaru**, 58 kilometres from the Raga junction on the North Lato or Lhartse road, 105 kilometres from Dzongka on the Zhangmu or South Lato road, and 146 kilometres from Drongpa on the southern route to Mount Kailash.*

Saga County (40)
萨嘎县
Saga
Population: 9,430
Area: 13,374 sq km
Colour map 1, grid C5

Tengkar

A jeep track leads 26 kilometres south from Raga to **Tengkar** township on the north bank of the Brahmaputra. Downstream from here (and still on the north bank) are the villages of Sharu, Salung and Taktse, the last of which has a hot spring. Fording the Brahmaputra at Tengkar, a trail continues from **Drakna** township on the south bank to Lake Pelkhu and Dzongka (see above, page 306).

Kyakyaru

Saga county town (*Tib* Kyakyaru) straddles the **Dargye Tsangpo** above its confluence with the Brahmaputra, 14 kilometres west of old **Kyakya** village and 58 kilometres southwest of the Raga road-junction. The river is crossed here via the **Saga Chakzam** bridge. The town is strategically located at the intersection of three motor routes: the Lhartse road from the east, the Dzongka road from the south, and the Purang and Drongpa road from the west. The town of Saga (ironically meaning 'Happy Land') has grown in recent years to service an important Chinese military garrison, which functions as the head-quarters of the border patrol force, monitoring the entire length of the Tibeto-Nepalese frontier as far west as the Indo-Nepalese border. Soldiers from the garrison also are likely to have target practice near the centre of town; so don't be surprised if you hear machine gun fire at any time of the day. As you leave town heading west they may give a friendly wave from the low side of the road while they shoot bullets over your head aiming at targets placed on the slope above. There is little of interest here in Saga, so rest well!

Facilities On the southern route to Mount Kailash, Saga is the last town with a rea-sonable transport station since it has a shop and restaurant at the west end of its courtyard. The transport station is located near the southeast corner of the main side street, which leaves the highway via a bridge leading directly to the town hall and cin-ema. It is important to reach the truck stop as early as possible since it usually fills up each night and there is little alternative accommodation. A short walk down the main road leads past local shops and the new Chinese small business ventures to a hospital and dispensary.

Dzongka & Zhungru roads A few kilometres south of Saga, the road reaches the **Kyakya Druka** ferry, leading to the south bank of the Brahmaputra. Heading south on this jeepable road, after 37 kilometres there is a turn-off on the right (west), which leads to **Zhungru** township. The main road continues due south for a further 32 kilo-metres, after which it again bifurcates, the right (west) branch leading to **Dzongka** (34 kilometres) in Kyirong county, and the left (east) branch leading around the southern shores of **Lake Pelkhu** to join the Dram (Zhangmu) highway. Take the latter route if you wish to reach Nepal quickly and avoid the Lhartse detour.

If you take the **Zhungru** turn-off, you will reach the township of Trhango after 75 kilometres. Trhango lies close to the south bank of the Brahmaputra, and it is also the roadhead for the renowned Gungtang La (Jang La) pass through which Padmasambhava first entered Tibet in the eighth century. A ferry crossing, **Zhungru Druka**, links Pudrak, Zhungru and other villages on the north bank with those on the south bank, including Trhango and Rila.

Dargyeling The **southern route to Mount Kailash** and Purang leaves Saga town, follow-ing the **Dargye Tsangpo** upstream in a northwest direction. After **Garshok**, it reaches the township of **Dargyeling**, 26 kilometres from Saga. Further upstream, the road passes the confluence of the combined waters of the **Rukyok Tsangpo** and **Kyibuk Tsangpo**, before following the **Men-chu** trib-utary of the Brahmaputra, via Lhaktsang, into Drongpa county. The valleys are rugged with little veg-etation. The distance from Dargyeling to Drongpa is 119 kilometres.

Saga County

Not to scale

Drongpa County འབྲོང་པ

*Drongpa county is the region around the source of the Brahmaputra River, which in its uppermost reaches is known as the **Tachok Tsangpo**. To the south lies the Nepalese enclave of **Lowo Matang** (Mustang) and the glacial sources of the Brahmaputra. To the north are some of the great Jangtang lakes – Ngangla Ringtso, Taro-tso, and the Drangyer saltfields. The main road following the course of the Brahmaputra through Drongpa county is the **southern route to Mount Kailash**, rich in nomadic grassland pastures. The county capital is located in the environs of **Drongpa Tradun**, 145 kilometres from Saga and 224 kilometres from Mayum La pass, which divides West Tibet from the Ngari region of Far-west Tibet.*

Drongpa County (41)
仲巴县
Zhongba
Population: 14,133
Area: 28,940 sq km
Colour map 1, grid C5

The road leading from the Men-chu valley of Saga county into Drongpa initially passes through vast sand dunes, and for a large part of the distance stays close to the north bank of the Brahmaputra. From the pass on the border which separates these two counties, there are fine views of **Mount Longpo Gangri** (7,095 metres) to the northeast and the Himalayan ranges to the south. The road thereafter deteriorates considerably, making travel much slower than before.

Drongpa Tradun

The Drongpa river valley, formed by the combined waters of the **Tsa-chu** and **Yur-chu**, is a broad delta of sand and low-lying scrub. The waters of the river flow south into the Brahmaputra. One of King Songtsen Gampo's geomantic temples of the 'further-taming' (*yangdul*) class, named **Jang Traduntse**, is said to have been located in this valley, on the 'right knee' of the supine ogress. It was from here and from neighbouring **Zhungru** that Tibetan traders and lamas would traditionally make their way into **Lowo Matang** (Mustang), via the **Lektse Tsongra** market and the **Chu'arok** river valley.

Like Saga, **Drongpa** county town was developed originally as a military base, and it was once the main check post for illegal traffic (such as hitchhiking tourists). It had no restaurant save a public kitchen where local people could come and pick up a bowl of rice and greasy gruel. It was located on the south side of a wind-swept sand dune and was singularly uninviting. Then, abruptly, in 1993, the town was moved about 25 kilometres west! That is, at least the military garrison and administrative buildings moved, leaving a semi-ghost town at the old site, which is inhabited mostly by local Tibetans. However, it is easy to miss the **new Drongpa** completely, in that it is concealed some distance away from the main road on the far west side of the Drongpa river valley. Look out for the turn-off some eight to 10 kilometres west of the new bridge and just before the road enters the Brahmaputra gorge. However, since there is nowhere to stay at new Drongpa, if it is not late you are advised to press on.

Drongpa Town

Drongpa County

▲ *To Mnt Kailash*   ○ Lungkar
Lake
Balungtso   105
Maryum La ○ Ribzhi
50   58
○ Satsam
50 ○ Horpa
20
Gacho
Baryang ○—14—○ 36 ○ (4,725m)
Drongpa Tradun
N   (7,095m)
▲
Brahmaputra   119
Dargyeling ○
Not to scale   26
Kyakyaru ○

From Drongpa, the main road continues to follow the Brahmaputra valley upstream, ever closer to its source. After 71 kilometres, it crosses **Soge La pass** (4,725 metres), and descends 36 kilometres to the small township of **Gacho**. Some nine kilometres

Baryang

Western Tibet

beyond Gacho, after crossing some of the large sand dunes, there is a small hamlet of Tibetan houses, known locally as **Dutu**. Located on the eastern side of a rocky ridge on the south side of the road it is the focus for a number of families who graze their animals on the rich surrounding pastures. Nomads pitch their tents here, and there is a fine water supply nearby. From this point on, healthy, growing herds of yaks and goats are to be seen on both sides of the road. The next main settlement is **Baryang**, 14 kilometres after Gacho; but since the township has little of interest, it may be better to camp. The *Yak Hotel* in Baryang is small but comfortable.

Horpa Some 20 kilometres after Baryang, the road fords the **Neu Tsangpo River** at **Horpa**. This river eventually flows into the Brahmaputra below Baryang. A new bridge has recently been constructed here. Formerly the crossing was dangerous and vehicles were often trapped midstream. Whether the whole **southern route to Mount Kailash** is open or not depends largely on this one crossing. If the weather is fine you should attempt to make the crossing as early as possible in the day, before the snow melt has swollen the river. If it has been raining it may be necessary to wait for assistance to arrive. It is always sensible to make this crossing together with other vehicles. Once across, the road continues through sandy grasslands.

Lungkar From Horpa, a side-road leaves the Brahmaputra valley to follow the **Neu Tsangpo** upstream. Crossing the high **Me La** watershed, it descends into the Jangtang Plateau after 58 kilometres. It then bypasses **Ribzhi** village on the east shore of Lake Balungtso, and after a further 105 kilometres it comes to a halt at **Lungkar** township on the southwest shore of **Lake Tarotso**. Recently Lungkar has been given an enhanced status as the capital of a new county bearing its own name (*Ch* Longe'er). There are old trade routes heading north from here to the **Drangyer saltfield** and the vast lake **Ngangra Ringtso**.

Mayum La pass From Horpa, the main road continues to follow the north bank of the Brahmaputra upstream to **Saṭsam** (50 kilometres) and, then, after crossing to the south bank, traces the course of the **Mayum Tsangpo** feeder river towards the **Mayum La pass**, which marks the frontier between West Tibet and Far-west Tibet. The distance from Satsam to the pass is 50 kilometres. The road across Mayum La may be impassable if it has been raining heavily. It is often practical to camp out before the pass and negotiate it in the morning while the earth may be frozen. It is a long, gradual pass that consists largely of marshy soil. Once over it, however, the road to **Barga** and **Mount Kailash** is straightforward.

On the northeast side of the **Ganglungri** range, which divides Drongpa county from the **Simikot** region of Northwest Nepal, there are the glaciers of **Jema Yungdrung**, **Ngangser** and **Gyama Langdzom** which are included among the sources of the Brahmaputra.

Northern Tibet

Jantang Plateau བྱང་ཐང་

7

316

Northern Tibet
Jangtang Plateau བྱང་ཐང

The northern plateau of Tibet, known as the Jangtang, is a vast lakeland wilderness, over 438,000 sq km in area. The average elevation is 4,500m, and the distance from the easternmost parts which adjoin Nakchu and Amdo counties to Lake Pang-gong in the far-west exceeds 1,300 km. The northern limits of the plateau are demarcated by the Kunlun Mountains and the southern edge by the Gangtise and Nyenchen Tanglha ranges. The basin of the upper Indus lies to the west, and those of the upper Salween and Yangtze are to the east and northeast. In general the western parts of the plateau are higher than the eastern parts.

The Jangtang plateau is mostly contained within the Tibetan Autonomous Region, although the extreme northeast parts currently fall within Qinghai province. Four counties form its heart: among them are **Tsochen** and **Gertse** counties in Ngari district, through which the northern route from Raga to Mount Kailash passes; and **Shentsa** and **Palgon** in Nakchu district, which link the Lhasa-Ziling highway with Far-west Tibet.
Recommended itineraries: 2, 6.

Geography of the Jangtang

The Jangtang plateau itself has no external drainage, but it is dotted with brackish salt lakes, some of which were once part of the Yangtze and Salween basins, and others remnants of the Neo-Tethys Sea. Most of these are at elevations of 4,500-5,000 metres; and among them the largest include **Namtso** and **Serling** (both 81 kilometres across), **Dangra Yutso** (64 kilometres long), **Ngangla Ringmo**, and **Lake Pang-gang** (48 kilometres by 113 kilometres). It is clear that these lakes are relics of once significantly larger bodies of water, the traces of which can be observed in the relief of the ancient shorelines. Certain lakes have become salt swamps, while others are connected by small streams.

The internal river network is largely undeveloped – the longest being the **Tsakya Tsangpo** which drains into Lake Serling. In winter, the rivers freeze to the bottom, thus confining drainage to the summer months. These processes and frost weathering have lead to the formation of colossal accumulations of friable material, which has levelled the relief. Due to the winnowing of fine particles, the coarser gravel-pebble material is gradually compacted and polished, forming a shiny mantle that is subject to no further deflation. In addition, the thickness of certain salt swamps is so great that they form entire beds which have acquired unique and strange shapes – pyramids, spheres and cones.

Flora of the Jangtang

At least 53 species of plants grow in the stony tundra landscape of the Jangtang. These belong to the genus of the Gramineae, Compositae, and Cruciferae. The **northern** portion of the **plateau** and the **Eastern Kunluns** are more desertified. On the better drained areas there are creeping shrubs of teresken, acantholiumn, capsella, astragalus, thermopsis, sage, and saussurea. Along the shores of certain lakes with internal drainage grow sedges and in poorly drained swampy areas Tibetan cobresia. In ravines sheltered from the winds there are poa, sheep's fescue and reaumurea.

In the **southern** and **south-eastern** parts of the **Jangtang** where the precipitation marginally increases, the alpine steppes encourage the growth of poa, sheep's fescue, feather grass, and quack grass; also sandwort, delphinium, sage, astragalus and saussurea. Juniper grows sparsely on the shores of Lake Namtso.

Overall, there are few creeping shrubs capable of growing in the salty Jangtang soils: caragana, myricaria, ephedra, and tansy among them, but extensive areas of salt swamp are completely devoid of vegetation cover.

Jangtang Nature Reserve
Colour map 6, grid C2

In 1993 the northernmost parts of the Jangtang were declared as the world's second largest nature reserve (300,000 square kilometres), exceeded only by the ice-caps of the Greenland National Park. Here roam the much depleted herds of wild ungulates (wild yak, wild ass, blue sheep, argali, gazelle and antelope); and the plateau's remaining large predators (snow leopard, wolf, lynx and brown bear). The ubiquitous pika predominates at the bottom of the food chain.

Tsochen county མཚོ་ཆེན་

*Tsochen county on the **northern route to Mount Kailash** is a nomadic region with road access to Gertse and Amdo in the north, and to Ngamring or Saga in the south. The county capital is located at **Mendong**, near the northwest shore of Lake Tashi Namtso. The distance from the capital to Raga is 242 kilometres, and to Gertse 257 kilometres.*

Tsochen County (42)
措勤县
Coqen
Population: 9,818
Area: 35,887 sq km
Colour map 6, grid C1

Sights

Heading north into the Jangtang Plateau from Raga on a long, deeply potholed straight road, a concrete bridge is crossed. Down the slope to the right of the road at this point there is a large geothermal area. If the water table is high enough geysers spout forth every few minutes or so. One shoots steaming water over 15 metres high. At one time it is said that there were over one hundred geysers here. Ruins of a bath house are now all that remain. The road skirts a small lake and then passes along the full length of **Lake Takyel-tso**, which is teeming with fish.

Snaking its way north up long valleys, the road crosses over small passes offering a vista of ever-changing scenery. Snow-capped peaks, among them **Mount Sanglung** (6,174 metres), rise far to the west through the occasional huddle of wind-whipped Chinese road gang buildings or small Tibetan hamlets nestled against the leeside of a stony ridge. The lake **Gyesar-tso** lies to the south of Mount Sanglung.

Late in the long day the road descends into the broad sandy plains of the **Yutra Tsangpo** valley – a river which drains into the small **Lake Lungkar-tso** to the southeast. The drivers must be careful to follow recent tracks since they can be led into treacherous quicksands. Some 35 kilometres before Mendong (Tsochen), there is a turn-off on the left (west) which leads 14 kilometres to **Kyangtreng** township, on the shore of **Lake Kering-tso**. The main road continues north, crossing the **Tsochen Tsangpo**, to reach the capital around dusk.

Mendong

Mendong is a barren town near the northwest corner of the large Lake Tashi Namtso. It consists of one main street and little else. Existing hotel space is taken up by Chinese soldiers or officials. It can be a somewhat frustrating exercise to find the truck stop at the north end of town, and then the manager, or the caretaker who has the key to the room after a long and tiring day on the road. All this has to be done before one can think about boiling water for tea, eating dinner and falling asleep. Therefore be prepared to pitch a tent in a sheltered courtyard! Recently, there were no restaurants in Tsochen, but this may well have changed owing to the constant influx of Chinese settlers, and there may even be a new guesthouse designated for foreign travellers.

Tsochen County

A motorable side-road from Tsochen leads 50 kilometres to **Tsitri** township, northeast of **Lake Tashi Namtso**. There are a number of small hamlets in this nomadic pastureland, interspersed between smaller lakes, such as Ngangkok-tso.

Northern Tibet

Tsochen Mendong Gonpa The most important monastery in Tsochen county is the Kagyu monastery of **Tsochen Mendong Gonpa** which lies west of Mendong in Tsitri township, by the banks of the Soma Tsangpo, in the nomadic area known as **Chokchu-me**. The mountain to the west is well known even now for its abundance of medicinal herbs. It is a branch of Tsurphu, founded by the students of the charismatic local lama, **Karma Ngedon Tengye** (1820-1889), whose embalmed remains were entombed here in a reliquary temple (**Kudung Lhakhang**). In the early decades of the present century assembly halls, a protector shrine, **Mani Lhakhang**, and nunnery were added, and at its height there were approximately 100 monks and nuns residing in its vicinity. The monastery developed under the supervision of a succession of *drubpon* trained at Tsurphu, and has been under reconstruction since 1984 following its destruction during the Cultural Revolution, and there are presently 41 monks and nuns altogether.

Other reconstructed monasteries in Tsitri include the **Tsochen Jomo Gonpa**, where there are 17 Kagyupa nuns, and the **Penda Lhakhang**, which is ministered by four monks and nuns, also of the Kagyu school.

Continuing on the northern route to Mount Kailash from Mendong, the trip now changes from a rugged journey to an arduous expedition. It soon reaches the shore of the wide **Lake Dawa-tso**, around which are clusters of nomad tents. This is a traditional grazing land for herds of yaks, goats and sheep. You may notice well-made cairns of rock up to two metres high. They are actually hollow and, if undamaged, hold cooking and camping equipment for a family of nomads who will have left it there the previous year before setting out for their winter dwelling. The goods will remain untouched until they return. After driving along the northeast shoreline, the road climbs through a narrow valley and comes out on the lush marshy plain of **Dawazhung**. Here there is an abundance of wildlife. Wild geese, storks and many other types of waterfowl share the area with yaks and gazelles as well as the occasional lammergeier. The Kagyu monastery of **Burkar Gon**, located in Dawazhung township, was founded in 1920 by Karma Sherab Ozer. Currently there are 35 monks and nuns residing here.

The road crosses a high pass, 98 kilometres north of Mendong, and then sweeps down 72 kilometres into a vast salt plain, where it spreads out into dozens of tracks. These eventually veer west for 16 kilometres, and, near **Dungtso**, meet up with the main Jangtang lateral road which links Amdo county in the east with the Far-west Tibet. The raw force of the late noon sun blasts the landscape into a bleached monochrome over a featureless terrain. The town of Lumaringpo, capital of Gertse county, lies 81 kilometres west of this road junction.

Mendong

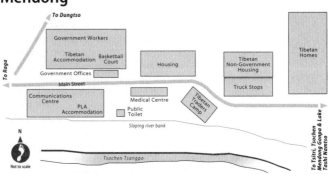

Gertse County སྒེར་རྩེ

Gertse is a large, desolate county bordering Drongpa in the south, Gegye in the west, and the Kunlun Mountains in the north. The capital is located at Lumaringpo, 257 kilometres from Mendong (Tsochen), 836 kilometres from Draknak (Amdo) in the upper Salween basin, and 385 kilometres from Napuk (Gegye) in the upper Indus valley. According to both oral tradition and archival sources, some 300 years ago there were seven villages of Kham, known as Teryik Drongdun, which migrated en masse to settle in the Gertse region. The very name Gertse is said to have been borrowed from their original locale, and many distinctive customs have been retained along with their unusual dialect.

Gertse County (43)
改则县
Gerze
Population: 13,964
Area: 97,771 sq km
Colour map 6, grid C1

Sights

Near Dungtso township where the roads from Tsochen and Amdo converge, you can head east in the direction of Nyima and Shentsa counties or west for Gegye on the northern route to Mount Kailash. Taking the latter route, you will pass **Lake Dungtso** to the north side of the road. The Karma Kagyu monastery of **Lowo Dechen Gon** can be visited nearby. Reconstructed in 1988-93, it was originally founded at the site of an ancient meditation cave complex, on the slopes of hill resembling the protector Mahakala in the form Bernak. Within the township the Gelukpa temple known as **Dungtso Lhakhang** has only two monk attendants. After 81 kilometres Lumaringpo, the county capital, suddenly appears in the distance beyond a conical, solitary hillock. It lies in the middle of nowhere; another one-street town.

Lumaringpo

Lumaringpo is larger than Mendong and it is the foremost administrative centre for the nomads of the Jangtang plateau. Its main street is bisected north-south by a second street down which, to the south, is the post office and the town hall. At the east end of the town is the hospital and dispensary (often strangely empty), the telecommunications centre and the larger government guesthouses. At the other end of town, a few hundred metres away, is the quarter occupied by Tibetan itinerants. This features the busiest and liveliest area of town: namely the pool halls, electric games parlours, 'chang' drinking houses, and gambling dens. Around here the traders from Kham, East Tibet, pitch their tents and sell all kinds of goods. The cheap truck stops are also to be found at this end of town.

Gertse County

Mikmar

There are side-roads extending from Lumaringpo into remote parts of the Jangtang plateau. One leads due south for 100 kilometres to **Mikmar** township, nestling between lakes Tsatso and Lakor-tso. From there, an old trade and trekking route runs further southwards, following the **Dobrong Tsangpo** valley into **Drongpa** county (see above, page 313). In this locality the most important monastery is **Mikmar Gonpa**, revered in oral tradition as the right eye of Lake Manasarovar. This monastery, which belongs to the Nyingma school, was founded by Orgyan Chopel, a student of Zhabkar

Northern Tibet

Tsokdruk Rangdrol, at the site of a meditation hermitage which had been frequented over the centuries by Gangri Lhatsen, Padmasambhava, Tsangpa Gyare, Gotsangpa, and others. Formerly the monastery contained images of Shakyamuni, Longchen Rabjampa, Jowo Yizhin Norbu, and Avalokiteshvara, all fashioned of East Indian bronze, as well as an image of Padmasambhava made of medicinal clay, and twenty-one lineage-holders of gilded copper. Following its destruction during the Cultural Revolution, reconstruction slowly began in 1985 and there are now some 16 monks at Mikmar Gonpa.

Another road leads northwards from Lumaringpo for 35 kilometres to **Khangtok** township in the **Mikpa Tsangpo** valley, and thence for 154 kilometres to the remote outpost of **Lugu** by the shore of **Lake Drakpo-tso**, where the Karma Kagyu temple known as Gonpa Luma once stood.

Gertse | At Khangtok, this Kagyu monastery, also known as Karma Drubgyu Tendar
Drakgyam Gon | Chokhorling, was founded in 1950 by Lama Karma Yonten (1926-88) and rebuilt in 1989. It comprises a meditation hermitage, established by lama Tsegon of Tsurphu, and an eight-pillared temple containing gilded copper images of Jowo Shakyamuni, Vajrapani and Vajradhara as well as copies of the *Rinchen Terdzo* and the *Collected Works* of both Mipham Rinpoche and Karmapa Khakhyab Dorje. Above the monastery in the uplands of Drakgyam valley there is the meditation cave known as **Tsenper Phuk**.

There are several 6,000 metres peaks in the region to the east of Lugu, bordering Shentsa county. Trekking routes also run from Lugu through the lakeland region bordering the Kunlun Mountains, and thence out of Tibet into Xinjiang. The northern parts of Gertse county are occupied by the Jangtang Nature Reserve (see above, page 318). The best area for wildlife observation is reputedly the **Aru Lake basin** (34°N, 82.5°E) and the environs of **Memar** and **Ngamong Lakes** (34.5°N, 82°E) which are located near the West Kunbun range. *Getting there:* to reach the Aru basin drive northwest from Lumaringpo via Khangtok, Lakar La pass and Gyatso hamlet .

The **northern route to Mount Kailash** runs northwest from Lumaringpo, passing Oma township after 90 kilometres. **Lake Tarab-tso** lies beyond, on the border of Gertse and Gegye counties. The town of **Napuk** is 295 kilometres from Oma, in the upper Indus valley.

Lumaringpo

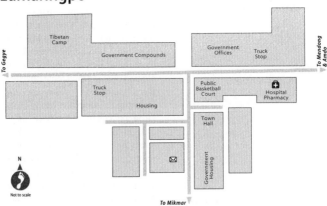

Shentsa County ཤན་རྩ

*From **Dungtso** where the Tsochen and Gertse roads intersect, head eastwards across the length of the Jangtang plateau towards the Lhasa-Ziling highway, passing through Shentsa and Palgon counties. Until recently **Shentsa** was by far the largest of the Jangtang counties, extending from the present day Xinjiang and Qinghai provincial borders in the north to the Brahmaputra watershed in the south. As such the county was larger than the United Kingdom! But now it has been subdivided into Nyima county and Shentsa proper, governed from Naktsang. In this region there are 67 lakes, including some of Tibet's largest: Serling, Dangra Yutso, Ngangtse-tso, Kering-tso, Taktse-tse and Uru-tso. In the northeast there are a number of 6,000 metres peaks including **Purok Gangri** (6,482 metres) and **Norlha Gangri** (6,136 metres), not to mention the Kunlun Mountains on the Xinjiang border further north. The entire northern region forms part of the Jangtang Nature Reserve. Ten large salt fields testify to the importance of this region for the traditional trading commodity of the Jangtang plateau. The county capital of Shentsa is located at **Naktsang** (Shentsa), 805 kilometres from Gertse, and 232 kilometres from Palgon. However, owing to the enormity of this sparsely populated region, there is a second administrative centre at **Tsonyi** (Twin Lakes) in the north. The distance from Naktsang (Shentsa) to Tsonyi is 442 kilometres.*

Shentsa County (44)
申扎县
Xainza
Population: 40,891
Area: 205,202 sq km
Colour map 6, grid C2

Dangra Yutso Lake

Driving eastwards from Dungtso, the road reaches **Kyewa** township in the valley of the **Boktsang Tsangpo** after 244 kilometres, and then passes south of Lake Taktse-tso for 78 kilometres to **Nyima** county town. Here, there is a turn-off which leaves the main road, heading southwest for 167 kilometres via Kanglung to **Ombu** township on the northern shore of **Lake Dangra Yutso**.

Getting there
Colour map 1, grid C2

The shores of Dangra Yutso sustained a relatively large population in ancient times. Research by John Belizza documents a number of ruined hamlets, fortifications and megaliths in its environs. The entire Dangra region is sacred to the Bonpo, and at Ombu itself there is a small Bonpo temple and hermitage complex, known as Ombu Zhangzhung Gon, which is affiliated to Menri Gonpa. Bonpo pilgrims come from afar to circumambulate the lake, most following their preferred anti-clockwise route. The trek takes 11 days (carry all essential supplies and camping equipment0. Three days into the trek, the trail passes through an area rich in wildlife and thence to the impressive **Serzhing Monastery**, beyond the southwest corner of the lake. This is revered as one of the most important ancient Bonpo monasteries in Tibet, although today it is largely in ruins. On the fifth day the trail passes through the **Tango Tsangpo** valley in view of the glaciers of **Mount Tangori** (6,450 metres), frequented largely by Bon hermits (and a few Nyingmapa). At **Tso-me** township in this valley, there is a motorable route to **Zangzang**, and a 14-day trek through the **Mu-chu** valley to **Phuntsoling**.

Shentsa County

Continuing on the circuit of the lake, on the tenth day the trail reaches **Orgyen Gonpa** – a small rebuilt Bonpo monastery with a cave temple containing a rock hand-print of Shenrab Miwoche, founder of the Bon religion. Nearby at **Khyungdzong**, there was once an important Bonpo terma-site and hermitage, as well as a seventh century castle belonging to the kings of Zhangzhung. There is also a trail leading due east from here to **Gyakok** township, on the shore of Lake Ngangtse-tso, and eventually to **Drowa** township.

Naktsang   To reach the county capital from Ombu, return to the turn-off at **Nyima** county town on the main Gertse-Amdo road, and continue driving eastwards, along the north shore of the enormous **Lake Serling**. Cross the **Tsakya Tsangpo** near its confluence with the lake, and after 204 kilometres, you will reach a major intersection, where side-roads branch off both to the north and south. The former leads to **Tsonyi** district. Taking the latter, the road cuts southwest via Zhung-me township to **Naktsang**, 180 kilometres distant. This is the largest settlement within the county, located southeast of the elongated lake Kering-tso, and there are simple but spartan guesthouse facilities. During the 17th century, Naktsang was the focus of a military campaign directed against the nomadic traditions of the Jangtang by the Mongolian governor Ganden Tsewang. An ancient trade and pilgrimage route leads from here southwards, through **Batsa** township into the **Shang** valley of Tsang (page 250).

Tsonyi   Head northwest from Dayul on the lateral Highway to **Tsonyi** (262 kilometres). There are excellent areas further west for wildlife observation - particularly around the **Yibuk Tsaka** salt basin and the **Rongma** hotsprings (33°N, 86.8°E).

Palgon County དཔལ་དགོན་

Palgon County (45)
班戈县
Baingoin
Population: 26,392
Area: 99,112 sq km
Colour map 6, grid B3

*Palgon county in the hinterland of **Lake Namtso Chukmo** is relatively close to the Lhasa-Ziling highway. The circuit of this amazing lake and its ancient Bon sites documented by John Belizza have already been mentioned (see above, pages 139-140). In addition, there are 46 lesser lakes and 21 rivers, of which the **Tsakya Tsangpo**, draining into Lake Serling, is the longest.*

If you approach the county capital, **Namru**, from the north, you should take the turn-off at **Dayul** which leads to Shentsa, and then after 10 kilometres cut southeast in the direction of Namru, 62 kilometres distant. Here there is simple transport station accommodation.

A jeepable trail leads directly south from Namru to Lake Namtso Chukmo, passing through the townships of **Poche** (52 kilometres) and **Dechen** (65 kilometres); and from Dechen due west to **Shelyer** along the Bo-chu valley (52 kilometres). Another jeep track heads from Namru directly for 226 kilometres to join the Lhasa-Ziling highway. Alternatively, from Dayul on the main road to Amdo county, the distance is 211 kilometres. In the north, the Jantang Nature Reserve occupies the part of Palgon County adjacent to the Qinghai border.

325

Far-west Tibet

Mount Kailash & Gu-ge Kingdom མངའ་རིས་རྫོང་

8

Far-west Tibet

Mount Kailash & Gu-ge Kingdom མངའ་རིས་ཆོ་ས།

*The vast region of Far-west Tibet, known as Ngari, in
Tibetan (Ch Ali), is, like the neighbouring Jangtang
plateau, one of the least populated parts of the country.
Access into this region can be made from the bordering
countries of Nepal, and India (the latter closed to
non-Indian nationals), or from Pakistan and
Kazakhstan via the Xinjiang Autonomous Region (East
Turkestan). Within Tibet, the region may be approached
via the northern route (Amdo or Tsochen, and Gertse),
or the southern route (Saga and Drongpa). At the heart
of the region is sacred Mount Kailash, the focal point for
most visitors, renowned for its natural beauty.
Furthermore, within the canyons and valleys of the
upper Sutlej River are numerous ruins of ancient cities
that once comprised the kingdom of Gu-ge. A number
of temples are still intact and contain exquisite murals
and decorative motifs, some dating back more than
1,000 years. Close to the Indian border this area has
only recently been opened for western travellers and is
well worth including in an itinerary.*

*In the description which follows, the northern route
to Kailash passing through the counties of the upper
Indus will be described first, followed by the southern
route from Tsang, the western route through Gu-ge, and
the north-western route through Xinjiang.*

Recommended itinerary: *2.*

Far-west Tibet

Ngari མངའ་རིས་

Colour map 1, A1 *Traditionally, the region of Ngari is said to have comprised three districts (Ngari Korsum): the district of* **Maryul** *including* **Rutok, Ladakh,** *and* **Zangkar;** *the district of* **Gu-ge,** *corresponding to the heartland of the ancient Zhangzhung kingdom; and the district of* **Purang.** *However, Tibetan influence in Central Asia was particularly strong during the periods of the Zhangzhung and Yarlung dynasties and some hold the three districts of Ngari to have been much larger.*

Ins and outs   The journey across the great Northern Plain into Far-west Tibet passes through a land where the lifestyle remains close to what it has been for centuries. The landscapes and vistas are vast and sparsely inhabited but exhilarating, like a treeless moonscape. Lone groups of nomads dwelling in low, black tents, tend flocks of sheep and goats as well as herds of the ubiquitous yak (the 'grunting ox' according to its Latin name).

Towns are few and far apart and generally consist of one main street bisected by another, neither being more than a few hundred metres long. The main building invariably is a Chinese communist party meeting hall, and one is not always assured of finding a shop or restaurant, hotel or water, or any facilities at all for the average intrepid traveller, let alone a tourist. However, one is continually assured that, "Next year we will have made much improvement in our service!" For example, every room in the district's premier hotel, the *Ali Hotel* at Senge Tsangpo, has been tastefully laid out in a universal motel design with en suite bathroom, toilet and shower, only lacking one element – water! Such a minor shortcoming, however, may not stop the manager (a party cadre and retired army captain) from charging the special double rate for western tourists. This situation and the lack of water has continued over the last 12 years, despite the hotel being located next to the bank of the Indus River!

Much of the journey consists often of little more than parallel tracks across the flat expanse of the plateau. The distances to be covered each day entail many hours of bumpy riding. Transport is usually arranged through the Tibetan (or Chinese) tour operator. It is likely to consist of a small convoy led by one or more four-wheel drive Toyota landcruisers accompanied by one or two support trucks carrying food, baggage and fuel. It will be the pace of the truck that determines how quickly the distances can be covered. Although this involves long, somewhat gruelling days, the faster the grand scope of the Northern Plateau is traversed the more time that can be spent within the environs of the sacred Mount Kailash.

NB   Special travel permits required for entry into Ngari and other 'closed' areas of Tibet. See Essentials page 34.

Nowadays, Far-west Tibet comprises five of the seven counties in Ngari district of the Tibetan Autonomous Region: **Gegye** and **Senge Tsangpo**, which are situated in the upper Indus valley, **Rutok** county in the Aksai Chin and Northern Plateau, **Tsamda** county in the upper Sutlej valley, and **Purang** county where the Karnali and Brahmaputra rivers have their sources to the south and west of Mount Kailash. The district capital is located at **Senge Tsangpo** (*Ch* Shiquanhe).

Geography   The region is demarcated by the Himalayas in the south, and the Gangtise Range (or Trans-Himalayan Range) in the north. The **Gangtise** Range (5,500-6,000 metres) forms a watershed between the upper Brahmaputra River and the land-locked plateau of Northern Tibet (Jangtang). The northern and southern slopes are gentle, marked by flat peaks, low elevations relative to the Tibet plateau, and intensive weathering, whereas the western slopes are broken by the deep gorges of the Indus and the heavily eroded sandstone canyons of the Sutlej.

Khampa traders of Ngari

The vast region is strikingly reminiscent of the wide open spaces of the American Wild West, especially as seen in countless Hollywood films. The inhabitants also bring to mind images of the Wild West. The nomads bear a strong physical resemblance to North American Indians, such as the Navaho. In the towns tall Khampa traders from East Tibet are like `macho' cowboys. They swagger about, gold teeth flashing behind a wide knowing smile, long hair wound in red or black braid embellished with a large gold and turquoise earring, their feet balanced on high-heeled riding boots or showing through holes in Chinese canvas trainers, and wearing a bulky gown or `chuba' (Tibet's national costume) tied loosely round the waist with a fat money belt from which dangles a long knife in a silver scabbard. They stand outside their tented shops on the edge of town selling everything from batteries to baseball hats, from music cassettes to motor spare parts. There is a similar sense of lawlessness to the cowboy west in this land that is free of any visible boundaries. It makes the accounts by previous travellers to Tibet of robbers raiding the caravans of traders and pilgrims all too real.

The unique 6,658 metre pinnacle of **Mount Kailash** (*Tib* Gang Ti-se/Gang Rinpoche), lies at the geographic watershed of South Asia. Before it, a few kilometres to the south, are two lakes, **Mapham Yutso** (Manasarovar) and **Lakngar** (Rakshas Tal), shaped respectively like the sun and the moon. The sources of four major rivers rise from this geomantic crown and flow in the four cardinal directions: the **Indus** (north), **Brahmaputra** (east), **Karnali** (south) and **Sutlej** (west). It is for this reason and because of the unique beauty of the region that Mount Kailash has been looked upon as a sacred realm – a goal of pilgrimage by peoples from India, Tibet and Asia for thousands of years.

Further north, the **Nganglung Gangri** range (elevation 5,700-6,300 metres) separates the upper Indus from the Jangtang plateau. The highest peak is **Ngari Gangri** (6,348 metres); and the range is less rugged than the Himalayas, with more rounded and weathered hills.

Climate Ngari is marked by the greatest extremes of dryness and the lowest temperatures. In Senge Tsangpo (4,600 metres) the annual precipitation is less than 100 millimetres and the mean January temperature -12°. In recent years, however, the climate has become more inconsistent. During the Indian monsoon from late June to mid-September heavy rains often reach as far as the northern slopes of the Gangtise range, causing rivers to become impassable and increasing erosion. Deforestation of the Himalayas is thought to be the main cause.

Flora & fauna The landscape is barren, reminiscent of the Jangtang steppes north of the Gangtise range, but there are some variations in flora. Here juniper grows, along with barberry and honeysuckle.

The region between the source of the Brahmaputra and Mount Kailash abounds with wildlife, especially after the rainy season of July and August. Apart from the herds of **yak** there are large herds of **wild ass** (*kyang*), a large and vividly marked creature which gallops away from the road when disturbed. You have to be quick to take photographs. More common throughout West Tibet are the Tibetan **gazelle** (*Tib* gowa; Procapra picticaudata) and **Hodgson's antelope** (*Tib* tso; Pantholops hodgsoni). The former is small and similar to the wild chamois of the European Alps. The latter is larger, distinguished by its long, slightly curved horns and white buttocks or hindquarters. Other animals commonly seen are the **marmot** (*chiwa*), which resembles a

Far-west Tibet

The Upper Indus Valley

The Indus is 2,900 km in length, encompassing a drainage area of 1,165,500 sq km (of which 453,248 sq km are within the mountain area). The annual flow is 207 billion cu m. The actual source of the Indus is the stream known in Tibet as the Senge Khabab or Jang Senge Khabab ("northern source from the lion-shaped rock"). This source lies to the north of Mount Kailash at 5,500m in a remote valley within the Sengto district of Gegye county. In its uppermost reaches the river which emerges from this glacial source is called the Senge Tsangpo. It flows northwest for about 320 km through Drakya Gonpa, Dongpa, and Napuk townships of Gegye county, and then west to Senge Tsangpo, where it converges with the Langchu Tsangpo and the Gar Tsangpo, before cutting northwest through Tashigang and Demchok. Here, the river leaves Tibet, crossing into India at about 4,570m. The river volume in Tibet is mainly snow-fed, but thereafter it passes through Ladakh, Baltistan, and the alluvial plains of Pakistan, where it provides the life support for millions of people. Over 5,000 years ago its waters sustained the Indus Valley Civilization, one of the earliest settlements of mankind. Major tributaries include the Zangskar, Shyok, Shigar, Gilgit, Astor, Kabul, and the five Punjab rivers.

brown, furry football with legs, and the **abra**, a small Tibetan rodent like a gerbil that lives in large colonies of burrows in the midst of healthy grasslands.

Huge flocks of migrating birds can also be seen throughout the late summer, making their way south over the Himalayas to India for the winter. In addition there are indigenous birds such as the graceful **Brahmany geese** which have golden coloured bodies and a black head, and which maintain a life-long mating relationship. They have become the subject of numerous love songs and poems in Tibet. It is well known that if one should die or be killed, the mate will pine and grieve until it too passes away.

Gegye County དགེ་རྒྱས།

Gegye County (46)
革吉县
Gegyai
Population: 10,340
Area: 54,885 sq km
Colour map 1, grid A2

*Gegye county on the **northern route to Mount Kailash** extends from Lake Tarab-tso, on the edge of the Jangtang plateau, as far as Dongpa and Gegye in the upper Indus valley. The capital is located at **Napuk**, 383 kilometres from Lumaringpo in Gertse, and 112 kilometres from Senge Tsangpo.*

Tsaka
Driving west from **Oma** township in Gertse county, the road passes south of **Lake Tarab-tso**, and on for 94 kilometres to **Tsaka** (*Ch* Yanba), where there are commercial salt fields. At Tsaka, the Karma Kagyu monastery of Tashi Choling was founded in 1894 by Kunga Tashi Rinpoche (1858-1918). All of its precious artefacts were destroyed during the Cultural Revolution, and restoration is proceeding slowly. There are now 23 monks and nuns residing there.

Zhungba
The road then cuts southwest for 96 kilometres to **Zhungba** township on the Shang-chu River, passing **Lake Nyer-tso** to the west. A jeepable side-road leads south from Zhungba to **Yakra** (130 kilometres) on the southeast shore of **Lake Tsonak**, and from here there is a trekking route to the large lake **Ngangla Ringtso** on the border of Drongpa county (see above, page 313). In Zhungba, there are two small reconstructed Kagyu temples, known as **Shang Lukhang** and **Kyawo Lhakhang**.

The main road from Zhungba cuts northwest, with **Mount Tsotra** (6,046   **Dongba**
metres) to the right. After 75 kilometres, it reaches **Dongba** township, descending into the valley of the upper Indus. There is a small Kagyu monastery,
Drirapuk Gon, here, ministered by only three monks. Trekking routes follow
the river upstream to the larger **Drakya Gonpa** and the broad **Yalung Selung**
range (largest peak 6,105 metres), giving access to Mount Kailash. During the
latter half of the 17th century a nomadic camper group of approximately 50 families under the leadership of Behu Agya was forced to leave its ancestral homeland in the Nangchen region of Kham, and they moved westwards, eventually to
occupy the upper Indus basin, comprising the three nomadic pasturelands of
Kongchen, **Seng-to** and **Senge-me** in Dongba. In return for military assistance
against Ladakh, the Tibetan government and their Mongol allies formally
appointed Behu Agya as the chieftain (*pon*) of this locality, inhabited by more
than 100 camper groups. His descendants maintained this hereditary succession, known as the Dongba Pon, through to the mid-20th century.

This monastery was founded near Seng-to in the Upper Indus valley during   **Drakya Drubgyu**
the 19th century by Karmapa XIV Tekchok Dorje (1797-1868) at the behest of   **Tengyeling**
its patron Ponmo Sonamtso, the estranged wife of the chieftain of Drongpa.
Formerly it contained an image of Karmapa VIII Mikyo Dorje, fashioned of
Chinese bronze, a bronze image of Manjughosa which was once the property
of Karmapa VI, a gold and silver image of Karmapa XV which was personally
donated by the late Karmapa XIV, Rikpei Dorje, and many other treasures.
The monastery which administered to the spiritual needs of the nomadic community, was utterly destroyed in 1968. The present restored temple dating
from 1986-1988 contains assorted clay images of the Karma Kagyu lineage,
and there are now 20 monks.

    The main motorable route continues northwest from Dongba, following
the Indus gorge downstream to **Napuk**, the county capital of Gegye, only 30
kilometres distant. **Mount Dongri** (5,825 metres), a major landmark, lies to
the east as the town is approached.

The present county capital is a completely new town, poorly located at the base   **Napuk**
of a cliff where the prevailing winds create a semi-permanent sand storm. Such   *Colour map 1, grid A2*
is the 'skill' of the latter-day Chinese geomancers who created it! This very
bleak town, which was set up mainly to control the nomads, will be reached in
the late afternoon if you have left Lumaringpo early in the morning. The road
now is quite straightforward and the average speed can be increased accordingly. It may be best to continue on to **Senge Tsangpo**, the district capital,
because accommodation is difficult to find. If the transport station is full camp
out against a sheltered bluff, two kilometres out of town. Perfectly adequate for

Gegye County

the few hours rest that one needs, this
bluff is formed by an uninhabited
complex of buildings, originally
made for the Muslim construction
workers who were brought down
from Xinjiang province.

To reach Senge Tsangpo from Gegye,
continue following the Indus downstream towards **Jangpa** (70 kilometres) and thence for 42 kilometres
to the district capital.

Far-west Tibet

Senge Tsangpo སེང་གེ་གཙང་པོ

Senge Tsangpo
County (47)
噶尔县
Shiquanhe
Population: 9,381
Area: 11,802 sq km
Colour map 1, grid A2

Senge Tsangpo county, formerly known as Gar, straddles the confluences of the Indus River and two of its tributaries: the Langchu Tsangpo, which converges at Senge Tsangpo town, and the Gar Tsangpo, which converges south of Tashigang. The former, which is both the district and county capital, is located 112 kilometres from Napuk in Gegye, 127 kilometres from Rutok, 255 kilometres from Toling, and 428 kilometres from Purang.

Senge Tsangpo

Colour map 1, grid A2

The **northern route to Mount Kailash** continues following the upper Indus valley through **Jangpa** village (70 kilometres beyond Gegye) and on to **Senge Tsangpo** (42 kilometres from Jangpa), which is by far the largest town in the entire region. It is a new Chinese built town, named after the **Indus River** (*Tib* Senge Tsangpo, *Ch* Shiquanhe), which has its confluence with the **Langchu Tsangpo** here. The traditional capital of the Ngari region was Gartok, a nomadic encampment in the Gar Tsangpo valley (see below, page 333).

After the long, arduous journey across the Northern Plateau this is an opportunity to spend one or two days washing clothes etc while preparing for the last, most important stage of the journey to Mount Kailash. One should also check or obtain **permits** for Tsaparang, Toling and Mount Kailash.

There are four roads which diverge at the capital: one leading northeast to Gegye and Gertse (see page 330 and page 321), another leading due north to Rutok (see below, page 368), a third leading west to the confluence of the Indus with the Gar Tsangpo, and a fourth which leads southeast to Tsotsho township.

From Senge Tsangpo you can go directly to Mount Kailash, but to reach it in one day it is essential to depart well before sunrise. Otherwise you should break the journey at Montser.

Sleeping In town, the ostentatious and 'modern' *Ali Hotel*, T0897-2821400, F0897-2821487, provides compulsory accommodation for foreign visitors (US$40/room). Since its inception, it has been generally managed by ex-public security or ex-PLA officers who know little about running a hotel. **NB** If you try to camp out at Senge Tsangpo, the police can arrest you and fine you the price of a night's stay at the hotel (US$10-33), and then charge the hotel's rate on top! Although the *Ali Hotel* has all the right fittings in its attached bathrooms, until now there has been no running water, despite promises of hot showers!

Eating The meals at the *Ali Hotel* are good (breakfast US$7; full meal plan US$28) but be sure to arrive on time otherwise you will miss out.

Shopping *Friendship Shop* at the town crossroads allows the purchase of food and other supplies.

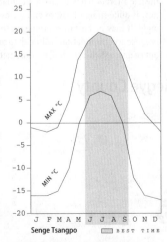

Senge Tsangpo   ☐ BEST TIME

Far-west Tibet

Directory Hospitals & medical services In town there is a modern hospital, which also dispenses Tibetan medicine. **Tour companies & travel agents** *Tibet Kailash Travel*, T(868073)21400/21799, F(868073)21496. Organize travel throughout Ngari, including the routes from Simikot in Nepal and Kashgar in Xinjiang.

Langchu Tsangpo Valley

A jeepable side-road goes southeast from Senge Tsangpo town, following the *Colour map 1, grid A2* **Langchu Tsangpo** upstream. After 40 kilometres it reaches its terminus at **Tsotsho** township, where the local chieftain had a hereditary status dating back to the appointment of his ancestor Jurik Chingwadur by the 17th century Mongol governor Ganden Tsewang in return for military assistance. An ancient trekking route leads from Tsotsho into the upper reaches of this valley to **Gotsang-me** and **Gotsang-to**.

Tashigang and Demchok

Taking the westerly road from Senge Tsangpo, you will reach the confluence of *Colour map 1, grid A1* the Indus with the Gar Tsangpo at **Ridong** after about 30 kilometres. From here the main road to Mount Kailash follows the Gar Tsangpo upstream (southeast), while a jeepable side-road continues northwest following the course of the Indus downstream to **Tashigang** (21 kilometres). Here, in a dramatic riverside location, is the monastery of Tashigang Gonpa, which was originally founded by the Drukpa Kagyu lama Taktsangwa of Ladakh, but converted to the Gelukpa school by Mongol force of arms during the 17th century when Ganden Tsewang placed it under the authority of Sera Je college in Lhasa. Nonetheless, there are extant murals at Tashigang indicative of its original Drukpa Kagyu heritage. The pot-holed surface of this side-road continues on through the upper Indus gorge to reach **Demchok** and the Indian frontier (closed to tourists), where the river flows into Ladakh.

Gar Tsangpo Valley

Turning southeast at **Ridong**, the confluence of the Indus with the Gar *Colour map 1, grid A2* Tsangpo, the main **northern route to Mount Kailash** follows the latter upstream. It passes through **Lungmar** and then bypasses **Gar Gunsa**, the ancient winter capital of Ngari district, 111 kilometres from Senge Tsangpo.

Far-west Tibet

Senge Tsangpo

To Xinjiang, Rutok & Leh

PLA HQ

Government Offices

Town Hall

Workers Quarries

Friendship Shop

Muslim Bakery

Hotel Canteen

Ali Hotel

Truck Stop

School

Shops & Stalls

New Office Blocks

To Lhasa

General Market

Indus River

N

To Mt Kailash & Tsamda

Not to scale

On old maps Gar Gunsa is referred to as Gartok. Following the military campaign of the Mongolian general Ganden Tsewang in Ngari against the invading forces of the king of Ladakh (circa 1681), the region was secured under the authority of Dalai Lama V. Gar Gunsa then became the seat of a viceroy appointed by the central government in Lhasa to whom all foreign travellers were supposed to apply for travel permission. It lay on one of the main caravan routes. Today it is nearly impossible to see where it once was situated. All that remains are mounds of rubble.

Further south, the road passes through **Namru** after 23 kilometres, where there is an important turn-off leading to Toling and Tsaparang in the upper Sutlej valley (see below, page 356 and page 360). Namru was formerly the seat of the Namru Chieftain (Namru Pon), a rank initially conferred on Hor Dodrak, chieftain of the Hor troops who migrated from Namru near Lake Namtso, after being mustered by the Mongol governor Ganden Tsewang in 1679. Continuing along the Gar Tsangpo valley, you will reach **Gar Yersa**, the ancient summer capital of the Ngari viceroy, and **Sogto** village.

After Sogto, the road crosses a watershed, leaving the source of the Gar Tsangpo behind, and following the southwest side of the **Gangtise** range into a wide sandy valley which forms part of the upper Sutlej basin. This road can be quite treacherous in the rainy season because it follows a poorly cut track along the sandy floor of the river valley. Bumpy ruts cut through the sandy surface, causing vehicles to toss about. Sections of the road also ford streams and rivers which can be deceptive as far as their depth is concerned. However an experienced driver should be familiar with hazards and cover the journey safely. Eventually the road reaches the new township of **Montser**, 237 kilometres from Senge Tsangpo.

Montser

Colour map 1, grid B2 Montser is a coal mining town with little of redeeming interest. There are no streets to speak of, nor a town centre, just housing compounds and open space. Therefore you need to enquire where the truck stops are. There are at least two truck stops in Montser, which is usually reached at dusk. The small **Dunchu Lhakhang** of the Gelukpa school has only six monks.

Sleeping One guesthouse is very basic, just beds with thin mattresses. The other is cleaner and better equipped, with beds, mattresses, and a quilted sheet, but may have no empty rooms.

Eating One restaurant will be open, if you arrive early enough.

Tirthapuri

Colour map 1, grid A2 Before setting out from Montser on the road to Darchen, you can take a detour to visit the hot springs, picnic ground and pilgrimage site of **Tirthapuri**. It is about six kilometres southwest of Montser. Here is a cave associated with Padmasambhava, the Indian master who established Buddhism in Tibet in the eighth century and his Tibetan consort Yeshe

Senge Tsangpo County

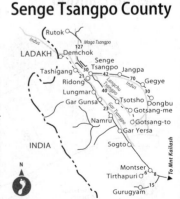

Far-west Tibet

Tsogyel. You may prefer just to spend a short time here and return after the circuits of Mount Kailash and Lake Manasarovar. Tirthapuri is one of the traditional pilgrimage sites visited after Mount Kailash (see below, page 349).

Gurugyam Monastery

The road to **Khyunglung**, which leaves the main road 8 kilometres south of Montser, passes southwest through a broad agricultural valley dotted with single family compounds. The Bonpo Monastery of **Gurugyam Dongak Drakgyeling** is located about 15 kilometres from the turn-off, at the western limit of this valley. Camp here!

Getting there
Colour map 1, grid A2

This is one of the most important Bonpo monasteries in Far-west Tibet, founded in 1936 by Khyungtrul Yungdrung Gyeltsen Pelzangpo below the Yungdrung Rinchen Barwa meditation cave, where the revered Bon masters of Zhangzhung: Gyerchen Drenpa Namka, Tsewang Rigzin and Pema Tongdrol had meditated in antiquity. Today it has a strong connection to the main Bonpo settlement at **Dolanji** in North India where many of its monks gathered after the Chinese invasion and have successfully re-established the Bon tradition in exile. Gurugyam was rebuilt in 1989-91 from walled ruins and is one of the finest examples of a Bon monastery within Ngari district. An earlier site, known as **Zhangzhung Gonpa**, is located at a square mound within a number of collapsed stupas a few hundred metres east of Gurugyam. This must have been active over the same era as Khyunglung.

The **Yungdrung Rinchen Barwa** cave hermitage, situated in the cliffs above, is particularly associated with the name of the Bonpo master **Gyerchen Drenpa Namka**, who lived and meditated here for centuries, according to the Bon chronicles. He was also renowned as a great doctor – his mortar and pestle for grinding herbs and medications can still be seen to the side of the pathway leading up to his room. A steep climb leads through a series of staircases and tunnels before reaching Drenpa Namka's meditation cave, cut deep into the cliff above the temple. Inside the cave there is a palpable sense of sanctity amidst a remarkable wealth of religious objects.

The other major temple associated with Drenpa Namka is a box-like shrine on the top of a canyon directly to the east. Inside is a statue of the master himself, which was decapitated by the Chinese and has now been given a new head by devotees. Unfortunately the replacement is two or three times larger than normal – obviously the devotion exceeded any sense of the conventional!

From Gurugyam, you can also make a secondary expedition to the ruins of one of Tibet's earliest cities, known as **Khyunglung** ('Garuda Valley'). Dating back to 2,000 BC or even earlier it was established by the first kings of Zhangzhung, the original name for Far-west Tibet, and it continued to be occupied for 3,000 years. For a description of Khyunglung (which is in Tsamda county), see below, page 355.

Khyunglung

Far-west Tibet

Purang County སྤུ་ཧྲེང་

*Purang county is the heart of Far-west Tibet, where the four great rivers of South Asia diverge from their glacial sources around Mount Kailash. It is the goal of the great pilgrimage routes which approach this sanctified mountain from the north (Gegye or Xinjiang), from the west (Kinnaur in India), from the south (Almora in India and Simikot in Nepal), and from the east (Drongpa). The county capital is located at **Purang**, known as Taklakot in Nepali, which lies 104 kilometres*

Purang County (48)
Bulan
普兰县
Population: 7,187
Area: 11,641 sq km
Colour map 1, grid B3

south of Barka township, in the valley of the Karnali River (Tib Mabcha Tsangpo). The distance from here to Senge Tsangpo, the district capital, is 428 kilometres, to Drongpa in Tsang 487 kilometres, and to Toling in the upper Sutlej valley 434 kilometres.

The 68 kilometres road from Montser to **Darchen**, where the circuit of Mount Kailash begins, follows the Gangtise or Trans-Himalayan Range directly down (southeast) to the **Barka** Plain between Mount Kailash and the two lakes. Before leaving Montser you may decide to take a detour to visit Tirthapuri and Gurugyam Monastery (in Senge Tsangpo county) and Khyunglung (in Tsamda county). Otherwise drive directly to Darchen.

Darchen

Colour map 1, grid B2   Darchen was formerly an important sheep station for the nomads and their flocks. Until the late 1980s it still consisted of only two permanent buildings. One had survived the mass destruction of religious shrines during the Cultural Revolution since it was said to have belonged to the Bhutanese government through the Drukpa Kagyu tradition which still claimed jurisdiction over it. Resembling a temple, it is coloured in red ochre and serves as a shelter for Tibetan pilgrims. The second building was created in the 1980s to accommodate the first wave of pilgrims from India. It is thus known as the *IP (Indian Pilgrim) Guest House.* In 1995 a medical centre and dispensary was inaugurated. Sponsored by a Swiss Tibetan benefactor it has since become a centre for training doctors and for dispensing medicine and treatment for the various illnesses that afflict the local nomadic community.

Sleeping The large *Darchen Guesthouse* has expanded from the *IP Guesthouse* with rooms available for mainly western travellers, each room has at least 5 beds for ¥25 each. The main compound also has a shop selling souvenirs, canned food, and the ever-present green-bottled beer.

Hospitals & medical services The recently opened *Swiss Medical Clinic* administered by one Dakpo Namgyel.

Mount Kailash   གངས་རིན་པོ་ཆེ

Colour map 1, grid B2   *For most travellers to Far-west Tibet the prime focus of their journey is the sacred peak of **Mount Kailash** (6,658 metres). This extraordinary mountain is regarded as the 'heart of the world', the 'axis Mundi', the centre of Asia, by Buddhists, Hindus, Jains and followers of other spiritual traditions. Of all the special destinations for the traveller to reach, Mount Kailash is surely one of the most sublime and sacred. Its geographical position as the watershed of South Asia is unique and it is this which gives it a cosmic geomantic power. From its slopes flow four great rivers in the four cardinal directions – the Indus north, the Brahmaputra east, the Karnali into the Ganges south, and the Sutlej west.*

Before Mount Kailash lie the twin lakes of **Manasarovar** (4,600 metres) and **Rakshas Tal** (4,584 metres), shaped respectively like the sun and moon, and which are said to have associations respectively with the forces of light and dark. Further south, just on the edge of the Tibetan plateau and near the Himalayas is another snow-capped peak, **Mount Nemo Nanyi** (Gurlamandhata; 7,728 metres), which is one of the highest inside Tibet. Its three peaks and four ridges form a swastika, an ancient symbol of the universe's infinity.

Mount Kailash itself is known in the Tibetan language as **Gangkar Ti-se** and informally as **Gang Rinpoche** ('Precious Snow Mountain'), and in Chinese as **Gang Rinboqe Feng**. Though only 6,714 metres high, it stands quite alone like a great white sentinel guarding the main routes into Tibet from India and Nepal in the south and west.

Traditionally a pilgrim undertakes the 58 kilometres trekking circuit or circumambulation (*khorlam*) around Mount Kailash commencing at **Darchen** (4,575 metres) and crossing the 5,723 metres high **Dolma La pass** on the second day of the three-day walk. This is followed by a trek of the same duration around the beautiful turquoise **Lake Mansarovar**. The journey is then completed with a rest and camp at the hot springs and geysers of **Tirthapuri**, a few hours' drive away and especially associated with Padmasambhava. All along the pilgrimage route are places of historical and spiritual interest.

The Rigour of the Routes to Mount Kailash

Although Mount Kailash and its environs are of exceptional natural beauty it can only be reached via lengthy and often arduous travel along one of several routes into the region. Rivalry for the tourist business between the authorities of various Chinese provinces and districts has led to the imposition of travel restrictions by Lhasa on foreigners travelling in outlying regions. Only the most determined or wealthy travellers can therefore hope to circumvent such obstacles.

Despite the lifting of some of these bureaucratic restrictions, facilities for the foreign traveller are sparse and the way itself, from whichever direction, is rugged and often tiring. Travel in this region takes one into contact with a lifestyle that has probably suffered the least change as a result of the Chinese occupation. Local food is basic and needs to be supplemented and a large degree of self-reliance and fortitude is essential. Furthermore, the sacred Mount Kailash has never easily allowed visitors into its sanctum, but with fortitude, patience and a pure, constant intention to reach and circle its snow-capped peak, one will succeed. For all these reasons, the journey to and through Far-west Tibet requires the appropriate preparation, both logistically and mentally.

Purang County

The traveller who is prepared to undergo the rigours of this journey will come into contact with a way of life that has undergone little change for centuries, and experience the wonder of a unique wilderness and culture largely untouched by the modern world. Therefore, despite all drawbacks and hardships, to participate in a pilgrimage to Mount Kailash or simply to travel in this unique and stunningly beautiful and unpolluted natural environment can be one of life's most rewarding experiences.

Five Routes to Mount Kailash

There are four main approaches, each of which roughly follows one of four great river valleys, located in the four

A pilgrim's view of Mount Kailash

The approach to Darchen from Montser, passing eastwards along the southern ridge of the Gantise range, offers a spectacular panoramic view where the most striking feature is the snow massif of **Mount Nemo Nanyi** (7,728m), one of Tibet's highest mountains, known in Nepali as Mount Gurlamandhata. It lies to the southeast of **Lake Rakshas Tal**. Do not be deceived into thinking this is Mount Kailash! The sacred mountain remains hidden for most of the journey. Mountain after mountain seem to be possible contenders until, finally, it rises above all those before it; a giant snow-capped pyramid when viewed from the west; majestically standing aloof from all those lesser peaks that surround it. Now these neighbouring mountains really do seem to bow down before its magnificence!

As one moves closer, its form seems to change with every mile passed; from a pyramid, to a breast, to a dome. Now one observes clearly how it rises alone, unique among mountains. Its dominance of the entire landscape is unlike anything in the mighty Himalayas. Its 6,658m is not touched or even glanced at by any mountain near it. As Darchen comes closer its form becomes rounded and the extraordinary black markings on its faces cut into the form of a universal cross or eternal swastika through its snow capped mass. It is not of this mundane world because it now makes even the Himalayas seem ordinary. It grew up through the depths of the great ocean, the **Tethys Sea**, some 50 million years ago. The **Great Himalayas** on the other hand are one of the newest ranges on the planet, arbitrarily wrenched out of the Asian landmass as it met the tectonic plate of the Indian subcontinent, buckling skyward from the massive forces unleashed below the surface some 20 million years ago.

Mount Kailash's very whiteness and convex south face, like a mirror, is said to reflect the sun's rays out, beyond the confines of the planet. Like a giant crystal, its three faceted sides encompass a trinity that rises glittering at the nexus of the Hindu and Buddhist planetary universe. From the stark duality of its white sheen and black mystery etched into its every face – the inner and outer, splits the triad of its faces, complete and self-contained. Grudgingly through the valleys and folds of the land it then manifests into four, the great rivers of the world flowing in the four cardinal directions: the sacred rivers which are the sources of civilizations and knowledge: north the **Indus**, spawning the earliest, the Indus Valley civilization; east, the **Brahmaputra** feeding the mystics of Tibet before cutting through the eastern Himalayas and cascading down into Bengal and the source of the great philosophy and knowledge of ancient India; south via the **Karnali** into the **Ganges**, India's life-blood and the well-spring of its spiritual inspiration and ongoing timeless presence; and west, along the **Sutlej**, little known but in fact the link with the mystics of the Indian Himalayas and the sustainer of the richness of life in the northwest of India. Thus the mountain would appear, just on its own to a viewer from afar.

cardinal directions of the mountain. It is only recently that such diverse routes have become available for the foreign traveller. In addition, there is a fifth traditional route reserved for Indian pilgrims. Yet another, the route from Simla and Kinnaur along the Hindustan Highway into Tsamda county, is still closed for political reasons.

Northern Plateau Route 2,021 km from Lhasa; 1,670 km from Lhartse: **1** Lhartse-Raga (241 km); **2** Raga-Tsochen (242 km); **3** Tsochen-Gertse (260 km); **4** Gertse-Gegye (370 km); **5** Gegye-Senge Tsangpo (112 km); **6** Senge Tsangpo-Montser (237 km); **7** Montser-Darchen (68 km).

Departing from Lhartse on the Lhasa-Dram highway, the northern route traverses the Jangtang Plateau to **Senge Tsangpo**, the district capital of Far-west Tibet (Ngari) in the upper Indus valley, and then cuts south to **Mount Kailash** directly or via Tsamda, where the great sites of **Tsaparang** and **Toling** can be visited. Until the 1990s this was the only legitimate route open to foreign travellers, and of the four main routes it is still the most commonly used since it remains open throughout the year.

1,338 km from Lhasa; 847 km from Lhartse: **1** Lhartse-Saga (293 km); **2** Saga-Drongpa (145 km); **3** Drongpa-Barka (387 km); and **4** Barka-Darchen (22 km). **Or** 993 km from Kathmandu: **1** Kathmandu-Dram (122 km); **2** Dram-Dzongka (204 km); **3** Dzongka-Saga (103 km); **4** Saga-Drongpa (145 km); **5** Drongpa-Barka (387 km); and **6** Barka-Darchen (22 km).

Southern Brahmaputra Route

Departing from Kathmandu via Dram and Kyirong, or from Lhartse via Ngamring, this route follows the course of the Brahmaputra upstream through Saga and Drongpa counties. The road is generally impassable from late June until early September due to snow-melt, or during the monsoon when heavy rainfall swells the several rivers which need to be forded.

This southern road is the most direct route to Mount Kailash, closely following the valley of the upper **Brahmaputra** to and past its source. However until recently it was off-limits because of the Chinese military presence and

Mount Kailash & Lake Manasarovar

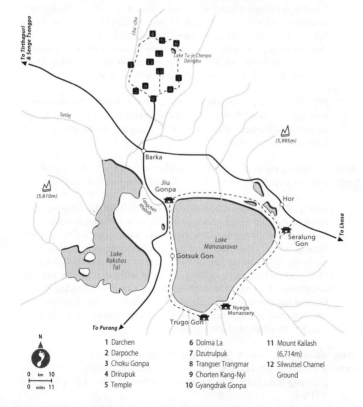

1 Darchen	6 Dolma La
2 Darpoche	7 Dzutrulpuk
3 Choku Gonpa	8 Trangser Trangmar
4 Drirupuk	9 Chorten Kang-Nyi
5 Temple	10 Gyangdrak Gonpa

11 Mount Kailash (6,714m)
12 Silwutsel Charnel Ground

Far-west Tibet

border patrols. Those setting out from Lhasa will take the route via Lhartse and Ngamring. Alternatively, if you make the journey direct from Kathmandu across the Nepal border, you will meet up with the Lhasa/Lhartse approach at Saga.

Northwestern Xinjiang Route 1,671 km from Kashgar: **1** Kashgar-Yarkand/Yecheng (249 km); **2** Yarkand-Mazar (249 km); **3** Mazar-Tserang Daban (456 km); **4** Tserang Daban-Domar (172 km); **5** Domar-Rutok (123 km); 6. Rutok-Senge Tsangpo (117 km); **7** Senge Tsangpo-Montser (237 km); and **8** Montser-Darchen (68 km).

Departing from **Hunza** in Pakistan via the Karakorum highway or from **Alma Aty** in Kazakhstan, this route effectively begins at **Kashgar** in the Xinjiang Autonomous Region, north of Tibet. Kashgar can also be reached by air from Beijing.

Leaving Kashgar, the road skirts the northern frontiers of Pakistan, Kashmir and Ladakh in Northwest India, cutting across the disputed territory known as the **Aksai Chin**, for which reason it has been strictly off limits for foreign travellers. The Aksai Chin is a large region claimed by India, and it can be difficult or impossible to obtain the necessary permits to leave Kashgar because there are also ongoing uprisings by the indigenous Uigur population. Although technically a 'closed' area, this can be circumvented either by guile and courage (just try your luck or hide in the back of a truck going to Senge Tsangpo), or by making prior arrangements with a tour operator who has connections with an authorized travel company either based in Ngari (Far-west Tibet) or in Kashgar. On the other hand if flying from Beijing to Kashgar it is possible to make all arrangements for permits to enter this region with a Beijing-based travel agent. If you enter China from Pakistan over the Kunjerab Pass and along the Karakoram Highway from Hunza to Kashgar it becomes a memorable and economic journey. Remember however to obtain a double entry permit to Pakistan if you wish to exit via the same way.

NB At present, this northwestern route is more commonly undertaken in reverse, to exit from Far-west Tibet into Pakistan or Kazakhstan. Nonetheless, the tourist authorities of Far-west Tibet are trying to have the approach from Kashgar officially opened.

West Nepal Route **1** Kathmandu-Nepalganj; **2** Nepalganj-Simikot-Tuling; **3** Tuling-Kermi; **4** Kermi-Yangar; **5** Yangar-Torea; **6** Torea-Sibsib; **7** Sibsib-Purang; **8** Purang-Darchen.

Over the last four years it has been possible to travel on this route under the auspices of certain trekking and travel agencies in Kathmandu, but is somewhat expensive. It begins with a flight from Kathmandu via Nepalganj to **Simikot**, a small village nestling on the spur of a mountain. An intense five or six day trek following the **Karnali river** valley takes one over the **Nak La** pass (4,877 metres) before crossing the Tibet border and going on to **Purang**. This ancient town at the base of Mount Nemo Nanyi (Gurlamandhata) has been the focus for Nepalese traders and pilgrims from India for thousands of years. One can then travel by bus, truck, or pre-arranged land-cruiser for a half-day to Darchen at the base of Mount Kailash.

Indian Pilgrim Route 866 km from Delhi: **1** Delhi-Almora (395 km); **2** Almora-Bhirinaga (68 km); **3** Bhirinaga-Dardu La pass (78 km); **4** Dardu La pass-Garyang (157 km); **5** Garyang-Jang La pass (38 km); **6** Jang La pass-Purang (18 km); **7** Purang-Darchen (112 km).

This was first reopened in 1980, a remarkable act resulting from the first international agreement between India and China since the Chinese invasion of Northern India and the ensuing 1962 war. Thus it was the Hindu pilgrims who were the first to make their way to Mount Kailash since the Cultural Revolution. Until 1980 even local Tibetans had been forbidden to circumambulate or visit the sacred mountain.

Today the Indian pilgrimage is organized as a lottery by the Delhi government. Each year 5,000-10,000 Hindus apply from all parts of India. Approximately 700 are chosen and after medical examinations and fitness tests this number is reduced to 300 to 400 pilgrims, the current annual quota. (Earlier, in the 1980s, only 200 could make the journey each year.) Departing from Delhi via Almora and Bhirnag, they travel in groups of 30-40, for 10 days commencing in June/July. After five days' trekking they cross the **Jang La** (Lipulekh) pass where they are exchanged with the outgoing group and met by Chinese tour guides, before being driven to **Purang** and the *Indian Pilgrim's Guest House*. Following a rest day, they journey to Mount Kailash where half commence the circuit of the mountain while the other half go to Lake Manasarovar. After three days they switch around before beginning their journey home three days later.

The pilgrims must bring all their supplies with them from India. Most are ill-prepared in terms of equipment and clothing however. Many arrive clad in light cotton clothes and flimsy canvas sneakers, usually topped by a woollen balaclava or plastic rainhat. Despite this, their strong and genuine devotion carries them through the experience. For Hindus, Mount Kailash is the abode of Shiva, the God of Destruction, and it has been one of the most sacred pilgrimage destinations for over 5,000 years.

The Circumambulation of Mount Kailash

Darchen is the starting and completion point for the general circuit of the sacred mountain. It is wise to spend at least a day here in preparation. **NB** It is possible to leave extra baggage at the *Darchen Guesthouse*.

Preparation

Weather Observe the weather conditions and ask those who have made the trek in the past few days the conditions you are likely to encounter. The weather will determine to a large extent the amount of baggage you need. Do not be concerned with a change of clothes for each day. Extra pairs of socks and underwear are the most that are needed. Do not forget a good raincoat, and parka all-weather jacket even if the sky is clear blue. A strong pair of walking shoes are essential.

Acclimatization By the time you arrive in Darchen (4,880 metres) you should be reasonably acclimatized to the altitude (it is said that over 3,660 metres it takes from 10 days to three weeks for the blood count to adjust to less oxygen). Remember the Dolma La pass is not far under 5,790 metres: plan to carry as little extra weight as possible.

Porter Arrange for a Tibetan porter or yak to carry your baggage in Darchen. The price ranges from around ¥45 for a yak, the same for a yak-herder or porter and ¥50 for a horse per day. This can be done by approaching likely looking people or by making arrangements through the guesthouse manager. If you have arranged your travel through an agency all will be handled by your tour guide.

Provisions   Water It is said that one should drink around four litres of liquid

Far-west Tibet

a day to replace the fluid lost through perspiration at high altitude. So it is important to stock up whenever you come across a spring or fresh stream. Dehydration leading to digestion problems is always possible at high altitude. Arrange to carry a good-sized water bottle with you and drink from it throughout the day. Orange or fruit flavour powders such as 'Tang' are good to mix in the water.

Food You need to plan the food to take. Each day the body burns a lot of energy so you need to start with a substantial breakfast of carbohydrates and glucose. Muesli, granola, and porridge oats are all beneficial. Do not hold back on sugar or glucose either. A large mug or two of tea, coffee or cocoa is vital. Carry at least six muesli-type bars (two a day) and when you feel your energy flagging, stop and enjoy. Glucose tabs are also helpful. In the evening you need to make up a thick soup or dehydrated stew and hot tea or chocolate.

Apparatus This means your luggage should include a stove, fuel and cooking utensils as well as cleaning soap and scourer. Also candles, matches, torches, batteries, ground sheet, sleeping bag and tent if you want to sleep outside the pilgrim shelters.

Gyangdrak Gonpa

Gyangdrak Gonpa is an easy trek from Darchen and can be done whilst waiting for porters etc. It is a Drigung Kagyu monastery in the central approach valley of Mount Kailash, which was reputedly founded some 800 years ago by Drubtob Guya Gangpa, and has been rebuilt in the 1980s. This is said to be the actual place where the founding master of the Bon tradition, Shenrab Miwoche, stayed when he came to Tibet several thousand years ago and imparted the prime Bon ritual practices. It is said that he was only able to teach basic rituals relating to the pacification of the spirits who control mountains and environment. The more advanced Bon teachings of Dzogchen arose much later. The ruins of the Drigung Kagyu monastery of **Selung** lie beyond Gyangdrak. Both these sites are located within the inner circuit (*nangkor*) of Mount Kailash and towards its south face. The inner circuit is usually undertaken only by those who have already made 12 circuits on the standard outer route!

Day One: Darchen to Drirapuk (22.5 kilometres)

Leave as soon as possible after breakfast. The trail follows along the western spur of the foothills before reaching a cairn of prayer stones where it turns north into the great western valley. After about one kilometre it reaches **Chorten Kang-nyi** ('Two Legged Stupa'). This was blown up in the 1960s and rebuilt in 1987, being the first Buddhist structure on the circuit to be replaced. A few hundred metres east of this is the **Darpoche** ('Great Prayer Flagpole') which is taken down and redecorated on the full moon day of the Buddha's Enlightenment Festival (around April/May each year). Hundreds of Tibetan pilgrims come for this event. It marks the beginning of the pilgrimage season since the Dolma La pass is blocked by snow until April.

Above the shallow depression of **Darpoche** is a large flat ledge of red rock. On the surface many prayers and mantras are carved. It was here that the Buddha came with 500 disciples from India. They were said to have flown there over the Himalayas by means of their supernatural powers. The view from this place looks down upon a wide flat expanse of the valley floor. Steep cliffs rise high on either side. The **Lha-chu** ('Divine River') flows down from the valley ahead and pours out onto the gentle slope of the **Barka Plain**, flowing into the waters of the **Rakshas Tal** ('Demonic Lake') in the far distance. On the valley floor are ruins of 13 stupas, dynamited in the 1960s.

A footbridge now crosses the river and above it, nestling in the cliff face is the rebuilt Kagyu monastery of **Choku Gonpa**, which was originally founded by Nyepo Drubtob in accordance with a prophesy of Gotsangpa. Below this but not discernible is the **Langchen Bepuk** ('Hidden Elephant Cave') where Padmasambhava stayed and meditated when he came to Mount Kailash.

One can climb down from the **Buddha's Platform** directly to the trail below, or return to the **Two Legged Stupa** and rejoin the circuit. If time permits a walk over the bridge to the **Choku Gonpa** is worth including in the trek. The view of the south face of the mountain, if clear, is striking. Do not be surprised if the attendant monk here is not very cooperative. Photos are strictly forbidden of the shrines. In 1991 a gang of art thieves from Nepal and working for western art dealers broke into the shrine and stole 16 ancient statues. Two of the gang were caught and told how they were stealing to order, using photos taken by 'tourists' the previous year. This helps one to understand the cool reception one often receives in such places.

The trail now continues up the valley. The path is not steep but climbs steadily. The red escarpments of the eastern wall tower above the valley obscuring the peak from view. After some time you pass the **Three Pinnacles of Longevity** above the opposite cliff face. They represent the Three Deities of Longevity: Amitayus, White Tara and Vijaya. Above the trail the right-hand cliffs become smooth and form what seems to be a giant seat. Rising higher behind this is the rock formation regarded by Hindus as the monkey god Hanuman in prayer to the mountain. Buddhists call it the "**Torma-offering of Padmasambhava**".

After some hours more one comes upon a grassy flat populated by marmots. Rivulets of pure sweet water cross the trail. There is a rock in the middle of this spot which is associated with **Mahakala**, one of the main Buddhist protectors. From here the valley begins to turn east and, as though gazing down from the heavens, directly above is the western face of Mount Kailash, a triangular facet of rock dripping with great drops of overhanging snow. This is a face of the mountain rarely seen in photos, yet it has a power and beauty of its own.

From this turn in the valley it is another two hours at least before reaching **Drirapuk**. At this point the going is not so easy and, if it is late afternoon or near sunset, each step seems a race against time. If your yaks and porters have not gone ahead (unlikely by now) you may prefer to camp along this northeastern part of the valley. It is best to proceed on and up.

NB Once Drirapuk is in sight it is important to keep to the trail. Do not be hasty. It actually passes your destination on the far side of the river. Unless you are prepared to remove shoes and socks and chance a wade through the river (which can be risky when the water is high) it is better to keep walking past Drirapuk and you will find a bridge which crosses the river over two spans. Many pilgrims drowned here before it was built in 1986. Now follow the trail down the opposite bank and traverse a second bridge of one span which crosses a tributary from the valley north. A short distance away is the *Indian Pilgrims' Rest House* at Drirapuk.

Drirapuk Temple This is further up the hill behind the rest house. It encloses a retreat cave associated with the great yogin Gotsangpa. Drirapuk ('Cave of the Female Yak Horn') is so named because its walls bear indentations of a *dri's* horn. Gotsangpa, who stayed here from 1213 to 1217 was a disciple of one of Milarepa's disciples and is known as the author of the first history and guide book of Mount Kailash.

The north face The location here presents one with a spectacular view of the great north face of the mountain. Unlike the south face which has a smooth slope, usually covered in snow apart from the unique vertical striations down its centre, the north face is a near-vertical sheer cliff some 1,520 metres high consisting of jet black rock. In only a few places does the snow cling to it, creating extraordinary oval panels like massive eyes sited within long mask-like bands of horizontal strata, all framed by the near-circular dome of the peak which itself is flanked by two symmetrical mountains. It is as though the gods rent the mountain with a cosmic sword and then swept the rubble of the one shattered half into two tidy piles.

The 'pile' to the right is the mountain associated with the bodhisattva **Vajrapani**, the one to the left, the peak associated with **Avalokiteshvara** and beyond that a third is known as the mountain of **Manjughosa**. These three patron bodhisattvas of Tibet respectively embody enlightened power, compassion and discriminative awareness.

The view of the north face is equally spectacular at midnight (under the moonlight) as at midday.

Day Two:
Drirapuk to
Dzutrulpuk
(22.9 kilometres)

This day is the climax of the pilgrimage. The **Dolma La pass** lies 6.4 kilometres ahead but 762 metres above Drirapuk. Physically it is the most arduous day. Breakfast early and set off as the sun's rays break over the ridges above. After the footbridge the trail rises up a rocky slope. Take this gently but steadily. It soon reaches a level walk. The peak of Mount Kailash rises to the right and can now be seen linked to a long spur which joins the eastern ridge. This is the top edge of the glacial valley from which the **Lha-chu** ('Divine River') flows.

Silwutsel charnel ground The trail continues to meander along levels and then up short staircases. At one point it passes by a broad pile of discarded clothes, utensils and personal items including hair and teeth. This is the Silwutsel charnel ground, the place of death. Named after a famous cremation ground near Bodh Gaya in India. Tibetan pilgrims discard something of their possessions here. It represents the renouncing of attachment to worldly objects and to this life. Without such an understanding death remains a moment to fear.

Just above Silwutsel is a knoll over which all loose rocks have been piled up into small cairns. This is a place linked to Vajrayogini, a *dakini* who inhabits fearsome places such as charnel grounds. She is the consort of the wrathful meditational deity Cakrasamvara (Khorlo Demchok), who is said to preside over Mount Kailash.

Dolma La All along the path now are special places connected to the history and mythology of the mountain. The air becomes more rarefied and it is essential to take short rests, breathing deeply, before continuing on. Shortly after passing a small azure pool below the trail it turns right and begins the ascent to the **Dolma La** ('Pass of Tara'). Now one's steps only cover a few metres before one must stop, gulping in air, before covering the next short distance. At last one reaches the 5,723 metres pass and is able to sit down and take in the meaning of that moment. At the pass is a large boulder depicting Tara, festooned with prayer flags. Here too Tibetans leave a momento of themselves such as a tooth, a lock of hair or even a personal snapshot.

Dolma La to Dzutrulpuk After perhaps 30 minutes and a warm drink we descend a steep, rock-strewn path to the valley below. Just below the pass is **Lake Tu-je Chenpo Dzingbu** (*Skt.* Gauri Kund; *Eng.* 'Pool of Great Compassion'). Take great care now because it is easy to sprain your ankle or worse. You must negotiate steep staircases down to a snowfield. The only way down is to jump from boulder to boulder across a large rockfall. On the ridge above is a formation known as the **Lekyi Ta-re** ('Axe of Karma'), as though one's previous actions, if ignored, may, at any moment ripen in an accident, suffering or death.

A final steep descending staircase brings you to the valley floor. From here it is still about five hours to the day's destination with no shelter in between. It is *vitally* important to remain on the right hand side of the river, the west bank. If not, you will get trapped, unable to cross it. The walk now becomes very pleasant and relaxing (as long as the weather is clear and there is no howling gale). The path follows the gentle slope of the valley over grassy fields and clear brooks for several kilometres before it narrows and turns further south to merge with another valley before reaching **Dzutrulpuk**, the 'Miracle Cave' of Milarepa.

Stay in the rest house and the next morning can be spent exploring the caves and visiting the temple and shrine that has been built around Milarepa's cave. A married elderly couple supervise the temple which is usually an active residence for over half a dozen Tibetan devotees, helpers, or relatives who continuously busy themselves with the tasks of maintaining the buildings. Perhaps for this reason they often seem quite impatient with visitors.

Day Three: Dzutrulpuk to Darchen (11.3 kilometres)

Milarepa's cave The main temple encloses Milarepa's cave which is capped by a large slab of rock, said to be impressed on its underside with the shape of Milarepa's shoulders and upper back. This was formed when he forced the huge rock higher to make the cave more roomy. Unfortunately it now was too high and draughty. So the top of the slab (which is encased inside a mud wall) is said to hold imprints of his feet and hands where he pressed down on the rock to make it lower and just right!

You may sit within the cave. A torch is useful. It is appropriate to make an offering either by placing money on the altar or giving it to a temple attendant. They may then offer you blessed relics which look like large white pills. These are made from deposits gathered during the cleaning of the rock roof of the shrine. Do not assume that they are freely given. The residents rely upon donations and gifts from pilgrims for their sustenance. Even then the 'price' of such relics is equal to perhaps five pence or 15 cents or less.

Outside the temple a few metres to the south is a huge hexagonal boulder. It stands upright as though placed there by hand. It once stood alone but has been half encircled by a stone wall built in the late 1980s. This wall now is beginning to collapse. It is said that Naro Bonchung hurled this boulder at Milarepa in the midst of their contest of magical powers. Milarepa caught it and placed it down gently, just above his meditation cave.

Surrounding the boulder and the temple complex are dozens of stacks of Mani Stones, rocks carved with prayers and quotations from the scriptures. Hardly a stone remains untouched. Hundreds of thousands of prayers cover the valley's slope. They continue in heaps up until reaching a vertical cliff face. Along its base is a strata into which retreat caves have been created. One imagines Milarepa's disciples meditating here, following his example by living off soup made from the abundant nettles that grow all about. Many of the caves contain meditation platforms, self-contained by dry stone walls which divide them from their cooking partitions and entrance areas. It is well worth the short climb up to these caves before beginning the final stage of the trek.

The return to Darchen The walk back to Darchen is easy and the exit from the valley can be reached within a few hours. Just as the valley allows the river to flow out into the Barka plain, the walls become steep and the trail passes through multicoloured stratas of rock changing from red to yellow, from black

Far-west Tibet

Milarepa and Mount Kailash

For Buddhists Milarepa's influence in the history of Mount Kailash is most important. Although the Buddha himself was said to have flown there with 500 saints by means of their miraculous powers the mountain had been the most sacred place for followers of the Bon religion for hundreds of years. It was to Mount Kailash that the founder of Bon, Shenrab Miwoche, first came and taught in Tibet perhaps several thousand years before Christ (his dates are imprecise). Even after Buddhism became established in Tibet by Padmasambhava and other Indian masters, Mount Kailash continued to be venerated especially by the Bonpos. This changed when Milarepa became a mendicant master and began teaching a small band of disciples. He travelled to Mount Kailash on the basis of a prophecy of the Buddha which states that "this mountain at the navel of the world ... like a crystal stupa is the abode of Cakrasamvara, a great place of accomplished yogins ... nowhere is more marvellous or wonderful ...".

When he arrived there Milarepa met a powerful Bonpo master called **Naro Bonchung** who presided over Mount Kailash and Lake Manasarovar. Each disputed the other's authority and they agreed to resolve this in a competition of their magical powers. First they tested each other at Lake Manasarovar. Naro Bonchung stood astride in one step. Milarepa spread his body over the whole surface and then balanced its waters on his finger. Not satisfied they went to the mountain and circumambulated it in their opposite directions. They met at Dolma La pass and thus began a series of feats of strength, power and magic which still left the contest unresolved.

Naro Bonchung then suggested the first to the summit after dawn on the full moon day would be the victor. Before sunrise Naro Bonchung appeared in the sky flying on his drum to the top. Despite the concern of his disciples Milarepa did not appear to be worried. Naro's ascent had ceased and he was just flying around on his drum at the same level. Then, as the rays of the sun first struck the top Milarepa joined with them and was instantly transported to the summit. Naro the shaman was shocked and fell from his drum. It dropped from the sky and tumbled down the south face of Kailash gouging out a vertical line of pits and crevices. The Bonpo conceded defeat and was given jurisdiction over a neighbouring mountain to the east.

From that contest by Milarepa until today the mountain has been influenced primarily by Buddhist adherents of Cakrasamvara, the wrathful meditational deity, who is the Buddhist tantric aspect of Great Compassion. At the same time Mount Kailash remains a major pilgrimage for Tibetan Bonpos whose custom is to circle it anticlockwise and who revere the Dalai Lama as strongly as other Tibetans. For Hindu pilgrims from India, Mount Kailash is the abode of Shiva, the Lord of Destruction and one of the triumvirate which includes Brahma and Vishnu. Jains too have traditionally made pilgrimage to Mount Kailash.

to purple. This section is known as the **Trangser Trangmar** ('Gold and Red Cliffs'). The trail now turns right as it skirts the base of the foothills before finally returning to Darchen.

NB There are many more sites of lesser significance on the three-day circuit of Mount Kailash, but those just described are all that an average pilgrim would be able to absorb in the short time available.

Circumambulation of Lake Manasarovar

Colour map 1, grid B2 After completing the circuit of Mount Kailash, the next day you can embark on

Blessed objects from the lake

*Apart from the numerous abra rodent colonies between Hor and Seralung, lapping the northeast shoreline are strange **egg-shaped bundles of lake grass**. They occur nowhere else, which is enough to confer on them sacred status. Devotees take one or two for their blessings. Also along this stretch it is possible to find small **stones of black jet**. These are treasured for their association with the Karmapas. The shoreline sand changes continuously. Along a short stretch just south of Seralung it is made of 5 coloured grains: black, white, red, yellow and greenish-blue. If you find such sands, they are of special value. Moreover one often finds the dried-out bodies of fish, which are highly treasured for their medicinal properties and are said to ease the pains of childbirth if just a small piece is eaten.*

the circuit of **Lake Manasarovar**. The Tibetan names for the lake are **Mapham Yutso** and **Tso Madropa**, the later being a translation of a secondary Sanskrit name, **Anavatapta**. From Darchen drive 22 kilometres to Barka township, at the crossroads.

Barka is a small administrative base for the people living in the environs of Mount Kailash and the lakes. It is newly made, replacing the original **Barka** hamlet, which is some eight kilometres to the west. Here, the roads from Senge Tsangpo, Drongpa and Purang all converge.

Day One To reach the starting point for the circuit of Lake Manasarovar, take the Drongpa (east) road, and continue on to **Hor** township 28 kilometres distant. Hor is a haphazard collection of mud-walled houses and assorted compounds, located slightly inland from the northeast corner of the lake. It may be possible to find the only store in town open if you wish to buy any extra provisions. Otherwise drive on to **Seralung Gon**, the so-called eastern gateway to the lake. The rebuilt compound here replaces a Kagyu monastery that originally was sited a few hundred metres up the valley behind. The family of a local lama and shaman live here and if possible they may have a room which you can use for the night. Don't forget to offer them a payment for the room before you leave. Otherwise it is better to camp out.

Day Two The trek now covers some 22.5 kilometres to reach **Trugo Gon**, a monastery at the southern gateway to the lake. Although level, the sandy trail becomes arduous by the day's end. For the first few kilometres you should keep to the shoreline but then the trail cuts across a sandy headland, heading towards the bridge which crosses the **Trak Tsangpo** River. Wildlife abounds and herds of wild ass (*kyang*) graze on the valley floor. Soon Trugo Gon comes into view. The distance is deceptive for now, no matter how much ground one seems to cover, it never appears to be any closer. It is best not to look ahead and instead to enjoy the grassy fields abounding with flowers and mosses. Eventually, the track passes the ruins of **Nyego Monastery** at the lake's edge. It once was associated with Atisha, the Indian master who revived Buddhism in 11th century Tibet. Trugo Gon is now a simple walk away.

Day Three **Trugo Gon** is the most active monastery around Lake Manasarovar. It is supervised by a young reincarnate Gelukpa monk from Northeast Tibet named Lama Lobzang. He is training a small number of young monks and has rebuilt the main compound as well as arranged the construction of a pilgrims' guest house nearby. He has also built a stupa outside the entrance. One can stay in the guest house if beds are available for around ¥25 per night. Be careful

Far-west Tibet

Lakes Manasarovar and Rakshas Tal

*Below the sacred Mount Kailash, there is the contrast and balance inherent in the two majestic lakes. Here the symbiosis is complete. One, **Lake Manasarovar** ("Lake Conceived from the Mind of God") is a disc of turquoise brilliance, passive, at peace, whole in its very nature and presence. Shimmering blue at 4,572m, it is one of the highest bodies of pure water on the surface of the earth. Its waters are not just fresh, they are pure beyond conventional scientific confirmation, remaining pure for at least 6 years. Upon its surface the great dome of Mount Kailash is reflected for much of the year. In the winter it then freezes over as great ice sheets explode like voices from the underworld. It is alive, sustaining a teeming richness of trout, carp and huge*

freshwater dolphins. Migrating birds from Europe, Central Asia and Siberia rest here on their journeys south to the Indian subcontinent.

*A short distance down the riverbed of the **Langchen Khabab**, which is the source of the Sutlej River, leads one to the dark and stormy shores of **Lake Rakshas Tal**, some 15m lower and totally disconnected from Lake Manasarovar. Shaped like the crescent moon it embodies the forces of the night, the dark and unknown side of the psyche, yet is essential for the wholeness of life. Without the cool mystery of the night and the presence of the lunar phases sunrise could not sustain the fullness of life. Life would be consumed by the solitary brilliance of the sun.*

with your possessions however since thefts have been reported. As in many similar places the Tibetans put in charge can be far from cooperative and have little idea of good public relations.

Trugo Gon is also a location where Nepalese Brahmins come to make ritual ablutions in the lake waters. They trek up from the Nepalese Terai on the Indian border and follow ancient trails right through the Himalayas. Most are very poor and only visit the lake. The main date for them is the full moon in August during the monsoon when the rain and wind is numbingly cold. These thin, frail men recite mantras and prayers building up the strength to walk naked into the lake and immerse themselves completely before rushing out to huddle around a small fire.

From Trugo Gon one follows the shoreline for most of the day. Before the southwest corner, however, be prepared to encounter swarms of mosquitoes or midges. It may be necessary to cover your mouth, nose and ears with a cloth or scarf for this section. Having turned north, the western shoreline becomes a low cliff face. After a few kilometres there is evidence of caves with blackened ceilings that once were inhabited. Above them is the rebuilt Gelukpa monastery of **Gotsuk Gon**, the original foundation of which is attributed to Gotsangpa and Kyapgon Jinpa Norbu. An elderly lama and a few monks reside here. It is well worth the climb since there is a superb view of the lake from its roof.

Continue following the shoreline and the trail will turn left, pointing almost directly to the peak of Mount Kailash in the distance. Again the shore swings north towards the final *Indian Pilgrims' Guest House*. It is said that some of Mahatma Gandhi's ashes were brought here and cast into the lake's waters. You can stop here since the road is nearby, or continue on to Jiu Monastery, the appropriate destination for the day.

Jiu Gonpa   **Jiu Gonpa** ('Sparrow Monastery') at the lake's western gateway sits atop a conical outcrop of red rock. Originally founded by the Kagyu lama Kyapgon Gangriwa, inside there is a small shrine and cave where Padmasambhava was said to have meditated with his consort Yeshe Tsogyel before leaving this

The grandest lightshow on earth

*The area around the source of the **Brahmaputra** is undeniably beautiful. Parallel to the road, the Tibetan plateau rolls south to the white jagged wall of the Himalayas. At dusk, as wisps of smoke drift above the black silhouettes of the nomads' tents, the herds of yak lumber back home to camp, spurned on by hoots and whistles from the yak-herders and their sons. The folds in the hills turn a deep indigo while the snow teeth of the Himalayas, now cobalt blue in the eastward shadowlands, gleam with gold caps across the horizon as the sun sets, giving its last caress of the day to these crown jewels of Asia.*

It sets, slipping away in the west and, if one turns toward the east a miraculous sign seems to hint at the sun's rise the next day – high in the sky above, vast rays of pink and red light streak across the deep blue stratosphere to converge on a now-vacant point in the distant east. It is the grandest lightshow on the planet; the shadows of peaks hundreds of miles away in the west are cast through the heavens, parallel to infinity but appearing to converge as the viewer perceives their perspective played out on a cosmic plane. This unique, awesome display may be seen just after sunset when few clouds remain, depending upon the conditions, along much of the Upper Brahmaputra, as well as at Lake Manasarovar and perhaps most vividly at Toling in the Upper Sutlej.

world. Various objects are to be found inside the cave, such as the granite rocks with clear imprints of Padmasambhava's hands and feet.

Here too is the **source of the Sutlej River**, known as the Ganga or Langchen Khabab, which at times links Lake Manasarovar with neighbouring Lake Raksas Tal (*Tib* Lakngar Tso). When the fortunes of Tibet are low, it is almost dry, as is the present situation. The only water that remains is the brackish cusp of hot springs behind Jiu Gonpa. The Tibetans however have created several open-air stone baths where one can wash body and clothes in the clean hot water.

Here one should meet up with one's transport and either begin the return journey (whichever way that may be) or go on to Tirthapuri, traditionally the third and final destination of the pilgrimage.

Tirthapuri: the Cave of Padmasambhava

Concluding the pilgrimage is a visit to **Tirthapuri**. Here hot springs and a gey- *Colour map 1, grid B2* ser add to the power of the place. Inside a temple enclosure is a small cave where Padmasambhava meditated with his Tibetan consort Yeshe Tsogyel. It contains two granite stones in which indentations of their footprints are clearly present, and a hole through which Padmasambhava is said to have extracted the consciousness of the ogress who previously inhabited the cave. Formerly it also contained as its main images Padmasambhava flanked by Amitabha and Shakyamuni. Photography inside is forbidden. The actual temple was originally constructed by the Nyingma lama Gonchen Chonyi Zangpo of Dorje Drak, but more recently it has been maintained by Kagyupa monks.

The surrounding landscape consists mainly of red and white earth. Around the cave are dozens of unusual rock formations, almost all of which have become imbued with religious significance. Events from the lives of the buddhas and bodhisattvas are associated and recounted with each place, in accordance with the Tibetan concept of 'sacred outlook'.

The hot springs at Tirthapuri are clean to bathe in. In the past there was a geyser that erupted every few minutes spraying water six metres or so into the air. The water table must be lowering because this has not happened since the

Far-west Tibet

late 1980s. From one of the blowholes, however, small white flecks or 'pills' of lime can be found. Tibetans strain the water for these and use them for medicinal purposes, since they are said to have a consecrated power to cure disease.

At Tirthapuri, the quiet waters of the Sutlej pass by grassy paddocks that are ideal for picnics or camping. The tranquillity of the place is the attraction for most Tibetan pilgrims who come here to rest and relax after the intensity of their Mount Kailash and Lake Manasarovar circuits. The pilgrim now has the opportunity to confirm and assimilate the experiences of the previous days. The spaciousness and blessings here provide a means for uniting the power and majesty of Kailash with the peace and beauty of Lake Manasarovar. In this way the pilgrimage is completed.

Tachok Khabab Source

From Hor township, drive southeast for 92 kilometres to reach the village of Nyoktse on the north shore of **Lake Gung-gyu**, and then continue climbing for 40 kilometres to reach the **Mayum La** pass. The source of the Brahmaputra, known as the **Pakshu** or **Tachok Khabab**, lies on the far side of the pass, in the glaciers of the **Ganglungri** range (see above, page 314).

Mabcha Tsangpo Valley

The **Mabcha Khabab**, rising near Shiri Langdor northwest of **Mount Nanda Devi** (7,815 metres), on the Tibetan side of the Indo-Tibetan border, is a major source of the **Karnali** River. It flows southeast from its source to **Rigong** township, where it becomes known as the Mabcha Tsangpo (Karnali). The motor road from Barka which cuts through the isthmus between Lake Manasarovar and Lake Raksas Tal enters the valley of the Mabcha Tsangpo at Rigong, and then continues downstream to Purang, the county capital, 104 kilometres from Barka.

Purang

Colour map 1, grid B2
About 112 kilometres south of Mount Kailash, past the twin lakes and Mount Nemo Nanyi, is the ancient township of **Purang** (*Ch* Bulan), which the Nepalis and Indians call **Taklakot** (a corruption of the Tibetan **Takla Khar**). It is the administrative base for the Kailash region and traditionally it has been the focus for pilgrims from India coming via **Almora** and the **Jang La** pass (Lipulekh; 5,090 metres). Purang lies on the Mabcha Tsangpo, the Tibetan tributary of the Karnali, which rises in the peacock-shaped rocks of the **Mabcha Khabab** ('Peacock Source'), south of lake **Rakshas Tal**. South of Purang, the river, now known as the **Mabcha Tsangpo** ('Peacock River') flows through the villages of **Khorzhak**, **Zher**, **Lemi** and **Omlho**, before cutting through a deep gorge into Nepal.

Purang is a fascinating trading station on the Tibetan border with India and Nepal. It was here that most of the early travellers from India would reach and make their first contact with the Tibetan authorities. It has been a capital of the early kingdoms of Far-west Tibet and has been inhabited for at least 3,000 years. It was where **Sudhana**, a previous incarnation of Buddha, reputedly lived. His exploits are recounted extensively in the *Gandhavyuhasutra*, a section of the voluminous *Avatamsakasutra*, which describes the events in a bodhisattva's life exemplifying the development of great compassion and the awakening of enlightened mind (*bodhicitta*).

Sleeping To rest and recuperate from the difficulties of travel one can stay in the *Pulan Hotel* (double room US$33 per night, breakfast US$7; full meal plan US$28). *Pulan Indian Pilgrim Guest House*, simple but comfortable, with individual bungalows and well-prepared Chinese meals.

The Ruins of Shepeling Monastery

Rising above the town of Purang is a high, steeply sloping ridge capped with a large complex of ruins. Before the Chinese invasion this was the residence of the regional administrator as well as the temple and monastic complex for several hundred monks. In those days it was referred to as the 'Dzong' or fortress of **Shepeling**. Such buildings on commanding positions were once common throughout Tibet. The main monastery was of the Gelukpa school but there was also one large part that held a Sakya monastery.

To walk up and explore the ruins gives one an excellent view taking in the north slopes of the Himalayas from Nepal to India and the **Jang La** pass as well as the whole southern face of **Mount Nemo Nanyi**. It takes less than an hour at leisurely pace from the cave dwellings to reach the top. Across the Karnali River is the Chinese cantonment and the military garrison.

Cave dwellings and Tsegu Gonpa

From the road on the east bank of the Karnali River you can cross a suspension bridge to the west side where, in the cliff above the Tibetan traders' houses, there are ancient cave dwellings. Remarkably many are still inhabited. This was probably the original town of **Purang** and it may date back several thousand years to the time when cave cities were created across Asia. It is likely that it was in such cave cities man first lived in secure settlements instead of following a nomadic lifestyle.

At the western end of the caves is an ancient temple cut into the cliff. It is known as **Tsegu Gonpa** ('Nine-Storey Monastery') and includes many terraced levels going up the cliff. It can be reached by steps, ladders and platforms hanging off the wall. In the lower levels there is a residence of the family who look after the temple. Be polite as you approach and wait to be asked to enter. You will have to walk through the house, which itself is fascinating, and then be lead up to the temples above. Take shoes off before entering. The walls are covered in highly polished murals that are unique in style. They have been darkened from the smoke of lamps over hundreds of years. It is helpful to bring a torch with you.

Far-west Tibet

Purang

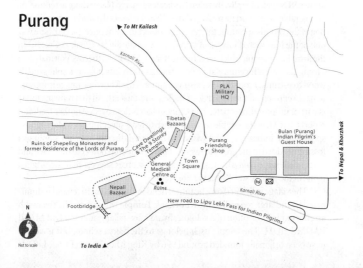

The temple belongs now to the Drigung Kagyu or Gelukpa school, yet it may even predate the founding of these schools of Buddhism.

NB Photography here is strictly forbidden and the supervisor gets very nervous if you bring cameras out so it is best not to intimidate him.

Trading markets At Purang one can still see how many of the Tibetan border towns were used as trading posts for the nomadic produce of the **Jangtang**, such as wool and salt which would be bartered for the rice and palm sugar of Nepal and the Indian plains. This centuries-old trade continues here today. Below the cave dwellings a trading camp forms over the summer and autumn months when large encampments of Nepalese appear. Those in front of the caves come for the salt and rice trade. Sheep and goats are loaded up with a double back-pack holding up to 30 kilos of produce before they make their way over the trail on a three week journey to the Indo-Nepalese Terai.

Tanga Follow the path past the caves to quickly reach the busy trading camp, known as Tanga. This larger camp below the Simbiling ruins consists of streets of temporary one room residences over which the traders must sling a tarpaulin for the roof. The prohibition against permanent roofs is said to date back to a 1904 treaty between Tibet and Britain! Here there is a fascinating glimpse of a bustling bazaar that has been barely touched by time. The Nepalese bring every kind of practical item, from cooking utensils to cotton cloth and manufactured goods from India, to sell or trade for the wool and salt brought by the Northern Plateau nomads. The wool bales, resembling giant doughnuts, are carried by yaks and, once sold are undone into long skeins which are stretched down the alleyways and prepared for transport south.

The Chinese authorities today let this small trade continue (although Indians are now excluded) probably because the traders barely eke out an existence from it.

Khorzhak Temple and Village

Colour map 1, grid B2 About 15 kilometres further down the Karnali river valley, the motorable road comes to an end at the small village of **Korzhak** (*Ch* Korqag), or Kojanath as it is known in Nepal. Literally, this name indicates a sacred place where a 'retinue' or 'a venerable object and its surroundings' (*khor*) is 'placed' (*zhak*). According to one of the various accounts, the venerable object that was once 'placed' here was one of the four sacred images of standing Avalokiteshvara (Phakpa Chezhi) in the form Padmapani, which were brought from Nepal to Tibet by Akarmatishila during the seventh century after he extracted them intact from a split sandalwood tree-trunk. From the few existing photos of the Khorzhak image it appears to have represented the Pala style of Indian Buddhist art. All that remains today is part of its lotus flower base. The Chinese had it destroyed. Another tradition reports that when the temple was first constructed a silver image of Manjughosa spoke aloud, indicating that it wished to be placed directly upon an amolingka fossil embedded in the ground, saying "I have wandered (*khor*) to this place and here I shall settle (*chags*)!" Yet, other literary sources suggest that the original name of the temple was Khvachar Lhakhang.

The village is situated on a beautiful bend in the Karnali River and is dominated by the large red wall of the **Khorzhak Temple** which faces the river with an enormous inscription of Avalokiteshvara's six-syllable mantra: OM MANI PADME HUM. The temple itself belongs to the Sakya school, but is said to have been originally founded around 996 by King Khor-re and Prince Lha-de

Ganges and Karnali Rivers

*The **Ganges**, sacred river of India, flows for 2,510 km from its sources to its confluence with the Brahmaputra in Bengal. There are five headwaters, namely: the Bhagirathi, Alaknanda, Mandakini, Dhauliganga, and Pindar, that all rise in **Uttarakand** in India, not in Tibet. Of these the two main sources, Alakanda and Bhagirathi, originate at an elevation of about 3,050m in an icy cavern below **Gangotri Glacier**. **Gaumukh**, 21 km southeast of Gangotri is often cited as the Ganges' actual source.*

*However, in close proximity to these, a major source of the **Karnali**, one of Ganges' main tributaries, does rise in Tibet, to the south of **Lake Rakshas Tal**. It flows through **Purang** to cut southeast of **Mount Nemo Nanyi** (Gurlamandhata) and enter Northwest Nepal. There it converges with other tributaries of the Karnali, and flows into India, where, as the **Gogra**, it eventually converges with the Ganges at **Patna**.*

of Purang. It has outer and inner gates with a spacious courtyard. The foremost image was of silver, depicting Jowo Shakyamuni in the form Manjuvajra. Later in the 13th century, images of Avalokiteshvara and Vajrapani were placed alongside it by King Namgonde and his consort Jabum Gyelmo. The temple has been damaged and reconstructed several times over the centuries, most recently following the Cultural Revolution, and there are currently some 17 monks. Beside the temple, a smaller eight-pillared temple attributed to Rinchen Zangpo, the great translator, once stood.

On certain special days of the month monks from the region come here to per- **Ritual masked**
form a day-long series of ritual masked dances. They still use many of the cos- **dances**
tumes and masks made before 1959. Local maidens who are betrothed come
out on such occasions and display their family jewellery and fine clothes. This
usually takes place in September or after the harvest in early October. Enquire
at the *IP Guest House* to see whether any festivals are coming up.

From Purang, you can trek out of Tibet via **Zhingpa** township and **Jang La** **Trekking**
pass (18 kilometres) into India, if you are an Indian pilgrim, or via Piling La,
Chema La, or **Nak La** passes into Nepal, providing you have the right permits
and visas. If you lack such travel documents, you will be placed under arrest
inside Nepal and sent back to Tibet. The alternative is to begin the return journey through Purang and then along one of the other routes described above. If
you haven't yet been to Gu-ge and have the time, it is a very worthwhile
side-trip on the way back to Senge Tsangpo.

Tsamda county རྩ་མདའ་

Tsamda county is the current name for the region which once was known as the *Tsamda County (49)*
***Gu-ge** kingdom. It extends along the banks of the upper **Sutlej** from Khyunglung,* 札达县
southwest of Montser, as far as the Indian border, where the river flows into *Zanda*
*Kinnaur below the Sibkyi La pass. The valley of the **Rashok Tsangpo**, which* *Population: 5,134*
gives access to Southern Ladakh and Spiti also lies within Tsamda, as does the *Area: 28,033 sq km*
*valley of the **Gyaza Kar-chu**, through which the Uttarakashi district of Uttar* *Colour map 1, grid B1*
*Pradesh can be reached. The county capital is located at **Toling**, 278 kilometres
from Senge Tsangpo, and 443 kilometres from Purang. The new county name,
Tsamda, is a contraction of **Tsa** (parang) and **Da** (wa-dzong), which are two of
the most important sites within the upper Sutlej valley.*

The Tsamda area is characterized by the striking complex of canyons cutting through the red sandstone composite of what was once an ocean floor, all descending into the upper Sutlej River. For much of the year these canyon tributaries are dry, only becoming impassable or hazardous in the monsoon. Those south of the Sutlej, such as the Manam Tsangpo, Dapa-chu, and Tophu-chu, arise in the Himalayas near the Indian border, which is heavily patrolled. The north is bounded by the Gar Tsangpo valley and southern slopes of the Gangtise Range.

It was in this region of Far-west Tibet that Tibetans appear to have first established permanently inhabited cities. At that time, in the antiquity of the pre-Christian era, the kingdom was known as **Zhangzhung**. From Bon chronicles that have recently come to light, the Far-west area was known (reputedly as far back as 2,800 BC!) as the 'heartland', in contrast to Central Tibet, which was known as the 'outlying' area, and the regions of Kham and Amdo, which were termed the 'gateway' lands. However Tibet was not a unified country at that time – the vast distances and geography being more conducive to the development of independent semi-feudal states.

Khyunglung Ngulkhar: the capital of Zhangzhung

Getting there
Colour map 1, grid B2
From **Montser** township on the main Senge Tsangpo-Darchen road, take the trail which cuts south for 8 kilometres to the **Tirthapuri** hot springs (see above, page 349) on the banks of the Sutlej. An alternative trekking route from **Jiu Gonpa** on the shore of Lake Manasarovar follows the Sutlej downstream from its source near Lake Raksas Tal for 79 kilometres via Gyanyima Dzong to reach Tirthapuri.

The road cuts westward from here, at first passing through a broad agricultural valley dotted with single family compounds. Camp at the Bonpo monastery of **Gurugyam** (see above, page 335), about 15 kilometres from Montser at the western limit of the valley. Thereafter the trail follows the Sutlej downstream into Tsamda county. Continue on this trail, via the Gerikyung camping ground, to **Khyunglung**.

Tsamda County

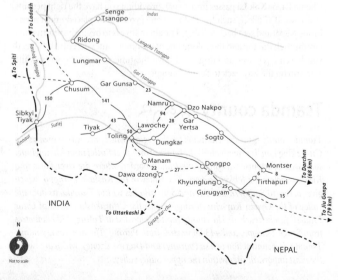

NB Since you must cross two passes above the steep cliffs on the north bank of the Sutlej and then descend back down to the river before fording its waters to the south bank, it is preferable to arrange the hire of horses and yaks before setting off from Gurugyam. Ensure that your local guide is allowed to cross this county border (since some local Tibetans may not be able to do so without first obtaining a special permit).

The ruins of Tibet's earliest inhabited city are located on the northern bank of **Khyunglung** the Sutlej at the western end of the Khyunglung valley, approximately 25 kilometres southwest of Tirthapuri. First noted by Prof Tucci in 1932 as a "troglydite settlement", it is a vast cave city sprawling over lesser valleys and canyons which, at its peak must have held a population of 2,000-3,000 people. In 1988, on the basis of recently discovered chronicles, Prof Namkei Norbu confirmed this as the location where the earliest kings of Zhangzhung such as Limichar had established their dynasty in antiquity.

On reaching the entrance of this valley, you will pass the small village of Khyunglung after approximately five kilometres, and from there it is another two kilometres to the western end of the valley, where you can camp near an outcrop of white limestone facing the broad complex of caves on the far bank of the river. A suspension bridge below the white limestone traverses the Sutlej at its narrowest point and leads left to the cave city. To the right another pathway leads towards a hot springs and a series of white and blue lime terraces.

The cave city itself extends one kilometre along a red cliff. The centre of the complex is reached via a valley at the western end of the city. This leads up past myriad cave dwellings cut into the conical formations of the red sandstone aggregate, to reach the ruins of the actual **Ngulkhar**, or the 'Silver Castle' of the kings. Here the multi-storeyed rooms are finely hewn from the earth, and there is evidence of outer wooden structures that would have made them very imposing. Below the king's residence, the city consists of pathways and tunnels winding past walls and cave habitations that cover every serviceable slope.

There is little evidence of anything related to Buddhism or even to the Bon tradition so that one has the sense of walking amidst the ruins of one of the world's oldest cultures.

Dawadzong མདའ་བ་རྫོང

From Khyunglung the trail continues on the south side of the Sutlej at some dis- *Colour map 1, grid B1* tance from the river, reaching the Gelukpa monastery of **Dongpo Gon** after 53 kilometres (three days). Dongpo Gon was once a large monastery, its foundation being attributed to Khewang Jamyang Shinti, but presently there are very few monks here. **Dawadzong** lies 27 kilometres further west on the Dawa-chu tributary. Here there is a fabled landscape of natural pyramid formations. The ridge-top Gelukpa monastery known as **Dawa Gon**, the foundation of which is also attributed to Khewang Jamyang Shinti, comprises an assembly hall, a Maitreya Temple (Jamkhang) and a Labrang. For a vivid description of this area, see Lama Govinda's account in *The Way of the White Clouds*.

Manam Tsangpo Valley

The trail continues from Dawadzong in the direction of the county capital, *Colour map 1, grid B1* crossing the **Manam Tsangpo** River after 22 kilometres. Here at **Manam Gonpa**, there is an enormous complex of ruins dating back to the period of Lha Lama Jangchub-o, which even now holds untold precious works of art, buried beneath the rubble. A further trek of 21 kilometres will bring you to Toling, capital of Tsamda county, on the left bank of the Sutlej.

Toling ᠉ᠲ᠋ᠪᠠᢅᠨᠵᡏᢉᠵᢉᠣᡵᢉᢥᡵ

Colour map 1, grid B1 *The county capital of Tsamda, known as **Toling** or Toding, may be reached by two motorable routes which turn south off the Senge Tsangpo-Darchen road to cross the watershed leading into the Sutlej valley.*

Getting there One turns off the main highway at **Namru**, 23 kilometres southeast of Gar Gunsa (see above, page 333), and the second at **Dzo Nakpo**, a few kilometres further south, where the Bauer Army Camp is also located. The latter road passes through **Dungkar** where spectacular caves have recently been discovered (see below, page 366). Taking the former, you will cross two passes, reaching the crossroads of **Lawoche** after 94 kilometres. Here there are three possible routes: one driving northwest via **Chusum** (141 kilometres) to **Sibkyi Tiyak** on the Kinnaur frontier (150 kilometres); a second leading west to **Jangtse** and **Tiyak** townships (48 kilometres); and a third heading southeast for 50 kilometres to **Toling** in the Sutlej valley.

Taking the last of these roads, you will soon see far down below in the valley floor the capital of the ancient kingdom of Gu-ge. From various vantage points on the descent into Toling, there are some of the most spectacular views in Tibet. The vast sweep of the Himalayas is discernible, as the range turns northwest from Nepal and along the Indian border as far as Ladakh and Kashmir, spanning several hundred kilometres. One of the marvels of this vista is the awareness that one is apparently looking down on the Himalayas. It gives one the real sense of Tibet as the roof of the world. If you are driving from Senge Tsangpo, you must leave early because it will take a full day to reach Toling.

Sleeping The *Tsamda Hotel* is about 500 metres down the only street on the left.

The Temples of Toling

History The temples and religious buildings of **Toling** are the most significant in Far-west Tibet. They were constructed under the guidance of the great Tibetan translator **Rinchen Zangpo** (985-1055), around 1014-25, although some sources suggest an earlier date (996). During his lifetime he is said to have built 108 temples throughout Far-west Tibet and Ladakh, and although few still exist, those at Toling and Tsaparang are considered to be the finest repositories of the **Gu-ge style** of Buddhist art. Even though the city was subsequently replaced as a political centre of power by the citadel of Tsaparang, where the later kings of Gu-ge established their capital, slightly closer to the Indo-Tibetan trade routes, the importance of the Toling temples for the cultural heritage of Ngari remained unsurpassed.

It was primarily due to the influence of Rinchen Zangpo that Toling had become the main religious centre of the Gu-ge kingdom prior to the visit of the great Indian master **Atisha** (982-1054) in 1042. The great translator was himself the monastic preceptor of Toling at the time of Atisha's arrival. Yet, without the support of the King of Gu-ge, **Yeshe-o**, the impact of these two great masters on Tibetan Buddhism would have been far less significant. The king, a devout patron of Rinchen Zangpo's activities, sacrificed everything over several years, culminating in his own life, to invite the illustrious and peerless 11th century pandita Atisha to Tibet. After refusing several requests made by those Tibetan translators and scholars studying at Vikramashila and Odantapuri monasteries in North India, Atisha finally agreed to travel when he heard of the death of the king. Yeshe-o had been captured by invading troops from a neighbouring tribe who demanded ransom. When his nephew Jangchub-o came to see him the king responded by saying, "I am an old man. My life now is short. Use the ransom to invite and assist Atisha to come to Tibet". Consequently, when Atisha arrived in Gu-ge he was amazed to see Buddhism flourishing.

He also must have been impressed with the architectural style of the Toling temples which were based upon the Kashmiri style and the Pala/Sena style of Bengal, his homeland in Northeast India. An effort had also been made to incorporate Indian elements found in Samye, Tibet's first monastery. The interiors were solidly embellished with paintings in the contemporary Indian and Nepalese styles, following formal conventions that within a few centuries were to be obliterated by the Muslim invasions of India. This artistic tradition that has come to be known as the Gu-ge style provides a unique link to the Buddhist art of North India that today can only be found in a few other temples exemplary of Rinchen Zangpo's work in Ladakh (at **Alchi**) and Spiti (at **Tabo**) during the early 11th century.

The Toling complex originally comprised six major buildings. The entrance **The site** was from the east where today is a run-down concrete town hall. Clockwise from here within the compound were the **Neten Temple** containing images of the 16 Elders; the **Mani Dungchyur Lhakhang**; the **Assembly Hall (Dukhang)**, still intact and commonly known as the Red Temple due to the colour of its outside walls; the **Mandala Chapel of Yeshe-o** (Kyilkhor Lhakhang or Gyatsa Lhakhang), which has sometimes confusingly been called the Golden Temple, at the west end of the compound (today only its walls remain); the **Lhakhang Karpo** (White Temple), which is still intact although vacant; and the **Serkhang**, the actual Golden Temple (a three storied temple, now destroyed, which formerly had exquisite images and murals depicting the assembled deities of the Kriyatantras and the Unsurpassed Yogatantras).

NB It is absolutely essential to bring with you a strong flashlight in order to see the paintings clearly.

This is the largest temple at Toling and would have been used by the monastic **The Dukhang** assembly for gatherings, discourses and collective ritual practices. Formerly it (Assembly Hall or had some 36 pillars, and its foremost images depicted the Buddhas of the Red Temple) Three Times in gilded copper. Distinguished by its red-washed outer walls, inside it contains the largest and earliest display of Indian and Gu-ge painting at Toling (c 13th-14th century, though some scholars cite 15th-16th century). The highly organic form of the decorative embellishments such as the flora which entwine each of the figures shows the overriding influence to be Indian/Kashmiri with a hint of Nepalese style. The artists must still have held the principles transmitted to them from the Kashmiri masters brought into Tibet by Rinchen Zangpo a century or two earlier.

Along the left-hand wall are floor-to-ceiling rows of deities entwined in wreath-like borders interweaving each into a whole organic complex across the entire space. Nearly all the deities are peaceful in form and many are in blissful union with their consorts (symbolizing the integration of skilful means and emptiness). These paintings were heavily coated with mud and dust on account of the temple's neglect, but they have now been partially cleaned.

The rear wall (west) held the main shrines and altars beneath a large statue of the Buddha (added long after the original construction). Within the inner pilgrim's walkway (*korlam*), which passes along the left, back and right sides of the altar, there is a series of paintings depicting the life of the Buddha. Nearly all are miniatures which include amusing details of rural and domestic life that reflect

Mandala Chapel of King Yeshe-O

The most impressive building at Toling is at the western focal point of the entire complex. The walled remains of King Yeshe-o's Mandala Chapel are unlike any seen elsewhere in Tibet. Superficially it resembles many other ruins from the Cultural Revolution and although there is an entrance from the east, the central shrine itself is given access through a gap in the southeast inner wall. One enters a square hall with secondary chapels opening off from the middle of each wall. Around the mud-streaked walls of the central and secondary shrines are aureoles in relief, spaced equally about 2m apart above metre-high pedestals which once must have supported life-size images of deities. At first there appears to be no main shrine, that is until one begins to imagine the object to which all these figures face, and one's gaze moves from the vivid blue sky above the walls to the mounds of earth and mud on the ground below. There in the rubble it is just possible to make out the shape of a broad lotus with a pedestal at its heart situated in the centre of the inner shrine.

At this point, one is, in fact, standing in the midst of the central sphere of a life-sized 3-dimensional mandala, which in most circumstances would only be represented in two dimensions on a mural or scroll painting. A large statue of the main tantric deity would have been on the lotus pedestal, facing east, embellished with gold, precious jewels, ornaments and robes, probably surrounded by four or eight secondary figures on the petals of the lotus. Initiates and devotees would have been led into this inner sanctum in a state of reverence and wonder, awed by the beauty, balance and harmony of this extraordinary display which would have been illuminated by soft light cascading from the windows in the bell-tower directly above the central deity. The figures on the surrounding walls would have been gilded and painted and the walls themselves no doubt embellished with buddhas, bodhisattvas and tantric deities along similar lines to those in the Dukhang (Red Temple) or the White Temple at Tsaparang (see below page 362). The mandala itself was most likely that of Vajradhatu or Vairocana, the main tantra practised by Rinchen Zangpo and one which encompasses and synthesizes many of the other Yogatantras.

The central hall is encircled by a series of shrines and chapels (similar to those in the Jokhang in Lhasa), facing inwards and today mainly filled with dirt and rubble through which here and there protrude

the individuality of the painter. The colours are still vivid and the expressions specific to each figure depicted in the paintings. Also included are stories from the early kings of Gu-ge and the development of Buddhism in Tibet.

The right (north) wall of the temple was once similar to its opposite wall but has been seriously ruined. A basic shrine now provides the focus for the temple with a few images and framed photos on it. In the early 1980s this was full of extremely precious images that had been donated during the period of 'relaxation'. It also then held over a dozen other statues and sacred images that had been released from storage by the authorities for reconsecration and worship. In the early 1990s it is alleged that a gang of art thieves based in Kathmandu stole everything, having sent photos around the world to determine the highest bidder. For this reason, the Tibetan people may object strongly to the photography of such objects today.

Lhakhang Karpo (The White Temple) Nearly opposite the red walled Assembly Hall there is an unimpressive, squat portico leading into what appears to be a shabby windowless block. Normally closed it is necessary to rouse the caretaker in the Red Temple or at his farm-house 100 metres south. This portico although painted is wooden, torsos and remnants of what once were objects of profound faith and devotion. In the centre of the west wall of this hall is a tall shrine that once held a 5m standing figure of Avalokiteshvara. There then follow a series of rooms which now contain the relief remains of two-dimensional mandalas.

According to literary sources, the central chapel was dedicated to Vairocana (Namnang Lhakhang), and it was surrounded by 18 other chapels, the names and foremost images of which are as follows (clockwise sequence): 1) Dudul Lhakhang (immediately in front, Shakyamuni Buddha); 2) Jikje Lhakhang (Vajrabhairava); 3) Atsara Lhakhang; 4) Tashi-o Lhakhang (Shakyamuni); 5) Menla Lhakhang (Eight Medicine Buddhas); 6) Tu-je Lhakhang (Eleven-faced Avalokiteshvara); 7) Dolma Lhakhang (White Tara); 8) Gyelma Riknga (Buddhas of the Five Families); 9) Sungma Lhakhang (Vajrabhairava, Dharmaraja and so forth); 10) Jampa Kerzheng Lhakhang (Maitreya); 11) Chakdor Lhakhang (Vajrapani); 12) Yum Lhakhang (Green Tara); 13) Jampa Ngalso Lhakhang (Maitreya); 14) Je Lhakhang (Tsongkhapa and students; obviously later installed!); 15) Tsepame Lhakhang (Amitayus); 16) Kangyur Lhakhang; 17) Tangyur Lhakhang; and 18) Jamyang Lhakhang (Manjughosa).

Towering above each of the four corners of the temple complex are the only stupas of the Indian prasada style in existence. They are also uncommon in being made up of terracotta units since most Tibetan stupas are made from mud and stone. Within each are chambers that contain pages from Buddhist manuscripts and hundreds of thousands of small, palm pressed votive images known as **Tsa-tsa**. Despite being only around 10 cm in size, the attention to detail is remarkable, including not only a perfect figure of the deity but a depiction of the appropriate mantra or tiny stupas in the background. Such objects are added to the `core' of any large stupa in order to enhance its sanctity and power.

These Tsa-tsa can also be found spilling out from the broken shell of many of the stupas that stand in rows of 108 outside the Toling complex on land adjacent to the cliffs above the Sutlej river. Sadly in the last few years even these have begun to be destroyed, or given an enhanced help in their collapse by local people wishing to gain more land.

Far-west Tibet

framed by two stout, short pillars and probably 500 years old. It opens into a long rectangular temple with a pebble stone floor and lines of 42 thin pillars supporting a multipanelled, multidecorated ceiling culminating in a large, one-eyed Buddha statue (the other eye having been broken).

Along the left and right walls are respectively a series of the main male and female bodhisattva deities. Over three metres high, each is seated within a framework which reflects specific attributes and qualities, whether these are presented within a formal aureole, a palace, or a representation of mountains and forests in a natural landscape. Arrayed along the left (west) wall is a pantheon of the male deities, and along the opposite wall are the female deities. Unfortunately most murals of the male deities have been seriously affected by water seepage which has caused streaking, pigment destruction and complete erosion of the figures. Those that remain however, such as Avalokiteshvara, Vajradhara, Vajrasattva, Vajrapani and Manjughosa are sublime examples of the Gu-ge art form.

Of greater value still is the intact wall depicting the female deities: they begin near the door with a depiction of the life of the Buddha above a graphic presentation of life in the world and, with the surface peeled back, in the underworld, bringing to mind images from Heironymous Bosch. The line of female deities includes Vijaya, ensurer of long life, wrathful White Tara an opponent to life's inner dangers; Bhuvatrayacalanatara, 'earth mother' and protector from dangers in forest, jungles and wild lands, Sarasvati the muse of music and poetry, Red Tara the protector over earthquakes and natural disasters, Mahaprajnaparamita the 'Great Mother' of discriminative awareness, bestower of intelligence and knowledge, and Green Tara the compassionate bestower of protection out of good actions.

Created in the 16th century they depict the major pantheon of peaceful and semi-wrathful deities that are central to the renaissance of Buddhism in Tibet as expressed by the Drigung Kargyu tradition (whose founder and disciples feature at the end of the line of female deities) and the Gelukpa (whose verses of praise to "*The Foundation of Good Qualities*" (*Yon-ten Shi-gyur-ma*) by its founder Tsongkhapa are inscribed below the entire freeze). Prior to the Chinese invasion Toling had 400 Gelukpa monks, most of whom later found sanctuary in India.

Hermitages above Toling Along the cliff walls of the canyons above Toling one can see the caves and now crumbling walls of what once were retreat quarters for the monks. These can be reached by road by turning left of the main route to Toling and climbing into the canyons. Once on top an entire new complex opens out, for along each ridge to the south is a series of temples and caves hardly seen by foreign eyes. Once they were reached by climbing through man-made tunnels and staircases cut into the cliff face. Paths zigzagged up to the top from where one was also afforded a vast panoramic view of the upper Sutlej valley. It may still be possible to reach the peak directly above Toling provided that one carries a shovel for cutting stairs and a rope for safety.

Routes to Uttarakashi and Chamoli

In addition to the two motorable routes into Toling from the Senge Tsangpo-Darchen road, the county capital can also be approached by trekking from Tirthapuri and Dawadzong (see above, page 334 and page 355). Another jeepable road leads out of town to the west, passing through Tsaparang (26 kilometres) and Puling (56 kilometres). From Puling there are trekking routes to **Uttarakashi** in North India via Tajak La pass, and to **Chamoli** via Dronyi La pass.

Tsaparang

History
Colour map 1, grid B1
The founding of the Gu-ge kingdom in the ninth century evolved as a result of the collapse of the Yarlung Dynasty under the anti-Buddhist ruler Langdarma. After his assassination, one of his sons, Namde Osung, who had fled to Far-west Tibet, founded the Gu-ge kingdom. Before he died he assigned rule over the three provinces of Far-west Tibet, or Ngari, comprising **Gu-ge**, **Purang** and **Ladakh/Rutok** to his three sons in the hope of binding the realm together. Later in the 10th and early 11th century the religious king Yeshe-o sponsored the great translator Rinchen Zangpo, who had built over 100 temples throughout Far-west Tibet, to construct temples at Tsaparang and Toling. These are generally regarded as the most sublime of his work. After the Indian master Atisha came to Gu-ge, Buddhism was further revitalized and the kingdom flourished.

However, in 1624 the first European to reach Tibet, a Portuguese Jesuit based in Goa named Antonio del Andrade, arrived at Tsaparang. At this time the kingdom had less than 50 years to endure before its total collapse. It is often said that because the king favoured Andrade and allowed him to build a church jealousies arose on the part of the Buddhist lamas and officials who entered into a conspiracy with the ruler of Ladakh to bring about the kingdom's untimely end. However, according to local historical knowledge, the downfall of the kingdom of Gu-ge is far more dramatic. Why the city was never reinhabited has always remained something of a mystery.

Apparently relationships between the rulers of the three kingdoms gradually deteriorated over the centuries. This was especially true in the case of the kings of Ladakh/Rutok. Battles had been fought between these rulers from the north and their cousins in the south at both Gu-ge and Purang. Over 40 years after the Jesuit was recalled to India in 1685 a youthful king in his early twenties was forced to confront armies from the north. Deeply loved by his subjects his own forces were able to repel the aggressors repeatedly. It became clear to the king of Ladakh that he could only succeed with help from outside forces. Thus the supposedly Buddhist king of Ladakh paid for the assistance of Muslim tribal mercenaries.

With this additional strength his army soon laid seige to the city, encircling the population of several thousand in Tsaparang town around the base of the citadel. With their army decimated the people had no protection. The Ladakhi ruler then threatened to slaughter 50 people a day until the young king capitulated. From the heights of the royal citadel, impregnable and secure with its own secret water source, the King volunteered to renounce his position and depart from the realm saying that he would devote himself to the anonymity of a monastic life. He promised never to lay claim to the throne in the future on the condition that his subjects be spared their lives and that his queen and family, along with the ministers of court be guaranteed free and safe passage out of the land. To the relief of the people of Tsaparang the invaders agreed to these conditions.

The young king, his queen and their children as well as the ministers and commanders of the army descended from the heights of the citadel, bypassing a huge seige tower that was being built up the side of the 170 metres high cliffs. They presented themselves to the invaders and were all immediately bound and taken prisoner. The young king and his family were slaughtered immediately in full view of the population. Members of the court, ministers and generals were led down the hillside where they were all beheaded, their bodies tossed into the ravine below. The heads were then impaled upon spears and poles, forming a circle around the entire town. In this way a Muslim army repeated its ruthless techniques of war, ensuring that the 'infidels' immediately departed and never returned. A tragic testimony to this episode still exists in a secret cave where the headless torsos of the ministers were laid to rest over 300 years ago.

From the 1680s until the first half of the 20th century, Tsaparang was a ruin intact in time, virtually untouched by human forces except for the removing of the valuable timbers for new accommodation. Its major temples such as the **White**, **Red**, **Vajrabhairava** and **Demchok** temples, were intact when Prof Tucci visited in 1932 and still later when Lama Govinda and Li Gotami documented them in 1948-49. However the ravages of the Cultural Revolution swept through in the 1960s and wrecked the finely detailed surroundings of the statues, broke open their hearts and reduced the main figures to rubble. It was as though the apparent physicality of the statues presented a greater threat to the new, abstract ideology of communism for the masses than plain two-dimensional murals. Today the ruins of Tsaparang, because they were already vacant when the Chinese invaded and thus were only lightly affected by the Cultural Revolution, are one of the finest examples of early historical ruins

Far-west Tibet

in Tibet, and now deemed part of the 'great artistic and historical treasures of ancient China'.

Citadel of Tsaparang To reach **Tsaparang**, 26 kilometres west from Toling, it is best to leave before sunrise. Exploring this vast ruin takes all day. In the lower reaches of the city there are four main temples. One of these dates back nearly 1,000 years. The wall paintings and statues display some of the earliest examples of Tantric Buddhist art in existence. High above these temples is the citadel of the kings. One must climb up through a secret tunnel cut into the interior of the hillside to reach the top of this natural fortress, which was the residence of the later kings of Gu-ge. All that now remains intact is a small temple known as the **Demchok Mandala**. It has exquisite tantric murals inside.

The entire complex is located around a spur in the canyons south of the Sutlej. Like Khyunglung further east and upstream, Tsaparang lies on one of the main trade routes linking India and Kashmir in the west with Central Tibet in the east or the Silk Road in the north. At its height Tsaparang was a bustling city and home to perhaps several thousand people, giving rest and support to caravans of traders, as well as a refuge and religious knowledge to members of the monastic community. The diversity of the population is vividly depicted in murals of the construction and consecration of the Red Temple.

Lhakhang Karpo (The White Temple) After passing through the newly-built gate at the base of the city's slopes the bulk of the **Lhakhang Karpo** looms immediately to the right. To the left is the small shrine dedicated to Shakyamuni Buddha. Bypassing this, a few steps higher one will reach a porch in front of the entrance to this temple.

One enters, stepping down the dusty floor of a high ceilinged hall, diffused with a soft white light that lingers on the particles of dust, covering the room with a silvery glow. The silence is total and yet it feels as though one is being watched. One begins to explore the corners of gloom and just as one turns around one's gaze is met by a ferocious set of eyes above a snarling mouth and fangs. Over three metres high it is joined by another so that either side of the doorway is protected. These would have been forms of Hayagriva and Acala.

Now as your eyes adjust you can begin to make out the extraordinary contents of this temple. Around the walls were once larger than lifesize statues of the Buddhas of the Five Families. Each was seated upon a one metre high pedestal that is individually appropriate to each deity. All once were framed in elaborate terracotta aureoles that were easily broken in the 1960s. The finest record we have is the photographic archive of Li Gotama and Lama Govinda, dated 1948-9.

On the background walls there is a series of painted panels stretching from floor to ceiling. Each is unique in its content and proportions. Some are merit-gaining repetitive images of hundreds or thousands of buddhas; others consist of a series of vignettes depicting the lives of the tantric masters, including one or two incomplete panels that reveal the means by which they were made; yet others include detailed large images of Thousand-armed Avalokiteshvara and other deities.

The main feature of the statues (and paintings) is that they are executed in a highly distinctive style found nowhere else in Tibet. The work certainly appears to have been influenced by India, if not actually supervised by Indian master artists from Kashmir or Bengal. The torsos are elongated, the robing of the figures is loose, the ornamentation and crowns are unlike the later form of deities in Tibetan art; and perhaps most of all, the rendering of the background wall design is flexible and varied within the confines of its purpose, to an extent that is paralleled only in the temples at **Alchi**, Ladakh, in a slightly more rigid form.

Sadly all the three-dimensional figures, in addition to the destroyed aureoles, have been broken in one way or another. Usually each had its heart ripped open, revealing little more than the sacred prayers of consecration and the life-pole which rises through the centre of the figure giving it strength and symbolic life. Most also had their arms and hands which were once displaying mudras, broken or torn off. Despite this destruction the statues retained a kind of dignity which today has been ruined by the botched attempt at restoration. Mud has been slapped into the cavities and smeared over the facial gashes without any skill such that now, with the addition of gold enamel paint, many of the figures appear to be afflicted by some disease.

The ceiling of the temple is composed of panels painted with individual decorative motifs, which are generally illustrative of Gu-ge art. At the altar end of the temple which once held a large statue of the Buddha there is a magnificent wooden skylight. Fashioned of painted beams forming a hollow square, it gradually reduces in size at 45 degree turns, making a small tower which allows a shaft of light to enter and illuminate the shrine. On its side walls the chapel has pedestals upon which still sit figures in armour. These are likely to be some of the religious kings of Gu-ge and Yarlung. Painted on the lower walls are episodes from the life of the Buddha.

NB   Photography inside the temples is forbidden and you are likely to be shadowed by a zealous Tibetan guide. Don't be surprised and do complain about this restriction if you wish to.

Directly above the White Temple, up some steep steps is the **Lhakhang Marpo** (Red Temple). The doors are original, possibly dating from the 13th century. They were either carved in Kashmir or under the guidance of Kashmiri artisans in Tsaparang. Each has three panels containing the Sanskrit seed syllables of the mantra of great compassion OM MA-NI PAD-ME HUM. The door frame has weather-beaten figures of kings and bodhisattvas. The only other comparable doorway is found in the inner sanctum of the Jokhang in Lhasa.

The doors open onto a tall hallway filled with piles of rubble in its centre merging with a broken stupa to the right. The back wall where the central shrine once stood is vacant except for the upper decorative tendriles that held offering gods and goddesses surrounding the three metres high central figure of Amitabha. To either side of the altar the rear walls of deep blue hue have deities seated on lotus platforms. A few of the figures still remain. They comprise some of the Thirty-five Confession Buddhas. The rubble in the centre of the room once was a throne supporting an image of Shakyamuni Buddha and was probably added some time after the completion of the temple. The stupa to the right was also a later addition and appears to be in the Kadam-style associated with Atisha.

The most outstanding feature of the Red Temple is the series of murals which rise from 0.6 metres above the floor to the ceiling. They are comprised of two levels. The lower 0.6 metres consists of a frieze while the remaining upper area contains a series of images which, together with their thrones and the surrounding aureoles, are approximately four metres high. Both the frieze and the deities are rendered in the highly decorative form of the Gu-ge style, covered in a high gloss varnish that perhaps has helped preserve their deep, rich colours.

The **frieze**, commencing on the north wall to the right of the altar, depicts episodes from the life story of the Buddha. Each story is contained in a panel of flat colour. The temptation of the demons and the Buddha's enlightenment are two of the most outstanding. Copies made by Lama Govinda are supposed to exist in the Prince of Wales Museum, Bombay. On the rear wall (east) there is a

Lhakhang
Marpo
(The Red
Temple)

Far-west Tibet

set of the eight stupas symbolizing the major acts of the Buddha. These are followed by the emblems of a universal emperor as encorporated in the mandala offering of the material world. On the right side of the door is a remarkable depiction of the construction of the Red Temple, and the dignitaries attending its inaugural consecration. Animals and humans are shown carrying wood and building materials; musicians and dancers celebrate the festivities; dignitaries from both Tibet and foreign lands dressed in their respective costumes are seated in ranks; ministers, generals, relatives and close family members sit in line before the king, who is flanked by his queens, princesses and princes; all turning in devotion to the radiant central image of Amitabha to whom the temple is dedicated. Amitabha himself is flanked on the far side by rows of monks, teachers and illustrious monastic preceptors.

The magnificent paintings above the frieze on the side walls are the Buddhas of the Five Families and the Medicine Buddhas. On the rear wall are the commonly known figures of Padmasambhava, Avalokiteshvara, Green Tara and a protector flanking either side of the doorway. To the right of the door are Manjughosa, White Tara, and Vijaya. All are seated on individually elaborate thrones and literally melting into the swirling decorative elements characteristic of the Gu-ge style.

Dorje Jigje Lhakhang (Vajrabhairava Temple) Just a few metres in front of the Red Temple's courtyard is a small protector chapel known as the Vajrabhairava shrine. This, together with the **Neten Lhakhang** below it, was created at a later date than either the White or Red temples. Both are distinctly decorated in accord with the pantheon of the Gelukpa tradition. On the altar, now vacant, once stood a large wrathful image of Yamantaka, the bull-headed tantric emanation of Manjughosa. This is most likely the deity that Lama Govinda saw from the skylight in 1948, the photo appearing in *The Way of the White Clouds*.

On the walls of the shrine are images of deities from the *Unsurpassed Yogatantras*, such as Cakrasamvara, Hevajra, Guhyasamaja; Green Tara and the protectors near the door: Mahakala, Shridevi, Dharmaraja, and so forth. The figures on the walls to the side of the altar are of Tsongkhapa and Atisha along with their closest disciples. All are interspersed with miniature paintings of the mahasiddhas and lineage masters. The extraordinary feature of this entire room is that all the paintings are reduced to a range of colours limited to black, red and pure gold. Every figure has been covered in gold leaf and the ornaments embossed in relief. Moreover the crowns and rendition of the jewels is strikingly real in the style peculiar to Gu-ge. The overall effect is one of light and richness despite the fact that the paintings are heavily covered with centuries of candle soot and dust. This combination of gold and grime is like the radiance of a jewel penetrating the gloom of fog at dusk.

Regent's Shrine This, the smallest shrine, is to the left of the main entrance to Tsaparang. Built around the late 16th century it was the private chapel of the Regent of Tsaparang, attached to his winter residence. It too follows the style of the Vajrabhairava Temple with the figures gilded and the remaining colours limited to black and red. Most of the paintings are heaviily coated in black soot from smoke and may even have been scorched by fire. It has no altar as such but the rear wall features a central image of the Buddha seated with his right hand in the gesture of calling the earth as a witness to his past merits (*bhumisparshamudra*). His main disciples, Sariputra and Maudgalyayana stand on the throne with him. On either side are two important masters of the *Lam-rim* teachings: Tsongkhapa, on the left and Atisha, on the right. These murals are seriously ruined and stylistically flat, lifeless and uninspiring.

The jail The lower slopes of Tsaparang are covered with pathways, staircases,
tall mud walls and caves cut into the soft sandstone. Some of the caves were
small shrines and still have paintings and charcoal drawings of the Buddha and
other figures. Some are repositories for **tsatsa** votive images. About half way up
the lower slope is a huge cave cut into the heart of the hillside which curves
down for at least 15-20 metres like a large well. Surprisingly it was used as a jail
or detention pit for men. Another for women was also excavated.

    The siege wall Near the top of the slope is a strange windowless structure
of dressed granite, the only one of its kind. Between three to five metres high it
is rectangular, about 15 metres wide and sited at the base of the cliff to the citadel. This was the base of a huge seige tower built by the invading Muslim army
who destroyed the kingdom on behalf of the King of Ladakh at the beginning
of the 18th century. It seems improbable that the tower would have reached a
height of over 150 metres, but perhaps it helped convince the king safe in the
citadel to give himself up to the invaders.

Above the siege tower there are a number of caves and tunnels. The one on the
extreme right is the entrance to a staircase that twists and turns upwards through
the interior of the citadel. The way is lit every now and then by shafts of light or
windows offering a view from the top of a sheer cliff down to a dry river valley.
The height of the citadel is 170 metres from the top of the slope. The exit opens
out onto a complex of collapsing walls and pathways that covers the top from
edge to edge. Along the western edge runs a pathway protected by a low wall.

    At the far end (south) the ridge narrows and becomes totally impassable.
Here the cliff has caved in; for once there was a narrow road that allowed horses
access to the top. The first structure to the south is a large open corral with
attached stables. Next to it is a deep well which provided water along an
aquaduct through a tunnel to the south. Walking back to the entrance one
passes the high walls of what once was an assembly hall before reaching the
only intact building, a square red walled temple known as the **Demchok Mandala**. Directly beneath this is a cave with dusty murals of wrathful deities. The
lower torso of a statue remains. This was a shrine of the protector Mahakala.

Built as late as the 16th century this small shrine was probably created under
the personal instructions of the king and his spiritual mentor. The walls are
covered from floor to ceiling in a precise arrangement of deities, corresponding to the mandalas of the *Unsurpassed Yogatantras*. Each of the roof panels
has one of the peaceful symbols of the Buddhist doctrine, such as the wheel, the
lotus, the three jewels, the eternal knot, the vajra, and so on.

    The temple takes its name from a miniature three-dimensional mandala
that once stood in the now vacant space in the centre of the room. It was dedicated to Cakrasamvara, considered by Buddhists to reside at Mount Kailash. It
once held 32 miniature figures of the peripheral deities and was about 2.5
metres in diameter. All that remains now are some of the outer walls and the
lotus petal floor of the mandala. It was partially intact when Govinda saw it in
1948 and it is widely believed that Prof Tucci removed most of the figurines of
deities and dakinis in 1932.

    The bands of figures on the walls begin at the base with a frieze depicting
the charnel grounds where Indian yogins would meditate on death and confront ghosts or spirits. These places of terrifying events are vividly rendered,
replete with corpses, beasts, demons, yogins, birds of prey, and atmospheric
jungle. Traditionally there were eight great cemeteries in India. Above these is
a frieze depicting the dakinis, the messengers of buddha-activity, embodying
emptiness. Next is the broad band of tantric deities.

Each wall has five main figures, representing the central figure of the mandala and those of the four cardinal directions. On the left (south) wall are the aspects of Cakrasamvara himself, on the rear (west) wall the forms of Guhyasamaja, on the right (north) side are the aspects of Hevajra, and on the rear walls on either side of the door the protector Mahakala as well as labelled images of the king, his retainers, and contemporary masters. Above the main deities, there is a long frieze depicting the mahasiddhas and important lamas from the Tibetan lineages.

The rendering of these deities is superb in its refinement of the torsos, the power and dynamism of the wrathful figures (Cakrasamvara and Hevajra) and the sublime gentility of the peaceful figures (Guhyasamaja). The ornaments and decorative elements in the fabric are as fine as the designs of a master jeweller. The pigments of the colours are still fresh and are not overwhelmed by an excess of gilding. Overall the content of this small temple amply rewards one for undertaking the rigours of the journey.

Outside the Demchok Mandala and adjacent to it is a newly built rest room where beer and soft drinks are served!

Winter Palace   Along the path toward the north end of the citadel is the entrance to the King's **Winter Palace**. This comprises a series of seven rooms branching off a central hallway dug from the very heart of the mountain approximately 12 metres below the surface. Access is down a nearly vertical tunnel with aid of an iron railing for support. The warmth of the earth sheltered the king and his retinue from the bitter cold of winter. Secret tunnels led to a water supply and could be used to make an escape in the event of danger. Windows are cut through the outside wall, providing light to the interior and a breathtaking view to the valley below.

From the northernmost ramparts one has a vertigo-inducing view down the cliff face to the complex of buildings and temples spread around the lower slopes. Stupas stand on the spurs of ridges and across the small stream to the east is another large stupa in an Indian style, as at Toling. The Sutlej valley's gorge cuts the broad vista from east to west and far in the distance under the bleached blue midday sky are the snow dusted peaks of the Gangtise Range.

Dungkar and Piyang

Colour map 1, grid B1   In 1992-93 a series of painted caves was discovered further east up the Sutlej from Toling at the small village of **Dungkar** and some six kilometres away amidst the ruins of **Piyang**.

Getting there   To reach Dungkar you must drive back out of Toling, follow the canyon north until the fork in the road. Take the branch leading east to **Dzo Nakpo** on the Senge Tsangpo-Darchen road (see above, page 356). After approximately 20 kilometres, turn off down a poorly marked side-road, heading south. After 8 kilometres the valley opens out into green pastures alongside a small village. You will have to find the caretaker to the caves. A surly character, he will lead you 2 kilometres down the valley and then up to caves at the base of a cliff. He will probably ask for ¥20-50 to open the doors to two of them.

Dungkar   Inside are possibly the earliest murals in Far-west Tibet, on walls carved in the form of a mandala interior. The shelves cut into the rear wall are altars which once held stucco statues of the Buddha and still have one or two images on them. Others are mingled with rubble on the floor.

The first feature that strike one is the similarity of the paintings with those of

TSAMDA COUNTY **367**

the early art at the caves of **Dunhuang** at the eastern edge of the Silk Route. In the first cave are large mandalas as well as repeated rows of Buddhas, whereas the second is almost totally covered in small Buddha figures. The figures have elongated torsos and sit on semi-spherical lotuses like those in the Dunhuang mandalas. The most distinctive feature is the manner in which the spaces surrounding the mandalas are encorporated. Instead of the precise decorative patterns of the Gu-ge style there are hosts of flying *apsara*, or offering goddesses. Their diaphonous gowns waft around them in soft breezes in a similar way to 10th century figures at Dunhuang. Even the colour of the murals is similar – a light blue overall, featuring pastel colours. Perhaps these works were created by Indian painters on their way to the cities of the Silk Route 1,000 years ago.

Other caves nearby which have not been locked up also contain paintings although seriously damaged by age and weathering. A small Gelukpa monastery was established alongside the caves at Dungkar in the early 16th century by Khewang Jamyang Shinti.

Down the valley at its far end is the extensive ruins of Piyang monastery. Like **Piyang** Dungkar, Piyang once had a Gelukpa monastery, under the control of Tashilhunpo in Zhigatse. There are also cave paintings at Piyang and perhaps more in the side valleys if one had the time to engage in a little exploration. Without doubt throughout the upper Sutlej valley there are other important sites waiting to be discovered.

Roads to Kinnaur, Spiti and Ladakh

Driving north from Toling, via the **Lawoche** intersection, you will reach **Chusum** township after 141 kilometres, and **Sibkyi Tiyak** in the Sutlej gorge after 150 kilometres. Here you reach the Indian border which is currently closed and across which lies the ethnic Tibetan region of **Kinnaur** (*Tib* Kunu). In Kinnaur, the Hindustan Highway leads through Kalpa to Simla in Himachal Pradesh. Within Chusum township there are six small reconstructed Gelukpa temples or monasteries, each of which now has only a handful of monks. Among them, **Barchok Puntsok Rabten Gon** was reputedly founded before 1600 by Khepo Lekpel.

The traditional trade route to Kinnaur is a caravan trail, leading directly from **Jangtse** township to **Tiyak** in the Sutlej valley and thence to Sibkyi Tiyak. Tiyak is renowned as the birthplace of Lha Lama Yeshe-O (b. 958), and there are 12 reconstructed temples or monasteries of which nine are Kagyupa, two Gelukpa and two Nyingmapa. Among them, **Ranyi Lhakhang** was reputedly founded by Rinchen Zangpo and now follows the Kagyu tradition, **Lhakpak Lhakhang** represents the Nyingma school, and **Nuwa Gon** the Gelukpa.

Trekking

From Chusum there is also another trekking route which leaves the Sutlej basin, crossing into the valley of the **Rushok Tsangpo**. Here there are two trails, one following the river downstream via Sumdo to **Tabo**, across the Indian border in Spiti, Himachal Pradesh; and the other following the river upstream via Khayungshing La pass into Southern **Ladakh**.

Rutok County རུ་ཐོག

*The county of Rutok in the extreme northwest of Tibet borders the Xinjiang Autonomous Region and Ladakh. Geographically it forms part of the Northern Plateau (Jangtang) in the sense that its rivers drain internally into lakes, such as the long tapering **Lake Pang-gong**, which lies half inside Tibet and half inside Ladakh. None of its waterways drain into the Indus basin, which lies just a short distance to the south. The county capital is located at **Rutok**, 127 kilometres from Senge Tsangpo and 1,239 kilometres from Kashgar in Xinjiang.*

Maga Tsangpo Valley

The road from **Senge Tsangpo**, the district capital of Far-west Tibet to Kashgar in Xinjiang province passes through Rutok county. It crosses **La-me La** pass after 31 kilometres, leaving the Indus basin to descend into the valley of the **Maga Tsangpo**. The township of **Chakgang** is 26 kilometres below the pass, and from there to **Risum** township it is a further 30 kilometres. At Risum there are remarkable prehistoric rock carvings (see below, page 369) and Tselung Lhakhang, a small Gelukpa temple. From here, a motorable side-road leads eastwards, following a tributary of the Maga Tsangpo upstream to Khulpa and **Rawang** (60 kilometres), where there are a number of small salt lakes, and the small Tsa'u Mani Lhakhang of the Gelukpa school.

The main road from Risum continues to follow the Maga Tsangpo downstream for 30 kilometres, as far as **Derub**, where a turn-off cuts northwest for Rutok, the county capital, 10 kilometres distant. The river itself flows immediately into Lake Pang-gong.

Rutok

In the ninth century Namde Osung, the younger Buddhist son of the apostate king Langdarma, fled Central Tibet and established Buddhism in Far-west Tibet. He divided Ngari into three regions at **Guge**, **Rutok** and **Purang**, giving authority to rule to each of his three sons and their descendants. Thus **Rutok** became the capital of the kings of northern Ngari. Over 500 years later political rivalries saw **Rutok** join with **Ladakh** to lay waste the kingdom of **Guge**, and wage war against the kingdom of **Purang**.

Today the newly built town of Rutok is basically a Chinese military garrison of harsh concrete buildings and satellite dishes. Located in a slight depression its two main thoroughfares hold a few small groups of laconic soldiers in their ill-fitting green uniforms. Apart from the army, the residents of this sleepy town seem to be mainly Tibetan as well as a few Muslim traders from Xinjiang. Dust-covered Tibetan children with spikey, uncut hair and ragged clothes are sometimes the only people one sees in the three broad and dusty avenues of the town. At Rutok, the hill-top citadel of **Lhundrub Choding Gon** was founded jointly by the charismatic yogin Drukpa Kunlek and the Gelukpa master Yonten Gyatso. Following the campaigns of the Mongol

Rutok

The Rutok prehistoric rock carvings

About 40 km south from **Rutok** *at* **Risum** *hamlet, the road crosses a low culvert and turns left around the corner of a cliff facing flat wet lands from which fresh springs bubble forth. On the cliff to the left of the road one suddenly comes across a mass of ancient carvings chiselled into the surface of the red and black schist rocks. These remarkable images were discovered only in 1985 by the Lhasa Cultural Relics Institute and are extremely important for the insight they give into the key elements in the ancient nomadic way of life.*

Included are stylized figures of deer, sheep, yak, antelope, wolf or dog, fish and men. Most are rendered in outline only and in many panels the figures are realistically portrayed rearing up or galloping. Their physicality is accented by spiral swirls and elaborate curving branches on the body, antlers or tail. Birds are also present although they are eagle-like, and yet in the midst of what seems a shower of sparks. In this way they reflect the features of the mythical Garuda, a half-man half-eagle that flies in the midst of a blazing fire eliminating all negativity. There are also abstract carvings of strange bicellular forms, evoking the cosmic egg, one of the images found in the Bon philosophy for the origin of existence.

These rock carvings are possibly the most significant prehistoric images in

Tibet. Petroglyphs in the same style have recently been unearthed inside burial mounds on the steppes of Central Asia.

On the main road there are two distinct groups of petroglyphs at the location known as **Rimotang***, 1.5 km southeast of* **Risum***. After crossing the culvert the first is a few hundred metres on the left. The second is about a hundred metres further on. The figures are cut into a dark red coloured schist or granite. Some were defaced recently by devout Buddhists carving mantras over portions of the petroglyphs. This Buddhist graffitti is most abundant at* **Rimotang***. The location is alongside a broad lush valley which may be a reason why the images are located here. It is ideal for the nomads to graze their animals while enroute. Directly beneath the rock face is a small, natural spring.*

Another set is located 32 km west of **Rutok** *town, on the north bank of the Chulung River and is known as* **Luri Langkar***. They are similar to those of* **Rimotang** *and are spread over six panels less than 4m above ground.*

One final group known as **Karke Sang** *lies 159 km northeast of Rutok and about 25 km south of* **Domar township***. They are sited in a cave and along a ridge west of the* **Karke Sang cave***. Downstream one can see evidence of a more intensively cultivated landscape.*

general Ganden Tsewang against Ladakh in the late 17th century, the eclectic traditions of Rutok, which also had a Sakyapa presence, were overruled and the monastery was handed over to the authority of Sera Je college in Lhasa.

Sleeping   There is a truck station with overnight accommodation. Electric ring heaters, blankets, hot water bottles and televisions are supplied.

A road leads due west from Rutok for 65 kilometres to **Retso** township, giving access to a traditional trade route via **Lake Mendong-tso** and across the Chugu La and Kharmar La passes into **Ladakh**.

Pang-gong Lake

The long (113 kilometres) **Lake Pang-gong**, located north of Rutok, straddles the Indo-Tibetan border and is said to be patrolled by the highest navy in the world! This is a Chinese claim boasted by eager officials. They also say that the waters at the Tibetan end are fresh and potable while those at the

Colour map 1, grid A1

Far-west Tibet

Ladakh end are saline. Be that as it may, the region surrounding the lake is renowned for its wildlife. Herds of asiatic wild ass graze along its shore line and massive flocks of migrating birds rest here on the way from Siberia south to India. In the late summer and autumn seasons thousands of birds can be seen. Muslim fishermen from **Xinjiang** are often seen paddling out from the shore on large inner tubes to net the fish that abound in the lake. Tibetan Buddhists generally never go fishing. The surrounding area is a natural habitat for various types of wild animals, for which reason there are now plans to establish a wild game hunting park, with a sliding scale of rates according to the rarity of the animal killed, along the lines of the Balung hunting park in Qinghai province (see below, page 515).

Domar

Rejoining the highway at Derub, 10 km southeast of Rutok, you can continue driving northwards to **Domar** township, 113 kilometres distant in the Northern Plateau. At the outset, the road follows the eastern shoreline of Lake Pang-gong, and the landscape along this stretch is breathtaking in its beauty. The extreme clarity of the atmosphere gives the strange, multicoloured earth of the hills, cliffs and plains a surreal visionary quality. Have your camera ready to take some memorable landscape photos.

The drive to Domar from Rutok takes only half a day. The surrounding terrain, as the name suggests, is deep red in colour. The township is a bleak settlement with a military garrison, that must be the last outpost for a soldier coming from remote mainland China. One could not get posted to a more remote location than here! It is also at the edge of the **Aksai Chin**, a disputed region claimed by India, who belatedly discovered a Chinese road traversing the middle of the territory in the 1960s. The Tibetan settlement of concrete buildings and nomadic tents is located at the southern end of the township. Here, on the left side of the road, there is the Domar transport station and a small Tibetan café, serving noodles, tsampa, and hot drinks. Some 100 metres left of the road, there are three stupas and a pile of mani stones which local devotees circumambulate. North of the Tibetan settlement, the road crosses a river, only 10 metres wide, and forks: left for the Xinjiang border, and right for the military barracks. At this junction, a small restaurant sells freshly prepared Chinese food. The military presence at the garrison is small, although many convoys appear to pass through. The only telephone in town, linked to Rutok and Hong Liu Tan in Xinjiang is in their possession and may be used by them alone.

Essentials *Domar Transport station*, has basic accommodation (¥20 per room) and is well located for hitch-hiking. *Domar Military Garrison*, has cleaner rooms (¥40 per room), excellent canteen food and nearby outdoor toilet facilities.

Xinjiang Border

From Domar township, the road continues up the Domar valley, and then turns right to cross the Aksai Chin and leave the Northern Plateau of Tibet for Xinjiang province. The last settlements on Tibetan territory are at **Sumzhi** and **Tserang Daban** transport station, 172 km from Domar, where it is possible to stay overnight. Just beyond Sumzhi on this road, there is a high 5,000 metre pass which local drivers wisely treat with caution. Tserang Daban has no military garrison, but there is a transport station, which is set 50 metres off the road and therefore inappropriate for potential hitch-hikers. Its concrete sheds have rickety beds and very dirty blankets. Yak-dung stoves are provided, along with hot water and dry instant noodles (¥ 60). It takes at least half a day to reach the bleak outpost of Tserang Daban from Domar, and the actual border, which is unguarded, lies 36 kilometres further north.

The road from the Tibet-Xinjiang border to Kashgar initially continues passing through the largely uninhabited Aksai Chin. Very occasionally, Tibetan nomads can be seen leading their herds of yak and sometimes two-humped camels across the plateau. Alongside the highway are many forms of flora which are unique to the region. A number of these plants have highly prized medicinal properties, considered to be especially efficacious in Tibetan pharmacopaea. After four hours there is a small Chinese transport station where truckers stop for lunch. Stir fry dishes are available (¥30). Some five hours further on, the road passes through the military garrison of **Hong Liu Tang**, situated at the lower edge of the Aksai Chin plateau, where the climate is significantly milder. Simple, clean accommodation is available in the barracks. Hong Liu Tan is situated in a deep brown valley, from where the road begins its descent into the Western Kunlun Mountains through deep gorges and across rushing rivers.

Some two to three hours after Hong Liu Tan, you will reach the turn-off for **Mazar**, and it is possible to spend the night here, Mazar, 456 kilometres from Tserang Daban, is a ghost town of long concrete compounds and if you are heading directly to Kashgar, it may be preferable to keep going and camp out somewhere near fresh water. Nowadays, Mazar is also the starting point for treks into the Karakorums (see below, page 685) on the Pakistan border, particularly the Base camp for the ascent of K2, the world's second highest peak. K2 is not, however, visible from the highway.

On the descent through the **Western Kunluns**, the road crosses three passes (between 3,000 and 4,000 metres), from the last of which there is a dramatic view of the Taklamakhan Desert. Leaving the Kunlun foothills, the landscape dramatically changes. The high altitude environment of the Tibetan plateau and the Aksai Chin is suddenly left behind, as sand dunes, camels, fruit orchards, and the Islamic culture of the Uighur people come into view. How little cultural exchange there has been in this border area over recent centuries!

The road then descends into the valley of the **Karakax River**, where a detour cuts through to **Khotan** at the southern extremity of the Taklamakhan Desert on the Silk Route. Perhaps as sparsely populated as the Arabian Desert, Khotan is a region comprised of barren wastelands and ethereal blue lakes which are among the last remnants of the Ice Age. As they melted and formed rivers flowing north through the Kunlun range they once fed the renowned Khotanese Buddhist civilization. The merchants and scholars of Khotan travelled along this route to India and China, trading in Chinese silk and other commodities, or studying and translating the Sanskrit Buddhist scriptures, several hundred years before Buddhism was established in Tibet. However, as the great rivers from Tibet's Northern Plateau dried up, the Khotanese civilization collapsed. It was buried under the desert sands until European explorers uncovered its traces at the turn of the century.

Modern Khotan is two hours' drive from Yecheng, and is famous for its carpets, jade and hand-made silk. Virtually nothing remains of its ancient Buddhist ruins (which were documented by Stein), but the markets and oases are of interest. Excursions to the fringe of the Taklamakhan Desert can be arranged here. **Sleeping** The *Hotan Hotel* is excellent, and preferable to the accommodation at Yecheng.

Khotan & Mazar

Far-west Tibet

Descending from the Karakax valley into the Yarkand River basin, the road soon reaches **Yecheng**, 249 kilometres from Mazar. Yecheng is a sprawling town which has become the main centre for Chinese immigration into Western Xinjiang. Extensive irrigation in this region has transformed huge areas of the desert. The *Yecheng Hotel*, where foreigners are obliged to stay, is overpriced and seedy. Normally one will arrive soon after lunchtime and, after a short stop for food, continue onto Kashgar, a further 249 km.

About one hour's drive north from Yecheng, you will reach the ancient town of **Yarkand**, which still has important historical significance for the Uighur people, despite the destruction of its old city during the Cultural Revolution. Of its ancient buildings, all that remains is the grand gate of the old palace, the central mosque, and the royal cemetery. These can easily be visited in one hour.

Kashgar

Phone code: 0998 Kashgar lies some 200 km north of Yarkand, and can be reached in three hours. On the approach to the city, one catches a glimpse of the Pamirs in the distance. Kashgar is a large conurbation, undergoing rapid development, but parts of the old city have remained intact. Almost everything is sold in the markets, including Tibetan jewelry and prayer wheels.

Essentials **Sleeping** *Seman Hotel* (the former Russian Consulate) is the best place to stay. Alternatively, try the *Qiniwake Hotel* (the former British Consulate), where a new block is expected to open in 1999. Outside town, accommodation is available at the *Xin Binguan Hotel*.

Transport **Air** There are daily flights to Urumqi, from where international flights operate as far as Almaty in Kazakhstan, Bishkek, Moscow, Islamabad, Tashkent and Sharjah, as well as major domestic destinations.

Road There are daily air-conditioned buses to **Urumqi**, and public buses over the Khunjerab pass leading into Pakistan. Foriegners are not presently permitted to use public transport to the **Torugart Pass** on the Kyrgyz border. Those wishing to enter Kyrgyzstan by road have to hire a jeep (about US$450) to reach the border and have a pre-arranged vehicle to rendezvous at the pass for the transfer to **Bishkek** (another US$500). Exit permits can be arranged for land travel into Pakistan or Kyrgyzstan through the Kashgar Mountaineering Association, and at *John's Information and Café* (open summer months only), next to the *Seman Hotel*. Expect to spend up to one week making these arrangements. **NB** Visas for Pakistan and Kyrgyzstan are required but not obtainable in Kashgar.

Rail There is a direct international rail link bewteen Urumqi and Almaty.

Eastern Tibet

The ranges and rivers of Kham ཁམས

9

Eastern Tibet

The ranges and rivers of Kham ཁམས

Eastern Tibet or Kham presents an amazing contrast to the landscape of the Brahmaputra valley and is characterized by extremely rugged mountains in parallel ranges extending from northwest to southeast, broken by very deep alpine gorges. The ranges are narrow and rocky with steep slopes and sharp ridges and high altitude nomadic grasslands, while some peaks are covered by glaciers. Eroded narrow valleys and deep forested limestone and sandstone gorges have been cut by the Salween, Mekong and Yangtze rivers and their numerous tributaries, hence the name traditionally given to the region of Kham: '**four rivers and six ranges**' (chuzhi gangdruk).

Nowadays this vast, fertile and most populated region of Tibet is divided for political and historical reasons between four Chinese provinces, comprising altogether 47 counties. **Tibetan Autonomous Region** includes 7 counties in Nakchu district, 15 in Chamdo district and 3 in Nyangtri district. **Yunnan province** includes the 3 counties of Dechen Tibetan Autonomous Prefecture; **Qinghai** includes the 6 counties of Yushu Tibetan Autonomous Prefecture; and **Sichuan** includes 16 counties of Kandze Tibetan Autonomous Prefecture, in addition to the Mili Tibetan Autonomous County.

The distance from Lhasa to Chamdo is 1,066 kilometres via Nakchu; and 1,179 kilometres via Kongpo. The distance from Chamdo to Chengdu is 1,325 kilometres; from Chamdo to Kunming 1,789 kilometres; and from Chamdo to Ziling 1,542 kilometres.

Eastern Tibet

Kham ཁམས

Land and life

Geography The four great rivers of Kham, all of which rise on the Tibetan plateau, are: the **Salween** (*Tib* Ngul-chu, *Ch* Nu jiang), **Mekong** (*Tib* Da-chu, *Ch* Lancang jiang), **Yangtze** (*Tib* Dri-chu, *Ch* Jinsha jiang), and **Yalong** (*Tib* Dza-chu/Nya-chu, *Ch* Yalong jiang). The six highland ranges (*chu-zhi gang-druk*) which form the watersheds for these river systems are as follows: **Tsawagang** range (5,100-6,700 metres) which includes the fabulous snow peaks and glaciers of **Mount Kawa Karpo** (6,702 metres) lies between the Salween and the Mekong; the **Markhamgang** range (*Ch* Ningjing Shan; 5,100-5,700 metres) lies between the Mekong and the Yangtze; the **Zelmogang** range (4,800-5,400 metres) lies between the northern reaches of the Yangtze and Yalong; the **Poborgang** range lies between the southern Yangtze and the lower Yalong; **Mardzagang** (5,100-5,700 metres) occupies the area between the upper Yalong and the Yellow River; and, lastly, the **Minyak Rabgang** range (4,800-7,750 metres) including **Mount Minyak Gangkar** (7,756 metres), the highest mountain in Kham, lies between the lower Yalong and the Gyarong.

Climate The climate is milder here than in West Tibet and Central Tibet owing to the penetration of monsoon winds and precipitation from Southeast Asia, yet the great ruggedness of the terrain contributes to localized climatic diversity. Generally, there is little precipitation in winter (with the exception of the higher grasslands), and abundant rainfall in summer; the annual average varying from 500 to 1,000 millimetres.

Flora and fauna of Kham

In the more **arid areas** of Northwest Kham adjacent to the Jangtang Plateau, alpine steppes and meadows predominate on rock soil. Cobresia grows, along with rock jasmine, arenaria, rhubarb, gentian, buffalo pen, saussurea, and astragalus. On lower mountain slopes are shrub thickets including rhododendron, willow, cinquefoil, spirea, and juniper. Towards the southeast, the precipitation increases and the alpine steppes give way to forest steppe. At 3,000-3,900 metres there are balfour spruce, purple cone spruce and fir trees. On dry slopes the forests include juniper, oak, and pine.

Within the **gorges** of Kham there are subalpine coniferous forests growing on podzolic soils. In the northeast these are characteristically mixed temperate and subtropical forests; and in the south and southwest mostly evergreen or laurel forests, with magnolia, michelia, and so forth. There is great variation within these subalpine coniferous forests: ie fir in humid areas, spruce in dry areas; with numerous shrubs, grasses and mosses. In the far north gorges where winter is cold and dry there are mixed forests of oak and pine; and in the wetter southeast with precipitation exceeding 2,000 millimetres, there are fir, spruce, hemlock, lithocarpus, birch, and poplar. As for fauna: there are fewer ungulates and rodents, but more badgers, lynxes, wild cats, monkeys, and, in some peripheral border areas, tigers or giant pandas.

Eastern Tibet

History of Kham

The kingdoms and tribal confederations of East Tibet, whether nomadic or sedentary, have been shaped by this vast and formidable terrain. Since the disintegration of the Tibetan Empire following the demise of King Langdarma, for most of their history, they have fiercely maintained their independence from Lhasa, China and indeed from each other. Among them the most important states in Kham were the five kingdoms ruled by hereditary kings (*gyelpo*), viz. **Chakla**, **Derge**, **Lingtsang**, **Nangchen**, and **Lhato**; the five Trehor states ruled by hereditary chieftains (*ponpo*), viz. **Drango**, **Kangsar**, **Mazur**, **Trewo** and **Beri**; the diverse grassland states of the upper **Yalong** and of **Nyarong**, **Sangen**, **Gonjo**, and **Khyungpo**, which were also ruled by hereditary chieftains; the southern states of **Batang**, **Litang**, **Markham**, **Tsawarong**, **Powo** and **Kongpo** which were governed by appointed regents; and the western states of **Chamdo**, **Drayab** and **Riwoche**, which along with **Gyarong** and **Mili**, were governed by lama dignitaries.

In Kham, religious and secular festivals have had great impact on the lives of the people since earliest times. Each region has its horse-riding festival at a fixed date in the calendar – an occasion for song, dance and various athletic competitions, at which the boisterous Khampa crowds display their local costume and traditions. Traders and spectators would often travel throughout Kham from one region to the next, planning their travels to coincide with local festivals.
Social history and religious impact

Similarly, each region also has its distinctive spiritual affinities. The pre-Buddhist Bonpo have their most important strongholds in the **Khyungpo** region of the present Tibetan Autonomous Region and the **Ngawa** (Aba), **Beri** and **Gyarong** regions of Sichuan.

Pilgrimage is as important here as in Central Tibet. When Buddhism was established in the eighth century, Padmasambhava roamed throughout East Tibet in the company of his students, and he is reputed to have concealed his teachings as *terma* in many parts of the country. Twenty five such ancient pilgrimage sites are esteemed above all others in East and Northeast Tibet. They are considered to have special affinity with either buddha-body, speech, mind, attributes or activities.

Buddha-body: Kyadrak Senge Dzong in the Upper Yalong valley is the main site. It has five aspects, viz. Chijam Nyinda Puk in the Yalong valley (body), Lotu Karma (speech), Nyen in the Yangtze valley (mind), Khala Rongo in Nangchen (attributes) and Hekar Drak (activities).

Buddha-speech: Powo Gawalung is the main site. It also has five aspects, viz. **Mount Kawa Karpo** in Tsawarong (body), **Pema Shelri** (speech), **Nabun Dzong** in Nangchen (mind), **Yegyel Namka Dzong** near Riwoche (attributes) and **Hor Tresho** or **Chakdu Khawa Lungring** near Kanze (activities).

Buddha-mind: Dentik Shelgi Drak in Ma-khok, Amdo, near the Huangho River is the main site. Its five aspects are: **Zhara Lhatse** in Minyak (body), **Warti Trak** (speech), **Dorje Drak** in lower Machu (mind), **Khandro Bumdzong** in lower Nangchen (attributes), and **Po-ne Drakar** near Riwoche (activities).

Buddha-attributes: Rudam Gangi Rawa, is the main site, ie the mountain Trori Dorje Ziltrom above Dzogchen. Its five aspects are: **Ngulda Podrang** in

Eastern Tibet

front of Derge Lhundrupteng (body), **Pema Shelphuk** in lower Mesho Dzomnang (speech), **Tsandra Rinchen Drak** at Pelpung (mind), **Dzongsho Deshek Dupa** in Dzing (attributes), and **Dzomtok Puseng Namdrak** by the Yangtze (activities). All these sites are in Derge district.

Buddha-activity: Katok Dorjeden is the main site. Its five aspects are: **Ngu** (body), **Tsangshi Dorje Trolo** (speech), Tashi or **Kampo Kangra** (mind), **Hyelgi Trak** (attributes), and **Drakri Dorje Pungpa** (activities). These sites are in and around Katok in southern Derge.

These power places later came to be closely associated with the Nyingma, Kagyu and Sakya traditions. Despite intertribal rivalries, the diverse states of Kham were noted for their religious tolerance until the 17th century. The Nyingma, Kagyu, Sakya and Geluk schools of Tibetan Buddhism were represented, alongside the adherents of Bon. Among areas of Kagyu influence, the strongest were **Nangchen** and **Derge**. For the Sakya school the most influential regions were **Jyekundo** and **Derge**, and for the Nyingmapa the **Zelmogang** and **Southern Derge** regions. Prior to the 17th century, the Gelukpa had their greatest centres at **Chamdo** and **Litang**.

The Mongols A fundamental change occurred in the 17th century, however, and this is closely connected with the rise to political power of Dalai Lama V in Lhasa. The long civil wars waged between the supporters of the Kagyu and Geluk schools in Central Tibet had some impact in the east. The zealous Mongol Gushri Qan of the Qosot tribe sought to intervene on behalf of the Gelukpa faction by sending his Mongol armies against Donyo Dorje, the king of **Beri** who adhered to the Bon religion. That kingdom was subdued between 1639-41, and the region from Beri to Drango was settled by Mongol tribesmen (Horpa), who forcibly converted and renamed some monasteries belonging to the Kagyu and other traditions. The **five Hor states** of Drango, Kandze and Beri district with their partisan affiliation thus came into being. Great monasteries were built at **Kandze** and **Dargye** near Rongpatsa. Gradually, the new administration at Lhasa was able to exert its influence on other regions to the south: **Drayab**, **Markham**, **Batang**, **Chaktreng**, **Chakla** and so forth. In the 18th century, the Changkya Qutuqtu conducted a campaign against the Bonpo of the **Gyarong** region. Only the kingdoms of Derge, Nangchen and Khyungpo with their strong traditions could withstand the sectarian attacks.

Mongol intervention in Tibetan politics had even more serious repercussions in the 18th century. In 1705-6, the Manchu emperor Kangxi had supported the Qosot leader Lhazang Qan in his abduction of Dalai Lama VI and murder of the regent Desi Sangye Gyatso. The Dzungar Mongols then intervened in 1717 to kill Lhazang and plunder Central Tibet. Although the Tibetan forces were eventually able to gain the upper hand, the Manchu emperor who had custody of the new Dalai Lama VII, sent armies to vanquish the Dzungars and instate Kelsang Gyatso (1720). Campaigns then followed against the Qosot in Amdo leading to the annexation of Amdo and Nangchen by the new Qinghai province in 1724. Finally, in 1727 the Manchus claimed much of Kham east of the Yangtze as their own protectorate, and from 1728 they posted two representatives in Lhasa.

Manchu Yet, while Manchu China unilaterally claimed a nominal suzerainty over much
Warlords & of Kham and Amdo, the reality of the situation was that the kingdoms and
occupation tribes of Eastern Tibet were de facto independent. When the forces of **Nyarong Gonpo Namgyel** overran the territories from Drango to Derge, it

was the Tibetan government of Lhasa which came to their assistance and subdued the power of Nyarong in the campaign of 1863-65. Sichuan warlords, among them Chao Erh Feng, began to intervene from 1894, but direct interference in the affairs of East Tibet by Beijing was precipitated by Chinese reaction to the arrival of the Younghusband expedition in Lhasa (1904). In 1909, Chao Erh Feng was dispatched to adopt a 'forward policy' which sought to carve out a new and governable 33 district province called **Xikang**. The proposed territory would encompass the entire region from **Gyamda** in Kongpo to **Dartsedo**. The 1909-18 campaign, which devastated much of Kham, resulted in the eventual Chinese withdrawal from the region, despite British diplomatic efforts to maintain the artificial boundaries devised by the Manchu emperors. The conflict was later resumed with the arrival in Kham of the PLA during the 1950s. The retribution exacted on Kham for its militancy resulted in the massacre of the population and the destruction of the region's great Buddhist artefacts. Only a few key sites, exemplified by the printery at Derge, were spared.

There are few well-informed works on these regions of Kham available in languages other than Tibetan. Among them the most important are RA Stein, *Les tribus anciennes des marches sino-tibetaines*, Eric Teichman, *Travels of a Consular Official in Eastern Tibet*, the writings of the botanist F Kingdon Ward who travelled throughout Konpo and Southern Kham between 1913-20, Warren Smith's recent historical opus *Tibetan Nation: A History of Tibetan Nationalism and Sino-Tibetan relations*, Steve Marshall and Suzette Cooke's *Tibet Outside the TAR* (on CD Rom) and the cartographic studies of Pieter Kestler in Rikon, Switzerland. Among travelogues, the most readable include A Migot, *Tibetan Marches*; C Trungpa, *Born in Tibet* and the works of the American evangelist M Duncan.

Further reading

Accessibility

In late 1998, Eastern Kham (Kandze and Dechen Prefectures) was officially opened to tourism. Previously, individual travellers had to venture through 'closed' areas with or without official sanction. The authorities of TAR, Qinghai, Yunnan, and Sichuan had been slow to accept the great potential for tourism in Kham. However, economic necessity has forced a reappraisal of government policy. The ban on lumbering, belatedly imposed following the severe flooding of the lower Yangtze in 1998, has lead the authorities to look to tourism as an alternative means of generating economic development.

Amdo is in a somewhat different situation: the peripheral areas of Northeast Tibet, around Ziling and Labrang have long been open to individual travel, and tour groups frequently traverse the rail and road link from Ziling in the northeast to Lhasa via Golmud, Amdo, Nakchu, Damzhung, and Yangpachen. This does, however, entail a 21-hour journey by train, followed by a 1,155 kilometres' drive across the desolate Qinghai plateau. One of the disadvantages of taking this route is that, apart from Kumbum, Labrang and so forth, the great cultural centres of Kham are bypassed.

With proper organization and travel permits – and a sufficiently large wallet to enable you to pay the high daily rates charged by the provincial tourism bureaux – it is even possible to travel throughout the areas of Kham which remain 'closed' (ie Chamdo prefecture). These routes through Eastern Tibet are often impassable in winter and in the rainy season (July-August). The best time to make this journey is therefore between April-June or September-November. Nonetheless, communication can be difficult and unexpected problems may occur at anyy time of the year.

At present, there are two fully motorable roads leading from Lhasa to Chamdo in the heart of Kham: the **northern route**, which passes through Nakchu, Sok Dzong, Hor Bachen, Khyungpo Tengchen, and Riwoche; the **southern route**, through Gyamda, Bayi, Powo, and Tsawa Pasho. The northern route is currently in greater use as it permits faster driving and is more reliable during the rainy season. The southern route is subject to recurring landslides due to the glacial snow-melt and deep river gorges around Powo. Soon, however, a more direct motorable route will be fully operational, following the **old caravan trail**, via Gyamda, Lhari, Pelbar, and Lhorong. Until the final section is completed between Lhari and Pelbar, this trail still requires some trekking through the Nyenchen Tanghla watershed. All three routes offer considerable variation in landscape and cultural programmes.

Lhasa to Chamdo:

the Northern Route via Nakchu

The northern route, described in this section, comprises the counties of Nakchu, Sok Dzong, Hor Bachen, Khyungpo Tengchen, Riwoche, and Chamdo. In addition, three outlying counties of Nakchu district: Amdo, Nyenrong, and Driru, are also included. **Recommended itineraries: 4, 5 and 7.**

Nakchu County རྣག་ཆུ

Nakchu district, traditionally known as **Jang Nakchuka***, is the name given to the high nomadic terrain of the East Jangtang Lakes and the Salween headwaters, average altitude 4,500 metres. This is a vast wilderness region through which the Nak-chu, Shak-chu, and Sok-chu tributaries flow to form the* **Salween** *(Tib Nak-chu): a 2,784 kilometres river rising in the Dangla range to the north, which has its estuary at the Gulf of Martaban, south of Burma. The city of* **Nakchu***, which has undergone unprecedented development within the last four years, is the administrative capital of nine counties within the upper Salween region, as well as having its own county-level bureaucracy. It is located on the Ziling-Lhasa highway 315 kilometres northeast of Lhasa, near the headwaters of the Nak-chu tributary, from which it derives its name. The actual sources of the Nak-chu are at* **Chutsen Narak** *(Jukchu), north of the Brahmaputra-Salween watershed, and at* **Galong** *on the southern shore of the freshwater* **Lake Tsonak** *to the northwest. The distance from Damzhung to Nakchu is 169 kilometres, and from Nakchu to Amdo township, 138 kilometres along the Ziling highway.*

Heading northeast from Lhasa via Yangpachen and Damzhung, the paved Ziling-Lhasa highway enters Nakchu county 27 kilometres beyond **Omatang**. The stupas of **Chorten Rango** lie just north of the county border. Passing through **Koluk** township after 14 kilometres, the road rises slowly towards

Nakchu County (51)
那曲县
Nagqu
Population: 61,404
Area: 17,194 sq km
Colour map 6, grid C5

Koluk & Lhoma

Eastern Tibet

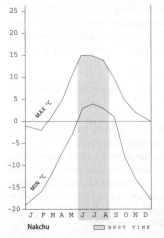

Nakchu, Amdo & Nyenrong

Zangzhung La pass (4,727 metres), which forms the watershed between the Brahmaputra and Salween river systems, and after crossing this divide, it bypasses **Sangzhung** township on the west. The road now crosses the Nak-chu southern source, and runs parallel to it. Light snowfall is a normal occurrence in this exposed and sparsely populated Jangtang region, even in summertime! The township of **Lhoma** straddles the highway, 66 kilometres northeast of Koluk, and 17 kilometres further on there is a turn-off on the right (east), which follows the Nak-chu through **Takring** and **Hor-me** townships in the direction of **Lhari**. This is part of the central Lhasa-Chamdo road network, on which see below, page 402.

Nakchu City   **Getting there** Continue along the highway for 10 kilometres, and soon the city of **Nakchu** comes into view, impressively large in its wilderness setting. Cross the Nakchu Zamchen bridge on the right (east), which leads off the highway into town.

The phenomenal growth of this city is due to its important location on the Lhasa-Ziling highway, and as the centre of trade for the entire nomadic region of North Tibet, which urban and farming communities refer to as **Hor**. There are strategic petrol stations, both civilian and military to the west of town, and to the south is the **Nakchu Race Course**, where an important horse festival is held each year, commencing on 10 August. More than 10,000 visitors from the Lhasa and Nakchu regions attend the events, which also provide an occasion for traditional barter, and regional folk dances. The colourful applique tents which surround the race track, some of them larger than houses, are particularly impressive.

Within the town the crossroads is the commercial centre. Here there are grocery, textile, and electrical stores, as well as shops selling traditional crafts. Local industry is mostly a derivative of nomadic animal husbandry: dairy products and meat processing, and cashmere wool production (also including yak and sheep wool). The Chinese population is less pronounced in this high inhospitable climate (4,509 metres) than in other Tibetan cities. The mean temperature is 10° in mid-summer and -10° in mid-winter, and the oxygen content only 61 percent. Muslim shopkeepers from the Ziling area do have their own quarter.

There are two main temples in town, one Nyingma and the other Gelukpa, both of which are extremely active and well-supported by the local community. Among them, **Zhabten Gonpa**, recently reconstructed and with outstanding murals, now houses 80 monks.

Sleeping The 3-storeyed *Nakchu Hotel* on 262 Senidong Rd, T(0896)3822463. Has 88 rooms at ¥480 per superior room, ¥288 per standard room, and ¥120 per inferior room. Accommodation is adequate, but the attached bathrooms lack running hot water, which has to be supplied by thermos bottles. The hotel has its own shop, karaoke bar, and 2 restaurants.

Eating There are a number of small street restaurants near the hotel: **Sichuan, Muslim**, and **Tibetan**.

From Nakchu, if you wish to continue travelling along the **Ziling** highway, retrace the route west out of town, and then turn north onto the highway. Those intending to take the **northern route to Chamdo** or visit **Driru** county should turn left (east) on exiting from the *Nakchu Hotel*, drive along the dirt track which leads out of town over the ridge, and across the **Langlu La** pass (4,300 metres), through **Khormang** township, and via the **Jangkhu La** pass (4,700 metres) to **Shakchuka**. The distance from Nakchu to Khormang is 49 kilometres, and from Khormang to Shakchuka township, another 49 kilometres.

Amdo County ཨ་མདོ

*The Ziling highway continues northwest from Nakchu, following the valley of its source tributary upstream to **Tsaring** (40 kilometres), and thence to **Draknak**, the capital of Amdo county, which is located to the northeast of **Lake Tsonak**, the fabled source of the Nak-chu branch of the Salween River. This town is 98 kilometres from Tsaring on a side-road, which leaves the Ziling highway after 81 kilometres. At an altitude of 4,600 metres, Draknak is even more inhospitable than Nakchu. Nonetheless, it is an important crossroads town.*

Amdo County (52)
安多县
Amdo
Population: 27,743
Area: 22,159 sq km
Colour map 6, grid C5

From here, a westerly route (see above, page 315) cuts across the exposed salt-pans and lakes of the **Jangtang Plateau** to **Senge Tsangpo**, near Mount Kailash (1,333 metres). The main highway runs north to cross the **Dang-La pass** (5,220 metres), a watershed between the Salween and Yangtze headwaters, which also marks the present-day boundary between the Tibetan Autonomous Region and Qinghai province. The Dangla mountains, where the highest peaks range from 5,700 to 6,300 metres, are rich in minerals, including iron-ore, coal, graphite, asbestos, and soapstone. From Draknak to Dang La pass the distance is 106 kilometres. Before reaching the pass, there is a turn-off on the west, 67 kilometres from Draknak, which leads to the coal mines at **Tumen Dosol Terka**. The mines are located near the source of the **Trakara-chu**, a tributary of the **Tsakya Tsangpo** River, which drains internally into the salt Lake Serling. The lifestyle of the Draknak region is nomadic. Economic activity is centred around animal husbandry, as well as coal-mining and salt-panning.

Nyenrong County སྙན་རོང

*Nyenrong county is a large sparsely populated area to the south of the Dangla Range. It comprises both the sources of the **Shak-chu** and the **Sok-chu** tributaries of the Salween. The townships of Serkhang and Dzamar are to be found near the source of the Shak-chu, and those of Bezhung and Trawola around the source of the Sok-chu.*

Nyenrong County (53)
聂荣县
Nyainrong
Population: 23,627
Area: 7,259 sq km
Colour map M6, grid C5

Taking the Ziling highway from Nakchu, after 11 kilometres there is a turn-off on the right (north), which leads to **Serkhang**, the capital of Nyenrong county, 82 kilometres distant. The watershed between the Nak-chu and Shak-chu is crossed at **Gyatsam La** pass, 38 kilometres along this road. **Shakchuka** is the name given to the barren upper reaches of the Shak-chu valley, which extends through both Nyenrong and Driru counties, as far as the confluence with the Nak-chu.

Driru County འབྲི་རུ

*Taking the Chamdo road from Nakchu, via the **Langlu La** and **Jangkhu La** passes (see above, page 382), you will reach the township of **Shakchuka**, 49 kilometres east of Khormang. Here the motor road cuts across the Shak-chu valley, which extends southeast from its upper reaches in Nyenrong county to its lower reaches and confluence with the Nak-chu in Driru county. The road follows a tributary of the Shak-chu upstream beyond **Drilung**, and after 22 kilometres there is a major turn-off on the right (southeast), which leads to the heart of Driru county.*

Driru County (54)
比如县
Biru
Population: 36,478
Area: 11,295 sq km
Colour map 6, grid C6

Eastern Tibet

Taking this branch road, you will pass through **Chaktse** township after 39 kilometres, and then cross the **Dam-ne La** (5,013 metres). The barren landscapes of the upper Salween tributaries now give way to a forested valley, passing through **Traring**, where the Ka-chu River comes in from the southwest to swell the combined waters of the Nak-chu and Shak-chu. **Naksho Driru**, the county capital, is located 16 kilometres downstream in the Salween gorge. Timber is the main industry and logging trucks can frequently be seen plying the road between Driru and Nakchu. The region is characterized by small Gelukpa monasteries interspersed with those of the Bonpo, representing two distinct phases of religious propagation.

From Driru, there are two tracks leading towards **Pelbar** county in Chamdo district, which link up with the Central Lhasa-Chamdo road (see below, page 402). Of these, the southeast track crosses **Zha La** pass (5,090 metres) after 27 kilometres, and descends via Sentsha (after 35 kilometres), and Benkar (after eight kilometres), to join the Kyil-chu

Driru

tributary of the Salween. It then heads due east to **Sateng** township in Chamdo district, 59 kilometres distant, where the Kyil-chu converges with the Salween. The other track is a trekking route, which heads east from **Naksho Driru**, following the main Salween gorge, through **Bompen** and **Chamda**, and on downstream to Sateng. The forests of this middle Salween region are delightful but rarely visited.

Sok County སོག་རྫོང་

Sok County (55)
索县
Sog Xian
Population: 28,753
Area: 5,839 sq km
Colour map 6, grid C6

If you continue due east on the main Chamdo road from Nakchu and Shakchuka, without taking the Driru turn-off, after 35 kilometres, the road soon crosses the **Gang La** *pass (4,811 metres), which forms a watershed between the Shak-chu and Sok-chu. A second slightly lower double pass named* **Shara La** *(4,744 metres) quickly follows, and the road then descends through the Si-chu gorge to enter the Sok-chu valley above* **Nyinpa** *(72 kilometres).*

Sok Tsanden Zhol

Colour map 6, grid C6 Sok Tsanden Zhol, the county town, is located some 22 kilometres upstream from Nyinpa within the Sok-chu valley. The terrain here is arid and barren. The lower reaches of the Sok-chu valley are administered from this town (whereas the upper reaches are within the neighbouring county of Hor Bachen).

Sleeping and eating The *Soktreng Yulkor Khang Guesthouse* has 9 clean rooms with comfortable beds (¥40 per bed, ¥160 per 4-bed room). The *Yigzam Guesthouse* has clean rooms (¥14 per bed) adjoining a small compound. Barking dogs are unavoidable at night. There is a good Sichuan restaurant, northeast of the guesthouse, on the main road.

Sok

Eastern Tibet

Sok Tsanden Gonpa

As you drive into town from Nakchu and Shakchuka, you will notice across the river the hilltop Gelukpa monastery of **Sok Tsanden Gonpa**, which was founded by the Mongol chieftain Gushi Qan Tendzin Chogyel during the 17th century. Prior to the civil war between Lhasa and Zhigatse, the region had been a stronghold of the Bon religion. The recently renovated temple, which once housed 600 monks, is currently home to 200 monks, and it has an impressive citadel-like façade, reminiscent of the Potala! It comprises the Lhakhang Marpo (Red Temple), the Rabselkhang, and the Lhakhang Karpo (White Temple). The ground floor of the **Lhakhang Marpo** contains a temple dedicated to Tsongkhapa. The main images are Shakyamuni flanked by his foremost students and the 16 Elders, along with 1,000 small Tsongkhapa images. The second floor houses the Gonkhang dedicated to Vajrabhairava and Shridevi; the Rinchen Lhakhang with images of the 33 Confession Buddhas, Tara, Avalokiteshvara, Jowo Shakyamuni, and Amitabha; and the Kangyur Lhakhang which contains the Lhasa edition of the Tibetan canon. Adjacent to the Gonkhang is the residence of the incumbent lama, Kangyur Rinpoche. In the 56 columned **Lhakhang Karpo**, there is a renowned sandalwood image of Avalokiteshvara, from which the monastery acquired its name ('tsanden' means sandalwood); and other images including Padmasambhava. The

Sok Tsanden Zhol

Sok Tsanden Gonpa

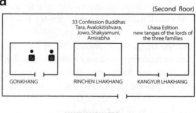

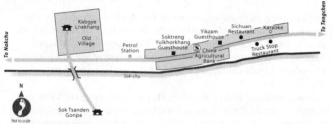

1 Shariputra
2 Maudgalyayana
3 16 elders
4 Shakyamuni
5 Vajrabhaiava
6 Shridevi

7 Phakpa Lokeshvara
8 Tsongkhapa with students
9 Ekavira Bhairava
10 Old Tangkas
11 Tsongkhapa with Gyaltsabje & Khedrupje

Eastern Tibet

present sandalwood image is a replica of the damaged original which has been inserted within the heart of the new image. On the lowest level, there is a *mani* wheel chamber.

Kabgye Lhakhang

Southwest of Sok Tsanden Gonpa, on the west side of the Sok-chu, within the old quarter of town, is the Nyingmapa temple known as **Kabgye Lhakhang**. This shrine was founded in 1169 by the renowned treasure-finder Nyangrel Nyima Ozer (1136-1204). Following its destruction by Gushi Qan's Mongol army in the 17th century, it was restored by *terton* Nyima Drakpa. There are 30 married *mantrins* now living around the temple, where the main spiritual practices followed are all derived from the *terma* traditions, including Nyangrel's *Kabgye Deshek Dupa*, the *terma* doctrines of Nyima Drakpa, the *Lama Gongdu* of Sangye Lingpa, and the *Rigdzin Dupa* of Jigme Lingpa. The temple is in need of further funds to complete its restoration.

Further downstream below Nyinpa, a trail leads towards the confluence of the Sok-chu and Salween at **Shamchu**. The townships in the southeast of the county include Chungpa and **Chamda**, where there are six cave hermitages associated with Padmasambhava. One of these, **Dorje Sherdzong**, has a cave temple complex. Rongpa township in the extreme east of the county will be described below with Hor Bachen, as it follows Hor Bachen on the motor road.

Bachen County སྦྲ་ཆེན

Bachen County (56)
巴青县
Baqen
Population: 28,835
Area: 13,738 sq km
Colour map 6, grid C6

*Bachen county, more properly known as **Hor Bachen**, comprises the upper reaches of the Sok-chu and its feeder rivers, the Bon-chu and Bachen-chu, all three of which converge above **Gurkhuk**. The county capital is located at **Tartang** in the Ye-chu valley, 37 kilometres northeast of Sok Dzong on the Chamdo road, and a short distance beyond **Patsang Monastery** (Yeta).*

Tartang

This area was formerly the centre of the **Hor Jyade** camper groups, who successfully maintained their nomadic lifestyle and relative independence until the present century. A large horse-festival is held on the **Tartang** plain in summer-time; and the Bon tradition survives, alongside a Gelukpa nunnery. The town has both civilian and military guesthouses, a petrol station, a few shops, and a small roadside restaurant cum tea-house.

The townships within Bachen county are located in the upper reaches of the various feeder rivers: **Bonsok** on the Bon-chu, **Bachen** township (not to be confused with Bachen county town at Tartang) on the Sok-chu, **Tsek-ne** on the Bachen-chu, and **Chang-me** on the Ye-chu.

Trekking North of Tartang

Trekking routes lead up these river valleys to the **Dangla** watershed range, crossing the Salween-Yangtze watershed into present day Qinghai (see below, page 490). Among these **Trawo La** pass (4,930 metres) crosses directly from the Sok-chu valley, and **Tsek-ne La** (5,140 metres) from the Bachen-chu valley.

Bachen

The main road East of Tartang

Taking the main **Chamdo highway**, 44 kilometres east of Tartang, at

Eastern Tibet (vertical side text)

Yangada, the road crosses yet another tributary of the Salween, which flows downstream through Chungpa to its confluence above **Chamda**. The road then cuts southeast via **Chak La** pass (4,502 metres) into the **Rongpo Gyarubtang** region, where an important battle was fought between the Tibetan government forces and the Kuomintang in the early decades of this century.

The township of **Rongpo Gyarubtang**, on the meandering Ri-chu tributary of the Salween, is 33 kilometres beyond Chak La pass, at the base of the **Pugyel Gangri** snow range (6,328 metres). There is a small guesthouse with a congenial attendant, but lacking in electricity. Southwest of town at **Sertram Drak**, there is a thriving Nyingmapa monastery; and accessible on a more remote but motorable trail is the Gelukpa residence of Zhiwalha, the second most important incarnation of Chamdo monastery. The road now ascends the high **Shel La** pass (4,830 metres) on a spur of the Pugyel Gangri range. The forested alpine terrain of the middle Salween is visible to the southwest. On reaching the pass, 44 kilometres from Rongpo, there is a spectacular view of the **Dangla** range to the northeast and the cragged **Tanyi Tawun** (*Ch* Tanlan Taweng) range to the southeast.

Rongpo Gyarubtang

Tengchen County སྟེང་ཆེན་

*On the descent from Shel La pass, the road enters the **Khyungpo** district of Kham, where the Bon tradition predominates. **Khyungpo Tengchen** county comprises the valleys of the south-flowing Ga-chu and Ru-chu tributaries of the Salween and those of their northwest-flowing feeder rivers, the Dak-chu and Kyilkhar-chu. The county capital is located at Khyungpo Tengchen, also known as **Gyamotang**, 271 kilometres southeast of Sok Dzong, 98 kilometres from Shel La pass, and 143 kilometres northwest of Riwoche.*

Tengchen County (57)
丁青县
Dengqen
Population: 49,971
Area: 11,175 sq km
Colour map 4, grid A1

18 kilometres from Shel La pass, the Chamdo road cuts across the Ga-chu River at **Trido**. A trekking route leads off on the left (north) through the upper Ga-chu valley to **Gata** township, and the river's source southeast of **Mount Lagen Zhushab**. Another trekking route leads due south from Trido to the river's confluence with the Salween in **Lhorong** county (see below, page 403). The **highway**, however, cuts southeast from Trido, following a tributary of the Ga-chu upstream to Sertsa (35 kilometres), where the Ru-chu also flows in from the north and the Dak-chu from the southeast.

Routes from Shel La

This small township of Sertsa has several monasteries. Among them, the

Sertsa

Eastern Tibet

Tengchen County

largest Bonpo monastery is **Sertsa Yongdzong**; and the largest Gelukpa monastery is **Sertsa Tashiling**. The latter is located across the **Tsuri La** pass (4,200 metres) from Sertsa township, and on the right (south) side of the motor road. Originally a Kagyupa monastery, Tashiling was converted to the Gelukpa school by the armies of Gushi Qan in the 17th century. It also has affinities with the Nyingma school, as evidenced by its main chapel, which contains large images of Padmasambhava flanked by Shantaraksita and King Trisong Detsen. The traditions of this renovated monastery which once housed 300 monks are being revived under the guidance of Tulku Ngawang Zangpo, who presides over a group of 80 monks. **Essentials** Sertsa has a government compound with guesthouse and dining facilities, a motor repair shop, and a petrol station.

Tengchen

Colour map 4, grid A1   Following the Dak-chu downstream from Sertsa, after 45 kilometres the road reaches **Tengchen**, the capital of the Khyungpo district, situated in a wide cultivated valley, hemmed in by red sandstone hills. The old Tibetan village of **Tengchen Kha** and the county town of **Tengchen** (*Altitude*: 3,750 metres) face each other across the river, as if worlds apart.

    The inhabitants of **Tengchen Kha** village are extremely hospitable, and display a remarkable sense of religious tolerance. At a Padmasambhava tenth day ceremony in 1988 attended by the author, Nyingmapa *mantrins*, Gelukpa monks, and Bonpo practitioners participated together with an exemplary sympathy. A branch road to the northwest leads 25 kilometres along the Zhe-chu valley to Zhezhung township.

Tengchen   The region of Khyungpo, as its name suggests, is one long connected with the
Monastery   Bon tradition; for **Khyunglung** ('Garuda Valley') in Far-west Tibet was an original Bon stronghold, and many later Bon communities also utilized this name. Most religious establishments in the region are Bon rather than Buddhist, and among them, there are two important monasteries situated side-by-side on the northern ridge which overlooks the town: **Tengchen Monastery** and **Ritro Lhakhang**. The former, also called Namdak Pema Long-yang, was founded in 1110 by Sherab Gyeltsen and Monlam Gyeltsen who hailed from the 'White Lineage of the Chen family'. The third lineage-holder (ie the successor of those two) greatly expanded the community of practitioners around Tengchen and established the **Ritro Lhakhang** hermitage above the temple in 1180. The two monasteries have had long close connections with the Bon communities of **Yungdrungling** and **Menri** in

Tengchen

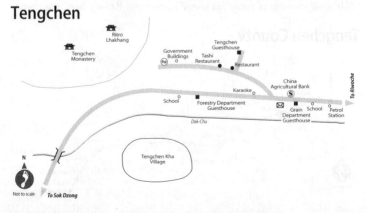

West Tibet, and with those of the **Ngawa** region of Amdo.

Renovations began in 1986; and are still continuing under the guidance of Lama Sherab Gelek. Of the original vast complex of buildings, two chapels have been restored in each monastery. The **Ritro Lhakhang** comprises the **Serdung Chewa**, a chamber containing the reliquary of the second lineage-holder, Monlam Gyeltsen; and the **Serdung Chungwa**, containing the reliquaries of the six other early lineage-holders: Nyima Gyeltsen (I), Kunga Gyeltsen (III), Jinpa Gyeltsen (IV), Tsultrim Gyeltsen (V), Yungdrung Gyeltsen (VI), and Tsultrim Nyima (VII). **Tengchen Monastery** contains the **Nampar Gyelwa Lhakhang** (downstairs) and the **Residence of Lama Monlam** and the library (upstairs), which are finely decorated with frescoes of Bon divinities and *mandalas*. The **Ritro Lhakhang** also has an abbot's residential chamber, in its upper storey, where the murals depict scenes from the life of Shenrab, and a copy of the *Bon Kangyur*, recently reprinted in Chengdu, is housed. Formerly both monasteries had 300 monks each, but now the Tengchen Monastery has only 85 and the Ritro Lhakhang a mere 23.

Sleeping

In town, the *Tengchen Government Guesthouse* (left of the square) has rooms (¥15 per bed, ¥60 room), including television. The *Grain Department Guesthouse (Drurik Dronkhang)* has newer rooms at ¥40 per bed and ¥160 per room), while the *Forestry Guesthouse* (next to the school below the motor road) has clean but simple accommodation (¥15 per bed, television included). Hot water is provided in thermos bottles. A Sichuan-style restaurant and shop are attached to the *Tengchen Guesthouse*, and in the square outside the hotel compound gates, there are karaoke bars, pool tables, etc. The government buildings and public security bureau are located on a side-road to the left, which adjoins the square near the *Guesthouse* entrance.

Kyilkhar Lhakhang

Continuing along the main highway from Tengchen, the route follows the Dak-chu downstream through **Sagang** (27 kilometres) and the valley of its feeder river, the Kyilkhar-chu, upstream through **Gyangon** (15 kilometres). This region contains a number of large Bon monasteries perched on remote precipices, high above the motor road. At **Kyilkhar**, where the Kyilkhar-chu thrusts its way out of a long narrow red sandstone gorge, there is a large *mani* stone mound and an important branch monastery of Chamdo Jampaling. Two temples have been restored in recent years and there are now 250 monks. Inside are fine murals and images depicting Shakyamuni, Tsongkhapa flanked by his foremost students, Green Tara, White Tara, and three meditational deities: Guhyasamaja, Carasamvara, and Vajrabhairava.

Rotung Nyedren Gonpa

This monastery of the Karma Kagyu school, adjacent to Kyilkhar Lhakhang, is currently undergoing renovation. Images include Mahakarunika, flanked by Padmasambhava and Vajrakila; and there are tangkas depicting the Karmapas. Recently a Mani Lhakhang has been constructed. In the past there were some 600 monks at Rotung, but nowadays there are only 70 under the direction of Tsepak Lama. Beyond Rotung, the road bypasses the grassy knoll of Kharje and plunges into the **Kyilkhar gorge**. The red sandstone walls rise sharply on both banks of the river. Only in the summer months is there evidence of vegetation. A hydro-electric power station has been constructed at **Meru** within the gorge.

Eastern Tibet

Riwoche County རི་བོ་ཆེ

Riwoche County (58)
类乌齐县
Riwoqe
Population: 32,937
Area: 5,699 sq km
Colour map 4, grid A2

*Riwoche county extends from the **Dzekri La** pass (4,809 metres), which forms the watershed between the Salween and Mekong river systems, as far as the **Zhopel La** or Trugu La pass (4,688 metres), which divides the Dzi-chu and Ngom-chu tributaries of the Mekong. The county capital is located at Ratsaka, 143 kilometres southeast of Tengchen and 105 kilometres east of Chamdo.*

Kharmardo

After passing through the Kyilkhar gorge, the highway to Riwoche and Chamdo crosses the **Dzekri La**, 66 kilometres from Gyangon in Tengchen county. Then, descending abruptly into the **Kharmardo** valley, the terrain is utterly transformed. High altitude barren landscape is replaced by juniper and conifer forests, and rolling alpine meadows, carpeted with blue gentian and white edelweiss. To the southeast large outcrops of red sandstone and white marble are strewn across the undulating slopes. After Kharmardo, the road drops due north into the lower Ke-chu valley at **Sibta**. A motorable side-trail follows the Ke-chu upstream (northwest) from Sibta, reaching **Tramoling** after 55 kilometres. The main road follows the Ke-chu downstream from Sibta to its confluence with the Dzi-chu at **Riwoche** (35 kilometres from Dzekri La pass).

Takzham Monastery

In the lower Ke-chu valley, some 20 kilometres before Riwoche county town, the road passes **Takzham Monastery** on the left. This was the residence of Takzham Nuden Dorje, an 18th century treasure-finder who discovered various texts hidden by Yeshe Tsogyel including her own biography, and who held the lineages of Katok Monastery and Choje Lingpa. The main temple, constructed in Zangdok Pelri style, contains images of Padmasambhava, Amitayus, Vajrasattva, and Shakyamuni, as well as several large prayer wheels replete with the mantras of Vajrasattva, Padmasambhava and Amitabha. The central throne bears a photograph of the present Takzham Rinpoche, who resides in Switzerland. The newly painted murals depict the Takzham lineage. Outside and to the left of the temple entrance there are sets of stupas symbolizing the deeds of the Buddha, both in traditional stone design and in the distinctive Khampa wooden style. A nomadic camper group occupies the grassland behind the monastery.

Ratsaka (Riwoche county town)

Colour map 4, grid A2   Entering the town of **Ratsaka** (*Altitude*: 3,690 metres) from the west, you first

Riwoche

pass the turn-off to the north which crossss the Dzi-chu bridge, heading in the direction of Riwoche Tsuklakhang. The paved main street, now known as Hiechen Gonglu, contains all the buildings of note: the Public Security Bureau and government buildings are at the west end, while the two hotels are at the east end. The largest general store is on the south side, to the west of the hotels, and the Post Office is on the north side. Entertainment is minimal, being confined to open-air pool tables and a video parlour.

Riwoche Government Guesthouse (Sizhung Nelen Khang) on the north side of the street. Recently refurbished, best rooms upstairs (¥8 per bed and ¥20 per room). *Grain Department Guesthouse (Drurik Dronkhang)* on the south side of the street, T(08050)2253. 8 recently refurbished and comfortable rooms (¥40 per bed). There are Sichuan-style restaurants and small shops on both sides of the street near the hotels.

Sleeping & eating

Riwoche Tsuklakhang

The great temple, known as **Riwoche Tsuklakhang**, was founded in 1276 by Sangye On, a student of Sangye Yarjon, the third lineage-holder and abbot of the Taklung branch of the Kagyu school. Following the death of Sangye Yarjon, who was interred at Taklung in a stupa reliquary alongside his two predecessors Taklung Tangpa Tashipel and Kuyalwa, Sangye On took charge of the mother monastery for some time, but then departed abruptly for Kham, leaving Taklung in the hands of Mangalaguru, in order to fulfil a prophecy to the effect that he should found an even greater branch of the monastery at Riwoche. As such it became the main branch of Taklung in Kham, and according to Go Lotsawa, author of the *Blue Annals*, it had the greatest reputation among Khampa monasteries, and it once housed 2,000 monks. From the time of its foundation, the Taklung Kagyu school was considered to have upper and lower branches, the former being the original monastery at Taklung and the latter the Riwoche Tsuklakhang. The lineages associated with both are recounted in the religious history called *Chojung Ngo-tsar Gyatso*, composed in 1648 by Ngawang Damcho Zangpo.

History
Colour map 4, grid A2

The temple at Riwoche is physically imposing in the manner of the main temples at Samye and Sakya, with enormous tree trunk columns supporting its three storeys. It is painted in the distinctive black, white and red vertical stripes, which are a hallmark of the Taklung lineage. In the early 15th century Tsongkhapa is known to have praised the community at the Tsuklakhang for their expertise in the meditation practices of Hevajra and other deities. The

The temple

Eastern Tibet

Ratsaka

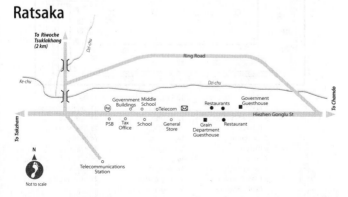

surrounding community of practitioners, married or monastic, adhered to both the Taklung Kagyu and the Nyingma lineages. The Nyingmapa element in Riwoche has been especially strong since the time of Jedrung Rinpoche (Trinle Jampa Jungne), who was the teacher of both the late Dudjom Rinpoche (1904-87) and the late Kangyur Rinpoche (1888-1975).

The temple dwarfs the surrounding Riwoche village, which contains the government compound, the residences of Jedrung Rinpoche and Panchuk Rinpoche to the northeast, that of Zhabdrung Rinpoche to the east, and the quarters of the monastery's 500 monks which extend between them. It is

Riwoche Tsuklakhang

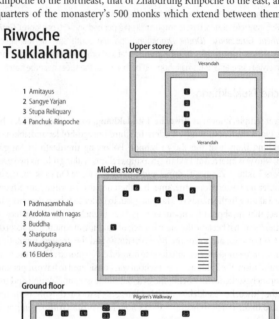

Upper storey

1 Amitayus
2 Sangye Yarjan
3 Stupa Reliquary
4 Panchuk Rinpoche

Middle storey

1 Padmasambhala
2 Ardokta with nagas
3 Buddha
4 Shariputra
5 Maudgalyayana
6 16 Elders

Ground floor

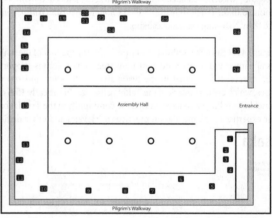

1 Maitreya	10 Shakyamuni	20 Derge Kangyur
2 Aksobhya	11 8 Stupas (small)	21 Sarvavaid Vairocana
3 11-faced Avalokiteshvara	12 Assorted small images	22 Dipamkara
4 8 Stupas	13 Buddhas of 3 Times	23 Shakyamuni
5 Shakyamuni	14 Munindra	24 Maitreya
6 Vajrapani	15 Sangye Yarjon	25 Bhaisajyaguru
7 Amitayus	16 Sangye Yarjon	26 11-faced Avalokitesvara
8 Padmasambhava	17 Munindra	27 Remati
9 8 Manifestations of Padmasambhava	18 Sangye Yarjon	28 Local Protector
	19 Sangye On	

N

Not to scale

*Riwoche
Tsuklakhang*

well-supported by those members of the local community who are engaged in the rebuilding project and in spiritual pursuits.

The three-storeyed temple has been undergoing restoration since 1985. The outer wall is surrounded by a pilgrim's walkway complete with rows of prayer-wheels on all four sides. The temple is entered from the east side. The **ground floor** comprises the assembly hall with enormous larger-than-life size images on all four walls, separated from the hall by wooden lattices. Proceeding clockwise from the left you will pass on the east wall: Maitreya, Aksobhya, 11-faced Avalokiteshvara, and Eight Stupas (symbolizing the deeds of the Buddha); then on the south wall: Shakyamuni, an original Vajrapani, Amitayus, Padmasambhava in the form Nangsi Zilnon, the Eight Manifestations of Padmasambhava, and another Shakyamuni. On the west wall, which is the **inner sanctum**, there are eight small stupas and assorted small statues, followed by the Buddhas of the Three Times and two images of Sangye Yarjon, flanked by two old Munindra images. On the north wall are: Shakyamuni, Sangye Yarjon, Sangye On, Sarvavid Vairocana, Dipamkara Buddha, Shakyamuni, and Bhaisajyaguru. Behind Sarvavid Vairocana is a full set of the Derge *Kangyur*. Lastly, on the east wall near the exit, you will pass Eleven-faced Avalokiteshvara and the protector deities including Remati. One thousand small statues of Padmasambhava surround these principal images.

The **middle storey**, which has recently undergone much restoration, contains images of Padmasambhava, Ardokta surrounded by naga-spirits, and Shakyamuni flanked by his foremost students and the 16 Elders. The murals here depict the Taklung lineage, the 100 Peaceful and Wrathful Deities, and 1,000 aspects of Amitayus. The **upper storey**, entered from the open rooftop gallery, contains images of Amitayus, the late Panchuk Rinpoche, and Sangye Yarjon, as well as a reliquary of the late preceptor, Khenpo Pema Rangdrol, who was instrumental in maintaining the tradition through recent difficult times. It also houses the Derge *Kangyur*, 400 small images, and the riding saddle of Ling Gesar, which is kept behind the beams. The rebuilding at Riwoche is currently supervised by Tendzin Tulku, Lama Orgyan, Mr Ngadra, who is a relative of the late Kangyur Rinpoche, and Kunga Tre, the son of the present Jedrung Rinpoche. In Toronto, Canada, the Riwoche Society founded by Lama Sonam Topgyel has actively sought to promote the Riwoche lineage overseas and contributes to the various restoration projects.

If you wish to visit **Riwoche Tsuklakhang**, situated in the old Riwoche valley (which is the only reason for spending time in Ratsaka), you should first obtain clearance from the Public Security Bureau in town. Take the turn-off at the west end of the main street, which leads across the Dzi-chu Bridge, and then head north, following the Dzi-chu upstream on its west bank for 29 kilometres. En route you will pass a turn-off on the right, across the river, which leads through a defile to the **Matsala Coal Mines**, located on a prominant spur of the **Tanyi Tawun** range, 64 kilometres distant. It is on

Getting there

Mekong River

The Mekong (Tib Da-chu, Ch Lancang jiang) is the world's 12th longest river, and the 7th longest in Asia, extending 4,350 kilometres from its high altitude Ngom-chu and Dza-chu sources (4,900 metres) in the Tangula Mountains of present-day Qinghai province, to its delta in Vietnam. The river has a total drainage area of 810,600 square kilometres. In its upper reaches, the Mekong flows through the deeply eroded narrow gorges of East Tibet and Yunnan for 1,955 kilometres. Its waters have a distinctly greenish hue, except during the rainy season, when its flow is faster and turbid silt abruptly turns it reddish brown. Overall, the river has an annual sediment of 187 million tons. The lower reaches of the Mekong are wide, meandering for 2,390 kilometres through the Khorat plateau of Thailand, Annamese Corderilla, and Cambodia, from where it eventually enters South Vietnam to form a wide delta.

account of these peaks that the valley received the name Riwoche. The track continues through **Nyinta**, and then opens out into a wide plain, where the resplendent Riwoche Tsuklakhang is visible in the distance.

Riwoche to Nangchen

From **Riwoche Tsuklakhang** the motorable road continues northwest for 76 kilometres, following the Dzi-chu upstream, before cutting northeast to **Jikto** and descending to **Chakzamka** on the Ngom-chu branch of the Mekong. Here there is a small Gelukpa monastery called **Gozhi Tubden Dorjeling**. After crossing the river at Chakzamka, the road traverses the TAR-Qinghai border at **Shoknga** to enter the Nangchen district of Kham. Immediately above the border checkpoint is **Netengang**, the seat of the great Nyingmapa *terton* Chogyur Dechen Zhikpo Lingpa (1829-70). For a description of the road from Nangchen to Riwoche, see below, page 489.

Chakzamka to Chamdo

From Chakzamka, there is also a trekking route which follows the Ngom-chu branch of the Mekong downstream to **Zamka** township. Below Zamka, the track becomes motorable as far as **Chamdo** (89 kilometres). A turn-off on this road at **Zo** village, between Zamka and Sagang leads to the **Matsala Coal Mines**.

Riwoche to Chamdo

The highway from Ratsaka to Chamdo (105 kilometres) follows the Dzi-chu downstream to the farming village of **Ngamda**, where a trail branches off to the southwest for Lhorong county via the **Yikdruk La** pass (4,998 metres). There is an attractive Gelukpa monastery here, with a series of the Eight Stupas by its entrance.

At **Teda** the highway leaves the Dzi-chu valley and ascends **Zholpel La** or Trugu La pass (4,688 metres), at the southern extremity of the high **Tanyi Tawun** range. The terrain beyond the pass is a spectacular fusion of alpine conifer and deciduous forest. If you cross in the summer or early autumn, the rich diversity of the forest hues never ceases to amaze. **Trugu Gonpa** of the Gelukpa school is located on a forested alpine crag, clearly visible on the descent. The road continues plunging deeply through this forest to emerge in the Ngom-chu valley at **Guro** (sometimes written Karu), an important neolithic site, 19 kilometres above Chamdo.

Chamdo County ཆབ་མདོ་

*Chamdo (literally meaning 'river confluence') usually refers to the **city of Chamdo** (Chamdo Drongkhyer) which straddles the Mekong at the point where its Ngom-chu and Dza-chu branches converge. It may also refer to **Chamdo district** (Chamdo sa-khul), which is the administrative headquarters for 15 counties of Kham, extending from Tengchen to Jomda in the north and from Pasho to Tsakalho in the south. In addition, it may refer specifically to **Chamdo county** (Chamdo Dzong), a triangular shaped wedge of territory which includes the upper reaches of these Mekong branch rivers, and the Lhato and Menda areas, which lie respectively on the Ri-chu and Ke-chu tributaries of the Dza-chu. It is expected that the recently taken decision to give Lhato and Menda a separate county status will soon be implemented, and at that time these areas will have their own county towns at **Topa** and **Sibda** respectively. At present, the county and district capitals are located in Chamdo city, one of the largest conurbations of East Tibet.*

Chamdo County (59)
昌都县
Qamdo
Population: 77,326
Area: 9,800 sq km
Colour map 4, grid A2

Chamdo

Distances The distance from Chamdo to Lhasa is 1,066 kilometres via Nakchu; and 1,179 kilometres via Kongpo. The distance from Chamdo to Derge is 345 kilometres; and to Kunming 1,789 kilometres.

Chamdo City

Orientation

Approaching Chamdo city from Riwoche (105 kilometres), you will reach the Ngom-chu valley at **Guro** and follow the west bank of that river downstream before crossing the east bank and entering the city on **Gyelsung lam** (Chotrika). Passing large military garrisons, you drive down into **Ozer lam** (Daratang), and then sharp left into **Dekyi lam** (Sarkyelam/Zetsongsing), which is the original commercial heart of the city. On the north (left) side of the street there is the *Xinhua Bookstore*, the Bank of China, the Chamdo City Government Buildings, the local police station; and a number of tea houses and coffee shops, including the *Derge Restaurant* (upstairs), which serves Tibetan butter tea and sweet Indian tea. On the south side (right) there is the Peoples' Cinema, and the open-air market (Tromzikhang), where Chamdo's stall-holders intermingle with Chinese traders. The costumes and coiffures of the people are a colourful spectacle in the market, but the diversity of traditional merchandise has diminished in recent years due to an increase in the availability of bland Chinese products. Look out for textiles, Tibetan books and the occasional trader who claims to possess antiques.

At the east end of Dekyi lam, there is a T-junction, leading on to **Mimang lam** (Gyelzam drong). Turning left and heading uphill, you now notice the Dza-chu River on the east (right). The road passes the **Chamdo Mentsikhang** on the left, and then runs due north as far as the **Dza-chu Suspension Bridge**,

Phone code: 0895
Colour map 4, grid A2
Dekyi lam

Eastern Tibet

Mimang lam

which leads northeast out of town towards Derge. A lane on the left side of the road called Gyelkalam (Barongka) leads steeply to **Kalden Jampaling Monastery** and the sky-burial ground, passing the Armed Police Compound on the right. If you turn right at the aforementioned T-junction, and follow the Dza-chu downstream, the road connects with the Ngom-chu Suspension Bridge. On the right (north) side, you will pass the *Panchen Lama Hotel*, the Chamdo County Theatre, and the Chamdo Area Transport Company, while the local bus station is on the left (south). On both sides of the street there are small restaurants, some of them Muslim owned.

Zetotang lam Crossing the Ngom-chu via the **Suspension Bridge** or **West Bridge** (Nubkyi Zamchen), you reach **Zetotang lam**, which follows the west bank of the Ngom-chu. At the intersection there is the largest karaoke establishment in Chamdo! Turn uphill for the *Chamdo Hotel*, or downhill to head out of town in the direction of Pomda, Drayab, and Markham. Heading uphill, you will pass on the left the *Grain Department Guesthouse*, the Bank of China and the Post Office, which has DDD connections to Lhasa and Chengdu. Opposite the Grain Department, there is a lane leading down to the river bank, where a foot-bridge (**Chaktak Zampa**) spans the Ngom-chu, leading directly into the aforementioned commercial area. On both sides of this street there are new glass-fronted department stores, schools, and electrical supply shops. At the upper end of the street, behind a high enclosure wall is the Chamdo District Government Compound. Here the road turns sharp right and then sharp left, as it continues following the river bank upstream. In this area there are a number of small Chinese restaurants and noodle bars. Passing the *Chamdo Hotel* on the right, you will reach the Public Security Bureau, also on the right, while *Guesthouse No 2*, the Long Distance Bus Station, and the Petrol Station are on the left.

If you head downhill on Zetotang lam from the **Ngom-chu Suspension Bridge**, you will pass the **Tatsatang Zamchen** bridge which leads across the combined Mekong waters to the Tatsatang grazing pasture. Continuing downstream on the west bank, you will reach the Chamdo Cement Factory complex, located on the west of this road on the outskirts of town near **Chaka** township. **Chamdo Airport** is also located on this latter road, 128 kilometres to the south, near Pomda.

History

Neolithic excavations at **Guro** suggest that the Chamdo area was one of the earliest centres of population on the Tibetan plateau. In **Drayab** county to the southeast there are rock carvings attributed to the royal dynastic period; and in the light of the second diffusion of Buddhism the area became a stronghold for the Karma Kagyu tradition. The obvious strategic importance of the Mekong confluence at Chamdo combined with the relatively low altitude, and the excellent climate to generate a considerable population density. The high ground above the monastery was chosen as the site for the

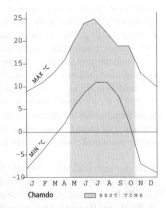

Chamdo   BEST TIME

construction of **Kalden Jampaling** during the 15th century; and ever since control of this area has been regarded as essential for the control of communications throughout Kham. Between 1909-18 Chamdo was occupied by the Chinese forces of Chao Erh Feng and General Peng, and later in 1950 the fall of Chamdo was a key even in the advance of the PLA into Tibet.

Sights

The great monastery of **Kalden Jampaling** was founded by Tsongkhapa's student Jangsem Sherab Zangpo between 1436-44. It formerly had over 1,000 monks and ranked alongside Litang and Kandze as the largest Gelukpa establishment in Kham. However, it had greater prestige and influence insofar as it was the oldest Gelukpa monastery in the region. The development of Kalden Jampaling was maintained over the centuries by the successive incarnations of

Kalden Jampaling Monastery

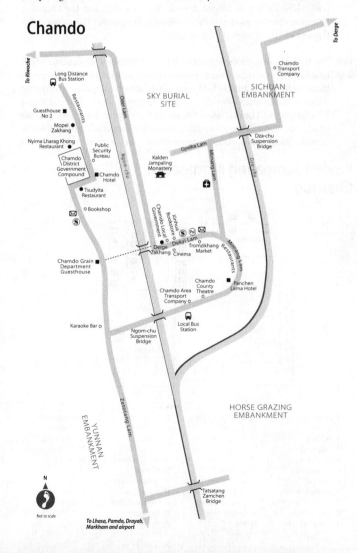

Chamdo

Eastern Tibet

Pakpalha; whose father, Kuchor Tokden, had been an actual disciple of Tsongkhapa. The other important incarnate successions associated with the monastery were those of Phakpalha's own disciples Zhiwalha and Chakra Tulku.

The original monastery was destroyed in 1912-13 by Chao Erh Feng, who had captured the town in 1909. After the Chinese retreat following the siege of Chamdo by the Tibetan army in 1917, the monastery was rebuilt, but it was again destroyed during the Cultural Revolution, along with a multitude of precious artefacts – 800-year-old tangkas among them.

During recent renovations, the site of the monastery, which formerly occupied the entire plateau above the town, has been considerably reduced in size. There are four major buildings on the north and east sides of the compound which have now been restored: the **Gonkhang** (northwest), the **Labrang** (north), the **Dukhang** (northeast), and the **Lhakhang Nyingba** (east). The kitchen is located between the Dukhang and the Lhakhang Nyingba, while the quarters of the monks who now number 700 are mostly on the west and south sides of the compound.

Assembly Hall (Dukhang) The largest building at the monastery is the wide three-storey **Assembly Hall** (*dukhang*), on the right. Its red columns and silk pendants lead to the central throne of the Dalai Lama, behind which, in the **inner sanctum**, is an exquisite image of Shakyamuni flanked by his foremost students Shariputra and Maudgalyayana. The altar below this image is in silver and inscribed with the words "Shakyamuni, supreme guide and matchless speaker". To the left of this central image are statues representing the earlier traditions of

Kalden Jampaling Monastery, Chamdo

1 Sarvavid Vairocana	12 Nechung Chokyong	22 Tsongkhapa	30 Guhyajamaja
2 Hevajra	13 Shridevi	23 Jangsem Sherab	31 Bhairava
3 Kalacakra	14 Two Guardian Kings	Zangpo	32 Dharmaraja
4 Guhyasamaja	15 Two Guardian Kings	24 Vaishravana	33 Tutor of Phakpalha
5 Vojrabhairava	16 Dudjom Dorje	25 Standing Manjughosa	34 Remati
6 Cakrasamvara	17 Kongstun Demo	26 4-armed	
7 Amitayus	18 Wheel of Rebirth	Avalokiteshvara	
8 8 Medicine Buddhas	19 Shakyamum flanked by	27 Tsongkhapa and	
9 Throne of Dalai Lamas	foremost students	foremost students	
10 Vinaya (mural)	20 Padmasambhava	28 Amitayus	
11 Tseringma (mural)	21 Atisha	29 Shridevi	

Eastern Tibet

Padmasambhava and Atisha, while to the right are representations of Tsongkhapa, Jangsem Sherab Zangpo and other Gelukpa lineage-holders. The outer main hall contains images of Sarvavid Vairocana, Hevajra, Kalacakra, Guhyasamaja, Vajrabhairava, Cakrasamvara, and Amitayus, while the murals depict the Eight Medicine Buddhas, and the protector deities. **Upstairs** there is a shrine dedicated to Jowo Rinpoche, containing an image of Jowo Yizhin Norbu, flanked by Maitreya and Guhyasamaja. The body of the Jowo image is original but the head has recently been replaced. Smaller images of Pakpalha are interspersed with these. There is also an inner chamber on this level where the present Dalai Lama resided in 1954 en route for Beijing.

The ante-chamber has posters describing the daily and monthly rituals performed at Chamdo.

To the right of the assembly hall and beyond the kitchen is the old temple (**Lhakhang Nyingba**), which is presently used as a college for dialectics (*tsenyi tratsang*). Inside (from left to right) are images depicting Vaishravana, Manjushri (standing), Four-armed Avalokiteshvara, Tsongkhapa flanked by his foremost students, Eleven-headed Avalokiteshvara, and Amitayus.

Old Temple (Lhakhang Nyingba)

Situated to the left (northwest side) of the compound, the **Gonkhang** contains images of Bhairava flanked by Four-armed Mahakala and Dharmaraja on the inner wall, Kongtsun Demo, Shridevi, and Guhyasamaja on the west wall, and Remati and the tutor of Phakpalha on the east wall. Upstairs is the library.

Protector Temple (Gonkhang)

The recently restored residence of Phakpalha and the other main tulkus of Chamdo is a tall four-storey building set further back to the north of the compound, between the Gonkhang and the Assembly Hall. This building, under reconstruction since 1988, was formerly known as the Palace of Chamdo. The present Phakpalha incarnation, Gelek Namgyel, resides in Lhasa.

Master's Residence (Labrang)

Essentials

C *Chamdo Hotel (Qamdo Hotel)*, T(0086)89521231 (reception), T(0086)89521026 (manager). 4 storeys, with comfortable rooms which are poorly maintained, attached bathrooms in various states of delapidation, and television, ¥50 per bed, hot water supplied in thermos bottles, no elevator, mediocre but expensive Chinese restaurant, large rooms available for special functions. **C** *Panchen Lama Hotel (Panziktsang)*, located 20 metres down an alleyway off Mimang lam in the downtown area. A clean new hotel with 15 rooftop hot shower cubicles, ¥50 per room, ¥5 per shower. *Grain Department Guesthouse*, on Zetotang lam. Well located but may not be open to foreigners. **D** *Guesthouse Number 2*, adjacent to the Bus Station. No attached baths, but communal showers are available.

Sleeping
■ *on map, page 397*
Price codes:
see inside front cover

There are many street restaurants in the upper and lower parts of town. For excellent Sichuan dishes, try *Nyima Lharag Khang*, or *Mopei Zakhang*, opposite the *Chamdo Hotel*. For noodles and Chinese dumpling dishes, the *Tsudyita Restaurant*, at the top of Zetotang lam.

Eating
● *on maps*

The main discotheque cum karaoke club is located on Zetotang lam, opposite the Ngom-chu Suspension Bridge. The *Peoples' Cinema* is located in Dekyi lam (Sarkyelam/Zetsongsing), west of the open-air market.

Entertainment

For the dates of certain traditional Tibetan festivals, see above, Essentials, page 26.

Festivals

Eastern Tibet

Shopping **Books** Books are available at *Xinhua Bookstore* on Dekyi lam. **Handi-crafts** Handicrafts for textiles, Khampa knives, metalwork, jewellery, and traditional religious or household artefacts, try the open-air market (Tromzikhang). **Modern goods** There are large glass-fronted department stores in Zetotang lam, selling groceries, electrical goods, ready-to-wear clothes, and so forth. Official currency exchange is impossible; but a few market traders will accept payment in US dollars. It is best to change currency in Lhasa, Kunming, or Chengdu long before reaching Chamdo. **Photography** Print film and processing are available at the department stores, and smaller electrical shops in town. **Stamps** Stamps are available at PO, on Zetotang lam, near Chamdo District Government Buildings.

Transport **Air** Chamdo Airport, located in Pomda township, 128 kilometres south of town, has been recently constructed, the radar equipment having been purchased from Austra-lia. There are twice weekly flights from Chengdu to Chamdo (Tuesday and Friday; US$83).

Road Most visitors to Chamdo, whether arriving via Lhasa, Kunming or Chengdu, will have their transportation organized by the travel services. Long distance car and jeep transportation is more easily available from Lhasa, but occasionally through the **Chamdo Transport Company**, near Dza-chu Suspension Bridge. The public bus sta-tion is located on Ozer lam, northwest of *Chamdo Hotel*. Buses runs northwest to Riwoche and Lhasa, east to Jomda and the Drichu Zampa, as well as south to Dzogang and Markham.

Directory **Banks** *Bank of China*, Dekyi lam. Subsidiary branch on Zetotang lam. **NB** Foreign exchange is not likely to be available. Best to change money in Lhasa or Chengdu. **Communications** Post Office: on Zetotang lam, adjacent to Chamdo District Government Buildings. DDD calls accepted. Chamdo area code: 0895. **Hospitals & medical services** *Peoples' Hospital*, T(0895)21745 (direct), T(0895)22965 (in-patients), T(0895)22947 (out-patients). *Military Hospital. Chamdo Hospital of Tibetan Medicine.* **Tour companies & travel agents** *Chamdo Travel Service, Chamdo Hotel.* **Useful addresses** Police & public security: *Chamdo District Police and Public Security Bureau*, near *Chamdo Hotel. Chamdo City Police*, Dekyi lam, opposite open-air market.

Ngom-chu Valley At the intersection above Guro, 19 kilometres north of Chamdo, take the river-side road which follows the Ngom-chu upstream. The road passes through the townships of **Sagang** (36 kilometres), where there is a small Gelukpa monas-tery, and **Zamka** (34 kilometres), after which it forks, one trail leading to **Chakzamka** (see above, page 394) and the other clinging to the west bank of the river. Both of these trails eventually lead into the Nangchen district of Kham (in present day Qinghai), but they are only passable when the river lev-els are at their lowest: from late September until March.

Dza-chu Valley Cross the Dza-chu Suspension Bridge to the northeast of Chamdo city, and take the road which follows the river upstream (rather than the highway to Derge). This route is motorable for 158 kilometres as far as **Tser-be**, passing through **Ridung** and **Kokhyam**, where the Ri-chu tributary flows into the Dza-chu from Lhato. Above Tser-be, a trekking trail continues following the river bank upstream to **Karma** township. En route, it passes through the important **Karma Gon**, the original Karma Kagyu monastery, which was founded in 1147 by Karmapa I Dusum Khyenpa (1110-93). Formerly, its 100-pillared Assembly Hall was one of the largest in Tibet, with 12 chapels and outstanding murals depicting the deeds of the Buddha and the history of the Karma Kagyu school. The inner sanctum contained enormous gilded brass images of the Buddhas of the Three Times. The central Shakyamuni image and the sandalwood throne were designed personally by Karmapa VIII. Little remains of these splendours.

Above Karma, the trail forks at the confluence of the Dza-chu and Ke-chu rivers, the former branch leading to **Nangchen** and the latter to **Zurmang Namgyeltse** – both in present-day Qinghai (see below, page 486).

One of the five formerly independent kingdoms of Kham, **Lhato** comprises the river valley of the Ri-chu and those of its tributaries: the Drugu-chu and the A-chu. According to a recent directive, this area will soon be governed from Topa county town, independent of Chamdo county. The Ri-chu rises northeast of Lhato township, in the stunning limestone crags of the **Tanyi Tawun** range (5,082 metres) which thrust upwards through the red sandstone landscape. It flows southeast to **Lhato**, where it is joined by the Drugu-chu, and then due west to converge with the Dza-chu at **Kokhyam**. The most important monastery in the upper Ri-chu valley is **Dzodzi Gon**.

The A-chu follows a parallel southeast course to enter the Drugu-chu, south of Lhato. In the nomadic grasslands of this **A-chu** valley, is the famous Drukpa Kagyu monastery of **Khampagar**, founded during the 18th century by Khamtrul IV Chokyi Nyima under the inspiration of his great predecessor Khamtrul III Ngawang Kunga Tendzin (1680-1728). Formerly there were two temples here and over 300 monks, with 200 affiliated branches throughout this part of Kham. An important college was founded at Khampagar by the late Khamtrul Dongyud Nyima, who also established a vital branch monastery in exile at Tashijong, Northwest India.

Getting there To reach **Lhato**, there is a trekking route from **Kokhyam**, but the easier road follows the Drugu-chu downstream from **Topa** on the main Chamdo-Derge highway. To reach Topa from Chamdo, follow the Derge highway on the east bank of the Dza-chu, and drive through Tayer township, and across the **Tama La** pass (4,511 metres), from where there are fine views of the city. A second pass, **Jape La** (4,680 metres) is then crossed, offering a clear vista of the ranges around Lhato and Nangchen (north) and around Drayab and Gonjo (south). Descending from this pass you arrive at Topa township, in the grasslands of the Drugu-chu valley. The distance from Chamdo to Topa is 109 kilometres.

Menda township is located in the extreme northeast of Chamdo county at the confluence of the Ke-chu and the Kyang-chu. The Ke-chu rises in southeast Lhato and flows northwest in an arc to Menda on the frontier of TAR and Qinghai, where its waters are swollen by the Kyang-chu, flowing south from **Zurmang Dutsitil** (see page 484). Southwest of Menda, the river is joined by the Tsi-chu, which flows south from **Zurmang Namgyeltse**, and the combined waters then converge with the Dza-chu branch of the Mekong above Karma. The entire region bounded by the Tsi-chu and Ke-chu rivers, including Zurmang, is sometimes known as **Tsike**. The landscape is typically nomadic, interspersed by these fast-flowing Mekong tributaries. Historically, the Karma Kagyu and the Nyingmapa have both had a strong presence in Tsike over the centuries.

Getting there Two trails lead to **Menda** from Chamdo – one via Lhato and Pangri; and the other following the Ke-chu downstream from its source near **Chunyido** and via **Sibda**, which has recently been designated as the county town from which the Ke-chu valley will soon be governed. Another jeepable approach can be made from Zurmang Dutsitil in Qinghai province (see below, page 484).

Lhato

Ke-chu Valley

Eastern Tibet

Lhasa to Chamdo:

the Central Route via Lhari

The central route from Lhasa to Chamdo, which is not yet fully motorable, corresponds to the old caravan trail, which was followed by pilgrims and traders alike for centuries before the construction of the northern and southern highways. The route eastwards into Kham begins at Artsa township in Lhari county, and cuts through the Nyenchen Tanglha range at Shargang La pass (5,037 metres) to enter the Salween basin. Artsa is accessible 202 kilometres driving distance from Nakchu City, following the Nak-chu valley southeast to Taksar, and thence across the Salween-Brahmaputra divide to Mitika.

Trekking Access Routes also lead to Artsa from Gyamda, Drigung and Reting. The trail from **Gyamda** (104 kilometres) in the south follows the Nyang-chu upstream to its source and across the **Tro La** pass (4,890 metres) and the scenic **Lake Artsa**. The latter trails follow the **Reting Tsangpo** upstream through the townships of **Sebrong**, **Drakar** and **Sangpa**.

This ancient direct trading route to Kham passes through three present-day counties: **Lhari**, which is administered from Nakchu, as well as **Pelbar** and **Lhorong**, which are administered from Chamdo. The overall distance from Artsa to Chamdo is 638 kilometres.

Lhari County སྒུ་རི

Lhari County (60)
嘉黎县
Lhari
Population: 19,719
Area: 7,483 sq km
Colour map 2, grid A6

*The county of Lhari comprises the upper reaches of the **Reting Tsangpo River** (which eventually flows into the Kyi-chu at Pondo) and the feeder rivers of the **Yi'ong Tsangpo** (which eventually joins with the Parlung Tsangpo to merge with the Brahmaputra northeast of Mount Gyala Pelri).*

This sparsely populated nomadic area holds strong allegiance to the Nyingmapa tradition, particularly the teachings of the treasure-finders Sangye Lingpa (14th century) and Nyima Drakpa.

Getting there 10 kilometres south of Nakchu on the Lhasa-Ziling highway, there is a turn-off on the east, which follows the Nak-chu River downstream and then cuts across the **Shilok La** pass (5,100 metres) and the **Apa La** pass (5,140 metres) in quick succession to enter the upper Reting Tsangpo valley. Ford the latter river at **Mitika**, via the Miti Tsangpo Zamchen bridge, and then cross the watershed to reach **Artsa**, on the banks of the Zhung-chu. The county capital is located at **Takmaru (Lhari)**, 38 kilometres downstream from Artsa.

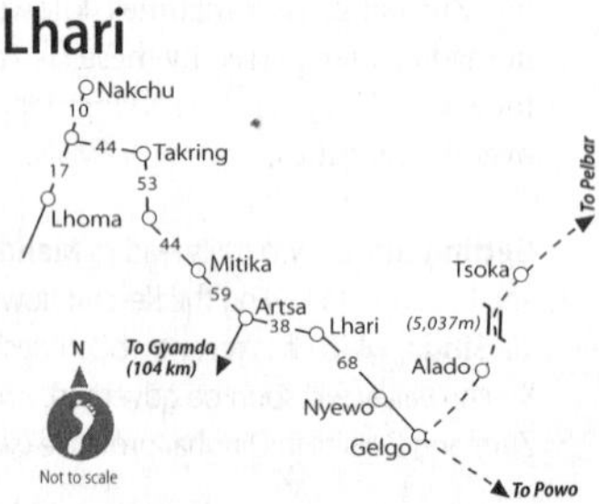

Below Takmaru the Zhung-chu merges with the Sung-chu (source above Lharigo), and thereafter is known as the **Nye-chu**. The road

Lhari

[Map: Not to scale]

Nakchu
10
44 — Takring
17   53
Lhoma
44 — Mitika
59
Artsa — Lhari   (5,037m)
38   68   Alado
To Gyamda   Nyewo
(104 km)
Gelgo
Tsoka
To Pelbar
To Powo

[Margin text, vertical: Eastern Tibet]

follows this river downstream for 68 kilometres to **Nyewo** township. Below Nyewo, the Zha-chu tributary joins the river from the northeast at **Gelgo**, and their combined waters are then known as the **Yi'ong Tsangpo**. The motor road presently does not continue beyond this point; but trekking routes follow the Yi'ong Tsangpo downstream into **Powo** and the Zha-chu tributary upstream through **Alado** to the Brahmaputra-Salween divide.

Taking the last mentioned trail, the Salween basin can be reached within four days' trek. From **Nyewo to Alado** the trail is particularly difficult and precipitous, passing through the gorge of the Zha-chu rapids. Above **Alado**, the trail through the upper Zha-chu valley becomes easier, passing Ngodroke township and the monasteries of **Arig** and **Namgyel**. Eventually it crosses the watershed pass of **Shargang La** (5,037 metres) in the Nyenchen Tanghla range, and connects once again with a motorable track at **Tsoka** in the Salween basin. On the ascent of Shargang La, there are wonderful views of the high 6,000 metres peaks of this barrier range.

Trekking

Pelbar County དཔལ་འབར

Pelbar county is the thickly forested region of the middle Salween basin, extending from Sateng township in the northwest as far as Rayul in the northeast, and including the north-flowing tributaries of the Me-chu and the Gye-chu.

Pelbar County (61)
边坝县
Banbar
Population: 25,973
Area: 8,641 sq km
Colour map 2, grid A6

To the south and west the county is bounded by the Nyenchen Tanglha watershed range. After crossing **Shargang La** pass, you rejoin the motorable road to Chamdo at **Tsoka**, below the village of **Orgyen Tamda**, where there was once an important Nyingmapa temple. The county capital is located at **Do Martang** (Pelbar) in the Me-chu valley, some four kilometres north of Tsoka. Trekking routes also reach the capital from **Sateng** on the border of Driru county (see above, page 383) and from **Tengchen** county (see above, page 387).

The Chamdo road runs east from Tsoka, traversing the upper reaches of the Me-chu and Gye-chu tributaries. En route it passes through **Pelbar** township (27 kilometres), and **Lhatse** township (three kilometres), each of which has a Gelukpa monastery. From Lhatse a southerly trekking route also crosses the watershed and follows the Jepu Tsangpo downstream to **Poto**.

Lhorong County ਲྷོ་རོང

The county of Lhorong is (in Tibetan terms) a densely populated area of the middle Salween basin through which the river completes its east-flowing course and turns south in the direction of Tsawagang. A trekking route follows the main Salween gorge downstream on the north bank from Rayul through Ngulsho and Shingrong townships, and thence to Zhabye.

Lhorong County (62)
洛隆县
Lhorong
Population: 33,731
Area: 6,728 sq km
Colour map 4, grid B1

The main central highway runs further south from Lhatse and crosses the Dakwang-chu tributary to reach Shopado and Dzitoru after 117 kilometres. **Shopado** was formerly the seat of the Martsang Kagyu school in Tibet, and its main monastery was extensive, with 12 chapels and over 200 monks at its height. **Dzitoru** (nowadays known as Lhorong town) is the county capital. Here, the Gelukpa tradition predominates, its monasteries for the most part being affiliated to Chamdo.

Eastern Tibet

Trekking A four-day trekking route follows the Dakwang-chu downstream from **Shopado** to its Salween confluence and thence via the Dak-chu valley on the north bank to **Khyungpo Tengchen** (see above, page 387). A motorable 55 kilometres side-road from **Dzitoru** heads southeast, initially following the Malatso-chu tributary, and then cutting across a watershed pass to **Nakchok**. Below Nakchok, the southeast flowing tributaries: Dzi-chu, Pel-chu, and Dungtso-chu converge with the Salween, now itself plunging southwards.

Dzitoru to Chamdo

The main road from Dzitoru to Chamdo continues eastwards as far as **old Lhorong township** (36 kilometres), and then fords the Salween at Zhabye Zampa bridge. After **Mar-ri** (90 kilometres from old Lhorong) it crosses the Salween/Yu-chu divide, and passes into the border area of Riwoche, Pasho and Drayab counties.

The 18th century **Dolma Lhakhang**, the seat of Akong Rinpoche, who resides at Samye Ling in Scotland, is located at **Dolma-ne**, near **Chakdado** in the upper Yu-chu valley, 24 kilometres beyond Mar-ri. Further south within its vicinity at **Kulha Drak**, there is a Padmasambhava meditation cave known as Zangtal Yeshe Puk, and a Bonpo power place with many grottoes. Generally in Tsawagang, Kulha Drak is revered as the power place of buddha-body, Dolma-ne as the power place of buddha-speech and **Dorje Drilkar** as the power-place of buddha-mind. A trail from here crosses the **Yikdruk La** pass (4,998 metres) to reach Riwoche; while a jeepable track leads south to **Tangkar** township in Pasho county (42 kilometres).

The main road follows the upper Yu-chu for 37 kilometres as far as **Shayak** township (in Pasho county), where it connects with the Chamdo-Kunming highway. From **Shayak to Chamdo via Kyitang** the distance is 87 kilometres.

Pelbar & Lhorong

Lhasa to Chamdo:

the Southern Route via Powo

The southern route from Lhasa to Chamdo is by all accounts the most scenic, and yet road conditions are often precarious, particularly in summer, when glacial melt and rainfall can cause havoc. Most drivers prefer to take the northern route via Nakchu and Riwoche. The route eastwards into Kham begins at Serkhyem La pass (4,515 metres) in Nyangtri county, and traverses the present-day counties of Po-me and Pasho. The virgin forests and subtropical areas of low-lying Po-me county are unique on the Tibetan plateau. Trails also lead south from the highway into Pemako (Metok), one of Tibet's remote 'hidden lands' and largest wildlife reserves; and into Dzayul where the Lohit River winds its course through tribal areas to join the Brahmaputra in India. The counties of this region are administered from Nyangtri, with the exception of Pasho and Drayab which are administered from Chamdo. The distance from Lhasa to Serkhyem La is 452 kilometres (via Kongpo Gyamda), and from Serkyim La to Chamdo 653 kilometres. Recommended itineraries: 4, 5 and 7.

Po-me County ⊂ོ་སྨད

The **Powo** *region, nowadays known as Po-me county, includes both* **Upper Powo** *(Poto) and* **Lower Powo** *(Po-me). The former comprises the valleys of the Poto-chu and its tributary, the Yarlung-chu, which converge below* **Chumdo**. *The latter comprises the lower reaches of the Yi'ong Tsangpo and Parlung Tsangpo rivers which converge above* **Tang-me** *to join the Rong-chu and the Brahmaputra in quick succession, northeast of* **Mount Gyala Pelri**. *The county capital is located at* **Tramog**, *182 kilometres beyond Serkhyem La pass in the lower gorge of the Parlung Tsangpo.*

Po-me County (63)
波密县
Bomi
Population: 24,798
Area: 16,072 sq km
Colour map 4, grid B1

Eastern Tibet

Po-me (Lower Powo) ⊂ོ་སྨད

The southern highway descends through a series of switchbacks from **Serkhyem La** into the flowering Rong-chu valley where **Tongjuk** (46 kilometres) is located. There are spectacular views of **Mount Namchak Barwa** (7,756 metres) and **Mount Gyala Pelri** (7,150 metres) to the east and northeast respectively. Below Tongjuk, the road reaches its lowest point at **Taktra**, where the Rong-chu converges with the Parlung Tsangpo to flow into the Brahmaputra gorges.

Slightly further on, at **Tang-me** (47 kilometres from Tongjuk), the Yi'ong Tsangpo and Parlung Tsangpo rivers converge. At Tang-me, a low-lying jungle settlement (1,700 metres), the road branches: a **trekking route** leads northwest up the Yi'ong Tsangpo valley to **Dra-ke** and **Nyewo** townships. Crossing the Tang-me Zampa bridge, the **highway**, by contrast, follows the east bank of the Parlung Tsangpo upstream in a southeast direction. After 73 kilometres it reaches **Kanam** (Khartak), the traditional seat of government in Powo.

The rulers of Kanam traditionally claimed descent from Prince Jatri Tsenpo, the younger son of Tibet's first 'mortal' king, Drigum Tsenpo, who fled here

Kanam

following the death of his father. Henceforth, the **Kanam Depa** was regarded as one of Tibet's princely states until the unification of the county was achieved by Songtsen Gampo in the seventh century. Special privileges were granted to the rulers of Kanam by the Yarlung Dynasty monarchs in recognition of their royal descent. The region maintained its independence from Lhasa in later centuries, despite the military intervention of 1834, which sought to quell civil unrest. Eventually, in 1928, Kanam was absorbed by the government of Dalai Lama XIII, and its ruler fled to India. In recent times, the most illustrious scion of the house of Kanam has been the late head of the Nyingmapa school Dudjom Rinpoche (1904-87).

At Kanam, the Khartak Zampa bridge crosses the Parlung Tsangpo to **Bakha**, where the Nyingmapa residence of Bakha Tulku is located.

Trekking A trekking route leads southwest across the **Zholwa La** pass to the Brahmaputra gorge, and thence downstream to **Pemako** (see below, page 407).

Tramog Continuing southeast from Kanam, the highway crosses the entrance to the Poto-chu valley and reaches **Tramog** (2,743 metres) the county capital after 16 kilometres, set deep within the thickly forested gorge of the Parlung Tsangpo. Timber is not surprisingly the primary source of wealth and industry. Southwest of town, and across the river, the **Galung La** pass leads southwest into Pemako (see below, page 407). There are guesthouse and restaurant facilities in this town.

The forested valleys of Powo are intimately connected with Padmasambhava. **Gawalung** is the main pilgrimage site of buddha-speech in Kham. The great treasure-finders Sanggye Lingpa (1340-96) and Dudul Dorje (1615-72) also meditated in the region and discovered treasures at **Pukmoche** and **Takdzong** respectively. Treasure-sites (*terkha*) of Dudul Dorje are to be found, additionally, in the environs of **Mount Namchak Barwa**.

Upstream from Tramog, another trail fords the Parlung Tsangpo and leads into Northeast Pemako via the **Chendruk La** pass.

Side-valleys of the Parlung Tsangpo in Po-me Continuing upstream from Tramog and Khamog, the somewhat treacherous road reaches the entrance to the **Chodzong** valley at **Sumdzom** after 41 kilometres. A motorable track branches off here, following the Chodzong Tsangpo upstream for 42 kilometres to **Dorje** township. From here, a trekking route leads across **Kudza La** pass to **Khangyul** in the Salween basin.

The side-valleys of the Moglung-chu, Yupuk-chu, and Midpa-chu rivers are similarly accessible from the highway. Of these, the entrance to **Yupuk valley** is at the township of the same name, located some 34 kilometres southeast of Sumdzom. Above Yupuk, the road continues southeast to the stunningly beautiful glacial lake known as **Ngan Tso** (see below, page 410).

Eastern Tibet

Po-me

Tramog

Poto (Upper Powo) བྲོ་སྟོད

Upper Powo comprises the valley of the Poto-chu, and those of its main tributaries: the Dong-chu (west) and Yarlung-chu (east), which converge at **Chumdo**.

From Kanam, leave the Parlung Tsangpo valley, and head north to Chumdo (23 kilometres).

Getting there

The **Dong-chu valley** is intimately associated with the activities of the treasure-finder Dudul Dorje. It was here that he discovered a *Guidebook to the Secret Land of Pemako*, and practices pertaining to the meditational deities Yamari and Bhairava. In the **Dechen Sangwa** cave in this same valley, he then discovered the text entitled *Gathering of the Entire Intention of the True Doctrine (Damcho Gongpa Yongdu)*. Below the cave, at **Dechen Tang** he established his main residence.

Dong-chu valley

Above Chumdo, the road follows the Dong-chu as far as **Shulmo** (29 kilometres) and **Yuri** (nine kilometres), before cutting northeast towards the **Zhartse La** pass for a further 30 kilometres. From here, you can trek across the watershed to Lhorong county in the Salween basin. At **Yuri Gango**, there was a second temple founded by Dudul Dorje.

Metok County མེ་ཏོག

*The **Pemako** region, one-third of which currently lies within Tibet and the remainder within the **Arunachal Pradesh** province of India, is the name given to the wild jungle terrain of the Brahmaputra valley, southeast of the foaming rapids formed where the river plunges 5,000 metres through the gorge between the East Himalayan peaks of **Mount Namchak Barwa** and **Mount Gyala Pelri**. Pemako is exposed to the full force of the Assamese monsoon (over 300 centimetres per annum), and its altitude is low (4,500 to 600 metres). The climate is hot, tropical and humid, and its virgin forests form one of the **largest wildlife preserves** on the Tibetan plateau. A haven for bears, wild cats, snakes, leeches, and countless species of insects, the region is even now extremely isolated. No proper motorable road links Pemako with the rest of the country. Most supplies are flown in by helicopter from **Nyangtri** to the county capital at **Metok**; and tractors sometimes negotiate the main trail from **Tramog** in Po-me, across the **Galung La** pass. The population is predominantly tribal, comprising the jungle-dwelling **Abor (Lhopa)**, who subsist as hunter-gatherers, and the **Monpa**, who also cultivate the land. Later influxes of Tibetan peoples from Kongpo and Powo have added to the population diversity, and the indigenous Abors have been pushed into peripheral border areas.*

Metok County (64)
墨脱县
Medog
Population: 8,714
Area: 6,787 sq km
Colour map 4, grid B1

Eastern Tibet

Pemako

Despite the inhospitability of the terrain and its inhabitants, the Pemako region has long been regarded as one of the prime pilgrimage sites in Tibet. When Padmasambhava propagated Buddhism during the eighth century, he included Pemako at the head of a select number of 'hidden lands' (*beyul*), as an ideal environment for Buddhist practice in the future. Even now there are caves and *terma*-sites in Pemako associated with the great master and his 25 Tibetan disciples.

Later, during the 17th century, the treasure-finder Dudul Dorje discovered a pilgrim's guide to Pemako near his hermitage in Poto. Accordingly, the valley was identified as the abode of Vajravarahi, her head at **Mount Gangri Karpo** (northeast), her neck at **Mount Dorjeyang**, her navel at **Mount Rinchenpung**, and her breasts as **Mount Gongdu Podrang** and **Pemasiri**. The gateway to the 'hidden land' is located at **Pemakochung** in the Brahmaputra gorge (see above, page 232). It was only during the late 18th century, that Pemako was formally opened as a place of pilgrimage by Gampopa Orgyen Drodul Lingpa (b 1757), Choling Garwang Chime Dorje (b 1763), and Rikdzin Dorje Tok-me (1746-97).

Trekking Various trekking routes lead into Pemako. From Tramog the most important are via Galung La, Chendruk La, and Pokhung La passes, and from Kanam via Bakha and the Zhowa La pass. From Pe in Kongpo there are most direct trekking routes from South Tibet, via the Tamnyen La, the Deyang La (3,713 metres), Buddha Tsepung La, Dozhong La (4,115 metres), and Nam La (5,225 metres). Of these latter passes, **Dozhong La** is the most direct, reaching Metok county town from Pe within four days. The best times to trek from Kongpo are in July or late September, but Pemako is a destination recommended only for pilgrims and explorers of great stamina and physical endurance.

Metok Trek across **Zhowa La** pass from Kanam to reach the east bank of the Brahmaputra at **Pangzhing** township, and continue south to **Takmo**, where the Chendruk Tsangpo flows in from the east. The trekking routes from Tramog via Galung La and Chendruk La also converge here.

The main trail continues to follow the east bank of the river downstream to the county capital at Metok. A trail also follows the west bank from **Jarasa** down through **Muknak Gonpa**, to Dezhing township, and thence to **Metok**, which is at the low altitude of 760 metres. A trail leads west from this riverside track towards **Mount Namchak Barwa**, and Dudjom Rinpoche's sacred *terma*-site known as **Phurparong**.

Zhumo Valley From the confluence of the Brahmaputra and Zhumo-chu at Metok, follow the latter upstream to reach **Mount Zangdok Pelri**, and **Rinchenpung Monastery**, where there is a sacred image of Hayagriva. A three-day trek from Rinchenpung leads southeast to **Gongdu Dorsem Podrang** a wildlife sanctuary close to the de-facto Indian border, consecrated to the meditational deity Vajrasattva.

Bipung **Bipung** or Drepung township lies southwest of Metok on the east bank of the Brahmaputra. Within this township, at **Tirkhung**, is the birthplace of the late Dudjom Rinpoche (1904-87), head of the Nyingmapa school. Across on the west bank is the village of **Patengtsa**, from where a three-day trek leads to **Buddha Tsepung La** pass. The valley approaching the pass is the location of the fabled talismanic lake **Chime Dutsi Latso**, otherwise known as **Lake Bokun**, which is set against the backdrop of a sheer forested mountain, its slopes harbouring temples dedicated to Vajravarahi. Phukmoche, a meditation cave of Padmasambhava, is also located here.

A parallel valley leads via **Harmi** and across **Dozhong La** to Kongpo. South of Bipung the trail follows the Brahmaputra downstream, passing through **Digdong** village and thence directly to the de-facto Indian border (closed and disputed). The river from this point on is known as the **Dihang**.

Dzayul County རྫ་ཡུལ་

*Dzayul county comprises the upper reaches of the Dzayul-chu (**Lohit**), which is fed by two main sources: the Zang-chu (east) and the Gangri Karpo-chu (west). These tributaries converge at Lower Dzayul township before flowing south into Arunachal Pradesh.*

*Towards the southeast of the county, is the valley of the Kyita-chu (Burmese: Nmai), a major source of the 2,170 kilometres long **Irrawaddy** River, which rises at the Languela glacier in Dzayul and enters Burma via Yunnan province.*

Dzayul County (65)
察隅县
Zayu
Population: 22,802
Area: 19,693 sq km
Colour map 4, grid B2

The county capital of Dzayul is located at **Kyigang** (formerly known as **Sangak Chodzong**) in the Zang-chu valley, 258 kilometres southeast of **Sumdzom**, and 172 kilometres southeast of **Rawok**. Dzayul shares its south borders with India (which controls one third of its territory), Burma, and Gongshan county of Yunnan. The sparse population is both Tibetan and tribal Lopa.

Kyigang

Getting there To reach Dzayul, leave the highway at **Rawok**, and drive southeast across **Demo La** pass. The road follows the Zang-chu tributary of the **Lohit** through **Goyul** township (92 kilometres from Rawok), and thence downstream to **Drowa Gon** (63 kilometres) and the county capital at **Kyigang** (17 kilometres).

After Kyigang, the river changes course southwest, and the motorable road follows it for 61 kilometres as far as its confluence with the Gangri Karpo-chu at **Lower Dzayul township (Dzayul Rong-me)**.

Lower Dzayul

The Gangri Karpo-chu, which rises in the snow range of the same name in Northeast Pemako, passes through **Upper Dzayul** township (Dzayul Rongto) and eventually merges with the Zang-chu at Lower Dzayul township (Dzayul Rong-me). The only motorable stretch is between these townships (66 kilometres), but there are also trekking routes leading northwest from Upper Dzayul to **Pemako** and southeast from Lower Dzayul to **Burma** and **India**.

Upper Dzayul

Eastern Tibet

Dzayul

The extreme east of the county comprises the lower Salween gorge, from the villages of **Golak** township on the Ralung-chu tributary as far south as Tsawarong, on the east bank of the Salween. According to one tradition, it was to **Gyelmo Taktse** in Tsawarong that Vairocana, the great translator, was exiled during the eighth century; and where he taught the Dzogchen practices to his foremost students Sangton Yeshe Lama and Pangen Sangye Gonpo. At **Wa Senge Puk (Wapuk)** in **Tsawarong**, three successive generations of Dzogchen masters, who had received teachings from Vairocana, attained the rainbow-light body.

Salween gorge

NB The Salween in this stretch is not

motorable, but trekking routes follow the river downstream from Pasho county, through Golak to Tsawarong. Below Tsawarong, the trail continues downstream into Yunnan.

Pasho County ৎ্པর་ৰঁ১

Pasho County (66)
八宿县
Baxoi
Population: 32,942
Area: 12,580 sq km
Colour map 4, grid B2

*The highway from Po-me to Chamdo continues to follow the Parlung Tsangpo upstream through alpine forested landscape for 127 kilometres as far as **Rawok** township, where it enters Pasho county. Rawok is located on the north shore of the blue lake **Ngan Tso**, dramatically girded by snow peaks. The ruins of the Gelukpa **Shukden Gonpa** lie to the south of the lake; and there is a turn-off for Dzayul in the southeast. Keep to the highway, which then turns abruptly north on its 23 kilometres ascent of **Ngajuk La** pass (4,468 metres).*

Pema

Colour map 4, grid B2

Crossing this pass, which forms a watershed between the Brahmaputra and Salween river systems, the beautiful alpine forests recede; and the road follows the barren Ling-chu valley downstream for 67 kilometres to **Pema (Pasho)**, the capital of **Tsawa Pasho** county, in the mid-Salween basin. En route it passes through **Chidar** township, **Tashitse Dzong** and **Rangbu Gonpa**. At Pema there are simple guesthouse and restaurant facilities. The highway continues to follow the Ling-chu downstream from Pema to its confluence with the Salween at **Po**, bypassing a turn-off on the right (south) which leads to **Lingka** township. The ruins of **Nera Gonsar** monastery are visible here. After crossing the Salween via the **Ngulchu Zampa** bridge, the highway then rises steeply from the gorge through 180 switchbacks to scale the **Gama La** pass (4,618 metres).

Pomda

The descent on the far side of the pass is much more gradual, leading down to the rolling grasslands of **Pomda** in the Yu-chu valley. Here, 92 kilometres from Pema, the southern highway from Lhasa finally connects with the Chamdo-Kunming highway. Pomda township (4,084 metres) lies 13 kilometres further upstream in the wide Yu-chu valley. It is an important cross-roads for traffic heading west to Lhasa, north to Chamdo, and south to Yunnan or Sichuan. A small Gelukpa monastery, named **Pomda Sangak Dechen**, was founded by Phakpalha Tongwa Donden as a branch of Chamdo. Destroyed by the Bonpo king of Beri in the 17th century, it was subsequently rebuilt by Phakpalha Gyelwa Gyatso. It had 70 monks, and was formerly the main attraction of the valley, prior to the construction of the highway.

Sleeping and eating The town has Sichuan restaurant facilities and a transport station guesthouse, beloved by truck drivers. When the southern highway to Lhasa is blocked by landslides or snowmelt in summer, the trucks often remain stationary at Pomda for prolonged periods.

The gently sloping grasslands of the Yu-chu valley (the principal tributary of the Salween) lie in the highlands of **Tsawagang**, north of the Tsawarong (Salween) gorges. The new **Chamdo Airport** (4,300 metres) has recently been constructed here, 25 kilometres north of Pomda and 128 kilometres

Pema

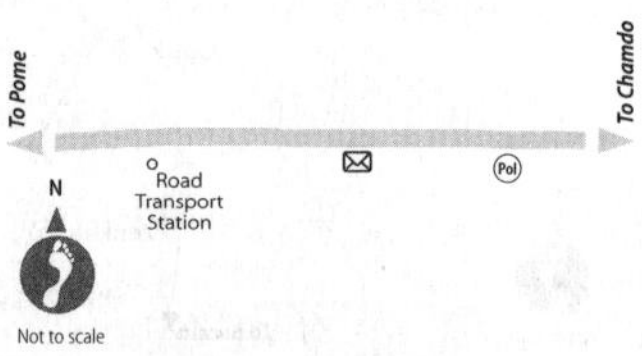

Eastern Tibet (side tab)

south of Chamdo, but it is generally not open to foreign travellers unless they have obtained a permit for Chamdo. Locals can fly to and from Chengdu twice weekly (Tuesday and Friday).

Pasho

To Chamdo
(128 km)

Chamdo Airport

25
Pomda
92 3

Pema 67 Po
4,618m

Tramog Lingka

Parlung Tsangpo
27

23 4,468m

Ngom-tso
Rawok

N

Not to scale

To Dzayul   To Dzogang

Salween

Yu-chu

Pomda to Chamdo

From Pomda the combined highway follows the Yu-chu valley upstream to **Shayag** (59 kilometres). A turn-off on the left (northwest) connects with the old caravan trail to Lhasa via Shabye Zampa and Lhorong (see above, page 403). The main road then cuts east across the **Lona La** pass (4,511 metres), which is a watershed between the Mekong and Salween river systems. **Kyitang** (Jyitang) village lies beyond the pass, above the Mekong valley, in Drayab county, and from here to Chamdo the distance is only 65 kilometres.

Drayab County བྲག་གཡབ

*Drayab county extends southeast from **Kyitang** on the Pomda-Chamdo highway through the valley of the Me-chu tributary of the Mekong and those of its small feeder rivers, the Leb-chu, Do-chu, and so forth. Kyitang township is distinguished by its sturdy houses with horizontal timbers: a typical feature of Khampa domestic architecture. Descend into the Mekong gorge, and follow the river downstream, reaching the Drayab turn-off at the Me-chu confluence after 10 kilometres. The county capital is located at **Endun** (Drayab town), 34 kilometres from Kyitang.*

Drayab County (67)
蔡雅县
Zhagyab
Population: 46,998
Area: 9,672 sq km
Colour map 4, grid B3

Returning to the Me-chu/Mekong confluence from Endun, take the right turn and follow the Mekong upstream on the highway. Soon you will pass the Dzi-chu (Riwoche) River confluence on the left (west) side of the road; and continue on to Chamdo. The entire 234 kilometres' drive from Pasho to Chamdo can be covered in a single day in optimum road conditions.

In **Nyagre** district of Drayab county, there are ancient rock carvings and statues which suggest that this area had close connections with the Yarlung Dynasty kings of Tibet. At **Denma Drag** (now known as Rinda Dekyiling) there is a relief carving of Vairocana Buddha, said in the *Mani Kabum* to have been commissioned by Princess Wengcheng in the seventh century. An important inscription suggests that the image was actually fashioned in the time of his descendant King Tride Songtsen (ninth century).

Nyagre Rock Carvings and Images

In 1621, Drayab Kyabgon I Ngupe Trakpa Gyatso (1572-1638) founded the Gelukpa monastery of **Drayab Tashi Chodzong**, and unified the surrounding areas: three agricultural valleys including Nyag-re, and two outlying nomadic tracts. The original monastery became known as the **Magon** ('mother monastery') following the foundation of the **Bugon** ('son monastery') at Jamdun in 1640; and since that time Drayab county has comprised both the **Endun** area, under the authority of the Magon, and the **Jamdun** area under the authority of the Bugon.

Drayab Endun (Mother Monastery)

Eastern Tibet

Drayab Tashi Chodzong The **Magon** monastery rapidly became one of the most influential cultural centres of East Tibet, developing under the guidance of the nine successive Drayab Kyabgon incarnations (also known as Tulku Chetsang) and the successive incarnations of Sangye Tashi, who are known as the Tulku Chungtsang. The monastery housed over 1,000 monks. It has been destroyed twice in the present century – once by Chao Erh Feng's forces and more recently by the Communists. Reconstruction is proceeding apace through the effort of the local populace and the development project initiated by Drayab Kyabgon IX who resides in Germany.

Of its former 32 temples, which symbolized the 32-deity mandala of Guhyasamaja, a three-storeyed **Assembly Hall (Dukhang)** has been restored. On the ground level, the spacious **Jamkhang temple** contains images of Drayab Kyabgon IX Loden Sherab, Ngok Lekpe Sherab, Atisha, and the protector Ksetrapala, among others. The residence of the Kyabgon is on the third floor of this building. Below the monastery the restored **Drayab Gonkhang** contains images of Dorje Drakden, Dorje Shukden, Ksetrapala (six forms), and Dorje Yudronma, as well as fine murals depicting the 12 *Tenma* protectors.

Formerly the Magon monastery had 33 branches throughout Drayab county, including the nunneries of **Dolma Ritro** and **Evam Ritro** hermitages. Currently there are about 100 registered monks at the Magon, and approximately 900 unofficial monks.

Sleeping and eating The town of **Drayab** (Endun), which lies at 3,660 metres, below the Magon Monastery, has simple guesthouse facilities. There are 3 small Sichuan-style restaurants on the main street, and small grocery stores. The government buildings and public security bureau are located within a compound at the end of the main street.

Jamdun Further south at Jamdun, there is a life-size stone image of Maitreya, said to have been the central image of a geomantic temple dating from the period of the royal dynasty. Formerly, it was flanked by smaller images of the Eight Bodhisattvas, Princess Wengcheng and Minister Gar. In 1265, when Chogyel Phakpa visited Drayab, he identified the main image as Maitreya. Other authorities, such as Karma Chak-me, have stated that a Maitreya temple existed there during the royal dynastic period. At **Kyilechu Nyal**, there is a large stone image of Bhaisajyaguru, the medicine buddha; and at **Langrung-ne Tramo** there is a relief image of Avalokiteshvara, nearby a temple dedicated to the same deity.

Jamdun Bugon Monastery The Bugon ('son monastery'), properly known as **Jamdun Ganden Shedrub Chokhor**, was founded at Jamdun, near the ancient stone Maitreya image, by Drayab Kyabgon II Ngawang Sonam Lhundrub in 1640. Formerly it housed 1,300 monks and had some 19 branches within the county, including the **Jorkhe Ritro** hermitage, which was once one of the largest nunneries in Tibet, housing 700 nuns at its height. The Bugon was also destroyed twice in the present century by Chao Erh

Drayab

Feng and the Communists. Current rebuilding is under the direction of Drayab Kyabgon IX.

Getting there   Jamdun is reached by jeep from Endun, via **Rangdrub** township. The other outlying townships of the county, such as **Khora**, are accessible on horseback from Endun or Jamdun. **Wakhar** can however be reached by jeep from Endun (27 kilometres). **Khargang** township is reached 14 kilometres from Kyitang, following the Mekong valley downstream.

Chamdo to Kunming:

Descent of the Yu-chu and Mekong Gorges

The motor route from Chamdo at the heart of Kham to Kunming in Southwest China follows the great waterways of East Tibet and the contours of the high ranges dividing them. The initial section runs along the west bank of the Mekong as far as Kyitang, and, after crossing the Lana La pass, hugs the Yu-chu through the grasslands as far south as Dzogang. Recrossing the Tsawagang range here via the Dungda La pass, the road then plunges down to cross the Mekong at Drukha Zampa. Reaching the east bank, it abruptly rises through the Markhamgang range and forks, the east branch leading to Batang (on which see below, page 430), and the south branch leading through Markham and Gartok. Taking the latter turning, the road eventually rejoins the Mekong at Lagyab Sho above Tasakalho, and follows its course downstream as far as Jol county (in present day Yunnan). On this section there are spectacular views of the Kawa Karpo glaciers (6,740 metres). From Jol, it cuts southeast across the watershed to enter the Yangtze river system, fording this mighty river twice: in Gyeltang and Jang Sadam (Lijiang) counties. Finally, the highway leaves the Tibetan area and re-enters the Mekong basin at Dali.

*Altogether, the highway traverses two counties which are administered from Chamdo (**Dzogang** and **Markham**), three which are administered from Gyeltang (ie **Jol**, **Gyeltang** and **Balung**), and the **Jang Sadam** (Ch Lijiang) region, before heading south to **Dali** and east to **Kunming** City. The overall distance from Chamdo to Kunming is 1,789 kilometres. **Recommended itinerary: 7.***

NB *This itinerary can be reversed, and those who have entered Tibet from Kunming have often been impressed by the proximity offered by this approach.*

Dzogang County མཛོ་སྒང་

Dzogang County (68)
左貢县
Zogang
Population: 35,960
Area: 12,320 sq km
Colour map 4, grid B2

Tsawa Dzogang *county comprises the valley of the Salween south of Pasho and those of its tributaries, the Le-chu and the Yu-chu (south of Pomda). At the intersection 13 kilometres south of **Pomda**, take the left (east) road, which continues to run through the Yu-chu valley. Gradually the wide grasslands narrow, and the Yu-chu tapers into a forested gorge. After 29 kilometres, you will pass on the left (east) a turn-off for **Meyul** township.*

Getting there The distance from the Pomda intersection to Dzogang is 94 kilometres; and from Chamdo 260 kilometres.

Temto The renovated Gelukpa monastery of **Temto** (founded as a branch of

Drepung Loseling) is one of the most impressive among the 13 Gelukpa monasteries of this area. Notice the distinctive roadside stupas of the Yu-chu valley, which have a protective wooden pavilion to ward off precipitation.

At Temto, 22 kilometres south of the Meyul turn-off, there are two branch roads: one to the east leading to **Sayul** (50 kilometres) and **Sanor** on the Mekong, and the other to the southwest leading to **Tobang** (22 kilometres).

Keeping to the main highway, continue south via Uyak to **Wamda**, the county capital, otherwise known as **Tsawa Dzogang**, which is located on a spur (3,780 metres) overlooking the Yu-chu, with a backdrop of forest. Timber is plentiful here and this is reflected in the local building construction.

Wamda

The monastery of **Tsawa Dzogang Sangakling** was founded by Phakpalha of Chamdo, consequent on the conversion of various local Bon monasteries to the Gelukpa tradition. Spend the night here at the *Dzogang Guesthouse* (¥15 per bed). The exceedingly long main street has a number of small shops and restaurants, government buildings, schools, and the inevitable karaoke bar, Tibetan-owned, and with a surprisingly sophisticated sound system. On the outskirts of town there is a petrol station.

South of Tsawa Dzogang the road branches. Keep to the main road, which leaves the Yu-chu valley to ascend the watershed **Dungda La** pass (5,008 metres) after 40 kilometres, and enter Markham county.

Dungda La

Dzogang & Markham

If instead you continue along the riverside south of Tsawa Dzogang, the Yu-chu gorge deepens and a jeepable dirt road follows the river downstream for 92 kilometres as far as **Drakyol** township, where there is a small Gelukpa monastery. Further south there is no vehicular access as the Yu-chu is abruptly forced to change course by the snow massives of the **Kawa Karpo Range**. The rapid river snakes back upon itself before flowing southwest into the Salween above **Tsawarong** (see above, page 409). It is, however, possible to trek south from Drakyol to Tsawarong, as the French adventurer Alexandra David-Neel did in reverse on her journey to Lhasa (1923). Upstream from this confluence are the remote Salween townships of **Kyil Lingka** (Trung Lingka) and **Zha Lingka**, which offer trekking access to Dzayul and to Pasho.

Drakyol

Eastern Tibet

Markham County སྨར་ཁམས

Markham County (69)
芒康县
Markham
Population: 66,060
Area: 12,258 sq km
Colour map 4, grid B3

*Markham county is a prosperous and densely populated part of Kham, occupying the high ground (**Markhamgang**) between the Mekong and Yangtze rivers. The farm houses of Markham are for the most part large three-storey detached buildings of whitewashed adobe and ornate wooden lintels. Trade has been a significant factor in its economy, in that the county straddles the crossroads from Lhasa (via Chamdo), Chengdu (via Batang), and Kunming (via Jol). The capital is located at **Gartok**, 168 kilometres from Tsawa Dzogang, and 104 kilometres from Batang.*

Descent from Dungda La pass to the Mekong

Ascending the **Dungda La** pass (5,008 metres) from Tsawa Dzogang, the highway offers spectacular views of **Mount Dungri Karpo** (6,090 metres) to the south. A second but lower pass **Joba La** (3,908 metres) is quickly crossed after **Dempa**, and then the road zigzags down the barren sandstone ravine to **Druka Zampa** bridge, which spans the Mekong. A gradual ascent on the east bank via **Rong-me** township leads across **Lao-shan** pass (4,060 metres) into the alpine meadows of Markhamgang.

Gartok

The prosperity of the region is instantly apparent. Passing the turn-off for Batang, you soon reach **Gartok**. Its main attraction is the Gelukpa **monastery of Markham**, a beautiful yellow building containing in its inner sanctum a large impressive image of Maitreya, flanked by smaller images of Tsongkhapa and his students. Markham Monastery is affiliated to Drayab, on which see above, page 411.

Sleeping & eating Stay at the *Markham Guesthouse*, where the superior rooms are ¥45 (¥15 per bed) and inferior dormitory-style beds are ¥8 per person. The town has a number of Sichuan-style restaurants.

South of Gartok Following the highway south from Gartok, along the Drong-chu (Markham Kyilchu) valley, you will pass **Biru** village and 63 kilometres south of Gartok, at **Bum-nye** a turn-off leads east across the river to the farming village of **Pangda**, home of Lhasa's famous merchant Pangdatsang. Motorable country roads link Pangda with **Bumpa** township (57 kilometres) and Jikdrong township (47 kilometres). The **Bum La** pass (4,115 metres) above Bumpa was held by the Qing emperors as the boundary between independent Tibet and Chinese occupied Tibet from the mid-18th century onwards (although this had little meaning on the ground until the present century).

Staying on the highway, you soon cross **Hung La** pass (4,470 metres), and the road rejoins the Mekong valley at **Lagyabsho**, some 48 kilometres north of Tsakalho. The descent into Tsakalho is impressive, overlooking the sheer Mekong gorge, and the road tunnels its way through precipitous cliffs.

Tsakalho

Tsakalho (*Ch* Yenching) lies 914 metres above the Mekong gorge, and the cliffs are so steep that the river cannot be seen from town! Near the riverside are the commercial salt-pans which give Tsakalho its name. The altitude here is relatively low (3,109 metres), and the climate is warm. Beware of mosquitos in summer. For centuries Tsakalho has been a staging post on the trading route from **Jang** (Lijiang) and **Jol** (Dechen) to Lhasa, and it has recently acquired the status of a county town in its own right. In addition to the Tibetan Khampa population, there is a substantial **Jang (Naxi)** community. South of town there is a checkpoint, 12 kilometres below which the road crosses the present day frontier between the TAR and Yunnan province.

Stay at the *Tsakalho Guesthouse* (¥6 per bed). There are small Sichuan and Tibetan-style restaurants in the market, which is well worth a visit.

Sleeping & eating

Dechen County བདེ་ཆེན་

Dechen County (70)
德钦县
Deqen
Population: 56,644
Area: 7,164 sq km
Colour map 4, grid C4

*Dechen county comprises the Mekong valley south of Tsakalho and the **Kawa Karpo** range (also known as the Minling range; Ch Meili) which divides it from the Salween. Its east boundary is formed by the Yangtze. The county capital is located at Jol, 112 kilometres south of Tsakalho.*

*The best seasons for driving from Tsakalho to Kunming are spring and autumn. In summer the road surface can be devastated by heavy landslides, necessitating a walk of over 2 days to reach **Jol**. Pack animals can be hired in Tsakalho.*

From Tsakalho, follow the east bank of the Mekong downstream to **Hongshan (Fuchang)** village (40 kilometres), where there is a hospitable roadside inn and the *Markham County Naxi Guesthouse* (beds at ¥2 per night). Continue downstream, crossing and recrossing the river, until reaching a point where the road rises high above the river and turns southeast for Jol.

Hongshan

Across the gorge as you approach Jol from Tsakalho and Hongshan, there are truly dramatic views of the Kawa Karpo glaciers (6,740m). The astonishing main glacier of **Mount Kawa Karpo** appears to plunge downwards, almost to the level of the Mekong in the gorge below. The snow range is an important focal point for pilgrimage, and it is revered as one of the 25 important meditation sites associated with Padmasambhava in Kham and Amdo. Specifically, this mountain symbolizes the body-aspect of buddha-speech. In the past it has been a stronghold of the Nyingmapa school. Vairocana gave teachings on Dzogchen to his followers at Tswarong, to the northwest of the range; and there are branches of **Katok Monastery** in its environs. The most renowned figure in this lineage was Kawakarpowa Namka Gyatso, who, with his teacher Khedrup Yeshe Gyeltsen, expounded the Katok lineage throughout this extreme south region of Kham.

Mount Kawa Karpo

At Km road marker 1,854, north of Jol, there is an observation pavilion from which the sunrise on Mount Kawa Karpo may be witnessed. Adjacent to the pavilion is a monument dedicated to 17 members of a Sino-Japanese mountaineering expedition who died on Kawa Karpo in 1990. Further south on this road is the **Namka Tashi Temple**, which was constructed in 1986 to commemorate the visit to Jol of the late Panchen Lama X. Inside the images depict (left to right): Tsongkhapa with his foremost students, Jowo Shakyamuni, Padmasambhava in the upright form Totrengtsel, and the protector deity Kawa Karpo. Above the door is a mural depicting the Lords of the Three Families, while those on the wall adjacent to the door portray the Nyingma protectors: Rahula, Ekajati and Dorje Lekpa, along with 6-armed Mahakala and Mahakala in the form Bernakchen. The left wall has murals of the meditational deities

Eastern Tibet

including Guhyasamaja, Cakrsamvara, and Vajrabhairava; while the right depicts the deities according to the *Konchok Chidu* revelation of Jatson Nyingpo.

At km road marker 1.838 a motorable trail leaves the main road at 2,700 metres, and descends to **Pandzara** village, where the head-man Mr Tsering Dorje and his sons can arrange porterage if you wish to trek to Kawa Karpo. Since 1997 it has also been possible to drive all the way to the glacier! Cross the Mekong by a concrete bridge below the village at 2,215 metres, and ascend a 45 degree incline to reach the Miyam valley. Cross the Miyam-chu river at 2,523 metres and climb through the forest to reach **Miyam Monastery**, located spectacularly below the glacier at 3,030 metres. This monastery is also known as **Go-me Gonpa**, in contrast to **Go-to Gonpa** which lies even higher up at the head of the valley. Formerly Miyam Monastery had 3 temples, an outer shrine dedicated to Avalokiteshvara, an inner shrine dedicated to Cakrasamvara, and an upper shrine dedicated to Shakyamuni. The small renovated temple which is supervised by Jampa Pema Dondrub has large images (left to right) depicting Manjughosa, Padmasambhava, Jowo Shakyamuni, 4-armed Avalokiteshvara, and Vajrasattva, along with smaller icons of Jowo Shakyamuni, Padmasambhava, Tara, Aksobhya, Vajradhara, and Vajrapani. Posters decorate the side-walls, depicting calendrical charts of the left and the 8 manifestations of Padmasambhava on the right. The portico has an inscription recounting the history of the monastery on the left and a large Mani Wheel on the right.

Starting from Miyam Monastery, the full inner pilgrimage circuit of the snow range takes 12 days, passing through **Aben Gon**, **Wapuk Gon**, and **He Gon**, which are all branches of Katok. This trail can also be reached from the village of **Meili Dungjang** on the west bank of the Mekong (accessible by ferry). The outer circuit, approached from Seji village, south of Jol, is extremely dangerous but can be completed by hardy pilgrims in 22 days. These routes are favoured by Japanese visitors and botanical groups.

Jol (Dechen; *Ch* Shenping) Pass the night at the county town of **Jol**, located on a
Phone code: 0887 steep hillside (3,480 metres), its slopes and climate strangely reminiscent of Darjiling in Northeast India.

The main street, leading uphill from the hotel towards the open market has a number of small Sichuan and Yunnan style restaurants. In the wet season, the local economy is centred on mushroom picking, since the **Songrong mushroom** which grows on the river banks and in the forests is exported to Japan, where it is reckoned to have curative effects for the treatment of certain cancers. The monasteries of Jol traditionally belonged to both the Karma Kagyu and the Gelukpa schools. Among them, the most important is **Ganden Dongdrubling**, where religious dances are held in mid-October. There are two nature conservation parks: at Kawa Karpo and at Padma, both of which are to be incorporated within the proposed Great Rivers National Park.

Sleeping The comfortable *Dechen Meili Hotel*, T(86)0887841204, has

Dechen & Gyeltang

To Derong

Salween

Tsakalho
40
Hongshon

6,740m

72

Jol

Tongtaling

Mekong

4,292m

Pontselang

184 (from Jol)

Gyeltang
193

To Jang Sadam
(Lijiang)

187

Dali
412
Kunming

N

Not to scale

The Great Rivers National Park

In 1998, following two years of negotiation, an agreement was signed between Yunnan province and the US Nature Conservancy, with a view to establishing the Great Rivers National Park. Covering an area of 66,000 sq km (four times the size of Yellowstone National Park), this is claimed to be China's first world class national park, extending from Shigu in the south to Tsakalho on the TAR border in the north, and from the Burmese border in the west to Lugu Lake in the east. As such, it will include the gorges of the Salween, Irrawady, Mekong, and Yangtze, amalgamating several former national parks under the jurisdiction of Dechen Prefecture, Ninglang county, and Lijiang. This vast region which is home to diverse ethnic groups, including the Khampa Tibetans, Naxi, Yi, Li, Nu, Moso, and Malimoso, has been described by the Royal Botanic gardens of Edinburgh as "one of the most significant resources of plant diversity in the northern temperate hemisphere". It sustains 10,000 of the 15,000 plant species found in Yunnan, including 60% of those used in traditional Chinese medicine and 75% of those used in Tibetan medicine. There are also more than 1000 species of bird, at least 30 endangered species of animal, including the snow leopard, the clouded leopard, the lesser panda, and the Yunnan golden monkey. A single tiger was reportedly spotted in 1979! The four mountain ranges within the proposed park, including Mt Kawa Karpo and Mt Padma, contain more than 30 major peaks, at least 5 of which are above 6,000m. It is hoped that the park, once established, will extend special protection for the biological and cultural diversity of the region.

---

double rooms (¥200) and single rooms (¥90). But the electricity supply is unreliable. The attached bathrooms currently have hot water supplied in thermos bottles. *Dechen Travel Company*, headed by Mr Tsering Nyima. Have an office in the hotel, T(0887)8412852/8413096, F(0086887)8413227. The *Dechen Tourism Hotel*, scheduled to open in January 1999, will have standard rooms, priced between ¥150-250. *Dechen Government Guesthouse*, opposite the *Meili Hotel*. Has cheaper but inferior accommodation, and hot showers.

Mount Padma

From Jol, the highway heads southeast (a turn-off at Seji village leads down to an old trekking route across the Mekong-Salween divide, from where one can undertake the 22 day outer circuit of Mount Kawa Karpo or head north into Dzogang county). It then crosses the watershed pass of **Yak La** (4,230 metres) between the Mekong and the Yangtze, offering to the south a spectacular view of the snow peaks of **Mount Padma** (*Ch* Baima Shan; 4,292 metres), where there is a forested nature reserve. Descending to the Yangtze basin, via three successive passes (two at 4,260 metres and one at 3,540 metres), you will reach the large Gelukpa monastery of **Tongtaling**.

Tongtaling Gonpa

This Gelukpa establishment contains images of Tsongkhapa flanked by his foremost students and to their left the reliquary of the monastery's founder, Kusho Tongta. The murals depict the Four Guarding Kings, the Gelukpa meditational deities, cosmological charts, and the Wheel of Rebirth. Outside in the courtyard there is a statue in Chinese style depicting the 'laughing buddha'. Formerly there were 456 monks at Tongtaling, but nowadays it is maintained by a mere 22 monks.

Pontselang

Downhill from Tongtaling, the road soon reaches the bustling town of Pontselang (Benzilan). Here, there are plentiful Chinese restaurants, among which the *Ga-ha Restaurant* is recommended.

Below Pontselang, a **branch road** crosses to the east bank of the Yangtze, and follows the river upstream to **Derong** county in present day Sichuan (see below, page 440). The **main road** continues south on the west bank for some distance before crossing the Yangtze and a southeast flowing tributary, at a point made famous by the Long March. From here, it proceeds through Gyeltang county.

Gyeltang County རྒྱལ་ཐང་

Gyeltang County (71)
中甸县
Zhongdian
Population: 122,108
Area: 11,869 sq km
Colour map 4, grid C4

*Gyeltang county is a densely populated area, bounded on the west, south, and east by the bending course of the Yangtze, and comprising the wide fertile plain of the Gyeltang-chu, a major tributary of the Yangtze. Both the county and prefectural capitals are located at **Gyeltangteng**. 184 kilometres southeast of Jol, and 193 kilometres northwest of Lijiang. Nowadays only 40 percent of the county's population is estimated to be Tibetan. The remainder are Han Chinese, Naxi, Lisu, Yi, Bai and Pumi. The Gyeltang region prospered over the centuries since it commanded the trade routes between East Tibet and Burma, Yunnan, and Northeast India. Brick tea from Yunnan, and the raw silk and cotton from British India were particularly valued. The summer horse festival of Gyeltang dates back to the 17th century equestrian master Topden.*

Napa Lake

Descending into the Gyeltang plain from the northeast, the road skirts the east shore of **Napa Lake**, which is occupied by nomadic camper groups. The **Napa Lake Nature Reserve** is a migratory home to the black-necked crane in winter. Large herds of yak are commonplace here, and the exposed plain has a number of windmills.

Gyeltangteng City

Phone code: 0887
Colour map 4, grid C4

The large city of **Gyeltangteng** (*Ch* Zhongdian) lies at the heart of the Gyeltang-chu plain, at an altitude of 3,344 metres, and four hours from Lijiang Airport. Nowadays, Gyeltangteng functions as the capital of the entire Dechen Autonomous Prefecture, a region of extraordinary biodiversity, which supports some 7,000 species of native plants including the blue poppy and other types of meconopsis, azelias and 200 types of rhododendron. Many of these have medicinal usage. This discovery was made known to the outside world through the work of George Forrest of the Royal Botanic Gardens in Edinburgh; and in recent years this Scottish connection has been renewed when a conservation programme was implemented by the Dechen Forestry Bureau, in liaison with the Royal Botanic Gardens, Edinburgh and a US-based local entrepreneur.

Gyeltang Sungtseling Monastery

The architecture of the city is largely drab and uninspiring Chinese provincial style. Badly damaged by a major earthquake which hit neighbouring Lijiang in early 1996, the dusty streets are now the scene of extensive and rapid reconstruction. Three buildings do however stand out. Among these, the **Hospital of Traditional Tibetan Medicine** located behind the *Dechen Guesthouse* is one of the largest in Tibet.

Hospital of Tibetan Medicine

An image of Shakyamuni has recently been reconstructed in the temple on the small hill, while the main assembly hall of the large Dokar Dzong is currently undergoing renovation. It contains images of Avalokiteshvara, Padmasambhava, Shakyamuni, Green Tara and White Tara, along with the Four Guardian Kings. In a side building there is a memorial exhibition to the Long March of the Red Army. Tibetan handicrafts are available, particularly the azalea wooden bowls, silver ornaments, and embroidered covers which are made locally.

Dokar Dzong

By far the most important site within the valley is **Gyeltang Sungtseling Monastery**, which is the largest Tibetan Buddhist complex in the prefecture, currently housing 600-700 monks. Located some eight kilometres from the city on an isolated ridge, known as Guardian Hill, it has the appearance of a small monastic town. The monastery was originally constructed in 1681 at the advice of Dalai Lama V, and it traditionally comprised an assembly hall flanked by eight residential colleges (*khangtsang*).

Gyeltang Sungtseling Monastery

Recently, the **Assembly Hall**, the **Drayab Khangtsang** and a Tsongkhapa temple have been renovated. The Assembly Hall (Dukhang) has an 80-pillared chamber, containing a teaching throne and a series of images depicting Tsongkhapa and his students, Dalai Lama V, and three past lamas of the monastery (Sambo Rinpoche, Kensur Rinpoche and the late Kangyur Rinpoche), along with the reliquary of Sambo Rinpoche. The **upper storey** has a gallery overlooking the main hall, and in its northwest corner a protector chapel with a large image of Dharmaraja, and others depicting Shridevi, Sertro, and Shukden. The private quarters of the Dalai Lama are also here.

The **Drayab Khangtsang** contains images of Tsongkhapa flanked by his students, and the mundane protector deities Gyel, Se, and Tsen. **Upstairs** is a room where a team of seamstresses occasionally prepare brocade hangings and ceremonial dance costumes for use at the monastery.

The **Jang Khangtsang**, currently being refurbished by Kyapje Pondro Rinpoche and Ngawang Tropel, is seeking to raise US$9,000 for restoration work.

South of town, the protector hills of Rutapo and Rutamo rise above the *Gyeltang Dzong Hotel*. A four-hour walk leads across the flower-carpeted hills to Riknga Lhakhang, where there are images of the Five Meditational Buddhas.

Rutapo & Rutamo Hills

Gyeltang Dzong Hotel (Ch Jentan Binguan, T0887-8223646/8227583/8227610, F86-887-8223620. Situated below the Rutapo and Rutamo hills which traditionally protect the Gyeltangteng valley, constructed in an attractive Tibetan dzong style, and under international management, has well-appointed rooms with private phone, TV, attached bathroom with running hot water, central heating, *Metok Pema Restaurant* serving Tibetan, Western, Chinese and Indian cuisine, cultural programmes highlighting botany and Tibetan medicine, and an in-house travel agency, T0887-82227493. There is a plan to extend the complex, adding 50 new rooms by 2000, along with a stable of riding horses, a craft and cultural centre, and a botanical landscape development. Poorer

Sleeping & eating

Eastern Tibet

accommodation is available at the spacious **Dechen Guesthouse** (¥120 per room, ¥60 per bed), and the **Zhongdian Kang Beng Minzu Jiulou**, T0887-8222091 (¥50 per room), while backpackers often prefer the privately run **Tashi Hotel**. Cheap restaurants are plentiful on the main street outside the *Dechen Guesthouse* and here you will also find the government buildings, public security bureau, bookshop and post office.

Festivals February/March: *Tibetan New Year* (Losar) is commemorated by a 15 day festival of prayers and religious dances at Ganden Sungtseling Monastery; **May/June**: *Gyeltang Horse Festival*; **1-4 October**: *Traditional Folk Dances* (Tibetan, Lisu and Yi).

Transport **Air** The new *Gyeltang Airport* is expected to open in April 1999, and 2 flights will be scheduled each week from Kunming.

Routes and excursions from Gyeltangteng There are four roads leading from Gyeltangteng city. One (already described) heads northwest towards **Dechen** county (184 kilometres); a second runs northeast via **Geza** and the rich nomadic grasslands of **Zhakdo** and **Mikzur** to **Wengshui** (156 kilometres) on the present-day Sichuan border and thence a further 69 kilometres to **Chaktreng** (see below, page 440); a third which is the **Kunming highway**, running south for 152 kilometres to **Jang Sadam** (Lijiang); and a fourth heading southeast to **Chukar** and the Haba Gangri range.

Hongshan Mountains Heading northeast via Geza in the direction of the Chaktreng county border, a rough side-road leads into the Hongshan Mountains (4,000 metres), which are well-known for their azaleas, rhododendrons, meadow and scree flowers.

Zhado and Beta Lakes If you take the last of these roads, heading southeast from town, there are turn-offs on the left leading to the pristine waters of Zhado Lake (*Ch* Shudu hai), the shores of which are famous for their alpine meadow flowers, and to the Beta Lake Nature Preserve and the Balgo Forest Nature Park. From the forested shores of Jehra Lake (*Ch* Jisha hai), near Beta Lake, a trail leads through the meadows to the spectacular high alpine glacial lake of Yangdo Ubdutso, also known as Lhamo Dungtso.

Chukar The main southeast road comes to an end below Mount Haba Gangri (5,425 metres) at the Chukar limestone platform (*Ch* Baishui), where the ridge formation resembles a terraced field or tiers of jade and silver.

Tiger Leaping Gorge The main Kunming highway running south from Gyeltangteng follows the west bank of the Shudu-chu or Yangpang Tsangpo, a tributary of the Yangtze, as far as its confluence below Mount Haba Gangri. Here, at the renowned Tiger Leaping Gorge (*Tib* Takchong Gak, *Ch* Hu Tiaoxia), the foaming Yangtze rapids cascade 3,250 metres down a precipitous ravine sloped at an angle of 75-80°. The spectacle is alluring for tourists but arrange to go with a local guide since rock slides and sheer cliffs are a hazard for the unprepared traveller.

At the south extremity of Gyeltang county the Yangtze makes a remarkable bend, flowing abruptly northeast as its torrents are channelled between the snow peaks of Haba Gangri and Yulong Shan (Mount Jade Dragon, 5,596 metres).

Balung County འབའ་ལུང

*Occupying the Mekong valley due south of Dechen county, it is a region of great ethnic diversity, the dominant group being the Li (Ch Lizu), intermingled with Jang (Naxi), Tibetan, and Han Chinese. Terraced farming is the mainstay of the economy here. The county capital is located at **Balung**, known in Naxi language as **Nyinak** and in Chinese as Baohezhen, in the extreme south of the county; and a road connects the capital with Jol, following the east bank of the Mekong. The most important site in Balung is the meditation cave associated with the Chan Buddhist master **Bodhi-dharma**; as well as the temple of **Shougou** and the ruins of **Gedeng**.*

Balung County (72)
维西县
Weixi
Population: 136,564
Area: 1,529 sq km
Colour map 4, grid C3

Jang Sadam འཇང་ས་དམ

*Jang Sadam, known as Lijiang in Chinese, is the Tibetan name for the narrow peninsula bounded on three sides by the bend of the Yangtze River, to the southeast of Gyeltang. The ancient kingdom of Jang Sadam, where the population is predominantly **Naxi** (Tib Jang) was for 253 years of its history directly absorbed within the Tibetan Empire from the reign of King Songtsen Gampo onwards, ie from 649 until the disintegration which followed the assassination of Langdarma in 902. Thirteen successive kings of Jang, who ruled from **Bumishi**, were regarded with fraternal respect by the Tibetan monarchs in recognition of their ethnic affinity.*

Jang Sadam
丽江纳西族自治县
Lijiang
Population: 1,041,676
Area: 19,594
Colour map 4, grid C4

The Naxi are a Qiangic people, said to have migrated here from the northeast in antiquity. They speak two dialects and are divided into four distinctive clans, with a combined population of 250,000. The Dongba culture and religion which the Naxi maintain is a synthesis of indigenous polytheism, Tibetan Bon, Chinese Daoism, and Buddhism. The word Dongba means priest or sorceror, ie the main carrier of the traditional culture. The scriptures of the Dongba comprise 20,000 extant volumes and rare scrolls preserved in the libraries of Yunnan, Nanjing, Beijing, Taiwan, USA and Europe. These concern philosophy, history, religion, medicine, astronomy, folklore, literature, and art. The Dongba script has some 1,400 ideographs and is considered to offer insights into the development of both Chinese traditional calligraphy and seal cutting. Contemporary research into this ancient culture has been internationally acclaimed, largely through the efforts of Dr Xuan Ke (*Tib* name: Tsering Wangdu), a well-travelled Dongba ethnomusicologist, and the Academy of Social Sciences in Lijiang county.

During the Yuan Dynasty (13th century), the capital of Jang was moved from Bumishi to **Lijiang** by Qubilai Qan; and Tibetan Buddhist influence on the indigenous Dongba culture of the Jang people gradually prevailed. The main beneficiaries of this early missionary activity were the Karma Kagyu and the Katokpa branch of the Nyingma school. During the Ming Dynasty, the authority of the successive kings of Jang Sadam was officially recognized; and their influence even spread north into the Dechen area of Kham and Mili. Presently, the majority of Jang (Naxi) people reside in the **Naxi Autonomous Prefecture** of Yunnan county, which has its capital at Lijiang, but there are also sizeable minority groups as far north as Tsakalho in Markham county of TAR.

Lijiang City

The city of Lijiang, dramatically situated below the snow peak of Mount Yulong Shan (Jade Dragon, 5,596 metres), was the setting for the award-winning television documentary series Beyond the Clouds. Despite its

Altitude: 2,000 metres
Phone code: 0888
Colour map 4, grid C4

Eastern Tibet

Lijiang: Gateway to South-eastern Tibet

*Travellers arriving in Lijiang from East Tibet are liable to experience culture shock, in that this is the first place on the itinerary completely open to unmonitored individual travel. Package tourists and backpackers come here in great numbers. For travellers intending to visit East Tibet or travel through East Tibet to Lhasa, the advantage of starting here is that it is now possible to fly directly to Lijiang from Hong Kong and principal Chinese cities. **Gyeltang** in Southeast Kham is therefore only 1 days drive from Lijiang Airport!*

status as the Naxi capital and the vigorous promotion of the local culture by the Naxi governor of Yunnan, the predominant influence here is clearly Chinese. The exception are the old narrow cobbled streets of the traditional market and Naxi music concerts which are an obvious attraction for visitors. During the winter of early 1996 the city was badly damaged by a severe earthquake.

Bumishi (Baisha) Monastery   Also known as **Liu Lidian Temple** in Chinese ('Coloured Glaze Temple'), the monastery of **Bumishi** stands at the site of the former capital of the Naxi Kingdom on the outskirts of Lijiang. The present building was constructed somewhat later between 1385-1619, in Chinese style. There are three successive halls, the **outermost** containing the temple office and a shop selling Naxi memorabilia. The second and third halls are particularly interesting because they contain original Tibetan-style frescoes. Within the **innermost hall** a central Buddha image has to its rear a series of outstanding murals depicting (left to right): Avalokiteshvara, Vajrasattva, Karmapa, Vajrasattva (again), and Vajrayogini. To the left near the entrance by contrast there are later Chinese-style paintings.

Tashi Gepel Gonpa   The monastery of **Tashi Gepel** (*Ch* Yufeng Si), in the Lijiang countryside, has been reconstructed and is currrently under the supervision of a Naxi caretaker, whose Tibetan name is Karma Chokyab. It contains images of Shakyamuni, flanked by his foremost students, as well as four-armed Avalokiteshvara and Tara.

Jade Dragon Mountain   The graceful snow peak of **Yulong Shan** (Jade Dragon) has become an important alpine resort for Yunnan and Sichuan tourists. There is a cable car to the summit from *Snowflower Village Hotel*, and another cable car runs between the *Jade Dragon Villas* (2,970 metres) and the Spruce Meadow.

Sleeping & eating   There are 5 good tourist hotels in Lijiang, namely: *Yu Quan Binguan*, T(0888)523927/5123925 (¥180 per double room), *Lijiang Binguan* (¥150 per room), *Yun San Pin Guesthouse*, Moxi Mountain Village, also known as *Jade Dragon Villas* (¥250 per chalet), *Guluwan Hotel*, Xinda St, T0888-5121446, F088-5121019 (¥80 per room), *Grand Hotel*, Xinyi St, Dayan, T088-5128888, F088-5127878 (¥45 per room, plus 15 percent service charge), and *Airport Hotel*, Fuhui St, T088-5120274 (¥180 per room). Restaurants are plentiful, including some, such as *Mama Fu* (damaged in the recent earthquake but now rebuilt), which cater specifically to the western backpacker market. Those located close to the old Naxi quarter are also popular, especially *Dindin Friendly Café*, *Lijiang Mi-mi Café*, *Simon Café*, and *Hom Lou Café*, which have English menus.

Directory   **Tourist offices** *Lijiang Culture Travel Service*, T/F(0888)5123462. *Naxi Dongba Cultural Museum*, Black Dragon Pool Park, Lijiang, T(08891)24172.

Eastern Tibet

Lugu Lake

Beautiful **Lugu Lake** straddles the present day frontier between Yunnan and _Colour map 4, grid C5_
Sichuan provinces. Its south shore lies within the Yi Autonomous County of
Ninglang, and the north shore within the **Mili Tibetan Autonomous County**
of Sichuan. The lake covers an area of 50 kilometres and is 2,900 metres above
sea level. The average depth is 45 metres and its transparency is as deep as 11
metres. There are five islands and four peninsulas. It is possible to go by canoe
from Luoshui village on the Yunnan side to Mukua village on the Sichuan side,
via Lama Island, and to trek around the lake shore back to Luoshui.

The local Tibeto-Burman people, known as Moxi, maintain the Tibetan
Buddhist religion. In the past there were important monasteries constructed
near its shores. Most of these were Gelukpa establishments: **Daming Gonpa**,
or **Yardzong Gonpa**, **Shubi Gonpa**, **Ozer Gonpa**, and **Galong Gonpa** (of
which only the first two have been renovated), but the Sakya monastery of
Dzembu was also noteworthy. The Buddhist traditions of Lugu have been
documented by the local lama Lobzang Yeshe Rinpoche. However, the area is
better known for its unique maintenance of an ancient matriarchal culture, in
which property is handed down from mother to daughter, rather than from
father to son. The maroon blouses and long white pleated skirts worn by the
women and girls of Lugu Lake are indeed striking, while the boldness and confidence they display reveals the secure basis of their authority. The Ninglang
region and Lugu Lake straddle a fault zone, and in 1998 an earthquake measuring 6.5 on the Richter scale severely damaged this pristine environment.

To reach Lugu Lake from the south, drive from Lijiang to **Yongsheng** (101 kilo- **Getting there**
metres), and thence to **Ninglang** (107 kilometres), which is the county capital,

Lugu Lake

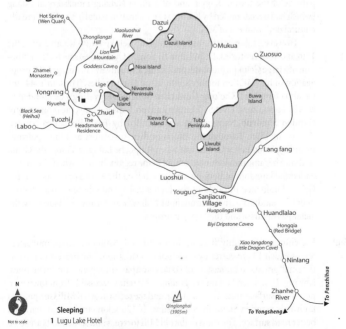

Eastern Tibet

Sleeping

1 Lugu Lake Hotel

Not to scale

predominantly inhabited by Yi people. From Nyinlang to Lugu Lake the distance is 80 kilometres and 4 passes are crossed, the first at 2,460 metres, after which the Yi territory is left behind, and the others respectively at 2,460 metres, 2,760 metres, and 3,240 metres. Lugu Lake may also be reached from the northwest, by following a rough motorable trail from Tong-nyi (see below, page 440) in South Dabpa county, or from **Xichang** via **Yanyuan** and **South Mili** (see below).

Essentials Ammenities for tourists have been improving in recent years; and local arrangements, including boating and horse-riding, can be made through the *Lugu Lake Travel Agency* (head office at Ninglang), or the *Lugu Lake Girls' Travel Company*, T(0888)5521169/5521999. Best accommodation is available at *Musuo Yuan Mountain Lodge*, contact Mrs Tsering Lhamo.

Mili County སྨི་ལི

Mili County (73)
木里
Muli
Population: 115,258
Area: 12,573 sq km
Colour map 4, grid B5

*The county of **Mili** lies to the north of Lugu Lake, near the confluence of the Li-chu and the Yalong River. It may be approached from **Ninglang** county in Yunnan, or by road from **Xichang**, the capital of the Yi Autonomous Prefecture of Liangshan in South Sichuan. Mili traditionally had an 80 percent Tibetan population and 20 percent Jang (Naxi) population, but nowadays Yi and Han immigration has radically altered the ethnic composition of the region. In town (Altitude: 2,310 metres), the Tibetan population now amounts to only 50 percent. Within the county as a whole there are three ethnic Tibetan concentrations: the majority (yi-chou) live in the north around old Mili fortress, the second largest group (er-chou) live in the town, and the smallest (san-chou) is more remote.*

History Prior to the 16th century the ancient kingdom of Mili was a stronghold of the Karma Kagyu school. The influence of the kings of Jang Sadam who were patrons of the Karma Kagyu, and of Kampo Nenang monastery at Litang (which had been founded by Karmapa I) was instrumental in shaping the early cultural development of Mili.

However, following the expansion of the Gelukpas into Kham during the 15th and 16th centuries, Dalai Lama III Sonam Gyatso oversaw the construction of a large Gelukpa monastery at Litang, and actively encouraged the propagation of his tradition further south in the Li-chu valley. Thus, in 1544, the Gelukpa temple of **Khe'ong Dewachen Sonam Dargyeling** was founded in Mili by Lama Dampa Neten Tsultrim Zangpo. Subsequently, the monastery of **Ganden Shedrub Namgyeling** was founded by Pakti Rabjampa Samten Zangpo in 1596. Through the efforts of their successors and their patrons, including Lama Peljor Gyatso and Khen Rinpoche Lobzang Tutob, the Geluk tradition became the dominant school in the region. In 1640 when Gushi Qan ended the kingdom of Beri, his armies subdued the Kagyu opposition to the Geluk dominance throughout the Litang valley and adjacent areas. Subsequently, Buddhist activity throughout Mili was uniformly sponsored by the Gelukpas of Lhasa and their Qing patrons.

Sights Presently in Mili county there are three main and 18 minor Gelukpa monasteries, of which 13 are currently undergoing restoration. The nearest to town is the small grassland monastery of **Dzikri Gonpa**. Among the three main ones, Khe'ong Dewachen Sonam Dargyeling is currently accessible from town on a poor road surface, near the Long Lake, and the reconstructed **Mili Gonpa**, also known as Ganden Shedrub Namgyeling, is 126 kilometres from town on a better road surface. The ruins of the old **Mili fortress** and settlements are to be found here. Important religious dances are held here (28-29 May, and 21-22 November 1999, or 17-18 May and 9-10 November 2000). **Warja Monastery** is a one or two day drive from town.

From **Ninglang** county town the Yunnan-Sichuan border is reached after 58 kilometres on a rough road, which is in a state of disrepair, particularly during the summer rainy season. Avoid night travel since the local Yi people may ambush vehicles and extract money for safe passage! One pass (3,150 metres) is crossed on the Yunnan side. After the provincial border, continue driving to the settlement of **Meiyu** (57 kilometres), where there is a local school guesthouse. From Meiyu to **Mili** (92 kilometres) the road crosses a 3,210 metres pass, before which there is a turn-off for the easy highway leading to **Xichang** (162 kilometres). Descending from the pass, the road enters a deep gorge, spanned by a high suspension bridge, which carries traffic into town. From Lugu Lake there is a more direct but rougher road, which reaches **Mili Gonpa** (*Ch* Muli Da Si), north of town, bypassing **De'ong Gonpa** of the Sakya school and a **Bon monastery**. It is also possible to trek from **Yongning** near Lugu Lake via **Wujiao** and **Xilinshan** to Mili (3-4 days).

Getting there

Further north, there is road access to **Litang** county via **Lato** and **Chaksum**, and to **Dabpa** county via **Jiulong**, north of the three sacred snow peaks of **Dabpa Lhari**, which are named after the three bodhisattvas, Manjushri, Avalokiteshvara, and Vajrapani, and are a focal point of pilgrimage for the inhabitants of Mili (see below, page 438).

Mili

To Chaksum

PSB
Muli County Guesthouse
CCP Office
Muntskhang Hospital
Bookshop
(S)
✉
To Mei Yu
Norgye Zakhang ●
N
Not to scale

Accommodation is available at the *Muli County Guesthouse*, ¥80 per room. Among the restaurants of Mili, the *Norgye Zakhang* is recommended. The main street also has a post office, bank, bookshop, communist party office, and public security bureau on the north side and the Mentsikhang traditional hospital on the south side.

Sleeping & eating

Eastern Tibet

Dali

Those not wishing to fly directly from Lijiang may travel by road to **Dali** and **Kunming**, capital of Yunnan province. **Dali**, 187 kilometres from Lijiang, is situated on the west shore of **Lake Erhai**, at the crossroads leading from Kunming to Tibet (north) and Burma (east). Eighteen streams cascade from the 19 symmetrical peaks of the Canshan Range to the east shore of the lake. The climate is pleasant (average temperature 15° and average rainfall 1,176 millimetres).

Phone code: 0872

During the period of the Tang and Song dynasties, Dali was the capital of the **Nan Chao Kingdom**, which came into conflict with the Tibetan Empire of Songtsen Gampo and his successors. The celebrated **Three Pagodas (Sanda)** of Dali date from this era. Later during the Yuan period, Dali county fell the authority of neighbouring Jang Sadam. Nowadays, the county (*Population*: 391,765. *Altitude*: 1,062 square kilometres) is home to more than 20 ethnic minorities, including the Bai, Yi, and Hui.

From Dali, it is possible to take an excursion west to **Chicken Foot Mountain**, where according to the Chinese Buddhist tradition, Kashyapa the student of Shakyamuni Buddha passed away, his body being sealed within the mountain until the advent of Buddha Maitreya.

Sleeping Stay at the *Red Camelia Hotel*, the *Erhai Guesthouse*, or *Dali City Number 2 Hotel* (best rooms ¥160, cheaper rooms ¥78 or 37), which are all close to the old part of town, or at the lakeside *Erhai Dragon Hotel*, T(0872)2125064 (¥100 per room), or else in the Xiguan new town at the *Jinhua Hotel*, T(0872)2134426/2134427 (¥150 per room). The town has western-style restaurants and bars catering to the tourist market.

Directory **Tourist offices** *Dali Travel Information*, 34 Dali Huguo Rd, T(0872)2671890. *Dali Chahua International Travel Service*, T(0872)2129504, F(0872)2134427. *Dali Merchants International Travel Service*, Cangshan Rd, Xiguan, Dali, T(0872)2178619, F(0871)2123292.

Kunming

Phone code: 0871 Kunming City, the capital of Yunnan province lies 412 kilometres east of Dali by rail or road. It is a large modern city with a pleasant climate, varying little from winter to summer. The inner city has a population of 165,562, and an area of 206 square kilometres; while Outer Kunming has a population of 1,168,320 and an area of 1,452 square kilometres. Three important Buddhist sites are located in and around Kunming: **Huating Si** in the western hills; **Qongzu Si**, which contains images of the 500 Elders; and **Yuantong Si**, which is the largest monastery within the city. However, most first-time visitors to Kunming will prefer to take a day trip to the **Stone Forest** (Shilin), where there are bizarre limestone pillar formations and narrow passageways.

Essentials

Sleeping **A** *Golden Dragon Hotel*, 575 Beijing Rd, T3133015, F(86871)3131082. 17 storeys, 290 rooms with attached bath (US$88 per standard, US$120 per single, surcharge 15 per-cent), 3 restaurants (*Lobby Lounge* for snacks, *Yunnan Kitchen Chinese Restaurant* for Chinese, and *Czarina* for international cuisine), room service available, swimming pool, fitness centre, shopping arcade, hairdresser, karaoke, airline offices, and business centre. *King World*, 28 Beijing Rd, T3138888, F(86871)3131910. 320 rooms with attached bathrooms (US$99 per standard, US$118 per single, surcharge 15 percent), a revolving

■ on maps
Price codes:
see inside front cover

Eastern Tibet

Kunming

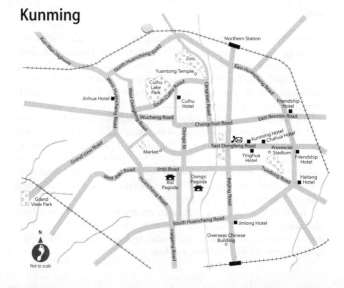

rooftop restaurant, Peony Banquet Hall, *Rose Garden Restaurant*, Magnolia function room, business centre and discotheque. ***Kunming Hotel***, W145 Dong Feng Dong Lu, T3169877, F(86871)3138220. 12 floors and spacious rooms (US$85 per standard and single, surcharge 15 percent), 5 restaurants, bar, shopping arcades, beauty parlour, gym and sauna, mahjong room, travel centre, and business centre. ***Holiday Inn***, 25 Dong Feng East Rd, T3130623. 252 rooms (US$159 per standard), 3 restaurants serving Chinese, Japanese, and Western cuisine, lobby lounge, disco/karaoke, swimming pool, sauna and massage centre, health and fitness centre, shopping arcade, and business centre. **B** *Green Lake Hotel*, 6 S Cui Hu Rd, T5158888, F(86871)5153286. 306 rooms with attached bathrooms (new building: US$104 per standard, US$94 per single, and old building: US$35 per standard, US$41 per single, surcharge 15 percent), Chinese restaurant, *Meldevere* coffee shop, *Mezzo Bar*, business centre, and beauty parlour. **C** *Pinnacle Tianhong Hotel*, 50 Milesi Rd, T(0871)4193984/4161888, F(86871)4161333. Under European and Thai management, with fine rooms (US$57 per standard) and excellent Thai restaurant. ***Red River Hotel (Honghe Binguan)***, 124 Chuncheng Rd, T(0871)3515666, F(0871)3515668. Well-maintained rooms (US$39 per standard, US$45 per superior, US$50 per executive, surcharge 15 percent) with business centre, Chinese restaurant, ticketing service, and shop. ***Kunming Camellia Hotel***, 15 E Dongfeng Rd, T(0871)3161204, F(0871)3162918. Standard rooms (US$18 or US$28), and 4 or 7-bed dormitories (US$4 per bed). ***Kunming Airport Hotel***, T7176965. Diverse rooms (US$36 with a/c, US$25-US$34 without a/c, US$25 per single, US$31 per triple).

Kunming has a number of specialist restaurants offering cuisine associated with the diverse nationalities of Yunnan province. Among them, the Dai and Wa restaurants are particularly renowned. Try the ***North Star Restaurant***, T(0871)4176898, which includes a cultural performance. Or the ***Liao Zhi Qing Dai Restaurant***, adjacent to the Green Lake Park (Cuihu Gongyuan). For western food, outside the big hotels, there are many restaurants of varying quality. Try ***Miaojie West Food***, 152 Dongfeng Road, T(0871)3123967. ***Forty-Seventh Street*** on Beijing Rd, or ***Sister Drum***, behind the *Red River Hotel*, which has a pseudo-Tibetan ambience. For local nightlife, try the ***Jacket Disco and Bar***, or the various nightclubs, adjacent to the *Red River Hotel*.

Eating
● *on maps*

For **Kunming Airport**, domestic flights connect daily with Lijiang, Dali, Chengdu, Chongqing, Xian, Beijing, Guangzhou, Guilin, Shanghai, and Hong Kong, and international flights arrive and depart daily for Bangkok. There are also flights to and from Singapore (Tuesday, Friday, Sunday), Vientianne (Thursday), and Rangoon (Wednesday). The **railway station** has connections to Hanoi. **Buses** from Kunming *Yunnan Provincial Bus Station*, has scehduled departures for Dali, Lijiang, Gyeltangteng, Jijiaoshan (Chicken-Foot Mountain), Ninglang and Lugu Lake.

Transport

Tourist offices *Yunnan Overseas Travel Corporation*, 154 E Dongfeng Rd, Kunming, T3188905, F(0086871) 3132508. *Yunnan Exploration & Amusement Travel*, 1/F Building B (North), 73 Renmin West Rd, T5312283, F(0871)5312324. Tourist office: *Yunnan Provincial Tourism Bureau*, Huancheng Nanlou St, Kunming, T(0871)3132895.

Directory

Eastern Tibet

Yunnan Bus Station Timetable

Kunming to:	Frequency	Cost
Dali	0730-2100 (every 2 hours)	¥51 (minibus)
		¥71 (couchette)
Lijiang	1530, 1600, 1700, 1730, 1830	¥105 (top couchette),
		¥116 (lower couchette)
Gyeltangteng	0530	¥123
Ninglang (Lugu Lake)	1630 (every other day)	¥114.50
Ji Jiaoshan	1730, 1830, 1900	¥69.50
(Chicken-Foot Mount)		

Chamdo to Chengdu:

the Southern Route via Litang

*There are two motor roads from Chamdo to Dartsedo and thence to Chengdu, the capital of Sichuan province. The northern route which leads through Derge and Kandze will be described below, page 457. The first section of the southern route via Batang and Litang follows the same road as the Chamdo-Kunming highway as far as the turn-off for Batang in Markham county (see above, page 416). The distance from Chamdo to the turn-off is 428 kilometres. On reaching the turn-off do not head south into Gartok on the road to Tsakalho. Instead, take the left (east) turning which leads 72 kilometres down to Druparong Zampa, the bridge spanning the Yangtze. Batang is a mere 32 kilometres on the far side of the bridge. The distance from there to Dartsedo (Ch Kangding) is 497 kilometres, and from Dartsedo to Chengdu 400 kilometres. All the counties of Kham described in this section are presently administered within the Kandze Autonomous Prefecture of Sichuan province. **Recommended itineraries: 5, 10.***

Batang County འབའ་ཐང

Batang County (74)
巴塘县
Batang
Population: 47,184
Area: 9,201 sq km
Colour map 4, grid B3

Batang (Altitude: 2,670 metres) lies 32 kilometres northeast of the confluence of the Batang-chu with the Yangtze. It is an important town, spread out across the fertile and densely populated Batang-chu valley.

The earliest habitation is attributed to a legendary garuda bird (*jakhyung*) whose modern sculpted form can be seen in the town centre. For this reason, the town was originally known as Jakhyung. From the 16th century onwards the Gelukpa tradition established itself in the valley, and two monasteries were constructed, **Batang Chode** (Tsesum Gyashok Kapu Gon) and **Jakhyung Rito Pendeling Gon**. During the Sino-Tibetan wars of the early 20th century, the former was destroyed along with the castles of the Batang chieftains, and gradually repaired over the following decades. One of the Potala Palace's massive applique tangkas was offered to Batang following this reconstruction.

The low-lying prosperous Batang valley (2,740 metres) was one of the few localities in Tibet which had a Chinese settlement prior to the 1950s. There were also American Protestant and French Catholic missions, which focussed largely on medical and educational projects. The work of Shelton at the American mission was particularly respected by the Tibetans. Many Bapa (natives of Batang) acquired high bureaucratic

Batang County

positions following the Chinese occupation in consequence of their familiarity with the Chinese language and modern education.

Nowadays, Batang resembles a modern provincial Chinese town. Entering Main Street from the Markham Road, you pass an important intersection at the west end. Head downhill for Batang Chode or the Hospital via the Grain Department, the Radio Station, and Health Clinic, or uphill via the Primary School, Public Security Bureau, and local tax office to Jakhyung Rito Pendeling, which lies within the old part of town. Returning to the intersection, head due east along Main Street, passing a number of shops. The Post Office, Agricultural Bank and *Batang Hotel* are on the left, while the Jakhyung Monument, the Local Government Offices, *Government Guesthouse* and National Tax Office are on the right. A second intersection is then passed. Head downhill via the Open Market to the riverside, or continue due east on the Litang Road to reach the long distance bus and truck station.

Orientation

Renovated most recently in the aftermath of the Cultural Revolution, **Batang Chode** now has some 400 monks under the guidance of Kusho Jamda and Geshe Pema Gyeltsen. The complex is entered from the street through a high gateway, which leads into a spacious courtyard. Murals here depict the motif known as the 'Mongolian leading a tiger' (Sokpo Taktri). The monastic kitchen is to the left and the Tsuklakhang in the far left corner of the courtyard. The **assembly hall** has faded murals on the left wall and 1,000 small Amitayus images inscribed on the right. The **inner sanctum** has large images of Tsongkhapa flanked by his foremost students and murals depicting 1,000 forms of Shakyamuni. **Upstairs**, accessible by an external staircase, is the Jampa Lhakhang, containing a large image of Maitreya, which was constructed in 1994 by a sculptor from Dartsedo.

Batang Chode

This small temple, which nowadays houses the Batang Dzong Buddhist Association, is a manifestly old building, located at the higher end of town, and approached via a steep stone staircase. There are only three monks residing here, but it contains, nonetheless, some original images. Beyond the portico, which has a Mani Wheel and a depiction of Green Tara, flanking the Four

Jakhyung Rito Pendeling

Eastern Tibet

Batang

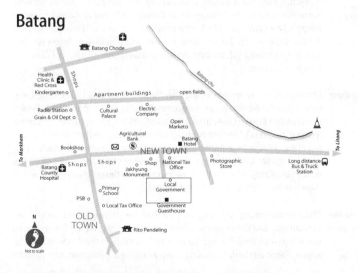

Guardian Kings, the temple has in its **inner sanctum** (left to right): Vajrayogini, Tsongkhapa with foremost students, Lakhor Lama, Shakyamuni flanked by his foremost students, Maitreya, 1,000-armed Avalokiteshvara, a small Padmasambhava, two small Tara images, a reliquary stupa, and the *Collected Works* of Panchen Lama IV and Tsongkhapa. The left wall has old and faded murals, some of which appear to depict Tara and Amitabha.

Sleeping & eating Accommodation and meals are available at the *Batang Hotel (Batang Bingun)*, T(113)22509. At ¥108 per single, ¥144 per double, and ¥108 per triple. The *Government Guesthouse*, on the opposite side of the road has superior VIP accommodation and ordinary rooms.

Routes from Batang

A trail follows the Yangtze upstream from the Batang-chu confluence into the gorge known as **Sangenrong** ('badlands'). Feeder rivers, such as the Karda-chu and the O-chu swell the river's flow on both banks of the inhospitable gorge. Another rough but motorable trail follows the Yangtze downstream to Zang-me in Derong county (see below, page 440). The **main highway** runs inland (northeast) from Batang, following the gorge of the Batang-chu upstream as far as **Taksho** (42 kilometres). Not far from town the road forks. Avoid taking the lower road which leads through a timber yard, and keep to the high road. A pass (3,450 metres) is crossed on the ascent and the tree-line left behind at 4,230 metres (Km marker 3,222). Two glacial lakes are visible below the road on the approach to the watershed pass (*Ch* Haizi Shan; 4,500 metres) which divides the Batang-chu and Li-chu (crossed at Km marker 3,214), and is effectively the county border. The distance from Batang to Litang is 195 kilometres.

Litang County ལི་ཐང་

Litang County (75)
理塘县
Litang
Population: 43,798
Area: 14,619 sq km

Litang county occupies the high **Puborgang** *range, which forms a watershed between the Yangtze around Batang and the lower Yalong basin (here called Nya-chu). The town of* **Litang**, *characterized by its large stone houses, lies near the source of the Li-chu tributary of the Yalong, and is one of the highest settlements in East Tibet (Altitude: 3,900 metres). The county has 31 monasteries; and the annual seven-day* Litang Horse Festival, *which nowadays begins on 10th July, is a great colourful spectacle, attracting visitors from all parts of Kham and even from overseas.*

Getting there Entering Litang county from Batang after the watershed pass (4,500 metres), the meadows of the Puborgang range are carpeted in eidelweiss and gentian. At **Ronko** township (Km marker 3,184), there is a turn-off which leads up country to **Kampo Nenang** (see below). Then, the main road enters the high Litang plain in the headwaters of the Li-chu. A large rusting yellow dredging machine sifts the Li-chu's silt for gold (Km marker 3,145). Making the gradual descent into Litang, a turn-off on the right, 11 kilometres before the town, leads southeast to **Getse** (81 kilometres), where there is an important branch of Katok Monastery.

Orientation
Phone code: 08470

Three roads converge at Litang: the west road from Batang, the east road from Pundadrong and the south road from Dabpa. Entering via the Batang Road, you will pass on the left a petrol station and on the right the Bus Station and a school. Shops line both sides of the road. Reaching a T-junction, turn left into

Main Street, which leads uphill to the Government Buildings. On the left you will pass the Post Office, the Agricultural Bank, and on the right the *Government Guesthouse*, the Merchandise Monitoring Office, and the Nationalities' Shop (Mirik Tsongkhang). Then, at an intersection, dominated by a tapering monument named 'Pearl of the Grassland' (*tsatang-gi mutik*), you can turn left (west) for the Transportation Company, right (east) for the School of Agriculture and Animal Husbandry, the Litang Hospital and Middle School, or continue uphill towards the Government Buildings. Heading uphill, you will pass on the left (west), the cinema and karaoke club, a number of good cheap Sichuan restaurants, and the Public Order Standing Committee Office, while on the right (east) you will pass the *High City Hotel*, and the law courts. At the top end of Main Street there is another T-junction, turn right (east) for the Public Security Bureau, or left (west) and sharp right to continue uphill to Litang Chode Monastery.

Returning to the T-junction formed by the Batang Road and Main Street, continue east, passing on the left the South Kham Unified Open Market (Khamlho'i Dutsongra) and a large clothing store, and on the right a second petrol station, a school, and the health clinic for the prevention of infectious diseases. Continue east out of town on the Pundadrong Road (125 kilometres), or turn right down a dirt road towards the Litang Festival Site and the Dabpa Road.

The **Puborgang** area was traditionally a stronghold of the Karma Kagyu and **Kampo Nenang** Katokpa branch of the Nyingmapa. In 1165 Karmapa I Dusum Khyenpa founded the monastery of **Kampo Nenang**, at a site where a large rock reputedly bears the letter KA whenever a new Karmapa appears in the world. He remained there until the age of 74 (ie 1184) and only in his later years did he go on to found the renowned **Karma Gon** monastery in Lhato (see above, page 400). Kampo Nenang is located in Ronko township, 80 kilometres from Litang (one hour driving) and one hour by horse from the Litang-Batang road. Later in the 15th century, Khedrub Yeshe Gyeltsen, a local lama and prolific author, propagated the Katokpa tradition of the Nyingmapa here. Nyingmapas in Litang at the present day maintain strong contacts with the Nyingma monasteries of Nyarong and Sertal.

The Karma Kagyu tradition however was eclipsed in 1580 when Dalai Lama III Sonam Gyatso founded **Litang Chode**. An outstanding image of Jowo Shakyamuni was placed in its Tsuklakhang. Subsequently, in 1640, opposition to the expansion of the Gelukpa order in Litang was suppressed by the Mongol armies of Gushi Qan, and, as an institution, the monastery quickly became the largest in Puborgang, and the dominant influence on local cultural life. Litang Chode rivals Chamdo and Kandze as the most influential Gelukpa monastery in Kham.

Litang County

Litang Chode, also known as **Ganden Tubchen Chokhorling**, was founded in 1580 by Dalai Lama III, and rebuilt in recent years in the aftermath of the Cultural Revolution, under the guidance of Litang Kyabgon Tulku Palden Dorje and Shodruk Tulku. The reconsecration was carried out in conjunction with the Litang Horse Festival in July, 1996. Entering the main gate from the

Litang Chode

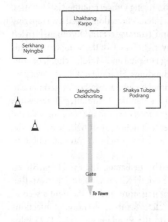

town, there are four main buildings within the precincts of the monastery. The assembly hall known as **Jangchub Chokhorling** and the **Shakya Tubpa Podrang** occupy the centre, while the **Serkhang Nyingba** and **Lhakhang Karpo** temples are higher up the hillside to the rear.

The door of the **Jangchub Chokhorling** is surmounted by murals depicting the lion, tiger and bear-headed protector deities (Sengdong, Takdong, and Domdong). Proceeding clockwise, the murals of the wall adjacent to the door depict Dharmaraja and the four-armed and six-armed forms of Mahakala. Those of the left wall depict two-armed Mahakala, Aksobhya, Guhyasamaja, Cakrasamvara, and Vajrabhairava. In the centre of the hall are the thrones of Dalai Lama III, Dalai Lama XIV, and Litang Kyapgon. Behind are murals depicting 1,000 forms of Tsongkhapa. To the left of the thrones there are images depicting Manjughosa, Avalokiteshvara and Shakyamuni, and a protector shrine-room approached via a steep wooden staircase. It contains images of (left to right): six-armed Mahakala, Shridevi, Dharmaraja, Senge Dongma, and Shukden. To the right of the thrones are images depicting Tsongkhapa, Avalokiteshvara, Maitreya and Tara, while to their rear there is an **inner sanctum**, also approached via a wooden staircase. It contains images of (left to right): Manjughosa, Maitreya, four-armed Avalokiteshvara, and Vajrapani Khorchen, while its murals depict the Buddhas of the Three Times. Continuing clockwise around the assembly hall, the right wall has images of Padmasambhava and Sarasvati, backed by murals depicting Manjughosa, Amitabha, Aksobhya, Cakrasamvara, and Marici. Finally, the right wall adjacent to the door depicts the protectors Shridevi,

Jangchub Chokhorling

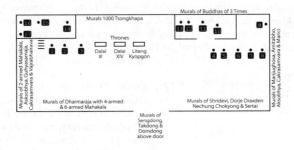

1	Manjughosa	7	Tara	13	Manjughosa
2	Avalokiteshvara	8	Sarasvati	14	Senge Dongma
3	Shakyamuni	9	Padmasambhava	15	Dharmaraja
4	Avalokiteshvara	10	Vajrapani Khorchen	16	Shridevi
5	Tsongkhapa	11	4-arms Avalokiteshvara	17	6-armed Mahakala
6	Maitreya	12	Maitreya		

Eastern Tibet

Dorje Drakden, Nechung Chokyong and Sertri.

To the right of the assembly hall, the **Shakya Tubpa Podrang**, constructed on the site of the original 1580 temple, has an **outer vestibule** with murals depicting the Four Guardian Kings. **Inside**, there is a large central image of Jowo Shakyamuni backed by others depicting Shakyamuni and his foremost students, and flanked by the reliquary stupas of two former preceptors of Litang Chode. The murals of the left wall depict Shakaymuni, Tsongkhapa, and Tara, each surrounded by 1,000 identical icons.

The **Serkhang Nyingba** is a three-storeyed building. On the **ground floor** there are images of (left to right): Tsongkhapa, Atisha, Jowo Shakyamuni and Panchen Sonam Drakpa. To the left there is a throne and a reliquary stupa, and against the innermost wall a full set of the 16 volumes of the *Shatasahasrika Prajnaparamita*. The **second floor** has an image of Shridevi and the reliquary stupa of Litang Kyapgon. The **third floor** has large images of Dalai Lama III and Dalai Lama VII, surrounded by smaller images of Phawangka, Litang

Shakya Tubpa Podrang

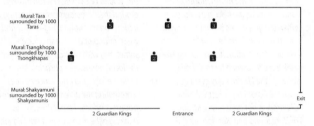

1 Reliquery of Litang Khenpo	4 Shakyamuni
2 Jowo Shakyamuni	5 Shariputra
3 Maudgalyayana	

Lhakhang Karpo

Serkhang Nyingba

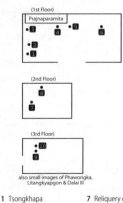

Lhakhang Karpo:

1 Je Yabsesum
2 Jowo Shakyamuni
3 Trinle Gyelpo

Serkhang Nyingba:

1 Tsongkhapa	7 Reliquery of Litang
2 Throne	Kyapgon
3 Reliquery	8 Shridevi
4 Atisha	9 Dalai Lama VII
5 Jowo Shakyamuni	10 Dalai Lama III
6 Panchen Sonam	
Drakpa	

Horse festivals

The horse festival (ta-gyuk du-chen) tradition in Central Tibet is said to trace its origins back to King Rabten Kunzang Phak of Gyantse in Western Tibet, who in 1408 organized a religious and secular festival on behalf of his grandfather's memory. It included wrestling, weightlifting, and horse-racing, to which archery on horseback was added in 1447. However, the festival tradition in the Amdo and Kham areas of Eastern Tibet, where horses abound and horse-riding remains a skill acquired at a young tender age, may have had an even longer history. Most festivals, with the exception of Gyantse which coincides with the fourth month of the lunar calendar, are held in the autumn when the grasslands begin to turn yellow and the harvest has been gathered in the villages. Among the sites in Central Tibet, which are renowned for their horse festivals, the Lhasa 4-day event coinciding with the Great Prayer Festival (Monlam Chenmo) is not presently held; but those of Damzhung and Kongpo are still extremely popular. The Damzhung Festival is particularly grand, the 10 kilometres site being covered with the blue appliqued tents of the riders, traders, and locals. The Yak Race is the comic highlight of the event.

In East Tibet, horse festivals nowadays tend to be organized according to the western or modern Chinese calendar. For instance, the well-known Jyekundo Festival begins on 25 July; and the Litang Festival on 10-16 July . In addition to speed-racing, there are other equestrian events, with riders stooping from their galloping steeds to pick up kataks from the ground or twirling Tibetan muskets around their shoulders before shooting at a target on the ground. Tug-of-war and weightlifting add to the spectacle – sometimes with strongarm monks from the local monasteries participating; and there are folk song and dance troupes representing the different regions. A brisk trade is conducted amid the copious drinking of beer, chang, and hard liquor.

Litang Town

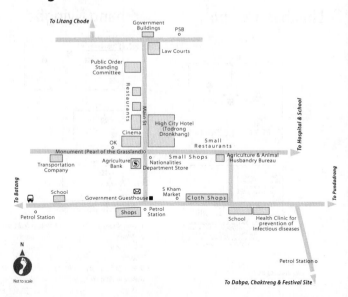

N

Not to scale

Kyapgon, and Dalai Lama III.

The large **Lhakhang Karpo** (White Temple) has a **vestibule** with murals depicting the Four Guardian Kings, the Wheel of Rebirth and the Vinaya code of discipline for monks. **Inside** on the **ground floor** there are images of Jowo Shakyamuni and Tsongkhapa flanked by his foremost students. The murals are dark and obscure. An **inner sanctum** on the left, approached via a wooden staircase, contains an image of the protector Pehar in the form Trinle Gyelpo. On the **second floor** there are the bedroom and dayroom of the late Panchen Lama X, the former containing a throne with photographs of Panchen IX and Panchen X, and the latter the robes of Dalai Lama III and Panchen Lama X, along with old original images of Amitayus, Avalokiteshvara and Shakyamuni.

Accommodation and meals are available at the *High City Hotel*, T(08470)22418. ¥180 per single, ¥240 per double, and ¥180 per triple. As well as at the *Government Guesthouse*, and the *Mirik Dronkhang*. The small Sichuan restaurants on the west side of Main Street are better value.

Sleeping & eating

From Litang, the highway leads east to **Pundadrong** in Nyakchuka county (125 kilometres). There is a massive radar station on the way (approximately N 30°08', E 100°55').

East of Litang

South of Litang to Dabpa and Mili

Another road leads due south from Litang, following the Li-chu valley downstream through the grasslands to **Gyawa** (32 kilometres). En route a 4,050 metres pass is crossed and the descent traverses forested and craggy terrain. A trail leads southeast from Gyewa to **Mola** (53 kilometres), where the local monastery, **Wa Gon**, was converted to the Gelukpa tradition during the 17th century.

The main road runs due south across a 3,600 metres pass to enter a wide north-flowing river valley. At **Chaksum** (15 kilometres) it branches, the wider track leading southwest to **Dabpa**, and a second continuing due south for a further 73 kilometres to **Lato**. At Lato the monastery of **Jangwar Lato Gon** can be visited. This was formerly a Karma Kagyu temple constructed by Karma Pakshi in the 12th century; but in the 17th century it was converted into a Gelukpa monastery by Serkong Onpo. From Lato, a trekking route leads south to **Mili** (see above, page 426).

Taking the **Dabpa** road from Chaksum, you leave the plain and ascend through a forested gorge (4,050 metres) to recross the Yalong-Yangtze watershed (4,320 metres) where there are a number of nomad encampments. Here, you will reach the border between Litang and Dabpa counties. The distance from Chaksum to Sumdo in Dabpa county is 80 kilometres.

Eastern Tibet

Dabpa County འདབ་པ

Dabpa County (76)
稻城县
Daocheng
Population: 25,496
Area: 5,870 sq km
Colour map 4, grid B4

*Dabpa county is a mountainous region in the south of Puborgang. The county town (Altitude: 3,735 metres) lies on the south bank of the Dab-chu (Ch Shuiluo he), a tributary of the Yangtze which rises in the Sangtobla uplands in the north of the county and flows south to merge with other Yangtze tributaries. In the south of the county there are the sacred snow peaks known as **Dabpa Lhari** or **Riksum Gonpo**, which are visited by pilgrims and mountaineers.*

Northern Dabpa County

Heading south from **Chaksum** in Litang county, the road crosses the watershed pass at the county border and traverses the **Sangtobla uplands** (*Ch* Haizhu), a bleak lakeland plateau containing the remnants of Tibet's oldest glaciers (*Altitude*: 3,600-5,000 metres), which are known locally as the 'ancient ice-cap of Dabpa'. Here, there are 1,145 lakes covering an area of 3,200 square kilometres. The eroded rocks assume grotesque shapes: dogs, flowers and so forth; and in 1982 fossilized dinosaur teeth and eucalyptus were discovered. The area is important for the scientific study of glaciation. On the periphery of this plateau there are monasteries: Niya of the Gelukpa school in the east, and adjacent to the motor road, a Bon monastery is passed on the far bank of the Dab-chu after a derelict old stupa on the right. On the approach to **Sumdo** township (80 kilometres from Chaksum), Dekyi Gonpa of the Drigung Kagyu school is visible across the Dab-chu river to the left. It has three stupas.

Sumdo

At Sumdo, there is a turn-off to the southwest which leads into Chaktreng county (67 kilometres). The valley abounds in rhododendrons, buttercups, peonies and daisies, and the village houses are of sturdy stone construction, as at Litang further north. The county capital lies 26 kilometres downstream from Sumdo and 152 kilometres south of Litang.

Dabpa Town

Heading into Dabpa town from Sumdo, most buildings are located on Main Street. On the left (east) you will pass the Public Security Bureau, the Electric Company, the Culture and Education Department, and the karaoke bar, while on the right (west) are the law courts, the local hospital, the open market, the tax office, the communist party offices, the dance hall and the bank. At the main intersection, turn left (east) for the *Government Guesthouse* and the road to Yangteng Gonpa, or continue due south on the Tong-nyi Road, passing the Government Buildings, the Post Office and the *Daocheng Binguan*.

Dabpa

To Sundo

Court · · PSB

Local Hospital · · Electric Company

Open Market

Tax Office · · Cultural Education Department

CCP ·

Dance Hall · · OK

$ · Shops & restaurants · Traffic Police

Dead end

Government Guesthouse

✉ Government

N

Derong Binguan

Not to scale

To Tongnyi

To Yanghgonpa

Dabpa Yangteng Gonpa

Dabpa Yangteng Gon was originally a Kagyu monastery, converted to the Gelukpa school by Lodro Namgyel, a student of Jetsun Jampal Nyingpo in the 17th century. Formerly it housed 100,000 texts and many images including a Shakyamuni presented to the monastery by Panchen Lama IX. As the most important of the 13 monasteries in Dabpa county, it was once even larger than Litang Chode. It is located on a hilltop approximately 20 kilometres east of town (*Altitude*: 4,080 metres) above the east (Sanmo-Litang) road, and depending on weather conditions, it may be possible to drive uphill all the way. In recent decades, the most important lamas associated with Yangteng Gonpa have been Dzeme Tulku who resides in Paris and Gosok Rinpoche who is based in India. Presently there are some 300/400 affiliated monks.

Within the reconstructed Tsuklakhang, the main images represent (L-R): Dharmaraja, the Buddhas of the Three Times, and Hayagriva, in front of which are smaller images of (L-R): Lodro Namgyel, Phabongka, and Tsongkhapa with his foremost students. A poster of Dorje Shukden is positioned in front of Hayagriva. Alongside the Tsuklakhang is a smaller recently renovated temple containing images of Dharmaraja, Tsongkhapa flanked by his foremost students, and Amitayus. An image of Dorje Shukden is covered in a corner recess. Here, there are also photographs of the monastery's lineage holders alongside the present Dalai Lama XIV, Panchen Lama X, and his communist-backed reincarnation. A Mani Wheel is located below the Labrang, which also functions as a tea-room for visiting guests.

Sleeping & eating

Accomodation and meals are available at the *Government Guesthouse*, ¥60 per single and ¥50 per double, as well as at the *Daocheng Binguan* on Main Street.

Southern Dabpa County

Heading south from Dabpa county town, two roads diverge before Zer La pass. One leads southeast in close proximity to **Mount Pari**, following the **Tsulrub Tsangpo**, its banks covered with grassy meadow and forest belts interspersed by feeder streams. In this beautiful valley the scenery changes throughout the four seasons. This side road continues southeast, passing through **Jiulong** to reach the border with Mili county (see above, 426). The main road, however, continues due south from **Zer La**, passing through **Chitu, Gonling**, and **Riwa** before skirting the west approaches of the Nyinteng (Yading) Nature Preserve. At Chitu, the **Kungaling Monastery** of the Gelukpa school contains an exquisite copper image of the bodhisattva Maitreya (reconstructed), which was originally presented by Dalai Lama V. The walls, ceilings and pillars are finely decorated.

Here, in South Dabpa county, the **Ngulso Range** (5,140 metres) hugs the east bank of the **Tong-nyi Tsangpo** river. The larch forests of the mountain slopes in autumn are a fusion of red, yellow and green, while the river banks are broken by copses of trees and jagged rocks, against which the rushing torrent noisily cascades.

Chaktreng, Dabpa & Derong Counties

The Three Sacred Snow Peaks of Dabpa Lhari

Lying to the east of the Ngulso Range is the most important site in Dabpa: the triple peaked mountain sanctuary, generally known as **Rigsum Gonpo**, but particularly named Dabpa Lhari by Dalai Lama V. **Mount Chenrezi** (6,032 metres) lies to the north, **Mount Jampeyang** (5,958 metres) to the south, and **Mount Chakna Dorje** (5,958 metres) to the east. These perennial snow peaks, which face each other like the legs of a tripod, cover an area of 800 square kilometres and are focal points for pilgrimage from Litang, Dabpa and Mili. In front of each peak there is a limpid lake, poetically described as the mirrors upon which the Lords of the Three Families shaved their hair. Wild goats, deer, monkeys, and black bears thrive in this protected environment.

The motor road continues to follow the Tong-nyi Tsangpo south via **Tong-nyi** township, 104 kilometres distant from Dabpa town, after which a rough motorable trail leads southeast to **Lugu Lake** on the Yunnan border (see above, 425).

Chaktreng County སྤྲུག་ཕྲེང་

Chaktreng County (77)
乡城县
Xiangcheng
Population: 23,923
Area: 4,712 sq km
Colour map 4, grid B4

*Chaktreng county, in the middle reaches of the Chaktreng-chu valley, has been a staunchly partisan Gelukpa area since the 17th century when the local Kagyu monastery **Gyazawei Gonpa** was razed to the ground by the Mongol army of Gushi Qan. Pon Khandro, a local chieftain, subsequently constructed the Gelukpa monastery of **Chaktreng Sampeling** on the same site.*

The inhabitants of Chaktreng vigorously resisted the Chinese occupation of Chao Erh Feng's army in the Batang area during the early decades of the present century.

Trijang Rinpoche, the late tutor of HH Dalai Lama XIV, was a native of Chaktreng, and many of his most devoted followers hailed from this part of East Tibet and the adjacent areas of Drayab and Gyeltang.

Getting there The road to Chaktreng from Sumdo in Dabpa county leaves the Dab-chu valley and crosses a grass-covered pass (4,560 metres), at Km marker 138 (from Litang). It then descends through a deep forested gorge, penetrating the tree-line at 4,140 metres. The distance from Dabpa to Chaktreng is 112 kilometres, and from Sumdo 86 kilometres.

Chaktreng Town The county town (*Altitude*: 3,180 metres) occupies a high ridge above the Chaktreng-chu gorge. The escarpment plunges steeply to the river banks below. On the long Main Street there are a number of small Sichuan restaurants, some of which now serve local fish, and there are two guesthouses towards the south end. A turn-off on the right leads uphill to the **Chaktreng Monastery**, which is now under reconstruction. On the way you will pass the Government Buildings and the Primary School.

Routes from Chaktreng Town From Chaktreng there is a 69 kilometres drive due south to **Wengshui** on the Yunnan border, after which **Gyeltangteng city** (see above, page 420) is only a further 156 kilometres distant.

Alternatively, drive west into Derong county. The distance from Chaktreng to **Derong** county town is 151 kilometres. Heading south from the town, the road climbs through a richly forested gorge to cross a 4,080 metres pass after 30 kilometres. This marks the county border between Chaktreng and Derong.

Derong County སྡེ་རོང་

Derong County (78)
得荣县
Derong
Population: 14,986
Area: 2,244 sq km
Colour map 4, grid B4

*Derong county includes the east bank of the Yangtze south of Batang and the valley of the Ding-chu along with its tributaries. It is a region of deep gorges and steep dusty river banks. The county town, otherwise known as **Lower Zang (Zang-me),** lies on the banks of the Ding-chu River, south of its confluence with the Mo-chu, and north of its confluence with the Mayi-chu. The distance from Chaktreng to Derong via **Zangang** is 151 kilometres.*

After crossing the pass 30 kilometres south of Chaktreng, which forms the county border, the road descends towards Zangang, via a 3,750 metres ridge. Here, it bifurcates, one trail leading north to the Yangtze and Batang (see above, page 432); and the other south to Zang-me, the county town, which sprawls along the banks of the Ding-chu in the Derong gorge. Taking the latter route, you will observe (at 2,880 metres) many roadside stupas in classical Tibetan style or in simple mani-stone or sog-shing styles. A final pass (3,300 metres) leads across a slate mountain into the county town.

Getting there

The road from Zangang leads into town on the east bank of the Ding-chu. The town hugs both banks of the river, which is spanned by three main bridges. Heading into town, you will pass on the left, the *Forestry Department Guesthouse*, the water and electric company, the post office, the police station and law courts, a post-natal health clinic, the Derong Hospital, and the primary school. Opposite the post office there is a small *Tibetan Guesthouse* overlooking the river. Across the upper bridge, on the west bank, there are the Government Buildings and a newly constructed *Government Guesthouse*. Heading downhill on the west bank you will pass the tax offce, the bank, barber shops and grocery stores, the Tashi Tsongkhang, which sells Tibetan artefacts, the cinema, and the open market. Trekking routes lead across from the west bank of the Ding-chu into the Yangtze gorge where the monasteries of Derong county are mostly located.

Zang-me
(Derong Town)

Accommodation and meals are available at the *Forestry Department Guesthouse (Lin Yie)*, ¥20 per bed and ¥80 per room. As well as at the *Government Guesthouse* and the *Tibetan Guesthouse*.

Sleeping & eating

Zang-me

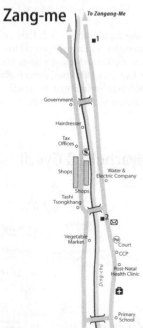

Leaving Derong by the south road on the west bank of the Ding-chu, you will soon cross another bridge leading over to the east bank and continue following the course of this river downstream to its confluence with the Yangtze at **Wakha** on the Yunnan border. Here at the provincial check-point, a suspension bridge crosses the Yangtze, and the road bifurcates: one branch heading northwest to **Pontselang** (*Ch* Benzilan) and **Dechen** (see above, page 417), and the other southeast to **Gyeltangteng** (see above, page 420).

Derong to Yunnan

Eastern Tibet

Not to scale

■ **Sleeping**
1 Forestry Department Guest House
2 Tibetan Guesthouse

Nyachuka County ཉག་ཆུ་ཁ

Nyachuka County (79)
雅江县
Yajiang
Population: 36,617
Area: 6,732 sq km
Colour map 4, grid B5

*Taking the main highway east from Litang, after 59 kilometres you will pass through verdant forested meadows to **Nub Golok** township (Ch Xi Golok), where a branch of Litang Chode named **Golok Gonsar** was founded in the 17th century by Ripa Sarampa. Hiku Nunnery is also passed on the right. Then, driving across two passes: the first (4,290 metres) which is grass-covered, and the second named **Lama La** (4,320 metres) which is forested, you reach the watershed between the Li-chu and Yalong. Here, there are spectacular views towards Nyarong (northeast) and the Batang-Litang divide (west). Then, after 66 kilometres the road descends into **Nyachuka** county, where there are important monasteries such as **Odozangpo Gonpa** of the Sakya school.*

Pundadrong The administrative capital is located at **Pundadrong** in the Yalong valley. Striking timber dwellings rise in tiers above the south bank of the Yalong river, as it surges out of the Nyarong gorge. A strategically important bridge spans the river here, and it is well guarded. The roads leading down to the bridge are steep, but there are a number of Sichuan-style restaurants, and a guesthouse.

Routes from
Pundadrong
Four roads diverge at Pundadrong: west to Litang, north to Nyarong and Tawu, south to Bawolung, and east to Minyak and Dartsedo. Among these the north-south roads follow the course of the Yalong River (known here as the Nyak-chu). For a description of the north roads to **Tawu** (121 kilometres) and **Nyarong** county (142 kilometres), which are important cultural areas for the Nyingmapa and the Bonpo, see below pages 498 and 501. The south road to **Bawolung** is only motorable in its initial 39 kilometres sector, as far as Lake Malangtso.

The east road ascends the **Minyak Rabgang** highlands, which form the watershed between the Yalong and the Gyarong basins. En route you will pass through **Kabzhi Monastery**, which represents the Karma Kagyu tradition. The ascent becomes drier and dusty, and **Kabzhi La** pass (4,140 metres) is eventually reached at Km marker 2,940. Then the road winds downhill to its intersection with the Dartsedo-Derge highway, four kilometres north of Dzongzhab.

Dzongzhab

Dzongzhab township (*Ch* Xinduqiao), 72 kilometres east of Pundadrong, is an important transport station. The valley in which it lies straddles the intersection of four main roads: north to Tawu, Kandze and Derge, south to Gyezil, and east to Dartsedo.

Sleeping &
eating
There are a number of small guesthouses in Dzongzhab, but the best and quietest is probably the *Kangding Xinduqiao Hongsheng Inn*, ¥20 per double and ¥36 per 4-bed rooms, which also has a downstairs restaurant. There are several other Sichuan-style restaurants in this bustling market town.

Nyachuka & Gyezil

Eastern Tibet

Gyezil County བརྒྱད་ཟིལ

*Taking the south route from Dzongzhab, you will arrive in **Gyezil** county, traditionally known as **Gyezur**. The road at first follows a feeder river of the Tung-chu
(itself a tributary of the Yalong) upstream through South Minyak district. There
are fine views of **Mount Minyak Gangkar** (7,556 metres), the highest snow
range in East Tibet; and six-day treks can be arranged from the Base Camp
(5,220 metres), approached via **Rindrubtang**, 95 kilometres south of
Dzongzhab, and **Lugba** (Ch Liuba) at the end of the motor road. After Lugba, a
horse trail leads via Muju and Zimei to **Gangkar Gonpa** (Ch Gongasi) and the
Base Camp, which lies to the south-west of the main peak.*

Gyezil County (80)
九龙县
Jiulong
Population: 43,216
Area: 7,478 sq km
Colour map 4, grid B5

This is the highest peak of the **Minyak Rabgang** range (*Ch* Daxue), which covers an area of 290 square kilometres, with more than 20 peaks over 6,000
metres and some 45 glaciers. In summer the mountain is shrouded in cloud,

**Mount Minyak
Gangkar**

Minyak Gangkar

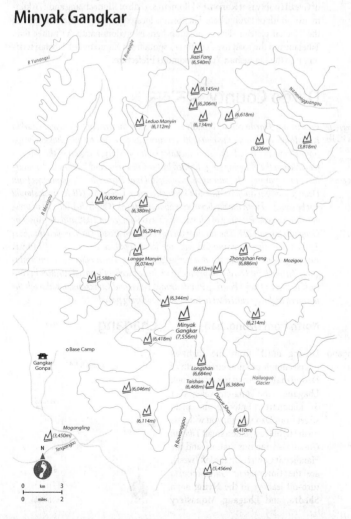

Eastern Tibet

the air temperature sometimes falling to -20°, and most of the annual precipitation (800-900 millimetres) occurs between July and September. The precipitous granite ridges of the mountain's north-west, north-east, south-west and south-east faces have attracted mountaineering expeditions since 1878. The first ascent was made by an American team in 1935. The optimum seasons for climbing are spring and autumn. **NB** The eastern ridges of Minkak Gangkar and the Base Camp are usually approached directly from **Chakzamka** (see below, page 451). Important monasteries in the vicinity of Minyak Gangkar include the Gelukpa monastery of **Giwakha Jampaling**, which was founded by Lama Gangringpa, a student of Dalai Lama II; the Karma Kagyu monastery of **Gangkar Gonpa**, located at the Base Camp; and the smaller monasteries of **Nego**, **Tongku** and **Chukmo**, which appear to have been originally of Kagyupa provenance, and later absorbed by the Sakya and Geluk traditions.

Karpo South of the Rindrubtang turn-off, the road enters the valley of the Gyezil-chu tributary of the Yalong, and follows it downstream. The administrative capital of Gyezil county is at **Karpo**, 83 kilometres south of Rindrubtang and 176 kilometres south of Dzongzhab. The town is located in the extreme southeast of the Tibetan plateau. The population here is predominantly **Yi** rather than Tibetan; and the road itself continues south from Karpo out of Tibetan territory into the **Liangshan** Yi Autonomous Prefecture.

Dardo County དར་མདོ

Dardo County (81)
康定县
Kangding
Population: 98,960
Area: 11,125 sq km
Colour map 4, grid B5

*Present-day **Dardo** county broadly corresponds to the area of the ancient **Chakla Kingdom**, which until the mid-20th century was governed by the Chakla Gyelpo from Dartsedo town. It therefore includes both the Minyak region of the Tibetan plateau and the plunging gorge formed by the Cheto-chu and Yakra-chu tributaries of the Gyarong. The administrative capital is at **Dartsedo**, 75 kilometres from Dzongzhab (Xinduqiao) and 400 kilometres from Chengdu. **NB** Minyak should not be confused with the medieval kingdom of Minyak (Ch Xixia), located in present-day Ningxia Province of China, which was founded in 1038 and destroyed by Genghiz Qan in 1227. The survivors of this kingdom are said to have fled into East Tibet, where they intermingled with the local populace in the west of Minyak Rabgang. Some say that the distinctive language of Tawu reflects this intermingling. Throughout Dardo county the roads have excellently paved surfaces in contrast to those of neighbouring Pundadrong, Tawu and Chakzamka, although the northern highway via Tawu to Kandze is now being paved.*

North from Dzongzhab

Lhagang
Colour map 4, grid B5

Driving north from the highway intersection four kilometres north of **Dzongzhab**, the road passes through **Lhagang** in the Tung-chu valley after 37 kilometres. Entering the main street from Dzongzhab, you will pass on the right (east) side a small *Tibetan Guesthouse*, the Bus Station, and the Handicraft Centre. On the left (west), are the *Government Guesthouse*, a turn-off leading to the **Nyingmapa Shedra**, and **Lhagang Monastery**

Lhagang

To Tawu

Lhagang Monastery

o Handicraft Centre

Nyingmapa Shedra

Government Guest House

Private Guest House

N
Not to scale

To Dzongzhab

itself. In town, a large orphanage has recently been opened under the auspices of the New York based Trace Foundation.

Sleeping Simple accommodation is available at the *Government Guesthouse*, ¥9 per bed, and the privately run *Tibetan Guesthouse*, but most visitors will prefer to camp near the monastery or stay at the Nyingmapa Shedra.

Lhagang Monastery At the north end of town surrounded by three hills symbolizing the bodhisattvas Manjushri, Avalokiteshvara, and Vajrapani, is **Lhagang Monastery**, formally known as **Lhagang Gon Tongdrol Samdrubling Chode**. The chapel to the right of the Assembly Hall contains a revered Jowo Shakyamuni image named Semnyi Ngalso (popularly called Lhagang Jowo). According to legend, when Princess Wencheng travelled to Tibet, she stayed overnight here, and the Jowo Shakyamuni image which she brought as her dowry to Lhasa is said to have spoken out aloud, requesting to be left in that idyllic setting! Subsequently King Songtsen Gampo constructed 108 temples in the direction of China, the last being Lhagang. Later in the 12th century, the original temple was expanded into the form of a monastery by the Kagyupas, and from the 13th century onwards under the influence of Chogyel Phakpa it was gradually absorbed by the Sakyapa school, to which it holds allegiance at the present day.

The renovated **Assembly Hall** in its **lower storey** contains images of the Buddhas of the Three Times, Manjughosa, three of the Five Founders of Sakya (Kunga Nyingpo, Sakya Pandita, and Chogyel Phakpa), and a set of the Eight Stupas symbolizing the deeds of the Buddha. The murals depict Mahakala, Remati, Panjaranatha and Tara (adjacent to the door), the meditational deities of the Sakya school (left wall), and the Sakyapa lineage (right wall). In its **upper storey** there are reliquary stupas containing the remains of past teachers associated with the monastery – including Do Khyentse Yeshe Dorje.

The **Jokhang Chapel**, containing the sacred Jowo Semnyi Ngalso image, has an air of great sanctity. Pilgrims from Kham who have seen this image will sometimes say that the blessing resembles that of seeing the Lhasa Jowo image itself! The main image is flanked by others depicting (L): Thousand-armed Avalokiteshvara, Four-armed Avalokiteshvara, and Buddha (twice); and (R): the previous Sakya Trizin, Padmasambhava flanked by Shantaraksita and King Trisong Detsen, Vajrasattva and Tara; and (to the rear): the Sixteen Elders. The ancient murals of this chapel depict the deities of the four *classes of tantra* and the Sukhavati paradise of Amitabha.

Behind the assembly hall compound, which is surrounded by a perimeter wall of prayer wheels, there is a large garden containing 124 stupas of various sizes. One ancient stupa housed here is said to vibrate of its own volition; and there are wonderful views of the snow peak of **Mount Zhara Lhatse** (5,820 metres) on a clear day to the northeast.

Dardo & Chakzamka

Nyingmapa Shedra On the left side of the road before reaching the monastery, there is a dirt road leading across the fields towards the Nyingmapa Shedra ('college') run by Khenpo Chodrak. Here there are over 100 monks of the Nyingma tradition engaged in the study of classical philosophical texts. The small temple of the college has recently been expanded into a large Lhakhang, capable of accommodating an increased number of students. The view from the plain below the college dramatically overlooks the snow range of **Minyak Gangkar** in the distance.

Minyak Pelri Gonpa A trail northwest from the college leads to **Minyak Pelri Gonpa**, a Nyingmapa monastery in a wonderful grassland setting, where the Northern Treasure (*Jangter*) tradition is maintained. For those not wishing to stay in the cramped guesthouse in town, there are wonderful camping grounds to be found beyond the town on the north side.

Mount Zhara Lhatse Crossing **Drepa La** (4,420 metres) on an excellent paved road, the sacred snow peak of **Mount Zhara Lhatse** (5,820 metres) is visible to the northeast. This mountain (*Ch* Haitzu Shan) is revered as one of the 25 Padmasambhava sites in East Tibet, specifically representing the body aspect of buddha-mind. According to the ancient pre-Buddhist tradition, the mountain is regarded as an off-spring of Nyenchen Tanglha. The beautiful lake **Zhara Yutso** is located on the northeast side of the mountain, and around it are many meditation caves associated with Do Khyentse Yeshe Dorje (19th century). On the southwest side of the mountain, there are as many as 15 medicinal hot springs. The snow peak remains visible far to the north for those crossing the **Mejesumdo** uplands.

Garthar Chode Monastery Garthar township (*Ch* Qianning) is located at a road junction, 16 kilometres north of Lhagang, and on the far side of **Drepa La**. There are many government compounds here; some providing guesthouse and dining facilities. Beyond the town the valley widens and the road forks: the left branch heading northwest towards **Tawu** (76 kilometres) and the right branch heading in the direction of **Rongtrak** (72 kilometres). Take the latter road and after nine kilometres you will reach **Garthar Chode Monastery**, located on a hilltop promontory (3,871 metres) to the north of the road. This renowned Gelukpa monastery, which formerly housed 300 monks, was founded in the 18th century by Dalai Lama VII Kalzang Gyatso, and its construction was sponsored by Emperor Qianlong of the Qing Dynasty. Subsequently, in 1838 Dalai Lama XI was born at Garthar. The road through the **Mejesumdo** uplands to Tawu will be described below, page 501.

Southeast to Dartsedo

Heading southeast from **Dzongzhab** (Xinduqiao), the highway branches after eight kilometres, the south dirt track leading to **Gyezil** (see above, page 443) and the east main road leading towards **Dartsedo**. Taking the latter, two minor passes are crossed, and the road enters a wide pasture, flanked by an avenue of planted poplars and willows. The farming villages of **Minyak** have distinctive detached three-storeyed stone mansions. At **Rilung Drongde** village there is a circular prayer flag formation wound around a central wooden axis, and some fine *mani* stone carvings.

Minyak Chakdra Chorten The main landmark in this part of East Minyak however is the enormous white stupa known as **Minyak Chakdra Chorten**, dedicated to the Eight Buddhas of Medicine. The stupa stands beside the highway to the east of the village called Minyak Dem Drongde. The original stupa is attributed to Tangtong Gyelpo; but it has been renovated and reconsecrated several times, by great masters such as the late Panchen Lama X. The adjacent Gelukpa monastery has a small temple depicting images of Shakyamuni and his foremost disciples.

From here, at nearby Lugba (*Ch* Liuba) village it is possible to trek via Dzumi **Trekking**
La pass (4,700 metres) towards **Mount Minyak Gangkar** and the various
Geluk and Sakya monasteries in its environs, including **Gangkar Gonpa**
where the Minyak Gangkar glacier is in close proximity. There is a further
three-day trek from Gangkar Gonpa which circuits part of the mountain
range, via **Jatse La** (4,000 metres). Expeditions and trekking groups for the
Minyak Gangkar Base Camp generally approach the mountain from
Chakzamka (see below, page 451).

The highway continues east to cross the **Gye La** pass (4,290 metres),
which the Chinese call Zheduo Shankou. This watershed, which divides the
Yalong and the Gyarong basins, is 42 kilometres east of Dzongzhab township
and 33 kilometres above Dartsedo.

Dartsedo དར་རྩེ་མདོ་

The town of Dartsedo (*Ch* Kangding) lies deep within a gorge at the confluence
Altitude: 2,590 metres
of the Cheto-chu and Yakra-chu tributaries which form the Dardo River. It was
Phone code: 0836
formerly the capital of the **Chakla** Kingdom – one of the five independent king-
Colour map 4, grid B5
doms of Kham, under the hereditary authority of the Chakla Gyelpo. The town
prospered as the centre for the tea-trade between Tibet and China. Traders
would travel long distances, carrying herbal medicines from the Tibetan plateau
to sell in exchange for the tea grown in the Ya'an region, which appealed to the
Tibetan palate when blended with salt and butter. The main streets were flanked
by large tea warehouses. Nowadays, the profitable tea trade continues, but the
town has grown into a large city, containing the Kandze prefectural government
as well as the local Dardo county administration. In the past Dartsedo always
had the air of a frontier town where Chinese and Tibetans would intermingle.
However, the Chinese element of the population has grown considerably in
recent years, far outweighing the indigenous element.

Descending from the **Gye La** pass, the road plunges into the Cheto-chu valley, **Orientation**
and on reaching the outskirts of town, passes the entrance to **Lhamotse** and

Eastern Tibet

Dartsedo

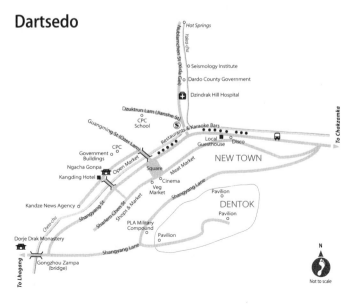

Dordrak monasteries on the left. At an important intersection above the town a barrier obstructs the traffic. Continue west of the barrier into the large military compound, located in the northwest part of town. Turn south passing through the barrier, and you will enter the city. The prefectural and county government buildings are located in the uptown area, near **Ngachu Monastery**, as is the *Kangding Hotel*.

Ngachu
Monastery
(Tenlo Gonsar)

Dartsedo formerly had seven monasteries – three Nyingma, two Sakya and two Geluk. Among these, the largest and best known was the Gelukpa monastery of **Ngachu Gonpa**, founded by Minyakpa Tenpel Nyima in the 17th century as a branch of Drepung Losaling College. The monastery once had over 100 monks. In 1954 the present Dalai Lama stayed there en route to Beijing.

The monastery is located close to the *Kangding Hotel* and its striking roofs in Sino-Tibetan style are visible from the balconies of that building. The restored **Assembly Hall** contains large images of (L-R): Jowo Shakyamuni flanked by his foremost students (Shariputra and Maudgalyayana), of Padmasambhava flanked by his foremost consorts Mandarava and Yeshe Tsogyel, and of Tsongkhapa flanked by his foremost students (Gyeltsabje and Khedrubje). Other images to the right depict Avalokiteshvara in the form Simhanada, Manjughosa, Vajrapani, White Tara, and Green Tara. On the side-walls are images of the protector deities: Dorje Drakden (left) and Shridevi and Dorje Drakden (right). The **Maitreya Hall**, which once housed an enormous three-storey high image of Maitreya, has recently been renovated. It contains a central image of Maitreya, flanked by the bodhisattvas Manjughosa and Samantabhadra. A new **Mani Wheel** chapel lies to the left of the courtyard portico. Presently, there are 18 monks here, most of them young novices. Kusho Dardo, the head lama, recently passed away at Nalanda in India.

If you walk down the main street (Shangyang Street), you will notice that the **Cheto-chu** River rushes through the middle of the town, hemmed in by steep concrete embankments and small ghats. The sound of its running waters is all-pervasive. Early in the morning the elderly Chinese populace can be seen practising Tai-Chi by the riverside. Shangyang Street has recently been rebuilt following its destruction by floods in 1995.

Several bridges span the river, linking the government building and open-air market (on the west bank), with the two parallel main streets (on the east bank). The wider of the two main streets (Shangyang Street), adjacent to the river, contains shops. The narrower of the two (Sharlam Chen Street) has a number of grocery and general stores, some of which sell Tibetan books, artefacts and ready-to-wear clothing. Look out for the Khampa style chubas (for both men and women).

At a large square on the east bank the two roads intersect and the Peoples' Cinema dominates one corner. The corresponding square further downhill on the west bank has government buildings, and below it the Yakra-chu River flows in from the north. In this area of town you will find some modern Chinese shops.

Returning to Shangyang Street on the east bank, heading downhill after the confluence, you will pass a series of seedy karaoke bars on the left and a series of tea warehouses and go-downs on the right.

There are several schools in town, including the **Tibetan Language University of East Tibet**, which moved here recently from Tawu. Mist permeates the steep walls of the valley, particularly in summertime, and in the winter icy conditions make the main street somewhat slippery.

Excursions   **Yakra-chu hot springs**   Continue out of town from the square on the east

Tibetan Tea

Tea has been an indispensable part of the Tibetan diet since the 7th century, and yet it has only recently been grown within the moist low-lying valleys of Dzayul and Pemako in the south-west of the country. Instead, the Tibetans have throughout their history relied upon imported tea from China. Following the arrival of the Chinese princesses Wengcheng and Jincheng in imperial Tibet, it was soon realized that the drinking of tea acted as an antidote to the cold and dryness at high altitudes, as well as compensating to some extent for the absence of fruit and vegetables in the Tibetan diet. Nomads and villagers alike drink tea throughout their working day; and, like alcohol in other lands, tea has developed an important social dimension. Whenever Tibetans have guests or visit their relatives or friends, they will offer tea as a courtesy. A cup, once offered, will never be left empty, and will constantly be replenished. If you do not wish to drink it is best to leave the cup full and drain it at the time of departure!

Chinese potentates and emperors, realizing the significance of the tea trade for Tibet, would sometimes exert economic pressures, obliging the Tibetans to trade horses for tea or to pay exorbitant tea taxes to avoid the anguish of a tea embargo! The preferred traditional brand of tea is black, with thick twigs and leaves, which would be imported from Ya'an in Sichuan and other border areas in the form of compressed bricks, packed inside long oblong bamboo cases, and transported by pack animals over immense distances. This tea would be consumed either as a clear black tea (ja-dang) to which a pinch of salt would be added, or as butter tea (so-ja), or more recently, due to Indian influence, as a sweet milk tea (ja ngar-mo). Butter tea is unique to Tibet and particularly well suited to the Tibetan climate. Contrary to the often bandied misconception, most people prefer fresh rather than rancid butter in their tea! The strained black tea is mixed with dri butter and salt in a wooden churn (dong-ma) and then poured into a kettle for heating and serving. Rounds of dri butter are packed and sewn into yak-skin cases (mar-ril) by nomad ladies for the village market and for their own use; and it is important that the supply should never run out! Tea churns made of pine or bamboo consist of an outer cylindrical tube tightly bound with brass hoops at both ends, and an inner wooden piston into which holes are drilled to enable the liquid and air to pass during churning. They come in various sizes: the largest over 1m in height and 30 cm in diameter, and the smaller types 60 cm or 30 cm in height, with proportionate diameters. Butter tea may be consumed from a wooden bowl (which one would normally carry in one's pocket), or mixed with ground roasted barley flour (tsampa) into a dough, which is the staple Tibetan meal.

Among the Muslim communities of Far-east Tibet, the preferred brew is known as 'eight treasure' tea (Ch baboa cha). This is a delicious concoction of chun jian tea, crystal sugar, and dry fruits such as red jujube, apricot, raisin and gui yuan. Nowadays, Chinese jasmin tea is also popular; and drivers will carry a screw-top jar, filled to the brim with this thirst-quenching brew when crossing the dusty roads of the plateau. To be prepared, bring your own screw-top or jam jar!

Eastern Tibet

bank of the river following the **Yakra-chu** upstream, and you will reach (after eight kilometres) the Yakra-chu hot springs which have been used as a medicinal spa for centuries. Private bathhouses have been constructed around the sulphurous pools.

Dordrak Gonpa Northeast of town on the **Gye La** road there is an inobtrusive passageway on the right leading to **Dordrak Gonpa**, a branch of the celebrated Dorje Drak monastery of South Tibet. Restoration is on-going; and inside the main temple is a new gilded-copper image of Padmasambhava, flanked by his foremost consorts Mandarava and Yeshe Tsogyel. To the left there are further images of White Tara, Amitabha, and Shantaraksita, and to the right King Trisong Detsen, Four-armed Avalokiteshvara and Green Tara. On the central throne there is an image of the monastery's founder, Dordrak Rigzin Pema Khyenrab. Of the original frescoes, only the magnificent torso of a blue Vajrasattva figure remains; but there are excellent new murals. The wall adjacent to the door depicts Padmasambhava, Nyenchen Tanglha, and Ekajati (left), and Rahula along with the Five Aspects of Pehar (right). On the left wall are Four-armed Avalokiteshvara, Padmasambhava, flanked by Shantaraksita and King Trisong Detsen, and Amitayus flanked by Vijaya and White Tara, along with Hayagriva. The murals of the right wall depict Padmasambhava in the form Tukdrub, Vajrakila, the Kabgye meditational deities, Tsedar, and Four-armed Mahakala. Other outstanding new murals are found in the upper-most gallery, depicting the 25 Disciples of Padmasambhava and Zangdokpelri, and in the upper gallery depicting the liturgical cycle known as *Lama Sangdu* and Dalai Lama V (left) and Rigzin Godemchen (right).

The adjacent **Jokhang** which once housed the canonical texts of the *Kangyur, Tangyur, Nyingma Gyubum* and commentaries, along with the **Gonkhang** and the residence of Gyelse Rinpoche (Kusho Putruk), the head lama, have yet to be restored. Of the original treasures nothing remains. There are presently only 15 monks, in contrast to the 70-100 who once lived here. However a large number of additional monks' quarters have been reconstructed.

In front of Dordrak Gonpa, by the roadside, is the renovated Gelukpa monastery of **Lhamotse**, which contains images of Shakyamuni and Tsongkhapa, each with their foremost students. Originally this monastery was located on the hilltop facing the town where the Dentok Stupa now stands, and it has been rebuilt on two subsequent occasions, most recently at its present site. Of the other former monasteries of Dartsedo, the **Dolma Lhakhang** is unrestored, and the **Sungmakhang**, which once contained an important image of Mahottara Heruka but has functioned in recent years as a guesthouse and a school, is soon to be restored.

Sleeping *Kangding Hotel*, 2 Kangding Guangming Road, T(0836)2823084. Comfortable new rooms at ¥210 per double and old rooms at ¥160. In reception a signboard proclaims that Hong Kong and Taiwan residents should pay a 30 percent surcharge, while foreigners should pay 300 percent. The many guesthouses on the east side of town are only for domestic visitors.

Eating Many Sichuan-style restaurants. The best is situated to the right outside the main entrance of the hotel. Try also the *Three Friends' Fish Restaurant (San You Yu Zhuang)* on Shangyang St, T(0836) 2822830. Tea houses are located on Shangyang St near the river, while other down-market restaurants can be found further downhill on the river's east bank.

Entertainment *Peoples' Cinema* is located on the main square of west bank of river. Karaoke bars can be found on the river's east bank.

Dartsedo Bus Station Timetable (early morning departures)

Rongtrak	Daily	¥46
Pundadrong	Daily	¥28
Litang	Daily	¥54
Dabpa	Every other day	¥87
Chaktreng	Every other day	¥98
Batang	Every other day	¥132
Tawu	Daily	¥40
Drango	Daily	¥52
Sertal	3 buses every 10 days	¥90
Kandze	Daily	¥96
Barshok	Every other day	¥95
Derge	3 buses every 10 days	¥114
Pelyul	3 buses every 10 days	¥120
Sershul	3 buses every 10 days	¥136

The bus station and petrol station lies at the lower end of town. Public buses run **Transport**
throughout the prefecture to destinations, including Litang, Batang, Tawu, Drango,
Sertal, Kandze, and Derge, but permit restrictions apply and tickets may not be sold to
foreigners. Bus tickets to Chengdu, however, are readily available.

Banks *Bank of China* is located in the square on the east bank of the river. **Hospitals & medical** **Directory**
services There is a hospital located on the square on the east bank of the river. **Tour companies**
& travel agents *Kangding Travel Service*, T(0836)22928, on main street near to the river.

Chakzamka County ལྷགས་ཟམ་ཁ

Below Dartsedo, the paved road follows the Dardo-chu downstream to its conflu-   *Chakzamka County (82)*
ence with the Gyarong Ngulchu (Ch Dadu) in **Chakzamka** *county. Here, the*   泸定县
road forks, a narrow branch on the left (north) following the rapids upstream to   *Luding*
Rongtrak in Gyarong (see below, page 621). The main road bears right (south)   *Population: 69,178*
and shortly thereafter crosses the Gyarong via a new bridge to enter the county   *Area: 1,570 sq km*
capital of **Chakzamka** *(Ch Luding). This is the last outpost of Tibetan territory*   *Colour map 4, grid B5*
(1,100 metres) on the long highway from Lhasa to Chengdu. The distance from
Dartsedo to Chakzamka is 48 kilometres; and from here to Ya'an 189 kilometres.

The old wooden suspension bridge, which marks the traditional frontier **Chakzam Bridge**
between Tibet and China, has a Chinese style temple on its west bank. Chinese
tourists now flock here in great numbers in memory of a heroic episode in the
Long March when the Red Army was obliged to take the bridge from the
Kuomintang in order to secure its passage northeast to Yenan. There is a small
museum and south of the bridge a tall but rather nondescript stone column
commemorating the martyrs of that occasion. Walk across the bridge, which
sways markedly towards the middle, and peer down through the slats of its
walkway to observe the torrents of the Gyarong below!

Hailuogou Glacier Park and Minyak Gangkar Base Camp

From Chakzamka, trekking and mountaineering groups set out for Hailuogou   *Colour map 4, grid 5*
and Mount Minyak Gangkar (see above, page 443). Drive from Chakzamka to
Mozhi (*Ch* Moxi) village, which is the base camp for the **Hailuogou Glacier**
Park (log cabin accommodation, accessible on horseback). The Hailougou
(Conch Ditch) Glacier is the longest of Mount Minyak Gangkar's five glaciers,
more than 10 kilometres in length, plunging steeply from snow-covered rocks
through primeval forest, to an elevation of only 2,600 metres. Here, the most
spectacular sight is the great ice cataract. More than 1,000 metres long and
wide. From Hailougou, the **Minyak Gangkar Base Camp** is accessible by a
two day/12 hour trek via Daozaizhong or a one day/six hour trek from
Xinxing. Camp I is located seven hours' trekking above the Base Camp, but
only serious and well prepared mountaineering expeditions can go further.
Most expeditions would spend 17 days on the ascent to the summit and the
descent to Xinxing, before driving back to Mozhi. Expeditions are organized
by the Sichuan Mountaineering Association in Chengdu.

Chakzamka to Chengdu (via Rongtrak, Ya'an, or Hanyuan)

There are three possible routes from Chakzamka to Chengdu, the capital of
Sichuan province. The **northern route** follows the west bank of the Gyarong
upstream to **Rongtrak** (112 kilometres), where it crosses to the east bank and

Eastern Tibet

☞ *Mount Emei Shan*

*An interesting detour to **Emei** which extends the journey to Chengdu by 1-2 days offers you an opportunity to visit the Chinese Buddhist shrines on **Mount Emei Shan** – one of the four sacred Buddhist mountains in China, which rises abruptly 2,600 metres from the Sichuan plain. This peak (admission: ¥50) is dedicated to the bodhisattva Samantabhadra. It has 70 temples and is a veritable treasure-store of medicinal herbs. Altogether, more than 3,000 tropical and temperate plants grow on Emei, many of them having medicinal properties. At the base of the mountain, the **Baoguo Temple** actively espouses the Chinese Vajrayana tradition, and it has a well-kept guesthouse. The peak monastery may be reached on foot or by cable car; and at sunrise the diffracted light sometimes produces the distinctive aura effect known as the "precious light of the Buddha". It is possible to spend several days making a complete pilgrimage circuit of the mountain. The main temple of **Wannian Si**, with its life-size image of Samantabhadra riding an elephant, is particularly renowned. Stay in Emei city at the splendidly tranquil Hongzhushan Hotel, T08426-525666, F08426-525666. After Emei, don't forget to visit the **Temple of the Great Buddha** at **Leshan**- site of the world's largest stone Buddha image (71 metres). The distance from Han Yuan to Emei is 237 kilometres; and from Emei to Chengdu 296 kilometres.*

follows the Tsenlha-chu upstream to the large town of **Tsenlha** (58 kilometres). The watershed pass known as **Balang Shan** (4,237 metres) is crossed 79 kilometres beyond Tsenlha, and thereafter, the road descends into **Wolong Panda Reserve**. Spend the night here, and drive the following morning to **Chengdu** via **Guan Xian** (156 kilometres).

The **central route**, which is the most direct, crosses **Mount Erlang Shan** via the 3,000 metres pass known to Tibetans as **Khakha Buddha La**. Prior to the communist period, the traders, pilgrims and adventurers who walked the tea-trail from Ya'an to Dartsedo via Mount Erlang Shan were constantly subjected to harassment by brigands. Later, the difficulties faced by the PLA while constructing this road in the 1950s came to inspire a new Chinese proverb comparing any particular hardship to the crossing of Erlang Shan. From the pass, on a clear day there is a magnificent view of **Mount Minyak Gangkar** (7,556 metres), the highest mountain in Kham. The distance from Chakzamka to **Ya'an** across the pass is 189 kilometres, and from Ya'an to **Chengdu** 170 kilometres. This road has been intermittently closed pending the construction of a new tunnel bore-hole through Mount Erlang. On its completion, the journey time from Dartsedo to Chengdu will be reduced to less than a single day.

The **southern route** from Chakzamka to Ya'an initially follows the Gyarong downstream on its east bank to **Han Yuan** (202 kilometres), crossing a 2,340 metres pass from which Mount Minyak Gangkar is visible in the distance, before cutting northeast to **Ya'an** (220 kilometres) and on to **Chengdu** (170 kilometres). Both Han Yuan and Ya'an are large uninspiring towns, although the latter is more prosperous, with better accommodation and restaurants. Try the *Yazhou Hotel*, 9 Wenhua Road, T(0835)223032, F(0835)222028, which has 238 rooms (¥240 room) with attached bath and running hot water!

Chengdu

*Chengdu lies on the Jinjiang (Brocade River), a major tributary of the Minjiang, which flows southwards from Amdo to converge with the Gyarong at Leshan. During the Eastern Han Dynasty, it was formerly known as Jincheng (Brocade City); and during the Five Dynasties period, it was one of the capitals of China. Later in the 13th century, the Mongol city of Chengdu was visited by Marco Polo. Nothing remains, however, of the old Tatar city walls and towers. The narrow streets of the old town rarely preserve their quaint traditional-style wooden houses, except for the old quarter in West Chengdu, and the former Ming Dynasty imperial palace was destroyed and replaced by a grotesque concrete building, known as the **Long-life Exhibition Hall** (Ch Wang Sui Zhan Lan Guan), in front of which is one of China's largest statues of Mao Zedong!*

Chengdu is nowadays the capital of Sichuan Province. As such, it marks the end of the overland road through East Tibet (Kham), but for many it is also the beginning. The routes from **Lhasa to Chamdo** and thence to **Chengdu via Litang or Derge** described in this section of the guide can easily be reversed;

Ins & outs
Phone code: 028

Eastern Tibet

Chengdu

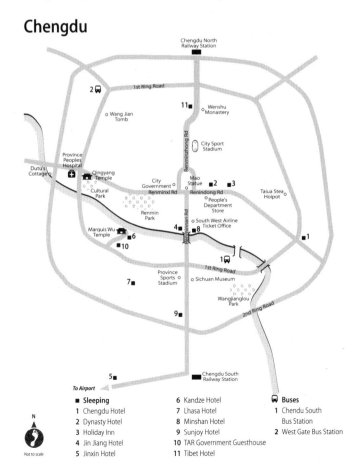

■ Sleeping
1 Chengdu Hotel
2 Dynasty Hotel
3 Holiday Inn
4 Jin Jiang Hotel
5 Jinxin Hotel

6 Kandze Hotel
7 Lhasa Hotel
8 Minshan Hotel
9 Sunjoy Hotel
10 TAR Government Guesthouse
11 Tibet Hotel

🚌 Buses
1 Chendu South
  Bus Station
2 West Gate Bus Station

N
Not to scale

and Chengdu has the advantage of being well-connected to the outside world.

As far as East Tibet is concerned, Chengdu is a city of great importance, in that the 19 counties of Kandze Autonomous Prefecture, the 13 counties of Ngawa Autonomous Prefecture; and the Mili Tibetan Autonomous County are all administered from Chengdu. Political and civil offices dealing with the affairs of East Tibet are therefore located here; as are the head offices of cultural organizations such as the Sichuan Nationalities Publishing House and the Southwest China Nationalities Institute.

Sights Central Chengdu is the commercial hub of the city, concentrated around the Renmin Road intersection, where the Ming Dynasty palace once stood. There are a number of five-star and four-star hotels, and good Sichuan restaurants. The Sichuan Nationalities Publishing House is located behind the *Minshan Hotel* on South Renmin Road, alongside a number of antique shops, some of which belong to traders from Ngawa. Also on South Renmin Road is the **Sichuan Provincial Museum**.

East Chengdu is the industrial sector of the city and largely of no interest to the casual visitor. However, in the southeast, the **Wan Jiang Pavilion Park** (River View Park) contains three Qing Dynasty buildings and a rare collection of 110 species of bamboo (including the 'mottled' and 'human face' varieties).

Most sites of cultural importance are to be found in the west of the city. Here, the **Dufu Caotang** contains the thatched cottage of the Tang Dynasty poet Du Fu (712-770). Du Fu was an impoverished nobleman from Shaoling near Xi'an; but as a poet he is regarded as the archetypal Confucian moralist. His difficult prose style, which focusses on creativity tempered by austere hardships contrasts with the style of his contemporary, Li Bai (701-762), a renowned exponent of the Daoist libertine style, emphasizing atmosphere and spontaneity. A Song Dynasty temple complex, reconstructed most recently during the Qing period, contains a stone tablet, a clay statue of Du Fu, and an exhibition with drawings and photographs illustrating his life and works.

Other temples can also be visited in West Chengdu: The **Wuhou Temple** is dedicated to Zhu Geliang, who appears as the greatest military strategist in the Chinese classic novel *Romance of the Three Kingdoms*. Nearby are the shops owned by Khampa and Ngawa traders, adjacent to the *Kandze Hotel* (Garze Binguan) and the *TAR Government Guesthouse*. The **Qing Yang Gong** is a Daoist temple, the original foundation of which is attributed to the ancient Zhou Dynasty, but most recently rebuilt between 1667-1671.

Near the West Gate Bus Station, there are shops owned by Ngawa traders and the *Ngawa Hotel* (Aba Binguan, T7768957). Further west, in Pi Xian satellite county, on the road to Dujunyan, the important Kangyur-Tangyur Collation Project has its headquarters.

Near Zhongbei in South Chengdu there is a US Consulate, the Sichuan University and Science University combined campus and a number of computer stores. It is here that the largest concentration of expatriates is to be found in the city. The SW China Nationalities Institute is also located nearby on First Ring Road (West Section).

In the north of Chengdu, the most important site is the **Wenshu Monastery** on Renmin Bei Road, an impressively large and active Chinese Buddhist temple, dedicated to Manjughosa, which contains a precious bone relic of Shakyamuni Buddha. On the site there is also an extraordinary vegetarian restaurant where the texture and shape of the food are prepared so as to resemble meat and eggs!

22 kilometres north of Chengdu in the countryside is the **Baoguangsi** (Blazing Jewel Temple), which was founded during the Tang Dynasty. The

Lohan Hall houses 500 arhat images from the Qing period, among the best of traditional Chinese sculpture.

Essentials

A *Holiday Inn Crown Plaza*, 31 Zongfu St, T6786666, F(028)6786599. 5-star, 33 floors, 433 rooms, under international management, with the best rooms in the city (US$320 per suite, US$203 per standard or single), business centre, and the best western buffet in town. **A** *Jinjiang Hotel*, 36 Renmin Nan Rd, T5582222, F(8628)5582348. 5-star (recently refurbished), has 9 storeys, 520 rooms, all with attached bath (US$148 per standard, US$120 per economic, US$98 or US$148 per single, US$248 per executive, US$210 VIP, plus 15 percent surcharge), 7 restaurants (lobby lounge for snacks, ground floor Japanese and Chinese restaurants, 2nd floor group restaurant and 9th floor Western and Chinese restaurants), room service available, excellent shopping arcade, hairdresser, karaoke, airline offices and business centre. **A** *Minshan Hotel*, 17 Renmin Nan Rd, T5583333, F(8628)5582154. 4-star high-rise hotel with 21 floors and 432 rooms (US$110 or US$96 per standard room with attached bath, US$110 per single), has lobby snack bar, 2nd floor Cantonese restaurant, among others, with shops, disco, karaoke, sauna and beauty salon. *Yinhe Dynasty Hotel*, Zongfu St, T6618888. 4-star, 26 floors, 348 rooms (US$166 per single, US$138 per standard), with excellent Guangdong restaurant.

B *Chengdu Hotel*, Shudu Dadao Dong Yi Duan, T4444112, F(8628)44416023. 4-star, has 11 storeys, standard room with attached bath at ¥880, 6 restaurants (Chinese, Japanese, Western, Korean BBQ, Beijing Imperial Food and Café de Orchid), bar, excellent shopping facilities on mezzanine and 9th floor, business centre, travel services, massage and sauna, karaoke and nightclub, swimming pool, billiards, and clinic.

C *Chengdu Tibet Hotel* (Xizang Fandian), 10 Renmin Bei Rd, T3333988, F(8628)3333526. 3-star, 15 floors, has 359 refurbished rooms, Japanese-style 426 rooms with attached bath or shower (US$65 per standard, US$46 per single, US$95 per deluxe double), 8 restaurants and banquet halls (including *Red Palace Dance-Dinner Restaurant*), lobby bar, business centre, massage and beauty salon, hairdresser, shops and travel services. **C** *Xili Hotel*, 237 Liberation Rd (Section 2), T3344997, 3340889, F(028)3343800. 3-star, new construction with 13 floors and 110 rooms (US$52 per standard). **C** *Sichuan Hotel*, 31 Zongfu Jie, T6661115, F(8628)66652633. 3-star, has standard rooms with attached bath (US$77 per standard), and good restaurants, centrally located. **C** *Jinxin Hotel*, 18 Airport Rd, T5190381, F(028)5189669. 3-star, under *Jinjiang Hotel* management, US$48 per standard, US$86 per deluxe). **C** *Sunjoy Inn (Xinzu Binguan)*, S Renmin Rd (Section 4), T5563388, F(028)5546598. 3-star, 7 floors, 189 rooms (US$50 per single, US$58 per standard), with Chinese restaurant, coffee lounge, shop, and business centre. **C** *Lhasa Hotel*, 88 Xiaojia He St, 4 Ring Rd (South), T5198998, F(028)5189973. 3-star (US$51 per standard, US$94 per suite).

D *Jinhe Hotel*, 18 Jinhe Jie, T6672888, F(8628)6662037.

E *Traffic Hotel*, 77 Linjiang Lu, T5552814. The backpackers' favourite, has 7 floors with 100 standard rooms and 22 triples (US$25 per standard, US$26 per triple).

Sleeping
■ *on map, page 453*
Price codes:
see inside front cover

Chengdu is famous for its spicy Sichuan cuisine. There are many excellent Sichuan restaurants throughout the city, but apart from the major hotels, try *Taipei Stone Hotpot*, near *Chengdu Hotel* which offers the best Sichuan hot-pot buffet in the city; and *Huang Cheng Lao Ma Restaurant* or the elegant *Wenjun Restaurant* both in Qintai Road, which is famous for its many eateries. For spicy bean-curd dishes, try the *Chen Ma Po Dou Fu Restaurant* which have many branches, including one outside the Daoist temple of Qing Yang Gong.

Eating
● *on map, page 453*

Eastern Tibet

Transport **Air** There are daily flights to and from Beijing, Lhasa, Hong Kong, Kunming, Lanzhou, Chongqing, Shanghai, Xian and Guangzhou; and also to and from Bangkok (Monday, Thursday, Saturday), Singapore (Tuesday, Saturday), Pomda (Tuesday, Friday), Ziling (Monday, Thursday), as well as Kathmandu via Lhasa (Tuesday, Thursday, Saturday).

Bus Long distance buses depart the South Bus Station outside the *Traffic Hotel* for Dartsedo (Kangding) daily: 0630 (4 buses), 0710 (2 buses); 0830 (minibus).

Directory **Airline offices** *China South-west Airlines*, 15 Renmin Nan Rd (Section Two), T6656991 (international), 6679663 (domestic). *Dragonair*, 65 Renmin Nan Rd (Section Two), T6679186 ext 363. *Chengdu Central Ticketing Centre*, T5190111. *Yunnan Air*, T6712822, F(028)6712833. **Tour companies & travel agents** *Trans Himalaya*, 97 Xida St, T/F(028)6248977. *China International Travel Service*, 65 S Renmin Rd (Section 2), T6679186, F(028)6672970. *Golden Bridge Travel Service*, 38 Jia Hua Yuan Rd, T7730708, F(028)7730728. *Guagda Everbright Travel*, 72 Shuangling Rd, T4337891, F(028)4313632. *Sichuan Mountaineering Association*, 2 S Ring Rd (Section 3), T5588047, F(028)5588042.

Chengdu West Gate Bus Station Timetable

Destination	Departure Time	Price
Wolong	0700	
Wenchuan	0640, 0800, 1030, 1230, 1300, 1430, 1530	¥15
Tashiling	0900	¥20.50
Maowen	0720, 1100, 1150, 1320, 1410, 1440	¥20 (standard) ¥21.50 (minibus)
Trochu	0640	¥32.50
Tsenlha	0640	¥37
Rongtrak	0640	¥47.50
Chuchen	0740	¥48
Zungchu	0700	¥37
Hongyuan	0820	¥44.50
Barkham	0700, 0740	¥39 (standard) ¥61 (deluxe)
Ngawa	0630	¥50.50(standard) ¥65 (couchette)
Nanping	0720, 1600	¥61
Dzitsa Degu	0800	¥45 (direct)
Dzoge	0820, 1400	¥58.50
Sertal	0800	¥84.30
Dzamtang	0700	¥59 (direct) ¥84 (Italian minibus)
Ganlho Dzong	1000	¥153

Chengdu: South Bus Station

Ya'an	0630-1550 (every 20 mins)	¥32
Chakzamka	Every morning	¥96 (top couchette) ¥104 (lower couchette) ¥58 (standard)
Dartsedo	0630, 0730, 0830	¥90 (express) ¥62 (2-days)

Ngawa Prefectural and County Bus Transport units; also Ngawa Prefectural No 1 Bus Transport Company

Chamdo to Derge:
the Cultural Heart of Kham

The northern route from Chamdo to Chengdu via Derge will be described in this and the following sections. The first part of the route follows the highway from Chamdo to Topa county and then passes through Jomda to cross the Yangtze and enter either Derge or Pelyul. From Jomda there is also a side-road leading south into Gonjo county. The distance from Chamdo to Derge is 345 kilometres, and from Topa to Derge, 230 kilometres. Of these five counties, Topa, which has already been described (see above, page 401), along with Jomda and Gonjo are currently administered from Chamdo district, within the Tibetan Autonomous Region; while Pelyul and Derge are administered from Dartsedo, within the Kandze Autonomous Prefecture of Sichuan Province.
Recommended itineraries: 5, 8, 10.

Jomda County འཇོ་མདའ

Jomda county comprises the upper reaches of the Ri-chu around **Chunyido** *and of the Ke-chu around* **Sibda***, as well as the Do-chu (Tsang-chu valley) and its tributary, the Dzi-chu, which eventually flow into the Yangtze at* **Bolo** *in Gonjo county. In the extreme northeast of the county,* **Denkhok Nubma** *is more accessible by ferry from Denkhok on the Sichuan side of the border. The county capital is located at* **Jomda***, still known locally as Derge Jomda in recognition of the fact that the kingdom of Derge once extended across the west bank of the Yangtze.*

Jomda County (83)
江达县
Jomda
Population: 59,993
Area: 13,384 sq km
Colour map 4, Grid A3

To reach Jomda from Chamdo, first follow the Derge highway out of town on the east bank of the Dza-chu, and cross the **Tama La** (4,511 metres) and **Jape La** (4,680 metres) passes to arrive at **Topa** township in the grasslands of the Drugu-chu valley. The distance from Chamdo to Topa is 109 kilometres. After Topa the highway crosses **Lazhi La** (4,450 metres) and enters Jomda county at **Chunyido** township, where there are excellent camping grounds. The distance from Topa to Chunyido is 63 kilometres, and from Lazhi La to Chunyido 40 kilometres.

Getting there

Jomda & Gonjo

The main monastery in the Chunyido nomadic area is **Dordzong Gonpa** of the Drukpa Kagyu school. The present incumbent lama resides at Tashijong in India. From Chunyido near the source of the Ri-chu, the highway continues east to **Khargang**, crossing Gele La pass (4,352 metres) en route and passing through **Tralso**, where there is a small Sakya Monastery. Khargang, on the banks of the Dzi-chu River, is 44 kilometres from Chunyido. A motorable road follows this river upstream for 33 kilometres to **Dzigar**, which is another

Dordzong & Dzigar

Eastern Tibet

stronghold of the Drukpa Kagyu school (a branch monastery has been established at Rewalsar in India through the efforts of Lama Wangdor and Dzigar Choktrul).

Trekking   A trekking route crosses Guru La from Dzigar to enter the Ke-chu valley, and head downstream to **Sibda**. Here there are important Kagyu monasteries: **Taklung Gon** and **Cho-ne Gon**. From Sibda, the trekking trail continues following the Ke-chu downstream to **Menda** area, where it merges with the Kyang-chu River of East Zurmang (see above, page 401 and below, page 485).

Jomda town   The highway runs east from Khargang, following the Dzi-chu downstream to the county capital (12 kilometres). **Jomda** is a large town, sprawling along both banks of the river. The main industries are timber and cement. The town with its finely decorated log cabin houses has an air of prosperity, particularly during the harvest season. There are guesthouse and restaurant facilities. At **Troru Gonpa** of the Karma Kagyu school, there is a small Tibetan hospital which supplies herbal medications throughout the county. The monastery is under the direction of Lagen Tulku VIII and Khenpo Tsenam, one of Tibet's foremost scholars and physicians who is based at the Tibet Medical University in Lhasa. After Jomda, the road descends to **Tangpu** (22 kilometres), where the Dzi-chu river flows into the Do-chu.

A motorable side-road runs north from Tangpu to **Terton** township (53 kilometres), where there are a number of important Kagyu monasteries: **Dokhar Gon**, **Gonsar Gon**, and **Kyapje Gon**, among them. It is also possible to trek northeast from Terton township to **Denkhok Nubma** on the banks of the Yangtze.

Below Tangpu, the Do-chu is known as the Tsang-chu as far as its confluence with the Yangtze at **Bolo**. The road to Bolo from Tangpu (55 kilometres) passes through **Kutse**, where many of the renowned Derge woodblocks were carved.

Wara Monastery   The highway continues east from Tangpu towards the **Nge La** pass (4,245 metres). En route you will drive through the beautiful **Wara Gonpa** (3,444 metres), a significant monastery of the Sakya school, which had its own woodblock edition of the *Kangyur*, prepared during the present century by Jamyang Khyentse Chokyi Lodro. The temple complex at Wara has undergone considerable restoration in recent years. Descending from Nge La pass, the road reaches **Kamtok** on the banks of the Yangtze. The distance from Tangpu to Kamtok is 63 kilometres.

Trekking   Trek upstream through the Yangtze gorge to visit **Onpo-to** township, or cross the Yangtze to enter Derge county at **Kamtok Drukha Zamchen** bridge.

Gonjo County གོན་འཇོ

Gonjo County (84)
贡觉县
Gonjo
Population: 38,271
Area: 4,994 sq km
Colour map 4, grid A4

*The county of Gonjo comprises the valleys of the southward-flowing Ri-chu and northward-flowing Mar-chu, which converge above **Akar**, and then flow due east to enter the Yangtze at **Motsa**. It also includes the valley of the Je-chu and adjacent rivers which flow into the Yangtze further southeast at **Sangenrong** (the 'badlands'). The county capital is located at **Akar (Gonjo)** on the Mar-chu. The distance from Chunyido to Akar is 82 kilometres.*

At **Tranak**, three kilometres east of Chunyido, there is a turn-off on the south **Akar**
side of the road, which runs parallel to the course of the Ri-chu River. Driving
along this road, you will cross a 4,064 metres pass after five kilometres, which
leads into **Pelha Gon**, and a second pass, **Gyelpo La** (4,472 metres) after 22
kilometres. Descend into **Kyabal** township (12 kilometres) and **Tsanda**,
where a trail follows the Ri-chu upstream to the Nyingmapa monastery of
Nyakla Gonpa. The motorable track continues downhill from Tsanda to the
confluence of the Ri-chu and Mar-chu, and then rises again to reach **Akar**, the
county town (40 kilometres from Kyabal), also known nowadays as **Gonjo**.
There are spartan guesthouse facilities at Akar.

You can continue driving southeast from Akar for 24 kilometres as far as
Lhagyel in the upper reaches of the Mar-chu, but beyond that point it is necessary to trek southeast to reach Lhato township.

Beyond northeast Gonjo county, the township of **Bolo** (55 kilometres drive **Sangenrong**
from Tangpu) lies on the west bank of the Yangtze. The township of **Tsepa** is
situated on the Tse-chu tributary of the Mar-chu. Further southeast, a trail
crosses **Pel-yi La pass** (4,642 metres) to enter the Je-chu valley. Passing
through **Jangsum** and **Bumkye** townships, this trail follows the Je-chu downstream to its confluence with the Yangtze in **Sangenrong** ('badlands'), a wild
and traditionally lawless part of Kham. The people of Gonjo are regarded as
barbarous, headstrong, and somewhat inhospitable, compared to the other
inhabitants of Kham.

Pelyul County ད་པལ་ཡུལ

*At **Kamtok Drukha** two bridges span the swift-flowing waters of the Yangtze.* Pelyul County (85)
The lower bridge is the original one constructed by the PLA during the occupation 白玉县
of Tibet in 1950. The other is the modern suspension bridge which carries all Baiyu
motor vehicles and pedestrians across the present day border between the Tibetan Population: 39,543
Autonomous Region and Sichuan. Traditionally, the areas on both banks of the Area: 10,646 sq km
*Yangtze belonged to the independent kingdom of **Derge**; and the peoples of* Colour map 4, grid A4
Jomda and Pelyul often refer to themselves even now as inhabitants of Derge.
Crossing to the east bank of the Yangtze (ie into the Kandze Prefecture of Sichuan
Province), there are two motorable roads, one following the river upstream
towards Derge (28 kilometres), and the other following the river downstream to
*Pelyul. Taking the latter road, you will reach **Pelyul** after 87 kilometres.*
    Pelyul county comprises the lateral valleys of the Horpo-chu and Ngu-chu
tributaries of the Yangtze, which between their estuaries demarcate a dramatic
section of the awesome gorge, where the river abruptly changes course from
southeast to southwest and again to northwest within the distance of 39 kilo-
metres. Two outstanding Nyingmapa monasteries, Katok and Pelyul, are located
within the county.

Horpo

Driving southwards down the east bank of the Yangtze on a narrow but Colour map 4, grid A3
jeepable road surface, after 32 kilometres you will traverse the estuary of the
Mesho-chu. Continue south for a further 10 kilometres to reach the confluence of the Horpo-chu and the Yangtze. **Horpo** township (3,170 metres) is
located a short distance upstream at a point where the Dzin-chu and
Horpo-chu streams flow together. The township was formerly one of the 25

Yangtze River

This mighty river (6,300 kilometres) is the longest in Asia and the third longest in the world. There are two main sources: the southern one, known as the Dam-chu (Ulan Muren) rises in the Dangla mountains at 5,486 metres; and the northern source, known as the Chumar-chu, rises in the Kunluns. These converge above Chumarleb, and flow initially through a spacious lakeland valley. The Yangtze has eight principal tributaries, of which the Yalong, Gyarong, Minjiang, and Jialing all originate on the Tibetan plateau. The upper reaches of the river are inhabited by nomadic peoples, who are largely pastoralists, but also engaged in subsistence farming. South of the Bayankala range, the river forms a narrow gorge, 3-5 kilometres deep in places, and with sheer river-bank peaks as high as 4,900 metres. Some remote villages are located high up on the river banks. For over 350 kilometres the river flows south through this gorge in close proximity to the Salween and Mekong (which are all within 25-40 kilometres of each other). In winter when the water level is lowest the river is deep blue in colour; but in the rainy season when coffee-coloured alluvium is carried downstream at the rate of 430-500 million tons per annum, its rapid flow increases to more than 2,000 cubic metres per second.

On reaching the territory of the Jang (Naxi) nationality, at the southernmost outpost of Tibetan culture (now in Yunnan province), the river loops sharply northeast to touch the Sichuan border near Mili, and bends back upon itself (southwest), before turning east into Dukou. Here, at the confluence of the Yalong, the river widens to 396 metres and increases to 9 metres in depth. The other major tributaries – the Gyarong (Dadu) and the Min, which both rise in Amdo, converge together at Leshan in Sichuan province, before emptying into the Yangtze at Yibin.

districts within the kingdom of Derge, and especially renowned in the past for the high quality of its metalwork. One can stay in the house of the local shopkeeper.

Katok Dorjeden Monastery གཏི་ཕྱོག་རྡོ་རྗེ་གདན་

History Katok Dorjeden Monastery (4,023 metres) is located some 853 metres above Horpo on a hilltop resembling the shape of the Tibetan letter KA, or that of an 'eight-footed lion'. Until 1993 visitors to Katok were obliged to walk five hours or ride on horseback from Horpo. The tranquillity of the remote hilltop monastery was rarely disturbed. Now, following the construction of a jeep track, the monastery can be reached with ease in 20 minutes!

The monastery was founded in 1159 by Katok Dampa Deshek (1122-92). Immediately below the site is a large boulder, in which a local Bonpo divinity is said to have been trapped at the time of the monastery's founding. According to legend, the student and successor of Dampa Deshek called Tsangtonpa helped drag it along to the river bank below the valley where it can still be seen today.

Katok is revered as the main pilgrimage site of buddha-activity in Kham and as the oldest surviving monastery of the Nyingma school, excluding Samye and the temples constructed by the early kings. Dampa Deshek gave teachings continuously to students from all parts of East Tibet and his monastery acquired great prestige both for philosophical studies and meditation practice. It is known to have maintained certain rare lineages of teaching from the 12th century at times when they were lost in central Tibet.

The development of the monastery from its inception was guided by the 13 successors of Katokpa Dampa Deshek, by their students, and the 13 successors of Mokton Jampel Senge. In the 13th century Mani Rinchen of Katok, an associate of the treasure-finder Guru Chowang, is said to have constructed reliquaries for the remains of the first three Katokpa, and then to have flown across to an adjacent hilltop before vanishing into light. During the time of Jampabum, Katokpa III, 100,000 students are said to have flown on their robes to another adjacent hilltop, which thereafter became known as 'Cloth Hill'. In the early years of this century, although the community of monks at Katok numbered only 400, the hermitages above Katok (Ritsip, Bartro and Dechen Choling) continued to produce great masters of meditation, and the monastery developed over a thousand far-flung branches in East Tibet and Central Tibet.

In the 16th century the monastery was expanded by Rigdzin Dudul Dorje, Longsel Nyingpo and Sonam Detsen. Sonam Detsen's successive incarnations, beginning with Drime Zhingkyong Gonpo, maintained the ancient lineage of Katok, and were ably assisted by great scholars of the calibre of Tsewang Norbu (1698-1755) and Gyurme Tsewang Chokdrub (late 18th/early 19th century). More recently, the monastery has been connected with respected figures such as Katok Situ II Chokyi Gyatso (1880-1925) and Khenpo Ngaga (1879-1941), as well as living meditation masters such as Chatrel Senge Dorje.

The site The track from Horpo to Katok crosses a wooden cantilever bridge over the Dzin-chu and proceeds through lush green countryside, initially on level ground but gradually rising to a steep ascent of 4,023 metres. On reaching the hilltop, a track to the right leads round the contour of the hill to Katok. On the way it passes a cremation ground, the site from which a former lama, Katok Mani Rinchen, is said to have flown off into space, and the seven damaged stupas which still contain relics of the founders of Katok.

Anyone viewing the majestic setting of Katok's red and white buildings which cover the peaceful mountaintop can appreciate why the concept of 'sacred outlook' or 'pure visionary perception of the landscape' is so significant here. To the right of the hillside are rocks in the shape of Vajrasattva's vase, and of Vajrakila and the Kabgye deities, while to the left of the last of these rocks is the **Bartro** hermitage. Beyond and behind that retreat centre are the **Ritsip** and **Dechen Choling** hermitages. Behind the mountain on the circumambulatory trail, there are impressions in stone of Hayagriva and Simhavaktra, as well as a Padmasambhava footprint.

Two temples have been renovated in recent years, under the auspices of Moktse Tulku, Getse Tulku, and the present Drime Zhingkyong incarnation (who lives in Chengdu). Of these, the large **Assembly Hall (Dukhang)** is for the most part unimpressive, housing new clay images of Padmasambhava and Shakyamuni. However, in the course of its reconstruction all the original

Eastern Tibet

Pelyul County

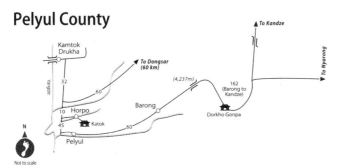

stones were utilized and thus an original blessing was preserved.

The **Zangdokpelri Temple** is a magnificent and ornate structure over-looking the open courtyard, where religious dances are performed on the tenth day (Tsechu) of the sixth month of the lunar calendar, commemorating the birth of Padmasambhava. Large applique tangkas depicting Katokpa Dampa Deshek and Longsal Nyingpo (founder and restorer of Katok) are erected to the side of the amphitheatre. If you decide to visit Katok at this time, the pageantry and colourful costumes of the dancers and spectators will for-ever haunt the memory. To visit Katok at other times of the year is to appreci-ate the tranquillity of this mountain-top bastion of Nyingmapa learning.

A new college (Shedra) is currently under construction on the opposite side of the courtyard from the Zangdokpelri temple. There are over 180 resi-dent monks and 300 affiliated monks, studying philosophical texts of the Nyingma tradition under Khenpo Jamyang, who has authored a *History of Katok Monastery*.

Trekking Returning to Horpo, you can drive south to Pelyul (45 kilometres), north to Derge (70 kilometres), or else trek through the upper reaches of the Dzin-chu valley to Dzenko and Manigango.

Pelyul

Getting there Crossing the Horpo-chu near its confluence with the Yangtze, the motor road contin-
Colour map 4, grid A3 ues down the east bank as far as **Barna**, where it spans the Ngu-chu tributary, flowing in from the southeast. It then follows the latter upstream to **Pelyul** (*Ch* Baiyu), the county capital, 45 kilometres from Horpo.

Pelyul (3,261 metres) is a large and rapidly expanding town with a consider-able Chinese population. Chinese traders and gold-miners fill the streets, alongside somewhat incongruous Khampa inhabitants. Slightly uphill, the **Hospital of Traditional Tibetan Medicine** and its college are presided over by Dr Phuntsok Rabten, who has struggled heroically to provide a service in great demand by the local Tibetan population.

Dominating the Ngu-chu valley, which is somewhat reminiscent of the Austrian Tyrol, the renovated **Pelyul Monastery** broods over the town on a verdant and picturesque hillside. The former tranquillity of the monastery will

Pelyul

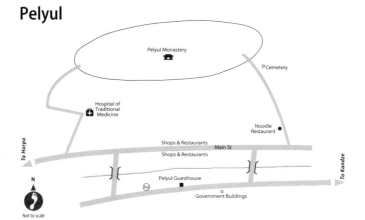

be hard to recapture since the sound of music and the radio broadcasts of the town permeate the hillside.

Stay at the *Pelyul Guesthouse*, on the south bank of the Ngu-chu, which has comfortable rooms, brilliant electrical lighting, a restaurant, and a bath-house with solar heated hot water. The Public Security Bureau is adjacent to the hotel. The main street, on the north bank of the Ngu-chu, has a number of smaller restaurants, serving both Tibetan and Sichuan cuisine. Several shops selling clothing, groceries, electrical goods, and luxury items.

Sleeping & eating

Pelyul Namgyel Jangchubling དཔལ་ཡུལ་རྣམ་རྒྱལ་བྱང་ཆུབ་གླིང་པ

The monastery of Namgyel Jangchubling was founded at Pelyul in 1665 by the king of Derge, Lachen Jampa Phuntsok, who appointed Rigdzin Kunzang Sherab (1636-99) as its first throne-holder. The location, sacred to the bodhisattva Vajrapani, had ancient associations with Garab Dorje, Padmasambhava and the latter's second generation disciple, Kyere Chokyong Wangpo. As such, it was an important power place for the discovery of *termas*. Prior to the 17th century, the site also had Kagyu connections.

History

At Pelyul, the teaching-cycles of the Nyingma school were maintained with a particular emphasis on the *terma*-tradition of Ratna Lingpa (1403-71). The monastery was also inspired from its foundation by the visionary teachings of Namcho Migyur Dorje (1645-67), who lived in nearby **Muksang** until his untimely death at the age of 23. Along with Katok, it played a major role in the dissemination of the Nyingma Kama (the oral teachings of the Nyingma school), and the xylograph blocks for this collection of oral teachings (20 vols) along with the *Collected Works of Namcho Mingyur Dorje* were prepared and published here under the guidance of the eighth throne-holder, Orgyen Dongak Chokyi Nyima (1854-1906).

The temples of Pelyul were constructed on the slopes below the peak of Dzongnang and the ridge of Dago Osel Lhari. Among them the most important was the **Lhasarkhang** or **Chagrakhang**, constructed by Kunzang Sherab himself and containing a gilded copper image of Shakyamuni in the form of Jowo Yizhin Norbu, as well as frescoes of the Namcho deities. Stupas and reliquary halls housed the remains of past masters including those of Namcho Migyur Dorje. The **Dorsem Lhakhang** with its enormous image of Vajrasattva was constructed by the seventh throne-holder, Gyatrul Pema Dongak Tenzin (1830-91), and the **Terdzokhang** or library by the eighth. The ridge-top temple of **Dago Osel Lhari** contained images, tangkas and frescoes of deities according to the Mahayoga and Anuyoga systems.

The expansion of Pelyul was supervised by 11 successive throne-holders, beginning with Rigdzin Kunzang Sherab and including the emanations of Drupwang Pema Norbu and Karma Kuchen. In past times the monastic population at Pelyul fluctuated greatly, but there were over 100 branches throughout East Tibet, the most important being the monastery of **Tarthang Dongak Shedrupling** in the Golok region of Amdo, which was founded in 1882 by the seventh throne-holder. A new branch of the monastery, **Namdroling**, was constructed in South India in 1963 under the guidance of the present throne holder, Pema Norbu Rinpoche III, who is also the actual Head of the Nyingmapa School.

The monastery (3,261 metres) is approached from the west end of town via the Hospital of Traditional Tibetan Medicine, and a lane which leads sharply uphill through a timber yard. The reconstruction at Pelyul began in 1981. The

The site

Eastern Tibet

new **Assembly Hall** (Dukhang) contains images of Padmasambhava flanked by Shantaraksita and King Trisong Detsen. The skylight murals are exquisitely crafted. In succession (left to right) they depict: (left wall) Karma Chakme, Rongzompa, and Trisong Detsen; (inner wall): Namcho Mingyur Dorje, Longchen Rabjampa, and Rigdzin Kunzang Sherab, and (right wall): Nubchen Sangye Yeshe; Ratnalingpa, and Jamyang Khyentse Wangpo.

150 monks currently live in houses across the hillside, studying under the supervision of Tulku Tubten Pelzang and Chi-me Tulku, who are responsible for the reconstruction pending the exile of Penor Rinpoche in India. Beside the new temple is a chapel containing four large *mani* wheels and a room containing the relics of Namcho Migyur Dorje. Hardly any of the aforementioned xylographs survive, and new blocks are expensive to make.

Higher up on the ridge, the ruined walls of the original massive two-storey temple are still prominent. Under close inspection, they reveal bullet-holes, as well as Marxist slogans in Chinese from the period of the Cultural Revolution. Above this ruin, on the northwest summit is the newly restored hermitage of the late Dzongnang Rinpoche. The meditation retreat centre lies on the upper east side of the ridge.

Pelyul to Kandze road

Following the Ngu-chu valley upstream from Pelyul, the road passes through **Lingtang** and **Barong** (60 kilometres), where forestry is the main industry; and **Zhang Chumdo**, where many small teams of Chinese gold prospectors can be seen spraying the hillside and panning the streams. Crossing the watershed pass (4,237 metres), the road cuts southeast to **Dorkho Gonpa** of the Sakya school (3,612 metres), before heading northeast towards Kandze. On this stretch, there are spectacular upland lakes and variegated grasslands of gentian, meconopsis and edelweiss. A turn-off on the right (east) leads towards Nyarong (see below, page 498). The final watershed pass cuts through the glacial **Kawalungring** range, which divides the Yangtze and Yalong basins. The overall distance from Pelyul to Kandze is 222 kilometres.

Derge County སྡེ་དགེ

Derge County (86)
德格县
Dege
Population: 59,486
Area: 11,711 sq km
Colour map 4, grid A4

*Derge is often regarded as the cultural, if not the geographical, heart of Kham. Traditionally it is the name given to a large independent kingdom, which occupied until recent times present-day Jomda, Pelyul, and Sershul counties, in addition to Derge county. The much diminished county of Derge now comprises only the valley of the Zi-chu tributary of the Yangtze, extending from its watershed in the **Tro La** range to its confluence with the Yangtze; and the outlying grasslands of **Yilhun** and **Dzachuka** to the north, and the valley of **Mesho** to the south. The county capital is located at **Derge Gonchen** in the Zi-chu valley – 28 kilometres northeast from the Kamtok Drukha Zamchen bridge, 345 kilometres from Chamdo, and 115 kilometres from Pelyul.*

Dzongsar རྫོང་གསར

Colour map 4, grid A3

10 kilometres north of **Horpo** township, and 32 kilometres south of the **Kamtok Drukha** bridge, on the east bank of the Yangtze, the road swerves into a ravine to span the estuary of the **Mesho-chu**. A derelict fortified machine-gun post beside the bridge bears witness to the vigorous resistence maintained by the Khampa Chuzhi Gangdruk organization against the

Win

a 7 night 'Bangkok & Beach' holiday for two courtesy of Hayes & Jarvis

20 runners up to win a Footprint Handbook of their choice

Footprint Handbooks are the most accurate and up-to-date travel guides available. There are over 38 books in the series and more in the pipeline. You can find out more by contacting us:
T +44 (0) 1225 469141
E handbooks@footprint.cix.co.uk
www.footprint-handbooks.co.uk

Well established as one of the UK's leading tour operators Hayes & Jarvis has been selling long haul holidays to the discerning traveller for over 40 years. Every Hayes & Jarvis holiday is the product of careful and meticulous planning where good quality and reliability go hand in hand with value for money.

HAYES and JARVIS
HOLIDAYS WORLDWIDE

To enter the Prize Draw fill in this form using a ball-point pen and return to us.

Mr ☐ Mrs ☐ Miss ☐ Ms ☐

First name _____

Surname _____

Permanent Address _____

_____

_____

Postcode/Zip _____ Country_____

Email _____

Occupation _____ Age _____

Title of Handbook _____

If you have any friends who would like to hear about Footprint Handbooks, fill in their details below.

Mr ☐ Mrs ☐ Miss ☐ Ms ☐

First name _____

Surname _____

Permanent Address_____

_____

_____

Postcode/Zip_____ Country _____

Which two destinations would you like to visit in the next two years?

_____

Travel guides for free spirits

Footprint Handbooks

Footprint Handbooks
6 Riverside Court
Lower Bristol Road
Bath
BA2 3DZ
England

which overlooks the confluence of the Pelpung-chu with the Yangtze (seven to nine hours). The distance from the White Chorten to Derge is 16 kilometres. A more direct but less frequented trekking route from Pelpung to Derge heads due north, crossing four 4,000 metres passes en route (13 hours).

Changra Podrang

A short distance north of the White Chorten which marks the beginning of the *Colour map 4, grid A3* Pelpung trail, the road passes below the ruins of **Changra Podrang**, the former summer palace of the kings of Derge, where a small temple [Changra Gonpa] has recently been restored. The short drive from here to Derge leaves the Yangtze at its confluence with the Zi-chu, and follows the latter upstream through a prosperous farming belt. The road markers from the Kamtok Drukha Zamchen bridge begin at 980 kilometres and run in descending order, all the way to Chengdu.

Derge

Derge was the largest and most influential of the five kingdoms of Kham. The *Altitude: 3,292 metres* crafts of Derge, particularly in printing and metal work were renowned *Colour map 4, grid A3* throughout Tibet. The independence of the kingdom was firmly maintained until 1865 and sporadically thereafter by its hereditary kings, who have been documented in J Kolmas, *A Genealogy of the Kings of Derge*. The town still has a majority Tibetan population; which is considerably increased in summertime when the **Rain Retreat Festival** attracts visitors from all parts of Kham.

The buildings of Derge are located in a sharp-sided ravine, which abuts the **Orientation** Zi-chu valley. At present, it appears to have lost much of its former grandeur. Two bridges span the Zi-chu, connecting the Chamdo-Kandze highway on the west bank with the town on the east bank. Along the highway you will find the county bus stop and bus station, the *Forestry Department Guesthouse*, which has hot public showers, a number of restaurants, shops, and bars, and two power stations, one at either end of the town.

The best view of the town is to be obtained from the cave of Tangtong Gyelpo, high up on the cliff-face across the Zi-chu. From this vantage point one can clearly discern the ruins of the royal palace and the reconstructed monastery of **Derge Gonchen** at the top end of Culture Street (*Tib* Rig-ne lam; *Ch* Wenhua Jie). Further downhill on Culture Street, the Derge Middle School, the renowned **Derge Parkhang** and its Guesthouse and Bookshop are located, while further to the south (right), accessible via a narrow lane, is the old Tibetan quarter where the houses are clustered around the **Temple of Tangtong Gyelpo**. Below the Derge Parkhang is a large reconstructed stupa – originally founded by Dudul Dorje and later rebuilt by Jamyang Khyentse Wangpo.

Heading downhill from Culture Street, a turn-off on the right leads north towards the County Hall, the Government Buildings and the cinema. Continuing downhill you will pass a number of shops and general stores, and arrive at an intersection. Turn south (left) on to Sanitation Street (*Ch* Weisheng Jie) for the Peoples' Hospital, the Tibetan Hospital, the petrol station and the PLA Base. Turn north (right), on to Main Street (*Ch* Zheng Jie), for the Xinhua Bookstore, the Post Office, the Public Security Bureau, the *Derge Hotel*, and the Festival Site. Alternatively, continue downhill on Commercial Street (*Ch* Shang Yie Jie) to the Chamdo-Kandze Highway on the west bank of the Zi-chu.

Eastern Tibet

Sights

Derge Gonchen Monastery The ruined monastery was rapidly reconstructed between 1987 and 1988, the internal structures and windows being rebuilt around the shell of the outer walls which largely remained from the past. The **Assembly Hall (Dukhang)** with its high fluted columns is illuminated by windows on the upper level. It contains images of the Five Founders of Sakya and relics of the previous Dzongsar Khyentse Rinpoche. The murals depict Buddha in the form Ardhokta and the meditational deities of the Sakya school. Towards the centre of the hall the grand throne of Sakya Trizin, the head of the Sakyapa school who currently resides at Rajpur in India, is prominent. Behind it there are three **inner sanctums** approached via steep wooden staircases, which respectively contain enormous clay images of the Eight Manifestations of Padmasambhava, a gilded Jowo Shakyamuni, and Maitreya flanked by the eight standing bodhisattvas. The antechamber contains on its walls a painting of the deer and dharma-wheel motif alongside a list of all those who have made donations towards the rebuilding programme.

Derge Parkhang Printing Press The celebrated printing press of **Derge Parkhang** is a magnificent three-storeyed building with original frescoes that were blackened by smoke during the wanton destruction of the 1960s, but recently restored with painstaking care. Beyond the portico, there is an inner courtyard, giving access to the **temple** on the ground level, **the printing works** on the second level, and

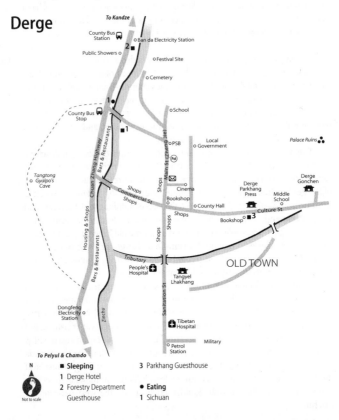

Derge

To Kandze

County Bus Station
Ban da Electricity Station
Public Showers
2
Festival Site
Cemetery

County Bus Stop
School
1
1

Chuan Zhang Highway
Bars & Restaurants

Main St (Zhenan)

PSB
Local Government
Palace Ruins

Housing & Shops
Shops
Commercial St
Shops
Cinema
Bookshop
County Hall
Shops
Bookshop
Derge Parkhang Press
Middle School
Derge Gonchen
3
Culture St

Bars & Restaurants

Tangtong Gyalpo's Cave

Tributary
People's Hospital
Tangyel Lhakhang
OLD TOWN

Sanitation St
Zinchu

Dongfeng Electricity Station
Tibetan Hospital
Petrol Station
Military

To Pelyul & Chamdo

N
Not to scale

■ **Sleeping**
1 Derge Hotel
2 Forestry Department Guesthouse

3 Parkhang Guesthouse

● **Eating**
1 Sichuan

Eastern Tibet

History of Derge

The Kings of Derge claimed descent from the ancient Gar family, the most illustrious representative of which was Songtsen Gampo's chief minister. Their early Bonpo religious affiliations appear to have been superseded first by the Nyingmapa, and then by Chogyel Pakpa and the Sakyapa who granted them authority in Kham.

In the 15th century, the 31st generation descendant, Lodro Tobden, moved his capital to the present site and constructed the royal palace. He also invited Tangtong Gyelpo to select an adjacent site for the new monastery of **Lhundrupteng** (or Derge Gonchen). Tangtong Gyelpo is said to have consecrated the site in 1448 while meditating in a cave high on the cliff-face across the Zi-chu River. The town has since had another temple dedicated to his memory. **Lhundrupteng** was eventually completed by the king Lachen Jampa Phuntsok in the mid-17th century. It became the most important centre for the Ngorpa order of the Sakya school in East Tibet and its branches were to extend throughout the kingdom from Khorlomdo and Dzongsar to Wara.

At Derge itself the monastic population was approximately 1700. In the 18th century the king Tenpa Tsering (1678-1738) brought Derge to the height of its power by conquering the outlying northern districts of **Dzachuka**. Under his auspices, the celebrated printery, **Derge Parkhang**, was established in 1729. Here, the Sakya scholar Zhuchen Tsultrim Rinchen produced his own edition of the Kangyur and Tangyur, generally regarded as the most accurate in Tibet. However, the collection of xylograph blocks housed at the printery, carved in the style of the **Kutse school**, was also regarded as the most eclectic in Tibet. Works of the Nyingma, Kagyu and Geluk schools were printed alongside those of the Sakyapa. The eclecticism of the kingdom was also reflected in the scope given to non-Sakya traditions, particularly of the Nyingma and Kagyu schools, for their own development.

The kingdom which had survived the campaign of Gushri Qan in the 17th century finally succumbed to Gonpo Namgyel, the chieftain of Nyarong in 1863. However, the latter was defeated by the Tibetan army in 1865 and after an interim period of administration from Lhasa, independence was restored. Later, the armies of Chao Erh Feng occupied the kingdom and it remained in Chinese possession between 1909-1918.

Eastern Tibet

the rooftop chapels on the third level. The temple contains original exquisite images of (L-R): the three emanations of Manjughosa, namely: Sakya Pandita, flanked by Tsongkhapa and Longchen Rabjampa; along with Four-armed Avalokiteshvara, Amitabha, Shakyamuni, Padmasambhava, Manjughosa, Tara, Pelpung Situ Chokyi Jungne, and King Tenpa Tsering. There is an old tangka depicting Milarepa and murals of the 1,000 buddhas of the aeon. **Upstairs**, is the precious collection of xylograph blocks, including the Derge editions of the *Kangyur, Tangyur, Nyingma Gyudbum* and other works, which are constantly in demand throughout the towns, villages and monasteries of Tibet. The entire printing process can be observed here: from the preparation of the paper and the ink to the carving of the woodblocks and the actual printing and collating of the various texts. The bookshop (open Monday to Saturday) is located in the south wing of the building opposite the Parkhang.

Surrounded by the timber and adobe residential houses of the Tibetan quarter, the **Tangyel Lhakhang** is dedicated to the memory of Tangtong Gyelpo, Tibet's multi-talented bridge-builder, dramatist, engineer and treasure-finder, who consecrated the site of the Gonchen Monastery in 1448. The temple, which was severely damaged during the 1960s, contains a fine

Tangyel
Lhakhang

characteristic image of this great figure – identified by his reddish brown complexion, white hair and white beard. There is also a large *Mani Wheel* in an adjacent building; and the elderly townspeople devote much time to the circumambulation of the entire complex.

Sleeping &   *Derge Hotel*, T22167/22044/22287. Excellent new rooms in the east building at ¥80
eating   per single, ¥108 per double, and ¥77 per bed in triple, and older cheaper rooms in the west building. The ***Forestry Department Guesthouse*** has poorer accommodation, but hot showers are available. For restaurants try the Chamdo-Kandze Highway, particularly the ***Sichuan Jiatong Restaurant*** on the corner below the *Derge Hotel*; or Main Street, opposite the PSB.

Festivals   *Rain Retreat Festival* This monastic festival is an occasion for religious dances, depicting the purification of negativity by Shakyamuni over his successive past lives. The performance is held on the open plain by the Zi-chu River, adjacent to the Chinese Martyrs' Cemetery; and colourful tents are pitched on this site for the duration of the festival.

Taxi   Contact Sonam Dondrub, T22448.

Upper Zi-chu Valley

The highway from Derge to Chengdu (952 kilometres) begins by following the Zi-chu River upstream to its source in the Drida Zelmogang range. This is the name given to the highland region forming a watershed between the upper Yangtze and the upper Yalong. En route it passes through **Khorlomdo**, where there is a small Sakya temple, and the **Kasado** gorge. The ascent to the watershed **Tro La** pass (4,916 metres), 69 kilometres northeast of Derge, is precipitous and switchback, gradually rising above the tree line into a world of jagged snow mountains. There are magnificent views of the Yangtze gorge to the southwest. On the far side of Tro La, the landscape is totally different, the enclosed forested valleys giving way to rugged open grassland. The crossroads town of **Manigango** is located in the grassland, 110 kilometres from Derge, and 41 kilometres from Tro La pass.

Yilhun

Colour map 4, grid A3   The grassland region to the northeast of Tro La pass is known as **Yilhun**. On the descent, take a turn-off on the right (south) to visit the sacred glacial lake of **Yilhun Lhatso** (*Ch* Xinluhai), situated some 30 kilometres below the pass. This lake is one of the most beautiful in all Tibet – its shores bedecked with carved *mani* stones. The mountains and rocks surrounding the lake are said to assume the divine form of the Cakrasamvara *mandala* to those who have the pure vision to perceive them as such. If you have time, pitch a tent here, and explore the pilgrim's trail along the lake shore. A lakeside retreat house and pavilion have recently been constructed.

Manigango   The town of **Manigango**, 11 kilometres below the lake, lies at the junction of three important roads. Derge lies 110 kilometres to the southwest, Jyekundo 429 kilometres to the northwest, and Kandze 84 kilometres to the southeast. In the meadow above the town there is a branch of Dzogchen Monastery, known as **Yazer Gon**. It was in this locale that Derge Yilhunpa Sonam Namgyel attained the rainbow body accomplishment in 1952. An interesting account of this event is described by Chogyam Trunpa in his autobiography, *Born in Tibet*.

Stay at either the *Qinghai Guesthouse* or *Sichuan Guesthouse* – the latter has electric blankets on the beds, and an excellent Sichuan-style kitchen beloved by truckers and bus drivers. There are 2 small general stores, selling groceries, liquor, and a few household necessities.

Sleeping & eating

Some 23 kilometres east of Manigango, a motorable road leaves the Kandze highway and the Yi-chu valley, via a side-bridge and heads north to **Yilhun** township. Here, in August, there is a small but interesting horse-festival, held on a wide plain below the local monastery and village.

Dzogchen Rudam Orgyen Samten Choling Monastery རྫོགས་ཆེན་དགོན་པ

From Manigango, take the northwest route for **Jyekundo**, and cross the Muri La pass (4,633 metres). After 50 kilometres, you will notice the hamlet of **Dzogchen** coming into view on the left (south) side of the road. Above it you will glimpse the **Mani Wheel Chapel** of Dzogchen Monastery on a ridge, protruding from a hidden valley to the southwest. Leave the highway here and drive across a stream, leading down to the hamlet. The road cuts across a low defile to enter the wonderful valley of **Rudam Kyitram**, where Dzogchen Monastery is located.

Getting there

Colour map 4, grid A3

Dzogchen is recognized as the major pilgrimage site of buddha-attributes in East Tibet and as one of the largest monasteries of the Nyingma school in Kham. It lies at an elevation of 4,023 metres, in the concealed valley of Rudam Kyitram, dominated to the southwest by the jagged snow peaks of **Trori Dorje Ziltrom** (5,816 metres).

History of Dzogchen Monastery

The monastery was founded in 1684-85 on the advice of the Dalai Lama V, by the charismatic Dzogchen I Pema Rigdzin (1625-97), and it was subsequently maintained by his students, including Zhechen Rapjam Tenpei Gyeltsen, and by his successive incarnations. Among the latter, Dzogchen II Gyurme Tekchok Tenzin (1699-1758) is known to have inspired the king of Derge to construct the famous **Derge Parkhang**, Dzogchen III Ngedon Tenzin Zangpo (1759-92) built 13 hermitages, colleges and mantra-wheels, Dzogchen IV Migyur Namkei Dorje (b 1793) presided over the monastery when its greatest college was founded, and Dzogchen V Tubten Chokyi Dorje (1872-1935) increased its branches to over 200 throughout Kham, Amdo, and Central Tibet. The mother monastery itself had a population of 1,000 monks. Dzogchen VI Jikdrel Jangchub Dorje (1935-59) died tragically during the resistance to the Chinese occupation of East Tibet, and his reliquary is even now revered in the main temple. Dzogchen Rinpoche VII lives in Karnataka in South India, where he has constructed a branch of the monastery.

At Dzogchen Monastery, two great temples were constructed. The **larger** housed exquisite images of Shakyamuni, Vajradhara and Padmasambhava, alongside the reliquaries of the past emanations of Pema Rigdzin. The **smaller** to the northeast contained enormous images of Padmasambhava, Shantaraksita and King Trisong Detsen. In the early 19th century, a college was constructed below the monastery by Gyelse Zhenpen Thaye at a site consecrated by the ancient Nyingma lineage-holder Shrisimha. The college, known thereafter as **Shrisimha**, became renowned for the study of philosophy and Vajrayana until the mid-20th century. It attracted some of the greatest literati of East Tibet, such as Peltrul Rinpoche (1808-87), Mipam Rinpoche (1846-1912) and Khenpo Zhenga (1871-1927), who wrote commentaries on 13 major texts.

Meditation hermitages The monastery was equally renowned for its

Eastern Tibet

meditation hermitages and the caves which were inhabited by hermits in the upper reaches of the Rudam Kyitram valley. Important figures such as Dodrub Trinle Ozer (1745-1821), Do Khyentse Yeshe Dorje (b 1800), Peltrul Rinpoche and Mipham Rinpoche passed many years in meditation in this region, the rocks of which are intimately connected with their visionary experiences. It was also here that Peltrul Rinpoche composed his great commentary on the preliminary practices of Buddhist meditation, the *Kunzang Lamei Zhelung* (translated into English under the title "Words of my Perfect Teacher").

The site The monastery is located on the north slopes of the Rudam Kyitram valley. The larger of the two temples which formerly housed the relics of past Dzogchen Rinpoches is yet to be restored. The **smaller** one, where the images of Padmasambhava, King Trisong Detsen and Shantaraksita were once enshrined, is undergoing restoration, having been destroyed during the Cultural Revolution, rebuilt, and yet again destroyed by fire! It has decorative columns at the entrance, protected by silk wrappings, and in its upper storey there is a chapel containing the relics of Dzogchen VI Jikdrel Jangchub Dorje, who was killed in 1959. Religious dancing is still held in the courtyard on the tenth day of the first month of the Tibetan calendar.

To the north of these temples is a **Mani Wheel** temple, and to the south are two lower elongated buildings on either side of an open courtyard. Approaching these from the temple, one passes the **Nga-khang** on the left and the **Podrang Khamsum Zilnon** on the right. The latter building, which once housed many chapels, contains in its upper storey the residence of Dzogchen Rinpoche named **Chime Drupei Gatsel**, a library, a printery, and a temporary residence where the present Dzogchen Rinpoche stayed during a recent visit.

Below the monastery and to the right is the **Shrisimha college**, so called because this ancient yogin is said to have appeared in a vision to the college's founder and to have left an impression in a nearby rock. A few buildings within the small campus have been restored by Tulku Kelzang, who has revitalized the college in collaboration with Khenpo Dazer and Khenpo Pentse.

The Cave Hermitages Heading up the valley from the college towards the cave hermitages and the **Trori** glacier (northwest face of Tro La), you first pass, in a clearing, a series of burial stones marking the graves of past monastic preceptors. Above and to the right as you ascend the valley is the ruined hermitage of the monastery where long regulated retreats were once held. Higher up the slope on the same side of the valley are firstly the cave – hermitage of Do Khyentse Yeshe Dorje, known as the **Tseringma cave** because he is said to have met the deity Tseringma here face to face, and secondly that of Peltrul Rinpoche.

Continuing up the central part of the valley you reach an elevated area where there are well-constructed and active hermitages. On the hillside to the left, high up and across the rushing river is the cave-hermitage known as **Shinje Drupuk** – a former retreat of Dodrub Jigme Trinle Ozer, containing a footprint of Yamantaka which gives the cave its name. Directly opposite the cave site on the right side of the valley is a rock into which the deity Palchen Dupa vanished after appearing in a vision to Dodrub Trinle Ozer. Below this cave is another, approached from the site where Peltrul Rinpoche first taught his celebrated text, *Kunzang Lamei Zhelung*. It contains the meditation-box of Peltrul Rinpoche and naturally produced impressions of Yamantaka which appeared while Dodrub Rinpoche was engaged in practice there. Yet lower down is a **cave of Mipam Rinpoche** containing original but damaged clay relief images of the 25 disciples of Padmasambhava.

From atop these caves one has an excellent view to the north beyond Dzogchen Monastery to the **Kyadrak Senge Dzong** retreat (4,872 metres) in Dzachuka, the major pilgrimage site representing buddha-body in Kham. There, Padmasambhava himself is reputed to have passed three months.

Above the valley in the Rudam Kangtro range are three sacred lakes and on their circuit is a place where Padmasambhava made medicinal myrobalan.

Zhechen Tenyi Dargyeling Monastery ཞེ་ཆེན་དར་རྒྱས་པ

Getting there
Colour map 4, grid A3

Returning to the highway from Dzogchen, drive west for 10 kilometres as far as the transport station at **Chusumdo** (*Ch* Sansaho). Here, a side-road follows the Nang-chu tributary of the Yalong downstream to its confluence. Some 10 kilometres along this road, you will reach **Zhechen Monastery** on the left (west). This monastery, located in the Nang-chu valley, is situated in a defile between **Bonri** and **Dolmari** hills (3,780 metres). The site was chosen because on the slopes of Dolmari there were many sacred hermitages and caves associated with Padmasambhava, Yeshe Tsogyel, Vajravarahi, Tangtong Gyelpo and so forth.

History of Zhechen Monastery

The monastery was founded in 1735 by Zhechen Rabjam II, Gyurme Kunzang Namgyel (1710-69). His predecessor, Zhechen Rabjam I Tenpei Gyeltsen (1654-1709), had been a student of Dalai Lama V and Dzogchen Pema Rigdzin. The seat was maintained by his successive emanations, including Zhechen Rabjam III Rigdzin Peljor Gyatso (1771-1809), who constructed the **Pema Choling** hermitage in 1794; and Zhechen Rapjam IV Garwang Chokyi Gyeltsen, as well as by a succession of regents. In the time of the regent Gyeltsab Tendzin Chogyel, 100,000 students gathered from all four Buddhist traditions and also from the Bon to receive his teachings. In more recent years however, the resident population of the mother monastery included about 300 monks. The present Zhechen Rabjam VII, under the guidance of the late HH Dingo Khyentse Rinpoche, constructed a new flourishing branch of the monastery at Boudha in Nepal.

The monastery was known for its fine sculptures, tangkas and murals. Formerly there were two temples with major images of Shakyamuni and Padmasambhava, respectively representing the sutra and mantra traditions. There was also a famous image made of herbs, representing Terdak Lingpa, the founder of Mindroling. Alongside these images were eight reliquaries containing the remains of past Zhechen Rabjam emanations and their regents.

A prestigious college at Zhechen was founded in this century by Gyeltsab III Pema Namgyel (1871-1927), and it rapidly became known in Kham for the excellence of its study programme, largely through the efforts of the late Zhechen Kongtrul (d 1959) and the late Zhechen Rabjam VI (d 1959). Woodblocks were kept for the works of Karma Lingpa and for liturgical texts associated with Mindroling Monastery.

The site

The hill to the right as one approaches from the Chusumdo-Nangdo road, is **Bonri** and the one to the left **Dolmari**. Of the former impressive structures on the slopes of Dolmari, nothing remains. The two original temples are currently undergoing reconstruction. At present there are approximately 200-300 monks affiliated with Zhechen, but few live permanently at the site.

Above the temple is the ruined hermitage, and below and beyond the stream is the **college**, restored through the efforts of the late Lama Gyenpel. The main building of the college contains a shrine with a new Padmasambhava image and a gold-painted footprint of its founder, Zhechen Gyeltsab III.

Eastern Tibet

Sacred caves Above the monastery on **Dolmari** are many sacred caves and hermitages associated with important historical figures and deities. Among them the following are most notable:

The **Kabgye Drupuk**, where Vajravarahi reputedly appeared in a rock during the meditations of Gyeltsab Gyurme Pema Namgyel. This cave was damaged during the Cultural Revolution, but the earth inside is held by pilgrims to be sacred.

The **Zangdok Pelri Drupuk** of Padmasambhava and Yeshe Tsogyel, where pilgrims go to gather natural medicinal nectar.

The **Khandro Bumgyi Drupuk**, which is adorned with a red and white stupa and a dark blue relief image of Tangtong Gyelpo.

The former **hermitage of Gyeltsab Tenzin Chogyel** and site of the destroyed hermitage of the previous Zhechen Rabjam VI.

The **Osel Drupuk** which has a naturally produced image of the deity Rigdzin Dupa.

Zhechen to Nangdo

Ten kilometres north of Zhechen, the Nang-chu flows into the Yalong at **Nangdo**. From here there are trekking routes following the Yalong downstream towards the farming settlements of **Rongpatsa**, and upstream into the sparse grasslands of **Sershul** county. The monasteries of **Drokda Gonpa** and **Samdrub Gonpa** are located downstream around the confluence of the Ding-chu with the Yalong, while **Peni Gonpa** and **Dzechen Gonpa** lie upstream.

Chusumdo to Denkhok

Another motorable trail leads southwest from Chusumdo to **Marong**, where Jamgon Kongtrul discovered *termas* in the 19th century. (A trekking route also leads from here across **Le La** pass to **Khorlomdo** near Derge.) The motorable trail then crosses the watershed **Latse Kare La** pass (4,298 metres) and enters **Lingtsang**, one of the former independent kingdoms of East Tibet, where the Gyelpo (king) claimed descent from Tibet's epic hero Ling Gesar. En route you pass the Nyingmapa monastery of **Dzungo** which spectacularly overlooks the Yangtze from its hilltop pinnacle.

At Lingtsang, there is a large distinctively striped Sakya monastery called **Gotse Gon**. A wide cultivated plain opens out 24 kilometres from Lingtsang, where the road reaches **Denkhok** on the east bank of the Yangtze. Denkhok, the birthplace of the late HH Dingo Khyentse Rinpoche, is nowadays divided into two main sectors – **Denkhok Nubma** lying within the jurisdiction of the Tibetan Autonomous Region on the west bank of the Yangtze, and **Denkhok Sharma** within Sichuan province on the east bank. The Gelukpa monastery of **Chunkor** (a branch of Sershul) is located on the west bank, and the celebrated **Langtang Dolma Lhakhang**, one of Songtsen Gampo's 12 major geomantic temples, is located on the east bank. As its name suggests, it contains an image of Tara, which was recently returned to the custodianship of the temple through the efforts and devotion of the Tibetan businessman Tenpa Dargye.

Grasslands of Dzachuka, Jyekundo and Nangchen

The upper reaches of the Yalong, Yangtze, and Mekong rivers in the extreme northwest of Kham flow through spacious grasslands, largely above the tree line. Here are some of the richest nomadic pastures in Tibet, and a surprisingly large number of monasteries, which minister to the spiritual needs of the nomadic population as well as to the inhabitants of the relatively few agricultural settlements. Driving across the watersheds of these mighty rivers, you will pass through seven counties, one of which (Sershul) is presently administered from Dartsedo (Sichuan), and the remaining six from Jyekundo (Qinghai).
Recommended itinerary: 8.

Sershul County གསེར་ཤུལ

*The rich nomadic pastures of **Sershul** extend through the upper reaches of the Yalong as far as the present day Sichuan-Qinghai provincial border. (The actual source of the Yalong lies across the border near **Domda**.) The county capital is located at **Jumang**, now a large sprawling frontier town (generally called Sershul), 139 kilometres from Jyekundo, and 219 kilometres from Manigango. There are 43 monasteries within Sershul county, reflecting all the diverse traditions of Tibetan Buddhism and Bon.*

Sershul County (87)
石渠县
Serxu
Population: 59,486
Area: 20,477 sq km
Colour map 5, grid C2

Eastern Tibet

From **Langtang Dolma Lhakhang** at Denkhok in the Yangtze valley, there is an old caravan trail following the Yangtze upstream via the ferry-crossing of **Drenda Druka** to approach Jyekundo from the southeast. The main highway however runs northwest from **Chusumdo** (*Ch* Sansaho) through the Nang-chu valley, crossing the **Magar Drokra** grassland. After passing the Gelukpa monastery of **Trugu Gonpa** (also pronounced as Jowo) on the left (36 kilometres from Chusumdo), the road leaves the Nang-chu and follows the Tra-chu downstream past the turn-off for **Ralung-kado** village on the right (42 kilometres from Trugu Gonpa), and the important Karma Kagyu monastery of **Tsatsha Gon** after 10 further kilometres.

Tsatsha Gon & Junyung

Here, there is a turn-off on the right, which follows the Tra-chu downstream for 40 kilometres as far as its confluence with the Yalong at **Tung** township. The Nyingmapa monastery of **Tashul** can be visited on this side-road. At Tung township, the Ngoshi-chu tributary also flows into the Yalong from the northwest.

Keep to the highway at **Tsatsha Gon**, and the road will continue north to reach the south bank of the Yalong. Following the course of this main waterway upstream, after 38 kilometres (at marker 186), you will arrive at **Rinyur**

Gonpa (on the left) and a turn-off (on the right) which leads east to **Arikdza Gonpa** of the Nyingma school, which is currently maintained by Khenpo Pentse.

Further north, the main road passes through **Junyung** township on the left (46 kilometres from Tsatsha Gon). Here there is the Nyingmapa monastery of **Junyung Mehor Sangak Choling** and its retreat hermitage, where the renowned Mipham Rinpoche (1846-1912) studied and practised. At **Junyung**, the Omchung-chu flows into the Yalong from the south via **Bumsar** township, and the Nyingma monastery of **Ponru Gonpa** is located up a lateral valley on the north bank.

The highway continues northwest from **Junyung**, following the river bank upstream for a short distance, and then abruptly heads southwest following the Om-chu tributary upstream to the county capital at **Jumang** (Sershul). If you prefer to continue following the Yalong, a trekking route leads upstream as far as **Gemang**, where there is an important branch of Dzogchen Monastery. Beyond Gemang, the Muge-chu tributary flows in from the northwest and you will reach the Gelukpa monastery of **Kabzhi**, where there are 250 monks. From here, you can cross the provincial border to reach the source of the Yalong at Domda.

Jumang

Colour map 5, grid C2   Driving south along the main road through the Om-chu valley, 19 kilometres after Junyung, the main road passes the Gelukpa monastery of **Bumnying Gonpa**, where there are 200 monks. The county capital of **Jumang** lies in the same valley, six kilometres further south. This is the largest Chinese settlement northwest of Kandze, and the nomadic peoples of the grasslands intermingle here with incongruous Chinese immigrants.

Essentials   The sprawling main street has a petrol station and bus station at the east end (south side). Across on the north side of the street you will pass in succession: the Cinema, the Book Store, the Post Office, the Public Security Bureau, and a number of general stores and simple Sichuan-style restaurants. At the west end of town, there are two hotels, one on either side of the main street. The hotel on the north side also owns the adjacent *Tiemushe Restaurant*.

Sershul Monastery

Getting there   Leaving the capital, the road also leaves the Om-chu valley, and heads northwest,
Colour map 5, grid C2   passing the small hamlets of Jumang and **Serlha** on the right. From **Deongma** township, 18 kilometres after Jumang, you can see the Nyingma monastery of **Dzakya Gonpa**, in the distance to the northwest. Here there are 50 monks.

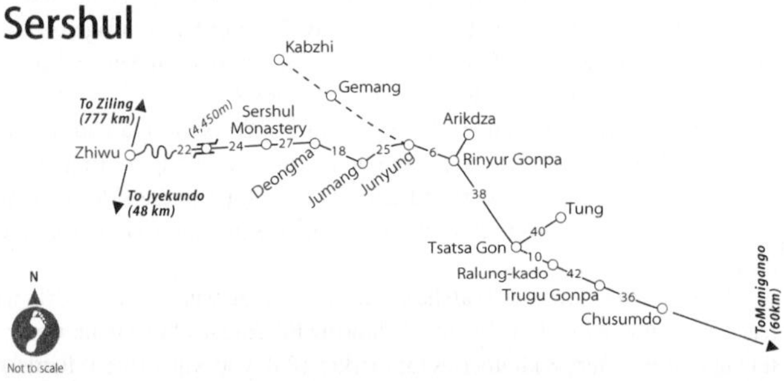

Sershul

Eastern Tibet (side tab)

The great **Sershul Monastery** of the Gelukpa school lies 27 kilometres east of Deongma, on the right side of the road. This is currently the largest monastery in Sershul county, with 800 monks, and a grand assembly hall. The rain retreat festival held in August is a magnificent spectacle, attracting nomad communities from afar. The hills and plains around the monastery (4,054 metres) are bare and spacious. Beyond the monastery, the highway heads west for 24 kilometres over a pot-holed and deeply rutted surface to cross the **Ngamba La** pass (4,450 metres), which divides the Yalong and Yangtze basins, as well as the present day provinces of Sichuan and Qinghai.

Trindu County ཁྲི་འདུ་

*Trindu county comprises the area around the southern source of the Yalong River, which now belongs to the Yushu Tibetan Autonomous Prefecture of Qinghai Province. The county capital is located at **Druchung**, 24 kilometres west of the Jyekundo-Ziling highway. Within the county which has a rich nomadic heritage, there are presently 26 monasteries representative of all the major schools: Sakya, Kagyu, Geluk and Nyingma.*

Trindu County (88)
称多县
Chindu
Population: 37,742
Area: 9,717 sq km
Colour map 5, grid C2

Zhiwu

Descending from the **Ngamba La** pass (4,450 metres) after Sershul, the highway zigzags downhill for 22 kilometres to the township of Zhiwu (*Ch* Xiwu), a low-lying (3,900 metres) settlement straddling an important crossroads. Cultivated fields appear around Zhiwu, in contrast to the high grasslands of Dzachuka to the east. The climate is several degrees warmer. On the descent from the pass there are magnificent views of **Drogon Monastery**, clinging to the sheer cliff-face above the town, and painted in the distinctive Sakya colours. At the crossroads, a barrier blocks the road, indicating that you are about to drive from Sichuan into Qinghai. The road to the north (right) leads 777 kilometres to Ziling, and the road to the south (left) leads 48 kilometres to Jyekundo. Southwest of town, is the hilltop monastery of **Nyidzong** (founded 1580), which belongs to the Drigung Kagyu school and has a revered charnal ground alongside.

Colour map 5, grid C2

The Sakyapa monastery known as **Dogon Puntsok Dargyeling** originally belonged to the Kadampa tradition, but was converted by Drogon Chogyel Phakpa in 1265 when he sojourned here on his return journey from Mongolia to Lhasa. From his time until the present, there have been 18 lineage-holders, bearing the title Do-la. The present incumbent is Do-la Jikme Chokyi Nyima, a son of the late HH Dudjom Rinpoche, and father of the present Dudjom Rinpoche. Do-la Jikme was recognized at the age of seven by the head of the Sakya school; and thereafter educated in Kham. Other teachers associated with Drogon Monastery include Gaden Wangchuk (Ga Tulku) and Ngakpa Ngoten. Currently there are about 70 monks here. The summer festival following the end of the rain retreat is a major event held in the plains below the monastery.

Dogon Puntsok Dargyeling

The **main temple** with 38 columns is now being restored. It is planned to install two storey images of Shakyamuni, Padmasambhava, and Maitreya in gilded bronze. At present, the smaller **Tsuklakhang** with 16 columns has been undergoing restoration and refurbishment since 1981. The central image, encased in glass, is of the previous Sakya Gongma, and the altar also has colour photographs of the present throne-holders of the Dolma and Phuntsok

Eastern Tibet

palaces of Sakya, who respectively reside at Rajpur in India and Seattle in the USA. Alongside these is a photograph of the present Dzongsar Khyentse, a nephew of Do-la Jikme, who now resides in Bhutan and the West. To the left of Sakya Gongma are images of Shakyamuni and the Sixteen Elders, while to the right are an assortment of images, including Tara, Padmasambhava, and Vajrasattva. Below the central image of Sakya Gongma (in the same glass case) are a number of old images including Vajrasattva. Tangkas which decorate the side-walls, including two very old ones depicting Two-armed Mahakala and Vajrabhairava. There are also new images which have been brought from Chamdo, including one of Padmasambhava. On the left is a large Maitreya in a glass case.

Among other restored chapels at Dogon Monastery, visit the **Gonkhang**, containing images of Panjaranatha and the eight classes of spirits (Lhade-gye), the **Mani Wheel Chapel**, and the revered **Vajrayogini Temple**. Below the complex, to the right, is a series of the Eight Stupas symbolizing the major events in the life of the Buddha.

Sleeping & eating There are 2 hotels at the north end of town, the *Transport Station Guesthouse* down an alleyway on the right, and a Tibetan family-run hotel called *Mirik Dronkhang* on the left. Stay at the latter! There are a number of small tea-shops and restaurants near the crossroads, some serving excellent Muslim tea and lamb dishes.

Northern Route from Zhiwu to Domda and Druchung

Heading north from Zhiwu, the National Highway 214 reaches the Drigung Kagyu monastery of Drubgyuling Gonpa after 51 kilometres. Here, a turn-off on the left (west) leads 24 kilometres to the county capital at Druchung. Alternatively, you can continue north on the highway from Drubgyuling for 51 kilometres to Domda (*Ch* Qingshuihe), near the northern source of the Yalong River. From Domda, the highway leaves Trindu county for Mato and Ziling (675 kilometres).

Drubgyuling Gonpa Prior to the 13th century it is said there was a Nyingmapa temple at this site overlooking the trails to Druchung, Zhiwu and Domda. It appears to have been converted to the Drigung Kagyu cause by a Mongol nobleman, after which it has always been considered as a branch of Drugungtil in Central Tibet. The **main temple** at Drubgyuling contains many new tangkas flanking a central applique which depicts Drigung Kyopa, with the protector deities below and Vajradhara above. There is a new image of Padmasambhava, as yet unpainted, and many small reliquary stupas. Within the **Gonkhang** there is a larger stupa inset with a photograph of the present Drigung Kyapgon, surrounded by the protector deities of the Drigung Kagyu lineage. There are two other buildings, one of which is the Labrang and the other the residence of Drubgyu Tulku (most senior of the five tulkus of this monastery). Currently there are 200 monks at Drubgyuling.

Druchung town The county town is small, and the community mostly pastoral farmers. In the vicinity of the town there are Sakyapa monasteries, such as

Trindu County

Karzang Peljor Gonpa, which was built by Drogon Chogyel Phakpa's student Ame Dampa in 1268. Formerly a revered eighth century Jowo Shakyamuni was housed in this monastery, but it was destroyed during the 1960s. There is, however, a small collection of original 15th century images, costumes and a chair used by Drogon Chogyel Phakpa in person. **Gatri Dudongtre Samten Chokhorling** was also founded at the behest of Chogyel Phakpa in 1269 and is affiliated to Ngor Monastery of the Sakya school. The Karma Kagyu also have a presence near the town at **Zhedzong Gonpa** (founded 1727), as do the Drigung Kagyu at **Khamjok Gonpa**.

Roads lead from Druchung, west to Sekhok (39 kilometres) and southeast to Ngonga Rinda (13 kilometres). Some 15 kilometres south of Sekhok (*Ch* Saihe), there is a Drigung Kagyu monastery known as **Tashi Gonpa**, while further north in the direction of Gato there is a Mongolian monastery, **Pangshar Gon**, which still espouses the Sakya tradition, and at Trado (*Ch* Zhaduo), an influential branch of Sera called **Zerkar Gonpa** (originally founded 1398). **Sekhok**

In this area, 13 kilometres south of Druchung county town, the Gelukpa school have long established a strong presence. **Lab Gon Ganden Dongak Shedrubling** was founded in 1419 and its images were said to have contained the hair and garments of Tsongkhapa which he personally donated; and at nearby **Yawa Gonpa** there is a small Gelukpa nunnery affiliated to Lab Gon. Smaller Sakya and Nyingma monasteries also co-exist here, north and west of the Dri-chu (Yangtze). **Ngonga Rinda**

Gold panning is extensive in this area, where the town of Domda has grown up to service the truckers and bus companies which ply the highway from Ziling to Jyekundo. There are several Sichuan and Muslim-style restaurants. There are small Nyingmapa communities at **A-me Gonpa**, **Yangshar Gon** and **Kyewo Gon**, these last two being itinerant nomadic camps which are affiliated to Dzogchen. **Domda**

Southern Route from Zhiwu to Yangtze Crossing

The highway from Zhiwu to Jyekundo heads south on an excellent paved surface, following the Zhiwuchi-chu downstream to its confluence with the Yangtze after 18 kilometres. En route you will bypass the Kagyupa monasteries of **Bage Gonpa** and **Bambi Gonpa**. From the bridge over the Yangtze which marks the county border, Jyekundo is only 30 kilometres distant.

Eastern Tibet

Jyekundo County སྐྱེ་དགུ་མདོ

Jyekundo County (89)
玉树县
Yushu
Population: 64,530
Area: 13,7384 sq km
Colour map 5, grid C1

*Jyekundo county is the northwest region of Kham, known locally as **Gawa**, which occupies the upper reaches and source feeder rivers of the Yangtze. At the present day the city of Jyekundo is not only the county capital, but also the administrative capital of six counties belonging to the Yushu Tibetan Autonomous Prefecture of Qinghai Province. Here the predominant traditions are those of the Sakyapa and Kagyupa.*

Getting there Crossing the bridge over the Yangtze at **Druda**, 18 kilometres south of Zhiwu, National Highway 214 reaches Jyekundo after 30 kilometres.

Labda Crossing the Yangtze bridge, you will notice a trail on the right (west) which follows the course of the Yangtze upstream for 35 kilometres to **Labda** township. En route, you can visit the 13th century **Tarlam Monastery** (4,000 metres), the residence of Pende Rinpoche of the Ngorpa branch of the Sakya school, who currently resides in France. Other monasteries on that road include **Samdrub Gonpa** of the Sakya school (22 kilometres further west), the 18th century **Palchung A-me** which is affiliated to Katok, and **Gargon Dechenling** (30 kilometres west of Labda), a 13th century Drigung Kagyu foundation which has functioned as a branch of Sera since the 15th century, when Tsongkhapa presented offerings to the monastic community.

Gyanak Mani At the beginning of the descent into Jyekundo valley, the road passes through **Gyanak Mani** – the largest field of mani stones in the whole of Tibet, approximately one square kilometre in area. Stop here to circumambulate the field and wander through the lanes between enormous piles of carved stones and prayer flags. Some stones are intricately inscribed with entire sections from the scriptures, and others have bas-relief images of certain meditational deities. The site is said to have been visited by Princess Wengcheng who presented three mani stones to a local devotee and when red rainbow light (jamar) appeared, her subject was given the appelation Gyanak Tsering Gyeltsen. According to one tradition, the original temple on this site was constructed in the late 13th century by Gyanak Tulku who came here from Chamdo on a return visit from China, although it has also been attributed to Tangtong Gyelpo. The field of stones bears witness to the faith of the Tibetan pilgrims who would travel along the trade routes from Ziling to Lhasa via Jyekundo and make offerings as an expression of their devotion. During the 1960s, many stones were removed for the construction of latrines, but the site has since been reconsecrated, and renovation is supervised by the present incumbent lama, Gyanak Tulku VII.

The **main temple** to the northeast of the site contains seven images, viz. (left to right): Doringpa, Shakyamuni, Avalokiteshvara, Padmasambhava, Vajrasattva, Green Tara, and White Tara. There are also stone footprints and handprints of Doringpa. The mani wheel chapel

Jyekundo County

called **Sengzer Dungkhar Chenpo**, reconstructed in 1987, has colour reproductions of the Indian Buddhist masters Vasubandu, Dignaga, Dharmakirti, Aryadeva, and so forth. The wall on the left has an inscription listing the donors who provided funds for the rebuilding.

Above Gyanak Mani at **Lebkhok** there are rock carvings of Maitreya and rock inscriptions from the royal dynastic period, which have recently been documented.

Jyekundo ཐྲྀ་དགུ་མདོ་

Jyekundo (*Ch* Yushu), meaning 'confluence of all attributes or growth', is named after the town's illustrious hilltop monastery, **Jyekundo Dondrubling**. In ancient times, the Bon religion was strong in the region. The earliest Buddhist contact appears to have coincided with the period of King Songtsen Gampo and his Chinese consort Princess Wengcheng, who passed some time at nearby **Bida** (see below, page 483). In the 13th century a small monastery and nunnery of the Karma Kagyu school were established here, but in 1398 the site was cleared to make way for a Sakyapa monastery, the foundation of which was encouraged by Dagchen Sherab Gyatso of Sakya. It was claimed that Drogon Chogyel Phakpa himself had given teachings here en route for Mongolia.

The town of **Jyekundo** (3,700 metres) quickly sprang up around the monastery as a trading centre, controlling the caravan trails between Ziling and Lhasa; and its traditional summer festival has for centuries attracted crowds of itinerant merchants and pilgrims. Teichman, travelling through Jyekundo in 1919, noticed all sorts of imported goods (tea, textiles, metalware, sugar etc) in the marketplace for sale at cheaper prices than in Dartsedo; and the products of Tibet's nomadic economy: hides, furs, wool, medicines, and so forth attracted the investment of Muslim traders and middlemen. In 1727 the area was nominally brought within the sphere of influence of the Kokonor Muslim territory; but prior to that it had held allegiance to the independent kingdom of Nangchen for centuries. Since 1951 the town has been the capital of Yushu Tibetan Autonomous Prefecture, comprising six counties with a total population of 237,000 and 121 monasteries; and it therefore has a two-tier bureaucracy. The town alone currently has a population of 37,000.

Following the Jyeku River upstream from its confluence with the Yangtze, you **Orientation**

Jyekundo Town

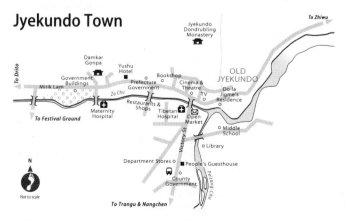

Eastern Tibet

will soon reach Jyekundo, noticing **Dondrubling Monastery** on the hill to the northeast of town. There are two main streets forming a T-junction; and nearby is the confluence of the Jyeku River's two tributaries: the Za-chu which flows from the northwest and the Peltang-chu flowing from the southeast. West of the T-junction is the monastery of **Damkar Lhundrub Dechen Sadon Chokhorling**. The town-residence of Dola Jikme Tulku and the present Dudjom Rinpoche is located down a lane to the southeast of town. The road to the south leads out of town in the direction of **Trangu** and **Nangchen**; while the road to the west leads to Lake **Rongpo** and **Drito**.

Jyekundo
Dondrubling
Monastery
Following the consecration of its site by Drogon Chogyel Phakpa who taught here, the monastery was gradually established in two phases: by Dagchen Sherab Gyatso of the Sakya school in 1398, and Karmapa VII Chodrak Gyatso of the Kagyu school. The construction was finally completed by Dagchen Palden Chokyong (Ngorpa) of the Ngorpa suborder of the Sakyapa, to which it now holds allegiance. Until recently there were 16 temples and 1,000 monks. One of these was restored in 1977 and there are currently 140 monks.

The monastery has been visited over its history by illustrious pilgrims, such as the Mongol prince Gaden Qan, and Panchen Lama IX who passed away here in 1937.

The **lower storey** of the temple houses the Delhi edition of the *Kangyur*, a large image of Padmasambhava, and several smaller images including one of Dagchen Palden Chokyong. Murals depict the meditational deities and lineage-holders of the Ngorpa Sakya tradition; and there are tangkas on the side-walls depicting Mahakala and Bhairava. Within its **inner sanctum**, there are images of the Buddhas of the Three Times, the central Shakyamuni being flanked by his foremost students and the Sixteen Elders. **Upstairs** is a small assembly hall, where rain retreat observances are held in summertime. Formerly, the monastery is said to have held one of the most revered representative objects of buddha-speech in Tibet, the **Chokorma** image, but this no longer survives.

A new protector shrine has recently been renovated to the west of the complex. It is dedicated to Panjaranatha, and has a number of macabre stuffed animals.

Dondrubling
Dungkhor
Below, on the approach road to the monastery, there is a Mani Wheel Chapel named **Dondrubling Dungkhor**, which was newly constructed in 1983 by one Tenkyong at the request of Dzongsar Khyentse Rinpoche. The chapel contains images of Avalokiteshvara, Padmasambhava, and White Tara; several tangkas depicting Green Tara, and murals of Vajrasattva, Padmasambhava, Shantaraksita, King Trisong Detsen, and Sachen Kunga Nyingpo. The mantras contained within the wheel include those of the deities Amitayus, Bhaisajyaguru, Vajrapani, Manjushri, Vajrasattva, Padmasambhava, and Sitatapatra; as well as the entire sutra texts of the *Bhadracaryapranidhanaraja* and the *Parinirvanasutra*. Outside the antechamber has paintings of the Four Guardian Kings and the Wheel of Rebirth, as well as a painting of Dondrubling Monastery as it once looked.

Damkar Lhundrub Dechen Sadon Chokhorling Situated to the west of town, this Karma Kagyu monastery has been in its present location since 1239. The original foundation is attributed to Pasang Tamdrin (1110-1193).

Sleeping The 5-storey *Yushu Hotel* lies to the west of the junction on the north side of the road. Hot showers are sometimes available on each floor of the building.

There is a restaurant in the hotel, but the best restaurants and shops are outside, clus- **Eating**
tered around the crossroads and near the open-air market.

East, beyond the crossroads are the theatre and city cinema. **Entertainment**

South of town, there is a wide plain – extending southwest from the confluence of the **Festivals**
Dzi-chu and Peltang-chu rivers. Here, starting on each **25 July**, the *Jyekundo Horse*
Festival is held. Throughout the last week of July and the 1st week of August, colourful applique tents are pitched across the plain, and a programme of horse-riding
events, and folk dancing attracts people from all corners of the prefecture, and other
parts of East Tibet, as far afield as Nakchu. Each year one of the six counties takes it in
turn to organize the event, and approximately 60 percent of the budget (average
¥160,000) is provided by the prefectural government, the balance being provided by
the organizing county. In 1991 all six counties held a joint festival to commemorate
the 40th anniversary of the prefecture, but during the summers of 1996 and 1997 the
festival was cancelled owing to the severe winter snows which have badly damaged
the pastoral economy.

Books can be purchased at a shop immediately to the east of the hotel. South of the **Shopping**
crossroads is the open air market. Look out here for nomadic produce: hides, furs,
chubas, fresh meat and butter; as well as imported Chinese goods.

Buses run from Jyekundo to Ziling. The bus station is located south of the crossroads. **Transport**

Communications Post Office: the Post Office is located south of the crossroads. **Directory**

Some seven kilometres south of Jyekundo, the road passes **Trangu Monas-** **Trangu**
tery on the left (east). This is the seat of the great contemporary Karma Kagyu **Monastery**
scholar and lineage-holder Trangu Rinpoche, who is now based at Rumtek in
Sikkim. Formerly there were two buildings, some 70 metres apart, known as
the lower and upper monasteries. The original foundation is attributed to
Karmapa I Dusum Khyenpa during the 12th century. The renovated **assem-**
bly hall at Trangu contains exquisite gilded brass images of the Buddhas of the
Three Times, flanked by murals depicting the 16 past Karmapas. The out-
buildings are still utilized as granaries by the neighbouring village.

At **Peltang**, 19 kilometres south of Jyekundo, the road branches: the left fork **Bida Nampar**
leading south towards **Nangchen** (174 kilometres via Kela or 280 kilometres **Nangdze**
via Zurmang) and the right leading west towards **Dzato** (237 kilometres). If **Lhakhang**
you take the former road, after 1 kilometre a dirt track on the left (east) leads
across streams to the **Bida gorge**. Here, surrounded by four sacred peaks,
there are rock inscriptions, some revered as naturally produced, which pro-
claim the site's ancient association with King Songtsen Gampo and Princess
Wencheng. According to one legend the princess stayed here for 1 month
while en route for Lhasa and she is said to have had stone relief images of
Vairocana flanked by the eight major bodhisattvas carved into the rocks. Subsequently, when the princess Jincheng passed through in 710, she made
arrangements for a hall to be constructed, and this was enlarged in 730.
According to another legend, the princess had a miscarriage here; and a temple
was subsequently commissioned by Lochen Yeshe Yang and erected as a
memorial during the reign of King Trisong Detsen.

The original images, which depict Vairocana Buddha flanked by the Eight
Bodhisattvas, have been 'restored' in recent years. Among them, the central
image, which some hold to be natural, is said to contain relics of Kasyapa

Eastern Tibet

Buddha and the remains of Princess Wengcheng's deceased child. Most of the rock inscriptions are located immediately behind the temple, and reached via a rear gate. Some have been documented; although there are many unclear expressions. Another set of inscriptions can be seen on a rock to the west of the site. The temple at Bida was traditionally maintained by the Drigung Kagyu school, but nowadays, it is in the care of monks from neighbouring Trangu Monastery.

Benchen Puntsok Dargyeling Returning to the road from the Bida gorge, turn south and drive past a disused airstrip through a wide plain. A trail then turns off the road to the left (east) to **Benchen Puntsok Dargyeling**, facing into the plain against a backdrop of grassy knolls. This is a monastery of the Karma Kagyu school, the seat of Sangye Nyenpa Rinpoche and Chime Rinpoche. The monastery was originally located on the hill at Jyekundo, but moved to its present site in 1398 when Dondrubling was consecrated. Later, in 1797, Karmapa XIII passed away here. The **Assembly Hall** at Benchen has been restored in recent years, and there is a finely crafted row of eight stupas outside, symbolizing the eight major deeds of the Buddha. Within the assembly hall are the reliquaries of previous lamas and the thrones of the present incumbents, both of whom are in exile – in India and England respectively.

Zurmang Dutsitil Monastery ཟུར་མང་བདུད་རྩི་མཐིལ

Colour map 4, grid A2 The village now known as **Xiao Zurmang** lies 120 kilometres south of the Peltang intersection. The road crosses the snow-carpeted Ku La watershed pass which divides the Yangtze and Mekong basins, and a second lesser pass, before descending into the valley of the Kyang-chu, a fast-flowing stream which eventually merges with the Ke-chu at Menda (see above, page 401). A difficult motorable trail follows the river downstream for a further 35 kilometres to reach Zurmang Dutsitil, on occasions fording it at places where bridges have been damaged by the summer rains. Notice that old carved *mani* stones have been used in places for road construction.

The monastery of **Zurmang Dutsitil** is located on high ground above the road to the right (west). Founded in the 15th century by Trungpa I Kunga Gyeltsen, a close disciple of Trungpa Ma-se of the Karma Kagyu school, the monastery developed into an important meditation and study centre for the nomads and pastoralists of the Nangchen grasslands and surrounding areas. The site was expanded by his successors Trungpa II Kunga Zangpo, Trungpa III Kunga Osel, and Trungpa IV Kunga Namgyel, the last of whom was renowned both for his meditation skills and prolific compositions. In the time of his successor, Trungpa V Tendzin Chogyel, the monastery reached the high point of its development. Exquisite murals depicting the lives of the Buddha were executed in gold line on a red background. After the lifetime of Trungpa VI Lodro Tenpel, in the time of Trungpa VII Jampal Chogyel the site was plundered in 1643 by the Mongol army of Gushi Qan, and the important lamas were briefly incarcerated. Reconstruction of the assembly hall, temples, and the founding of the Zurmang library were undertaken during the late 17th and early 18th century by Trungpa VIII Gyurme Tenpel, who was himself a reputable artist of the Karma Gadri school. His successors, Trungpa IX Karma Tenpel and Trungpa X Chokyi Nyima, ensured that the Karma Kagyu tradition was maintained and revitalized in this part of Tibet during a time of increasing strife as Muslim overlords from Kokonor rivalled the Tibetan government and Chinese warlords for control of this important region. Trungpa XI Chokyi Gyatso (1939-87) left Tibet in 1959 and established the **Samye Ling**

Eastern Tibet

Monastery in **Scotland**. Later, he founded the worldwide Buddhist organization known as **Dharmadhatu**. The present Trungpa XII is now being educated at **Pelpung** Monastery, near Derge.

Little remains of the grandure of this site, which not so long ago housed
300 monks. The main **assembly hall** is currently undergoing reconstruction.
Upstairs are the residential quarters of the Trungpa Tulku and the Chetsang
Tulku. There is an image of Four-armed Mahakala. Above the site is the retreat
centre known as **Repuk Dorje Chodzong**; and a ruined fortress.

Below the monastery, the jeepable road continues southwest through
pine forest for some 30 kilometres, crossing the present-day Qinghai-TAR
border, to reach **Menda** and the **Lhato** region of Kham. Other monasteries in
this area include **Dongtsang Gon** of the Sakya school, four kilometres north of
Xiao Zurmang township, which possesses a mask and conch shell donated by
Drogon Chogyel Phakpa; and **Ladro Samdrub Lhaden Chokhorling** (eight
kilometres west of Xiao Zurmang township), which was founded by a student
of Karmapa V during the 15th century.

Nangchen County ནང་ཆེན་

*Nangchen was formerly one of the five independent kingdoms of East Tibet. Its
territory corresponds to the upper reaches of the five main Mekong feeder rivers:
the Ngom-chu, Do-chu, Dza-chu, Tsi-chu and Kyang-chu. As such it includes
the region of **Zurmang** in the east and **Nangchen** proper in the west (although
the easterly parts of Zurmang in the Kyang-chu valley are now administered
directly from Jyekundo). This area was able to maintain its Kagyupa heritage
despite the onslaught of Gushi Qan's armies during the 17th century; and it may
in fact have been spared the fate of Litang owing to the nomadic lifestyle of its
inhabitants and the inhospitability of the terrain for settlement. Only in a few
lower sheltered areas are cultivated fields to be seen; yet the rolling grasslands,
dramatic limestone and sandstone cliffs, and pristine nature reserves combine to
make Nangchen one of the most interesting and unspoilt parts of Kham. Currently it is estimated there are 78 monasteries within the county, of which some 70
percent are Kagyupa and the remainder Sakyapa, Nyingmapa and Gelukpa in
descending order. The capital is located at **Sharda**, 193 kilometres from
Jyekundo (via Ke La), 160 kilometres from Zurmang Dutsitil, and 189 kilometres
from Riwoche.*

Nangchen County (90)
囊谦县
Nangqen
Population: 55,432
Area: 15,014 sq km
Colour map 4, grid A1

Upper Tsi-chu

To reach Nangchen from Jyekundo by the more direct route, drive west from
the **Peltang** intersection for 46 kilometres to **Rato** (*Ch* Duolamakang), crossing the high **Zhung La** watershed pass (4,816 metres). Then turn south, following the Tsi-chu downstream for 35 kilometres to **Rabshi Lungsho
Ganden Chokhorling**, one of the very few Gelukpa monasteries in Nangchen.
This site is said to have been frequented by Lhalung Pelgyi Dorje during the
ninth century when he fled to Amdo from Lhasa, having slain the evil king
Langdarma. Subsequently, a temple was constructed by the Drigung
Kagyupas, and later, during the 18th century, it was converted to the Gelukpa
school with the encouragement of Dalai Lama VII. The **Rabshi** area (*Ch*
Xialaixue) also has Drukpa Kagyu communities at **Drukpa Gon** and **Ajung
Gon**, which fled persecution in 16th century Central Tibet, as well as smaller
Sakyapa, Drigungpa and Nyingmapa temples.

Two trails lead from Rabshi: the main road crossing the Ke La (4,267 metres) which divides the Tsi-chu from the Dza-chu, to arrive at **Kharda** in the Dza-chu valley (93 kilometres), and the latter following the Tsi-chu downstream towards **Zurmang Namgyeltse** (73 kilometres).

Zurmang Namgyeltse Monastery ཟུར་མང་རྣམ་རྒྱལ་རྩེ

Getting there
Colour map 4, grid A2

The monastery of **Zurmang Namgyeltse** lies 60 kilometres west of Zurmang Dutsitil in the Tsi-chu valley. It may also be approached from the turn-off south of Rabshi, following the Tsi-chu downstream for 67 kilometres to the **Tsi-chu bridge** (*Ch* Maozhuang Qiao). If you are travelling from Zurmang Dutsitil, follow the Kyang-chu back upstream in the direction of Xiao Zurmang for 15 kilometres and then turn left (west) after the first pass. The road runs through rich pasturelands where the herds of yak and dri are particularly impressive; and crosses a second pass to enter a narrow gorge. Flowers and medicinal herbs abound in this area. Descending into the Tsi-chu valley, you will pass the Sakyapa monastery of **Dordu Gon**.

On reaching the Tsi-chu bridge, leave this trail (which heads downstream on the east bank for **Karma Gon** via Lintrang) and cross the river. The road then forks: upstream (to the right) for **Rabshi** (67 kilometres) and downstream to the left for **Da Zurmang** township. The forested Tsi-chu valley is an important nature reserve and you will notice roadside signs prohibiting the killing of animals. Da Zurmang, also known as Maozhuang in Chinese, lies only 6 kilometres from the bridge. Here are the grand ruins of the monastery known as Zurmang Namgyeltse.

The original foundation dates from the 15th century when Trungpa Ma-se, a disciple of Karmapa V constructed a 'many-cornered' (*zurmang*) meditation hut here. His disciples gathered in numbers and the local chieftain Adru Shelubum donated his castles (at both Namgyeltse and Dutsitil) to Trungpa Ma-se and his followers. The ruins of the large **assembly hall**, founded by Trungpa V Tendzin Chogyel, convey an impression of the former magnificence of the monastery. It once contained large images of the Buddha of the Three Times and over 40 images of the Karma Kagyu lineage-holders. Three colleges also once existed here: the **Dechen Dratsang** (450 monks) on the higher slopes, the **Lingpa Dratsang** (350 monks) on the lower slopes, and the **Lama Dratsang** (300 monks) adjacent to the assembly hall.

Nowadays there are between 100-200 monks affiliated to Zurmang Namgyeltse, and one temple has been reconstructed. It contains murals depicting Padmasambhava, Simhavaktra, Vajrayogini, Vajravarahi, Cakrasamvara, and various Kagyu lineage-holders including the Zhamarpas. Upstairs a chapel contains newly sculpted clay images of the 16 previous Karmapas.

At the township, near Zurmang Namgyeltse, there is another noteworthy monastery named **Ganden Gontsi Zurmang Ganden Tubten Ngelekling**, which was founded by a Nyingmapa lama in 1535 and later converted to the Gelukpa school in 1652 when Dalai Lama V passed through on his return from Beijing to Lhasa.

Nangchen & Dzato Counties

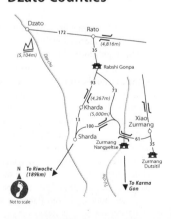

Zurmang Namgyeltse to Sharda

From Namgyeltse, the distance to Sharda (Nangchen county town) is 100 kilometres. The road crosses the precipitous **Yi gu La pass** (5,000 metres) – its difficult surface both narrow and gravel-covered. Drive slowly! This is the watershed between the Tsi-chu and Dza-chu rivers, and on the far side, the descent cuts across rolling meadows towards Kharda. Here you rejoin the direct Jyekundo-Nangchen road and enter the wide valley of the Dza-chu, the greatest of the Mekong source rivers. The tableland limestone crags of **Rakjangri** stand out across the sandbanks of the meandering river.

Rabshi to Sharda

If you take the highway from Rabshi into Nangchen, avoiding the turn-off to **Ke La** Zurmang Namgyeltse, the road crosses the Ke La watershed (4,267 metres) between the Tsi-chu and Dza-chu rivers, and gradually descends to reach **Kharda** township after 93 kilometres. This wilderness is a stronghold of the Barom Kagyu school, the most prestigious of its monasteries being **Kyodrak Gonpa**, where Tashi Rolpa, the student of Barom Darma Wangchuk, passed away in the 14th century, and the affiliated nunnery at **Metil Gegon**.

Sharda

After Kharda, the highway descends to **Sharda**, the county capital of Nangchen, after a further 13 kilometres. Here, the Dza-chu river meanders around sandbanks and the tableland mountain known as **Rakjangri** dominates its west bank. This is a natural habitat and breeding ground of the macoque. Sharda comprises one long and broad main street, where dust and tumbleweed are blown in sporadic gusts. Formerly this town was the heart of the independent kingdom of Nangchen, to which the 25 clans of the Mekong grasslands held allegiance. The inhabitants of the town are largely engaged in trade, and you may find some interesting Tibetan artefacts here. There are some cultivated barley fields, but agriculture is generally less important to the economy than animal husbandry and lumbering.

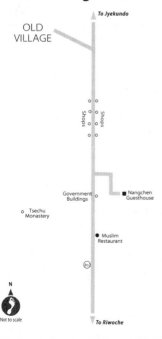

Sharda (Nangchen)

To Jyekundo

OLD VILLAGE

Shops

Shops

Government Buildings

■ Nangchen Guesthouse

Tsechu Monastery

● Muslim Restaurant

N

Not to scale

To Riwoche

Eastern Tibet

Some six kilometres north of town, in **Excursions** the hills, there is an important Barom Kagyu nunnery at **Merchen Gegon Tashi Choling**. During the 1920s it was absorbed by the Drigungpas, and recently it has undergone reconstruction. Nearby is the Barom Kagyu monastery of **Dzamo Gon Tubten Metok Choling** which was founded by Lama Tashi Rolpa (1128-1201), and further to the northwest (15 kilometres from town), there is a small Sakyapa monastery called **Nyayakyul Gonpa**.

Southwest of the county town near **Palme** village, there are 17th century Drigung Kagyu monasteries named **Tekchen Evam Gatseling** and **Chibub Gonpa,** while to the southeast of town there is a Sakyapa presence at **Taksar Gonpa** and, three kilometres from town, a Drukpa Kagyu presence at **Tashi Gatseling** (founded 1923). Also, **Go-che Gonpa** is an important branch of Yangpachen, the seat of the Zhamarpas in Central Tibet.

Sleeping & The *Nangchen Guesthouse*, where there are comfortable rooms and friendly maids, is
eating located in a compound on the east side of the main street, near its middle section, and the Public Security Bureau is on the west side at the extreme south end of the street. Outside the hotel, there are small restaurants, some of them Muslim owned (distinguished by their green banners).

Roads from Sharda

From Sharda there is a road heading northwest for 46 kilometres to Yeyondo (*Ch* Sigeton), from where trails lead to **Drokshok** (44 kilometres) and west to **Dompa** (94 kilometres) in the Ngom-chu valley. The highway, rough as it is, leads south to **Treltsa** township (nine kilometres), where it forks: southeast for **Nyagla** (43 kilometres) in the Dza-chu valley, and southwest across the mountains to **Chichu** (72 kilometres) in the Ngom-chu valley. All these roads lead towards **Tengchen**, **Riwoche** and **Lhato** counties in the present-day Tibetan Autonomous Region.

Drokshok The most influential monastery in the vicinity of Drokshok township (*Ch* Zhuoxiao) is **Karma Dargyeling**, the seat of Beru Khyentse Rinpoche who has established branch monasteries in India and USA. The monastery here was founded in the 1950s by the previous Karmapa XVI Rikpei Dorje. Other sites of interest in this region include **Tilyak Gonpa** (18th century) and **Nege Gegon** nunnery of the Karma Kagyu school, **Rabjor Gonpa** which maintains the Nedo lineage of Karma Chakme, and **Beru Lachen Gon**, a 13th century Barom Kagyu centre.

Dompa There are nine monasteries around Dompa township, the most significant being the 14th century **Tongnak Gonpa** which converted from the Barompa to the Karma Kagyu tradition, **Domyo Kalzang Gon** (Karma Kagyu), **Rela Gonpa** (Sakyapa), and further west towards the Tengchen county border, the Nyingmapa nunnery of **Dechen Ting Gegon**.

Tsashul At Tsashul township (*Ch* Jienesai) on the east bank of the Ngom-chu, approached on a 63 kilometres detour southwest from the Shadra-Yeyondo road, the Barom Kagyu tradition is present in strength. One of their monasteries, **Chiradzago Gonpa** (six kilometres west of the township), is revered as the place where Sachen Kunga Nyingpo, the first of the Five Founders of Sakya, passed away. Others have maintained their allegiance to the Drukpa Kagyu school at **Totrari Gonpa** and the Yelpa Kagyu school at **Tana Senge Gon**, which was founded in 1180 by Yeshe Tsekpa. Some 20 kilometres downstream in the direction of Chichu, there is the largest nunnery of the Nyingma school in present day Qinghai province at **Gechak Gegon** (founded in 1893 by Gechak Tsangyang Gyatso).

Treltsa Following the highway south from Sharda through the Dza-chu valley, you will reach the township of Treltsa after nine kilometres. Here, there are also influential Kagyu monasteries: **Tsechu Gonpa** of the Drukpa Kagyu school and **Gonzhab Gonpa**, founded in the 15th century by a student of Karmapa VII Chodrak Gyatso, are both close to the township, while **Nedo Sangak Dechenling**, the main seat of Karma Chakme's student Nedo Karma Losung, lies five kilometres east.

If you take the Dza-chu river road from Treltsa to Nyagla, you will reach the **Nyagla** Lhato county after 43 kilometres. **Karma Gon**, the oldest of all the Karma Kagyu monasteries in Tibet, lies across the border (see above, page 400). Around Nyagla, on the **Qinghai** side of the border, there were three small monasteries affiliated to Zurmang Namgyeltse, of which **Trikso Gonpa** and **Jereda** have been rebuilt.

From Nangchen, you can drive south to **Riwoche** (189 kilometres) when the **Chichu** river levels are low. The road heads southwest from Treltsa, crossing the triple pass of **Tsedri La** (4,277 metres) and **Churi Meri La** pass (4,504 metres) which form the watershed between the Dza-chu and the Do-chu. Driving conditions rapidly deteriorate in the Do-chu gorge, as the road becomes a narrow rocky slope hugging the cliffs beside the swift flowing river. At one point it becomes a wooden log bridge, jammed between sharp canyon walls on both sides, with the river rushing below. **NB** This route is not passable in the rainy season (June-early September) or when the water level is high. Leaving the Do-chu valley, the road soon descends to Chichu township on the east bank of the Ngom-chu. The distance from Treltsa to Chichu is 72 kilometres.

Most of the monasteries around Chichu represent the Drukpa Kagyu school, which survived persecution on 16th and 17th century Central Tibet in these remote outposts. Among them are, **Jam-me Gon**, 30 kilometres northeast of the township, **Chopuk Gon** (30 kilometres west), and **Tsabzhi Gon**, which was eventually outgrown by its branch monastery at Tsechu Gonpa (see above). Exiles from Chichu established a thriving centre for Tibetan culture at Mainpath in Madhya Pradesh, India during the 1960s and 1970s, under the leadership of their chieftain, Namka Dorje. A new Tibetan school has recently been established at Chichu for young nomadic children through the efforts of the Nangchen Children's Trust, Mukairn, Taynuilt, Argyll, Scotland PA35 1JN, T44-1866-822241).

From Chichu, a rough road follows the east bank of the Ngom-chu down- **Nangchen to** stream to the provincial border, crossing into Riwoche county above Shoknga **Riwoche** (see above, page 394). In the hills above (approximately 80 kilometres from Chichu), there is influential Nyingma monastery of **Neten Gang**, the seat of Chogyur Dechen Zhikpo Lingpa (1820-70), which was founded in 1858. In its vicinity there are sacred Padmasambhava meditation caves and *terma*-sites in the range known as **Yegyel Namkadzo**. This is the power place representing the attributes-aspect of buddha-speech in East Tibet, where this lama discovered important *terma*-texts and representative images of Padmasambhava. The overall distance from Sharda to Riwoche Tsuklakhang is 189 kilometres.

Eastern Tibet

Dzato County རྫ་སྟོད

Dzato County (91)
杂多县
Zadoi
Population: 31,307
Area: 33,127 sq km
Colour map 5, grid C1

*Dzato county is the area around the source of the Dza-chu tributary of the Mekong, far upstream from Nangchen. To reach Dzato, drive west from Peltang in the direction of Nangchen, but do not turn south at the **Rato** turn-off (46 kilometres). Continue due west for a further 172 kilometres, en route crossing the Tsi-chu valley to the north of **Mount Sharpu Karpur** (5,104 metres), and entering the Dza-chu basin at **Chidza**. Apart from a few coal mines, this is a sparsely populated nomadic area. Nonetheless, there are 24 small monasteries within the county, mostly representing the Kagyu and Nyingma schools.*

Chidza   In the hills above the Dza-chu, close to **Chidza** township (*Ch* Jiezha), there are five Karma Kagyu monasteries, including **Pelbeu Gon**, which originally belonged to the Barong Kagyu tradition. A small branch of Dzogchen monastery known as **Tubten Samdrub Gatseling** was also founded here by Dzogchen I Pema Rigdzin in 1685. Below Chidza, the road descends to the banks of the Dza-chu, where in modern Angsai township, there are Nyingmapa monasteries affiliated to Pelyul, and Choling Gonpa, including **Chogyege Gon**, a nunnery which was founded in 1910 by Choling Rinpoche. At **Tobchu Gonpa** there are both Bon and Nyingmapa practitioners living alongside one another.

Dzato town   The county town, 60 kilometres upstream from Chidza on the bank of the Dza-chu, is one of the most isolated on the plateau. Yet there are Drigung and Karma Kagyu monasteries which have survived here, including a 13th century Barong Kagyu establishment at **Geuna Gon**, which converted to the Karma Kagyu school in 1673. To the west of town, there are trails leading south via Ato township, through the Dangla range, into the Tengchen, Bachen and Sok Dzong counties of the present day Tibetan Autonomous Region (see above, page 384).

Ato & Sangchen   From Dzato county town, two roads diverge: northwest for 59 kilometres to **Sangchen** (*Ch* Zhaqin) and southwest for 36 kilometres to **Ato** township, which lies in the hills to the south of the Dza-chu river. The monasteries and nunneries in these remote parts are mostly tented camps, affiliated to the Drigung or Karma Kagyu, although the Nyingmapa and Gelukpa do have some representation at **Damzhung Terton** and **Tashi Lhapuk Gon** respectively.

Drito County འབྲི་སྟོད

Drito County (92)
治多县
Zhidoi
Population: 19,313
Area: 78,945 sq km
Colour map 5, grid C1

*Drito county is the area around the southern source of the Yangtze, the county capital being located at **Gyelje Podrang**, 194 kilometres northwest of Jyekundo. To reach Drito, drive west from **Jyekundo** following the Za-chu tributary upstream and passing a grass seed escarpment on the road out of town. On a hill to the north there is a sky burial site.*

Ato Monastery   Above **Jalakda**, the road crosses a pass, and descends through an isolated area to **Lake Rongpo** and the township of **Gyelring**, 73 kilometres from Jyekundo. En route, there is also a turn-off on the left, which leads south to the Karma Kagyu monastery of **Ato Gonpa**, the seat of Ato Rinpoche who now resides in England.

In the vicinity of Lake Rongpo, the **Rongpo Nature Reserve** has the most **Rongpo Nature** important breeding site in present-day Qinghai province for the Black Necked **Reserve** Crane. There are approximately 69 adult birds and 18 chicks within the reserve, where the marsh is up to two metres deep in places. Other protected species here include the ruddy sheldrake, the bar-head goose, the brown-headed gull, the redshank, and various types of wader and song bird. There is a small barrack-style guesthouse, where the wardens also live. The nests of the Black Necked Crane are protected for several days after hatching by the wardens who camp near the nests to ward off hostile nomad dogs. A guide and photographic permit are available for ¥150 (officially per hour but generally per day!).

Northwest of the marshy lake, there is a *mani* stone wall and **Rongzhi Monas-** **Gyelring** **tery** stands on a hilltop opposite **Gyelring** township. Gyelring itself is 73 kilo-metres from Jyekundo, and there are two significant Gelukpa monasteries here. **Bumgon Chokle Gyelnamling**, one kilometre east of the township, was originally a Bon temple, which converted to the Drigung Kagyu school in the 13th century, and subsequently in the 16th century to the Gelukpa school. A branch monastery, **Gyezang Gonpa**, was constructed in the township in 1957. At Gyelring the road forks: the main route heading northwest into Drito county, and a side road running north for 55 kilometres towards **Hashul** (*Ch* Haxie) and **Anchong** townships, which are a stronghold of the Sakyapa and Karma Kagyu schools, exemplified by **Purang Sakya Gon** and **Nezang** **Gonpa** respectively.

Continuing on the main road from **Gyelring**, you will cross a pass to enter **Gyelje Podrang** Drito county, and head downstream through the sparsely populated Jong-chu valley, where marmots, hares and pika abound. The Yelung-chu flows in from the southwest, and the valley opens out. There are horses in the pastures here and the eroded terrain is evidence of intensive grazing. **Damjong** township is 61 kilometres northwest of Gyelring and southeast of the Jong-chu valley. **Drito** county town, known as **Gyelje Podrang**, lies above the confluence of this river and the Nechak-chu, 60 kilometres further northwest. It is an unat-tractive town with a few compounds and a dozen shops. A gravel works depot is located by the riverside.

Eastern Tibet

From Drito, there are routes lead-ing west towards the southern source of the Yangtze in the Dangla range. These eventually link up with the road from Dzato at **Mukzhung** to head south across the range into **Bachen** and **Sok Dzong** counties of the Tibetan Autonomous Region. About 19 kilometres along this road from the county town there is a Gelukpa mon-astery known as **Gonsar Gonpa**, which currently has 150 monks.

A more frequently travelled road follows the Nechak-chu downstream to its confluence with the Yangtze, and the latter upstream to Chumarleb county, 45 kilometres to the northwest.

Drito & Chumarleb Counties

To Toma
Serpo Lungpa
16
74
Bagon
16
To Domda (93 km)

To Mukzhung

45

Gyelje
Podrang

Ba Gonpa

Yangtze

60

Damjong
61

N

Not to scale

Lake
Rongpo

To Jyekundo

Chumarleb County རྒྱ་དམར་ལེབ

Chumarleb
County (93)
曲麻莱县
Qumarleb
Population: 18,983
Area: 43,123 sq km
Colour map 5, grid C1

*The county of **Chumarleb** comprises the area around the northern source of the Yangtze, which flows in a southeast course from the Kunlun Mountains. The county capital is located at **Serpo Lungpa**, a new town 45 kilometres from Drito and 270 kilometres from Jyekundo (via Domda). Nowadays there are 12 monasteries within the county, of which at least five are itinerant Nyingmapa camps. At **Chizhi** (Ch Qiuzhi) village, 121 kilometres north of the county town there is the Nyingmapa monastery of **Khorama Gonpa**, affiliated to Katok, while to the southeast of town there is a Gelukpa monastery at **Kyabdung Gonpa**.*

The hills around Chumarleb have been heavily eroded by the itinerant 70,000 or 80,000 Chinese gold miners who come here during the summer months. The lawlessness of these prospectors is encouraged by the paucity of the police force assigned to monitor them – presently only 40 officers. The town is larger than Drito, and is a centre for the wool and meat trade. Muslim traders come here on trucks to kill sheep; and there are a number of restaurants which have been opened in Chumarleb to serve these butchers and the itinerant mining population.

Formerly there were many herds of wild yak (*drong*), wild ass (*kyang*), and antelope in the Chumarleb River valley to the northwest of **Serpo Lungp**a, but now only a small number of herds remain. There is, however, another Black Necked Crane Nature Reserve to the northwest of the river.

A trail leads into the remote interior of the Yangtze source region to link up with the Lhasa-Kermu road near Toma.

NB This route is not passable in summer when the river levels are high, and at other times only in a four-wheel drive jeep with a high-axled support truck.

Chumarleb to Domda

South of the town, there is a good motorable road which runs southeast for 199 kilometres to **Domda** (*Ch* Qingshuihe), where it connects with the main Jyekundo-Ziling highway. Head east out of town and turn southeast at the road junction. After 16 kilometres (at marker 174) a pass is crossed. To the south, between the road and the Yangtze there are some argali mountain sheep and gazelle. The road now passes through a gorge, where goldminers are encamped near **Bagon** township, 74 kilometres from the pass (around marker 100). A four hours' trek west from Bagon leads for nine kilometres to **Ba Gonpa** of the Gelukpa school, where there are 100 monks, and thence to **Sharu Gonpa** (25 kilometres from Bagon township), which is a branch of Zerkar, founded in 1447 by Choje Palden Gyatso.

Staying on the main road, after **Bagon** you climb steeply, crossing a pass after 16 kilometres (marker 84), and then after 20 kilometres, reaching a well-equipped government goldmine. Then, after 12 kilometres (marker 42), the road crosses the south-flowing Gara-chu tributary of the Yangtze, before heading northeast up a lateral valley to **Trado** (*Ch* Zhaduo) township. The final watershed pass crosses the Yangtze-Yalong divide, offering fine views of the rounded peaks of the **Bayankala** range to the north. Thereafter the road descends to the main highway, and **Domda** township (*Ch* Qingshuihe) lies only nine kilometres to the north, near the northern source of the Yalong River.

Trehor and Nyarong:

the Yalong Valleys and Gorges

The middle reaches of the Yalong and the valley of its main tributary, the Zhe-chu, together form the widest cultivated tract of land in Kham, sustaining a large sedentary population, as well as nomadic pastoralists on the high ground. Emerging from the Dzachuka region at Rongpatsa, the Yalong flows through this wide valley as far as Kandze, where the massive snow range of Kawalungring forces it to change course, cutting south through the Nyarong gorge to converge with the Yangtze at Dukou.

The Zhe-chu and its Nyi-chu tributary both rise in the Dzachuka area to the east of Sershul county, and flow southeast in parallel courses to converge at Drango, and then, after meandering through the pleasant Tawu valley, their combined waters flow south to merge with the Yalong above Nyachuka.

*Prior to the 17th century, the **Nyarong** valley was a stronghold of the Nyingma and Bon traditions, while the plains to the north were also important for the Sakya and Kagyupa. Further east the peoples of **Tawu**, who speak an extremely idiosyncratic dialect or language, may well be descended from the migrant Minyak (Xixia) population, following the destruction of their kingdom by Genghiz Qan in the 13th century. However, from 1638-41 the Qosot Mongol armies of Gushi Qan forcibly converted many of these Yalong settlements to the Gelukpa tradition, eventually defeating the Bonpo king of Beri in 1641. They then established the five Trehor states: **Beri**, **Kangsar**, **Mazur**, **Trewo**, and **Drango**, which supported a large number of new Gelukpa institutions. Settling there, they intermarried with the local populace, from which time on the inhabitants have been known as the **Trehor Khampa**. Secular arts and crafts also flourished; and the renowned metal work of the region still exhibits many distinctive features – animal motifs and so forth – reminiscent of Scythian or Ordos bronzes.*

*Nowadays this region includes four counties administered from Dartsedo namely **Kandze** and **Nyarong** in the Yalong valley, and **Drango** and **Tawu** in the Zhe-chu valley.*

Recommended itineraries: 5, 8, 10.

Kandze County དཀར་མཛེས

Kandze County (94)
甘孜县
Garze
Population: 53,458
Area: 6,232 sq km
Colour map 4, grid A4

*Kandze county extends from the lower Yi-chu valley and **Rongpatsa** township as far as the **Latseka** watershed pass (also known as **Dresel La**) in Trehor. The county capital is located at **Kandze** town, 94 kilometres east of Manigango, and 158 kilometres northwest of Tawu.*

Yi-chu Valley

Following the Yi-chu downstream from **Manigango**, the highway passes the turn-off for Yilhun township after 15 kilometres and continues along the south bank of the river. Sometimes in the rainy season the river level rises above that of the road! Soon the **Pak-tse Mani Wall** comes into view on the right (south), while, on the distant hilltop across the river, you can see the **Nyaduka Retreat Hermitage**, a branch of Dzogchen Monastery, bedecked in streaming red prayer flags. Thereafter the river cuts northeast to join the Yalong, while the road continues due east to Rongpatsa.

Yangkar Dorje Phakmo

Some 50 kilometres east of Manigango, the road passes on the left a cave containing an image of the deity Vajravarahi. The pathway leading down to the cave is adorned with prayer flags, but the cave itself lies across a stream and is only accessible in the dry season when the water level is low. This is the most important power place of the Rongpatsa valley.

Rongpatsa

Driving east from Yangkar, the road soon crosses an almost indiscernible pass to enter the wide fertile valley of **Rongpatsa**. Fields of golden barley extend on both sides as far as the distant foothills. To the right (south) you will pass the side-valley leading from **Dzengko** and **Horpo** and the village of **Lakhar**. Just before entering Rongpatsa town (57 kilometres east of Manigango), a turn-off on the left leads towards a ridge overlooking the valley. Here you can visit **Bongen Gonpa**, a finely reconstructed temple in the midst of a flower garden, which is the seat of the late Kalu Rinpoche of the Kagyu and Shangpa Kagyu traditions. The ruins of the original temple still occupy the hillside far to the northeast. The present Kalu Rinpoche is currently being educated at Sonada in Darjiling, where his predecessor passed away.

Trekking Trekking routes follow the Yalong upstream from Rongpatsa in the direction of **Dzachuka**, where there are many monasteries of all the Buddhist traditions and the Bon. The largest Gelukpa Monastery in that vicinity is **Samdrub Gonpa**, a 17th century foundation, which formerly had 700 monks, while the **Lingtsang Katok Gonpa** of the Nyingma school and **Ripu Gonpa** of the Sakya school are also prominent.

Kandze & Nyarong

Eastern Tibet

Dargye Gonpa

Leaving Rongpatsa, the road passes through **Yartsa** village, where there is a hot spring, and after six kilometres runs through a tree-lined avenue to **Dargye Gonpa**. This monastery (3,536 metres) which represents the Gelukpa school and was founded in 1642, is the oldest of all the 13 so-called Horpa monasteries established by the victorious Mongol forces of Gushi Qan in the 17th century. Its traditional precedence continues, although it is smaller than Kandze Monastery.

The Ngakpa Tratsang has not yet been rebuilt, but the quality of reconstruction in the **Tsenyi Tratsang** (Dialectical College) is outstanding. The most impressive feature is its enormous three-storeyed **assembly hall**, approached from named gates in each of the building's four directions. Large teams of volunteer and commissioned craftsmen have been working on the reconstruction of the buildings since 1988. The **main hall** contains a throne of the Dalai Lama, flanked by images of the 16 Elders. Side murals depict scenes from the *Avadanakalpalata*, and Tara who protects from the eight fears. The murals adjacent to the entrance doorway depict the protectors and meditational deities: Guhyasamaja, Cakrasamvara, Vajrabhairava, and Shridevi (L); and Dralha, Dharmaraja, Vaishravana, Avalokiteshvara, and Manjughosa (R). The **inner sanctum** contains images of (L-R): Tsongkhapa, Maitreya, Sarvavid Vairocana, Dalai Lama XIV, Tsongkhapa, Atisha, Simhanada, and Jowo Yizhin Norbu, all flanked by the eight Standing Bodhisattvas and the eight Medicine Buddhas, with Hayagriva and Vajrapani guarding the gate.

Upstairs, on the second floor, there is a Gonkhang containing images of (left to right): Shridevi, Modak, Six-armed Mahakala, Three-faced Vajrabhairava, Two-armed Mahakala, Four-armed Mahakala, Vaishravana, Jo-se, and the Five Aspects of Pehar.

Beri

Located 17 kilometres east of Dargye Gonpa on the **Horko plain** (3,536 metres), **Beri** was the capital of an important Bonpo Kingdom and the cultural centre of this part of Kham until the 17th century. The king of Beri, Donyo Dorje, was defeated by the armies of Gushri Qan between 1639-41, and this event led to the formation of the Trehor states. At Beri, the Bonpo temple was converted into a Gelukpa Monastery, housing 100 monks.

The strategic importance of the town overlooking a narrow part of the Yalong valley, continued to be recognized. In 1918, it was occupied as the front line of defence by the Chinese army, and this subsequently attracted the animosity of the villagers around Dargye Gonpa, who held the Tibetan front line. In 1931 when Beri was assisted in its dispute with Dargye Gonpa by the Chinese governor of Sichuan, the Tibetan forces stationed at Derge came to the assistance of Dargye Gonpa and the attackers were thrust back to Kandze.

Approaching the Beri acropolis from Dargye, the reconstructed buildings of **Beri Gonpa**, where there are more than 200 Gelukpa monks, are visible afar on the north bank of the Yalong. The citadel dominates the road overlooking the river valley from the south bank. Here within a walled town are the ruins of the **Beri Castle** and the renovated **Kablung Monastery**, where there are 50 monks. Kablung, which represents the Nyingma school, is a combined branch of both Katok and Dzogchen, the former tradition being maintained by Norbu Tulku and the latter by Babu Tulku. Extant murals at Kablung depict the *Longchen Nyingtig* tradition. Inland from Beri is the power place of **O Tashi Pema Tsepel** at Lake Tashi Tso, which is frequented by pilgrims at the present day.

Colour map 4, grid A4

Eastern Tibet

Kandze

Altitude: 3,581 metres
Phone code: 0836
Colour map 4, grid A4

Kandze (*Ch* Garze), the county capital, is a large provincial town located in the loses hills close to the banks of the Yalong, 13 kilometres east of Beri and nine kilometres east of the Pelyul turn-off. Two of the five Hor states, Kangsar and Mazur, were formerly located above the gently sloping plain of Kandze; and since the construction of their castles in the 17th century, the town has been the largest and most important in the Trehor region. During the 1909-18 war, the castles were occupied by Chinese garrisons; and today they lie in ruins below **Kandze Monastery**. Apart from this monastery and the historically important **Den Gonpa**, there were several other monasteries of note in the valley. These include Drakar, Nyatso, Khangmar, and Tsitso monasteries of the Gelukpa school; Dontok Monastery of the Sakya school, and Rirak Gonpa of the Kagyu school. Since 1950 the name Kandze has also been given to the Autonomous Prefecture administered from Dartsedo.

Orientation

At the entrance to town, a bridge spans the Yalong, carrying all traffic across to the north bank. The road then climbs to the north leaving the river, and winds downhill to the crossroads, which marks the town centre. The bus station lies to the right, near the crossroads.

The road to the left from the crossroads leads uphill towards the hilltop **Kandze Monastery**, passing en route a large number of shops, selling traditional Tibetan artefacts and modern Chinese or Indian goods. Further uphill (on the left) there are electrical stores, a photographic studio, the *Post Office Hotel*, and on the right a middle school. At the top of this road, you will pass residential town houses – their horizontal red timbers adorned with flower pots – and climb sharply to the monastery. Alternatively, you can take one of the bridges which span the Kandze-chu to the right of this road. These lead across to a parallel residential street offering good photographic views of the monastery. Here, there is a public bathhouse (with hot showers).

Returning downhill to the crossroads, if you go straight ahead, you will pass by the Post Office, which has DDD connections to Chengdu, and through the vegetable and meat market. There are some restaurants on this street also, and small shops selling Tibetan artefacts, including old carpets. After the market, a lane to the left leads into the compound of **Den Gonpa**, the oldest temple of Kandze. If you continue along the street from the market you can head out of town right (southeast) for Nyarong and Latseka pass, or left along the main paved avenue where the government buildings and the *Kandze Guesthouse* are to be found. The distance from Kandze to Pelyul is 232 kilometres and to Tawu 158 kilometres.

Kandze Gonpa

Kandze Monastery was originally constructed by the Qosot Mongols circa 1642 on a hilltop overlooking their castles of Mazur and Khangsar. It once had a population of 1,500 monks, making it the largest in Kham alongside Chamdo; and the pilgrimage circuit around the monastery was nearly eight kilometres long. The monastery has been undergoing extensive repairs since 1981. Currently it has an estimated population of 700 monks and three tulkus, including Lamdrak Rinpoche who recently returned from Switzerland and has established a local girls' school.

The main **Assembly Hall** is approached by a long flight of steps. It is a striking building in wood and stone, with a golden roof. Downstairs, the passageways between the red columns lead to the **inner sanctum**, where the images are raised high within glass cabinets. There are three sets of three images, representing the founders of the Kadampa, Gelukpa and Nyingma lineages of Tibetan Buddhism. There are also fine tangkas depicting the meditational deities Guhyasamaja, Cakrasamvara and Yamantaka.

Upstairs are a *Kangyur* library containing old images of Tsongkhapa and Eleven-faced Avalokiteshvara and a **Gonkhang**, entered through a striking black and gold painted doorway, which contains new protector images and a new set of images representing the three aforementioned meditational deities. The **Maitreya Hall** has an enormous central image of Maitreya, flanked by Tsongkhapa, Shakyamuni, Dipamkara and Sitatapatra. On the hillside to the northeast of the monastery is a reconstructed white stupa.

Den Gonpa

In the southeast of Kandze town there is an important protector temple which survived the events of the 1960s relatively unscathed since it was utilized as a granary during that period. The temple, containing a revered image of Mahakala in the form Panjaranatha, is said to have been constructed at the suggestion of Drogon Chogyel Phakpa in the 13th century while en route for Mongolia. Since the 17th century the temple has been maintained by the Gelukpas. There is a circumambulatory walkway replete with prayer wheels. Upstairs a number of original woodblocks are preserved.

Sleeping

The *Kandze Guesthouse* has comfortable rooms in its 2-storey main building, and less comfortable rooms in a rear annex. There is a clean restaurant, where local officials like to hold banquets, and a washroom. The *Kandze County Youdianju Yinge Hotel (Post Office Hotel)*, T0836-22332. Has clean new rooms, at ¥80 per room (foreigners' price), and ¥50 per bed in triple, and a good restaurant downstairs, but foreigners may be discouraged from staying here. There is also accommodation at the bus station.

Eating

Several small restaurants are also to be found adjacent to the bus station, around the intersection, and in the market street. These invariably serve noodles and dumplings, as well as Sichuan dishes. Small tea houses on the road up to Kandze monastery also sell delicious home made bread.

Kandze

Eastern Tibet

Kandze to Latseka

The highway leaves Kandze and heads southeast, rejoining the course of the Yalong. The outlying Gelukpa monasteries of **Drakar**, **Nyatso**, **Khangmar**, and **Tsitso**; and the Sakyapa monastery of **Dontok**, are all to be found in this part of the valley. After nine kilometres, a side-road leaves the highway on the right, following the river as it changes course to head into **Nyarong**. The highway itself veers steeply to the east, passing through the picturesque farming village of **Puyulung** (*Ch* Lozhling), and you can then see rising on the southeast horizon the snow peaks of **Kawalungring** (5,082 metres), which conceal the entrance to Nyarong. 16 kilometres after the Nyarong turn-off, the road enters a nomadic grassland area and reaches the high Latseka pass (3,962 metres), which forms a watershed between the Yalong and Zhe-chu rivers.

Nyarong County ཉག་རོང

Nyarong County (95)
新龙县
Xinlong
Population: 39,842
Area: 9,821 sq km
Colour map 4, grid A4

Nyarong county is the name given to the traditional tribal area of ***Upper Nyarong****, in contrast to that of* ***Lower Nyarong****, which is now under the jurisdiction of* ***Nyachuka*** *county. The Yalong River flows through both Upper Nyarong and Lower Nyarong on a southerly course towards its confluence with the Yangtze at* ***Dukou****. The county capital is located at* ***Barshok****, 109 kilometres from Kandze.*

The isolated Nyarong valley has always been a stronghold of the Nyingmapa school and the pre-Buddhist Bon tradition. During the 19th century, the chieftain of Nyarong, Gonpo Namgyel subdued most of Kham, unifying much of East Tibet under his command in the military campaigns of 1837-63. He was eventually defeated in 1865 by the Tibetan government and forced to withdraw into the citadels of Nyarong, where he came to an untimely end.

Chakdu Kawalungring Driving into Nyarong from Kandze, the road follows the east bank of the Yalong downstream through a deep gorge. The most important power-place associated with Padmasambhava in the Nyarong valley is at **Hor Tresho**, also called **Chakdu Kawalungring**, within the Kawalungring range (5,082 metres). It represents the activity aspect of buddha-speech; and a nearby monastery is the seat of Chakdu Tulku, who has in recent years established retreat centres in Oregon and Brazil. At **Da-ge Drongtok Gon**, 46 kilometres from the turn-off, there is an important branch of Katok Monastery.

Barshok The county capital, **Barshok**, lies 54 kilometres further south, at the heart of Nyarong (*Ch* Xinlong). Here there are guesthouse and restaurant facilities. This was formerly the residence of Nyarong Gonpo Namgyel who unified the upper and lower districts of Nyarong under his command and embarked on a military campaign against the neighbouring independent kingdoms and provinces of Kham. Trehor, Derge, Dzachuka, Lhato, Nangchen, and Jyekundo all succumbed to his forces, as did Batang, Litang, Chaktreng, and Gyeltang in the far south, and Chakla, Trokhyab and Tawu in the east. Only the intervention of the Tibetan government army in 1865 brought an end to this expansion; and Gonpo Namgyel was himself burnt to death when the government forces set fire to his fortress.

Nyarong has produced two outstanding Buddhist masters: the treasure-finder Nyakla Pema Dudul, who lived at **Shunlung** 17 kilometres west of Barshok during the 19th century; and Lerab Lingpa, also known as Terton Sogyel (1856-1926), who hailed from **Karzang Gonpa** and was a close associate of Dalai Lama XIII. The former was one of the few lamas venerated personally by Nyarong Gonpo Namgyel.

From Barshok there is a difficult motorable trail to **Pundadrong**, the capital of Nyachuka county in lower Nyarong, which straddles the Litang-Dardo highway. The road follows the Yalong downstream southeast to its confluence with the Zhe-chu and then due south to Pundadrong (see above, page 442). An alternative route from **Tawu to Pundadrong**, following the Zhe-chu (*Ch Xianshui*) downstream, offers easier access to lower Nyarong.

Barshok to Nyachuka

Drango County ब्रग་འરོ་

Drango county comprises the valley of the Zhe-chu as far as its confluence with the Nyi-chu tributary, at the county town of the same name. The distance from Kandze to Drango is 93 kilometres, and from Drango to Tawu 72 kilometres.

Drango County (96)
炉霍县
Luhuo
Population: 37,312
Area: 4,764 sq km
Colour map 4, grid A4

Joro Lake

On the descent from the watershed **Latseka Pass** (3,962 metres), also called **Dresel La**, the road passes through sparsely populated nomadic country, dotted with dark yak wool tents. Soon you will reach the ruins of **Joro Gonpa**, a Gelukpa Monastery dating from 1642, where there were once 300 monks. Below the ruins there is a beautiful panorama of an idyllic blue lake, which was once a thriving bird sanctuary. A farming village is located by the lakeside near the road.

Below Joro Lake, the road descends for 19 kilometres to **Trewo** (3,612 metres), where it meets up with the Zhe-chu valley. Trewo, like Khangsar and Mazur at Kandze, was one of the five Trehor kingdoms set up by the Qosot Mongols in this part of Kham. Formerly it had a large citadel with impressive walls, which was the residence of the chieftain of Hor Trewo. The flat-roofed earthen houses of the Tibetan village are now clustered around the ruins of the castle, and alongside new Chinese compounds with white walls and sloping roofs. Across the river on the north bank of the Zhe-chu is the rebuilt temple of **Dzaleb Gonpa**.

Trewo

Eastern Tibet

Drango

As the name ('head of the rock') suggests, **Drango** is a strategic location on the mountain slope at the confluence of the Zhe-chu and Nyi-chu rivers. The castle of **Drango Dzong** formerly stood at this vantage point at an elevation of 3,475 metres. Above it in the 17th century, the Gelukpa monastery of **Drango Gonpa** was constructed. At its high point, this monastery housed 1,000 monks, making it the largest in Kham east of Litang and Kandze. In 1863 Drango along with the other Trehor kingdoms and Derge was overwhelmed by the tribal forces of Nyarong Gonpo Namgyel. Then, in 1865 on the defeat of Gonpo Namgyel, the town became a protectorate of Lhasa. Subsequently, the Chinese settlement, **Luho Xian**, was founded in 1894 by Lu Ch'uan-lin who ended the succession of local chieftains.

Phone code: 0836
Colour map 4, grid A4

Drango County

Orientation Most buildings in Drango are newly constructed, the older town having been devastated by an earthquake in recent decades. Entering the town from the west (49 kilometres from Trewo), the main street runs past a prison and then, on a paved surface, a number of high-rise concrete buildings, including the Bank of China. Reaching the crossroads, which marks the town centre, there are two parallel streets running uphill, both filled with small shops and restaurants. At the upper end of the westernmost of these two streets, turn right and then left to enter the *Drango Government Guesthouse* compound. The Government Buildings are to its rear.

Outside the hotel, turn right and walk along the boulevard running along the upper end of the two parallel market streets. There are several video parlours, and karaoke bars. Head downhill on this main road, and you will pass the main commercial centre: glass-fronted shops selling textiles, ready-to-wear clothing, shoes etc, as well as the China Agricultural Bank, the Public Security Bureau and the law courts. The bus station and cinema are located at a roundabout at the bottom of this road – a barrier on the right pointing the way out of town in the direction of Tawu.

The town evidently has a large Chinese population. Returning uphill to the parallel market streets, turn right and follow the road downhill to the bridge which spans the Zhe-chu River. This is the road leading north to **Serwa** (71 kilometres) and thence to **Sertal** or **Dzamtang** (see below, pages 609 and 612). Before reaching the bridge you will pass a *Forestry Department Guesthouse* on the right.

Drango Gonpa The monastery which gives the town its name is located across the river on the 'head of the rock' promontory. The **main hall** which has 63 pillars contains images of Tsongkhapa and his foremost students, Buddha in the form Gyelwa Yizhin Norbu, and the Buddhas of the Five Families, with a teaching throne in front. Along the side walls are tapestries in Chengdu brocade depicting the 1,000 buddhas of the aeon, while adjacent to the door there are depictions of Six-armed Mahakala and the 33 Confession Buddhas. The **inner sanctum** has images of Tsongkhapa and Jowo Shakyamuni, the latter crafted in India. On the **second floor**, there is a rear section containing the **Reliquary Chapel** of Geshe Yeshe Norbu and Geshe Kentsang, both former preceptors of Drango Monastery; the **Jamyang Lhakhang**, containing the reliquary of the late Umdze Jamyang who rebuilt Drango Monastery in recent years; and the

Eastern Tibet

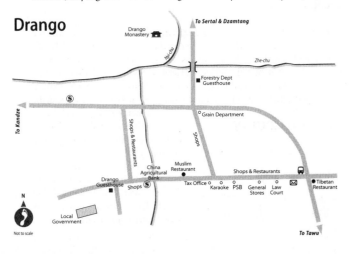

private apartments of the Dalai Lama (as yet unused). The front section contains the **Dolma Lhakhang** and the **Guru Lhakhang**, which respectively house images of Tara and Padmasambhava, as well as a chamber where the late Panchen Lama X once resided. Below the monastery, the confluence of the Zhe-chu and the Nyi-chu is clearly visible.

Drango Government Guesthouse, T0836-22332. Has good clean rooms with electric **Sleeping**
heaters and hot water or showers on each floor, at ¥24 per bed, and ¥72 per triple, but
foreigners must pay 100 percent surcharge! *Forestry Department Guesthouse*, just
before the bridge to Drango Monastery.

The guesthouses have a slow service and are more expensive than the roadside res-   **Eating**
taurants and noodle bars, which serve Sichuan, Tibetan and Muslim cuisine.

Tawu County རྟའུ

*The county of **Tawu** comprises the valley of the Zhe-chu (Ch Xianshui) below*   Tawu County (97)
Drango, extending as far south as the river's confluence with the Yalong, and the   道孚县
Mejesumdo uplands, which form a watershed between it and the Tung-chu Daofu
*River of Minyak. The county capital is located at **Tawu**, 72 kilometres from*   Population: 44,117
Drango and 76 kilometres from Garthar.   Area: 5,099 sq km
    The distinctive dialect spoken here may well accord with the legend stating   Colour map 4, grid A5
that the displaced inhabitants of Xixia (Minyak) migrated to these parts following
ing their defeat by Genghiz Qan in 1227.

The Tawu valley is one of the most attractive parts of Tibet, the neatly constructed white flat-roofed houses with their horizontal red timbers exuding an air of quiet prosperity. The low altitude of Tawu (3,125 metres) and the prosperity of the valley have attracted Chinese immigrants since the first Chinese settlement was founded here in 1911 by Chao Erh Feng. Catholic and protestant missions were also based here prior to 1949 with the support of this Chinese community.

Eastern Tibet

Tawu

Entering Tawu from Drango via the **Trongmi** goldfields (72 kilometres), the   **Orientation**
road crosses to the north bank of the Zhe-chu and passes the *Forestry Depart-*   Colour map 4, grid A5
ment Guesthouse at the west end of town. Above the main street, on the hillside
to the northwest you will notice the white gravestones of the Chinese cemetery
and the renovated buildings of **Nyitso Gonpa** – a monastery of the Gelukpa
school which formerly housed 400 monks.

On both sides of the main street there are small Sichuan-style restaurants. Pass   **The town**

Tawu County

the compound on the right where the
Tibetan Language University of East
Tibet was based until recently, and on
the left a lumber yard. The road forks
here; the left branch leading towards
the government buildings, the post
office, and courts; and the right
branch leading to the bus station and
the main crossroads at the centre of
the town.

Reaching the crossroads, a turning on the left leads uphill to connect with the left branch opposite the law courts. General stores, grocery stores, and vegetable sellers line the main street, near the crossroads. Continue due east from the crossroads to head out of town in the directions of Garthar, southeast for Nyachuka and northeast for Barkam. A petrol station lies at the extreme east end of town.

Sleeping & eating *Tawu Government Guesthouse*, close to the law courts. The rooms are very basic, the toilets outside (as is the norm for transport stations), and the restaurant mediocre. Better to dine outside at the simple street restaurants. The *Forestry Department Guesthouse*, also has rooms, but may not accept foreign guests.

Tawu to Nyachuka, Tu-je Chenpo, and Garthar

Three different roads lead east from Tawu, diverging beyond the petrol station. To the south, a motorable trail follows the Zhe-chu downstream, leaving the Tawu valley at a large white stupa, and heading in the direction of **Drawa** (69 kilometres), where there is a Gelukpa Monastery, and thence to **Nyachuka** (56 kilometres) via the confluence of the Zhe-chu and the Yalong. To the north a trail abruptly crosses the watershed and follows a tributary of the Do-chu River upstream to **Tu-je Chenpo** (*Ch* Qanyiqao) (152 kilometres), from where there are roads east to **Barkham**, and west to **Dzamtang** or **Sertal** (see below, pages 612 and 609). Lastly, the main highway runs southeast from Tawu, ascending the richly forested watershed region of Mejesumdo, where there are wonderful picnic spots in view of **Mount Zhara Lhatse**. It then crosses the **Nedreheka La pass** (4,115 metres) to enter the Minyak region of East Tibet at **Garthar**. The distance from Tawu to Dartsedo via Garthar is 240 kilometres.

Tawu

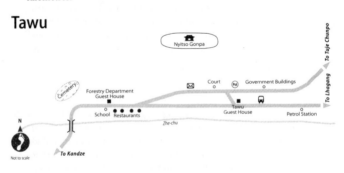

Far-east Tibet
Amdo ཨ་མདོ and Gyarong རྒྱལ་རོང

10

Far-east Tibet

Amdo ཨ་མདོ and Gyarong རྒྱལ་རོང

Far-east Tibet includes Amdo or the grassland region around the upper reaches of the Yellow, Min, and Jialing rivers in the northeast, and the deep gorges of the Gyarong feeder rivers: Ser-chu, Do-chu and Mar-chu further south. Amdo is the region in which the Tibetan population has been most exposed over the centuries to cultural contacts with neighbouring peoples: Tu, Salar, Mongol, Hui, and Chinese; and this intermingling is reflected in the demographic composition of the grasslands. By contrast, the isolated Gyarong valleys remained aloof for centuries from all outside influences and their inhabitants were known for their expressed hostility towards intruders, whether Tibetan, Mongol, Manchu, or Chinese.

Amdo ཨ་མདོ and Gyarong རྒྱལ་རོང

*There are seven sections in the following description of Far-east Tibet: the first details the route from **Lhasa to Ziling** (Xining) across the West Kokonor plateau; the second, third and fourth trace the old caravan trails and the densely populated valleys to the north, east, southeast and southwest of **Lake Kokonor**; the fifth and sixth follow the upper reaches of the Yellow River through **Golok** and the Gyarong feeder rivers through **Sertal** and **Ngawa** as far as **Rongtrak** and **Tsenlha**; and finally, the seventh follows the upper reaches of the Min and Jialing rivers from **Lanzhou to Chengdu** via **Labrang, Dzoge,** and **Zungchuka** (Ch Songpan).*

Presently this entire region of Far-east Tibet comprises 60 counties, of which 37 are within Qinghai province, eight within Gansu province, and the remainder in Sichuan (13 in the Ngawa Autonomous Prefecture and two in the Kandze Autonomous Prefecture).

Getting there The nearest points of access are the large provincial capital cities: Chengdu, Lanzhou, and Ziling.

History

Tibetan-speaking tribes played an important role in the formation of several Chinese dynasties in the northeast; but during the Tang Dynasty, the Tibetan Empire of the **Yarlung kings** consolidated its control over the whole region of Far-east Tibet. Culturally, the peoples of the region have remained within the Tibetan orbit ever since, influenced by both the Bon and the Buddhist traditions. The unifying influence of Tibetan culture withstood the political fragmentation of the region which followed the collapse of the Yarlung Empire in the ninth century; and it was through contact with the Sakyapa and Kagyupa traditions in the grasslands that the Mongol tribes of **Genghiz Qan** and his successors were brought within the fold of Tibetan Buddhism.

For some 500 years (13th-18th century) the Mongol tribes dominated the grasslands, and following the conversion of **Altan Qan** to the Gelukpa school by **Dalai Lama III** in 1580, successive *qans* zealously sought to impose the acceptance of the Gelukpa order upon the diverse cultural traditions of the region. **Gushi Qan** of the Qosot Mongols established his kingdom around Lake Kokonor, and in 1641 aided Dalai Lama V to unify spiritual and temporal power under his authority in Lhasa. His military campaigns directed against the Bonpo and Kagyupa monasteries of Kham in particular were extended into the Gyarong region during the 18th century by **Changkya Qutuktu Rolpei Dorje**, who targeted the Bonpo and Nyingmapa in particular. Despite these efforts, the traditions of the Bonpo, Nyingmapa and Jonangpa remain strong in Gyarong and neighbouring areas at the present day.

Following the pacification of the Mongols by the Manchu emperor **Qianlong** in the 18th century, the political vacuum in the Amdo area was filled by the Muslims, who encroached southwest from Ziling towards Jyekundo, dominating the trade routes. From 1727 until the mid-20th century the towns of the grasslands and Tsong-chu valley were controlled by the **Ma** family who looked upon the Kokonor Territory as their own protectorate. Gradually their influence filtered south from Jyekundo into Nangchen, but the nomadic areas of Golok, Sertal, and Gyarong always remained beyond their jurisdiction in the hands of the local Tibetan populace. The present Dalai Lama was born in the Tsongkha Khar area of Amdo in 1935, firmly under the control of the Muslim warlord **Ma Pu-feng**. The Tibetan government had to pay a large ransom to ensure his release and safe passage to Lhasa. In 1950, Ma Pu-feng succumbed to the PLA, leaving most of Amdo in the hands of the Communists.

Land and environment

The southern border of Amdo is divided from the Salween basin of West Kham by the **Dangla** Mountains, and from the Yangzte and Yalong basins of East Kham by the rolling **Bayankala** Mountains, which form a southeast spur of the Kunluns. In the northwest, the **Altyn Tagh** range divides the Tsaidam basin of Northwest Amdo from East Turkestan (*Ch* Xinjiang); and in the northeast the jagged **Chokle Namgyel** Mountains (*Ch* Qilian) divide the Kokonor basin of Northeast Amdo from the Gansu corridor and Mongolia. In the extreme east, the **Min**, **Longmen**, and **Qionglai** mountains divide the Amdo grasslands and Gyarong gorges from the mainland Chinese parts of Sichuan and Gansu.

Other ranges internally demarcate the distinct regions of Amdo and Gyarong: the **Kunluns**, which divide the Jangtang Lakes and Yangtze headwaters from the Tsaidam basin; the **Amnye Machen** range which forms the bend of the Yellow River, dividing the nomadic tribes of Golok (south) from those of Banak (north); the **Nyenpo Yurtse** range dividing Golok from Gyarong; and the **Nanshan** range, which divides Kokonor from the Yellow River basin.

The terrain of Far-east Tibet is characterized by its broad valleys, rolling hills and extensive flat tableland. However, there are considerable variations between the deserts of the **Tsaidam** and **Jangtang**, the rich grasslands of **Amdo**, and the forested gorges of **Gyarong**.

In the northwest of the region, the intramontane depression of the **Tsaidam** basin is extremely low. The north-westerly parts of the Tsaidam (2,700-3,000 metres) are characterized by denuded plains of bedrock; while in the lower southeast (2,600-2,700 metres) there are thick Meso-Cenozoic deposits. The terrain therefore varies between gravel, sand and clay deserts, semi-desert tundra, and salt wastelands.

The **Altyn Tagh** Mountains, which divide the northwest border of the Tsaidam from the Tarim basin of East Turkestan, extend over 805 kilometres. The western hills are rugged and rocky, above 5,700 metres with perennial snow peaks and glaciers. The central part of the range is lower at 4,000 metres; but is higher in the northeast, 5,000 metres. There are few rivers except in the southwest, and the central portion which adjoins the Tsaidam is arid and waterless.

The **Chokle Namgyel** (Qilian) range, dividing the Kokonor basin from the Gobi desert of Mongolia, runs from northwest to southeast at an average altitude of 5,100 metres. Many rivers originate from its glaciated peaks, especially the Ruo Shui (known as Etzingol River in Mongolian) which flows northwards into Mongolia. Around 4,200 metres there is high altitude pastureland. The area is rich in minerals including iron, chromium, copper, lead, zinc, gold, and coal.

Geography

Far-east Tibet

Yellow River

The **Yellow River**, known in Tibetan as **Ma-chu** and in Chinese as **Huang He**, is often regarded (in its lower reaches) as the cradle of Chinese civilization. The world's sixth longest river, it flows 5,464 kilometres (1,167 kilometres in Tibet) from its source in the Bayankala Mountains to its estuary in the East China Sea; and has a drainage area of 745,000 square kilometres (of which 77,249 km are within Tibet). From its source, the river flows east, traversing **Kyaring** and **Ngoring** Lakes, then turning westwards through the hairpin bend (khug-pa), it crosses the **Amnye Machen** range, and flows northwards from **Rabgya**, descending in a series of rapids (fall 2m per km) to **Lanzhou**. From Lanzhou, the river flows east through Ningxia, Mongolia, and the Shanxi, Henan and Shandong provinces of mainland China. The river averages a flow of 1,530 cubic metres per second, an annual volume of 48.2 cubic kilometres, and an precipitation of 470 millimetres (mostly snow-melt in the upper reaches). It is the world's muddiest river, carrying 1.52 billion tons of silt per year.

The **Nanshan** range, which divides the Kokonor basin from the Yellow River, has an average altitude of 4,000-5,000 metres; the higher western peaks being glaciated and exceeding 6,000 metres. There are a number of tectonic intermontane depressions on both sides of the range, the largest being that of Lake Kokonor to the north. In the lower eastern parts of the range, where the intermontane valleys are more open, humid and warm rains penetrate. Tributaries of the Yellow River rise to the south of the range.

In the south, the **Bayankala** range divides Amdo from Kham. The northwest peaks of this range lie south of Kyareng and Ngoreng lakes, at an average altitude of 4,600-5,100 metres; and they are the source of the Yellow River. The central hills of the range are rounded and rolling. The most renowned peak in the southeast is **Mount Nyenpo Yurtse** (5,369 metres), the sacred mountain of the Golok, which is surrounded by five lakes.

The **Amnye Machen** range, which forms the bend of the Yellow River, extends from higher northwest peaks to lower southeast peaks. This range, which is revered as the sacred abode of the protector deity Machen Pomra, has 21 major snow peaks: the three main ones are situated towards the northwest end. Mount Dradul Lungshok (6,154 metres) is the northernmost peak; Mount Amnye Machen (6,282 metres) is the central peak; and Mount Chenrezik (6,127 metres) is the southernmost peak. The northern Golok foothills between the Bayankala and Amnyen Machen ranges average 4,200 metres.

The **Min Shan** range, which demarcates the eastern extremity of the Amdo grasslands, forms the river basins of the Minjiang and Jialing, characterized by strata of red clay, red sandstone and gypsum. This part of the plateau is exposed to higher levels of precipitation, as much as 508 millimetres.

Flora and fauna

The upper reaches of the Yellow River are predominantly a region of grassy hills and marshlands; but they are not entirely without trees. Small patches of spruce and fir are often found on north-facing slopes, and their presence is important in maintaining the watertables, preventing soil erosion and protecting the local micro-climates. The best quality grassland also contains a wide range of flowers and grasses, but sadly many areas are now becoming overgrazed, and exhibit only a limited diversity of species. Large wild animals have almost disappeared from this region, but smaller mammals such as the pika, mole, vole, rabbit and marmot have proliferated in the absence of preda-tors. Before 1950, this area did support some large herds of yak and sheep, but banditry was rife, and many side-valleys were rarely used for grazing. The modern emphasis on animal husbandry, the new road network and changes in stock management techniques have led to increasingly intensive use of the grasslands and a deterioration in pasture quality.

Many of the marshes have shrunk in size, threatening the habitat of wad-ing birds, including the well-known Black-necked Crane. In a few places, the thin top-soil has been completely eroded by the action of wind and water, causing some of this rich grassland to turn into semi-desert. Around Lake Kokonor, the plateau vegetation includes tamarisk, haloxylon, feather grass, white willow, craxyweed, astragalus, gentian and allium. Spruce forests are found on the northern slopes of the Nanshan Mountains.

Peoples

The Tibetan population of Amdo comprises the **Drok-ke** speaking nomads of Banak, Golok, and Ngawa; the **Rong-ke** speaking towns of the Tsong-chu val-ley, and the **semi Drok-ke** (also called Rongma Drok-ke) speaking settle-ments of Repkong, Labrang, Luchu and Jo-ne areas. Non-Tibetan languages are also spoken within the Amdo area: particularly among the **Salar** Muslims of Dowi county, the **Tu** of Gonlung and Pari counties, and the **Mongols** of Sogwo county. Further south, in the Gyarong gorges and the lower Min valley, there are Tibeto-Burman populations of the ancient **Qiangic** speaking lan-guage group, including those who speak **Tawu-ke** (in Tawu and Rongtrak), **Gyarong-ke** (in Chuchen and Tsenlha), and **Qiang-ke** in Maowen.

The **Qiang** were forced into the mountain fastnesses of the Gyarong and Min valleys by the Qin and Han Emperors following their unification of China in the pre-Christian era. Their **Qiang Long** stone culture is characterized by the construction of large stone watchtowers and sturdy stone dwellings, often containing white quartz rocks which were regarded as sacred artefacts.

The rich pastures of the Amdo grasslands sustain a nomadic population larger than in any other part of Tibet. These nomads, including the **Golok** (south of Amnye Machen) and the **Banak** (north of Amnye Machen) have recently benefited economically from the reforms in China, but face a long-term threat to their future from environmental deterioration. The education system is basic at best, with Tibetans forced to study Chinese if they wish to advance in their cho-sen career. There are few employment opportunities in this region, so most chil-dren follow their parents and become nomadic pastoralists, while a few, mostly boys, join one of the numerous monasteries that have been rebuilt in the last 13 years. Government funds have been allotted to help rebuild these monasteries, and each site is given a quota of timber and building materials, as well as a con-struction team, usually composed of Chinese craftsmen. This official help how-ever covers little more than the basic building, and the Tibetans are forced to look to the local communities for the cost of internal and external decoration, and the construction of monastic residences. As a result, most of these monas-teries are little more than a concrete shed, only the timber entrance and porch roof supports being made in traditional style. Shrines, statues and murals are generally very poorly executed, although there is now a small body of well-trained artists, centred at the excellent **Schools of Painting in Repkong**. With the exception of the main temples in **Repkong**, **Labrang** and **Kumbum**, virtually all the original monasteries of Amdo were destroyed in the Maoist era, and the vast bulk of Amdo's artistic heritage has been lost.

Far-east Tibet

The West Kokonor Plateau

The main highway from Lhasa crosses the border between the Tibetan Autonomous Region and Qinghai at Dang La pass (5,220 metres), 85 kilometres north of Amdo township; and then runs through the Autonomous Prefecture of West Kokonor to Kermo (Ch Golmud) and Ziling. The West Kokonor area, so-called because it lies to the west of Lake Kokonor (Tib Tsongon), comprises the sparsely populated and spacious terrain of the Jangtang Lakes and the Tsaidam basin, as well as the source of the Yangtze River. There are eight counties within the prefecture, which is administered from Kermo, 837 kilometres northeast of Nakchu and 782 kilometres west of Ziling. The indigenous population of Mongols, Tibetans, and Kazakhs must nowadays contend with widespread Chinese immigration, both official and unofficial. One of the great concerns is the increase in the number of lawless and unaccountable Chinese gold prospectors.
Recommended itinerary: 6.

South Kermo County ལྷོ་གི་ར་མོ

South Kermo County (98)
南 格尔木
Golmud Nan
Population: 49,939
Area: 44,278
Colour map 6, grid B4

The highway from Lhasa breaches the **Dangla Mountains** at Dang La pass (5,220 metres), 85 kilometres north of Amdo township, where there is a memorial depicting Chinese soldiers. To the west of the pass, Mount Dangula (6,022 metres) is clearly visible, and the higher Mount Longyala (6,104 metres) soars to the east. It then enters the Yangtze basin, following the Bu-chu tributary as far as its confluence with the Kar-chu at **Karchudram Babtsuk** (*Ch* Gaerquyan). En route it passes through Dangla Maktsuk after 19 kilometres, the hot springs of Chutsen, and **Toma** township (*Ch* Wenquan) after 54 further kilometres. From Toma a seasonal side-road leads southwest for 88 kilometres to the crystal mines between the glaciers of Mount Jang-gyen Deuruk Gangri (6,548 metres) and Mount Kolha Dardong (6,621 metres) in the Dangla range. Here and around Lake Mirik Gyadram to the southwest are the main **southern sources of the Yangtze**: the Kar-chu and the Mar-chu (*Ch* Tuotuohe).

Continuing on the highway from Toma, you will reach **Yanshiping** after 25 kilometres and **Marchudram Babtsuk** (*Ch* Tuotuohe) on the banks of the Mar-chu after 90 kilometres. This last settlement has guesthouse and restaurant facilities; and just to the north of town the road crosses the **first bridge over the Yangtze**.

Northeast of Marchudram Babtsuk, the highway reaches the

South Kermo County

county border after 64 kilometres; and then traverses the extreme northwest of Drito county (see above, page 490) to cross the Chumar River, the **northern source of the Yangtze** which rises in the Kunluns. The main settlement in the Chumar valley is **Chumarhe**, 141 kilometres northeast of the border. To the west lie the Jangtang Lakes, and the road in places bypasses small isolated lakes dotted over a fairly barren plain. Occasionally gazelle and kyang (wild ass) can be seen from the road, but wild yak, antelope and argali can only be found in the high plains to the west. Buses reach this area from the Norbulingka Bus Station in Lhasa, while expeditions to the sources of the Yangtze are organized by the Qinghai Mountaineering Association.

Kermo County ཀེར་མོ

*Kermo county lies between the Kunlun and Tsaidam Pendi ranges. Its rivers which rise on the southern slopes of the Kunluns flow into the salt lakes of the South Tsaidam. The county capital, **Kermo**, is located on the banks of the Kermo-chu at the Qinghai railway terminus. It is an important intersection, in that roads lead north to Gansu and northwest to Xinjiang provinces, as well as south to Lhasa and east to Ziling.*

Kermo County (99)
洛尔木市
Golmud
Population: 83,017
Area: 51,484
Colour map 6, grid B5

Eastern Kunluns

The highway from **Chumarhe** reaches **Budongquan** after 65 kilometres, and, leaving the Yangtze basin, crosses the pass through the Eastern Kunlun Mountains after a further 21 kilometres. To the west lies the snow peak of **Mount Yuxu** (5,933 metres), revered by Chinese Daoists as the abode of the celestial princess Yuxu, and to the east is **Mount Hohosai Kenmenho** (*Ch* Yuzhu, 5,989 metres).

Distinct from the Western Kunluns, which divide the Jangtang Plateau of Northwest Tibet from the Tarim basin of Central Asia (see above, page 315), the Eastern Kunluns are characterized by their high perennial snow line (5,700-6,000 metres), low temperatures, aridness, strong winds, intense solar radiation, and brief summers with precipitation under 100 millimetres. The mean July temperature in the higher parts of the range is less than 10°, and the nights can be bitterly cold. The winter is long with severe frosts and strong dust storms (minimum temperature -35°, and wind speed exceeding 20 metres per second). The Kunlun landscape largely consists of rock desert and stagnant water pools. **Geography**

This is more plentiful here than in the Himalayas and other ranges which have been exploited more on account of their proximity to large centres of popula- **Wildlife**

Kermo County

To Mangnai (200 km)
Urt Moron
180
Altenquoke
To Da Tsaidam (185 km)
30
Kermo
To Ziling (782 km)
90
Dronglung
68
E Kunluns
21
Budongquan
N
Not to scale
To Chamarhe (65 km)

tion. The ungulates of the Kunluns include the gazelle, wild ass, wild goat, wild yak, blue sheep and argali, while brown bears and wolves are also found in fewer numbers. Waterfowl are frequently seen on the saline lakes around the Kunluns during the migratory season.

The Qinghai Mountaineering Association organizes expeditions to the major peaks of the range, including **Mount Pukhala Ritse** (*Ch*

Far-east Tibet

Xinqing, 6,860 metres), **Mount Achen Gangchen** (*Ch* Daxuefeng, 5,863 metres), and **Mount Wuxuefeng** (5,804 metres), all of which lie southwest of Kermo.

Dronglung

From the pass through the East Kunluns, the road descends into the valley known as **Dronglung** ('Wild Yak Valley') to its Tibetan herders (*Mong* Niaj Gol). The Kunlun foothills to the south of this valley still have most of the Jangtang range of mammals in their upper reaches, despite hunting from passing goldminers and occasional professional hunters. Here the temperature range is also extreme: averaging 25-28° in mid-summer, and -9° in mid-winter. After **Naij Tal** township (68 kilometres from the pass), the highway leaves the spectacular plain of the Kunlun snow ranges and, below the Naij Gol River's confluence with the **Kermo-chu**, it descends through a gorge with a hydro-power station to emerge after. 90 kilometres at Kermo city on the southern fringe of the Tsaidam desert.

Kermo City

Altitude 2,800 metres
Phone code: 0979
Colour map 6, grid B6

Kermo (*Ch* Golmud) is a large new town which has developed in recent decades as a centre for potash mining, and (even more recently) oil-refining. Formerly there were barely a dozen houses here! The sprawling concrete buildings and barrack-style compounds abut straight avenues, but there is little of interest in the city itself, its population largely comprising Chinese immigrants. It is however an important transit point for visitors to Lhasa, Ziling or Dunhuang.

Orientation Approaching the city from the Lhasa/Nakchu road, you will pass a turn-off on the right (Huanghe Street), which leads to the **railway station** and the **Ziling Bus Station**, and continues east out of town in the direction of Ziling. If you stay on the main road, you will head north onto **Xizang Street**, passing to the left the TAR government shops and the **Lhasa Bus Station.**

A second right-turn leads from Xizang Street along **Tsaidam Street**. Take this turn-off and you will soon reach the intersections of **Zhongshan Street**, **Kunlun Street**, and **Jiangyuan Street** in quick succession. The Bank of China is located on the south side of Tsaidam Street after its intersection with Kunlun Street. On the east side of Kunlun Street itself you will find (in succession) the *Best Café*, the *Golmud Hotel*, the *Golmud Hotel Restaurant*, and the open-air market. The Post Office is located on the corner of the Tsaidam Street and Jiangyuan Street intersection.

Returning to Xizang Street, if you head north, you will soon reach an important crossroad, from where you can head west out of town in the direction of **Mangnai** and the Xinjiang border, east via **Jinfeng Street** to the **downtown** area, or north via **Yanqiao Street**, out of town in the direction of **Dunhuang**.

Kermo

1 Buses for Lhasa
2 Buses for Ziling

Sleeping C *Kermo Hotel (Golmud Binguan)*, 160 Kunlun Rd, T(0979)412061. New   **Essentials**
standard rooms (¥300), with erratic hot showers and the *Golmud Hotel Restaurant*.

Eating *Golmud Hotel Restaurant*, on Kunlun St. Good and reasonably priced Chinese food. For western food, try the ***Best Café***, also on Kunlun St (2nd Floor).

Entertainment The only forms of entertainment are pool, karaoke, and tourist baiting!

Shopping Try the open-air market on Kunlun St and the *Department Store* on Tsaidam St.

Transport Road *Tibet Bus Station*, Xizang Street, has daily departures for Lhasa. The basic fare is ¥180, but foreigners should expect to pay around ¥1,000 including a hefty foreigners' registration fee. The bus station has a foreigners' registration desk. The 1,150 kilometres journey takes between 28 and 35 hours. **NB** The *Kermo Hotel* is used to foreigners attempting to get to Lhasa and CITS here has had a somewhat chequered history over the years.
  Main Bus Station, opposite the *Kermo Railway Station*, has daily bus departures for Ziling and Dunhuang (¥50, 13 hours).

Train There are express and local services to and from Ziling. The former departs *Kermo Railway Station* around 1400, and the latter around 2030. Plans to extend the railway from Kermo to Lhasa have so far floundered on account of the difficulty of laying tracks on a permafrost surface and boring ice tunnels through the Kunluns. An official announcement, broadcast on 3 December 1998, indicates that this costly project will soon begin. Some 1,110 kilometres of track will be laid via Kermo, Amdo, Nakchu, Damzhung and Toling counties, including 30.6 kilometres of tunnels.

Directory Banks *Bank of China*, Tsaidam St. **Hospitals & medical services** *Golmud Hospital*, 43 Kunlun Rd, T(0979)412677. **Tour companies & travel agents** *CITS, Golmud Branch*, 160 Kunlun Rd, T(0979)413003. **Useful addresses** Police and Public Security: *Golmud City Police and Public Security Bureau*, Tsaidam St.

Northern Routes from Kermo

From Kermo, you can drive due east to **Ziling** (782 kilometres), via Dulan; or due north through the Tsaidam Pendi range to **Dunhuang** (524 kilometres) via Lenghu and Aksay. A third and more difficult drive follows the 568 kilometres road to **Mangya** on the Xinjiang border, but parts of this road are seasonal and sealed by the military. Alternatively, take the **train to Ziling**, which runs parallel to the Dunhuang road, before cutting east through Greater Tsaidam, Ulan, and Tianjun counties and skirting the north shore of Lake Kokonor.

Mangnai District

A road runs northwest from Kermo via **Altenqoke** *(30 kilometres) and* **Urt**   Mangnai District (100)
Moron *(180 kilometres), where there are borax mines. It then continues across*   芒 崖
the Kermo-Mangnai border, following a seasonal track for some 200 kilometres   Mangnai
as it traverses the northwest area of the **Tsaidam** *desert.*   Population: 60,665
                                                                   Area: 53,788
                                                                   Colour map 6, grid A5

The terrain here is low-lying, arid, waterless, and unpopulated. Sand is blown

Far-east Tibet

southwest from the Mongolian plateau, and the climate is one of extremes: dry, cold, and windy winters, followed by hot summers. The road surface improves around **Mangnai** (where a side-road from neighbouring Lenghu district connects). The distance from here to the Xinjiang border is 159 kilometres. En route you will pass to the north of Gasikule Lake, where there is a Black-necked Crane reserve.

Onwards to Xinjiang From the border, the road crosses the **Altyn Tagh** range to reach **Ruoqiang** in the Qaraqan valley of Xinjiang province, and thence to Korla and **Urumqi**.

Greater Tsaidam District

Greater Tsaidam District (101)
大柴旦
Daqaidam
Population: 40,927
Area: 36,287
Colour map 6, grid A5

*The main road north from Kermo follows the railway line through the **Tsaidam Pendi** range. En route it crosses a spectacularly long 32 kilometres bridge of salt (Ch **Wangzhang** salt-bridge), which is the main scenic attraction of Kermo. The railway then cuts eastwards through south Tsaidam for **Ulan**, while the road heads north for the town of **Da Tsaidam** (185 kilometres from Kermo). About 43 kilometres beyond Da Tsaidam, at **Yuqia**, there is a branch road leading west towards **Mangnai** (351 kilometres), while another branch road heads southeast from Da Tsaidam to **Delingha** (201 kilometres) and thence to **Ulan** (142 kilometres).*

The only fertile tracts are those around the Da Tsaidam and Xiao Tsaidam Lakes; and further east at Hurleg and Toson lakes near **Delingha** railway station. The oil industry has recently become a significant factor for the local economy.

The complexity of the Tsaidam landscape has engendered great variation in climate, soil and vegetation. In general, there is a continental climate, the average precipitation being less than 100 millimetres (mostly in summer). The northwest is particularly arid and waterless. The winters are dry, cold, and windy; while the summers are hot. Strong winds from the Mongolian plateau cover the region with sand. There are, however, some fertile tracts in the piedmont and lakeside areas of this basin; while the southeast is a broad saline swamp formed by the rivers draining internally from the Kunluns. Only in the northeast, towards the East Nanshan mountains does the climate become milder.

Mangnai & Greater Tsaidam Districts

Lenghu District

Lenghu District

The **Kermo to Dunhuang** highway enters **Lenghu** district to the north of Da Tsaidam town and Yuqia. It passes through the unpopulated north part of the Tsaidam desert, and after 112 kilometres reaches the township of **Huahaizi**. From here it continues for 55 kilometres to the Qinghai-Gansu provincial border at **Dangjin Shankou** pass, located in a defile between the Altyn Tagh and Chokle Namgyel ranges. The only oasis in these parts is the area close to the shores of **Lake Suhai**. This part of the Tsaidam is largely uninhabited, but there are occasional Kazakh settlements, related to those from neighbouring Aksay in Gansu.

Lenghu District (102)
冷湖
Lenghu
Population: 21,113
Area: 18,720
Colour map 6, grid A5

Panchen Zhingde County པན་ཆེན་ཞིང་སྡེ

The main highway from Kermo to Ziling runs due east for 782 kilometres. En route, it passes through **Panchen Zhingde (Dulan)** *county, which has its capital at Dulan, 354 kilometres from Kermo. The initial stretch of 250 kilometres passes through the barren southeast fringe of the Tsaidam. Only occasional desert vegetation on low sand-dunes and stony desert break the horizon as the road runs parallel to the Kunlun. Some 150 kilometres after Kermo, a line of trees to the north marks* **Nomahung**, *one of the prison farms for which Qinghai is renowned, located nearby a prehistoric archaeological site.*

Panchen Zhingde County (103)
都兰县
Dulan
Population: 56,090
Area: 53,518 sq km
Colour map 5, grid B2

Balung Hunting Ground

Leaving the desert, at Balung hamlet, there is a side-road on the right (south), which leads south into the **Balung Hunting Reserve** of the Kunlun Mountains. Here, over a 127 square kilometres area (*average altitude*: 4,200 metres), the few remaining large mammals of the Tibetan plateau, including argali, gazelle, white-lipped deer, red deer, corsac foxes, wolves, and marmots, can be shot for hefty fees (ranging from US$10,000 for a white-lipped deer to US$60 for a marmot). Hunting trips are organized from mid-August until late-November; and from April until late-May. Much better to leave them in

Colour map 5, grid B2

Panchen Zhingde County

peace. Organized hunting of this scale could be halted if ecologically sensitive wildlife tourism could be promoted successfully throughout the region. There is also a small Gelukpa monastery at Balung, which is regarded as a branch of Tashilhunpo.

Accommodation is provided in Mongolian-style yurts and proper kitchen facilities including refrigeration are available.

Sleeping

Far-east Tibet

Panchen Zhingde Monastery After Balung, the highway passes through **Shang** (*Ch* Xiang Ride), where there are interesting stone carvings and cliff paintings. A major river cuts through the Kunlun range here, its two sources rising in Alag Lake and Dongi Tsona Lake to the south. This area is the ancestral home of several nomadic Tibetan groups presently living north of Lake Kokonor. These Shang Tibetans were forced northwards en masse into Mongol territory during the 18th century, probably due to pressure from the Goloks. **Panchen Zhingde Monastery**, which was given as a concession to the Dalai Lama, is close to the road. It is run by monks from Tashilhunpo in Zhigatse, while its patrons are Mongol herdsmen. Further south, at **Guri**, a second hunting park can be visited. The local Nyingmapa monastery, **Guri Gonpa Samten Choling** (founded circa 1690) is 15 kilometres southeast of Guri village. From **Lake Dongi Tsona** there is a route leading to **Tsogyenrawa** on the main Jyekundo-Ziling highway (see below, page 598).

Dulan

Colour map 5, grid B2 The county capital is located 60 kilometres north of Panchen Zhingde, on the banks of the **Qagan Us** River. Situated in the southeast corner of the Tsaidam, where irrigated fields and tree plantations have brightened the marshy desert, it is a growing town, inhabited largely by Han Chinese and Hui Muslims. In the hinterland, there are Mongol herdsmen; while Tibetans inhabit the high mountains further south, where three monasteries are located: **Puntsok Dargyeling** and **Aten Tsamkhang** of the Gelukpa school, and **Lungmar Gonpa** which is maintained by both Gelukpa and Nyingmapa monks.

Ulan Sok County ཁྲུ་ལན་

Ulan Sok County (104)
乌兰县
Ulan
Population: 88,515
Area: 32,959 sq km
Colour map 5, grid A2

*The road and railway links from Da Tsaidam area to Ziling pass through **Ulan Sok Dzong** county. At **Keluke Lake**, between the road and the railway tracks, there are large fish reserves. The only functioning monasteries in the west of the county are **Gormo Gonpa** and **Tenpa Pelgyeling** of the Gelukpa school, while those at Tototala are still in ruins. **Delingha** city, 56 kilometres further east, where the road rejoins the railway track, is a burgeoning Chinese town, which has recently been granted a separate municipal status in Qinghai province.*

Delingha

Orientation
Population: 52,771
Phone code: 0977
Colour map 5, grid A2

Heading into town from Da Tsaidam, you reach **Dexin Street**, which is the main thoroughfare. Continue due east on Dexin Street, crossing the Bayan river, to reach the bus station and the railway station, and thereafter head out of town in the direction of **Ulan, Tianjun** and **Ziling**. A turn-off on the left (**Qingxin Street**) leads towards the Delingha Mosque, the Post Office, the City Government Buildings, and the downtown area, where there are department stores and the *Nationalities Hotel* (Minzu Fandian). A second turn-off on the left (**Kunlun Street**) leads north

Delingha

Mong Zang Hospital

Prefectural Government

Kunlun St

People's Department Store

Prefectural Hospital

Tuan Jie St

Bayan River

Mosque

City Government

Qing Xin Road

Nationalities Hotel

Bus Station

Dexin Street

N

Not to scale

Delingha Station

Far-east Tibet

towards the Gansu border, while the hospitals and prefectural government offices are in the north of the city, between Kunlun Street and Tuanjie Street.

C *Delingha Guesthouse* (*Nationalities Hotel*), T(0977)222781. Standard rooms (¥100). **Sleeping**

Ulan

Ulan, the county capital, lies 142 kilometres southeast from Delingha, at the *Colour map 5, grid A2* next major intersection of the road and railway tracks. In this area there are several Mongol settlements which have been hugely expanded by recent Chinese immigration. The important Mongol monastery of **Ganden Sangak Yarpeling** was established to the northeast during the late 18th century, and near **Tsaka**, the monastery of **Ganden Gepeling** was founded in 1800 below Mount Changjie. Both of these are branches of Ganden Namgyeling Monastery at Lhasa. West from Tsaka, there is also the monastery of **Pekhokho Gon Gendun Dekyiling**, which was originally founded by Panchen Lama IV, Lobzang Chokyi Gyeltsen (1570-1660). Further north in Ulan county, the Northeast Tsaidam desert is largely unpopulated, apart from a few nomadic groups in the upper reaches of the **Yangkang-chu** valley, and to the west of **Hara Lake**.

Ulan County

From Ulan to **Tsaka**, on the northeast **Getting there** corner of **Tsaka Lake**, the distance is 37 kilometres by road or rail. This road then connects with the main Kermo-Ziling highway and passes into Chabcha county (see below, pages 523 and 588).

Bongtak Tianjun County
 བོང་སྟག་ཐེམ་ཆེན་རྫོང་

Tianjun county, which lies to the east of the Tsaidam fringe, comprises the valleys of the northwest flowing Shu-le River and the southeast flowing Yangkang-chu. The county capital is located at Bongtak Tianjun, on the Ziling-Kermo railway.

Bongtak Tianjun County (105)
天峻县
Tianjun
Population: 15,915
Area: 22,396 sq km
Colour map 5, grid A2

Bongtak Tianjun

This desolate town is located in a windswept plain where the Tsaidam tableland rolls gently down towards the west shore of Lake Kokonor. The town has grown in recent years with the development of the railway network. There is a wool and textile factory, processing the produce of the nomadic inhabitants of the Lake Kokonor hinterland who maintain large flocks of sheep as well as yaks. Despite its 'wild west' ambience, the town boasts guesthouses, schools, a hospital, cinema, TV station, and assorted government buildings.

Altitude: 3,420 metres
Phone code 09833
Colour map 5, grid A3

Getting there A road link also connects the town with **Tsaka**, 81 kilometres to the southwest, and from Tianjun to **Kangtsa** on the north shore of Lake Kokonor, the distance is 114 kilometres.

Heading into Bontak Tianjun county from Tsaka or Delingha, you will pass

(60 kilometres before the town), the Gelukpa monastery of **Bongtak Gonpa Gendun Shedrubling**, which is a branch of Rabgya Gonpa in Golok (see below, page 602). Then, reaching the outskirts of town, the road crosses the railway tracks, and continues north in the direction of the Yangkang valley and the Gansu border. There are two turn-offs on the right, leading downtown. The first will bring you to the bus station, the railway station, and the *Tianjun Government Guesthouse*. Continue past the guesthouse, heading due east for Kangtsa. There are no monasteries in close proximity to the town, but further north there are Nyingmapa temples at **Mari Gonpa**, **Changho Ngakhang**, and **Drakmar Gon Mindrol Dargyeling**, the last being affiliated to Dzogchen Monastery in Kham.

Sleeping C *Tianjun Government Guesthouse*, T(09833)66280. Reasonably well-maintained and heated rooms (no attached bathrooms) at ¥54 per room. You are advised to keep a watchful eye on your possessions. Even the spare tyre of a Toyota land-cruiser can disappear overnight from the secure car park! Alternative accommodation can also be found at the *Tianjun Guesthouse* across the road, and at the *Truckers' Transport Station*.

Eating *Tianjun Government Guesthouse*, has the best restaurant in town, frequented nightly by Chinese and Tibetan government officials. Outside, there are small Muslim and Tibetan street restaurants.

A jeepable trail follows the **Yangkang** valley upstream from Bongtak Tianjun, and across the watershed into the Shu-le river basin. From here it runs

Bongtak Tianjun

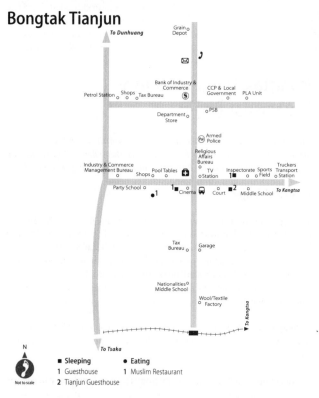

Far-east Tibet

Tsaka Salt Lake

*From Dulan, a pass leads northeast across the attractive Erla hills, to Wang Gaxun and the salt city of **Tsaka** (130 km). Tsaka is encased in salt; vast heaps of it cover the plain, buildings are encrusted, and it is even in the air you breathe. The lake offers spectacular mirages. There is a Mongolian festival here in spring connected to the small monastery in the northern hills. A network of trolley trains carries salt over the lake and a branch line (and road) leads northwest to Ulan on the Ziling-Kermo railway. Beyond Tsaka, the highway climbs southeast through a semi-desert landscape with spiky tuftgrass, into the grassy pastures of the **Nanshan** (South Kokonor) range. Mongol tents can be seen on this plain and camels are typical. After some 80 km you will reach the Chabcha county border, leaving the West Kokonor region behind.*

northwest, past an area of sulphur mines, and through the **Shu-le Nanshan** branch of the Chokle Namgyel Mountains, into Gansu province.

The flat gravel road east from Tianjun to **Kangtsa** bypasses a range of rolling hills to the south, where the snowline is low, even in May. Large flocks of sheep studiously avoid the railway tracks. After 19 kilometres, it reaches the railway station near **Ping** township. Some six kilometres to the northwest there is the small Nyingmapa monastery of **Tempung Ngakhang**, located north of the railway and south of the road. Continuing along the Kangtsa road, after 30 kilometres, you will reach a long bridge spanning a seasonal river. From here, you pass into Kangtsa county.

Bongtak Tianjun

To Gansu
Shu-le Valley
Kangtsa
114
Bongtak Tianjun
Jadabling
Ulan
81
Lake Kokonor
37
53
Tsonying
Mahadeva
To Dulan (130km)
Tsaka
80
Tanakma
N
Not to scale

Far-east Tibet

North Kokonor and Tsongkha

This route follows the course of the Qinghai-Gansu railway, and its adjacent valleys. It includes the environs of Lake Kokonor, Tibet's largest lake, and the densely populated Tsong-chu valley, the main artery between the cities of Ziling and Lanzhou, where Tibetan, Mongol, Muslim and Chinese traders have intermingled over the centuries. Also included are the lateral valleys of the Tsong-chu's south-flowing tributaries: Serkhok-chu, Julak-chu, and Zhuanglang.

A few city-states, ruled by Tibetans, had fleetingly existed in this area from the fourth century onwards, but it was not until the Yarlung Dynasty arose in Central Tibet during the seventh century that Tibetan power was consistently applied throughout the region. During the reign of Relpachen in 823 a peace treaty was signed between Tibet and China, demarcating the border at **Chorten Karpo**, near present day **Yongjing** in Gansu.

The sacred abode of **Dentik** is included among the 25 power places of Amdo and Kham, which were frequented by Padmasambhava and his disciples; and it was here that the refugee monks from Central Tibet fled following the persecution of Buddhism by King Langdarma. Here they transmitted the monastic lineage of Tibetan Buddhism to Lachen Gongpa Rabsel and ensured its continuity through to the present day.

The power vacuum, left in the wake of the Yarlung Empire's disintegration in the ninth century, was subsequently filled by the Tangut Kingdom of **Minyak** (*Ch* Xixia) which emerged towards the end of the 10th century, with its capital in the Ordos desert (modern Ningxia Province). Reaching its zenith in 1038 during the reign of King Si'u Gyelpo, the Tangut Kingdom ruled over Tibetans, Mongols, Turks, Arabs and Chinese. During the last century, Russian explorers discovered relics and books from this little-known civilization, which Genghiz Qan and his armies completely wiped out in 1227. The surviving population are said to have fled to the Tawu and Minyak areas of Kham (on which see above, page 501).

The Mongols ruled the area through a system of princeling chieftains called the **Tu**, who were mostly of Mongol and Arab descent; but who acquired Tibetan Buddhism under the influence of their Tibetan subjects. Important lamas of the Karma Kagyu and Sakya schools visited Amdo during this period, and, so, by the time of Tsongkhapa, several large monasteries and many small ones had been established in the Ziling valley and north of the Yellow River. Tsongkhapa himself was taught at the most important of these, **Jakhyung Gonpa**, but it is his birthplace, **Kumbum** in modern Rushar (Huangzhong) county, that later grew into one of the major monasteries of Tibet under both Mongol and Manchu patronage.

Political power remained in the hands of Mongol tribes who became zealous patrons of the Gelukpa school. During the 17th and 18th century, Gushi Qan of the Qosot Mongols and Sonam Rabten of the Dzungars both launched sectarian assaults on Tibet. By the time the Mongol tribes were brought to heel by the Manchus in the mid-18th century, the Kokonor and Tsong-chu areas had fallen under the control of Muslim warlords; and so they remained until the Communist occupation of the present century. It is important to note that despite the variable political climate in Amdo, it was the Tibetan culture which provided a common ground to these disparate populations.

Nowadays, this region comprises 13 counties, of which 12 are in Qinghai and only one in Gansu. The former include all four counties of the Tibetan Autonomous Prefecture of North Kokonor, and all eight counties of Ziling district; while the latter is the remote Pari autonomous county on the Zhuanglang River.

Recommended itineraries: 6 and 8.

Kangtsa County ཀྲང་ཚ

The county of Kangtsa occupies the area around the west and northwest shores of Lake Kokonor and its hinterland. The county capital, Kangtsa, which is part of the North Kokonor Tibetan Autonomous Prefecture, lies 114 kilometres east of Bongtak Tianjun and 110 kilometres northwest of Dabzhi, on the railway line and northern shore road to Ziling.

Kangtsa County (106)
刚察县
Gangca
Population: 39,601
Area: 9,155 sq km
Colour map 5, grid A3

Lake Kokonor

The largest lake on the Tibet plateau, 4,456 metres in area, known in Mongolian as **Kokonor** and in Tibetan as **Tsongon** (*Ch* Qinghai, *Eng* Blue Lake), gives its name to the present-day province of Qinghai. In former times the wide-open shores of this saline lake provided rich pastures for both Tibetan and Mongol nomads. However, the 'vast and magnificent pasturage of Kokonor', where Abbé Huc reported 'vegetation so vigorous that the grass grows up to the stomachs of our camels' and where other visitors of old reported sightings of gazelle and Tibetan wild ass, has been sadly degraded by intensive grazing and a spread of cultivation near the lake shore. The fields of

Lake Kokonor

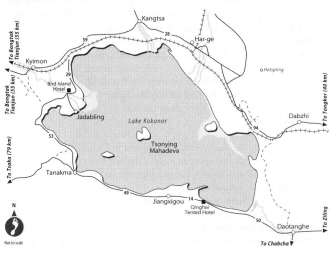

Far-east Tibet

Legends of Lake Kokonor

This island has several legendary origins. One, encountered by Abbé Huc, details how the lake was connected to Lhasa by an underground sea, which caused a temple being constructed there to constantly fall down. An old Mongolian shepherd carelessly gave away his secret to a passing lama and the sea flooded out as Kokonor. Another, recounted by Sven Hedin and Dr Rijnhart, recalls a great lama who dug up one white and one black root. He cut the black root, out of which the lake's water fortunately emerged. If he had cut the white root, the lake would have been full of milk and thus unsuitable for use as pastureland! In these legends the island forms the plug which dams the underground sea. In Chinese chronicles over 2,000 years, the island is regarded as the breeding place of the fastest horses on earth; the dragon colts, which were born from mares released on the island. Throughout the centuries important lamas, such as Zhabkar Tsokdruk Rangdrol, have passed periods of time in retreat on Tsonying Mahadeva.

yellow rape in the summer attract numerous bee-keepers from the eastern provinces of China, and groups of hives are scattered all over the plains. At this time, most of the local Tibetans have moved their herds south into the mountains, but a few tents remain near the lake for the whole year. In August, a delicious yellow mushroom is sold to passing traffic by Tibetans at the roadside. Fish is also occasionally offered but the official fishing fleet, based at the southeast corner of the lake, takes the bulk of the 5,000 ton annual catch of scaleless carp. Nowadays, the shores of the lake and their environs are administered from four counties: Kangtsa in the west and northwest, Dabzhi in the northeast, Tongkor in the east, and Chabcha in the south.

Hetugang

Driving from Bongtak Tianjun, the gravel road enters Kangtsa county after 49 kilometres. At **Kyimon** township, six kilometres further, the road crosses south of the railway tracks, and gradually descends towards the northwest shore of Lake Kokonor. A trail leads north to the Nyingmapa monasteries of **Pontsang Gongma Gonpa** (10 kilometres) and **Chuknor Gon Dongak Shedrub Dargyeling** (17 kilometres), which is located at the foot of a table mountain, while another leads northeast (20 kilometres) to **Rumang Gonpa**, a branch of distant Dzitsa Monastery in Bayan Khar county. After Kyimon, the blue atmospheric haze of the lake rises in the distance, contrasting with the barren landscape, and after 22 kilometres, the highway intersects with the road leading along the west shore, frequently criss-crossing the railway line en route. The west shore of the lake is known as **Hetugang**, and, here, there are two noteworthy sites: the **Bird Island Sanctuary** (*Tib* Jadabling, *Ch* Niao Dao), and the nearby Nyingmapa monastery of **Sato Kalden Tashi Chokhorling**.

Jadabling
Phone code: 0984 The bird island sanctuary (Jadabling), known in Chinese as Niao Dao, is a national reserve located on a peninsula of the west shore of the lake, 29 kilometres south of the Tianjun/Kangtsa highway and 53 kilometres north of **Tanakma** (*Ch* Heimahe) in Chabcha county. It is also accessible by train from the rail head at **Sixin**. There are local inhabitants of Hetugang who can still recall the days when the site was a true island, but the waters of the lake have receded in recent decades, forming a narrow peninsula. The sanctuary is open 0830-1730 daily. The admission fee is ¥28 per person, payable at the Bird

Sanctuary Management Office (*Ch* Guanlicu) in the *Bird Island Hotel* outside the park, and there is a further ¥2 charge for entry to the hatching room, though the best nesting sites are 16 kilometres further along the peninsula. In spring, more than 100,000 birds of 26 diverse species, including brown-headed gulls, fish gulls, speckle-headed wild geese, cormorants, and red-spotted ducks, converge at this peninsula, their tumult reminiscent of a crowded sport's stadium. April, May, June, and early July are the best months for nesting bar-headed geese, gulls, terns and even an occasional black-necked crane. At nearby **Cormorant Island** (*Ch* Liuci Diao), a black rocky outcrop is home to nesting cormorants throughout the summer.

Sleeping At *Bird Island Hotel*, T(0984)7652447. Newly refurbished superior rooms are now available (¥220 per standard), and there are also triples (¥30 per bed) and 4-bed rooms (¥25 per bed).

Eating *Bird Island Hotel Restaurant* offers good quality Chinese food, and in the village there is an abundant supply of fresh fish (*Ch* Huangyu) for sale.

Above the village of Jadabling and its tented camp, there is an important Nyingmapa monastery. **Sato Kalden Tashi Chokhorling** is a branch of Dzogchen Monastery (see above, page 471), originally founded in 1665 on a site sanctified by Dalai Lama V on his return journey to Lhasa from Beijing, where he had gone to visit the Manchu emperor, Shun Zhi. There are four stupas and four large temples, and a hillside where the rocks are carved with the syllables of the Vajra Guru mantra of Padmasambhava. The most important buildings are located to the left of the complex. Adjacent to the assembly hall there is the **Padmasambhava Lhakhang**, containing a large image of Padmakara, and murals depicting Aksobhya, Bhaisajyaguru, Tara, Mahakarunika, Sitatapatra, Shakyamuni Buddha, and the 16 Elders. To its left is the residence of the monastery's presiding lamas and tulkus, its temple containing an image of Padmakara, and excellent murals of the Peaceful and Wrathful Deities, Bhaisajyaguru, and Zangdokpelri. Nowadays, there are 60-70 monks at Sato.

Sato Kalden Tashi Chokhorling

Hetugang to Tanakma

An excellent paved road leads from the bird sanctuary at Jadabling along the west shore of the lake to Tanakma. The road owes its construction to the patronage of an Australian visitor whose wife died in a car accident close to the sanctuary, some 10 years ago (her tomb is located within the grounds of the sanctuary). After 27 kilometres, the road crosses a pass (3,240 metres) and winds its way through excellent lakeside grazing pastures to Tanakma, 37 kilometres distant, in Chabcha county (see below). Here, it links up with the Ziling-Lhasa highway (National Road 109), giving access to Tsaka and to the southern shore of Lake.

Kangtsa County

Tanakma

Tanakma (Heimahe) is a modern roadside town on the southwest edge of Kokonor. From here, public buses run to Kermo on the highway to Lhasa, and directly to Ziling. Tsaka

Altitude: 3,060 metres
Colour map 5, grid A3

Far-east Tibet

(see above, page 517) lies 79 kilometres to the west. Excellent grazing pastures sustain large herds of yak and sheep. Near the town, there are two small monasteries: the newly-founded Gelukpa Gonpa of **Lamoti**, two hours' walk away, and **Gyasho Benkhar**, also called Gyayi Ngotsar Tardrenling, founded by Jeu Neten Lobzang Nyima in the 16th century, which is several hours' walk to the southeast. About 35 kilometres northwest of Tanakma is **Karsho (Garla) Gonpa** of the Gelukpa school, which was founded by Tashi Gyatso.

Sleeping Try the **C** *Drolsu Dronkhang Guesthouse* in town, or the **C** *Traffic Guesthouse* on the Tsaka Rd.

Eating There are a number of small Muslim restaurants and shops.

Southern Shore of Lake Kokonor

Driving along the southern shore of Lake Kokonor from Tanakma through rich grassland, after 49 kilometres the road passes through the township of **Jiangxigou**. Accommodation is available at the *Electric Company Hotel* (Lokhang Dronkhang), and there are a few shops and Muslim restaurants alongside. The island of **Tsonying Mahadeva** now comes into view. In July and August the shore is carpeted with brilliant yellow rape flowers, and the Kokonor range (*Ch* Nanshan), which once met the waters of the lake, divides the lowlands (3,240 metres) from the Yellow River basin beyond. Some 14 kilometres further east, at **Khyamri**, there is the *Qinghai Tented Hotel* (*Tib* Bagur Dronkhang).

Essentials *Qinghai Tented Hotel*, T(0974)513520/513874. Constructed on the site of a former military camp (Number 151), this complex has been transformed over recent years into a tourist resort. Entered through an ornate gateway with the inscription 'Turquoise Mirror' (Yu'i Melong), the hotel is even now laid out as a camp. There are rooms in mock Tibetan-tent style at US$35, standard rooms at US$28, and inferior rooms at US$25 a night. Facilities include a dining hall, dance floor, and sea-jetty giving access to Tsonying Mahadeva island. Tourists are encouraged to visit the local nomad tents to have some experience of the daily life and the typical nomadic diet of curd, mutton, butter tea, and barley-ale (chang). Horse-riding and camel-riding activities are provided, as well as boating and shooting facilities. Khyamri village, outside the hotel, has Muslim restaurants and jewellery shops.

Tsonying Mahadeva

Colour map 5, grid A3 There are several small Gelukpa and Nyingma monasteries in the hills around the lake, but the most important religious site is on a small island in the centre, known as **Tsonying Mahadeva**, the 'heart of the lake' (*Ch* Haixin Shan). This temple, inhabited only by a handful of monks, used to be isolated for most of the year, since boats were not permitted on the lake. The monks could therefore only be reached during the three month winter period when the lake froze sufficiently deeply for it to be safely crossed.

Nowadays, the island receives regular tourboats from the *Qinghai Tented Hotel* and is occasionally visited by fishing vessels. The tour-boat has a capacity of around 60 people and costs about US$200 to hire for the day, so casual visitors must hope to be able to join a pre-existing tour. Barely an hour is spent on the hill island, but the boat continues to other rocky outcrops where colonies of birds can be found.

Khyamri to Daotonghe

Driving 15 kilometres east from Khyamri, the road reaches a fish farm, and the Kokonor fishing fleet, which is stationed near the southeast corner of the lake. After a further seven kilometres, a turn-off leads 15 kilometres north to the **Qinghai Farming Commune** on the east shore of the lake. The highway abruptly leaves Lake Kokonor for the **Daotonghe** intersection, 28 kilometres distant (see below, page 588). Northwest of Daotonghe, close to the east shore of the lake, there are two small monasteries, the most significant being **Ganden Tashi Rabgyeling**, 15 kilometres from Daotonghe, which was originally a Mongol tented monastery before becoming a branch of Jakhyung, under the guidance of the female incarnation Tulku Damdo Dolma.

Kangtsa Town

Returning from the Jadabling Bird Sanctuary north to the intersection (see above), turn right, and follow the railway line along the north shore of Lake Kokonor. The gravel road quickly turns to hard earth and mud, and the grazing pastures are of poorer quality. After 15 kilometres, the road passes through **Tsokyil** township, from where the Nyingmapa monastery of **Jokor Gon Puntsok Namgyeling** and the Gelukpa monastery of **Khotse Gonpa** are accessible to the north. Both were founded in the 1930s are currently under reconstruction. The villages after Tsokyil are bedecked with colourful prayer flags, as you negotiate the muddy road surface through to the county town.

Colour map 5, grid A3

About two kilometres before reaching town, a turn-off on the left leads inland to Kangtsa Gonchen, a branch of the Gelukpa monastery of Dzitsa in Bayan Khar county (see below, page 558). This impressive establishment, some 20 kilometres inland, is considered to be the oldest monastery in the county.

Orientation Approaching the town from Tianjun (114 kilometres distant) or the Bird Island Sanctuary (62 kilometres), the road crosses the Kangtsa river, which flows south into Lake Kokonor. A turn-off on the right, just before the bridge, leads to Kangtsa railway station (10 kilometres) and the Qinghai Agricultural Farm. After the bridge, you will pass (left): the petrol station, the leather factory, and the tax bureau, and (right): muslim restaurants, the bus station and the China Construction Bank. Then, reaching an intersection, turn left (north) for the road out of town to **Kangtsa Gonchen**, right (south) for **Dabzhi** county, or continue straight ahead for the Xinhua bookstore, the pharmacy, or primary

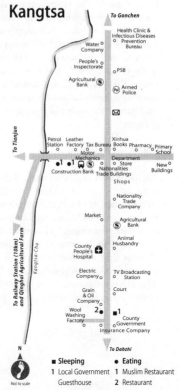

Kangtsa

To Gonchen

Health Clinic & Infectious Diseases Prevention Bureau

Water Company

People's Inspectorate

PSB

Agricultural Bank

Armed Police

To Tianjun

Petrol Station | Leather Factory | Tax Bureau

Motor Mechanics

Xinhua Books | Pharmacy | Primary School

Construction Bank

Department Store

Nationalities Trade Buildings

New Buildings

Shops

Nationality Trade Company

Market

Agricultural Bank

Animal Husbandry

County People's Hospital

To Railway Station (10km) and Qinghai Agricultural Farm

Kangtsa-Chu

Electric Company

TV Broadcasting Station

Grain & Oil Company

Court

Wool Washing Factory

County Government

Insurance Company

N

Not to scale

To Dabzhi

■ **Sleeping**
1 Local Government Guesthouse

● **Eating**
1 Muslim Restaurant
2 Restaurant

school. Taking the Gonchen Road, you will pass (left): the China Agricultural Bank, the Peoples' Inspectorate, and the Water Company, and (right): the post office, the armed police, the PSB, and a health clinic. On the Dabzhi Road, you will pass (left): shops, the Nationalities Trading Company, the China Agricultural Bank, the department of animal huisbandry, the TV and broadcasting stations, the government buildings and the Nationalities' Middle School, while to the right are: the Nationalities' Trade Building, the market, the County Peoples' Hospital, the electric company, a wool washing factory, and a newly opened restaurant.

Kangtsa
Gonchen

Kangtsa Gonchen of the Gelukpa school, is located 25 kilometres northwest of the town. Follow the east bank of the Kangtsa river upstream from town, to cross a pass (3,240 metres). The surface is rough and broken by several streams which have to be forded. After 10 kilometres a stupa is passed above the river bank on the right, and the extensive buildings of **Kangtsa Gonchung** are visible on a distant ridge above the west bank. After a further two kilometres, the small Gelukpa monastery of **Gyanyak Gonpa** comes into view in a side-valley adjacent to Kangtsa Gonchung. Then, after 11 kilometres, you will reach an intersection. Continue north for the **Chilen** region (see below, page 530) on an extremely rough surface, or turn right for Kangtsa Gonchen (two kilometres).

The monastery of **Kangtsa Gonchen Ganden Chopeling** (*Altitude*: 3,450 metres), like its sister monasteries across the valley, is a branch of Dzitsa. The **assembly hall**, approached through a cluster of stupas and *mani* wheels has a façade draped with blue and black yak hair canopies. Its portico has images of the Four Guardian Kings and an inscription outlining the history of the monastery. The central images are of Tsongkhapa and Shakyamuni, flanked by their students and the volumes of the Buddhist canon, along with Vajrasattva, Vajrapani, Padmasambhava, Maitreya, Hayagriva, and local lamas. The central throne has photographs of Dalai Lama XIV and Panchen Lama X, while the murals, in Repkong style, depict (left): Shridevi, Tara, Sarvavid Vairocana, Mahakarunika, and Guhyasamaja; and (right): Lama Chopa, Shakyamuni, Bhaisajyaguru (twice), and Six-armed Mahakala. To the left of the assembly hall, which currently houses 80 monks, there is the **Dukhar Lhakhang**, containing a large image of Sitatapatra, and the residence of Alak Shenyen.

Kangtsa to Dabzhi

The road from Kangtsa to Dabzhi (122 kilometres) runs some distance north of the lake, which is no longer visible. A pass (3,300 metres) is crossed after three kilometres, and several motorable trails lead down to the lakeside. The roadside fields are increasingly cultivated in these parts. **Har-ge** township soon comes into view, 28 kilometres from Kangtsa. From here trails lead north for 16 kilometres to the ruined Gelukpa monastery of **Pontsang Zholma Gon** and northeast for 16 kilometres to **Tashi Chokhorling**, another Gelukpa establishment, which is now undergoing reconstruction. After Har-ge, the road crosses the railway line and soon, after seven kilometres, enters Dabzhi county.

Dabzhi County མདའ་གཞི

The county of Dabzhi (Ch Haiyan) occupies the northeast shore of Lake Kokonor and in its hinterland there is the source of the Tsong-chu River, which flows through the area traditionally known as Tsongkha via Ziling city to its confluence with the Yellow River near Lanzhou.

Dabzhi County (107)
海晏县
Haiyan
Population: 38,185
Area: 4,195 sq km
Colour map 5, grid A3

The county capital is located at **Haiyan town** (Sanjiaocheng), 122 kilometres southeast of Kangtsa and 40 kilometres northwest of Tongkor (*Ch* Huangyuan). Only 13 kilometres inland from Haiyan, at **Nubtso** (*Ch* Xihai) the ghost town of China's defunct nuclear bomb factory was transformed in 1996 into the administrative capital of the North Kokonor Tibetan Autonomous Prefecture, formerly located at Mongyon.

Har-ge to Haiyan Town

Entering Dabzhi county from Kangtsa, the road crosses a long bridge, and after 10 kilometres reaches an important intersection. Both roads lead to Ziling! The sourthern approach (152 kilometres) passes through the Dabzhi county town of Haiyan and the northern one is an excellent paved road (146 kilometres), which appears on no published maps because it passes through Nubtso, the first manufacturing plant of China's nuclear arsenal! Taking the longer route, a second intersection is reached after 11 kilometres. Turn north for the mining town of **Reshui** in upper Kangtsa (68 kilometres) or continue southeast for 65 kilometres to reach Haiyan town.

On the shorter route, you quickly cross a pass (3,240 metres) and descend to the shore of **Lake Tsochung Norbu** (*Ch* Ga hai). After skirting the north shore of this lake for 28 kilometres, another pass (3,270 metres) bedecked with prayer flags is crossed, and on the descent, the ruins of the Gelukpa monastery of **Ngod Ariktang**, which was built by Rushokpa to fulfil a prophecy made by Dalai Lama III Sonam Gyatso during the 16th century, can be seen to the right. Some four kilometres south of **Qinghaihu** village, near the northeast shore of the Lake Kokonor there is the Gelukpa monastery of **Lamo Gartok Kuntu Deweiling**, a branch of Lamo Dechen Monastery in Jentsa county (see below, page 565), which was founded in 1916 and rebuilt from 1981 onwards. The

Far-east Tibet

Haiyan Town

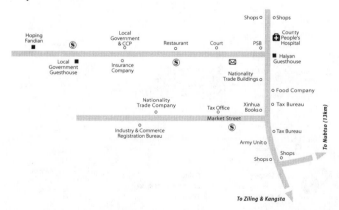

Hudong pastures by the lake shore provide excellent grazing for nomadic live-stock. Near Lamo Gartok, there is also a newly established Gelukpa monas-tery, called **Dabzhi Gonsar Namgyeling**, yet another branch of Lhamo Dechen, which was relocated in 1987 from a monastery of the same name in the **Bayan** township of adjacent Tongkor county.

Bridges now carry the railway line back and forth across the road. A brick kiln factory is passed on the left, followed by two intersections, only one kilo-metre apart. Take the left turn on both occasions, and you will arrive immedi-ately in Haiyan town.

Haiyan Town

Orientation

Altitude: 3,000 metres

Entering from the main Kangtsa and Ziling road, you will pass on the right: government tax buildings, the *Haiyan Guesthouse*, and the County Peoples' Hospital. On the left, after the PLA barracks, there is a turn-off leading into **Market Street** where banks, the Nationalities Trade Company and the *Xinhua Bookstore* are located, alongside a number of well-stocked fruit and vegetable stalls. A second turn-off on the left leads to the PSB, the post office, the local government, more banks, restaurants, and the *Peace Hotel* (*Ch* Hoping Fandian).

Nubtso

Phone code: 0970

If you turn right at the intersection before Haiyan town, you will enter the val-ley between the hills which Chinese inhabitants have named Reclining Buddha and Dragon peaks, and after 13 kilometres, you will reach **Nubtso** (*Ch* Xihai), a large surreal town of Soviet-style factories and residential buildings which was constructed during the 1950s as a manufacturing plant for China's first nuclear arsenal. The town (*Altitude*: 3,090 metres) was apparently constructed on the site of an ancient Han Dynasty military garrison, although the 18th cen-tury Gelukpa monastery of Machak Gon Ganden Puntsoling had to be destroyed to make way for a factory. The monks have more recently been relo-cated at Lamo Gartok. In 1996 this ghost town with its excellent infrastructure of paved roads was officially opened, though conspicuously absent from the maps, and it was given the status of prefectural capital of North Kokonor.

Nubtso Tsojang Prefectural Town (Xihai Zhen)

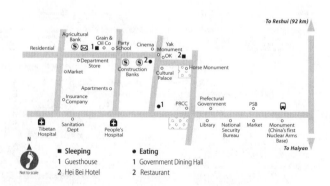

Far-east Tibet

Entering Nubtso from Haiyan, you will pass on the right a race track, where the North Kokonor inaugural horse festival was held in 1997. Continue north along this road for the mining town of **Reshui**, 92 kilometres distant, or turn left into **Main Street**. Here, on the right are the bus station, the PSB and prefectural government buildings, while on the left you will pass a monument dedicated to China's first nuclear arsenal, the market, the National Security Bureau, and the library. Reaching a crossroads, you can continue straight ahead for the Communist Party building, the Government Dining Hall, the Peoples' Hospital, Sanitation Dept and Tibetan Hospital; or else turn right for the *North Kokonor Hotel* (Heibei Binguan). Nearby this hotel, there is a large park, dominated by a horse sculpture commemorating the national unity of China, and beyond the park, there is the Cultural Palace and a number of banks, restaurants, and cinemas. Nonetheless, the population is small, and the broad, well-paved, streets, flanked by Soviet-style buildings still have the air of a desolate ghost town. One can easily imagine them filled with the throngs of factory workers who were sent here to manufacture the bomb. Radiating out from the town into the hinterland there is a complex network of paved roads, some leading to factory buildings, others into solid rock, or underground bunkers! Industrial workers, engineers and scientists were once bussed from nondescript apartment buildings to their respective work sites, but tight security ensured that very few personnel had access to the whole labyrinth.

C *North Kokonor Hotel*, T(0970)642648. Standard rooms, with attached bathrooms, but no hot running water, at ¥80 per room. There are cheaper rooms, ranging from ¥8-¥25 per bed, and suites or VIP rooms (also without hot running water!), ranging from ¥120-¥888.

Try the street restaurants, adjacent to the park.

Dabzhi to Reshui and Chilen

The road north from Nubtso to **Reshui** (98 kilometres) initially passes through the outlying factories of this former nuclear manufacturing zone. Air raid shelters are now used as donkey stables! After 25 kilometres, it crosses a pass (3,390 metres), on both sides of which there are excellent grasslands for sheep. Descending from the pass, after nine kilometres, an intersection is reached. Turn left for Haiyan town, continue straight ahead for Kangtsa, or turn right for Reshui. Heading towards Reshui, the road re-enters Kangtsa county, and begins its gradual ascent towards the **Chokle Namgyel** (Chilen) range. Many trucks pass by, weighed down with coal from the Reshui mines, and after 45 kilometres the paved surface gives way to an old familiar dirt road. The distant snowline now comes into view, and the Reshui branch railway line is crossed on the way into town. After following this dirt road for 16 kilo-

Dabzhi County

metres, you will arrive at **Reshui** (*Altitude*: 3,510 metres), a drab mining town, where several side roads lead directly to the pits. Continuing uphill, north out of town, after 10 kilometres the road surface becomes extremely rough. An intersection now looms: turn left for the Jiangcu coal mine (97 kilometres) or right for Chilen (104 kilometres).

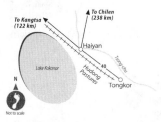

Far-east Tibet

Taking the latter route, you drive through pastures where yaks are grazing, and a pass (3,810 metres) is crossed after 4 kilometres, leading downhill for 17 kilometres to the upper reaches of the Julak-chu. Crossing the river, the road forks yet again, a rough track heading north-east for Chilen (82 kilometres) and a better surface leading east to **Mo-le** township (10 kilometres). The Chilen road follows a tributary of the Julak-chu upstream into the Chokle Namgyel range, crossing five passes and frozen streams. The highest of these passes (4,050 metres) forms a watershed between the Julak-chu and a tributary of the Rui Shui, which flows northwards through Gansu and Inner Mongolia. The snowline is low, and the road is often impassable, even in April. Buses also run from Ziling to this remote border area.

Chilen County ཆེ་འཉེན

Chilen County (114)
祁连县
Qilian
Population: 42,392
Area: 13,575 sq km
Colour map 5, grid A3

Chilen county lies across the watershed, deep within the Chokle Namgyel range, and is administered nowadays from Nubtso, within the North Kokonor Autonomous Prefecture. This is a culturally diverse region, and prior to 1958 there were six Gelukpa monasteries in the county, which have all been permitted to reopen in recent years. The largest and most renowned among them is Arik Gon Ganden Chopeling. The county town, which derives its name from the Chinese name for the Chokle Namgyel Mountains, is 170 kilometres north-west of Mongyon, and 212 kilometres from Nubtso. Buses also run from Ziling to this remote border area.

Chilen has been identified with the ancient kingdom of **Bhatahor**, from which the Tibetan imperial armies acquired Shingjachen, a sacred bird-image of the protector deity Pehar, during the eighth century.

Reshui to Chilen

After crossing the watershed from Reshui (see above), the road enters a deep glacial gorge. The tree line begins at 3,360 metres after 16 kilometres, and soon red sandstone cliffs appear, but the upper reaches of the valley are still dominated by the snow peaks of the **West Chokle Namgyel**. Tibetan nomadic camper groups pitch their tents amid the evergreens. The first village is bypassed after a further 11 kilometres, decorated with a small mosque in Chinese style. Then, following the river downstream, after five kilometres, the road reaches an intersection at the outskirts of **Chilen** town. Turn left for the defunct monastery of **Huangzangsi** (eight kilometres), which is now a mosque, or left for the town, which is only two kilometres distant.

Mongyen & Chilen Counties

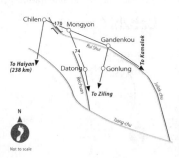

Chilen

Altitude: 2,760 metres
Phone code: 09846
Colour map 5, A3

Chilen town is a picturesque alpine settlement, overlooked by the high snow peaks of the West Chokle Namgyel range. A bridge spans a small tributary of the Hei River and leads into the long main street. Here, there are shops, banks, guesthouses, and the bus station, as well as the usual government buildings, police station, and hospitals. The population is predominantly Muslim, but there are also Mongols, Tibetans and Chinese traders in the marketplace.

Sleeping C *Baboa Hotel*, T(09846) 672547. Standard rooms (¥22 per bed) and single rooms (¥30 per bed). There are also 4 guesthouses in town.

Eating The best and newest restaurant, offering local seafood and standard Chinese and Muslim dishes, appears to be the **C** *Yue Lai Shun Restaurant*, T(09846) 672368, also on Main Street.

Arik Gonchen

Heading southeast from Chilen, along a dusty road, you ascend gradually into the alpine forest, with the high snow peaks to the south. After 11 kilometres the road crosses a pass (3,000 metres) and on the descent it bifurcates. Turn left for **Ebao** (52 kilometres) or right for **Xiaobao** (18 kilometres). Taking the former road, the valley soon widens and the monastery of **Arik Gonchen Ganden Chopeling** is reached after seven kilometres on the high ground to the left.

Chilen Town

This isolated Gelukpa monastery was constructed during the 17th century by the Arik mongols of Sogwo county (Henan), to commemorate the site where both Dalai Lama III and Dalai Lama V had sojourned. There is a protector shrine room and to its rear, approached via an ornate gateway, an **assembly hall** with a trilingual inscription above the door. Inside the latter, the throne has photographs of the late Panchen Lama X and Lama Gari, who currently presides over the monastery's 40 monks from his residence at Nubtso. The murals, which are in Repkong style, depict (left): Amnye Nyizang, Shridevi, Vaishravana, Mahakarunika, Sarvavid Vairocana, Tara and Guhyasamaja; along with (right): Shakyamuni, Lama Chopa, the Thirty-three Confession Buddhas, Bhaisajyaguru, two local protectors, Dharmaraja, and Dorje Lekpa. Along the innermost wall are reliquaries containing the remains of Arik Dorje Chang of Repkong and other lamas, as well as a full set of the *Kanjur*, and images of Vajrabhairava, Shakyamuni, Manjughosa, and Vajrasattva in union with consort.

Ebao

After Arik, the road continues to follow the north side of the West Chokle

Far-east Tibet

Namgyel range through excellent grazing pastures which sustain large herds of yak. A small temple and the ruins of **Demang Ganden Samtenling** monastery (founded 1940s) are passed on the left. Ebao township, dominated by a bizarre mock castle, is eventually reached after 45 kilometres. Here the paved road begins, and there is an important intersection. Head north on highway 227 for Zhangye and **Dunhuang** in Gansu, or left for **Mongyon** and Ziling. Taking the latter route, the valley soon narrows into a gorge, with snow peaks rising both to the south and the north. The watershed pass (3,720 metres) is reached 24 kilometres after Ebao, and at this point the road enters Mongyon county.

Mongyon Hui Autonomous County མོང་ཡོན

Mongyon Hui AC (113)
门源回族自治县
Menyuan
Population: 138,284
Area: 5,497 sq km
Colour map 5, grid A4

*Mongyon county occupies the mid-reaches of the **Julak-chu**, which converges with the Tsong-chu at Minhe, after flowing through a gorge between the East Chokle Namgyel range to the north and Mount Dawa to the south. Further north lie the Gansu corridor and Mongolia, so this is truly the northeast extremity of Amdo. Mongyon county, which occupies much of the Julak-chu valley, was until 1996 the prefectural capital of North Kokonor. Its county town is located 74 kilometres north of Datong in **Serkhok**, and it is largely an area populated by Muslims. There are, however, isolated Gelukpa monasteries, located southeast of the county town, on or near the north bank of the Julak-chu.*

Ebao to Mongyon

Crossing the watershed from Ebao in Chilen county, the road re-enters the Julak-chu valley. The streams here are frozen, even in May, but the road surface is excellent. Gold dredging machines can be seen at work in this area. A second pass (3,420 metres) is crossed after 25 kilometres, and the only inhabitants of this snowbound terrain are a few groups of hardy Tibetan nomads. On its descent the road enters the Julak-chu valley, following the north bank of the

Mongyon Town

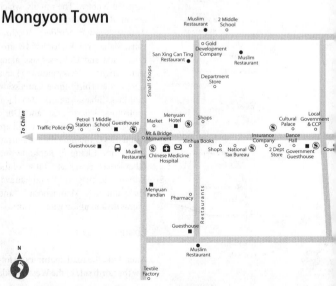

river down to **Qingshizui** township (32 kilometres), where it forks: the high-way on the right leading to **Ziling** (132 kilometres) and the branch road to the left leading into **Mongyon** (20 kilometres). **NB** The highway to Ziling is currently impassable due to the construction of a long tunnel, which, on its completion, will reduce the distance to Ziling by approximately 100 kilometres. Taking the potholed branch road into Mongyon, you cross to the south bank of the Julak-chu.

Mongyon Town

The county town is still coming to terms with its much diminished status, following the recent move of the prefectural government to Nubtso. Many large official buildings appear to be empty and unused. Entering **Main Street** from the Chilen/Ebao road, you will pass two guesthouses and the bus station, before reaching a roundabout. Continuing on Main Street, the *Mongyon Hotel* is on the left with the post office and Chinese Medicine Hospital on the right. Turning right or left at the next crossroads, you will find some good inexpensive Muslim restaurants, alongside the offices of the Gold Development Company. If you continue straight ahead, via the next block which houses local government buildings, banks and insurance offices, you will reach the Serkhok road.

Altitude: 2,880 metres
Phone code: 0978

Sleeping C *Menyuan Hotel*, T(0978)612226. Standard rooms (¥120 per room, ¥28 per bed). There are also 3 guesthouses located on Main St.

Eating For Chinese food, try the **C** *San Xing Can Ting Restaurant*, situated behind the *Menyuan Hotel*, or else sample the local Muslim dishes at one of the many small Muslim eateries.

Transport Public buses run from Ziling via Datong into the Mongyon area.

Mongyon to Kamalok

Three roads lead from Mongyon to Ziling. Among them, the high road (via **Ebao**) will remain closed until the completion of a new tunnel. The low road passes through **Gonlung** (see below, page 547), and the middle road crosses **Mount Dawa** to reach the **Serkhok** valley. Taking the middle road, you continue following the Julak-chu downstream through a well-cultivated valley. The snowline is noticeably low on both the East Chokle Namgyel range to the north and Mount Dawa to the south. After 18 kilometres, the road reaches an intersection at **Shengli**. Continue heading southeast for **Julak** (*Ch* Minhe) and **Gonlung**, or turn right for **Serkhok**.

If you continue in the direction of Julak, after 28 kilometres you will reach the T-junction at Serkhok-chu Bridge. Turn right (south) for Julak

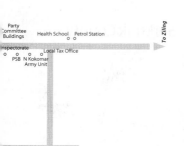

Party
Committee
Buildings   Health School   Petrol Station
                                o o
nspectorate
   o   o   o   Local Tax Office
     PSB N Kokomar
         Army Unit

To Ziling

Far-east Tibet

and Gonlung or left (north) to reach **Semnyi** (Xianmi) township. Taking the latter option, you may visit the Gelukpa monasteries of **Drugu Gon Ganden Chokhorling** (founded 1644), **Semnyi Gon Ganden Dargyeling**, which was founded in 1623 by a monk from Yerpa near Lhasa, and **Bengyu Gon Mindrol Tosam Dargyeling**, which was founded circa 1607-82. If you turn right (south) at the bridge, you will pass the turn-off for Gonlung (see below, page 547) after 69 kilometres at Gandenkou. The Kamalok county border lies some 42 kilometres southeast of here in the lower Julak-chu valley.

Mongyon to Serkhok via Mount Dawa

Taking the middle road to **Ziling** from Mongyon, the road leaves the Mongyon-Julak road at the **Shengli** intersection, crossing the **Julak-chu** (*Altitude*: 2,700 metres), and then follows the course of a tributary upstream through Muslim villages and verdant hills towards the snowline. On the ascent of Mount Dawa, there are wonderful views of the jagged East Chokle Namgyel peaks to the north and the Gansu corridor beyond. Three passes are crossed in quick succession, but driving can be hazardous owing to ice and snow. The snowline is reached at 3,120 metres and the watershed at **Dawa La** pass (3,960 metres), 25 kilometres from the intersection, is frequently shrouded in mist and swept by hailstones.

Serkhok County གསེར་ཁོག

Serkhok County (112)
大通县
Datong
Population: 389,371
Area: 2,945 sq km
Colour map 5, grid A4

*The **Serkhok** valley (Ch Beichuan) extends from the watershed pass on Mount Dawa to the river's confluence with the Tsong-chu at Ziling. The county capital, **Datong**, is an industrial city, situated 39 kilometres north of Ziling. Formerly, there were eight Gelukpa monasteries in Serkhok, of which three have been reopened in recent years. The largest and most renowned among them is **Tsenpo Gon**. **Minyag Hermitage** is under the authority of Kumbum Jampaling, while **Ganden Rinchenling** is a branch of Gonlung Monastery.*

Upper Serkhok Valley

The descent into the **Serkhok-chu** valley from **Dawa La** pass is made on a treacherous muddy road surface. Nomads can be seen herding sheep across the hillsides. Gradually, the tree line appears, followed by small hamlets and cultivated fields. Then, some 23 kilometres below the pass, the dirt road comes to an abrupt end, and a paved road leading to **Datong** and **Ziling** begins.

Tsenpo Gon

The principal monastery of the county is **Tsenpo Gon Ganden Damcholing** (*Ch* Guanhuasi), which was founded in the Serkhok area in 1649 by Tsenpo Dondrub Gyatso, an abbot of Gonlung. Later, it became the seat of the Mindrol Nomenqan incarnations. The site is located 32 kilometres below Dawa La pass and six kilometres below Zhanghua township, along a narrow track to the

Serkhok County

To Mongyon
(74 km)
Datong
Beichuan River
39
To Gonlung
(44 km)
To Tongkor
(40 km)
N
Ziling
To Airport
(29 km)
Not to scale

west of the road. Only two temples still stand within its courtyard: the **Jokhang**, which has elegant door panels and a Chinese inscription donated by Emperor Qianlong above the door, and the **Protector Shrine**. The former contains images of Tsongkhapa with his students and Jowo Shakyamuni, and an inscription and seal offered by Panchen Lama IX, while the murals depict the 1,000 buddhas of the aeon. Behind the Jokhang, there are extensive ruins. Currently there are 30 monks and two incarnate lamas at Tsenpo Gon, which appears as a highly sinicized enclave within a Muslim dominated valley.

Datong

The large city of **Datong** lies only 19 kilometres south of Tsenpo Gon, in the lower reaches of the valley. This is a polluted, heavy industrial zone, with a large aluminium smelting plant, cement factory, and power station. To the east of town, on **Mount Laoye Shan** (Old Grandfather Mountain), the Flower Song Festival (*Ch* Huarhui) is held by the **Tu** nationality each year on the sixth day of the sixth lunar month. Song, dance, and serious drinking take place against the backdrop of a brisk trade fair. Festival dates are 28-30 July, 1998 and 18-20 July, 1999. Driving south from Datong, the road crosses the Ziling-Datong railway line after five kilometres, and from here the provincial capital is only 28 kilometres distant.

Phone code: 09811

Colour map 5, grid A4

Tongkor County སྟོང་སྐོར་

*The county of **Tongkor**, which occupies the upper reaches of the Tsong-chu valley and the east shore of Lake Kokonor, nowadays belongs to the East Kokonor Prefecture, governed from Ziling. The county capital, **Tongkor**, is 40 kilometres equidistant between Dabzhi in the northwest and Ziling City in the southeast.*

Tongkor County (108)
湟源县
Huangyuan
Population: 127,083
Area: 1,293 sq km
Colour map 5, grid A4

Dabzhi to Tongkor

The road from Haiyan town in Dabzhi to Tongkor follows the banks of the **Tsong-chu** downstream. It passes through **Bayan** township, where two monasteries were once sited. **Gonpa Soma** is now derelict, its monks having been relocated at Dabzhi Gonsar Namgyeling (see above, page 528). **Dratsang Gon Ganden Chokhorling**, which was built to commemorate the visit of Dalai Lama III in 1578, formerly housed the sword and armour of the Mongol king Gushi Qan and a precious trilingual *Kanjur*. It is an important monastery for the Mongol tribes and has undergone reconstruction since 1984. Driving on from Bayan, after 15 kilometres, you will reach **Tongkor**. The ruins of **Ladrol-ne Gonpa** and **Rali Hermitage** are passed en route near **Dahua** township.

Tongkor Town

For centuries, this has been an important trading post for the Mongols and Tibetans of Kokonor. Abbé Huc joined a large caravan to Lhasa here in the 1860s, and noted how, even then, the Chinese were 'encroaching on the desert, building houses, and bringing into cultivation portions of the land of grass'. 30 years later, Dr Susie Rijnhart witnessed the second major Muslim rebellion when almost 10,000 Muslims were massacred in the town by a combined force of local Tibetans and the Chinese army sent from Lanzhou. Just to the northwest of town are the ruins of **Ganden Tengyeling** (*Ch* Cinghosi), which was

Colour map 5, grid A4

founded as a branch of Tongkor Monastery in 1783.

Here in Tongkor, the rail/road links to the north of Lake Kokonor connect with the Lhasa-Ziling highway (Route 109) from the south.

Tongkor Gonpa

Colour map 5, grid A4

Following the highway southwest from town, you will pass through several small Chinese farming villages. Then, about 30 kilometres from the town, you will reach the ruins of **Tongkor Gonpa**, **Ganden Chokhorling**, which was founded by Tongkor IV, Yonten Gyatso in 1648. This was formerly the largest monastery in the county, and an American visitor, WW Rockhill, noted that it housed 500 monks at the turn of the century. A few kilometres further on, the tarmac road splits, with the west branch leading over the famous **Nyima Dawa La** ('sun-moon') pass, and the east branch leading to **Trika** county (see below, page 579).

Nyima Dawa La Pass

The **Nyima Dawa La** pass (3,399 metres), situated 38 kilometres south of Tongkor, was made famous when Princess Wengcheng, en route for Tibet to marry King Songtsen Gampo in the seventh century, looked in a magic mirror with a sun-moon design, which was supposed to show her family home in Changan (modern Xi'an). On seeing only her own reflection, the princess smashed the mirror in despair. The river near the pass, unusually flowing from east to west, is said to be formed from the princess' tears as she continued on her journey to meet Songsten Gampo. Nowadays, two small concrete temples have been constructed on the pass, and the murals are modern, depicting nomad life and the royal couple. A Flower Song Festival (*Ch Huarhui*) is held here every summer around the sixth day of the sixth lunar month, which in 1998 will coincide with July 28-30, and in 1999 with July 18-20. On the far side of the pass, the road descends into Chabcha county (see below, page 588).

Tongkor County

Tongkor to Ziling

Driving east from Tongkor on Highway 109 the road follows the north bank of the Tsang-chu downstream to Ziling. On this 40 kilometres stretch, it bypasses the Chinese townships of **Zhama, Duoba, Hezui,** and **Mafang**.

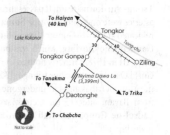

Ziling City ཟི་ལིང་

Ziling (Ch Xining) is the capital of Qinghai province, located at 2,200 metres on the edge of the Tibetan plateau, in a wide section of the **Tsong-chu** valley, where the **Serkhok-chu** (Ch Beichuan) River joins from the northwest. The valley floors are well irrigated into a patchwork of fields and trees but the hills nearby are barren, affording only poor grazing. Most heavy industry is located further north in Serkhok (Ch Datong), which also possesses a coal mine, but Ziling itself is largely a residential and market town. The population of Ziling is mostly Muslim (25 per cent), Chinese, Mongol or Tu, and very few Tibetans live in the town itself. It has, however, become an important centre for Tibetan Studies. The Tibetan Nationalities College, the Tsongon Publishing House, and the Gesar Research Institute are in the vanguard of this movement. Ziling has a mean January temperature of -7° (minimum -27°), and a mean July temperature of 18° (maximum 34°). The annual precipitation is 366 millimetres (mostly in summer), and there is little winter precipitation.

Ziling City (109)
西宁市
Xining Shiqu
Population: 697,784
Area: 430 sq km
Phone code: 0971
Colour map 5, grid A4

The distance from Ziling to Tongkor is 40 kilometres, to Repkong 185 kilometres, to Gonlung (Huzhu) 41 kilometres, to Serkhok (Datong) 39 kilometres, and to Lanzhou 280 kilometres.

Getting there

The city developed on the basis of trade between China and Persia, linking with the famous Silk Route to the north. Buddhist pilgrims such as Fa Xian passed this way en route for India, and both the Han and North Wei Dynasties sponsored the construction of Chinese-style Buddhist and Daoist temples. Tibetan influence increased following the consolidation of the Yarlung Empire in the seventh century, and during the ninth century it was here that the three ordained monks from Central Tibet passed away, having fled the persecution of the apostate king Langdarma. Later, there were influxes of Mongol, Tu, and Muslim groups. Muslim migrants from Central Asia gradually became the dominant sector of the population; and from 1860 onwards, successive uprisings among the Muslims resulted in the destruction of many old settlements in the region. Even Kumbum Monastery itself was badly damaged. The Chinese, calling on their Tu and Tibetan allies, managed to suppress each insurrection with great loss of life, and for decades Muslims were not allowed to reside within the walled city of Ziling. However, by the 1930s, Muslim warlords, in agreement with the Nationalists, once again controlled the entire valley down to the Yellow River.

History

The Tibetans, to whom the region is known as Tsongkha, largely continued to govern their own affairs, but were forced to allow Muslim trade as far south to Jyekundo. The Mongols were concentrated in outlying parts of Kokonor, Tsaidam and the Kunlun mountains, and were organized into banners or districts, which owed only nominal allegiance to the Ziling *amban* and Muslim government. In recent years there has been an increasing influx of Chinese immigrants from Nanjing in Southeast China.

Approaching Ziling city from Tongkor (*Ch* Huangyuan), the road, known as **Qilian Street**, follows the railway and the Tsong-chu River (*Ch* Huangshui) on the north bank and crosses the Beichuan tributary, just upstream from its confluence with the Tsong-chu. **Renmin Park** lies to the south overlooking the confluence. Soon the road passes a turn-off (**Chaoyang Donglu**) which heads north out of town for Serkhok and the Datong branch railway. The Daoist temple of **Beishan** is located 45 minutes walking distance up the mountainside to the

Orientation

Far-east Tibet

north of the road. Continue east along Qilian Street, following the north bank of the Tsong-chu, to reach the main **Xining Railway Station**.

Four bridges span the Tsong-chu within the city: the westernmost bridge leads into the west part of town. Here, Xining Street, Tongren Street, and Huanghe Street all run north-south and the lateral roads known as Shengli Street, Wusi Street, Xiguan Street, and Kunlun Street bisect them on an east-west axis. **Tongren Street**, in particular, leads south out of town in the direction of Repkong. **Huanghe Street** runs parallel to the west bank of the north-flowing Nanchuan River. **Erlang Park** in the south of the city can be reached via either Tongren Street or Huangehe Street. The city's best hotel, *Qinghai Hotel*, is located beside the grounds of the park.

Three bridges span the Nanchuan River, leading into the commercial and administrative heart of Ziling. All three of them link up with **Changjiang Street** on the east bank of the Nanchuan, which extends all the way from Qilian Street (on the north bank of the Tsong-chu) to the south end of town. The **West Gate Bus Station** (Ximen) is located on this street.

At the city centre is the **Da Shizi** (Great Cross) intersection, alongside the Xining Sports' Stadium and the provincial government buildings. The old city which lies to the east of Changjiang Street, contains the municipality buildings, the open-air market (one of the most interesting in China), and the **Post Office**.

The municipality buildings on **Xida Street** (west of Da Shizi), in particular were constructed on the site of a 13th century Buddhist temple, built to commemorate the place where Mar Shakyamuni and his two colleagues maintained the Tibetan monastic tradition and finally passed away, during the

Ziling

Sleeping
1 Qinghai Hotel & CAAC
2 Xining Dasha
3 Xining Hotel
4 Yongfu Hotel

Eating
1 Muslim Restaurant
2 Peace Restaurant

Buses
1 Long Distance Station
2 Ximen Bus Station

Far-east Tibet

persecution of Buddhism in Central Tibet by Langdarma. Formerly it contained exquisite images of the three great monks. The temple, known in Chinese as **Dafusi**, was levelled to make way for the government offices, but one small section was rebuilt in the mid-1980s, and further rebuilding is being carried out at the site. It is only a few hundred metres west of the main Post Office. None of the other three Tibetan Buddhist temples of Ziling survive at the present day. Among these, Hongjuesi which was founded in 1390, and Jintasi, which was a branch of Kumbum Jampaling, were formerly located further south on **Hongjuesi Street**, while the Tu nationality monastery of Cangjinsi, founded in 1412, was situated to the west of **Nanda Street**.

North from the main Post Office on Beida Street lies the **Public Security Bureau** and at the head of the same road, the *Xining Hotel*.

The **Bank of China** lies further east on Dongguan Street in the Muslim quarter. The **Great Mosque**, built originally in the 14th century, is one of the largest in the region; and there are a number of excellent small Muslim restaurants. From here, follow **Jianguo Street** northeast to cross the Tsong-chu at the entrance to the main **Xining Railway Station**. The long-distance bus station is located just before the bridge on the right (east) side of the road. The *Yongfu Hotel* is on the opposite side of the road. From the railway station follow Qilian Street out of town (north) in the direction of Gonlung (Huzhu) county; or follow Bayi Street southeast in the direction of Lanzhou.

The *Qinghai Institute for Nationalities* has an interesting exhibition hall; also the *Qinhgai Provincial Museum* houses some of the province's greatest archaeological treasures, including ancient Persian and Chinese artefacts, as well as Buddhist manuscripts.   **Museums**

Sleeping
■ *on map, page 538*
Price codes:
see inside front cover

A *Qinghai Hotel (Qinghai Binguan)*, 20 Huanghe Rd, T(0971)6144888, F(86971)6144145. A 3-star hotel with 395 rooms, the best in town, with attached bath (range: US$30-59 per double room and US$61-850 per suite), but some distance from city centre in Erlang Park. There is an excellent Chinese restaurant on the 2nd Floor, and a lobby bar cum coffee shop. CAAC airline office is located on the 1st Floor. Also tour agencies, excellent shopping arcades, business centre, hairdressing and massage service. The karaoke bar and dance hall are located to the rear on the ground floor. **B** *Xining Hotel*, T(0971)8238701. Located 5 kilometres west of the railway station. A Russian-style building with double rooms (range: ¥120-¥280), and triples (¥35 per bed). It has attached bathrooms (be careful not to stub your toes on the bathroom door threshold!). The hotel restaurant serves excellent hotpot. **C** *Yongfu Hotel*, on Jianguo St near railway station, has best value. Double rooms at ¥50, with attached bathrooms and good hot water supply, and a coffee shop. **D** *Xining Mansion* (Xining Dasha), T(0971)8149991. On the corner of Jianguo St and Dongguan Dajie, in Muslim quarter, 10 minutes walking distance from railway station, has standard rooms (range: ¥56-¥162), singles (range: ¥181-239), and triples (¥165 per room).

Eating

Among the major hotels, the *Qinghai Hotel* is expensive, but offers excellent Chinese cuisine and adequate service. The restaurant of the *Xining Hotel* offers an excellent Mongolian hotpot.

Nearby the *Qinghai Hotel*, there are reasonably priced local Chinese restaurants of good quality, and in *Wenhua Jie Meishi Cheng*, there are a number of plush restaurants offering a wide range of high-class cuisine, including seafood, Korean barbecue, and spicy Hunan dishes. Ziling also has many simple street restaurants, of which the cheapest are in the open-air market area near the **West Gate Bus Station** and the kebab stalls in the Muslim quarter. For good inexpensive Chinese food, try the *Peace Restaurant*. For excellent Muslim food, try the *Muslim Restaurant*, on the corner of

Far-east Tibet

Jianguo St and Dongguan Dajie, for noodle dishes, try the restaurant run by the *Yongfu Hotel*, near the railway station, and for local mutton specialities, try the **Zhuang Guo Yang Gao Rou** restaurant, opposite the petrol station on the Pingan road.

Entertainment Ziling has the usual turbid nightlife of provincial or frontier towns. The main forms of entertainment are karaoke, disco, and cinema – all located in the downtown area near Da Shizi, or in the major hotels. In all, the city has more than 7 theatres and cinemas.

Festivals The **Spring Festival** (*Ch* Chunjie) is held on the 1st day of the 1st month of the lunar calendar; and the **Flower Song Festival** (*Ch* Huarhui) on the 6th day of the 6th month. For the 1998 dates of certain traditional Tibetan festivals, see above, Essentials, page 26.

Shopping The large open-air market near the West Gate Bus Station on Changjiang St, has handicraft stalls selling crystal salt carvings and Kunlun jade products, bookshops, traditional medicines, dried fruit, *babao* tea, and meat and vegetable markets, as well as textiles of great variety. **NB** Pickpockets are rampant! For luxury items, including the hugely popular yak wool sweaters made in the Repkong area, try the shopping arcade in the *Qinghai Hotel*. A visit to the carpet factory is also worthwhile.

Photography Print film and processing are available at photographic shops in town and in the larger hotels.

Stamps Stamps are available at **GPO**, on Dongda St, and also at the reception counters or shops in the major hotels.

Sport **Mountaineering:** *Qinghai Mountaineering Association*, 1 Shan Shaan Tai, Xining 810000, T0971-8238877, F0086-9718238933.

Transport **Air** Ziling is connected to Beijing, Shanghai, Guangzhou, Chongqing, Chengdu, Xi'an, Kermo, Lhasa and other cities. The airport lies 29 kilometres east of town on the north bank of the Tsong-chu River.

Road Buses run throughout Qinghai province to and from Kermo (Golmud), Repkong, Lanzhou, Mato, and the Xinjiang border. Long-distance buses leave from the *Main Bus Station* near the railway station (see schedule), and in addition there are frequent buses departing throughout the day for all county towns in East Kokonor prefecture, including Tongkor, Rushar, Serkhok, Gonlung, Tsongkha Khar, Drotsang and Minhe; while local buses leave from the *West Gate (Ximen) Bus Station*. Minibuses and landcoasters can be hired (with driver) from CITS. Some bus fares from Ziling: Tsongkha Khar (Pingan) ¥4.10; Gonlung (Huzhu) ¥4.80; Drotsang (Ledu) ¥6.70; Dowi (Xunhua) ¥16.50; Minhe ¥11.40; Tongkor (Huangyuan) ¥5.50; Bayan Khar (Hualong) ¥12; Daotonghe ¥10.50; Tanakma (Hemahe) ¥21; Tsaka (Chaka) ¥28.30; Shang (Xiang Ride) ¥47; Nomahung (Nuomuhong) ¥102.60; Kangtsa (Gangca) ¥19.10; Longyang Xia Dam ¥14.60; Padma (Baima) ¥81; Trika (Guide) ¥12.50; Tsogyenrawa (Huashixia) ¥63.30; Mato (Maduo) ¥75.30; Dabzhi (Haiyan) ¥8.70; Zhiwu (Xiewu) ¥117; and Yeniugou ¥55.60. For other destinations, please consult the table.
Ziling long-distance bus station information office: T8149690.

Taxi T6142393.

Train There are frequent train connections to Lanzhou (4½ hours); as well as to Beijing, Shanghai, Qingdao, Xi'an, and Kermo (both afternoon express, and morning local services).
Railway station automatic answerphone: T8149970.

Far-east Tibet

Qinghai and Gansu Provincial Railway Schedules

Train No	Depart	Time	Arrival	Time	Hard seat	Soft seat	Hard Sleeper	Soft Sleeper
Y201	Lanzhou	1516	Ziling	1903	¥17	¥29	N/A	N/A
Y202	Ziling	0800	Lanzhou	1130	¥17	¥29	N/A	N/A
Y203	Yinchuan	2145	Ziling	1200	¥51	¥87	¥108	¥168
Y204	Ziling	1815	Yinchuan	0720	¥51	¥87	¥108	¥168
T75	Beijing	0850	Ziling	1723	¥133	¥226	¥264	¥417
T76	Ziling	0849	Beijing	1653	¥133	¥226	¥264	¥417
T575	Xi'an	1922	Ziling	1530	¥64	¥110	¥133	¥208
T576	Ziling	1758	Xi'an	1457	¥64	¥110	¥133	¥208
T603	Ziling	1830	Kermo	1200	¥62	¥106	¥129	¥201
T604	Kermo	1430	Ziling	0746	¥62	¥106	¥129	¥201

Qinghai Regional Long Distance Bus Schedule from Ziling Bus Station

Destination	Schedule	Information	Price
Mangra (Guinan)	0830-0930	2 buses daily	¥28.00
Kawasumdo (Tongde)	0800-0830	2 buses daily	¥41.30
Machen (Dawu)	0845	1 bus daily	¥70.70
Sogwo (Henan)	0715	1 bus daily	¥30.90
Repkong (Tongren)	0730-1200	7 buses daily	¥18.40
Jentsa (Jianzai)	0845-1530	3 buses daily	¥12.70
Chilen (Qilian)	0815-0930	2 buses daily	¥26.00
Linxia	0730-0830	3 buses daily	¥25.00
Ganlho Dzong (Hezuo)	0715	1 bus daily	¥32.80
Monyon (Menyuan)	0745-1300	5 buses daily	¥16.00
Zhangye	0730-0845	2 buses daily	¥33.70
Wuwei	0715-0900	2 buses daily	¥35.00
Lijiaxia	0720-1615	30 buses daily	¥11.80
Lanzhou	0800-1600	14 buses daily	¥29.10
Bongtak Tianjun	0745	1 bus every other day	¥31.00
Lhasa	1600	1 bus daily	¥300.00
Delingha	1600	1 bus every other day	¥50.00
Da Tsaidam	0715	1 bus every other day	¥69.40
Panchen Zhingde (Dulan)	1730	1 bus daily	¥40.60
Ulan	0745	1 bus every other day	¥36.20
Kermo (Golmud)	1600	3 buses daily	¥72.50
Chabcha (Gonghe)	0800	2 buses daily	¥23.00
Tsigortang (Xinghai)	0800-1015	2 buses every other day	¥26.40
Darlag (Dari)	1015	2nd, 5th, 8th, 12th, 15th, 18th, 22nd, 25th, 28th of each month	¥62.20
Jyekundo (Yushu)	1100-1300	2 buses daily	¥85.90

Far-east Tibet

Airline offices *Minghang Flight Ticket Centre*, 85/1, Bayi St, T(0971)8174616. Books flights to **Directory**
Golmud, Xi'an, Chengdu, Chongqing, Guangzhou, Beijing, Shanghai, Shenyang, Ururnqi, and
Wuhan. *CAAC*, *Qinghai Hotel*, 1st Flr, also has a flight booking service. **Banks** *Bank of China*,
Dongguan Dajie. Exchange facilities are also available at the *Qinghai Hotel*, and *Xining Hotel*, while
credit card payments are accepted at the *Qinghai Hotel*. **Communications** General Post Office:
Beida St. Postal facilities also available in major hotels. **Fax:** *Qinghai Hotel Business Centre, Xining
Hotel Business Centre.* **Hospitals & medical services** *Peoples' Hospital*, Gonghe St. **Tour**

companies & travel agents *China International Travel Service: Ziling Branch (CITS)*, 156 Huanghe Rd, T(0971)6143950, F(0086)9716131080/8238721. *Beijing Longmen International Tours*, A9 Daquideng Lane, Meishuguan Houjie East District, Beijing, T(010)84010085, F(0086)10-64012180. *Qinghai International Sports Travel Service (QIST)*, 1 Shan Shaan Tai, Xining 810000, T(0971)8238877, F(0086)9718238933. **Tourist offices** *Qinghai Tourist Corporation (QTC)*, *Qinghai Hotel*, 156 Huanghe Rd, T(0971)6143711, F(0086)9718238721. **Useful addresses and telephone numbers** Police and Public Security: *Foreigners Registration Office*, Beida St, north of post office. Lost or stolen property: T110. Automatic weather forecast: T6145121. Traffic accident unit: T6146027.

Rushar County ᠌᠌

Rushar County (110)
湟中县
Huangzhong
Population: 427,530
Area: 2,488 sq km
Colour map 5, grid A4

*The county of Rushar (Ch Huangzhong) lies 26 kilometres southwest of Ziling city; only a 40 minute bus ride away. The county capital, **Huangzhong**, is a town dominated by Muslim traders, and much of the countryside around consists of Chinese farming villages. Prior to 1950 there were 29 Tibetan monasteries, temples and hermitages of the Gelukpa school within Rushar, the largest and best known being **Kumbum Jampaling**. Nowadays three of these have reopened with official permission, and eight have done so privately. The remainder are in ruins. Among them, **Ame Zhidak Lhakhang** lies one kilometre south of Kumbum, **Chesho Ritro Samtenling**, a small branch of Kumbum Jampaling, lies 28 kilometres southeast of the county town, while to the northwest are **Zurgyi Chokhang** (18 kilometres) which contains revered relics of Tsongkhapa, **Lasar Gonchung** (27 kilometres), and **Sertok Gon** (43 kilometres).*

Kumbum Jampaling Monastery

History At **Rushar Drongdal**, the county boasts the most renowned monastery in Tsongkha, and one of the greatest in all Tibet: that of **Kumbum Jampaling** (*Ch* Taersi), which was founded to commemorate the birthplace of Tsongkhapa in 1560 by Rinchen Tsondru Gyeltsen. The monastery is built around the tree which marks his actual birthplace, where Tsongkhapa's mother, Shingza Acho, had herself built a stupa (*kumbum*) in 1379. Later, in 1583, Dalai Lama III Sonam Gyatso sojourned here, and encouraged Rinchen Tsondru Gyeltsen to build a **Maitreya Temple (Jampa Lhakhang)**, after which the site became known as Kumbum Jampaling. Over subsequent centuries, the monastery developed into a large complex, 41 hectares in area.

Kumbum has been sacked and rebuilt several times in its history, particularly during the Muslim rebellion of 1860, when hundreds of monks died protecting the main chapels. It has recently undergone major restoration work, which was finished in 1997. Only half of the monks in Kumbum are Tibetan, and most of these come from the Kokonor region or areas to the south of the Yellow River, while Mongol, Tu, and a few Chinese make up the remainder of the monastery's 400 monks. Despite the obvious sanctity and grandeur of the complex at Kumbum, the monastery at times has the sad air of a museum, and this is enhanced by the arrival of strident Chinese tourists from Ziling, Lanzhou and other urban areas.

Far-east Tibet

Ziling & Rushar

To Datong
(39 km)

To Gonlung
(44 km)

Rechoan River

To Tongkor
(40 km)

Ziling   Ziling Airport

N

Rushar
(Kumbum)   26   15   14   18   Pingan

To Trika (99 km)

Not to scale

As one approaches the monastery from town, there are a large number of sou- **The site**
venir stalls selling a range of Tibetan jewellery, both old and new, as well as
tangkas and other religious artefacts. By the side of the road you will pass the
Chorten Gobzhi (1), which is a large stupa with four gates. Then, at the
entrance to the monastery are the **Chorten Degye** (2), the eight stupas symbolizing the deeds of the Buddha. The originals were destroyed during the Cultural Revolution, the present set having been reconstructed in the early 1980s.
The ticket office and a small guesthouse, known as **Nelenkhang Kakun Gon**
(5) are located beside the stupas, and entrance to the following nine main temples and halls is granted for ¥16.

The gold-tiled **Tsenkhang Chenmo** (7), constructed in 1692 and rebuilt in **Main temples**
1802, is a protector chapel dedicated
to the five aspects of the protector
deity Pehar known as Gyelpo Kunga.
The **Zhabten Lhakhang** (9), which
was completed in 1717 and consecrated by Dalai Lama VII, contains
images of Shakyamuni Buddha with
his foremost disciples, along with the
Sixteen Elders. The **Jokhang** (17),
constructed in 1604, has an exquisite
image of Shakyamuni in bodhisattva
form, inlaid with pearls and gems, as
well as the reliquary of its founder,
Ozer Gyatso; and the adjacent **Gonkhang** (29), dated 1594, has images of
Tsongkhapa and Yamantaka.

The most sacred temples are
those at the heart of the complex: the
Serdong Chenmo (18) was originally
built by Tsongkhapa's mother in 1379
on the spot where a sandalwood tree is
said to have sprung from the ground
where Tsongkhapa's placenta fell at
the time of his birth. The walls are
made of aquamarine tiles, and the central gold image of the master, which
overlooks the branches of the original
tree, is housed in the upper storey
below a gilded roof. Adjacent to it is
the **Jamkhang** (19), the temple dedicated to Maitreya, containing an image
of Maitreya at the age of 12 and the reliquary stupa of Rinchen Tsondru
Gyeltsen, which dates from 1583.

The lavish grand assembly hall,
Tsokchen Dukhang (20), was originally constructed in 1611, but rebuilt
in 1776 and again in 1912. The present
building has a spacious outer courtyard, and a vast hall with 166 pillars in
ornate yellow dragon motifs, and
murals depicting the 1,000 buddhas

Kumbum Jampaling Monastery

To Town

N

Not to scale

1 Chorten Gobzhi
2 Chorten Degye
3 Champa Dratsang
4 Minyak Garwa
5 Nelenkhang
   Kakun Gon (ticket
   office)
6 Gomangwei
   Gyencho Zhengsa
7 Tsenkhang
   Chenmo
8 Dukhor Chorten
9 Zhabten Lhakhang
10 Labrang Tse Tashi
   Khangsar
11 Patrik Garwa
12 Gonkya Garwa
13 Sertok Garwa
14 Parkhang

15 Chichen (admin)
16 Menpa Dratsang
17 Jokhang
18 Serdong Chenmo
19 Jamkhang
20 Tsokchen Dukhang
21 Jamyang Kunzik
   Lhakang
22 Thamche Khyenpei
   Lhakhang
23 Dukhor Dratsang
24 Chesho Garwa
25 Gyupa Dratsang
26 Jetsunpei Gyencho
   Zhengsa
27 Yarcho Chora
28 Akya Garwa
29 Gonkhang
30 Dukhor Lolang
   Kyilkhor

Far-east Tibet

Festivals at Kumbum Jampaling (1999)

Festival	Starting Time	1999
Masked Dance of Dharma King	*1230*	*1 March*
Butter Sculpture Display	*1730*	*2 March*
Marked Dance of Mahacakra	*1200*	*28 May*
Display of Buddha Tangka	*0800*	*29 May*
Dance of Hayagriva	*1200*	*29 May*
Display of Buddha Tangka	*0800*	*19 July*
Dance of Mahacakra	*1200*	*20 July*
Dance of Hayagriva	*1200*	*20 July*
Anniversary of Tsongkhapa		*31 October*
Masked Dance of Hayagriva		*31 October*

of this age. The volumes of the Tibetan canon are stacked up on the side-walls. The **Jamyang Kunzik Lhakhang** (21) is an elongated building with a Chinese-style roof, dating from 1592. In the centre of its shrine are large images depicting the bodhisattvas, Manjughosa, Avalokiteshvara and peaceful Vajrapani; while to the right are the trio: Simhanada, Sitatapatra and Sarasvati; and to the left, Tsongkhapa flanked by his students and the great scholars of ancient India known as the 'Six Ornaments and Two Supreme Ones'. The protector Dharmaraja stands guard at the side. Lastly, the **Thamche Khyenpei Lhakhang** (22) contains a reliquary stupa of Dalai Lama III (not to be confused with his principal reliquary at Drepung in Lhasa).

The colleges   In addition to those temples there are four colleges: **Champa Dratsang** (3) is for the study of religious dancing. **Menpa Dratsang** (16), the medical college, was built in 1757 and contains images of Tsongkhapa, Bhaisajyaguru, and Shakyamuni, along with a three-dimensional mandala of the Eight Medicine Buddhas. **Gyupa Dratsang** (25), the tantric college, dating from 1649, contains images of Shakyamuni and Maitreya buddhas, the meditational deities Guhyasamaja, Cakrasamvara and Bhairava, and murals depicting the 1,000 buddhas of this age. Finally, **Dukhor Dratsang** (23) for the study of Kalacakra-based astrology and esoteric practices, founded in 1817, contains images of Kalacakra, Shakyamuni, and Avalokiteshvara, as well as some fine old tangkas.

Residential buildings   The building known as **Labrang Tse Tashi Khangsar** (10) is the residence of the presiding abbot of Kumbum; and it was where Dalai Lama V and Panchen Lama VI resided during their historic visits. The original structure dates from 1650 and it was further renovated in 1687.

There are six other residential buildings, each associated with one of the great incarnating lamas of the monastery. The largest is that of the Tulku Akya (**Akya Garwa**; 28), followed by those of Tulku Chesho (**Chesho Garwa**; 24), Tulku Minyak (**Minyak Garwa**; 4), Tulku Patrik (**Patrik Garwa**; 11), Tulku Sertok (**Sertok Garwa**; 13), and the monastic supervisor (**Gonkya Garwa**; 12). Next to the residence of Tulku Akya is the **Dukhor Lolang Kyilkhor** (30), containing a 40 cubit sized three-dimensional mandala of the meditational deity Kalacakra, which was built in 1987 by Gyabak Lobzang Tenpei Gyeltsen to mark the beginning of the 17th sexagenary year cycle.

Other buildings   Other buildings include the **Parkhang** (14) where woodblock editions of the *Tibetan Canon* and the *Collected Works of Tsongkhapa* are housed; the hillside

Yarcho Chora (27) or 'summer debating courtyard', the **Dukhor Chorten** (8), the general administrative office known as **Chichen** (15), and two small rooms for moulding tormas and so-called 'butter-sculptures' – the **Gomangwei Gyencho Zhengsa** (6) and the **Jetsunpei Gyencho Zhengsa** (26).

Stay at the *Taer Hotel* (Taersi Binguan), where double rooms are ¥100, and the food is excellent. Muslim street restaurants are also good value.   **Sleeping**

Festivals and important ceremonies are still held here, notably the Great Prayer Festi-   **Festivals**
val during the first month of the lunar calendar, the masked dances held in the 4th month, 7th and 9th months; the *Dharmacakra anniversary* (4th day of the 6th month); and the *Anniversary of Tsongkhapa* (25th day of the 10th month), followed by the *Dance of Hayagriva* (26th day).

Tsongkha Khar County ཚོང་ཁ་མཁར

*Tsongkha Khar (Pingan) county occupies the banks of the Tsong-chu river and their hinterland southeast of Ziling. The county town is located at **Pingan** (Altitude: 2,070 metres), 33 kilometres from Ziling, and 29 kilometres northwest of Ledu in Drotsang county. The Ziling-Lanzhou highway follows the Tsong-chu downstream, parallel to the railway line. To the east of the city, it becomes a toll road, which forks after five kilometres: north for **Ziling Airport** (14 kilometres) and east for Pingan (18 kilometres). Continuing towards Pingan, after one kilometre, you will pass on the right (south) the Xiha Du Jia Cun bungalows (no attached bathrooms). Pingan town lies three kilometres further along this road. There are five Gelukpa monasteries within the county, one of which, **Martsangdrak Gonpa**, originally dates from the ninth century.*

Tsongkha Khar
County (115)
平安县
Pingan
Population: 102,013
Area: 671 sq km
Colour map 5, grid A5

Taktser and Sanhe

Just before entering Pingan, a turn-off leads southwest for 15 kilometres to   *Colour map 5, grid A5*
Taktser, the birthplace of the present Dalai Lama XIV near **Sanhe** township. The Dalai Lama's house was reconstructed in 1986, and some of his distant relatives, including the local school teacher, still live in the area. Until recently, this village was the only destination in the county which required the foreign traveller to obtain an Alien Travel Permit prior to visiting! Also near Sanhe township, some 28 kilometres southwest of Pingan, below Mount Amnye Gyeli there is the **Shadzong Hermitage** which once housed relics associated with the Chinese pilgrim Fa Xian who passed through en route for India in 399AD. There are also small branches of Kumbum Jampaling and Labrang monasteries located in neighbouring townships.

Far-east Tibet

Pingan

Tsongkha Khar

Entering **Pingan** from Ziling, you will   *Phone code: 0972*
pass a turn-off on the left (north) which leads across the Tsong-chu river for Gonlung Monastery (see below, page 547). The historic red-walled temple of **Martsangdrak** is visible high against the cliff-face on the north bank. Continuing along the highway, you will pass restaurants

and the Bank of China, opposite which a side-road leads south for Jentsa, Dowi, Linxia (211 kilometres) and Labrang. Facing an open square at the town centre are the bus station and the railway station, along with other banks and the *Pingan Guesthouse*. Then, reaching the crossroads at the east end of town, you can turn right (south) for the East Kokonor Prefectural Government Buildings and the *Haidong Hotel*, or continue on the highway in the direction of **Lanzhou** (195 kilometres).

Martsangdrak Gonpa

When, during the ninth century, Buddhism was persecuted in central Tibet by the king Langdarma, the three monks Mar Shakyamuni, Tsang Rapsel and Yo-ge Jung fled to Amdo where they maintained the monastic lineage intact for the sake of posterity. They lived for some time at Martsangdrak and passed away at Ziling. During their sojourn, they ordained **Lachen Gongpa Rapsel** (892-975), who was later to transfer the lineage of Buddhism monasticism back to 10 monks from Central Tibet. Lachen himself is said to have passed away at Martsangdrak and his mortal remains are entombed here.

To reach the site, turn left (north) to cross the Tsong-chu on the Gonlung road, and after a second smaller bridge, turn right along a narrow but motorable track towards a large stupa. High above, the temple sites precariously on the ledge of a steep red cliff, which is is danger of subsidence due to heavy rainfall. A Maitreya image guards the approach to the complex, warding off the flooding waters of the Tsong-chu with his defiant hand-gesture. There are two chambers: the upper one housing the embalmed remains of Lachen Gongpa Rapsel and the lower one a shrine replete with images of the three Tibetan monks and their two fellow Chinese monks who formed the quorum to ordain Lachen during the early 10th century. Alongside these are images of Lhalung Peldor, the yogin who assassinated the apostate king Langdarma before fleeing to Amdo, and Makarunika, the compassionate bodhisattva. Nowadays, the temple is under the management of Gonlung Monastery.

Martsangdrak is known in Chinese as Baimasi ('White Horse' temple) either because in 1584 the riding horse of Dalai Lama III died here, or else it was the earliest Tibetan Buddhist temple in Amdo, just as the famed White Horse Monastery in Honan was the the earliest Buddhist monastery in China.

Pingan

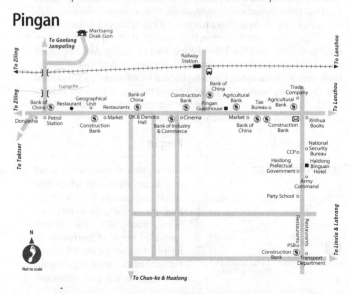

Far-east Tibet

C *Haidong Hotel*, T0972-613516/6135. ¥120 per rooms, standard rooms. There are **Sleeping** also 2 guesthouses located on Main St, but most visitors will prefer to stay in Ziling.

Pingan to Ledu

Leaving Pingan on the highway, the road criss-crosses the railway line, passing through more intensively cultivated fields. After 13 kilometres, a turn-off on the right (south) leads to **Xiaying** township, while the highway continues on to **Ledu** (19 kilometres).

Gonlung County ད་གོན་ལུང་

Gonlung county (Huzhu) lies 44 kilometres northeast of Ziling in a minor side-valley of the Tsong-chu River. Here the **Tu** *peoples, who are of Turkic origin but practitioners of Tibetan Buddhism, are to be found in one of their greatest concentrations. Most of the people wear Chinese clothes, but occasionally Tu women wearing distinctively striped dresses can be seen in the villages. The county capital is located at* **Huzhu,** *54 kilometres north of Pingan town and 60 kilometres south of Gandenkou on the Mongyon/Minhe road. Traditionally, there were 14 Tibetan and Tu monasteries within the county, of which two were Nyingmapa and the remainder all Gelukpa.*

Gonlung County (111)
互助土族自治县
Huzhu
Population: 345,068
Area: 3,133 sq km
Colour map 5, grid A4

Pingan to Gonlung

Driving from Pingan in Tsongkha Khar county, you will bypass a turn-off on the right for Martsangdrak Gon (see above, page 546), and continue north through a prosperous valley where there are plentiful bee-hives and the best potatoes grown in the Ziling area. The villages in the lower reaches of the valley are all Chinese. After 25 kilometres, the road forks, right (six kilometres) for **Sangdu** and left (28 kilometres) for Huzhu town. Taking the former, you will reach **Chozang** hermitage of the Gelukpa school and **Kata Lhakhang** of the Nyingma school, which are four kilometres east of Sangdu township. Following the latter road north towards **Huzhu,** after one kilometre, a branch road leads east for six kilometres to the renowned Gelukpa monastery of Gonlung Jampaling.

Gonlung County

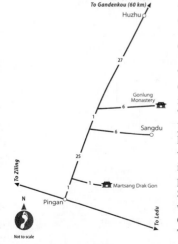

To Gandenkou (60 km)
Huzhu

27

Gonlung
Monastery

6

6   Sangdu

25

1   Martsang Drak Gon

1

Pingan

N

Not to scale

To Ziling

To Ledu

Gonlung Jampaling

The most important monastery of Gonlung and probably the most influential one north of the Tsong-chu river is **Gonlung Jampaling**. The picturesque and lightly forested valley of Gonlung was visited in 1584 by Dalai Lama IV and in 1602 Dalai Lama IV Yonten Gyatso passed through en route for Lhasa. Subsequently, in 1604, the monastery was founded by Gyelse Donyo Chokyi Gyatso and supported by 13 Tu and Tibetan tribes. Later,

Altitude: 2,850 metres
Colour map 5, grid A4

Changkya II, Ngawang Lobzang Chokden (1642-1714), revered as the incarnation of Jamchen Choje Shakya Yeshe (founder of **Sera Monastery** at Lhasa) was invited here by the Manchu emperor, and he constructed a number of temples. His incarnation was Changkya III Rolpei Dorje (1717-1786), the sectarian author and zealot who waged war against the kingdoms of Gyarong (on whom see below, page 619). The monastery was destroyed by the Manchus in 1724 during the suppression of Lhazang Qan, but rebuilt officially in 1732. During this period, the most influential scholars of Gonlung were Sumpa Yeshe (1704-1787), Tuken II Ngawang Chokyi Gyatso (1680-1736), and the latter's renowned incarnation, Tuken III Lobzang Chokyi Nyima (1737-1802), who composed his celebrated philosophical treatise on the schools of Buddhism entitled *Crystal Mirror of Philosophical Systems (Drubta Shelgyi Melong)* at Gonlung in 1801.

The monastery, which has some 49 branches presently houses 300 monks of Tu, Tibetan, and Mongol origin. Nowadays there are two important tulkus: Tuken IX, a youth of 20 years, who is being educated at Labrang Monastery, and Yonten Sumpa IX, who lives in Ziling.

The monastery stretches over the north ridge of the valley, and there are 11 main buildings. To the left of the car park and the reception building there is a hall for religious dancing and a stupa, while to its left there is the **Gyupa Tratsang**, containing images of the meditational deities Guhyasamaja, Cakrasamvara and Vajrabhairava. Heading up hill from here, you will pass (R) the **residence of Tuken** and (L) the **residence of Changkya**. The former has an image of Tuken VIII, the throne of the present lineage-holder Tuken IX, and a fine mural depicting the complete Tuken lineage. Further uphill, there is the **Assembly Hall** (Dukhang), a building of 108 pillars with a central throne holding a portrait of the previous and last Changkya, who died in Taiwan. To its rear there are images (L-R) of Jowo Shakyamuni, Tubpa Chokhorma, Tara, Tsongkhapa with his students, the Buddhas of the Three Times, Vajrasattva, Amitabha, and Vajradhara. Behind the Assembly Hall, and higher up the

Gonlung Jampaling

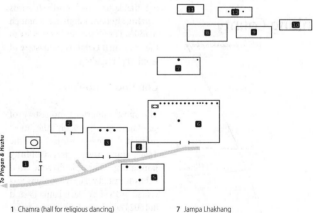

1 Chamra (hall for religious dancing)
2 Reception
3 Gyupa Tratsang
4 Changkya Tsang
5 Tuken Tsang
6 Dukhang (Assembly Hall)
7 Jampa Lhakhang
8 Zhidak Lhakhang
9 Tomb of Changkya II
10 Gyelsekhang
11 Tuken Zimchung
12 Sumpa Zimchung

ridge, there is the **Jampa Lhakhang**, containing a precious image known as Jampa Yelogma, along with small images of the Sixteen Elders, the 1,000 buddhas of the aeon and the eight bodhisattvas. Climbing further, you will reach the **Zhidak Lhakhang**, a protector shrine built by Changkya II, and the adjacent tomb of Changkya II which lies within a walled garden. Towards the top the ridge, there is the **Gyelsekhang**, with an image of Maitreya, the **Tuken Hermitage** (Tuken Zimchung) and the **Sumpa Hermitage** (Sumpa Zimchung), the last of which has an image of Atisa within. Two kilometres distant from Gonlung is the **Gyelse Hermitage**, affiliated to the monastery, while other branches exist within the valley at **Sangdu** and **Denma** townships.

An important ceremony is held at Gonlung Monastery during the **prayer festival** of the first month of the lunar calendar; while masked dances are held during the first, third and fourth months. On 10 May 1998, a large tangka will be displayed at Gonlung, in conjunction with the masked dances.

Huzhu Town and Chubzang

The burgeoning county town of **Huzhu** lies 33 kilometres north of Gonlung Monastery. In nearby **Bazha** township there is the Gelukpa monastery of **Kanchen Gon**, which was founded in 1654 by a student of Panchen IV Lobzang Chokyi Gyeltsen. To the northwest of Bazha (3.5 kilometres), there is also a small Nyingma monastery called **Kanchung Gon** which was founded during the 1930s. About 20 kilometres north of town, on the plain of **Bumlung Tashithang**, there is another influential Gelukpa monastery known as **Chubzang Ganden Migyurling**, which was founded in 1649 by Tolung Chubzang Lalebpa Namgyel Peljor (1578-1651). Like Gonlung, this establishment was destroyed in 1724 and subsequently rebuilt in 1765 and refurbished in 1887. Its branches extend as far as Trika and Ulan Sok counties.

Festivals

The *Lantern Festival*, including local song and dance performances, will be held in **Huzhu** from **10-11 February 1998** and **1-2 March 1999**. The *Broad Bean Festival*, in which local costumes and embroidery are exhibited along with local opera and folk art performances, and the consumption of the local delicacy: broad beans, will be held from **28 February-3 March 1998**. The *Flower Song* festival (Haurhui) will be held at **Wufeng** temple in Gonlung county from **28-30 July 1998** and **18-20 July 1999**. Other song and dance fairs of the Tu nationality are held within the county at **Songshuiwan** and *Weiyuan* in **July**, and at **Tuguan** in **August**.

Drotsang County གྲོ་ཚང

*Drotsang county comprises the section of the Tsong-chu downstream from Tsongkha Khar, and its lateral valleys to the north and south, where **Drotsang Monastery** is located. This region was formerly known as **Neu-be**. Traditionally, the county had 31 Tibetan monasteries, or temples, representing the Gelukpa school, and of these Drotsang is still the most important. Now eight have been officially reopened and four have privately reopened. The county town, Ledu, lies 32 kilometres southeast of Pingan and 47 kilometres northwest of Minhe in Kamalok.*

Drotsang County (116)
乐都县
Ledu
Population: 279,280
Area: 2,520 sq km
Colour map 5, grid A5

Ledu

Driving southeast from the Xiaying intersection in Tsongkha Khar into Drotsang county, after five kilometres, a branch road leads across to the north

Altitude: 2,010 metres
Phone code: 0972

Far-east Tibet

bank of the Tsong-chu for 15 kilometres to reach the old market of Ledu town. Instead, if you continue on the highway, after eight kilometres, a turn-off leading south to **Fengdu** will be reached. The county capital is only six kilometres distant at this point.

Drotsang County

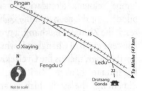

Ledu is a rapidly growing Chinese market town, situated on both banks of the river. No street signs at all appear to be written in Tibetan! Entering town, you will pass the Peoples' Park and the South Bus Station on the left, and a petrol station, carpet factory and the *Ledu Hotel* on the right. Here, a side-road leads across the Tsong-chu through a banking and commercial street towards the old market and the Ledu bus and railway stations. If you continue along the highway, you will pass the local bus station and a teacher training school on the right, after which a side-road leads inland to **Drotsang Monastery**, following the Drotsang-chu tributary upstream.

In the north of the county, the largest monastery is **Tongshak Tashi Choling**, a branch of Gonlung, founded by Gendun Lodro, which once held 300 monks, and has been rebuilt since 1981.

Sleeping **C** *Ledu Hotel*, T(0972)622888/622868. Newly constructed, with standard rooms at ¥160, suites at ¥380, and deluxe doubles and triples at ¥480 and ¥680 respectively.

Festivals The *Lantern Festival* is held annually in Ledu, coinciding with **10-11 February 1998** and **1-2 March 1999**.

Ledu

Drotsang Monastery

Drotsang Monastery (*Ch* Qutansi), formally known as Drotsang Lhakhang Gautamde Gegye Dechenling, is located 22 kilometres from the intersection at the east end of Ledu town. A generally well-paved road with occasional pot-holes leads gradually uphill through the farming villages of the Drotsang valley. After 14 kilometres, it bypasses a dam and an artificial lake. The monastery is located six kilometres further on in **Drotsang** township (Qutan; *Altitude*: 2,430 metres). This remarkably symmetrical complex of temples in Sino-Tibetan style, 10,000 square metres in area, dates from 1392 and originally belonged to the Karma Kagyu school. It was founded by Samlo Lama Sangye Tashi and funded by his patron, the Ming emperor Zhu Yuan Zhang. Although the temple has the air of a museum, it is worthy of a visit since it does contain original images and unique murals. Entering the front gate (admission: ¥15), there are two tablet pavilions, beyond which four main halls are entered in succession, in typical Chinese temple design. These are known respectively as the **Vairocana Hall** (*Ch* Jing Gang), the **Vajradhara Hall** (*Ch* Qutansi), the **Amitabha Hall** (*Ch* Bao Guang) and the **National Protection Hall** (*Ch* Longguo). Flanking the Amitabha Hall are two small assembly halls and surrounding the Vajradhara Hall are four stupas. The perimeter wall, which has two temples (a protector shrine and the **Temple of the Buddhas of the Three Times**, *Ch* Sanshi), and four drum towers, is remarkable for its covered side-corridors decorated with 400 square metres of spectacularly vivid murals depicting the life of Shakyamuni Buddha. These paintings, some of which have been lost and other now undergoing restoration, are of an ingenious composition, full of vibrant detail, and subtle in both colour and perspective.

Colour map 5, grid A5

Drotsang Gonpa

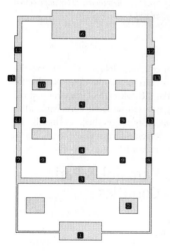

1 Front Gate
2 Tablet Pavilion
3 Vairocana Hall
4 Gautama/Vajradhara Hall
5 Amitabha Hall
6 National Protection Hall
7 Protector Temple
8 Hall of Buddhas of the Three Times
9 Stupas
10 Small Hall of Scripture
11 Small Bell-Drum Tower
12 Big Bell -Drum Tower
13 Side Corridor

The oldest building is the Vajradhara Hall (170 square metres), dated 1392, which has a central image of Jowo Shakyamuni in the form Vajradhara, known as Drotsang Dorjechang. This original image is flanked by the Sixteen Elders, while the murals of the hall are in Tibetan style and relatively unscathed. The Amitabha or Middle Hall (400 square metres), dated 1418, contains four marble seats inscribed with characters from the Yongle period. The Great Hall (912 square metres), dated 1427, has a large stone throne, once occupied by images of Maitreya. Later, in 1564 the complex was refurbished as a Gelukpa monastery by Sherab Chokden (Drepung Samlo Rabjampa), in accordance with a prediction made by Dalai Lama III. Three tulkus were recognized here, and 17

Far-east Tibet

branches developed throughout Drotsang and adjacent counties. However, the influence of the monastery sharply declined during the late 17th century for political reasons.

The hermitage of Drotsang known as **Tashilhunpo** lies nine kilometres from the temple in the remote uplands. It was founded in 1619 at the behest of Dalai Lama III who had visited the site in 1583. Also, five kilometres southwest of nearby **Zhongba** township, there is the historic hermitage of **Pula Yangdzong**, where the ninth century monks Mar Shakyamuni and Tsang Rabsel sought refuge from persecution in Central Tibet.

Festivals In addition to the Buddhist festivals held during the 1st and 4th months of the lunar calendar, a secular *Flower Song Fair* (*Ch* Huarhui) is also held here on the 6th day of the 6th lunar month, which in 1999 corresponds to **18-20 July**.

Kamalok County བཀའ་མ་ལོག

Kamalok County (117)
民和县
Minhe
Population: 327,488
Area: 1,681 sq km
Colour map 5, grid B5

Kamalok county lies 48 kilometres downstream from Drotsang on the border of present day Qinghai and Gansu provinces. ***Minhe****, the new county town, which is situated near the confluence of the Tsong-chu and the* ***Julak-chu*** *tributary (Ch Datong he), is 47 kilometres southeast of Ledu and 121 kilometres from Lanzhou. Traditionally, the county had 61 Tibetan monasteries or temples, most of them in the lower* ***Julak*** *valley, but the vast majority of these were small, with a mere handful of monks. In recent years, some 55 have been rebuilt, approximately half with official permission and half funded privately. All of them are Gelukpa (circa 16th-19th centuries), and many house monks of Tu nationality.*

Minhe

Phone code: 0972
Colour map 5, grid A5

The road from Ledu to **Minhe** town continues following the Tsong-chu downstream. After 10 kilometres, a turn-off leads right (south) for **Yahongying**. The hills in this section of the valley are of grass-covered red sandstone. After 15 kilometres, the highway crosses to the north bank, while the railway line is on the south bank. The valley narrows here, and the hills are barren. The **Songzhi** intersection, 12 kilometres further downstream, marks the beginning of the polluted Minhe industrial zone. The monastery of **Lenhate Ganden Nechu Pelgyeling**, which is the most influential in Julak county, overlooks the north bank of the Tsong-chu at this point. Many of the small temples and monasteries of the county hold allegiance to this mother monastery.

The county town itself (*Altitude*: 1,830 metres) is located two kilometres off the highway. It is a large and growing town with a considerable Muslim and Tu population, rendered unattractive by a large ferrochrome smelting plant. Local landmarks include a hill-top temple, with a stupa at its base, and a mosque.

In the far south of the county, in the vicinity of **Chuangkou** township,

Kamalok & Pari Counties

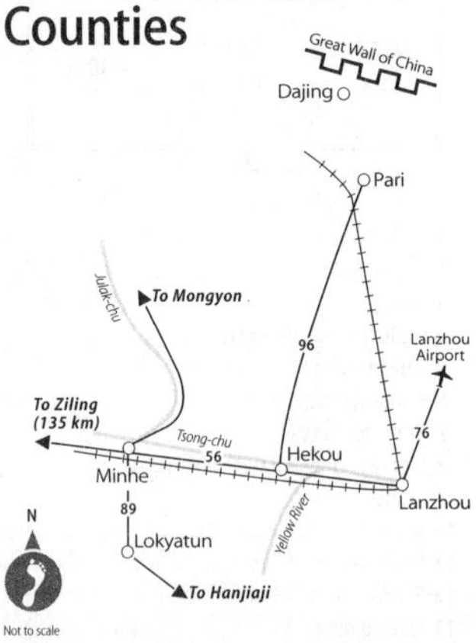

64 kilometres from town, there are several monasteries and shrines. These include **Shangparsi Samten Dargyeling**, 35 kilometres to the southwest of Chuangkou, which was founded by Tsongkhapa's student Jamyang Choje Shakya Yeshe en route for Beijing, and later renovated in 1895. Some three kilometres south of **Gankou** township, there is another major monastery, known as **Khataka Gonpa**, which was founded by Tsongkhapa's student Sonam Zangpo, and subsequently visited by Dalai Lama III.

Sleeping C *Minhe Hotel*, 38 Chuan Kou Zhen Xin Cheng St, T(0972)522149. Standard rooms at ¥164, suites at ¥204, and triples at ¥186, although a 100 per cent mark-up is charged to foreigners. There are many small Muslim restaurants in town and by the highway.

Liuwan North of the highway, at **Liuwan** cemetery, 1,600 tombs and 30,000 relics have been excavated, including a celebrated clay pot with dancing figurines, which is regarded as a national treasure. This is the largest of many archaeological sites, which have been opened in the Qinghai area. A detailed report was published in 1980, including extensive illustrations of the unearthed pottery.

Another road leads southeast from Minhe to cross the Yellow River at **Lokyatun** (*Ch* Guanting, 89 kilometres via Gushan and Maying), and then to reach the **Sang-chu** river valley at **Hanjiaji**, southwest of Linxia in Gansu province.

Pari County དཔའ་རིས

After Kamalok, the highway crosses the present Qinghai-Gansu border and heads for Lanzhou. At Hekou (78 kilometres from Minhe town), it passes the confluence of the Tsong-chu and Yellow rivers (Altitude: 1,650 metres), and from there it is but a short drive into the city on a toll road. From Hekou, there is also a side-road which heads due north, following the Zhuanglang tributary upstream for 96 kilometres to Pari (Ch Tianzhu). This autonomous county is the furthest outpost of Tibetan habitation in Northeast Amdo, and lies not far to the south of Dajing on the Great Wall of China. It is also accessible via the Lanzhou-Wuwei railway line, but unlike neighbouring Ziling and Labrang districts it is not yet classed as an open area. Alien travel permit restrictions still apply.

Pari County (118)
天祝藏族自治县
Tianzhu
Population: 210,845
Area: 6,633 sq km
Phone code: 0938
Colour map 5, grid B6

The Pari region has been occupied by Tibetan tribes since the period of the Yarlung Dynasty. The monastery of **Chorten Tang Tashi Dargyeling**, situated to the west of the county town, was originally a Bon monastery constructed during that period (806-820). Subsequently, during the 11th century the Amdowa Tibetan tribe known in Chinese as Liang Zhou Liu Gu conquered the region. When Sakya Pandita passed through en route for Mongolia in the 13th century, the Sakyapa monastery of **Chorten Tang** was built upon the earlier Bon foundation. Later still, when visited by Karmapa IV Rolpei Dorje in 1360, the monastery was converted to the Karma Kagyu school, and following its destruction by Mongol tribes, it finally resurfaced as a Gelukpa establishment.

Prior to 1958 there were over 800 monks in Pari, but nowadays there are no more than 70 monks affiliated to the eight temples or monasteries, which have recently been reopened. Apart from Chorten Tang, the most important of these are **Paling Tosam Dargyeling**, 11 kilometres west of the county town, which still houses its precious artefacts, including an ivory image of Avalokiteshvara presented by Dalai Lama VII and a costume worn by Dalai

Far-east Tibet

Lama VI. The monastery of **Taklung Gon Ganden Choling** originally, as its name suggests, represented the Taklung Kagyu school since its founding by Lobzang Tenpa Chokyi Nyima during the late 14th century. However, it too was subsequently converted to the Gelukpa tradition.

Lanzhou

Altitude: 1,600 metres
Phone code: 0931
Colour map 5, grid A5

*Like Chengdu, Kunming, and Kathmandu, **Lanzhou** is an important starting point for travellers visiting the Tibetan plateau. It is the hub of the communications network for China's Northwestern provinces, and most travellers to Amdo in Tibet or the Silk Road in Xinjiang will pass through here. Two areas of Amdo are currently administered within Gansu province with their centre of government at Lanzhou: the Ganlho Tibetan Autonomous Prefecture (on which see below, page 632) and the Pari Tibetan Autonomous County, which has just been described.*

Lanzhou is a large elongated industrial town set on the edge of the Tibetan plateau and Ordos desert. Many of the nearby hills are covered in thick deposits of loess, which can be very fertile where irrigated. However, the area around Lanzhou receives little rain, and many parts of Gansu are constantly challenged by desert encroachment.

Orientation

Lanzhou itself sprawls along the south bank of the Yellow River, and grew in importance after the construction of the first bridge in 1385. During the present

Lanzhou

■ Sleeping
1 Friendship Hotel
2 Jincheng Hotel
3 Lanzhou Hotel
4 Lanzhou Legend Hotel
5 Ningwozhuang Guesthouse
6 Victory Hotel

Far-east Tibet

century, the advent of the railways brought heavy industry to Lanzhou and the urban population rapidly increased. The 500 square kilometres of the inner city now has a population of 423,875; and its surrounding district (area 1,712 square kilometres) has a population of 1,450,809. The **airport** is two hours' drive (76 kilometres) from the city itself, up a northern valley, and the journey down to the Yellow River reveals typical small farming of the loess hills.

The **West Railway Station** and the **West Bus Station** (for buses to Labrang) are located at the northwest end of town, and nearby are the Gansu Provincial Museum, and the *Friendship Hotel*. The **Main Railway Station** is to the southwest of the main shopping area, and connected to it by Pinglian Street (where the Post Office is located) and Tianshui Avenue. Most hotels are clustered in the area around the Xuguan Traffic Circle on Tianshui Avenue, notably the *Lanzhou Fandian*, the *Jingcheng Hotel*, and the *Ningwozhuang Guesthouse*. CITS and CAAC are conveniently here also. Across Central Square on Qingyang Street you will find the Bank of China and the Public Security Bureau.

The **Gansu Provincial Museum**, near *Friendship Hotel*, has an interesting collection of artefacts from the Silk Road, including neolithic painted pottery. Open 0900 to 1130 and from 1430-1700. Closed on Sun, admission ¥10.

Museums

Essentials

A *Lanzhou Legend Hotel (Lanzhou Feitian)*, 599 Tianshui Ave, T8882876, F(86931)8887876. The best and most modern hotel in Lanzhou. There are standard rooms at ¥800, deluxe rooms at ¥860, and suites ranging from ¥1,900 upwards, plus 15 per cent surcharge. **A** *Jincheng Hotel (Jincheng Fandian)*, 601 Tianshui Ave, T8416638, F(86931)8418438. 136 rooms, with attached bath, ¥440-¥520 per standard room, ¥650-2,000 per suite, ¥40 per dorm-style accommodation in rear annex. **A** *Lanzhou Fandian*, 434 Dongangxilu St, T8416321. A 1950s Russian-style building with 80 double rooms at ¥180-¥333 (with attached bath), single rooms at ¥230 (with attached bath), and triples at ¥30 (without attached bath). **A** *Ningwozhuang Binguan*, 366 Tianshui Ave, T8416221. A splendid garden hotel, once reserved for party cadres and visiting dignitaries. Standard double rooms with attached bath are at ¥328, and deluxe single rooms at ¥980. **B** *Friendship Hotel (Youyi Fandian)*, 16 Xijin St, T8334711. 43 double rooms at ¥150-¥382, and triples at ¥93. The hotel has postal and shopping facilities. **C** *Victory Hotel (Shengli Fandian)*, 133 Zhongshan St, T8465221. 168 double rooms at ¥180-¥260, and triples with attached bath at ¥153, and without attached bath at ¥93.

Sleeping
■ *on map, page 554*
Price codes:
see inside front cover

Among the major hotels, the *Lanzhou Legend* and the *Jincheng* have both Chinese and Western menus, and the *Friendship Hotel* has inexpensive set meals. For local street food, try the restaurants in the lane behind the *Jincheng Hotel*, around the Main Railway Station or in the lane due east of the Bank of China. Local specialities including *ruojiabing*, a fiery lamb or pork kebab served in a pitta bread, and *tianpeizi*, a fermented barley dish prepared by Muslims.

Eating

Air There are daily flights to and from Beijing, Chengdu, Dunhuang, Guangzhou, Shanghai, Urumqi, and Xi'an. Also less frequent flights to Chongqing, Guilin, Wuhan, Nanjing, Kunming, and Hangzhou.

Transport

Road Buses run from the *West Bus Station* to Linxia, Xiahe, and Ganlho Dzong (Hezuo), as well as Wuwei; and from the *East Bus Station* to more remote destinations in Shaanxi and Ningxia provinces. **NB** Foreigners travelling by public bus must pay

Far-east Tibet

Lanzhou West Bus Station Schedule

Destination	Time	Price
Labrang (Xiahe)	0730	¥19.40
Luchu	1430 (1 bus every 2 days)	¥49.10
Cho-ne	0630	¥22.50
Lintan	0800	¥25.20
Ganlho Dzong (Hezhuo)	0700, 0800, 0930	¥19.30
Tewo	1600	¥71.90 (lower couchette)
		¥63.70 (upper couchette)
Drukchu	0700	¥31.90
Ziling	0730, 0900, 1000, 1200,	
	1330, 1430, 1630	¥17.60

local travel insurance through the Public Insurance Company of China, 150 Qingyang Street, T8416422 ext 114, or from CITS directly.

Train There are frequent train connections to Kermo via Ziling, and also to Urumqi, Beijing, Chengdu, and Xi'an (see above, page 541).

Directory **Airline offices** *Jing Lan Flight Centre*, 8 Qinan St, T(0931)8831184. *CAAC*, 46 Dongang Xilu, T821964, 828174. **Banks** *Bank of China*, Pingliang St, T8485354. Exchange facilities. **Communications** General Post Office: Pingliang St. Open 0830-1900, and has parcel wrapping service. The Telephone and Telegram Office, on Qingyang St, has IDD facilities. Postal facilities also available in major hotels. **Tour companies & travel agents** *Gansu CITS*, 361 Tianshui Ave, T8826181/8861333, F0931-8418556. *Gansu Silk Road Travel*, T8414498/8416638, F0931-8418457/8414589. **Useful addresses** Police and Public Security: *Gansu Province Foreigners Registration Office*, 38 Qingyang St. *Lanzhou City Foreigners Registration Office*, 132 Wudu St.

The Yellow River Bend:

Repkong and Sogwo

There are three routes from Ziling to the Golok region in South Amdo: one via Tsongkha Khar, Bayan Khar or Jentsa, and Repkong; a second via Rushar and Trika; and a third via Chabcha and Mato. The first is described in this section, and the others in the following section.

The ethnic mix to the north and east of **Repkong** *is the most complex in Amdo. The Hsuing-nu, distant relatives of the Sodgians, once ruled here, in constant conflict with neighbouring Han China, after which came the Tuyunhun (Tib Azha), the Qiang, and then, during the seventh to the ninth century, the Central Tibetans. The Tangut state to the north and the Mongolian Empire also encompassed this area during the 10th-14th century. There were, additionally, pockets of Hor or Uighur tribes of Turkic origin, who had been dispersed along the oases of the Silk Road very early, and from the eighth century Arabs and Persians. The Hui Muslims of China, who are mostly of Turkic origin, and the Salar, a distinct tribe exiled from Samarkand, all had a presence. The earlier conquering armies had a tendency to disband at the end of their campaigns, frequently displacing the locals.*

After the Ming emperors of China had rescinded the ancient imperial policy of 'using barbarians to rule barbarians', colonial settlements were gradually established in the grasslands, and the agricultural Chinese began to push back the nomadic tribes. Many outlying groups of Amdowa Tibetans became isolated from the rest of the Tibetan population by these large settlements, and at the start of this century in a few regions, Tibetans were becoming a minority. To complicate matters, some Tibetans converted to Islam, often at the point of a sword, and racial intermarriage was commonplace.

The route described in this section comprises six counties, of which three belong to the Tibetan Autonomous Prefecture of South Yellow River (Jentsa, Repkong and Tsekok), two (Bayan Khar and Dowi) are administered directly from Ziling, and one (Sogwo) is a Mongolian Autonomous Prefecture in its own right.

Recommended itineraries: 6, 8, 9, 11.

Far-east Tibet

Bayan Khar County བ་ཡན་མཁར

Bayan Khar County (119)
化隆回族自治县
Hualong Hui AC
Population: 200,488
Area: 2,732 sq km
Colour map 5, grid B5

From **Pingan** town, a branch road leads south from the Ziling-Lanzhou high-way. Leaving the Tsong-chu valley it crosses into **Bayan Khar** (Hualong) county, where virtually half the population is Muslim. Nonetheless, 41,000 Tibetans also live here, the third highest concentration of Tibetans in the part of Amdo controlled by Qinghai. Most of these Tibetans are in villages far to the east and west of the county, with the town itself being predominantly Hui and Han. The county capital, known as **Hualong**, lies 84 kilometres southeast of Pingan, on a south-flowing tributary of the Yellow River, or 56 kilometres from Dowi and 58 kilometres from Jentsa. In the northeast of the county, there is also an impor-tant north-flowing tributary of the Tsong-chu. Traditionally, there were 44 tem-ples or monasteries within the county, the most historically important being **Jakhyung** and **Dentik**. Twenty-seven of these survived the Cultural Revolution, havibg been used as granaries and storerooms. Presently, the county has 34 mon-asteries, four of which are Nyingmapa and the remainder Gelukpa.

Jakhyung Shedrubling Monastery

Getting there
Colour map 5, grid B5

The southern road from Pingan bypasses a stupa on the right and the *Jimbu Restau-rant* (where Hu Yao Ban once dined), before crossing the watershed pass (*Altitude*: 3,210 metres) on Mount Chingsha, which marks the county border. Entering Bayan Khar county, the road then passes through **Zawa** (*Ch* Quanzhuang) township (39 kilo-metres), from where a rough side-road heads west to **Chapu** and **Zhongshen** (*Ch* Xiongxian) villages. Both Jakhyung and Detsa monasteries are accessible south of this branch road, which, after Zhongshen, links up with the Ziling-Trika road (see below, page 579).

The monastery of **Jakhyung Shedrubling** lies to the south of the Zawa-Zhongshen road on a ridge overlooking the Yellow River, 19 kilometres beyond Zawa or 10 kilometres from Chapu. This is one of the most historic and renowned Gelukpa monasteries of Amdo, founded in 1349 by Lama Dondrub Rinchen, the teacher of Tsongkhapa. The attractive monastery is sit-uated in a smalp forest zone, quite popular with Chinese picnickers from Ziling at weekends. Small tractors wait for passengers at the turn-off, and will charge about ¥12 for the 30 kilometres trip to the monastery.

Prior to the Gelukpa foundation, an earlier monastery had been founded on the same site by Karmapa II, Karmapakshi in the 12th century. Later, following the Gelukpa founda-tion in 1349, the monastery was listed, along with Serkhok, Chubzang and Gonlung, as one of the 'four great monasteries of the north', a phrase used in Amdo to signify the oldest and most significant Gelukpa institu-tions of the region. It was here that Tsongkhapa became ordained as a renunciate, and studied until leaving Amdo for Lhasa at the age of 16. The small forest on the eastern slope of the ridge on which Jakhyung lies is said to

Bayan Khar & Jentsa Counties

Far-east Tibet

be formed from his hair, and is included on the two hours circumambulation of the monastery. There are currently about 500 monks and 10 reconstructed temples. The large assembly hall is brand new and unimpressive, but the small temples to the rear have more character. A green-glazed brick temple houses images of Shakyamuni, Maitreya, and Tsongkhapa; while another houses a stupa reliquary (the destroyed original once held the hair relics of Tsongkhapa), flanked by large images of Jowo Rinpoche, Maitreya and Manjughosa.

From Jakhyung, a two hour walk heads steeply down the barren 'bad-lands' to the Yellow River.

Detsa Tashi Choding Monastery

There are two Gelukpa monasteries in the northwest vicinity of Detsa township, some 40 kilometres beyond Jakhyung along the spur road. The lower one, **Detsa Gonpa**, is a branch of Jakhyung, founded by Lama Wangchuk (fl. 17th century). The upper one, known as **Detsa Tashi Choding**, is a well-respected Gelukpa monastery that was founded in 1903 by Sharma Pandita IV Gendun Tendzin Gyatso. It has two temples, the larger with a stupa and statue of the founder, along with modern images depicting Jowo Rinpoche, Atisha and Tsongkhapa, and mural panels created by artists from Repkong. The smaller holds a large Avalokiteshvara, a small Manjughosa, and a White Tara. There are currently four lamas and about 300 monks, many of whom come from far afield drawn by the quality of teaching here. Further up-valley en route to **Trika** (*Ch* Guide) is a patch of coniferous forest that must have once covered much of the Lhamori mountain and the small hermitage of **Zhongshen Ritro**, connected to Kumbum, which was originally a 13th-century Sakyapa foundation.

Colour map 5, grid B4

Bayan and Dehinglang

Returning to the main road from Jakhyung, turn southeast and after 11 kilometres there is a major fork at **Nakchutang** (*Ch* Laqutan). The large water-powered prayer wheel of **Jentsa Mani**, dedicated to the deity Cintamanicakra and dating from the early 20th century, is located nearby. The southwest branch road leads directly from Nakchutang to **Chunke** township on the north bank of the Yellow River where bridges cross to Lugyagak, Jentsa and the Gu-chu valley; and the southeast branch to **Dowi** (Xunhua) after first bypassing Hualong county town. Taking the latter route via **Ertang**, where **Gechuk Gonpa**, a branch of Lamo Dechen is located, after 17 kilometres you will reach another intersection, where a turn-off on the right (south) leads downhill to **Bayan** and **Dehinglang** townships. The few monasteries along this road are mostly branches of Jakhyung, although **Ngosa Gon**, eight kilometres southeast of Dehinglang, is affiliated to Lamo Dechen. Continuing along the highway, you will soon reach the turn-off for **Hualong** (32 kilometres from Nakchutang). The town lies only two kilometres east along this branch road.

Colour map 5, grid B5

Far-east Tibet

Hualong County Town

Entering Main Street from the north, you will pass the Tibetan Hospital on the left. A turn-off on the right leads to the County Hospital, the *Nationalities Hotel* (Minzu Binguan), the government buildings, and a number of small Muslim restaurants. Continuing south on Main Street you will pass the post

Colour map 5, grid B5

office, bank and tax office, along with the bus station, court and police station. At the south end of Main Street, the road forks. Turn left (east) for **Dentik** (63 kilometres), or southwest for **Dowi** (58 kilometres).

Sleeping C *Nationalities Hotel (Minzu Binguan)*, T0972-712299/712199. Standard rooms at ¥90 per room. There are also 3 guesthouses in town.

Eating The Muslim noodle restaurants adjacent to the *Nationalities Hotel* are the best in town. Alternatively, try the small restaurants situated by the highway outside town.

Transport Bus routes link this town with Ziling, Jentsa, and Rongpo Gyakhar.

Hualong Town

Hualong to Dentik

Heading east from Hualong town, the road passes through **Shidachang** and **Chuma** townships, where the monasteries are mostly affiliated to Lenhate Gonpa in neighbouring Kamalok (see above, page 552). However, south of **Jinyuan** township (45 kilometres east of Hualong), on the approach to Dentik, you will pass the 17th century **Drakargya Ngakhang**, which is the largest Nyingmapa monastery in the county, and its retreat hermitage at **Khorpa Ngakhang**.

Dentik

Colour map 5, grid B5 Some 63 kilometres from Hualong town and 18 kilometres due south of Jinyuan township, there is the most important pilgrimage site and power place in all of Amdo. **Dentik Sheldrak**, also known as **Dentik Shelgyi Bamgon**, has been revered since the time of Padmasambhava as the foremost power place associated with buddha-mind throughout Kham and Amdo. Later, it was here that Mar Shakyamuni and his colleagues first accepted Lachen Gongpa Rabsel (892-975) as their student, thereby saving the monastic tradition for the sake of posterity. Later, Lu-me and the 10 men of Utsang arrived to receive ordination from Lachen, and on their return to Lhasa, they revived monastic Buddhism in Central Tibet. Lachen himself is said to have built a monastery here, and the site has been visited by Tibetan pilgrims over the centuries, including Dalai Lama III.

Getting there Driving south from Jinyuan, the motorable road comes to an end at the village of Korba, 1 hour walking distance from Dentik. Traffic is very infrequent and if you have no transportation, it may be easier to access the site on foot from Dowi (see below, page 561).

The monastery is spread along the floor of a small side-valley with two simple temples and a number of caves and sacred springs. One of the caves is associated with Lachen Gongpa Rabsel, while Lhalung Pelgyi Dorje, the monk who assassinated Langdarma with an arrow, also spent his last years here, although he refused to take part in the ordination of Lachen Gongpa Rabsel because of his crimes. Most of the original pre-1958 buildings (approximately 200 rooms) are still standing, and some contain undamaged images. The

Far-east Tibet

hermitage of **Yangtig Ritro**, one kilometre east of Dentik, which was first opened by Dalai Lama III in the 16th century, contains natural stone representations of the eight bodhisattvas and the eight auspicious symbols.

There are several other monasteries in East Bayan Khar county, including two which represent the Bon tradition, and the **Jampa Bumling** – an extensive Gelukpa establishment, founded by Rinchen Gyatso in the 16th century alongside an earlier Maitreya temple.

Hualong to Dowi

Heading south from the Hualong intersection on the Pingan-Dowi road, you will cross a pass (2,400 metres) after four kilometres, followed by an artificial lake to the east. The descent leads for 32 kilometres down to **Kado** township, and eventually reaches the north bank of the Yellow River at **Kado Tashi Chodzong** (*Ch* Gando), where it crosses over into Dowi county (44 kilometres). This monastery is a branch of Labrang, founded in 1791, when Jamyang Zhepa II Konchok Jikme Wangpo passed away here.

Dowi County རྡོ་སྦིས་

*The county capital of Dowi (Xunhua), traditionally known in Tibetan as Dowi Khar, lies on the south bank of the Yellow River, 56 kilometres southeast of Hualong, and 113 kilometres west of Linxia. Since the 14th century the county has been predominantly inhabited by the **Salar**, a very tight-knit band of Central Asian Muslims. A legendary camel carried bags of earth from home, which were matched with earth around a nearby spring, and the tribe's long migration came to an end. The camel appropriately turned to stone!*

Dowi County (120)
循化撒拉族自治县
Xunhua Salar AC
Population: 99,471
Area: 2,132 sq km
Colour map 5, grid B5

By the 19th century, the Salar had expanded to include several villages north of the Yellow River, but they were badly defeated by the Chinese armies during the intermittent Muslim wars. The quite large county town is surrounded by fields, both open and enclosed in mud-walled houses, where fruit trees are a speciality.

Despite the Salars' overwhelming dominance in the agriculturally rich valleys, the Tibetans continue to occupy the upper valleys, and several important monasteries can be visited. Prior to 1958 there were altogether 33 Tibetan shrines or monasteries within the county, the most important being **Bimdo Gonpa** and **Gori Gonpa**.

Dowi County

Xunhua Town

Crossing the bridge over the Yellow River which leads into Dowi county from Bayan Khar, after five kilometres you will reach the Camel Spring Mosque at Lutuo. This is where the stone camel, talisman of the Salar people, is to be seen. The highway to Repkong, Labrang and Linxia continues south from the mosque, bypassing the town, while a branch road leads left (east), five kilometres into town.

Altitude: 1,920 metres
Phone code: 0972
Colour map 5, grid B5

Taking the latter road, you will pass on the right the *Abdul* and *Chenglai* restaurants, and the West Gate Market, while on the left you will pass the *Tianchi Hotel* (Tianchi Fandian), banks, and government buildings. The bus station is next to the *Traffic Guesthouse*, towards the south end of town. Although the town has excellent Muslim restaurants, the sanitation of the hotels leaves much to be desired.

Sleeping C *Tianchi Fandian (Minzu Binguan)*, T0972-813068, has standard rooms. *Huanxia Fuandian*, located on the bypass road, while the *Government Guesthouse*, T(0972)812323, has suites at ¥70-¥80. Standard rooms at ¥25 per bed, triples at ¥12 per bed, and 4-bedded rooms at ¥8 per bed. Foreigners have to pay a 100 per cent surcharge.

Eating The best cuisine in town is to be found at the *Chenglai Restaurant*. However, there are many other options.

Dowi to Dentik

A small bridge leads across the Yellow River from Xunhua town in the direction of **Dentik** (see above, page 560), but the journey has to be made on foot and will take a full day. To reach Dentik on foot head northeast from Dowi and cross the Yellow River by a small bridge. Then, leave the motor road, and take a footpath which heads up a narrow rocky gorge straight ahead, climbing steeply through a series of ridges, 610 metres above the valley. This trail eventually descends into a narrow side-valley where Dentik is located, five hours' walk uphill and three hours' walk downhill.

Dowi to Linxia

Mengda Tianchi Lake If you take the southeast road from Xunhua town, which initially follows the Yellow River downstream, and then crosses the mountains, you will reach

Xunhua

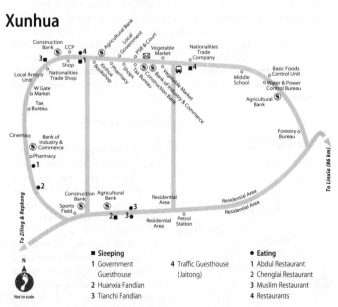

■ Sleeping		● Eating
1 Government Guesthouse	4 Traffic Guesthouse (Jaitong)	1 Abdul Restaurant
2 Huanxia Fandian		2 Chenglai Restaurant
3 Tianchi Fandian		3 Muslim Restaurant
		4 Restaurants

N

Not to scale

Far-east Tibet

Linxia after 86 kilometres. Some eight kilometres due east of Dowi on this road at **Qingshui**, three trails diverge, east for the small dam on the Qinghai-Gansu border (17 kilometres), southeast for Linxia, or southwest to **Mengda Tianchi Lake**. The last of these cuts through a lateral gorge for 12 kilometres to reach the lake, which is revered by Tibetans who view it as a talismanic power place, and it is now a nature reserve, although its woods are still extensively used by the last Salar village. There is a guesthouse before the lake which hires out horses for the four hours' trail through a craggy mountain gorge to the lakeside.

Heading southeast towards Linxia from the Qingshui intersection, the road passes through **Dawei** township, where there are some 13 monasteries, the most important being **Gori Dratsang Ganden Pelgyeling**. This was originally a Sakyapa establishment, which converted to the Gelukpa school during the 17th century. Most of the small monasteries of **Dawei valley** are affiliated to Gori. The exceptions are **Sechang Gar** which is a small branch of Labrang, **Dabma Gon**, which is a 19th century Nyingmapa nunnery eight kilometres northwest of the township, and **Changshar Gar**, nine kilometres southeast of the township, which was founded in 1626. After Dawei, the road crosses **Darje La** pass, which forms the current Qinghai-Gansu border and descends via **Gangshun Gon**, **Chorten Rangma**, and **Hanjiaji** to reach Linxia. A few hours' walking distance on the west side of the pass leads to **Darje Yumtso**, an oracle lake sited at the base of a high mountain.

Dowi to Repkong

At the Camel Spring Mosque of Lutuo, five kilometres west of Xunhua town, you can head north across the Yellow River to Hualong and Pingan (see above, page 558), or southwest for 57 kilometres to **Baoan**, where roads lead into **Repkong** (16 kilometres) and **Labrang** (78 kilometres). The latter, known as Highway 214, is currently under reconstruction. The road climbs from Lutuo for 12 kilometres to reach **Bimdo** village (*Altitude*: 2,280 metres), which is the most important Tibetan settlement in Dowi, and the birthplace of the late Panchen Lama.

Bimdo

Entering **Bimdo**, on the right (west) there is an impressive large building in classical Tibetan style with sloping white walls and architrave of red potentilla wood. This is a Tibetan primary school, which was funded by Tibetan residents of India. A stupa is passed on the left (east) and soon, on the right (west) you will reach the well-preserved farmhouse, which was the **birthplace of late Panchen Lama X**. It contains a small shrine attended by a caretaker and a courtyard is surrounded by wood-panelled rooms with packed-mud roofs, typical of Amdo hamlets. A footpath leads one hour walk over a spur from here to **Bimdo Gonchen Tashi Chokhorling**, which was rebuilt quite lavishly in the late 1980s but has not yet regained its religious atmosphere and former importance. Around Bimdo, there are six other monasteries, including **Kyilkhor Sangak Choding**, a branch of Labrang founded in 1777, and a Bonpo power place at **Wangtsangma**.

Higher up, in the mountains northwest of Bimdo, at **Karing**, there were formerly 11 monasteries, of which the Gelukpa **Lungyontang Hermitage**, **Bitang Lakhagar**, and **Ronpo Yershong** have been rebuilt, along with the Nyingma temples at **Dampoche Ngakhang** and **Rato Ngakhang**.

After Bimdo, the highway continues to follow a tributary of the Yellow

River upstream to the watershed (eight kilometres), Kangtsa (10 kilometres) and down to **Baoan** (22 kilometres), where the Repkong and Labrang roads diverge. At **Kangtsa**, there is another small 17th century Gelukpa monastery of the same name.

Jentsa County ᠎᠎᠎᠎᠎

Jantsa County (121)
尖扎县
Jainca
Population: 46,083
Area: 1,601 sq km
Colour map 5, grid B5

*Jentsa county straddles the Yellow River, between Trika to the west, and Bayan Khar and Repkong to the east. The county town is situated 18 kilometres southwest of Chunke and 58 kilometres from Hualong town, overlooking the south bank of the river. Though small and largely Tibetan, it has seen much encroachment from the Hui Muslim traders in recent years. Traditionally, there were 18 Tibetan monasteries in the county, the most important being **Lamo Dechen** of the Gelukpa school and **Achung Namdzong** of the Nyingmapa school.*

Hualong to Chunke township

From the Nakchutang intersection, 34 kilometres northwest of Hualong town, you can head north into Pingan (see above, page 545), or south towards the Yellow River. **Chunke** (*Ch* Qunke) township (*Altitude*: 2,040 metres) lies 18 kilometres due south of the intersection on the north bank of the Yellow River. Many of the small quiet hamlets passed on the descent are inhabited by Muslims, and each has its own village mosque. Tibetan monasteries were destroyed by Muslim zealots here as recently as 1952 (Gomzhi Gonpa). Chungke, however, has an air of activity; for three busy roads leads across the Yellow River from here in different directions: west to Lugyagak (*Ch* Lijiaxia), southeast to Jentsa town and east to Rongpo Gyakhar in Repkong. Slightly south of Chunke, and overlooking the north bank of the Yellow River is **Andarchagen Kharnang Monastery**, where a large image of Miatreya was recently rebuilt.

Jentsa town

Altitude: 2,040 metres
Phone code: 09828
Colour map 5, grid B5

To reach the county town, turn east at the Chunke T-junction, and after 16 kilometres on an excellent paved road surface which follows the north bank of the Yellow River, you will arrive at a turn-off which heads south across the river

Far-east Tibet

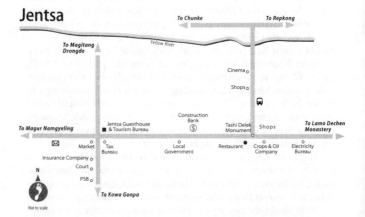

Jentsa

to **Jentsa**, two kilometres distant. (The main road continues east into Repkong, reaching **Rongpo Gyakhar** after 62 kilometres.) Crossing the bridge into town, you will pass a cinema and shops on the right and the bus station on the left, before reaching an intersection, dominated by a monument bearing the inscribed legend Tashidelek. Turn left here and head south for **Lamo Dechen Monastery**, or right (west) to the downtown area, where there are banks, government buildings and the *Jentsa Guesthouse* where the local tourism bureau is based. Then, turn south for **Kowa Gonpa** or head due west, following the river bank upstream to **Magur Namgyeling** monastery.

Sleeping C *Jentsa Government Guesthouse*, T(09828)32503. Rooms at ¥88 (deluxe), ¥60 (standard), ¥90 (triple), and ¥40 (ordinary).

Eating There is a newly constructed Sichuan restaurant at the crossroads, which has the best and cleanest food in town.

Lamo Dechen Monastery

Lamo Dechen Gonpa, with around 250 monks, is the largest monastery of *Colour map 5, grid B5* Jentsa county, located high on a ridge about 25 kilometres, south of town near **Lengke** township, and approached on a soft earth surface which can be treacherous during the rainy season. The monastery is sited amidst high altitude Tibetan farming villages with some nearby patches of original forest.

    Lamo Dechen Chokhorling was founded by Lamo III Ngawang Lobzang Tenpei Gyeltsen (1660-1728). Although it subsequently developed into the largest monastery of Jentsa county, the **Magur Namgyeling** monastery which was founded by his predecessor Lamo II Lodro Gyatso (1610-1659) is still revered as its mother monastery. Gradually Lamo Dechen's influence increased throughout the region, until at its zenith there were 40 affiliated branch monasteries, extending from Dabzhi southwards, and as many as 51 recognized tulkus, presiding over the main temple complex of two assembly halls and 26 additional shrines.

    The principal line of incarnations here is that of the Lamo succession. The first of the line was Zhabdrung Karpo (fl. late 16th century) from Lamo Rinchengang in Central Tibet, who is formally known by the title Lamo I Tsoknyi Gyatso. The line was extended back retrospectively to include the great Kadampa masters Chengawa Tsultrim Bar (1038-1103), Lama Dampa Sonm Gyeltsen (1312-1375), and Chengawa Lodro Gyeltsen (1402-1472). His successors were scions of the Tumed and Arik Mongol clans, who had occupied much of Amdo since the military campaigns of Gushi Qan, namely: Lamo II Lodro Gyatso (1610-1659) who established Magur Namgyeling; Lamo III Ngawang Lobzang Tenpei Gyeltsen (1660-1728) who was recognized by Dalai Lama V; Lamo IV Lobzang Tendzin Gelek Gyeltsen (1729-1796); Lamo V Pende Wangchuk Khetsun Gyatso (1797-1831); Lamo VI Ngawang Chokdrub Tenpei Gyeltsen (1832-1872); Lamo VII Tendzin Norbu Pelzangpo (1873-1927); Lamo VIII Lobzang Lungrik Tenpei Gyatso (1928-1951), who was also known as Alak Sharak; and the present incumbent, Lamo IX Lobzang Tendzin Chokyi Gyeltsen, who is currently being educated at the Dabzhi Gonsar branch monastery (see above), to the northeast of Lake Kokonor.

    Although there are six newly constructed temples and one assembly hall at Lamo Dechen, they are all extremely basic, with the Repkong mural panels as the main point of interest. In the vicinity of **Dangshun** township which is passed on the way to Lamo Dechen, there are two affiliated monasteries at **Gyertang Ritro** and **Trika Gonpa**. Also, at **Angla** township, 12 kilometres

Far-east Tibet

south of town, there is the **Nangra Serkhang**, which was founded in 1341 by Dondrub Rinchen before he went on to establish the more illustrious Jakhyung Shedrubling (see above, page 558). Some original buildings in Sino-Tibetan style have been preserved here.

Magur Namgyeling

The monastery of **Magur Namgyeling**, also known as **Gurgon**, is located five kilometres north of Jentsa town, on a ridge overlooking the north bank of the Yellow River. The original foundation is attributed to Zhabdrung Karpo who received an injunction from Dalai Lama III, but it appears to have been rebuilt by his incarnation Lamo II Lodro Gyatso in 1646, and to have been refurbished in later centuries following periodic damage inflicted by the flooding waters of the Yellow River. Nowadays, there are 40 monks at Gurgon. Two buildings now stand: the newly constructed **assembly hall** (Dukhang) and a magnificent **Jokhang temple**, which survived the Cultural Revolution unscathed when it was used as a granary. The former contains images of Tsongkhapa, Alak Sharak and his reliquary, and Repkong murals depicting (left): Shridevi, Vaishravana, Vajrapani, Kalacakra, Guhyasamaja, Cakrasamvara, and Vajrabhairava, and also (right): the paradises of Abhirati, Sukhavati and Sudarshana, along with Sarvavid Vairocana, Six-armed Mahakala, and Dharmaraja. In the vestibule, there is an inscription outlining the lineage of the Lamo Rinpoche. The **protector temple** to the rear is still incomplete, but above its entrance there are fine murals depicting Tsongkhapa, the Gurgon lineage, the 16 Elders, and the 35 Confession Buddhas. To the west of the courtyard stands the undamaged **Jokhang temple**. Inside there are images of the Buddhas of the Three Times, flanked by the eight standing bodhisattvas, with Songtsen Gampo near the door. Murals also depict the Six Ornaments and Two Supreme Masters of Ancient India (left) and the 10 teachers of Tsongkhapa (right).

Kowa Gon and Ngagrong Gon

There are several smaller monasteries in Jentsa county, most of them set high up the side-valley between Lugyagak and Jentsa. These can be accessed on a hill-road, which connects the bridge at **Dongma** with the county town. Some four kilometres west of town, there is the **Lo Dorjedrak cave**, where Lhalung Pelgyi Dorje stayed in retreat after his assassination of the Tibetan king Langdarma in the ninth century. Nearby is the mountain hermitage of **Bumkhang Ja'oma**, which is said to have been founded in the 13th century by Sakya Pandita, and which contains relics of the Nyingma treasure-finder Sangye Lingpa and the bow used by Lhalung Pelgyi Dorje to slay Langdarma. Then, 10 kilometres west of modern **Cuo Zhou** township, there is the monastery of **Kowa Gonsar**, founded in the 14th century by the Sakyapa master Kowa Shinglu Jangchub Osel, who acted as a quorum member when Tsongkhapa was ordained at Jakhyung. The Gelukpa monastery of **Ngangrong Tashi Chopeling**, (founded 1738) lies five kilometres further southwest from here.

Sangdrok Gon and Dzongang Gon

Continuing northwest on the hill road, a turn-off on the left leads inland to modern **Jiajia** township and **Sangdrok Dechenling**, another 14th century Sakyapa monastery which was absorbed by the Gelukpas of Lamo Dechen.

Then, just five kilometres south of Lugyagak there is the Gelukpa institution of **Gawu Dzongnang**, which houses a fine set of old tangkas. All of these smaller monasteries in Jentsa county have 50-100 monks each.

Lugyagak

If you drive west from the Chunke intersection on the north bank of the Yellow River, you will cross to the south bank at **Dongma** after eight kilometres and reach **Lugyagak**, after a further 10 kilometres. Just before entering town the Gelukpa monastery of **Jakhyung** (see above, page 558) comes into view on the opposite north bank. Lugyagak, also known in Tibetan as **Ngagyagak** (*Ch* Lijiaxia), is a rapidly growing town located alongside the largest hydroelectric construction project on the Tibetan plateau. The dam at Lugyakag is 155 metre high and 411 metre long, creating a 320 square kilometres reservoir lake. From here it is possible to visit the **Khamra National Park** (*Ch* Kanbula) and the historically important monasteries and caves of **Achung Namdzong**.

Sleeping **C** *Lijiaxia Hotel*, T099830-42888. Excellent standard double rooms at ¥94. There are also smaller guesthouses in the town, including the *Mirik Dronkhang*.

Eating There are many small restaurants catering to dam workers and engineers. However, the best cuisine on offer is undoubtedly at the *Lijiaxia Hotel*.

Khamra National Park and Achung Namdzong

Khamra National Park (*Ch* Kanbula) is a spectacularly forested region to the south of the Yellow river, covering an area of 1,525,000 square kilometres. The forest is named after the homeland of the Nub clan who moved here from Central Tibet via Kham. Approximately 80 per cent of the park is virgin forest. Some 276 species of plants and trees have been identified, including pine, cypress and birch. However, the park is characterized by its extraordinary peaks, many of which rise abruptly from the verdant valley floor in the form of bare red rock pinnacles. The central peak is known as **Namdzong** (approximately 2,000 metres) and around it spread throughout the park there are 18 identifiable peaks. Among these, the highest group of six are revered as the snow-white abodes of the gods (ie Gopodzong, Nepodzong, Bashingdzong, Trichdzong, Jomodzong and Ngadzong); the middle group of six are known as the red-rock abodes of the hunting spirits (ie Razhudzong, Gonpodzong, Lamtrengdzong, Tadzong, Degyedzong, and Lugdzong); while the lowest group of six are known as the verdant abodes of the serpentine water spirits (ie Mukpodzong, Nordzong, Shadzong, Radzong, Sermodzong, and Zordzong). The name Achung Namdzong is an amalgam of Mount Namka, and the hill blocking its approach, which is said to resemble the Tibetan letter "a-chung"; while the term "dzong" here implies that the peaks are citadel hermitages for meditation.

■ *Admission: ¥10*
Colour map 5, grid B4

Far-east Tibet

Getting there Khamra National Park is accessible by road on a long 32 kilometres detour to the south. The easier option is to drive 7 kilometres to the jetty on the shore of the vast artificial lake created by the dam, and cross by ferry boat (4 kilometres). The road from the town to the jetty recrosses the Yellow River just below the dam, offering a close view of this ambitious construction project in progress, and then traverses a pass (2,220 metres) before descending to the lakeside. There are several boats moored at the jetty (¥5-¥7.5 per person, and the crossing of the lake itself will take about 15 minutes. On reaching the southeast shore, jeeps are available (¥40) to negotiate the rough 4 kilometres track uphill to the Gate of the Khamra National Park (*Ch* Kanbula). The road divides here, with the right fork heading into the protected forest area of the National Park, and the left heading up to Achung Namdzong. In 1998 when the construction of the dam is completed, the water level will rise a further 30 metres, enabling the ferry boats to moor alongside the gate. An admission fee of ¥10 is charged for entrance to the park.

Achung Namdzong

Colour map 5, grid B4   The historically important site of **Malho Dorje Drakra Achung Namdzong** is located within the Khamra National Park. During the eighth century this sacred abode was entrusted by Padmasambhava to the protector deity Mesang, and it was revered as one of the 25 important power places of Kham and Amdo, specifically symbolizing the mind aspect of buddha-mind. Later, when Buddhism was persecuted in Central Tibet by the king Langdarma, the three wise monks: Tsang Rabsel of Chuwori, Mar Shakyamuni of Tolung and Yo-ge Jung of Bodong fled via Qarloq to Amdo, where they initially stayed for 20 years in the cave hermitage of Achung Namdzong. Lhalung Pelgyi Dorje followed them here, after his assassination of Langdarma, and the meditation hermitage on the adjacent Ugdzong Hill, known as Shamalung, is said to contain the remains of his robe. It was here, and in other power places of Amdo, such as Dentik, that the monastic lineage was preserved from persecution and eventually restored intact to Central Tibet by their disciples and successors. In later centuries, Achung Namdzong was visited by important lamas, including Zhabkar Tsokdruk Rangdrol who likened the red-rock terrain to a red ruby. Four monasteries were built around Namdzong, along with the 13 residences of the great lamas who lived here, namely: Sangak Tengyeling, Dzatro Dorjeling, Tashi Namgyeling, and Samten Chopeling. Lama Gurong Tsan, the chief Nyingmapa master of the region, whose 80-year-old mother also lives here, has overseen the construction, but funds are now short and the temples still require interior decoration.

Samten Chopeling   Overlooking the gateway to the Khamra National Park, the nunnery of **Samten Chopeling** occupies the flat tableland of **Chorten Tang** on Jomodzong Hill. Tibetan Buddhist nuns had lived here since 1710 during the lifetime of the famed meditation teacher Yeshe Drolma. The actual monastery was founded in 1870 by Gurong Natsok Rangdrol, and the ornate roof of the assembly hall was added by Gurong Orgyan Jikdrel Choying Dorje in 1899. Samten Chopeling quickly became the most important nunnery of the Nyingma school in Amdo, visited by great Dzogchen masters of Kham and Amdo alike. The present reconstructed buildings, which date from 1979, were completed due to the efforts of Gurong Gyelse, Lama Drolo, Tulku Pema Namdrol, and Ane Rigzin who presides over some 200 nuns. The approach to the nunnery is marked by a large stupa and a set of the eight stupas symbolizing the major events in the life of Shakyamuni Buddha. It contains images of Padmakara, flanked by his two consorts, along with Manjughosa and Tara. The murals, in Repkong style, depict (left): the 35 Confession Buddhas, Shakyamuni with the 16 Elders, and the *Longchen Nyingtig* lineage, and (right): Sarvavid Vairocana, Sitatapatra, and Ekajati.

Tashi Namgyeling   About two kilometres up valley from the nunnery on the **Tashitang** tableland, there is a small Gelukpa temple, named **Tashi Namgyeling**. This establishment was founded in 1794 by Kapukpa Pandita Lobzang Dondrub, and subsequently rebuilt in 1809 and 1821. The present structure dates from the 1980s, and there are only a few monks in residence. The assembly hall contains images of Tsongkhapa with his students, the reliquary of Serkhang Rinpoche Lobzang Tendzin Gyatso, and murals depicting the 35 Confession Buddhas, Vaishravana, Shakyamuni with the 16 Elders, Khacari, Sarvavid Vairocana, and the life story of Milarepa.

The original Nyingma temples were constructed on the table hill of **Namtar Tang** in conjunction with the adjacent mountain hermitages of Lhalung Pelgyi Dorje and the three wise monks. Later, in 1814, a large temple was founded here by Palchen Namka Jikme, and in 1848 it was refurbished by Gurong Natsok Rangdrol. In 1898, Gurong Orgyan Jikdrel Choying Dorje extended the complex of buildings and added a golden spire to the roof. During the 19th century and early 20th century, the monastery was visited by most of the great Nyingma lamas of Kham, and it had the reputation for being the most active teaching and meditation centre of the Nyingma school in Amdo, with some 25 branches under its authority. From 1932 onwards the lineage has been maintained by Gurong Gyelse and his successors, and the present buildings date from 1981 onwards. There are about 100 monks and a variable number of long-haired mantrins, known as *ngakpa* in Tibetan (pronounced 'ngukwa' or 'hwon' in local Amdo dialect). The mantrins at Sangak Tengyeling are generally older men who have received some religious instruction in the past, and take a limited number of Vinaya vows in conjunction with their bodhisattva and mantra vows. Most are married farmers or, less frequently, nomads, and one who lives nearby acts as the caretaker.

Sangak Tengyeling is rare amongst the monasteries of Amdo for the high quality of its construction, particularly the woodwork, which is excellent. There are two main temples: the **Dolma Lhakhang** and the **Assembly Hall** (Dukhang). The former, contains large images of Padmakara flanked by his two consorts, along with Manjughosa, Shakyamuni with his foremost students, the Lords of the Three Enlightened Families, and Tara, along with 1,000 smaller images of Tara. There is a throne bearing a portrait of Gurong IV, the current incumbent who resides in Jentsa county town, and fine murals depicting (left): Amritakundalin, Vaishravana, Zangdokpelri, and the *Nyingtig* lineage, and (right): Sukhavati, the Kabgye meditational deities, Gonpo Maning, Ekajati, Rahula, and Dorje Lekpa. The balcony has images of Longchen Rabjampa, Padmasambhava and Zhabkar Tsokdruk Rangdrol, while towards the roof there are murals depicting the 35 Confession Buddhas and the Nyingma lineage.

The **Assembly Hall** contains images of Padmakara with his two foremost consorts, along with Manjughosa and Tara, and the volumes of the *Kangyur* and *Tengyur*. The murals here depict (left): Amritakundalin, Kabgye, Vajrakila, the Lords of the Three Enlightened Families, and Sukhavati, and (right): Vajrasattva with consort, Khorwa Yongdul, Bhaisajyaguru, Guru Drakpo, and Hayagriva. The balcony has images of the Eight Manifestations of Padmasambhava, and the eight stupas symbolizing events in the life of Shakyamuni Buddha.

Dzatro Dorjeling

The reliquary temple of Gurong Choying Dorje was originally founded in 1913, and named **Dzatro Dorjeling** in 1923. It functioned as an important hermitage for Nyingma practice until its destruction during the Cultural Revolution. In 1993 it was relocated at **Namdzong Tse**, the summit of Mount Namka, near the caves of the three wise monks. Within the caves, which are spectacularly located on a ledge near the summit of Namkadzong Tse, there

Sangak Tengyeling

Far-east Tibet

are traces of original murals to be seen. This site is accessible by a steep track on the north side, which should not be attempted during or just after heavy rain.

Below Sangak Tengyeling, there is the residence of Lama Drolo, which has a finely constructed Mani Lhakhang. There are images of Amitayus, White Tara and Vijaya, tangkas depicting Vajrakila and Zangdokpelri, and nine large water-powered prayer wheels.

Repkong County རེབ་གོང་

Repkong County (122)
同仁县
Tongren
Population: 68,349
Area: 3,353 sq km
Colour map 5, grid B5

Central Amdo, the region south of Tsongkha, comprises a large proportion of the Tibetan population of Amdo. Farmers and nomads are spread through the verdant valleys and plains, and there are many monasteries dotted throughout the region. **Repkong** *in Central Amdo, just south of the Yellow River, can in many ways be considered the heart of Amdo. Its principal monastery predates Labrang and Kumbum by at least two centuries, and the county itself possesses 36 smaller monasteries, mostly of the Gelukpa school, although there are also important Nyingmapa hermitages here.*

The main river of Repkong is the Gu-chu, which flows north to converge with the Yellow River near Lamo Dechen. The 'nine side-valleys' that make up the Gu-chu basin vary from rolling grasslands which support nomadic camper groups, through forested gorges, to an agricultural zone near the county town itself. The ethnic mix is also fascinating, for there are four villages inhabited by thoroughly Tibetanized Tu people in the valley while to the east lies Dowi (Xunhua), home of the Muslim Salar and to the north Bayan Khar (Hualong), a Hui autonomous county, and to the south, Sogwo (*Ch* Henan), a Mongol autonomous county.

The capital, **Rongpo Gyakhar**, is both the administrative centre for Repkong County and for the South Yellow River Prefecture. The distance to the capital from Jadir in Tsekok is 97 kilometres, from Jentsa 64 kilometres, and from Dowi 67 kilometres (both via the Bao'an intersection). Another road leads southeast via Bao'an for 115 kilometres from Rongpo Gyakhar to Labrang Monastery.

Lower Gu-chu Valley

Driving east from the Chunke intersection on the north bank of the Yellow River (see above, page 564), you will bypass the turn-off for Jentsa town after 16 kilometres, and continue on to cross the Yellow River and head into the Gu-chu valley. Rongpo Gyakhar lies 62 kilometres from the Jentsa turn-off. Driving into the valley, there are branch monasteries of Rongpo Gonchen close to the road at **Rongpo Gon Chopeling** (18th century) and **Tashikyil** (founded 1625-1648). The road follows the spectacular Gu-chu gorges upstream, and gradually the valley broadens

Repkong County

into a fertile plain, dotted with villages and monasteries, that stretches all the way to Rongpo Gyakhar, the county and prefectural capital. About 22 kilometres south of the bridge, a side road cuts southwest for 25 kilometres to **Yershong Gon**, another branch of Rongpo Gonchen. Continuing south on the main road, after five kilometres you will reach **Maba** township, in the vicinity of which there are three monasteries, the most significant being **Yiga Chodzinling**, which was converted from the Nyingmapa to the Gelukpa tradition in 1685. Some five kilometres south of Maba, the road intersects with the highway from Dowi (see above) at **Bao'an** 16 kilometres north of the county capital.

If, instead of driving south to Rongpo Gyakhar, you take the highway toward Dowi, leaving the central Gu-chu valley, it splits after seven kilometres at a cement factory near **Tokya**: the highway on the left fork heading northeast to Dowi (52 kilometres) and a branch road on the right heading southeast to Labrang (100 kilometres). Up a side valley to the south, before reaching this junction, the small monastery of **Tokya Tashi Chopeling** is set on a cliff at the entrance to a vast cave network. The extensive caves (some 20 kilometres from Tokya) are said to link up with the cave at Drakar near Labrang in an eight-day underground pothole. There is a natural cave temple dedicated to Cakrasamvara here, and it is one of the 'eight places of spiritual attainment' sited around the Gu-chu valley. A roadside stupa marks the approach to the caves.

Tokya Tashi Chopeling

Yarma Tashikyil

The road to Labrang climbs for 12 kilometres from the Dowi turn-off, leaving the Gu-chu valley, and entering a beautiful red sandstone gorge, which is forested in its upper reaches. Here, it reaches the township of **Zhongpang Chi** (*Ch* Shuangpengxi), a farming village with two temples, one of which (20 minutes' walk north of the road) marks the birthplace of Zhabkar Tsokdruk Rangdrol (1781-1851). Driving six kilometres uphill from the township, you will reach a clearing on the left, from where a trekking trail leads sharply uphill towards the ridge of the valley. The climb takes approximately 50 minutes, and leads to a flat tableland where the monastery of **Yarma Tashikyil**, an important hermitage of the Nyingma tradition, maintained by a strong community of monks and *ngakpas*, is located. On the approach to the monastery, you will pass three stupas, built by Zhabkar Tsokdruk Rangdrol in person, and the empty spot where the house of Gendun Chopel, one of Tibet's greatest 20th century writers, once stood. The temple itself has images of Padmakara flanked by Shantaraksita and King Trisong Detsen, with Vajrasattva to the left and the volumes of the *Kangyur* and *Tengyur* on the side walls. Murals depict (left): Ekajati, Guru Drakpo, Zangdokpelri, and Vajrasattva with consort, and (right): Dompa Trungri, Hayagriva, Tara, White Jambhala, and Shridevi. The gallery has images of Zhabkar III, Shakyamuni with his foremost students and Atisha with his foremost students. The murals below the roof depict the 84 Mahasiddhas.

    From the vantage point of Yarma Tashikyil, there are wide panoramic views of the Repkong region with the snow peak of **Mount Amnye Nyenri** to the left. Zhabkar spent many years teaching here, and his stone chairs are still enclosed in ancient groves. There is a small government compound truckstop at **Zhongpang Chi**, where it may be possible to stay. The present incumbent, Zhabkar IV is 18 years old, undergoing education at Rongpo Gyakhar.

Colour map 5, grid B5

Far-east Tibet

Gartse Gonpa

Colour map 5, grid B5 Continuing through the heavily logged gorge from Zhongpang township, and crossing a spur, the road ascends 12 kilometres to the attractive **Gartse Gonpa**. This is revered as one of the eight foremost places of spiritual attainment in Repkong, and it currently has 140 monks. There is a Jokhang temple, a protector temple, and an assembly hall (Tsokchen Dukhang), all decorated in the Labrang style. Within the **assembly hall**, there are images of Tsongkhapa with his foremost students, along with images of Alak Gangzang, Shar Kalden Gyatso, Jamyang Zhepa V (b. 1916), and Alak Sertsang, as well as murals depicting (left): Shridevi, Vaishravana, White Tara, Green Tara, Amitabha, Sarvavid Vairocana, and Vajrabhairava, and (right): Vajrapani, Hayagriva, Sitatapatra, Tsegyel, Six-armed Mahakala, and Dharmaraja.

After Gartse, the road traverses a broad grassy plain beside **Mount Amnye Nyemri**, and continues six kilometres to the watershed pass (3,600 metres) which marks the current provincial frontier between Qinghai and Gansu. From here, Labrang (see page 626) in Sangchu county is only 48 kilometres distant (via Kangya and Drakar Gonpa). A more indirect trekking route continues southeast across the plain from Gartse to **Dowa** (42 kilometres), and thence to Labrang via Sangke. A branch of Rongpo Gonchen, named **Dowa Dongak Dargyeling**, was also established at remote Dowa.

Rongpo Gyakhar

Phone code: 0973
Colour map 5, grid B5 According to 1989 statistics, the population of the town is almost 70 per cent Tibetan, but the buildings have a very Chinese appearance. The town has not yet developed as a tourist destination, but this is changing following the completion in 1997 of the new high-rise *Huangnan Hotel*, at the top of Main Street. The open air market, entered by a passageway opposite the old *Huangnan Hotel* is well worth a visit.

Festivals Local village folk dances are held in Rongpo Gyakhar and outlying villages in summertime. The 1998 dates for these festivals are: 8-16 August.

Rongpo Gonchen Monastery **Rongpo Gonchen**, the principal monastery of Repkong, lies in the southern part of town. The original buildings were constructed in 1301 by the Sakyapa master Sangda Rinchen, who was an emissary of Drogon Chogyel Phakpa. Later, it was reconstituted as a Gelukpa monastery by Shar Kalden Gyatso during the 16th century. The monastery currently has nine temples and around 400 monks; headed by the important incarnate lamas of Rongpo. The principal tulku, Rongpo Kyabgon VIII, is now a young boy. The previous incumbent passed away in 1978.

There are 35 branch monasteries, most of them in Repkong county, and these are often associated with the other lamas affiliated to the mother monastery: Alak Re Yerchung, Alak Kutso, Alak Rongwo, Alak Tson-de, and so forth. The main north-south road runs between the monastery and a small cliff below which is the old village, complete with Chinese temple and a mosque, on the banks of the Gu-chu.

The site At its high point, Rongpo Gonchen had four major colleges: a general college known as **Dratsang Tosam Namgyeling**, a tantric college known as **Gyudra Sangchen Chokyi Bangzo**, a Kalacakra college known as **Dudra Sangak Dargyeling**, and a meditation college called **Drubdra Nechok Tashikyil**. Among the renovated buildings, the **Great Assembly Hall (Tsokchen**

Dukhang) is close to the main road, behind a shrine dedicated to the gate-keeper Acala (containing an enormous image of this sword-wielding deity). The main entrance of the monastery is located some distance further south, through a chapel gateway decorated with modern murals. The interior of the Great Assembly Hall is vast and spartan; but its porch contains some interesting murals, which depict the ubiquitous Four Guardian Kings, the dress code for monks, and in addition, the local protector deities of Amdo, known as Amnye Machen and Amnye Jakhyung. The latter is the name of a sacred snow peak 20 kilometres due east of Repkong.

To the south and slightly uphill from the Great Assembly Hall is the **Khardong Chapel**, containing the reliquary stupa of Rongpo Kyapgon VII. The renovated **Kalacakra College (Du-khor Dratsang)** lies behind it, and contains some beautiful new murals executed by the master artist, Kharsham Gyal, in the Repkong style. There are new images of the kings of Shambhala, yet to be installed, and a few old tangkas, notably a large Tsongkhapa and a depiction of Tsongkhapa flanked by his followers (Je Yabsesum). One of the statues depicts Shar Kalden Gyatso, who established the Gelukpa tradition here in the 16th century. Far to the right of the Kalacakra College is the **Jampeyang Lhakhang** with its distinctive *gyabib*-style roof. It contains an exquisitely fashioned clay image of Manjughosa, which exhibits all the best hallmarks of Repkong clay sculpture. Above this temple is the **Podrang**, or residence of the present Rongpo Kyapgon VIII, and the restored tantric college or **Gyupa Dratsang**.

Ceremonies, including the unveiling of a large tangka, debates and religious dances, will be held at Rongpo Gonchen during the 1st month of the lunar calendar on 28 February-3 March 1999.

Festivals

Rongpo Gonchen was formerly renowned for its expertise in Tibetan medicine and in painting. Two painting schools known as Sengeshong Yagotsang and Sengeshong Magotsang were established to the north of the monastery and these were given responsibility for the painting and embellishing of different temples and colleges.

Painting schools of Repkong

At the monastery of Palden Chokhorling in **Sengeshong Yagotsang** (founded 1385) there is an **Assembly Hall** containing exquisite clay statues, the foremost representing Repkong Kyapgon VII and the founder of Yagotsang. The work is recent, the original having been destroyed by fire in 1946 and replaced in 1949. Alongside the assembly hall is a temple dedicated to the Buddhas of the Three Times, in which the enormous figures of the three buddhas are flanked by the eight standing bodhisattvas. A side chapel dedicated to Tsongkhapa is currently under construction.

Sengeshong Yagotsang

Ceremonies, including the unveiling of a large tangka and religious dances, will be held here during the 1st month of the lunar calendar on 20-24 February 1999.

Festivals

At the monastery of **Gendun Puntsok Choling** in Sengeshong Magotsang (founded 16th century), where there are currently 150 monks, the **Assembly Hall** has original ceiling panels, dating to the 1910s. These survived the ravages of the Cultural Revolution because the building was used as a wheat granary during that turbulent period. Alongside it is a Maitreya temple containing enormous and outstanding clay images: Maitreya, flanked by Manjushri (twice), Mahakarunika, and Tsongkhapa. The image of Manjushri to the left is upright, as is that of Mahakarunika to the right.

Sengeshong Magotsang

Sengeshong Art Schools

Slightly north of the town, the two renowned painting schools of Repkong, known as **Sengeshong Yagotsang** and **Sengeshong Magotsang**, are located within their unique idyllic village settings. Almost every house is an artist's studio, and in recent years four artists have become celebrities in their own right: Shawu Tsering of Sengeshong Yagotsang, Gyatso of Sengeshong Magotsang, Kunzang (who resides across the Gu-chu river) and Jigme (now deceased). Their works are on display in the Repkong Art Centre of the Huangnan Tibetan Nationality Autonomous Prefecture in town. More importantly, their work is represented in the exquisitely decorated temples of Sengeshong Yagotsang and Magotsang monasteries.

The Repkong school of art, known as Wutun to the Chinese, was established by the 15th century and, by the 18th century, it had spread to cover much of Amdo, as indeed it does today. Almost all of the work executed here over the centuries was lost, unseen by the outside world, during the destruction of Amdo's monasteries in the Cultural Revolution; but due to the dedication of a few elderly masters the tradition is now being carefully handed down to the next generation. The style broadly follows that of Central Tibet, but the infusion of cultures brought by contact with the Mongols, Tu and neighbouring Chinese makes the work distinct. This is reflected in the ethnic origins of the people of Sengeshong themselves, who are said to have come from Western Tibet and to have intermingled over the centuries with neighbouring communities.

Sleeping *Huangnan Hotel*, T0973-722684/722293. ¥220 per room. The best rooms and cuisine in town. The old *Tongren County Guesthouse* also has a range of rooms from ¥20 upwards, the best with attached baths and running hot water in the evenings. There is a good 2nd Floor Chinese restaurant, and a cheaper one on the ground floor (sharing the same kitchen).

Eating As with most Amdo towns, there are mostly Muslim noodle restaurants, and a few more upmarket Chinese ones.

Festivals Religious dances will be held here on **25 February 1999**.

Middle Gu-chu Valley

Gomar Gonpa On the valley floor north of Repkong are the Gelukpa monasteries of **Nyentok** and **Gomar**, both populated with Tu rather than Tibetan monks. Nyentok (founded 1740-94) is small and close to town, while Gomar is five kilometres further north and much more impressive. The three-storey **Jampa Lhakhang** built in 1741 by Alak Yeshe Jang still stands. There are also newly-built temples, all of a much higher artistic and architectural standard than the normal concrete and brick, and a colourful seven-tiered stupa with temples atop with a good view of the valley. A large tangka will be displayed on 25-26 February, 1999.

From **Rongpo Gyakhar**, a branch road extends northwest for 10 kilometres to **Shadrang Gon Puntsok Choling**, which was built by Tsongkhapa's teacher Dondrub Rinchen in 1341 before he founded **Jakhyung Monastery**. En route, at **Dangpozhi Magon Tubten Chokhorling**, four kilometres from town, the original foundation is attributed to one of Lhalung Pelgyi Dorje's students (10th century). Another branch road runs southeast from town towards **Tsagyel Tarpaling**, 25 kilometres to southeast, and thence to **Dechen Ritro** hermitage.

Upper Gu-chu Valley

Jangkya

Due south of Rongpo Gyakhar town, the main road continues to follow the Gu-chu upstream, into the broad grassy plains of Tobden, Tsekok, and Sogwo. **Jangkya** is the first village, seven kilometres out of Repkong, and it has a tiny Nyingmapa temple. A few rather tattered original Repkong wall hangings are preserved here, reputedly thanks to them being hidden on **Mount Amnye Mori** behind the village during the 1960s. The valley to the east contains the affiliated **Janglung Khyung Gonpa**, also of the Nyingmapa school, which once housed 125 monks, and a small Gelukpa monastery, named **Janglung Garsar Ganden Chopeling**.

Chukhol Khartse Gonpa

Further south, at **Chukhol Khartse Gonpa**, 18 kilometres from town, there are sacred hot springs. **Dardzom Gonpa**, a 17th century branch of Rongpo Gonchen, lies higher, above the valley, giving unparalleled views and a tantalizing glimpse of **Mount Amnye Jakhyung**, the prime holy mountain of Central Amdo. There are many other significant hills and mountains in the vicinity, and almost every village will have its arrow shrines on a nearby hill, which are attended annually. A few like **Amnye Taklung**, close to Repkong, are more broadly recognized; and Amnye Jakhyung is renowned all over Amdo.

Chuku

Also in the Upper Gu-chu region, near **Chuku** township, there are old Nyingmapa hermitages at **Kodegon Dzogchen Namgyeling** and **Muselgar**, the former having been an original 13th century Kadampa foundation, and the latter affiliated to Katok. There appear to be no traces, however, of the two largest Nyingmapa monasteries in the area: **Repkong Nyingon** of the Mindroling tradition, which had over 1,000 monks; and **Repkong Sibgon** of the *Longchen Nyingtig* tradition, which had over 1,500 monks.

After Dardzom Gonpa, the road continues through partially forested hills to cross the county border into **Tsekok**, 20 kilometres above Chuku township. The distance from the county border to Jadir town in Tsekok is only 62 kilometres.

Tsekok County རྩེ་ཁོག

Tsekok County (123)
泽库县
Zekog
Population: 42,489
Area: 6,858 sq km
Colour map 5, grid B4

The county of Tsekok is a broad grassland which extends hundreds of kilometres through the upper reaches of the Tse-chu, north of the sharp bend in the Yellow River. The county town, known as ***Jadir****, has an air of the Wild West. Nomads in shaggy sheepskin coats typical of Amdo ride into town on a yak or horse to do the shopping, play pool, and sell a sheep or yakskin. The town has simple guesthouse and restaurant facilities. Within Tsekok county, Nyingmapa and Gelukpa nomadic communities have co-existed since the 15th century. Presently, there are 13 monasteries, of which six are Nyingmapa, and the remainder mostly affiliated to Rongpo Gonchen in Repkong.*

Getting there

The distance from Repkong to Jadir is 98 kilometres, from Jadir to Henan in Sogwo county, 39 kilometres, and from Jadir to Tungte in Kawasumdo 111 kilometres.

Repkong to Jadir

The road from Jadir leads across the watershed into a forested area, where in the vicinity of Tobden township there are three monasteries of note:

Karashong Gon was founded as a branch of Labrang in the 1950s. **Karong Sangchen Gatsel Choling** is a largish Nyingmapa monastery, founded in 1944 by Lama Tsering Dondrub; and **Dzongmar Tashi Choling** is an 18th century branch of Rongpo Gonchen. The township of **Tobden** (*Ch* Duofudun), 25 kilometres down valley, is little more than a restaurant and checkpost on the grasslands, and the distance from here to Jadir in the upper Tse-chu valley is only 37 kilometres.

Jadir

The Gelukpa monastery of **Sonak Geden Tashi Choling**, four kilometres south of town, lies on the north bank of the Tse-chu. It was originally a tented monastery, its first adobe buildings being constructed by Tendzin Gyatso (1616-1687). About one kilometre distant, also on the north bank of the river, there is a small Nyingmapa temple called **Sonak Tersar**, and another small Gelukpa monastery, named **Tukchen Yonden Dargyeling**, which is affiliated to Rongpo Gonchen. One of its temples is built of stone, all too rare in modern Amdo, and decorated with Repkong-style tangkas which depict Tara, Bhaisajyaguru, Avalokiteshvara, Sitatapatra, Tsongkhapa, and the protectress Shridevi, alongside the standard set of images. At **Chakor** township, 10 kilometres southeast of town on a branch road, the Gelukpa monastery of **Gartse Gonpa** is located on the north bank of the Tse-chu.

East of Jadir

Heading east from Jadir town on a branch road to the north, you will reach **Chisa** (*Ch* Xibusha) township after eight kilometres. In the hills above Chisa, there is the Gelukpa monastery of **Chisa Drubde Gecheling**, formerly a tented camp, where the first adobe temples were constructed in 1936 by Chisa Lodro Gyatso (d. 1957). A small Nyingmapa hermitage known as **Chisa Ngakhang** was founded nearby in 1950 by Rekong Tulku. The motorable trail continues into the hills from Chisa as far as **Dokar Ngakhang**, where the small Nyingma hermitage dates from 1955. Some 20 kilometres further north in a remote area of **Dorjedzong**, there is a Gelukpa hermitage affiliated to Rongpo Gonchen, where the **Dzikar Caves** contain a natural stone image of Maitreya.

Hor township

Colour map 5, grid B4 — Southwest of Jadir, a rough 72 kilometres trail leads to **Hor** township, where some two kilometres south in the grassland, there is a Nyingmapa monastery known as **Terton Chogar** or Hor Gon Tekchok Tashiling. Originally a tented camp, the first solid buildings were constructed here by Hor Tulku in 1831. Now, mantrins and monks of the Nyingma school both attend a three-storeyed temple and its 200 metre long Mani Wall, the most famous in all of Amdo. A religious opera enacting the life of King Songtsen Gampo is performed here in season. Slightly further northwest, close to the county border of

Tsekok & Sogwo

Kawasumdo, at **Bongya**, there is an eclectic community in which Nyingma, Geluk and Bon monks all participate, and at **A-me Gur**, there is a sacred image from Sakya which was originally offered to Repkong by an emissary of Chogyel Phakpa during the 13th century, and later brought here by the nomads of the grassland.

Hor to Tungte

Two roads diverge at Hor township, southwest for **Tungte** (*Ch* Tongde) in Kawasumdo (40 kilometres) and northwest to **Bongya** (11 kilometres), from where you can drive through the grasslands southwest into Tungte (44 kilometres) and **Golok** (via Rabgya), or northeast to **Mangra** and **Trika** (see below, page 579).

Sogwo Prefecture ཤོག་བོ

*Sogwo prefecture is a region where the dominant population is ethnically Mongol, but so thoroughly integrated with the Amdowa, that only a few distinctive cultural traits remain. The yurt, the round felt tent of the Mongols, is found in abundance here, and slight differences in dress and jewellery can be detected. The best sheepskin coats (*Tib *chuba) are made from the skins of blue sheep, and this region is famous for their production. All four monasteries within the prefecture are Gelukpa.*

Sogwo Prefecture (124)
河南蒙古族自治县
Henan
Population: 25,074
Area: 6,072 sq km
Colour map 5, grid B4

Henan

The county capital is located at **Henan** on the lower Tse-chu River, 39 kilometres south of Tsekok. The small monastery of **Laka Gon Ganden Shedrub Dargyeling**, two kilometres south of town on the banks of the Tse-chu, was founded at the behest of Panchen Lama IX by Laka Tulku VI Lobzang Jinpa Tubten Gyatso (1926-1969). The present incumbent, Laka Tulku VII, is now a boy aged 18. The monastery is affiliated to **Tsang-gar Monastery** near Rabgya (see below, page 587).

Colour map 5, grid B4

Chogar Tashi Chodzong

Some 31 kilometres southwest of Henan town, below Mount Dongwu and facing the Tse-chu river, there is the Mongol monastery of **Chogar Tashi Chodzong** (*Ch* Qugesi), which was founded by the mother of a local chieftain in 1937. The monastery has been considered a branch of Labrang since 1948.

Colour map 5, grid B4

Taklung Shingza Gon

A difficult trail leads south for 75 kilometres from Henan town to **Taklung Shingza Monastery** (*Ch* Xiangza) on the north bank of the Yellow River. This monastery, founded in 1905 by Shingza Lobzang Chokyi Gyatso, is also known as Tashi Delekyil, and it is affiliated to Labrang. Originally it was a tented camp, the first solid adobe buildings dating only from 1930. This grassland locale is particularly well known for its beautiful riding horses. Rough unreliable trails lead upstream to **Rabgya** (and thence to Machen in Golok) and downstream for 40 kilometres through marshland and gorges to **Machu** in present-day Gansu province.

Colour map 5, grid B4

Far-east Tibet

Serlung and the Eastern Grasslands

Colour map 5, grid B5 At **Serlung**, 61 kilometres southeast of Henan town, the monastery of **Datsengon Tashi Gandenling** overlooks the banks of the upper Lu-chu. A branch of Labrang, its foundation dates to 1924, and it actually marks the end of Mongol territory in Sogwo. The eastern grasslands on the road from Sogwo to Luchu are as good as they get in Amdo, but the density of livestock is high and several species of pika (small herbivores) burrow extensively over the terrain. They prefer not to use steeper land, rough shrub or marshlands, so the extension of pastures and drainage of marshes suits them well. As the last remaining mammal predators are eliminated by hunting, they, along with the marmot, have often prospered. Several birds of prey, led by the steppe eagle and the huge lammergeier vulture, as well as songbirds, inhabit the steppe for most of the year nesting in deserted holes and roosting on telephone poles.

The shrub-covered hills between Sogwo and Luchu contain a disputed border, one of many among the present-day provincial, prefectural, or county borders throughout the plateau.

Getting there The distance from Serlung to Luchu is only 48 kilometres on a road which follows the upper reaches of the Lu-chu downstream. Public buses also run from Henan, the county capital, via Luchu to Ganlho Dzong (184 kilometres).

Ziling to Mato:

South Kokonor and Yellow River Basin

*The second and third routes from Ziling to the Golok area of South Amdo are
described in this section. The second runs from Ziling via Rushar through Trika
and Kawasumdo to cross the Yellow River at Rabgya Gonpa. The third runs from
Ziling via Tongkor and Nyima Dawa La pass to Daotong and thence via
Chabcha to Tsigortang and Mato. This entire area, presently administered
within the Tibetan Autonomous Prefecture of South Kokonor, comprises five
counties: Trika, Mangra, Kawasumdo, Chabcha and Tsigortang.*
Recommended itineraries: 8, 9, 11.

Trika County ཁྲི་ཀ

*Trika is the traditional name for the region straddling the banks of the Yellow
River, west of Jentsa. The county capital is located at **Guide** town, 117 kilometres
south of Ziling, and 55 kilometres northeast of Guinan town in Mangra. Within the
county there are approximately 56 monasteries, of which 33 represent the Gelukpa
school, 20 the Nyingmapa, and three the Bon tradition. Regular buses leave Ziling
for Trika, taking the Kumbum road for 18 kilometres and then heading south
across the **Lhamori** mountains, which comprise three prominent craggy black
peaks on the watershed of the Yellow River. The pass (Altitude: 3,750 metres),
where snow can fall even in May, is 16 kilometres from Rushar. Just 17 kilometres
down from the pass, a rough road heads east to Detsa monastery and **Bayan Khar**
(see above, page 558), but the main road continues south through a few small Muslim and Tibetan villages – including **Garang** and **Akong**, to the Yellow River, 43
kilometres below the watershed. The final stretch is through some very barren rusty
brown hills, typical Yellow River scenery.*

Trika County (125)
贵德县
Guide
Population: 85,563
Area: 3,408 sq km
Colour map 5, grid B4

Far-east Tibet

Trika County

Ziling
18
To Tongkor
Rushar
16
17
To Detsa
Lhakhangtang
26
10
Horkya
13
Garang
Rohangtang
Yellow River
E Guide
W Guide
Jojo
Lhakhang
12
16
Rungan
Gonpa
Dongkou

N
To Mangra (43 km)
Not to scale

Garang township, just 10 kilometres
after the turn-off for Detsa, has a high
concentration of Nyingmapa monasteries. Among them, **Yutsa Ngakhang** is within the township, while
the biggest, **Karju Damkazhar
Ngakhang Namdrol Pemaling**, lies
three kilometres to the southwest.
Sumbha Ngakhang, 22 kilometres
south of the township, faces towards
the Yellow river, while **Akong
Ngakhang** overlooks the north bank
of the Yellow River. In addition, one
of the largest Gelukpa monasteries of
Trika is located 1.5 kilometres northwest of the township at **Chorten Ki
Ganden Tashi Dargyeling**. This is a
branch of Kumbum Jampaling,
founded in 1706.

Garang

Horkya After Garang, the road follows the north bank of the Yellow River upstream. Narrow strips of cultivated land flank the tree-lined road, but the steep canyon walls of the Yellow River at this point are pale yellow, reminiscent of the North African Mahgreb. Some 13 kilometres further on, at **Horkya** township, a rough side road heads west in the direction of Chabcha and Tongkor counties via Lhakhangtang, while the highway crosses to the south bank, where West Guide (Hexi) is only two kilometres distant. At Horkya, on the north bank of the Yellow River, there is the Gelukpa monastery of **Horkya Dratsang Samtenling**, which was founded by Minyak Tulku I Losel Dargye. A small Nyingmapa temple, **Horkya Ngakhang** is located nearby within the village. About eight kilometres north from here, **Go-me Do-re Dratsang**, founded in the 16th century by Do-re Tulku Rongkor, was reopened in 1983, and alongside it is the Nyingmapa temple of **Do-re Ngakhang**.

Lhakhangtang **Lhakhangtang** township, 26 kilometres west of the bridge in the direction of Tongkor, has three Gelukpa and four Nyingmapa monasteries within its jurisdiction. The Nyingmapa temples are all located close to the township, the largest being **Lhakhangtang Wangchen Drupei Gatsel**, which currently has 70 monks. Among the Gelukpa establishments, which lie further north, the most noteworthy is **Dechen Gon Sangak Rabgyeling**, a branch of Labrang.

Guide

Altitude: 2,280 metres
Phone code: 0984
Colour map 5, grid B4

The county town of Trika is nowadays known as **Guide**, two kilometres south of the bridge and 117 kilometres from Ziling. Guide is a fairly large town spread along the south bank of the Yellow River, where it has absorbed several farming villages. Tibetans account for 32 per cent of the population, but only a few live in the town itself, which is predominantly Chinese and Muslim. The houses of this region have very tall outer walls enclosing a courtyard with a few fruit trees or a vegetable plot, and a single-storey house built of mud brick. Guide is a town of two distinct halves, separated by the waters of the Trika-chu, which flows into the Yellow River here. **West Guide** (Hexi) has guesthouses, banks and a larger volume of through traffic, whereas **East Guide** (Heyin) has

West Guide

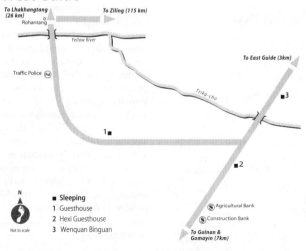

To Lhakhangtang (26 km)
Rohantang
To Ziling (115 km)
Yellow River
Traffic Police
To East Guide (3km)
Trika-chu
■3
1■
■2

N
Not to scale

■ Sleeping
1 Guesthouse
2 Hexi Guesthouse
3 Wenquan Binguan

Ⓢ Agricultural Bank
Ⓢ Construction Bank

To Guinan & Gomayin (7km)

parks, government buildings, guesthouses, a hospital, bus station, opera theatre, mosque and an old Daoist temple called Yihuangsi.

Formerly the most important site in Guide was the ancient stupa, founded by Tibetan kings during the ninth century, and gilded in 1806 by Tsewang Tenpei Nyima. The stupa, which did not survive the Cultural Revolution, was 30 metres high with a five-tier base. Alongside it, Minyak Tulku I Losel Dargye (1675-1753) founded the Gelukpa monastery of **Minyak Dratsang Tashi Chopeling**. A small 14th century protector temple affiliated to this monastery no longer exists. Nowadays, the greatest attraction of Guide and the outlying villages of Trika county is the large number of medicinal hot springs, which have been documented for over 600 years. These are particularly recommended in the treatment of muscular and stomach disorders.

Sleeping C *Hotsprings Hotel (Wenquan Binguan)*, T(09841)553234. Standard rooms at ¥59 and suites at ¥140, capable of accommodating 113 clients. Each room has a private bath and shower with 24 hour piping hot mineral water (average temperature 76°). Cheaper accommodation is available at the *Hexi Guesthouse* in West Guide and the *Gyelnyer Dronkhang* in East Guide.

Eating There are many small Muslim noodle restaurants in both West and East Guide.

East Guide

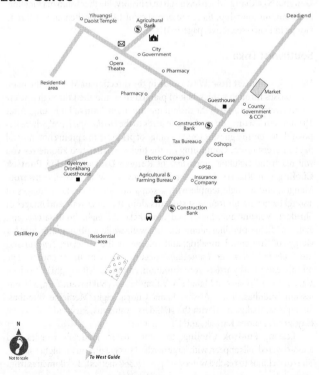

East Trika

Heading east of the county town, after two kilometres, you will reach the rebuilt **Jojo Lhakhang**. This temple was originally constructed in the 13th century, and funded by Sakya Pandita in person who visited the great stupa of Guide en route for Mongolia, and donated a set of pearls offered to him by Godan Qan. Nearby, there are also Nyingmapa temples at **Kepa Ngakhang**, **Gongpa Ngakhang**, and **Mepa Ngakhang**, while **Gongwa Dratsang** of the Gelukpa school is now regarded as a branch of Tashilhunpo, although it was originally constructed by the Sakyapa lama Kunga Kechuwa (1387-1446) who amalgamated two separate temples here.

South Trika

Dongkou   The greatest concentration of monasteries in Trika is found in **Dongkou** township, 16 kilometres south of the county town. It is in the upper valleys around here that most Tibetans can be found, and there are numerous small monasteries, mostly Gelukpa but including five Nyingma temples and even a Bon presence. Among them, the most renowned are **Rabza Dratsang Samten Choling**, five kilometres northwest of the township, which is an 18th century branch of Lamo Dechen in neighbouring Jentsa county, and **Rongzhi Dratsang**, in the same locale, which was reopened in 1986. Other branches of Lamo Dechen are found here: **Gyabtsa Dratsang** (two kilometres southwest of the township), **Drom Dratsang** (some kilometres southeast), and **Nyedrubde Lhundrub Chodzong** (7.5 kilometres southeast). The Nyingmapa temples include **Lingtsa Ngakhang**, founded in 1939, and **Lanju Gongma Ngakhang**, which has a 700 year history. Further south of Dongkou, at **Changmu** township, there are branches of Lamo Dechen and of Bimdo Gonpa in Dowi (see above, page 563).

Southwest Trika

Heading southwest from West Guide in the direction of Mangra, the main road passes through a thick belt of planted trees and then through a stony desert stretching towards the distant mountains of **Amnye Jakhyung**. After 10 kilometres, a turn-off on the right leads to the *Health Spa Hotel*, where it is possible to stay in a guesthouse, at a range of prices, with a piping hot mineral bath in every room. Continuing on the highway, after two kilometres you will reach the Gelukpa monastery of **Rungan Dratsang Dekyi Puntsok Choling** (*Ch* Riansi). Here, there are only a few monks, mostly from Mangra, and a single temple with a stupa outside. It contains images of Tsongkhapa with his foremost students along the inner wall, and images of Shridevi, Vaishravana, Six-armed Mahakala, the eight bodhisattvas and eight medicine buddhas along the left wall, while a photograph of Alak Gergya of Kumbum Jampaling, and volumes of the *Kangyur*, *Tengyur* and the *Collected Works of Tsongkhapa* occupy the right inner corner. The murals, executed by artists from Kumbum, comprise (left to right): Shridevi, Vaishravana, Six-armed Mahakala, Vajrabhairava, Sukhavati, Tara, 35 Confession Buddhas, Tara, Atisha, Lama Chopa, eight Medicine Buddhas, Sitatapatra, Shakyamuni with the 16 Elders, Amitayus, Sarvavid Vairocana, Hayagriva, Dampa Karnak, and Dharmaraja.

Leaving **Puntsok Choling**, the stony desert gradually recedes and grass-covered hills appear, with large herds of yak grazing on the higher slopes. The road climbs to reach a watershed pass (3,360 metres), 30 kilometres from

Puntsok Choling, within the green hills of the Amnye Jakhyung range. This demarcates the border between Trika and Mangra counties. The distance from Guide to Guinan town in Mangra is 55 kilometres.

Mangra County མང་ར

Mangra county occupies the bend of the Yellow River, southwest of Trika and southeast of the dam and hydro-electric power plant at **Longyang Xia.** *Here, the Mangra-chu tributary flows west towards its confluence with the Yellow River. Mangra is a county of two halves, the northern part being barren, sandy desert, while south of the Mangra-chu, towards the low mountain range that divides it from Kawasumdo, there is some lush grassland. Prior to 1958 there were 19 monasteries and temples within the county, including one Gelukpa nunnery and one Nyingmapa centre. Of these, approximately 13 have been rebuilt and two (Ati Gon and Rungan Dratsang) allocated to neighbouring Trika county. The county town lies 144 kilometres from Guide town in Trika and 96 kilometres from Tungte in Kawasumdo, and until recently it was the only county in this prefecture still closed to foreigners.*

Mangra County (126)
贵南县
Guinan
Population: 57,141
Area: 5,585 sq km
Colour map 5, grid B4

Gomayin

After crossing the watershed pass of the Amnye Jakhyung range, the road from Trika descends through a windswept plain where sheep and goats are grazing freely. At **Gomayin** township, 15 kilometres below the pass, there is an intersection, from where two roads head south towards Mangra and Kawasumdo, and a lesser track heads northwest in the direction of Longyang Xia. If you take the southeast road, you will reach the Gelukpa monastery of **Ati Gon Samtenling** after 35 kilometres. This branch of Lamo Dechen is nowadays administered from Trika, and may be accessed directly from Guide town on a southerly trail (37 kilometres). In its vicinity, there are three other Gelukpa monasteries, of which **Wanshul Gon Shedrub Rinchenling**, founded in 1895 by Wangshul Lobzang Tashi Gyatso, is also a branch of Lamo Dechen. Northwest from Gomayin, some 13 kilometres distant, there is a small Gelukpa temple at **Kharngon Garka**, originally constructed in the 1940s.

Gomayin to Mangra

Continuing south, the rough road gradually climbs through sandy hills and desert landscape to reach the grasslands and pass (*Altitude*: 3,765 metres) after 31 kilometres. The descent on an excellent paved road surface is through wide open grassland, which extends towards the horizon. Strong winds blow from the Amnye Jakhyung range to the southeast. About 22 kilometres below the pass, the two southerly roads from Gomayin converge at another intersection, from where you can also head west to Mangra town or southwest to Kawasumdo. If you take the

Mangra & Kawasumdo Counties

Far-east Tibet

former option, you will pass **Shengdor** township after 15 kilometres, where a trail leads 19 kilometres northeast to **Wanshul Garka** monastery, and reach the county town after a further 19 kilometres. The terrain here is arid, but for narrow strips of cultivation close to the dirt road.

Mangra town

Altitude: 3,090 metres
Colour map 5, grid B4

Mangra town (*Ch* Guinan), comprises one main street with two intersections. Entering from the east, you will pass the bus station and post office on the left, and a guesthouse, hospital, and banks on the right. Then, continuing along Main Street, after the first intersection, you will pass the *Government Guesthouse* and clothing market on the left and the government buildings on the right. Three roads radiate outwards from the west end of Main Street, southwest to **Tarshul Monastery**, due west to **Atsok Gon**, and northwest to the police station, cinema, and **Lu Gonpa**, which is the only monastery within the town, three kilometres distant. The best and cleanest place to eat in town is the *Chongqing Restaurant* on Main Street.

Lu Gonpa   This monastery, more formally known as **Lutsang Gon Shedrub Gepeling**, currently has 150 monks. It was founded in 1889 by Alak Nyenzang IV Lobzang Chokyi Nyima, whose present incarnation, Alak Nyenzang VI is 20 years old. The reconstructed **Assembly Hall** (Tsokchen) has 56 pillars, and it has been redecorated by sculptors from mainland China and artists from Repkong. The central images are of Tsongkhapa and his foremost students, to their left is a photograph of the present Panchen Lama XI, Gendun Chokyi Nyima, and to their rear the volumes of the *Kangyur* and *Tengyur*. The murals here depict (left): Shridevi, Vaishravana, Tara, Sarvavid Vairocana, and Vajrabhairava; and (right): Vajrapani, Mahakarunika, Sitatapatra, and Dharmaraja. The **Jampa Lhakhang** to its rear contains a large image of

Mangra

N
Not to scale

■ **Sleeping**
1 Guesthouse
2 Government Guesthouse

● **Eating**
1 Chonging Restaurant
2 Restaurants

Maitreya, flanked by smaller images of Dalai Lama XIV and Panchen Lama X. The volumes of the *Kangyur* are to the left, along with encased images of Shakyamuni and his students flanked by the six ornaments and two supreme masters of ancient India. The *Tengyur* is stacked along the right wall, along with encased images of Tsongkhapa and his foremost students, flanked by the 35 Confession Buddhas.

Mangra township

Heading west from Guinan town, a turn-off leads north to **Mangra** township after 16 kilometres. This township, from which the county derives its name, lies 15 kilometres along this side road, on the banks of the Mangra-chu. Here, the **Podu Garka** temple, affiliated to Bimdo Gonpa in Dowi, can be visited, along with the Nyingmapa monastery of **Turol Ngakhang** (nine kilometres west). About 19 kilometres northwest of the township, there is the monastery of **To-le Gon Namgyel Puntsoling**, a branch of Lamo Dechen, founded in 1916, which was recently moved to this location following the construction of the Longyang Xia Dam.

Tarshul Gonpa

Continuing due west from the intersection south of Mangra township, you will pass through **Tarshul** township after 16 kilometres. Southeast of here (approximately 25 kilometres from the county town), there is the Gelukpa monastery of **Tarshul Gonpa Namdak Trimdenling**, pleasantly located in the grassy hills. There are approximately 80 monks here, under the guidance of the charismatic Alak Yongdzin I Lobzang Khedrub Gyatso (b. 1908), now 91 years old, who founded the monastery in 1935 with the support of Tarshul Tulku Gelek Wangchen Choying Gyatso. Previously, a tented monastery had been founded here in 1671 by Tarshul Tulku I Choying Gyatso. Alak Yongdzin is revered by many as the best lama in Mangra and one of the most learned in all of Amdo. He himself was formerly a tutor at Labrang, although his own monastery is affiliated to Lamo Dechen. Near Tarshul, there are the ruins of the Gelukpa nunnery of **Maril Jomo Tsamkhang** and the **Chubzang Tsamkhang**, a branch of Labrang founded in the early 19th century by Jamyang Zhepa III.

Mangra to Tsigortang

A rough road extends west from Guinan via Tarshul township to cross the Yellow River at Atsok Gonpa after 63 kilometres. From **Atsok Gonpa**, two roads connect with the main Ziling-Jyekundo highway in Tsigortang county (see below, page 591). Another rough road cuts northwest, crossing the Yellow River at Kyikyug to arrive in Chabcha county.

Mangra to Kawasumdo

Returning to the paved highway 34 kilometres east of Guinan town, you can turn northeast for Guide (110 kilometres) or southwest for Tungte in Kawasumdo (62 kilometres). Taking the latter road, you drive quickly through lush grasslands to cross the pass (*Altitude*: 3,480 metres) after 15 kilometres, and reach the county border.

Far-east Tibet

Kawasumdo County ཀ་བ་སུམ་མདོ

Kawasumdo County (127)
同德县
Tongde
Population: 40,834
Area: 5,331 sq km
Colour map 5, grid B4

*Kawasumdo is the traditional name given to the grasslands within the bend of the Yellow River to the south of Mangra. As the name suggests, it lies at the junction of three main routes: northeast to Guide and Ziling, west to Tsigortang and Chabcha, and south to Tsekok and Machen. There are 14 monasteries within the county, of which 10 are Gelukpa and four Nyingmapa. The county capital is located at **Tungte** (Ch Tongde), 96 kilometres from Guinan, 102 kilometres from Xinghai in Tsigortang, and 111 kilometres from Jadir in Tsekok.*

North Kawasumdo

The paved highway descends from the pass on the Mangra-Kawasumdo county border through rolling green hills and rich wide open pastures, which now sustain large herds of yak. The grasslands are dotted with nomadic tents, and in summer there are occasional grassland festivals, when scores of tents, including tented monasteries, are pitched together. After 12 kilometres, a dirt road branches to the southeast in the direction of Jadir (82 kilometres), and then after a further 13 kilometres, it forks again at a petrol station, the highway leading south to Rabgya Gonpa and Tawo in Machen county (180 kilometres), and a bumpy gravel road heading west into Tungte, the county town. A smoother dirt road, which bypasses the petrol station from the south, runs parallel to the gravel road for most of the 22 kilometres' drive into town, crisscrossing it occasionally. This offers a much better driving surface than the gravel.

Tungte

Altitude: 3,180 metres
Phone code: 09844
Colour map 5, grid B4

The county town is located in the Ba-chu gorge below the level of the surrounding tableland, affording some protection from the strong winds. There is one long main street, which forks at the west end. Entering from the east (Mangra, Guide or Jadir), you will pass on the right a petrol station, the martyrs' cemetery, assorted banks, a Tibetan hospital, government buildings and the *Government Guesthouse*, while on the left you will pass the *Traffic Guesthouse*, the bus station, market, banks, post office, bookstore and cinema. At the west end of Main Street, you can head south on a rough trail for **Gumang** township and **Serlak Gonpa** or northwest for **Xinghai** in Tsigortang, crossing the Yellow River.

Sleeping C *Tongde Government Guesthouse*, T(09844)592630. Standard rooms at ¥50, suites at ¥120, and 4-bedded rooms at ¥10.50 per bed. The rooms are surprisingly well maintained, but there are no attached bathrooms. Cheaper accommodation is available at the *Traffic Guesthouse*.

Eating The best is a Sichuan noodle restaurant, near the *Tibetan Hospital* on the north side of Main St.

Gumang

Gumang township can be reached via a six-hour trek over a pass to the southwest, or more easily by returning to the intersection 22 kilometres east of the county town and driving southwest for 15 kilometres, after which a dirt road leads west for 20 kilometres to Gumang. On the way you will pass through **Serlak Gon Ganden Puntsok Tengyeling**, the largest monastery in North

Far-east Tibet

Kawasumdo. Affiliated to Sera Monastery at Lhasa, it was founded during the 17th century at the behest of Panchen Lama V by two monastic preceptors from Sera and Tashilhunpo. Currently, there are around 180 monks here, headed by Do-me Rinpoche. The small brick and concrete temple of **Gochen Dzong Gon** lies 15 kilometres east of Serlak, and is visible from the main road across a small river. Also, 12 kilometres southeast of Gumang, there is a Nyingmapa hermitage at **Drakto Tsamkhang**.

Southern Kawasumdo

From the intersection 22 kilometres east of the county town, you can drive northeast to Mangra and Guide, or continue south towards Rabgya Gonpa and Machen county. Taking the latter road, which is currently undergoing reconstruction, you continue heading south through the rich flat grasslands. Motorable dirt roads cross the highway after eight kilometres and again (for Gumang and Serlak) after seven kilometres. Heading further south, the terrain soon becomes hilly, prayer flags are suspended across the road, and a clinic serving road maintenance workers is passed on the left (east). Climbing gradually, passes are crossed after 23 kilometres and again after 12 kilometres, the second (3,930 metres) traversing the snow range to the north of the Yellow River. On the descent into the valley of the Serchung Nang-chu, which flows due south into the Yellow River, there are grasslands where caterpillar fungus abounds. After five kilometres, a rough track leaves the highway, heading east through a broad side-valley and crossing a southerly pass to reach **Hedong** township and **Tsang-gar Gonpa**, about 20 kilometres from the main road.

Tsang-gar Dondrub Rabtenling was founded in 1765 by a monk from Tashilhunpo known as Tsang Pandita. In 1941 the monastery was destroyed by Muslim warlords, and the monks were forced to flee east into the Sangke grasslands near Labrang. Subsequently, the original site was reclaimed and the monastery reopened in 1981. Currently, it is the largest monastery in Kawasumdo county, housing over 400 monks. Several temples have been constructed, but not yet fully decorated. Some of the monks are 'Sogwo Arik', a Mongolian clan whose main base is in Sogwo (*Ch* 'Henan') Prefecture to the east, but who have now fully adopted Tibetan language and culture.

Tsang-gar Gonpa

The descent to Rabgya

In order to avoid the steep gorges as the tributaries plunge sharply towards the Yellow River, the main road crosses several small ridges before descending to

Far-east Tibet

Tungte Town

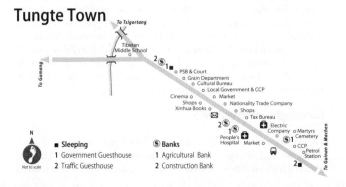

Rabgya Gonpa, 137 kilometres from Tungte (and 371 kilometres from Ziling). About 22 kilometres after the turn-off for Tsang-gar Gonpa, the road enters a red-rock canyon, interspersed with good grazing pastures and forested copses. **Majang** township (*Altitude*: 3,360 metres) lies four kilometres within the canyon, and there are a number of inexpensive roadside Muslim restaurants here. Four ridges, the highest at 3,630 metres, are crossed before the road finally descends into full view of the Yellow River. The distance from Majang township to Rabgya Gonpa is 33 kilometres. Below Rabgya, there is a bridge crossing the Yellow River which leads from Rabgya to Tawo, the capital of Machen county, 43 kilometres to the south. There is a small Muslim-run truckstop near the bridge, where it is possible to stay. Although Rabgya is on the north bank of the river, it technically falls within the Machen county of Golok, for which reason it is described below, page 602.

Tungte to Tsigortang

Heading west from Tungte county town, after one kilometre, the road forks, the south trail leading across a bridge which spans the Ba-chu in the direction of Gumang, and the west trail following the river downstream towards its confluence with the Yellow River. Taking the latter, the gorge gradually opens out into a wide cultivated valley, and the road becomes a tree-lined avenue. After 15 kilometres, a side-road crosses the Ba-chu to the south bank, where it follows the course of an aquaduct. The main road, however, continues on the north bank, passing through a series of small farming villages, such as **Bagu**, where the houses have typical courtyards and adobe perimeter walls. Some 24 kilometres west of town, the road bypasses **Sumdo Gon**, a branch of the Gelukpa monastery of Drakar Tredzong (see below, page 593), which was founded in 1925.

After Bagu township, the road cuts northwest for 27 kilometres to reach the suspension ridge (2,760 metres) spanning the Yellow River and enter Tsigortang county (see below, page 591). In this area there are a number of small shrines and monasteries, the most important being **Shartsang Rigzin Jigme Kalzangling**, a branch of Kowa Gon in Jentsa, which was founded in 1945, and the Nyingmapa hermitage at **Togen Nagar**, founded 1935.

Chabcha County ཆབ་ཆ

Chabcha County (128)
共和县
Gonghe
Population: 127,903
Area: 16,313 sq km
Colour map 5, grid B3

The third route from Ziling to Golok, follows the highway southwest from the city, through Tongkor county and **Nyima Dawa La** *pass (see above, page 536), to enter Chabcha county.* **Chabcha** *(Ch Gonghe) occupies the exposed basin between Lake Kokonor and the Yellow River. As such, it includes the southern shore of Lake Kokonor as far west as Tanakma, and the plain through which National Highway 214 cuts its way southwest towards Mato and Jyekundo. The county capital is located at Chabcha town, 143 kilometres from Ziling, and 350 kilometres northeast of Mato in Golok. There are 21 monasteries within the county, 10 of which are Gelukpa, eight Nyingmapa, two Bonpo, and one,* **Sokpo Gon**, *which is both Gelukpa and Nyingmapa.*

Daotonghe intersection

Descending from Nyima Dawa La pass, at **Daotonghe**, 102 kilometres from Ziling, two roads diverge. Head west for **Lake Kokonor**, **Kermo** and **Lhasa** on National Highway 109; or alternatively, head southwest for Chabcha town on

National Highway 214. The former route via Tanakma and Tsaka has already been described (see above, page 517-526).

Longyang Xia Dam

Heading southwest from Daotonghe, the highway crosses a pass, known in Chinese as Liu Shankou (3,580 metres), and then descends through the rolling green hills of the South Kokonor range. About 18 kilometres south of Daotonghe, a turn-off on the left leads east for 61 kilometres to the Longyang Xia Dam on the Yellow River. This is one of China's largest dams but the reservoir has silted up fast under the heavy sediment load of the river. A smaller reservoir dam to the west of Chabcha burst in 1993 due to an earthquake, killing over 200 people. Earthquakes are common in this region, and a powerful one also struck in the mid-1980s. Monasteries in this area are largely Nyingmapa, including the 13th century **Tingkya Sangak Choling**, which subsequently became a branch of Zhechen (see above, page 473), and **Tsotolung Ngakhang**, which had to be moved to its present location when the dam was constructed. Continuing southwest on the highway, you will cross three passes in quick succession, the highest at 3,210 metres, to arrive at the county town, 41 kilometres from Daotonghe.

Colour map 5, grid B4

Chabcha

Chabcha is a surprisingly large modern town on the fringe of a semi-desert, and nowadays it functions as the administrative capital of the entire South Kokonor Prefecture. Entering from the northeast, a bypass takes through traffic around the town en route for Mato and Jyekundo. If you turn left at the petrol station, you will pass on the left a memorial temple and stupa dedicated to King Songtsen Gampo, which was constructed recently by Panchen Lama

Altitude: 2,940 metres

Phone code: 0974

Colour map 5, grid B4

Chabcha & Tsigortang Counties

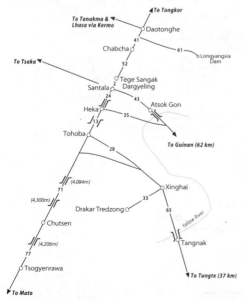

Far-east Tibet

X. The road curves past the South Kokonor Prefectural government buildings and the *Hainan Hotel* to reach a roundabout, dominated by the police and communist party buildings. Three roads diverge here. Turn left (west) across a bridge for the Tibetan Nursing school, the carpet factory, the Hainan Peoples' Hospital, the bus station, and some smaller guesthouses. Turn right (east) for the *Government Guesthouse*, the Birth Control Unit, and the bypass, or continue straight ahead (south) on Main Street, where you will find the post office, supermarkets, department stores, street markets, cinemas, schools, banks and the hospitals of both Chinese and Tibetan traditional medicine.

North of Chabcha there are several monasteries which can be visited, including **Gonpa Soma** of the Gelukpa school (founded 1902), **Kyildong Ngakhang** of the Nyingma school (founded 1942), and at **Gandi** township, 13 kilometres northwest of town, **Khyamru Gon Tashi Gepeling**, a branch of Labrang founded by Jamyang Zhepa III, which is the biggest monastery within

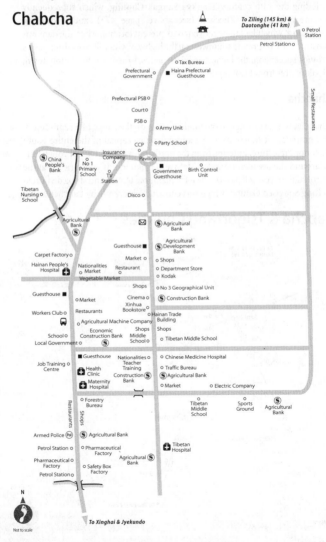

Chabcha

To Ziling (145 km) &
Daotonghe (41 km)

To Xinghai & Jyekundo

Not to scale

the county. Some six kilometres south of Chabcha there is another important Gelukpa centre at **Sachuk Sangak Tengyeling** (founded 1943).

Sleeping C *Hainan Prefectural Government Hotel*, T(0974)512773. Suites at ¥50, triples at ¥18 per bed, and hot showers at ¥2.50. Cheaper accommodation is available at the other guesthouses in town.

Eating Try the upmarket Sichuan restaurant, located on the 2nd Floor of a building to the north of the vegetable market.

Santala

Driving southwest from Chabcha, the highway climbs gradually through the plains to reach the **Santala** intersection after 54 kilometres. En route it is intersected by tall electricity pylons, connected to the power station at Longyangxia Dam. About two kilometres before Santala, there is a small Nyingmapa temple called **Tege Sangak Dargyeling**, located to the right (west) of the road. The building, founded only in 1984, is of an excellent construction, surrounded by large heavy prayer wheels on three sides. There are 20 monks here under the guidance of Lama Kham Kunkhyab. On the horizon some 40 kilometres to the west, one can clearly discern the fault line formed where the Yellow River gorge meets the high tableland plateau. The blue haze of the river filters into the atmosphere. At Santala, four roads diverge. Turn right (northwest) for Tsaka (see above, page 517), left (southeast) for Atsok Gonpa and Mangra (105 kilometres), or continue southwest for Mato (296 kilometres). At this point the highway enters Tsigortang county.

Colour map 5, grid B3

Tsigortang County རྩི་གོར་ཐང་

*The county of Tsigortang (Ch Xinghai) occupies the tableland west of the bend of the Yellow River, formed by the Amnye Machen range. The county capital is located at **Xinghai** new town, 65 kilometres southeast of the Santala intersection on a branch road, which leaves the highway at the Tohoba bridge. The town is also accessible from Tungte in Kawasumdo, 102 kilometres to the southeast. Altogether, there are 14 monasteries within the county: nine Gelukpa, four Nyingmapa and one Kagyupa.*

Tsigortang County (129)
兴海县
Xinghai
Population: 49,914
Area: 11,621 sq km
Colour map 5, grid B3

Far-east Tibet

Atsok Gon

From the Santala crossroads, you can head southeast for 43 kilometres to **Atsok Gon**, where a bridge crosses the Yellow River to enter Mangra county (see above, page 583). This bridge may also be reached from Heka, 24 kilometres further along the highway, over a rougher 35 kilometres road. **Atsok Gon Dechen Chokhorling** is an important but small Gelukpa monastery, located some two kilometres south of the bridge which spans the Yellow River into Mangra. It has an impressively sited set of the eight stupas symbolizing the deeds of Shakyamuni Buddha, and several old tangkas. The monastic community here was founded in 1889 and currently numbers 70.

Heka

From Santala, National Highway 214 continues southwest for **Heka** (24 kilometres), crossing four passes (range 3,180-3,300 metres) on the way. Heka

Colour map 5, grid B3

township (*Altitude*: 3,330) is a busy road junction for truckers and there are several Muslim restaurants and shops. The attraction here, and in similar roadside towns throughout Amdo, lies in the local Tibetans who frequently visit to purchase supplies from the Chinese, Hui and Salar shopkeepers. Northwest of Heka, there are small Nyingma monasteries at **Yulung Drakar** (three kilometres), **Cholung Ngakhang** (26 kilometres), and **Tsidung Ngakhang** (26 kilometres), all of which have only a few monks or mantrins. From the Heka crosssroads, there is also a branch road leading 35 kilometres southeast to Atsok Gon.

Leaving Heka, the highway crosses a higher pass (3,900 metres) on **Mount Heka** after six kilometres, and then descends to the Tohoba bridge after a further seven kilometres, where a well paved side-road branches off the highway to the left, heading 28 kilometres for the county town.

Xinghai town

Phone code: 09843
Colour map 5, grid B3

Turning-off the highway at **Tohoba**, the side-road crosses a pass (3,450 metres) after 10 kilometres, and reaches the town after a further 18 kilometres on an excellent paved surface. **Xinghai** is surprisingly attractive, large and situated near the scenic power place of **Drakar Tredzong**. The surrounding tableland is intermittently broken by the deeply eroded gorges of its Yellow River tributaries. Entering town from the Chabcha side (north), you will pass on the left the local government guesthouse and tax bureau, while on the right are the carpet factory, the *Xiashuidian Guesthouse* and various commercial buildings. Reaching the crossroads, turn left for the police station, the Peoples' Hospital, and the road to Tungte, right for the *Xinghai Hotel* and the road to Drakar Tredzong, or continue straight ahead (south) for the *Allah Restaurant*, the bus station, cinema, market and the road to **Chutsen** (*Ch* Wenquan).

Sleeping **C** *Xiao Shuidian Guesthouse*, T(09843)581271. Superior double rooms at ¥24 per bed, and standard rooms at ¥20 per bed (without attached bathroom). Accommodation is available at the *Xinghai Fandian* and the *Electric Company Guesthouse*.

Eating The best Muslim food in town is found at *Allah's Restaurant*, and the best Sichuan fare at the *Shuidian Dajiujia*.

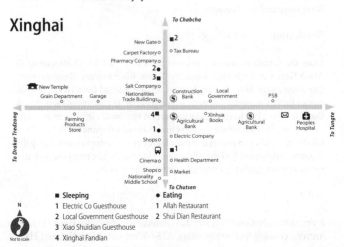

Xinghai

To Chabcha

New Gate ○ ■2
Carpet Factory ○ ○ Tax Bureau
Pharmacy Company ○
2●
3■
🏯 New Temple Salt Company ○
Grain Department Garage Nationalities Construction ⓈBank Local Government PSB ○
○ Garage Trade Buildings ○ Bank
4■ Ⓢ ○ Xinhua ⓈAgricultural Books Bank ✉ ✚ Peoples Hospital
Farming Products Store
○ Electric Company
Shops ○
Cinema ○ ■1
Shops ○ ○ Health Department
Nationality ○ Market
Middle School
To Chutsen

To Drakar Tredzong

To Tungte

N
Not to scale

■ Sleeping	● Eating
1 Electric Co Guesthouse	1 Allah Restaurant
2 Local Government Guesthouse	2 Shui Dian Restaurant
3 Xiao Shuidian Guesthouse	
4 Xinghai Fandian	

Drakar Tredzong

Drakar Tredzong, the celebrated 'white monkey fortress' is classed along with *Colour map 5, grid B3*
Dentik and Achung Namdzong, as one of the three most important sacred
sites in Amdo. A high 5,000 metres peak with thickly forested slopes and abundant wildlife, it is located only 33 kilometres southwest of Xinghai town, but
transport is irregular. Heading west out of town, after three kilometres a
grass-covered motorable road leaves the main dirt road heading west. Take
this trail, and after seven kilometres, descend from the high tableland plateau
into a steep arid gorge which extends downhill for four kilometres. Then, ford
the river and follow another tributary upstream for six kilometres to regain the
tableland (*Altitude*: 3,390 metres). Drakar Tredzong peak now comes into
view. The approach on foot is impressive, crossing a final 3,606 metres pass,
and for the last six kilometres the trail joins the pilgrim's route, which is one of
the most renowned in Amdo. The air is permeated by aromatic herbs and
incense.

The large Gelukpa monastery of **Tosam Yonten Dargyeling**, located on the   **Tosam Yonten**
south side of the mountain, was constructed in 1923 by Arik Tsang, and its   **Dargyeling**
present incumbent Arik Tsang IV (aged 22), who resides in Xinghai town, currently presides over 400 monks, although it is capable of holding 1,000.
Approaching the entrance to the monastery, on the left there is a large stone
wall where a large ceremonial tangka is displayed on the 14th day of the first
lunar month, and on the right, a fine set of the eight stupas representing major
events in the life of Shakyamuni Buddha. The residential buildings are located
to the left of the entrance. The courtyard is entered via a steep flight of stone
stairs, and within there are three buildings: the Assembly Hall in front, and the
Jampa Lhakhang and Gonkhang to the left. The **Assembly Hall** is particularly
impressive. It has 100 carpeted pillars and Repkong style murals. The main
gilded images represent (L-R): Acala, Sitatapatra, Acala, Arik Tsang II,
Padmasambhava, Shar Kalden Gyatso of Repkong, Arik Tsang III,
Manjughosa, Vajrapani, and Avalokiteshvara. The throne bears a photograph
of Arik Tsang III. The murals of the ground floor depict (L): Shridevi,
Six-armed Mahakala, Cakrasamvara, 21 Taras, Vairocana, Bhaisajyaguru,
Guhyasamaja, and Kalacakra, and (R): Vajrapani, Hevajra, 35 Confession
Buddhas, Sukhavati, Abhirati, Mahakarunika, and Dorje Lekpa. **Upstairs**,
alongside the residence of Arik Tsang IV and the large tangka banner, there are
images replicating those of the ground floor, while the murals include the Lama
Chopa refuge tree, Padmasambhava and Panchen Lama X. Within the **Jampa**

Lhakhang, there is a large Maitreya
image, flanked by Aksobhya, Amitabha, and Shakyamuni, along with
tangkas depicting the Lords of the
Three Enlightened Families and the
Three Deities of Longevity, while the
murals depict the 16 Elders, the eight
Medicine Buddhas, Sukhavati and
Abhirati.

Drakar Tredzong Gonpa

Tosam Yonten Dargyeling is one of   **Pilgrimage**
the so-called 18 sacred sites of Drakar   **circuit of Drakar**
Tredzong. Others, which can all be   **Tredzong**
seen on the five-hour pilgrimage circuit around the mountain, include a

(margin, vertical text) Far-east Tibet

Drakar Tredzong: abode of solitude

*The attractions of **Drakar Tredzong** for the meditator are summarized in the following verse by Zhabkar Tsokdruk Rangdrol:*

*"Ema! The Trakar Dredzong mountain
Is as beautiful as a heap of precious white crystals.
It is a supreme abode of solitude
Blessed by Padmakara, the Lord of the Victorious Ones.
There are countless miraculously arisen images of deities,
The refuge of all beings, men and gods.
Almost all the practitioners who, after renouncing the world,
Meditated in this place, attained realisation"*

M Ricard (transl) The Life of Shabkar

natural image of Tara said to cure infertility (**Dolma Bujin**), the rock impressions of Ling Gesar's horse; a stone image of Avalokiteshvara which is said to have saved the life of an old native inhabitant of Arik; a renowned charnel ground associated with Vajrasana in India; a passageway through which pilgrims squeeze to test their karma in the face of the Lord of Death (**Chogyel Nang**); a hermitage of Yeshe Tsogyel (**Khandro Tsokhang**); a cave where Padmasambhava meditated (**Yamatarkhung**); and the site where he tamed the hostile spirits (**Dresin Tulsa**); a medicinal spring (**menchu**); the summit (**nego**) where there are stone footprints of Padmasambhava and many *mani* stones; a natural pillar of crystal in a bottomless cave; the auspicious pass (**Tashi La**) where Tsongkhapa gave wondrous teachings; the place where Tsongkhapa rested; a cave containing a wish-granting 'cow'; the vase and begging bowl of Padmasambhava; and the deep cave (**Dorje Puklam**) at the centre of a natural amphitheatre where Padmasambhava hurled his vajra into the air to create a natural skylight in the cave-roof.

A number of active retreat hermitages are also found on the mountain, as well as a small camp of Nyingma nuns. Formerly there were also 400 Nyingmapa monks at Drakar Tredzong.

Tsigortang to Kawasumdo

Heading east from Xinghai town, the road cuts across the tableland plateau, descending steeply over 300 metres on two occasions to ford tributaries of the Yellow River, and climbing back to the high plateau. On the tableland itself driving is easier on the dirt road which runs parallel to the gravel road surface. After 53 kilometres, the road finally begins its descent towards the Yellow River canyon. There are magnificent views of its confluence with the Ba-chu below. A power station is passed on the left and the suspension bridge at **Tangnak** is eventually crossed after a further 12 kilometres. This marks the border between Tsigortang and Kawasumdo counties, and from here the road leads to Tungte (see above, page 586). The overall distance from Xinghai to Tungte is 102 kilometres.

Tsigortang to Chutsen

A rough trail leads south for nine kilometres from Xinghai to **Daheba** township, and then cuts across the grassland towards **Chutsen** (*Ch* Wenquan), on the highway.

Tohoba to Tsogyenrawa

Continuing southwest on National Highway 214 from the intersection at

Tohoba (see above, page 592), the road eventually leaves the plateau to cross the higher **Ngalo La** pass (4,084 metres), known in Chinese as Waka Sankou, followed by a second pass on **Mount Erlan** (4,300 metres). The township of **Chutsen** (3,400 metres) is 71 kilometres southwest from Ngalo La pass.

The main attraction here is the hot spring, which is yet to be developed. Outlying monasteries include **Gyesa Detsa Gonsar**, which is a branch of Jakhyung founded in 1938 (18 kilometres northeast), and **Tokden Gonpa** of the Kagyu school, which was founded in 1887 (12 kilometres southeast).

Chutsen

Sleeping There is a small guesthouse (¥12 per bed) amid the usual truckstops and restaurants.

From Chutsen, continue across another pass (4,206 metres), which leads into the basin of a small lake and over a stony plain to the road junction at **Tsogyenrawa** (*Ch* Huashixia, 77 kilometres). There is a small tented Nyingma monastery at **Tsorik Chogar**, 24 kilometres to the southwest of Tsogyenrawa, but the main interest is the proximity of Golok. The various routes from here into Amnye Machen, Central Golok, and Mato in Upper Golok are all described in the following section.

Golok-Sertal and Ngawa:

Amnye Machen Range and the Gyarong Headwaters

The Bayankala and Amnye Machen ranges of Amdo demarcate the upper reaches of the Yellow River, homeland of the Golok; while the Mardzagang range forms a watershed between the Yellow River and the three main sources of the Gyarong: the Ser-chu, Do-chu, and Mar-chu. This entire region is the domain of independently minded nomadic peoples who have maintained their distinctive cultural traditions for centuries.

Four of the six counties currently included in the Golok Tibetan Autonomous Prefecture of Qinghai occupy the valley of the Yellow River, whereas the other two, Padma and Jigdril along with those of Sertal, Dzamtang, and Ngawa, all lie within the gorges and valleys of the Gyarong source rivers. Nowadays the counties of the Golok Tibetan Autonomous Prefecture are administered from Machen, Sertal from Dartsedo (in the Kandze Tibetan Autonomous Prefecture), and the last two from Barkham, within the Ngawa Tibetan Autonomous Prefecture of Sichuan province.

Recommended itineraries: 9, 11 (also 8).

Mato County མ་སྟོད

Mato County (130)
玛多县
Madoi
Population: 10,539
Area: 25,263 sq km
Colour map 5, grid B2

*This county, also known as **Machuka**, contains the source of the Yellow River, and lies north of the Bayankala watershed. There are a few small Nyingma shrines and monasteries, of which the largest and most influential is **Horkor Gon**. The county town, **Mato**, lies 331 kilometres northeast of Jyekundo and 494 kilometres southwest of Ziling.*

Bayankala Watershed

Approaching Mato from Kham (ie from Jyekundo or Sershul via Zhiwu, on which see above, page 478), National Highway 214 gradually ascends through the rolling swamplands of the upper Yalong to cross the **Bayankala Pass** (5,082 metres), 61 kilometres beyond **Domda** (*Ch* Qingshuihe). There are fine views of the rolling humps of the Bayankala range to the east of the road; and yellow poppies are commonplace around the pass. After crossing this

Mato County

Far-east Tibet

Pilgrimage

Throughout the Buddhist world, pilgrimage is an important means of affirming the faith of devotees and above all of accumulating merit (punya) and virtuous actions (kushala), without which progress to enlightenment or buddhahood would not be possible. In Tibet, pilgrimage (ne-khor) has assumed a significant social role, and there is a distinct genre of literature, the pilgrimage guidebook (ne-yig), which describes both the historical background and development of any given site, as well as the manner in which its rocks and contours are to be viewed from the perspective of 'pure vision'. For, the peaks, stones, and rivulets of the most sacred sites are properly viewed as deities or consecrated objects in their own right!

While travelling through remote areas of Tibet, you will occasionally come upon remarkable individuals who are in the course of prostrating hundreds or even thousands of kilometres, all the way from their local villages to Lhasa, the most magnetic of Tibet's pilgrimage places. Often elected by village communities to undertake the pilgrimage, their journey may take several years to complete. Such pilgrims frequently wear leather aprons, knee pads, and hand pads to protect their bodies from exposure to the rough road surfaces, and they may travel in a group, accompanied by an assistant who will arrange food and shelter on their behalf. On reaching the goal of their pilgrimage, the sacred image of Jowo Rinpoche in Lhasa, they will make offerings, and then return home by motor vehicle.

The act of prostration (phyag-tshal) is generally combined with the recitation of the refuge prayer (kyab-dro), through which the Buddhist meditator or practitioner reduces pride, generates humility, and becomes confident in the goals and methods of Buddhism. Outside the Jokhang temple in Lhasa, the flagstones have been worn smooth by centuries of prostrations. Inside, pilgrims will add lumps of butter to the lamps as they proceed from one shrine to the next in a clockwise sequence, occasionally also making monetary offerings, or attaching some metalic or precious object to the wire mesh of a shrine as an act of simple devotion.

---

watershed, a bleak expanse of high altitude lakeland unfolds. The road descends gradually for 121 kilometres, passing en route a blue stone obelisk (after 29 kilometres) and nomadic camper groups at **Yeniugdo** (51 kilometres). Foxes are a common sight by the roadside. Soon small lakes appear close to the road on the left and right; and there is a charnel ground marked by prayer-flags. A turn-off on the right leads southeast to **Huanghe** township and **Horkor Gon Shedrub Dargyeling** (69 kilometres), an important branch of Dzogchen, which was founded in 1927 by Dzogchen Rinpoche V Tubten Chokyi Dorje. Then, skirting a larger lake on the left, the highway enters the valley of the Yellow River. It soon crosses the **first bridge over the Yellow River** and after a further five kilometres arrives at **Mato** town (70 kilometres from Yeniugdo).

Mato Town

Mato is a high altitude town, where snow is not uncommon in summertime! Entering the town from the southwest, a bypass leads directly ahead, and beyond, to continue in the direction of Ziling. A turn-off on the left leads into the centre of town. Here, on the left side of Main Street are the *Mato Military Guesthouse* and the general store; while the post office is on the right. At the head of this road, commanding a T-junction, is the Mato Theatre/Cinema. Turn left for the *Government Guesthouse* (rooms at ¥25) and Lake Ngoring Tso, and right for

Altitude: 4,300 metres

Colour map 5, grid B2

Far-east Tibet

the Mato Hospital. Returning to the bypass, the bus station is located on the left towards the Ziling end of the road. The open-air market has an interesting selection of nomadic produce and Golok style clothing. The town itself is small, but its bus station and market are important for the locals.

Ngoring and Kyaring Lakes

Colour map 5, grid B2 Mato county has several marshy plains dotted with tiny lakes and meandering rivers which provide good grasslands for the many nomads around the source of the Yellow River. There are, however, two particularly large lakes, known as **Kyaring Tso** and **Ngoring Tso**, through which the Yellow River itself flows. To reach these lakes, take the jeepable road from Mato which follows the Yellow River upstream, for 57 kilometres to Ngoring Tso, the closer of the two lakes (area 618 square kilometres, average depth 17 metres). There is a bird sanctuary at the southwest corner of Kyaring Lake (area 526 square kilometres, average depth nine metres), where swans, gulls, wild geese and ducks can be seen nesting. Both lakes provide a rich fishing ground for Chinese immigrants. Tibetans, even in these remote parts, are reluctant to eat fish.

On a hilltop (4,610 metres) between the lakes there is a very small reconstructed monastery, **Tsowar Kartse Doka**, said to mark the unknown site of **Kartse Palace**, which, according to old Chinese sources, is where Songsten Gampo met and married Princess Wencheng. It contains the mortal remains of Mani Lama, who passed away at Jyekundo in the late 1950s, and is maintained by Nyingma and Geluk monks, despite having been built originally by a Bon lama. The region west of the lakes is in places very marshy and an excellent breeding ground for many of the plateau's bird species, including the rare black-necked crane. It leads over the 'plain of stars' to **Mount Yakra Tatse** (5,442 metres), near the hamlet of **Dzomo Manang**, which is just inside Chumarleb county (see above, page 492). This is **Machuka**, the true source of the Yellow River.

Tsogyenrawa

Colour map 5, grid B3 National highway 214 from Mato to Ziling cuts northeast through a fairly flat plain, following a tributary of the Yellow River upstream for 75 kilometres to reach the gorge of **Tsogyenrawa** (*Ch* Huashixia, 4,039 metres). The town is named after the colourful mountain range below which it lies. It is a small town, with Muslim tea shops, Chinese restaurants, and a simple guesthouse.

Four roads converge at Tsogyenrawa: a side-road leading northwest to **Lake Dongi Tsona** and the **Shang** area (on which see above, page 516); another jeep track leading east for 45 kilometres to **Tawo Zholma** village on the Amnye Machen trail; the main highway leading northeast to **Ziling** or southwest to **Mato**, and a wide gravel road, which leads southeast into **Machen** and **Darlag** counties. Tsogyenrawa marks the extremity of the Golok penetration. Further north from here, the nomads belong to the Banak group rather than the Golok.

Machen County རྨ་ཆེན

Machen County (131)
玛沁县
Maqen
Population: 30,718
Area: 16,625 sq km
Colour map 5, grid B4

The ***Amnye Machen*** *range, which forms the large bend of the Yellow River, is the ancestral homeland of the* ***Golok****; and the sacred abode of the protector deity,* ***Machen Pomra****, revered by Bonpo and Buddhists alike. As recently as 1949 there had been reports suggesting that the highest peak of this isolated range exceeded the height of Mount Everest; and it was only during the 1950s and 1960s that the height was fixed at 6,282 metres. The county of Machen includes the entire pilgrim's circuit around the range. The county capital is located at* ***Tawo*** *(Machen), 209 kilometres from* ***Tsogyenrawa*** *(Ch Huashixia) and 68 kilometres from* ***Rabgya Monastery*** *on the banks of the Yellow River (see below, page 602).*

Amnye Machen Circuit ཨ་མྱེ་རྨ་ཆེན

The traditional starting point for the Bon and Buddhist pilgrims, who all circumambulate the range in a clockwise direction, is the **Chorten Karpo** near **Chuwarna** (*Ch* Xueshan) village; although most pilgrims presently set out from **Tawo Zholma** village, 45 kilometres due east of Tsogyenrawa. On the rough road approaching this village, the Amnye Machen range comes into sight in the distance. There are wonderful sunsets to be seen here.

Tawo Zholma (*Ch* Xiao Dawu) is a pastoral commune with only 77 inhabitants, of whom 30 are children attending the local primary school, where there are five teachers. Most of the commune members are of Banak origin, but a transient workforce from Labrang area, and as far away as Shanxi province, contributes to the ethnic mix of the commune. Pack animals for the circuit of the mountain can be arranged in this village. See Dolma Tsering, a native of Dzachuka who has lived here since the late 1950s.

Guri Gonpa

Fording the **Qushian** River below the village, the trail leads five kilometres to **Guri Gonpa**, a branch of Dzogchen and Dodrub Chode of the Nyingma school, which until recently was the seat of the late Thubten Tsering, a charismatic lama descended from Lhalung Peldor, who was also a contemporary of Dodrupchen Rinpoche and a qualified Dzogchen master in his own right. It was he who founded the original tented camp at the beginning of this century, and who supervised the temple's construction from 1985 onwards. The local community in the monastery and surrounding village numbers approximately 100. There are a few monks, but the majority of practitioners here are mantrins.

The complex comprises three main buildings, in addition to the lama's residence. Among these, the **main temple** contains excellent new images of Padmasambhava, Shantaraksita and King Trisong Detsen, as well as White Tara, Green Tara, Vairocana, Vajrasattva, Four-armed Avalokiteshvara, Eleven- faced Avalokiteshvara, Machen Pomra, and Tangtong Gyelpo. The vestibule has a large Mani Wheel Chapel in addition to the murals depicting the four guardian kings.

To the left of the temple is a **Reliquary Chapel** containing the consecrated remains of Lama Gyatso (d 1987) and Lama Thubten Tsering. It also has images of Padmasambhava and of the three deities symbolizing longevity: Amitayus, White Tara, and Vijaya. The **Gonkhang**, situated behind the lama's residence, contains a revered central image of Ling Gesar, the hero of Tibetan epic poetry who has many associations with Amnye Machen. Its murals depict (left) Tangtong Gyelpo, and (right) Machen Pomra, complete with retinue. In the **lama's residence** there are images of Padmasambhava, Jigme Lingpa, and Tangtong Gyelpo. Texts are kept here which describe both the Buddhist and Bonpo pilgrimage guides to Amnye Machen.

Approaching the Snow Peaks   The trail climbs steadily from the monastery following the **Niwagu** River upstream. A large *latse* bedecked with mantra-engraved stones and colourful prayer-flags is passed before the low pass of **Drado Wangchuk La**. A trail of steeper gradient then ascends the high **Drakdo Latse Chogon** pass (4,328 metres), close to the glaciers. The walk from the monastery to this pass takes eight hours. A ridge above the pass leads towards the glaciers and the icy **Tso Karpo** ('white lake'), otherwise known as **Drodu Nyaka** (4,600 metres). Slightly below the pass, on the south side, there is a field of protuberant glaciers, known as **Rigar Tongka** or **Rigar Tongjung**. This is revered as a sacred site symbolic of the Thousand Buddhas of the present aeon, or of the Sixteen Elders. Golok camper groups are to be found in this vicinity in summertime.

The view of the main peaks of the range is genuinely impressive from this vantage point. The highest of the 14 peaks forming the range are **Dradul Lungshok** (6,154 metres), the northernmost peak, which lies close to the trail across the Rigar Tongjung glacier field. The next peak is the dome-shaped **Mount Amnye Machen** itself (6,282 metres), followed by the pyramid-shaped **Mount Chenrezig** (6,127 metres), down the valley, towards Chuwarna.

Descending from the pass through the **Zhideka** valley, after three hours, the side-valley of the **Yekhok-chu** joins the circuit from the north. The trail then descends through flower-carpeted grassland to the junction of the **Halong-chu** valley, which leads northwest towards the **Amnye Machen Base Camp** (4,600 metres). Gazelles can frequently be seen in these parts, and there is a sky burial terrace. Deep within the Halong-chu valley near the rocks of **Phawang Serka** and **Phawang Hekar**, there is the **Terdak Phawang Drubzhi**, containing the *termas* of Ling Gesar, the warrior king of Tibetan epic poetry, who is said to have hidden his sword here, pledging one day to retrieve it. Even closer to the mountain are the **Ser Tso** ('golden lake') and **Ngon Tso** ('blue lake').

Eastern Part of the Circuit   From the Halong-chu junction to the **Chorten Karpo** at **Chuwarna** (*Ch* Xueshan) village it is an easy six-hour trek. Here, the **Yonkhok-chu** (*Ch* Qiemuqu) flows from the southwest to join the Yekhok-chu, thereby forming the **Tshab-chu** which flows east into the Yellow River. At **Chuwarna** (*Ch* Xueshan) village there are small shops and a motorable track. Adjacent to the Chorten Karpo is a large wall, known as **Gonying Mani Lhartse**, inscribed with the mantra of the meditational deity Vajrakila. Traditionally, this is the starting point of the circuit for many pilgrims.

Follow the motor road for four hours from Chorten Karpo, passing several nomad houses set among

Machen County

sparse juniper woods in the hills around. At **Tselnak Khamdo**, the road leaves the circuit, and cuts southeast for 116 kilometres to **Tawo** (Machen), the capital of the Golok region. Prayer-flags and stone cairns bedeck the trail and the trees along this section of road.

Continuing on to the southwest sector of the pilgrims' circuit, the trail passes the entrance to the **Halong Langri-chu** valley, which leads north towards the Base Camp, and then gradually ascends the **Yonkhok-chu** valley, to eventually reach the **Tamchok Gongkha la** pass after some seven hours. The broad saddle of the pass stretches for a further 10 kilometres (three hours). In summer this area is a carpet of wild flowers set against the imposing snow peaks and many nomads establish camps here. After the saddle one comes to a curious rock formation in the middle of the valley called **Mowatowa**, which houses several meditation caves, including that of the great Nyingmapa meditation master Zhabkar Tsokdruk Rangdrol (1781-1851). The variegated cliffs of **Goku Chenmo** are said to mark the entrance to the 'palace' of the protector **Machen Pomra**.

Southern Part of the Circuit

Some four hours later, the trail reaches the **Dolma Gur-chu** spring, which demarcates the final part of the circuit. Rather than follow the gorge of the Qushian River, the path heads over a spur, where Ling Gesar tied his horse, and then descends back down to **Guri Gonpa**, about five hours away.

The best months to make this circuit are May/June and September/October, avoiding the summer rains and the biting cold of winter. A tent and sleeping bag are essential as well as a good supply of food, for apart from being offered tea, tsampa and yoghurt by the occasional nomad, there is no chance of restocking. It is advisable to allow at least a week for the full circuit.

Practicalities

Tawo (Machen) Town

The Golok capital at **Tawo** is an archetypal image conjured out of the Wild West! Prior to the 1960s when a concerted policy was adopted with a view to settling the nomadic Golok and Banak populations of Amdo, Tawo was but a small hamlet. The prefecture even now has an estimated 88 per cent Tibetan population. Almost half the non-Tibetan population of Golok, ie Han Chinese, Hui and Salar, live here in Tawo, alongside the indigenous Tibetan groups. There are also many itinerant traders and work-unit appointees who come during the seasonable months, for in winter temperatures of -20° are common. Most of the Tibetan nomad families currently have a small disposable income and Tawo, situated on a tributary of the Tshab-chu, is a natural gathering place.

Phone code: 0975
Colour map 5, grid B4

Far-east Tibet

Sleeping & eating Stay at the *Xueshan Hotel*, T0975-382142. ¥300 per room. There are a few Muslim and Chinese-style restaurants, apart from the hotel restaurant. Take a walk down the main street to inspect the Golok markets, the dusty pool tables, and the Stalinist concrete blocks from which the prefecture is administered.

Various roads diverge at Tawo: west for 122 kilometres to **Temahe** (*Ch* Qamalung) on the Tsogyenrawa-Darlag road; northwest for 118 kilometres to **Chuwarna** (*Ch* Xueshan) on the Amnye Machen pilgrimage circuit; northeast for 73 kilometres to **Rabgya Monastery** on the banks of the Yellow River; southwest for 83 kilometres to **Gabde**; and southeast for 109 kilometres to **Xia Zangke** on the Yellow River. Heading southeast on the last of these roads, there is a small monastery affiliated to Dzogchen called **Tokden Gon Dongak Shedrubling**, 210 kilometres from town.

Roads from Tawo

Rabgya Monastery

Altitude: 3,090 metres
Colour map 5, grid B4

Taking the northeast road, a southern pass is crossed and this leads into a series of small, lightly-forested gorges to the Yellow River opposite Rabgya. A small enclave on the north bank of the Yellow River belongs to Machen rather than Kawasumdo. It includes the bridge spanning the Yellow River (73 kilometres from Tawo), **Rabgya Monastery**, which is two kilometres beyond the bridge and **Mount Khyung-ngon**.

Rabgya Monastery, otherwise known as **Tashi Kundeling**, is an important branch of Sera monastery, founded at the advice of Dalai Lama VII in 1769 by a Mongol from Kokonor named Arik Geshe (1726-1803). Even today there are several monks from the Sogwo Mongol prefecture just to the east. The second abbot, Shingza Pandita Lobzang Dargye (1753-1824), is regarded as an incarnation of Tsongkhapa's mother, Shingza Acho, and his subsequent incarnations have presided over the monastery.

The complex has been substantially rebuilt during the last decade, but a few old artworks did survive, including a handful of pillar carpets in the main prayer hall and a set of tangkas. The architecture of the modern temples is functional but unimaginative, except for the artwork which is in the wonderful Repkong style. Approaching the main entrance of the **Assembly Hall** (Tsenkhangling), marked by two ornate stone lions, there is a large stupa and the **Menpa Dratsang** to the left, with an unrestored residential building to its rear, and to the right the **Dukhor Lhakhang**. The college of Rabgya lies one kilometre east, adjacent to the motor road.

The **Assembly Hall** which has a trilingual inscription above the door, contains 64 carpeted pillars and an original flagstoned floor. The **inner sanctum** contains (left to right): images of Amitabha, Arik Geshe, the Buddhas of the Three Times, Tara and Aksobhya, along with the volumes of the *Kangyur*. The **main hall** has truly wonderful murals executed in silver, which depict Shakyamuni surrounded by the 1,000 buddhas of the aeon, as well as Padmasambhava flanked by the masters of the Kadampa and Kagyupa lineages, and Tsongkhapa surrounded by his students. The hall still holds an air of antiquity.

The **Menpa Lhakhang** contains a throne bearing the portrait of Alak Yongdzin of Tarshul in Kawasumdo (see above, page 586), and images of the eight Medicine Buddhas and the Lords of the Three Enlightened Families. The murals here depict (left to right): Mahakala, Sitatapatra, Havagriva, Eight Medicine Buddhas, Amitabha, Aksobhya, Mahakarunika, Uchusmakrodha, and Simhavaktra.

The broad cliff behind Rabgya is known as **Mount Khyung-ngon** (Blue Garuda) and the walk to the hilltop shrine passes several smaller shrines and caves, giving a good view of the Yellow River.

Temahe

To reach the main Jyekundo-Ziling highway from **Machen**, take the west road out of town and on reaching **Domkhok** (*Ch* Dongqingguo) after 33 kilometres, do not turn northwest for Chuwarna and Amnye Machen. Instead, turn southwest across the **Dramani La** pass (4,760 metres) for **Temahe** (*Ch* Qamalung), reaching that township after 89 kilometres. **Trangmar Chogar**, a small Nyingma monastery, is located here to the west of the township.

Then, head northwest over a shallow pass, which can be muddy in summer and snow-bound in winter, to arrive at **Tsogyenrawa** (87 kilometres). This road runs parallel to the southern and western sectors of the Amnye Machen circuit. Alternatively, from Temahe, you can head southeast towards **Darlag**, passing

Far-east Tibet

through **Dangxiang** township, where a small monastery, **Dangzhung Makar Chogar**, holds allegiance to Katok and Rabgya simultaneously!

Gabde County དགའ་བདེ

*Gabde county lies in Central Golok to the south of the Amnye Machen range and within the bend of the Yellow River. It is an important breeding area for the black-necked crane. The county capital is located at **Bakchen** (Ch Gabde) on the Shi-ke-chu, a southeast flowing tributary of the Yellow River. Bakchen lies 83 kilometres southwest of the prefectural capital **Tawo** (Machen), and 53 kilometres from **Darlag**. There are seven monasteries within the county, including some representing the Jonangpa school.*

Gabde County (132)
甘德县
Gade
Population: 21,973
Area: 6,554 sq km
Colour map 5, grid C4

Bakchen can also be approached from Tsogyenrawa on the Jyekundo-Ziling highway. A turn-off at Tsogyenrawa leads southeast through **Temahe** (87 kilometres), and **Jang-gegye** (91 kilometres) in the direction of Darlag. Turn northeast at Jang-gegye to reach Bakchen after 35 kilometres.

Getting there

Jonangpa Monasteries of Eastern Gabde ཇོ་ནང་དགོན་པ

Towards the end of the 19th century, the Jonangpa lamas of Dzamtang began to establish branches within the Gabde region of **Golok**. Three monasteries were constructed here to represent that unique lineage of Tibetan Buddhism. Among them, **Lungkya Gonpa**, only 10 kilometres from town, is affiliated to Dzamtang Tsangpa Gon. **Tashi Choling**, 75 kilometres east of town is affiliated to Dzamtang Chode, and **Trayaklung Gon**, which is the largest monastery within the county is a branch of Lungkya Gonpa, founded by a Jonangpa monk from Sertal. The last of these is located near Jiangqian, in a side-valley southeast of Qingzhen on the Gabde-Machen road, about 15 kilometres before the Yellow River. The head lama here is Tashi Gyatso, currently residing in New York.

Southern Gabde

A little used side-road leads southeast from Bachen to the north bank of the Yellow River at **Sharo Gonpa** (*Ch* Xiagongma). Here, the Gelukpa monastery of **Sharo** is noted for its strict discipline and excellent teachings. The monastery which was founded in 1922 as a branch of Rabgya, is situated on the ridge north of the Yellow River, 46 kilometres down-valley from the county town.

Also in this vicinity is **Washul Lama Chogar**, the largest Nyingmapa community of Gabde, which was founded in the 19th century as a branch of Dzogchen.

Darlag County དར་ལག

*Darlag county straddles the Yellow River due south of the Amnye Machen range in Golok, and extends further south as far as the Mardzagang watersheds, which separate the Yellow River basin from the Ser-chu, Do-chu and Mar-chu tributaries of the Gyarong. The county capital is located at **Gyu-me** on the banks of the Yellow River. The distance from Gyu-me to Gabde is 53 kilometres, to Machen 118 kilometres; to Tsogyenrawa 196 kilometres, to Padma 168 kilometres, and to Jigdril 261 kilometres. There are currently 10 monasteries within the county, eight of which are Nyingmapa.*

Darlag County (133)
达日县
Darlag
Population: 21,539
Area: 14,351 sq km
Colour map 5, grid C3

Far-east Tibet

Gyu-me Town

Altitude: 3,993 metres **Gyu-me** town has two long and wide intersecting streets. Beside the bridge over the Yellow River at **Darlag** is a small Nyingma monastery, **Wachin Gonpa**, an easy walk from town. The *Government Guesthouse* has reasonable rooms (¥30-150), and an excellent restaurant. There are other guesthouses, restaurants and a public cinema lining the two streets.

Traling Monastery

The Nyingmapa monastery of **Traling Gon Tashi Chodenling**, which is the largest and best known in the county, is situated 15 kilometres west of town in the direction of **Dzuktrun** (*Ch* Jianshe), and a further seven kilometres along a side-road. For much of the journey the road follows the Yellow River upstream through rich pasture lands. This monastery, which has over 300 monks, was founded in 1895, and is affiliated to Katok in Kham. It has been visited by Moktse Tulku of Katok, who in recent years has been responsible for the reconstruction of the mother monastery (see above, page 461). Within the **main temple** there are large cast images of Shakyamuni and Padmasambhava, and old tangkas representing the Eight Manifestations of Padmasambhava, as well as the **reliquary stupa** containing the remains of the previous Lingtrul Rinpoche. The present incumbent, also called Ya Tulku, currently resides in Vancouver. In his absence, monastic affairs including reconstruction are in the hands of Tulku Taknyi and Khenpo Peljor.

Above the monastery is a renowned **charnel ground** (*durtro*), to which corpses will be brought for dismemberment and sky burial from all parts of Golok. Here there is a raised platform above the circular dismemberment stones, and on its rear wall there are individually framed paintings of the Hundred Peaceful and Wrathful Deities, who appear to the deceased following death and before rebirth.

Roads from Dzuktrun

Dzuktrun lies 23 kilometres west of Gyu-me, and two roads diverge here: southwest to **Sangruma** (50 kilometres) on the Khanglong-chu and **Taktok** on the Yellow River (40 kilometres); and southeast for 110 kilometres to **Ponkor** (*Ch* Xiahongke) on the Darlag-chu. **Sangruma Gonpa** is affiliated to Traling Gon, while **Taktok Gonpa** was founded in 1890. The Bayankala watersheds are crossed on both these roads: trekking southwest to **Arikdza Gonpa** and the Yalong River from Sangruma (see above, page 476), or southeast from **Ponkor** into the Nyi-chu valley (50 kilometres). The latter is the main road to Sertal which crosses the Qinghai-Sichuan border, 17 kilometres beyond Ponkor. At Ponkor itself, the local monastery, founded in 1920, is affiliated to Katok.

South of Darlag

Taking the main road southeast from **Gyu-me**, you will pass through the

Far-east Tibet

valley of the **Gyu-chu**, a tributary of the Yellow River, reaching **Ozer** (*Ch* Wesai) after 21 kilometres, and **Dernang Gonpa** after a further 39 kilometres. **Dungchung Gonpa** at Ozer is a small Nyingmapa monastery, founded in 1940 as a tented camp, while **Dernang** is a branch of Katok, founded in 1910. Continuing south from Dernang, you will cross the watershed (4,465 metres) between the Gyu-chu and the Mar-chu tributary of the Gyarong. At **Mangdrang**, 46 kilometres further southeast, where the small **Budon Gonpa** is a branch of Katok, the road bifurcates, leading southeast into Padma county and northeast into Jigdril county.

Jigdril County གཅིག་སྒྲིལ་

*Jigdril county, at the southeast extremity of Golok, occupies the watershed between the Yellow River basin and the Nga-chu tributary of the Gyarong. The county capital is located at **Drukchen Sumdo**, 155 kilometres from Mangdrang, and 75 kilometres from Ngawa.*

Jigdril County (134)
久治县
Jigzhi
Population: 16,422
Area: 7,963 sq km
Colour map 5, grid C4

Tarthang Monastery དར་ཐང་དགོན་པ

From **Mangdrang**, where the road branches, take the left fork which heads east over an occasionally snowy pass. In the distance there are views of the Nyenpo Yurtse mountain range. Reaching **Warje** village after 22 kilometres, the road divides again, east for Sogruma and south for Tarthang. Taking the latter, you will enter a side-valley which follows the **Mar-chu** downstream. After travelling along this rough road for 18 kilometres (sometimes it is impassable in the rainy season), you will arrive at **Tarthang Monastery** (*Ch* Baiyu), which is the largest in the county.

This monastery, properly known as **Tarthang Dongak Shedrub Dargyeling**, **History** was founded in 1857 or 1882 by Gyatrul Rinpoche, Pema Dongak Tendzin (1830-91), the seventh throne-holder of the great Nyingmapa monastery of Pelyul in Kham. It quickly became the largest and most influential branch of Pelyul in the entire Golok-Sertal area, with 1,210 monks and 30 incarnate lamas, headed by the Pelyul Choktrul incarnation, who presently resides in Nepal. Among the other important figures connected with this monastery in recent times, special mention should be made of Lama Kunga or Tarthang Tulku, who has established a Nyingma institute and publishing centre (Dharma Publishing) in California. In addition, the charismatic tulku Garwang Nyima is presently responsible for the reconstruction and revitalization of the monastery, which houses over 1,000 monks.

The **Great Assembly Hall (Tsokchen)** has 140 pillars, and contains large cast **The complex** images of Jowo Shakyamuni, Padmasambhava, and Amitabha. There are important murals in the Repkong style, the work of the master artist Kalzang, which focus on the meditational deities of the Nyingma lineage.

Alongside the assembly hall, there are two other buildings: the **Serdung Lhakhang**, containing the reliquary stupas of the previous

Jigdril County

Far-east Tibet

Pelyul Choktrul and of two former monastic preceptors of Tarthang; and the **Teaching Hall (Dukhang)**, with Repkong-style murals which depict the *terma* visions of the Nyingma school, such as the Peaceful and Wrathful Deities according to Karma Lingpa's *Tibetan Book of the Dead*. In front of this complex of buildings there is a **wall of prayer wheels**, over two kilometres in length; and beyond that, further down the valley, there is a new **Buddhist Studies College (Shedra)**, sponsored by Tarthang Tulku in the United States.

After the college and close to the road, there is the magnificent **Zangdok Pelri Lhakhang**. On its **ground floor** there are cast images of the Eight Manifestations of Padmasambhava (made by Chamdo artisans) and clay images of the Twenty-five Disciples of Padmasambhava (made by the Repkong artist Kalzang). The surrounding corridors depict scenes from the *Biography of Padmasambhava (Pema Katang)*. On the **second floor**, there are images of the Lords of the Three Enlightened Families (ie Manjughosa, Avalokiteshvara, and Vajrapani), along with Tara and Acala. Amitabha is the central image on the **third floor**.

Behind the Zangdok Pelri Lhakhang, there is another temple known as the **Phurba Lhakhang**, dedicated to the meditational deity Vajrakila. Here, the central image depicting Vajrakumara is made of wood and its facial features of clay. To the right of the last two temples and close to the road, there is the residence of Tarthang Tulku (now in the United States) and his sisters.

The township lies beyond the monastery lower down the Mar-chu valley. It contains a small guesthouse run by a Tibetan medical practitioner and his family (¥10 per bed).

From Tarthang, it is possible to trek further, following the Mar-chu downstream into Padma county.

Mount Nyenpo Yurtse

Colour map 5, grid C4 From Tarthang Monastery, the trail continues southeast to **Lungkar Gonpa**, a branch of Rabgya founded in 1785, where there are over 200 monks. It then leads to the western edge of **Mount Nyenpo Yurtse** (5,369 metres), the principal holy mountain of southern Golok, which is revered as the birthplace of the Golok tribes. The range has 14 peaks over 5,000 metres, and the 10-15 day pilgrimage circuit is much harder than at Mount Amnye Machen. The snow-capped steep ridges of the mountain are surrounded by marshland and glacial lakes, such as **Tsochen** and **Tsochung** which feed streams flowing north into the Yellow River, or **Tso Nagma** and **Nojin Tso**, which feed streams flowing south into the headwaters of the Gyarong. The **Base Camp** is located at 4,000 metres, and climbing expeditions are organized by the Qinghai Mountaineering Association. On the south side of the mountain there are three hot springs and a nature reserve for the macaque.

Drukchen Sumdo (Jigdril) Town

Colour map 5, grid C5 After **Warje**, where the hermitage of **Yakra Nagar** dates from the 1940s, another steep pass leads to Sogruma (58 kilometres). Just eight kilometres before reaching this township, the Jonangpa monastery of **Cham Gonpa** is visible on the left of the road. A trail leads northwest from here to **Wasai** (48 kilometres), where there are branch monasteries of Zhechen, Katok and Pelyul, but the main road turns southeast, crossing five more major passes, which offer increasingly spectacular views of Mount Nyenpo Yurtse's glaciers. After traversing the glacial rivers which flow northwards from this sacred mountain, the road eventually reaches **Drukchen Sumdo**, the county capital of Southeast Golok.

The town has a population of only a few thousand, but there are comfortable guest-house facilities, and a fine Sichuan-style restaurant with a chef who once worked at the *Jinjiang Hotel* in Chengdu!

Essentials

Taklung Gonpa

Located just to the south of Drukchen Sumdo town, and on a side-road, this Nyingma monastery is a branch of Pelyul, under the supervision of Dampuk Rinpoche who has dedicated his recent years to its reconstruction. There is an Assembly Hall, a Zangdok Pelri-style temple; a Potala-style temple, named after the residence of Avalokiteshvara on Mount Potalaka; a protector chapel (Gonkhang), and a large Tara stupa.

Colour map 5, grid C5

The road to Ngawa

A poorly serviced road heads south across the watershed to **Ngawa** (75 kilometres) in the Nga-chu valley, while another with even less traffic heads north-east to **Mantang** (43 kilometres) and **Awantsang**, from where it crosses the Yellow River twice en route to Machu in present day Gansu (see below, page 638). Along the Ngawa road, apart from Taklung, there are two other small monasteries: **Khangsar** (Nyingma) and **Nyinyu** (Jonangpa and Gelukpa combined).

Padma County ‌པདྨ

Padma county, locally pronounced Parma, *is one of the most beautiful parts of Tibet. It lies on the south side of the watershed between the rolling grasslands of the Yellow River basin and the forested gorges of the Gyarong. Specifically it occupies the upper reaches of the Mar-chu and Do-chu rivers. The county capital is located at* **Selitang** *on the Mar-chu, 168 kilometres southeast of Darlag, 217 kilometres southwest of Jigdril, and 202 kilometres northwest of Ngawa. There are 23 monasteries scattered throughout the valleys of the county, 20 of which are Nyingmapa establishments, and the remainder Kagyupa and Jonangpa.*

Padma County (135)
班玛县
Baima
Population: 18,782
Area: 6,437 sq km
Colour map 5, grid C4

Far-east Tibet

Padma County

Do Gongma Gonpa

Colour map 5, grid C3

Crossing the watershed from **Mangdrang** in Darlag or Jigril county, after 26 kilometres the road reaches **Do Gongma Gonpa** in the valley of the **Kyilho-chu**, a tributary of the Mar-chu. This important monastery is a branch of Katok, founded in 1840, with over 200 affiliated monks. Outside the temple by the river banks, there is a fine set of stupas symbolizing the deeds of Shakyamuni Buddha. Nearby, there is also another branch of Katok, called **Wemda Gonpa**, which was founded in 1830 and expanded in 1942.

Padma Bum

At Do Gongma Gonpa, an incomplete nine-storey tower marks the entrance to the **Padma Bum** region, and a side-trail leads southwest, into the upper reaches of the Do-chu valley. Trekking routes also give access to this region from Ozer and Dernang Gonpa on the north side of the watershed (see above, page 605). It is possible to drive along the side-road from Do Gongma Gon for 17 kilometres as far as **Makehe** township, where **Pangyu Gon**, yet another branch of Katok, is located. From here trails lead to the birthplace of Do Khyentse at **Wangchen Drok Gon** and the spectacularly located **Tsimda Gonchen**.

Upper Do-chu Region

At Makehe, a rough road leads west across the watershed into the upper Do-chu valley, where trails diverge: northwest to Daka, southwest to Dodrub Chode, and west towards **Mapa** (*Ch* Maba) in the valley of the Darlag-chu. Apart from **Langwu Gon** in Mapa, which is a Jonangpa branch of Dzamtang Tsangpa Gon, the entire region is a stronghold of the Nyingmapa. The most important establishments here are **Nyagen Gonpa**, affiliated to Zhechen in Kham (70 kilometres from the county town), which was founded in 1904, and **Dodrub Chode** (*Ch* Zhiqinsi) which holds allegiance to Dzogchen and maintains the tradition of Rigzin Jigme Lingpa (90 kilometres from the county town).

Dodrub Chode Monastery ཪྫོ་གྲུབ་དགོན་པ

The upper reaches of the Do-chu valley are rich in gold and there is a major mine eight kilometres south of the village of **Dankar**, where **Kharnang Gonpa** (founded 1840), an active, newly-constructed Nyingmapa monastery with about 150 monks, may be visited. The nomads of this region appear wild and unkempt with most men having long hair and heavy silver earrings. There is a trekking route but no motorable road leading down the valley to Dodrub Chode.

History   This monastery, properly known as **Tsangchen Ngodrub Pelbarling**, was founded by Dodrub Chen II Jigme Phuntsok Jungne in the mid-19th century when the monks of its mother monastery, **Yarlung Pemako** in Sertal, fled north to escape the marauding army of Nyarong Gonpo Namgyel (see above, page 378). An older tented monastery had been founded here in 1527 but destroyed by Mongol forces during the civil war. At Dodrub Chode the tradition which is maintained is that of the 18th century treasure-finder Jigme Lingpa, whose *Longchen Nyingtig* cycle is widely practised throughout Tibet. Jigme Lingpa's disciples Dodrubchen I Jigme Trinle Ozer (1745-1821) and Jigme Gyelwei Nyugu returned to their native Kham after receiving the teachings from Jigme Lingpa, and they founded the monasteries of **Dzagya** in Dzachuka and **Drodon Lhundrub** at Sukchen Tago in the Do valley. Dzagya was where the great Paltrul Rinpoche (1808-87) studied under Jigme Gyelwei Nyugu. Dodrubchen then went on to found **Tseringjong Monastery** at Yarlung Pemako (also called **Pemako Tsasum Khandroling**) in neighbouring Sertal. It was his successor who moved the monastic community to its present location in Padma county, seeking to avoid the Nyarong incursions, and building anew on the site of an ancient 13th century Sakyapa monastery (once visited by Drogon Chogyel Phakpa).

Subsequently, the new monastery was developed and expanded by Dodrubchen III Tenpei Nyima (1865-1926), the son of the great treasure-finder

Dudjom Lingpa (1835-1904). He was a renowned scholar who built the great temples of **Dodrub Chode**, and established a non-sectarian college as well as a meditation hermitage. The woodblocks for his published works were formerly housed here. In all, the monastery had 13 incarnate lamas and 250 monks until the 1950s. The present Dodrubchen Rinpoche IV, Thubten Trinle Pelzangpo (b 1927), resides at the Chorten Monastery in Gangtok, Sikkim; and he has also established a Buddhist Temple in Massachusetts.

From Dodrub Chode, a seasonal jeep track heads south to **Nyenlung** in Sertal county, and thence to Gogentang (65 kilometres from Nyenlung).

Selitang

Selitang, the county capital, lies 62 kilometres below **Mangdrang**, in the upper Mar-chu valley. It is a small garden town, pleasantly situated amidst coniferous forest, which is being exploited for timber. A branch road leads northeast to **Tarthang Monastery**, following the Mar-chu upstream. There is a spartan guesthouse and a number of Sichuan-style roadside restaurants.

Colour map 5, grid C4

Mar-chu Gorge

Heading south from Selitang, the Mar-chu plunges through virgin forest, one of the most spectacular locations in all Tibet. The road runs parallel to the river, passing the villages of **Jangritang**, **Yartang** (30 kilometres), **Bengen**, and **Tinta** (35 kilometres), before crossing the current Qinghai-Sichuan border to enter Ngawa county. Along this road, you will bypass the Jonangpa monastery of **Ekyonggya Gonpa** after 10 kilometres. This was originally a Nyingmapa site, founded in 1367, which subsequently converted to the Jonangpa school. Some 20 kilometres further south, around **Yartang** and **Bengen**, there are several branch monasteries of Pelyul and Katok, including **Butsa Gon** (founded 1887), **Tralo Gonpa** (founded 1849), and **Raya Gonpa** (founded 1650). An isolated Kagyupa monastery also survives here, 58 kilometres south of Selitang at **Gyude Gonpa**, which was founded at the behest of Karmapa VIII Mikyo Dorje in 1520. Finally, before crossing the county border into Ngawa, at **Tinta** there are branch monasteries of Pelyul: **Dhida Gon** and **Getse Gon**, both of which were founded in the early decades of this century.

The town of **Ngawa**, 108 kilometres further northeast on the Sichuan side of the border, is approached via the Dze-chu tributary which flows into the Mar-chu near **Khokpo**.

Sertal County གསེར་ཐལ

*Sertal county occupies the valley of the Ser-chu, a major source river of the Gyarong, which drains the grasslands from the northwest and, as in neighbouring Dzamtang, its southern portions are densely forested. Since these hills are less steep than the gorges downstream, they have been quite heavily logged, and until the recently imposed ban on logging, many convoys of timber trucks could be seen transporting logs to Chengdu. The Pelyul branch of the Nyingmapa school predominates in Sertal county and there are several small monasteries in the villages and on the grasslands further north. The county capital is located at **Gogentang**, within the Kandze prefecture, 126 kilometres southeast of the Qinghai-Sichuan border. The distance from Gogentang to Dzamtang is 152 kilometres, to Nyenlung 65 kilometres, and to Drango 149 kilometres.*

Sertal County (136)
色达县
Sertar
Population: 33,646
Area: 7,454 sq km
Colour map 5, grid C4

Far-east Tibet

Getting there Two motorable roads lead into Sertal county from Golok. The first crosses the Bayankala north of **Ponkor Me-ma** (50 kilometres) on the Nyi-chu, and then, after crossing the Qinghai-Sichuan border, enters the Ser-chu valley above **Nyichu** township. Below Nyichu it follows the Ser-chu downstream to **Gogentang**, the county capital, and thence to **Serwa**, where the Drango road branches off to the south and the Dzamthang/Barkham road to the east.

The second crosses from **Dodrub Chode** into **Nyenlung** township, and thence downstream to Gogentang. Between these two border crossings, equidistant between the Ser-chu and Do-chu valleys is the monastery known as **Dartsang Gonpa**, the seat of Dudjom Lingpa (1835-1904).

Nyichu and Yarlung Pemako

Colour map 5, grid C4 At **Nyichu**, 53 kilometres southeast of the border, there are two Nyingma monasteries of note: **Zhichen Kharmar Sang-me Gon** is a branch of Katok, with over 1,000 monks. Beru Rinpoche, the head lama, currently resides in Nepal. He is the father of the present head of the Drukpa Kagyu school. The smaller monastery of **Taklung Gon** is located nearby. About nine kilometres further southeast is the small **Khenleb Gonpa**, a branch of Pelyul, in Khenleb township.

From Khenleb, the road cuts east to **Yarlung**, 45 kilometres distant. Here is the celebrated **Yarlung Pemako Monastery**, founded by Dodrubchen I on his return from Central Tibet. The tradition followed at Yarlung is that of Rigdzin Jigme Lingpa. Nearby, there are smaller branches of Pelyul at **Serto Gonpo Drongrir Nego Gon** and **Ser Shorok Gon**, where there are fewer than 200 and 300 monks respectively.

Gogentang and Ser

Colour map 5, grid C4 Gogentang, the county capital of Sertal, is 19 kilometres east of Yarlung. Here the major landmark is the large white stupa, known as **Gogen Chorten**. A small monastery, named **Ser Gogen Chorten Gon**, lies alongside the stupa.

Essentials The town has the standard up-country guesthouse and restaurant facilities. Buses also run from here to Drango and Barkham.

The neighbouring township of **Ser** has a number of grassland monasteries, which are nearly all branches of Pelyul. Among them the largest are **Raktrom Jampaling**, and **Singsing Dungkar Gon**, which both once had over 1,000 monks. The latter is located not far from the Chorten. Smaller monasteries in this same township include **Jekar Luklha Gon** in Sholeb (450 monks), **Sangsang Dradra Gon** (100 monks), **Tashul Barmi Gon**, **Tashul Ogmi Gon**, **Washul Pon Gonsum**, and **A'u Sera Gon**.

Sertal County

Nyenlung

At Gogentang, a poor road leads north over the grasslands via **Nyenlung** (65 kilometres) to **Dodrub Chode** in Padma county (see above, page 608), but it receives very little traffic. The monasteries of **Nyenlung Gon** and **Bochung Rusal Me Gon** are located here.

Nubzur and Larung

The main road follows the Ser-chu downstream to an important intersection at **Serwa**, above its confluence with the Do-chu. **NB** In the summer months this road can be cut off by the flooding waters of the Ser-chu.

Getting there

Nubzur (*Ch* Loro) township lies along this road, 27 kilometres southeast of Gogentang. Here, the principal monastery is **Ser Nubzur Gon**, which was the original seat of Khenpo Jikpun, also known as Terton Sogyel, the incarnation of Lerab Lingpa. This charismatic lama subsequently founded the monastery of **Larung Gar**, located in a side valley about 15 kilometres south of Gogentang, which has over 2,000 monks and 1,000 nuns. There are no temples as such, since the lama has registered the institution as an educational establishment rather than a monastery. Khenpo Jikpun is well-known for obtaining the 'bird-dogs' of Tibet, a tiny dog which is reputably found in the nest of cliff-nesting birds, and has the power to detect poison in food! He presented one to the Dalai Lama on a recent visit to India. He has also travelled widely in Europe and North America.

Serwa and Lhartse Sangak Tenpeling

Passing through **Horshe** township after 13 kilometres, where the monastery of **Horshe Gon** is a branch of Pelyul, the road continues to follow the river downstream via **Sheldrub** (16 kilometres), and **Yango** (10 kilometres), before reaching **Serwa** township (12 kilometres). This important crossroads village has a large guesthouse, small shops, and a restaurant. The monastery of **Serlha Tsechu Jar Gon** is located here.

Colour map 4, grid C4

Taking the east road from Serwa which leads to Dzamtang and Barkham, you will pass through **Gyasho** after nine kilometres, and **Golatang** after 20 kilometres. Barley is cultivated in these lower reaches of the Ser-chu; and before reaching the wooden barrier which demarcates Kandze and Ngawa prefectures, you will pass by a **Mantra Wheel Chapel (Dungkor)** containing the mantras of Padmasambhava, a white stupa containing an image of Padmasambhava, and 13 kilometres from Serwa, the Pelyul branch monastery of **Lhartse Sangak Tenpeling**, which has a high tower replica of **Sekhar Gutok** (see above, page 211), the tower of Milarepa. The tower was rebuilt by the late Panchen Lama X. The monastery is located above this tower on the ridge. The road then passes into Dzamtang county.

Likhok and Tsang-chu Valleys

Taking the south road from Serwa, you will reach Drango after 71 kilometres. A verdant pass crosses the watershed (4,115 metres) between the Ser-chu and Nyi-chu rivers after 17 kilometres. The nomads of this area are tough and not particularly hospitable to strangers. Sometimes they will block the road with logs and extract protection money from passing drivers! At **Nyipa**, a branch road on the left leads sharply northeast into the **Likhok** and **Tsang-chu** valleys. There are many Nyingmapa monasteries in this area, including **Rahor Gonpa**, in Tsangto township, a branch of Dzogchen which is the seat of Rahor Khenpo Thubten, now resident in Switzerland; and **Khardong Monastery**, the Jangter seat of Lama Chime Rigdzin who also resides in Europe. Other

Far-east Tibet

Nyingmapa monasteries in this small area include: **Shukgang Gon**, **Tsangda Gon**, **Senge Dzong** (a branch of Katok in Tsang-me township), **Sago Gon**, **Domang Gon**, **Dicham Gon**, **Jangang Gon**, and **Gochen Gon**.

Dzamtang County ឧ័ঝ་ঘ८

*Dzamtang
County (137)*
琅塘县
*Zamtang
Population: 30,072
Area: 7,650 sq km
Colour map 4, grid A4*

*Dzamtang county occupies the valley of the Do-chu, from the grasslands and gorges of its mid-reaches, through its confluence with the Ser-chu, and as far as its confluence with the Mar-chu, at which point it becomes known as the **Gyarong** (Ch Dadu) River. It also includes the valley of the north-flowing Dzi-chu, a tributary of the Mar-chu. The county capital is located at **Dzamtang**, 152 kilometres from Sertal, 213 kilometres from Barkham, and 155 kilometres from Drango.*

Access

Driving into Dzamtang county from Sertal or Drango, via Serwa, a wooden barrier marks the modern border between Kandze and Ngawa prefectures. At the confluence of the Ser-chu and Do-chu rivers, 39 kilometres beyond Serwa, there is a turn-off on the left which follows the Do-chu upstream through a precipitous gorge. In the summer season this road can become impassable due to the damage caused by the swollen river banks. Turn left for Dzamtang or continue due east for Barkham.

Jonangpa Monasteries of the Middle Do-chu Valley

If you head north through the Do-chu gorge, you will pass **Drukje** township after 18 kilometres and reach **Dzamtang**, the county capital, after a further 27 kilometres. There are two main monasteries, both representing the Jonangpa school. Among them, **Dzamtang Chode Gonpa** was founded by Drung Kazhi Rinchenpel, and **Dzamtang Tsangpa Gon**, where there are 1,500 monks, was founded by Ngawang Tendzin Namgyel, whose uncle had been an actual student of Taranatha. Isolated in their remote sanctuaries, the Jonangpas of Dokhok and Markhok successfully survived the persecution and conversion of their mother monastery in Tsang by the Gelukpas during the 17th century. There are guesthouse and restaurant facilities.

There are also several small monasteries of the Kagyupa and Nyingmapa schools in the main Do-chu valley.

Yutok

Colour map 4, grid A4

The road bifurcates at Dzamtang, the left branch heading northwest to **Doto** (32 kilometres) and **Yutok** (24 kilometres); and the right branch heading northeast across the watershed to **Nada** (28 kilometres) and **Dzongda** (18 kilometres) in the Dzi-chu valley. Around Yutok, the Nyingmapa monasteries of **Do Shukchung Gon** and **Do Yutok Gon** each have about 500 monks. A trail leads from Yutok via Shukchung to **Dodrub Chode** (see above, page 608) across the Qinghai border.

Dzamtang

Dzi-chu Valley

Driving northeast into the Dzi-chu valley, there are minor Nyingma monasteries, such as **Dzika-me Akye Gon**, most of which are branches of Dodrub Chode. The most important sites in this valley, however, are the numerous monasteries of the Jonangpa school, each with around 100 monks, which are affiliated with the two main Jonangpa monasteries at Dzamtang. The land is flatter here, and quite suddenly the forested gorges with their stone and wooded houses blend into the rolling hilly grasslands inhabited only by yak herding nomads.

Lower Do-chu Valley

Heading east from the aforementioned confluence of the Do-chu and Ser-chu rivers (2,896 metres), the road follows the combined waters of these Gyarong feeder rivers downstream for 122 kilometres as far as their confluence with the Mar-chu. On this route through the gorges, there are only a very few small roadside settlements. After 26 kilometres, the road passes through **To-de** (2,743 metres), where a side-road leads southwest to **Tsangkhok** (20 kilometres), and after a further 40 kilometres it leaves Dzamtang county for Barkham county.

Ngawa County རྔ་བ

*Ngawa county, named after the Nga-chu tributary of the Mar-chu, which flows south from **Mount Nyenpo Yurtse**, is an area where nomadic groups and long-established sedentary communities intermingle. The villages are characterized by large detached adobe farming houses with tapering walls and windows all on one side of the building! Agricultural produce is limited to valley floors and alluvial fans, where fields of barley, rapeseed and beans are planted, but it is animal husbandry and forestry that provide the principal economic outputs. Ngawa has also thrived on trade for centuries; and its inhabitants even now frequently undertake business trips to Chengdu and Lhasa. Several antique stores in Chengdu are owned by traders from Ngawa. The county capital is located at **Ngawa** (Ch Aba); 75 kilometres from Jigdril, 254 kilometres from Barkham, and 157 kilometres from Mewa (Ch Hong Yuan).*

Ngawa County (138)
阿坝县
Aba
Population: 50,996
Area: 8,776 sq km
Colour map 5, grid C5

Upper Ngawa (Ngawa To)

Two roads approach Ngawa from Golok, one following the Mar-chu downstream from Padma, across the Qinghai-Sichuan border, as far as **Khokpo**, where a side-road leaves the Mar-chu and heads northeast for 55 kilometres to Ngawa town (total distance 192 kilometres). The other follows the Nga-chu downstream from Jigdril on the southeast side of Mount Nyenpo Yurtse, via **Ngato** (total distance 75 kilometres).

The monasteries of Upper Ngawa (Ngato) include **Tsinang Gon** of the Jonang school, and Gelukpa institutions such as T**segon Sangchen Tashiling** (founded by

Ngawa

Khenchen Ngawang Drakpa), and **Ziwei Ritro Ganden Tashi Choling**. Just before reaching the town, the road leaves a narrow gorge marked by a vast stone cairn in the open hills that lead up towards the sacred Mount Nyenpo Yurtse, just visible in the distance. 15 kilometres northeast of town is the famous **Gomang Gonpa**, also known as Gomang Gar Ganden Labsum Zungjuk Dechenling. Most of the Nyingma monasteries of Ngawa are small and located in this northern part of the county.

Middle Ngawa (Ngawa Barma)

The town of **Ngawa** itself (population approximately 15,000) is a typical mix of Chinese compounds, department stores and simple shops, but despite its remote location, it remains an important thriving trading town. In common with most of Amdo, gold is a predominant local product, and large numbers of itinerant Chinese workers visit the area to pan for gold in summer. As in Dzamtang and Sertal, the forested hills on the upper reaches of the Nga-chu tributaries have proved easier to log than the gorges further south, and many hillsides have been stripped bare. There is little evidence of replanting except beside the roads of the valley floor, and the denuded slopes are soon covered with herds of yaks and sheep, making regeneration almost impossible. The Public Security Bureau are over-vigilant and may restrict one's movements, even when all travel permits are in order. The town has an interesting leather goods factory and a teacher training college.

Essentials In town there is a large *Government Guesthouse* and several Sichuan-style restaurants. There is a varied nightlife with lively karaoke bars and discotheques.

Monasteries and temples

Kirti Gonpa The hills around the town are dotted with more than 30 monasteries of the Nyingma, Sakya, Geluk and Jonang schools of Buddhism, as well as major Bonpo institutions. The largest monastery, Kirti Gonpa, properly known as **Kirti Kalari Gon Tashi Lhundrub**, is located on the western edge of town. It was founded in 1472 by Rongpa Chenakpa, a disciple of Tsongkhapa; and has well over 1,000 monks. The head lama Kirti Tsenzhab Rinpoche currently resides in India. At its entrance is a huge stupa, one of the largest in Amdo, and this is a major destination for pilgrims from all parts of Tibet. The restored murals and images display a high standard of craftsmanship.

Other Gelukpa monasteries near the town include **Khashi Ritro Tashi Gepeling, Dongkhu Gon Yulgyel Samtenling,** and **Namkyak Ritro Namdakling**, the last having been founded by a student of Dalai Lama VII, named Gyakhe Lama.

Ngawa

The Bonpo monasteries of **Narshi** and **Topgyel** lie just northeast of town. Narshi Gonpa
Both represent the so-called 'old Bon' tradition, which remains aloof from the
19th century ecumenical movement, according to which great Bonpa masters
such as Sharza Tashi Gyeltshen juxtaposed their realizations with those of the
various Buddhist traditions. **Narshi Gonpa** is the larger of the two, and its
monks are well-versed in dialectics, composition, and the decorative arts.

The Jonangpa tradition is also represented in the valley itself at **Setenling** Setenling
Gonpa, which was established by Namnang Dorje. There are 800 affiliated Gonpa
monks, some currently practising retreat in Dzamtang under the guidance of
Sangye Dorje. The head lama here is Thubten Dorje Hwon Rinpoche. The
restored **Assembly Hall** contains new tangkas and images of Kunkhyen
Dolpopa, Jetsun Kunga Drolchok, Taranatha, Namnang Dorje and the deities
Cakrasamvara and Kalacakra. The large central image depicts Maitreya, and in
a glass case there are 1,000 small images of Dolpopa, along with others depict-
ing Padmasambhava, Maitreya and so forth. Relics include the boot of
Taranatha. There are various collections of texts including the *Kangyur* from
Derge and *The Collected Works of Taranatha* (28 vols). Woodblocks for the *Six
Yogas of Niguma* are also preserved here.

The **Gonkhang** has a central image of Mahakala in the 'tiger-riding form'
Takkiraja; while the **meditation hermitage** has images of Dolpopa,
Taranatha, Namnang Dorje, and the meditational deity Vajrakila. In the
lama's residence, there is a Jokhang Chapel with fine images, tangkas and
books, including one tangka depicting Taranatha surrounded by the so-called
Rinjung Gyatsa deities.

Lower Ngawa (Nga-me)

The 108 kilometres descent from Ngawa town to **Lungzi** (*Ch* Longriwa)
crosses six passes, offering fine views (north) of Mount Nyenpo Yurtse after 20
kilometres, and (south) of the deforested hillsides towards Barkham. Gelukpa
monasteries in this area include **Tsakho Gon Ganden Dargyeling**. The highest of the passes on this route (3,764 metres) is the main watershed dividing the
Mar-chu/Nga-chu basin from the Yellow River basin, 56 kilometres south of
the town. Crossing this pass, on a hillside just north of the road, is the Gelukpa
monastery of **Darchen**, with around 200 monks.

Amchu Gonpa

Further on, about 40 kilometres from the pass, the monastery of **Amchu** Colour map 5, grid C5
Gonpa comes into view in the valley floor far below. At **Lungzi** (*Ch* Longriwa)
roads lead south into **Barkham** county (136 kilometres) and northeast follow-
ing the Ger-chu tributary of the Yellow River upstream for 49 kilometres to
Mewa (*Ch* Hongyuan). If you take the latter route, you will reach **Amchu**
Gonpa after 19 kilometres. This is a particularly large Gelukpa monastery with
two complexes: the **Tsenyi Lhakhang** for the study of dialectics and the **Tenyi**
Lhakhang for the study of sutra and tantra. Altogether there are over 1,000
monks, under the guidance of Amchu Rinpoche. The present incumbent,
Amchu Rinpoche IV, returns regularly from exile.

Gyarong Gorges

རྒྱལ་རོང་

*South of Ngawa, in the precipitous rugged gorges of Trokhyab, the source rivers of the Gyarong converge. This is the beginning of the Gyarong region, which extends through the lower reaches of this river valley as far as Chakzamka, and includes the lateral valleys of the Tsenlha-chu and Somang-chu, as well as the upper reaches of the Trosung-chu. This section, outlining the Gyarong gorge and its adjacent valleys, comprises five present-day counties: **Barkham**, **Chuchen**, **Rongtrak**, **Tsenlha**, and **Tashiling**, of which only Rongtrak falls within the Kandze prefecture – the others all being within the Ngawa prefecture. Dardo has already been described (see above, page 444).*
Recommended itinerary: 9 (also 5).

History   In Gyarong, the indigenous population speak a distinctively archaic Qiangic dialect called **Gyarong-ke**, and they maintained their unique way of life and culture for centuries. Until 1949, the tribes of Gyarong were organized into **eighteen petty kingdoms**. Among them, the **northern group** includes Trokhyab (Zhousejia), Dzongak (Songang), Barkham, Choktse (Zhoukeji), Somang (Suomo), Zida, Tsakhok (Li dzong/Zagunao), Gyelkha, and Wasi. These are all located around the Do-chu/Somang-chu confluence and in the upper Trosung-chu valley.

The **central group** comprises Rabten (Chuchen/Jinchuan), Badi, Pawang (Chuchen), Geshitra, Rongtrak, and Dardo (Chakla), which are all located in or around the main Gyarong valley; and the **south-eastern group** includes Tsenlha, Dawei, Hva-hva (Hanniu), and Dronba (Muping), which are all located in the Tsenlha valley and the mountains further south.

Traditionally, **Trokyab, Rabden, Tsenlha,** and **Dardo** were the most influential among these 18 kingdoms, which kept the powerful Sino-Manchu armies of Emperor Qianlong at bay for 10 years during the 18th century. Nowadays, both Barkham and Dardo are prefectural capitals, responsible for the administration of those parts of Kham, Amdo and Gyarong presently under the control of Sichuan province.

Barkham County   འབར་ཁམས།

Barkham County (139)
马尔康县
Markam
Population: 57,341
Area: 7,327 sq km
Colour map 4, grid A5

Barkham county is the northern limit of the Gyarong region and the language here (considered a branch of the archaic Qangic group of Tibeto-Burman) is almost unintelligible to the Amdowa populations further north, and the Khampa peoples to the west. The dress is also distinctive. Most of the women wear multi-coloured embroidered headscarfs and elaborate belts and aprons. Fewer men wear the traditional felt tunic, which is quite distinct from the Tibetan chuba or bulky sheepskin coat. The vast majority of men now wear Chinese clothes, and only a small number of traditionalists can be observed in the market. There are almost 40 monasteries in the county, representing the Nyingma, Gelukpa, Sakya, Jonang and Bonpo traditions, several of them in attractive mountain locations.

Ga-ne and Tuje Chenpo Gon

Entering Barkham county from Dzamtang, the road passes first through *Colour map 4, grid A5* **Ga-ne** (2,590 metres), where a bridge spans the river and a side-road leads south to **Tawu** (see above, page 501) in Kham. On the far bank of the Do-chu at Ga-ne, there is a **Mani Wheel Chapel**.

Continuing downstream from Ga-ne for 13 kilometres, the road passes through **Tuje Chenpo** township (*Ch* Guanyinqiao), where another motorable bridge cuts south across the river. Above the town (one and a half hours' walking distance), there rises the Nyingmapa monastery of **Tuje Chenpo Gon**, which formerly had over 300 monks, and is revered as one of the major pilgrimage sites in Far-east Tibet. There is a small reconstructed monastery here, with about 70 monks, and although the building itself is unimpressive, the winding path up to it is covered in small shrines where pilgrims leave old bits of clothes, tufts of wool from their sheep and broken jewellery.

The side-road leading southwards from Tuje Chenpo leads to **Akhori Gon** (41 kilometres), a branch of Dzogchen monastery. Across the pass from here (in Rongtrak county), is **Maha Kyilung Gon**, the seat of Zenkar Rinpoche, the incarnation of Do Khyentse Yeshe Dorje. The present incumbent is currently based in England.

Trokhyab

Following the main road downstream for four kilometres from Tuje Chenpo, *Colour map 4, grid A5* you will arrive at **Trokhyab**, once one of the most powerful of the 18 ancient kingdoms of Gyarong, but nowadays having the appearance of a small country village. Some houses have the Tibetan syllable 'Tro' (written *khro*) inscribed on the doors!

Some 34 kilometres further east at **Tro-ye**, the road reaches the confluence of the Do-chu and Mar-chu rivers (2,073 metres). The gorge here is one of the steepest in Tibet; and a sturdy bridge spans the rapids. Crossing over to the east bank, the main road heads upstream and then east through the valley of the Somang-chu tributary to **Barkham**, the prefectural capital. The distance from the confluence to Barkham is 55 kilometres.

Alternatively, from the confluence at **Tro-ye**, you can take a side-road which leads upstream to **Tsedun Sobdun Gonpa** – the largest Gelukpa monastery in the county, and Khangsar; as well as Jonangpa monasteries such as

Far-east Tibet

Barkham

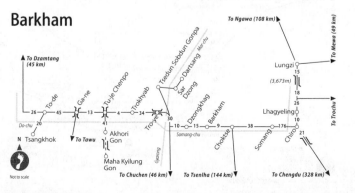

Dzago, Bala, and Tashigang, all of which are in the Mar-chu valley (and its side-valleys). The Gelukpa monastery of **Datsang**, located above **Sar Dzong** on a west-flowing tributary of the Mar-chu, is also accessible by this route. There are fine views from here of **Mount Shukgopuk** (4,906 metres) to the southwest. Unfortunately, the road does not continue upriver to the junction of the Mar-chu and Nga-chu. Visitors and pilgrims to Ngawa are therefore forced to backtrack to Barkham and head for Ngawa via the Somang valley.

Barkham City

Getting there

Population: 20,000

Phone code: 0837

Colour map 4, grid A5

At **Tro-ye** where the combined waters of the Mar-chu and Do-chu are crossed, the road bifurcates: one trail (south) following the Gyarong downstream into Chuchen county (see below, page 619), and the other (east) following the Somang-chu upstream. The latter passes through several of the ancient Gyarong kingdoms: **Dzonggak** lies 10 kilometres east of turn-off, **Barkham** (15 kilometres further east), **Choktse** (9 kilometres further east), and **Somang** (38 kilometres further east). Of these Barkham, which was once one of the smaller of the ancient kingdoms, is now a city replete with high-rise apartment buildings. As the capital of both Barkham county and Ngawa Prefecture, the city is now comparable to Dartsedo in its importance.

The steep-sided valley of the fast-flowing Somang-chu, almost denuded of its original forest, constricts the town into a long thin corridor. Much of the town is composed of administrative buildings and compounds, of uninspired design (large high-rise concrete apartments), but nearby village houses are still constructed in the traditional three-storey stone and wood fashion characteristic of most of Gyarong. Alluvial fans on the valley floor and the less steep slopes high above the river provide some rich agricultural land and terraced fields, irrigated by cleverly contoured canals which surround the small hamlets throughout this area.

Sights

The small Gelukpa monastery which overlooks the town is little more than a concrete shed, with about 30 attendant monks. **Gyidruk Monastery** of the Nyingma school is located some three hours' climb southwest of town. It offers spectacular valley views, although the building and its contents are disappointing artistically.

Far-east Tibet

Barkham City

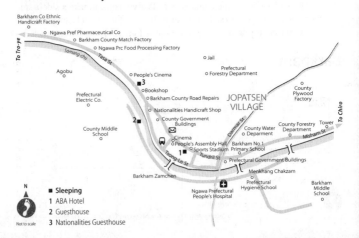

Barkham Co Ethnic Handicraft Factory

To Tro-ye

Ngawa Pref Pharmaceutical Co
Barkham County Match Factory
Somang-chu
Tasa St
Ngawa Prc Food Processing Factory

Jail

Agobu

People's Cinema

Prefectural Forestry Department

■3
Bookshop

Prefectural Electric Co.

Barkham County Road Repairs
Nationalities Handicraft Shop
2■
County Government Buildings

JOPATSEN VILLAGE

County Plywood Factory

To Chiro

County Middle School

Cinema
■1
People's Assembly Hall
Sports Stadium
Tsong Le St

County Water Department
Barkham No 1 Primary School

County Forestry Department
Misham St
Tower

Barkham Zamchen

Jundril St
Prefectural Government Buildings

Ngawa Prefectural People's Hospital

Prefectural Hygiene School

Menkhang Chakzam

Barkham Middle School

N

Not to scale

■ **Sleeping**
1 ABA Hotel
2 Guesthouse
3 Nationalities Guesthouse

The more upmarket *Aba Hotel* (Aba Binguan). With its expensive attached bathrooms, and restaurant/karaoke wing. The cheaper *Minshan Hotel* (*Aba Zhou Minshan Hotel*) which has 4-bedded rooms (¥20 per bed) and functional hot showers on each floor. There are a number of small guesthouses and street restaurants. **Sleeping**

The town has several industries: handicrafts, Tibetan medicines, matches, and wooden furniture; located alongside the ubiquitous government buildings and shops. Look out for the *Minority Handicrafts Shop* (*Ch* Minzu Yongpin Shangdian) for traditional products, and the *Xinhua Bookstore* for books on the region. A cinema and sports stadium provide local entertainment. **Shopping**

Upper Somang Valley

From Barkham the road continues to follow the Somang-chu gorge upstream, passing the ancient kingdom of **Choktse** after nine kilometres. Here there is a turn-off to the south which crosses a pass and then follows the Tsenlha River (*Ch* Xiaojin) downstream for 144 kilometres to Tsenlha county (see page 622).

Continuing east along the Somang-chu, you will pass through the area where, according to one tradition, the great translator Vairocana is said to have meditated and transmitted the Dzogchen teachings during his exile from Central Tibet in the eighth century. Passing **Somang**, another of these ancient kingdoms, after 47 kilometres, you will then after eight further kilometres reach the major intersection at **Chiro**. The road to the southeast leads via **Tashiling** (Lixian) and **Lungu** (Wenchuan) to **Chengdu** (328 kilometres) and the road to the north continues to follow the Somang-chu upstream to the watershed area.

Taking the latter, you drive through a narrow gorge for 10 kilometres to emerge at **Lhagyeling**. This important Gelukpa monastery once specialized in gold-printed texts, and is one of the oldest in Amdo. The area is densely forested and rugged. After a further 26 kilometres, there is a turn-off on the right (east) which leads to **Trochu** (*Ch* Hei shui) county. Continuing on the main road for a further 18 kilometres, you will cross the watershed between the Gyarong and Yellow river basins (3,673 metres), and then after 15 kilometres reach **Lungzi** (Longriwa) in the grasslands. From here you can drive northwest for 108 kilometres to Ngawa (see above, page 613), or northeast through the Ger-chu grasslands to Mewa (Hongyuan).

Chuchen County ཆུ་ཆེན་

*Chuchen county lies deep in the awesome and unwelcoming Gyarong gorge. Formerly known as **Rabden**, it was at times the most powerful of all the Gyarong kingdoms, and its king was a vigorous proponent of the Bon religion. At **Yungdrung Lhateng**, 15 kilometres south of Rabden, there was the largest and most important Bonpo monastery in this part of Tibet. Between 1746-49 and 1771-76 the Sino-Manchu armies of Emperor Qianlong (1736-95) marched into Gyarong, sustained by the messianic zeal of the Gonlung lama Changkya Qutuqtu Rolpei Dorje (1717-86) who sought to convert the Bon and other communities of Gyarong to the Gelukpa school by force of arms. The heroic resistance of the Gyarong people owed much to the isolation of the terrain and to their skill at constructing fortified towers – a tradition indicative of their Qiang ancestry. The imperial forces were driven back across the **Balang Shan** pass (see below, page 623) in disgrace before eventually returning to destroy the Bonpo monastery with their Portuguese cannons, and achieving a partial conversion to the Gelukpa*

Far-east Tibet

Chuchen County (140)
金川县
Jinchuan
Population: 68,291
Area: 5,435 sq km
Colour map 4, grid A5

Gyarong Farmhouse

cause. The present county capital is located at **Chuchen** *(Ch Jinchuan), formerly Rabden, 46 kilometres south of Tro-ye and 84 kilometres north of Rongtrak.*

Rabden Town

Phone code: 08499
Colour map 4, grid A5 The road from the north enters the Gyarong valley at the **Tro-ye** intersection, and heads downstream for 46 kilometres to **Chuchen** (Rabden), passing through **Drukzur** (*Ch* Xiazhai) and **Chingnying**. The small county town has simple guesthouse and Sichuan restaurant facilities. There are also hot springs near the town.

Side-roads lead northeast from the town for 21 kilometres to **Rihruntang** (via Kalingka), and for 15 kilometres to **Retiping** (via Wenlin).

Yungdrung Lhateng

Colour map 4, grid A5 Further south, the road passes **Hozhi** after 10 kilometres; and then, after **Dosum**, it reaches the site of the Bon monastery of **Yungdrung Lhateng** (near Kharatang). Following the subjugation of Chuchen and the destruction of this monastery by the forces of Qianlong, a Gelukpa monastery named **Tenpel Gonpa** (*Ch* Guangfasi) was constructed in 1776, and developed with funds directly from the imperial coffers. Its golden roofs were among the most lavish in Tibet. The wealthy monastery was destroyed during the 1960s and has subsequently been reclaimed by the Bonpos, who have once again resurrected Yundrung Lhateng.

Chuchen County

Anying and Tsemda

Colour map 4, grid A5 From here, the road follows the river south. Tall fortified towers are commonplace on both banks of the river, particularly at strategic confluences. Passing through **Anying**, the road reaches the town of **Tsemda** (59 kilometres south of Chuchen), and from here it crosses the modern prefectural boundary to enter Rongtrak county and the Kandze prefecture.

Far-east Tibet

Rongtrak County རོང་བྲག

*Rongtrak county occupies the Gyarong valley further south from Chuchen. Here the rapids are strong and the sound of rushing waters all-pervasive. The most important pilgrimage centre and power place is **Mount Gyelmo Murdo**, from which the Gyarong region gets its name. Gyarong is a contraction of Gyelmo Tsawarong. This mountain of solid quartz which once reputedly had mantra syllables inscribed in the rock crystal, has sadly been fully exploited for its minerals. The county capital is located at **Rongmi Drango**, 84 kilometres south of Chuchen and 112 kilometres north of Chakzamka.*

Rongtrak County (141)
丹巴县
Danba
Population: 57,923
Area: 6,887 sq km
Colour map 4, grid A5

Dragteng and Pawang

From **Tsemda** in Chuchen county, the road runs due south, passing the sacred **Mount Gyelmo Murdo** on the east bank. Two of the ancient Gyarong kingdoms are passed along this stretch – **Dragteng** after 10 kilometres, and **Pawang** after seven kilometres. At **Dragteng** there are two major monasteries: the Gelukpa monastery of **Phuntsoling** and a large Bonpo monastery, which was once the principle shrine of the Dragteng kings. Near **Pawang** there is another 18th century Gelukpa monastery and the **Bumzhi Hermitage**, associated with the great translator Vairocana, who is said to have built 100,000 stupas here during the eighth century.

Colour map 4, grid A5

Geshitra

Continuing south from Pawang, after three kilometres, a branch road on the northwest leads over a high pass to **Geshitra**, another of the ancient Gyarong kingdoms, 44 kilometres distant. In Lower Geshitra there is the Gelukpa monastery of **Yangra Gon** and the Bon monastery of **Chadolo Gon**. Middle Geshitra has a large Bonpo monastery named **Taksum Gonpa** (at Cherba township) and a ruined Jangter monastery of the Nyingma school. In Upper Geshitra there is a Bon monastery named **Halo Gonpa**. Two trails lead from here to **Maha Kyilung Gon**, the seat of Zenkar Rinpoche, incarnation of Do Khyentse Yeshe Dorje (see above, page 617). The first crosses high passes and a hot springs, while the second, the easier route, passes through the Nyingma monastery of **Odu Gonpa**, birthplace of the present Gyatrul Rinpoche.

Colour map 4, grid A5

Far-east Tibet

Rongmi Drango

Some four kilometres south of the turn-off from Geshitra, the road reaches the county capital of **Rongmi Drango**, at the confluence of the Gyarong and Tsenlha rivers. Tall 18th century fortifications dominate the landscape of this ancient Gyarong Kingdom. The nearby **Mount Lateng** has three monasteries, situated one above the other on the hillside. The lowest of these is Gelukpa, the second is Nyingma, and the third is **Norbupuk Hermitage**, located at the site of Vairocana's eighth century

Rongtrak County

To Rabden
(59 km)

Tsemda

10
Mt Gyelmo Murdo

Dragteng

7

To Geshitra
(44 km)

Pawang

3

4
To Tsenlha
(58 km)

Rongmi Drango

N

To Garthar
(74 km)

Sokpa

5

20

Gudzong

To Chakzamka
(87 km)

Not to scale

Gyarong River

cave, where a *drubchu* stream attributed to that great master remains ice-cold even in summer.

On the west bank of the Gyarong, near Rongmi Drango the main road leads downstream to **Sokpa** (five kilometres) and **Gudzong** (20 kilometres). Sokpa has a Bonpo monastery named **Taktse Gon**.

Moving on Four roads diverge at Rongmi Drango (including the road just described from Chuchen). Head downstream (southeast) on the west bank of the Gyarong to reach **Chakzamka** (112 kilometres); southwest following the Dungku-chu tributary to **Garthar** (74 kilometres); or cross the Gyarong and head northeast following the Tsenlha-chu valley to **Tsenlha** (58 kilometres).

Among these, the main road to Chakzamka passes through small villages at kilometres markers 85 and 28. Here there were labour camps during the Cultural Revolution. The low-lying county of Chakzamka (1,829 metres) has already been described (see above, page 451).

The southwest road passes through **Tong-gu** township and reaches **Garthar** after 74 kilometres. This was formerly the main motor road to Garthar and Tawu prior to the construction of the **Gya La** route above Dartsedo (see above, page 447).

Tsenlha County བཙན་ལྷ

Tsenlha County (142)
小金县
Xiaojin
Population: 72,820
Area: 5,074 sq km
Colour map 4, grid A6

Tsenlha county occupies the valley of the Gyarong river's main tributary, the Tsenlha-chu (Ch Xiaojin), which nowadays lies within Ngawa prefecture. The population here is mixed Tibetan and Qiang, and both the Bonpo and Gelukpa traditions have co-existed since the 18th century. The county capital is located at ***Drongdal Mezhing***, *58 kilometres northeast of Rongtrak, 143 kilometres south of Barkham, and 146 kilometres west of the Wolong Panda Reserve.*

Dronang and Tselung

Colour map 4, grid A5
The road from Rongtrak to Tsenlha crosses the Gyarong River above its confluence with the Tsenlha-chu, and follows the latter upstream. At **Dronang**, eight kilometres east of Rongmi Drongo, there is **Langchen Gonpa** of the Gelukpa school and a small Jangter monastery of the Nyingma school, as well as a hot spring. Continuing on to **Tselung** (31 kilometres), the road crosses the prefectural border, and after a further 19 kilometres reaches the county capital.

Drongdal Mezhing Town

Colour map 4, grid A5
Drongdal Mezhing (*Ch* Xiaojin) is a picturesque town, located on the steep slopes of the Tsenlha valley, below its confluence with the Bupen-chu. Even the government buildings have assumed the appearance of a pagoda, and the local municipality has taken over the old Catholic Church. Traditionally one of the important kingdoms of Gyarong, Tsenlha entered the mythology of Chinese 20th century history as the place where the participants of the Long March met up with the Fourth Front Army on 21 June 1935. Some 11 kilometres south of Tsenlha a side-road leads to **Huanniu**, one of the minor kingdoms of ancient Gyarong.

Sleeping Stay at the *Xiaojin Government Zhaodaisuo*, 3 Zhengfu Jie. Which has double rooms at ¥20 per bed.

Bupen-chu Valley

About seven kilometres east of town at **Masangtra**, the two tributaries of the Tsenlha-chu converge: the Bupen-chu flowing from the north and the Wangzhing-chu flowing from the east. Taking the former, a road follows the tributary upstream and across the watershed to **Choktse** (143 kilometres from Tsenlha) and **Barkham** (see above, page 616). On this road you will pass **Bupen** (36 kilometres), **Chugar** (26 kilometres), **Tapon** (23 kilometres), and **Tsakho Gon**, the seat of Tsongkhapa's great student Tsakho Ngawang Drakpa (15 kilometres). This road appears to get much less traffic than the main Rongtrak route.

Wangzhing-chu Valley

Following the Wangzhing-chu tributary upstream, the road passes through **Wangzhing** township (10 kilometres), **Zur** (18 kilometres), **Dawei** (five kilometres), and **Zhilung** (23 kilometres). Among these, Dawei is one of the old Gyarong kingdoms. The valleys here are extremely mountainous, with raging rivers flowing through steep-sided gorges. Only a few side-valleys still contain patches of original forest. Many of the villages, often with small Gelukpa or Bonpo temples, are on the flatter slopes, high above the road and are only visible on account of the numerous tall watchtowers found beside nearly every settlement. The village houses of the mixed Tibetan and Qiang population who inhabit this region are characteristically made of stone, their small windows decorated with swastikas.

Balang Shan

From **Dawei**, the road rises gradually over a rough pot-holed surface to cross the high **Balang Shan** pass (4,487 metres) after 25 kilometres (marker 203). The pass is often shrouded in mist, obscuring the view of the snow peaks of **Mount Siguniang** (6,250 metres) to the north, and it is not difficult to visualize the demoralized armies of Qianlong retreating across Balang Shan watershed in disarray.

After crossing the pass, the road enters **Lungu** (Wenchuan) county, and passes through the **Wolong Panda Reserve** (see below, page 664).

Tsenlha County

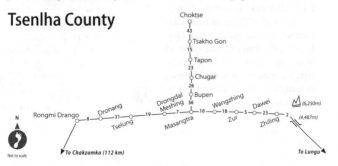

Far-east Tibet

Tashiling County བཀྲ་ཤིས་གླིང་

Tashiling County (143)
理县
Li Xian
Population: 42,418
Area: 4,569 sq km
Colour map 4, grid A6

The county of **Tashiling** occupies the valley of the Troksung-chu, a tributary of the Minjiang, which rises south of the Trakar Shankou (Partridge Pass) watershed below Chiro in Barkham county (see above, page 616). Four of the ancient Gyarong kingdoms are located in this valley. The county capital is located at **Li Dzong**, 186 kilometres southeast of Barkham (via Chiro) and 56 kilometres southwest of Lungu (Wenchuan).

Trosung-chu Valley

Getting there

From **Chiro**, 64 kilometres east of Barkham, there is an important intersection. Head north for Lhagyeling, Ngawa and the grasslands of Mewa within the Ger-chu valley (a tributary of the Yellow River); or head south across the Gyarong-Minjiang watershed to Chengdu (328 kilometres). The watershed **Trakar Shankou pass** (4,110 metres) is 21 kilometres from Chiro. Take this latter road, and after crossing the watershed, you will enter the long valley of the Trosung-chu, a major tributary of the Minjiang. Passing **Hrenchopa** (15 kilometres), **Teu Rampa** (18 kilometres), and **Nyaglo** (9 kilometres), where the attractive Nyaglo Lungpa valley extends northeast, the road eventually, after a further 23 kilometres, reaches Hrapa, the site of the ancient **Zida** Kingdom of Gyarong.

Li Dzong
Phone code: 08407

Continue on to **Phudu** (27 kilometres) and then climb to **Li Dzong**, the county capital after 15 kilometres. The village stone houses are typical of the Tibeto-Qiang culture. The main monastery is **Tashiling** of the Gelukpa school. Across the south bank of the Trosung-chu from Li Dzong, there was the ancient Gyarong Kingdom of **Tsakhok** (*Ch* Zagunao). There are simple guesthouse and restaurant facilities.

After Li Dzong, the valley leads northeast for 23 kilometres to **Zhutreng** (Ch Xuecheng), where the ancient Gyarong kingdoms of **Gyelkha** and **Wasi** were once located. A side-road leads northwest for 27 kilometres to Shuko.

Then, after **Tonghua** (nine kilometres), and **Lungchin** (nine kilometres), the road eventually after 15 kilometres reaches the Trosung-chu river's confluence with the Minjiang at **Lungu** or Wenchuan (see below, page 663).

Tashiling

Far-east Tibet

Labrang to Chengdu:

the Upper Minjiang and Jialing Valleys

The road from Lanzhou to Chengdu passes through rich grasslands and nature parks interspersed with areas of high Chinese population density. The basins of the Yellow River, the Jialing, and the Minjiang are crossed and recrossed by the network of roads which cover this most easterly region of Amdo. 14 counties are visited, the first seven of them currently in the Ganlho Tibetan Autonomous Prefecture of Gansu province, and the others in the Ngawa Tibetan Autonomous Prefecture of Sichuan.
Recommended itineraries: 11 (also 6, 8, 9).

Bilingsi

The road from Lanzhou to Labrang heads west through **Yongjing** county, where the major attraction is the **Bilingsi Cave** complex. Here there are 183 Buddhist grottoes containing 694 statues and many terracotta sculptures and frescoes. The oldest date from the Western Qin Dynasty, and the greatest period of development occurred during the Tang Dynasty. The largest image is a 27 metres seated Maitreya.

The caves are situated in a 60 metres high ravine beside the **Liujiaxia** reservoir on the Yellow River, and are accessible by boat. An average 2-way journey from Lanzhou to Bilingsi takes 12 hours, of which half the time is spent in the boat. Boats depart from the reservoir, 30 minutes' walk above Yongjing county town. A round-trip will cost around ¥150 for a group of three or four people, but entrance charges to certain groups of caves are extra. It is easy to link up with other Chinese or foreign tour groups at the lake, but the local bus only goes twice a day. Alternatively, stay overnight at *Lidian Hotel* in Yongjing (¥70 per double with attached bathroom), or the *Huanghe Hotel* (¥50 per room).

Getting there

Far-east Tibet

Chorten Karpo

South of the Liujiaxia reservoir in Yongjing county, there is the site where **Chorten Karpo** once stood. This structure, constructed in 823, formerly marked the official frontier between Tibet and China, as determined by a peace treaty approved by the Tibetan monarch Relpachen. There is no trace of the stupa today!

Linxia

A newly constructed one and a half kilometres tunnel provides easy access to Linxia county from Lanzhou, avoiding the former route which entailed crossing the reservoir by ferry boat. The direct route from the northeast links up with the older road after passing through the fertile loess-covered hills of **Dongxiang** county. The drive is interesting, climbing through high terraces and small villages, each with its distinctive mosque.

Phone code: 0930
Colour map 5, grid B5

Linxia, located in the lower valley of the Sang-chu (*Ch* Daxia), is an extensive county town renowned for its hundreds of mosques and as a trading town throughout the centuries. It is currently accorded priority development as a Special Economic Zone. Brick carving among the Hui community has a long history here, and the houses are well-decorated with flowers. The population pressure is obvious – the markets and bus stations are crowded, and modern construction rampant.

Sleeping Stay at the *Linxia Hotel*. Local arrangements can be handled by the *Linxia Travel Company*, T(0930)214496 ext 2888.

Linxia to Dowi

At **Hanjiaji**, 20 kilometres southwest of Linxia county town, a side-road heads northwest over **Darje La** pass to **Dowi** (Xunhua) county (80 kilometres), and thence to Ziling, while the main road continues upriver into the mountains of Central Amdo. Taking the former road, the first stretch is exclusively Muslim. At **Dowi Chorten**, also known as Chorten Rangma, there is a small community of nuns, founded during the 15th century by one Nakjin Rangron. Then, after the pass, in Dawei township, there are several small Gelukpa monasteries, the most renowned being Gori Dratsang (see above, page 563). Dowi county which lies on the far side of the pass has already been described (page 561).

Sangchu County བསང་ཆུ

Sangchu County (144)
夏河县
Xiahe
Population: 139,637
Area: 8,562 sq km
Colour map 5, grid B5

*Sangchu county, as its name suggests, occupies the grasslands around the upper reaches of the Sang-chu (Ch Daxia) river. The county capital is located at **Xiahe**, 280 kilometres from Lanzhou, and it is accessible from Lanzhou via Linxia on National Highway 213. The Tibetan population of the county is nowadays estimated at 45 per cent and there are six Tibetan monasteries along with 29 lesser shrines, the most important being **Labrang Tashikyil**, the largest monastery in Amdo, which dwarfs all the others. Labrang is located only three kilometres west of Xiahe town.*

The winter here is severe, down to -20°, but in the short spring season the hillsides bloom, providing excellent hill walks or horse riding, and summer is very pleasant despite the rain. Autumn is cool and clear, and in this season the dirt roads of Central Amdo are more comfortable to travel along.

Getting there Driving southwest from Linxia, at Km marker 201 there is a gateway indicating that you are leaving the Muslim area for that of the Tibetans. Then, 6 kilometres further on, a large stupa comes into view, opposite a small monastery. To reach Labrang, follow the Sang-chu upstream from Linxia city for 71 kilometres to **Wandotang**, where National Highway 213 leaves the Sang-chu valley, heading southeast for **Ganlho Dzong (Hezuoshen)**. Take the branch road which extends west from Wandotang, and continue to follow the river upstream all the way to Xiahe (36 kilometres), crossing **Da-me La** pass (3,698 metres) en route. In this steep gorge,

Sangchu County

Far-east Tibet (vertical sidebar)

there are a few houses, on either side of the pass, and a few small Gelukpa monasteries are interspersed among the hamlets. Among them the most noteworthy is **Terlung Yiga Chodzinling**, founded in 1760, which long sought to distance itself from Labrang, its dominant neighbour.

Xiahe Town

Xiahe sprawls along the banks of the Sang-chu, for over two kilometres, and is predominantly Hui Muslim at the east end and Tibetan at the west end. In all, the town is well-developed for tourism with several guesthouses, restaurants and souvenir stalls.

Altitude: 2,920 metres
Phone code: 0941
Colour map 5, grid B5

Entering from the east, a turn-off on the right leads southwest to Repkong across the present-day Gansu-Qinghai border. There is a petrol station near this intersection, and the distances given here are 221 kilometres to Lanzhou, 28 kilometres to Kangya (Ganja), and five kilometres to Xiahe. Continuing into town, the interesting Tibetan quarter is towards the west of Main Street. Passing the bus station and post office on the right, two roads diverge: **Gonpa lam** continuing due west for the entrance to Labrang Monastery and **Rigdra lam** bypassing the monastery to the south en route for the *Labrang Hotel* and the Sangke grasslands. Continuing along **Gonpa lam**, you will pass on the left the *White Conch Hotel*, the *Tashi Dagye Overseas Tibetan Guesthouse*, Tibetan bookshops, and the *Tara Restaurant*, after which a lane runs down towards Rigdra lam. Continuing west on Gonpa lam, you will pass the *Tibetan Restaurant* on the left, and crossing a small bridge, a health clinic, the *Labrang Monastery Guesthouse*, and the Mentsikhang. Now, on the right the walls of Labrang Monastery appear: the debating hall (Sokshing Chora), the School of Buddhist Studies (Nangten Lobdra), and the Main Gate (Zhung-go). From here, Gonpa lam continues due west until reaching a large two-storeyed restaurant at the west end beyond the precincts of the monastery. Here, it turns sharply to the left (south), past a Tibetan school, to cross the Sang-chu river and rejoin Rigdra lam.

Orientation

    Rigdra lam, heading south from the *White Conch Hotel*, crosses the Sang-chu and turns abruptly west, passing on the right the residential buildings of Alak Dema Sertri and Gontang Rinpoche, and the spectacular Gongtang Chorten, accessed via a motorable bridge (Gongtang zam). It then bypasses to the right the Labrang Metal Press, before reuniting with Gonpa lam south of another bridge which spans the Sang-chu. On the left (south) side of Rigdra lam, there is a hilltop offering a panoramic view of the entire complex of buildings at Labrang. Continuing west from the junction, you will soon reach the turn-off on the right for the *Labrang Hotel*, or else continue out of town, southwest into the Sangke grasslands. Development west of the monastery is restricted, leaving the splendid *Labrang Hotel* attractively isolated in the midst of fields and hamlets. Cycle rickshaws and taxis operate along the tarmac road, and on the 40-minute walk to the hotel, you can detour north along a muddy track to visit the Nyingma Gonpa amd Labrang nunnery.

Far-east Tibet

Labrang Tashikyil Monastery བླ་བྲང་བཀྲ་ཤིས་འཁྱིལ

Labrang Tashikyil is one of six great Gelukpa monasteries in Tibet and, although 90 damaged temples have yet to be restored, it is amongst the handful anywhere in Tibet that survived the Cultural Revolution relatively intact. It was founded in 1709 by Jamyang Zhepa I Ngawang Tsondru (1648-1721), who was revered as an emanation of Tsongkhapa's teacher Umapa Pawo

History
Altitude: 2,820 metres
Colour map 5, grid B5

Dorje. Within the Gelukpa hierarchy, the incarnations of Jamyang Zhepa are superceded only by the Dalai Lama and the Panchen Lama. During his studies in Lhasa, where he was a contemporary of Desi Sangye Gyatso, he received his title 'Jamyang Zhepa' (laughing Manjughosa), when a statue of Manjughosa (Jamyang) laughed at his prostrations. Returning to his homeland, he then founded the most powerful monastery in Amdo.

Main buildings   The great temples and colleges of Labrang Tashikyil were constructed by Jamyang Zhepa and his successors. He himself founded the **Tsokchen Dukhang Tosamling** (3) or assembly hall in 1709, the **Gyu-me Dratsang** (9) or lower tantric college in 1716, the **Sokshing Chora** (12) or college of dialectics, and the **Jokhang temple** (1), containing a much revered Jowo Rinpoche image (flanked by 108 others) in 1718.

His successor, Jamyang Zhepa II Konchok Jigme Wangpo (1728-91) founded the **Serkhang Chenmo** (2), also known as Tsegaling, containing an eight-storey high cross-legged image of Maitreya, murals of the three deities of longevity (Amitayus, White Tara and Vijaya) as well as Shakyamuni flanked by the Eight Bodhisattvas, and Tsongkhapa. Then, in 1763 he founded the **Dukhor Dratsang Evam Chogarling** (10) for the study of Kalacakra chronology and astrology. Towards the end of his life in 1784 he instituted the medical college, **Menpa Dratsang Sorik Zhenpenling** (7), which has a fine image of Aksobhya Buddha and is currently the most active of Labrang's colleges.

The tradition was maintained by his successors, Jamyang Zhepa III Kyabchok Jigme Gyatsode (b 1792) and Jamyang Zhepa IV Kalzang Thupten Wangchuk (b 1855). The latter founded the **Kyedor Dratsang Sangak Dargyeling** (11) for the practice of the Hevajra meditational cycle in 1879. It contains images of Hevajra flanked by Guhyasamaja, Kalacakra, Cakrasamvara, and Vajrapani in the form Chakdor Khorchen, as well as

Labrang Tashikyil Monastery

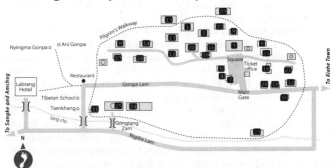

1 Jokhang Temple	11 Kyedor Dratsang Sangak	23 Library
2 Serkhang Chenmo Tsegaling	Dargyeling	24 Gongtang tsang Nangchen
3 Tsokchen Dukhang Tosamling	12 Sokshing Chora	25 Alak Dewa Sertri Nangchen
4 Jamyang Lhakhang	13 Dukhar Lhakhang	26 Alak tsang Nangchen
5 Dedenling Senge Ngaro	14 Dolkar Lhakhang	27 Gongma tsang Nangchen
6 Je Rinpoche Lhakhang	15 Gongtang Chorten	28 Nangten Lobdra (School of
7 Menpa Dratsang Sorik	16 2 Printing Presses	Buddhist Studies)
Zhenpenling	17 Deyang Podrang	29 Gyume Tsamkhang
8 Gyuto Dratsang Sangchen	18 Cham Jangsa	30 Mentsikhang
Dorjeling	19 Labrang Museum	31 Metal Press
9 Gyume Dratsang	20 Dolma Lhakhang	
10 Dukhar Dratsang Evam	21 Tuje Chenpo Lhakhang	
Chogarling	22 Zhabten Lhakhang	

Festivals at Labrang Tashikhyil Monastery

Festival	Starting Time	1999
Freeing of Animals from Death	0800-1000	23 February
Display of Buddha Tangka	0900-1100	28 February
Marked Dance	0800-1300	1 March
Butter Sculpture Display	2000-0000	2 March
Public Teaching	0900-1200	3 March
Enlightenment Prayer Days	All day	28,29 May
Mountain Festival	All day	18-24 July
Prayers and Debates	1100-1400	11-25 August
Tibetan Opera	1000-1600	18 August
Horse Races	All day	23 August
Debates	0730-1000	13-24 September
Debates	2100-0500	22 September
Anniversary of Tsongkhapa	All day	31 October

Maitreya. The **Gyuto Dratsang Sangchen Dorjeling** (8) or Upper Tantric College, was built by Jamyang Zhepa V Je Tenpei Gyeltsen Pelzangpo (b 1916), in 1928, as was the **Dolkar Lhakhang** (14) in 1940.

Other important temples at Labrang include **Jamyang Lhakhang** (4), which has a large image of Manjughosa flanked by Maitreya and White Manjushri; the **Dedenling** (5) temple, dedicated to Sukhavati buddhafield and containing an image of Avalokiteshvara in the form Simhanada; **Je Rinpoche Lhakhang** (6), which contains images of Tsongkhapa and Kharsapani; **Dukhar Lhakhang** (13), dedicated to Sitatapatra; the still closed **Dolma Lhakhang** (20), which is dedicated to Tara, **Tujechenpo Lhakhang** (21), dedicated to Mahakarunika, **Zhabten Lhakhang** (22), and the **library** (23).

Other temples and buildings

There are also two printing presses (16): one for woodblocks and the other for texts printed in movable type. The former contains the *Collected Works of Tsongkhapa* and those of his closest students. The residence of the Jamyang Zhepas called **Deyang Podrang** (17), the **Cham Jangsa** or religious dancing school (18), and the **Labrang Museum and Butter-Sculpture Collections** (19) are also worth a visit. The entire complex can be circumambulated by pilgrims over a three kilometres circuit.

At its high-point Labrang Tashikyil Monastery housed 4,000 monks, and when Jamyang Zhepa V passed away in 1947 there were 300 geshes, 3,000 monks and 50-100 incarnate lamas. The present incumbent, Jamyang Zhepa VI, who lives in Lanzhou, presides over a much depleted monastery where there are barely more than 1,000 monks, of whom half are engaged in the study of dialectics and the rest in tantric meditation practice. In April 1985 the **Assembly Hall** (Dukhang) had been destroyed by fire, and the renovated hall (3), which can now be visited, was consecrated only in 1990. It contains a central image of Maitreya, with images of Tsongkhapa, the Eight Bodhisattvas, and Shakyamuni with his two foremost students to the left, and the five stupa reliquaries of the previous Jamyang Zhepa incarnations to the right. The hall itself has 140 pillars and 1,000 small buddha images.

Recent renovations at Labrang

The restored **Gongtang Chorten** (15) is one of the most recent buildings within the complex. Funded by a Chinese American devotee and consecrated in 1992 by Gongtang Rinpoche, its **ground floor** contains resplendent images of Sarvavid Vairocana, Manjughosa, Maitreya, and an exquisite reclining

Far-east Tibet

white jade Buddha from Burma. There are 21,000 volumes of texts encorporated within the structure. On the **second floor** there is an image of Amitabha, along with the Thousand Buddhas of the Aeon. The gallery offers a wonderful view of the murals downstairs, which depict the diversity of the Buddhist lineages in Tibet. On the **uppermost level** there is an inscription bearing the name of the sponsor.

Admission fees Guided tours of the monastery (the only means of access) are available at ¥23 per person from the ticket office (closed from noon until 1400), ¥5 per person for the printing press, and at ¥5 per person for the Gontang Chorten. The supervisor, Konchok Gyatso, is a close aide of Gontang Rinpoche. **NB** Internal photography is generally prohibited, except in the museum.

School of Buddhist Studies Outside the main gate of the monastery, there is an important **School of Buddhist Studies** (Nangten Lobdra), where some of the great contemporary teachers of Labrang, such as Geshe Gendun Gyatso and Geshe Jamyang Gyatso continue to teach.

Festivals at Labrang The major festivals of the Buddhist calendar are observed at Labrang. During the *Great Prayer Festival*, reminiscent of the identical ceremonies held at Lhasa, on the 13th day of the first lunar month, a large (30 by 20 metres) applique tangka is displayed on the **Tangka Wall** on the south bank of the Sang-chu River, opposite the monastery. This is followed on the 14th by religious marked dances, on the 15th or full-moon day by *torma* (butter sculpture) offerings, and on the 16th by the procession of a Maitreya image around the monastery (see table).

Sangke Grasslands

Colour map 5, grid B5 The open **Sangke** grasslands, where large horse-racing festivals are held, are located 14 kilometres southwest of Labrang. The main festival falls in the seventh month of the lunar calendar and is a highly-organized display of sports in which teams of Tibetans from settlements far and near participate, each with a distinctive hat and coat. A rough road leads over to **Amchog Gonpa** from Sangke's huge open grassy bowl and a large crowd attends, swelled by Chinese and western photographers. White tents mushroom on the hills and a great deal of beer is drunk. The *Labrang Hotel* has a traditional tented camp here on the grasslands, enabling tourists to sample the nomadic life.

Getting there The Sangke grasslands are some 31 kilometres southwest of the *Labrang Hotel*, just before the watershed pass at the head of the Sang-chu valley. The distance from the grasslands to Amchog Gonpa is 32 kilometres.

Essentials

Sleeping The most charming *Labrang Hotel* (T0941-7121849, F0941-7121328) lies at the extreme west end of town, beyond the monastery and this is recommended above all others. Formerly the Summer Palace of Jamyang Zhepa, it has been renovated as a Tibetan-style hotel with all modern comforts, set within its own tranquil grounds. There are 36 3-star chalets constructed in the style of an ornate Tibetan tented-camp (¥300 per room), 61 standard rooms with attached bath (¥220 per night), 4 restaurants with seating for 22, bar, dance hall, business centre, shop, laundry service, and local *Gansu Silk Road Travel* office. In town, the best hotel is the *White Conch Hotel* (Baihailuo Fandian), T0941-7122486. 35 standard rooms at ¥250 (with attached bath)

Far-east Tibet

and ¥100 per bed, or without attached bath at ¥70 per bed, and triples at ¥50 per bed. For budget travellers, the *Labrang Monastery Guesthouse* has beds for ¥10 per night (no showers), and *Tashi Dagye Overseas Tibetan Hotel*, T0941-7121345. 15 clean and well-maintained rooms (best upstairs).

The Muslim commercial end of town (east) has less appealing hotels: the *Daxia Hotel*, the *Xinhua Hotel*, the *Waterworks Hostel*, and the *Minzu Hotel.* All are inexpensive.

Tibetan carpets may be a good buy here. Some traders and shopkeepers have **Shopping** returned from exile in India over recent years.

To reach Xiahe by bus from Lanzhou be prepared for a 7 hour journey, departing at **Transport** 0730 and stopping over for lunch at Linxia.

Kangya Drakar Gonpa

Buses leave Xiahe every other day for the 115 kilometres (6 hours) journey to **Getting there** **Repkong** although during heavy summer rain the muddy track can become almost impassable. From the intersection, 5 kilometres east of town, a winding road gradu-ally cimbs for 7 kilometres to cross a pass (3,360 metres) leading into the **Tsilung** val-ley. There are several small villages on both sides of the pass, and rich grazing pastures, with a panoramic view of the distant snow range of Mount Amnye Nyemri.

The township of **Kangya** (locally pronounced Kanja) lies 19 kilometres **Kangya** beyond the pass. Here, **Kangya Drakar Gonpa**, a monastery affiliated to Labrang, dominates the approach to a complex of caves, visible on the cliff face, as far as 17 kilometres northeast. Unusually, this establishment is pre-sided over by a female incarnation, Gongri Khandroma. The main cavern descends along steep muddy tracks through a vast fractured pothole which has legendary underground connections to caves in the Repkong and Sogwo areas (see above, page 557).

A long pilgrim's circuit of the mountain passing several lakes starts from the **Trekking** monastery but requires camping equipment for one night at least. There is also a small Bonpo temple on the opposite mountainside.

From Kangya, the road crosses two further passes, the second (3,600 metres) after 20 kilometres, with a cairn of *mani* stones marking the current Gansu-Qinghai provincial frontier. In these upper grasslands marmots can be seen in great numbers. The road then descends to **Gartse, Yarma Tashikyil**, and **Repkong** (see above, page 570).

Amchog Gonpa

The Gelukpa monastery of **Amchog Demotang Ganden Chokhorling** (2,835 *Colour map 5, grid B5* metres) is an important branch of Labrang, located in the grasslands further southeast. The monastery was founded in 1760 by Jamyang Zhepa II, and the recently reconstructed complex has two temples, a large stone wall where tangkas are ceremonially displayed, and a long *mani* wall. The **Dukhang** (Assembly Hall) contains images of Guhyasamaja, Tsongkhapa and Cakrasamvara, and, within the **inner sanctum**, an image of Maitreya flanked by Alak Yongdzin of Amchog, Jamyang Zhepa I, Jamyang Zhepa IV, and the reliquary of Alak Yongdzin. The murals of the main hall depict (L-R): Vaishravana, Tsegyal, six-armed Mahakala, Guhyasamaja, Vajrabhairava,

Far-east Tibet

Cakrasamvara, Kalacakra, Sitatapatra, Nechung Chokyong, Shridevi, four-armed Mahakala, and Dharmaraja. Amchog is an active monastery, with much local support among the nomads and villagers of the grasslands, and curently houses 300 monks.

Getting there   Amchog can be reached directly from Labrang by driving 59 kilometres southeast through the **Sangke grasslands** on a rough seasonal road, and across the watershed pass (3,570 metres) which lies at the head of the Sang-chu valley. Four small Tibetan villages are passed en route, but the grasslands here are largely the preserve of nomads, marmots and wild hares. A longer but better road (National Highway 213) leads 107 kilometres from Labrang via Wangdotang, **Pongartang** village, and across a pass to the prefectural capital of **Ganlho Dzong** (*Ch* Hezuoshen), from where it traverses a 3,048 metres pass to reach Amchog.

Roads from   Three roads lead from Amchog: north to **Labrang** (59 kilometres), south to
Amchog   **Luchu** (43 kilometres), and northeast to **Ganlho Dzong** (34 kilometres). Taking the last of these you will pass through **Bora Gonpa** after 13 kilometres, to the right (east) of the highway. Yet another branch of Labrang, Bora was founded in 1757. After a further six kilometres a side-road leaves the highway at **Dzatsa**, heading northwest for the **Sangke grasslands**, while the main road crosses a pass (3,240 metres) and cuts through the hills to the prefectural capital, 15 kilometres distant.

Ganlho Dzong

Ganlho Dzong (Ch *Hezuoshen*) *is a large city of recent development, 36 kilometres south of* ***Wandotang*** *(the turn-off for Labrang) on National Highway 213, and 34 kilometres northeast of Amchog. Nowadays it functions as the prefectural capital of South Gansu.*

Orientation

Altitude: 2,895 metres   Entering the city from the north (ie Lanzhou or Labrang side), you will pass the
Phone code: 0941   monastery of **Tsogon Geden Choling** and the Geology and Mining Bureau on
Colour map 5, grid B5   the right. A turn-off next to the bus station and petrol station then leads west, enabling through traffic to avoid the city en route for Luchu (southwest) or Lintan (southeast). Along this ring road, you will pass the Peoples' Hospital, the Hezhuo Mosque, and the Tibetan clinic. Continuing straight ahead, you will enter the busy thoroughfare of **Tengzhi Street**, where there are shops, banks, government buildings, and tax offices, as well as restaurants and hotels. On the left you will pass the Tibetan Hospital (Mentsikhang), the *Bayi Hotel*, the Ganlho market, the *Jinling Dajiudian Hotel*, the *Minzu Hotel*, and the *Gansu Hotel*, while the bus station is on the right. After the first roundabout, you will pass the *Xinhua bookstore*, an insurance company, and pharmacy on the left, with the cinema and police station on the right. The next two blocks are lined by an avenue of trees which divides the road from its cycle lanes. Here, on the left are the post office, and the local government buildings. Then, after the Yak Roundabout, you will pass the communist party offices, Tibetan middle and primary schools, and the *Muslim Wengsan* restaurant on the left, with the *Ganlho Hotel*, and assorted schools on the right. Crossing a bridge, the road forks at the south end of town, heading southeast for Lintan (78 kilometres), or southwest for Luchu (81 kilometres).

Tsogon Geden Choling

The local monastery, **Tsogon Geden Choling** on the outskirts of town has a nine-storey tower replica of Sekhar Gutok (see above, page 211), which dominates the skyline. The original foundation of this monastery is dated 1673 and an inspirational self-originated image of Milarepa, which had been offered by Shar Kalden Gyatso of Repkong to the local lama Gyeltsen Senge (the 53rd Ganden Tripon) was installed in 1678. The complex was first renovated as a nine-storeyed building in 1888 by Lobzang Dargye, himself revered an incarnation of Milarepa, and it survived until its destruction during the Cultural Revolution (1967). The newly constructed tower, funded by local resources as well as by donations from Mongolia and Tibetan exiles in India, was built between 1988 and 1994. It ranks among the greatest modern temples of Tibet for its exquisite design and art. The perimeter wall is surmounted by 1,500 brick stupas and the building itself is surrounded by 130 large prayer wheels.

Inside, the well-carpeted **ground floor** contains images of the principal bodhisattvas, accomplished masters and ancient kings of Tibet. The central images are of Maitreya, Manjughosa and Vajrapani, flanked on the left by Machik Labdron, Padampa Sangye, Tangtong Gyelpo, Tsangnyon Heruka, Dacharuwa, Ralotsawa, Nyimadzin, the Three Deities of Longevity, White Tara, Bhaisajyaguru, Shakyamuni, Milarepa and Mahakarunika. To the right of the central images are: Tonmi Sambhota, Relpachen, Trisong Detsen, Tride Tsukten, Nyatri Tsenpo, Bhrikuti, Wencheng, Songtsen Gampo, Rudracakra, Simhanada, Jowo Shakyamuni, Aksobhya, Prajnaparamita, Green Tara, and Sitatapatra.

On the **second storey**, there are images depicting the historic figures associated with the New Translation Schools of the Kadampa, Sakyapa and Gelukpa orders. The central images depict Atisha and Tsongkhapa, flanked by their foremost respective students, along with Remdawa, Lhodrak Namka Gyeltsen, Umpapa Pawo Dorje, Sherab Senge, Drakpa Gyeltsen, Dalai Lamas I, V, and XIV, Panchen Lamas IV, IX, and X, the eight foremost students of Tsongkhapa, Potowa, Chengawa Tsultrim Bar, Puchungwa, Tsang Rabsel, Yo Gejung, Mar Shakyamuni, Lachen Gongpa Rabsel, Shakyashri, the Five Founders of Sakya, and the five major throneholders of Ganden including Gyeltsen Senge, Dzopa Aten Tenpa Gyeltsen, Sera Jetsun Chogyen, Rongpo Shar I Kalden Gyatso and Rongpo Shar VII, Kirti Tenpa Rabgye, Kirti Lobzang Trinle, Jamyang Zhepa I, VI, Gungtang VI, the successive emanations of Drubchen Choying Dorje, Sherab Chokden and other lamas affiliated to Tsogon Monastery.

The images from the third to eighth stories upwards are all fashioned of wood, and each storey also contains 1,000 small images of Milarepa. Among them, the **third storey** is dedicated to the lineage masters of the Nyingmapa school, with Padmasabhava, Shantaraksita and King Trisong Detsen in the centre, flanked by Mandarava, Yeshe Tsogyel, the Eight Manifestations of Padmasambhava, Vairotsana, Garab Dorje, Vimalamitra, Terdak Lingpa, Rigzin IV Pema Trinle, Jikme Lingpa, Longchen Rabjampa, Minling Terchen, Hayagriva, Vajrakila and other meditational deities, along with Zangdokpelri. The **fourth storey** is dedicated to the assembled deities of the lower tantras: the Lords of the Three Enlightened Families, flanked by Vairocana, Amitabha, and Amoghapasha; as well as to the ancient Indian masters Asanga, Vasubandhu, Dignaga, and Dharmakirti. The **fifth storey** is dedicated to the lineage holders of the Kagyupa school, and above all to Marpa, Milarepa and Gampopa, each flanked by their foremost students, along with Karmapa I,

Ganlho Dzong

To Labrang

Tsosm Gonpa
Petrol Station ○ ○ Geology & Mining Bureau

Shops | Shops

City CCP ○ ⓢ Agricultural Bank

ⓢ Agricultural Bank

Tax Bureau ○ ○ Mentsikhang

Transport Police ⓟⓞ

○ Ganlho Market

■ Jingling Dajudian

○ Public Notay

Restaurants ■ Minzu Hotel

■ Jindum Hotel

■ Gansu Hotel

○ Trade & Industry Market

Goat

Hospital ✚

Agricultural Bank ⓢ ○ Xinhua Bookshop

Construction Bank ⓢ ○ PLCC Insurance

Cinema ○ ✚ Pharmacy

ⓢ Construction Bank

PSB ○

○ Kindergarden

Market ○ Shops ✉

Bank of Industry & Commerce ⓢ

Tibetan Clinic ✚

Avenue of Trees

Avenue of Trees

Local Government ○

Bank of Industry & Commerce ⓢ

Yak

Ganlho Fandian ■ ○ CCP

✚ Maternity Care Unit

Shops

CCP School ○ ○ Tibetan Middle School

Shops

No1 Middle School ○

● Muslim Wengsan Restaurant

Teacher Training School ○

○ Tibetan Primary School

Workers Committee ○ ○ Electric Company

○ Tibetan Middle School

To Chengdu (820 km)

To Linton (788 km)

Far-east Tibet

N

Not to scale

Ganlho Dzong Bus Station Schedule

From	Via	To	Schedule	Price
Ganlho (Hezuo)		Lintan	1530	
Ganlho (Hezuo)		Lanzhou	0900, 1200, 1400	
Ganlho (Hezuo)		Linxia	1630	
Ganlho (Hezuo)		Chone	0800, 1030	
Ganlho (Hezuo)		Minxian	0720	
Ganlho (Hezuo)		Labrang	1000, 1050, 1140,	
		(Xiahe)	1430, 1600	¥5.30-¥6.30
Ganlho (Hezuo)		Lanzhou	0630, 0730, 0900,	
			1200, 2200	¥18.80-¥20
				¥31 (sleeper)
Machu	Ganlho (Hezuo)	Linfa	1330	
Linfa	Ganlho (Hezuo)	Chone	1300	
Chone	Ganlho (Hezuo)	Linxia	0930	
Linxia	Ganlho (Hezuo)	Lintan	1150	
Lintan	Ganlho (Hezuo)	Linfa	1100	
Luchu	Ganlho (Hezuo)	Linxia	1030	

Phakmodrupa, Tokden Darma Wangchuk, Zhang Drogonpo, Drigung Jikten Gonpo, Taklung Tangpa, Lingrepa, Tsangpa Gyare, Karmapa II, Gotsangpa, and Dakpo Gomtsul, who all founded the great Kagyu monasteries of Central Tibet. Murals here and in the floor immediately above depict the life-story of Milarepa. The **sixth floor** is dedicated to the deities of the Ngok transmission of Unsurpassed Tantra, including Guhyasamaja, Cakrasamvara, Vajrabhairava, Hevajra, Nairatmya, Mahamaya, Caturvajrapitha, Jnaneshvara, and Vajrapanjara; along with four of the eight bodhisattvas. The **seventh storey** is dedicated to Vajradhara and the ancient Indian lineage holders of the unsurpassed tantras, namely: Tilopa, Naropa, Indrabhuti, Saraha, Nagarjuna, Aryadeva, Shantideva, Candrakirti, Luipa, Ganthapada, Krisnacarin, Lalitavajra, Amoghabhadra, Padmavajra, Jalandaripa, Guhyaka, Maitripa, Dombipa, Kurmikapada and Vijayapada. The **eighth storey** is dedicated to Buddhas of the Five Enlightened Families, along with Shakyamuni, Kurukulla, Uchusmakrodha, Acala, Avalokiteshvara, and Maitreya. Finally, at the centre of the **ninth storey**, there is a large tangka depicting the mandala of Hevajra.

Outside, to the right there is the Protector Temple, dedicated to Tseringma, Cimara, and the Twelve Tenma Goddesses, while to the left there is a temple in honour of Jambhala. Nowadays, 200 monks reside here. The ticket office is located outside the main gate (admission: ¥2).

Essentials

C *Jindun Hotel*, 60 Tengzhi St, T(09411)8211135. Standard rooms at ¥130, and suites at ¥220, and triples at ¥90. Other accommodation is available at the many cheaper hotels on Tengzhi St, including the **C** *Gansu Hotel*, the **C** *Minzu Hotel*, and the **C** *Gannan Fandian*. | **Sleeping**

Try the Muslim **C** *Wengsan Restaurant* on the east side of Tengzhi St. | **Eating**

The bus station is an important hub for passengers heading north to Lanzhou, and into the Tibetan areas of Labrang, Luchu, Lintan, and Dzoge. There is also a private bus station which runs frequent minibuses to Linxia and Labrang. | **Transport**

Far-east Tibet

Roads from Ganlho Dzong

National Highway 213 connects with **Lanzhou** to the north (258 kilometres) and **Luchu** to the south (81 kilometres), while a lesser road cuts southeast for **Lintan** (78 kilometres).

Luchu County རྒྱ་ཆུ

Luchu County (145)
碌曲县
Luqu
Population: 25,804
Area: 4,253 sq km
Colour map 5, grid B5

*The county of **Luchu** occupies the upper reaches of the Lu-chu (Ch Tao), which is the principal tributary of the Yellow River in Ganlho prefecture, from **Serlung** near the river's source (on the Qinghai frontier) through to the borders of **Lintan** county in its mid-reaches. The grassland roads leading south from Labrang and Ganlho Dzong converge at **Amchog**, 43 kilometres north of Luchu town. Further south, beyond the Lu-chu valley, National Highway 213 extends for 95 kilometres as far as **Taktsang Lhamo** on the present Gansu-Sichuan border. Here, important roads diverge: southwest to **Machu** (71 kilometres) near the first bend of the Yellow River, south to Dzoge (90 kilometres), and southeast across the watershed to **Tewo** (90 kilometres). Formerly, there were eight monasteries within the county, of which the two most important have been reconstructed.*

Luchu Dzong

Colour map 5, grid B5

The pleasant county town of **Luchu** lies 43 kilometres south of the nomadic pastures of Amchog and in the sheltered Lu-chu valley (2,957 metres). En route you will pass through **Nyimalung** village where there are interesting stone houses and the turn-off for the **Kotse** grassland, before crossing a 3,200 metres pass. The 106 kilometres' drive from Labrang takes approximately three hours.

Formerly Luchu was a stronghold of the Bon tradition, and a major Bonpo monastery survived here until its final conversion by the Gelukpa in 1688, at which time it was renamed **Gegon Ganden Phuntsoling** by Lobzang Dondrub, the lord of neighbouring Cho-ne. The town's tranquil setting, four kilometres off the highway, and the mild climate add to its attractions. The population is even now largely Tibetan.

Sleeping The town has simple but clean guesthouse and restaurant facilities.

A side-road from Luchu leads upstream from a junction just north of the town for 45 kilometres through a rugged and wide range of hills to **Serlung** on the edge of the Sogwo region (see above, page 577). The exact provincial border is marked differently on maps published in Qinghai and Gansu provinces. Yet another side-road heads downstream following the river bank to **Ala** and then via Mapusola to **Lintan** (185 kilometres). The reconstructed Gelukpa monastery of **Shitsang Ganden Chokhorling** is located along this road, 13 kilometres

Luchu & Machu Counties

down-valley from Luchu. It is a branch of Labrang, founded in 1839 by Dewatsang III Jamyang Tubten Nyima.

Heading south from Luchu, the highway leaves the Lu-chu valley and crosses the watershed (3,414 metres) between the Lu-chu and Yellow River, eventually reaching the rugged mountain terrain of **Taktsang Lhamo** after 95 kilometres. About 10 kilometres out of town on this section of the road there are superb views of the **Dzichen** range to the southwest, which hides the Yellow River from view. Three further passes are crossed in close proximity, the highest (4,054 metres) offering a vista of verdant and cragged terrain as the Dzichen range draws near. Then, at Lake **Drangto Tso**, 79 kilometres south of Luchu (at marker 414), there is a dirt trail on the west (right) which leads through the range to **Machu** on the bank of the Yellow River (see below, page 638).

Taktsang Lhamo

About 19 kilometres south of the Machu turn-off (at marker 433), a spectacular mountain view heralds the valley of the **Druk-chu** (*Ch* Bailong), which stretches from the cliffs of Taksang Lhamo at its source through Tewo and Drukchu counties to converge with the Jialing River in **Guangyuan**, Sichuan. The turn-off for Tewo is on the left (east) of the highway, only four kilometres north of **Taktsang Lhamo**.

Colour map 5, grid B5

Continuing south into the hilly township of Taktsang Lhamo, two major monasteries can be visited. **Gerda Gonpa**, also called **Ganden Shedrub Pekar Drolweiling**, the higher of the two, currently falls within Gansu province, while neighbouring **Sertang Gonpa** is under the jurisdiction of Sichuan. Although Taktsang Lhamo (*Ch* Lamosi) itself is the name traditionally given to the cave-shrine beside Gerda Gonpa, nowadays it is applied to both monasteries and the township which they share.

Gerda Gonpa

The origins of Gerda Monastery have been attributed to the disciples of Tsongkhapa who around 1413 spread throughout Tibet. The present complex of buildings, some of which survived the Cultural Revolution, was founded in 1748 by Gyeltsen Senge, the 53rd throne-holder of Ganden, and four colleges were developed for the study of dialectics, medicine, Kalacakra and tantra. Reconstruction began here in 1981, and there are now some 700 monks. The current Gerda Rinpoche XI is now in his mid-fifties and lives in India. His residence is being carefully rebuilt and the architecture of the whole monastery is of a higher standard than most new Amdo monasteries.

Sertang Gonpa

Sertang Gonpa, which currently has 300 monks, is situated slightly below Gerda Gonpa, to the southeast. The **Assembly Hall** (Dukhang) here contains gilded clay images of Shakyamuni and Tsongkhapa, each flanked by their foremost students, along with the 16 Elders, the six ornaments and two supreme masters of Ancient India, the Three Deities of Longevity, and the preferred meditational deities of the Gelukpa school. The **Trichen Lhakhang** contains the throne of the Ganden Tripa, who presides over the Gelukpa order, and there are other impressive buildings, including the **Protector Temple** (**Gonkhang**) and the residence of Alak Chetsang.

A small trading village, 4 kilometres south of the main Luchu-Tewo/Dzoge road, **Sleeping**

Far-east Tibet

Taktsang Lhamo can provide basic food and accommodation and the area has already become a popular stop-over for travellers between Dzoge and Labrang. There is a small post office, a Tibetan language primary school, and roadside restaurants with English menus, offering Italian spaghetti, and American apple pie!

Roads from Takstang Lhamo

The road from Taktsang Lhamo to **Machu** (71 kilometres) heads east from a turn-off opposite the post office. Alternatively, for **Tewo** and **Dzoge**, drive north for four kilometres on the highway, and then turn right into the upper Druk-chu valley. After a further eight kilometres, the road forks: south for Dzoge and southeast for Tewo.

Machu County ཨ་ཆུ

Machu County (146)
玛曲县
Maqu
Population: 30,314
Area: 10,249 sq km
Colour map 5, grid C5

*Machu county is traditionally regarded as the southeast extremity of Golok, although nowadays it falls within Gansu province. Its hinterland contains almost all of the Yellow River's first bend as it makes its 'south' curve through Amdo. Much of the terrain is flat, marshy grassland, but a spine of mountains runs down to **Sogtsang** monastery, at the apex of the bend. The county capital, recently opened to outsiders, is located at **Dzoge Nyima**, 71 kilometres west of Taktsang Lhamo, 22 kilometres southeast of the Sogwo border, and 143 kilometres northwest of Dzoge. Prior to 1958 there were eight monasteries in the county, all holding allegiance to Labrang. These were originally tented monasteries, and they subsequently remained small in scale since the nomadic population of the region were constantly moving from one pasture to the next. The riding horses raised by the nomads here are highly prized throughout Amdo.*

Lake Drangto Tso

Some 23 kilometres north of Taktsang Lhamo and 79 kilometres south of Luchu, a dirt road leads west from National Highway 213 into Machu county. Three kilometres along this side-road, at **Lake Drangto Tso** (*Ch* Gahe), there is a small bird sanctuary.

Takstang Lhamo to Machu

The main road into Machu heads directly west from the high watershed at Taktsang Lhamo on the Sichuan side of the current provincial border. It undulates through the **Amnye Lhago** range, rising to 3,540 metres before reaching the flat grasslands. After 29 kilometres, a turn-off leaves the road, heading south for Dzoge. The main road continues through the grassland, passing **Mazhi** (*Ch* Maizhi) village and then crossing the border to re-enter **Gansu**. On the way into town, it bypasses Dashui Military Farm (21 kilometres from town) and a gold mining complex.

Dzoge Nyima

Altitude: 3,480 metres
Phone code: 0941
Colour map 5, grid B5

The capital, **Dzoge Nyima**, is a fairly large town, located five kilometres north of the Yellow River. Entering from the east, you will pass the Tibetan Hospital on the right, after which a turn-off on the left leads five kilometres southwest to the bridge over the Yellow River. Continuing on **Main Street**, you will pass on the left the *Government Guesthouse*, the Primary School and tax office, while on the right are the China Agricultural Bank, a number of small restaurants and shops, and the *Gangjong Hotel*. Now, a turn-off on the right leads northwest towards the border of Sogwo county (22 kilometres). Taking this road, you will pass on the left the Peoples' Hospital, and on the right the *Tashi Dronkhang Hotel* (*Ch* Ji Xiong Fandian), and the *Mirik Dronkhang Hotel*, followed by the police station and the county government buildings. A gate spans the road marking the limits of town. Beyond it, on the left, a side-road winds its way uphill to **Dzoge Nyima Monastery**, two kilometres distant.

Returning to the intersection on Main Street, continue heading west, and you will pass on the left the bus station, the *Gangri Dronkhang Hotel*, the open market, and another turning on the left, which leads down to the Yellow River. On the right, there are banks and government buildings.

The monastery of **Dzoge Nyima**, which currently has 90 monks, is located on high ground above the town, offering a distant panoramic view of the first bend of the Yellow River. It is a branch of Labrang, founded by Jamyang Zhepa II Konchok Jikme Wangpo (1728-91). The **Dukhang** (**Assembly Hall**), decorated in Repkong style, contains images of (left to right): Tsongkhapa, Jamyang Zhepa II, Avalokiteshvara, Maitreya and Vajrapani, along with a stone footprint of Jamyang Zhepa II, and the volumes of the *Kangyur* and the *Collected Works of Jamyang Zhepa*. The murals here depict (left to right): six-armed Mahakala, Hayagriva, Cakrasamvara, Vajrabhairava, Bhaisajyaguru, Guhyasamaja, Kalacakra, Sarvavid Vairocana and Dharmaraja. Other temples located to the rear of the Assembly Hall include the **Tamdrin Lhakhang** on the right, dedicated to Hayagriva, and the **Gongtang Zimchung** on the left, which is the residence of Gongtang Rinpoche and contains a natural stone *mani* inscription.

Dzoge Nyima Gonpa

Essentials

C *Tashi Dronkhang* has newly constructed standard rooms at ¥17-¥18 per bed, and triples at ¥7 per bed. More expensive rooms are available elsewhere, including **C** *Machu Government Guesthouse*, T(0941)6121466.

Sleeping

Try the Muslim noodle restaurant on Main St, opposite the *Machu Government Guesthouse*.

Eating

Far-east Tibet

Dzoge Nyima

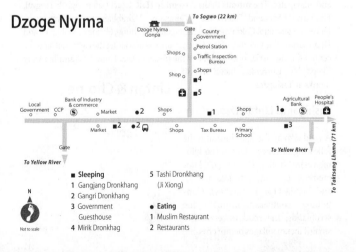

Sleeping
1 Gangjang Dronkhang
2 Gangri Dronkhang
3 Government Guesthouse
4 Mirik Dronkhag

5 Tashi Dronkhang (Ji Xiong)

• Eating
1 Muslim Restaurant
2 Restaurants

West of the Yellow River

Crossing the Yellow River from Dzoge Nyima (five kilometres) two roads diverge at Duku: southwest to **Awantsang** (54 kilometres), from where a trail leads across the lower part of the Yellow River bend to Jikdril county in Golok (see above, page 607), and southeast via a PLA breeding station for Golok riding horses to cross the Yellow River north of **Gihama**, and enter **Ngawa** county (see above, page 613). A number of small Gelukpa monasteries have been reconstructed in these outlying parts, including **Ngora**.

Lintan County ལིན་ཐན

Lintan County (147)
临潭县
Lintan
Population: 131,112
Area: 1,399 sq km
Colour map 5, grid B5

*The fertile counties of **Lintan** and **Cho-ne** in the mid-reaches of the Lu-chu valley can be reached from Lanzhou (via Linfa on National Highway 212 and Kangle), from Drukchu (via Minxian on National Highway 212), from Tewo on a rough hill road, or from Lanzhou and Labrang via Ganlho Dzong on National Highway 213. The Tibetans of this area claim descent from the disbanded Tibetan army of the Yarlung kings, which occupied the region in the eighth and ninth centuries. The county town of **Lintan**, set some kilometres back from the Lu-chu river, lies 29 kilometres northwest of Cho-ne and 78 kilometres southeast of Ganlho Dzong.*

Tashigar Monastery

Heading southeast from Ganlho Dzong (see above, page 613), through rugged grassland, after 12 kilometres the road passes the monastery of **Tashigar** on the right (south). It is affiliated to Labrang and follows the tradition of Jamyang Zhepa, despite having been founded prior to Labrang, by Lama Tri Gompa, almost 300 years ago. There is a large complex of buildings here, among which the Kungarawa monastic residential building to the left and the Assembly Hall to the right are the most prominent. The **assembly hall** contains images of (left to right): Manjughosa, Guhyasamaja, Jowo Shakyamuni, Jamyang Zhepa I-VI (encased in glass along with orange and white aspects of Manjughosa), Tara, and Sarvavid Vairocana. An **inner sanctum** to the rear contains (left to right): the reliquaries of Lama Tri Gompa and another local lama, and images of Mahakarunika, Maitreya and Sitatapatra. The **murals** of the **Assembly Hall** depict (left to right): Tsegyal, Hayagriva, Sarvavid Vairocana, Vajrapani, Vajrabhairava, Guhyasamaja, Hevajra, Kalacakra, Cakrasamvara, Sitatapatra, Nechung, Shridevi, Mahakala and Dharmaraja. The volumes of the *Kangyur* are stacked along the right wall, and the central throne carries photographs of the present Dalai Lama XIV and Jamyang Zhepa VI. Currently, there are 80 monks at Tashigar.

Tashigar to Lintan Dzong

A road sign at Tashigar indicates the following distances: Lintan (66 kilometres), Ganlho Dzong (12 kilometres), Labrang (60 kilometres), and Linxia (117 kilometres). Continuing southeast through the scrublands, the road traverses five small Tibetan villages before crossing

Lintan & Cho-ne

To Ganlho Dzong (Hezuosher)(76 km)
To Shitsang (185 km)
Lintan
30
Cho-ne
Min Xian
Dengka Gon
150
Drukchu
To Wudu
N
Not to scale

two passes, the second of which (3,300 metres) is 32 kilometres from Tashigar. The descent leads after nine kilometres to an open plain and an intersection, where a branch road cuts south to **Mezho** village (15 kilometres) and over the hills to Tewo county (see below, page 644). During the period of the Yarlung Empire, a major battle was waged here between the Tibetan and Chinese armies. Further southeast (15 kilometres northwest of town), there is the Gelukpa monastery of **Gyakhar Gon Shedrub Dargeling**, which was founded during the 18th century by Gyakhar Gongma I Lobzang Damcho, and now has approximately 100 monks. After Gyakhar Gon, a 2,880 metres pass is crossed, and a roadside stupa is bypassed six kilometres before the town. The outlying villages in this stretch are primarily agricultural, and some have public phone booths.

Lintan town

The county town, which is built upon hilly terrain, has a large Muslim and Chinese population. Few Tibetans are in evidence. Entering the top end of town from Ganlho Dzong in the west, the road forks: northwest to outlying villages and southeast downhill to the downtown area. Taking the latter road, you will pass on both sides of the road banks, Muslim restaurants, and shops. The *Minzu Fiandian* and the cinema are on the left. At the first of two crossroads, turn left for the Lintan Mosque and the road to Kanle/Linfa, or continue downhill through the commercial part of town, passing the post office on the left and the *Lintan Guesthouse* on the right. Then, at the second crossroads, turn right for the trail leading down to the north bank of the Lu-chu (a Christian church is located at this corner), or left for the local government buildings and the bus station. Then, continuing downhill, you will head out of town in the direction of Cho-ne. The town itself has little of interest, and visitors generally pass through en route for Cho-ne, 29 kilometres to the southeast on the north bank of the Luchu.

Altitude: 2,790 metres

Colour map 5, grid B5

Yerwa Gon Samdrubling

Heading southeast from town, the road crosses two passes (2,880 metres) to reach the Cho-ne intersection after 24 kilometres. From the high ground there are excellent views of the range to the southwest which forms the watershed between the Yellow River and the Jialing. If, instead of turning south for Cho-ne (only six kilometres distant), you traverse a third pass (2,850 metres), you descend via a Chinese fort to **Yerwa Samdrubling**, five kilometres northeast of the intersection. Approached via a large earthen stupa, this monastery, constructed in Sino-Tibetan style, was originally a Sakyapa foundation. It has been dated 1146, or else classed among the 108 border temples constructed by Qubilai Qan (13th century) to atone for his war crimes. The monastery has been reopened since 1985 and there are 12 monks.

Lintan Town

People's Bank
Agricultural Bank
Agricultural & Forestry Department
Agricultural Bank
Cinema
Construction Bank
Tax Bureau
Birth Control Unit
Muslim Restaurant
Shops
Minzu Fiandian
Muslim Restaurant
Shops
PPIC Insurance
Brocade Shop
Pharmacy
Shops
Agricultural Bank
Guesthouse
Tax Bureau
Shops
Small Shops
Agricultural Bank
To Ganlho Dzong
To Luchu
To Cho-ne
N
Not to scale

Far-east Tibet

Lintan to Minxian

After Yerwa Gon, the road climbs again to cross another pass (2,940 metres), leading down to another intersection. The landscape is one of green terraced fields and red soil. Here, you can turn left (north) for Xiliguan (77 kilometres) or southeast, crossing yet another pass (2,865 metres) to reach the border of Lintan and Minxian counties after a further 19 kilometres. Leaving the Tibetan ethnic area behind, the road then crosses a 3,000 metres pass and follows a tributary downstream to its confluence with the Lu-chu at Minxian, 40 kilometres from the pass. On this descent, the villages are entirely Muslim and Chinese, some with small mosques and temples. The only Tibetan landmark is a ruined stupa in Tibetan style, which lies just above the confluence of the two rivers, indicating the easternmost limit of Tibetan penetration at the height of the Yarlung Dynasty.

Minxian Cross the Lu-chu via the Yefu Qiao bridge to enter the largely Muslim city of **Minxian** (2,340 metres), where the road links up with National Highway 212. Head north on the highway for Linfa and Lanzhou, or south, across the watershed, for Drukchu county (137 kilometres). The latter road will be described below, page 647.

Sleeping **C** *Minxian Garden Hotel (Huayuan Fandian)*, T(0932)7723509. Comfortable standard rooms at ¥50, and suites at ¥120, with attached bathrooms and hot running water.

Eating The hotel has an excellent restaurant. Alternatively, try the many small Muslim noodle restaurants in town.

Cho-ne County ཅོ་ནེ

Cho-ne County (148)
卓尼县
Jone
Population: 87,241
Area: 4,954 sq km
Colour map 5, grid B5

Cho-ne county straddles the banks of the Lu-chu in its mid-reaches. The county town, which is located on the north bank, is renowned for its ancient monastery, and across the river, there are lateral valleys where branches of Cho-ne were located. Presently there are only six monasteries within the county, all of them Gelukpa.

Cho-ne town

Altitude: 2,610 metres
Colour map 5, grid B6

The **town of Cho-ne**, adjacent to the monastery, is fairly large, 374 square kilometres in area, with a predominantly non-Tibetan population (7,022). Entering town from the Lintan intersection, five kilometres to the north, the road descends towards the bank of the Lu-chu. After a bridge which spans a small tributary, a turn-off on the left leads into Main Street. As you drive downhill on Main Street, you will pass on the left the Cho-ne Printing press, the Bank of Industry and Commerce, and the *Xinhua Bookstore*, while on the right are the Peoples' Bank, the *Commercial* guesthouse, and a turn-off leading to the local government buildings and police station. At the foot of the hill, the road meets the north bank of the river, where it forms a T-junction with the riverbank road. Turn left here (east) for the bus station and bridge spanning the Lu-chu, or right (west) for access to the monastery.

Cho-ne
Gonchen

Cho-ne Gonchen Ganden Shedrubling was originally a Sakyapa monastery, founded by Drogon Chogyel Phakpa and his patron Qubilai Qan in 1269.

Subsequently, it was converted to the Gelukpa tradition in 1459 by Choje Rinchen Lhunpo. The colleges at Cho-ne were established in the 18th century by Kunkyen Jigme Wangpo: the school of dialectics (**Tsenyi Dratsang**) in 1714, and the tantric college (**Gyupa Dratsang**) in 1729. The monastery was renowned for its woodblock collection of the *Kangyur* and *Tangyur*, prepared in 1773. Printed copies of this collection are still extant, in the United States and elsewhere, although the woodblocks have been irreparably damaged.

At the entrance to the complex, there is a Chinese pavilion, containing a stele inscribed in Tibetan and Chinese which commemorates the history of the monastery and its expansion with Manchu patronage during the 18th century. Within the precincts, there are six original grand buildings, only one of which is in ruins (to the left). The Dukhang (Assembly Hall) is in the centre, and the Gyupa Dratsang to the right, while to their rear are the Tsenyi Dratsang, the Debating Garden (Chora), the Taknyi Lhakhang, dedicated to Hevajra, and the Sariwa Lhakhang.

Among them, the **Assembly Hall** contains large images of Tsongkhapa with his students, flanked by Mahakarunika and four-armed Avalokiteshvara (left) and Manjughosa (right). Within the **inner sanctum**, there are large images of Jowo Shakyamuni and Maitreya with 1,000 small images of Tsongkhapa, a library and two stacked recensions of the *Kangyur*. The murals depict the meditational deities and lineage-holders of the Gelukpa school, executed in Repkong style.

Cho-ne Monastery

To the right of the Assembly Hall, the **Gyupa Dratsang** contains images (left to right) of Padmasambhava, Jowo Shakyamuni, Vajrabhairava, Tsongkhapa with his students, Maitreya, Guhyasamaja, and Cakrasamvara. The murals, also in Repkong style, depict the *tantra* lineage of the Gelukpa school. Presently, there are only 120 monks at the monastery,

Cho-ne

Far-east Tibet

which means that, considering its scale, former prestige, and grandeur, it cannot avoid having the air of a ghost town.

South Bank of the Lu-chu

Some 31 kilometres west of Cho-ne on the south bank of the Lu-chu, at Ka-che township, there is the monastery of **Marnyung Jampaling**, which is currently under reconstruction. As recently as 1962, this site was transferred from Cho-ne to Lintan county. Closer to the county town, there are other branch monasteries of Cho-ne Gon, notably: **Nakdo Gon** (founded 1676), **Kyage Gon** (founded 1587), and **Showa Khedrubling** (founded 1685 at the behest of Dalai Lama V). Only **Ganden Tashi Sambrubling** at **Azitang**, founded in 1789, is affiliated to Labrang.

Tewo County ཐེ་བོ

Tewo County (149)
迭部县
Tebo
Population: 50,217
Area: 4,927 sq km
Colour map 5, grid B6

*Tewo county occupies the upper reaches of the Druk-chu, a major tributary of the Jialing, which rises near the watershed at **Taktsang Lhamo**, and flows into the Jialing 18 kilometres below **Drukchu** town. This valley is the eastern extremity of Amdo and most of the population is highly sinicized. Nonetheless, it is a scenic and historic route, visiting pockets of Amdowa who trace their ancestry back to border armies from the time of the Tibetan kings. Formerly the Sakyapa school had a strong presence in these parts, but since the 18th century, most Buddhist monasteries have espoused the Gelukpa order. The exceptions are those of the ancient Bon tradition which have survived in remote corners of the Drukchu valley. The county capital is located at **Dengka Gon** (Ch Tebo), 90 kilometres southeast of Taktsang Lhamo and 157 kilometres northwest of Drukchu town at the lower end of the valley.*

Taktsang Lhamo to Tewo

As an alternative to going due south through the grasslands from Taktsang Lhamo to Dzoge, it is possible to detour through the forested counties of **Tewo** and **Drukchu** within the valley of the Druk-chu (*Ch* Bailong), a tributary of the Jialing. To enter the Druk-chu ('white dragon') valley, turn right (east) at the road junction four kilometres north of Taktsang Lhamo, and then left (southeast) after eight kilometres at the Tewo/Dzoge intersection. Bee hives are plentiful in this area, and in season you will be able to buy fresh honey at the roadside.

The first section of this road currently falls within the borders of Dzoge county in Sichuan province. The township of **Khoser**, located at the Tewo/Dzoge intersection, has a Ngawa Prefectural Tibetan Language Middle School and a small Gelukpa monastery. Here, the tree line begins and a hot

Tewo Dzong

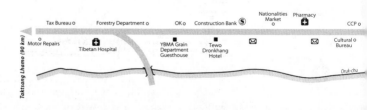

Far-east Tibet

spring is passed on the left. There is also some evidence of roadside cultivation, usually of wheat and beans. Some other small Gelukpa monasteries can be visited on this stretch, including **Keri Gon**, **Trinpa Gon**, and **Bompo Gon**, and there is a turn-off on the right which leads south to the Bon monastery of **Tatsa Gon**. Eventually, at Km Marker 175, the county border is crossed and the road now re-enters **Gansu**, on a better paved surface.

Dengka Gon town (Tewo Dzong)

The county town at **Dengka Gon** lies only eight kilometres southeast of the county border, and deep within the forested gorge of the Druk-chu. The town is a narrow strip of urban development, hugging the north bank of the river. Entering from Taktsang Lhamo (west), you will pass on the left side of **Main Street,** the tax office, the forestry department, the Nationalities Market, government buildings, the *Tewo Hotel*, *Xinhua Bookstore*, police station, Peoples' Hospital, *Yohou Hotel*, and the Tibetan Middle School. On the right side of Main Street, close to the river, you will pass the Tibetan Hospital, the *Grain Department Guesthouse*, the *Tewo Dronkhang*, the post office, cultural bureau, sports hall, assorted banks and schools, and the bus station. Two small bridges span the Druk-chu, leading to outlying lateral valleys on the south side; and in this vicinity, there is the hermitage of **Tratsang Ritro**, which was founded by a lama named Tewo Rabjampa Palden Senge.

Altitude: 2,370 metres
Colour map 5, grid B5

The monastery of **Pal-she Denka Gon**, which gives the town its name, lies 2.5 kilometres northwest. Its foundation is originally attributed to Pakshi Rolpa, a student of Drogon Chogyel Phakpa in the 13th century, and later it converted to the Gelukpa tradition. In 1982 this monastery was reopened, and it currently supports 100 monks.

Pal-she Dengka Gon

C *Tewo Hotel (Tebo Fandian)*. Comfortable standard rooms ¥52 (w/o attached bathrooms), with clean communal toilets and washrooms (hot showers: ¥2).

Sleeping

The best food appears to be on offer at the large *Muslim Restaurant* adjacent to the *Tewo Hotel*.

Eating

Tewo to Lintan

About five kilometres northwest of town, at a turn-off on the right (north), a side road leaves the Druk-chu valley, for **Lintan** (91 kilometres), via **Yiwa, Niba**, and **Jango** (Gyakhar Gon). This rough trail crosses the hills forming the watershed between the Yellow and Jialing river systems, and there are some peaks exceeding 4,000 metres.

Far-east Tibet

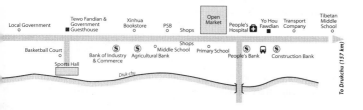

Tewo to Drukchu Some 10 kilometres southeast of town, the Bon monastery of **Tsotsang Gon** lies on a ridge to the north of the road. This complex was reconstructed in 1990, amalgamating within it three local Bon monasteries. There are currently 40 monks, who uphold the Khyungpo Tengchen lineage. The foremost image within the main hall is that of Shenrab Miwoche, while the murals, in Repkong style, depict Namka Gyelmo, Drenpa Namka, Shenrab Miwoche, and protector deities such as Machen Pomra.

Continuing down valley, the rapids of the Druk-chu begin in earnest 18 kilometres below town at the Drukchu Dam. A power station is located seven kilometres below the dam, and seven kilometres further on at Khapa village there is the hill-top Gelukpa monastery of **Tashi Dagye Gon**. The undecorated newly constructed assembly hall contains images of Tsongkhapa and students, flanked by Maitreya, Manjughosa, and 1,000 small images of Tsongkhapa. A full set of the *Kangyur* is kept here. Below Tashi Dagye Gon, the road surface suddenly becomes rough, and the gorge deepens. A turn-off on the left (three kilometres after Tashi Dagye) leads for 20 kilometres to **Gyeli Gon** of the Bon tradition. Continuing on the main road, you will pass a dam under construction. The cliffs here are red and white and the river bed is strewn with large rocks of the same hues. About 20 kilometres below the gorge in **Maya** township, there is the monastery of **Wangtsang Gon Tashi Puntsoling**, an 18th century branch of Cho-ne, which has 32 monks. Then, after a further 15 kilometres, a paved road branches off on the left, heading for **Minxian** (Km Marker 86). Keeping right, and continuing uphill on the rough dirt road, you will reach **Tsenyi Gon** of the Gelukpa school after three kilometres. There are 45 monks here, and the assembly hall is large. Continuing along this road, you will reach the county border after 18 kilometres, and enter the territory of **Drukchu**.

Drukchu County འབྲུག་ཆུ

Drukchu County (150)
舟曲县
Zhuqqu
Population: 116,336
Area: 2,972 sq km
Colour map 5, grid C6

Drukchu county is the name given to the lower reaches of the Druk-chu river around its confluence with the Yao tributary, where the terrain ranges from 3,000-4,000 metres. The Tibetan population of Drukchu is now confined to rural areas. The county capital is located 157 kilometres southeast of Dengka Gon in Tewo, 137 kilometres south of Minxian, and 78 kilometres northwest of Wudu.

Tewo to Drukchu

The dirt road from Tewo enters Drukchu county at Km Marker 65, ie 46 kilometres above the town of Drukchu. The descent into town is disappointing. The hills are largely deforested, and there is some evidence of inbreeding among the population. The narrow river banks are cultivated in places, but the only cultural sites of note appear to be two small village temples at **Nyiga** and **Peltsang**, located 10 and 32 kilometres above the town respectively.

Drukchu town

Altitude: 1,380 metres
Colour map 5, grid B6

Entering the town from the north-west, the **Main Street** leads downhill

Tewo & Drukchu

To Luchu (98 km)

To Dzoge Nyima (71 km)

Taktsang Lhamo

To Dzoge (78 km)

To Min Xian & Cho-ne

Tewo Dzong

To Wudu (78 km)

Drukchu

Druk-chu

N

Not to scale

Far-east Tibet

The forest dwellers of Drukchu

Formerly this was the wealthiest part of the prefecture because it was an important forest region with a reserve of 156 million cubic metres of wood. The local people had lived by lumbering generation after generation and, at the same time, taken care of the forest which sustained them, so that it never deteriorated and provided a beautiful green environment with scenic waters and roaming pandas. The forest dwellers of Drukchu had a higher living standard than the peasants and nomads. However, great changes have occurred since the establishment of the Bailong Forest Administration Bureau in 1966, and the immigration of 10,000-20,000 lumber workers from Manchuria and Sichuan,

plus their families. These alien people have no affinity toward this heavily wooded region. They have actively cut down trees but had no intention to replant. Consequently, the hills on both sides of the Druk-chu are denuded, and the ecological system endangered. The Tibetan inhabitants are gradually being marginalized and empowered – all that is left for them is the cultivation of mountain barley. Since the 1950s, the area of forest has shrank by 30% and the reserve of timber has been reduced by 25% due to overcutting. The sand in the river water has increased by 60%, and the water flow volume has reduced by 8%, resulting in increased flooding and drought.

towards a T-junction on the north bank of the river. On the left, you will pass a small guesthouse, the Workers' Hospital, the Forestry Department *Guest-house*, assorted banks, the bus station, and the vegetable market, while on the right there are only a few shops, and a lane leading down to the bridge which spans the Druk-chu here. After the T-junction, you will pass on the left, a restaurant, the local government buildings and the local transport company, while on the right are the traffic police, the *Zhengda Hotel*, a small dance hall, and a Muslim restaurant.

Drukchu to Minxian and Wudu

From Drukchu, you can continue following the river road downstream to its confluence with the smaller Yao River at **Lianhekou**. Here, our road unites with National Highway 212, which can be followed downstream to **Wudu** (59 kilometres), or upstream through the Yao valley to the watershed (2,550 metres) and thence to **Minxian** in the Lu-chu valley (118 kilometres), from which the Tibetan areas of **Lintan** and **Cho-ne** can be reached (see above, page 640).

Far-east Tibet

Drukchu Town

Sleeping
1 Forestry Department Guesthouse
2 Guesthouse
3 Zhengda Binguan Hotel

Eating
1 Muslim Restaurant
2 Restaurant & OK

Not to scale

Dzoge County མཛོད་དགེ

Dzoge County (151)
若尔盖县
Zoige
Population: 57,527
Area: 11,226 sq km
Colour map 5, grid C5

*The county of Dzoge lies south of the craggy **Amnye Lhago** range (Ch Erlong Shan), which in parts forms the provincial divide between present-day Gansu and Sichuan. It is an area of high grassland, corresponding to the valley of the Me-chu, a tributary of the Yellow River, which rises in the Minshan range and flows northwest to converge with the Yellow River below Machu. The county capital is located at **Taktsha Gondrong**, in the mid-reaches of the Me-chu valley, 90 kilometres south of Taktsang Lhamo (via **Zhakdom**), 140 kilometres northeast of Hongyuan, and 174 kilometres northwest of Zungchu. There are altogether 80 monasteries in Dzoge county, of which only three are Sakya and one Bonpo, the remainder are all Gelukpa. Among them, the best known (but not the largest) is **Dzoge Gonsar Ganden Rabgyeling**.*

Northern Dzoge

In the extreme north of the county, there are important lateral roads which carry traffic from Taktsang Lhamo along the south fringe of the Amnye Lhago range to Machu in Gansu, and also to Tewo in the Drukchu valley. These routes have already been described (page 638 and 644). The main road, National Highway 213 continues south from Taktsang Lhamo, following the Me-chu upstream to Dzoge. After 20 kilometres, another dirt road converges from the west. This turn-off leads southwest to the banks of the Me-chu from where motorable trails lead northwest to Machu (48 kilometres via Mazhi), and southwest to Tangkor (77 kilometres) in the Ger-chu valley. Continuing south on the highway, you will reach Taktsha Gondrong after 58 kilometres, crossing one pass (3,480 metres) en route.

Some small remaining clumps of forest are visible on the steeper hills, but the landscape is still primarily grassland, and the terrain around **Taktsha Gondrong** consists of high windswept marshland and open grasslands (3,292 metres), with an abundance of medicinal herbs. The horizon is dotted with nomad camps ringed by piles of yak-dung. The topsoil is thin and grazing land is intensively used, which has resulted in severe wind and water erosion in several areas. Everywhere there are molehills and the small holes made by pika, a voracious herbivore, which have added to the deterioration of the range.

Taktsha Gondrong

Phone code: 08476
Colour map 5, grid C5

The land around **Taktsha Gondrong** (*Ch* Roergai) is classic yak-herding country: shaggy-haired nomads, dressed in little more than filthy sheepskin *chubas* edged with fur, ride into town to barter skins or shoot pool in the market square, and fights are commonplace. Muslims from Gansu visit regularly to buy wool and carcasses which they transport northwards on ancient Chinese lorries, some of them settling to run the noodle restaurants and tea houses, which are found all over northern Amdo. Most of the Chinese here are administrators or shopkeepers selling a range of cheap nylon and plastic goods, and it is evident that few enjoy their stay. There are local industries based on the traditional nomadic produce: especially milk powder processing and meat canning

Dzoge County

Far-east Tibet

factories; while at **Chukcho** near town there is an international joint-venture gold mining development project.

Orientation

Entering town from Taktsang Lhamo (northwest) on the highway, turn left at the T-junction, or else continue southwest towards Hongyuan, bypassing the town. If you turn left, you will pass on the left the Tibetan Medical College (Mentsikhang) and the *Agriculture and Animal Husbandry Guesthouse*, while on the right there is the forestry department, and a number of small restaurants. At the next intersection, turn left onto **Main Street** or continue east towards the Education Bureau and the bus station, close to the banks of the Me-chu. On the left side of Main Street you will pass the cinema, *Xinhua Bookstore*, the post office, the *Dzoge Hotel*, the *County Government Guesthouse*, the Communist Party offices, and the police station, while on the right are banks, small restaurants and the County Peoples' Hospital. At the far end of Main Street, turn left for Dzoge Gonsar monastery or right, heading out of town in the direction of Zungchu.

Mentsikhang

The town is most famous, however, for its hospital of traditional medicine. This **Mentsikhang** is a teaching hospital with a four-year study course run by Lopon Tenko, a former pupil of Geshe Lobzang Palden of Labrang who died in 1963 at the age of 88. The medicinal compounding room, the grinding machine, the dispensary, and the library are all open to visitors. On average the hospital treats 80 patients each day, mostly for stomach and liver ailments, as well as arthritis and bronchitis.

Taktsha Gondrong

Far-east Tibet

<table>
<tr><td>Dzoge Gonsar
Ganden
Rabgyeling</td><td>The Gelukpa monastery of Dzoge Gonsar Ganden Rabgyeling was founded in 1798, the site having been offered by Konchok Rabten, the chieftain of neighbouring **Mewa** (*Ch* Hongyuan). Presently there are 100 monks here. Entering the precincts of the monastery via an ornate gateway and a large white stupa, the residential buildings (Labrang) are on the right, while the Protector Temple (Gonkhang), Medical College (Menpa Dratsang), Mani Wheel Chapel, and **Assembly Hall** (Dukhang) are to the left. Among them, the assembly hall has images of Shakyamuni, Tsongkhapa and Maitreya. In the **Gonkhang** there is a Four-armed Mahakala, while the **Mani Wheel Chapel (Dungkhor)** was constructed in 1988. The monastery has an important medical college (Menpa Dratsang), under the guidance of Akhu Puntsok.</td></tr>
<tr><td>Sleeping</td><td>**C** *Dzoge Hotel (Roergai Binguan)*, T(08476)218360. Doubles at ¥25 per bed, triples at ¥22 per bed, suites at ¥60, and cheaper rooms on the 2nd and 3rd floors (¥9-¥22). Foreigners pay ¥25 surcharge. **C** *County Government Guesthouse*, T(08476)218234. Doubles with electric heaters at ¥21 per room and doubles with radiators and electric blankets at ¥50 per room.</td></tr>
<tr><td>Eating</td><td>Try the **C** *Nordzin Restaurant and Bar* on Main St, or the Muslim noodle restaurant, opposite the police station. Cheaper menus are on offer opposite the post office.</td></tr>
<tr><td>Festivals</td><td>Small grassland festivals are held in Dzoge county throughout the summer with horse and yak races, weightlifting and traditional dances. The monastery establishes a small tent temple and numerous visitors bring tents in which a great deal of alcohol is consumed.</td></tr>
</table>

Minshan Region

Crossing the bridge to the east of town, you pass through pastures where sheep and goats graze in large numbers, and after 25 kilometres, the road forks, its branches following the tributaries of the Me-chu upstream to **Bozo** (33 kilometres) in the Minshan range, and **Choje Nangwa** (20 kilometres) in the grasslands. The former leads deep into the Minshan range, and gives access to **Dzitsa Degu** in Nampel county (see below page 658). The latter is a rough pot-holed surface, which bypasses the monastery at Choje Nangwa and stockaded villages and crosses two passes (3,600 metres and 3,570 metres) to enter a disputed grassland region. Here, the nomads of Mewa, Dzoge and Zungchu have resumed their age-old dispute concerning ownership of these border grasslands. Every year there are fatalities as marauding camper groups assault their neighbours. Taking the latter road, after 107 kilometres, you will reach the intersection of the three border roads at **Garita** (*Ch* Galitai). Turn northwest for **Bachen** (115 kilometres) in the Ger-chu valley (see below, page 652), or southeast for **Zungchu** (62 kilometres), in the upper valley of the Zung-chu (*Ch* Min) river.

Ger-chu Valley

National Highway 213 heads southwest from the bypass west of Taktsha Gondrong town, and gradually climbs through the grasslands, leaving the Me-chu valley behind en route for **Tangkor** (57 kilometres). Here, it enters the valley of the Ger-chu, a north-flowing tributary of the Yellow River, which merges with the latter at nearby **Sogtsang Gonpa**. This is beehive country and the monastery is visible just to the north of the road. There are also ancient camouflaged village dwellings, their roofs covered in grass and earth for protection. From here to **Mewa** (*Ch* Hongyuan) is only 76 kilometres upstream.

Mewa County ཨེ་བ

*Mewa is the traditional name for this grassland region, lying south of the Ngawa hills and the Amnye Lhago range. Chinese immigrants have flocked to the towns in this area, buoyed by their recent historic associations with the Long March. The county capital is located at Hongyuan in the mid-reaches of the Ger-chu, 59 kilometres from **Lungzi** (Ch Longriba) which is the gateway to Ngawa and Barkham, 177 kilometres west of **Zungchu**, and 136 kilometres southwest of Takstha Gondrong in Dzoge county. The monasteries here principally represent the Nyingmapa and the Gelukpa schools.*

Mewa County (152)
红原县
Hongyuan
Population: 30,796
Area: 7,328 sq km
Colour map 5, grid C5

Mewa Gonpa

Following the Ger-chu tributary of the Yellow River upstream from **Tangkor**, the road reaches **Bachen** (pronounced Wachen) after 33 kilometres. Here a road branches southeast across the watershed between the Yellow River and Zung-chu basins towards **Zungchu** (*Ch* Songpan), 186 kilometres distant via Changla. Some 18 kilometres along this road, you can visit **Mewa Gonpa** of the Nyingma school, the largest monastery in the county, where the *Longchen Nyingtig* and *Choling Tersar* traditions are maintained. The monastery was founded in the 19th century by Do Rinpoche. Presently, there are over 1,300 monks here.

Colour map 5, grid C5

Razhitang Mani Khorlo

Continuing on the main road southwest from Bachen, the Ger-chu valley flattens out, and on pools beside the meandering river black-necked cranes can occasionally be seen nesting in summer. At **Razhitang Mani Khorlo**, two kilometres south of Bachen, there is a Gelukpa monastery under the guidance of Zhabtra Rinpoche, with a teaching throne of the late Panchen Lama X.

At **Amokok**, 25 kilometres southwest of Bachen, a turn-off on the east (marked by stupas and prayer flags to the right of the road) follows the course of the Amo-chu tributary upstream to **Gonlung** and the **Mu-ge** grasslands (25 kilometres).

Gongtang Temple

Back on the main road, the marshy plain around the county town (*Ch* Hongyuan) supports large numbers of nomads, but the numerous Gelukpa and Nyingmapa monasteries, such as **Regur**, are little more than concrete sheds whose most attractive feature is the decorative field of prayer-flags, sometimes pyramid-shaped, that are found beside them. Approaching the town, just above a little village to the west, is the small **Gongtang Lhakhang**, the summer residence of Gongtang Rinpoche of Labrang, whose lineage is traced back to Je Gongtangba (1762-1823). Except during his visits, only a handful of monks, of Bon and Nyingma traditions as well as Gelukpa, inhabit this site.

Mewa County

Far-east Tibet

Hongyuan

Phone code: 08475
Colour map 5, grid C5

Hongyuan

The burgeoning county town of Hongyuan (Km Marker 647) is a place where Chinese settlers have established themselves in great numbers, alongside the indigenous nomadic population. It is not uncommon to see horses and yaks tethered in front of shop doorways. The name Hongyuan ('red plain') refers to the associations of the county with the Long March. Within the town there is an important Grasslands Research Institute.

Sleeping   Stay at the *Hongyuan Zhaodaisuo* (IDD: 08475), which has simple rooms in the main concrete building, alongside an uninspiring restaurant, in an annexe to the rear.

Transport   Public transport runs from here to Dzoge, Ngawa, Barkham, and Chengdu from the large bus station.

From Mewa, the main road leads southwest via **Amchu Gonpa** to **Lungzi** (49 kilometres) where it bifurcates: one branch heading northwest to Ngawa and the other due south to Barkham (see above, page 616).

Zungchu County ᠊ᠵᠤᠩ᠊ᠴᠦ

Zungchu County (153)
松潘县
Songpan
Population: 65,023
Area: 6,517 sq km
Colour map 5, grid C6

*Zungchu (Ch Songpan) county occupies the upper valley of the Zung-chu (Ch Minjiang) river, from its source in the Minshan range to the deep gorges north of Maowen county in the south. The county capital is located at **Zungchu (Songpan)**, 177 kilometres southwest of Hongyuan, 174 kilometres south of Dzoge, and 142 kilometres north of Maowen. The region is a stronghold of the Bon tradition, although there are also some Gelukpa monasteries.*

Grassland Watershed

Roads lead south into Zungchu county from Hongyuan via Bachen and from Dzoge via Choje Nangwa. The latter heads south through disputed grassland terrain as far as the Garita intersection, while the former route leaves National Highway 213 and the Ger-chu valley at **Bachen** (90 kilometres south of Dzoge and 43 kilometres north of Hongyuan), and cuts southwest to Mewa Gonpa (see above, page 651), after which it enters Zungchu county. On the first part of this route from Mewa, you will pass through classic Amdo country: low hills, broad grassy valleys and meandering rivers with patches of marsh. Black yak-hair tents, typical of all Tibetan nomads, are abundant here, and the rich grazing land supports vast herds of yak and many sheep and goats. Much of

Zungchu & Nampel Counties

the milk produced in this region is collected in large churns and taken by truck to Hongyuan, Dzoge, and other centres where it is processed into powdered milk. The remainder is used by the nomads to make butter, cheese and yoghurt, some of which is sold or bartered for tsampa, wheat, tea and salt, the principal constituents of the Tibetan diet.

About 70 kilometres from Bachen, the road passes through **Serdutang**, where there is an attractive Nyingmapa monastery, known locally as **Sergyi Gon** or **Decha Gon**, and then traverses the source of the Me-chu to reach the intersection with the Dzoge road at **Garita**, after a further 55 kilometres. From here, it crosses the watershed pass (3,624 metres) between the Yellow River and Zung-chu (Minjiang) basins, and winds its way down from the grasslands through **Pangzang** village, to enter the forested Zung-chu valley at **Chunda** (*Ch* Chuanzhusi), 46 kilometres southeast of Garita.

Chunda

Chunda, on the banks of the river, is a small, but important crossroads town. The attractive timber houses with carved gables, seen here for the first time, are typical of many Zungchu villages. Formerly, there was a monastery at Chunda, as the Chinese name still suggests. This was destroyed during the Second World War when the Japanese airforce bombed a Guomintang airstrip, slightly north of town. A smaller monastery, known as **Tsotso Gon**, has however been rebuilt. From Chunda, you can follow the Zung-chu valley upstream to visit **Nampel** (Nanping) county and the **Dzitsa Degu** (*Ch* Jiuzhaigou) **National Park** (128 kilometres), or cross the Minshan range to reach the **Sertso National Park** (56 kilometres). Alternatively, you may continue downstream to reach the county town after 16 kilometres.

Altitude: 2,880 metres
Phone code: 08493

C *Chunda Yinyuan Hotel (Chuanzhusi Yinyuan Fandian)*, T(08493)242166. Doubles at ¥280, triples at ¥200, and suites at ¥600 per room. Cheaper accommodation is available at the Tibetan run **C** *Chunda Dronkhang*.

Sleeping

Try the hotel restaurants for Sichuan cuisine, or the roadside Muslim restaurants and tea-houses.

Eating

Sertso National Park (*Ch* Huanglong)

Crossing the Zung-chu (Minjiang) river at Chunda, the road forks after two kilometres: northeast towards Dzitsa Degu, following the Zung-chu upstream to its source, and due east, across the Minshan watershed to **Sertso National Park** (*Tib* Sertso Rangjung Sungkyong Sakul). Taking the latter route, which was once followed by the PLA during the Long March (a monument has been erected here), to the right, you will pass the Bon monastery of **Lingpo Gon**, situated below the road on the right. Two passes are crossed on this winding hill road, the second, known in Chinese as Xue Bading Shankou (4,420 metres), being in the heart of the Minshan range, near the holy Bon mountain called **Mount Shar Dungri** (5,588 metres), which is the main peak of the Minshan range. After crossing the watershed, the road descends to the **entrance of the park** at Sertso village on the road to **Pingwu**. From Sertso, the distance is 56 kilometres to Chunda and 114 kilometres to Pingwu.

■ *Admission: ¥75*
Colour map 5, grid C6

The park, a steep valley which extends for nine kilometres, was established as a nature reserve in 1983. It contains a series of variegated lakes suffused with minerals and algae, and (according to one tradition) received its name from the yellowish karst limestone formations which cover the

Far-east Tibet

landscape. Visitors should be aware, however, that the lower pools, close to the entrance, are dry until July, which is the best month here. The trail from the entrance leads past a series of small lakes and steep coniferous forests to an impressive alpine meadow (1,080 metres), with numerous rhododendron species, at the eastern foot of **Mount Shar Dungri**. The climb takes approximately one hour 30 minutes, and there are local guides available to escort groups or individual travellers to the summit. The lakes and pools have been given fanciful names: Flying Fall, Golden Fall, Potted Landscape Pool, Cuckoo-Reflecting Colourful Pool, Green Jade Colourful Pool, and Zhuanhua Jade Pool, which is the highest. Reaching the meadow, there are three small reconstructed Chinese temples which can be visited in turn: Zhongsi, Huanglongsi, and Longwangsi, all of which have Tibetan shrines in front, where juniper is burnt, and *lungta* (Tibetan printed prayers) are scattered. Among them the most famous is **Huanglongsi** (*Tib* Sertso Gon), a Daoist temple with one resident Chinese monk, where local Tibetan and Qiang peoples of the Bon tradition gather during a summer festival, held over a three-day period from the 15th day of the sixth lunar month.

Several protected species, including the red panda, golden monkey, takin and water deer are supposedly found in the Sertso National Park, but in such small numbers they are unlikely to be seen by the casual visitor. The park has become a popular destination, particularly for Chinese tourists, and it is

Sertso National Park

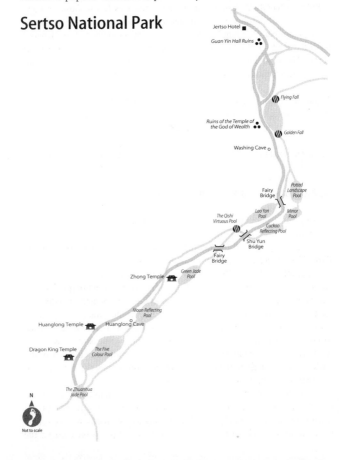

Jertso Hotel

Guan Yin Hall Ruins

Flying Fall

Ruins of the Temple of
the God of Wealth

Golden Fall

Washing Cave

Potted
Landscape
Pool

Fairy
Bridge

Lao Yan
Pool

Mirror
Pool

The Qishi
Virtuous Pool

Cuckoo
Reflecting Pool

Shu Yun
Bridge

Fairy
Bridge

Zhong Temple

Green Jade
Pool

Moon Reflecting
Pool

Huanglong Temple

Huanglong Cave

Dragon King Temple

The Five
Colour Pool

The Zhuanhua
Jade Pool

N

Not to scale

possible to stay at the *Sertso Hotel* (Sercuo Fandian), near the entrance. Cheaper guesthouse accommodation is also available, and there are restaurants close to the car park.

From **Zungchu** town, there is also a trekking route to **Sertso**, which follows a tributary of the Minjiang upstream through **Dongna** to **Rongkok**, where you can visit **Rongpa** monastery of the Sakyapa school and **Sebo** monastery of the Gelukpa school. En route are the small villages with Bonpo temples, such as **Rinpung** and **Kharchung**.

Source of the Min River

If from the intersection two kilometres east of Chunda, you turn north for **Dzitsa Degu National Park** (85 kilometres), the road follows the east bank of the Zung-chu (Minjiang) upstream towards its source in the Minshan hills. At **Tsangla** village, there are gold mines, attested by the extravagant house of the wealthiest local prospector, and across the river from here there is the unused Guomintang airstrip, which was bombed by Japanese planes during the Second World War. Continuing upstream, there is a Bon monastery at **Nangzhi**, and several affiliated nearby temples, notably **Lenri** and **Kyang**, the last having been founded by Kyang Lobzang Gyatso.

Gamil Gonpa

Further north, just before reaching the source of the Zung-chu, the road passes through the village of **Shadri**, below the sacred **Mount Jadur**. The largest Bon monastery of the region, known as **Gamil Gonchen** or Pal Shenten Dechenling, is located by the roadside, and has an enormous prayer wheel at its entrance. The monastery was founded some 600 years ago by Rinchen Gyeltsen of the Khyung family, and so it is affiliated to Tengchen Monastery in Kham. Currently there are 450 monks and one *tulku* in residence. The complex has an Assembly Hall (Dukhang), and three colleges: Tsenyi Dratsang (Dialectics), Gyupa Dratsang (Tantric), and Dongak (Scriptural). The **Tsenyi Dratsang** has images of Shenrab Miwoche flanked by the Bon equivalents of Vajrapani and Vajrakila (Vasin), while in the main hall of the **Dukhang** there are images of Shenrab Miwoche, Sherab Nampar Gyelwa, and the Bon equivalent of Tara. A **stupa reliquary** here contains the remains of Khenpo Tendzin Dargye. Since it is beside the main road to **Dzitsa Degu National Park** (*Ch* Jiuzhaigou), Gamil Gonpa receives many Chinese tour buses, although most visitors stay only a short while. After Shadri, the road crosses the Zung-chu river near its source, and crosses the watershed to enter Nampel county (see below, page 658).

Zungchu Town

Driving south from Chunda township, the road follows the east bank of the Zung-chu downstream for 16 kilometres to **Zungchu** (*Ch* Songpan), the county capital. Zungchu has long been an important trading town for Tibetans, Qiang, Chinese and Muslims. Much of the tea trade for Amdo was centred here, with wool, furs, musk, medicinal herbs and gold also providing important markets. The old city walls, now crumbling and overshadowed by new construction, can still be seen, and the extensive market area still attracts a wide selection of visitors from the hills. The Zung-chu river runs through the town, until recently carrying an abundance of logs downstream in defiance of the posters urging conservation and restraint. The population is diverse, but

Phone code: 08493
Colour map 5, grid C6

Far-east Tibet

predominantly Muslim, and worshippers can frequently be seen at **Qingzhen Si Mosque** near the north end of town.

Orientation   Entering the city from Chunda, you will reach the North Gate. A ring road follows the old city wall round towards the East Gate, passing the *Linyu Hotel* and the Agricultural Bureau. Continuing through the North Gate into **Main Street**, there are shops and grain department offices on both sides. An elegant old covered bridge then spans the Zung-chu, which bisects the town here. Crossing the bridge, you will notice the Qingzhen Si Mosque on a forested ridge to the north. Now, on the right side of Main Street, you will pass the *Xinhua Bookstore*, the *Songpan Department Store* and the *Mingsong Restaurant*, while on the left is the *Songpan Hotel* and a kindergarten. The main crossroad now looms ahead. Turn left through the market towards the ruins of the West Gate (destroyed by Japanese bombs in the Second World War), or right towards the East Gate, where the local government buildings and banks are located. Continuing straight ahead on Main Street from the crossroads, you will pass on the right the *Huanglong Hotel*, and the *Songpan Government Guesthouse*, while on the left are the police station, the post office (which had a fax bureau to the rear), and the *Taiyanghe Hotel*. Then, leaving town via the

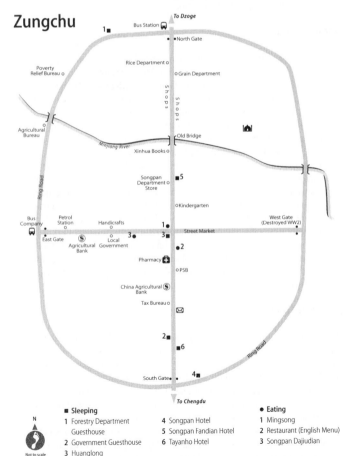

Zungchu

Sleeping
1 Forestry Department Guesthouse
2 Government Guesthouse
3 Huanglong
4 Songpan Hotel
5 Songpan Fandian Hotel
6 Tayanho Hotel

Eating
1 Mingsong
2 Restaurant (English Menu)
3 Songpan Dajiudian

N
Not to scale

Far-east Tibet

South Gate, the road continues following the steep gorge of the Zung-chu downstream towards Maowen county.

Zungchu is rapidly becoming an important tourist centre for domestic and foreign visitors; and in summer, dozens of minibuses leave daily for the nearby national parks. It is also possible to hire horses and guides for trips into the mountains, lasting up to a week, but be sure you understand the itinerary, what services (eg food and accommodation) are included, and that you see the horses before parting with any money.

C *Songpan Hotel (Songpan Fandian)*, T(08493)232531. Doubles at ¥60 and triples at **Sleeping** ¥75 (all without attached bathroom), and singles at ¥100, doubles at ¥160, and triples at ¥180 (with attached bathroom). C *Taiyanghe Dajiudian*, T(08493)232742. Doubles at ¥280, and triples at ¥390. Cheaper accommodation is available at the C *Songpan Government Guesthouse*, which has double rooms with attached bath at ¥25 per bed, or ¥16 per bed without.

There are several restaurants in town, mostly serving Muslim and Sichuan cuisine, but **Eating** one next to the police station has an English menu. Alternatively, try the *Mingsong Restaurant* or the *Songpan Dajuxan Restaurant*, both on the East Gate road.

Nyenyul Valley

To the west of town, a steep climb and descent leads into the picturesque **Nyenyul** valley, which can also be approached by road from a turn-off at **Anhong** township, 33 kilometres south of Zungchu. Here, there are several Bonpo temples, including the important **Gyagar Mandi**, which is built on an Indian model, and the Sakya monastery of **Jara**. **Muni Gulley** to the west of Nyenyul has its own scenic lakes, hot springs, and a famous waterfall called **Zhaga Purbu**, which are increasingly visited by tourists. Here, as at Sertso, the lakes have been given fanciful Chinese names: Ginseng Lake, Hundred Flower Lake, Wild Duck Lake, and so forth.

Zung-chu Gorge

Heading south from Zungchu and Anhong, the main road follows the east bank of the Zung-chu downstream, passing through **Pata**, **Dongna**, and **Zhenjiangquan** after 45 kilometres. The village houses on this stretch are constructed of plain timber and accompanied by wooden frames where barley is dried during the harvest season before threshing. Some 27 kilometres further south, it passes through **Tungping** (*Ch* Taiping), a lumber control checkpoint, after which it climbs along the upper ridge of the increasingly deep Zung-chu gorge to reach the roadside monument at Diexihaici, commemorating the inhabitants of a Qiang village which vanished from the face of the earth during the 1953 earthquake, when a large lake formed on the Zung-chu below. The lake is clearly visible from the high road. Descending to **Jiaochangba**, the road reaches a turn-off on the right, which leads 21 kilometres to **Songpingkou** village in the Yungping valley. Continuing south on the main road, you will then cross two 2,400 metres ridges, before arriving at **Lianghekou**, 107 kilometres south of the county town, where an important branch road spans the river, giving access to the Zhangdu-chu valley, and connecting with the neighbouring Metsa valley in Tro-chu county (see below, page 662). South of Lianghekou, the main road soon passes the confluence of the Zung-chu and Tro-chu rivers to enter Maowen county, only 29 kilometres north of Mao Xian town.

Far-east Tibet

Nampel County རྨ་འཕེལ།

Nampel County (154)
南坪县
Nanping
Population: 53,001
Area: 6,175 sq km
Colour map 5, grid C6

The county of Nampel occupies the upper reaches of the Baishui and Fujiang tributaries of the Jialing River, from their watershed in the Minshan range towards Wudu in mainland China. This region, which was once a stronghold of the Bon religion, has become culturally threadbare in recent years, despite having some parks of outstanding natural beauty. The county town of Nampel is located at **Nanping** town, on the Baishui, 142 kilometres northeast of Zungchu, 61 kilometres northwest of Wen Xian in Gansu, and 132 kilometres northeast of Pingwu in Sichuan.

Dzitsa Degu National Park (Jiuzhaigou)

Colour map 5, grid C6

Named after its nine largest settlements, this national park is one of the most beautiful areas of the Tibetan plateau. **Dzitsa Degu** is a Y-shaped forested ravine, 30 kilometres long, within the Minshan range. Numerous mineral-tinted pools and lakes, connected by small waterfalls, line the valley bottom, while the forest extends to the snow peaks above. The total area of the park is 720 square kilometres, and its altitude is in the range 2,000-3,100 metres. The park is rich is flora including wild roses, clematis, honeysuckle, violet, wild ginger, and above all rhododendron; and in recent years, it has been developed as the major tourist destination of northern Sichuan.

Getting there

After Gamil Gonpa, the road from Zungchu and Chunda reaches **Tatsang** near the source of the Zung-chu, and crosses the **Gang Gutok La** pass (3,510 metres) in the Minshan range, which form the watershed between the Zung-chu (Minjiang) and Jialing basins. There are fine views of the snow peaks of the sacred Bon mountain, **Shar Dungri**, to the south. On the descent from the pass to Chukar, the excellent paved road cuts through juniper forests, passing **Dzole**, the first scenic spot in Dzitsa Degu to have been discovered and opened by local inhabitants. On the right there is a school and a crystal trinklet factory, both funded by a Taiwanese entrepreneur. **Dartse Gonpa** of the Bon tradition is then passed on the left. This is one of only two monasteries in the area, and currently there are 91 monks, studying under a *khenpo* from Menri near Zhigatse. From here the road descends to **Chukar** at the entrance to the Dzitsa Degu National Park.

Chukar

Chukar (2,100 metres), 42 kilometres west of the county town, has undergone considerable development in recent years since it lies at the gateway to the park, and is the focal point for the vast legions of Chinese and Taiwanese tourists who come here by bus from Chengdu. It has several hotels and guesthouses, restaurants, and a heliport, 3.5 kilometres to the south. The ticket office is located at **Penpo** (Goukou) where the Fujiang River makes a hairpin bend. Admission: ¥106 per person. It is also possible to hire a horse and local guide: ¥350 per day.

Tsaru Village

Entering the park, after six kilometres, the road forks at **Tsaru** village. Tsaru has the only monastery located within the grounds of the park, **Rabwen Gonpa Tashi Puntsoling** of the Bon religion. The buildings were restored about eight years ago, having been damaged by fire, and the main temple now has a large image of Shenrab Miwoche, surrounded by 1,000 small identical images. Presently, there are 67 monks at Rabwen Gon.

From Tsaru, the road continues following the west bank of the Fujiang River, **Mangsolde** on the far bank of which a number of scenic lakes are passed: Dumtsa Tso **Village** (Reed Lake), Tsozhi Nangchu (Four-Lake Waterfall), Mebar Tso (Burning Lake), Takchen Tso (Tiger Lake), and Seru Tso (Rhino Lake). **Mangsolde** village (*Ch* Shuzheng) lies 11 kilometres upstream from the park entrance, and there are a number of tourist handicraft shops, small tea houses and restaurants, one of which (uphill from the car park) is smartly decorated in Tibetan style. About three kilometres after Mangsolde, at **Laga**, the road forks below **Mount Senmo** (4,100 metres): southeast for Tsoring (18 kilometres), and southwest for Ri-tse and Domei Naktsal (17 kilometres). *Nurilang Guesthouse*, just west of this intersection is a focal point for many visitors to Dzitsa Degu since buses run inside the grounds of the park, several times a day, from the entrance as far as this road junction. It takes about three hours to walk from the entrance to Laga (14 kilometres). From the guesthouse, there are two public buses per day running back and forth (southwest) to **Ri-tse** (17 kilometres),

Dzitsa Degu Valley

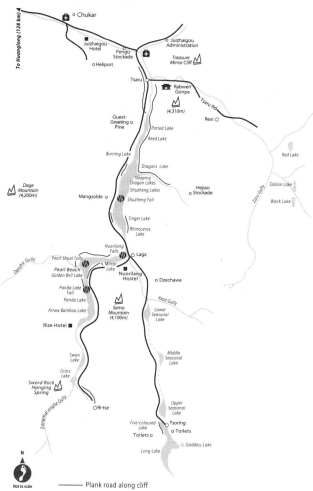

and a more infrequent public bus service to **Tsoring Lake** (18 kilometres) in the southeast. Most of the buses operating within the park are private tour buses from Chengdu, which will not pick up individual travellers.

Dzechawa Gully Taking the left gulley from the Laga intersection, the road passes through **Dzechawa** village and three seasonal lakes on the left, before reaching **Doknga Tso** (Five-coloured Lake). It is said that the seasonal lakes have been ruined in consequence of the ecological imbalance caused by mass tourism in Dzitsa Degu. A steep flight of stone steps leads down to the shore of Doknga Tso, where yellow, blue, green and white hues are reflected through the clear calm waters, and submerged ancient tree trunks are sharply discerned. The motor road ends after 18 kilometres at **Tsoring** (Long Lake), which is the park's largest lake (*Altitude*: 3,150 metres). Another steep stone staircase leads down to the lake shore, where local Tibetans are waiting with their docile yaks to dress eager Chinese tourists in Tibetan garb for their personal yak photographs. The clear blue waters of the lake reveal all their secrets, including a pattern of submerged trees.

Ri-tse Gully From the Laga intersection buses run for 17 kilometres, as far as **Domei Naktsal** (Primeval Forest) in the upper reaches of the southwest gully. This is undoubtedly the most spectacular section of the park. To the right of the road you will pass the resplendent **Shel Tso** (Mirror Lake) and the **Mutik Chu** (Pearl Shoal Waterfall), where white surf cascades over the white boulders of the Fujiang River, approached at their base via a long wooden bridge and stone staircase. Further on, **Gyila Domgyi Tso** (Panda Lake) has, at its southeast corner, shoals of fish which are fed by passing tourists, while **Tso Mukdachen** (Arrow Bamboo Lake), **Tso Ngangpachen** (Swan Lake), and **Tsa Tso** (Grass Lake) were formerly part of the giant panda's natural habitat. The motor road comes to an end at **Domei Naktsal**, the primeval forest (2,970 metres), where horses are available to transport tourists uphill through the woods at ¥30 per person.

Sleeping Inside the park: *Nuorilang Guesthouse* at Laga has double rooms with attached bath at ¥120, and there are three restaurants. *Lotus Leaf Guesthouse (Heyezai Guesthouse)* at Mangsolde village. Doubles at ¥140 and triples at ¥100-¥110. Accommodation is also available within the park at *Rhinoceros Lake Lodgings (Xiniu Hai Shishudian)*, the *Ri-tse Guesthouse*, or the Tibetan-run *Minzufeng Hostel*, all of these with minimal facilities but inexpensive.

Accommodation outside the park: at the entrance to the park there is the *Jiuzhaigou Hotel*, T(08494)234023, F(08494)234024. 3-star, has 112 rooms (superior double in A Wing at ¥800 per room, superior double in B Wing at ¥600 per room, and standard double in A Wing at ¥320). The hotel also has Chinese and Western restaurants, café, beauty salon, disco, karaoke, massage service, and Tibetan camp fire parties at which freshly roasted mutton and chang are offered to Chinese tourists (¥1,400 for a group less than 5). *Linxiagyuan Hotel*, T(08494)234030. 57 rooms at ¥240 per standard, ¥280 per triple (with attached bathroom). With Sichuan restaurant, café, massage service, car rental service, hairdresser, and shops; and the excellent Hong Kong managed *Jiuzhaigou Sangzhuang Hotel*.

Directory **Tour companies & travel agents** The *Jiuzhaigou International Travel Service*, Room 207 *Hualong Hotel*, 18 Yingmenkou St, Chengdu, T(028)7778699, F(028)7778696. Offers package tours to Dzitsa Degu National Park by bus, via Zungchu and Pingwu. Try the hotel restaurants for Sichuan cuisine, or the roadside Muslim restaurants and tea-houses.

Nanping

The county town, **Nanping**, is located 42 kilometres from Chukar at the entrance to the Dzitsa Degu National Park, in the valley of the Baishui river. The Tibetan population is small, and for the most part representative of the Bon tradition. There are guesthouse and restaurant facilities, although most visitors will proceed directly to Dzitsa Degu.

Phone code: 08494
Colour map 5, grid C6

From Nanping, a rough motorable road heads upstream through the Baishui valley to the northwest extremity of the Minshan range, and thence through the grasslands to **Bozo** in Dzoge county (see above, page 648). The main road, however, follows the Baishui downstream for 61 kilometres to **Wen Xian** in Gansu province, from where there are connections to **Pingwu** and **Wudu**. Buses run from these cities to connect with the Chengdu-Lanzhou railway line.

Tangjiahe National Park

Although Dzitsa Degu is still notionally a panda park, most of the few remaining giant pandas are found further southwest at the junction of Pingwu, Nampel, and Qingchuan counties, especially in the **Tangjiahe National Park**. This represents the westernmost penetration of Tibetan influence. But nowadays this tiny Tibetan population is isolated in the mountain regions, greatly outnumbered by Chinese and Muslim settlements lower down.

Colour map 5, grid C5

Maowen County མ་རོ་ཕྱུན་

Maowen is the county inhabited by the Qiang nationality, who are believed to be descendants of ancient Tibetan tribes that ranged widely across the extreme north and east of the plateau before and during the period of the Tibetan kings.

Maowen Qiang Autonomous County (155)
茂汶羌族自治县
Maowen
Population: 91,229
Area: 4,373 sq km
Colour map 5, grid C6

The Qiang women still proudly wear their national dress: long brightly coloured (often blue) slit dresses, with blue or black trousers underneath, and intricately embroidered collars adorned with heavy amber jewellery. Most wear a black or white turban, or a decorative headscarf.

The Qiang are renowned for their stone buildings and watchtowers, a culture which they share with the apparently related Qiangic peoples of East Tibet, such as those of Gyarong, and of Tawu and Minyak in Kham. Nowadays they are principally agriculturalists, with wheat and maize as their main crops, with a few domestic animals stabled in large courtyards or the ground floor of their three-storey stone and timber houses. A large number of these houses have been rebuilt in the last 15 years, and most window and door-frames are painted in bright colours with traditional designs.

Maowen, Trochu & Lungu Counties

Higher up, above the tree-line, on alpine meadows, yak, sheep and goats are pastured by mixed populations of Qiang and Tibetan nomads living in traditional black yak wool tents.

Far-east Tibet

Mao Xian town

Altitude: 1,590 metres
Phone code: 08491
Colour map 4, grid A6

South of the Zung-chu's confleunce with the Tro-chu at Lianghekou (see above, page 662), the road from the north begins to criss-cross the river on its 29 kilometres descent into **Mao Xian** county town. Here, the waters of the Zung-chu are silvery in colour and the mountains are rich repositories of quartz and other minerals. The local people grow *hua jao* spice bushes and maintain bee hives by the roadside. The town itself, which lies 142 kilometres south of Zungchu and 55 kilometres north of Wenchuan, has a population of 60,000 – mostly Muslim and Qiang. The open market is active, although the *Qiang Handicrafts Shop* on Main Street is disappointing. From Mao Xian a branch road leads northeast to **Beichuan** (199 kilometres).

Sleeping   Stay at the comfortable *Lingye Binguan*, on the west side of Main St, where double rooms with attached showers are ¥520 per room. Or at the cheaper *Renmin Guesthouse* near the crossroads, which has rooms at ¥25 per bed.

Trochu County ཁྲོ་ཆུ

Trochu County (156)
黑水县
Heishui
Population: 57,072
Area: 2,952 sq km
Phone code: 08492
Colour map 4, grid A6

*At **Lianghekou**, 29 kilometres north of Mao Xian town, where the Tro-chu (Ch Heishui) River flows into the Zung-chu, there is a road branching off the Maowen-Zungchu highway, which follows the Tro-chu upstream. To reach **Trochu** county, head west up this side-valley, passing through Pichi, Serkyu, Gagu, and Shiwar Kazi. The county capital, also known as **Trochu**, is 94 kilometres from the junction at Lianghekou, on a tributary of the Tro-chu. Until the recent ban, many logs were floated downstream, continuing evidence of the massive deforestation which has halved the area's forest cover since 1950.*

Muge-chu Valley

Some 26 kilometres before reaching the county capital, the road forks: the west branch leading to the capital and the north branch continuing to climb north through the Tro-chu gorge to **Tsimule**. At Tsimule, two valleys converge: the Muge-chu valley (west) and the Tsagi-chu valley (east). Taking the former, the road (69 kilometres) passes through **Chunak**, the Bonpo monastery of **Yungdrung Gon**, **Muge** and **Norwa**. **Muge Gonpa** in particular is an important Gelukpa institution, and was visited by Mao Zedong during the Long March.

Tsagi-chu Valley

The east branch runs north to **Mechu**, where a jeepable loop road heads southeast through the Tungping valley to rejoin the Zungchu-Maowen highway at **Jiaochangba** (30 kilometres). Further north of Mechu, the road through the Tsagi-chu valley continues for 41 kilometres, via **Natsi** and **Tsege**. These valleys are characterized by small village temples, all recently rebuilt, and mostly of Bonpo origin. There are also a few very small Gelukpa temples, usually attended by a single caretaker or a handful of monks, and which only come to life during village festivals.

The giant pandas of Wolong

This nature reserve (2,000 sq km) has acquired international renown as the principal breeding ground for the **Giant Panda**, an endangered species whose natural habitat in now confined to a few forested areas of Sichuan, Gansu and Shaanxi provinces. Established in 1983, the **Hetaoping** breeding station within the reserve monitors the greatest concentration of the panda population (overall less than 1,000), but their survival is constantly under threat due to rampant deforestation and the peculiarity of their diet. The arrow bamboo and umbrella bamboo on which they depend have a 50/60 year cycle, at the end of which many pandas die due to starvation.

Apart from the pandas, there are almost 100 species of animals, 230 species of birds, and 4,000 species of plants within the reserve; and the Wolong Museum of Natural History at **Shawan** (Wolong town) is well worth a visit. Here, the Wolong Nature Reserve Administration Office runs a bungalow-style lodge and restaurant. Single rooms with attached baths are ¥30; and doubles without bath ¥15. To reach Shawan from Balang Shan pass, the road follows the **Pitiao** River, a tributary of the Minjiang, downstream for 67 km. From Shawan to the east entrance of the reserve the distance is 40 km, and from there to Chengdu only 136 km. In the northwest of the reserve near **Mount Siguniang** (6,250m) there are trekking and camping facilities. The local population is a mix of Tibetan and Qiang.

Lungu County ལུང་དགུ

From Maowen the main road to Chengdu continues to follow the steep Zung-chu gorge downstream into **Lungu**. This is a traditional Tibetan name for the area around Wenchuan town and the confluence of the Trosung-chu with the Zung-chu. The Chinese name Wenchuan means Wen River, which is an ancient local name for the Zung-chu (Minjiang) River. Although there are patches of forest left on the steeper slopes, most of the mountains were deforested long ago and now exhibit a rich and varied selection of shrubs and wild flowers. Apple bushes now grow by the roadside. The road lies only a few hundred metres above the raging river, and in many places is prone to landslides, particularly in early summer. Precarious bamboo and pulley type suspension bridges span the chasm at intervals, and these are nonchalantly crossed by the locals.

Lungu County (157)
汶川县
Wenchuan
Population: 99,194
Area: 3,537 sq km
Colour map 4, grid A6

Wenchuan

The county capital, **Wenchuan**, is located 55 kilometres southwest of Mao Xian town at a point where the Troksung-chu flows in from the west. The attractive setting and colourful markets are memorable, but although undeniably a major industrial town, Wenchuan is architecturally uninspiring. More importantly, it is a gateway to Ngawa and the Gyarong region.

Altitude: 1,326 metres
Phone code: 08489
Colour map 4, grid A6

Stay at the **Wenchuan County Government Guesthouse**, where there are beds at ¥25; or north of town at the roadside **Shan Zhuang Hotel**.

Sleeping

Try the roadside **Yutian Restaurant**, T(08489)554289. Sichuan cuisine.

Eating

An important bridge (Wei Zhou Da Qiao) crosses the Zung-chu at Wenchuan, and a road leads west to Tashiling (Li Xian), Nyaglo and Barkham (244 kilometres), following the Troksung-chu upstream (see above, page 616). Most villages in this area are situated on flatter ground high above the road, and a few

Far-east Tibet

possess the tall stone watchtowers characteristic of the regional Qiang culture.

Xiasuo Qiao The road from Wenchuan to Chengdu continues following the course of the Zung-chu (Minjiang) south from Wenchuan. A new road tunnel is currently under construction on this stretch, and after 30 kilometres it reaches a bridge called Xiasuo Qiuao, which gives access to the last Qiang village, located on a hill-top promontory above the west bank of the river. The watchtower and stone houses of this village have been well maintained, and the inhabitants have kept their local cottage industries.

Wolong Panda Some 29 kilometres south of the Xiasuo Qiao bridge, the road reaches
Reserve **Yenzhing**, where the Pitiao River flows in from the Wolong Panda Reserve.
      Wolong lies only 25 kilometres to the east of Yenzhing, and 67 kilometres west of Tsenlha across the **Balang Shan** pass (see above, page 623).

Guan Xian

Colour map 4, grid A6 *After the turn-off for Wolong at Yenzhing, the road leaves Lungu (Wenchuan) county and in doing so it simultaneously leaves the Tibetan world for that of mainland China. It bypasses a dam and power station on the Zung-chu and crosses the Yinxiu Yenzhou hills, and descends to **Xuankou** village, where there is an 18th century stone tower.*

Qingcheng Just 23 kilometres south of the Yenzhing, on the outskirts of the city of
Shan **Dujiangyan**, a turn-off leads 15 kilometres uphill to the Daoist holy mountain, **Qingcheng Qian Shan** and the adjacent Buddhist holy mountain of **Qingcheng Hou Shan**. Both sites are worth visiting. The four hours' ascent of Qingcheng Qian Shan (Front mountain) passes several temples and caves which once housed over 500 Daoist monks. Historically, the most important temple here is Tianshi Dong, revered as a major source of the Daoist religion. It is possible to sleep at **Shangqing Gong Temple** and rise early to see dawn at the summit (■*Admission fee: ¥10*). At nearby Qingchen Hou Shan (Back Mountain), there is a two-day pilgrimage circuit of Buddhist shrines and caves, the most memorable sites being the scenic White Cloud Temple, Goddess of Mercy Cave, and the double waterfall passed on the descent. Stay overnight at **Youyi Cun** village (■*Admission fee: ¥20*).

Dujiangyan The county town, **Dujiangyan**, is only 55 kilometres northwest of Chengdu. Here there is an important irrigation system which has been in use since the Han Dynasty (256 BC). The then governor of Chengdu, Li Bing, constructed a weir in the Minjiang River in order to split the river into two channels, diverting much of its flow through the irrigation network of the Chengdu Plain (6,500 square kilometres). This reduced the annual summer flooding of the valley, and, from that time on, Chengdu became a significant farming region. Models and inscriptions here commemorate Li Bing and his son. The nearby **Two Princes Temple (Erwangmiao)** was built in their honour, and there is also a Daoist temple (**Fulongguan**) commanding the weir.

Dujiangyan to At Dujiangyan the road from Taktsang Lhamo and Zungchu meets the
Chengdu National Highway 213 from the northeast, and a toll road takes traffic towards Chengdu, 55 kilometres distant. In **Pixian** county along this road, the Tibetan Kangyur-Tangyur Collation Project have their offices.

Background

11

Background

Isolated by formidable mountain barriers, the peoples of the Tibetan plateau uniquely carried a sophisticated, living, medieval culture into the 20th century. The allure of Tibet's pristine high-altitude environment and profound Buddhist traditions attracted intrepid travellers and explorers from Europe, India, and America throughout the 19th and early 20th centuries. Many faced great physical and mental hardships in their journeys to Lhasa and elsewhere; and some tragically lost their lives, without reaching their goal. The Tibetans actively discouraged such contacts and, with the exception of a few far-sighted intellectuals and lamas, no-one inside Tibet realized the implications that Tibet's self-imposed isolation would come to have in the latter half of the 20th century.

Following the Chinese occupation of the plateau and the abortive Tibetan uprising of 1959, the country was plunged into the long dark night of the Cultural Revolution. Then, quite unexpectedly, in the early 1980s, Tibet opened its doors to the outside world as a tourist destination.

Although there are still restrictions imposed on individual travel in many parts of Tibet for political reasons, ensuring that only the well-endowed traveller can afford to undertake full-scale guaranteed itineraries, bureaucracy has not deterred the adventurous hardy backpacker who can often be seen trudging through remote parts of the country, following in the footsteps of his or her illustrious predecessors.

History

Legend

The Tibetan Buddhist historical work known as the *Mani Kabum* mentions both the dehydration of the Tibetan lakelands and the legendary ape-like origins of the Tibetan race. The first Tibetans are said to have been the offspring of a monkey emanation of Avalokiteshvara (the patron deity of Tibet) – representing compassion and sensitivity – who mated with an ogress of the rocks – symbolizing the harshness of the Tibetan environment – at Zodang Gongpori Cave above Tsetang in South Tibet. They gave birth to six children, indicative of six types of sentient being, which later multiplied to 400, divided into four large tribes and two smaller groups. Gradually the monkeys evolved into humans, displaying both their paternal compassion and maternal aggression.

Other Bonpo (pre-Buddhist) legends, found in the *Lang Poti Seru*, trace the origin of the early tribes not to the monkey descendants of Avalokiteshvara, but to sub-human or primitive groups. Here, O-de Gung-gyel intermarries with various types of spirit – a *lhamo*, a *nyenmo*, a *mumo*, and a *lumo*, thereby giving birth to the Tibetan kings, demons, and human beings.

Meanwhile, there are other legends referring to the 10 groups of primeval non-human beings who held sway over Tibet prior to the dominion of the Tibetan monkey-tribes. Appearing in succession these were: Nojin Nagpo of Zangyul Gyen-me (who used bows and arrows), Dud of Dudyul Kharak Rong-gu (using battle axes), Sin of Sinpo Nagpo Guyul (using animal bone slings and catapults), Lha of Lhayul Gung-tang (using sharp swords), Mu-gyel (using lassoes with hooks and black magic rituals), canyon-dwelling Dre (using bolos with rocks attached), the Masang brothers of Bod (using armour and shields), the Lu of Bo-kham Ling-gu (using metamorphosis), the Gyelpo of Dempotse, and the 18 classes of bewitcher demons or Gongpo (using guile but squandering good fortune). Subsequently, the monkey descendants of Zodang Gongpori emerged, perhaps indicating a shift from the primitive human culture of the Old Stone Age to a more advanced neolithic culture.

Archaeology

There has been no systematic archaeological survey of the Tibetan plateau, but the evidence that does emerge from the disparate excavated sites suggests that Tibet was inhabited during the Old Stone Age (2 mya-10,000 ya). Crude pebble choppers have been unearthed at Kukushili, flake tools at Dingri, and stone scrapers, knives, drills, and axes at Lake Xiaochaili in the Tsaidam – the last dated to 33,000 BC. There are also primitive cave and 'nest' dwellings in Kongpo, Powo, Lhartse, Yamdrok, and the Jangtang Plateau.

A number of finely chipped blades from the Middle Stone Age (10,000 ya) have been excavated at Serling Lake, Nyalam, Chamdo and Nakchu, indicating the prevalence of a hunting culture. Nonetheless, there are also indications of early farming communities in eastern areas: at the neolithic settlement of **Go-ru** north of Chamdo, dated 3,500 BC, where the remains of two-storey dwellings partitioned, as now, into human habitation upstairs and animal barns downstairs, have been discovered, along with stone artefacts, pottery and bone needles. Similar sites containing stone artefacts and pottery shards have been located in Nyangtri (disc

1958/1975), and above all in Amdo, where the authorities of Qinghai and Gansu have supported a number of archaeological digs. Among them are the farming villages of Ma-chia-yao and Pan-shan in Cho-ne, respectively dated 3,000 BC and 2,500 BC; the village of Ma-ch'ang to the east of Lake Kokonor dated 2,000 BC; and the sites in the Sang-chu and Lu-chu valleys dated 1,850 BC. Evidence suggests that the yak became a domesticated animal around 2,500 BC and that there was an early interdependence of the hunting, nomadic and farming lifestyles.

Megaliths, generally dated 3,000-1,000 BC, have been discovered at Reting, Sakya, Shab **Megalithic sites** Geding, Zhide Khar, Chi'u near Lake Manasarovar, and Dangra Lake in the Jangtang. Sometimes these stones have an obvious formation: at Pang-gong Lake in Far-west Tibet there are 18 parallel rows of standing stones with circles at end of each row; while at Saga is a large grey stone slab surrounded by pillars of white quartz. Unusually shaped and coloured stones are found also in Kongpo, Powo, and Tsari.

Tibetan historians refer to either four or six distinct Tibetan clans, which claimed **The early** descent from the legendary monkey and ogress. The former comprise the Se clan, **Tibetan Clans** the Mu clan, the Dong clan, and the Tong clan (collectively known as the Ruchen Zhi). Sometimes, the Ba and Da clans are added to these. As the power of the 'non-human' rulers declined, the indigenous tribes took control of the land, eventually forming 12 kingdoms and 40 principalities. The 12 kingdoms were: Chimyul Drushul, Zhangzhung, Nyangdo Chongkar, Nubyul Lingu, Nyangro Shambo, Gyiri Jongdon, Ngamsho Tranar, Olphu Pangkhar, Simrong Lamogong, Kongyul Drena, Nyangyul Namsum, and Dakyul Druzhi. Only three of the 40 principalities are now known: Drokmo Namsum, Gyemo Yuldruk, and Semo Druzhi. These kingdoms and principalities are reckoned to have existed from the period before the first king of the Yarlung Dynasty (third/fourth BC), and some, notably Zhangzhung in Far-west Tibet, maintained their independence from around 3,000 BC (according to Bonpo sources) until their absorption by Songtsen Gampo in the seventh century.
    Some sources associate the four original clans with four important Tibetan cultures of antiquity: the Dong with that of Minyak (Far-east Tibet and Ningxia), the Tong with Sumpa (Jangtang), the Mu with Zhangzhung (Far-west Tibet), and the Se with Azha (Lake Kokonor). Among the aristocratic family names of Tibet, those of Lang, Gar, Khyungpo, and Khon are said to have been descendants of the Se clan. Illustrious descendants of this clan therefore include Amnye Jangchub Drekhol, who was the teacher of the epic warrior Ling Gesar, the ruling houses of Sakya and Phakmodru, Gar Tongtsen (the minister of Songtsen Gampo) and the Derge royal family, the great yogin Milarepa and Khungpo Neljor. By contrast, the Ba family, which assumed important military and civil positions during the period of the Yarlung Dynasty, claims descent from the Dong clan. Its members include Marpa, Phakmodrupa and Drigungpa who were all seminal figures in the development of the Kagyu school of Buddhism. The Kyura and Nyura families of Driigung and Mindroling respectively claim descent from the Tong clan, as do the Achakdru of Golok. Lastly, the ruling house of Zhangzhung in Far-west Tibet claimed descent from the Mu clan, as attested in important Bonpo historical works.

Chinese annals suggest that the Qiang or Ti tribes inhabiting the western periphery **Qiang Tribes** of the Chinese Empire were of Tibetan extraction. These tribes were established by 1,500 BC west of the Shang settlements near Chang-an (modern Xi'an), from where they would raid the farming communities. By 500 BC the Qiang were organizing themselves into agricultural and cattle-rearing societies, gradually developing into 150 sub-tribes, along the easternmost borderlands of the Tibetan plateau. They are said to have constituted a significant percentage of the region's population during the Zhou and Qin dynasties. Around the fifth century (CE) the Qiang tribe known as

Background

the Tang-hsiang (identified with the Dong clan) appear to have subdivided into western and northern groups, which Chinese sources identify respectively with the Tibetan (Ch T'u-fan) tribes (dominant from the seventh century) and the Tanguts (dominant in Xixia during the 11th century). Remnants of the Qiang tribes are found today around Maowen, and in those parts of East Tibet where the so-called Qiangic languages are spoken. Some sources suggest that it was an intermingling of Qiang tribes with the Yueh-chih and Hsiung-nu in the northeast (c 175-115 BC) which gave rise to the tall aqualine Tibetans of the northeast, who are distinct from the short Mongoloid type of western and southern origin.

The Yarlung Dynasty

The chronology of early Tibet is not easily determined with any degree of certainty. There are sources suggesting that by 781 BC the aforementioned primitive groups had been supplanted by the descendants of the four clans, and that until 247 BC the 12 kingdoms and 40 principalities formed by those clans held sway alone.

Seven Heavenly Kings called Tri The first king of the Yarlung Dynasty, Nyatri Tsenpo (1) is said to have had divine origin and to have been immortal – ascending to the heavens on a sky-cord (*mu*) at the appointed time for his passing. Other sources suggest an Indian origin for the royal family – the lord Rupati who fled North India during the Pandava wars, and who is said to derive from the mountain-dwelling Shakya clan, or the Licchavi clan of Nepal – connecting him with the family line of Shakyamuni Buddha. Descending on **Mount Lhari Yangto** in Kongpo, he proceeded to **Mount Lhari Rolpa** in Yarlung around 247 BC (the time of Ashoka) and thence to **Tsentang Gozhi** where he encountered the local Tibetan tribes who made him their king. Carried shoulder-high, he was bourne to the site of the **Yumbu Lagang** palace, which he himself had constructed. Utilizing magical weaponry and powers, Nyatri Tsenpo defeated the shaman Oyong Gyelwa of Sumpa and the ruler of Nub.

The first seven kings of this Yarlung Dynasty, circa 247-100 BC, including Nyatri Tsenpo himself, are known as the 'seven heavenly kings called Tri', in that they all passed away in the celestial manner, without the need for tombs. Nyatri's successors were: Mutri (2), Dingtri (3), Sotri (4), Mertri (5), Daktri (6), and Sibtri (7). Towards the end of this period, the Silk Road was opened to the north of Tibet.

Two Celestial Kings called Teng Sibtri's son, Drigum Tsenpo (8), is said to have fallen under the influence of the Iranian shaman Azha of Gurnavatra; who persuaded the king to adopt the fatalist line suggested by his own name 'sword-slain'. Deceived by his royal horse keeper Longam, the king accidentally cuts his own sky-cord in a contest of swordsmanship. Bereft of his divine powers the king is then killed by Longam's arrow, and thus has the dubious distinction of becoming the first mortal king of the Yarlung Dynasty. The king's three sons, Chatri, Nyatri and Shatri fled to the Powo area of Southeast Tibet, while the king's body was sent downstream to Kongpo in a copper casket, and Longam usurped the throne. Chatri later regained the throne in battle with Longam and adopted the name Pude Gungyel (9), after which he built the **Chingwa Taktse Castle** in Chongye.

Pude Gyungyel's ministers, including his own nephew Rulakye who had helped him regain the throne, are accredited with the introduction of charcoal, smelting, metalwork, bridge-building, and agriculture. The rituals of the Bonpo shamans of Zhangzhung also gained prominence during this period on account of their elaborate funerary rites. Henceforth, the mortal kings of Tibet would be buried in locations such as the **Chongye tombs**. Drigum Tsenpo and his son Pude Gungyel, collectively known as the 'two celestial kings called Teng', reigned approximately from 100 BC-50 BC, making them contemporaries of Han Wu Ti (140-85 BC).

The six 'earthly kings called Lek' like their predecessors mortal or otherwise, continued to marry into 'non-human' or rarified aristocratic lines only. Pude Gungyel's son Esho Lek (10) was the first in this line, followed by his son, Desho Lek (11), the latter's son Tisho Lek (12); and so on through Gongru Lek (13), Drongzher Lek (14), and Isho Lek (15). Their castles were all located in and around Chongye Taktse; and their tombs were located on adjacent rocky peaks or foothills. During this period (c 50 BC-100 CE) farm animals were domesticated, and irrigation and taxation developed.

Six Earthly Kings called Lek

The eight 'middle kings called De' (c 100-300 AD) are little known, apart from their burial sites at river banks. They were: Za Namzin De (16), De Trulnam Zhungtsen (17), Senolnam De (18), Senolpo De (19), De Nolnam (20), De Nolpo (21), De Gyelpo (22), and De Tringtsen (23). Tibetan trade prospered with the neighbouring Shu Han Dynasty (221-263 AD), which had its capital at Chengdu. Large trade marts were established in the Kokonor region, and Tibetan horses were highly valued.

Eight Middle Kings called De

The 'five linking kings called Tsen' are significant in that it was during their reigns (c 300-493 AD) that the kings of Tibet first married among their Tibetan subjects. The ancient title lha-se ('divine prince') was now replaced with the title tsenpo ('king'/'potentate'). The first in this line was Tore Longtsen (24); followed by Trhitsun Nam (25), Trhidra Pungtsen (26), Trhi Tokje Toktsen (27), and Lhatotori Nyentsen (28). The important ministers during this period hailed from the Tonmi, Nub and Gar clans, and the rich heritage of Tibetan folklore was established through the activities of the Bonpo priests known as Shen, the bards who narrated epic tales (*drung*), and singers of enigmatic riddles (*de'u*).

Five Linking Kings called Tsen

During the reign of the last of these kings, Lhatotori Nyentsen (374-493), Buddhism was introduced to Tibet. According to legend, in 433 certain Buddhist sutras including the *Karandavyuha* (dedicated to Tibet's patron deity Avalokiteshvara) landed on the palace roof at Yumbu Lagang, along with a mould engraving of the six-syllabled mantra of Avalokiteshvara and other sacred objects, but these were given the name '**awesome secret**' because no-one could understand their meaning. Lhatotori was rejuvenated and lived to the ripe old age of 120. His tomb is said to be at Dartang near the Chongye River, though others say he vanished into space.

More sober historians, such as Nelpa Pandita, assert that these texts were brought to Tibet by Buddharaksita and Tilise of Khotan. It appears from this and other sources, such as Fa-hien's records of Buddhism in Central Asia (dated 400 AD), that Lhatotori's discovery of Buddhism was predated by Buddhist contacts in East Tibet, where the Tibetan P'u (Fu) family formed the ruling house during the Earlier Chin Dynasty (351-394). Later, the seccasionist Later Chin Dynasty (384-417), also Tibetan, offered patronage to the renowned Buddhist scholar Kumarajiva, and its rulers were well acquainted with Buddhism.

Meantime, an administrator of the P'u family named Lu Kuang was sent to Xinjiang where he ruled over a mixed Tibetan and Turkic population (T'u yu-hun), and founded the Later Liang Dynasty (386-403) on the trade routes to the west.

The kings of this period were contemporaries of the Toba Wei emperors in China and the Gupta Empire in India.

The four immediate ancestors of the great religious kings of Tibet (493-630) were: Lhatotori's son Trhinyen Zung-tsen (29), Drong Nyendeu (30), Mulong or Takri Nyenzik (31), and Namri Songtsen (32). During these reigns the principal ministerial families were those of Shudpu, Nyen, Nyang, Be, and Tsepong. Lhatotori's son was the first king to be entombed in the **Dongkar** valley, east of Chongye. His consort gave birth to a blind son named Mulong, whose sight was subsequently restored by a Bonpo doctor from Azha. Taking the name Takri Nyenzik, the new king reoccupied the ancestral castle at Chingwa Taktse, and seized control of about half of the 12

Four Ancestors of the Religious Kings

Taming the Ogress: the geomantic temples of Tibet

When the Tang princess Wencheng arrived in Tibet, she introduced Chinese divination texts including the so-called Portang scrolls. According to the ancient Chinese model of government, spheres of influence were based on 6 concentric zones, namely: an imperial centre, a royal domain zone, a princes' domain, a pacification zone, a zone of allied barbarians, and a zone of cultureless savagery. The Tibetan geomantic temples were laid out according to 4 such zones, corresponding to the imperial centre, the royal domain zone, the pacification zone, and that of the allied barbarians. Just as China was conceived of as a supine turtle, so the Tibetan terrain was seen as a supine ogress or demoness, and geomantic temples were to be constructed at focal points on her body: the **Jokhang** temple at the heart, the 4 'district controlling' temples (**runon**) on her shoulders and hips, the 4 'border taming' temples (**tadul**) on her elbows and knees, and the 4 'further taming' temples (**yangdul**) on her hands and feet.

According to literary sources such as the Mani Kabum, Buton, Longdol Lama, and Drukpa Pekar, the 4 'district controlling' temples are: **Tradruk** (left shoulder), **Katsel** (right shoulder), **Yeru Tsangdram** (right hip), and **Rulak Drompagyang** (left hip). These same authors list the 4 'border taming' temples as: **Khomting** (left elbow), **Buchu** (right elbow), **Jang Traduntse** (near Saga, right knee); and **Mon Bumtang** (left knee); while the 4 further taming temples are listed as: **Jang Tsangpa Lungnon** (left hand), **Den Langtang Dronma** (right hand), **Mangyul Jamtrin** (right foot), and **Paro Kyerchu** (left foot).

Other authors such as Sakya Sonam Gyeltsen, Pawo Tsuklag and Dalai Lama V list the 'district controlling' temples as: **Langtang Dronma, Kyerchu, Tselrik Sherab Dronma**, and **Jang Tsangpa Lungnon**; the 4 'border taming' temples as: **Uru Katsel, Lhodrak Khomthing, Den Langtang Dronma**, and **Yeru Tsangtram**; and the 4 'further taming' temples as: **Lhodrak Khomting, Kongpo Buchu, Mangyul Jamtrin**, and **Jang Traduntse**. These are the central temples among the 108 reputedly built in this period throughout Tibet.

ancient kingdoms that constituted Tibet. Following his untimely death circa 560, the task of conquering Tri Pangsum, the usurper king of the **Kyi-chu** valley, fell to his son Namri Songtsen. The usurper was successfully expelled to the north and the newly acquired territory named **Phenyul**. Namri Songtsen established an important political network of aristocratic families. He promoted the horse and salt trade; and secured diplomatic relations with the Toba Wei Dynasty (386-534), with the Turkish Khanates established by the sons of Bumin Khagan in Mongolia and Dzungaria, and finally with the Sui Dynasty which reunified China in 589. Following the Sui Emperor's annihilation of the T'u yu-un (c 600), the Tibetans of the Yarlung Dynasty (known in Chinese as T'u-fan) expanded into North Tibet to fill the vacuum. In 630, the king was poisoned by discontented nobles.

The Tibetan Empire and the Nine Religious Kings It is not surprising that the unification of Tibet and its imperial expansion should have coincided with the adoption of Buddhism as the dominant civilizing influence in Tibetan life. This is the age of the nine great religious kings (630-836) and the most powerful political figures in the whole course of Tibetan history, namely: Songtsen Gampo (33), Gungsong Gungtsen (34), Mangsong Mangtsen (35), Dusong Mangpoje (36), Tride Tsukten or Me'agtsom (37), Trisong Detsen (38), Mune Tsepo (39); Tride Songtsen, also known as Mutik Tsenpo or Senalek Jinyon (40), and Tri Relpachen (41).

When Songtsen Gampo (617-650) acceded to the throne and conquered the far-western kingdom of Zhangzhung, he succeeded in unifying the whole of Tibet for the fist time in its recorded history. **Lhasa** became the capital of this grand empire, and the original **Potala Palace** was constructed as his foremost residence. In the course of establishing his empire, Songtsen Gampo came into contact with the Buddhist traditions of India, Khotan, and China, and quickly immersed himself in spiritual pursuits, reportedly under the influence of his foreign queens Bhrikuti, the daughter of Amshuvarman, king of Nepal; and Wencheng, daughter of Tang Tai-tsung, Emperor of China. These queens are said to have brought as their dowry the two foremost images of Buddha Shakyamuni – one in the form of Aksobhya,

Position of Geomantic Temples

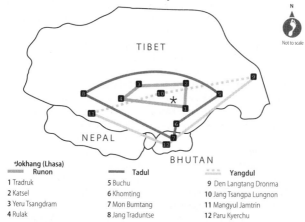

*Jokhang (Lhasa)			
Runon	**Tadul**		**Yangdul**
1 Tradruk	5 Buchu		9 Den Langtang Dronma
2 Katsel	6 Khomting		10 Jang Tsangpa Lungnon
3 Yeru Tsangdram	7 Mon Bumtang		11 Mangyul Jamtrin
4 Rulak	8 Jang Traduntse		12 Paru Kyerchu

Geomantic Temples of Tibet

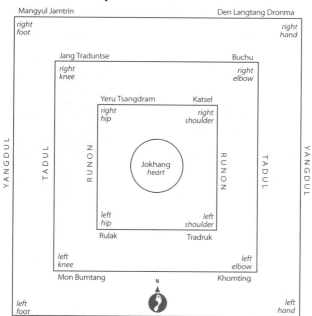

After M.Aris, Bhutan

which Bhrikuti introduced from Nepal and one in the bodhisattva form known as Jowo Rinpoche, which was introduced from China.

The king constructed a series of geomantic temples at important power-places across the length and breadth of the land, and these are revered as the earliest Buddhist temples of Tibet. He sent his able minister Tonmi Sambhota to India where the Uchen (capital letter) script was developed from an Indian prototype to represent the Tibetan language. In later years, the king abdicated in favour first of his son and later in favour of his grandson; passing his final years in spiritual retreat. His tomb is the celebrated **Banso Marpo** in the Chongye valley (although other traditions claim him to have been interred in the Jokhang).

The years immediately following Songtsen Gampo's unification of Tibet saw engagement in wide-ranging military campaigns. From 665-692 the Yarlung kings controlled the Central Asian oases and cities, and this Tibetan influence is reflected in the manuscripts and paintings preserved in the **Dunhuang** caves, which have been dated 650-747. Conflict with Tang China began in 670 and by 680 the Tibetan army had advanced as far southeast as the **Nan-chao** Kingdom (modern Dali in Yunnan province). King Tride Tsukten (b 704) constructed a number of Buddhist shrines, including the temple of **Kachu**, and extended his imperial influence westwards into **Brusha** (the Burushaski region of Gilgit) by 737.

In 730, Tride Tsukten's Chinese consort Jincheng gave birth to a son – Trisong Detsen, perhaps the greatest of all the Tibetan kings, in whose reign Buddhism was formally established as the state religion. In the early years of his reign Trisong Detsen sent his armies against Tang China, eventually occupying the imperial capital **Xi'an** in 763. The **Zhol pillar** was erected at Lhasa to commemorate this event. Increasingly, the king sought to promote Buddhism, and he invited the Indian preceptor Shantaraksita to found the country's first monastery at **Samye**. Owing to obstacles instigated by hostile non-Buddhist forces, the king accepted Shantaraksita's advice and invited Padmasambhava, the foremost exponent of the tantras and the Dzogchen meditative tradition in India to participate in the establishing of Buddhism. Padmasambhava bound the hostile demons of Tibet under an oath of allegiance to Buddhism, enabling the monastery's construction to be completed and the first monks to be ordained.

The king then instituted a methodical translation programme for the rendering of Sanskrit and Chinese Buddhist texts in Tibet. Intelligent children were sent to India to be trained as translators, and their prolific work ranks among the greatest literary endeavours of all time. Meanwhile Padmasambhava, Vimalamitra, and other accomplished masters of the Indian tantra traditions imparted their meditative instructions and lineages to the custodianship of their Tibetan disciples in remote but spectacularly located mountain caves, **Chimpu**, **Sheldrak**, **Kharchu**, **Drak Yangdzong**, **Monka Senge Dzong**, and so forth. In this way their Tibetan followers were brought to spiritual maturity and attained the highest realizations concerning the nature of mind and the nature of reality. Chinese Buddhist influence receded to some extent in the aftermath of the great debate held at Samye in 792 between Kamalasila of the Indian tradition and Hoshang Mo-ho-yen of the Chinese tradition.

The establishment of Buddhism as the state religion of Tibet, commemorated by an inscribed pillar at the entrance to Samye Monastery, was a threshold of enormous significance, in that the demilitarization of Tibet can be be traced back to that event. The great empire forged by the religious kings gradually began to recede. In 781, Dunhuang was lost, and following the king's death, conflict with China resumed.

His successors all acted as lavish patrons of Buddhism, sometimes at the expense of the older Bon tradition and the status of Tibet's ancient aristocratic families. This trend reached its zenith during the reign of Tri Relpachen (r 816-836), who had each monk supported by seven households of his subjects. Among Tri Relpachen's many achievements, the most important one politically is the peace treaty agreed with

China in 823; which clearly defined the Sino-Tibetan border at **Chorten Karpo** in the Sang-chu valley of Amdo. Obelisks were erected there and in Lhasa to commemorate this momentous event, the one in Lhasa surviving intact until today. The strong Buddhist sympathies of the king attracted an inevitable backlash on the past of disgruntled Bonpo and aristocratic groups. This resulted in his assassination at the hands of his elder brother, the apostate Langdarma Udumtsen; and with this act, the period of the great religious kings came to an abrupt end.

Persecution of Buddhism and disintegration of Empire

When Langdarma (42) came to power following the assassination of his brother, the Bonpo suddenly found themselves once more in the ascendancy. Old scores against the Buddhists were settled and a widespread persecution ensued. The monasteries and temples were desecrated or closed down and Buddhist practice was driven underground. Only practitioners of the tantras survived in Central Tibet, whether in their remote mountain retreats or by living their lives incognito in small village communities. The monastic tradition could only survive in the remote northeast of Amdo, where at **Dentik** and **Achung Namdzong**, three far-sighted monks transmitted the Vinaya lineage to Lachen Gongpa Rabsel, ensuring that the lineage of monastic ordination would continue unbroken for the benefit of posterity.

Langdarma's severe persecution of Buddhism was itself brought to an abrupt end in 841/2, when he was assassinated by the Buddhist master Lhalung Pelgyi Dorje, a black-hatted and black-clothed figure, who shot the apostate king with an arrow and fled in disguise, reversing his clothes to reveal their white lining! This act is commemorated in the famous black hat dance (*shanak*). Lhalung Pelgyi Dorje eventually reached the safety of **Achung Namdzong** in Amdo where he remained in penance for the rest of his life.

The succession to the throne was then disputed by Langdarma's two sons, Tride Yumten, the son of his senior consort, and Namde Osung, the son of his junior consort. Osung gained control of Lhasa while Yumten moved to Yarlung, and this event marked the beginning of the disintegration of the royal dynasty and the corresponding disintegration of Tibet's political unity (869). The line of 42 kings which began with Nyatri Tsenpo had come to an end, and Tibet was left without central authority for over 300 years.

The later diffusion of Buddhism

While anarchy prevailed in much of Central Tibet, the kingdoms of **Tsongkha** (c 900-1100) and **Xixia** (990-1227) maintained the Buddhist heritage in the remote northeast parts of Amdo and the adjacent province of Ningxia. Around 953 or 978 Lu-me and his fellow monks from Utsang brought the monastic ordination back from Amdo to Central Tibet, having received it from Lachen Gongpa Rabsel. They embarked upon an extensive temple building programme in the Kyi-chu and Brahmaputra valleys, which laid the basis for the later diffusion of Buddhism.

Further west, descendants of the royal family had effectively maintained the traditional royal sponsorship of Buddhism. The kingdom of **Gu-ge** had been established on trade routes with North and Northwest India along the canyons of the upper Sutlej River. One of the most important kings Lha Lama Yeshe-o and his nephew Lha Lama Jangchub-o were the patrons of both Rinchen Zangpo (958-1055), the great translator of the later diffusion, and Atisha (982-1054), the renowned Bengali Buddhist master. He reinforced the ethical discipline of the gradual path to enlightenment and its compassionate ideals, rather than the practices of the tantras, which apparently had been dangerously misapplied by some corrupt practitioners.

Background

During this period, Tibetan translators once again began travelling to India to study Sanskrit and receive teachings in the various aspects of the Indian Buddhist tradition. The texts which they brought back to Tibet were naturally those in vogue in 11th century India, in contrast to those previously introduced during the eighth century by Padmasambhava and his followers. Consequently a distinction was recognized between the 'old translations' of the early period and the 'new translations' of the later period. Among this new wave of translators were Rinchen Zangpo and Ngok Lotsawa who represented the **Kadampa** tradition (associated with Atisha), Drokmi Lotsawa (992-1074) who represented the **Sakyapa** tradition (of Gayadhara and Virupa), and Marpa Lotsawa (1012-97) who represented the **Kagyupa** tradition (of Tilopa and Naropa). By contrast the practitioners of the earlier teachings became known as the **Nyingmapa**, and among them, during this period was the outstanding translator Rongzom Pandita (11th century).

The foundation of large temples and monasteries soon followed: **Zhalu** in 1040, **Reting** in 1054; **Sakya** in 1073, **Ukpalung** in the 11th century, **Katok** in 1159, and the Kagyu monasteries of **Daklha Gampo, Kampo Nenang, Karma Gon, Tsurphu, Densatil, Drigung, Taklung,** and **Ralung** – all in the 12th century.

Sakyapa Administration (1235-1349)

A new sense of militancy was introduced into Tibetan life during the 13th century when, in common with most peoples of Asia, the Tibetans had to come to terms with the phenomenal rise to power of the Mongols who, unified by Genghiz Qan (r 1189-1227) swept across Asia, combining great horsemanship and mobility with astute strategy. In 1206 the Mongols reached Tibet, and suzerainty was offered to **Sakya**. In order to avoid the fate of Xixia, the Tangut Kingdom, which was annihilated in 1227, the Tibetans decided to accommodate themselves to Mongol aspirations by filling a unique role – that of spiritual advisors seeking imperial patronage. Consequently, after the Mongol general Dorta Nakpo had sacked **Reting** and other northern monasteries in 1240, Sakya Pandita (1182-1251) proceeded to **Lake Kokonor** in 1244 to meet Guyug and Godan, the son and grandson of Genghiz Qan, accompanied by his nephew, Drogon Chogyel Phakpa (1235-80). A 'patron-priest relationship' was established and Godan transferred the hegemony of Utsang to Sakya Pandita in 1249.

Later, in 1253, Prince Qubilai once again offered this hegemony to his new advisor, Drogon Chogyel Phakpa. Central Tibet (Utsang) was divided into four horns (*ru*) and 13 myriarchies (*trikhor*). Among these, the horn of **Uru** was centred at **Ramoche** in Lhasa with Olka Shukpa Pundun to the east, Mala Lagyu to the south, Zhu Nyemo to the west, and Drakyi Langma Gurpub to the north, including the myriarchies of Gyama, Drigung, and Shalpa. The horn of **Yoru** was centred at **Tradruk**, with Kongpo Drena in the east, Shawuk Tago in the south, Kharak Gangtse in the west, and Mala gyu in the north, including the myriarchies of Tangpoche, Pangpoche, Phakdru, and Yabzang. The horn of **Yeru** in Tsang was centred on **Namling** in Shang, with Drakyi Langma Gurpub in the east, Nyangang Yagpo'i Na in the south, Jemalagu in the west, and Smriti Chunak in the north, including the myriarchies of Chumik, Shang, and Zhalu. Lastly, the horn of **Rulak** was centred in **Drekyi Durwana**, with Jamnatra in the east, Belpo Langna in the south, Kem Yagmik in the west, and Jema Langon in the north, including the myriarchies of South Lhato, North Lhato, and Gurmo. Although the Mongols sought to govern Tibet and actually held a census there in 1268 and 1287, power remained effectively in the hands of the Sakyapas.

Drogon Chogyel Phakpa thus became the most powerful Tibetan ruler since the assassination of Tri Relpachen in 836. Although the tribal confederations and kingdoms of East Tibet maintained a degree of independence, the power of Sakya even extended deeply into Kham and Amdo. When Qubilai Qan subsequently invaded China and established the Yuan Dynasty (1260-1368), Phakpa was given the rank of Tishri, imperial preceptor, and remained in **Dadu**, the imperial capital of Qubilai Qan (Beijing), where he devised a script for the Mongolian language, based on the Tibetan script. Executive decisions on the ground were made by the Ponchen, or administrator, who was appointed to head the 13 myriarchies. Ponchen Shakya Zangpo (r 1265-68) and Ponchen Kunga Zangpo (r 1268-80) held this office during the lifetime of Phakpa; and following the latter's death in 1280, Dharmapala (r 1280-87) was appointed as imperial preceptor and Shang Tsun as Ponchen. Later, following the lifetime of the imperial preceptor Danyi Zangpo Pal (r 1305-22), the ruling house of Sakya split into four branches, two of which – the Phuntsok Palace and the Dolma Palace, took turns at holding supreme authority in Tibet. Actual power was however exercized by the successive Ponchen.

Nonetheless, some of the other Buddhist non-Sakya traditions inside Tibet did not accept this situation with ease: Emperor Mongke had been the patron of Karma Pakshi until his death in 1260; while the Drigungpa were backed by Hulegu of the Ilkhan Dynasty (1258-1335) – a brother of Qubilai Qan, who launched an abortive attack on Sakya in 1285. This resulted in the burning of **Drigung** and its sacred artefacts in 1290. Later, in 1350, during the reign of Sonam Gyeltsen and his Ponchen, Gawa Zangpo, power was usurped by one of the myriarchs, Tai Situ Jangchub Gyeltsen of Phakmodru. The power of the Sakyapa rulers rose and fell in proportion to the rise and fall in the power of the Mongol qans in China.

Phakmodrupa Administration (1350-1435)

The Tibetan nationalist movement which wrested power from the Mongol-backed Sakyapas in 1350 was headed by Jangchub Gyeltsen (r 1350-71), the myriarch of Phakmodru, and based at **Nedong** in South Tibet. On acquiring supreme power in Tibet, he and his successors assumed the title gongma ('king'). His power was belatedly recognized by the Mongol emperors, who additionally conferred the title Tai Situ upon him. Jangchub Gyeltsen reorganized the myriarchy system into a system of dzong or county fortresses, which persisted down to the present century. Local dzongpon officials, such as Rabten Kunzang Phak at Gyantse, came to hold considerable autonomy under this administration. During this period the rulers of Tibet firmly backed the Kagyupa school of Tibetan Buddhism, but it also coincided with the rise of the Gelukpa tradition. Jangchub Gyeltsen's successors were Sakya Gyeltsen (1372-84), Drakpa Jangchub (1385-90), Sonam Drakpa (1391-1408), Drakpa Gyeltsen (1409-34), Sangye Gyeltsen (1435-39), Drakpa Jungne (1440-68), Kunga Lekpa (1469-73), Rinchen Dorje (1474-1513), Chenga Ngagi Wangpo (1514-64), Ngawang Tashi Drakpa (1565-78), and Drowei Gonpo (1579-1617). The power of the later gongma was gradually eclipsed by the house of Ringpung in Tsang, until by 1478 the position had little more than nominal or titular significance.

Rinpung Administration (1478-1565)

The Rinpung princes first came to prominence during the reign of the Phakmodrupa king Drakpa Gyeltsen (r 1409-34), who appointed Namka Gyeltsen as lord of the **Rinpung** estates and governor of Sakya and Chumik. In 1435, his relation Rinpung Norbu Zangpo seized power from Phakmodru in West Tibet, gradually bringing to an end the influence of Nedong in that region. His son Donyo Dorje in 1478 finally inflicted a decisive defeat on the kings of Phakmodru; and he became the most powerful ruler in Tibet. He was a principal patron of the Zhamarpa branch of the Karma Kagyu school. The family's power was eventually eclipsed in 1565 by Zhingzhakpa Tseten Dorje of the Samdrubtse fiefdom at Zhigatse.

Background

Tsangpa Administration (1565-1642)

The princes of **Samdrubtse** (modern Zhigatse) became powerful patrons of the Karma Kagyu school, particularly following the foundation of the Zhamarpa's residence at Yangpachen. In 1565, the power of the Rinpungpas was usurped by Karma Tseten (Zhingshakpa Tseten Dorje) of the Nyak family. He made **Zhigatse** the capital of Tibet. In religious affairs, he adopted a sectarian posture, which favoured the Karma Kagyu school at the expense of others. When he persecuted the Northern Treasures (Jangter) community of the Nyingmapa school, he is said to have been ritually slain in 1599 by Jangdak Tashi Topgyel; but the son who succeeded him, Karma Tensung Wangpo, maintained the same policy. He forged an alliance with the Chogthu Mongols and captured Lhasa and Phenyul in 1605. On his death (1611), he was succeeded by his son, Karma Phuntsok Namgyel, who, in 1613, established a new 15-point legal system for Tibet. His imposing castle at Zhigatse is said to have been a prototype for the present Potala Palace at Lhasa.

In 1616 he forced Zhabdrung Ngawang Namgyel to flee **Ralung** Monastery for Bhutan, and following the latter's establishment there of a theocratic Drukpa state, the kings of Tsang engaged in a series of unsuccessful military campaigns against Bhutan. In 1618 he also established a Karma Kagyu Monastery, known as **Tashi Zilnon**, on the hill above Tashilhunpo, and once again sent Mongol armies against Lhasa.

Following his death in 1621, he was succeeded by his son, Karma Tenkyong Wangpo (1604-42). From 1635-42 much of Tibet was plunged into civil war, the power of the Tsangpa kings of Zhigatse and their Chogthu allies being challenged by the Gelukpas of Lhasa, who were backed by the powerful Mongol armies of Gushri Qan. Mongol forces sacked Zhigatse in 1635, and eventually occupied the city in 1642, slaying Karma Tenkyong. From this point on until the present Lhasa has functioned as the capital of Tibet.

Depa Zhung (1642-1959)

From the 13th century onwards, the hierarchies of a number of Buddhist schools – the Sakyapas, the Drigungpas, the Karmapas and later, the Gelukpas vied for political control of the country, relying upon the military power of Mongol princes, with whom they established a 'patron-priest relationship'. The most famous of these princes were Godan, Qubilai Qan, Altan Qan, Arsalang, and Gushri Qan. While these schools managed to gain control of the country in succeeding centuries and established their capitals at Sakya, Nedong, Zhigatse and Lhasa, none of them exercised temporal authority over the whole of the Tibetan plateau in the manner of the early kings. The remote kingdoms and tribal confederations of East Tibet, whether nomadic or settled, fiercely maintained their independence and permitted a high degree of eclecticism in religious expression. The willingness of Tibetan potentates to involve Mongol princes in Tibetan political life had serious consequences for the nation's integrity.

In 1639-41, during the prolonged civil war between Zhigatse and Lhasa with their partisan religious affiliations, the Qosot Mongols decisively intervened on the side of Lhasa, enabling Dalai Lama V to establish political power for the Gelukpa school.

Reconstruction of the **Potala Palace**, symbol of Songtsen Gampo's seventh century imperial power, was undertaken by Dalai Lama V and the regent Desi Sangye Gyatso; and this building once again became the outstanding symbol of the Tibetan national identity. The new Lhasa administration gradually extended its influence over many parts of East Tibet through the agency of Gushri Qan's Mongol armies, imposing a religious and political order which was often at variance with the local traditions. Kagyu monasteries suffered in particular, and many were converted to the Gelukpa school. Nonetheless, this was the first period since the early kings in which a strong national identity and political cohesion could develop. The Dalai Lama soon became an all-embracing national figurehead, representing not only the Gelukpa school but the aspirations of all the other traditions. As the embodiment of Avalokiteshvara, the patron bodhisattva of Tibet, his compassion permeated the land and provided a compassionate stabilizing influence in times of strife.

The predecessors of Dalai Lama V had been important figures for the early development of the Gelukpa school. Dalai Lama I (1391-1474) had been a close disciple of Tsongkhapa, founder of the Gelukpa school, and he himself had established **Tashilhunpo** monastery in Zhigatse in 1447. His mortal remains are interred in a stupa within that monastery. His successors were based at **Drepung** to the northwest of Lhasa, and the Ganden Palace of Drepung remained their private residence and political power base until the construction of the Potala. The stupas containing the embalmed remains of Dalai Lamas II, III and IV are housed at Drepung. Among them, Dalai Lama III Sonam Gyatso (1543-88) travelled to Mongolia where he became spiritual advisor to Altan Qan, king of the Mongols, and received the Mongol title Dalai Lama, 'ocean of wisdom'.

The Dalai Lamas of Tibet

Dalai Lama I	*Gendun Drupa (1391-1474)*
Dalai Lama II	*Gendun Gyatso (1475-1542)*
Dalai Lama III	*Sonam Gyatso (1543-1588)*
Dalai Lama IV	*Yonten Gyatso (1589-1616)*
Dalai Lama V	*Ngawang Lobzang Gyatso (1617-1682)*
Dalai Lama VI	*Tsangyang Gyatso (1683- ?)*
Dalai Lama VII	*Kalzang Gyatso (1708-1757)*
Dalai Lama VIII	*Jampal Gyatso (1758-1804)*
Dalai Lama IX	*Lungtok Gyatso (1805-1815)*
Dalai Lama X	*Tsultrim Gyatso (1816-1837)*
Dalai Lama XI	*Khedrub Gyatso (1838-1855)*
Dalai Lama XII	*Trinle Gyatso (1856-1875)*
Dalai Lama XIII	*Tubten Gyatso (1876-1933)*
Dalai Lama XIV	*Tendzin Gyatso (b 1934)*

Subsequently he was reborn as the grandson of Altan Qan. Dalai Lama IV Yonten Gyatso is therefore the only Dalai Lama to have been born a Mongol rather than a Tibetan. From that time onwards, the backing of the Mongol armies was secured, and victory over Zhigatse in the civil war guaranteed.

The regents of the Dalai Lamas and external intrigues

The succession of Dalai Lamas who ruled Tibet from the Potala Palace were assisted by powerful regents. During the time of Dalai Lama V, there were four regents: Sonam Rabten (1642-58), Trinle Gyatso (1660-68), Lobzang Tutob (1669-74), and Sangye Gyatso (1679-1705) – the last of whom was a prolific scholar in the fields of Tibetan medicine, astrology and history. He concealed the death of Dalai Lama V in 1682 in the interests of national stability, but was himself tragically killed by the Mongol prince Lhazang Qan who interfered to depose the libertine poet Dalai Lama VI in 1706. Lhazang was later slain by the invading Dzungarwa armies of the Mongol prince Sonam Rabten in 1717; and it was the turmoil caused by this invasion that prompted Kangxi, the Manchu emperor of China to become embroiled in Tibetan politics. Ostensibly supporting the Mongol faction of Lhazang Qan, which had abducted Dalai Lama VI and murdered the regent in Lhasa, and opposing that of the Dzungarwa, which had invaded Lhasa in response to that abduction, the Manchu armies effectively put an end to Mongol influence on Tibetan affairs.

In 1720, during the regency of Taktsewa (1717-20), the Manchus instated Dalai

Lama VII, who was in their custody. **Amdo** and **Nangchen** were annexed by the new **Kokonor territory** in 1724, and in 1727 the Manchus claimed much of Kham, east of the Yangtze as their own protectorate.

The next 150 years saw periodic intervention by the Manchus in the affairs of the Lhasa government, assisting it in its wars with Nepal and intriguing against it by ensuring that few Dalai Lamas ever reached the age of majority! This was the age when powerful regents and Manchu ambassadors (*amban*) held sway during the infancy and childhood of the Dalai Lamas. Some such as Miwang Sonam Topgyel (1728-47) were highly regarded for their political acumen and secular stance; while others connived against the young Dalai Lamas within their charge.

During the lifetime of Dalai Lama VII alone there were four important regents: Taktsewa (1717-20), Khangyel (1720-27), Miwang Sonam Topgyel (1728-47), and Gyurme Namgyel (1747-50). During the lifetime of Dalai Lama VIII, there were three main regents, Delek Gyatso (1757-77), Ngawang Tsultrim (1777-91) and Tenpei Gonpo (1791-1810). The next four Dalai Lamas all passed away prematurely before reaching the age of majority. During this period the following regents held sway: Jigme Gyatso (1811-19), Jampal Tsultrim (1819-44), Panchen Lama VII Tenpei Nyima (1844-45), Ngawang Yeshe Tsultrim (1845-62), Wangchuk Gyelpo (1862-64), and Khyenrab Wangchuk (1864-73). Despite those unilateral machinations of the Manchus which were designed to divide Tibet and weaken the rule of the Dalai Lamas, it is important to note that the Tibetans still controlled their own affairs and that apart from a diplomatic legation in Lhasa there was virtually no Chinese presence on the Tibetan plateau, even in those supposedly partitioned eastern regions.

This 19th century pattern of regency power continued for a while during the childhood of Dalai Lama XIII, when Tatshak Jedrung Ngawang Palden (1875-86) and Trinle Rabgye (1886-95) held power, but the Dalai Lama himself soon took control and gained respect, not only for his spiritual status, but as the first Dalai Lama since the Great Fifth to hold genuine political power. Later regents during his lifetime, such as Lobzang Gyeltsen (1906-09) and Tsemonling (1910-34) acted more as the instruments of his policy. However, from the late 19th century onwards, Sichuan warlords began to intervene and establish military garrisons in East Tibet, wary of the declining power of the Manchu Dynasty and of the enhanced power of Lhasa in the region.

Global political concerns had a dramatic impact upon Tibet during the reign of Dalai Lama XIII. The Younghusband expedition from British India in 1904 forced the Dalai Lama to flee to Mongolia; and precipitated a new Chinese 'forward policy' in Tibet. The warlords Chao Erh-feng and Liu Wen-hui in their aggressive campaigns of 1909-18 and 1928-33 respectively attacked East Tibet, seeking to carve out a new Chinese province which they would call Xikang (West Kham). The Dalai Lama again fled into exile, this time to Calcutta (1910) and the ill-equipped Tibetan forces bitterly resisted the invaders. In 1912-13 all Chinese were expelled from Lhasa and the Dalai Lama XIII began a period of internal reform and external independence from China. However, he was unable to change the deeply ingrained conservatism and xenophobia of the monastic and aristocratic hierarchy. Despite his warnings of what might befall the Tibetan nation if they did not heed his prophesies and change accordingly Tibet continued in blind isolation from the world forces swirling about it. The 13th Dalai Lama died in 1933.

During the infancy and childhood of HH Dalai Lama XIV (b 1934), political events were in the hands of the regents Reting (1934-40), Takdra (1941-51), and Lukhangwa Tsewang Rabten (1951/2).

Chinese Administration (1951-)

The conflict between the Tibetan forces and the Chinese Communists under Mao Zedong and the warlords in East Tibet resumed after the First World War, resulting in

Early Western contacts with Tibet

1603	Portuguese merchant d'Almeida in Ladakh
1624-32	Jesuit missionaries d'Andrade, Cabral and Cacella in Gu-ge and Tsang
1661	Missionaries Grueber and d'Orville visit Lhasa from China
1707-45	Capuchins in Lhasa; d'Ascoli and de Toursdella Penna and da Fano compile Tibetan dictionary
1715-17	Jesuit cartographers survey Tibet
1716-33	Jesuit Desideri in Lhasa
1774-75	George Bogel of British East India Co visits Zhigatse
1783-92	Samuel Turner's trade mission from British India
1811	Thomas Manning visits Lhasa
1823	Csoma de Koros in Zangskar
1846	Lazarist fathers Huc and Gabet visit Lhasa from Amdo
1879-80	Przevalski visits Amdo, Kham, and Tsaidam
1885-86	Carey from British India visits Tsaidam and Dunhuang
1889-90	Bonvalot visits Amdo and Kham via Lop Nor
1890	De Rhins and Grenard travel to Namtso
1895	Sven Hedin in Jangtang
1896	Wellby and Malcolm travel to Kokonor and Kunluns and thence to Kashmir
1900-1906	Hedin in West Tibet
1900	Koslov in Kokonor, Tsaidam and South Amdo
1904	Francis Younghusband leads a British military force to Lhasa
1906-7	Stein and Pelliot in Dunhuang
1906-48	British Trade Mission in Gyantse and Lhasa

the invasion of Tibet by the communist forces from 1951, and culminating in the forceful seizure of the country by the People's Liberation Army. The Tibetan government in Lhasa was obliged to sign a 17-point agreement in 1951, outlining the policies for the 'peaceful integration of Tibet' into the 'motherland'. In 1959 an apparent attempt to kidnap the Dalai Lama by Communist generals in Lhasa resulted in a spontaneous revolt by the Tibetan people against the Chinese invaders. The Chinese People's Liberation Army ruthlessly suppressed the Lhasa uprising, resulting in the exodus of over 100,000 refugees to India, Nepal and Bhutan.

In 1965, those parts of the country under direct control of Lhasa were proclaimed an Autonomous Region of China, known as the Tibetan Autonomous Region (TAR), while East Tibet had already been divided between four other provinces – Qinghai, Gansu, Sichuan, and Yunnan. During the dark years of suppression and the insanity of the Cultural Revolution and its aftermath (1966-77) which followed the communist invasion systematic attempts were made to obliterate Tibetan culture. Thousands of monasteries were destroyed, along with their precious artefacts and vast libraries of great literary works. Some sources suggest that as many as one million Tibetans died in consequence of these events, whether directly through war and persecution, or indirectly through famine and material hardships. Accusations of genocide against the People's Republic of China were upheld by the International Commission of Jurists at The Hague.

Yet Tibetans, both inside and outside Tibet, never lost their strong sense of national identity, and at every opportunity they have striven to preserve and restore their precious culture. Under the guidance of the Dalai Lama in India a Tibetan Government-in-exile has been established, and developed broadly upon democratic principles. Moreover the main centres of Buddhist learning have been

Background

re-established in refugee settlements in Nepal and India and many of the great Buddhist masters of Tibet who followed the Dalai Lama into exile have established worldwide communities of Buddhist practitioners, holding allegiance to one or another of the schools of Tibetan Buddhism.

The influence of HH Dalai Lama XIV as an international statesman and Nobel Peace Prize holder of the Gandhian persuasion is widely acclaimed. Meanwhile, until a genuine political solution to the problems engendered by occupation can be found and the rulers of China are willing to engage in a dialogue with the Dalai Lama or his representatives, the signs of internal dissension and discontent within the country known to the world at large as 'Tibet' will remain as great as ever.

Tibetan Government in exile

In the aftermath of the suppression of the Lhasa Uprising in 1959, HH Dalai Lama XIV fled into exile, followed by some 80,000 Tibetan refugees, who sought sanctuary in India, Nepal, Bhutan and Sikkim. By 1970 there were some 100,000 Tibetan refugees dispersed throughout 45 settlements – extending from North India through Madhya Pradesh and Orissa, to Karnataka in the south. The Dalai Lama first settled in Mussoorie, but soon moved to Dharamsala, where the Government-in-exile was established.

In exile the Tibetan Government was reorganized according to modern democratic principles. Elections were called in 1960 for the establishment of a new body known as the Commission of People's Deputies; and in 1963 a draft Constitution of Tibet was promulgated, combining the aspirations of Buddhism with the needs of modern government. This constitution was eventually published in Tibetan in 1991; and awaits the final approval of the Tibetan people.

The Government-in-exile administers all matters pertaining to Tibetans in exile, including the re-establishment, preservation and development of Tibetan culture and education, and, internationally, it leads the struggle for the restoration of Tibet's freedom. The Tibetan community in exile functions in accordance with the Charter for Tibetans in exile and is administered by the Kashag (Council of Ministers), which is accountable to the Assembly of Tibetan People's Deputies (a democratically elected parliament). The Tibetan Supreme Justice Commission is an independent judiciary body.

The Central Tibetan Administration (CTA) is comprised of three autonomous commissions – Election, Public Service and Audit, seven departments – Religion & Culture, Home Affairs, Education, Information and International Relations, Security, Health, and one council for planning.

The CTA mainly through the assistance of the Government of India and various international voluntary organizations, has successfully rehabilitated Tibetan refugees in 14 major and eight minor agricultural centres, 21 agro-industrial settlements and 10 handicraft centres throughout India and Nepal. There are also 83 Tibetan schools in India, Nepal, and Bhutan, with an approximate 23,000 children currently enrolled.

More than 117 monasteries have been re-established in exile; also a number of institutions including the Tibetan Medical and Astrological Institute; the Library of Tibetan Works and Archives, the Tibetan Institute of Performing Arts, the Centre for Tibetan Arts and Crafts – all based in Dharamsala, the Central Institute for Higher Tibetan Studies in Sarnath, and Tibet House in New Delhi. These institutions help to preserve and promote the ancient Tibetan heritage and culture, whilst enhancing the cultural life of the exiled community.

The CTA also maintains Offices of Tibet in New Delhi, New York, Zurich, Tokyo, London, Kathmandu, Geneva, Moscow, Budapest, Paris, Canberra, Washington DC, and Taipei. These Offices of Tibet are the official agencies representing the HH Dalai Lama and the Tibetan Government-in-exile.

Land and environment

Geology and landscape

The area covered by the Tibetan plateau and the adjacent Sino-Tibetan border ranges (latitude: 39-27°N; longitude: 78-104°E), which are sometimes poetically referred to as the 'roof of the world' or the 'third pole', forms an enormous land-locked region in Central Asia, 2,300,000 square kilometres in area. It encompasses Tibet (including the eastern provinces of Kham and Amdo) which is the cultural heartland of Inner Asia, and the countries to its south, Bhutan and the Kathmandu Valley of Nepal, where the cultures of the Tibetan world and the Indian subcontinent converge. The Tibetan plateau is an immense region (as large as Western Europe); and has considerable importance within the biosphere as the highest region on the planet and the source of virtually all the important waterways of South and East Asia.

Location

The indigenous name given to this region is **Bod** or **Bod-Kham**; the English equivalent (Tibet) being derived from the Mongolian *Thubet*, the Chinese *Tufan*, and the Arabic *Tubbat*.

Yet, the plateau includes, in addition to Tibet, the peripheral mountain areas to the south, which are defined by the Karakorum and Himalayan ranges: Gilgit and Baltistan (now in Pakistan); Ladakh, Lahoul, Spiti, Kinnaur, Tehri-Garwal, Kumaon, Sikkim, and Arunachal (now in India); Manang, Dolpo, Mustang, Langtang, Helambu, and Khumbhu (now in Nepal); and the mountainous areas of Bhutan. The formidable terrain and its communication difficulties have ensured that the plateau has rarely been politically united in the course of its history. The defining characteristics of the region are made, rather, on the basis of topography, ethnicity, language, and religion, which together form the distinct Tibetan cultural millieu.

Traditionally, Tibet has been divided into three provinces (*Tib* cholkha sum), namely: **Utsang** (extending from Ngari Korsum in Far-western Tibet as far as Sokla Kyawo in the upper reaches of the Salween); **Kham** (extending eastwards from Sokla Kyawo to the watershed of the Yellow and Yangtze basins); and **Amdo** (extending eastwards and north-eastwards from the source of the Yellow River and the Sertal region to Chorten Karpo on the Sang-chu tributary of the Yellow River).

Provinces & terrain

Currently, the plateau is administratively divided between the **Tibetan Autonomous Region** (1,106,780 square kilometres) of China, and four other Chinese provinces – Qinghai, Gansu, Sichuan, and Yunnan. Of these latter provinces, the plateau incorporates virtually the entire land-mass of **Qinghai** (676,851 square kilometres, excluding Ziling district), the **Ganlho Autonomous Prefecture** and **Pari (Tianzhu) Autonomous County** (44,323 square kilometres) of Gansu province, the **Kandze** and **Ngawa Autonomous Prefectures** of West Sichuan (240,154 square kilometres), and the **Dechen Autonomous Prefecture** of Northeast Yunnan (20,562 square kilometres). The region is bordered on the west by India, on the north and northwest by Xinjiang (Chinese Turkestan), on the

Background

northeast, east and southeast by mainland China, and on the south by India, Nepal, Bhutan and Burma.

NB   Many of the bordering regions of these neighbouring countries, ie Baltistan, Gilgit, Ladakh, Zangskar, Lahoul, Spiti, Kinnaur, northern Nepal, Sikkim, Bhutan and Arunachal Pradesh, have at one time or another been considered Tibetan territory and their cultures, languages, and ethnic composition are still predominantly Tibetan. Taken as a whole, Tibet occupies about one fourth of China's territory.

Terrain   The Tibetan plateau covers an area as large as Western Europe, or seven times the size of France, with an elevation ranging from the low-lying southern gorges at 1,700 metres to the massive 8,000 metres Himalayan peaks. The country can conveniently be divided into four distinct geographical regions – the Northern lakeland plateau (**Jangtang**) which is sparsely populated by nomadic herdsmen, the dry far-western highlands (**Ngari**) which are the source of the Indus, Sutlej and Brahmaputra rivers, the urbanized central valleys of Lhasa and Zhigatse (**Utsang**) which form the Brahmaputra River system, and the most fertile and populated eastern region (**Kham and Amdo**), which is characterized by the deep river gorges of the Salween, Mekong, Yangtze, Yalong, and Gyarong and by the high rolling pastures around the upper reaches of these rivers, as well as around the upper reaches of the Yellow River, Minjiang and Jialing.

Origins of Tibet's landscape   Most of the Tibetan plateau is considered to have formed the bed of the **Neo-tethys Ocean**, which was destroyed some 210-50 million years ago as the Indian sub-continental plate moved to throw up the mountains of the Himalayan region. This however is a comparatively recent geological event, and it is predated in the peripheral north and east areas of the plateau, where the oldest rocks are Precambrian granite, known to be about one billion years old. Unfortunately, the geological correlations of these earlier strata have been complicated by subsequent neotectonic development.

During the **Palaeozoic** era (570-245 million years ago) the **Kunlun ranges** of Tibet's northern frontier, which are largely composed of Cambrian and Triassic granites, granodiorites, and andesites, began accumulating along the southern margin of the Tarim Basin. This developing mountain range continued westwards into the Pamirs and the Hindu Kush. Then, during the **Mesozoic** era (245-66.4 million years ago), the **Jangtang** plain of North Tibet became separated from the South Tibet block by an ocean; evidence of this can be found in the Dangla mountains of North Tibet. Further movement involving the breakup of the southern supercontinent 'Pangaea' produced the granite **Gangtise**, **Nyenchen Tanglha**, and **Karakorum ranges** (180-100 million years ago).

The process continued until, during the **Cenozoic** period (66.4 million years ago – onwards), the Tibetan plateau was finally formed. The all-important collision of the drifting Indian subcontinent with Eurasia is considered to have taken place some 2,012 kilometres south of the Indus-Brahmaputra watershed on the northern side of the Inner Himalayan range. Since then some 805 kilometres of this horizontal movement of the continental crust northwards have been contracted to form the Himalayas – the world's highest mountain range and the largest concentration of continental crust on earth (69 kilometres thick in places). Further south, the collision created the Gangetic basin. The massive plateau, subject to widespread volcanicity, continues to extend upwards and outwards under its own weight, as the Indian sub-continental plate moves ever northwards at a speed of about 6.1 centimetres per year.

Geological history of the Tibetan Plateau

Precambrian

4,000-2,500 mya (million years ago): oldest stable continental rock.
660 mya: oldest Tibetan rock

Palaeozoic

500 mya: Gondwanaland included India and South Tibet.
Earliest South Tibetan fossils (1979) suggest latitude of modern Australia.
400/300 mya: Pangaea (4th) supercontinent forms; and Old Thethys Sea contracts.
300 mya: formation of Kunlun, Pamir, and Altyn Tagh ranges.

Mezozoic

200 mya: fusion of Jangtang plain and Indochina with Asia, along two connection zones of the Salween and Yangtze respectively. Consequent rising of plateau from seabed.

140 mya: India separates from Africa.
100 mya: tectonic pressure raises Kangtise and Nyenchen Thangla ranges.

Cenozoic

45 mya: Himalayas begin to form as India fully collides with Asia, subducting the Neo-Tethys sea.
20 mya: older Himalayan rock thrust upward through younger strata over 2,000 km central fault.
15-10 mya: Himalayas at 3,000 metres; plateau at 1,000 metres.
2 mya: rapid uplift of plateau and Himalayas along main boundary fault.

Pleistocene Epoch

1 mya: Himalayas at 4,500 metres; plateau at 3,000 metres.
10,000 ya: Himalayas at 6,000 metres; plateau at 4,700 metres.

The entire region is subject to intense geological activity. Satellite photos reveal widespread thrust fault zones throughout the plateau; deep fault zones in the Himalayas, the Jangtang lakeland plain, and the river gorges of East Tibet; as well as strike-slip fault zones in the Kunlun and Altyn Tagh ranges, and in the Yalong, Yangtze, and Yellow River valleys. From 1870-1999 over 50 major earthquakes (measuring over six on the Richter scale) have occurred along these fault lines.

Earthquake & geothermal activity

Over the plateau as a whole, there are more than 600 geothermal areas including hot springs, geysers and hydrothermal explosions. The majority of these are found in the region between the southern Himalayan watershed and the northern Gangtise/Nyenchen Tanglha watersheds.

Mountain ranges

Two principal mountain belts extend eastwards in a pincer-like manner from the **Pamir knot**. To the north, the ranges stretch through the **Kunluns** to the **Altyn Tagh** and **Chole Namgyel** mountains. In the south, they extend through the **Karakorums** and **Himalayas**, and thence southeast to the **Arakan** mountains of Burma. These frontier mountain ranges are imposingly high, with individual peaks rising above 7,000-8,000 metres. They have gentle interior slopes and rugged precipitous exterior slopes. This has ensured the geographic isolation of the region and its unique landscape complexes. The **plateau** extending between these two formidable mountain barriers is located between 3,990-5,000 metres above sea level; and its surface is a complex combination of ranges and plains, generally tilting from northwest to southeast. The permanent snow-line averages 4,510-5,000 metres; and may reach 6,400 metres in Central Tibet.

The Karakorum mountains (*Ch* Kala Kunlun Shan) extend southeast from the borders of **Afghanistan** for 800 kilometres as far as the **Pang-gong** Tibet range and **Chang Chenmo Ladakh** ranges. Approximately 240 kilometres wide, and characterized by craggy peaks with steep slopes and ravine-like transverse valleys,

Karakorum mountains

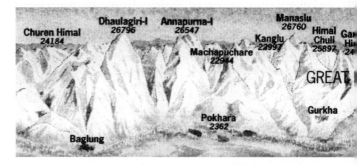

the Karakorums form a watershed between the **Indus River** to the south and the **Tarim basin** in the north. The average elevation is 6,100 metres, and there are four peaks which rise above 7,925 metres, the highest being **K2 (Dapsang)** at 8,611 metres.

The Karakorum glaciers, along with those of the Himalayas, are renowned for their immensity.

Himalayan mountains   The world's highest mountain range, which comprises 110 peaks above 7,300 metres, and more than 10 above 8,000 metres, the highest being **Mount Everest** (8,848 metres; 29,029 feet), extends 2,450 kilometres from **Mount Nanga Parbat** (8,126 metres) in the extreme west to **Mount Namchak Barwa** (7,756 metres) in the extreme east. From south to north the range covers an area of 200-400 kilometres; and the total area is 594,400 square kilometres.

The range is a drainage area for 19 major rivers, the greatest of which – the **Indus**, **Sutlej**, **Karnali**, and **Brahmaputra**, rise north of the Himalayan range and are fed by some of the world's highest glaciers (eg the 32 kilometres long Gangotri glacier and the Kumbhu glacier of Nepal). They flow through deep gorges between 1,524-4,877 metres deep and 10-48 kilometres wide.

Kunlun mountains   The **Kunlun** mountains forming Tibet's northern frontier extend 2,000 kilometres from the **Pamirs** in the west to the **Bayankala** and **Amnye Machen** mountains in the east. The range rarely exceeds 200 kilometres in its width. The southern slopes, which rise only 1,500 metres above the plateau, are contrasted with the steep northern slopes, which form a massive rampart as they are approached from the Tarim basin and its low-lying oases of **Khotan, Keriya** and **Qarqan**, only 900-1,500 metres above sea level.

The highest peaks are located in the West Kunluns, eg **Mount Muztagh** (7,723 metres), **Mount Keriya** (7,120 metres), **Mount Kongur** (7,719 metres), and **Mount Muztagh Ata** (7,546 metres). The Central and East Kunluns are lower, including the parallel ranges of the Kukushili (some peaks above 6,300 metres) and the Bayankala, characterized by their flat dome-shaped peaks and gently broken slopes. The region has long been subject to erosion, causing large sand dunes, and producing steppe and desert soils with low organic content. The high degree of evaporation has produced frequent saline depressions and largely undeveloped river systems.

Main features of the plateau

Hemmed in by those formidable mountain barriers, in the western part of the plateau, high plains predominate; while in the eastern part, there is a predominance of ranges and deep gorges.

In the northwest lie the **Northern Plateau (Jangtang)** and the **Tsaidam basin**. Both are hemmed in by mountain ranges with individual peaks which rise above

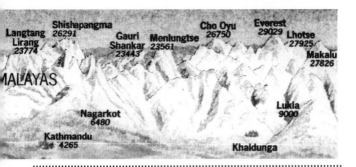

Himalaya: highest peak in the world

The main Himalayan range, known as the Inner or Great Himalayas, is paralleled to the south by two minor latitudinal ranges, the southernmost being the sub-Himalayan or Outer Himalayan range of the Shiwaliks (274-760 metres); followed by the Lesser Himalayas (4,572 metres, valleys at 914 metres) of Kashmir and Central Nepal. The Great Himalayas comprise nine of the 14 highest peaks in the world. The most prominent peaks are (from west to east): Nanga Parbat in Azad Kashmir (8,126 metres), Gangotri (6,726 metres), Kamet (7,756 metres), and Nanda Devi (7,817 metres) all in Northwest India, Nemo Nanyi (Gurla Mandhata, 7,728 metres) in Far-west Tibet, Dhaulagiri (8,172 metres), Annapurna (8,078 metres), Manaslu (8,160 metres), and Himal Chuli (7,898 metres), all in West Nepal; Ganesh Himal (7,411 metres), Langtang (7,250 metres), and Shishapangma (Gosainathan, 8,012 metres) all bordering Central Nepal and West Tibet; Jowo Tseringma (Gauri Shangkar, 7,148 metres), Jowo Guru (Menlungtse, 7,181 metres), Jowo Oyuk (8,153 metres), Jomolangma (Everest, 8,848 metres), Lhotse (8,501 metres), and Makalu (8,463 metres), all bordering East Nepal and West Tibet; Kangchendzonga (8,598 metres), Jomolhari (7,313 metres), and Kulha Kangri (7,554 metres) all of which border Sikkim or Bhutan and South Tibet; and finally Phulahari (7,410 metres) and Namchak Barwa (7,756 metres), which divide Arunachal Pradesh from South Tibet.

6,000 metres but, in general, their soft and smooth outlines tend not to dominate the surrounding landscape.

By contrast, the eastern sandstone ranges are deeply eroded, so that they have come to dominate the surrounding landscape. Such are: the eastern extremity of the **Nyenchen Tanglha** range dividing the Brahmaputra from the Salween River; the **Gaoligong Mountains** on the Burmese border, dividing the Irrawaddy from the Salween; the **Tshawagang** uplands and **Kawa Karpo** range (*Ch* Taniantaweng, Hengduan and Nushan), dividing the Salween from the Mekong River; the **Markhamgang** uplands (*Ch* Ningjing and Yunling), dividing the Mekong from the Yangtze; the **Drida Zelmogang** and **Puburgang** uplands including the Tro La (*Ch* Cholashan) and **Kawalungring** (*Ch* Shaluli) ranges, which divide the Yangtze from the Yalong River; the **Minyak Rabgang** uplands (*Ch* Daxue) dividing the Yalong from the Gyarong; the **Mardzagang** uplands along with the **Bayankala** and **Amnye Machen** ranges, dividing the Yangtze, Yalong, and Gyarong from the Yellow River and the **Minshan** range at the eastern extremity of the plateau, which divides the Yellow River from the upper Yangtze tributaries – the Minjiang and Jialing.

The far-western and northern highland regions are largely covered with detrital

Soil

desert; while the deeply cut mountain ranges of the frontiers and east are subject in places to extensive glaciation, or dissected by severe erosion. The **high-altitude plateau** in the Far-west and north, sustains soils which are either weakly developed embryonic soils of detritus and stony fragments, varying from light brown to grey in colour according to the humus content; or sandy soil subject to aeolian wind-relief, thus forming a thin surface layer above gravel or shingle. Here, the vegetation is extremely sparse, and the amount of humus reduced, increasing the content of unbleached mineral salts, and intensifying the upward flow of salt solutions to the surface.

In the south, the upper reaches of the **Indus** and **Brahmaputra** River valleys lie in a deep marginal depression running parallel to the frontier Himalayan range. This is a region of immature subsidence in which thick accumulations of earlier marine sediments and later continental deposits washed down from the mountains have been transformed into sandy deserts flanked by lateral valleys of alluvial deposits, enabling specialized agriculture to flourish in sheltered lower elevations.

South of this river system, the **Himalayas** have the most complex variety of vegetation and soil types. On a vertical axis, low-lying forested areas or desert steppe (ie mountain chestnut soils and mountain chernozems) give way to alpine meadow or mountain tundra, and thence to detritus, snow and glaciation. Soil tends to be thicker on the north-facing slopes, which support dense forests at lower altitudes and grasslands at higher altitudes. Predominant is the alluvial soil associated with mountain tundra, which has been deposited by the gorge rivers onto the **Gangetic** plain of India.

Further east and northeast the erosion processes have exposed the sandstone rocks, producing the alluvial soils of the **Mekong** and **Yangtze** gorges, the bleached podzolic grey-brown soils of the mountain slopes, the dark-coloured chernozem soils of the **Amdo** grasslands with their deep rich humus, and the thick loess deposits of the ranges around the upper reaches of the **Yellow** River. Among these the alluvial soils and chernozems, like those of the **Gangetic** plain, are more fertile than the deficient lithosols of the west and north. Generally, the major threat to agriculture in the region is the increasing salinization of the soil and the increasing erosion of the Indo-Tibetan and Sino-Tibetan rivers, as the plateau continues to be pushed upwards by tectonic movement.

Minerals Geological surveys suggest that the Tibetan plateau is extremely rich in its accumulation of ores within the folded zone – from the **Karakorums** in the Far-west through the **Himalayas** to the **Kawa Karpo** ranges – due to intrusions of granites and igneous rock. Such deposits include ores of copper, iron, lead and zinc, as well as antimony, arsenic, molybdenum, borax, sulphur, coal, bauxite, mica, gypsum, and sapphire. Throughout the plateau, many alluvial and vein deposits of gold are to be found.

Around **Lhasa** there is hard coal and alabaster; while magnetite is common in the eastern **Brahmaputra** valley.

Further north, in the **Dangla** range, iron ore, hard coal, graphite, asbestos, and soapstone have been discovered.

The **Northern Plateau/Jangtang** lakelands have an unlimited reserve of salts: borax, gypsum, common salt, quartz, and soda.

The **Chole Namgyel** mountains on the extreme northeast frontier of the plateau contain iron, chromium, copper, lead, zinc, gold, and coal from the Carboniferous and Jurassic ages.

The **Tsaidam** depression is known for its Jurassic coal and oil, which are deposited within Lower Tertiary sandstone.

Rivers The land-locked Tibetan plateau is the primary source of the water supply for most of Central, East and South Asia. **Internal drainage** is rare, being almost invariably confined to the short rivers and saline lakes of the Northern Plateau (Jangtang) and the Lake Kokonor region of the northeast.

Those rivers originating in Tibet which drain into the **Pacific Ocean** include the **Yellow** River (*Tib* Machu; *Ch* Huang Ho), the **Yangtze** (*Tib* Drichu; *Ch* Jinsha), and the **Mekong** (*Tib* Dachu; *Ch* Lancang); along with important tributaries of the **Yangtze**, namely the **Yalong** (*Tib* Dzachu/Nyachu), **Gyarong** (*Ch* Dadu), **Min** (*Tib* Zungchu), and **Jialing**.

Those rivers which drain into the **Indian Ocean** are the **Salween** (*Tib* Gyelmo Ngulchu; *Ch* Nujiang), **Irrawaddy** (*Burmese* Nmai Hka), **Brahmaputra** (*Tib* Tsangpo; *Ch* Zangbo), **Sutlej** (*Tib* Langchen Tsangpo), **Indus** (*Tib* Senge Tsangpo), and certain **Gangetic feeder rivers** including the **Karnali** (*Tib* Mabcha Tsangpo), **Trishuli** (*Tib* Kyirong Tsangpo), **Sunkosi** (*Tib* Matsang Tsangpo), and **Arun** (*Tib* Bum-chu).

Other tributaries of the Ganges and Brahmaputra have their sources further south in Nepal and Bhutan. Among these, important **Gangetic tributaries** include the Chamlia, Seti, Bheti, and Kali-Gandaki, while those of the **Brahmaputra** include the Wang-chu, the Puna Tsang-chu, the Mangde-chu and the Bumtang-chu.

Lakes

Many inland lakes have been formed on the plateau by the filling of geological basins, from volcanic debris, silting, and glacial retreat. Dehydration, however, suggests that the lakes of the Northern Plateau (Jangtang) south of the Kunlun range were once part of the Yangtze, and the lakes from Pang-gong Lake eastwards once part of the Salween. Some smaller lakes were once connected to larger lakes (eg Rakshas to Manasarovar, and Zigetang to Serling). The process of salination is more prominant in the northern lakes; the deep blue colour being due to paucity of silt and the intense sunlight. In general, the lakes of the plateau are important sources of minerals: mirabilite, gypsum, borax, magnesium, potassium, lithium, strontium, uranium and so forth. Among the largest are: **Kokonor** (97 kilometres across), **Ngoring** and **Kyaring** (40 kilometres across), **Namtso** and **Serling** (81 kilometres across), **Dangra** (64 kilometres long), **Yamdrok** (64 kilometres across), **Manasarovar** (24 kilometres across and 73 metres deep), **Rakshas** (24 kilometres long), and **Pang-gong** (48 kilometres by 113 kilometres).

Climate

The climate of the plateau, conditioned by the terrain, is generally severe, dry, and continental, with strong winds, low humidity, a rarified atmosphere, and a great fluctuation in the annual and summer daytime temperatures. The region is exposed to an unimpeded access of arctic air from the north; while the southern tropical and equatorial air masses barely penetrate the Himalayan barrier into Central Asia. The contrast between the strong heating of the land in summer months and the chilling in winter produces sharp seasonal variations in atmospheric circulation and enhances the role of local centres of atmospheric activity.

In winter, the polar continental air mass originating in Siberia dominates East and Central Asia, forming a persistent high-pressure anticyclone over Tibet. Cold dry air therefore moves eastward and southward out of the continent during the winter; and the plateau experiences cold but calm weather, with little snowfall. This pattern is occasionally interspersed by cyclonic storms moving eastwards from the Mediterranean, which give rise to short periods of low-pressure, bringing snow to the higher ranges. By contrast, **in summertime**, the heating caused by the dry and dusty continental wind creates a low-pressure area, which contributes to the onset of the monsoon rains in South Asia. Nearly all the plateau's precipitation (average 460 millimetres) falls in summer and in specific areas.

Background

The higher western and northern regions are less exposed to this monsoon weather pattern than the lower regions to the east and south. Thus, the former characteristically endure frost weathering for all but 45 days per annum, along with severe salt accumulation and wind activity.

In the **Kunlun** mountains to the north, where strong winds, dry dusty heat, and frost weathering predominate, the annual precipitation averages only 50-100 millimetres; and the temperature fluctuates between extremes: 25-28°C (foothills, in mid-summer) and -9°C (foothills, in mid-winter); 10°C (higher slopes, mid-summer) and -35°C (higher slopes, in mid-winter).

Further west, in the **Karakorum** Mountains, the climate is characterized by rarified air, intense solar radiation, and strong winds. Precipitation (100 millimetres per annum) is largely confined to high-altitude snow-fields above 4,877 metres, and to immense glaciers, which plunge on the southern slopes from 4,694-2,896 metres, and on northern slopes from 5,913-3,536 metres.

In the **Jangtang** plateau, rainfall is less than 100 millimetres. July temperatures fluctuate from 30°C in daytime to -15°C at night. Winter temperatures may drop to -35°C. Snow evaporates due to dryness, and wind speed exceeds 20 metres per second, causing severe dust storms.

Further south, in the **Himalayas**, a series of dramatic well-defined vertical climatic zones presents considerable variation in temperature and environment. The formidable mountain barrier obstructs the passage of cold continental air southwards and equally impedes the passage of warm monsoon air northwards, so that, on the southern side, precipitation varies from 1,530 millimetres in West Nepal to 3,060 millimetres in parts of Bhutan; whereas on the northwest slopes (around Ladakh) the figure drops to 765 -153 millimetres, and in Tibet proper to even less. Winter precipitation is heavier in the West Himalayas, which are more exposed to weather patterns from West Asia, than in the East Himalayas; but this is reversed in summer when the east is directly exposed to southwest monsoon currents.

Different altitudinal climatic zones are clearly defined on the southern slopes of the Himalayas, varying from the sub-equatorial and tropical climates of the foothills at the lowest level to the snowy climate of the peaks. The degree of exposure is also significant – the sunny southern slopes differing from the shady northern ones, and windward slopes exposed to moist ocean winds differing from leeward slopes. The barrier effect is most pronounced in areas where rain-bearing monsoon winds have a constant direction. Temperatures vary accordingly, so that the average pre-monsoon temperature is 11°C at 1,945 metres, -8°C at 5,029 metres, and -22°C at 5,944 metres.

The **gorges of Eastern Tibet** are much more accessible to South and Southeast Asian weather patterns. Here there is marked contrast between perennially snow-capped peaks, the temperate zone (1,829-3,353 metres), and the mild weather prevailing in the valleys below, some of which in the southernmost part of **Kham** are subject to a sultry heat and high level of humidity. Annual precipitation approximates 51 centimetres; and there is heavy snowfall in the mountain uplands during winter.

In **Nepal and Bhutan**, the contrast between those vertical climatic zones is seen at its greatest extent: the subtropical **Terai** has minimum 5°C (mid-winter) and maximum 45°C (mid-summer); the temperate **mid-mountain belt**, eg Kathmandu has minimum -3°C (mid-winter) and maximum 37°C (mid-summer); and the **alpine Himalayan belt**, eg Khumbhu has minimum -15°C (mid-winter) and maximum 35°C (mid-summer).

Flora and Fauna

The ancient environment of the plateau can be known from the fossils discovered in recent decades. These suggest a very different landscape from the one we have today. Marine fossils, including trilobites and brachiopods, characteristic of those found on ocean beds have been dated to 500 million years ago (mya). Marine plant fossils (dated 400-300 mya) suggest there was once warm water over northern Tibet and cold water over southern Tibet. In the **Chamdo** area, fossils of tropical plants, giant horsetail plants, and the *changdusaurus* (2.7 metres high and 6.1 metres long) have been dated to 200-150 mya, as has the *ichthyosaur* fossil (9.1 metres long), discovered at **Nyalam** in the Himalayas. Later fossils (dated 100 mya) suggest that swampland was gradually replaced by tropical plants and broadleaf forests, which still covered much of the **Tsaidam**, the **Kunluns**, and **Jangtang** as late as 25 mya.

Gradually (10-5 mya), those forests became drier grasslands as the temperature dropped, leaving only the subtropical eastern gorges and moister Himalayas forested. The plateau was frequented by gazelles, giraffes, deer, rhino, wild cats, hyenas, three-toed horses, and rodents. African mammal fossil remains (hippo, giraffe) have also been discovered in the **Shiwalik Hills** of southern Nepal.

During the **Ice Age** (3 mya-14,000 ya), the dry cold steppe increased and the forests decreased, causing Central Asian animals, such as cattle, sheep, goats; marmots, kiang and wild yak to reach the Tibetan plateau, and other animals such as the badger, hyena, tiger, horse, porcupine, elephant, panda, and leopard to migrate south to warmer climates. Glaciation reached its maximum during this period, with some glaciers being 130 kilometres long in **Kham**, 20-30 kilometres long on **Kailash**, and 40 kilometres long in the **Himalayas**! After a subsequent period of interglacial warming (14,000 ya – 1,000 BC) during which forests again increased, the **New Ice Age** (1,000 BC) brought a harsher climate, drier lakes and fewer forests. Unfortunately, there are no surviving vegetation relics from previous geological eras due to the relative youth of the plateau and the subsequent glaciation of the Quaternary Age, which destroyed the pre-glacial vegetation.

The present species of flora found of the plateau appeared in the wake of the retreating glaciers and are related through migration to the adjacent desert flora of Central Asia and the mesophyte flora of East Asia. The vegetation of the region, like its climate, reflects the diversity of the topography.

The very high altitude, dryness and complex land forms create a local climatic zone on the Tibetan plateau which runs counter to the worldwide pattern. Thus, the south is more heavily forested than the north, which is mostly rocky desert; the southeast is more densely forested than the Central parts, and the northeast is grassland. Mountain ranges also exhibit their own vegetation and vertical climatic zones, ie from tropical forest through deciduous forest, grassland, pine forest, alpine scrub and barren rock. However this pattern is broken in the southeast where mountain zones divide forest and meadowland; and on the plateau where steppe and desert prevail.

In the north and west, where there is a predominance of cold alpine desert, the soil cover is shallow and only perennial hard-frost resistant plants with roots reaching the parent rock survive. The arid climate of the **Jangtang** plateau, devoid of trees and larger plant forms, supports only grasses and a scattered vegetation of salt-tolerant bushes and Artemisia plants. The environment of the **Kunluns** is one of stark and barren desert rock, and stagnant pools. More variation is found in the **Karakorums**, where the lower river valleys (below 3,048 metres) abound in willow, poplar, and oleander; the lower slopes in artemisia, and the upper slopes in juniper.

Prehistoric flora & fauna

Vegetation

Background

Yak, Dri, Drong, Dzo: The Highland cattle of Tibet

No creature exemplifies the uniqueness of the Tibetan plateau like the yak. From whichever of the gateway cities you approach Tibet: Kathmandu, Chengdu, Kunming, Lanzhou, or Kashgar, the initial appearance of the yak at altitudes of 8,000-9,000 feet indicates that you have arrived within the ethnic Tibetan area. For the Tibetan people and the yak are inseparable. Hardy, stubborn, frisky, and apparently clumsy though deceptively agile on precipitous rugged terrain, this 'grunting ox' (Bos grunniens) comes in many shapes and sizes: the male of the species is known as the yak, and the female as the dri. These animals have been domesticated and tended by Tibetan nomads for thousands of years, giving rise also to the hybrid dzo (a cross between a bull and a dri), which has become an ideal ploughing animal in Tibetan farming villages. By contrast, the wild yak (drong), like the American bison, once roamed the grasslands of Northern and Eastern Tibet, in large herds, but their numbers have been severely depleted within the last few decades, falling prey to Chinese hunters and modern weaponry.

Since antiquity, the yak has been used as a pack animal and is rarely ridden in the manner of a horse. Prior to the construction of motorable roads, yak caravans were the principal means for the transportation of freight, and they still are in many remote parts of the country. Though slow, they are untiringly capable of carrying loads of over 50 kilos across 5,000 metres passes, and they withstand temperatures of -30°C. For the nomads who rear the yak, this creature is the source of their wealth and livelihood. The flesh provides meat (tsak-sha), which may be cooked or freeze dried; the milk of the dri provides butter (mar) and cheese (chura). Some Amdo towns now have meat and dairy processing factories supplied by the local nomadic communities. The hide is used for high-calved Tibetan boots, clothing, and traditional coracle construction. The soft inner hair (ku-lu) is now used for the production of high quality sweaters, particularly in the Repkong area of Amdo, and these are exported worldwide. The coarse outer hair (tsid-pa) is spun by the nomads themselves and used for making their black yak wool tent dwellings, known in Tibetan as 'ba' (bra).

Himalayan flora (as found in Tibet, Nepal, and Bhutan) are differentiated according to four complex vertical zones: the **tropical foothills** of the East and Central Himalayas (180-730 metres), which are covered in evergreens such as mesua ferrea, oak, chestnut, alder, and pandanus furcatus; the **subtropical zone** (910-1,370 metres) in which are found deciduous sal trees, steppe forest, and thorn steppe; the **temperate zone** (1,370-3,350 metres) in which grow pine, cedar, spruce, oak, and birch; and the **alpine zone** (3,200-4,450 metres) where juniper, rhododendron, flowering plants, moss and lichen grow.

A richer plant life is found in the river valleys and low-lying gorges of **South** and **Southeast Tibet**, where the humidity level is higher. Here, there are willows, poplars, conifers, teak, rhododendron, oak, birch, elm, bamboo, sugar cane, tea, tamarisk, and so forth.

On the mountain slopes dominating the **gorges** of **East Tibet** are rich virgin forests, abounding in spruce, fir, larch, juniper, pine, and medicinal herbs. The floral **grasslands of Amdo** and the **uplands of Kham** support grasses such as cobresia and sedge, which provide fodder and pasture for livestock.

Regional variations occur within the vertical climatic zones of **Kham**. For example, in the **Yangtze**, **Yalong** and **Gyarong gorges** of East Kham, below 610 metres there grow cypress, palm, bamboo, citrus fruits; from 610-1,520 metres there grow evergreens and oaks; from 1,520-2,430 metres grow mixed conifers; from 2,590-3,500 metres grow sub-alpine coniferous forests; and from 3,500-4,880 metres grow alpine shrub and meadow. Further south of Kham, in the **lower Salween** and **Mekong gorges** of **Dechen** county, the vertical zones have a more pronounced subtropical vegetation: below 1,830 metres there is conifer forest, from 1,830-3,350 metres there is an abundance of azaleas, rhododendrons, camelias, roses, and primroses and from 3,350-4,570 metres grow fir, bamboo, dwarf juniper, and flowering herbs.

In general, therefore, a transition is clearly observable from the grassy-shrub landscapes of the uplands, through the sub-alpine coniferous forests, to the forest landscapes of the warmly temperate and subtropical belts.

Wildlife

Over 530 species of birds, 190 species of mammals, more than 40 species of reptiles, and 30 species of amphibians, and 2,300 species of insects are found in the region as a whole.

In general it is said that **East Himalayan** fauna have an affinity with those of the Chinese and Indo-Chinese region, whereas **West Himalayan** fauna are more closely related to Turkmenian and Mediterranean fauna. In the **western** and **northern Tibet plains**, there are many animal specimens, predominantly hoofed mammals (ungulates), who thrive in this open habitat, and rodents. Within the **Kunlun** ranges, these include gazelle, wild ass, wild goat, wild yak, blue sheep, urial, ibex, brown bear, and wolf.

The **saline lakes** of the **Jangtang Plateau** are home to varieties of waterfowl in seasonal migration. In the **Karakorums**, the urial, wild yak, ibex, and wild ass are found; while birds of prey such as the lammergeier, griffon, and golden eagle are commonplace.

In the **Himalayan** region, **above the tree-line**, are found a number of endemic species adapted to cold, such as the snow leopard, brown bear, red panda, and yak. The **lower forests** are home to the black bear, clouded leopard, and terai langur; and the **southern foothills** are frequented by the rhino, musk deer, stag, and elephant. There are distinctive varieties of fish, such as the glyptothorax, and reptiles, such as the japalura lizard, the blind snake (*typhlops*), and unusual species of insects, such as the troides butterfly. Over 800 species of birds have been identified in **Nepal** alone – including the magpie, titmouse, chough, thrush, redstart, lammergeier, kite, vulture, and snow partridge.

The deep valleys of **Southeast Tibet**, which are exposed to the moist humidity of the monsoon, support dense forests with a plethora of animals and birds. Here there are found the leopard, bear, wild boar, wild goat, langur, lynx, jackal, wild dog, and spotted cat. Distinctive species such as the lesser panda and ling yang antelope are found in the **Gyarong** region. In the high **grasslands of Amdo** and the **Kham uplands** are brown bears, wild and bighorn sheep, mountain antelope, musk deer, wild ass, wild yak, snake, scorpion, and mountain lizard. Waterfowl is abundant in the lakes of **East and Northeast Tibet**, as are fish, frog, crab, otter, and turtle. Birds include the hoopoe, hawk, mynah, gull, crane, sheldrake, teal, owl, and magpie.

Wildlife reserves

These are extremely well developed in both **Nepal** and **Bhutan**, where ecological and environmental considerations have been given more of a priority. Among the current administrative divisions of Tibet, **Qinghai** province in the northeast has advanced furthest in the establishing of wildlife reserves. The world's second largest reserve was established in the **Jangtang** region in 1993. Details on these reserves will be found below, in their relevant chapters. In addition, the Great Rivers National Park, covering an area of 66,000 sq km is soon to be established in the Dechen Prefecture of Yunnan Province.

Background

Culture

People

The racial origins of the Tibetans are little known and still remain a matter of scientific speculation. A systematic research into their origins has been limited on account of the isolation and inaccessibility of the country, an instinctive in-built resistance to anthropometric examination, and the comparative lack of skeletal remains due to the paucity of archaeological excavations and perhaps to the funeral custom of dismemberment and 'sky burial'.

Ethnologists, whose opinions vary and disagree, have distinguished **two main racial types** among the **Tibetans** – one tall with long limbs and heads, and often distinct aqualine features; and another of shorter stature, with high cheekbones and round heads. The former type, found mainly among the northern and eastern nomads of Kham and Amdo, like the modern Turkic and Mongolian peoples, is considered to be descended from a tall dolicocephalous race of great antiquity. The latter, inhabiting mostly the central and western parts of the country, as well as the Himalayan valleys of Northern Nepal and Bhutan, is regarded as a descendant of the Proto-Chinese of the Paroean group from which the modern Han Chinese, Thais and Burmese are also descended.

However, this hypothesis appears oversimplified. There is evidence of great ethnic and linguistic diversity within the tribal confederations of Eastern Tibet, probably as a result of the process of intermingling with the neighbouring peoples and minority nationalities. The Tibetans themselves, according to legend, trace their ancestry to the union of an intelligent monkey and a demonic ogress, and for their part, the Chinese have always considered the Tibetans to be racially distinct.

Despite the demographic movements of the 20th century which have resulted in the widespread population transfer of ethnic Han Chinese into the Tibetan plateau, and of the Indo-Aryan Nepalese into the Himalayan valleys of Northern Nepal, Sikkim and Bhutan, the region as a whole is even now largely inhabited by a population of Tibetan origin. When the three countries are taken individually however, there are considerable variations.

The following statistics are based on 1995 projections made by the Global Demography Project, at the University of California in Santa Barbara.

Tibet (*Area*: 2,108,700 square kilometres) is one of the mostly sparsely populated regions on earth with an estimated population of only eight million (1998 estimate, excluding Ziling and Jang Sadam areas). Modern census figures are complicated, owing to the current partition of Tibet into five diverse Chinese provinces, but even conservative Chinese publications have given the overall ethnic Tibetan population at 4.5 million, suggesting that they comprise 56 percent of the plateau's population. Tibetans in exile and a number of Tibetologists, who hold these figures to be underestimated, both on account of the non-registration of many nomadic peoples and the large number of refugees now in neighbouring countries, such as India, have given the total Tibetan ethnic population between five to six million. Of the remainder (maximum 44 per cent), the majority (approximately 37 per cent) are accounted for by the recent rapid influx of Han Chinese from Sichuan and other provinces of mainland China into urban areas of Tibet and the more gradual demographic movement of Hui Muslims from the Ziling region. **NB** These figures do not take into account the transient Chinese population in Tibet (including the army), who are mostly registered in other provinces of mainland China.

Among the two larger groups, the Tibetans include within their numbers the **Topa** of the highland region (Far-west Tibet); the **Tsangpa** of West Tibet, the **Upa** of Central Tibet, the **Horpa** of North Tibet, the **Khampa** of East Tibet, the **Amdowa** of Northeast Tibet, and the **Gyarongwa** of Far-east Tibet. In all these areas of Tibet there are both sedentary communities (*rongpa*) and nomadic groups (*drokpa*).

The situation differs in the remote border areas where smaller nationalities have lived for centuries. These minorities, comprising approximately seven percent of the total population, include peoples closely related to the Tibetans, such as the **Monpas** (6,200) and **Lhopas** (2,100) – about 0.15 percent who inhabit Metok and the adjacent counties of the extreme south; the **Qiangs** (102,000, 1.6 percent) of Maowen and adjacent counties in the extreme east; and the **Jang** (Naxi; 245,000) and Li of Jang Sadam (Lijiang) who also inhabit the adjacent Tibetan counties of Markham, Dechen, Gyeltang, Balung, and Mili in the extreme southeast. Other nationalities (totalling about five percent) found in the extreme northeast are of Mongol or Turkic origin: some 2.5 percent (23,750) of China's estimated **Kazakhs** (ie 0.35 percent) inhabit West Kokonor. Some 90 percent of the 69,100 (one percent) **Salar** population inhabits Dowi (Xunhua Salar AC); and the 159,400 **Tu** (2.4 percent) are mostly found in Huzhu Tu AC and in the upper reaches of the Tsong-chu and Datong valleys. **Mongolian** populations are confined to certain parts of West Kokonor and Sogwo AC.

Language

The Tibetan language is classified as one of the 23 Tibeto-Burman languages spoken within the borders of present-day China, the others including Yi, Bai, Hani, Liau, Lahu, Jang (Naxi), and Qiang. There are great variations in dialect from Ladakh in the Far-west to the Golok, Gyarong and Gyeltang dialects of the east. With remarkable differences in pronunciation and vocabulary, these dialects have sometimes been mistaken for distinct languages in their own right.

Broadly speaking, the Tibetan language comprises the Utsang, Kham and Amdo groups of dialects. The first of these includes the **U-ke** spoken in Lhasa and Lhokha, the **Tsang-ke** spoken around Zhigatse and Gyantse, the **To-ke** spoken in the highland areas and Ngari (Far-west), and the **Sharpa-ke** spoken by the peoples of the Northeast Nepal border. **Kham dialects** include those of Nangchen and Jyekundo in the north, Nakchu in the west, Dechen and Mili in the south, and Chamdo, Drayab, Batang, Derge, and so forth in the east. **Amdo dialects** include **drokpa-ke**, spoken by the nomads of Golok, and the adjacent areas of Sertal, Dzamtang, and Ngawa; **rongpa-ke**, spoken by the settled farming communities of Tsongkha, Bayan Khar (Hualong) and Dowi (Xunhua); and the **semi-nomadic semi-sedentary** dialects spoken in Repkong, Labrang, and Luchu areas.

In general, the Tibetan language has constructed its specialized Buddhist vocabulary under Indian influence, while freely borrowing from Chinese commonplace words of everyday usage – food, drink, clothing. Tibetan writing has never made use of ideograms. The standard block-lettered script derives from the seventh century Ranjana script of North India, and the more cursive handwriting script, it has been suggested, may have an even older origin in the Northwest Indian Vartula script.

National language The great disparity in pronunciation and vocabulary between the various Tibetan dialects creates many problems of communication, even for native Tibetan speakers. Nowadays, Tibetans from Amdo and Lhasa often find it easier to converse in Chinese rather than Tibetan, so that the former has become something of a lingua franca for Tibetans inside Tibet. The Tibetan Government-in-exile has for many years now been promoting the ideal of a standard form of Tibetan in its schools; and even within Tibet the need for a national Tibetan language is well understood, even if it seems a remote goal. By contrast, the written language has remained remarkably constant since the orthographic revisions of the ninth century.

Tibetan language is an important medium of instruction in primary schools and, to a lesser extent, in middle schools. Higher education almost invariably is imparted in Chinese, and there are very few scientific textbooks published in Tibetan. The situation is slightly better among the exiled community, where efforts have been made to establish a wide-ranging technical terminology for modern scientific subjects.

Chinese speakers include those of the east and southeast who speak Sichuan dialect and those of the northeast who speak Putonghua (standard Mandarin) or Ziling dialect. Very few Chinese living or working in Tibet have attempted to master the Tibetan language, most assuming that the indigenous peoples will have to accommodate themselves to communicate with the newcomers, who control the urban economy. This is undoubtedly the prevailing trend among the young in particular, and in parts of East Tibet it has become commonplace to see educated Tibetans adopt Chinese names in order to secure their own advancement. The greatest fear confronting the Tibetan people is not the prospect of another persecution or cultural revolution, so much as being outnumbered by an influx of Chinese immigrants in their own land. After all, there are obvious precedents in Manchuria and Inner Mongolia!

Daily life

Social customs and life   Tibetan daily life and social customs have for centuries been highly influenced by Buddhism. Whenever child-naming rituals, wedding ceremonies or funerals and so forth are held, it is important that an auspicious day is chosen.

The **Tibetan calendar** is based on the 60-year cycle of the *Kalacakra Tantra* (rather than the century of the western system). Each of the years within a 60-year cycle has its own distinctive name according to the *Kalacakra Tantra*, and a derivative name formed by combining the 12 animals and five elements of Chinese divination. Each cycle thus begins with the fire hare year and ends with the fire tiger year. Presently we are in the 17th cycle counting from the year 1027 when this system was introduced to Tibet. Auspicious days within the lunar calendar may fall on the 15th or 30th days of any month, which are associated with Shakyamuni Buddha, or on the eighth (Medicine Buddha Day), the 10th (Padmasambhava Day), or 25th (Dakini Day). Specific events, such as the Buddha's first promulgation of the Buddhist teachings, are commemorated on set days of the year (ie the fourth day of the sixth month). In addition to such general auspicious days, there are also those which may be specific to a given individual, determined on the basis of the time of birth.

During all the important ceremonies of daily life, the offering of auspicious white scarfs along with tea or barley ale and tsampa (roasted barley flour), is a prerequisite.

Ceremonial scarfs

During the 13th century, Drogon Chogyel Phakpa, advisor to Emperor Qubilai Qan, introduced the custom of offering ceremonial scarfs (katak) on special occasions. This practice subsequently became the principal means of expressing courtesy, greetings, or respect in Tibet. Often the scarfs are presented to spiritual masters or sacred images, to the victors of sporting contests or divas of theatrical performances, or to dignitaries when being granted an audience, making a petition, or receiving tidings. Commonly, kataks are also offered to those about to embark on a long journey, and to new-born babies, newly weds, or deceased persons.

Simple ceremonial scarfs are made of loosely woven cotton, and superior scarfs of silk. The shorter ones may be 1-1½ metres long, and the longer up to 7 metres in length! Most are white in colour, indicative of purity, but blue, yellow, red, and green scarfs are not unknown. Generally 5-coloured scarfs are offered only to Buddha-images, or else wrapped around a ceremonial arrow (dadar), used in longevity empowerments (tsewang) and marriage ceremonies. Most are plain, but some may be inscribed with the words 'good auspices' (tashidelek), or designed with the 'eight auspicious symbols' (tashi da-gye), the motif of the Great Wall of China, and so forth.

Naming ceremonies consequent on the birth of a child follow the Buddhist naming system rather than the western patronymic system. Surnames are rarely found, with the exception of aristocratic families who add their clan name as a prefix to their given Buddhist names. Weddings are generally arranged by the parents of the bride and groom, taking into account important issues such as compatability of birth-sign, social class, and absence of consanguinity. Gifts are mutually exchanged – the 'milk price' being paid by the groom's family and the 'dowry' by the bride's family.

Funeral ceremonies assume varied forms: sky burial being the most common and compassionate form of corpse disposal in Central Tibet and West Tibet, and cremation an equally popular method in East Tibet where wood is more plentiful. The former entails the dismembering of the body and its distribution to celestial vultures. Important lamas may be cremated or embalmed within stupa reliquaries. Lesser persons may be given water burial (particularly in the fast-flowing gorges of the southeast), or earth burial. The latter, which carried high prestige during the Bonpo period when the early Chongye tombs were constructed, gradually came to have inferior associations from the Buddhist perspective.

Diet The traditional staple diet of the Tibetans is somewhat bland, consisting of butter tea, tsampa (roasted barley flour), dried meat, barley ale (*chang*), and dairy products – milk, curd, and cheese. Many nomadic families still survive on this diet alone today; whereas urban communities also have rice, noodles, millet and a wide range of fresh vegetables and pulses.

Animal husbandry is still the main occupation of rural and nomadic communities, while subsistence farming is possible only in the low-lying valleys. Although Tibetans have traditionally displayed a compassionate Buddhist attitude to all forms of wildlife, the eating of meat is widespread (both out of choice and necessity) in view of the fact that, until very recently, the country was not known for its abundance of vegetables.

National dress

The inhabitants of different parts of the Tibetan plateau may be recognized by their distinctive dress, notwithstanding the ubiquitous Chinese clothing which is all too prevalent nowadays. Both men and women wear the **chuba**, a long-sleeved gown, tied at the waist with a sash. Farmers often wear sleeveless chubas and nomads sheepskin chubas. Local designs are distinctive: the black smock design of Kongpo, the otter-skin bordered chuba of Amdo, the shorter length but longer sleeved chuba of Kham, the brocade-bordered black tunic of Tsang and To, and so forth.

Head-wear is also distinctive: the coiffure of both men and women indicating the part of the country to which they belong. For example, Khampa men with black hair braids generally come from Chamdo and those with red braids from Derge. Brocade hats lined with fur are popular in Central Tibet while stetsons or Bolivian-style bowlers are widely used in East Tibet. In general Tibetans wear subdued colours, but there are areas of East Tibet in particular where maroons and shocking pinks are preferred, above all on festival days.

Jewellery   Both men and women wear jewellery, the most highly prized stone being the uniquely Tibetan **zi** (banded agate or chalcedony). Ornaments of gold, silver, coral, turquoise, amber, beryl, and ivory are also worn, but none compare in value to the zi stone.

Tibetan houses

These vary in their design and material from one part of the country to the next. In Central Tibet and West Tibet, village houses are flat-roofed and made of adobe, in Kongpo and adjacent areas, they are made with wooden shingles and decorative features, reminiscent of Bhutanese architecture, in Kham horizontal timbers painted red with intricate window sills are typical, and in Minyak, Litang or Gyarong the sturdy stone houses of Qiangic construction are commonplace. Perhaps the most beautiful village and small town architecture is to be seen in the Tawu area of East Tibet, where the building technique combines the horizontal red timber construction with pristine whitewashed adobe, and finely carved windows. In general, village houses have a lower floor for animals; and an upper floor for human habitation. Shuttered windows with a trefoil arch shape are colourfully painted. Electricity is now commonplace in towns and cities, but in the countryside oil lamps are still in use. The nomadic communities throughout Tibet live in large sturdy tents (*ba*) made of black yak wool.

Minority groups

Among the smaller minority groups within Tibet, the **Monpa** inhabit the counties of Metok, Nyangtri, and Tsona. Their customs, religion and culture are fully integrated with those of the Tibetans through long-standing political, economic and marital links. Many speak Tibetan in addition to their own dialects. Both men and women wear robes with aprons, black yak hair caps, and soft-soled leather boots with red and black stripes. Women wear white aprons, earrings, rings and bracelets. In subtropical Metok women and men both wear jackets – the women with long striped skirts. The slash and burn method of agriculture is practised here, and the staple diet consists of rice, maize, millet, buckwheat, and chilli pepper, in addition to

Ba and Gur: Tibetan tents

There are basically two types of Tibetan tent: the black yak wool tent (ba) used as a dwelling by the nomadic populace, and the white canvas tent with blue appliqué (gur) used by villagers and townspeople for picnics and recreation. The former are dotted around the high grasslands and pastures where the nomads tend their herds of yak and flocks of sheep. They are made of a coarse yak wool tweed, which is capable of withstanding the elements: wind, rain, and snow; and the design has changed little in centuries. There is a central tent pole, from which the four corners are pegged out in a rectangle and a low inner wall of earth and clumps of grass constructed on three sides. The door flap may be kept open or closed. The stove is in the centre of the tent, with a ventilation opening immediately above – the size of the opening being controlled by pulley ropes. The nomads occupy the high ground in the spring and summer seasons; and by mid-autumn, they begin their age-old transhumance, exchanging

the snow-bound pastures for the comparatively well sheltered dwellings of the lower valleys. During the 1960s efforts were made to settle the nomads permanently in camps, but they have now reverted to their original lifestyle. A few of the permanent camps are still used as a winter residence for the elderly and the young. Alongside the black tents, there are sometimes small white tepee-style tents to be seen. These are occasionally used for storage, but often for the daughter of a nomadic family while entertaining suitors.

The picnic tents of the townspeople are used during the festival season. Some are very large and ornate, with decorative blue appliqué designs, depicting the eight auspicious symbols (tashi da-gye) and so forth. The horse festivals of Gyantse and Damzhung, and those of Kham (eg at Jyekundo and Nakchu) provide an ideal opportunity for visitors to see the large variety of Tibetan picnic tents in use. Also, in Lhasa, there is a tent factory producing decorative tents and awnings to order.

---

tsampa and tea. Hunting is still important in these areas where the virgin forest is dense, and species of wild boar, bears, foxes, and langurs are to be found. Monpa houses are made of wood with bamboo/thatched roofs.

The **Lhopa** of Menling, Metok, Lhuntse, and Nang counties are largely forest dwelling hunter gatherers and fishermen. Few of them speak Tibetan; and intermarriage is rare. The standard dress is a sleeveless buttonless knee-length smock of black sheep wool with a helmet-like hat made of bearskin or bamboo/rattan laced with bearskin, and no shoes. Men wear bamboo earrings and necklaces, and bows and arrows, while the women wear silver or brass earrings, bracelets, necklaces, and ornate waist belts. The staple diet is a dumpling made of maize or millet, as well as rice and buckwheat, in addition to tsampa, potatoes, buttered tea and chilli peppers.

In Far-east Tibet, the **Qiang** and related groups occupy fertile land and good mountain pastures. The adjacent forests are home to the giant panda, langur, and flying fox. Men and women wear long blue gowns over trousers with sheepskin jackets. The women have laced collars and sharp-pointed embroidered shoes, embroidered waistbands, and earrings. The staples are millet, barley, potatoes, wheat, buckwheat; and they have finely constructed stone blockhouses, two/three storeys high.

In Southeast Tibet the **Jang** or **Naxi** inhabit the Lijiang area and adjacent counties in Dechen, Markham and Mili. Here, the women wear wide-sleeved gowns with jackets and long trousers with an ornate waistband. The men tend to wear standard Chinese clothing. Naxi society is mostly patriarchal, but a few matriarchal elements survive in Yongining (Yunnan) and Yanyuan (Sichuan) counties. There, the children live with the mother and women comprise the main labour force.

Background

In the extreme northwest of Amdo, there are **Kazakhs** inhabiting the West Kokonor prefecture. These Turkic speaking peoples have a distinctive vocabulary assimilated from Chinese, Uighur, and Mongol. The written language is based on Arabic. Most Kazakhs are engaged in nomadic animal husbandry, dwelling in yurts (*yu*) during the spring, summer and autumn seasons. The men wear loose long-sleeved furs and skin garments, with sheepskin shawls or camel-hair stuffed overcoats in winter, and sheepskin trousers. The women wear red dresses with cotton padded coats in winter, and white-shawls embroidered with red and yellow designs. Dairy products such as milk dough, milk skin, cheese, and butter are plentiful. The diet also includes butter tea, mutton stewed in water without salt, smoked meat, horse sausage, fermented mare's milk, and sweets made of rice or wheat. Kazakh society is Muslim and patriarchal, while both monogamous and polygamous types of marriage are found.

In Dowi (Xunhua) county of Amdo, the **Salar** people of Turkic origin have lived since their arrival from Samarkhand during the Mongol period (1271-1368). Theirs is a strict Muslim society and the women are rarely permitted to appear in public. Predominantly a farming community, the Salar grow barley, wheat, buckwheat and potatoes, with secondary stock-breeding, lumbering, wool-weaving and salt production.

The **Tu** peoples of Gonglung and Pari (Tianzhu) counties in the northeast extremities of Amdo are said to be Chahan Mongols descended from the army of the Mongol general Gerilite, who intermarried with indigenous Turkic nomads (Horpa) during the time of Genghiz Qan. Later, they again intermingled with other Mongol groups who settled in those areas during the Ming period. Their language belongs to Mongolian branch of Altaic family and the script devised for the Mongol language by Drogon Chogyel Phakpa is still in use among them for certain literary functions. Both men and women wear shirts with finely embroidered collars and bright colours. Traditionally livestock breeders, the Tu adapted to farming from the 13th century onwards, and became converts to the Gelukpa school of Tibetan Buddhism.

The **Hui Muslim** community inhabit much of Amdo and the northeast. They are predominantly Chinese-speaking urban dwellers, but maintain their distinctive religion, names, and (sometimes) dress. In Central Tibet they are often known as Zilingpa; and have a reputation for unscrupulous trading.

Mongols inhabit the West Kokonor and Sogwo areas of Amdo. They wear fur coats in winter and loose chubas in summer, generally red, yellow or dark blue in colour, with a green or red waistband, knee-length boots, and conical hats (in winter) or silk/cloth turbans (in summer). The girls have hair parted in the middle, with agate, coral and turquoise ornaments. Mongol peoples are renowned for their excellent horsemanship and archery. Their staple diet consists of beef, mutton, dairy products, and tea; and they live in felt yurts. Both traditional shamanism and Buddhism are practised.

Background

Art

Tibetan painting and sculpture date from the seventh century onwards, coinciding with the unification of Tibet by King Songtsen Gampo and the gradual absorption of Buddhism from the neighbouring cultures of India, Nepal, China, and Central Asia. There is little evidence of Tibetan art prior to the seventh century and the earliest surviving examples so fully absorbed the impact of the surrounding artistic traditions that it is difficult to discern pre-Buddhist elements, should an earlier, purely indigenous tradition have existed.

Tibetan painting found three principal expressions: manuscript illumination (*peri*), mural painting (*debri*), and cloth-painted scrolls (*tangka*), each inexorably linked to the goals and practices of Buddhism. Appliqué tangkas and sand-painted mandalas also evolved as by-products. Sculpted images of deities and historical figures were mostly produced in metal, clay or stucco, and to a lesser extent in wood, stone, or even butter. In theory, Tibetan works of art served primarily as icon, intermediary between man and divinity, a function underscored by the indigenous term 'tongdrol' (liberation by seeing the deity). In conjunction with ritual, a painting or a sculpted image housed a deity consecrated for purposes of worship, offering, and spiritual communication.

Among the various stylistic influences which have been observed in the art of Tibet, the oldest strand seems to be that of **Newar Nepal** (and Guptan India) as seen in the oldest door frames and pillars of the Jokhang temple in Lhasa. Early Central Asian or Khotanese influence has been discerned in the extant images of Kachu Lhakhang, Yemar, and Dratang – the last of these also containing murals indicative of the Pala style of Bengal (eighth to 12th century). **Kashmiri art styles** are noticeable at Tsaparang in the Gu-ge Kingdom of Far-west Tibet, although the earlier murals of nearby Toling did not survive the Cultural Revolution. Better examples can be found at Tabo and Alchi in the adjacent Indian areas of Spiti and Ladakh. During the period of Mongol influence, the monasteries of Sakya and Zhalu were lavishly decorated by Newar artists from Nepal. Subsequent indigenous developments included: the 15th century **Lato** style (eg the murals of Chung Riwoche stupa), the **Gyantse** style (of Kumbum and Pelkor Chode), the **Uri** style of Lhasa, which became the prevalent style from the 17th century onwards, the exquisite **Repkong** style of Amdo, and the **Karma Gadri** style of Kham which incorporated landscape elements and perspective from Chinese art, and later exerted considerable influence on the mainstream Central Tibetan style.

Crafts

Traditional handicrafts are made largely for the indigenous market rather than the tourist trade. Among the most widely available items are: the wooden churns (*dongmo*) used for making butter tea; birchwood bowls (sometimes inlaid with silver or pewter); jade bowls from Rinpung area; knifes and daggers with ornately carved scabbards; gold and silverware engraved with motifs such as the Eight Auspicious Symbols; engraved amulet boxes; carpets from Gyantse and other towns, the weaving of which has become the principal cottage industry in Tibet and the Tibetan communities of North India and Nepal; blankets which may be finely woven, striped or shaggy; stuffed mattresses with decorative covers; wooden household furniture including shrines, cabinets, and tables – all with decorative panelling; striped aprons from Chidezhol; bamboo artefacts from the southern counties of Nyangtri, Menling, Metok, and Dzayul; and pastoral artefacts, such as the yak hair sling and the sheepskin bellows.

Background

Music and dance

Song and dance have always been an important vehicle for social contact in Tibet. Apart from the epics of **Ling Gesar**, which have already been mentioned, there are free-form mountain and nomadic ballads; lyric poems such as the *Hundred Thousand Songs of Milarepa*; and regional folk-songs from To, Batang, Kham and so forth. The folk songs have a thematic character: there are wedding songs, labour songs, round dance songs, archery songs, drinking songs, love songs (such as those composed by Dalai Lama VI), and songs in the form of repartee or playful rejoinders.

These songs are expressed in simple language which evokes an immediate mood or imagery, and employs both metaphor and hidden analogy. Modern songs are continually being written and performed in this traditional style, utilizing the sophisticated technology of the recording studio. Tibetan pop singers, such as Datron, Kalzang Chodron, and Tseten Dolma, are well known both inside and outside Tibet. Currently the vitality of the Tibetan folk song is under threat from the phenomenal development of Chinese karaoke throughout Tibet over the last eight years.

Songs are frequently accompanied by folk dances. Among the most popular are the round dances known as *gor-zhe* in Lhasa, Tsang and Lhokha, and as *gor-dong* in Chamdo area. Men and women form two concentric circles around a bonfire, singing alternate choruses, while the stamping of the feet keeps the rhythm. There are other distinctive dances, such as the drum dance of Lhokha, the bell-and-drum dance of Chamdo and Kongpo, the tap dance of the highland region (*to-zhe*), and the synchronized labour songs (*le-zhe*). For a description of the religious dances (*cham*), which are distinct from these, see the section on Bhutan (see below, page 878).

The first **opera** troupe in Tibet was founded in the 15th century by Tangtong Gyelpo, the celebrated bridge-builder who may be regarded as the Leonardo da Vinci of Tibet. By the 17th century opera (*dogar*) had become an art form in its own right. A stylistic distinction developed between the traditional **White Masked Sect** and the innovatory **Blue Masked Sect**. The former, which included troupes such as the Bingdungpa from Chongye, the Nangzipa from Tolung, and the Tashi Zholpa from Nedong, were gradually supplanted by the more sophisticated exponents of the latter style, such as those of Gyelkar based at Rinpung, Shangpa and Jungpa, both based at Namling, and Kyormolung based at Lhasa. Nowadays there are numerous troupes throughout the country, and the best time to see their performances is during the Zhoton festival in Norbulingka at Lhasa during the month of August.

Literature

The Tibetan language is the source of one of the world's greatest and most prolific literary heritages, rivalling those of China, India, Greece or Rome. Although most works are of a Buddhist nature, the secular tradition of poetics and drama continues to flourish. The epic poems of **Ling Gesar** are more voluminous than the great *Mahabharata* of ancient India – some 72 volumes having already been redacted and published in Tibet by the provincial publishing houses and the Chinese Academy of Social Sciences. Three million copies of these texts have been distributed throughout the Tibetan world! The development of secular Tibetan literature has also been given a new impetus by the **Amnye Machen Institute**, recently established at Dharamsala in Northwest India to promote the work of contemporary Tibetan writers.

The classical literature, which remains highly popular at the present day, includes the canonical texts of Buddhism and their indigenous Tibetan commentaries – amounting to hundreds of thousands of volumes; as well as the great works on the traditional sciences – grammar, medicine, logic, art, astrology, poetics, prosody, synonymics, and drama. Religious histories, biographies and hagiographies provide an important frame of reference for the adherents of the various Buddhist schools and the Bon tradition. The works are too numerous to detail here, but mention should be made of the great canonical compilations.

The Buddhist tantras translated into Tibetan during the early diffusion of Buddhism are contained in the *Nyingma Gyudbum*, the best known edition of which is preserved in woodblock form at the Derge Parkhang in Kham. The later translations of the tantras, as well as some earlier translations of both sutras and

Woodblock printing

The technique of woodblock or xylographic printing (shingpar) which was developed in Tang China predates the invention of movable type in Western Europe. A copy of the world's earliest extant printed book, the Chinese translation of the Diamond Cutter Sutra (Vajracchedikasutra), dated 868, is preserved in the British Museum in London. This technique was slow to reach Tibet, where from the introduction of the written script by Tonmi Sambhota in the 7th century until the intervention of the Manchu emperors in Tibetan affairs during the 18th, the vast Buddhist literature – both translated and indigenous, was recorded in manuscript form only. Some precious manuscript versions of the Buddhist Canon inscribed in gold ink (sertri) or silver ink (ngultri) on black paper have survived; and the general custom of utilizing red ink for canonical works and black ink for non-canonical commentaries persists even now. The oldest woodblock edition of the Tibetan canon, prepared in China by the Ming Emperor Yongle no longer exists (although one printed copy has been preserved in Sera Monastery).

During the 18th century, woodblock versions of the Kangyur and Tangyur – the compilations forming the Buddhist Canon, were commissioned at Nartang near Zhigatse, at Zhol Parkhang in Lhasa, at Derge in Kham, at Cho-ne in Amdo, and at Beijing. The letters are carved in reverse in oblong blocks of wood, and the paper, cut to size, is printed by impressing it with a roller against the inked surface of the woodblock. There are several teams, each of two persons, often monks, who work together, rhythmically printing multiple copies of a single page. The pages of the book (pe-cha) are then collated and the edges dyed red or yellow, in accordance with tradition. The pages are not bound but kept loose leaf, and wrapped in a cloth book cover (pe-re). This printing technique came to permeate most of the Tibetan plateau; and many small monasteries had their own distinctive woodblock collections, often reflecting their own traditions. At the present day, the largest woodblock collections are housed at Derge, Cho-ne, Lhasa, Labrang Tashikyil, and Kumbum. Copies of the Buddhist Canon and related works once again are being actively distributed throughout the plateau in this time-honoured method.

The storage of woodblocks of course requires a large amount of space. By contrast, the techniques of modern printing, including movable type, photo-offset, and computer typesetting are now in vogue, and the various nationalities' publishing houses of the TAR, Sichuan, Qinghai, and Gansu are particularly active in the printing and distribution of conveniently bound copies of classical and modern works of Tibetan literature at affordable prices.

tantras, are contained in the 104 volume *Kangyur*, compiled in the 14th century by Buton Rinchendrub (1290-1364). Most extant commentaries of Indian origin are contained in a companion anthology, the 185 volume *Tangyur*, which he also compiled. There are several extant manuscript versions of these canonical texts – most of them housed in the great monasteries around Lhasa, but seven woodblock editions of the *Kangyur* survive, along with four of the *Tangyur*. At present these are being collated and republished in a new master edition by the Kangyur-Tangyur Collation Project in Chengdu.

Background

Religion

Tibetan religious traditions may conveniently be considered in three categories – animism, Bon and Buddhism. The first concerns the control of animistic forces by bards and storytellers, and the second emphasizes the purity of space, funerary rituals, and certain meditative practices, which may have originated in either Zoroastrianism or Kashmiri Buddhism; and the third is the means of liberation from the sufferings of cyclic existence as propounded in ancient India by Shakyamuni Buddha.

Animism and the 'Religion of Humans'

The earliest form of Tibetan religion, which RA Stein has termed the 'nameless religion', is a type of animism based upon the worship of the elements and mountain deities. Incense offerings would be made to appease local mountain spirits, and 'wind-horse' (*lungta*) prayer flags or cairns affixed on prominent passes to ensure good auspices. Solemn declarations of truth (*dentsik*) and oaths would be made in the presence of local deities, to invoke good fortune (*gyang-khug*); and talismanic objects or places (*la-ne*) were revered as life-supporting forces. Enemies or hostile forces could then be overpowered by drawing in their life-supporting talisman in a ceremony known as *la-guk*.

The so-called 'religion of humans' (*mi-cho*) which evolved out of this early animism relied upon storytellers (*drung*) and singers of riddles (*de'u*) or epic poems to provide an ethical framework for social behaviour. According to a late 14th century chronicle, the religion of humans had nine aspects, represented in the body of a lion – the right foot symbolizes tales of the world's origin; the left foot symbolizes tales of the appearance of living beings; the hindquarters symbolize tales of the divisions of the earth; the right hand symbolizes tales of the geneology of rulers; the left hand those of subjects; the middle finger those concerning the origin of Buddhism; the neck those of the tribes holding allegiance to each ruler, the head those concerning patrilinear and matrilinear lines of descent, and the tail symbolizing paeans of joy.

Bon

The religion of Tazik (Persia) which was introduced into the Zhangzhung Kingdom of Far-west Tibet and thence into Central Tibet during the period of the early kings is generally considered to have evolved in three distinct phases, known as 'revealed Bon' (*dol-bon*), 'deviant Bon' (*khyar-bon*) and 'transformed Bon' (*gyur-bon*). The original importance which Bon held for the Tibetan kings probably lay in its elaborate funerary rites and veneration of space. The earliest kings of Tibet are said to have been immortals who would descend from and ascend into the heavens on a sky-cord (*mu*); but following the death of Drigum Tsenpo, the mortal kings increasingly focussed upon funerary rites and rituals for the averting of death through 'ransom' (*lud*).

The '**revealed Bon**' refers to those rituals which were prevalent in Tibet from the time of Drigum Tsenpo until the time of King Lhatotori Nyentsen. The '**deviant Bon**' included a new wave of rituals and practices derived from Zhangzhung and Brusha in Far-west Tibet; and the '**transformed Bon**' refers to the synthesis which developed following the introduction of Buddhism to Tibet and its establishment as the state religion. Contemporary research into the earliest ritual and philosophical texts of Bon has been galvanized by the work of Professor Norbu in Italy. However, the Bon orders which have survived until the present are thoroughly imbued with Buddhist imagery and symbolism; and they have evolved their own parallel literature to counterbalance that of the Buddhists, ranging from exoteric teachings on ethics to highly esoteric teachings on the Great Perfection (Dzogchen).

Since the late 19th century there have been two camps: the traditionalists who claim to reject all contacts with other Buddhist schools (as at **Menri** in Tsang and **Narshi** in Ngawa), and the modernists who accept the ecumenical approach followed in Kham towards the turn of the century by Jamgon Kongtrul, Zharza Tashi Gyeltsen, and others. Certain parts of Tibet remain strongholds of this tradition, notably the **Menri** area around the Shang valley in West Tibet, the **Bonri** area of Kongpo, the **Jangtang** lakelands, the **Tengchen** area of Kham, the **Ngawa** and **Zungchu** areas of Amdo, and **Gyarong**.

In exile the principal Bon community is based at **Solon** in Himachal Pradesh, India.

Buddhism

Buddhism evolved from the teachings of Siddhartha Gautama of the Shakya clan (known as the Buddha, the 'Awakened One'), who lived in northern India in the sixth or fifth century BC. The Buddha's teachings are rooted in a compelling existential observation: despite all persons' efforts to find happiness and avoid pain, their lives are filled with suffering and dissatisfaction. However, the Buddha did not stop there. He recognized the causes of suffering to be the dissonant mental states – delusion, attachment, aversion, pride, and envy, and realized that it is possible to free oneself permanently from such sufferings through a rigorous and well-structured training in ethics, meditation, and insight, which leads to a profound understanding of the way things really are, that is, enlightenment.

Brief introduction

The Buddha was born a prince and had known great opulence but had also experienced great deprivations when he renounced his life of luxury to seek salvation through ascetic practice. He concluded that both sensual indulgence and physical deprivations are hinderances to spiritual evolution. He taught the Middle Way, a salvific path which was initially interpreted to mean isolation from the normal distractions of daily life, by living in communities devoted to the pursuit of spiritual liberation, which were disciplined but did not involve extreme deprivation. These communities, consisting of both monks and nuns, preserved and put into practice the Buddhist teachings. Initially, the teachings were preserved through an oral transmission, but by the first century BC were increasingly committed to written form. Unlike other of the world's leading religious traditions, Buddhism does not rely on a single literary source (eg the Bible, Koran, or Talmut), but on a vast, rich, sophisticated literary corpus. The preservation of Buddhism brought literacy to hundreds of millions in Asia.

Buddhism's path to salvation depended largely on the individual's own efforts. Its emphasis on self-reliance and non-violence appealed to the merchant class in India, and thus it spread along trade routes – north through Central Asia, into China and then into the Far-east, Korea and Japan. It also spread south to Sri Lanka and Southeast Asia: Burma, Thailand, Indo-China, and Indonesia. Later, Nepal and Tibet embraced Buddhism at the zenith of its development in India, and it was this tradition which eventually came to permeate Mongolia, Manchuria and Kalmukya. In recent years Buddhism has also found adherents in the West.

A Buddhist is one who takes refuge in the **Three Precious Jewels** (Triratna):

Background

The Wheel of Existence

The Wheel of Existence (Skt bhavacakra, Tib sidpei khorlo), sometimes known as the wheel of life or the wheel of the rebirth process, is a motif widely depicted among the vestibule murals of Tibetan temples. Its graphic visual imagery symbolizes the modes of suffering endured by sentient beings of the 6 realms along with the causes of their sufferings, which generate a perpetual cycle of mundane rebirths. The wheel is firmly held in the jaws and clutches of Yama Dharmaraja, the lord of death who presides over all cyclic existence. It comprises four concentric rings, the outermost one representing the **twelve successive links of dependent origination** (Skt pratitya-samutpada, Tib tendrel) through which all forms of mundane existence come into being. The fundamental ignorance (1), propensities (2) and consciousness (3) which are the successive resonances of a past life continue to project their effects in a subsequent life in the following sequence: name and form (4), sensory activity fields (5), contact (6), sensation (7), attachment (8), grasping (9), and rebirth process (10), which in turn actualize birth (11) along with old age and death (12). The **second ring** depicts the actual sufferings endured by the gods (13), antigods (14), humans (15), animals (16), tormented spirits (17) and hell-bound beings (18), who are respectively dominated by pride, envy, diverse defilements, delusion, attachment, and hatred; along with the corresponding Six Sages (Buddhas) who manifest in order to demonstrate the paths leading to liberation from cyclic existence. The **third ring** indicates the dynamic of the rebirth process (19): an upward momentum through the three higher modes of rebirth (gods, antigods and humans) and a downward spiral through the three lower destinies (animals, tormented spirits and hell-bound beings). The **innermost ring** (20) depicts the three primary defilements or dissonant mental states underlying the entire cycle, namely: the delusion, attachment and hatred, which are self-perpetuating. It is important to remember that, in the Buddhist view, the sufferings endured by the 6 realms of sentient existence are never considered to be eternal. Indeed the impermanence of all conditioned phenomena may be observed from moment to moment, as well as from death to rebirth. The wheel serves to remind its observer of the nature and causes of suffering and of the remedial actions to be followed in order to attain liberation from cyclic existence.

Buddha, Dharma (his teachings), and Sangha (the monastic community). Beyond this, Buddhism has evolved remarkably different practices to bring about liberation, its teachings having been interpreted and reinterpreted by commentators in each new generation and in each cultural milieu. Buddhism's brilliance lies in its universality – its compelling existential appeal and, crucially, its efficacy. Historically it has appealed to peasants and to kings, to philosophers and to the illiterate, to prostitutes and murderers, and to those already close to sainthood. And though it was not its intention, Buddhism has transformed the cultures in its path – imbuing them with its ideals of universal compassion and profound insight.

Buddhist teachings The Buddhist teachings are broadly said to have developed in three distinct phases: (1) the sutra, vinaya and abhidharma texts (ie Tripitaka) of the **Lesser Vehicle** (Hinayana), which were maintained by the four great monastic orders founded in diverse parts of India by Katayayana, Rahula, Upali, and Kashyapa; (2) the sutra teachings of the **Greater Vehicle** (Mahayana), which were maintained by the followers of Nagarjuna and Asanga; and (3) the tantras or esoteric teachings of the **Indestructible Vehicle** (Vajrayana), which were transmitted by accomplished masters such as Manjushrimitra, Indrabhuti, and Padmasambhava. These different vehicles have their distinctive points of emphasis: the **Lesser Vehicle** holding that

Background

obscurations and defilements are eliminated by renunciation; the **Greater Vehicle**
holding that enlightenment can be cultivated through compassion and insight
which comprehends the emptiness underlying all phenomena, including those
obscurations; and the **Indestructible Vehicle** holding that all obscurations are
originally pure and transmutable into their pristine nature.

A primary distinction is made between the **sutra** texts which emphasize the
gradual or causal approach to enlightenment; and the **tantras** with their emphasis
on the immediate or resultant approach.

Tibetan Buddhism

Among all the Buddhist countries of Asia, the highest developments of Indian
Buddhism were preserved in Tibet. This was due partly to geographical proximity,
partly to temporal considerations, and partly to the aptitude which the Tibetans
themselves displayed for the diversity of Indian Buddhist traditions. The sparse
population, the slow measured pace of daily life and an almost anarchical disdain
for political involvement have encouraged the spiritual cultivation of Buddhism to
such an extent that it came to permeate the entire culture.

All schools of Buddhism in Tibet maintain the monastic discipline of the **vinaya**,
the graduated spiritual practices and philosophical systems based on the **sutras** and

Background

their commentaries, the shastras, and the esoteric meditative practices associated with the **tantras**. Different schools developed in different periods of Tibetan history, each derived from distinctive lineages or transmissions of Indian Buddhism.

The oldest, the Nyingmapa, are associated with the early dissemination of Buddhism during the period of the Yarlung Dynasty. The Sakyapa and the Kagyupa, along with the Kadampa, appeared in the 11th century on the basis of later developments in Indian Buddhism. The Gelukpa originated in Tibet during the 14th century, but can claim descent from the others, particularly the Kadampa and the Sakyapa. Each of these schools has had its great teachers and personalities over the centuries. Each has held political power at one time or another and each continues to exert influence in different parts of the country. Witness, for example, the strength of the Sakyapa in **Derge** and **Jyekundo**, the Kagyupa in **Tolung** and **Nangchen**, the Gelukpa in **Lhasa**, **Zhigatse**, **Chamdo** and **Tsongkha**, or the Nyingmapa in **Lhokha**, **Derge**, and **Golok-Sertal**.

NB   The Mongol and Chinese custom of referring to the major schools of Tibetan Buddhism by the colours of the ceremonial hats worn by their monks has been avoided in this book because it is an absurd oversimplification, containing a number of anomalies, as the great scholar Tseten Zhabdrung clearly pointed out in an article in *China Tibetology*.

Nyingmapa

The Nyingmapa school maintains the teachings introduced into Tibet by Shantaraksita, Padmasambhava, Vimalamitra and their contemporaries during the eighth century. The entire range of the Buddhist teachings are graded by the Nyingmapa according to nine hierarchical vehicles, starting from the exoteric sutras of the Lesser Vehicle and the Greater Vehicle and continuing through the classes of Outer Tantras to those of the Inner Tantras. It is the Inner Tantras known as Mahayoga, Anuyoga and Atiyoga (or Dzogchen) which are the teachings of the Nyingmapa par excellence.

Following the establishment of Buddhism in Tibet by King Trisong Detsen, the Nyingma literature was systematically translated into Tibetan at **Samye** Monastery. The tradition survived the persecution of Langdarma thanks to the activities of yogins such as Lhalung Pelgyi Dorje, Nyak Jnanakumara and Nubchen Sangye Yeshe; and the monks who preserved the Vinaya lineage in Amdo. When Buddhism was restored in Central Tibet, the unbroken aural tradition of the Nyingmapa flourished at **Ukpalung** in Tsang under the guidance of the Zur family, and the terma traditions (comprising teachings concealed in the past by Padmasambhava and his followers to be revealed for the benefit of future generations) developed their own local allegiances throughout the country. The most outstanding scholar and promulgator of this tradition was Longchen Rabjampa (1308-63). The six main monasteries of the Nyingma school, each of which has hundreds of branches throughout the land, are: **Katok**, founded in 1159 by Katokpa Dampa Deshek (1122-92); **Dorje Drak**, founded in 1632 by Rigdzin III Ngagi Wangpo (1580-1639); **Mindroling** founded in 1670 by Rigdzin Terdak Lingpa (1646-1714); **Pelyul**, founded in 1665 by Rigdzin Kunzang Sherab (1636-98); **Dzokchen**, founded in 1685 by Dzogchen Pema Rigdzin (1625-97); and **Zhechen**, founded in 1735 by Zhechen Rabjam II Gyurme Kunzang Namgyel.

Kagyupa

The Kagyupa school maintains the lineages of the Indian masters Tilopa, Naropa, and Maitripa, which emphasize the perfection stage of meditation

Sky Burial

The Tibetan custom of 'sky burial' in which corpses are dismembered and fed to vultures has attracted mixed feelings of revulsion, fear, and awe among outside observers. Yet it is important that the custom is seen properly in context. Firstly, 'sky-burial' is not the only means of disposing of the dead in Tibet; but it is the most popular.

Following the moment of death, the body of the deceased should be left untouched for 3 days, during which time an officiating lama should perform the transference of consciousness (pho-wa) which emancipates the consciousness (nam-she) of the deceased into a buddha-field or pure land; or else whisper advice into the ear of the deceased, informing him or her of the nature of the inner radiance experienced in the first of the successive intermediate states (bar-do) to be experienced after death. If the body is at all touched, it should be touched at the crown of the head, because the anterior fontanelle is the optimum point of exit for the consciousness. Touching the body elsewhere could result in the consciousness exiting from a lower unfavourable orifice. Relatives are encouraged neither to laugh and shout, nor to weep and cry during the period when the deceased's consciousness traverses the intermediate states. After 3 days, the officiating lama should continue offering advice to the deceased over the following 7 weeks, during which the consciousness may attain liberation from rebirth, or assume a subsequent rebirth. On the last day of each of the 7 weeks special prayers are recited and offerings made, culminating in the final ceremony. The purpose is to accumulate merits on behalf of the deceased, and to ensure his or her future well being, to which end a special tangka or image may be commissioned.

The disposal of the body is generally regarded as a separate, lesser matter. 'Sky-burial' in which the corpse is dismembered, the inner organs removed, the flesh cut into shreds, and the bones crushed and mixed with tsampa-flour, before being fed to the vultures is said to offer great merit. The vultures, who frequent the most popular 'sky-burial' sites and are summoned by an offering of incense, are revered as birds of purity, subsisting only on corpses and casting their droppings onto high mountain peaks. There are several well-known charnel grounds (durtro) on the plateau, including those at Sera and Drigung in Central Tibet; and Darling Monastery in Golok. Corpses may be carried long distances for dismemberment at one of the preferred sites.

Alternative forms of funeral are also current. 'Water burial' is regarded as a pure but inferior method of disposal in that fish are traditionally protected by the Buddhist community. 'Earth burial' is less frequently used, but preferred by the Chinese and Muslim communities. Traditionally earth burial was in vogue in Tibet during the period of the Yarlung Dynasty, when massive tumluli were constructed in Chongye and elsewhere. However, later it came to be regarded as a lower form of burial reserved for robbers, murderers, and plague victims. Cremation is utilized in parts of Eastern Tibet where wood is more plentiful; and particularly for lamas and aristocrats. Lastly, the embalmed mortal remains of certain great lamas may be interred within a reliquary stupa, or 'golden reliquary' (serdung), as an object of offering for the sake of posterity.

(sampannakrama) and the practice of the Great Seal (Mahamudra). These were introduced to Tibet by Marpa Lo-tsawa (1012-96) and Zhang Tselpa (1122-93). Marpa, who lived in the **Lhodrak** area bordering Bhutan, had four main disciples including the renowned yogin Milarepa (1040-1123), who passed many years in retreat in the mountain caves of **Labchi**, and adjacent Himalayan valleys. Milarepa is one of a select group of Tibetan masters revered for their attainment of enlightenment or buddhahood within a single lifetime. His biography and songs are classic texts, available in English translation, but it was his principal student, Gampopa (1079-1153), who founded the first monastery of that school at **Daklha Gampo** in the early 12th century. Gampopa's principal students Phakmodrupa Dorje Gyelpo (1110-70) and Karmapa I Dusum Khyenpa (1110-93) respectively founded the influential monasteries of **Densatil** and **Tsurphu**. The former was the source of the eight minor Kagyu schools, including those of **Drigung** (founded by Drigung Kyopa, 1143-1217), **Taklung** (founded by Taklung Tangpa Tashipel, 1142-1210), and **Druk** (founded by Lingje Repa, 1128-88). Later, in 1717 the great monastery of **Pelpung** was founded in East Tibet by Situ Chokyi Jungne.

Kadampa

When the Bengali master Atisha (982-1054) reintroduced the teachings of the gradual path to enlightenment into Tibet in 1042, he transmitted the doctrines of his teacher Dharmakirti of **Sumatra**, which focussed on the cultivation of compassion and the propitiation of the deities Tara, Avalokiteshvara, Acala and Shakyamuni Buddha. His disciples included Ngok Lotsawa (1059-1109) and Dromton Gyelwei Jungne (1004-64) who respectively founded the important monasteries of **Sangphu Neutok** and **Reting**. During the early 15th century this tradition was absorbed within the indigenous Gelukpa school.

Sakyapa

The Sakyapa tradition represents a unique synthesis of early eighth century Buddhism and the later diffusion of the 11th century. The members of the Khon family had been adherents of Buddhism since the time of Khon Luiwangpo Sungwa, a student of Padmasambhava. Then, in 1073, his descendant Khon Konchok Gyelpo, who had received teachings of the new tradition from Drokmi Lotsawa, founded the **Gorum** temple at **Sakya**. His tradition therefore came to emphasize the ancient teachings on Vajrakila, as well as the new teachings on Hevajra, Cakrasamvara, and the esoteric instruction known as the Path and its Fruit. The monastery was initially developed and expanded by the so-called five founders of Sakya: Sachen Kunga Nyingpo (1092-1158), Jetsun Sonam Tsemo (1142-82), Drakpa Gyeltsen (1147-1216), Sakya Pandita (1182-1251), and Drogon Chogyel Phakpa (1235-80). During the latter's lifetime, the **Lhakhang Chenmo** was built (1268) and, with the patronage of the Mongol Empire secured, a network of monasteries and temples was established throughout Central and East Tibet, comprising **Gongkar Chode**, **Jyekundo**, **Zhiwu**, **Dzongsar**, and **Lhagang**, to name but a few. After the death of the Sakya hierarch Danyi Zangpo Pal (r 1305-22), the ruling house of Sakya split into two main branches – the Phuntsok Palace and the Dolma Palace, which have until the present shared their authority on a rotational basis.

Other important sub-schools of Sakya also developed. Among them, **Ngor** was founded in 1429 by Ngorchen Kunga Zangpo, **Nalendra** in 1435 by Rongton Sheja Kunzik, **Derge Lhundrupteng** in 1448 by Tangtong Gyelpo; **Tanak Tubten Namgyeling** monastery in 1478 by Gorampa Sonam Senge; and **Dra Drangmochen** during the early 16th century by Tsarchen Losel Gyatso, who was a student of the great Doringpa.

Gelukpa

The Gelukpa school maintains the teachings and lineage of Je Tsongkhapa (1357-1419), who established a uniquely indigenous tradition on the basis of his Sakyapa and Kadampa background. Born in the **Tsongkha** valley of Amdo, he

Stupas

The stupa (Tib chorten) is a receptacle of offerings, symbolizing the buddha-mind, and the 'actual reality' (dharmata) or 'emptiness' (shunyata) behind the phenomenal appearance of the buddha-body in the world. When Shakyamuni Buddha passed away, poignantly offering his disciples a final instruction on the impermanence of conditioned phenomena, the funerary relics were interred in eight stupas, symbolic of that underlying reality, and distributed among the princes of the eight kingdoms which were his devotees: Kushinagara, Magadha, Vaishali, Kapilavastu, Calakalpa, Ramagrama, Visnudvipa, and Papa. Later, the practice of erecting such stupas as repository of offerings at crossroads and geomantic sites became popular in ancient India, particularly among some of the Mahasanghika schools. Emperor Ashoka then is credited with the multiplication of the original buddha-relics, which he reputedly inserted within 84,000 stupas constructed throughout the far-flung reaches of his Mauryan Empire and adjacent kingdoms. Some of these are said to survive at the present day, at Patan in Nepal and elsewhere.

The original stupas appear to have had a central axis, with an outer dome shape, forming a bulbous container where the relics would be interred. Books and sacred artefacts would also be inserted. As a ubiquitous Buddhism monument, the stupa has taken on a diversity of forms throughout the Buddhist world, in Southeast Asia, China, Japan, and so forth. The later stupas of Tibetan and Nepalese design came to have five characteristic parts: a squarish plinth or base, a rounded dome, an oblong harmika, a tiered triangular spire, and a bindu-shaped finial, respectively symbolizing the five elements: earth, water, fire, air, and space. Tibetan stupas also adopted eight distinct motifs, which together form a set, indicative of the eight principal deeds of Shakyamuni Buddha: his birth, victory over cyclic existence, enlightenment, teaching, descent from Tusita, resolution of schism, performance of miracles, and final nirvana. Such sets can be seen throughout the Tibetan plateau: for example, at Kumbum in Amdo, Zhiwu and Takzham in Kham, and at Chorten Rang-go north of Damzhung in Central Tibet. The original functionality of the stupa was never forgotten, and in Tibet the custom of cremating important lamas in a temporary funerary stupa (purdung), or of interring their embalmed bodies within a reliquary stupa (dungten) or 'golden reliquary stupa' (serdung) is still widely practised. The golden reliquaries of the Potala Palace, in which past Dalai Lamas are interred, are particularly renowned.

moved to Central Tibet and founded the monastery of **Ganden** in 1409. He instituted the Great Prayer Festival at Lhasa, and propagated his important treatises on the sutra and tantra traditions in and around the Tibetan capital. Two of his foremost students, Jamyang Choje Tashi Palden and Jamchen Choje Shakya Yeshe, respectively founded **Drepung** (1416) and **Sera** (1419); while others such as Gyeltsab Je and Khedrup Je, became the prime teachers of the new Gelukpa order. The latter was retrospectively recognized as Panchen Lama I. Another of Tsongkhapa's students was Dalai Lama I Gendun Drupa, who founded **Tashilhunpo** at Zhigatse in 1447.

The successive emanations of the Dalai and Panchen Lamas enhanced the prestige of the Gelukpa school, which swiftly gained allegiances among the Mongol forces of the northeast. Following the civil wars of the 17th century, many Kagyu monasteries were converted to the Gelukpa tradition, and the regent Sangye Gyatso compiled his *Yellow Beryl (Vaidurya Serpo)* history of the Gelukpa tradition.

The six greatest monasteries of the Gelukpa school are those of **Ganden**, **Drepung**, and **Sera**, in addition to **Tashilhunpo**, **Kumbum Jampaling**, and

Background

Labrang Tashikhyil in Amdo. Along with **Chamdo**, **Litang, Dargye, Kandze** and many other important centres, these became important institutions for the study of dialectics and the serious practice of the sutras and tantras.

Others

The lineages of certain minor Buddhist traditions have also survived intact – among them the **Zhiche** ('pacification') and **Chodyul** ('object of cutting') which were expounded by the South Indian yogin Padampa Sangye and his female Tibetan disciple Machik Labdron (1031-1126). The rituals of the latter are particularly popular among adherents of the Nyingma and Kagyu traditions.

The **Jonangpa** tradition was founded at Jonang in Tsang by Kunpang Tu-je Tsondru (b 1243), and widely propagated through the writings of its great exponents: Dolpopa Sherab Gyeltsen (1292-1361), Jestun Kunga Drolchok (1507-66), and Taranatha (1575-1634). Its teachings combined an in-depth knowledge of the *Kalacakra Tantra* and other tantra-texts of the new translation period, with a distinctive view concerning the nature of the emptiness (*shunyata*) which, according to Buddhism, underlies all phenomena. The Jonangpa differentiated between mundane phenomena which are regarded as being 'inherently empty' and the attributes of the Buddha which are regarded as being 'extraneously empty' of mundane impurities. The school was persecuted – ostensibly for holding this view, during the 17th century and its adherents have only survived in remote parts of **Dzamtang** and **Ngawa** in the Amdo area, where there are many Jonangpa monasteries.

The **Zhalupa** tradition is that associated with **Zhalu** monastery in Tsang and particularly with Buton Rinchendrub (1290-1364) who was one of Tibet's most prolific authors and the compiler of the modern Tibetan canon – known as the *Kangyur* and *Tangyur*. The **Bodong** tradition was founded, also in Tsang, by Bodong Cho-le Namgyel, who authored 132 volumes of texts on all the subjects of classical science including Buddhism. Lastly, the **Shangpa Kagyu** lineage was based on the tantric teachings which the yogin Khyungpo Neljor (b 978) received from the Indian yogini Niguma, and the masters Maitripa and Sukhasiddhi.

Buddhism today

The Buddhist traditions permeated the social life of Tibet until the destruction of the country's 6,000 monasteries during the suppression of the recent Tibetan uprising and the Cultural Revolution. Only a few temples and shrines of historic importance survived intact, along with a small number of temples which were used as granaries. Since the demise of the Gang of Four heroic efforts have been made by the people to restore the buildings which represent their Buddhist heritage, with or without the support of the government. More difficult is the reintroduction of systematic Buddhist learning and meditation practice. Many of the great Tibetan masters who reside in exile have returned home for visits to encourage a Buddhist renaissance; but some authorities often continue to react with suspicion and misunderstanding. This is particularly noticeable in and around Lhasa, where the political indoctrination of monks and nuns is widespread and a renewed hard-line attitude prevails against government employees who overtly support monasticism or even maintain their traditional household shrines.

Islam

The Muslim community of Tibet includes the descendants of medieval converts and merchants from **Ladakh**; as well as more recent migrants from the **Ziling** area. In Lhasa, there are mosques, such as **Gyel Lhakhang**, and Muslim cemeteries. In Northeast Amdo there are counties such as Bayan Khar (Hualong) and Dowi (Xunhua), where the Hui and Salar Muslim communities are predominant.

Religious and secular festivals

Religious festivals are important events throughout the Tibetan Buddhist world – commemorating the deeds of the Buddha, or those of the great masters of the past associated with one tradition or another. For a more detailed account, see the section on the religious festivals and religious dances of Bhutan in the present book (page 877), most of which also applies to Tibet.

Secular festivals include the traditional new year (*losar*) festival, the summer horse-festivals held throughout the country between the fifth and seventh months of the lunar calendar, and the more recent national festivals adopted from the Chinese calendar.

The following are the main festivals observed according to the traditional calendar:

	M	*D*
Losar, Tibetan New Year	1	1
Monlam, the Great Prayer Festival	1	1
Day of Offerings	1	15
Enlightenment of Buddha	4	15
Local Deities' Day	5	15
Dharmacakra Day	6	4
Birth of Padmasambhava	6	10
Yoghurt Festival	6	29
Rain Retreating Festival	7	1
Bathing Festival	7	27
Damzhung Horse Festival	7	30
Ongkor Festival	8	1
Descent from the God Realms	9	22
Anniversary of Tsongkhapa	10	25

M = Month; D = Day

Government and the modern country

Statistics

Official Name Bod

Capital Lhasa

National Flag Tibetan: white snow mountain extending from lower corners to centre, with two snow-lions supporting a gemstone (symbolic of Buddhism) and *gakhyil* (symbolic of prosperity), and a yellow sun which rises behind the summit, emanating alternate red and blue rays of light representing 12 traditional regions of Tibet which reach the upper borders; bound on three edges with a yellow border symbolic of Buddhism binding the cultural life of Tibet while remaining open to other religions with one edge of the flag open.

   Chinese: the red flag of the People's Republic of China with one large yellow star representing the Chinese Communist Party, and four minor stars representing the peasants, industrial workers, intellectuals and military.

Official Languages Tibetan, Chinese

Key Statistics 1998 *Estimated Population*: 8,106,613 (excluding Ziling and Jang Sadam districts), of which approximately 56 percent are Tibetan, 37 percent Han and Hui, and seven percent minority nationalities (including Monpa, Lhopa, Qiang, Jang, Mongol, Salar, Tu, Khazak, and Sarik). *Area*: 2,088,670 square kilometres (excluding Ziling and Jang Sadam districts). *Population density*: 3.403 per square kilometres. *Birth rate*: 30:1,000. *Death rate*: 14:1,000. *Life expectancy*: 62. *Literacy*: 40 percent. *Land use*: forested 11.2 million hectares, nomadic pasture 167 million acres (TAR only), agriculture 0.55 million acres (TAR only). *GNP per capita* (approximate): US$200. *Religion*: Buddhist 57 per cent, Atheist 32 per cent, Muslim eight per cent, Bon three per cent.

Government

Following the Chinese Communist occupation of East Tibet and Central Tibet, the country was divided between five Chinese provinces, administered, on the Soviet model, as autonomous regions, prefectures and counties. In this context it should be known that the word 'autonomous' is something of a euphemism. The Kandze area was initially an autonomous region in its own right (1950), but by 1955 it had been encorporated into Sichuan province as an autonomous prefecture. The Nagwa area was established as an autonomous prefecture of Sichuan province in 1953, and in the same year the Ganlho area of Amdo was encorporated as an autonomous prefecture of Gansu province, and the Dechen area of Kham into Yunnan province.

After the seizure of Utsang and West Kham by the PLA in 1951, and the signing of the 17-Point Agreement (see above, page 681), a preparatory committee was established to oversee the integration of Tibet into the 'motherland' in 1956. The abortive uprising against Chinese rule and policy in 1959 led to the enforced exile of HH Dalai Lama and many of his people, including Tibet's greatest lamas and spiritual masters. In 1965, the Tibetan Autonomous Region was inaugurated, and since then the areas of Utsang and West Kham have been so known.

Supreme authority lies in the hands of the Communist Party and the Army rather than in the civilian administration, many members of which appear to act as a rubber-stamp for decisions made elsewhere. There are numerous working committees and consultative bodies beneath the Communist Party right down to local village level. Since October 1992, the chairman of the party in the TAR has been Chen Kaiyuan, a technocrat who encourages economic reforms while repressing pro-independence sympathizers. There are indications that the TAR government is adopting a more rigid and hard-line stance against traditional Tibetan culture and Buddhist values, in the belief that the populace will be won over solely by economic development!

Economy

The economy of Tibet has undergone considerable reform in the last few years, though not to the same extent as mainland China. The infrastructure of the country is still dependent on inferior road surfaces which are often washed away in the rainy season. Nonetheless some modest effort has been made to extend the paved road from Gongkar Airport to Tsetang and Shelkar, and the recent opening of Chamdo Airport is likely to have a great impact on economic and social life in East Tibet – for better or worse.

The **Tibet Development Fund** is encouraged to promote foreign investment in the economy, in education, and in health. However, such changes tend to have their impact in urban areas alone, and often benefit the educated Chinese immigrants and shopkeepers rather than the economically dispossessed Tibetan population. This urban development is sustained by the vast number of branches of the Bank of Industry and Commerce, China Construction Bank and China Agricultural Bank throughout the county towns of the Tibetan Plateau. Tibetans employed in cement production and mining seem to have benefited more than most. The Lhasa Cement Factory, founded in 1960, is said to have an annual production of 110,000 tons, while the Lhasa Beer brewery, founded 1989, has an annual production of 5,000 tons. Mobile phones abound in government offices and trading circles, and IDD connections can be made from Lhasa, Ziling and other cities.

Rural economy The rural economy has changed little. There are greenhouses in the suburbs supplying vegetables to the urban communities, but most farmers are engaged in subsistence agriculture. Highland barley is the crop; supplemented in certain areas by wheat, peas, buckwheat, and broad beans, and in more sheltered valleys by rape seed, potato, turnip, apple, and walnut. Rice and cotton grow in the warmer parts of South Tibet. Nomadic groups are often better off, in that their livestock sustains the dairy and meat processing industry, as well as wool and leather production. Traditional imports from China, including tea, porcelain, and metals, are now supplemented by oil, textiles, and plastics.

Background

Importance to China Despite the often-proclaimed expense of Chinese investment in Tibet, the advantages to China of Tibet's occupation are indeed great – providing space for China's burgeoning population and enormous exploitable resources – particularly in water, timber, livestock, herbal medications, and minerals. As the source of East and South Asia's greatest rivers, the Tibetan plateau has an enormous hydro-electric and geo-thermal potential which even now has hardly been exploited. There are large reserves of natural gas, and the landlocked lakes abound in borax, salt, mirabilite, and soda. The mining of gold, copper, iron, coal, chromite, mica, and sulphur has become widespread; and unregistered economic migrants from China have created serious law and order problems in the remote mining areas of East and Northeast Tibet. Oilfields have been opened in the Tsaidam basin of Northern Tibet.

Even prior to 1911, Sichuan had begun to export Chakla timber to China. However, since 1950 lumbering has become a systematic and incessant occupation throughout Kham. Prior to the ban on logging which was introduced throughout the Kandze Prefecture in 1998, anyone entering Kham from the east will have encountered constant truck convoys from Darstedo, Batang and elsewhere carrying timber into China. Tawu became an important centre for the lumber industry and the hillsides from Drango to Riwoche and Kongpo are scarred and devastated with little sign of reforestation, causing considerable ecological damage.

The wildlife of East Tibet which once flourished is severely depleted and some species are on the verge of extinction, while only a few nature reserves administered within Qinghai appear to have taken the idea of conservation on board seriously. The lure of highly prized furs, including that of the Chiru antelope, valuable medications such as bear bile, musk, and caterpillar fungus often proves to be irresistible to the illegal hunter.

Economic life and minority nationalities The national minorities within Tibet have their own traditional economy: the **Monpa** grow rice, maize, buckwheat, barley, wheat, soya, and sesame. The **Lhopa** largely follow their traditional barter based economy, in which animal products and hides are traded for salt, wool, tools, clothing and tea. The **Qiang** of Far-east Tibet produce herbal medications such as caterpillar fungus, while their lands are rich in oil, coal, crystal, mica, and plaster. The **Jang** (Naxi) of Southeast Tibet live in a region of plentiful rainfall (average 2,700 millimetres), which sustains cash crops of rice, maize, wheat, potatoes, beans, hemp, and cotton; and minerals such as gold, silver, copper, aluminium, and manganese. The **Salars** of Dowi in Northeast Amdo grow barley, wheat, buckwheat and potatoes, with secondary occupations in stock-breeding, lumbering, wool-weaving and salt production. There is also a well-developed fruit-growing sector, including pears, apricots, grapes, jujube, apples, walnuts, and red peppers.

Tourism

This sector of the economy has been developed since the mid-1980s and reached its highpoint in 1987 prior to the recent political movement in Lhasa. Since then the movement of individual travellers has been restricted in most parts of Tibet and their activities closely monitored. However, organized cultural and trekking tours are available throughout the Tibetan plateau – mostly at premium rates but some with the budget traveller in mind. See the Information for visitors, page 26 for details. In December 1998, Kandze Prefecture was officially opened to individual foreign travellers, and it is now hoped that those areas of East and Far-east Tibet, outside of the Tibetan Autonomous Region, will soon generate considerable income from tourism to replace the losses incurred by the ban on the lumbering industry.

Kathmandu Valley

12

Kathmandu Valley

The Kathmandu Valley is the cultural and political heart of Nepal. After a long period of isolation throughout the 19th and early 20th centuries (which followed Nepal's unification in the late 17th century), Kathmandu has rapidly become an international centre for tourism. The first surfaced road to reach Kathmandu, that from Raxaul Bazar, was only completed in 1956. Now it also has direct road connections with Uttar Pradesh, Bihar and West Bengal in India, Lhasa in Tibet and Pokhara to its west. Thus, in recent years Kathmandu has become one of the important gateway cities for travel to and from Tibet (along with Chengdu, Lanzhou, Kunming, and Kashgar). Apart from the Kathmandu-Lhasa air route (Tuesday/Saturday), there are two main land routes - via the Arniko Highway (Kathmandu-Dhulikhel-Lamosangu-Barabise-Tatopani-Kodari) and via West Nepal (Kathmandu-Nepalganj- Simikot- Til-Khojarnath). **NB** *Each of the three historic towns of the Kathmandu Valley will be described in turn, beginning with Kathmandu, and then continuing with Patan (Lalitpur) and Badgaon (Bhaktapur).*

Essentials

Before you travel

Getting in   **Visas**   Visas are required by most nationalities. They are available from Nepalese embassies or consulates, and at the Indian border and Kathmandu airport. The cost of a visa varies according to your country of origin (£25 from UK), and is valid for 30 days. A visa issued on arrival is only valid for 30 days (US$20) but may be extended.

Warning   Visa extensions are very time consuming so it is best to get a 30-day visa in advance. From outside your home country it is easiest in Bangkok, Calcutta, Lhasa and New Delhi.

Extensions   Beyond one month, costs US$2 per day. Visas can only be extended further than three months through special application. The fourth month is granted at US$3 per day. Theoretically only four months residence per year is allowed on a tourist visa. It may, however, be possible to return after one month stay in India, Thailand or

---

 Nepali embassies and consulates

Australia, 3rd Level, 377 Sussex St, Sydney, NSW 2000 (T02-2647197); 66 High St, Toowong, Queensland 4006 (T07-3780124); Suite 23, 18-20 Bank Place, Melbourne, Vic 3000 (T03-6021271); 4th Floor, Airways House, 195 Adelaide Tce, Perth, WA 6000 (T09-2211207).

Bangladesh, Lake Rd, Road No 2, Baridhara Diplomatic Enclave, Dhaka.

Belgium, M25 Ballegeer, RNCG Office, 20/8 Antwerp.

Burma, 16 Natmauk Yeiktha (Park Ave), PO Box 84, Rangoon.

Denmark, 36 Kronprinsessegade, DK 1006, Copenhagen K (T01-143175).

France, 7 Rue de Washington, Paris 75008.

Germany, Im Hag 15, 5300 Bonn, Bad Godesberg 2 (T34-3097); Flinschtrasse 63, 6000 Frankfurt am Main (T06-1140871); Landsbergerstrasse 191, 8000 Munchen 21 (T089-5704406); Handwerkstrasse 5-7, 7000 Stuttgart 80 (T0711-7864614617).

India, 1 Barakhamba Rd, New Delhi 110001 (T381484); 19 Woodlands, Sterndale Rd, Alipore, Calcutta 700027 (T452024).

Italy, Piassa Medaglie d'Orro 20, Rome (T348176).

Japan, 16-23 Highashi-Gotanda, 3 chome, Shinagawa-ku, Tokyo 141.

Netherlands, Prinsengracht 687, Gelderland Bdg, NI 1017 J V Amsterdam (T020-250388).

Norway, Hakon, VIIs gt-5, 0116 Oslo (T2-414743).

Pakistan, 506 84th St, Ataturk Ave, Ramna 6/4, Islamabad 23; Karachi, Memon Cooperative Housing Society, Block 7-8 Modem Club Rd, Karachi 29 (T201908).

Sri Lanka, 290 R A de Mel Mawatha, Colombo 7.

Sweden, Birger Jarlsgatan 64, Karlavagen 97 S-115 22, Stockholm.

Switzerland, Schanzeigasse 22, CH-8044 Zurich (T816023).

UK, 12A Kensington Palace Gardens, London W8 4QU (T0171-2296231).

USA, 1500 Lake Shore Dr, Chicago, IL 60610; Heidelberg College, Tiffin, OH 44883 (T419-4482202); 473 Jackson St, San Francisco, CA 94111 (T415-4341111); 16250 Dallas Parkway, Suite 110, Dallas, Tx75248 (T214-9311212); 212 15th St NE, Atlanta, GA 30309 (T404-8928152); 2131 Leroy Place NW, Washington, DC 20008 (T202-6674550).

Tibet. Studying, teaching, research (University or Government Institute) may provide grounds for exemption. Kathmandu Immigration Office, Keshar Mahal, Tridevi Marg, Thamel, T412337. Pokhara Immigration Office is near the lake (extensions up to six weeks only). In an emergency local police stations may extend visas or trekking permits for up to seven days.

Validity   A visa is officially only valid for the Kathmandu and Pokhara valleys, and the Royal Chitwan National Park, although in practice this includes all major roads through the country.

Trekking permits   You must apply for a trekking permit to use trekking routes. This automatically extends your visa. Trekking in two areas requires separate permits. Trekking permits cost anything from US$10-US$700 per week, depending on your destination. Mustang and upper Dolpo are the most expensive. Two photographs are required.

Work permits   Work permits are required in Nepal which should normally be obtained before entering the country. Your employer applies for the permit, which can take months. If you arrange to work after arriving in Nepal, you should leave the country while the paperwork is negotiated. It is almost impossible to change a tourist visa into a work permit.

Driving   If you are considering driving a car or motorcycle in Nepal you should have an International Drivers Permit.

Student cards   An International Student Identity Card (ISIC) can be of help to get travel discounts.

Onward travel   Visa section of the Chinese Embassy in Kathmandu is open 1000-1200 Monday and Wednesday. Visas take four to five days and cost about US$20; extra US$20 if embassy has to telex Beijing. For special Tibet visa procedures, see above, page 34. Visas for India are required of every nationality, best obtained in your country of origin where possible. Visas for Thailand are issued without complication, they can be issued at Bangkok Airport for stays of 14 days or less.

Vaccinations   In Kathmandu you can get certain vaccinations free of charge from the Infectious Diseases Clinic (T215550) in Teku or from the CIWEC Clinic (T410983) and Kalimati Clinic (T214743) for a charge.

Money

Credit cards   Visa, MasterCard and AmEx are widely accepted in main centres, but not outside. In Kathmandu, Visa and MasterCard: Alpine Travel, Durbar Marg, T225020; AmEx: Jamal, Ratna Park, T226172 (Sunday-Thursday 0800-2000, Saturday 0930-1700).

Currency   The Nepalese Rupee (Rs) is divided into 100 paisa (p). Major international currencies are readily accepted (many hotels and travel agents ask to be paid in US$). The Indian Rupee is usually accepted at a recognized market rate (NRs 1.6 in 1996). Coins are 5, 10, 25 and 50 paisa and 1 rupee. Notes are 1, 2, 5, 10, 20, 50, 100, 500 and 1,000 Rupees. The last two are often difficult to change outside major towns, so carry smaller notes.

Cost of living   Cost of living in Nepal is low by western standards. The top of the range hotels and the best restaurants are considerably cheaper than their equivalent in the West.

Exchange   If travelling or trekking individually you will need cash, as it is impossible to exchange foreign currency or travellers' cheques. (Beware of pickpockets at start of trek.) Most travellers' cheques are accepted at banks and major hotels.

NB Only exchange currency at banks and authorized hotels and keep encashment

Kathmandu Valley

receipts. You need these if you wish to extend your visa and need proof of exchange (US$20 per day). You also require the form if you wish to exchange your rupees to US$ on departure. Only 15 percent of the total or the last amount exchanged, whichever is greater, will be exchanged. Airport Departure Lounge has a bank.

Getting there

Air From Europe, North America and Australasia a change of plane and/or airline en route is often necessary. Foreigners must pay for tickets in foreign exchange.

From Europe RNAC fly London, Frankfurt, Paris, Dubai, Kathmandu. Aeroflot flights via Moscow. Qatar have connections from London.

From North America Flights from US East coast usually require transferring in New Delhi to RNAC or Indian Airlines; from west coast in Hong Kong or Singapore. Fares from Canada are similar to USA, westbound from Vancouver or eastbound from Toronto or Montreal. Bangladesh Biman and PIA offer discounted fairs through small agents.

From Southeast Asia Thai International and RNAC connect Bangkok with Kathmandu. Direct flights from Singapore (Singapore Airlines) and Hong Kong (also RNAC).

From India New Delhi (IA, RNAC, Druk Air) is the main departure point (one hour). Calcutta (IA, RNAC), Bombay (RNAC) and Varanasi (IA) have direct connections with Kathmandu.

From other Asian cities Other departure points for Kathmandu include: Dhaka (Biman, Singapore Airlines), Dubai (RNAC), Karachi (PIA, Qatar), Paro (Druk Air), Osaka, Shanghai (both RNAC) and Lhasa (CSWA).

Discounts ISIC card holders under 26 years are eligible for 25 percent reduction on RNAC on domestic and international flights. Similar discount on certain RNAC and Indian Airlines routes for anyone under 30 years.

Land There are 21 recognized border crossing points. Eight are normally open, but only three are used by most foreign travellers. **Warning** At Immigration, clerks may demand an unauthorized 'fee' – do not pay unless a receipt is given.

Both the Sonauli/Bhairawa and Raxaul Bazar/Birganj border posts can be reached from Varanasi and Patna respectively by train or bus. Bus travel is quicker though crowded. In Nepal the government-owned Saja Sewa are a little less crowded than most – good value, 'Tourist Buses' allow seat reservation and have fewer stops. See also Kathmandu section.

From Tibet The route from Tibet across the Kodari/Khasa border point was opened in 1984 allowing access to Lhasa along the Friendship Highway. However in 1989 this crossing was closed again to individual travellers due to political troubles in Tibet. In June 1991 this road route was reopened to tourists. From the Friendship Bridge on the Nepal side of the border buses run twice a day to Kathmandu and taxis are also available. The road may be blocked by either landslides or snow.

Touching down

Airport tax Departure tax for international flights, Rs 1,000, for South Asian departures, Rs 800, and for domestic flights, Rs 30. Please confirm on arrival.

Tourist information No official government tourist office overseas, though some tour operators have backing, eg *Promotion Nepal (Europe) Ltd*, 3 Wellington Terrace, Bayswater Rd, London W2 4LW, T0171-2993528.

Touching down

Official time *Nepal is 15 minutes ahead of Indian Standard Time, and 5 hours 45 minutes ahead of GMT.*

Business hours *Bank holidays – 8 and 22 March, 13 April, 8 November, 25 and 28 December. Government Offices 1000-1700, Sunday to Thursday. Winter 1000-1600. Friday till 1500.* **NB** *Saturday in Nepal is a rest day and Sunday is a full working day for offices and banks. Embassies and international organizations take a 2-day weekend but are open 0900 or 0930 to 1700 or 1730 during the week. Shops are open on Saturday and holidays from 1000-1900 or 2000. For information on banking hours, see under Kathmandu.*

Voltage *Major towns in Nepal have electricity, 220 volt AC; fluctuations in current are common. A few major hotels have their own generators, as there are frequent power cuts.*

Weights and measures *Nepal uses the decimal system, but people often use traditional measures for some purposes, counting in lakhs (100,000) and crores (10 million). For rice, cereals, milk and sugar: 1 mana equals about ½ a litre; 1 pathi equals 3.75 litres, which contains 8 mana; 1 muri equals 20 pathi (75 litres). For vegetables and fruit: 1 pau equals 250 grammes; 1 ser equals 1 kilo (4 pau); 1 dharmi equals 3 kilos (3 ser). The term mutthara means 'a handful', for vegetables or firewood. For all metals 1 tola equals 11.5 grammes. For precious stones 1 carat equals 0.2 grammes.*

Kathmandu Valley

Rules, customs & etiquette

The weather ranges from sticky heat in the Terai to freezing in Himalaya. Therefore you should have clothing that will suit your travels. If you intend to trek you should have the correct clothing.

Clothing

When trekking, do not give money, cigarettes, sweets or other items indiscriminately, but do give to pilgrims and holy men who live on alms. Do not swim or bathe nude in rivers or hot springs. Help Nepal retain its beauty and its forests. Burn or bury litter. Do not use firewood or encourage its use. See 'Code of Practice' on page 47.

Conduct

Some Hindu temples are open to non-Hindus, most are not. Look for signs or ask. Remove shoes and any leather items before entering. Walk on the left of shrines and stupas. Also walk on the left hand side inside monasteries. Buddhist monasteries are open to all. You may even visit the resident lama (priest), offering him a khatak (white ceremonial scarf of silk or cotton – available in Asan, Kathmandu). If you wish to make a contribution, put money in the donation box. It will be used for the upkeep of the temple or monastery.

Visiting temples or monasteries

Many Nepalese like being photographed, particularly if you have a Polaroid and can give them a copy. If in any doubt, ask, but you are encouraged not to pay. Most festivals allow photography. Participants sometimes go into a trance and may act unpredictably. It is safest to avoid taking photographs under such circumstances.

Photography

Tipping is becoming more prevalent in Kathmandu. In expensive establishments tip up to 10 percent, in smaller places the loose change or Rs 10 will be appreciated. **NB** Taxi drivers do not expect a tip.

Tipping

Where to stay

Accommodation has been graded from **AL** down to **F**. The price is a guide to what you would pay for the best room (double) remembering that taxes vary and can sometimes add considerably to the basic price. However, hotels in some centres such as Pokhara offer large seasonal discounts. It is always worth asking. Prices in Nepal are almost always now quoted in dollars. **NB** In small towns and villages, hot water is provided in buckets. Some places have no electricity.

Keeping in touch

For information on postal and telecommunication services, see above, under Kathmandu.

Media **Newspapers** Nepal's daily English-language paper Rising Nepal, is often difficult to find. The International Herald Tribune, Time, Newsweek, Statesman, and Times of India, are sold in Kathmandu. Nepal Traveller, is a free monthly tourist magazine distributed at many hotels. Himal Magazine (six issues annually) is devoted to development and environment issues throughout the Himalaya.

Radio Radio broadcasts English news at 0800 and 2000.

Television Nepal TV, morning and evening transmissions only, Star TV.

Food and drink

Food Real Nepalese food consists of dhal (lentils), bhat (rice) and tarkari (vegetable curry). It can get monotonous. However, Kathmandu has a genuinely cosmopolitan cuisine.

Water buffalo is the usual substitute for beef since cows are sacred and cannot be eaten. You will come across 'buff' curry and even 'buff' burgers or steaks. Potatoes are the staple food of the Sherpa although they are a relatively recent introduction. Momo or Kothe – Tibetan 'dumplings' – steamed or fried meat or vegetables wrapped in dough (like Chinese 'dim sum' or Italian ravioli). Tsampa – staple hill country dish of ground barley usually mixed with tea, water or milk. Tama – a traditional Nepalese soup made from dried bamboo shoots. Thukpa – Tibetan pasta, meat and vegetable soup. Gundruk – soup made from dried vegetables.

Other popular local dishes: Charako sekwa (grilled chicken) and charako achar (marinated, spiced chicken); golbheda bari (meatballs); banel tareko (fried wild boar).

Desserts: Dahi – yoghurt or curd (usually from rich buffalo milk); Sikarni (sweet spiced yoghurt); khuwa (cheese curd dessert).

Drink Chiya is local tea prepared with milk and sugar. Coke as well as orange and lemon bottled drinks, are available in the main towns. Lassi is a refreshing drink made of curd mixed with water, but make sure the water is safe. The locally produced beer is generally good, especially refreshing after a day trekking. 'Iceberg' regarded as the best, is the most expensive. 'Leo' and 'Star' beers are good. Chang – the home brew made from barley, rye or maize, is the popular alcoholic drink. Arak is made from potato and rakshi from wheat or rice. Tongba, made from millet, is the South Tibetan and Sikkimese drink.

Warning See Health section in Introduction for detailed health advice.

You must not touch somebody else's food. You will notice that the Nepalese, when drinking water from a bottle or tumbler, may pour the liquid into their mouth without their mouth touching the container. In this way they avoid ritual pollution. You should only use your right hand for eating or passing food. The left is considered unclean as it is associated with washing after defecating. **Eating & drinking customs**

A cup of tea usually starts the morning, followed by a substantial 'brunch' late morning. If you are invited for a meal, socializing takes place before dinner (which may be served late by Western standards), and guests often leave soon after finishing the meal.

The kitchen in a Hindu home is sacred so non-Hindus should ask before entering.

Shopping

See under Kathmandu, Patan and Bhaktapur.

Sending Purchases Home If you cannot carry your goods with you, you can ship them, though it can be risky and expensive. The Foreign Post Office requires inspection by officials before you wrap your purchases for mailing. Reliable packing companies in Kathmandu include Sharma and Sons Packers & Movers (T411474) and Atlas Packers & Movers (T221402). DHL international couriers has an office in Durbar Marg.

Holidays and festivals

September/		**9 February**	Martyrs' Day
October	Dasain	**18 February**	National Democracy Day
October	Deepavali	**February/**	
7 November	Queen Aishworya's	**March**	Siva Ratri
	Birthday	**March**	Holi
17 December	Constitution and King	**8 March**	Nepalese Women's Day
	Mahendra Day	**10 April**	Teachers' Day
28 December	King Birendra's Birthday.		
11 January	Unity Day (King Prithivi Natham Shah's death anniversary)		

Useful addresses

UK: *Exodus*, T0181-6755550. *Explorasia*, T0171-6307102. *Himalayan Kingdoms*, T0117-9237163. *Promotion Nepal (Europe) Ltd*, T0171-2293528, *Trans Himalaya*, T01373-455518. **Tours and tour operators**

USA: *Abercrombie & Kent*, T312-9542944. *Archaeological Tours*, T212-9863054. *Distant Horizons*, T617-2675343. *Mountain Travel*, T415-5278100. *Tiger Tops International*, T415-3463402.

The Valley

Roughly oval in shape, the fertile valley is neatly and attractively enclosed by terraced hills. Little more than 30 kilometres in circumference at its widest, it contains not only the cities of Kathmandu, Patan and Bhaktapur – each with their own rich cultural heritage – but also many smaller villages, traditional cultivating communities that give the valley its lush patchwork appearance, and a concentration of important Hindu and Buddhist religious sites. It is the extraordinary blend of developing urbanism, continuing traditional lifestyles and an historic and prominent religious culture which still retains a high level of contemporary relevance, all set in magnificent surroundings and combined with a genuinely friendly people, that gives the Kathmandu Valley its dynamism and universal appeal. Slightly offset to the west from the geographical centre of the valley, Kathmandu now has roads extending out to all cardinal points, making the valley easily accessible by car, cycle or on foot.

Geography

At 1,340 metres above sea level, the Kathmandu Valley covers an area of some 905 square kilometres (estimates vary according to boundary demarcations) in the broadly latitudinal midland zone of Nepal, between the Mahabharat Mountain ranges to the south and the high Himalayan massifs to the north. The region is affected by its location at the junction of two of the world's major geological plates, and this continues to make the whole region vulnerable to significant seismic activity. The last great earthquake occurred in 1934 and caused immense devastation both within the Valley and further afield. Since the late 1970s, two seismic monitoring stations have been established in the Valley: at Phulchowki to the south, and at Kakani to the north.

The original Valley lake created by the Himalayan uplift of the late Pleisto-cene became the focus of a centripetal **drainage** system, in which a network of rivers from the north converged upon the Valley. Later seismic activity led to the breaching of the Valley wall at Chobhar, allowing the lake to drain out to the south through the Bagmati River. The resultant lacustrine **soils** were highly fertile, permitting cultivation and human settlement. Soils vary considerably with altitude, but include a range of red soils in addition to the alluvial deposits.

Temperate and subtropical wet hill vegetation dominates the valley's **flora**, with species of pine, cedar, fir, spruce, bamboo and rhododendron especially conspicuous. There are few species of large mammals among the valley's **fauna**, but deer are not uncommon in the broader tracts of forested

Kathmandu Valley

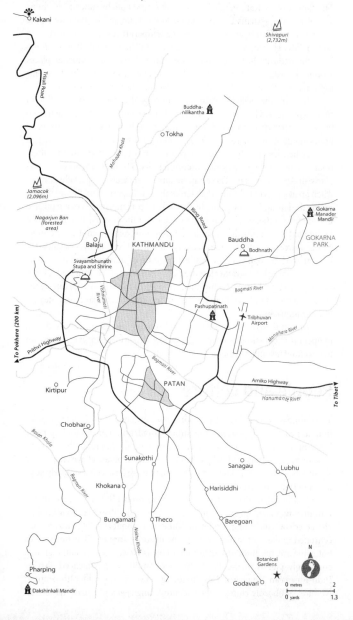

slopes. Monkeys (including the Rhesus Macaque and Common Langur) are also prevalent in some areas. The valley's main rivers have now become so polluted that they are unable to support any significant populations of fish. Commonly visible birds include species of kite and egret. Colourful species, such as parakeets and kingfishers, are concentrated in the forested periphery.

Climate

The climate of the Kathmandu Valley is influenced both by subtropical, monsoonal weather systems that prevail up to the Terai and by the cool alpine regime of the Himalayan region. Average **temperatures** range from 10°C to 26°C in July. The extremes are -3°C in January and 37°C in July. It never snows in Kathmandu itself, though there are winter flurries in the higher places around the valley, eg Nagarkot, Phulchowki and Kakani. Evening temperatures in these places are also noticeably lower at other times of the year.

Most of the valley's **rain** falls during the monsoon months of June-September. Though less severe than in lower latitudes, it is characterized by periodic **heavy** showers and storms of anything from five minutes to several hours duration and can result in local flooding. The months of July and August have the heaviest rain. In June and September, most rain falls from early afternoon and overnight, leaving many mornings dry. **Thunderstorms** occur regularly in April and May. These can be quite spectacular, especially at night when great shafts of lightning dart across the sky, lingering briefly and illuminating the city and countryside. By the end of April, moist air is being pushed in from the southeast. The **humidity** remains for the next five months. Much excitement surrounds the onset of the monsoon rains in mid to late June. Newspapers speculate as to the exact day on which it is officially proclaimed to have arrived, though with the gradual build up of humidity and occasional showers from April it is rather less dramatic than sometimes professed. Even if you are on a tight budget, taking the time to find a room with a fan during the warm, humid months of May until early September can make your stay far more comfortable.

From mid-November to the end of February, nights are very cold with temperatures occasionally dropping to below zero. Most budget hotels do not have central heating, so ask for extra blankets.

People and culture

The Kathmandu Valley is home to some five per cent of Nepal's total population and to over 34 percent of its urban population. On the trading route between the Gangetic plains and Tibet, two entirely different ethnic strains have mingled. Mongoloid peoples from the Tibetan plateau have entered the country from the north whilst from the south there has been a similarly large influx of Indo-Aryan people.

Of Mongolian origin, the **Newars** have probably been settled in the Kathmandu Valley for over 2,000 years. They have absorbed many Indian characteristics, including Hinduism. Numbering about 700,000, they are concentrated in the Kathmandu Valley. The majority are now Shaivite Hindus, but some are still Buddhist. Their **language** is Newari which, although it is commonly placed in the Tibeto-Burmese family, was influenced also by Indo-European languages. Despite losing power in the mid-18th century, Newaris stubbornly clung to their identity, language and rituals that are an agglomeration of Hinduism, Buddhism and Animism.

Traditionally Nepal's leading traders, the Newaris once organized trains of basket carrying porters over the trans-Himalayan passes to Tibet. They are also successful craftsmen and developed the unique building style that successfully blends influences from India, China and Tibet, with carved wood beams and pagoda-like temple roofs.

Kathmandu

History

Kathmandu was founded in 723 AD by the Licchavi king Gunakamadeva at the confluence of the Bagmati and Vishnumati rivers. The hub of the city is the oldest building, the Kasthamandap, which stood at the crossroads of two important trade routes. The name Kathmandu is itself derived from this temple, but did not enter customary usage until after Prithivi Narayana Shah's conquest in 1768; previously it was the valley and surrounding areas that were known as *Nepala* or *Nepal Mandala*. Later, following Jayasthiti Malla's 14th century unification of the three medieval Newar towns (Kathmandu, Patan and Badgaon or Bhaktapur) which occupy the valley, Kathmandu became an important administrative centre, but the medieval character of the three towns was well preserved. Then, in the late 17th century, following on the Gorkha unification of the kingdom by King Prithivi Narayana Shah, it naturally became the capital of the newly formed country. This sparked off a long period of expansion.

Population: 727,794
Area: 453 sq km
Altitude: 1,370m
Phone code: 1

In the 19th century, the ruling Rana family travelled frequently overseas, as a result of which new European building styles were introduced. The palaces that Jung Bahadur built from 1850 onwards were European in concept and contrasted sharply with the indigenous Newari style. Singha Durbar, a palace with 17 courtyards and over 1,500 rooms, was built within a year (1901). Reputed to have been the largest contemporary building in Asia, it was severely damaged by fire in 1974. Other palaces were built at Patan and Kathmandu, but with the eclipse of the Rana family's power in 1951 and the strengthening of the monarchy, these became neglected. Many are now used as offices.

European influences

The phenomenal growth of Kathmandu, especially over the last decade, has brought with it the new problem of pollution, one that is exacerbated by the seeming inability of the city's narrow streets to disperse the fumes of daytime traffic congestion. It is particularly difficult for asthma sufferers. In 1997, there were almost 100,000 motor vehicles on the 341 kilometres of roads in the valley, most concentrated in the capital itself. Since the early 1990s, more and more pedestrians and cyclists have taken to wearing protective masks. While anti-pollution laws do exist, they are often ambiguously applied. A vehicle's maximum permitted carbon monoxide emission is three percent. In June 1996, the Prime Minister's Mercedes failed a routine, though high profile test. The penalty: fix it within two months, or be banned from driving in the valley!

Pollution

Kathmandu Valley

Sights

Durbar Square Area

This astonishing area of religious and regal architecture and monuments is the spiritual and cultural heart of Kathmandu. It emerged from the crossroads of important trading routes. The old royal palace was at the centre of the city, surrounded by temples and other important buildings. The Durbar Square area in fact comprises three large open areas or squares and contains more than 50 monuments, the oldest dating back over 800 years. Many of the old buildings were rebuilt after the 1934 earthquake, but not always to the original design. Visit it early in the morning to see men start work and Hindu women arrive to make their offerings of flowers to the gods; or after dark, when candles, small electric lights, shadows and wisps of incense give the temples an altogether different perspective.

Kasthamandap (1) In the southwest corner is one of Kathmandu's most famous buildings, the Kasthamandap (*Kastha*, wood; *mandap*, platform or pavilion) which straddles the crossroads of the ancient trade routes, and is one of the grandest temples in Kathmandu. This is the real central point around which the city developed. Widely believed to have been built in 1596 by King Lakshmina Narasimha Malla from the wood of one enormous sal tree (*Shorea robusta*), it is now known to have a much earlier origin, as references to the temple have been found in a manuscript dating from the 12th century. It was originally a resthouse or community centre for merchants trading with Tibet and so has an open ground floor. Later it was made more ornate and converted into a temple dedicated to Gorakhnath. His shrine is at the centre of a small enclosure, although the temple also houses a few smaller shrines to other deities. For some years devotees lived here using the temple for tantric *chakra puja*. The Malla kings greatly embellished it. Nowadays, two bronze lions guard the entrance, scenes from Hindu epics are portrayed along the cornices of the first floor, and at the four corners there are figures of Ganesh. People gather to recite devotional songs, although the early morning is the time of greatest activity.

Mahadeva Mandir (2) (*Maju Deval* or *Shiva Mandir*) Just behind the Kasthamandap to the north-west, the smaller *shikhara* style Mahadeva Temple is considered to be especially auspicious for singers and dancers who come to worship here. Built in around 1690 by Queen Riddhi Laxmi, the terracotta edifice contains an image of the *linga*, symboliszing the creative male force of Shiva, in its usual combination with *yoni*, symbol of the feminine genitalia. Local lore has it that a golden image of Natyeshvara was stolen from the temple. Natyeshvara is the name given to the many-armed dancing Shiva enclosed in a circle of fire, and is particularly revered by Newars as patron of music and dance.

Singha Satal Immediately to the south of the Kasthamandap, the Singha Satal is said to have been built from wood remaining after the construction of the Kasthamandap. *Singha*, or *Singh*, means lion, and the temple takes its name from the four lions guarding it at each corner. Inside, the four handed image of Vishnu in his incarnation as Krishna is considered to be among the finest in Nepal. Vishnu is riding Garuda, the half-man half-bird god, on his way to slaying Bhaumasura, the demon king of Assam, and releasing 1,600 captive girls.

The 'Living Goddess'

*Hindus worship the **Kumari** as the reincarnation of Shiva's consort **Parvati**, Buddhists as **Tara**. The cult was instituted just over 200 years ago by Jaya Prakash Malla. All Kumaris are drawn from the Newar Shakya clan of gold and silversmiths and are initiated into the role at the age of 4 or 5. They must meet 32 requirements, including being at least 2 years old, walking, a virgin, in immaculate health, and having an unblemished skin, black or blue eyes, black hair with curls turning to the right, a flawless and robust body, soft and firm hands, eye lashes 'like those of a cow', slender arms, brilliant white teeth and the 'voice of a sparrow'.*

*   **Initiation** *The final examination is a test of nerve. Each suitable candidate is led to the **Taleju temple** at Kalratri in the dead of night and must remain calm and fearless as she walks amidst severed buffalo and goat heads. She confirms her divine right by identifying the clothes of her predecessor from a large assortment of similar articles. The installation ceremony is private. Astrologers then match her horoscope with the king's and she is ensconced in the bahal. The royal family consult her before important festive occasions. The bahal is her home until she menstruates or loses her perfection through haemorrhage from a wound or from losing a tooth. To maintain her purity, she is only allowed to leave the bahal for religious ceremonies when she is carried through the street in a palanquin or walks on cloth. Her feet must not touch the ground as this would be polluting. Whenever she appears she is dressed in red and has a 'third eye' painted on her forehead. When her reign ends, she leaves the temple with a handsome dowry, is free to marry and live a normal life. Nowadays she is taught to read and write to prepare her for the future.*

Also known as the Maru Ganesh Temple, this is dedicated to Ganesh (Vinayaka/Ganapati). As the god of success and good fortune, Ganesh is propitiated by departing travellers at this small but important golden temple, which has a continual flow of worshippers especially on Saturday and Tuesday. The gilded roof was added in 1874 by King Surendra Bikram Shah Dev, and each new King of Nepal comes to worship Ganesh here immediately following his coronation.

Ashok Vinayaka (3)

(*Natyeshvara* or *Nasal Devata* or *Dhansa Deval* mandirs) Opposite the Kasthamandap to the east, this temple is dedicated to Shiva in his Natyeshvara dancing form and is another temple favoured by Kathmandu's dancers. The broad, three-storeyed structure was renovated in the mid-1980s. The ground floor is enclosed by wooden latice screening through which you can see various images of the dancing Shiva which constitute the temple's focal point. The second floor in particular has some finely carved wooden struts supporting a protruding verandah whose seven windows testify to equally skilled and intricate craftsmanship. The smaller top storey is surmounted by three white vase-type pinnacles.

Kabindrapur Mandir (4)

Offset to the north between the Kasthamandap and Kabindrapur Mandir, the Lakshmi Narayana Mandir is a two-storeyed temple conspicuous by its decorative banality in Durbar Square's concentration of artistic and architectural masterpieces. Like the Kasthamandap, it was built as a rest house for pilgrims and travellers and only later did it assume religious significance. Inside there are two shrines which can be seen from the northern facing entrance: one appropriately dedicated to Lakshmi Narayana riding his vehicle, Garuda, while an image of Avalokiteshvara representing the infinite compassion

Lakshmi Narayana Mandir (5)

occupies the other. Today, souvenir vendors have also established themselves inside and around the temple.

Trailokya Mohan Narayana Mandir (6) This temple directly to the east of the Kasthamandap is dedicted to Vishnu and was built in the 1680s by King Parthibendra Malla as a memorial to his elder brother, Nripendra. A five-stepped platform supports the three-tiered building which has finely carved roofs, struts and window screens. Carvings illustrate the 10 incarnations of Vishnu.

On the Kasthamandap side of the temple is a **statue** of the winged **Garuda (7)**, exquisitely sculptured in stone. The faithful vehicle of Vishnu is kneeling with hands folded in prayerful homage of Vishnu. The statue was erected circa 1689 either by Queen Riddhi Lakshmi, widow of Parthibendra Malla or by her son Bhupalendra.

Kathmandu Durbar Square

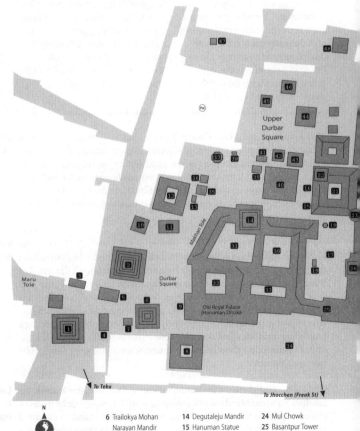

6 Trailokya Mohan Narayan Mandir	**14** Degutaleju Mandir	**24** Mul Chowk
	15 Hanuman Statue	**25** Basantpur Tower
7 Garuda Statue	**16** Stone Inscription	**26** Kirtipur Tower
8 Kumari Bahal & Chowk	**17** Nasal Chowk	**27** Lalitpur Tower
1 Kasthamandap	**18** Narasimha Statue	**28** Bhadgaon Tower
2 Mahadeva Mandir	**9** Gaddi Baithak	**19** Coronation Platform	**29** Lohan Chowk
10 Narayana Mandir	**20** Sundari Chowk	**30** Dahk Chowk
3 Ashok Vinayaka	**11** Asta Yogini Mandir	**21** Mohan chowk	**31** Masan chowk

(map labels in left margin: Kathmandu Valley)

N

0 metres 20
0 yards 22

To the southeast of the Trailokya Mohan Narayana Mandir is the Kumari Bahal and Kumari Chowk, where a living goddess (Kumari) resides for up to a dozen years until reaching the age of puberty. The stucco façade has a number of intricately carved windows on its three floors. This 18th century building and monastic courtyard is guarded by two large painted lions either side of the entrance. Note how the lintels are carved with laughing skulls while deities, doves and peacocks decorate the balcony windows. The building is in the style of the Buddhist monasteries of the valley, and was constructed by King Jaya Prakash Malla who instituted this tradition of virgin worship, reputedly as an act of penance. Inside, four large and beautifully carved windows look over the quadrangular courtyard where there is also a small stupa that marks the Buddhist worship of the Kumari as Vajrayogini. Hindus come here to receive *darshan*, a glimpse considered to be propitious, from the Kumari. Non-Hindus are allowed into the courtyard, but not upstairs.

Kumari Bahal & Chowk (8)

NB You may not photograph the Kumari who appears on cue at the middle window. Entrance Rs 2.

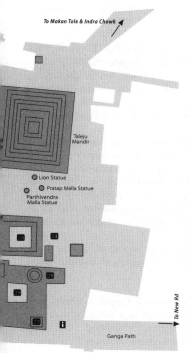

To the north of the Kumari Bahal, this palatial annex of the Hanuman Dhoka complex was built in 1908 by Chandra Sham Sher, a Rana prime minister under King Prithivi Bir Bikram Shah Dev. A product of the influence of European travels on the Nepali aristocracy of the time, it is a large white colonnaded building in the European neo-classical style and, although magnificent in its own right, sits uncomfortably amidst the area's indigenous Nepalese architecture. It houses a royal throne together with life sized portraits of all the Shah kings, and large chandeliers complete the opulence. It is used for state functions and the royal family come here to pay their respects to the Kumari and other deities.

Gaddi Baithak (9)

To the north of the Mahadeva Mandir, the much smaller Narayana Mandir is three-storeyed and built on a three-stepped platform. Each roof is tiled and small bells dangle from the top roof, ringing gently in a breeze.

Narayana Mandir (10)

(*Shiva Parvati Mandir*) Next to the Narayana Mandir, the wooden images of Shiva and Parvati observing life from an upper window have given this temple its alternative nomenclature. Asta Yogini refers to the eight mother goddesses whose images are contained within the rectangular building, and two large

Asta Yogini Mandir (11)

35 Stone Vishnu Mandir
36 Sarasvati Mandir
37 Krishna Mandir
38 Great Drums
39 King Pratap Malla's Column
40 Jayannath Mandir
41 Kala Bhairava

44 Kakeshvara Mahadeva Mandir
45 Kotilingeshvara Mahadeva Mandir
46 Mahavishnu Mandir
47 Kot Square
48 Mahendreshvara Mandir

painted, stone lions guard it from the bottom of the steps. Built in 1750 by the grandson of the great King Prithivi Narayana Shah, its architecture is similar in style to a traditional Newari house. Wonderfully carved ornamental doors and latticed windows allow a glimpse of the interior, while Shiva and Parvati look out arm in arm from the shade of the temple's overhanging tiled roof adorned by three decorative pinnacles.

Navakot Bhagavati Mandir (12) Directly to the north of the Asta Yogini Mandir, this small temple has some of Durbar Square's most beautiful wooden window and balcony carvings – if you can ignore the gaggle of souvenir sellers beneath. The upper two roofs are gilded while the first floor is tiled. Wooden figures of various female deities lavishly decorate the struts supporting each roof. Built during the first half of the 18th century by King Jagatjaya Malla in honour of his grandfather Mahapatindra whose image it contained. But the image was stolen in 1766 and the shrine remained empty for more than a century until it was again occupied, this time by a small image of the goddess Bhagavati installed at the behest of King Prithivi Narayana Shah. The image is taken to the village of Navakot, 57 kilometres north, for an annual festival. A ceremony takes place each morning in which sweet cooked rice is offered to the deity.

Makhan Tole Proceeding up Makhan Tole, on your left is the **Great Bell (13)**, installed by Bahadur Shah in 1797 which is rung whenever ceremonies are held at the adjacent **Degutaleju Mandir** (see below). It is popularly believed that the ringing of the bell wards off evil spirits, and in its early days it was used also as a general alarm. Suspended by metal chains from its decorative pagoda-style roof shade, it arrived in Kathmandu some 50 years later than similar bells in the Durbar Squares of Bhaktapur and Patan.

Ivory Windows and Sveta Bhairava Mask Opposite the Great Bell on Makhan Tole, the beautifully carved **windows** giving onto the corner balcony are another example of the fine craftsmanship concentrated in this area. The middle window is of polished copper while those flanking it are carved from ivory. The six wooden struts supporting the balcony are embellished with figures of Shiva and other deities. It is said that this was a perch from which early Malla rulers of Kathmandu would watch as processions passed through Durbar Square.

Adjacent to the balcony and behind a large wooden grill is a huge and fiercely grimacing mask of Shiva in the form of **Bhairava**, which was commissioned by Rana Bahadur Shah in 1796.

Degutaleju Mandir (14) Beside the Bhairava Mask to the east, this three-tiered pagoda style temple is a smaller and visually less impressive version of the huge Taleju temple dominating the northeast of the square. Standing some 15 metres high, it is built on top of a house and the wooden struts below its gilded roofs are once again decorated with elaborate carvings.

Hanuman Dhoka (The Old Royal Palace)

The Old Royal Palace is a collection of buildings which takes their name from the **Hanuman Statue (15)** at the entrance, installed by Pratap Malla in 1672. The monkey god is wrapped in a red cloak, his face smeared with red vermillion powder and mustard oil, and has a golden umbrella above. Nearby, outside the palace wall, is a **stone inscription (16)** in 15 languages, including French and English, in praise of the goddess Kalika. It was carved on 14 January 1664 during the reign of Pratap Malla, a talented poet and linguist.

The palace was originally built around more than 30 courtyards (*chowks*), but the addition of new buildings by successive royals through the centuries have left just 10 today. The site is believed to date back to the late Licchavi era. Mahendra Malla started the present buildings in the 16th century, and during the 17th century Pratap Malla added many temples. The south wing was added by Prithivi Narayana Shah in 1771, and the southwest wing by King Prithivi Bikram Shah in 1908.

The **Golden Gate** of the palace is brightly painted in green, blue and gold and is flanked by two stone lions, one carrying Shiva, the other his consort Parvati. The door itself is thought to have been installed by King Girvana Yuddha Bikram Shah in 1810, while the entrance dates back to the Mallas. In the niche above the gate is Krishna in his ferocious tantric aspect, flanked by the more gentle, amorous Krishna surrounded by the *gopi* (cowgirls), and by King Pratap Malla (believed to be an incarnation of Vishnu) playing a lute, and his queen. Open 1030-1600 daily, admission Rs 10.

In the west wing of Hanuman Dhoka is the Tribhuvan Museum dedicated to the king who led a revolt against the Ranas who built it. (See also under **Museums**.)

The Golden Gate (Suvarnadvara) leads to Nasal Chowk, meaning the 'courtyard of the dancing one', after the small figure of the dancing Shiva (Natyeshvara or *Nasaleshvara*) in a white temple on the east side of the courtyard; it is the largest of the 10 palace courtyards and is where coronations take place. Malla rulers used Nasal Chowk as both a theatre and a forum where the king would meet his subjects. Immediately on the left as you enter, a wooden door with exquisitely carved panelling leads to the former Malla living quarters. Images of the Mallas' protecting deities, Jaya and Vijaya, stand on either side. An interesting story lies behind the framed, dark and aminated statue of the half-man – half-lion god **Narasimha (18)** in the act of destroying the demon Hiranyakashipu: the silver-inlaid stone image was placed there by King Pratap Malla in 1673 as penance for publically dancing while dressed in Narasimha costume. Just beyond the image, there is a line of portraits of all Shah kings, the **Sisa Baithak**, beneath which is a ceremonial throne used by the king during official functions – a sword takes the monarch's place in his absence. The present king, Birendra, was crowned on the **Coronation Platform (19)** in the centre.

Nasal Chowk, along with the **Sundari Chowk (20)**, **Mohan Chowk (21)** and the **Mohan Tower (22)**, was originally built by Pratap Malla in the 17th century. Mohan Chowk, to the northwest of Nasal Chowk, was renovated by Rajendra Bikram Shah in the early 19th century and was used exclusively by the king to entertain visiting royalty. It is said that the occasional recalcitrant royal would be brought here to spend a little time at His Majesty's pleasure behind bars. Carved wooden **verandahs** illustrating the exploits of Krishna look down on the chowk on three sides. Intriguingly, there are also some depictions of figures in western costume along the north wall. The decorated golden waterspout named **Sundhara** was also built by Pratap Malla, who brought cool clear water from Budhanilakantha to a bath three and a half metres below ground level. Sculpted portrayals of the mythical Indian king, Bhagirath, who is credited with bringing the Ganges river from Heaven to its earthly course, adorn the waterspout, while various deities decorate the surrounding walls. Thus Pratap Malla was able to combine bathing with daily puja.

In the northeast corner of the complex is the **Panch Mukhi Hanuman (23)**, a round five-storeyed building which only the temple priests may enter

Nasal Chowk (17)

for worship. The five faces of Hanuman are portrayed on the mid-17th century structure.

Mul Chowk (24), beside this round tower and at the northeast of the complex, is unfortunately not open to visitors, but contains numerous statues, images and carvings, and was used for coronations by the Mallas. Mass animal sacrifices apparently take place here during Dasain.

You can climb to the top of the 18th century **Basantpur Tower (25)**, or Kathmandu Tower, that overlooks the square. It is the nine-storeyed palace in the southwest corner of Nasal Chowk with beautiful wooden windows and superb carvings on the roof struts. Prithivi Narayana Shah renovated many of the earlier buildings and from 1768 onwards extended the palace to the east. He introduced the fortified tower to Durbar Square, adding the smaller towers which are named after the ancient cities of **Kirtipur (26)** to the northwest with its superb copper roof, **Lalitpur (27)** to the southeast, and **Bhadgaon (28)** to the northeast. It once overlooked beautiful gardens with a clear view of the Taleju Temple, all set around the **Lohan Chowk (29)**.

The area west of Nasal Chowk was built in the latter half of the 19th century. This includes the **Dahk Chowk (30)**, **Masan Chowk (31)**, **Hunluche Chowk (32)** and **Lam Chowk (33)**. The **Degutaleju Temple**, dedicated to the Mallas' personal goddess, was erected by Shiva Singh Malla who reigned from 1578-1620.

Running south from **Basantpur Square (34)** is **Jhocchen**, or **Freak Street**, where cheap hotels, restaurants and hashish retailers made it a centre for hippies in the 1960s. The dope peddlars are still active, here and throughout the wider Thamel area.

Stone Vishnu Mandir (35) Returning to the west of Hanuman Dhoka, next to the Great Bell stands the Stone Vishnu Mandir, a square red columned structure supporting a grey stone and bell shaped upper portion, and standing on a three-tiered platform. The temple was badly damaged in the 1934 earthquake and has only recently been fully restored. Its origins are unknown. An image of Vishnu atop Garuda stands in the earth floored interior.

Sarasvati Mandir (36) Also recently renovated after earthquake damage, this small single-storeyed temple has an image of Sarasvati, goddess of knowledge and education, flanked by four-armed Lakshmi, goddess of wealth, and Ganesh, the elephant headed god of success and good fortune.

Krishna Mandir (37) This is one of the few octagonal temples here and was built by King Pratap Malla in 1648, either in response to the impressive Krishna Mandir in Patan, or as a religious consolation for his earlier failure to conquer the city, or in memory of his two wives, or a combination of all three. The three-tiered traditional Newari building is supported by stone columns around the circumference of the base. The image of Krishna inside the temple is accompanied by his two wives, Satyabhama and Rukmani, all of which, according to a Sanskrit inscription, bear deliberate resemblance to Pratap Malla and his own two queens. Beside the temple, a pair of **Great Drums (38)** mark worship at the temple. Added by King Girvana Yuddha Bikram Shah in 1800, they were formally used in combination with the Great Bell (see above) to sound alarm or as a call for people to congregate, but are now used only twice a year and accompany the sacrifice of a goat and a buffalo.

(*Pratap Dhvaja*) Opposite the Krishna Mandir to the east, this beautifully decorated column with statues of Pratap Malla, his two wives and four sons, was modestly erected by Pratap Malla himself in 1670. It shares a platform with several smaller religious objects, while the figures on top of the column are seated and looking directly into the prayer room used by Pratap on the third floor of the Degutaleju Mandir.

King Pratap Malla's Column (39)

This two-storeyed temple is the oldest in Durbar Square. Built on a three-tiered platform in 1563 by King Mahendra Malla, it contains images of Vishnu and Jagannath. A total of 48 wooden struts support the tiled roofs and are decorated with an amazing variety of sexually explicit carvings. Eight miniature shrines are affixed to the ground floor walls, but the dieties they once contained are missing.

Jagannath Mandir (40)

Opposite the Jagannath Mandir and immediately to the north of the Pratap Malla Column, the Kala Bhairava (Black Bhairava) is a fearful image of Shiva the destroyer, carved out of a single stone. Opposite and to the west, the Durbar Square police station now stands on a site formerly occupied by law courts.

Kala Bhairava (41)

Standing to the northeast of the Kala Bhairava, this temple is recognizable by the small but typically Newari open balcony of its first floor where an image of Indra was traditionally shown during Indrajata. A Shiva lingam stands inside the temple, but the image of Garuda is conspicuously positioned outside to the south, suggesting that it may once have been a Vishnu temple that was subsequently rededicated to Shiva.

Indrapur Mandir (42)

Immediately adjacent to the Indrapur Mandir to the east, this Vishnu temple is constructed on a four-tiered plinth and its three storeys rise attractively above its neighbour. Its exact origins are also unclear, although it is believed to have existed during Pratap Malla's reign. Its black and gold image of Vishnu as Narayana is seated. Its posture suggests that it was originally playing a flute.

Vishnu Mandir (43)

This small temple was built in 1681 by Queen Bhubhan Lakshmi and is an interesting combination of Newari and Indian architectural styles. On a two-tiered platform, the ground floor has wooden columns supporting the sloping red-tiled roof, while the upper portion contrasts totally with its bright white shikhara style edifice. The whole is surmounted by the *kalasa*, a vase of primeval water or divine elixir.

Kakeshvara Mahadeva Mandir (44)

In the northwest corner of the Durbar Square, this temple was built by Mahendra Malla in the 16th century and is one of the square's oldest temples. It is dedicated to Shiva and, with a Nandi bull, it differs from the surrounding temples. It is a cube with a bulbous dome in the Gumbhaj style, similar to early Muslim tombs in India. Attractively built of stone brick on a three-tiered platform, it also has a smaller adjoining dome above a square columned porch.

Kotilingeshvara Mahadeva Mandir (45)

Heading east from the Kotilingeshvara temple, the Mahavishnu Mandir nearby was built by Jaya Jagat Malla in the first half of the 18th century. The eponymous golden image of Mahavishnu was moved to the Royal Palace following the damage caused by the 1934 earthquake to the temple. It has remained there since, and the Mahavishnu Mandir has no replacement image. The temple has a miniature shikhara-type spire topped by a golden umbrella, a royal insignia.

Mahavishnu Mandir (46)

Kathmandu Valley

Kot Square (47) Just off the northwest corner of Durbar Square is the Kot Square. In 1846 Jung Bahadur Rana, the founder of the Rana Dynasty, murdered all his potential opponents from the local nobility before seizing power. As if commemorating that event, during Durga Puja each year, at this spot, young soldiers attempt to cut off a buffalo head with a single stroke of their khukuri.

Mahendreshvara Mandir (48) Just to the east of the Mahavishnu Mandir, this two-storeyed temple was built by Mahendra Malla in 1561. Steps lead beneath a simple metal arch to its main entrance from where the Shiva image can be seen.

Taleju Mandir (49) This is the tallest and the most magnificent of all the temples in the Durbar Square area, and stands in **Trishul Chowk**, a courtyard named after Shiva's trident which is stationed at its entrance. It stands 36 metres high, soaring above the Hanuman Durbar complex. The Taleju Mandir is closed to the public except on the ninth day of the annual Dasain festival in autumn when Hindus may enter. It was built in 1564 and only the royal family and important priests are allowed regular access. **Taleju** was a patron goddess of the Malla kings from the time of Jayasthiti Malla in the late 14th century. The image is said to have come from Ayodhya. One story recounts how it was damaged by an unnamed king in his fury at not being allowed to marry the wife of his choice, because she was not of his caste. The rulers of **Bhaktapur** and **Patan** followed suit and established their own Taleju temples beside their palaces, though neither could match this original for beauty and grandeur.

The entrance on the east side, on **Indra Chowk**, has a large peepul tree which gives shade to an image of **Vishnu** accompanied by his vehicle, **Garuda**. The main entrance (**Singha Dhoka**) on the south side of the temple has two stone lions guarding it and its arched frame is decorated with numerous brightly painted terracotta carvings, some of which were apparently pillaged from Bhaktapur by Pratap Malla in 1663. On the broad eighth stage of the elaborate 12 stage plinth a wall providing additional protection has 12 miniature two-storeyed temples outside it, while another four are placed at each of the four corners within. At the top of the platform are two large **bells**, one installed by Pratap Malla in 1564, the other by Bhaskar Malla in 1714, which are rung during temple worship. Smaller bells hang from the edges of all three roofs and ring gently in the breeze. Metal **flags** engraved with portraits of various deities are suspended from the corners of the first two roofs, while four vases (*kalasa*) hang from the corners of the top roof. It has ornately carved wooden beams, brackets and lattices, and superb wood and engraved bronze window decoration on each side. The extensive use of copper gilt makes it an even more attractive sight at **sunset**. The finial decoration, in keeping with the lavishness of the rest of the temple, has four small bell-shaped spires surrounding a larger central spire of gold which is topped by a golden umbrella.

Tanu Deval Mandir In the northeast extremity of the square, this small temple is comprised of two shrines, one dedicated to Vishnu, the other a Newari style house complete with brightly coloured carved window struts and a five point.

Beyond Durbar Square

Northeast from Durbar Square From the northeast corner of Durbar Square, you can walk to Indra Chowk, Asan Tole and the Rani Pokhari tank. This thoroughfare is the old artery of the city. An enclosed old stone image of the **Shiva linga** and **yoni** is supposed to be a smaller replica of the one at Pashupatinath. It is referred to as a five faced image, but only four are visible. On your left in the corner of the square is a statue of **Garuda**.

Makhan Tole was the start of the trade route to Tibet and is lined with interesting temples and shops. After the earthquake, much of its traffic was diverted along **New Road**. There are medieval houses with colourful façades, overhanging carved wooden balconies and carved windows. Many of the shops sell tangkas, clothes and paintings.

Indra Chowk, the first crossroads, is at the intersection of Makhan Tole and Shukra Path. The southwest corner has a small brass **Ganesh** shrine. The **Akash Bhairava Mandir** to the west has a silver image of the rain god which is displayed outside for a week during the Indrajatra festival. Non Hindus are not allowed in. The square was a textile market and many shops still specialize in blankets, shawls and cloth. In the northeast corner is a **Shiva Mandir** as the street runs towards Khel Tole, another market square with Tibetan carpet shops.

Off to the west past a small shrine often smeared with fresh blood, almost halfway between Indra Chowk and Asan, is the **Sveta Matsyendranath Mandir** (or *Jana Bahal*), one of the most venerated Buddhist shrines in Kathmandu (equally popular with Hindus). It has a two-tiered bronze roof and two brass lions guard the entrance. The courtyard is filled with small shrines, carved pillars and statues. The white-faced image inside the elaborately carved shrine is **Padmapani Avalokiteshvara**, in the form of the compassionate and benevolent divinity Matsyendra (*Tib* Phakpa Jamali; see above, page 893). There are an astonishing 108 paintings of Avalokiteshvara throughout the temple. A colourful procession of the main image around town takes place during the **Rath Yatra**, or chariot festival, in March/April. The pagoda-style Hindu temple next door on the left is the **Lunchun Lumbun Ajima**, a *shakti* temple with erotic carvings. Dedicated to Ajima, protecting goddess of children, it also contains an image of Ganesh.

Leave Khel Tole and continue walking northeast until you reach the next square, **Asan Tole**. Three temples dedicated to Annapurna, Ganesh and Narayana line the square which is regarded as the commercial heart of the old city with the rice market and bicycle and rickshaw repair shops. The **Annapurna Mandir**, also known as Yoganvara, is an attractive three-storeyed temple with copper gilt roofs whose rounded up-turning corners give a distinctly oriental impression and have copper birds attached to the end of each. Lions once again stand guard at the entrance and the divinity (an abstract silver form of *pathi*, a unit of weight) is worshipped by local traders for success and prosperity. On the opposite side of the square to the east, the **Ganesh Mandir** is a two-storeyed temple with a fine golden bell-shaped spire topped by an elaborately carved umbrella. It is also a shrine popular with Buddhists. The smaller **Narayana Mandir** is slightly offset from the centre of the square and is considered less significant locally than the above two. Its main image of Vishnu as Narayana is accompanied by those of Uma Maheshvara and Lakshmi Narayana. A tiny temple or shrine dedicated to **Uma Maheshvara** stands beside the Ganesh temple, while on the east side of the square a small water **tank** contains a statue of a **fish**.

Central Kathmandu

Heading west from Asan Tole, you will reach the crossroads of Bangemudha on Shukra Path. Continue south to return to **Indra Chowk**, or north to reach the tourist heartland of the old city. If you head north you will pass on your left a recessed square containing the large **Kathesimbhu Stupa**, and soon reach **Thahiti Tole** where the traffic moves around yet another stupa. From here you

**Thamel &
Chetrapati**

can turn east along Jyatha Road to Kantipath, passing on the right the entrance to the **Chusya Bahal**. Alternatively, proceeding north from the stupa you will enter the **Thamel** area, which takes its name from a former Buddhist monastery and resthouse here (*Tham Bahal*) and has become the undisputed focal point of the city for tourists. Or, heading west, you will reach the frenetic intersection of **Chetrapati** where traffic converges from six directions. This is the city's tourist centre with numerous budget hotels and exotic restaurants featuring cuisines from the four corners of the world. The intersection of Thamel Chowk can be reached from the **Thahiti Stupa** in the south via Kwa Bahal Road, or from Tridevi Marg and the Royal Palace to the east. Two parallel north-south running roads are particularly geared to the tourist industry: Kwa Bahal Road to the east and Thamel Road to the west. The former has more shops, selling Nepalese, Tibetan and Bhutanese handicrafts and second-hand trekking equipment, while the latter has many hotels, guesthouses and restaurants. Heading south, east or north from the junction near the *Kathmandu Guest House*, you will be mesmerized by the density of facilities available for the budget tourist – far removed from the ancient culture of the surrounding city. By contrast, at **Bhagavan Bahal** in Northeast Thamel, there are three active Newar Buddhist shrines which are particularly colourful during Dasain.

Around **Chetrapati** there are many more low-priced guesthouses, interspersed with authentic street life. This area is also interesting as the neighbourhood of brass bandsmen who are in demand during local festivals and Nepalese weddings, especially in February. Heading south from the Chetrapati intersection onto Pyaphal Road, you will eventually reach the Kasthamandap at the southwest end of Durbar Square.

Tridevi Mandir
(or Thamel Bahal) Heading east from central Thamel, diagonally opposite the immigration office on Tridevi Marg, there is a cluster of three small but attractive temples which give the road its name (*tri* is three, and *devi* refers to feminine divinity) and are dedicated to the goddesses Dakshinkali, Jawalamai and Mankamna.

New Road and Kantipath

New Road, extending southeast from Durbar Square, was constructed in the aftermath of the devastating 1934 earthquake, and is now the city's main commercial thoroughfare. Here, there are supermarkets, textile and clothing stores, jewellers, the **Nepal Bank**, and **Royal Nepal Airlines** on its intersection with Kantipath, opposite Ratna Park.

Mahabuddha
Stupa Heading north along Kantipath from the New Road intersection, you pass the **Bir Hospital** on the left, and **Ratna Park** on the right. To the west of Ratna Park and near the Bir Hospital, this impressive stupa standing in the centre of a busy market square measures over 10 metres in height. Entrance to the square through arches on the west and east sides. Four statues of Buddha, each in a different pose, stand around the stupa at the cardinal points. Beside the east entrance arch, a three-pinnacled shrine built by Newari Buddhists encloses another statue of Buddha and its wooden porch is decorated with carvings of Buddha and various mythological animals.

Rani Pokhari Continuing north on Kantipath, and bypassing the lane on the left which leads to Asan, you reach Rani Pokhari (*Queen's Pond*), a huge tank with a white temple dedicated to Shiva in the middle. The Rani in question was Pratap Malla's queen who in 1667 commissioned its construction in memory of their son, **Chakravartendra**, who, following his father's abdication in favour of his four sons each of whom would rule for one year, died on the second day of his reign, apparently having been trampled by an elephant. The pagoda temple originally installed by the Mallas fell into disrepair and was replaced by the current edifice in 1908 by Jung Bahadur Rana. The water with which the pond was originally filled was taken from 51 sacred rivers throughout Nepal, thus ensuring its sanctity.

Access to the temple is along a white stone walkway from Kantipath, but the area is kept locked except for one day during the Tihar festival (October-November). The **temple** has a domed roof reminiscent of classical Indian Mughal architecture and is surmounted by a copper spire. The main **image** is of the Shiva lingam, but other deities also feature. Four small **shrines** at each corner contain images of Bhairava, Harishankar, Shakti and Tarkeshvari.

Not surprisingly, various myths and legends have come to be associated with Rani Pokhari over the years. It is said to be haunted by ghosts, including one especially seductive female spectre which managed to unnerve even the great Pratap Malla. The pond was also used for a time for 'ducking': suspected criminals were immersed and if they drowned they were guilty, but their innocence was proven if they survived. Fortunately, it seems that most suspects were innocent.

The large clocktower (**Ghantaghar**) to the east of Rani Pokhari stands in the grounds of a college and serves as a useful local landmark. The tank contains fish whose numbers are said to be increasing following their serious depletion in the 1960s when toxic chemicals were emptied into it. The pond also attracts small numbers of ducks, herons and the occasional migratory waterfowl, as well as snakes, otters and frogs.

Tundikhel

If you turn south from the New Road/Kantipath intersection, you pass the GPO, Bhimsen Tower, Sundhara bathing area, and the **Central Telegraph Office** to the right, with the Tundikhel, the Martyr's Gate and the **National Stadium** on the left. Immediately to the south of Ratna Park and about one kilometre south of Rani Pokhari, Tundikhel means literally 'open grassy field'. The Royal Pavilion is to its north and has statues of six Gurkha recipients of the Victoria Cross, awarded for outstanding bravery during the two world wars. The Tundikhel has traditionally been used for army parades and major ceremonies (eg National Day in February, and Dosain in October/November) which are often attended by the King, who may use the opportunity to impart a Message to the Nation, by the Prime Minister, military leaders and other senior civil servants. Many thousands of people throng the Tundikhel on such occasions, but if you can find a strategic viewing place (standing on a wall has been recommended) the colour and pageantry is well worth the effort. Army drill sessions take place here early most mornings, when much of the Tundikhel is off limits.

Mahakal Mandir

On the west side of the Tundikhel, this attractive three-storeyed pagoda temple is venerated by Hindus and Buddhists alike. Gilded copper covers all three roofs which have divine images carved on the beams. The main entrance is an arched gate topped by a *kalasa*.

Bhimsen Tower
(Dharahara)

South of the Tundikhel and the GPO, this 60 metres tall column was built as a watchtower, one of two erected by Bhimsen Tappa in 1832. The other collapsed soon after construction, but this, although damaged in the 1934 earthquake, still serves as one of the city's most prominent landmarks. It resembles a Muslim minaret and the design seems to have been strongly influenced by Calcutta's Ochterlony Monument (now renamed *Shahid Minar*) which was constructed in 1828 as a memorial to Sir David Ochterlony who led East India Company troops against the Nepalese in the war of 1814-1816.

The revered **Sundhara**, a below ground level quadrangle with spring water flowing from the mouth of a gilded crocodile statue, is located beside the base of the Bhimsen Tower.

Prithivi Path

Shahid Smarak On Prithivi Path just east of the GPO, this memorial arch encloses a statue of
(Martyr's Gate) King Tribhuvan and is dedicated to those who fell or were executed during the struggle for democracy and against the Ranas in 1940. Wreaths are customarily placed here by visiting foreign dignitaries. Just to the east is the **Bhadrakali Mandir**, a small temple dedicated to the goddess Kali.

Beyond the Martyr's Gate, at the south end of Ratna Park and the Tundikhel, there is a large and well kept military camp, while along Prithivi Path, there is the **Singha Durbar** government buildings, the Supreme Court, and the **Archaeology Department** which must issue certificates before antiques or apparent antiques can be exported.

Singha Durbar Heading east from the Martyr's Gate, you reach this magnificent former Rana residence set in a 30 hectare complex which, since 1951, has been used as the central government's bureaucratic headquarters. Built by Chandra Shamsher Rana in 1901, the splendid neo-classical façade reflects the influence of the Ranas' newly found taste for European sojourns. The palace contains over 1,000 rooms and a similar number of servants were retained for its upkeep. Inside, the huge marble floored Durbar Hall was used to host lavish receptions: illuminated by giant crystal chandeliers, its walls were hung with ornate mirrors and portraits of previous Rana rulers, while stuffed tigers stood in each corner and richly embroidered carpets were rolled out for the guests. In July 1973 much of the eastern part of the building was destroyed by fire and has since been only partially restored. The complex also includes the Supreme Court.

Durbar Marg

Durbar Marg runs parallel to Kantipath, extending southwards from the Royal Palace as far as the Army Camp at the southeast corner of the Tundikhel. At its northern end, the road forms a T junction with **Tridevi Marg** heading towards the Immigration Office and Thamel to the west, and towards Nag Pokhari and Bodhnath to the east. Proceeding southwards along Durbar Marg, you pass the magnificent *Yak and Yeti* hotel at the end of a lane on your left, and the somewhat less grand *Annapurna* hotel on your right. At the crossroads ahead of you, Jamal Road cuts southwest towards Rani Pokhari, while to the east lie **Kamaladi and Bagh Bazar** leading on to the Naxal and Maitidevi districts respectively. In this area there are a number of upmarket hotels and expensive restaurants, various airline offices and travel agencies.

The Royal Returning to the intersection of Prithivi Path and Durbar Marg and heading
Palace north you reach the southern gate of the Royal Palace at the top end of Durbar Marg. Its official name is **Narayanahiti Durbar**, after a Vishnu temple to the east and the adjacent waterspout (*hiti*). The original palace buildings were constructed in 1915 for Rana Bahadur Shah and are situated behind the ultra modern pagoda extension seen from Durbar Marg which was completed for the wedding of King Birendra Bir Bikram Shah (then heir to the throne) in

1970. The grounds cover more than 30 hectares and are guarded on all sides. There is no admission to the private residence, though parts are open to visitors on Thursday during the winter, open 1000-1700, admission Rs 300. Look out for the throngs of giant bats hanging from the trees all along the northern extension of Kantipath to the east of the palace. A little further south along Durbar Marg, a prominent statue of **King Mahendra** in full ceremonial attire gazes down on Kathmandu's most exclusive thoroughfare.

On the north side of Tridevi Marg about one kilometre east of Durbar Marg towards Pashupatinath, Nag Pokhari is a water temple where people have traditionally prayed to the serpent deities, for rainfall. A fine gold serpent image stands atop a tall narrow plinth in the centre of the tank. **Nag Pokhari**

South Kathmandu

The area of South Kathmandu, extending from Jhocchen (**Freak Street**) towards the Vishnumati and Bagmati rivers is predominantly an untouristed area, where Hindu traditions thrive. There are temples dedicated to Bhimasena, one of the five Pandava brothers whose epic tales are recounted in the *Mahabharata*; the *Jaisi Deval* (dedicated to Shiva), and Panchali Bhairava near the ghats of the Bagmati River.

Although the **Bagmati River** has been abused and neglected in recent years, it has traditionally been a major source of irrigation for the valley's agriculture and of domestic water for its settlements, in addition to its historical religious significance to which various Nepali sacred texts (eg the Varaha Purana, the Pashupati Purana and the Nepal Mahatmya) bear witness. But the city's rapid growth has led to its transformation into a repository for sewage and other urban waste. Nevertheless, there is a multitude of temples, shrines, relics and other monuments along its northern bank, from **Teku** to **Tripureshvar**.

On the right side of the Bagmati River lies the **Tripureshvar Temple**. Built in 1818 by Queen Lalitatripurasundari Devi Shah, this is a three-storey temple in pagoda style, surrounded on four sides by small temples dedicated to Vishnu, Surya, Ganesh and Devi. In the centre of the main temple is a shapeless Shiva lingam without any facial features, which is circumambulated by worshippers.

West Kathmandu

From Thamel and Chetrapati you can head west to the banks of the Vishnumati River and on to one of the most sacred sites of the Kathmandu Valley on its far bank. The **Svayambhunath Stupa** (*Tib* Phakpa Shangku) is revered as the oldest and one of the two most important sites of Buddhist worship in Kathmandu. It is a major landmark, towering above **Padmachala Hill**, 175 metres above the valley and three kilometres west of the city centre. According to legend, the hill and stupa occupy the site where the Buddha of the previous aeon, Vipashyin, is said to have thrown a lotus seed into the lake which then filled the valley, causing it to bloom and radiate with a 'self-arising' luminosity, identified with that of the primordial Buddha, Vajradhara. The *bodhisatva* Manjushri is believed to have made this lotus light accessible to worshippers by using his sword to cleave a watercourse for the rivers of the valley, and thereby draining the lake. Newar Buddhists hold that the primordial Buddha Vajradhara is even now embodied in the timber axis of the stupa. **Svayambhunath**

The earliest historical associations of the site are linked to **Vrishadeva**, the patriarch of the Licchavi Dynasty, who is said to have built the first shrine, perhaps using a pre-existing projecting stone. Later inscriptions attribute the stupa's construction to his great-grandson King **Manadeva I** (c. 450 AD) and its reconstruction to the Indian master **Shantikara**, a contemporary of King **Amshuvarman**. It became a focal point for Indian pilgrims and was frequented by Padmasambhava, Atisha and others. By 1234 it had become an important centre of Buddhist learning, with close ties to Tibet. In 1349 Muslim troops from Bengal ravaged the shrine, but it was soon rebuilt with its now familiar tall spire. In 1614 additions and renovations were made by Zhamarpa VI during the reign of Pratap Malla. Access from Kathmandu was improved with the construction of a long stairway and a bridge across the Vishnumati. Pratap Malla also added two new temple spires and a large vajra placed in front of the stupa. Later repairs were carried out by Katok Tsewang Norbu (1750), Pawo Rinpoche VII (1758), and the Shah kings (1825 and 1983).

The Eastern Stairway The climb up the 400 stone steps is more impressive than the modern road. At the bottom are three painted images symbolizing the Three Precious Jewels of Buddhism, which were erected in 1637 by Pratap Malla and his son, Lakshmandra Singh Malla. A large **footprint** in the stone is said to be that of either the Buddha or Manjushri. At regular intervals are pairs of eagles, lions, horses and peacocks, the vehicles of the peaceful meditational buddhas.

NB The numerous **monkeys** here can be aggressive: treat with caution and take care of bags.

On entering the compound from the main stairway, you see the **Great Vajra** set upon its drum base, symbolizing male skilful means, and the **Bell** alongside, symbolizing female discernment. Around the pedestal are the 12 animals from the Tibetan calendar: hare, dragon, snake, horse, sheep, monkey, bird, dog, pig, mouse, ox, and tiger.

The Stupa With a diameter of 20 metres and standing 10 metres high, it has been a model for subsequent stupas constructed throughout Nepal. It was seriously damaged by a storm in the summer of 1816, coinciding with the instalment of an official British Resident in Kathmandu, an association not lost on the suspicious Nepalis. Repairs were carried out a decade later. The various tiers of its base and dome respectively symbolize the elements: earth, water, fire, air, and space. Above the dome is the square *harmika*, each side of which has the eyes of the Buddha, gazing compassionately from beneath heavy black eyebrows, fringed by a curtain of blue, green, red and gold material. The shape of the nose is considered by some to represent the number '1' in Nepali script, symbolizing unity. The 13 steps of the spire surmounting the *harmika* represent the successive bodhisattva and buddha levels and the crowning canopy represents the goal of buddhahood. On each of the four sides of the stupa, at the cardinal points, there is a niche containing a shrine dedicated to one of the meditational buddhas, each with its distinct posture and gesture, deeply recessed and barely visible within a richly decorated gilded copper repoussé. Aksobhya is in the east, Ratnasambhava in the south, Amitabha in the west, and Amoghasiddhi in the north. Vairocana, the deity in the centre, is actually depicted on the east side, along with Aksobhya. The female counterparts of these buddhas are located within the niches of the intermediate directions. The faithful turn the prayer-wheel as they walk clockwise around the shrine.

The Vajra at the top of the stairs is flanked by the two white *shikhara* temples, known as Anantapur (southeast) and Pratapur (northeast), which were built by Pratap Malla in 1646 to house the protector deities Bhairava and Bhairavai. Circumambulating the stupa clockwise, on the south side you will pass Newar shrines dedicated to Vasudhara and the nagas (rebuilt in 1983). On the west side, after the rear entrance, there is a museum, a Bhutanese temple of the Drukpa Kagyu school, and Newar temples dedicated to Manjushri and Ajima Hariti. Lastly, on the north side, is a Newar temple dedicated to Cakrasamvara, and a Karma Kagyu temple of the Zhamar school, built in the 1960s by Sabchu Rinpoche. An International Buddhist Library and Pilgrim Guest House are located on a side pathway. On a neighbouring hill is another stupa dedicated to Sarasvati, the goddess of discriminative awareness and learning.

Local festivals The two most popular festivals celebrated at Svayambhunath mark the Tibetan New Year (Losar) in February or March, a time of joyous revelry, and Buddha Jayanta in April or May which commemorates the Buddha's birthday. Both are very crowded, but colourful and worth a visit.

Getting there Svayambhunath is a comfortable one-hour walking distance from Durbar Square, along Maruhiti Tole to the river which you cross by a footbridge. There are cremation ghats on the riverbank. The path then leads through a built-up area with a sizeable Tibetan carpet weaving community, to a meadow. Or take a taxi or rickshaw to the south entrance at the bottom of the hill. **NB** If you hire a cycle, it is worth paying Rs 1-Rs 2 to have it 'minded' by one of the small boys hanging around: this avoids tyres being let down.

Balaju Water Gardens

If you head northwest from Thamel, passing through Naya Bazar, you will cross the Vishnumati River and the Ring Road to reach Balaju, some two kilometres north of Paknajol. This small park was created by Rana Bahadur Saha in the last century as a place of recreation easily accessible from Kathmandu, but the city's recent expansion and the building of the Ring Road has effectively brought it within the bounds of Kathmandu itself. Paths lead around numerous small fountains in the centre of the park. Statues commemorate Nepal's foremost poet **Bhanu Bhakta**, and King **Mahendra** with his **queen** overlooking over a pool of exotic fish. By the tank is a typical Nepalese temple flanked by a row of images of Hindu deities including one of the three supine Narayana images attributed to King Vishnugupta (seventh century). At three metres in length it is smaller than – and, some say, a copy of – the one at Budhanilikantha.

Along the whole of the north wall, natural **spring** water gushes from 22 open jawed crocodile taps, while the nearby seating area is shaded by a large peepul tree and surrounded by aromatic beds of rose and jasmine. At the far side a path leads up a small hillock wooded with pine, sal and bamboo. This is a popular spot for birdwatchers – 450 species are said to congregate here – and offers good **views** of the valley. The park also encloses a large **swimming pool**, formerly for the exclusive use of the Royal Family, but now open to the public, admission Rs 20.

Saturdays are especially crowded. Best time to visit is from April to June when flowers are in bloom. Refreshments available. Pleasant, but too popular to be really peaceful. Open 0700-2000, admission Rs 2, plus a further Rs 2 if accompanied by a camera.

East Kathmandu

Pashupatinath

Heading east four kilometres from the city centre towards Bodhnath, you reach **Goshala** (where there is a road leading south towards Pashupati and the airport). Pashupati is Nepal's most important Hindu pilgrimage site, located on the banks of the Bagmati River, which in the dry season is no more than a trickle of badly polluted water. It covers an area of more than 260 hectares with almost as many temples and religious monuments. Pashupatinath has been designated a World Heritage Site by UNESCO and its location allows a visit to be combined with a trip to Bodhnath. There is a Tourist Information Unit. Radio Nepal begins its daily transmission with a hymn to Pashupatinath, while the god's name is frequently invoked in the course of a royal blessing.

Pashupatinath belongs to **Shiva**, here in his peaceful form as Pashupati, the shepherd or lord of beasts, and to Narayana. The temple is one of the most important to Hindus in the subcontinent and has been closely associated with orthodox south Indian Shaivism since the visit of Shankaracharya. The **Pashupati linga**, over one metre in height, is among South Asia's most important linga sites for Hindu pilgrims.

The original temple was reputedly built by a Licchavi king, **Supuspadeva**, 39 generations before Mandadeva (464-505 AD), but later underwent considerable repair and reconstruction. The main temple was renovated by Queen **Gangadevi** during the period 1578-1620, turning it into a pagoda of brass and gilt with silver plated gateways. Upon her death the Pashupati linga is said to have emitted a cry of lamentation so loud that local residents were deafened. **NB** Non Hindus, which in practice usually also includes Western converts to

Pashupatinath

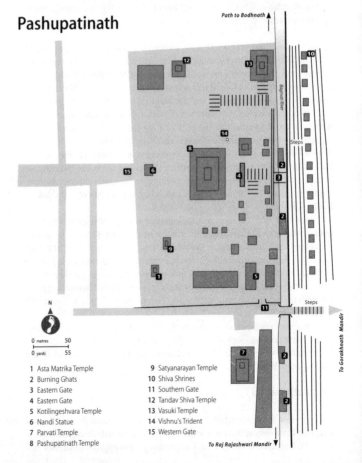

1 Asta Matrika Temple
2 Burning Ghats
3 Eastern Gate
4 Eastern Gate
5 Kotilingeshvara Temple
6 Nandi Statue
7 Parvati Temple
8 Pashupatinath Temple
9 Satyanarayan Temple
10 Shiva Shrines
11 Southern Gate
12 Tandav Shiva Temple
13 Vasuki Temple
14 Vishnu's Trident
15 Western Gate

Kathmandu Valley

Hinduism, are not allowed into this 17th century temple, but from the southern entrance you may get a glimpse of the gilt **Nandi** bull, Shiva's vehicle. It is thought to be around 300 years old, though it was not placed here until 1879. The black, four-headed image of Pashupati inside the temple is older, and it replaced one destroyed by Muslim invaders in the 14th century.

In the northeast of the courtyard is the **Vasuki Temple**, dedicated to the image of the *naga* king Vasuki, whose lower body appears as an intricate tangled body of snakes. Devotees generally circumambulate the Vasuki Temple before worshipping Pashupatinath, as Vasuki is considered the main temple's protector. It was constructed by King Pratap Malla during the Malla period. In the northwest corner, images of Shiva's consort Parvati decorate the **Tandav Shiva Temple**, while to the southeast the **Kotilingeshvara Temple** is a three-storey circular building surrounded at its base by a large number of stone lingas and yonis. Just to the west of the main temple, a large white building with a sloping grey roof (visible from the east bank of the Bagmati) houses a collection of religious images.

Outside the temple courtyard Surrounding the main Pashupatinath temple complex are numerous structures and temples which are open to non Hindus. Just west of Pashupatinath is a cluster of white temples called **Panchadeval** ('five temples'). Built in 1870, the central temple and the four surrounding it all have Shiva lingas as their central shrines. The pilgrim resthouses around the temple are used for homeless old people, and outside vendors sell an array of puja accessories including a colourful selection of powdered dyes. To the south and near the river is the sixth century **Parvati** (or **Baccheresvarai**) **Temple**, another two-storeyed pagoda with a crescent moon unusually forming part of the pinnacle. This contains a number of erotic Hindu tantric carvings and it is thought that in the past human sacrifices were made here during the Shivaratri festival. The adjoining **Narayana Temple** is said to have been constructed in the course of a single night in 1929, a memorial to the late prime minister Chandra Shamsher Rana. Nearby is a fine but neglected seventh century Buddha statue while a little further down the river is the **Raj Rajeshvari Temple**, notable for its carved windows and roof struts, and where many congregate during the Shivaratri celebration. It contains life-sized images of Rama, his consort and three brothers, and at the entrance is a huge Shiva linga image. The upper floor has five dome-like structures with gilt finials and commands a very good view of Kathmandu.

Along the western riverbank are the **Royal Cremation Ghats**, four on either side of the footbridge by the Parvati Temple. Cremations follow prescribed rituals and are presided over by a *pandit*, or Hindu priest, with family members also playing an active role in the ceremony. You can observe ceremonies from the opposite bank or from the roof above the southern ghats. Although conducted in the open air, a funeral is, as in the West, a profoundly emotional occasion, so sensitivity to the grief of the mourners is recommended. Conspicuous photography of a cremation is intrusive and is considered, at best, impolite.

Near the top of the stepped ghats on the eastern bank of the Bagmati is the **Hermit's Cave**. Further up is the **Gorakhnath Temple**, a tall brick *shikhara* structure with a brass trident in front, surrounded by lingas. This is one of the oldest temples dedicated to Gorakhnath, a semi-mythical figure who is considered a guardian deity of the Nath sect. The temple was built by Jayasthiti Malla in the late 14th century on a site dating several hundred years further back and is believed to contain the footprints of Gorakhnath. A track leads off to the right past the **Mankamna Temple** to the **Vishvarupa Temple** (non

Hindus are not allowed inside). Inside the onion domed edifice is a huge image of Shiva in union with his Shakti, almost six metres high. Beyond the Gorakhnath Temple and down by the Bagmati river on the other side of its meandering loop is the **Guhesvarai Temple**, built in the 17th century and dedicated to Kali, the goddess of destruction and re-birth. The arched tubular metal construction covers the main temple. Near the top, four gilded snakes support the roof apex illustrating the *yantra* diagram (geometric triangle). In the centre of the temple is a pool covered at the base in gold and silver. At the head of the pool is a jar which is worshipped as the goddess Guheshvari and the water from the pool is accepted as her offering. Again, only Hindus are allowed inside to see the gilded shrine room. Thousands of devotees visit Guheshvari daily.

Warning   The 400 or so **monkeys** living in the area should be treated with caution. Rabies is not unheard of. Keep a tight hold of bags and avoid tempting them with food, as they will not hesitate to assert their perceived right to your packed lunch. In the late afternoon they are fed inside the temple courtyard – the sight of the advancing simeon mob is memorable indeed.

Getting there   You follow an ancient road which in medieval times linked the old royal palace in Durbar Square with the temple complex, crossing the Dhobi Khola by a steel bridge. The road then traverses the Pashupatinath plateau which was the probable site of the Licchavi capital of **Deopatan**. You will pass a large pilgrims' rest house and a small village before reaching the temple to the right of the road. From the Royal Palace, head east towards the airport which, with Pashupati, is well signposted. Allow one hour by foot. Auto-rickshaws should charge about Rs 50, taxis Rs 100.

Chabahil   Heading northeast from the **Goshala** intersection (see above), you will pass through **Chabahil** where there is a small but elegant stupa known as **Dhanju Chaitya**. Believed to pre-date the Bodhnath stupa, it is widely thought to have been built by King Dharmadeva who also contributed to the early growth of the Pashupati complex. During Licchavi times, Chabahil was a village at the crossroads of a major trade route between India and Tibet. Ashoka's daughter, **Charamuti**, is said to have lived here and, with her husband Devapala, founded two monasteries. Some sources also credit her with construction of the stupa itself, which is occasionally still known locally as **Charamuti**. Tantric Buddhist monks were based here during the early ninth century. The stupa was rebuilt during the seventh century and again renovated during the 17th century, and stands over 12 metres high. There are even now some old chaityas, their form possibly influenced by that of the Shiva linga, and statuary at the site, including a ninth century free-standing Bodhisattva. Images of four meditational buddhas are found on each of the four sides around the stupa; and on the northern side, there is a three and a half metres statue of Buddha in the earth-touching gesture (*bhumisparshamudra*). It is said that the copper gilt in which the stupa was originally plated was removed and sold by the Mallas to raise funds for their ultimately futile defence of the valley against the invading forces from Gorkha.

The Chabahil area is also well known for its **Ganesh Temple**, which is one of the four Ganesh temples protecting the Kathmandu Valley. For the local people, this temple has the reputation of curing sores and pimples. The Ganesh image is reputed to date from the eighth to ninth centuries and once a year is taken around locally in a chariot. Tuesday are the most popular days for devotees.

Bodhnath Stupa   (*Tib* Chorten Jarung Khashor) About one kilometre east of Chabahil, the

Bodhnath Stupa is 38 metres high and 100 metres in circumference, and looms above the road dominating the ancient trade route between Kathmandu and Lhasa. It is the largest stupa in Nepal and is revered by both Tibetan and Newar Buddhists.

Origins Tibetans believe the stupa to contain the bone relics of the past Buddha Kashyapa and to have been built by a lowly poultry keeper and widow four times over named **Jadzimo**. Wishing to utilize her meagre resources in an offering to the Buddha, Jadzimo sought and received permission from the king to begin construction. When they saw what was being built, the local nobility became jealous and resentful that such a great stupa was being constructed by one of such humble social standing. They demanded that the king order its immediate destruction, but the good hearted monarch refused with the words '*Jarung Kashor*' ('The permission given shall not be revoked') from which comes the stupa's Tibetan name, Chorten Jarung Kashor. Jadzimo's sons are said to have been subsequently reborn as King Trisong Dtesen, Shantaraksita, and Padmasambhava, who together established Buddhism in eighth century Tibet, while the widow herself is said to have attained buddhahood and is known as the protectress Pramohadevi.

Newar chronicles, in contrast, hold the stupa to have been constructed by the Licchavi king **Manadeva** in the latter half of the fifth century AD in order to atone for his crime of patricide. The stupa's Newari name, Khasti Chaitya (Dewdrop Stupa), comes from the drought that accompanied its construction when workers put out cloths at night to be able to drink the dewdrops which accumulated.

The structure was subsequently restored (some sources say reconstructed) by the Nyingmapa lama Shakya Zangpo in the early 16th century. Later, following the 1852 treaty between Nepal and the Manchus, which ended the Tibeto-Nepalese border wars, the abbotship of Boudha was granted in 1859 to a Chinese delegate whose descendants, known as the **Chini Lama** (*Tib* Gya Lama), continued until recently to hold a privileged position in local affairs.

By its sheer size, the Bodhnath stupa may seem even more impressive than that at Svayambhunath. It too has a hemispherical dome, symbolic of emptiness, topped by a square *harmika* painted on each side with the eyes of the Buddha symbolizing awareness, above which rises the spire with its 13 steps leading up to the canopy, which symbolizes the goal of Buddhahood. However, it is now almost hidden from distant view by the surrounding buildings, which create an attractive courtyard effect for the stupa itself.

Around the octagonal three-tiered base of the stupa there is a brick wall with 147 niches and 108 images of the meditational buddhas, inset behind copper prayer-wheels. Each section of the wall holds four to five such prayer-wheels. The main entrance to the stupa is on the south side, and the principal shrine dedicated to the female protectress Ajima/Hariti on the west. Around the stupa there is a pilgrim's circuit which is densely thronged in the early mornings and evenings by local Tibetan residents and by pilgrims from far-flung parts of the Himalayan region and beyond. Numerous shrines, bookstores and handicraft shops surround the circuit, the speciality being Newar silverware cast by the *ciré perdue* ('lost wax') process.

In recent years Boudha, once a remote village, has become a densely populated suburb of Kathmandu. There is a particularly high concentration of Tibetans here, alongside the older Newar and Tamang communities, and this is reflected in the prolific temple building in which the various Tibetan traditions have engaged since the late 1960s. These shrines and monasteries are too numerous to describe here, but a few of the most important among them can be mentioned, some with well structured **teaching programmes**.

The only temple of importance on the south side of the main road is **Orgyen Dongak Choling**, the seat of the late Dudjom Rinpoche, a charismatic meditation master and scholarly head of the Nyingmapa school, whose mortal remains are interred here in a stupa. Those located to the **west** of the stupa include **Jamchen Monastery** (Sakya; under the guidance of Chogyel Trichen), **Sharpa Monastery** and Trulzhik Rinpoche's Monastery (both Nyingma), **Tsechen Shedrubling** (Kagyu), and **Shelkar Chode** (Geluk).

Heading **northwest** of the stupa, the following are the most important: **Tharlam Monastery** (Sakya), **Karnying Shedrubling** (Karma Kagyu; under the guidance of Chokyi Nyima Rinpoche), **Zhechen Tenyi Dargyeling** (Nyingma; under the guidance of the late Dilgo Khyentse Rinpoche and Zhechen Rabjam Rinpoche); Bairo Khyentse Rinpoche's monastery (Kagyu), and **Marpa House** (Kagyu; under the guidance of Khenpo Tsultrim Gyatso).

Close to the stupa on the **north** side are: **Dabsang Monastery** (Kagyu), **Trangu Tashi Choling** (Kagyu), and **Kyirong Samtenling** (Geluk).

To the **east** are: **Tashi Migyur Dorje Gyeltsen Ling** (Sakya; under Tarik Tulku), **Dezhung Monastery** (Sakya), **Leksheling** (Sakya/Kagyu; under Karma Trinle Rinpoche), **Thubten Ngedon Shedrubling** (Kagyu), and **Karma Chokhor Tekchen Leksheling** (Kagyu).

Further **north** on or near Mahankal Road are: **Mahayana Prakash Pelyul Dharmalaya** (Nyingma; under Penor Rinpoche), **To Pullahari** (Kagyu; under Jamgon Kongtrul Rinpoche), **International Buddhist Academy** (Sakya; under Khenpo Abe), and the **Drukpa Kagyu Monastery** (under Tsoknyi Rinpoche). Mahankal Road extends **northeast** to **Kopan Monastery** (Geluk; under Lama Zopa and Lama Yeshe), and **Ngagi Gonpa** (Kagyu; under Tulku Orgyan). To the extreme east of Boudha, on the north side of the main road, is **Chubsang Monastery** (Geluk; under Tsibri Chubzang Rinpoche).

Sleeping and eating D *Maya Guest House*, T470866. Has good, expensive rooms, but wonderful garden and trekking service to Langtang. *Stupa Hotel*, T470400. Large with a spacious garden. **E** *Snowlion Lodge*, T447043. Large building with 2 blocks and restaurant facilities. *Lotus Guest House*. Clean but simple rooms in excellent location. The *Hotel Tashi Delek*, T471380, and *Bir Restaurant*, T470790, are both located close to the noisy bus stand.

Festivals A lively procession carrying the goddess Mamla around the Bodhnath area is the main attraction of the *Mamla Jatra* festival (**January/February**). The Tibetan New Year, *Losar* (usually **February**) is celebrated here on the 3rd day of the new moon with special prayers, processions, masked dances and a feast. The Tamang festival of *Timal Jatra* (**March/April**) attracts Tamangs from throughout the country and begins with an all night celebration of music and dancing before a procession heads for ritual bathing at Balaju and continues on to Svayambhunath. Though honouring in particular those who have died during the past year, the vivacious *Gonai* festival (**July/August**) is celebrated with processions and much revelry and humour by Tamangs. Bodhnath's largest festival attracts Tibetans from all parts and takes place on the day of the first full moon of the year of the bird which next falls in 2005.

Transport Crowded buses to Boudha leave from Ratna Park and Bagh Bazar. Better to take a taxi (about Rs 150 by meter from central Thamel), or an auto-rickshaw (Rs 80). Alternatively, walk from the Guhesvarai Temple at Pashupati, head to your left downstream to the bridge, or from Pashupatinath Temple upstream along the west bank. Both paths meet on the north side of the bridge. A footpath leads northeast to Boudha, one and a half kilometres.

Museums

(*See also* **Patan** and **Bhaktapur**.)

Located within the grounds of the Ministry of Education on the corner of **Keshar Library**
Kantipath and Tridevi Marg. ■ *Open 1000-1700, Sunday-Thursday,
1000-1430 Friday. Entrance free.*

Situated just outside the Svayambhunath complex, it has a fine art gallery. **National**
■ *Open 1000-1700, Friday 1000-1430. Entrance Rs 10. Guided tour: Rs 50-100.* **Museum**

Near the National Museum, this is run by the Tribhuvan University and has a **Natural History**
notable collection of butterflies, as well as displays of birds, reptiles and mam- **Museum**
mals. ■ *Open 1000-1700, Sunday-Friday. Entrance free.*

Inside the old Royal Palace on the west side of Nasal Chowk, this museum **Tribhuvan**
houses a small but interesting collection of the chattels of King Tribhuvan. **Museum**
■ *T215613. Open 0800-1600, Wednesday-Monday. Admission Rs 10.* Also
includes the *Mahendra* and the recently added *Birendra* museums.

Essentials

Sleeping & eating

The hotels are grouped by area together with places to eat which are close at hand.

Sleeping AL *Soaltee Holiday Inn Crowne Plaza*, T272555, F272205. Pagoda-style **Durbar**
building, formerly the Oberoi and the first and largest 5-star hotel in Nepal, 286 rooms **Square/New**
most with excellent views of mountains, suites at US$675 per night, swimming pool, **Road**
tennis court, 24-hour casino, 4 restaurants including French, Italian, Indian, good
Indian and Western buffet breakfast in coffee shop, located at Tahachal, 10 minutes
southwest from Durbar Square, free bus service to New Rd and Durbar Marg at 1000,
1230, 1500, 1800 and 1930, all return 30 minutes later.
   B *Classic*, New Rd, T222630, F224889. 84 rooms, superb views of the city and
mountains from the top floor *Tower* restaurant, and live music in the *Natraj*, large
building in the centre of the city's main shopping and commercial area, near Durbar
Square. **B** *Saphire*, Shukrapath, corner of New Rd, near Durbar Square, T223636. Formerly known as the *Crystal*, has 52 rooms, all a/c, right by Durbar Square, good views
of town from roof terrace and convenient for temple visits, price reflects location, restaurant (Indian and continental).
   E *Kumari Guest House*. Basic, hot showers, but no safes for luggage, hence inse-
cure, unsatisfactory laundry.

Sleeping A central area with some excellent hotels and fine restaurants. **Durbar Marg**
   AL *Yak and Yeti*, T413999, F227782, off Durbar Marg. 255 rooms, set in charming
Japanese-style landscaped gardens, *Sunrise Café* coffee shop also does buffet breakfast, lunch and dinner, Rs 450, restaurants in Lal Durbar wing, a fine mid-19th century,
neo-classical Rana palace, *Nachghar*, elegant, colonnaded and crystal chandeliered
Nepali/Indian vegetarian restaurant with stage for nightly cultural programmes,
2000-2100, reservations usually essential; *Chimney*, Russian and Continental food in
fine rustic east European ambience, huge brass chimney fireplace and wall decor,
established by first owner Boris Lissanevitch, meal for 2 costs around Rs 2,000, comfortable bar, some exquisite wood carvings in reception and throughout.
Recommended.

Kathmandu

■ **Sleeping**
1 Ambassador
2 Asia
3 Blue Diamond
4 Blue Star
5 de l'Annupurna
6 Dreamland
7 Kathmandu Guesthouse
8 Kathmandu Lodge
9 Malla
10 Manang
11 Marshiyangdi
12 Mayalu & AMEX
13 Mt Makalu
14 Nook

15 Saphire
16 Shankar
17 Sherpa & Café de la Paix
18 Siddharth & Himalaya View
19 Valley View
20 Woodlands & Greenlands
    Restaurant
21 Yak & Yeti
22 Yellow Pagoda

● **Eating**
1 Bhanchha-ghar
2 German Bakery
3 Ghar-e-Kabab & Kushi Fuji
4 Jasmine & New Mandarin

5 KC's
6 Nirula's & Nanglo
7 Rumdoodle

🚌 **Bus stations**
1 Bhaktapur Minibuses
2 Bhaktapur Trolleybus
3 Central Bus Stand
4 Pokhara Minibus
5 Ratna Park (for Patan)
6 Sundhara Bus Stand
7 Trishuli Buses (Sorokhuti)
8 Trivedi Marg Bus Stand

A *Hotel de l'Annapurna*, Durbar Marg, T221711, F225236. 159 rooms, the best overlooking garden and pool, good Indian restaurant and coffee shop for buffet breakfast, swimming pool open to non-residents at Rs 450, also tennis court and billiards room at Rs 100 per hour, live Nepali and Western music every evening in foyer/bar, exclusive shops and cultural centre, extensively remodelled in 1993, refurbished rooms recommended. **A** *Dynasty Plaza Woodlands*, Durbar Marg, T220623, F223083. 125 rooms, restaurant and bar, health club, sauna, squash courts, and pool open to non residents at Rs 250. **A** *Sherpa*, Durbar Marg, T227000, F222026. 83 rooms and 2 restaurants: *Sherpa Grill* for Indian and continental food, evenings only, and *Café de la Paix* coffee shop with breakfast, lunch and dinner buffets, hours 0700-2300, rooftop swimming pool open to non-residents at Rs 300, regular Sherpa and Tamang cultural programmes.

D *Mayalu*, T223596, F220820. With 28 rooms all with bath, Punjabi restaurant also does some continental dishes.

Eating   Indian: *Amber*, T225938. For the best Indian food, live ghazals every evening 1930-2130. Recommended. *Niramar Restaurant and Bar* on the corner of Jamal Rd, near the statue of King Mahendra. Does good South Indian vegetarian food, ghazals every evening 1900-2200, 'no dancing', also has coffee house. *Taj*, T240744. In a basement at the southern end of Durbar Marg, near the two mosques, good tandoori Indian and Chinese food at reasonable prices.

Nepali/Tibetan: *Bhanccha Ghar*, on Kamaladi, off Durbar Marg, T225172. Excellent authentic Nepali food. *Saino Restaurant*, T230682. At the northern end of the road, set Nepali and Tibetan meals including local rice wine at US$10, also Indian, continental and Chinese food.

Fastfood: *Hot Breads*, T221331, F228816. For fresh bread, cakes and pastries, also ice creams. *Wimpy*, T220299, F414184. For lamb burgers, fries and shakes.

Sleeping   This is Kathmandu's tourist heartland, a mass of hotels, restaurants and shops densely concentrated along narrow and often congested lanes. This is the place to stay if you want the closest proximity to the rest of the transient population and to the steaks and cakes for which the area has become renowned, not to mention the perennial wallahs of tiger balm, khukuri knives, hashish and more. You won't go far wrong with most of the hotels and guesthouses here.   **Central Thamel**

C *Excelsior*, T411566, F410853. 50 rooms all with bath, some with tub, very central but reasonably quiet, lift, continental restaurant. **C** *Horizon*, T220904, F423855. 20 comfortable and well furnished rooms, breakfast served on the terrace. **C** *Karma*, T417897. 15 rooms all with bath, some with tub, breakfast only in restaurant. **C** *Kathmandu Guest House*, T413632, F417133. 115 comfortable rooms including some larger rooms, most with TV and some with a/c, relaxed restaurant with pleasant shaded garden sitting area, it even has a small 'business centre', one of the first hotels to open in Kathmandu and a Thamel reference point for many, prices reflect its reputation, so you can get a similar room nearby for a third of the price. **C** *MM International*, T411847, F412945. 31 rooms all with bath, Indian and continental restaurant, around the corner from supermarket. **C** *Newa Guest House*, T415781, F420055. 20 rooms all with bath and phone, good Indian restaurant, comfortable and helpful. **C-D** *Garuda*, T416340, F413614. 34 rooms, all with bath, some a/c, continental restaurant and deli counter.

D *A-One Guest House*, T229302, F227333. 9 rooms, some with bath, no food. **D** *The Earth*, T228850, F228890. 14 rooms, all with attached bath and TV, and a large dorm, snacks available, credit cards accepted. Recommended. **D** *Fuji Guest House*, T/F229234. 14 rooms, some with bath, good food nearby. **D** *Himal Cottage*, T229187. 10 rooms, some with bath, credit cards accepted. **D** *Lovers' Nest*, T220541, F227795. 15 rooms, some with bath, rooftop restaurant with movies, rates highly negotiable.

D *Mont Blanc*, T222447. 17 rooms, food on request. **D** *My Home*, T231788, F224466. 20 rooms, all with bath, no food, expensive. **D** *Nightingale*, T225038. 25 rooms, most with bath, cheaper rooms with common bath, breakfast only. **D** *Puska*, T225027, F227795. 22 rooms, most with bath (small), '*Big Belly Restaurant*', clean and pleasant. **D** *Sonna*, T418399, F471375. 20 rooms, all with bath, movies shown in restaurant, helpful staff. **D** *Star*, T411004, F411442. 55 rooms, restaurant, carpeted but gloomy. **D** *Tashi Dhele*, T217446. 24 rooms, restaurant, clean and comfortable. **D** *Thamel Guest House*, T411520. 13 rooms, all with bath, good restaurant also shows videos, very central. **D** *Thorung Peak*, T224656, F229304. 27 rooms, some with bath, rooftop restaurant tries everything, quiet, off road location. **D** *Universal Guest House*, T240930, F227333. 32 rooms, most with bath, restaurant downstairs. **D-E** *Down Town Guest House*, T224189, F419870. 19 rooms, all with bath, no food, close to many handicraft shops. **D-E** *Gorkha Guest House*, T214243, F240292. 10 rooms, some with bath and tub, also *Johnny Gorkha Restaurant*. Recommended. **D-E** *Guest Palace*, T/F225593. 8 rooms, some with bath, attached steak house also does breakfast. **D-E** *Namaskar*, T421060, F420678. 12 rooms, all with bath, no food, clean and good value. **D-E** *Range Guest House*, T410182, F420678. 10 rooms, some with bath, no food. **D-E** *Sagarmatha*, T410214. 28 rooms, some with bath.

E *Cosy Corner Lodge*, T411957, F417799. 14 rooms, all common bath, no food, central. **E** *Fortune*, T411874. 4 rooms, all with bath, no food, cheap. **E** *Friendly Guest House*, T414033. 12 rooms, no food, good value. **E** *Gurkha Soldier Guest House*, T221275. 9 rooms, all common bath, no food. **E** *Kunal's Guest House*, T411050. 21 rooms a few with bath and some with TV, comfortable and reasonably priced. **E** *Memorable Guest House*, T243683. 12 rooms, forgettable. **E** *Mom's House*. 10 rooms, some with bath, no food. **E** *N Pooja Guest House*, T416657. 12 basic but good rooms, reception on 2nd Floor above *Red Rock* restaurant. **E** *Pheasant Guest House*, T417415. 15 rooms, all common bath, no food, impressive entrance with old Gurkha family weapons and some pet pheasants. Recommended. **E** *Potala*, T416680, F419317. 25 rooms, all common bath, some with balcony, no food, clean and friendly, bookshop on 1st Floor. Recommended.

Eating Central Thamel has the bulk of the restaurants that have made Kathmandu famous for culinary excellence. Sticking to the restaurant's speciality can avoid disappointment.

Austrian: *Gourmet Vienna*, T419183, F415488, E gourmet@vienna.wlink.com.np. Has one branch just north of Pilgrim's Bookshop, a deli counter for take-away sandwiches, salamis and cakes, and a couple of tables for eating in; a similar branch towards Tridevi Marg at the front of the outstanding *Old Vienna Inn*, a superior Austrian restaurant and one of Thamel's best. Recommended.

Chinese: *Oriental Kitchen*, T416683. For average Chinese food, central.

Indian: *Shalimar*, T423606. Indian restaurant, try the Kathi rolls. *Third Eye*, T227478. Has excellent Indian food, also some continental, huge club sandwiches, more expensive than average, credit cards accepted.

Italian: *Al Pollo Pizzeria*. Some excellent Italian food using home grown herbs, proprietor lived in Florence, also herbal teas, south of Thamel Chowk near Chetrapati. Recommended. *Mamma Mia*. Does pizzas and some of the best and most reasonably priced Italian food in Kathmandu, candlelit tables, located at the west end of a lane leading off from JP School Rd about 300 metres south of *Kathmandu Guest House*. Recommended. *Pizzeria Panorama*, T216863. Shows free movies in separate 'jungle room'.

Japanese: *Aji No Silk Road*, just north of Thamel Chowk, T423681. For Japanese food, set meals, relatively expensive. *Fuji Restaurant*, Kantipath, near Grindlays Bank, T225272. Lovely Japanese restaurant in a peaceful off-road location, surrounded on 3 sides by a small moat, set meals from Rs 500, regular customers keep their unfinished bottles of Scotch in locked glass cabinets, expensive. Recommended.

Multi-cuisine: *Hotel Marshyangdi's* **Cozy Garden** restaurant. Specializes in open-air barbecues and grills, elegant rooftop *Palace* restaurant has an eclectic menu, expensive. *Manang Hotel's* **Jewels of Manang**, in basement. Exclusive, intimate atmosphere, Continental, Italian, Chinese, Indian food, live bands play Western and Indian music, dinner only, expensive. Recommended. The *Holiday Inn* has 3 speciality restaurants: an expensive **Al Fresco** for authentic Italian food; **Gurkha Grill**, despite the name, for candlelit *haute cuisine française* and a live band, and **Himalchuli** for the best of Nepali and Indian food accompanied by live music and dance. **Berale** is opposite *Helena's* and does continental and Israeli style (not Kosher) food. **Le Bistro**, T411170, F419734. Right in the heart of Thamel, delightful outdoor seating, good breakfasts, sandwiches, apple pie, and continental food, avoid the steaks. Recommended. **Green Leaves**, T224067. Multi-cuisine, live Nepali folk music every night. **Helena's**, T412135. Continental food and cakes in congenial rustic surroundings, very central. **In Himalayan**, jack of all foods, master of none. Also Nirula's ice cream. **KC's Restaurant and Bambooze Bar**, T416911. An established favourite in the middle of Thamel, good breakfasts, salads and continental dishes, sandwiches on a variety of breads, cheese and meat fondu for minimum 4 persons, Rs 250, spectacular but indifferent sizzlers, more expensive than average, pleasant bar upstairs. **New Orleans Café**, T416351, F418436. Mexican and continental food, outdoor and indoor seating, jazz. About 200 metres south of the *Kathmandu Guest House*, opposite the *Hungry Eye* restaurant, the **Ying Yang Restaurant**, T227478, F425510, E amma@apsons.mos.com.np. A smart Thai and continental restaurant with delightful courtyard seating area, excellent food and buffet breakfast at Rs 170, quality bakery stand has excellent lemon meringue pie, perhaps Thamel's best restaurant but expensive. Highly recommended.

Nepali/Tibetan: *Thamel House*, T410388. A charming, traditional Newari house, extensively renovated, and has a comprehensive excellent Nepali menu, a huge 9-course set meal costs Rs 450, bar, some floor cushion seating, credit cards accepted, expensive. Recommended. **Newar Kitchen**. Simple but good Nepali food, at the east end of a small lane off JP School Rd, near *Green Leaves* restaurant. **Tashi Deleg**, is centrally located opposite Namche Bazar building. Tibetan food. **Typical Nepali Restaurant**, near the *Green Leaves* restaurant. Small and friendly, typical tourist prices.

Fastfood: *Northfield Café*, T424884. Does snacks, excellent Mexican food, good sandwiches, free chips with beer during nightly happy hour, next to *Pilgrim's Bookshop*. **Old Spam's Space**, T412713. Good English breakfast, snacks and light meals, steam bath and massage next door, Thamel's version of a British pub, 100 metres north of *Pilgrim's Bookshop*. **Roadhouse Café**, T229187. Snacks, meals and bar.

Vegetarian: *Skala*, T223155, F229459. Does good vegetarian food.

Thai: *BKS Restaurant*, T415420. For Thai food, opposite *Helena's*.

Sleeping This area south of central Thamel takes its name from the busy intersection **Chetrapati** of 'six roads' where there is now a bandstand and a large city map. From here, the main north-south road heads south to Durbar Square. Most hotels here are situated along the main east-west road where there are also a number of good restaurants to choose from.

B *Marshyangdi*, T414105, F410008. 60 rooms, modern, courteous, well located, fine views from roof terrace, 24-hour coffee shop, 'Palace' restaurant has extensive menu, bar, popular with groups. Recommended.

C *Harati*, T226527, F223329. 59 rooms, good restaurant with Indian and continental menu, reasonably priced, bar, attractive garden, popular with groups. **C** *Lai Lai*, T240419. 32 rooms, restaurant, very clean, excellent views from rooftop, peaceful. **C** *Nirvana Garden*, T/F222668. 55 rooms, some with a/c, TV, balcony and bathtub, good Chinese food in restaurant, tastefully decorated, also quiet garden with small waterfall. Recommended. **C** *Tibet Guest House*, T214383, F220518. 38 rooms, most with bath, some a/c, Tibetan and continental restaurant and rooftop sitting area, family run, friendly and always helpful. Recommended. **C-D** *Park*, T214053. 36 rooms, all with bath, small rooftop eating area, 2 adjoining buildings, clean and comfortable. **C-D** *Shambala*, T225986, F414024. 32 rooms, most with bath and phone, water filters on each floor, restaurant does good Tibetan food, bar, clean and modern. Recommended.

D *Base Camp*, T212224, F221344. 17 rooms, some with bath, small restaurant, also 2 simple apartments, one with an occasionally functional sauna. **D** *Kathmandu Holiday*, T220334, F229459. 18 rooms, all with bath, tiny restaurant. **D** *Kathmandu View Guest House*, T244624. 27 rooms, some with bath, rooftop terrace, food available on request. **D** *Potala Guest House*, T220467. 60 rooms, all with bath, some have TV and phone, one of Kathmandu's long standing favourites, popular restaurant for steaks, Italian and Mexican. **D** *Tara Guest House*, T220634. 24 rooms, many with bath, some triples and good value cheaper rooms, boiled water available, roof terrace, breakfast only. **D** *Thahity Guest House*. 15 rooms, all with bath, small restaurant for snacks and light meals, between the Chetrapati bandstand and Thahity Tole. **D** *Trans Himalaya*, T245324. 30 rooms, most with bath, some with balcony, roof terrace and excellent adjoining restaurant. Recommended. **D** *White Lotus Guest House*, T224563, F229967. 16 comfortable rooms, most with bath, restaurant shows videos daily.

E *Norling Guest House*, T221534. 16 simple but clean rooms, common bath, very reasonable Tibetan food on request. **E** *Polo Guest House*, T242356, F245323. 16 rooms, some with simple bath, no food, central location.

Eating Chetrapati has some excellent eateries spilling over from Central Thamel.

Nepali/Tibetan: *Nepalese Kitchen*, near the *Base Camp* hotel. Has good Nepali dishes (buffet on Saturday, Wednesday and Monday less than Rs 200), also Tibetan and continental, also some interesting alcoholic hot drinks, stunning black and white photographs of Nepali life throughout, central fireplace, music and dance programme on alternate evenings from 1830-2100. Recommended. *Yulo* in the eastern part of Chetrapati is small, but does good and reasonably priced Tibetan food. More Tibetan food at the *Tibet Canteena*, T212224, in the *Base Camp* hotel, at the *Tibet Guest House*, and at the *Yak Lodge*.

Indian: *Cabin* restaurant, T214769. On the eastern side of Chetrapati towards Thahiti Tole, does cheap Chinese, Nepali and Indian food, including a plate of Dal-Bhat-Tarkari at Rs 25.

Steaks: *The Bluebell Inn*, T244084. Just to the west of *Walden's Bookshop* on the main Chetrapati road, does average steaks, pizzas, Mexican, etc. *Everest Steak House*, T217471. Has by far the best steaks in all Nepal, a carnivore's dream, superb fillet steak and grilled chicken, the Chateaubriand for 2 (Rs 650) is magnificent and enough for 4, also Italian, Tibetan and Mexican, but stick to the steaks. Recommended.

Multi-cuisine: *Himalayan Kitchen*, T214683, opposite *Everest Steak House*. Good for breakfast, Chinese, Tibetan, Mexican and continental menu, excellent enchilladas. *Pierre*, T228667. South of the Chetrapati intersection and near the *Harati* hotel, does Indian and palatable continental food.

Jyatha and Kantipath

Sleeping There is a scattering of hotels in the Jyatha area and a couple on Kantipath, slightly removed to the southeast from central Thamel, and close to the pick-up point for tourist buses to Pokhara and Chitwan. One or two superb eating places are located on Kantipath which makes the walk there or back a little shorter; otherwise, head into central Thamel for food.

B *Mountain*, Kantipath, T224498, F227736. 56 comfortable rooms in modern building, expensive coffee shop, restaurant and small bar, lovely rooftop lawn with seating and fine views of city and surrounding areas, but service is unexceptional. **B** *Yellow Pagoda*, Kantipath, T220337, F228914. 56 rooms and 3 rooftop apartments,

Indian restaurant, lobby bar and 24-hour coffee shop, also a small gift shop, central location, but like its neighbour, the *Hotel Mountain*, expensive and pretentious.

C *Hotel Utse*, Jyatha, Thamel, T226946, F226945. With Tibetan-style rooms and attached showers or baths, is very pleasant and popular, rooftop garden, excellent restaurant, small library with newspapers and magazines, helpful staff. Recommended. **C** *Gautam*, T244515, F228467. 20 rooms, all with bath and some a/c, restaurant does Indian, Chinese and continental food. **C** *Rara*, T222436, F229158. 32 rooms, all with bath (and tubs) and TV, some a/c rooms, unexceptional restaurant and bar, rooftop beer garden, credit cards accepted.

D *Himalayan View*, T216531, F221656. 24 rooms, all with bath, small restaurant. **D** *Kohinoor*, T213930. 25 rooms, all with bath, no food. **D** *Mt Kailash*, T232819. 40 rooms, all with bath, chaotic restaurant for Indian food. **D** *Blue Diamond*, T226320, F226392. Preferred by Indian visitors.

Eating A couple of fine restaurants on Kantipath, and one in the Jyatha area.

Old Vienna Delicatessen Centre, on Kantipath, T419183, F415488, E gourmet@vienna. wlink.com.np. Excellent Austrian deli with seating, cheeses, breads and pastries, cold meats. Light meals including Bratwurst and chips, and fish and chips. Smoked salmon also available. Recommended. *Café Lungta*, T217804, F227600. Around the corner from the *Yellow Pagoda* hotel, reasonable but rather expensive pizzas and continental food. *Royal Kasturi Restaurant*, in Jyatha, T212082. For Thai, Chinese, Indian and continental dishes, moderately priced. *Utse Restaurant and Bar*, in Jyatha, T212082. For Tibetan, Nepali and continental dishes, good value.

Sleeping To the northwest of central Thamel, there are a number of good value, **Paknajol** mid-range hotels and guesthouses. It is, for the most part, less congested than central Thamel with one or two quiet corners (a distinct advantage if you want some distance from overflowing, narrow laned commerciality), but is easily accessible and has some good restaurants.

A *Malla*, Lekhnath Marg near the Royal Palace, T410620, F418382. 125 rooms and 20 apartments for long stay guests, 3 restaurants, including Chinese and the pleasant garden terrace looking out across well kept lawns and a raised Buddhist stupa. Modern bar.

B-C *Norbhu-Linka*, T414799, F419005. 40 rooms, 24-hour coffee shop, restaurant, rooftop bar and snacks, nicely decorated.

C *Buddha*, T413366, F413194. 37 rooms, all with bath, restaurant (veg and non veg), bar, attractive garden and rooftop sitting area, surprisingly named, will confirm reservations by fax. **C** *Gauri Shankar*, T417181, F411878. 36 rooms, most with bath, quiet location off Lekhnath Marg, restaurant, bar, owned by Asian Trekking Ltd. **C** *Shakti*, T410121, F418897. 39 rooms, most with bath, continental restaurant, opened in 1976, the second oldest budget tourist hotel in Kathmandu. **C-D** *Blue Ocean*, T418499, F410079. 30 rooms, all with bath, most with TV, free local calls, restaurant and roof garden, quiet. **C-D** *Iceland View*, T416686, F420678. 16 rooms, all with bath, rooftop bar and snacks, central. **C-D** *Lily*, T415640. 17 rooms, all with bath, small restaurant will serve almost anything on request, rooftop garden, quiet, comfortable and friendly, rates are highly negotiable. **C-D** *Mandap*, T413321, F419734. 23 rooms, all with bath and with heating, rooftop garden, pleasant restaurant with central fireplace, bar, attached travel agency. **C-D** *Rimal*, T410317, F417121. 28 rooms, all with bath and TV, rooftop restaurant, bar, some rooms have exotic fish tanks, but many fish expire if room key is not handed to reception for feeding and maintenance during guests' absence. **C-D** *Shree Tibet*, T419902, F412026. 25 rooms, all with bath, small restaurant only does breakfast. **C-D** *Tashi Dhargey*, T417030, F423543. 22 rooms, restaurant does breakfast only, poor value. **C-D** *Tenki*, T414483, F412571. 35 rooms, some with bath, restaurant, rooftop garden. **C-D** *Villa Everest*, T413471, F423558. 10 rooms, some with bath, also 3 bed dorms for Rs 150, Korean restaurant, quiet. Recommended.

D *Capital*, T414150. 21 rooms, some with bath, convenient location. **D** *Florid*, T416155, F412747. 25 rooms, some with bath, basic but clean, no food, no entry after 2330. **D** *Greeting Palace*, T417212, F417197. 27 rooms, most with bath, small restaurant, gloomy interior but friendly. **D** *Holyland*, T411588. 15 rooms, all with bath, no food. **D** *Holy Lodge*, T416265. Unrelated to *Holyland*, 24 rooms, some with bath, breakfast only on roof terrace, good value. **D** *Kathmandu Peace Guest House*, T415239. 24 rooms, most with bath, small restaurant, comprises 2 buildings either side of the end of the track, good views across valley, friendly, popular with travellers so early booking advised in season. Recommended. **D** *Mount Fuji*, T413794. 16 rooms, all with bath, quiet but expensive. **D** *Namche Nepal*, T417067, F229459. 32 rooms, most with bath, restaurant does Indian/Nepali food, average. **D** *Prince*, T414456, F415158. 13 rooms, all with bath, pleasant rooftop garden restaurant. Recommended. **D** *Shikhar*, T415558, F220143. 15 rooms, all with bath, 2 restaurants (Indian and Chinese), rooftop garden, quiet, friendly. **D** *Souvenir*, 8 rooms, some with bath, small restaurant, friendly. **D** *Tibet Peace Guest House*. 19 rooms, some with TV and bath, all with phone, restaurant which expands to include 'traditional' floor seating at peak times, attractive garden, good views, despite the name is run by a Bengali. Recommended. **D** *Tridevi*. 14 rooms, most with bath, restaurant, best rooms at the back.

E *Ajanta*. 8 rooms, no food. Recommended only for the experienced budget traveller. **E** *Annapurna*. 15 rooms, dark but cheap, isolated. **E** *Arumdaye*. Small and noisy, very basic. **E** *Chitwan Tulasi Peace Guest House*. 6 rooms, spartan, best avoided. **E** *Earth House*. 15 rooms, most with bath, rooftop garden restaurant, clean. Recommended. **E** *Green Peace Guest House*, T420333. 12 rooms, some with bath, breakfast on rooftop terrace, friendly, quiet. **E** *Kalika Lodge*. Small, noisy and very basic. **E** *Lonely Planet*, T418918. 14 rooms, some with bath, small restaurant not recommended, has what claims to be a 'Tibetan Ayurvedic Yoga Massage Clinic', unexceptional. **E** *Mona*, T422151, F415158. 4 rooms, all with bath, no food, good views from rooftop terrace. **E** *Mustang*, T/F419361. 15 rooms, 24-hour room service, rooftop garden. **E** *Nippon*. 5 rooms, basic. **E** *Yeti*, T419789. 14 rooms, some with bath, reasonable rates.

Eating Although nowhere near as extensive a selection as in central Thamel, there is nevertheless a reasonably good range of restaurants in Paknajol. Some of the better hotels in particular are worth trying for ambience and variety.

Delima Garden Café, T414456, F415158. Continental, Chinese and Indian meals and snacks in a quiet pleasant setting. *Hungry Eye*, next to *Capital Guest House*. Reasonable Indian, Chinese and continental food. *Pradhan's San Francisco Pizza Restaurant*, T412314. Pizza, pasta and ice cream, popular among travellers, actual size paintings of menu items on the wall. Recommended. *Rum Doodle*, T414336, F227068. Among Kathmandu's best known eating and drinking spots, excellent steaks (try the Steak Breakfast), continental, Mexican, Chinese and Indian food, wonderful rum and raisin cheesecake, cocktails, named after WE Bowman's account of the conquest of the 40,000 foot fictional mountain, available for purchase at Rs 150, signatures of mountaineering expeditions and eminent visitors on display including Sir Edmund Hillary and Jimmy Carter, considered by a 1985 edition of *Newsweek* magazine as among the world's best drinking places but this has increased prices, large fireplace. Recommended.

Jhocchen
(Freak Street) **Sleeping** Leading off from the southeast corner of Basantpur Square, near Durbar Square, this area has attained minor celebrity status (or notoriety) as the place where budget travellers of the hippie generation stayed. Although Freak Street's popularity decreased markedly with the emergence of central Thamel as the travellers' heartland

from the late 1970s, there are still several smaller hotels and restaurants along its length with some of the cheapest rooms in town.

D *Eden*, T213863. 16 rooms, all with bath, tall narrow building with lift, located at the southern end of Freak St, good views from the rooftop. **D** *Sugat*, T216656, F241576. 11 rooms, most with bath, attractive wooden carved reception area, at the top end of Jhocchen overlooking Basantpur Square and the Hanuman Dhoka palace. Recommended.

E *Annapurna Lodge*, T213684. 20 rooms, some with bath, its *Diyalo* restaurant does reasonable Indian and continental food, large portions. **E** *Buddha Guest House*, T240071. 8 rooms, all common (squat) bath, cheap, basic and clean. **E** *Century Lodge*, T247641. 25 rooms, all common (squat) bath, cheaper dorm, parrots and budgies in reception, a traditional favourite also popular with cockroaches. **E** *Himalaya's Guest House*, T246555. 16 rooms, 3 with bath, basic and sometimes clean. **E** *Pagoda Lodge*, T212029. 17 rooms, all common bath, boiled and filtered water on request. **E** *Pokhara Guest House*, T241773. 14 rooms, all common bath, cheap and awful. **E** *Traveller's Paradise*, T240602. 8 rooms, all common bath, with good vegetarian *Paradise* restaurant.

Eating A few restaurants in and around Freak St, popular with budget travellers.

Tibetan: *New Mandarin Tibetan Restaurant*, opposite the *Eden* hotel to the south of Freak St. Small, dimly lit, and serves Tibetan food to Western music.

Multi-cuisine: *Diyalo* restaurant in the *Annapurna Lodge* does generous portions of Indian and continental food. *The Meeting Place*, T244984. Does Chinese, Indian and continental food, some low seating. *Meggi Restaurant*, T213643. On the 1st Floor, for Japanese and continental dishes.

Vegetarian: *Oasis*, T214392. Towards the south of Freak St, is good for vegetarian food, indoor and courtyard seating. *Paradise Restaurant*, T240602, in the *Traveller's Paradise Guest House* is good for vegetarian food.

Fastfood: *Carpe Diem Music Café* is a small trendy place for snacks, lassis, juices and beers. *The Old Palace Café*, T225246. On the southern side of Basantpur Square does most types of food at very reasonable prices, also snacks and cocktails, some floor cushion seating, pleasant, friendly and helpful. Recommended.

Sleeping Leads north from the Royal Palace, almost as an extension of Kantipath.   **Lazimpath**
The road passes through the main embassy area before continuing on towards the statue of the sleeping Vishnu at Budhanilikantha. There are a couple of luxury hotels here as well as some in the middle price range. Central Thamel is about 20 minutes' walk. Offices of a number of foreign NGOs are also located in this area, as well as some excellent supermarkets and a few restaurants and bookshops.

AL *Shangri La*, Lazimpath, T412999, F414184. 82 rooms, best face garden, Tibetan style decor, cultural programmes, good French and Chinese restaurants, garden café and small pool open to non-residents at Rs 250, conference facilities including tiny library/meeting room with Desmond Doig sketches, shopping arcade.

A *Kathmandu*, Maharajganj, Embassy area, T410786, F416574. Modern, clean, friendly, all Nepali staff. **A** *Shankar*, T410151, F412691. Located at the southern end of Lazimpath, 94 rooms, delightfully converted Rana palace, sumptuous, intimate and atmospheric, 1 large restaurant serves all types of food, comfortable bar with fire-place, lovely exterior and gardens. Recommended.

C *Ambassador*, T414432, F413641. 44 rooms, all with TV, phone and bathtubs, small restaurant does continental, Indian and Chinese food, bar, modern hotel at the south-ern end of Lazimpath, popular with groups. **C** *Lion*, T419395, F415307. 26 rooms, all with a/c, TV, phone and bathtub, restaurant and bar does good Chinese and continental food, rooftop terrace. **C** *Manaslu*, T410071, F416516. 56 rooms, multi-cuisine restaurant, bar, modern decor, peaceful though somewhat inconvenient location at the end of a small lane that can get very muddy in the monsoon.

Eating In addition to the major hotels here, there are a couple of smaller restaurants and fast food outlets.

China Town for Chinese food, bar. *Himtai Restaurant*, is 100 metres north of the *Ambassador* hotel and does good Thai food. *New Peace Restaurant* is small, but has a reasonable Chinese and continental menu. The *Tandoori Fast Food Café* is cleanish and has good tandoori meat preparations, 'burgers', 'pizzas', and momos also available to take away.

Other areas **Sleeping** Two of the more expensive hotels are to the east of the main city. **AL** *Everest*, New Banesvara, near the airport, T220567, F226088. 162 large rooms and 9 restaurants including *The Café*, all day coffee shop, *Sherpaland* for Tibetan and Chinese food; and Indian cuisine in *The Far Pavilion* on the 7th Floor with classical Indian music and excellent views, 2 bars, swimming pool and disco, tennis courts, international conference centre next door.

B *Dwarika's Kathmandu Village*, Batisputali, near Pashupatinath, T470770, F472328. 32 rooms, all individually decorated with hand carved, traditional Newari windows, won PATA Heritage Award for cultural sensitivity, excellent Nepali restaurant, 9 courses, reservations essential. **B** *Manang*, T410993, F415821. 39 rooms, coffee shop, 360° views of valley from rooftop terrace lawn, bar, elegant '*Jewels of Manang*' restaurant does dinner only, but has live Western and Indian/Nepali music.

A couple of good hotels in **Lainchaur**, the area north of Lekhnath Marg, near the Royal Palace and about 10 minutes' walk to central Thamel. **D** *Namaste*, T410459, F418578. Has 17 comfortable modern rooms, all with bath, multi cuisine restaurant is best for Indian dishes, bar facilities, TV lounge area, rooftop terrace, and helpful and friendly staff, good value. Recommended. *Sungawa*, T418217, F424457. Opposite the *Namaste* and has 15 rooms some with bath, small dining room does Nepali/Indian food.

Bhagavan Bahal: is the area between central Thamel and Kantipath and has a couple of decent places to stay. **D** *Shakti*, T410121, F418897. Has rooms with bath, restaurant. *Earth House*, T418197, F416351. Comfortable rooms, some with bath.

A few hotels also in **Tripureshvar**, along the main road running parallel to the Bagmati River in the south of the city. This area can be noisy and is removed from the principal places of interest. **B-C** *Bluestar*, T228833, F226820. 106 rooms, coffee shop (0700-2200) and 2 restaurants: *Vaishali* for Indian and continental food, and *Gompa* for Chinese, bar closes at 2200, conference facilities.

In the direction of **Svayambhunath**, **C** *Vajra*, Bijeshwari, T224719, F271695. 51 rooms, best with bath in new extension, restaurant, rooftop bar, library, river view, distinctive Newari architecture, excellent hotel, built 1980 using traditional designs and materials, surrounded by gardens and trees, centre for cultural programmes, heavily booked, very good value. Highly recommended. **E** *Catnap*, T272392, and *Peace Lodge* at Chauni. Both are fairly quiet.

In **Bhote Bahal**: **D** *Janak*. Large rooms, restaurant. *Sayapatri*, T223398. Breakfast, pleasant garden. **E** *Valley View*, T216771. Some rooms have bath, terrace, clean.

There are a few very basic guesthouses in the **Bag Bazar** area to the east of the city centre, but they have little experience of foreign visitors.

Numerous bakeries claiming various national identities throughout **Thamel**. The **Bakeries**
Bretzel Bakery, opposite *Kathmandu Guest House*, always has fresh bread in the morn-
ing and is recommended. The *Ying Yang* restaurant, 200 metres south towards
Chetrapati, has an excellent bakery stall (lemon meringue pie a speciality). *Helena's*,
in central Thamel has an alluring window display, but the cakes can flatter to deceive.
Good apple pie at *Le Bistro*, and excellent cheesecake at *Rum Doodle's*. Try *Old
Vienna Delicatessen*, in Thamel and on **Kantipath** for apple strudel and good sandwiches. The *German Bakery* in **Jhocchen** (Freak St) has a good line in bread and
cakes. On **Durbar Marg**, *Hot Breads* has fresh bread and pastries. The *Annapurna
Bakery* in the *Hotel de l'Annapurna* has a good selection. The nearby *Nanglo Bakery
and Café* is apparently the hip place for Kathmandu's bright young things to hang out
and be seen, but the food is unexceptional. On **Lazimpath**, the *Shangri La* hotel has a
good bakery. Other shops recommended for cakes, bread and pies along **Maru Tole**
('pie alley').

There are few pub-type bars in Kathmandu, though just about every restaurant has its **Bars**
own bar. Several have happy hours. All the big hotels have bars, including that at the
Malla Hotel, peacefully looking across at a Buddhist stupa in the middle of its well
maintained gardens. The *Yak and Yeti's* bar has a fireplace and an atmosphere of old
world comfort. Recommended. The *Shankar* hotel at the southern end of Lazimpath
has a cosy bar delightfully decorated with traditional Newari carving and fireplace.
Also, try upstairs at the ever popular *Rum Doodle's*. *Tom and Jerry's*, opposite *Pilgrim's Bookshop* in central Thamel has regular theme nights and happy hours. In
Paknajol, try the *Himalayan Cocktail Bar* for a range of surprisingly good cocktails
(including the 'Thamel Tiger'!).

Entertainment

Beauty Parlours and Massage All the 'AL' and 'A' hotels have in-house beauty
parlours for ladies (open to non residents) with Western trained staff and the latest
equipment. Appointments not always necessary. Others including *Enigma Beauty
Parlour*, T411131, *Hotel Garden*, Naya Bazar. *Sipi Beauty Club*, T244768, Putali Sadak,
Kamaladi (closed Monday). *Veena's Hair and Beauty Clinic*, with branches at Hattisar
(T422095) and Old Banesvara (T473511).

Cinemas The city has 5 cinemas, all showing hugely popular Bombay produced
Hindi movies as well as occasional **Nepali** films. *Biswajyoti*, in Jamal, T221837. East of
Rani Pokhari and near the clock tower. *Gopikrishna*, in Chabahil, T479893. On the east
side of town. *Jai Nepal*, T411014. Near the Royal Palace. *Kumari*, in Putali, T414932;
and *Ranjana*, New Rd, T221191. Most have shows in the late morning, early and late
afternoon and, occasionally, an evening showing. Tickets from Rs 2 to Rs 25. Buy in
advance or queue. An increasing number of restaurants in **Thamel** have begun
showing Western videos in an effort to attract more customers. Their menus can be
slightly more expensive.

Gambling Kathmandu has 4 casinos, all open 24 hours and especially popular with
Indian tourists. *Anna*, at the *Hotel de l'Annapurna* on Durbar Marg. *Everest*, at the *Everest Hotel*, New Banesvara, near the airport. *Nepal*, at the *Soaltee Holiday Inn*. *Royale*, at
the *Yak and Yeti Hotel* off Durbar Marg. Games include roulette, blackjack, poker and
slot machines. All have bars where drinks and food are reasonably priced or free. If you
have flown into Nepal within the past week, you can get Rs 100 worth of free chips on
production of your passport and ticket or boarding pass. US dollars and Indian rupees
accepted. Free transport to your hotel or the centre of town is provided from 2300 to
0300. Nepalis are not admitted – a visit to any of the casinos will confirm this to be an

Kathmandu Valley

insignificant deprivation.

Music and dance For performances of traditional Nepali dances and music, see below. Otherwise, Kathmandu offers little in the way of late night entertainment. The *Dynasty Plaza Woodlands Hotel*, T225650, on Durbar Marg has a **nightclub**, *Woody's Place*. The *Everest Hotel* also has a **disco**, *Galaxy*, supposed to be for foreigners only, open 2200-0400. Some Thamel restaurants have live **bands**. *Amber Restaurant* on Durbar Marg has live **ghazals** on some evenings. Recommended.

Sports Billiards: at *Hotel de l'Annapurna*, Rs 100 per hour. **Chess**: a chess club meets occasionally at the British Council library on Kantipath, T221305. **Golf**: the 18-hole *Royal Nepal Golf Club*, T472836, is next to the airport and is the country's only major golf course. Temporary members, any handicap, are welcome. 1 month membership costs around Rs 2,500, but can take 2 or 3 days to arrange. Club hire costs Rs 500 per day. Alternatively, a 1 day visitor can pay about US$40 which includes temporary membership, clubs, balls and caddy. Facilities including a small club house with bar, changing room and showers. The course is frequented by numerous monkeys from the nearby Pashupatinath Temple with a propensity for making off with flags and balls. Ongoing plans exist to build a new 18-hole course on the other side of the airport. **Squash**: at *Dynasty Plaza Woodlands Hotel* on Durbar Marg. **Swimming**: the *National Stadium* at Tripureshvar has a large pool, open daily except Sunday for members (temporary membership is available – enquire) and guests, Monday, women only, open 1000-1230 and 1330-1600 daily (Friday opens at 0830), Rs 30 women, Rs 35 men. There is also a large public pool by the *Balaju Water Garden*, formerly the Royal family's private pool, northwest of the ring road, open 1000-1600 daily, Rs 20, modest swimming costumes recommended. The *Yak and Yeti*, *Everest*, *Narayana* and *Soaltee Holiday Inn* hotels all have private pools which are open to non-residents on payment of a fee. **Trekking**: see under **Tour companies and travel agents**.

Theatre With occasional drama performances and concerts, the *National Theatre* (Rashtriya Nach Ghar) on Kantipath, is Kathmandu's only theatre.

Festivals

More than 50 festivals covering a total of over 100 days are celebrated in Kathmandu. Many are occasions for brightly coloured processions and gatherings, offering the visitor a vivid insight into the Valley's culture and customs. Festivals are set according to the lunar calendar and dates therefore vary each year. The most important include:

January-February: *Magh*, the 10th month of the Nepali calendar, is marked by women who dedicate their month long 'fast' of 1 meal per day to Shiva; *Ghyo Chaku Sanlhu*, on the winter solstice, takes its name from the clarified butter (*ghyo*) and molasses (*chaku*) which are essential ingredients in the festival meal that also includes yams and sesame seeds; *Basanta Panchami* at the Hanuman Dhoka palace, Svayambhunath, Budhanilikantha and other Vishnu shrines, marks the coming of spring and is dedicated particularly to Sarasvati, goddess of learning and creativity; *Losar*, the Tibetan new year at Boudha and Svayambhunath; *Maha Shivaratri* at Pashupatinath attracts pilgrims from throughout Nepal and India to an all night vigil.

March-April: *Holi* celebrates the victory of Narasimha over the demon Hiranyakashipu. Its most conspicuous feature is the coloured water and powders which are thrown over friends, acquaintances and passers by – beware!

May: *Buddha Jayanti* (or *Swanya Punhi*) at Svayambhunath and Bodhnath, commemorates the birth, enlightenment and parinirvana of the Buddha and is marked throughout the valley by colourful processions and burning candles. At Bodhnath, an elephant is elaborately decorated and paraded around the stupa, while musicians gather at Svayambhunath and the stupa is surrounded by thousands of small ghee lamps.

June-July: *Jya Punhi* at Svayambhunath, where devotees offer rice and flowers to mark the Buddha's departure from his family and the start of his quest for spiritual enlightenment; *Tribhuvan Jayanti* at Tripureshvar; *Trishul Jatra*, a Shaivite festival, processions and music to Deopatan, near Pashupatinath; *Guru Purnima* is held in honour of teachers, celebrated by Newar Buddhists as *Dilla Punhi*, marking the conception of Shakyamuni Buddha.

August: *Gathemangal* marks the end of monsoon rice planting and exorcizes evil spirits; *Pancha Dan* at Svayambhunath, Boudha and elsewhere, a Buddhist festival of charity when rice and other consumables are ritually offered to Buddhist monks; *Bahidyo Bwoegu*, a Newar Buddhist festival meaning 'displaying the gods'; *Gunhi Punhi* (or *Janai Purnima*) takes place throughout the valley and is the day when Hindus ceremonially bathe before tying their new sacred thread for the coming year; *Gaijatra* (or *Saparu*) is marked by recently bereaved families who trek around the city with a decorated cow which is believed to assist the departed into their next life.

September: *Indrajatra*, one of the most dynamic and colourful celebrations, marks the passing of the summer monsoon. Masked dances and processions of chariots and lamps start from Durbar Square. The Kumari begins her 2-day procession through the city streets on the 3rd day. *Krishna Janmastami*, in honour of Krishna. Processions to the Krishna Temple in Patan's Durbar Square; *Teej*, the festival of women, at Pashupatinath and other Shiva shrines. A huge feast is followed by a 24-hour fast during which many women wear red wedding saris.

October: *Dasain*, the major festival of the year, celebrates the triumph of good over evil as represented by the goddess Durga's victory over the demon Mahishasur. Animal sacrifices at many temples. Mechanical devices are venerated during the final days – if you are at the airport at this time, watch as Nepali aircraft become the objects of *puja* worship. Government offices remain closed for a week and the city is very busy and crowded. Accommodation and transport is difficult.

November: *Tihar*, the 5-day festival of lights (approximating *Diwali* in India), the 4th of which coincides with the Nepali new year; *Ekadasi* at Budhanilikantha and Pashupatinath.

December: *Bala Chaturdasi* at Pashupatinath; *Indrayani Jatra*, in honour of a mother goddess is celebrated at Kirtipur with musical processions, animal sacrifices and a feast; *Yomari Punhi* marks the end of the rice harvest. Yomari is a sweet made of rice flour, sugar and sesame seeds.

Shopping

Eventually, it is said, you can find anything you are looking for in Kathmandu. From an astonishing array of handicrafts sold in the huge Basantpur Square market and hundreds of smaller shops throughout the city to Western fashions and imported luxury goods in the expensive Durbar Marg and New Rd stores, as well as imported foodstuffs in the increasing number of supermarkets on Lazimpath and New Road. First thing in the morning try wandering around the colourful and hectic local markets –

Asan Tole, Indra Chowk and Bagh Bazar for instance – and watch as the locals haggle with stallholders for the best prices of vegetables, clothes and pots and pans. Most markets are open from dawn to dusk, though shops (especially in the Thamel area) often don't open until after 0900. Saturday is the main weekly holiday and many shops open late or remain closed.

Antiques Reliable antiques are available from the *Tibet Ritual Art Gallery* above the *Sunkosi Restaurant*, and from the *Potala Gallery*, opposite the *Yak and Yeti Hotel*, off Durbar Marg; or through various expatriate and Tibetan art dealers resident in Kathmandu and Boudha. There is also a thriving trade in fake antiques, with masks, woodcarvings, metalwork etc made to look considerably older than they actually are. **NB** Genuine antiques require a clearance certificate from the Dept of Archaeology (National Archives Building, Ramshah Path) permitting them to be exported. All reputable dealers will help in getting this.

Bookshops Central Thamel: *Pilgrims Book House*, T424942, F424943. The largest in Kathmandu. *Prajna Book Hut*, opposite *Pilgrims*. Manages to pack a surprising amount of stock into its small premises, good for maps and Himalaya and philosophy books, postcards. *Kathmandu Book House*, T412367. Next to *Helena's* restaurant. Further along, the *Global Book Centre*, T412180. Mostly travel and Nepali culture titles, maps, also tapes and CDs. *Walden's Bookshop* in Chetrapati.

Tridevi Marg: *Tibet Book Store*, T415126. The city's best selection of Buddhist titles, as well as books on other religions and guidebooks. Recommended. *Bookland* is opposite the Immigration Office and has a smaller range.

Other areas: *Kailash* by the *Yak and Yeti Hotel's* main entrance is good but rather expensive. *Mandala*, Bidhur, Kantipath. *Himalayan Booksellers*, near Clock Tower. Small but good range. *Everest Books* and *Asia Book House*, off Durbar Marg near National Theatre and Rani Pokhari. *Ratna Books*, Bagh Bazar, near French Cultural Centre. Wide range, informed, helpful. *Educational Bookshop*, Kantipath, opposite New Rd. Excellent for educational books. There are also a couple of smaller bookshops on **Lazimpath**.

Carpets There are two main types of carpet on the market: Tibetan woollen and the better quality Kashmiri silk. Manufacture of the woollen ones is concentrated in Patan, Jawalakhel, Boudha, Jorbati, and Bhaktapur, where they can be bought directly from the makers, but there are numerous shops in Thamel, Indra Chowk and Durbar Marg stocking a wide range of sizes, designs and qualities. The best of these use handspun yarn, sometimes with a mix of Tibetan and New Zealand wools. Since the increased political instability all but decimated Kashmir's tourist industry, there has been something of a minor influx of Kashmiri carpet emporia to Kathmandu, resulting in a degree of hostility aimed towards Kashmiris here. Nevertheless, Kashmiri silk carpets are among the finest in the world, and the best ones will last well over a hundred years and are sometimes bought as investments. Shops on Durbar Marg, and in Thamel try *Worst Arts*, T223778, F419419, next to the *Al Pollo* restaurant, 2 minutes walk south of Thamel Chowk, and *Q Enterprises*, T214940. In Jyatha, try *Tashi Rabten* for Tibetan tiger rugs, T250650, F416697.

Clothing & Pashmina shawls: a lightweight but very soft and insulating kid's wool from the Nep-
textiles alese and Tibetan Himalayas or from Kashmir, are a speciality. The best quality are so delicate that they can be passed through a ring, and, it is claimed, so warm that an egg wrapped in a shawl overnight will be partly boiled the following morning! Lambswool shawls are also popular. Best bargains at Asan and Indra Chowk. **Blankets** and **bedspreads** are sold throughout the city and are much cheaper outside Thamel. There are a couple of non profit making, fixed price shops on Lazimpath: *Women's*

Skill Development Project, near the French Embassy, and *Community Craft Centre*. Elsewhere, try the UNCF's *Hastakala*, opposite *Himalaya Hotel*, and *Mahaguthi*, on Durbar Marg. Attractive and excellent quality embroidered **cushion covers** are best value in numerous shops in the Kamaladi area, to the east of Rani Pokhari. You can buy **saris**, **salwar kameez** (Indian-style loose trousers and tops for women) and **topis** (traditional Nepali hat worn by men, an essential part of the national dress) made from a variety of material in most parts of the city, but try Asan Tole and the areas around Indra Chowk. Bottom end saris start at around Rs 200, while at the top end gold embroidered silk saris can sell for many hundreds of dollars. A decent salwar kameez will cost between Rs 300 and Rs 1,000, while you can get a nice little topi for Rs 30. For top of the range clothing, South Asian and Western, try the various department stores on Dharmapath, near New Road.

Foreign goods

The area around New Rd is the centre of Kathmandu's upmarket shopping, with modern Western-style department stores and shopping malls appearing in total contrast to the nearby Durbar Square. On one side of New Rd, on the corner of Shukrapath, is *Bishal Bazar*, a 4-storeyed shopping centre. Close by are **Dharmapath**, **Kicha Pokhari** and **Bhugol Park**. All have shops selling imported Western brand name goods and give the impression of an expansive duty free shopping complex where you can get French perfumes and fashion, cosmetics, electronic items, foods, etc. Prices are competitive and appeal especially to Indian tourists. *Bishal Bazar Supermarket*, T222423, New Rd. *Bluebells Fashion Wearhouse*, T217501, and *Central Department Store*, T222028, Kicha Pokhari. *La Dynasty*, T220859, Bughol Park. In addition to the shops in Thamel which sell mainly European and North American foods, there are a few supermarkets along **Durbar Marg** and **Lazimpath** well stocked with familiar consumables, wines and trekking food. On Lazimpath, try the excellent *Bluebells*, T415181, which has another branch in Tripureshvar, T245726.

Handicrafts

Jewellery: ranges in both style and quality, the latter being largely concerned with trinkets and semi-precious stones. If you are continuing on to India, it may be better to postpone any major gem purchases until you arrive in one of its main cities, though silver items can be good value in Kathmandu. Typically, gem stones and turquoise and coral are used in settings. Thamel shops and the stalls in Basantpur Square offer everything from coral necklaces to aquamarine animal figures. The *Namkha Craft Collection*, T243636, F423543, 100 metres west of *Walden's Bookshop* on Chetrapati is good for advice and is recommended for some of the most honest prices for its trinkets, silver and necklaces. The purity of gold and silver has been questioned, though the upmarket jewellers on and near New Rd are generally reliable.

Markets

Basantpur Square, in the shadow of Durbar Square. This busy market area has many shops and stalls selling handicrafts, precious and semi-precious stones, statues, khukuri knives and jewellery. Also *munga*, coral necklaces worn by married women, and jewellery favoured by women of the Gurung caste. **Warning** Beware of pickpockets, especially as evening approaches. **Indra Chowk** is one of the city's three ancient centres of trade (with Asan and Bhotahiti), its reputation as a place of commerce dating as far back as the 14th century. Situated on the old trade route that linked India with Tibet, probably Malla Kathmandu's equivalent of today's New Rd. The market supplies the local populace with fruit and vegetables and its tourist interest is now mainly anthropological and historical. **Asan**, on a busy thoroughfare linking Kantipath with Durbar Square, has shops and stalls selling everything from souvenir khukuri knives to cucumbers. **Putalisadak**, meaning 'street of butterflies', is near the City Bus Park and is known for its quality furniture and foreign clothes shops. It takes its name from the hordes of butterflies which descended annually on an erstwhile park at this site. **Bagh Bazar** is a typical example of a bustling urban South Asian market area. Here you can watch as all the ingredients for dal-bhat-takari are bargained for; look out for the many varieties of rice being sold. There are also a number of private language institutes along the road offering courses in English, Japanese, Spanish, etc. **Kicha Pokhari** extends along Exhibition Rd from the Bhimsen Tower to New Rd, with shops selling 'fancy goods': decorations, curios, ready made garments and cosmetics. The name means 'dog pool'.

Metalwork Patan is the centre for bronze casting by the *cire perdue* ('lost wax') process. Metal figures of deities, gameboards and pieces for the traditional Nepalese game *bagh chal* are also available. **NB** The word 'bronze' is often used as a general term for any bronze coloured metal. Buddhist ritual **bells** and **vajras** are popular, as are miniature **prayer wheels**. Basantpur Square and Thamel once again have the widest ranges, but you can probably get the best prices from individual stalls, particularly in Chetrapati. Otherwise, try Jawalakhel in Patan or Boudha.

Paintings *Tangkas*, traditional Tibetan Buddhist religious paintings on cotton scrolls, together with *paubhas*, their Nepali equivalent, are available in most handicraft shops. Durbar Marg has a number of such retail outlets, including *Dawa Arts*, T228938, and *Mannies Arts*, T223715, in Sakya Arcade. In Thamel, try **Amrita Craft Collection**, T244345, in Chetrapati, and **Tibetan Thangka Treasures**, T418177. On Lazimpath, the *Tibetan Thangka Gallery*, T417300, is near the *Ambassador Hotel*. Try also Jhocchen (Freak St). **Rice paper prints** are available in Thamel, near the *Kathmandu Guest House*. **The Print Shop** has a good selection of batik, small oil paintings, and greeting cards made of peepul leaf are popular and reasonably priced. The *Kathmandu Handicrafts* shop, opposite the *Malla Hotel* on Lekhnath Marg, also stocks **Mithila art**, a traditional form of painting from the Janakpur area. There are a couple of small shops ('museums') selling excellent **watercolours** by local artists on the road leading from the main Chetrapati intersection to Durbar Square. These shops do not yet feature on the main tourist shopping circuit and if you are lucky you can pick up something really impressive here for around Rs 500 or less.

Papier mâché Masks and puppets made from a combination of rice paper, cotton rag paper, ordinary wood paper, brush shavings and newspapers are widely available in all three of the valley's cities. **Thimi** is the manufacturing centre for masks (Ganesh, Bhairava and the Kumari are popular), and Patan's artisan district of **Jawalakhel** also produces puppets and masks. Some come from Kashmir and other parts of India. The best are water resistant and hand painted, sometimes decorated with gold and silver or with brass dust or bronze powder, though the two latter will eventually blacken through oxidation. Some masks are used in the traditional masked dances during the Indrajatra festival in September/October.

Photography Kodak and Fuji films are readily available in Kathmandu and developing and printing can be done with confidence. There are numerous processing labs in the Thamel area. Film costs about Rs 110 for 24 exposures and Rs 160 for 36. Developing the negatives costs about Rs 40 with an additional Rs 10 per print. Most shops will give discounts in the region of 20 percent for processing a 36 exposure film, more for bulk orders. Single use disposable cameras are also available at about Rs 400 for 36 exposures. Send pre-paid processing films home.

T-shirts Kathmandu has acquired something of a reputation for its made-to-order logo T-shirts, and you can find any number of shops in the central area displaying their newly embroidered products while sewing machines tick away inside. You can create your own design and enlarge it, if required, by photocopy; the options are limited only by the bounds of good taste. Prices depend on the amount of embroidery involved, but are generally very reasonable and start at around Rs 120, including the price of the shirt, for simple embroidery and go up to Rs 300 for intricate, multi-coloured designs. Orders placed in the morning are usually ready by the same evening or the following morning. The 'Double Apple' and 'Shangri la' makes have been recommended.

This is particularly good in Bhaktapur and Thimi (en route) which specialize in little flower pots, often in animal shapes. You can also get the increasingly popular clay pipes. One variety is alleged to result in less harmful smoking by passing the smoke through a water filter. Decorative wall designs are also available. **Terracotta Pottery**

You can get everything you need for a trek in Kathmandu. Numerous shops in Thamel and along Freak St stock clothing including warm jackets, sleeping bags, rucksacks, footwear, rainwear and other supplies. You can also rent many larger and more expensive items, for which a deposit is required. Some shops demand a passport as deposit, but this is not advised. Rates increase in peak season. If you buy cooking equipment, you can usually sell it on to other trekkers when you return. **NB** Large shoe sizes can be difficult to obtain. **Trekking equipment**

Miniature replicas of carved windows and doors are popular souvenirs and are available in all the city's tourist areas. You can also get some superb furniture, including beautifully carved screens, writing desks, coffee tables, etc, from the upmarket shops on Durbar Marg and on and just off Kantipath. The best will be made from seasoned hardwoods such as teak and walnut, both of which are long lasting but expensive. Try Basantpur Square for masks and jewellery boxes, or Bhaktapur for miniature windows, picture frames and screens. You can also get small exquisitely carved **statues** made of heavy yak bone. **Woodcarvings**

Transport

Five main highways converge on Kathmandu: the Tribhuvan Raj Path linking Kathmandu with Birgunj and Raxaul Bazar at the Indian border (200 kilometres); the Arniko Highway linking Kathmandu with Kodari on the Tibet border (114 kilometres); the Prithivi Highway linking Kathmandu and Pokhara (206 kilometres); the Mahendra Highway covering the Terai from east to west (1,000 kilometres); and the Kathmandu city Ring Road built by the Chinese in 1975 (32 kilometres).

Auto-rickshaws (Tempos) These also have meters which they should use and are a good way of getting around the narrow streets and alleys of the city. They are more manoeuvrable than cars and can often squeeze through impossible gaps in Kathmandu's traffic jams. The meter starts at Rs 1.50 and increases by 50 pence for each 50 metres. Fares are highly negotiable, but should be fixed before starting the journey if not using the meter. A long trip across town costs about Rs 50 by meter, with a journey from Thamel to the airport roughly the same. Prices rise sharply in wet weather and late at night. **Local**

Bus Local buses are cheap but very crowded and do not allow good views of the journey. There is little point in taking a bus within Kathmandu, as most parts of the city are easily accessible on foot. To **Patan**, **Bhaktapur**, **Dhulikhel**, **Kirtipur** and other parts of the valley, buses leave from the City Bus Park and from Shahid Gate. Regular departures from 0600 and throughout the day. Buses leave when they are full. **NB** Last buses leave at about 2000. Fares are cheap: to Bhaktapur Rs 10, and to Patan Rs 4.

Trolley buses: an intriguing cross between a bus and a tram, link Kathmandu with Bhaktapur. Their slow journey begins near the National Stadium at Tripureshvar. **Car**

hire: car hire is available in Kathmandu. Most come with a driver. Private car hire can be expensive – upwards of US$50 per day, and it is usually cheaper to hire a taxi for the day. If you do this, negotiate with the taxi driver in advance, explaining where you want to go and for how long you want the vehicle. There are official government set rates for certain routes and distances which the driver will show, but with discussion these can be substantially reduced.

Cycle and motorcycle hire: available from numerous points in Thamel and else-where. Prices are always negotiable, but increase in peak season. You can get a very basic and old bike for about Rs 30 a day; this increases to about Rs 90 for a mountain bike. Deposit not usually required. **NB** Check tyres, pump, gears, lock, etc before set-ting off. **Motorcycle hire**: from Rs 400 to Rs 600 per day. Japanese and Indian models available, including the excellent Indian made Enfield. You should carry your interna-tional driving licence with you. **NB** Make sure that your travel **insurance** covers you for motorcycling, liability, etc. This is not available locally.

There are several private hire companies in Kathmandu offering a variety of vehi-cles from the Indian made Premier (similar to an ancient Fiat) to Land Rovers and Toy-ota Land Cruisers. Book through your hotel or direct. They include Prajapati Transport Services, Bhagawan Bahal, T424692, and Transportation Mediator Services, Kamaladi, T610220, F220161.

Cycle Rickshaws: an interesting way to cover short distances. Fares are negotiable, but should always be fixed **before** setting off. Rates are generally Rs 3 per kilometre, but rickshaw wallahs have become accustomed to extracting considerably more from tourists, particularly if the journey starts or ends in Thamel.

Taxis: in early 1997 the meter started at Rs 7 with an additional Rs 2 for each 200 metres. Radio controlled taxi companies are beginning to make an appearance in Kathmandu and include Dial-a-Cab (T417978) and Kathmandu Yellow Cabs (T420987). Fares increase dramatically after 2230 and when it is raining, and it can be difficult to find a taxi after midnight. A long trip across town costs in the region of Rs 80, while for travel into town from the airport expect to pay about Rs 150-200.

Long distance connections

Air Overbooking can be especially problematic during peak tourist seasons, so it is advis-able to re-confirm your flight at least once and preferably twice.

Check-in times for domestic flights are 1 hour, and 2 hours for international departures.

On arrival: there are separate queues for those with and without **visas**. Visa forms are available here and the fee is payable at the counter. **NB** Only US dollars are accepted. Ironically, the 'Without Visa' queue can be quicker than that for those who already hold a visa.

If you have a new passport but already hold a valid visa in your old one, you can get it transferred. Both passports will have to be surrendered and an official receipt given. After the inevitable form filling and payment of US$1, it will be ready at the Immigra-tion Office on Tridevi Marg the following day. **NB** Be sure to change money at the bank counter in the immigration hall before surrendering your passport.

Departure formalities: are relatively straightforward. Before checking-in for Royal Nepal Airlines flights, the **departure tax** (Rs 800 within South Asia, Rs 1,000 for all other destinations) must be paid for which 2 coupons are issued, one of which is retained at check-in. For other airlines, this tax is payed at the check-in counter itself. Some baggage handlers have been known to ask for a tip after you have checked in. An embarkation form is required to be filled out and this is handed to the immigration official when entering the departure lounge. For security reasons you usually have to identify your checked-in luggage before boarding the aircraft, either behind the check-in counters or beside the aircraft.

Duty Free: there is a small duty free shop in the departure lounge. It stocks a limited range of alcohol, tobacco and perfumes as well as handicrafts. Prices are competitive for tobacco and alcohol, but are otherwise expensive. The shop accepts Nepalese and Indian Rupees, Sterling, US Dollars and some other major currencies. Amex, Mastercard and Visa credit cards (except those issued in India, even if printed 'Valid in India and Nepal') are also accepted. It is possible to make duty free purchases on arrival as well as when leaving.

Banks: you can change money in the arrivals' hall where there is an efficient Nabil Bank counter. Another Nabil Bank is located in the main terminal concourse, but this has unreliable opening hours. **NB** Remember to keep the exchange certificate so that you can change back any unused money when you leave.

International 10 international airlines operate regular scheduled services to Europe and Asia. **NB** It is essential to reconfirm your return or onward flight at least 72 hours before departure (see also below).

Schedules vary slightly according to season. The following applied in 1999: **Aeroflot Russian Airlines** (SU), 1 weekly flight to Moscow (Tupolev 154), Kamaladi, Kathmandu (T227399); **Biman Bangladesh Airlines** (BG), 5 flights to Dhaka per week (Fokker 27), Kamal Pokhari, Kathmandu (T422669); **China Southwest Airlines** (SZ), thrice weekly services to Lhasa (Boeing 757), Kamaladi, Kathmandu (T419770, F419778); **Druk Air** (KB), twice weekly flights to Paro (Bhutan) (BAe 146), Durbar Marg, Kathmandu (T225166, F227229); **Indian Airlines** (IC), daily flights to Delhi and Varanasi, 4 times a week to Calcutta (Airbus A300, A320 and Boeing 737-200), **reconfirm** your flight at the Indian Airlines/Air India office, Hattisar, Kathmandu (T419649). **Ticket sales**: at World Travels, Durbar Marg, Kathmandu (T226275, F226088); **Pakistan International Airlines** (PK), 4 flights a week to Karachi (Boeing 737), Durbar Marg, Kathmandu (T227429); **Qatar Airways** (Q7), 3 weekly flights to Doha and Europe (Boeing 727), General Sales Agent: High Mountain Tours, Durbar Marg, Kathmandu (T417812); **Royal Nepal Airlines** (RA), daily flights to Delhi, 4 times a week to Bangkok, 3 flights a week to Patna, Hong Kong, Frankfurt and Dubai, twice weekly to Calcutta, Bombay, Singapore, Shanghai, Osaka and London, and weekly flights to Paris (Boeing 757 and Boeing 727), Kantipath, Kathmandu (T220757, F225348); **Singapore Airlines** (SQ), 2 flights a week to Singapore (Airbus A300), Durbar Marg, Kathmandu (T220759, F226795); **Thai Airways** (TG), 5 flights a week to Bangkok (Airbus A300), Durbar Marg, Kathmandu (T221316, F221130).

The following fares applied for one way flights in early 1997: **Bangkok** US$220; **Bombay** US$257; **Calcutta** US$96; **Dhaka** US$96; **Frankfurt** US$575; **Hong Kong** US$310; **London** US$630; **Osaka** US$500; **Paris** US$575; **Patna** US$70; **Shanghai** US$320; **Singapore** US$310; **Varanasi** US$96.

Several airlines not flying to Kathmandu also have offices or representatives here where you can make reservations, amend or confirm flights, etc.

Air Canada, Durbar Marg (T222838); **Air France**, Durbar Marg (T223339); **Air India**, Kantipath (T211730); **British Airways**, Durbar Marg (T222266); **Burma Airways**, Durbar Marg (T224839); **Cathay Pacific**, Kamaladi (T411725); **China Airlines**, Hattisar (T412778); **Dragon Air**, Durbar Marg (T227064); **Emirates**, Kantipath (T220579); **Gulf Air**, Durbar Marg (T228288); **Japan Airlines**, Durbar Marg (T222838); **KLM**, Durbar Marg (T224895); **Korean Airlines**, Kantipath (T212080); **Kuwait Air**, Kantipath (T222884); **Lauda Air**, Hattisar (T419573); **Northwest Airlines**, Lekhnath Marg (T410089); **Philippine Airlines**, Durbar Marg (T226262); **Qantas**, Durbar Marg

(T220245); **Royal Brunei Airlines**, Kamaladi (T410208); **SAS**, Kupondole (T524232); **Saudia**, Kantipath (T222787); **Swiss Air**, Durbar Marg (T222452); **TWA**, Kamaladi (T411725).

Domestic Three private carriers in addition to Royal Nepal Airlines operate 'fixed wing' domestic services. All offer the popular '**Mountain Flight**', a tour of the Himalayas, from Kathmandu at US$99. All domestic fares are set by the government and are identical. Those under the age of 26 qualify for **discounts** of 25 percent; a valid passport or student identity card is required. Children under 12 years old pay 50 percent of the adult fare, and infants below 2 years pay 10 percent. **Refunds**: a 5 percent charge is made for refunds submitted more than 48 hours before departure; this increases to 10 percent up to 24 hours before and 33 percent up to 1 hour before the flight. **NB** No refunds are given after the flight has left or for lost tickets. No **airport tax** is payable on dollar fare domestic flights. On flights longer than 1 hour, a couple of the private airlines have a lucky dip with the prize of a free flight.

(*Denotes non all weather airport, seasonal services.*)

Everest Air (E2), regular scheduled flights on HS748 (Avro), Dornier 228 and Twin Otter aircraft from Kathmandu to Bhadrapur, Bhairahawa, Bharatpur, Biratnagar, Jomsom and Pokhara. Helicopter (MI-17) charters from Kathmandu to Lukla. Outstations include Athrai, Aiselukharka, Bhojpur, Chainpur, Dharan, Diktel, Dingla, Khandbari, *Taplejung and Tehrathum. Durbar Marg, Kathmandu (T222290, F228392; Helicopter Reservations 473127).

Necon Air (3Z), regular scheduled flights on HS748 and Cessna Caravan aircraft from Kathmandu to Bhairahava, Biratnagar, Janakpur, Nepalgunj and Pokhara. Kalimatidole, Kathmandu (T473860, F471459, E into@necon.mos.com.np).

Nepal Airways (7E), regular scheduled flights on HS748 and Yak Harbinger aircraft from Kathmandu to Bhairahava, Bharatpur, Biratnagar, Jomsom, Nepalgunj, Pokhara and Simra. Also operate helicopter charters. Hattisar, Kathmandu (T412388, F420585).

Royal Nepal Airlines (RA) Nepal's most extensive network of regular scheduled flights on HS748, Twin Otter and a Pilatus Porter aircraft from Kathmandu to Bajura, Bhadrapur, Bhairahava, Bharatpur, Bhojpur, Biratnagar, Dang, Janakpur, Jomsom, Jumla, Lamidanda, Lukla, *Meghauli, Nepalgunj, *Phaplu, Pokhara, *Rajbiraj, Ramjatar, Simara, Surkhet, *Taplejung, Tikapur and Tumlingtar. From its smaller base at Nepalgunj, there are connections to several lowland and mountain destinations in the far west.

Reservations for Pokhara, Bharatpur and Lukla are handled by the RNAC head office on Kantipath (T220757), while the New Rd office deals with all other domestic destinations (T224497). It is easiest to book through a reliable travel agent.

The following fares applied for one way flights to selected destinations from Kathmandu in early 1997: **Bhadrapur** US$99; **Bhairahava** US$72; **Bharatpur** US$50; **Biratnagar** US$77; **Janakpur** US$55; **Jomsom** US$110; **Lukla** US$83; **Nepalgunj** US$99; **Pokhara** US$61; **Taplejung** US$99; **Tumlingtar** US$48.

Helicopters There are several companies operating helicopters. Their great advantage lies in their adaptability which allows them to reach some of the more remote parts of the Himalayas where fixed wing aircraft are unable to land. Most companies use the sturdy Russian MI-17 helicopter which can carry up to 22 passengers. The French Ecureil machines, meanwhile, are smaller, holding just 5 passengers, but are rather more comfortable and can reach altitudes of up to 19,000 feet. Helicoptor operators are increasingly targeting the top end of the tourist market, offering tailor made group charters. This can be an excellent way for a group to arrange their own itinerary, eg for trekking or sightseeing (including Everest), particularly if you are on a tight schedule. As ever, there is room for negotiating rates, but reckon on about US$1,000 per block per hour for the MI-17, and proportionately more per person on the Ecureil. Always arrange directly with the company or through an approved, recommended broker.

(**NB** In 1996, the government suspended some MI-17 flights, accusing their operators of loading them beyond safety levels. Industrial agitation followed and services were soon resumed.)

Asian Airlines, regular charter flights to Everest, Lhotse and Simikot. Also ad hoc charters (MI-17), Tridevi Marg, Kathmandu (T410086, F423315). **Dynasty Aviation**, tourist charters (Ecureil), Lazimpat, Kathmandu (T414626, F414627). **Everest Air**, tourist charters, emergency flights (MI-17), Babar Mahal, Kathmandu (T477174, F228266). **Gorkha Airlines**, tourist charters (MI-17), tourist and cargo services, new Banesvara, Kathmandu (T471136, F414102). **Himalayan Helicopters**, tourist charters mainly to Langtang, Everest, Annapurna and Lumbini (Ecureil), Durbar Marg, Kathmandu (T414596, F225150). **Manakamana Airways**, tourist charters (MI-17, Bell 206), Lazimpat, Kathmandu (T416434, F420422). **Nepal Airways**, tourist charters (MI-17 and Ecureil), Lal Durbar, Naxal, Kathmandu (T420421, F411610).

Buses Tourist buses to **Pokhara** and **Chitwan** leave from Kantipath, opposite Grindlays Bank, all long distance Sajha government buses go from the new central bus station near Balaju. You can make reservations either at your hotel or from any of the innumerable travel agents in the city. Although they use Indian made Tata vehicles, the *Swiss Travels* company, with an office near the Immigration Office on Tridevi Marg, has been recommended as running some of the more comfortable buses to Pokhara. During peak seasons it is essential to book early – at least a couple of days in advance is usually enough – particularly for the more popular destinations such as Pokhara and Tadi Bazar (Chitwan). Fares on **tourist buses** are always subject to commission, so are negotiable. Freelance baggage loaders are often loitering around the Kantipath bus stop and have been known to demand (and get) ludicrous sums from tourists for putting their bags on the roof: Rs 5 is about twice as much as a local would pay and is reasonable. **NB** Beware of pickpockets. **Warning** A video coach is one that shows an uninterrupted series of Bombay movies, usually at maximum volume.

Buses leave either from the **New Bus Park** at Balaju, or from the **City Bus Park**, east of Ratna Park on the southern extension of Durbar Marg.

Pokhara (202 kilometres): several tourist buses run daily from Kantipath, departing at around 0700 for the 8-hour journey, Rs 200. When you book, ask for a seat on the right hand side of the bus for best views. Cheaper government buses leave at the same time from the central bus station, but are slower and less comfortable than tourist buses, Rs 110. Night buses also operate from here, but miss out on the breathtaking scenery en route.

Tadi Bazar (for Chitwan) (156 kilometres) Also served by tourist buses leaving the Kantipath stop at about 0700. The 8-hour journey goes through Mugling and Narayanaghat and costs Rs 175.

The following destinations are all served by Sajha government buses departing from the new central bus station near Balaju.

Biratnagar (541 kilometres): mid-afternoon departure, 16 hours, Rs 275. **Birganj** (270 kilometres): early morning and night buses, 10 hours, Rs 140. **Dharan** (539 kilometres): mid-afternoon departure, 16 hours, Rs 275. **Janakpur** (375 kilometres): evening departures, 12 hours, Rs 190, a good place to break the long Kathmandu to Kakarbhitta journey. **Kakarbhitta** (610 kilometres): early afternoon departures, 18-20 gruelling hours, Rs 341. **Kodari** (114 kilometres): departures from early morning, 6 hours. **Mahendranagar** (713 kilometres): morning departures, 24 arduous hours, Rs 397. **Narayanaghat** (146 kilometres): several buses leave from early to mid-morning, also night buses, 8-9 hours, Rs 90. You can also take a tourist bus to Tadi Bazar (Chitwan) and get off at Narayanaghat. **Nepalganj** (531 kilometres): mid-afternoon departures, 16 hours, Rs 275. **Sunauli (Belahiya)** (282 kilometres): early morning and night buses, 9 hours, Rs 150.

Directory

Banks There are several banks and authorized money changers in the Thamel area. Rates and commission may vary, so check if you are changing a lot of money. (The *Nepal Rastra* bank often has better rates and/or lower commission than *Grindlays*.) Bank rates are always better than those offered by hotels. You will need your passport to change money. Normal banking hours are 1000-1400 Sun-Thur, 1000-1230 Fri, closed Sat. **NB** Keep your exchange certificates which are required to change money back when you leave. The main branch of *Grindlays Bank* is on Kantipath, with a Thamel branch, T233128, F228692. 100m south of *Le Bistro* restaurant, Mastercard and Visa withdrawals, telegraphic money transfer, open 1000-1600, Sun-Fri, closed Sat. Most of Thamel's various authorized money changers are open daily, 0800-2000. **On Kantipath:** *Nepal Bank*, T227375. Sat 0930-1230, closed Sun. *Nabil Bank*, T227181. **On Durbar Marg:** *Everest Bank*, T214878. *Nepal Indosuez Bank*, T228229. *State Bank of India*, T225326. **On New Rd:** *Nepal Bank*, T221185. Open daily, 0800-1900. *Himalayan Bank*, T224787. At Bishal Bazar, 0800-2000 Sun-Fri, closed Sat. *Rastra Banijya Bank*, T228335. At Bishal Bazar.

   Credit cards: *American Express*, T226172. Has an office in Jamal, between Durbar Marg and Kantipath. Also deals with Amex TC enquiries and travel services. Open 0800-2000 Sun-Fri, 0930-1600 Sat. **Mastercard** and **Visa** are at *Alpine Travel*, T225020, on Durbar Marg, 0800-2000 Sun-Fri, 0930-1600 Sat.

Communications **Kathmandu area code:** 1 (01 if dialling from within Nepal). Dozens of public call offices have sprung up in Thamel and throughout Kathmandu and offer international direct dialling, fax and, increasingly, email facilities. **Phone** calls from Nepal are set by the government and are expensive by international standards. In 1997, a call to **India** cost Rs 40 per minute, and Rs 180 to **Europe** and **North America**. Similar rates apply for faxing. **NB Calls are charged per minute**, not per second, so 1 min and 1 sec is charged as 2 mins – dial with care! You may be able to negotiate a small discount as a regular user – try the friendly and obliging *Moonlight Communications* quietly located near the *Rainbow Guest House* 200m north of Thamel Chowk. Most are open until 2230 and you can also receive calls ('callback'), at Rs 5-10 per minute. The *Central Telegraph Office* at Tripureshvar, 200m south of the GPO. Has an international telephone service counter open 24 hrs and is a little cheaper than the private bureaux, but charges a minimum of 3 mins, even if answerphone. Phone calls, telex and fax messages may be sent. For international calls, T186, domestic information T197, and domestic trunk calls T186. **Post Offices:** are open 1000-1430 Sun-Thur, 1000-1230 Fri, closed Sat. **GPO:** at Sundhara, near Bhimsen Tower. Open Sun-Thur 1000-1700, Fri 1000-1500, closed Sat. **NB** Make sure that cards and letters are franked in your presence. There is a small post office in Durbar Square, often overlooked by visitors and therefore quicker. Major hotels sell stamps and have letter boxes. **Poste Restante:** at the GPO (not efficient for forwarding mail), and a philately counter. The American Express office on Jamal has a poste restante service for cardholders. **NB** Have your mail addressed with your surname in capitals and underlined. Bring your passport for identification. **Courier and Freight Services:** *Das Worldwide Freight International*, T244097, Thamel. *DHL*, T223222, F220215, Kamaladi. *Ritual Freight*, T241842, F220842, Thamel. *Speedway Cargo*, T410595, F412679, E raju@speedway.mos.com.np, Thamel. *United Parcel Service* at Nepal Air Courier Express, T221588, F225915, Putali Sadak. **Telecommunications:** Nepal country code: T977. To send **email** costs about Rs 50 per Kb (approximately 1,000 characters), and Rs 25 per page to receive. Operators including *ATM Telelinks*, T411127, F411055, E postfax@atm.mos.com.np, opposite Le Bistro restaurant in central Thamel. Some places accept credit cards, but a surcharge is made.

Cultural centres The *Hotel Mandap* has programmes of Nepali classical music every evening Tues-Sun, 1900-2130, including flute, sarangi, harmonium and musical drama, free admission.

Nepali music and dance at *Hotel Marshyangdi* twice a week, check days and timings. The *Soaltee Holiday Inn* also has a good dance and music programme every evening in the Himalchuli restaurant, 1900-2245, but you have to eat and transport to central Kathmandu can be problematic late in the evening. The **New Himalchuli Cultural Group** is one of the country's leading groups and has performed extensively in South Asia as well as in Europe and has nightly music and dance shows at the *Hotel Shankar*, 1900-2000 in summer and 1830-1930 in winter (Rs 250). The **Gandharba Culture and Art Organization** has programmes of music, song and dance every day at *Spam's Restaurant* from 1500. The **Everest Cultural Society** has Nepali folk dances at the *Hotel de l'Annapurna* at 1900 (Rs 250). The *Hotel Everest* has a programme of Indian classical music most nights, while there are also nightly performances in the magnificent setting of the *Yak and Yeti's Nachgar* restaurant (recommended). The **Chimal Cultural Group** in the *Manaslu Hotel* and the *Hotel Vajra* also organize regular shows. *Ghazal* programmes are good at the *Amber Restaurant* on Durbar Marg (most evenings), and at the *Jewels of Manang* restaurant in the *Hotel Manang* in Paknajol, 1900-2200 Tues-Sun. Regular theatre performances are staged at Kantipath and Rani Pokhari. Details from Rashtriya Nach Ghar, Kantipath, near Rani Pokhari (T211900). A further possibility is the **Royal Nepal Academy** at Kamaladi and the City Hall, opposite the Exhibition Ground. The **Arniko Cultural Society** is in Dilli Bazar.

Foreign Cultural Centres and Libraries: *Alliance Francaise*, Dillibazar, Kathmandu, T410193/411076, F417694 (Postal address: c/o French Embassy, Lazimpat, PO Box 452, Kathmandu). *The British Council*, Kantipath, PO Box 640, Kathmandu, T221305/223796, F224076. *The Goethe Institut* (Germany), Ganabahal, PO Box 1103, Kathmandu, T220528, F222967. *Russian Centre of Science and Culture*, Kamalpokhari, PO Box 1433, Kathmandu, T415453/410503, F412249. *United States Information Service*, Gyaneshwore, PO Box 58, Kathmandu, T415845, F415847. Additionally, the following organization promotes Nepali culture and conducts cultural tours for visitors: *International Community Services*, Lazimpath, Kathmandu, T415353.

Australia, T411578, Bansbari. **Austria*, T410891, Hattisar. *Bangladesh*, T414943, Maharajganj. **Belgium*, T228925, Durbar Marg. *Burma*, Myanmar, T524788, Chakupath, Patan. **Canada*, T415193, Lazimpath. *China*, T411740, Baluwatar. *Denmark*, T413010, Baluwatar. *Egypt*, T524844, Pulchowk, Patan. *Finland*, T471221, Lazimpath. *France*, T418034, Lazimpath. *Germany*, T416832, Gyanesvara. **Greece*, T233113, Tripuresvara. **Hungary*, T525015, Pulchowk, Patan. *India*, T414990, Lainchaur. *Israel*, T411811, Lazimpath. *Italy*, T412280, Baluwatar. *Japan*, T226061, off Durbar Marg. *North Korea*, T521855, Jhamsikhel, Patan. *South Korea*, T270172, Tahachal. **Maldives*, T223045, Durbar Marg. **Mexico*, T412971, Pani Pokhari, Lazimpath. **Netherlands*, T523444, Kumaripati, Patan. *Pakistan*, T411421, Pani Pokhari, Lazimpath. **Philippines*, T474409, Shinamangal. **Poland*, T221101, Ganabahal; *Russia*, T412155, Baluwatar. **Spain*, T472328, Batisputali. *Sri Lanka*, T417406, Baluwatar. **Sweden*, T220939, Kicha Pokhari. **Switzerland*, T523468, Jawalakhel, Patan. *Thailand*, T420410, Bansbari. **Turkey*, T232711, Bijuli Bazar. *United Kingdom*, T411590, Lainchaur. *USA*, T411179, Pani Pokhari, Lazimpath. (* Consular service.)

Embassies & consulates

Hospitals & medical services If you fall ill, there are numerous **pharmacies** throughout Kathmandu where you can buy medicines without prescription. If you require a stool, blood or urine **test**, it is advisable to get this done at a reputable clinic. Results are usually ready the same day or by the following morning. For vaccinations, lab tests, health information and surgical or GP consultations, the *Himalayan International Clinic*, T225455, F220143, is in Chetrapati. The *Mt Everest International Clinic*, T421540, F412728, is 400m west of the Immigration Office in Thamel. The *Synergy International Clinic*, T415836, is tucked away opposite the *Excelsior Hotel* in central Thamel. These are private clinics aiming to provide Western standards of care and travel medicine. Government hospitals include the *Bir Hospital*, T221988, on Kantipath near the Tundikhel. The Japanese assisted *Teaching Hospital*, T412303, and the *Kanti Hospital*, T411550, are both in Maharajaganj. If you fall sick whilst **trekking** and require evacuation, the *Himalayan Rescue Association* (T416828) can advise on helicopter rescue. This is expensive and requires proof of sufficient insurance or a written guarantee of full payment. **NB** Remember to keep receipts for insurance claims.

The *National Library* houses a collection of about 70,000 books, many in English but with a small and useful Sanskrit section. It is situated in Pulchowk, Patan (T521322). Open Sun-Fri, 1000-1700. The *National Archives* on Ramshah Path and the smaller *Asa Archives* (*Asa Saphu Kuthi*), T223817, at Kulambhulu in the city's western suburbs have scholarly collections of historical manuscripts in

Libraries

Sanskrit, Nepali and other regional languages. Elsewhere, the *Nepal Bharat Sanskritik Kendra* in the RNAC Building is on New Rd, and the imaginatively named *Book Library* is on Ramshah Path. The *Keshar Library*, in the HMG Ministry of Education premises on the corner of Kantipath and Tridevi Marg, is more of a museum than a library, but is definitely worth a visit. The *SARC* headquarters on Tridevi Marg has a small library, containing reference materials and newspapers from the 7 SARC countries. You can also buy SARC publications from here. Temporary membership may be available at some of the foreign cultural centre libraries, see below.

Tour companies & travel agents

NB Check all tickets, travel documents, etc, carefully. Many agencies in **Thamel**. *Wayfarers*, T229110, F245875, E wayfarer@mos.com.np. 50m south of Le Bistro restaurant is efficient, trendy and good for advice, with a branch in Pokhara. Recommended. Credit cards accepted. Many quality agencies on **Durbar Marg**: *Everest Express*, T220759, F226795. *Himalayan Travels*, T223045, F224001. Karthak, T227223. *Modern Travels*, near *Yak and Yeti Hotel*, T244357, F242388. Natraj, Ghantaghar, T222014. *President*, T220245, F221180. *Shambhala*, T225166, F227229. Specialists in Bhutan. *Team Tours*, T227057, F243561. Wonderland, near *Yak and Yeti Hotel*, T244643, F231116. *Nepal Kamaz Tours*, T241811, F223370. For connections to **Central Asia and Russia**. *World Travels*. For Indian Airlines reservations, T226275, F226088. *Yeti*, T221234. **Tridevi Marg**: *Ying Yang Travels*, T423358, F421701. Specializes in ornithological and topographical expeditions throughout the Himalayas. *Sita World Travel*, T418363, F227557, E sitaktm@sitanep.mos.com. np. *Swiss Travels*, T412964, F423336. Has branch in Pokhara. *Tibet Travel and Tours*, T231130, F228986. Leaders in Tibet tours, all arrangements made. Recommended. **Elsewhere:** *Fourteen Peaks*, Jyatha, T/F255370. Everest, Ganga Path, T222217, F249896 (Kantipath T249216). *Holy Land Travels*, Bodhnath, T479019, F478592. *Kathmandu Travel and Tours,* Tripureshvar, T222511, F471379. *Marco Polo*, Kamal Pokharai, T414192. *Namaste*, Maitighar, Ramsha Path, T227484, F226590. *Nepal Travel Agency*, Ramshah Path, T413188, F420203. *Paramount Nepal Tours*, Lazimpath, T/F415078. *Great Escape Trekking*, F411533. *Pashupati Travels*, Kantipath, T248598, F224695.

NB Making reservations on *Indian Airlines* is best done early and in Kathmandu, as there is no Indian Airlines office outside Kathmandu. Numerous other travel agents on Durbar Marg, Thamel and Kantipath where you might find very competitive rates for short tours and treks.

National Parks & 'Jungle Safari'

Packages to **Chitwan** and **Bardia** National Parks and to **Koshi Tappu** Wildlife Reserve are offered by almost every tour operator and travel agent in Kathmandu.

Chitwan: *(Inside the park)*: *Chitwan Jungle Lodge*, T440918, F228349, Durbar Marg. *Island Jungle Resort*, T226002, F223184, Durbar Marg. *Gaida Wildlife Jungle Camp*, T220940, F227292, Durbar Marg. *Machan Wildlife Resort*, T225001, F220475, Durbar Marg. *Tiger Tops*, T222706, F412920, Durbar Marg.

Chitwan *(Sauraha, outside the park)*: *Alka Resort Camp*, T224771. *Hermitage*, T/F424390, Tridevi Marg, near Immigration Office. *Jungle Camp*, T/F222132, Thamel. *Rainforest Guest House*, T60235. *Rhino Lodge*, T420316, F417146, Thamel. *Royal Park*, T229028, F412987, Thamel.

Bardia National Park: *Tiger Tops* (see above), *Bardia Jungle Lodge*, T417395, F229459. *Forest Hideaway*, T423586, F226763, Thamel.

Koshi Tappu Wildlife Reserve: *Koshi Tappu Wildlife Camp*, T226130, F224237, Kamaladi.

Sukla Phanta Wildlife Reserve: *Silent Safari*, T520523, F536941.

Tourist offices

There are two government tourist information offices in Kathmandu, one at the airport (T470537), the other just off Basantpur Square (T220818). Open 0900-1700 Sun-Thur, 0900-1500 Fri, closed Sat. The Department of Tourism headquarters (T523692) is situated behind the National Stadium in Tripureshvar and also has a supply of leaflets. Open Sun-Thur 1100-1600, Fri 1100-1500, Sat closed. There are a number of free **magazines** for tourists which carry interesting articles on various aspects of Nepali life as well as maps and compendious lists of useful and useless phone numbers. Titles include *Adventure Nepal, Image Nepal, Nepal Visitor* and *Travellers Nepal* and are available at the airport and in good travel agents. **Noticeboards** at various locations in Thamel are a good way to find out about any special events, as well as courses (eg language, yoga, massage), lost and found, travel companions wanted, trekking gear for sale, etc. Officially registered **tourist guides** can be hired, rates start from US$5 for half a day. *Himalayan Rescue Association (HRA)*: a non profit organization promoting safety in trekking and mountaineering. The HRA office is 100m west of the Immigration Office on Tridevi Marg (T419755). Open 1000-1700, Sun-Fri, closed Sat. *Kathmandu Environmental Education Programme (KEEP)*: this excellent organization was established to promote awareness of environmental problems facing the Himalayas and to reduce the negative impact of tourism on their ecology and culture through education and by maintaining a high profile for its wider agenda of conservation and development. Its publications include the informative *Himalayan First Aid Manual* and *Trekking Gently in the Himalaya*, both of which are recommended reading for all trekkers. There is a small library and regular presentations, video and slide shows are held at its office and travellers' information centre is located on Bhagavan Bahal in the eastern part of Thamel, around the corner from the Immigration Office, PO Box 9178, Thamel, Kathmandu, T410303, F411533.

Useful information

NGOs: for information about NGOs based in Kathmandu, contact the *Social Welfare Council*, Lekhnath Marg, Kathmandu, T418111, F410279. A booklet, NGO Profile, listing the activities and contact addresses of 42 NGOs is published by IUCN and USAID, and is available from the KEEP office in Thamel. **Useful numbers** Emergency Phone Numbers: *Emergency*, T100. *Police*, T216999. *Tourist Police* (Babar Mahal) T211293. *Fire* T221177. *Ambulance*, Bishal Bazar T211121. *Nepal Chamber* T230213; Bhimsenthan T211959. *Red Cross* (Brikhuti Mandap), T228094. Government Offices: *Dept of Tourism*, Babar Mahal, T223581. *Immigration Office*, Tridevi Marg, T412337. *Kathmandu Municipality*, Dharma Path, T221280. *Ministry of Tourism and Civil Aviation*, Singha Durbar, T211286.

Kathmandu Valley

Patan

Population: 257,086
Area: 385 square
kilometres

*Also known as **Lalitpur** ('beautiful town'), Patan (pronounced Pa-tan, with the emphasis on the first, long, syllable) is officially the valley's second largest city, although it has now been effectively absorbed into Kathmandu, separated from the capital by the Bagmati River. It has a long history and has traditionally been an important centre of Newar Buddhism. The four earth and brick directional stupas at its four corners are attributed to Emperor Ashoka.*

Like Kathmandu, the development of the city centred around its Durbar Square which marks the point at which all major roads to the city converge and around which a grid of other roads has been built. This is the oldest, most traditional and lively area of the city, while the growth of the newer residential area to the west has been more recent and, until now, more ordered than that of Kathmandu's eastern districts. Bounded to the north by the Bagmati River, the Ring Road effectively encloses the city on all other sides. It is easily reached from Kathmandu with three bridges spanning the Bagmati to Teku, Tripureshvar and New Baneshvar, while the Ring Road crosses the Bagmati to the west and to the east into Koteshvar and on to the airport. The city is easily navigable on foot: it is about three kilometres from the Teku bridge in the northwest to the Patan Industrial Estate to the southeast. Although it has far fewer options for accommodation than its northern neighbour, there are a number of hotels catering for most budgets and the number of travellers choosing to spend at least one night in Patan has increased over recent years. There are wonderful views over Kathmandu from the **Kopundol** area, which has some good hotels. Apart from the fact that several international and non-governmental aid organizations have their offices in Patan, many Westerners working in Kathmandu have chosen to live in Patan for what they consider to be its more peaceful and attractive environment.

To the southeast of Durbar Square, **Jawalakhel** is the valley's artisan centre where, together with the nearby **Patan Industrial Estate**, the majority of its handicrafts are produced as well as being the focus of Nepal's carpet manufacture, the country's largest single export. Carpets and handicrafts are produced mainly by the large population of Tibetans who have settled in this area, a former refugee camp, following their migration from their homeland from 1959. You can go and watch as carpets are woven and see statues take shape in the smiths' workshops.

History

Although disputed by a number of historians, it is popularly held that Patan owes its origins to the visit of Emperor **Ashoka** to the Kathmandu Valley during the third century BC. Regardless of its veracity, it has been convenient to believe that such a pilgrimage did indeed take place and this has served to promote the city's worthiness as an historical Buddhist centre, a perception which assumes added significance in the context of the cultural heritage of the valley's other two cities. Patan was probably founded during the early Licchavi period, from the fifth century AD, when its was known as **Yupagrama Dranga**. Amongst the earliest written records, there are allusions to a fifth century 'palace' belonging to one of the **Mangaladhipati** kings, after which **Mangal Bazar** to the south of Durbar Square may have been named. There is, however, little or no archaeological evidence to confirm either its existence or exact location, though there is a natural spring (**Manga Hiti**) in Durbar Square which may have provided drinking water to early residents. Inscriptions dating from the seventh century refer to changes made by the Licchavi king **Narendra Deva** to the taxation system, which suggests that the town had been fully established by then.

The medieval period brought political changes with the **Mallas** assuming a hegemony in the valley in about 1200, while the town's old name was replaced by **Lalitpur**. During the rule of **Yaksha Malla** in the mid-15th century the valley was divided into three city states, with Patan ruled by Yaksha Malla's son and daughter, respectively named **Dharmavati** and **Ratna**. There followed a period of unprecedented growth for the city, by now the valley's largest. Many of Durbar Square's magnificent temples, monuments and other architecture were built during the reigns of three generations of Malla kings: **Siddhi Narasimha Malla** (1618-1658), **Sri Nivas Malla** (1658-1685) and **Yoganarendra Malla** (1685-1706).

Patan remained one of the valley's three independent kingdoms until discord and rivalry between the ruling Mallas of Kathmandu, Patan and Bhaktapur allowed their eventual conquest and the unification of Nepal by the King of Gorkha, **Prithivi Narayana Shah**, in 1768. Patan's political importance decreased with the choice of Kathmandu as the Shah capital.

Sights

Durbar Square Area

More compact, more concentrated and more the city's focal point than either of its namesakes in Kathmandu and Bhaktapur, Patan's Durbar Square is a celebration of Newari architecture, its distinct character a product of the traditionally pivotal role of religion in society combined with the rivalry that existed between 17th and 18th century Malla rulers of the valley's three city states for the most resplendent reflection of their authority. It ranks between Kathmandu and Bhaktapur in both size and number of monuments, although there are similarities in conception insofar as most temples and structures are built facing the royal palace complex which completely dominates one side of the square, separated by an avenue or tangible open space. Further temples and Buddhist monuments are located to the north and south of Durbar Square.

Bhimsen Mandir (1)

This three-storeyed marble and gilt-faced building at the north end of Durbar Square has twice been restored: once by King Sri Nivas Malla in 1682 after a fire and again in the late 1960s following the damage it suffered in the 1934 earthquake. In front of the temple stands a pillar surmounted by a lion. Bhimsen in the *Mahabharata* is the exceptionally strong god of traders and the temple is propitiated accordingly by local businessmen.

Vishvanath Shiva Mandir (2)

Standing on a three stage plinth, this two-storeyed temple is dedicated to Shiva and was built in 1627 by King Siddhi Narasimha Malla. It has a large linga-yoni throne and the beams and brackets are profusely carved with erotic motifs. Two stone elephants guard the entrance to the east, while a statue of the Nandi bull stands to the west.

Kathmandu Valley

Krishna Mandir (3)	Standing beside the Vishvanath Shiva Mandir and set further back from the main thoroughfare, this is one of two temples in the square dedicated to Krishna and is sometimes referred to as the Krishna-Radha Mandir. This impressive shikhara design structure, built by King Siddhi Narasimha Malla and completed in 1637, is unlike the other Malla temples in using stone in a combination of early Mughal and Nagara architecture. It is one of the best known temples in Nepal, noted for the high quality of its stone work. The first three floors have *chattri* pavilions and open colonnaded sides reminiscent of the great Emperor Akbar's Panch Mahal at Fatehpur Sikri in India. On the second floor is a Shiva linga. Capping it is the curvilinear Hindu shikhara which contrasts with the traditional pagoda temples dominating most of the square and is similar to those in the Kangra Valley of Himachal Pradesh. A golden **Garuda**, the faithful bird headed vehicle of Vishnu, faces the temple from atop a pillar on the east and was erected on completion of the temple by King Narendra Malla. Inside are superb stone bas relief carvings of scenes from the Hindu epics with fine details, with stories from the *Mahabharata* depicted on the first floor and from the *Ramayana* on the second. A popular festival is held on Krishna Janmastami in August/September when devotees gather to pay homage to Krishna.

Jagan Narayana Mandir (4)	Also dedicated to Vishnu (as Narayana), this is said to be the oldest temple in the square dating from about 1566, although some scholars date it from the late 17th century. It is also known as Char Narayana Mandir. Two stone lions proudly guard the entrance. The red brick edifice contrasts attractively with the beautifully carved wooden doors, windows and roof struts. The latter are abundantly illustrated with erotic carvings.

Yoganarendra Pillar & Statue (5)	To the south of the Jagan Narayana Mandir, a bronze statue of King Yoganarendra Malla, complete with headwear, sits in a gilded basket on top of a six metres tall stone pillar gazing into the Taleju Mandir opposite. A bronze *naga*, or cobra, rises behind him, its head forming a protective umbrella for the king, on which stands a small bird. A local legend recounts how the god fearing Yoganarendra left his palace one night for the ascetic life and that as long as the bird remains, the king may return to his palace. A window is kept open for his return, and a hookah (pipe) ready for his use!

Hari Shankar Mandir (6)	The three-storeyed Hari Shankar Mandir was built by Yogamati, King Yoganarendra Malla's daughter, and was completed in 1705. The temple is notable for its elaborately carved roof struts and arches.

Taleju Bell (7)	Moving south, this large bell hanging between two thick pillars was cast by King Vishnu Malla and his wife Rani Chandra Lakshmi in 1736. It was the first of the great bells to be installed in all three of the valley's Durbar Squares. Although now largely ceremonial, it was rung during worship at the temples and could also be used to sound an alarm. Some accounts assert that by ringing the bell, citizens could draw the king's attention to injustices suffered by them.

Krishna Mandir(8)	At the southern corner of the main thoroughfare, this is the only octagonal temple in Durbar Square and was built by Yogamati, daughter of King Yoganarendra, in 1723. It is also known as Chyasim Deval.

Bhai Dega Mandir (9)	This is a small Shiva temple containing an image of the linga and is situated behind the Taleju Bell. A Mughal-style dome surmounts the cube-like main structure.

Occupying the entire area to the east of the main thoroughfare is the Royal Palace which gives the square its name. The exact origins of this magnificent complex are unclear, but date back as far as the 14th century which makes it the first of the valley's Durbar Square palaces to be built. The bulk of its construction occurred during the 17th century in the latter Malla period when the palace complex is said to have been comprised of at least seven *chowks*, or courtyards: Agan Chowk, Dafoshan Chowk, Kisi Chowk, Kumari Chowk, Nasal Chowk, Nuche Agan Chowk, and Sahapau Chowk. The complex was badly damaged during Prithivi Narayana Shah's conquest of the Kathmandu Valley in 1768 and again in the 1934 earthquake. Some renovations were made by the early Shah occupants, but today there are three main chowks (Sundari Chowk, Mul Chowk and Mani Keshar Chowk) each enclosed by a palace building.

Sundari Chowk (10) The name means 'beautiful courtyard' and it is the smallest and southernmost of the three chowks. The entrance is guarded by stone statues of Narasimha, Ganesh and Hanuman. The fine three-storey palace has carved roof struts and windows. The central window above the

The Royal Palace

Kathmandu Valley

Patan Durbar Square

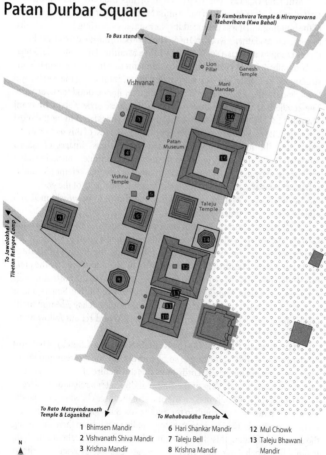

To Kumbeshvara Temple & Hiranyavarna
Mahavihara (Kwa Bahal)

To Bus stand

Lion Pillar

Ganesh Temple

Vishvanat

Mani Mandap

Patan Museum

Vishnu Temple

Taleju Temple

To Jawalakhel &
Tibetan Refugee Camp

To Rato Matsyendranath
Temple & Lagankhel

To Mahabauddha Temple

N

Not to scale

1 Bhimsen Mandir	6 Hari Shankar Mandir	12 Mul Chowk
2 Vishvanath Shiva Mandir	7 Taleju Bell	13 Taleju Bhawani
3 Krishna Mandir	8 Krishna Mandir	Mandir
4 Jagan Narayan Mandir	9 Bhai Dega Mandir	14 Degu Taleju Mandir
5 Yoganarendra Pillar &	10 Sundari Chowk	15 Mani Keshab Chowk
Statue	11 Tusha Hiti	16 Manga Hiti

entrance was originally gold plated, while those on either side are of ivory. The ground floor *dalans*, or open areas, surrounding the courtyard were used by the Malla kings for official functions. The numerous pillars here are ornately carved. Seventeen images of Hindu deities carved from wood are set in niches around the courtyard.

The centre of the chowk is occupied by the magnificent **Tusha Hiti (11)**, a sunken royal bath decorated with fine stone and bronze carvings. There is an incomplete set of carved stone eight divine mother goddesses (Asta Matrika), the eight Bhairava incarnations of Vishnu, and the eight naga kings. The bath is shaped as a yoni. The bronze plated water tap is formed in the shape of a conch shell and has a small figure of Lakshmi Narayana on it. Beside it are stone statues of Hanuman and Krishna. Sadly, the source that supplied water to the bath dried up in the 1970s. The stone block by the steps leading down into the bath was used by King Siddhi Narasimha Malla, who is credited with the construction of this part of the palace and chowk in 1670, and his descendants for meditation and prayer following ritual bathing.

Mul Chowk (12) The construction of this building and chowk was started in 1627 by King Siddhi Narasimha Malla. A major fire destroyed much of the building and it was left to Siddhi Narasimha's son, King Sri Nivas Malla, to complete his father's work in 1666. The chowk forms the core of the Royal Palace complex and has a small gilded **Vidhya Mandir** at the centre dedicated to the family deity and placed there to commemorate the completion of construction. The cloister is a two-storeyed building, comprising the Patan royal family's erstwhile residence, with three **Taleju** temples around the courtyard. The smallest of these, the three-storeyed Bhutanese-style **Taleju Bhavani Mandir (13)** on the south side of the chowk, is considered to be the most important. It was built at around the same time as the rest of this section of the palace and the main entrance is flanked by two brass images of Ganga mounted on a turtle and Yamuna on the mythical crocodile. The main courtyard was used by the Mallas for the performance of religious ceremonies and is still used today when, during the Dasain festival, the image of the goddess of the Taleju Bhavani Mandir is carried into the chowk to be worshipped and offered sacrifices of buffaloes and goats.

To the east of the chowk, but not open to visitors, is the **Bhandarkhal Garden**, dedicated to the family deity and containing a pond of lotuses and a number of images. On the northern side, meanwhile, the original structure of the **Degu Taleju Mandir (14)** was built in 1640, then destroyed by the great fire of 1662 before being renovated four years later. Just to the north, the large five-storeyed **Taleju Mandir** soars majestically above Durbar Square and is the largest and most spectacular of the palace's temples. A late addition to the main palace buildings, it was constructed in 1736 and rebuilt following its destruction by the 1934 earthquake.

Mani Keshab Chowk (15) (or **Keshab Narayana Chowk**) The most northerly chowk and, according to some sources, the most recent, though its exact dates are not known. Records show that a structure of some sort on this site was used for a gathering of the Kathmandu Valley's religious leaders in 1631 (which could actually make it the oldest of the three chowks) and that the chowk was renovated or rebuilt in the mid-1670s. Substantial alterations were carried out again in 1733 and much of the building dates from then. Following the conquest of Patan, this chowk became the residence of Dalmardan Shah, Patan's first Shah king and, by consummate chance, brother of Prithivi Narayana Shah.

The main entrance to the chowk is through the splendid **golden gate** from Durbar Square's main north-south thoroughfare. An inscription on the gate chronicles its restoration under Jung Bahadur Rana in 1854 at a cost of Rs 321. Above the gate is a fine golden *torana* engraved with images of Shiva and Parvati, while a **golden window** shows Avalokiteshvara. A small shrine dedicated to Keshab Narayana stands in the courtyard and gives the chowk its name. Since the mid-1990s, the chowk has been home to the **National Bronze Museum**.

Directly to the north of the Royal Palace complex is the Manga Hiti, the conduit of spring water which may have existed at the time of the founding of Patan from the fifth century. Steps lead down to the pool shaped as a lotus and water comes from three stone spouts carved in the shape of crocodiles. The **Mani Mandap**, or Royal Pavilion, built in 1700, stands beside it.

Manga Hiti (16)

Kathmandu Valley

Beyond Durbar Square

Just to the north of Durbar Square, this three-tiered temple has recently been renovated by a trust concerned with the conservation and restoration of the valley's architectural heritage.

Radha Krishna Mandir

Continuing north from Durbar Square, about 300 metres beyond the Radha Krishna Mandir you reach this two-storeyed temple on your right. A black stone frieze inside the shrine depicts the Uma Maheshvara, the name popularly given to this peaceful representation of Shiva and Parvati sitting closely together on Mount Kailash.

Uma Maheshvara Mandir

Leaving Durbar Square to the south, this three-tiered temple is situated on the first road on the right after about 200 metres. Vishvakarma means 'Creator of the World' and is the patron deity of this locality's artisans whose own creations on and in the temple pay seemly homage to the god. The temple's frontage is lavishly screened with embossed copper plate, while suspended bells flank the entrance and a large stone lion stands guard just outside.

Vishvakarma Mandir

Some 300 metres along the road which leads north from Durbar Square stands this imposing five-storey temple. Dedicated to Shiva, it is the oldest existing temple in the city and, with Bhaktapur's Nyatapola Mandir, is the other of the two detached five-storeyed temples in the valley. Construction of the original temple on this site is credited to Bhaskaradeva in 1392. A small tank on the northern side of the temple is said to be fed by an underground stream having the sacred Lake Gosainkund in the Himalayas (about a week's walk in each direction from Patan), as its source: immersion is believed to confer great merit upon the bather. During the Janai Purnima festival in July/August, large crowds of pilgrims take a ritual bath and worship a silver and gold linga, placed in the tank. Brahmins and Chetris replace their sacred threads at the festival amidst frenetic dancing by strikingly dressed *jhankri*, witch doctors.

Kumbheshvara Mandir

To the south of the temple is the **Baglamukhi Mandir**, a Newari house in which devotees implore the eponymous crane-headed goddess for succour in times of adversity.

Buddhist Patan

Patan is steeped in Buddhist history, tradition and legend, stretching back as far as the disputed visit of the great emperor Ashoka in the third century BC. More than half of the city's population is Buddhist. Shrines and temples were often built to become the geographical focus of the local community. Many of the temples and bahals are open to visitors, their monks happy to explain their traditions and to show the exquisite craftsmanship which decorates some of the buildings. A number of other Buddhist monasteries not mentioned here are located throughout the city which, sadly, have fallen into disrepair and now lie as defunct relics of a former age. With the exception of the Ashokan stupas and the Golden Temple, all of the following are situated south of Durbar Square.

The Golden Temple
(or Hiranyavarna Mahivihara)

Also known as **Kwa Bahal** and **Suvarna Mahavihara**, this Buddhist temple and monastery is two minutes' walk north of Durbar Square and its fabulous craftsmanship and lavish decoration should not be missed. Though first documented in 1409, it was renovated by the 11th century King Bhaskaradeva. It was presumably constructed some time before then – some sources say by a local trader in gratitude for the wealth he had accumulated in Tibet. **NB** The temple is open to visitors, but leather items, including belts and watch straps, are not allowed inside.

Behind the inconspicuous entrance (look for the street sign) guarded by a pair of decorative stone lions, the complex is surprisingly compact. The central courtyard contains a small but spectacular shrine dedicated to Svayambhunath. Mythical, griffin-like creatures stand on pillars at its four corners, and each side has wooden lattice windows. The golden pagoda roof is brightly polished and four *nagas* combine to support the *kalasa* at its pinnacle. On one side is a rack of prayer-wheels. This shrine is a late addition and, because it is no longer possible to view the fine façade of the main temple from across the courtyard, is considered by some purists to have diminished the earlier aesthetic appeal of the complex. The courtyard, circumambulated in a clockwise direction, is surrounded on three sides by lines of prayer-wheels which form the inner enclosure of a continuous verandah.

A large bell hangs beneath a gilded canopy near the entrance to the main temple, while above the entrance is a series of 12 carved images of Shakyamuni Buddha. On either side, the eyes of the Buddha are engraved into the bronze border and two richly decorated elephants stand guard. The temple itself is a marvellous three-storeyed pagoda building with each roof covered in copper whose colour gives the temple its popular name. Small statues of birds in flight are attached to the four corners of each roof, while bells hang along the length of their rims. Latticed window screens and carved roof struts are found on the first two floors. The 13 steps forming the pinnacle represent the Buddhist stages on the path to enlightenment. Two bronze lions shown carrying the goddess Tara flank the entrance to the sanctum, which has a frieze depicting the life of Shakyamuni Buddha where a strong Hindu component of some images indicate the extent of religious cross-fertilization in the valley.

Rato Matsyendranath

Heading southwest from Durbar Square, you reach the Rato Matsyendranath temple, another major religious site revered by both Hindus and Buddhists. It is also known as **Taha Bahal** and **Bungadhya**, the latter name linking it with Bungamati, regarded as the 'home village' of Matsyendranath. The construction of the original temple is attributed to Narendradeva in 1408, though the present temple dates from 1673. It is venerated as an abode of the Bungamati Matsyendranath, also called Karunamaya Avalokiteshvara or, in Tibetan, Bukham Lokeshvara. Legend has it that when Gorakhnath, a disciple of Karunamaya, visited Kathmandu, he was not shown due respect. In his anger he cursed the people and consequently they suffered drought and famine lasting 12 years. When Karunamaya learnt of this, he told Gorakhnath to pardon the people and lift the curse; this was done and rain poured down. In honour of

Karunamaya's kindness, King Narendra Deva built this temple. He also instigated the annual chariot race.

A number of pillars supporting statues of various creatures related to the
Tibetan calendar stand in front of the elaborately decorated main north
entrance, and a large bell hanging from a Tibetan-style shaft is to the left. The
revered image is made of sandalwood and clay, is repainted in red (hence *rato*)
before each annual chariot race, and is further embellished with jewellery and
garlands. It is worshipped as a god of rain and Hindus also believe that simply
seeing the chariot festival of Rato Matsyendranath is enough to attain salvation.
The courtyard is filled with sculptures of animals including horses, lions and
bulls. For several weeks from April onwards (in the month of Vaisakh), the deity
is trundled through the streets of Patan in an enormous chariot. This culminates
in the Boro Jatra festival, strategically timed prior to the onset of the monsoon,
when the chariot reaches Jawalakhel. The lower roof of the temple is tiled, while
the upper two are overlayed with copper. Carvings on the struts of each roof
depict various deities with lesser beings placed deferentially at their feet.

On the main road leading south from Durbar Square, the Minanath Mandir is
smaller than the Rato Matsyendranath Mandir opposite, but both are dedicated to forms of Avalokiteshvara and the bronze image of its deity, Bodhisattva Lokeshvara, also has a place in the annual Boro Jatra festival. A temple
was first built on this site during the Licchavi era. Two bronze lions stand
guard on either side of the entrance and a large prayerwheel stands beneath a
canopy to one side. Like its neighbour, the lower roof is tiled while the upper is
overlayed with copper.

Minanath Mandir

Dedicated to Mayadevi, the revered mother of Shakyamuni Buddha, this temple and monastery is located at Bhimche Bahal, near the Rato Matsyendranath
Mandir. Feline guardians at the entrance are flanked by two suspended bells
and the bronze torana above the main entrance depicts scenes from the lives of
Mayadevi and the Buddha. Inside are three stupas. Both roofs are tiled. Legend
has it that the group of chaityas here were commissioned by the emperor
Ashoka.

Mayurvarna Mahavihara

To the southeast of Durbar Square, and along a southwest leading alleyway, is
the 16th century shikhara-style Mahabouddha Mandir, dedicated to the thousand buddhas of the auspicious aeon (*Tib* Sangye Tongsta) whose names are
enumerated in the *Bhadrakalpikasutra*. Among these, Shakyamuna Buddha
was the fourth, and the next to appear in the world will be Maitreya. Tightly
hemmed in by surrounding buildings, the terracotta and tile building is difficult to locate. It is somewhat reminiscent of the great Mahabodhi Temple at
Bodhgaya in India, and its construction is said to have been completed in 1585
by Pandit Abhaya Raja during the reign of Mahendra Malla. This is a masterpiece of terracotta and each of the 9,000 or so bricks is said to carry an image of
the Buddha, and the face of Buddha is portrayed on blocks of the shikhara
structure. In the centre is a gold image of the Buddha, which, some sources
maintain, was brought here from Bodhgaya. Surrounding the shrine are
numerous friezes depicting scenes from the Buddha's life, while the many oil
lamps here are lit also in honour of Mayadevi. A narrow staircase leads to the
upper part. Although it was completely destroyed in the 1934 earthquake, it
has been rebuilt exactly like the original. The small shrine standing behind the
main temple is said to have been built with bricks remaining from the post
earthquake reconstruction. The temple is surrounded by Newar Buddhist
craft shops, most of them selling images of Buddhist deities fashioned in the

Mahabouddha Mandir

renowned *ciré perdue* ('lost wax') process.

Rudravarna Mahavihara About 100 metres south of the Mahabouddha Mandir, this temple (also known as Oku Bahal, or Bankali Rudravarna Mahavihara) and former monastery is one of the – if not the – oldest in Patan. The use of the site for religious purposes probably dates back to the early Malla period and some of the fixtures of the present building are said to be from the 13th century. The main temple rises from the centre of the monastery buildings. The tiled lower roof of the two-storeyed pagoda temple is topped by five decorative stupas and small statues of peacocks, and the copper upper roof has beams trimmed with images of antigods. Above the richly adorned entrance are bronze friezes with various Buddhist representations, including Mayadevi. Inside the rectangular complex are courtyards alive with reflections of the culture of Patan, with bronze and stone statues of elephants, peacocks, Garudas and (remarkably many) lions, as well as mirrors, woodcarvings, bells, *vajras*, minor deities and a statue of the Rana prime minister responsible for rebuilding much of Kathmandu after the earthquake, Juddha Shamsher. The courtyard also contains a central statue of the Buddha and a line of oil lamps.

Ratnakar Mahavihara (or Ga Bahal) Southwest of Durbar Square, this attractive three-storeyed temple and monastery is notable for the double row of Buddha images above the main entrance and, either side, the guardian lions which carry statues of the Buddha. Patan has its own 'living goddess', the *Kumari*, though the role does not have the profile of Kathmandu's Kumari nor does it come with palatial accommodation. Patan's Kumari is chosen from amongst the daughters of the priests of the Ga Bahal and lives with her family. Her major duty of the year is to take part in the Boro Jatra festival of Rato Matsyendranath.

Haka Bahal West of Durbar Square, this monastery includes a small temple and a Buddhist shrine contained in an inner courtyard.

Ibaha Bahal Located to the south of Durbar Square, between the square and the Rato Matsyendranath Mandir, this monastery has recently been renovated with Japanese assistance and now includes a school.

Ashokan Stupas The remains of four stupas, their construction attributed to the Mauryan emperor Ashoka in the third century BC, are located approximately at the cardinal points delineating the ancient boundaries of Patan. All but the Northern stupa are now mostly grassed over, though still recognizable.

Northern Stupa (Bahai Thura) Located north of Durbar Square, beyond the Uma Maheshvara Mandir on the road towards the bridge to Southeast Kathmandu, this is the best preserved of the four stupas. A lotus-shaped adornment supports the *kalasa* pinnacle above the spire's 13 steps, and a group of chaityas form part of the circumference wall at the base of the stupa. A natural spring, active only during the monsoon, is said to exist on one side. A small shrine dedicated to Sarasvati stands on the northern side. The exterior of the stupa has recently been renovated.

Eastern Stupa (Bhate Thura) This is the most out of the way of the four stupas and lies beyond the Ring Road to the southeast of Durbar Square at Imadole. Four chaityas are fitted into the brick perimeter wall at the cardinal points and a small stone structure, the remains of the pinnacle, projects from the top of the grassy hillock. The stupa is a landmark of sorts, but outwardly is otherwise undistinguished and attracts few visitors.

Southern Stupa (Lagan Thura) This, the largest of the four, is situated by a lotus pond just to the east of the main road leading south from Durbar Square and gives this area of Patan (Lagankhel) its name. Protruding from the top of the stupa is a small hemispherical stone edifice painted with the eyes of Buddha, replacing an earlier wooden structure, and supporting a compact spire representing the 13 stages on the path to enlightenment. The circumference wall is interesting for its inset hewn images of Buddha. A stone mandala, representing the 'palace' of the meditational deity, stands beside the eastern chaitya, while the western chaitya has a shrine containing images of Amitabha (*Tib* Opame).

Western Stupa (Pulchowk Thura) Situated in Pulchowk, about one kilometre along the main Mangal Bazar road heading west from Durbar Square. A large mound topped by a stone structure painted with the eyes of Buddha and with four chaityas in the base. This is where the annual Boro Jatra festival of Rato Matsyendranath begins its procession.

Jawalakhel

This area of Southeast Patan, pronounced *Jowl-a-kel*, is renowned for its large Tibetan community and the **Tibetan Refugee Camp**, now occupied by only the poorest of the exiles. Nepal's only **zoo** is also located here.

The refugee camp, with those in Pokhara and at Bodhnath was one of three major camps established by the Red Cross to accommodate the influx of Tibetans from the early 1950s, and over time it has developed from a transit camp into a focus for the manufacture of **handicrafts** and **carpets**. With further help from the Swiss Association for Technical Assistance, the production of Tibetan carpets blossomed, growing so rapidly that by the early 1990s carpet export accounted for more than half of Nepal's total export earnings. You can watch all stages of their production, from the dyeing and spinning of yarns to the weaving and final trimming. There are fixed price shops where you can buy the carpets made here along with blankets, jackets and pullovers.

From Durbar Square, you can get here by following the road south of the square, then turn right (west) onto the main road just past the Rato Matsyendranath Mandir. Continue along here for about one kilometre until you reach a major crossroads with a roundabout, just beyond the Haka Bahal. Turn left and follow this road south and past the zoo for less than one kilometre and the handicraft centre is on your left, just inside the Ring Road. If you continue south along this route, you will reach the village of **Bungamati**, the other home of the Rato Matsyendranath deity, after about four kilometres.

Just south of the busy Jawalakhel Chowk is Nepal's only zoo. Though not recommended as a special trip, it has pleasant gardens and its inmates include tigers, lions, leopards, rhinos, elephants, deer, monkeys, antelopes, snakes and an aviary. Elephant rides are available at Rs 100 inside the park and at Rs 2,000 for a stroll through the streets of Patan. ■ *Open 1000-1630, daily. Saturday is very busy with long queues. Entrance Rs 20, camera charge Rs 10, video camera charge Rs 50.* Vendors of peanuts (you may feed the animals) congregate outside the zoo, where there are also small snack stalls and even fortune tellers.

Zoo

Museums and Libraries

This is situated inside **Mani Keshab Chowk**, the northernmost of the three courtyards comprising the Royal Palace complex in Durbar Square. It houses

National Bronze Art Museum

900 exhibits, the oldest reputedly dating back to the Licchavi (seventh century). ■ *Entrance Rs 10. Open 1000-1600, Wednesday-Monday (1000-1500 Friday), closed Tuesday.*

National Library Situated in the Harihar Bhavan building near the *Hotel Narayanai*, northwest of Pulchowk, it contains Nepal's national collection with a total of approximately 70,000 volumes, the oldest of which (in English and Sanskrit) date from the 17th century. ■ *Open 1000-1700, Sunday-Friday, T521332.*

South of Patan

The roads heading directly south of Patan lead past some typically Newari villages, including **Bungamati** with its Rato Matsyendranath Temple and **Chapagaon** with the nearby **Vajravarahi Mandir**, and through forest and open countryside to the tranquil settings of **Lele**. This is a good mountain biking route. Two parallel roads run from the Patan Ring Road, the western one going as far as Bungamati and the eastern one to Chapagaon. There are a couple of easily walked trails leading from Bungamati to Chapagaon.

Khokana and Leaving the Patan Ring Road south of Jawalakhel, you first reach the village of
Bungamati **Khokana** after five kilometres. About one kilometre from the main road to the west of the village stands the **Shekali Mai Mandir**, a three-storeyed temple dedicated to a local female deity.

It is one kilometre from Khokana to Bungamati. Just before you reach Bungamati, you can visit another temple, the **Karya Binayak Mandir**, about 200 metres to the west of the road. The small temple is one of the four most important Ganesh shrines in the Kathmandu Valley and is attractively set in woodland with marvellous views of the Bagmati River beyond.

Some five kilometres from Patan, **Bungamati** is a compact village standing on a plateau just above the valley floor, its limits surprisingly precisely demarcated as if by a giant swathe, and surrounded by gently terraced slopes. A traditional farming village it is also noted for its weaving and, more recently, for its numerous tiny woodcarving workshops which supply Kathmandu's shops with interesting souvenirs. It is best known, however, as the other residence of **Rato Matsyendranath** during the six months over winter when this deity's image is not installed in its Patan temple. Every 12 years (next in 2003) the whole village takes part as the god is carried on a huge chariot in a journey which can take weeks. The imposing Rato Matsyendranath temple is the focal point of the village, with a large shikhara structure painted white, stands in the middle of a wide courtyard.

Getting there There is an irregular bus service from Patan's Jawalakhel bus stop to Bungamati.

The Road to The seven kilometres road to Chapagaon leaves Patan's Ring Road southwest
Chapagaon of the Industrial Estate. The first village you come to, after three kilometres, is **Sunakothi** with its **Jaganath Mandir** and **Vringareshvara Mahadeva Mandir**. The latter dates from the 16th century and is a two-storeyed temple. Although in a sadly neglected condition, there remain sufficient indicators to suggest that it was once another fine example of Newari temple architecture. It is renowned for containing the valley's 64 most holy lingas. Some 600 metres south of Sunakothi there is a footpath heading west to Bungamati (one and a a half kilometres).

Chapagaon is one kilometre further uphill to the south and marks the end of the sealed part of the road from Patan. The village has three temples of note. The first you come to is a Vishnu shrine, while just to the south is a small shrine dedicated to Bhairava. As you enter the village, a path leads off to your left (east) for some 600 metres to the **Vajravarahi Temple**. The structure, delightfully situated in a clearing amid woodland, dates from the mid-17th century on a site which had traditionally been used for religious worship. The temple also contains images of the eight mother goddesses, the *Asta Matrika*.

Lele is a small village that lies in a minor valley hemmed in by the 1,774 metres peak of Bhaga Ban and by the southern slopes of Kathmandu Valley. It is a walk of two kilometres from Chapagaon to the base of Bhaga Ban where you have the option of two routes around the peak. There are fine views across the Bagmati River valley from the western route. When you have almost reached the other side of the mountain, you will see the **Tika Bhairava Mandir**. A little way to the east is the **Lele Kunda**, an important but rather dishevelled pool fed by sacred spring water. The village of Lele is one and a half kilometres further east, while another *kunda* dedicated to the goddess Sarasvati lies by a 17th century shrine another one and a half kilometres east.

Lele

Kathmandu Valley

Essentials

Patan has neither the abundance nor range of accommodation on offer in Kathmandu, particularly of bottom end budget hotels. Most hotels are situated to the west of Durbar Square. Kopundol is the elevated area of Northwest Patan from where you can get magnificent views of Kathmandu and of the mountains beyond.

Sleeping

A *Himalaya*, T423900, F523909. 95 rooms, many with balcony and excellent views across Kathmandu and to the Himalayas, pleasant *Chalet* restaurant for multi cuisine and good views, 1000-2300, *Base Camp* coffee shop, breakfast buffet and a la carte, 0700-2200, bar, business centre and conference facilities, handicraft and book shops, swimming pool (residents only), tennis and badminton, situated some 700 metres from the bridge to South Kathmandu and about 1.5 kilometres northwest of Durbar Square.

B *Summit*, T521894, F523737. 72 rooms and 4 apartments, multi cuisine restaurant, bar, lovely building with traditional Newari touches, and beautiful garden, small swimming pool, some of Patan's best views of Kathmandu, Svayambhunath and the mountains, travel agent and trekking operator in hotel, an old wing has cheaper rooms, common bath, located in the high Kopundol area of Northwest Patan. Recommended. **B** *Greenwich Village*, T521780, F526683. 43 rooms, coffee shop, rooftop garden restaurant and larger dining room, bar and swimming pool, small conference room has a wonderfully carved 3 piece wooden window, off-season rates are very competitive and are negotiable, situated in Kopundol 'Heights', Northwest Patan. **B** *Narayanai*, T525015, F521291, E nbe@ nbepc.mos. com.np. 88 rooms, restaurant and coffee shop (0600-2200), free coffee in reception, pleasant garden and swimming pool (residents only), conference facilities, beauty parlour (ladies only). Located in Pulchowk, west of Durbar Square.

C *Aloha Inn*, T522796, F524571. 42 rooms, all with bath, TV and fridge, restaurant does Chinese, Indian and continental food, in-house travel agency, quietly situated in Jawalakhel, near the zoo, there is a good bakery shop opposite and Grindlays Bank next door. Recommended.

D *Café de Patan*, T525499. 14 rooms, most with bath, situated on the Mangal Bazar Rd just west of Durbar Square, this is one of Patan's favourite budget guesthouses and has an excellent restaurant downstairs.

E *Mahendra Youth Hostel*, T521003. The valley's only youth hostel, situated in

Jawalakhel 200 metres north of the zoo, this uninspiring establishment has the cheapest accommodation in Patan: double rooms with bath, a 4 bed dorm and another with 32 beds, no food, arrivals accepted only between 1700-2200, check out by 1000, closed from 1000 to 1700, lights out at 2200, no smoking, no alcohol, 10 percent discount for YHA members.

Eating   Once again, there are far fewer options for eating than in the capital. Durbar Square has a smattering of small restaurants and there are a couple more along the road leading to the bridge to Thapathali, South Kathmandu.

Expensive restaurants: the *Summit Hotel* has excellent Nepali, Indian, Western and Tibetan cuisine, and the neighbouring *Hotel Greenwich Village* has an attractive terrace restaurant by its garden and swimming pool. The *Chalet Restaurant* in the *Hotel Himalaya* overlooks Kathmandu and the mountains and does good Indian and continental food.

Budget Restaurants: on the main Mangal Bazar road just west of **Durbar Square**, the *Café de Patan*, T525499. Has a small outdoor 'garden' area while various masks of Bhairava peer down as you eat indoors. Excellent Indian, Newari and Tibetan food, good salads. Large portions. Chilli chicken and momos with mint sauce are recommended. The *Café Pagoda*, T536629, is tucked away in the northwest corner of Durbar Square and has good views from the 1st floor. It does a bit of everything including light meals, drinks and ridiculously overpriced dal-bhad-tarkari. Just opposite the *Café Pagoda*, and with marginally better views of the square, the *Café de Temple*, T527127. Does good snacks and meals, and cheaper dal-bhad-tarkari. On the south side of the square, the *Taleju Restaurant and Bar*, T525558, is a Tibetan restaurant, but also does a few continental dishes. The 3rd floor section has traditional floor cushion seating, while tables and chairs are on the 4th floor which has excellent views of Durbar Square and the valley.

In **Jawalakhel**, *Hot Breads*, T524359. Has seating and does good cakes, breads, ice cream, soft drinks and hot snacks. The *Pumpernickel German Bakery*, is just north of the main Jawalakhel crossroads towards **Pulchowk** and sells breads, good doughnuts (Rs 4) and rum and raisin balls (Rs 10). Diagonally opposite is the *Serene Hut Café*, T522568, which does reasonably priced grilled sandwiches, pizzas, steaks, and Chinese food. Further north and on the left hand side (west), the *Three Sisters Restaurant*, does reasonable pizzas and pastas, closed Sunday. Next door is the *Second Step Kitchen*, T535311, which has good value Chinese and Indian food, and has a bar. Heading downhill towards the main junction and the *Hotel Himalaya*, the **Downtown Restaurant**, T522451, on your left, is clean and does relatively cheap Chinese and Indian food. The *Ashoka Restaurant* is next door.

Bars & nightclubs   All the large hotels have their own bars. Most of the restaurants mentioned above have bar facilities.

Festivals   **February**: *Ilhan Samyek*, is held every 4 years in Patan (next in 2000), every 12 years in Kathmandu and annually in Bhaktapur. It celebrates the role of almsgiving in Buddhism and is marked by devotees offering rice and coins to images of the Buddha especially at Nag Bahal.

April-May: *Rato Matsyendranath* is the month-long festival when the red faced image of the patron deity of the valley, the god of rain and harvest, is taken around the city. His chariot moves by daily stages and may not return for some months. The image is prepared for the event in Pulchowk, when it is washed and repainted awaiting the assembling of the remarkably tall chariot. The procession through the streets is accompanied by musicians and soldiers and the nightly halts are marked by worship and feasting. The arrival in Jawalakhel several weeks later is witnessed not only by the royal family but also by Patan's Kumari, the 'living goddess'. Every 12 years the procession continues on to Bungamati, a village 5 kilometres south of Patan where the image is ensconced in a second home for 6 months. This next occurs in 2003.

July: *Janai Purnima* celebrates the annual changing of their sacred thread, the *janai*, by Hindus. At the Kumbeshvara Mandir the occasion is marked by the placing of a linga on the platform in the centre of its holy tank. Rice is also offered symbolically to frogs here following the monsoon rains.

August/September: *Krishna Janmastami* (or *Krishnastami*) celebrates the birth of Krishna, the 8th incarnation of Vishnu. It centres around the Krishna Mandir in Durbar Square, where, on the '8th day of the dark moon', an all night candlelit vigil is held by devotees from throughout the valley and prayers recited. Much of Durbar Square is beautifully illuminated. *Mat Ya* is a Buddhist festival in which processions carrying candles and incense tour the city's Buddhist sites, accompanied by musicians. Patan residents are expected to partake at least once during their life.

Shopping Patan is regarded as the best place for handicrafts in the valley. It has a long metal working tradition and produces fine statues of buddhas, bodhisattvas, and the Buddhist meditational deities. Prices for gold plated bronze figurines range from Rs 2,000 to over Rs 10,000. There are three main areas that concentrate on handicraft retail: Jawalakhel, the Patan Industrial Estate with some of the best prices in town, and the old city area south and southeast of Durbar Square.

Bookshops Patan has surprisingly few bookshops. Try the large hotels. The *Christian Bookshop* is located on the main road between the large Jawalakhel intersection and the crossroads south of the Rato Matsyendranath Mandir.

Carpets The centre for carpet manufacture is the Tibetan area of Jawalakhel where you can watch the entire production process.
Jawalakhel retailers include *Carpet Trading Company*, T521241, F527727, which was among the first businesses to export carpets from here. *Senon Carpets*, T522665, F524029; and *Sharma Carpet Manufacturing Co*, T525147. The last also has a showroom in Thamel.
At the Patan Industrial Estate, *Mahabaudha Carpet Industry*, T526110, F522291. Try also around the Durbar Square area and along Mangal Bazar.

Jewellery Trinkets are available in and around Durbar Square as well as Jawalakhel, Patan Industrial Estate and Oku Bahal.

Metalwork The **Patan Industrial Estate** is a collection of manufacturing units and retail outlets in **Lagankhel**, about 2 kilometres south of Durbar Square, and you can watch craftsmen creating images and decorative items in their workshops. Try *Nepalese Crafts*, T521412.
The **Mahabaudha (Oku Bahal)** area, south of Durbar Square, has a tradition of high quality metallurgy. Here you can get some of the best bronze, brass, copper and other metallic available in the valley and also high quality goods not usually available in Thamel. Various outlets include *Ganga Handicrafts*, T525857. *Goodwill Handicrafts*, T521912, F522406. *Gyan Hastakala Udhyog*, T525051. *Kishor Handicrafts*, T522294, F525098. *Mahabaudha Art Concern*, T522431, F226590, and *Mahabaudha*

Kathmandu Valley

Art Enterprises, T526229, F522431.

For **khukuri knives**, the best are available from *The Khukuri House*, T522116, F526185, at the Tibetan Refugee Camp in **Jawalakhel**.

Painting Tangkas are available in the Oku Bahal area. Try *Mahabaudha Art Enterprises*, T526229, F522431. The area around the Golden Temple, north of Durbar Square, also has a number of shops dealing in thangkas as well as other Nepali paintings and arts. There is a smaller selection in Jawalakhel.

Woodcarvings There are few outstanding woodcarving shops in Patan (see Bhaktapur), but try *Om Woodcarving Industries*, T426710, in the Patan Industrial Estate.

Other Shopping There are a small number of 'supermarkets' scattered around the western part of the city which also sell some foreign foods. On the road heading east from the large intersection at **Jawalakhel**, there is the *Lalitpur Shopping Centre*. Some 300 metres north of this intersection, where the road forks, is the *Namaste Supermarket*. If you take the right hand fork, just to the north is the *Dai Chi Supermarket* and, diagonally opposite, the *Landmark Supermarket*.

Transport **Local** All areas of Patan are within walking distance of each other. **Taxis** as well as **cycle-** and **auto-rickshaws** are readily available. A taxi from Durbar Square to Thamel in Kathmandu will cost around Rs 180 one way. There is a regular and cheap **bus** service from Patan Gate to Kathmandu City Bus Park (last departure at around 2000). There are few cycle hire places in Patan; better choice in Kathmandu.

Long Distance Connections Government *Sajha* buses link Patan with all major destinations. The Patan Central Bus Station is located near the UN complex and bookings are made here. Most long distance buses go via Kathmandu's new bus station at Balaju, departures are 1 hour earlier.

Directory **Communications** **Post Office:** the main post office is situated at Patan Gate, northwest of Durbar Square. *Speedway Cargo Service*, Jawalakhel, T525930. **Telecommunications:** there are a number of places in the Durbar Square area where you can make international phone calls. **Useful addresses Aid and development agencies:** a number of NGOs, national and international, have Patan as their administrative base in Nepal. For information, contact the *Social Welfare Council*, Lekhnath Marg, Kathmandu, T418111, F410279. **Embassies & consulates** *Norwegian Consulate*, Jawalakhel, T521646. *Swiss Consulate*, Jawalakhel, T523468. **Hospitals & medical services** *Patan Hospital*, Lagankhel, T522266.

Thimi

Thimi is the first town you come to after leaving Kathmandu, some three kilometres before Bhaktapur, and although often overlooked it is actually the fourth largest in the valley. It is renowned for its craftsmanship, especially **pottery** and **papier mâché masks**. Indeed, its name is a derivation of the Newari for 'capable people'. The majority of the masks sold in Kathmandu are produced here, though some are also used during local festivals. The surrounding land is a rich source of clay and, as in Bhaktapur, it is fascinating to watch as potters throughout the town prepare and turn the clay on large manually operated wheels. You can buy their wares – anything from practical water pots to ornamental candlesticks – direct from the potters themselves or from the several shops scattered throughout the town. With a little bargaining, prices are amongst the cheapest that you will find, though these are assuredly set to rise as the number of visitors to Thimi also increases.

The architecture is very much Newari in character, but the town is rather run down and there are few buildings of general tourist interest. The **Balkumari Mandir** in the square at the southern end of town is a 16th century structure and is dedicated to the *kumari* in her child form, but the temple has no 'living goddess'. A main road runs through Thimi and links the Arniko Highway to the south with a minor road running from the airport to Bhaktapur to the north. Just north of this smaller road lies the three-storeyed **Ganesh Mandir** which you can reach via a stone stairway. Less than one kilometre further north towards the **Manohara Khola** is the village of **Bode** with its 16th century **Mahalakshmi Mandir**.

Getting there You can get to Thimi by **trolley bus** which leaves Kathmandu from Tripureshvar and runs along the Arniko Highway and on to Bhaktapur. **Public buses** from the City Bus Park stand are quicker. You can **cycle** to Thimi either along the Arniko Highway or by turning left (north) just after you pass the southern end of the airport. After one and a half kilometres turn right (east) for the three kilometres' ride which takes you to the northern end of Thimi with the Ganesh Mandir on your left.

Kathmandu Valley

Bhaktapur

Population: 172,952
Area: 119 sq km
Altitude: 1,400 metres.

Bhaktapur ('city of devotees'), or Bhadgoan, lies some 10 kilometres east of Kathmandu. Built on a plateau (1,400 metres) on the northern banks of the **Hanumante River**, *it is the smallest of the valley's three cities. Its geographical separation from Kathmandu is deceptive, for it retains a simplicity far removed from the trappings of 20th century life which pervade the capital. The city exudes a sense of the past which is not so much medieval as traditional and, despite the gradual emergence of satellite dishes and other contemporary icons, gives the impression that little has changed here for centuries, that little is set to change and, happily, that it is a city at ease with itself. In its Durbar Square, Taumadhi Square and Dattatraya Square, it has arguably the valley's finest panoply of Newari temple architecture, including the magnificent five-storeyed* **Nyatapola Mandir**, *the tallest pagoda temple in Nepal.*

With Durbar Square less unequivocally a nucleus than its namesakes in either of the valley's other two cities, these three squares together form the point from which all other areas have developed and are connected by a newly paved main road, the city's central artery. Either side is a network of narrow, occasionally cobbled but mostly earthen, lanes proceeding through the main residential areas down to the river to the south and to open countryside to the north. Earthy red colours dominate the cityscape and the architecture is, almost without exception, traditional Newari: typically, two- or three-storey wooden or brick houses with protruding upper floors or roofs, decorative window frames, and a low entrance leading to a small courtyard perhaps containing a shrine or small image. The German funded Bhaktapur Development Project has led to much new building taking place, though traditional styles have successfully been maintained.

In contrast to the greater variety of ethnic groups found in Kathmandu and Patan, Bhaktapur's population is dominated by **Newars** who constitute more than 90 percent of its people. The independent development of Bhaktapur within the valley has resulted in a strong sense of identity for its people which is illustrated in the use of a dialect of Newari distinct from that spoken in Kathmandu and Patan. More than half of the population is directly or indirectly involved in agriculture.

The city's **tourist facilities** are minimal, consisting largely of a handful of guesthouses and restaurants catering mainly to the budget traveller. Most people come for the day from Kathmandu, an hour away by bus. The city is renowned for its curd (yoghurt) which, as vendors will not hesitate to tell you, is made from full cream milk (cow or buffalo).

Getting there Bhaktapur is approached from Kathmandu via the Ring Road, passing to the south of the airport and along the undulating, marijuana lined road and past the walled city of **Thimi**. Entering Bhaktapur from the west, you pass through a lovely pine grove on a low hill where two tanks once supplied the population with drinking water. The bus stop is near the walled tank known as **Siddha Pokhari**, considered holy by both Hindus and Buddhists. Beyond this, the road divides, the left fork continuing into Durbar Square.

History

The early history of Bhaktapur is vague. Its origins lie in the Licchavi period, but credit for its founding is widely attributed to King Ananda Malla in the late ninth century AD. The city began as a trading centre known as **Khopring** and was renamed *Bhaktagrama* ('village of devotees') in the early Malla period. The city is said to have been layed out in the shape of a conch shell and the main road which still winds its way through the centre of the city may (with a little imagination) be thought to resemble the outline of a conch shell. It will be noted, however, that the road also approximately parallels the course contours of the Hanumante River to the south.

The peak of the city's influence was between the 14th and 16th centuries when it became the valley's de facto capital. It was fortified in the 15th century. Many sources suggest that the royal palace was originally situated in Dattatraya Square before being relocated subsequently to its present Durbar Square location. Internecine rivalry among the valley's Malla rulers from the 17th century was expressed also in the arts with each city striving to exalt itself and endorse the authority of its rulers through the character and splendour of its architecture. Many of the temples and monuments adorning the three squares date from the late 17th and early 18th centuries, during the rule of King **Bhupatindra Malla**. With the Gorkha unification of Nepal and the selection of Kathmandu as the national capital by Prithivi Narayana Shah in 1768, Bhaktapur's influence declined dramatically and the city's development continued largely independently from then.

The city's architectural heritage was significantly damaged by the 1934 earthquake. Some restoration has taken place. A major development project was initiated with German funding in 1974. This resulted in further restoration and renovation of many of Bhaktapur's buildings as well as road construction and improvement and the establishment of sewerage and drinking water systems.

Sights

Durbar Square Area

The 1934 earthquake caused considerable damage to buildings in the square. In consequence, it appears more spacious than its two namesakes in Kathmandu and Patan. It is still an architectural showpiece, exhibiting numerous superb examples of the skills of Newari artists and craftsmen over several centuries.

Shiva/Parvati Mandir

As you approach Durbar Square from the west, in front of you is this small, two-roofed temple dedicated to Shiva who is depicted with his consort, Parvati. The main **gate** to the square is just beyond. Erected by King Bhupatindra Malla in the early 18th century, it is elaborately decorated with various auspicious symbols, images of Kartikeya, a son of Shiva and god of war, as well as large carved images of Bhairava on the left and Hanuman on the right.

Statues of Ugrachandi Durga & Bhairava (1)

On your left after entering the square a pair of large stone lions stand either side of the entrance to a school and guard these fine stone statues representing the 18-armed goddess Ugrachandi Durga and the 12-armed Bhairava. Both are garlanded with human heads and were commissioned in 1707 by Bhupatindra Malla. So pleased was the king with these sculptures, and so concerned that neither Kathmandu nor Patan should acquire their equal, that he ordered the hands of the unfortunate sculptor to be cut off.

Rameshvara (2), Bhadri (3) & Krishna Mandirs (4) Opposite the two statues are three temples of lesser importance, dedicated respectively to incarnations of Shiva (Rameshvara), Vishnu/Narayana (Bhadri) and again Vishnu as Krishna. The Krishna Mandir is the largest of the three, a two-storeyed simple pagoda design with a statue of Garuda, Vishnu's faithful vehicle, placed on a column facing the main entrance.

Shiva Mandir (5) Heading on towards the middle of the square, this shikhara-style temple was constructed in 1674 by King Jita Mitra Malla. Images of various deities adorn the exterior on all sides.

The Royal Palace (6) The original Royal Palace, built in 1427 by King Yaksha Malla, was situated in Dattatraya Square but was reconstructed in Durbar Square during the reign of Bhupatindra Malla (1696-1722). It was completed by King Jaya Ranjit Malla in 1754 and the result bore little resemblance to the original structure. The complex is said to have consisted of no fewer than 99 *chowks*, or courtyards. It was badly damaged in the 1934 earthquake and, despite extensive renovations, much of the artwork was lost and only six chowks remain (Bhairava Chowk, Igta Chowk, Kumari Chowk, Malagti Chowk, Mul Chowk and Siddhi Chowk). The palace is renowned for fabulous **55 carved windows** (after

Bhaktapur Durbar Square

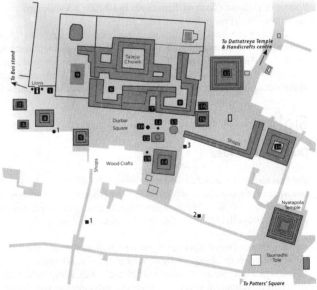

N

Not to scale

1 Ugrachandi, Durga & Bhairava statues
2 Rameshvara Mandir
3 Bhadri Mandir
4 Krishna Mandir
5 Shiva Mandir
6 The Royal Palace Complex
7 The Golden Gate (Sun Dhoka)
8 Palace of 55 Windows
9 Sundari Chowk
10 King Bhupatindra Malla's Column
11 Taleju Bell
12 Vatsala Durga Mandir
13 Chayasilin Mandapa
14 Pashupatinath Mandir

15 Siddhi Lakshmi Mandir
16 Vatsala Mandir
17 Fasidega Shiva Mandir
18 Tadhunchen Bahal
19 Small Nandi Pillar

■ Sleeping
1 Golden Gate Guesthouse
2 New Nyatapola
3 Shiva Guesthouse

● Eating
1 Temple Town

which it is sometimes known) as well as its **Golden Gate** (Sun Dhoka), **Taleju Mandir** and the **National Art Gallery** (see under **Museums**).

Widely regarded as one of the most important artefacts in the valley's heritage, this stunning portal to the middle section of the complex and the Taleju Mandir was commissioned by Ranjit Malla in 1745. Actually made of brass, it is set into and contrasts attractively with the main brick edifice. A pair of small gilded lions stand on their own miniature plinths either side of the remarkably small door, which is surrounded by images of six deities engraved in each side of the vertical brasswork. The large tilting torana above the door has a central image of a multiple limbed Taleju, above which it is crowned by a dynamic image of Garuda, vehicle of Vishnu. The surrounding masonry is framed with brass, with the upper portion having small finials of elephants and lions, flags, three central *kalasas* and a larger *kalasa* rising to form the pinnacle.

The Golden Gate (Sun Dhoka) (7)

Completing the trio of major temples dedicated to the Malla patron deity, Taleju, in the valley's three Durbar Squares, this temple has its origins in the early 14th century which makes it the oldest of the three. It and the courtyard (Mul Chowk) in which it stands are not open to visitors, although the guard may allow you to look from the open entrance. Hindus may enter only on one day of the year, during Dasain. The temple itself is a lavishly decorated, one-storey structure, and is considered to be Bhaktapur's holiest religious site. It is believed to have some of the valley's finest artwork. There are statues of various deities. One window of the temple is said to have been carved by Bhupatindra Malla himself. Squeezed between Taleju Chowk and Sundari Chowk is the tiny **Kumari Chowk**, again richly decorated.

Taleju Mandir

This is the eastern section of the complex and is named after the superbly carved balcony of windows in the red and black outer wall of the large Durbar Hall, the centre of what remains of the original Royal Palace after the 1934 earthquake. Widely considered to be the finest examples of decorative woodcarving in the valley, they were commissioned in the early 18th century by Bhupatindra Malla.

The Palace of Fifty Five Windows (8)

This is the westernmost chowk of the palace complex. The name means 'beautiful courtyard'. Like its namesake in Patan, it contains a bathing tank used by the ruling Malla family, but is bigger than the one in Patan. An upright brass *naga*, or serpentine spirit, is situated on your right as you enter, with another fixed to the base of the tank. The sides of the stone tank are elaborately adorned with carvings of various deities.

Sundari Chowk (9)

The mastermind behind the major development and beautification of Durbar Square is immortalized in brass opposite the Golden Gate. Reverentially seated in a bushel atop a stone pillar, the life size statue of the king wears a turban-like headpiece, while a shield and sword lie at his side. His gaze is directed towards the Taleju Mandir within.

King Bhupatindra Malla's Column (10)

This large bell, like those in Patan and Kathmandu's Durbar Squares, was used during temple worship and could double as an alarm. It was installed in 1737 by King Jaya Ranjit Malla, apparently in an attempt to thwart the nightmares that plagued him. It is also known as the 'Barking Dogs Bell', because its timbre seemingly incites the local canine population to collective bellowing.

Taleju Bell (11)

Beside the Taleju Bell is this shikhara-style temple, one of two dedicated to Vatsala in Durbar Square. Steps flanked on either side by five stone animals

Vatsala Durga Mandir (12)

lead to the shrine which is attractively surrounded by a pillored porch or verandah. Towards the top of the shikhara are further stone representations of minor deities. The temple was built in 1737 by King Jaya Ranjit Malla.

Chayasilin Mandapa (13)
Standing in front of the Palace of Fifty Five Windows and beside a small tank is Durbar Square's only octagonal structure. The original pavilion was probably used by members of the ruling Malla family to sit and watch Durbar Square life, but it was destroyed in the 1934 earthquake. The present pavilion, an attractive double-storeyed pagoda, was a gift from Germany in the 1990s. It was modelled from a 19th century photograph and is an exact replica of the original. It is one of the few structures here to contain steel rather than brass or copper.

Pashupatinath Mandir (14)
The exact origins of this temple are disputed: some say it dates from the late 15th century, a posthumous tribute to King Yaksha by his widow and son, while others maintain it was built much later, in 1682 by King Jita Mitra Malla. The design of the two-storeyed pagoda is based on the central shrine of the more famous Pashupatinath Mandir on the banks of the Bagmati River in Kathmandu. The roof struts have carvings depicting scenes from the *Ramayana* as well as some erotic themes. The shrine contains a Shiva linga.

Siddhi Lakshmi Mandir (15)
Returning to the eastern corner of the Royal Palace, this stone temple has statues of various animals as well as of men, women and children either side of the steps leading up to the entrance. The eponymous deity is the same as that to whom the shrine of the magnificent Nyatapola Mandir in Taumadhi Square is dedicated. Its construction was started by King Jita Mitra Malla and completed by Bhupatindra Malla after the death of the former in 1696.

Vatsala Mandir (16)
The second Vatsala temple in Durbar Square stands on a three stage plinth beside the Siddhi Lakshmi Mandir. It is again of shikhara design and was built by King Jaya Ranjit Malla in 1737, an especially productive year in the history of Durbar Square. The central shikhara is surrounded by three smaller shrines. Southeast of the temple are a pair of stone lions.

Fasidega Shiva Mandir (17)
To the north of the Vatsala Mandir, this temple stands prominently on a six stage plinth. Steps leading up to the main entrance are once again flanked by elephants and other animals. In contrast to the surrounding monuments, the shrine itself is plain, a cuboid structure topped by a small dome. It contains an image of the linga and yoni, which apparently replaced the originally intended deity, Matsyendranath.

Tadhunchen Bahal (18)
From the Fasidega temple, the square narrows to become an alley leading southeast to the neighbouring Taumadhi Tole. On your right (south) after the line of shops is this large 15th century monastery, the only Buddhist building here. The shops occupy what were dharamsalas, pilgrims' rest houses. Its design is classical Newari, and has some finely carved supports. If you continue west from the bahal, this paved road, the city's central artery, leads to Dattatraya Square after about one kilometre.

Taumadhi Square

From Durbar Square's Pashupatinath Mandir, follow the alleyway round to the south of the Tadhunchen Bahal and after 100 metres you arrive in Taumadhi Square. It is effectively an extension of Durbar Square to the southeast and, though much smaller, it contains Bhaktapur's finest and most impressive temple, the Nyatapola Mandir. From here you can head south to the city's famous pottery area, or east to join the road leading to Dattatraya Square. Around the Nyatapola Mandir is a small bazar, or market area, where various handicrafts as well as local produce are sold.

With a height of 30 metres, this is the tallest free-standing pagoda temple in Nepal, and is unquestionably the city's most superb example of temple architecture. It stands in the northern part of the square and completely dominates the area. The five-storeyed temple was constructed by King Bhupatindra Malla in 1708 and, remarkably, emerged almost unscathed from the 1934 earthquake, the only damage being experienced by a section of the uppermost roof. Some say that Bhupatindra built the temple as a foil to the terror of Bhairava, to whom a neighbouring temple is dedicated.

Nyatapola Mandir

The successive tiled roofs are supported by fabulously carved and painted beams and struts, with equally decorative windows. Five pairs of stone carved figures line the steps of the five plinths. Each figure is considered to be 10 times stronger than the one below. The images of the fabled Bhaktapur wrestlers, Jaya Malla and Phatta Malla, who are reputed to have had the strength of 10 men, kneel at the base and are followed in ascending order of strength by elephants, lions, griffins, and finally the goddesses Baghini and Singhini respectively depicted in the form of tiger and lion. The metaphor of strength serves to underline the power of the temple deity. The interior is accessible only to priests, is Sino-Thai in character. It contains a shrine (but no idol) dedicated to the Hindu Tantric goddess Siddhi Lakshmi who is also carved into the 108 roof struts. The temple has a well planned geometry, with the size of each roof smaller than the one beneath by a constant proportion. Similarly, extrapolations of lines drawn to connect the corners of the supporting plinths will meet at the top of the entrance doors on each side.

To the southeast of the Nyatapola Mandir and contrasting markedly with it, this three-storeyed temple owes its rather stocky appearance to its unusual rectangular base and to its originally intended design as a single storeyed place of worship. It was built during the reign of King Jagat Jyoti Malla (1613-1637). The second and third roofs were added by King Bhupatindra Malla in 1718. The whole building collapsed in the 1934 earthquake; the present structure is a replica which used those pieces of masonry and wood that could be salvaged from the remains of the original. A large prayer bell is suspended in front of the main entrance. The nearby image of Bhairava is surprisingly small, standing just 30 centimetres high, and is the focus of worship during the chariot processions of the annual *Bisket* festival. The main entrance to the temple is through the small **Vetala Mandir**, located behind the temple. Vetala is a protecting deity. There is a raised **platform** in front of the temple covering most of the southern part of the square which was used for performances of dance and drama, and shrines dedicated to Shiva and Narayana behind. Immediately south of the Bhairavanath Mandir is a small spring and tank, the **Lun Hiti**.

Bhairavanath Mandir

Inconspicuously situated in the southeast corner of the square, this two-storeyed temple is one of the oldest in Bhaktapur. A stone inscription refers to this as a site of religious importance since 1080. The image of Narayana in the shrine is said to date from the 12th century. A statue of Garuda, vehicle of Vishnu (Narayana), stands on a pillar in front of the entrance, as does a *chakra* (wheel) and a delicately poised representation of a conch shell, both images associated with Vaishnavism. Next to it is a shrine dedicated to **Shiva** which includes a linga and yoni, the former being carved with four faces while the 'fifth'

Til Mahadeva Narayana Mandir

is 'invisible'. To get here, take the lane south of the Bhairavanath Mandir and turn right into the courtyard behind the block of red houses.

Café Nyatapola   This popular restaurant now occupies a former pagoda temple. Renovated in the late 1970s as part of the Bhaktapur Development Project, it has some fine carved wooden beams and lattices. The roof strut carvings are dominated by erotic imagery.

Walking east from Taumadhi Square   Leaving Taumadhi Square by a lane at the northeast end of the square, you join the main road through Bhaktapur which leads to Dattatraya Square after barely one kilometre. The road is unusually and attractively paved with red brick, again a result of the Bhaktapur Development Project, and this is also the city's main commercial thoroughfare where most consumer items are available.

As the road bends to the right after Taumadhi Square, there is the **Sukul Dhoka** on your right. The *math* is home to some of the local temple priests, and was built as a monastery by King Jaya Ranjit Malla in the mid-18th century. Bhaktapur's last Malla king before Prithivi Narayana Shah led the Gorkhas to victory over the valley's cities. It was renovated in the late 1980s and the first floor in particular is decorated with some accomplished woodcarving. The **Lun Bahal** just beyond was built as a Buddhist monastery in the 16th century, but in 1592 was transformed into a Hindu temple dedicated to Bhimsen, a deity of exceptional strength and courage. A little further on you arrive at **Golmadhi Tole**, a minor square with a small three-storeyed temple dedicated jointly to Ganesh and Bhairava who feature on the carved roof struts. There is also a *chaitya*, or small Buddhist shrine, small Shiva and Vishnu shrines, and a sacred water tank. Continuing along the main road and just before it veers north, there is a good view south to the burning ghats on the **Hanumante River** and beyond. You then pass the small and variously decorated **Inacho Bahal** on your left. From here it is a short stroll into **Dattatraya Square**. The road continues on through Bhaktapur's eastern suburbs towards Nagarkot.

Dattatraya Square (Tachupal Tole)

The easternmost of Bhaktapur's three main squares is also the oldest. It is widely thought that the original Royal Palace was built here in 1427 by King Yaksha Malla and later relocated to its present location in Durbar Square. The square is dominated by the large **Dattatraya Mandir** and has a good restaurant with excellent views across the square. In an alley southeast of the square is the remarkable and justifiably celebrated **peacock window**, a masterpiece of woodcarving. It also has two interesting museums (see **Museums**) with exhibitions of bronze and woodcarving.

Bhimsen Mandir   This 17th century rectangular temple sits at the western end of the square in front of a small spring and tank. The ground floor is open while lattice windows enclose most of the middle floor. The much smaller second roof appears like an afterthought and is copper covered. In front of the temple to the east is a raised brick platform which was used, like that in Taumadhi Square, for performances of drama and dance.

Salan Ganesh Mandir   Behind a large, old house on the northern side of the square, this small temple has roof struts carved with images of Ganesh and Bhairava as well as representations of the *Asta Matrika*, or eight 'mother-goddesses'. It also dates from the 17th century. Its main image is a rock said to be a likeness of the elephant headed Ganesh.

Dominating Dattatraya Square from the eastern side, the construction of this temple was started by King Yaksha Malla in 1427 and completed in 1458. The temple is dedicated to Dattatraya, a syncretistic deity believed to be either an incarnation of Vishnu, a teacher of Shiva or a cousin of the Buddha. The presence of the winged Garuda standing on a tall pillar opposite the main entrance and, beside it, of a conch shell atop a smaller column, indicate that in this case the deity is worshipped primarily as Vishnu. The structure of the temple is reminiscent of the Kasthamandap in Kathmandu's Durbar Square and, similarly, the Dattatraya Mandir is said to have been built from the wood of a single tree. Its original purpose is unclear, but a further parallel with the Kasthamandap is suggested by those who argue that it was built as a pilgrim's rest house and was only later developed into a temple by the addition of the second and third floors. Its unique and somewhat ungainly second floor protrusion seems to serve only as embellishment. A large bell hangs suspended at the southwest corner of the temple and two huge painted statues of Jaya Malla and Phatta Malla, Bhaktapur's legendary wrestlers, stand guard at the main entrance.

Dattatraya Mandir

Forming the southeast corner of the square is a complex of former residences for local priests (*math*). The original structure dates from the 15th century. It was renovated and further buildings were added by King Jaya Ranjit Malla in 1763, five years before the Mallas were ousted from power by Prithivi Narayana Shah. The complex now houses the Woodcarving Museum. It was once more renovated in the 1980s as part of the German funded Bhaktapur Development Project.

Pujari Math & the Peacock Window

Of the many examples of magnificent woodcarving here, the **peacock window** is the best known. It is situated on the first floor of the east facing façade, a few metres along the narrow street leading off from the southeast corner of the square. The small window depicts a peacock displaying its fan of 19 feathers in a circular arrangement, surrounded by foliation and cherubic figures in the top corners. Thirty-five smaller birds form a border on three sides while deities are carved into the base. Three delicately carved eaves form the vertex. Hawkers are invariably on hand on the street below to offer some surprisingly good miniature replicas of the window.

Buddhist Bhaktapur

Although Bhaktapur has a predominantly Hindu tradition, a Buddhist presence is maintained in the city's shrines and monasteries (*viharas*). Unfortunately, many show the signs of years of neglect and the Bhaktapur Development Project has largely passed them by. Some have been converted and others have fallen into disuse. The following description runs from west to east.

Two *vyalas*, or lion-like statues, guard the front entrance of this shrine and the expansive metal door frame is ornately engraved. Inside is a modern statue of the Buddha. The surrounding walls have attractive representations of episodes of his life and were commissioned by a group of Buddhist monks from Thailand. To the right after you enter are the monastic living quarters. The tiled roof is supported by carved struts. The vihara is located on the next street running south after the bus stop.

Sammakrit Vihara

Heading into town from the bus stop, take the right hand fork just east of the bus stop and after about 300 metres there are two Buddhist sites on opposite sides of the road. In a courtyard on the right hand side (south), the Jetvarna

Jetvarna Vihara

Kathmandu Valley

Vihara has a raised platform on which two small chaityas, or shrines, stand. Two *vyala*s are placed at the front corners. The pagoda-like shrines contain images of Shakyamuni and Avalokiteshvara. Squeezed between the two is a small white chaitya and behind it stands an ornamental pillar.

Lokeshvara Vihara On the northern side of the road, this is probably the city's most attractive Buddhist structure and its only three-storeyed pagoda temple. In front of the entrance, a Buddha statue is surrounded by several smaller chaityas and other objects. Two large bells are installed on either side of the main doorway which is also guarded by stone lions. The temple is noteworthy for the *jangha*-like arrangement of household utensils between the first two floors, which are symbolically offered to the temple deity with the petitions of the faithful.

Mangal Dharma Deep Vihara Located on a side street just southwest of Dattatraya Square, this small vihara is memorable only for its ornately attired image of Dipamkara Buddha.

Indravrata Mahavihara South of Dattatraya Square and on the northeast side of Khancha Pokhari, is this uniquely designed vihara. Below the small upper pagoda roof, the square building has three floors. The middle one is compressed, giving the whole an almost sandwich-like appearance. The decorative main entrance has the ubiquitous lion guardians which in turn are flanked by racks of prayerwheels. A beautifully carved window frame above the architrave is the centrepiece of the stunted second floor.

Muni Vihara Following the main road as it leaves Dattatraya Square to the east on its way to Dhulikhel and eventually Tibet, you arrive at this active monastery after about 700 metres. It has an attractively columned verandah. Inside, the shrine has a large statue of the meditating Buddha accompanied by two smaller Buddha statues in different poses.

The Ghats

There is no actual footpath that follows the slender Hanumante River, but you can reach its ghats along streets leading from the centre of town. **Mangal Ghat**, the westernmost of the main ghats, is surrounded by a number of small buildings and religious monuments. You can cross the river here and after 200 metres there is the small **Varahi Mandir**. **Ram Ghat** is about 200 metres downstream. It is used for cremations and bathing and has a temple, the **Ram Mandir**. If you arrive from Kathmandu by trolley bus and head northeast from the bus stop, you will cross a bridge beside Ram Ghat. This road continues north through the pottery area and on towards Taumadhi and Durbar Squares.

If you leave Taumadhi Square heading east (near the entrance to the Til Mahadev Narayana Mandir) the road passes two temples (**Bhagvati Mandir** and **Kumari Mandir**) as it loops south and crosses the river to **Chuping Ghat**, a mélange of small run-down monuments and a cremation site.

You can reach the largest and busiest ghat, **Hanuman Ghat**, from either Taumadhi Square or Dattatraya Square. The ghat is used for bathing, washing and burning. It is surrounded by numerous small monuments and lingas, and there is an image of Hanuman beside a Rama shrine. On one side is a *dharamsala*, a pilgrims' rest house. The site also marks the junction of two channels of the Hanumante River and is thus considered to be endowed with greater holiness.

Getting there Leave Taumadhi Square at its northeast corner, by the Nyatapola Mandir, then take the first right turning. This road (southeast) continues straight to the ghat after some 700 metres. From Dattatraya Square, take the road heading south from the centre of the square. After 100 metres turn right then left around the rectangular Khancha Pokhari. Follow this road in a south-southwestern direction for a further 400 metres.

Furthest northeast is the much smaller **Maheshvari Ghat**, situated on the northern bend of the river. There is a small **Maheshvari Mandir** over the bridge. Leave Dattatraya Square as above for Hanuman Ghat. Just south of Khancha Pokhari, take the left hand fork which leads to the ghat after 100 metres.

Kumha Twa – Potters Square

Bhaktapur has earned a reputation for its pottery and produces much of the valley's terracotta pots, vases and souvenirs. The main pottery area (*Kumha Twa*, or Potters' Square) is south of Durbar Square and you can go there to watch the wheels go round in its open courtyards and verandahs. A visit is well worthwhile and you can buy souvenirs – anything from an ornamental candlestick to the traditional round water containers used by women in villages throughout the subcontinent – both in the square and from hawkers lining the street from Taumadhi Square.

As you enter the square from the north, there is a shrine dedicated to Ganesh, the patron deity of the local potters. Built by a Kumha Twa potter, the two-storeyed **Jeth Ganesh Mandir** dates from 1646 and tradition has it that its priest comes from this potter community.

Getting there Follow the street leading downhill from the southwest corner of Taumadhi Square and take the first turning on your left (southwest). After about 100 metres, the square opens to your right. You can continue along this street for a further 400 metres and arrive at the small **Ram Mandir** and **Ram Ghat** (bathing and cremation) by the **Hanumante River**.

Other areas

While the splendour of Bhaktapur lies most conspicuously in its three major squares, its rustic charms extend both north and south of the city's central artery. Just before the main western entrance to Durbar Square, you can turn left (north) down a long set of steps with small houses on either side and agricultural countryside beyond. Half-way down on your left (west) is the **Indrayani Mandir**, dedicated to the king of gods and god of rain. After 150 metres you reach the junction of the road that heads east to Nagarkot and west to Kathmandu. Turn right (southeast) and this street leads back towards the eastern side of Durbar Square, but if you head east on the Nagarkot road, you will see the raised **Mahakali Mandir** on your left (north) after 400 metres. Just beyond and again on your left is a dirt road that leads north to Changu Narayana (seven kilometres).

Changu Narayana Mandir

The ancient Hindu temple of Changu Narayana ranks as one of the finest and most dramatic of all sites in the valley and is a UNESCO designated World Heritage Site. Perched on the Dolagiri hill some 125 metres above the valley floor and 13 kilometres east of Kathmandu, it has superb views across the valley. Its origins are widely believed to date back to the fifth century AD. Some sources suggest an earlier beginning and that it was built by King Hari Dutta

Varma in 325 AD, while others say the temple was built on an erstwhile animist place of worship. Before the 18th century unification of Nepal it was part of the independent Malla kingdom of Bhaktapur. The temple is acknowledged to be the oldest extant example of the Nepalese style of pagoda architecture, though much of the present structure dates from 1702 when it was rebuilt following a fire. A programme for its conservation and development was initiated in 1985 under the auspices of HMG Dept of Archaeology.

From the Changu Narayana road junction, you can turn right (south) and after 300 metres turn left (southeast) at the second crossroads you come to Dattatraya Square after 300 metres, passing the **Nag Pokhari**, a small holy tank dedicated to the serpentine spirits which control rainfall. You can continue through the maze of narrow streets north and northeast of Dattatraya Square and the large **Kamal Pokhari** which lies at the northeast corner of the city. There are lovely views across both sides of the valley from here. From the pokhari, head south to join with the city's main central thoroughfare after 300 metres. Turn right (west) and the **Vakupati Narayan Mandir** is ahead of you. This is an attractive two-storeyed pagoda temple with a shrine containing an image of Vishnu as Narayana. Facing the entrance are numerous pillars with images of Garuda, a *chakra* and a conch shell.

Surya Vinayaka Mandir This *shikhara* temple is located on a ridge about one kilometre south of Bhaktapur. The temple is dedicated to Ganesh. Two bells are suspended on either side of the entrance and the image is believed to help cure children of learning disabilities. To get there from Bhaktapur, follow the road leading southwest from the potters' area and cross the river at Ram Ghat. Continue down over the Arniko Highway past the trolley bus stop and a stone stairway leads up to the temple.

Museums

National Woodcarving Museum This small museum is in the restored **Pujari Math** in the southeast corner of Dattatraya Square, and it includes the famous Peacock Window. **NB** The museum is closed on Tuesday, but if the main door is open you may be able to persuade the security guards to let you in. ■ *T610005. Open 1000-1530, daily except Tuesday and holidays. Friday closes at 1430. Entrance Rs 10, camera charge Rs 10.*

National Art Gallery Located on the first floor of the old part of the Royal Palace ('Palace of Fifty Five Windows') in Durbar Square and opened in 1961, this is the most recent of the valley's 'national' museums. Its collections include some especially fine displays of tangkas and paubhas, palm leaf manuscripts and examples of Bhaktapur's craft heritage. The entrance is flanked by statues of Hanuman in the Tantric form of Bhairava, and Vishnu as Narasimha. These were commissioned in circa 1698 by King Bhupatindra Malla, who purportedly wanted to combine the deities' respective powers in an effort to maintain law and order in the city. On either side of the entrance are inscriptions in stone: one dates from the Licchavi king, Shiva Deva, the other is more recent and was carved during the reign of one of the first Malla rulers, King Yaksha Malla (1428-1482).

The collection includes exquisitely painted tangkas and pal leaf manuscripts, include the Prajnaparamita penned in golden ink and lavishly illustrated throughout, and a hand painted/written 'biography' of the much revered King Pratap Malla (reigned in Kathmandu 1640-1674) who was responsible for the construction of many of the temples and monuments in

Kathmandu's Durbar Square. ■ *T610004. Open 1000-1530, daily except Tuesday and holidays, Friday closes at 1430. Entrance Rs 5, camera charge Rs 10.*

Located in a 15th century math on the northern side of Dattatraya Square, opposite the Pujari Math. ■ *T610448. Open 1000-1330, daily except Tuesday and holidays, Friday closes at 1430. Entrance Rs 5, camera charge Rs 10.*

The Bronze & Brass Museum

Essentials

Although Bhaktapur has even less accommodation than Patan, there are still a few places where you can stay in reasonable comfort. All are in the lower price range, catering for the budget traveller, and most are fairly central. It is not really an alternative to Kathmandu for a longer stay, but the advantage of staying overnight is that you get to see the place in its stimulatingly natural state, unencumbered by daytime touts and tourist buses.

Sleeping

Kathmandu Valley

C-D *Bhaktapur Resort Guest House*, T610670, F610267. Located outside Bhaktapur, on a hill overlooking the city from the south, follow the road south from the trolley bus stop, 20 rooms, most with bath, restaurant does Nepali and Chinese food, pleasant grounds, parking area, traditionally decorated hall.

D *Bhadgaon Guest House*, T610488, F610481. 9 rooms, all with bath, some with tub, good rooftop restaurant for all types of food, modern, clean, comfortable and bright, excellent location in the southwest corner of Taumadhi Square. **D** *Dattatraya Guest House*, no phone. 10 rooms, all common bath, large modern building on the west side of Dattatraya Square, bright and clean, rooftop restaurant has Bhaktapur's best views looking out over the Dattatraya Mandir and the southern valley. **D** *Golden Gate Guest House*, T610534. 15 rooms, some with bath, clean, basic Indian, Chinese, continental food, rooftop terrace. **D** *Nyatapola Inn*, T611323. 9 rooms, all with bath, small eating area, clean and comfortable, luminous green bed sheets throughout, small handicraft shop, prices ripe for negotiation, Taumadhi Square. **D** *Royal East Inn*, no phone. 18 rooms, some with bath, same food as *Café de Peacock*, northeast of Dattatraya Square, near the Dhulikhel bus stop. **D** *Shiva Guest House*, T610740, F(Kathmandu) 228600. 10 rooms (including 3 triples), all common bath, good Chinese and continental food, basic but clean, friendly family atmosphere, excellent views over Durbar Square from dining room and roof. Recommended.

E *Bhaktapur Lodge*, no phone. 10 rooms, all common bath, very dark and basic, simple eating area downstairs, no English spoken, near the bus stop. **E** *Nyatapola Rest House*. 5 basic rooms, all common bath, attached restaurant, superb location just north of the Nyatapola Mandir, but the only view from the rooms is of a brick wall. **E** *Traditional Guest House*, T611057. 10 basic rooms, all common bath, a typical large Newari house built around a sociologically intriguing courtyard containing a number of small shrines and an extremely large satellite dish, some food available, rooftop terrace, located between Durbar Square and Taumadhi Square.

Bhaktapur is by no means overburdened with restaurants, but there are enough in and around the three main squares to cater for most tastes.

Eating

Bhadgaon Kitchen Restaurant and Jom Bar, T610094. Located on the main road just west of Dattatraya Square, clean and bright, reasonably priced Nepali, Chinese and continental food. *Café de Peacock*, T610684. Probably the best place to eat in Bhaktapur, a popular restaurant on the 1st floor of a well maintained Newari wooden building with commanding views of the Dattatraya Mandir and square. Good menu including continental, Mexican and Nepali food, Kathmandu prices, cheaper liquor.

Café Nyatapola, T610346. This is the large pagoda building (sometimes confused for a temple) in the middle of Taumadhi Square, and is said to have been built using materials remaining from the reconstruction of the Bhairava Mandir opposite, popular for snacks and meals, also sells Kodak film and Western cigarettes. *Marco Polo*, is at the northwest corner of Taumadhi Square and there are good views over the square from the balcony. Italian, Indian, Chinese. *Nyatapola Restaurant*, just north of the Nyatapola Mandir in Taumadhi Square. Reasonable Nepali and Indian food, some 'continental' snacks, top floor has views of the square. *Temple Town*, T/F610782. Situated in the southwest corner of Durbar Square, semi-Thamel menu including Chinese, continental, Indian snacks and meals, more expensive than average, good views over Durbar Square from roof.

Entertainment **Cinema** A cinema showing mainly Bombay produced Hindi films is located northeast of the Kathmandu minibus stop, west of Durbar Square.

Festivals **January:** *Basant Panchami* marks the coming of spring and is dedicated to Sarasvati. In Bhaktapur it is celebrated particularly by craftsmen.

April: *Bisket* (Snake Slaughter). Special celebrations to commemorate the great battle in the Hindu epic *Mahabharata*. Chariots carrying Bhairava and Bhadrakali are drawn through the narrow streets. A tug-of-war between the upper and lower parts of town decides who will be fortunate for the coming year. A tall wooden pole (sometimes up to 20 metres high) is erected near the riverside at Chuping Ghat with cross beams from which two banners, signifying snake demons, are hung. On the following day (New Year), it is brought crashing down after another tug-of-war. There is dancing and singing in the streets over 4 days.

May: *Sithi Nakha* celebrates the victory of Kumar, god of war, over the demons, as well as marking the onset of the monsoon rains. A palanquin carrying an image of the goddess Bhagavati is the focus of a procession through Taumadhi Square.

August: *Gathan Muga* (or *Ghantakarna* or *Gathe Mangal*) This festival is a ritual exorcism of evil spirits which protects the forthcoming harvest. Effigies of the demon, Gathan Muga, are made of straw or dried rice stalks and in the evening are immersed in the river. Offerings of cooked rice are placed along the streets to placate the demons and iron are driven into the horizontal beam above the doorway of each house.

August/September: *Gai Jatra* A folk dance unique to Bhaktapur is performed during this festival. Families which have been bereaved during the past year are supposed to send a cow to join the procession, in the belief that the sacred cow will assist the departed soul in its onward journey. Alternatively, they will attire themselves in fancy dress resembling a cow. The procession is jovial and accompanied by music and dancing. Evening feasts centre around *kwati*, a type of bean soup.

September: *Panja Dan* A Buddhist festival of charity when rice and other consumables are ritually offered to Buddhist monks. Uniquely in the valley, Bhaktapur celebrates the day with colourful processions carrying five images of Dipamkara Buddha. The festival is also marked at Svayambhunath and Bodhnath.

Shopping Most of Bhaktapur's handicraft shops are concentrated around the 3 main squares. If you wander along the side streets leading off from the main road that runs through the centre of the city, you will come across numerous small shops where artisans demonstrate a remarkable degree of dexterity by simultaneously using hands, feet and tools to fashion metal **statues**, pieces of **jewellery** and other souvenir handicrafts

– follow the gentle tapping noises. You can find the wonderful **woodcarvings** for which Bhaktapur is acclaimed sold on the street below and near the peacock window, off Dattatraya Square. Try also *Antique Wood Carving* in Dattatraya Square. (**NB** Genuine antiques require certified permission from the Dept of Archaeology, Singha Durbar, Kathmandu, in order to be exported.) Miniature reproductions of the window are popular, but if you want a full size replica carved to order by a skilled craftsman, this can be done within 25 days for Rs 20,000!

For **terracotta** and **earthenware** products, the best place to go is the pottery area, south of Durbar Square where you can buy direct from the potter. Although the mainstay of the area's output has traditionally been water pots and other household containers for local sale, attractive ornamental items are increasingly being produced. You can get anything from decorative candlesticks to masks of various deities here.

Puppets Made in Bhaktapur often show tribal people with tools of their trade or many armed deities clutching little wooden weapons in each hand. Try the *Handicrafts Centre*, near the Dattatraya Mandir. For **cushion covers**, **napkins**, etc, try *S Laxmi Crafts*, T611323, in the *New Nyatapola Inn*, in Taumadhi Square. *Radha Krishna Dhaubhadel*, T612002, is at Suryabinayak, west of Dattatraya Square, and has export quality **pashmina shawls**, **rice paper prints** and textiles. You can get good **tangkas/paubhas** in Durbar Square, and **topis** (traditional Nepali caps worn by men) from shops near the Bhairavanath Mandir in Taumadhi Square. A range of locally produced handicrafts at *Valley Handicrafts and Workshop*, T610946, in Durbar Square.

If you can't find what you're looking for in Bhaktapur, it's all available in Kathmandu as well.

The only long distance route operated from Bhaktapur is via Dhulikhel to **Kodari** on the Nepal-Tibet border, but this begins its journey in Kathmandu. **Transport**

Local Minibus: the terminus for minibuses to and from **Kathmandu** (Bagh Bazar, City Bus Park and Martyrs' Gate bus stops) is at **Siddhi Pokhari**, about 800 metres west of Durbar Square. Regular departures throughout the day at approximately 15 minute intervals or when the bus is full. Last bus leaves Bhaktapur at about 1900 – check. Fare Rs 5. Journey time approximately 50 minutes. **Trolley Bus**: this is an intriguing cross between a bus and a tram and runs only between **Kathmandu** and Bhaktapur. It is slow and can be unreliable. It leaves Kathmandu from Tripureshvar, near the National Stadium. The Bhaktapur terminus is south of the Hanumante River: head south from Durbar and Taumadhi Squares, through the pottery area and across the river at Ram Ghat. Regular departures. Fare Rs 3. Journey time approximately 2 hours. **Taxi**: the official rate set by the government for the journey from Kathmandu is about Rs 800 each way, but this can be substantially reduced with negotiation. Hiring a taxi for the day is usually cheaper than going to a car rental firm. It allows flexibility and you can easily combine Bhaktapur with Thimi (en route), Dhulikhel or Nagarkot on a whistle stop tour of the eastern valley. Make sure that you fix the price with the taxi driver before setting off.

Hospitals & medical services There is a hospital at Doodh Pati, T610676. Several pharmacies in the centre of town, no prescriptions required. **Tourist offices** There is a small tourist information office at the western entrance to Durbar Square, but you will only get photocopied city maps here. **Useful services** Public toilets: serviceable ladies and gents WCs in the tourist information office at the western entrance of Durbar Square. (Gents has an impractically high urinal.) Wash basins sometimes have water. Two more public WCs opposite here, next to the *Temple Town* restaurant. **Directory**

Kathmandu Valley

Close to Kathmandu

To the Southeast

See map, page727 *An attractive route to the southeast of Kathmandu leads past one of the valley's more important Vishnu shrines, Vishanku Narayana, through the small town of Godavari with its botanical gardens, and up through delightful forests and rural scenery to Phulchowki, the tallest of the hills enclosing the Kathmandu Valley.*

Vishanku Narayana This temple marks the place where Vishnu is said to have delivered Shiva of the malevolent intentions of the demon Bhamasur. The temple, amongst the most revered by the valley's Vaishnavites, is a natural cave set into the hillside. The entrance is a narrow fissure through which you crawl to reach a spiral set of stone steps that lead down to the shrine. Here is a statue of Hanuman and of Vishnu.

Getting there Follow the Godavari Road as far as the village of **Baregaon**, six kilometres from the Ring Road at Patan. Take the dirt road that forks off to the left past a Tibetan carpet workshop and continue for one kilometre to the village of **Godamchaur**. Continue straight over the minor 'crossroads' (northeast) and up the hill. The temple is on your right after another one kilometre. There are also regular buses from Kathmandu's City Bus Park and from Lagankhel in Patan.

Godavari This small town, 10 kilometres southeast of Patan's Ring Road, is notable principally for its botanical gardens and as a stopover on the way up to Mount Pulchowki. On the approach along the Godavari Road, you will see a large marble quarry on your right (west) just before you get to the town. Though oft berated as an eyesore and pollutant by some environmentalists, its 'pink marble' is of importance to the local economy. St Xavier's College, one of several in the subcontinent with the same name and run by Jesuits, is a useful local landmark.

The **Royal Botanical Gardens** lie to the northeast of Godavari. Follow the main road northeast from St Xavier's for 800 metres then turn left. An inexpensive map together with a guide to the gardens are sold at the main entrance. There are several small ponds and streams, a Japanese garden, a rockery and the National Herbarium where research into the medicinal use of plants is carried out. A number of tropical species are on display in the greenhouses, including various cactii and orchids. It is also a popular picnic spot. ■ *The best times to visit are March-April and September-November when the gardens are at their most colourful. Admission Rs 5. Open 1000-1600 daily.*

The **Godavari Kunda**, a sacred water tank, is located on the main road just beyond the turning to the botanical gardens. Fed by natural spring water, whose source some believe to be spiritually if not physically associated with the Godavari River in India, it is regarded as an important holy bathing place. A special festival is held every 12 years (next in 2003) when pilgrims attain merit by bathing in its waters.

A large fish farm is situated 400 metres further along the main road. About 100 metres south of St Xavier's is the **Phulchowki Mai Mandir**. This is one of two similarly named temples dedicated to the local female deity, *Phulchowki Mai*. The other is situated at the summit of Phulchowki.

At a height of 2,762 metres (1,200 metres higher than Godavari) it's a hard **Phulchowki** climb, but the rewards are awesome. Phulchowki boasts breathtaking views of the entire Valley with a Himalayan panorama beyond which, on a clear day, stretches from Dhaulagiri in the west to Everest and Kangchendzonga in the east.

Forest covers much of the mountain slopes and provides a habitat for deer and other wild animals. It remains relatively undiminished by human settlement. The area is renowned for its flowers and you pass through wide rhododendron tracts on your way up as well as orchids and a host of other wild flowers, most of which bloom from March-April. At the top is a telecommunications tower which serves the Kathmandu Valley, and the area's other Pulchowki Mai shrine. During winter, the summit is usually snow capped.

You can reach the summit by a motorable road. The car journey takes about 45 minutes. There are also a couple of footpaths which can take up to four hours to climb up and about three hours for the way down. **NB** This is a steep ascent. If you do walk up, ensure that you start the day early enough and calculate your return to Godavari within daylight hours.

This scenic route to the southwest corner of the Kathmandu Valley has plenty to offer for a full day excursion from the capital. With a possible diversion to Kirtipur en route, the road runs alongside the Bagmati River for much of the way and passes the attractive Chobhar Gorge, also an important Buddhist site, before climbing through lush forest with superb views and through the scattered settlements of Pharping before reaching the fascinating temple site of Dakshinkali.

The small village of Chobhar stands on a hill on the west side of the Bagmati **Chobhar** River, four kilometres from the Patan Ring Road. The village is dominated by a three-tiered **Adinath Lokeshvara Mandir**, an unusual Buddhist temple adorned by an extraordinary number of metal pots, pans, mirrors and other household items nailed to wooden boards. These utensils are supposed to have been offered to the temple deity by recently married couples and others in a prayer for domestic contentment. The temple was built in the 15th century and renovated in 1640. Its origins as a religious site, however, are said to date further back to an earlier temple dedicated to Matsyendranath. The inner sanctum contains an image of Anadadi Lokeshvara (replacing the original Phakpa Wati image). The roof of the temple is of gilded copper and the copper torana above the entrance to the shrine has six engraved images of the Buddha.

At the picturesque Chobhar Gorge the Bagmati River narrows to cut its way **Chobhar Gorge** through the rocky hills. The gorge has an important place in Newari Buddhist lore. Legend recounts how the *bodhisatva* Manjushri, wishing to make the sacred lotus flame of Svayambhu accessible to devotees, drained the huge lake that was the Kathmandu Valley of its waters by renting the hills to the south with his flaming sword of discriminative awareness (*prajna*). He thus created the Chobhar Gorge and a fertile valley fit for human habitation. Spanning the gorge is an old iron suspension bridge, built in Aberdeen and installed here in 1903.

Just to the south and standing majestically on the bank of the Bagmati is the beautiful **Jal Vinayaka Mandir**. Built in 1602, this is one of the valley's four most important **Ganesh temples**. The main three-storeyed temple is incorporated into the western flank of the complex edifice and has a copper upper roof. In the centre of the courtyard facing the shrine is a rare bronze image of a divine shrew, the mount of Ganesh. The main image of Ganesh, meanwhile, is a large rock which is believed to resemble the shape of an elephant. There is also an image of Uma Maheshvara, a depiction of Shiva and Parvati, which is thought to have been made in the early 12th century. The pagoda roof struts are carved with images of the eight mother goddesses, the *Asta Matrika*, and of Ganesh. Steps lead from the main entrance of the complex to the river ghat, and on its southern side is a large cement factory.

Sadly, the **Bagmati River** carries the pollution of Kathmandu – sewage and other urban waste – for much of its course south. A further two kilometres south of Chobhar, between the Dakshinkali Road and the river, is the small **Taudaha Lake**. This is the only residue of the valley's original lake and was the mythical repository of the *nagas* released during Manjushri's draining of the valley.

Pharping
(Tib Yanglesho) After Chobhar, the condition of the road deteriorates as it climbs the eight kilometres to the small village of Pikhel and a number of scattered settlements collectively known as Pharping. From Pikhel, there is a walking trail heading four kilometres northwest to **Champadevi**, a 2,278 metres peak with excellent views across the valley and to the Himalayas beyond. About one kilometre along this route is the (**B**) *Himalayan Heights Hatiban Resort Hotel*, T290623, F418561, in a delightful setting and with excellent views. From Pikhel, it is another three kilometres along the main road to **Pharping** which, before the 18th century unification of Nepal, was an independent kingdom.

The **Shekha Narayana Mandir** stands below a steep limestone cliff at the first of Pharping's settlements. This Vaishnavite temple, dedicated to the fifth incarnation of Vishnu as the dwarf Vamana, contains statues said to date from the seventh century and has several water tanks at road level below the colourful main temple building. The current structure dates from the 17th century. There are a couple of shops and tea stalls here.

The place is also sacred to Tibetan Buddhists to whom it is known as **Yanglesho**. The cave alongside the temple is revered as the place where Padmasambhava attained his realization of the Mahamudra teachings. It has an as yet 'unopened' *terma* in its rock walls. Adjacent to the Shekha Narayana Mandir and approached via a flight of steps is the **Buddhist Monastery** under the guidance of Chatrel Rinpoche Sangye Dorje, one of the greatest living masters of the Nyingma school who maintains the Katok and *Longchen Nyintig* traditions, among others.

On a ridge a few hundred metres beyond, there is an ancient Newari pagoda dedicated to **Phamting Vajrayogini**. This 17th century temple is one of the four main Vajrayogini sites of the valley. Higher up the hillside, there is the **Asura Cave**, where Padmasambhava attained realizations by propitiating the meditational deity Vajrakila combined with Yangdak Heruka. There are several Tibetan Buddhist temples and monasteries which have been constructed on the hillside around and below this cave in recent decades and which principally represent the Nyingma and Kagyu traditions. Among them are those under the guidance of Zatrul Rinpoche and Lama Ralo. An exquisite 'self arising' rock image of Tara, which was not so long ago exposed to the elements, has now been incorporated within a large temple complex.

Dakshinkali
Mandir Leaving Pharping, the road snakes down the hill for three kilometres towards Dakshinkali at the bottom of a steep ravine. Just before you get there, the (**D**)

Ashoka Hotel on your left is popular with Indian tourists and offers basic accommodation if you want to stay overnight. A car park at the bottom of the hill charges Rs 8 for cars and Rs 2 for cycles and motorbikes. From here you can get to the temple by walking along the road lined by vendors of red *sindur* and other coloured powder dyes, fruits, vegetables, chickens and lucrative souvenir carvings and paintings.

The temple was built by a Malla king in the 14th century to appease Kali with a great sacrifice of buffaloes when the country was in the grip of a cholera epidemic. The path down from the car park crosses a bridge leading to the temple guarded by a pair of stone lions. The gilded canopy roof is supported by four bronze nagas, while the shrine beneath contains the image of the goddess formed of black stone. A bloodthirsty slaughter (usually the beheading of chickens or goats) takes place here on Tuesday and Saturday mornings in front of the goddess, whose image is on the left of the temple entrance.

Getting there There are frequent **bus** services on Tuesday and Saturday from the City Bus Park from 0600 for the two-hour journey, Rs 20. You can also join a group or hire a taxi. There are hourly bus services daily as far as Pharping and it is a three kilometres' walk on to Dakshinkali. By **taxi**, the journey from Kathmandu takes a little under an hour. Expect to pay around Rs 500 for the return trip. You can also make your way by mountain **bike**, but it is uphill all the way to Pharping and much of the road is in poor condition.

To the West

Kirtipur

From Kalimati in the western suburbs of Kathmandu, the main Prithivi Highway to Pokhara extends westwards before bifurcating at Naubase. At Thankot, there is a police checkpoint which frequently results in lengthy queues of traffic heading to and from Pokhara. Turning southwest from this highway, a side-road leads from Kalimati one and a half kilometres west of the confluence of the Bagmati and Vishnumati rivers to the medieval hilltop town of **Kirtipur** (1,400 metres). Formerly classed as one of the four cities of the valley, and with a predominantly Newar Buddhist population, Kirtipur has a proud though bittersweet place in the history of the valley. *See map, page727*

Its origins are traced back to the 12th century when it belonged to the kingdom of Patan. By the 15th century it had broken its links with Patan and was established as an independent Malla kingdom. Its hilltop location gave Kirtipur a strategic advantage over attackers and its defence was increased by the building of a fortified wall around the town, the remains of which can still be seen today. The wall had 12 gates which opened to each of the town's precincts. It was the last of the valley's towns to fall to the invading and ultimately unifying armies of Gorkha under Prithivi Narayana Shah. So fierce was the town's resistance, aided by its strategically high location, that it withstood the Gorkhas three times before eventually falling in 1769, a year after the submission of Kathmandu, Patan and Bhaktapur. Retribution for the town's opposition came swiftly, however, as Prithivi Narayana Shah famously ordered the noses of all men to be cut off, save those who could play wind instruments. It was reported that the severed noses filled two baskets with a combined weight of 40 kilos!

Kirtipur is often considered to be among the most quintessentially Newari of the valley's towns. In some ways it bears comparison with old Bhakatpur: an

Kathmandu Valley

undulating maze of narrow cobbled streets typically hemmed in by terraces of three-storeyed earthy-red houses often with fabulously carved windows and doors. Unlike Bhaktapur, however, many of its buildings are in an advanced stage of disrepair and this has only recently been addressed with efforts aimed at restoration and development of infrastructure. The town's people have traditionally been involved in agriculture though the manufacture of handicrafts, particularly carpets and textiles under the auspices of the **Kirtipur Cottage Industry Centre**, increasingly occupy many.

The town offers some fine views of Kathmandu and the mountains as well as a number of pleasant walking opportunities from and including Kirtipur.

Sights **Uma Maheshvara Mandir** This temple stands on a high point on the western side of the town from where you have marvellous views of Kathmandu. Two elephants stand guard on either side of the impressive stone stairway that leads up from the east. The three-storeyed temple was built in the 17th century. The smaller Vaishnavite shrine nearby is dedicated to Narayana together with his consort Lakshmi in an interesting complement to the Uma Maheshvara image of Shiva and Parvati.

Bagh Bhairava Mandir In the centre of town, just north of the main square, this is Kirtipur's best known temple. Its principal attractions are the swords and shields which adorn the temple, fascinating vestiges of the battle in which Kirtipur fell to Prithivi Narayana Shah. The Bagh Bhairava festival takes place in Autumn when the image is carried on a palanquin through the village and down to the river.

Chilancho Vihara Also known as **Chilandeva Bahal** and **Jagatpal Mahavihara**, this stupa stands in a square on Kirtipur's southern hilltop. Like those of Patan, its construction is widely attributed to the emperor Ashoka, though it is strongly disputed whether Ashoka ever actually visited the Kathmandu Valley. The oldest known reference to the stupa, pertaining to its enlargement and renovation, dates to 1509.

The central stupa is 11 metres high and above the dome 13 circular brass steps lead to the *chatra*. A bamboo structure supports an additional umbrella above the stupa. At the cardinal points around the base are smaller chaityas and between these are other shrines, some containing images of the meditational buddhas and various depictions of Tara. A bell, installed here in 1755, is suspended on one side. Around the stupa are a number of dharamsalas as well as the buildings of a disused monastery.

Leaving the stupa, a path leads south towards the market area of **Naya Bazar**. Just beyond is the new **Nagara Mandapa Kirtivihara**, a temple gifted to Kirtipur by the Thai government in the 1980s and built in the Thai style. At the extreme western end of town is the **Kirtipur Cottage Industry Centre**.

Getting there From Kathmandu's Durbar Square, it is a five kilometres' walk or bike ride to Kirtipur. Take the main road (which becomes the Prithivi Highway) out of the city. At Kalimati, one and a half kilometres after crossing the Vishnumati River, take the left hand turning (southwest) and follow this road all the way to the northern side of Kirtipur. From Patan, follow the Ring Road and immediately after crossing the Bagmati River turn left (south) onto the Dakshinkali Road. Continue south along here for just under one kilometre then turn right (west) for the two kilometres into the town past the road leading up to Tribhuvan University. There are regular buses throughout the day from Kathmandu's City Bus Park. The Kirtipur bus stop is on the link road between the town and the Dakshinkali Road at the junction of the road leading to the university.

The main campus of Nepal's only university occupies the area to the north of **Tribhuvan** the town. With more than 5,000 students, it was established in 1959 and **University** named after King Tribhuvan (d 1955). The university also has affiliated institutions in other parts of Nepal. Library facilities are available. To get there, follow the main road out of Kirtipur towards the Dakshinkali Road. About 200 metres outside the built up area of town, take the left hand turning which takes you to the campus.

To the Northwest

This small temple site, a good destination for a half day mountain bike ride, lies **Ichangu** beyond the village of **Ichangu**, some three kilometres northwest of the **Narayana** Svayambhunath stupa. The road from Svayambhunath leads uphill towards a **Mandir** Bhairava shrine at the village of **Halchowk** on a hill where there are excellent *See map, page727* views of the stupa with Kathmandu in the background. Beyond Halchowk, the road becomes a dirt track as it descends the one kilometre to Ichangu village. The temple lies at the far end of the village and is one of the quartet of the valley's most important Vishnu/Narayana shrines (with Changu Narayana near Bhaktapur, Vishankhu Narayana at Chapagaon, and Shekha Narayana at Pharping). In October/November each year, many thousands of Vaishnavites begin a one day pilgrimage of all these sites with a visit to the Ichangu Narayana Mandir.

(*Tib* Langru Lungten) Overlooking Balaju, five kilometres northwest of the **Nagarjuna Ban** city, and covering Nagarjuna Hill (2,188 metres) to the north of the Ichangu **& Rani Ban** Narayana Mandir is the delightful forest reserve of **Nagarjuna Ban** (*ban* = forest) and **Rani Ban** ('Queen's Forest'). The wide expanse of forest is virtually unspoiled by the latter day urbanization of Kathmandu and provides a natural habitat for a range of wildlife, including deer, pheasant, leopard and wild pigs. There are some lovely walks through tracts of rhododendron and oak, and the higher you climb the better are the views of both Kathmandu and the Himalayas to the north. Woodcutting is prohibited and penalties are strictly enforced. The hill is reputedly named after the Indian Buddhist master Nagarjuna, who is said to have lived in the caves inside the hill, and it is revered in the Tibetan tradition as the site where the Buddha delivered the *Prophetic Declaration of Goshringa*, although other sources locate this peak in Khotan. The hilltop stupa of **Jamachu** marks the site of this sermon. Legend also has it that prayers for rain made from here are particularly efficacious. The stupa is a simple white structure standing on an exposed windswept stone platform, and numerous prayerflags are attached to it. A dharamsala offers simple accommodation for pilgrims. **NB** Bring your own supply of water, as none is available either on the way up or at the top. An observation tower at the summit offers excellent panoramic views of the Himalayan range to the north.

Getting there You can drive to the summit via a dirt road, or go to Balaju by bicycle or bus (from Rani Pokhari) and hike about two hours on a trail. **NB** Trails can be very slippery during the monsoon. The main entry gate is just to the north of Balaju. ■ *Open 0700-2200. Admission Rs 10 (including bike), Rs 20 (motorbike), Rs 50 (car).*

From Balaju below the hill, a road leads northwest into the Trisuli Valley and **Kakani** towards Kakani. With breathtaking views of the Annapurnas, Manaslu, Ganesh Himal, and Langtang, the village of **Kakani** stands on a 2,067 metres ridge in the northwest corner of the valley, 23 kilometres from Kathmandu's

Ring Road. Like Nagarkot, with which it is frequently compared, Kakani appears on the tourist map almost exclusively for the views. Though spectacular, these are impeded somewhat by the valley's northern hills and are considered by many to be inferior to those from Nagarkot. Nevertheless, the road from Kathmandu passes through beautiful countryside and there are some pleasant short walks around Kakani, including one leading north to the **Kakani Memorial Park**, where a hilltop monument commemorates the victims of a 1992 air crash. To the east of the village is an army camp. Kakani was famously the entry point into the valley for the armies of Prithivi Narayana Shah in the mid-1760s.

The government run (**C/D**) *Tara Gaon Hotel*, T290812, has a reasonable restaurant and a delightful garden.

Getting there Kakani is easily accessible from Kathmandu via the Trisuli Road. **Buses** bound for Trisuli and Dhunche have regular morning departures from the City Bus Park for the two-hour journey. Ask to be dropped off at **Kaulia** from where it is a two kilometres walk east along a paved road. By **taxi**, the drive up takes less than an hour. Negotiate the fare in advance and expect to pay in the region of Rs 450 each way. Kakani is often recommended as a good route for (dedicated) **mountain bikers**, though it is uphill all the way from Kathmandu. Join the Trisuli Road at the northwest Ring Road and continue through Balaju. From Balaju, the road runs alongside the Nagarjun Ban for six kilometres before twisting the rest of the way up through lush paddy terraces and forest, particularly attractive in spring and late autumn when a wide variety of flowers are in bloom.

Trisuli Road From the Kakani turn-off, the road meanders dramatically first west out of the Kathmandu Valley then north for a total of 42 kilometres to the town of **Trisuli**, previously a popular starting point for treks into Langtang. Most of these treks now start at Dhunche, 50 kilometres further north. Beyond Kakani, the road descends steeply to meet with the **Tadi Khola** river, a southwest flowing tributary of the **Trisuli River**. The road then veers in a northerly direction before reaching Trisuli Bazar. There are numerous police checkpoints along the road where you may be required to show your **trekking permit**.

Navakot Just to the south of Trisuli Bazar, this small village is set high on a ridge overlooking its neighbour and also has majestic views of the mountains and surrounding valley. The *kot*, or fort, was another of Prithivi Narayana Shah's encampments between Gorkha and the Kathmandu Valley. Like all great military tacticians, Prithivi always chose such locations for strategic reasons and for the ease with which they could be defended. Three towers dominate the ruins of the walled fort, one of which is open to visitors. The village also has a two-storeyed temple dedicated to Bhairava.

Trisuli Bazar As an old trailhead for treks into Langtang, Trisuli Bazar served to amplify the contrast between the beauty to come and that which was left behind. The town is very much a functional centre, a market town where buses from Kathmandu to Dhunche stop for tea. No longer accustomed to catering for large numbers of visitors staying overnight, **accommodation** is limited to a few trekking standard guesthouses, including the *Pratistha Lodge*, *Shakyar Lodge*, *Ranjit Lodge* and the *Trisuli Guest House*, all located on the other side of the bridge. All **food** available here is Nepali – the *Ranjit Lodge* has been recommended.

Getting there From City Bus Park, there are regular morning departures by **bus**. Because of the poor condition of the narrow road and its constant twists and turns, the 65 kilometres journey takes around four and a half hours (longer in the monsoon), Rs 50.

To the North

(*Tib* Lu Gang-gyel) Heading northwest from the Royal Palace along Lazimpath, you enter Kathmandu's diplomatic enclave. Turn left at the *Hotel Ambassador* to reach the British and Indian embassies, or right on Lazimpath to reach the US embassy. Continuing north out of town, you will eventually reach Budhanilikantha, some nine kilometres north of the city centre, which is one of the valley's most photographed sites. Revered as an emanation of Avalokiteshvara by Newar Buddhists, and by Hindus as Narayana, an incarnation of Vishnu lying on a bed of naga spirits or snakes, this remarkable supine image is the largest stone sculpture of the Kathmandu Valley and one of three fashioned by King Vishnugupta in the seventh century. Another lies at Balaju, while the third was installed in the old Royal Palace for King Pratap Malla. It draws large crowds at **Haribodhini Ekadasi** and **Kartik Purnima**. The five metres monolithic statue is in a small tank at the foot of the Shivapuri Hills and is thought to have come from beyond the valley. In his four hands the deity holds the four attributes: a discus (symbol of the mind), a mace (primeval knowledge), a conch shell (the five elements), and a lotus seed (the universe). Pilgrims descend to the tank by a stone causeway. A priest washes the god's face each morning at around 0900. Jayasthiti Malla revived the Vishnu cult at the end of the 14th century, pronouncing himself to be an incarnation of Vishnu, a belief held by successive rulers to the present day. Since the time of King Pratap Malla (17th century), who dreamt that his successors would die if they were to visit the image, no king of Nepal has ventured into its presence. According to legend, Vishnu sleeps for four months of the year and the festival of Budhanilikantha, held in November, celebrates the deity waking from his monsoon repose.

Budhanila-kantha
See map, page 727

Getting there Buses run from the City Bus Park to Bansbari. From here it's about an hour's walk. Alternatively, you can walk from Kathmandu or cycle. Further north, the road heads from Budhanilikantha into the Shivapuri hills.

This small Buddhist site is actually situated outside the valley, beyond the Shivapuri Hills to the north of Budhanilikantha. It is revered by Buddhist legend as the place where the Buddha Krakuchhanda preached and effected the origin of the Bagmati River.

Baghdwar

To the Northeast

Continuing some three kilometres northeast of Boudha, on the banks of the Bagmati River, the royal game reserve at Gokarna used to be a favourite picnic spot, but since the mid-1990s is being developed into an exclusive hotel and golf resort. Work was expected to have been completed by 1998. Meanwhile, the park sadly remains closed to visitors.

    Overlooking the Bagmati River (and approached from Jorbati via the turn-off to Sundarijal) is the **Gokarneshvara Temple**. Founded prior to the 14th century and rebuilt in the late 16th century, this temple in Nepalese pagoda style exhibits some of the finest wood carvings. It is dedicated to Shiva and the shrine contains a linga. Above the main eastern entrance is a *torana*, or metal plaque, depicting Shiva with his consort, Parvati. Leading to the temple and surrounding it is an unusual collection of religious statuary, the extent of which is possibly unique in Nepal. In August-September each year thousands

Gokarna Park
See map, page 727

Kathmandu Valley

of people pay homage here to the memory of their forefathers. **Jorbati** has become an important base for the Tibetan carpet industry.

Getting there Gokarna is a good cycling destination. From Kathmandu, follow the road east from Chabahil. You pass the Bodhnath stupa on your left (north). After a further one kilometre, the road forks. Take the left hand fork (northeast) which becomes the Sundarijal Road. Climb for about two kilometres until you arrive at the temple. On your right is the small Bagmati River valley and on the opposite slope is the Gokarna park. **Buses** run regularly from City Bus Park to Bodhnath from where it is a pleasant walk. Alternatively, auto-rickshaws will charge about Rs 120 from central Thamel, and taxis about Rs 220 by meter. **Kopan**, with its monastery and spiritual retreat centre, can be reached by turning left (northwest) along a track just before the Gokarna temple. Follow the track for about 800 metres to the tiny village of Jagdol from where a path leads south to Kopan.

Sundarijal   This is a popular starting point for treks heading into the **Helambu** (*Tib* Yolmo) region, but also makes for an accessible excursion from Kathmandu. The Bhagmati here is only a stream, but there are a series of small waterfalls which are particularly attractive during and after the monsoon. If you continue some kilometres north of Sundarijal you will reach a reservoir which supplies much of Kathmandu's drinking water. A large and unsightly overland pipe channels the water from the watershed to the capital. Although it rather spoils the picturesque environment, it does serve as a useful landmark for walkers.

Getting there From Gokarna, the Sundarijal Road continues in a northeast direction for about three kilometres until the road becomes a track.

Sankhu   Sankhu, 15 kilometres east of Kathmandu, emerged as a result of its position
Vajrayogini   on the ancient trade route that linked India and Tibet. A permanent settlement was first established here during Licchavi times. Today, Sankhu is a village which in many ways typifies rural life in the Kathmandu Valley: an agglomeration of old Newari houses, their structural woodwork often dilapidated whilst simultaneously displaying the fine carvings which seem to have been taken so much for granted in traditional Newari architecture. The village is surrounded also by fertile agricultural land, the basis for the village's existence.

A large and colourfully decorated arched gateway marks the village limits. There are a couple of shops in the village selling cold drinks and snacks, but there are no restaurants. From Sankhu, you can head north to **Vajrayogini Temple**, or continue east towards **Nagarkot**.

Getting there Sankhu is 14 kilometres from Kathmandu on the main road heading east from Chabahil past Bodhnath. There are irregular **bus** services from Kathmandu's City Bus Park – it is a slow journey of about two hours and the fare is Rs 10. If you hire a car or **taxi**, it is possible to combine a visit to Vajrayogini with an excursion to Nagarkot. Negotiate the rate in advance. Alternatively, you can hire a mountain **bike**, though it is a long and steep climb onwards to Nagarkot, and the condition of the road deteriorates east of Sankhu. You can also take the bus as far as Sankhu then **walk** to and spend the night at Nagarkot.

Vajrayogini   This delightful three-storeyed pagoda temple, built by King Prakash Malla
Mandir   who was responsible for many of the buildings and monuments standing in Kathmandu's Durbar Square, is situated some two kilometres north of Sankhu and commands magnificent views of the valley. The uppermost roof is said to

be of gold, while the two lower roofs are copper gilded. The struts of all three roofs are lavishly carved with depictions of various deities and mythical animal figures. The main entrance of richly engraved copper is guarded by two large and brightly coloured stone lions. Just below and on plinths on either side of the steps are two smaller metallic lions. The current temple structure dates from the 17th century, but it is widely believed that the location was used as a place of worship even during Licchavi times.

Around this main temple is a variety of statuary and religious icons and to the west another smaller temple with some fine woodcarvings is dedicated to one of the Buddhist Taras. Beware of the numerous monkeys here. Basic dharamsala accommodation is available for devotees.

Getting there From Sankhu it is a 30-minute (two kilometres) uphill walk. North of the village, you can either follow the bumpy but more or less motorable road or, after one kilometre, take the footpath that forks off to the right (northeast) and parallels the road. En route you will pass an old dharamsala, or pilgrims' rest house, and just before you reach the stone steps that lead to the temple courtyard there is a site where sacrifices take place. There are several trails leading from Vajrayogini to the north and west. It is possible to climb to the top of the ridge that encloses the valley to the northeast, but although only about four kilometres as the crow flies it involves an ascent of some 800 metres through dense woodland in parts. You can also head northeast and join up with trails that will eventually reach Budhanilikantha. Sufficient supplies of food and water as well as a local guide are recommended.

Treks from Sankhu and Sundarijal One road leads from Sankhu to **Nagarkot** in the east, where there are superb views of the Himalayas as well as accommodation, and another leads west from Sundarijal before veering sharply to the north and climbing steeply to join a minor road which follows the contours west for three kilometres to **Nagi Gonpa**, a retreat centre affiliated to Karnying Shedrubling in Bodhnath. From here there is another trail leading two kilometres west to **Budhanilikantha.**

Nagarkot

See map, page 820

At the far east of the valley, 32 kilometres from Kathmandu and at an altitude of 2,190 metres, Nagarkot is widely considered to have the best views of the Himalayas from the Kathmandu Valley. On a clear day, there are panoramas extending from the Annapurnas – Annapurna S (7,273 metres), Annapurna III (7,557 metres), Annapurna I (8,090 metres) and Annapurna II (7,937 metres) – in the west, to Everest (8,848 metres) and Kangchendzonga (8,597 metres) in the east. The best months are from November to February. In October and March views may be obscured, while at other times the mountains remained concealed for most of the time by clouds. The views can be exceptional at sunrise and sunset when the mountains are bathed in perceptibly changing hues of pink, red and crimson. To the east, the Indravati and Chok rivers are visible.

Nagarkot itself is barely a village, though it has an army camp, a shrine and an increasing number of small hotels of varying standards. The army camp is a legacy of history: Nagarkot's strategic location allowing clear lines of vision through almost 360° led to a military presence being established here several centuries ago. Its recent growth – especially in the number of hotels – is almost entirely the result of tourism. A visit is highly recommended and the place is particularly relaxing after Kathmandu. Due to the altitude, temperatures are invariably lower than in Kathmandu (by as much as 10°C) and warm clothing is advised outside the hot summer months. It can also be very windy, so popular with kite flyers. The spring flowers and unusual rock formations make the short and undemanding treks from Nagarkot to Sankhu, Changu Narayana, Bhaktapur or Banepa and Dhulikhel particularly attractive. It is also a popular picnic spot for Nepalis and you may come across groups singing and dancing in traditional Nepali style.

Essentials

Sleeping **A** *Club Himalaya Nagarkot Resort*, T413632, F417133. 42 rooms, coffee shop with panoramic views, good *Tea House* restaurant next door does buffet lunches and dinners, bar, facilities including indoor pool, sauna and gym, modern building that sticks out like a sore thumb in a central location, but with superb views, has its own helicopter landing pad (10 minutes from Kathmandu's Tribhuvan airport), most guests come on a 1 night/2 day package from Kathmandu, inclusive prices from US$130 per person, book through *Kathmandu Guest House* in central Thamel.

B *Chautari*, T419718. 30 rooms, restaurant. **B** *Country Villa*, T228014. 28 rooms, some with verandah, restaurant, Japanese-style bar and prices. **B** *The Fort*, T290869. An extensive modern building traditionally decorated, good views, popular with groups. **B-C** *Space Mountain Holiday Resort*, T290871. 20 rooms, restaurant, modern, expensive, inexplicably built to face away from the mountains.

C *Flora Hill*, T226893, 13 rooms, restaurant. Government owned, modest but relatively comfortable, though inconvenient location to the south, on the road to Bhaktapur. **C** *Nagarkot Farm House*, T228087, 9 rooms, all with bath (best room: No 9), restaurant, conceived and built by an American in conjunction with a Tibetan, open fireplace in dining room, good food, 3 meals included in room rate, small hall for yoga, meditation or small conferences of about 20 people, solar heated water, about 10,000 trees have been planted, including 2,000 peach and apple trees, delightful and secluded location to the north, good value, reservations through *Hotel Vajra* in Kathmandu (T272719, F271695). Highly recommended.

D *Nagarkot Cottage*, T222532, F227372. 15 rooms in individual cottages, restaurant, hot water available in buckets, remote location 15 minutes' walk south of bus stop, simple but clean. **D** *Taragaon Resort*, T221768. Government owned, 8 minutes' walk south of bus stop, recently re-opened. **D** *View Point*, T290870. Clean if basic rooms with bath in cottages on a hillside, restaurant, electricity, hot water, excellent views from some rooms, now partially blocked by *The Fort* hotel, heavily booked in season, offers bus service from Kantipath, depart 1330, return 1030 the following morning.

E *At The End Of The Universe*, T Bhaktapur 610874. Cottage/hut accommodation, dining room, good views, another of Nagarkot's hotels whose name is inexplicably influenced by astronomy – to attract star trekkers? **E** *Galaxy*, T290870. 9 rooms, some with bath, cheaper dorm accommodation, food available, electricity, better views from upstairs rooms. **E** *Madhuban Village*. Rooms in bamboo cottages/huts, has electricity. **E** *The Niva*. Cottage/hut accommodation, dining room. **E** *Peaceful Cottage*, T290877. 8 rooms, some with bath, excellent views from dining room. Recommended.

Eating All hotels and guest houses have some dining facilities, but Nagarkot is by no means known for culinary excellence. The one, shining exception is the *Tea House*, T413632, F417133. Operated by and in a separate building next to the *Club Himalaya Nagarkot Resort* hotel. Good Nepalese, Indian and Chinese buffet lunches and dinners are available most days in season, as well as an à la carte menu, snacks and set teas. The restaurant has superb panoramic views of the mountains and an outdoor terrace seating area. Open 0600-2000. *The Fort* hotel has a good restaurant. Try also the *Flora Hill*, and the *Nagarkot Farm House* has good vegetarian dishes.

Tour companies & travel agents Package tours: widely available at travel agents in Kathmandu and include transport and overnight accommodation. Prices start at around US$20.

Directory

Road Buses: run to irregular schedules from Bhaktapur, leaving the Siddhi Pokhari stop when they are full. From Kathmandu, buses leave from the City Bus Park and go via Bhaktapur. With plenty of stops en route this can be a very slow journey of up to 4 hours, Rs 15. There is also one tourist bus service leaving Kantipath (near the British Council) at lunchtime for its 3-hour journey, Rs 60 each way. The return leaves Nagarkot after breakfast. Book in advance through your hotel or any good travel agent.

Transport

The official **taxi** fare from Kathmandu is around Rs 800 each way, but a little bargaining will normally reduce this by half. The journey takes about 1 hour. You can usually find a taxi to take you back to Kathmandu just below the *Club Himalaya Nagarkot Resort* hotel.

A **helicopter** service from Kathmandu is operated by the *Club Himalaya Nagarkot Resort* hotel as part of their 1 or 2 night package deals. Book through the *Kathmandu Guest House*. **Mountain bike**: you can mountain bike up the main road and descend down the track to Sankhu. **Hiking**: the adventurous can hike from Bhaktapur (about 4 hours). It is also possible to walk back to Bhaktapur (3½ hours) and Kathmandu (6 hours). Take plenty of drinking water – it can be hot from March onwards.

Kathmandu Valley

Arniko Highway to Tibet

*The Arniko Highway connects Kathmandu with Kodari, 81 kilometres northeast of the valley on the Nepal-Tibet border, where after some rough sections, it connects with National Highway 318 to Lhasa. From Kathmandu, the road passes just to the south of **Thimi** and **Bhaktapur** before continuing through **Banepa** and climbing on up to the old Newari hilltop village of Dhulikhel. There are some interesting stop-offs en route. **Dhulikhel** has a reasonable variety of accommodation available and also offers some fine walking opportunities.*

Banepa

Banepa is a small, uninspiring town 24 kilometres from Kathmandu at the base of the valley's southeast hills. It was briefly a capital of the Kathmandu Valley during the 14th century. A large statue of King Tribhuvan forms a roundabout in the eastern part of town, an ideal point from which to view the numerous police checkpoints along this stretch of the Arniko Highway. The town has a number of small guesthouses and restaurants serving Nepali food and light refreshments. The nearby three-storeyed **Chandeshvara Temple** is pleasantly situated in woodland about one kilometre to the northeast and connected to Banepa by a dirt road. The temple is named after a Shiva *shakti* who, legend has it, came here to destroy a demon named Chand.

Dhulikhel

Dhulikhel is the last major village in the Kathmandu Valley through which the **Arniko Highway** passes on its way to Kodari on the Nepal/Tibet border. About 30 kilometres from Kathmandu, it stands on the southeast slopes of the valley at an altitude of 1,585 metres and is a popular daytrip and overnight destination with good mountain views. In contrast to Nagarkot with which it is often compared, however, Dhulikhel is an established village with a history of settlement that goes back to its days as a stopover on the India-Tibet trade route. Its people are predominantly Newaris. The main part of the village lies to the west of the Arniko Highway, where the winding street leads up through the old and rustic residential areas before descending down towards Banepa. The Arniko Highway continues its eastward progress, but a major police checkpoint just after the road begins to dip outside Dhulikhel ensures often lengthy traffic queues. Views of the valley from here, though, can be magnificent, particularly if your visit coincides with the expanse of fields below appearing as a glorious patchwork of lush green and golden crops. To the east you can see the **Indravati River** meandering down from the Himalayas towards the Terai. As elsewhere, mountain views are dependent on the weather. The best months to visit are from October to March. During and around the monsoon time you will be lucky to get a glimpse of the mountains, though the otherwise entirely occlusive cloud cover is most likely to break in the early morning and late afternoon.

Entering the village from the east, you come to a junction and square where roads branch off to the southeast and northwest. A small *pokhari*, or tank, of rather forlorn appearance lies beside a statue of King Mahendra and the square is used as something of a local meeting point. Heading southeast the road climbs and you will pass a couple of budget guesthouses. Continuing directly along here you will reach an open space from where there are good **mountain views**, recommended for sunrise and sunset visits. After about one kilometre a road to the southeast leads up to a small temple/shrine standing on a hillock, another popular viewpoint. If you continue downhill to the bottom of the gorge, there is a small **Shiva Mandir** standing beside a stream.

If you take the northwest road from the square, you pass the architecturally unimpressive **Ganesh Mandir** partially hidden by trees to your right before entering another square, again with a small *pokhari* and two three-storeyed pagoda temples dedicated to Vishnu. The **Harisiddhi Mandir** is the first on your right, while just beyond is the colourful **Narayana Mandir** with two distinctive statues of Garuda, the bird headed vehicle of Vishnu, in front.

Essentials

Sleeping

A *Himalayan Horizon Sun-n-Snow*, T011-61260, F011-61476, reservations from Durbar Marg, Kathmandu T/F225092. 28 rooms (deluxe or standard), 2 restaurants, bar, excellent mountain views from all rooms and good food, room only and full board tariffs available. **A** *Dhulikhel Mountain Resort*, above the village, T Kathmandu 220031. 35 twin-bedded rooms with large windows in thatched cottages, attached bathrooms have running water heated by solar energy, good restaurant and bar in the main house which is built in typical Nepali style, delightful terraced gardens, the Mountain Resort has its own fleet of vehicles plus trekking and rafting equipment for excursions. **A** *Himalayan Shangri La Resort*, T/F Kathmandu 423939. 16 large rooms, all with mountain views, restaurant, bar, conference room, modern building in a secluded location south of the main village, all rooms attractively decorated in traditional Newari style.

B *Dhulikhel Lodge Resort*, T011-61114, reservations from Kamaladi, Kathmandu T247663, F222926. 25 rooms, Nepali, Tibetan and continental restaurants, bar, large and comfortable with good views of valley and peaks.

C *Himalayan Mountain Resort*, T011-61158, reservations from Tridevi Marg, Kathmandu T225388 ext 358, F220161. 18 rooms, restaurant and bar. Traditional Chhetri decor, pleasant terraced gardens with seating and fine views. **C** *New Mirabel Resort*, was still under construction in early 1997. **C** *Royal East Inn*. Large hotel near bus stop, comfortable, good restaurant, bar.

D *Dhulikhel Lodge*, T61114. Large building centrally located and the oldest budget hotel in Dhulikhel, reasonable food in restaurant with floor cushion seating, hot water in common bathrooms, ISD facilities, top floor rooms recommended, photocopies of the 1 day trek to Namobuddha available from reception. **D** *Peace Paradise*. 8 rooms, some with bath, restaurant, modern red brick building with some good value rooms.

E *Nawranga*, T61226. 6 rooms, all common bath, small but good budget restaurant, sells postcards and the paintings of a self taught local artist. **E** *Silk Road*, T61269. 6 rooms, some with bath, food available, central location but basic. **E** *Snow View*, T61229. 6 rooms, all common bath, food available. **E** *Sun Rise*, T61482. 4 rooms, all common bath.

Eating

All of Dhulikhel's eating places are attached to its hotels and guesthouses. If you are here on a day trip, the *Royal East Inn*, conveniently situated near the bus stop, has a good restaurant serving Nepali/Indian and continental food. The **Nawranga** guest-house has a small restaurant serving huge portions of Nepali food and has several excellent *tarkaris* and pickles. Try also the **Dhulikhel Lodge** restaurant for good, tried and tested Nepali food. Seating is on floor cushions.

Transport There are regular **bus** services to Dhulikhel leaving from the City Bus Park in **Kathmandu** from early morning. The journey goes via Bhaktapur and takes 2 hours or

Arniko Highway: the road to Tibet

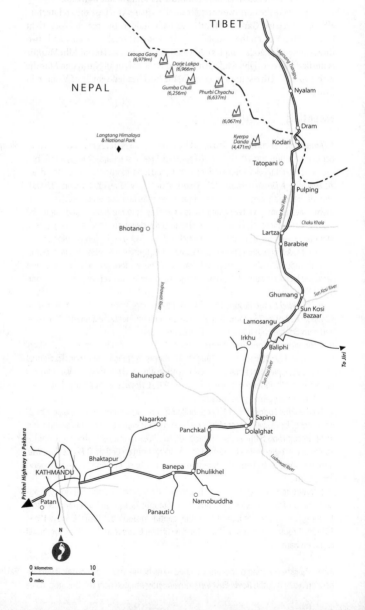

more, Rs 15. The bus stop is on the main road east of the village. To get into the village either turn right just after the bus stop or walk 200 metres and turn right as the road bends. You can make the journey in less than half the time by **taxi**. Once again, negotiation is essential after which expect to pay around Rs 450 one way and Rs 800 for a return trip with 2 hours' waiting. **NB** Check that the taxi has the necessary documentation to allow it to go as far as Dhulikhel. There are numerous police checkpoints along the Arniko Highway and the administration of on-or-near-the-spot fines can be a lengthy affair.

Walks from Dhulikhel

There are numerous interesting walks around Dhulikhel. For the more adventurous, there are trails leading all the way via Banepa to Nagarkot (16 kilometres), and thence to Sankhu and Budhanilikantha.

Other trails provide pleasant day hikes to Panauti, an ancient riverside town of temples which is a place of pilgrimage for Hindus, or to **Namobuddha** (*Tib* Tagmo Lujin), via Kavre Banjyang and the Tamang village of Phulbari. **Namobuddha** is one of Nepal's holiest Buddhist sites and commemorates the supreme compassion of the Buddha in his legendary self-sacrifice to a starving tigress at Panauti. The origins of the hilltop site are unknown, though some sources suggest that the architectural style is indicative of construction in the 17th or 18th centuries. It is dominated by a large stupa (Dharma Dhatu), and to one side is a small monastery, built by Trangu Rinpoche.

Sunkosi Valley

After Dhulikhel, the road descends into the **Panchkal Valley**, a picturesque expanse of scattered agricultural communities. A patchwork of fields dominates the valley floor while innumerable minutely terraced fields cover the slopes. The road winds its way northeast to reach the village of **Panchkal** after 21 kilometres. From here it is eight kilometres east to **Dolalghat**, a small town where the Indravati and Sunkosi rivers meet. This is where the Sunkosi rafting trips put in and some Helambu treks begin. The road then continues northeast following the river valley upstream. Just beyond the village of **Baliphi**, 16 kilometres from Dolalghat, there is the turn off for the road to **Jiri**, a stunningly beautiful though arduous 65 kilometres to the east. The area around Baliphi is effectively an ethnic transition zone where you leave behind the Newari dominated area to the south for the peoples of the mountainous country to the north. **Lamosangu** is five kilometres north of Baliphi, a quiet Sherpa village with a few shops and a basic guesthouse. Next comes **Barabise**, a functional town and the final destination for many buses from Kathmandu. For those continuing to Kodari it is a popular refreshment stop. Although it has several basic guesthouses, the town offers little else of tourist interest. Just before you reach Barabise you pass the confluence of the Sunkosi and Bhotkosi rivers. The source of the Bhotkosi (*Tib* Rongshar Tsangpo) lies in the mountains to the east and for the rest of the journey to Kodari the road runs alongside the Sunkosi (*Tib* Matsang Tsangpo) tributary.

Some 24 kilometres north of Barabise and about three kilometres before Kodari is **Tatopani**, a relaxed village which takes its name from the hot springs here. To get to the springs, follow the road heading north from the central market for 700 metres. The steps to the springs are then signposted. **NB** Modesty is the rule and nude bathing is prohibited. The village has a number of small basic guesthouses including the *Sherpa Lodge*, the *Sonam Lodge* and the *Tibet Lodge*. All do simple Nepali food. Local buses run between Barabise and Tatopani. **NB** The scenery on this route is spectacular with the clear waters flowing through ancient, deep cut gorges, but it is especially vulnerable to **landslides** during and after the monsoon, and these can leave sections of the road (particularly north of Barabise) unpassable for days at a time.

Kathmandu Valley

Tibetan border Balanced on one side of the deep gorge that separates Nepal from Tibet, **Kodari** is the last village you reach before passing through Nepali immigration and crossing the **Friendship Bridge** (*Tib* Dzadrok Zampa) into Tibet. Although the views from here are spectacular, Kodari itself is a motley assortment of huts and houses and its interest lies mainly in its strategic location. If no buses are running, you may have to walk the eight kilometres from the Friendship Bridge to reach the Chinese immigration and customs checkpoint at Khasa (*Tib* Dram). Porters are available on both sides. The border is currently Tibet's most important land border with the outside world.

Immigration The Dram **customs and immigration** posts open at 1000 Beijing time (GMT +8; Nepal = GMT +5.45), while those at Kodari open at 0930.

Bhutan

A self-imposed isolation and undeveloped infrastructure have ensured that Bhutan remains the most mysterious country in South Asia, notwithstanding recent moves towards modernization. Never colonized, the country is today fully independent and maintains excellent relations with India. Consistently cautious with respect to contact with the outside world, the flow of tourists is tightly controlled by the imposition of high package fees, which provide sufficient foreign exchange to aid development without over-extending the basic ammenities of the country. Less than 6,000 tourists visit Bhutan every year; and the government continues to make great efforts to uphold the country's religious and cultural traditions.

The country, dwarfed by its great neighbours India and Tibet, and only one third the size of Nepal, is nonetheless slightly larger than Switzerland. Its official name, Druk-Yul, means 'Land of the Thunder Dragon' (the emblem portrayed on the national flag), and also 'Land of the Drukpa Kagyu school', indicating the tradition of Tibetan Buddhism which has come to dominate Bhutanese religious life since the 17th century. The name Bhutan is probably derived from the Sanskrit bhotanta, meaning ' The End of Tibet'; while the Tibetans often refer to the land as 'Lhomon', or 'Southern Mon'.

Essentials

Bhutan

Planning your trip

In some respects Bhutan may be regarded as a microcosm of Tibetan culture, preserving intact traditions, life-styles, and architecture, which have been devastated in Tibet itself over the last forty-five years. Equally, it is important to recognise that Bhutan has evolved its own distinctive national identity over the last three hundred and fifty years during which time it has resolutely maintained its independence from both Tibet and India. As in Nepal, the terrain forms three clearly defined zones: the highland border region formed by the Himalayan range, which is frequented by nomadic drokpa and accessible largely on trekking trails; the central hills inhabited by sedentary Drukpa, Monpa and Sharchokpa communities; and the jungle terrain of the south, bordering the Assamese Duars, where the Lhotsampa of Nepalese origin form a majority.

Where to go

Among these zones, the areas of greatest importance for Bhutanese culture are to be found in the central hills. **Kyerchu Lhakhang** in Paro and **Jampa Lhakhang** in Bumtang are revered as seventh century geomantic temples, reputedly dating from the reign of the Tibetan king Songtsen Gampo, whose empire included Bhutan. **Lhakhang Karpo** in Ha and **Taktsang** hermitage in Paro, along with the temples of **Kurje Lhakhang** and **Konchoksum Lhakhang** in Bumtang are all associated with

Bhutan Essentials

Padmasambhava, and the establishment of Tibetan Buddhism throughout the Yarlung empire during the eighth century. From **Gangteng Monastery** in the Black Mountains through to the central valleys of Bumtang, there are several important sites associated with the three great Nyingmapa masters Longchen Rabjampa, Dorje Lingpa and Pema Lingpa (13-16th centuries) who sojourned in Bhutan. Among them, the temples of **Tharpaling**, **Trakar**, **Tamzhing**, and **Rimochen**, along with the monasteries of **Kungzandra** and **Thowadra** are particularly renowned.

Perhaps the most striking cultural resonance of this small Himalayan kingdom is found in the strategic fortifications or dzong founded by the Drukpa Kagyu hierarchs from the mid-seventeenth century onwards. Constructed in a distinctively Bhutanese style, these buildings combine administrative and religious functions, as did the Potala Palace in Lhasa. The best known are **Tashi Chodzong** in Thimphu, **Rinpung Dzong** and **Drugyel Dzong** in Paro, and **Dechen Phodrang Dzong** in Punaka, but those of **Wangdu Phodrang**, **Trongsar**, **Shemgang**, **Jakar**, **Lhuntse**, **Tashigang**, **and Tashi Yangtse** are also architecturally impressive and culturally significant.

The colourful pageantry and religious dances of the **Tsechu** festivals held throughout Bhutan in the district towns have in recent years attracted the interest of foreign visitors in ever increasing numbers. For the schedule of these festivals in 1999, see below, page 833.

Trekking The north and the more remote central and southerly parts of Bhutan are even now only accessible by trekking, which offers not only spectacular scenery but also a chance to see the village people maintaining their ancient skills and crafts. Bhutan is really off-the-beaten-track, has wonderful landscapes, amazing flora and kind, affectionate people who are very proud of their lifestyle.

Planning a trek Trekking conditions are very different from Nepal since it is much wetter; the season is much shorter and for some high-altitude treks choosing a period between snow and rain can be difficult. The best months are March-April and October-November. Treks start at 2,400 metres generally rising to 4,000 metres quite rapidly. With Bhutan's small, scattered population you might trek for hours, and sometimes days, without seeing a single house, and only passing the odd person with pack animals along the track. The trails are not mapped or well-defined so it is easy to lose one's way; high-altitude rescue is non-existent. It is therefore essential to trek with a reliable local guide.

The fast mountain streams are crossed by ingenious log or liana and split bamboo bridges, while wider rivers may have more substantial wooden ones – often protected by prayer flags. The famous 15th century iron chain bridges were built by Tangtong Gyelpo. The chains were often made in Bhutan (using a small quantity of arsenic to reduce the melting point of iron) and transported great distances. Over 50 bridges were erected across the Himalaya; some had nine lengths of chain suspended to form the frame of a bridge which would then be tied with wire and have matting placed underfoot.

For **accommodation** there are no 'tea houses' or cosy lodges with hot water to welcome you after a hard day's trek. In the countryside the Bhutanese are fully occupied tending animals and with work in the fields and do not have time, or the need, to take in guests, be they Bhutanese or foreigners – the traces of fire camps in rock shelters provide ample proof of this. Because of the inaccessibility of most of the countryside, people are reluctant to sell any food since a shop could be three days' walk away. In remote areas, barter is a standard mode of exchange; salt or edible oil are more likely to see eggs materialize than a bank-note! It is therefore essential to have tents and provisions.

The economy is not dependent on tourism and so the Bhutanese do not hire themselves as porters; yaks and mules carry all belongings on treks. Since the trekking months coincide with the busy period in the fields, the owners of pack animals have to be contacted well in advance, and be flattered and cajoled before they agree. Moreover, in the course of a single trek, the pack animals will also be changed at the district frontiers.

Trekking in Bhutan is logistically complicated because it is still a wild country. However, tour operators here know the problems well; they will help you with the choice of trek and the season, taking into account your own preferences and physical fitness. Small groups are provided with a guide, helpers, a wonderful cook, tents, mattresses, pack-animals and all the food needed, as there is nothing available on the way; you are advised to bring your own sleeping bags, walking boots and clothing (Gortex recommended), umbrella, flashlight (head lamp recommended), medications, sun hat, sun lotion and sunglasses, water flask, and film, batteries etc. In the monsoons some paths can be very muddy and below 2,000 metres, leeches are problematic.

Ecology and the environment have recently become the main concern of tour operators who do not want trekkers (and local staff) to litter the still pristine countryside. Many treks will take place in the national parks, such as the Jigme Dorje Wangchuck Sanctuary (7,813 square kilometres) which occupies the entire northern belt of the country. Conservation of flora and fauna is the responsibility of the Royal Society for the Protection of Nature. Please follow the Himalayan Code of Practice, cited above, page .

Mountaineering There are 21 peaks above 7,000 metres, but mountaineering is no longer allowed. Peaks below this elevation can be climbed by trekkers without seeking special permission. For details of climbing fees and organization, refer to TAB's Bhutan Mountaineering Regulations.

When to go **Best time for a visit** March-May and September-November, either side of the rainy season.

Finding out more **Tourist authority** The Tourism Authority of Bhutan (TAB) is the only government body; all other outlets are private travel agents. There is no tourism office abroad. You can write for information to TAB, PO Box 126, Thimphu, T975-223251, F223695. Information can also be obtained from Bhutan Embassies/Missions in Dhaka, Kuwait, Delhi, Geneva and New York.

There are a number of tour operators leading treks in Bhutan. These are listed under useful addresses in page 833

Before you travel

Getting in **Visas** Valid passports and entry visa are essential. Virtually the only way to see Bhutan is as a member of a commercially organized tour group. As of 1 February 1999, tour prices, all inclusive, average US$200 in the high season (March to May and September to November) and US$165 in the other months. After 10 nights in the country, a declining rate is applied.

Visas cannot be obtained at Bhutanese embassies. Foreigners can only go through a travel agent abroad or one in Bhutan who will obtain a visa for you and make all your bookings. This can take about three weeks (Fax is very reliable within Bhutan). You pay for the visa (US$20, validity 15 days) on arrival in Bhutan. The regulations are simpler for Indian nationals who do not need to go through a travel agent. **NB** Special permission is needed to visit monasteries and dzongs, with the exception of the following: Ta Dzong, Drugyel Dzong and Takstang viewpoint in Paro; Tashi Chodzong, Memorial Chorten, Changlimithang, and Jigmeling temples in Thimphu; Kamji, Chasilakha, Zangdokpelri and Kharbandhi temples in Phuntsoling; Damphu and Lamidara temples in Tsirang; Punakha Dzong in Punakha; Wangdu Choling Dzong, Mebartsho gorge, and Ura temple in Bumtang; Mongar Dzong in Mongar; Chorten Kora, Tashi Yangtse Dzong, and Kanglung Zangdokpelri temple in Tashigang; and the

Zangdokpelri temple in Samdrup Jongkhar. **Buddhists** may be given special permits to some restricted dzongs and gonpas, permission being granted by the Secretary of the Special Commission for Cultural Affairs.

Embassies abroad Royal Bhutan Embassy: *India*: Chandra Gupta Marg, Chanakyapuri, T6889807/05, F6876710, New Delhi 11021; 48 Tivoli Court, 1A Ballygunge Circular Rd, Calcutta. *Bangladesh*: 58, Rd No 3A, Dhanmondi RA, Dhaka, T545018. *USA*: 120 E 56th St, New York, NY 10022, T212-8261919, 826 1990, F212-8262998. *Switzerland*: 17-19 Chemin Du Champ D'Anier, Ch-12209 Geneva, T022-7987971-73, F022-7882593.

Friendship Associations For general information on Bhutan, contact: *Bhutan Society*, Friary View, Drummond Rd, Guildford, Surrey GU1 4NS, UK T/F44-1483538189. *Amis du Bhoutan*, 2 rue d'Enghien, 75010 Paris, France T/F33-1-45234177.

Customs Eight millimetre cameras are allowed. No 16 millimetre cameras. Permits are needed for video cameras used for professional filming (for a fee). Contact Tourism Authority of Bhutan (TAB), F223251. You may not take antiquities, religious artefacts, plants or animal products out of the country – all old items and new tangkas must have a certificate clearing them from the Dept of Antiquities, and all sales receipts should be kept for inspection.

Money

Currency The national currency is the Ngultrum (Nu). 100 Chetrum = 1 Nu. Exchange rate is approximately US$1 = Nu 40. Indian Rupees circulate at par. American Express credit card accepted in a few shops. No other credit card is accepted so far.

Exchange *Bank of Bhutan* and *Bhutan National Bank* in Thimphu and Phuntsoling will change TCs and hard currency. The *Bank of Bhutan* has 26 branches across the country. Head Office is at Phuntsoling. Money-changers prefer TCs to currency notes. Carry enough Nu when trekking or touring.

Health

Protection is recommended against cholera, typhoid, tetanus, polio, hepatitis, malaria and rabies, and optional for meningitis and altitude sickness. Avoid unboiled water and ice-cubes, as well as uncooked vegetables and unpeeled fruit since dysentery is commonplace. At high altitude, drink more liquid to avoid dehydration. See Health in Tibet Essentials, page 49.

Warning Thimphu Valley has been experiencing increased incidence of rabies because of the growing number of stray dogs.

Getting there

Air The airport is at Paro. **Transport to Thimphu**: one and a half hours' drive by Druk Air coach. **Druk Air**, the national carrier (2 BAe 146), has connections with Delhi (three hours), via Kathmandu (45 minutes) on Monday and Thursday; and with Bangkok (four hours), via Calcutta (one and a half hours): inbound to Paro on Wednesday, Friday and Sunday, and outbound to Calcutta and Bangkok on Tuesday, Thursday and Saturday. Approximate price: Delhi-Paro return US$580, Kathmandu-Paro return US$330,

Touching down

Official time *Bhutanese time is 30 minutes ahead of Indian National Time or GMT +6 hours.*
Voltage *220-240 volts, 50 cycles AC. The*

current is variable and supply sometimes erratic. Flashlights are useful.
Weights and measures *Metric – the same as in India.*

Bangkok-Paro return US$750, Calcutta-Paro return US$330. **NB** Bad weather can delay flights during monsoons. Druk Air change their schedule at least twice a year and are not very reliable. Always check the day and time with your travel agent before departure. Current departure from Paro 0730; to Paro from Delhi 1125; from Kathmandu 1410; from Bangkok 0800; and from Calcutta 0945. **Druk Air** have offices in Calcutta, Delhi, Bangkok and Kathmandu, but note bookings must be made through your travel agent. A visa fee of US$20 is payable upon entry at Paro airport, and two passport photographs are required. Airport tax of Nu 300 is payable on departure.

The road from Bagdogra (the nearest Indian airport) enters Bhutan at Phuntsoling, the border town. It is a three to four hour drive from Bagdogra airport which can be reached by plane from Calcutta and Delhi. From Darjiling or Gangtok, it can take seven hours to Phuntsoling. It takes about six hours to negotiate the winding 179 kilometres road from Phuntsoling through to Thimphu (or Paro). **Road**

Touching down

Clothing Cottons and light woollens in summer (June-September). Heavy woollens and jackets the rest of the year. Take an umbrella for the monsoons and comfortable shoes. Shorts, revealing clothes or T-shirts are not suitable. For trekking gear, see above, page 829. **Rules, customs & etiquette**

Hints on social behaviour Useful words include – *Kadrinche* (thank you), *Kusuzangpo* (greetings) and *Lasso* (when leavetaking). The interiors of some monasteries were closed because the tourists were disturbing the monks and stealing mementos. When visiting a dzong, **do not** smoke, wear a hat, interrupt prayers or enter the dance area during the *Tsechu* ceremony. Ask before photographing. See also the section on planning a trek, page 828.

Tipping Tipping is forbidden by law, but an acknowledgement of good services is always appreciated.

The crime rate in this unspoilt country is very low. However, it is safest to lock precious belongings and money inside a suitcase or a bag before leaving the room. **Safety**

Where to stay

Bhutan has only been accepting foreign visitors since 1974 and the number admitted is currently 6,000 per annum, so there is neither a well developed hotel industry nor category **A-C** hotels. In Phuntsoling, Thimphu and Paro there are some comfortable hotels with Bhutanese decor and modern facilities. BTCL accommodation in Bumtang, Trongsar, Mongar and Tashigang is simpler but has modern plumbing and helpful staff (water and electricity supply can be erratic). Elsewhere guesthouses are very

Bhutan Essentials

basic. Hotel prices vary considerably from Nu 2,000 for the large hotels in Thimphu and Paro to Nu 800/1,000 for the smaller ones. Outside these towns, the prices range from Nu 450 to Nu 1,000. Breakfast is generally excluded.

Getting around

Road The road network is not extensive since construction only began in the 1960s. The main lateral road links Thimphu with Tashigang (1965-85); and there are now four main roads linking the mountain areas with the plains: Thimphu-Phuntsoling (1982); Wangdu Phodrang-Khalikhola; Trongsar-Gelekphuk; and Tashigang-Samdrup Jongkhar (1963-65). The principal means of road transport is by public bus. Four-wheel drive and Japanese cars are available for hire. Cars are always hired with driver.

Keeping in touch

Postal services A postal service was introduced in 1962 which covers most of the country. Allow at least 14 days for delivery to Australia and Europe and longer for the Americas. Attractive and highly prized national stamps are sold at the GPO, Thimphu and Philatelic Bureau, Phuntsoling. Courier services, such as DHL, now operate out of Thimphu.

Telephone services Most of the country is now internally connected and international phone calls can be made from all the district headquarters. The connections are excellent and the fax services are also very reliable.

Bhutan international dialling code is 975. *Area codes*: Thimphu and Paro 2; Trongsar, Bumtang and Gelekphuk 3; Mongar, Tashigang and Samdrup Jongkhar 4.

Media *Kuensel* is the only national weekly (English) but international magazines are on sale. BBS is the national radio. BBC and VOA reception is good. Video but no TV.

Food and drink

Food Rice is the staple, eaten with spicy and hot vegetables and meat curries; buckwheat pancakes or noodles, and barley or wheat flour are eaten in some high valleys. Hot chillies and melted cheese (*emadasi*) is the national dish. The Tibetan dishes, dumplings (*momo*), and noodle soup (*thukpa*) are great favourites. Pork and beef are the most common meat; chicken is also becoming popular. Yak meat is the favourite but available only in the winter. Delicious fruits are available in season.

Drink Sweet milk tea, beer and fruit juices are available but no real coffee, only Nescafé. Butter tea is drunk at home for special occasions and local alcoholic drinks (*chang, arak* and *tomba*) are brewed or distilled at home. Bottled mineral water can be bought in the towns. Spirits (whisky, gin, fruit brandies and rum) are produced in Bhutan.

Shopping

Traditional handicrafts, jewellery, baskets, masks, textiles. Paintings and woodcarving make good buys. See Thimphu Shopping above. Get a receipt and please do not attempt to bargain.

There is some spectacular scenery, but if you go during the wet season make sure to **Photography**
protect film against humidity. Carry plenty of films and batteries. No photography
allowed inside temples and dzongs.

Holidays and festivals

Dates of national holidays sometimes vary according to the lunar calendar.   **Holidays**

1999

19 February	Bhutanese New Year	**23 September**	Blessed Rainy Day
27 April	Death Anniversary of Zhabdrung Ngawang Namgyel	**21 October**	Dasain
		2 November	Descent of Lord Buddha from Tushita
2 May	Birth anniversary of the third King	**11-13 November**	Birthday of the present King
2 June	Coronation Day		
21 July	Death anniversary of the third King	**16 December**	Meeting of Nine Evils
17 December	National Day		

Most religious festivals take place in the spring and autumn, see page 877. Check with **Festivals**
your travel agent who is sent a list by TAB, well ahead of time. Only authorized festivals
are listed.

1999

Punakha
Dromcho 20-24 February
Serda 24 February
Chorten Kora
2 March
16-17 March
Gomkora
25-26 March
Paro
Tsechu 27-31 March
Thimphu
Tsechu 20-22 September
Wangdu Phodrang
Tsechu 17-20 September
Tsechu 17-19 December

Trongsar
Tsechu 17-20 December
Bumtang
Tamzhing Phala Chopa 19-21 September
Tangbi Manicham 24-26 September
Jampa Lhakhang 24-28 October
Kurje Tsechu 23 June
Prakhar Tsechu 25-28 October
Mongar
Tsechu 15-18 November
Tashigang
Tsechu 16-19 November
Lhuntse

Useful addresses

Bhutan, in Thimphu: *Bhutan Himalaya Trekking*, PO Box 236, (code 975) T223293, **Tours & tour**
F222897. *BTCL* (Bhutan Tourism Corp Ltd), PO Box 159, T222854, F223392/222479. **operators**
Chhundu Travels, PO Box 149, T222592, F222645. *Ethometho Tours*, PO Box 360,
T223162, F222884. *Lhomen Tours and Trekking*, T/F23243. *Mandala Tours*, PO Box
397, T223676, F223675. *Reekor Tours*, PO Box 304, T222733, F223541. *Takin Tours*, PO
Box 454, T223129, F223130. *Yangphel Tours*, PO Box 326, T223293, F222897. *YuDruk*,
PO Box 140, T223461, F222116.

Nepal: *President Travels & Tours*, Durbar Marg, Kathmandu, T977-1226744.

Shambhala Travels and Tours, Durbar Marg, Kathmandu, T977-1225166, F977-1227229.

India: *Malbros Travels*, 415 Antriksh Bhawan, 22 Kastruba Gandhi Marg, New Delhi, T91-113722031, F91-113723292. *Stic Travel Pvt Ltd*, 6 Maker Arcade (GF), Bombay 400005, T9122-2181431. *Stic Travel Pvt Ltd*, 142 Nungambakkam Sigh Rd, Madras 600034, T91-44475332.

Bangladesh: *Vantage Tours & Travels Ltd*, L-270 Office Arcade, *Sonargaon Hotel*, Dhaka, T880-2326920.

Thailand: *Oriole Travel & Tour Co Ltd*, 10/12-13 SS Building, Convent Rd, Bangkok 10500, T66-22350411/2, F66-22367186.

UK: *Trans Himalaya*, 54 Croscombe Gdns, Frome, Somerset BA11 2YF, T01373-455518, F01373-455594. *Himalayan Kingdoms*, 20 The Mall, Clifton, Bristol, BS8 4DR, T0117-9237163, F0117-9744993. Leading specialist in Bhutan treks, including private itineraries for individuals and groups. *Worldwide Safaris*, Chelsea Reach, 2nd Floor, 79-89 Lots Rd, London SW10 0RN, T0171-3510298. *Karakorum Experience*, 32 Lake Rd, Keswick, Cumbria, CA12 5DQ, T017687-73966.

USA: *Bhutan Travel*, 120E, 56th St, Suite 1430, New York, NY 10022, T212-8386382. *Erickson Travel, Inc*, PO Box 99242, Seattle, USA, T800-208-8129, F206-285-9252, nepal@aa.net. *Geographic Expeditions*, 2627 Lombard St, San Francisco, Ca 94123, T415-9220448, F415-3465535. *Mountain Travel*, 6420 Fairmount Ave, El Cerrito, CA 94530, T415-5278100.

Bhutan Essentials

Districts of Bhutan

Thimphu City ཐིམ་ཕུ

Altitude: 2,350 metres
Population: 35,000
approximately
Phone code: (975) 2
Colour map 2, grid C3

Located 55 kilometres from Paro airport, Thimphu is a relatively new town, having been built by the late King Jigme Dorje Wangchuck to become the new permanent capital from 1955 onwards (the old capital was Punakha). By Bhutanese standards Thimphu is busy and lively, though to an outsider it may appear an uncrowded haven. The population largely comprises civil servants and shopkeepers, although a few families have maintained the traditional agricultural pursuits of the Thimphu valley. The city has seen unprecedented urban development over the recent decades, but the old place names remain, bearing witness to the past history of the valley: Mutigtang (Bh Motithang) and Kawangjangsa to the west; Chang Zamtog, Zamar Zingkhar, Yangchenphuk, and Lungtenphuk to the south, and Zilunkha, Langjuphakha, Hejo, Tagbab (Bh Taba), and Dechen Choling to the north.

Orientation

The major roads through the city run from south to north. **Dechen lam**, the only main road following the east bank of the Thimphu River, runs from the **Simtokha** intersection south of Thimphu to the **Dechen Choling Palace** complex in the far north of the valley. Bridges link this road with the **Chogyal lam** on the west bank or city side of the river at a southern intersection (known as **Lungten Zampa**) near the Bus Station, and also at a northern intersection near the Tashi Chodzong and the new central secretariat building, opposite the dzong.

On the west bank, the principal street is **Nordzin lam**, which is the commercial heart of the city. Nordzin lam is intersected by three roundabouts at its southern, central, and northern points. The southern roundabout (the **Dzogchen lam** intersection) is located near an ornate petrol station, after which the traffic moves through a one-way system, passing grocery stores, the famed Swiss Bakery, and the *Taktsang Hotel*. After the second roundabout (the **Chorten lam/Odzin lam** intersection), the traffic moves in both directions. Shops on the left side include handicraft, textile, pharmaceutical and video-rental stores, as well as the *Hotel Norling*, and the Public Library. On the right side, a large square is delimited by the cinema, a bookshop, and a building housing a small bakery as well as Ethometho Handicrafts and Ethometho Tours and Treks. The Druk Shopping-complex closes the square, and has shops selling imported goods as well as a handicraft outlet and a stamp counter. The Bank of Bhutan and the State Handicrafts Emporium are still further uphill on the right side. The final roundabout (at the **Dobum lam/Desi lam** intersection) marks the north end of Nordzin lam, where the old *Bhutan Hotel* is located, now housing Druk Air, the Bhutanese national carrier. Close by is the Bhutan Chamber of Commerce and Industry. Heading north beyond the *Bhutan Hotel*, on the right there is a golf course and on the left the Bhutan Broadcasting Service, the Telecommunication Office, the Satellite Station, and the National Library. A small road branching from the National Library leads to the Ministry of Education and Health, the Survey Department, the wireless station, the Painting school, Choeki Handicrafts, and the Hospital of Traditional Medicine.

There are a number of parallel streets, located between Nordzin lam and

Chogyal lam (the river road), among which **Odzin lam** is approachable from the second roundabout. Here are the *Druk Hotel*, the *Jomolhari Hotel*, and the *Druk Sherig Hotel*, as well as some smaller travel agencies, a bookshop and a stationer. On **Gaton lam**, which leads downhill from the north end of Odzin lam to the **Changlingmethang** weekend market and the adjacent riverside sport's field, are the *Druktrin Handicrafts* and *Wangchuk Hotel*. Then, on **Drenton lam**, northeast after the second roundabout on Nordzin lam, are the General Post Office, the UN buildings, the Bhutan National Bank and the Police Station, as well as a restaurant.

All three roads branching westwards from the roundabouts on Nordzin lam lead to the **Memorial Chorten**. Among these, on Chorten lam, approached from the second roundabout, there are the *89 Hotel*, the *Yidzin*

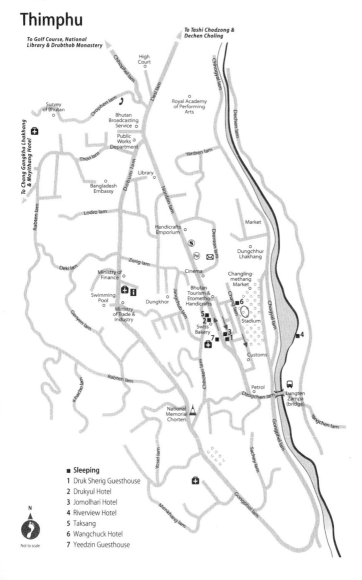

Thimphu

To Golf Course, National Library & Drubthob Monastery

To Tashi Chodzong & Dechen Choling

High Court

Chhophel lam

Desi lam

Chogyal lam

Survey of Bhutan

Drophen lam

Royal Academy of Performing Arts

Bhutan Broadcasting Service

Public Works Department

Dechen lam

To Chang Gangkha Lhakhang & Moyithang Hotel

Thori lam

Dobum lam

Library

Yardren lam

Bangladesh Embassy

Rabten lam

Lodro lam

Nordzin lam

Handicrafts Emporium

Market

Deki lam

Zorig lam

Drenton lam

Dungchhur Lhakhang

Cinema

Changling-methang Market

Ministry of Finance

Swimming Pool

Dungkhor

Bhutan Tourism & Etometho Handicrafts

Jangchhub lam

5

6

Gatön lam

Chogyal lam

Ministry of Trade & Industry

2

Swiss Bakery

7

3

1

Stadium

4

Genyen lam

Customs

Rabten lam

Chorten lam

Petrol

Doegchen lam

Lungten Zampa (bridge)

Khachen lam

Gongphel lam

Tangchen lam

National Memorial Chorten

Yoesel lam

Sechen lam

Menkhang lam

Gongphel lam

N

Not to scale

■ **Sleeping**
1 Druk Sherig Guesthouse
2 Drukyul Hotel
3 Jomolhari Hotel
4 Riverview Hotel
5 Taksang
6 Wangchuck Hotel
7 Yeedzin Guesthouse

Bhutan

Guesthouse, and the Jichudrake Bakery. **Dobum lam**, approached from the third roundabout, is a residential road, where one will also find the Ministry of Trade and Industries, the Tourism Authority of Bhutan, and a swimming pool complex. A southern ring road, called **Gongphel lam**, links the Memorial Chorten with the southern bridge across the Thimphu River, passing through the southern suburbs of Thimphu, known as **Chang Zamtog**. Here are the General Hospital, the Education Department, Save the Children, and the Fire Brigade.

In north Thimphu, the central government buildings of **Tashi Chodzong** are approached, via **Desi lam**, the High Court, and the nine-hole Golf Course (the only one in the country). **Chophel lam**, which demarcates the west side of the Golf course, leads northwards out of town to **Dechen Phodrang**, the original dzong of Thimphu valley (until 1772) and current site of the Central Monastic School. En route, one can visit the **National Library**, where precious Tibetan manuscripts and xylographs are stored, and the Painting School, where traditional tangka painting is taught. **Drubthob Monastery**, a recently reconstructed nunnery, the original 15th century foundation of which is attributed to Tangtong Gyelpo, is located higher up on Ganden lam, on a spur overlooking the Tashi Chodzong.

The western approach roads known as **Ganden lam** and **Thori lam**, run through West Thimphu, where the city's most fashionable residential area, Mutigthang (*Bh* Motithang), has undergone great development in recent years. Here are the new *Motithang Hotel*, the Embassy of Bangladesh, the *Kungacholing State Guesthouse*, and the Mutigtang Zoo. Southeast of Mutigthang, is the **Changangkha Lhakhang**, a celebrated 15th century temple of the Drukpa Kagyu school overlooking the entire city, which can also be approached from the Memorial Chorten (via Rabten lam).

Sights

Tashi Chodzong, the seat of the Bhutanese central government, was originally constructed on its present site in 1772, following the destruction by fire of the previous complex at Dechen Phodrang. Further restorations were carried out in 1870 and 1897 in the wake of natural disasters; and the present sprawling building with its tiered roof was built between 1962-69 using traditional techniques and modelled on the original after Thimphu had been recognized as the permanent capital. The adobe walls are two metres thick in places. Approached by an avenue of fine rose bushes, the **Dzong** is entered via the eastern gate, where ornate frescoes depict the four guardian kings, flanked by the gatekeepers Acala and Hayagriva, and the yogin Drukpa Kun-le. The distinctive Bhutanese architectural style, with its ornately carved wooden columns and ceilings is seen here at its best advantage. A large central tower, housing temples, separates the southern courtyard of the central administration (flanked by the royal offices and the **Secretariat for Religious Affairs** from the northern courtyard of the state clergy. The latter contains the **New Temple** (*lhakhang sarpa*), with its impressive Padmasambhava image, originally constructed in 1907, and the **Monastic Assembly Hall**, with its portico depicting elaborate cosmological diagrams and the Wheel of Rebirth. The lower storey of this latter building functions as the summer headquarters of the Central Monk Authority, and it contains a large image of Buddha Shakyamuni; while its upper storey functions as a state tailoring workshop. The gilded throne room and the King's Headquarters are also here. Half of the Dzong is an active monastery to which non-Buddhists are not allowed when monks are in residence during summer. **NB** This is true of all major monasteries.

Opposite the Dzong and adjacent to the SAARC Building on the other side of the river, a **New Central Secretariat** which also functions as a conference centre has been constructed in traditional style in 1993. The **Chamber of the National Assembly**, is now located here.

Four kilometres north of Tashi Chodzong is the **Dechen Choling** royal palace, where the government goldsmiths and silversmiths may be observed at work. (**NB** Silversmiths are now also at work in Thimphu itself.) En route, it is possible to visit the Forestry Institute at Tagbab (*Bh* Taba). In a meadow further northeast of Dechen Choling is the **Pangri Zampa** temple, where Zhabdrung Ngawang Namgyel first lived following his arrival in Bhutan from Tibet in 1616.

In downtown Thimphu, the most significant building of interest is the **Memorial Chorten**, constructed in 1974 by Dung-se Rinpoche Trinle Norbu, to commemorate the late third king, Jigme Dorje Wangchuck, at the behest of the Royal Grandmother Ashi Phuntsok Chodron. The chorten in its three storeys contains enormous three-dimensional mandalas of deities, representing three of the most important 'treasure-cycles' (*terma*) of the Nyingma school of Tibetan Buddhism, namely: the cycle of *Vajrakila: Dagger of Razor-sharp Meteorite (Phurpa namchak putri)*, which was revealed during the 19th century by Dudjom Lingpa; the cycle of the *Eight Wrathful Meditational Deities: Gathering of the Sugatas (Kabgye deshek dupa)*, revealed during the 12th century by Nyangrel Nyima Ozer; and the cycle of the *Gathering of the Guru's Intention (Lama gongdu)*, revealed during the 14th century by Sangye Lingpa.

The 15th century temple known as **Changangkha Lhakhang** in Southwest Thimphu contains a central image of Avalokiteshvara, and the paintings inside depict, amongst others, Tsangpa Gya-re (1161-1211), the founder of the Drukpa Kagyu school in Tibet.

Essentials

In West Thimphu: the new *Motithang Hotel*, off Thori lam, is small and cozy; and in **Sleeping** South Thimphu, the *Pinewood* has pleasant rooms and a fine view, while the large *Riverview Hotel* is comfortable, though somewhat lacking in character. Further away, the tiny *Sambhara Lodge* in Simtokha has lavishly decorated rooms.

In town: *Jomolhari*, T22747, *Druk*, *Drukyul* (formerly Peling), and *Taksang* hotels are all conveniently located, and all have modern facilities. Above the sports field, the new *Wangchuk Hotel* has beautifully decorated rooms. The smaller family-run *Yeedzin* and *Druk Sherig* are the favourites of frequent visitors and expatriates. The former is now considered to be the best hotel in Thimphu. All these have rooms with attached bath, restaurant, bar, fax, and laundry service. Other more modest downtown hotels include the *89*, the *Tamdrin* and the *Norling*.

All major hotels offer Indian, Chinese, Continental and a few local dishes including the **Eating** fiery *emadasi* (cheese with hot peppers). For *momo*, *chowmien* and *thukpa* the tiny and spartan *Beneez*, *Wangdi*, and *Lhanam*, near the post office, are very good. *89* is the favourite of many for continental and Indian cuisine. For Bhutanese delicacies *Rabten* is the place (on order only). The ever popular *Swiss Bakery*, near the central roundabout, is a good place to meet, serving snacks, fresh pasta, and cakes (closed Sunday); while *Jichudrake Bakery* offers good Viennese-style pastries. *Plum Café*, on the 1st floor of a building overlooking the central roundabout, is the meeting place for civil servants and expats.

Thimphu is very quiet by Western standards, although some local bars stay open **Entertainment** quite late and there are many parties held in private houses. At weekends, mix with the local yuppie crowd at Thimphu's trendiest nightclub in the *Drukyul Hotel* or at the spartan *Club X*. On the traditional side, the *Royal Academy of Performing Arts* holds performances on request.

Shopping Nordzin lam and adjacent streets have rows of neat, traditionally painted shops. Most accept only Bhutanese or Indian currency. Usually open 0800-1900, Monday-Sunday. Closed on Tuesday. There is an interesting market at Changlingmethang on Saturday and Sunday morning.

Books & cards The *DPS Bookshop*, the *Handicrafts Emporium*, *Ethometho Handicrafts*, and *Druktrin Handicrafts*. *Pekhang* in the cinema building, is a 'hole in the wall', but stocks an excellent selection of books, including foreign magazines. *Megah Bookshop*, on Nordzin lam, sells magazines, Western, Bhutanese and Tibetan books, as well as prayer-flags and other new ritual objects.

Imported goods A lot of shops sell toiletries and clothes imported from Thailand and Bangladesh. For foreign alcohol, cigarettes, French wine, chocolates, and other goodies, the duty-free shop has a surprising selection at reasonable prices. An outlet has been opened in the same building as the post office. Payment in dollars only (0900-1600, closed Saturday afternoon and Sunday).

Handicrafts *Handicrafts Emporium*, Nordzin lam, has an extensive range including sculptures, textiles, masks, bamboo and wood work, jewellery, paintings, and books. An excellent choice (including old textiles) is also available at *Druktrin Handicrafts*, a large shop on the 2nd floor of a large building on Gaton lam, and at a good outlet in the *Druk Hotel*. For water-colours on Bhutan, visit the *Yudruk Gallery*, near the *Druk Hotel*. For woodwork, masks, and tangkas, try *Choeki Handicrafts* or the *Painting School*, which has its own shop. For ethnic jewellery, try *Norling Handicrafts* and *Tsering Dolkar*, which are located in the same building on Nordzin lam, opposite the cinema; or *Kelzang Handicrafts* in the Druk Shopping Complex. For exquisite textiles, go to the shop in the *Yeedzin Hotel* or to *Druktrin Handicrafts*; and for Bhutanese music, the *Norling Music Shop*. Next to it are two good jewellery shops, including *Tshering Dolkar Handicrafts*. Some of these shops now accept American Express cards. Otherwise, payment can always be made in Bhutanese currency or US dollars. The handicraft section of the Changlimithang weekend market is also worth a visit, but beware of the prices of the mask seller there!

Health club, beautician, and hairdresser *Sakteng Salon* in the same building as *Druktrin Handicrafts* on Gaton lam. There is also a health-club and a hairdresser in the *Druk Hotel*.

Maps *Pekhang* in the cinema building sells maps of Paro, Thimphu, and others.

Photography Print films and batteries are available at photo shops situated in the basement of the Druk Shopping Complex, as well as at *Photofield* and *Sunrise*. Slide film is not available. Better to carry a sufficient supply of films and batteries. There are processing facilities for prints, but not of a high standard.

Stamps *GPO*, and, for collectors, the *Philatelic Bureau* in the same building. Stamps and postcards are also sold at a small counter inside the Druk Shopping Complex.

Textiles Handwoven textiles are sold in all the handicraft shops at prices ranging from 10 USD to 5,000 USD. The most beautiful selection is available through *Druktrin*

Handicrafts and *Yeedzin Hotel* shop. For Bhutanese machine woven textiles, which are much cheaper, check *Sephu Gyeltshen*, Shop 35, on Nordzin lam, and its outlet in the Druk Shopping Complex, as well as the shop adjacent to *Tsering Dolkar's* handicrafts.

Warning   Do not bargain since prices are generally comparable. An exception might be made in the case of certain outstanding pieces which are highly priced. It is not allowed to buy antiques, and for any purchase, one should always ask for and keep the receipt.

Golf Entrance on Chophel lam, behind Tashi Chodzong. There are also 2 tennis courts, a squash court, and swimming pool. Archery is practised widely, but with such style that it requires some training.   **Sports**

Road Most places of interest are now linked by bus. Private vehicle hire with a driver is possible. Paro (59 kilometres, 1½ hours); Punakha and Wangdu 2 hours; Phuntsoling, 6 hours.   **Transport**

Airline offices *Druk Air*, Nordzin lam, in old *Bhutan Hotel*. **Banks** *American Express*, *Bank of Bhutan*, and *Bhutan National Bank*, 0900-1600. As for credit cards, only *American Express* are accepted at present and only by a very few shops and hotels in Thimphu. Druk Air does not accept payment by credit card. **Hospitals & medical services** *General Hospital*, T22496. **Communications** Couriers & fax: fax machines are available everywhere, and work well. *DHL* have an office at the intersection of Thori lam and Rabten lam, on the way to the new *Motithang Hotel*. **Post Office:** Drenton lam, in the same building at the Bhutan National Bank, 0830-1230, 1330-1630, Sat 0900-1230. **Tour companies & travel agents** See **Essentials** above. **Tourist offices** *Tourist Authority of Bhutan* (TAB), PO Box 126, T23251, F23695.   **Directory**

Bhutan

Western Bhutan

Thimphu district ཐིམ་ཕུ

Area: 1,620 sq km *This is the district named after the Thimphu River, a tributary of the Wang-chu (Raidak), from which the national capital also gets its name. The district administrative capital (dzongkhag) is located in Thimphu city, north of the Changlingmethang market, and beside the river.*

Sights

North of the city Across the river from **Dechen Choling** palace complex is the picturesque monastery of **Pangri Zampa**, built in the early 16th century by Ngawang Chogyel, and the original residence of Zhabdrung Ngawang Namgyel in Bhutan. Some 20 kilometres further north, the motor road abruptly ends, close by the monasteries of **Cheri** (dated 1619) and **Tango** (original construction 13th century, rebuilt 1688). It is from the former that the difficult trekking route to **Lingzhi** in northern Thimphu district begins, crossing the Yele La pass (4,900 metres) via Shodu and Barshong. Lingzhi, largely a nomadic area, contains the ruins of one of the Zhabdrung's non-monastic fortresses at Yulgyel Dzong, close to the Tibetan frontier.

From Pangri Zampa there is an old trekking route (40 kilometres) which leads into the **Punakha** district to the east. The trek climbs through beautiful rhododendron forests via Kabjisa to Sinchu La pass (3,400 metres), and thence downhill via Tonshinkha to Sirigang (1,350 metres), from where there is a motorable road into Punakha.

Simtokha Dzong Five kilometres downstream from Thimphu city, strategically located at the junction of the Paro, Punakha, and Thimphu roads is **Simtokha Dzong** (*srinmo dokha*). Dated 1627, this was the first dzong to be constructed by Zhabdrung Ngawang Namgyel in Bhutan, and since 1961 it has functioned as the national Dzongkha language teacher training centre (foreign tourists not permitted access). The inner sanctum of the dzong's central tower contains large metal images of Shakyamuni Buddha and his foremost disciples Shariputra and Maudgalyayana, flanked by standing images of the Eight Bodhisattvas. Exquisite frescoes depict the Sixteen Elders (*neten chudruk*). The shrines to the left and right of this central temple respectively depict Avalokiteshvara, the bodhisattva of compassion, and the protector deities of the Drukpa Kagyu school.

Walking uphill from Simtokha Dzong, after approximately one and a half hours one will reach **Tala Monastery** (19th century), which offers a spectacular view of the peaks north of Thimphu. The main motorable road east from Simtokha to Punakha climbs rapidly, passing after 15 kilometres the village of Oesepang (from which there is a short trekking route to **Tashigang** nunnery (built 1768), and the police checkpoint at **Hongtso** with its 16th century temple, to **Dochu La** pass (3,050 metres), which from mid-October to February offers spectacular views of the Himalayan snow peaks to the north: Gyelpo Matsen (7,158 metres), Kangphugang (7,170 metres), and Gangkar Punsum (7,497 metres), among others. The road then descends approximately 42 kilometres to **Lobeysa**, giving access to both Punakha and Wangdu Phodrang districts.

West of the city, and approached from Mutigtang (behind the *Motithang Hotel*), there is a trekking route which ascends to 3,700 metres. and **Phajoding** monastery, named after the 13th century Drukpa Kagyu master Phajo Drugom Zhikpo, who frequented this site, where there are two fine 18th century temples. The ridge above (4,100 metres) contains the hermitage of

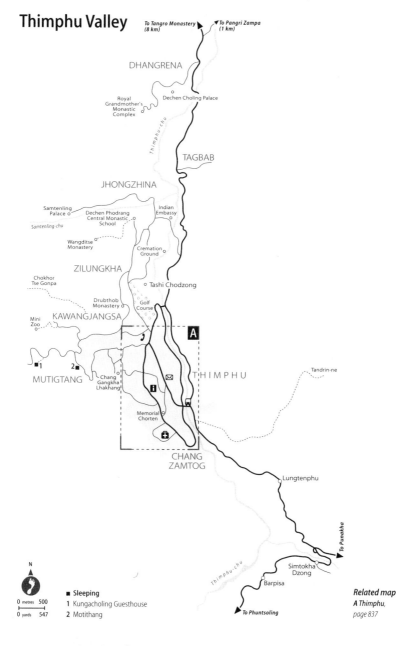

Thimphu Valley

To Tangro Monastery (8 km)

To Pangri Zampa (1 km)

DHANGRENA

Royal Grandmother's Monastic Complex

Dechen Choling Palace

Thimphu-chu

TAGBAB

JHONGZHINA

Samtenling Palace

Dechen Phodrang Central Monastic School

Indian Embassy

Samtenling-chu

Wangditse Monastery

Cremation Ground

ZILUNGKHA

Chokhor Tse Gonpa

Drubthob Monastery

Tashi Chodzong

Golf Course

Mini Zoo

KAWANGJANGSA

A

■1   ■2

MUTIGTANG

Chang Gangkha Lhakhang

THIMPHU

Tandrin-ne

Memorial Chorten

CHANG ZAMTOG

Lungtenphu

To Punakha

Thimphu-chu

Simtokha Dzong

Barpisa

To Phuntsoling

N

0 metres 500
0 yards 547

■ **Sleeping**
1 Kungacholing Guesthouse
2 Motithang

Related map
A Thimphu,
page 837

Thujedra, haunt of the aforementioned master, and give access to the Jimilangtsho lakes.

The motor road west from Simtokha to Paro passes through the conifer forest of **Namseling**, and then follows the Thimphu River gorge downstream to Khasadrapchu and on to **Chuzom**, where it converges with the roads into Paro and Ha districts, as well as those leading to Chukha and Phuntsoling in the south.

Paro district སྤ་རོ

Area: 1,285 sq km *This is the district named after the Paro River, a tributary of the Wang-chu (Raidak), which rises below the snow-peak of Jomolhari on the Tibetan frontier. The administrative capital is located in Paro town.*

Most foreign visitors to Bhutan arrive by air at Paro which has the only airport in the country. Thimphu is a 90 minutes drive away. The tranquil and unpolluted Paro valley is one of the most prosperous in Bhutan, characterized by ornate three-storey farm houses with shingle-roofs and beautiful forests of blue pine. The valley extends from the Wang River confluence at Chuzom, following the Paro-chu upstream to the airport and Rinpung Dzong, from where it divides into two: the main Paro valley leading northwest to Drugyel Dzong and Jomolhari base camp, and **Dopchari**, a very rural side valley. The former is motorable as far as Drugyel Dzong 16 kilometres above Paro town, and the

Paro Valley

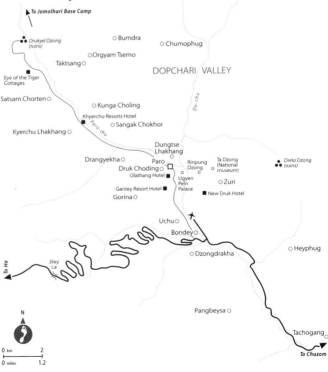

latter has an unpaved 15 kilometres road. The two oldest sites in Paro valley are the seventh century Kyerchu geomantic temple and the eighth century cave hermitage of Taktsang.

The town of Paro situated at the confluence of the Paro-chu and Do-chu valleys, some distance north of the airport, has been under construction only since 1985. The main street is lined by traditional ornately decorated houses, many of which have shop fronts to provide basic supplies to the local populace – cooking utensils, groceries, and so forth. The presence of an archery range testifies to the importance of the national sport of the Bhutanese people; and to its right, there is a lane leading gently uphill toward the impressive cantilever bridge of Paro Dzong, which is strikingly roofed with shingles.

Sights

The vast white **Paro Dzong**, formally known as Rinpung Dzong, dominates the skyline and life of Paro. The original building on this site had been constructed by a descendant of Phajo Drugom Zhikpo, who founded the Drukpa Kagyu school in Bhutan, and it had been the castle of the lords of Humrel until 1645 when it was offered to Zhabdrung Ngawang Namgyel. The following year (1646) the Zhabrung then constructed a more imposing five-storeyed fortress with a covered drawbridge on one wall, and, on the other three walls, dungeons, the narrow window slits of which are clearly visible. For 250 years it served as a bastion against invasions from the north. It burnt down in 1905 and all the treasures except the enormous **Tongdrol tangka** (30 metres x 45 metres) were destroyed. This tangka depicts Padmasambhava flanked by his two foremost consorts and surrounded by his eight manifestations. On the last day of the Paro Tsechu festival, it is unfurled for a few hours and dances are performed in front of it.

The present dzong was built immediately after the fire and has fine woodwork, large sections of logs slotted into each other, held together without any nails. It houses a state-sponsored monastic community of approximately 200 monks; and also functions as the administrative centre of Paro district.

The interior of the dzong (closed at present to foreign visitors) comprises two main courtyards and a central tower. The first courtyard contains administrative buildings, while the second houses the monastic community and an assembly hall, where the main image is that of Jowo Rinpoche and the frescoes depict Padmasambhava, the Buddhas of the Three Times, and Zhabdrung Ngawang Namgyel. The entrance to this assembly hall is decorated with three cosmological diagrams, representing the world according to the view of the *Kalacakra Tantra*, and the *Treasury of the Abhi-dharma*. The central tower (*u-tse*) contains temples dedicated to the masters of the Drukpa Kagyu lineage, to the eight stupas symbolizing major events in the life of Shakyamuni Buddha, and to the meditational deities Havagriva and Tara.

Above the dzong is the largest of the original watchtowers (c 1651), or **Ta Dzong**, which since 1968 has housed the **National Museum of Bhutan**. The building commands an excellent view of Paro Dzong and the valley. The museum has a varied collection of painted scrolls, applique, postage stamps, sculpture and engraving, silverwork, armour, stuffed animals, and traditional articles in daily use, as well as ancient and modern costumes and jewellery. Outside is a collection of iron chains derived from the eight iron bridges constructed in Bhutan by Tangtong Gyelpo. 0900-1600. Closed Monday. Carry a flashlight (erratic electric supply) and allow at least one hour to see all floors.

Paro Dzong

Bhutan

Dungtse Lhakhang The approach road to the National Museum passes in front of **Dungtse Lhakhang**, which lies across the river from Paro town on a geomantic promontory between the Paro and Do rivers. Constructed in 1421 by the celebrated bridge builder Tangtong Gyelpo on the head of a demoness, this temple, like the Memorial Chorten in Thimphu, is located within a stupa. The building was restored in 1841 and is a unique repository of the Buddhist iconography of the Drukpa Kagyu school. The three storeys, connected by a steep ladder, contain precious images and paintings, including: the Buddhas of the Five Enlightened Families, as well as Avalokiteshvara, Padmasambhava, and Tangtong Gyelpo on the ground floor, Mahakala along with the hundred peaceful and wrathful deities on the second floor, and meditational deities such as Guhyasamaja, Vajrabhairava, Cakrasamvara, Hevajra, and Kalacakra on the third floor. Permission needed for a visit; flashlight essential.

On the west bank of the river confluence at Paro, you can catch a glimpse of the lovely **Ugyen Pelri Palace** modelled on the heavenly Zangdokpelri palace of Padmasambhava and built circa 1930 by the then district governor of Paro, Tshering Peljor. Slightly upstream and to the left of the main road is the 16th century temple of **Druk Choding**, and south of that building, close to the *Olathang Hotel* turn-off, is **Gantey Resort**, the splendid former residence of the governors of Paro, now also converted into a hotel.

Kyerchu Lhakhang Heading northwest up the Paro valley, one reaches the two most sacred sites of this district: **Kyerchu Lhakhang**, and Taktsang hermitage. The former, which is presently closed to foreigners, is located a few kilometres north of Paro town and to the left side of the road amid masses of prayer flags. It is revered as one of the four further-taming geomantic temples (*yangdul lhakhang*) built by the Tibetan king **Songtsen Gampo** during the seventh century see above, page 672). Kyerchu is considered to have been constructed specifically on 'the left foot of the supine ogress', who, geomantically speaking, represents the rigours and hostility of the Tibetan landscape, which was to be tamed and civilized by the construction of Buddhist temples at selected power points on its surface. Later in the 13th century, the temple was administered in succession by the Lhapa and the Drukpa Kagyu schools. The gold roof was added in 1830, and in 1839, the site was restored by Sherab Gyeltsen, the 25th Je Khenpo of Bhutan, who commissioned the large central image of Avalokiteshvara. More recently, in 1968, the Queen Mother of Bhutan, had a second temple constructed alongside the original in the same style, but dedicated to Padmasambhava and the eight meditational deities of the Nyingma school, known as the 'eight transmitted precepts' (*kabgye*). The entire complex of buildings is situated within a decorative courtyard. The ancient temple (closed to the public) has murals depicting the 12 deeds and past lives of Shaykamuni Buddha, the Sixteen Elders, the protectors Tsheringma and Genyen Dorje Dradul, as well as Padmasambhava, Zhabdrung Ngawang Namgyel, and the aforementioned 25th Je Khenpo. The images include a celebrated Jowo image similar to that of the Jokhang in Lhasa, flanked by the eight standing bodhisattvas, as well as numerous images of Avalokiteshvara and his emanation, the Tibetan king Songtsen Gampo.

Taktsang hermitage The **Taktsang hermitage** (Tiger's Lair) is located on the face of a sheer 1,000 metres cliff above the Paro valley, and to the right side of the road, some five kilometres north of Kyerchu. It is an impressive sight but far from inaccessible. During the eighth century, Padmasambhava, the great Buddhist master of Oddiyana, is said to have travelled the length and breadth of the Himalayan regions, from Zahor in the northwest through Central Tibet, Nepal, and

Paro Taktsang in Bhutan

Bhutan, as far as Kham and Amdo in Eastern Tibet, establishing Buddhism en route. The sacred sites associated with Padmasambhava include some of the most dramatic and remote power places in the region. Taktsang is one of a number of awesome tiger lairs frequented by this master, who, according to legend, is said to have flown there from **Khenpajong** in Northeast Bhutan on the back of a tigress, in order to subdue negative demons, hostile to Buddhism, through his tiger-riding emanation, known as Dorje Drolod. In 853, one of Padmasambhava's Tibetan students known as Langchen Pelgyi Senge meditated in the main cave at Taktsang, which later came to be known as Taktsang Pelphuk, after his own name. A recently restored stupa at the entrance to this cave contains his mortal remains. Subsequently many great spiritual masters of Tibet passed periods here in profound meditation – notably 11th and 12th century figures such as Milarepa, Phadampa Sangye, and Machik Labdron, and 14th-15th century figures, such as Tangtong Gyelpo.

On the ascent to Taktsang from the road, you can rest at the *Taktsang Tea House*, which has breathtaking views of the hermitage; it serves refreshments, warm lunches, and sells handicrafts. Although horses can be arranged on request, it is better to walk up as Bhutanese saddles are memorably uncomfortable. The beautiful walk up from the motor road, past the **Satsam Chorten** (10 minutes' drive from Paro village; two hours from Thimphu) through oak and pine trees to the *Tea House*, is quite strenuous and usually takes two hours. A further one hour walk climbs steeply to a vantage point above Taktsang, from which a flight of cliff-hanging steps leads down towards the cave (three hours to reach the highest point).

The entire complex of Taktsang includes 13 holy places, and the earliest buildings (no longer extant) were constructed by Sonam Gyeltsen, a 14th century Nyingmapa lama of Katok monastery in East Tibet. Until the site was offered to Zhabdrung Ngawang Namgyel in 1645, it remained under the authority of Katok, and even in recent centuries its close association with the latter have been maintained.

The three temples at Taktsang, dating from 1692, were subsequently restored in 1861-5 and in 1982. However, disaster struck the main building at Taktsang in April, 1998, when a criminal act reduced two of the three temples to ruins, creating a shock-wave inside and outside the country. The government is currently making plans to rebuild these shrines, although their splendid paintings are lost forever. In the meantime, it is still worthwhile walking uphill as far as the small cafeteria.

Among the three temples, the most important and only surviving one is the smallest, containing the sacred cave of Padmasambhava. Here a wrathful image of Dorje Drolod riding the tigress guards the approach to the cave, while adjacent murals depict the meditational deity Vajrakila.

Above this shrine are the ruins of the second temple, which once contained a 'speaking' image of Padmasambhava, smaller images of the temple's founder Desi IV Tendzin Rabgye (1638-96) and Langchen Pelgyi Senge, and a variety of fine murals, depicting Shakyamuni Buddha, Zhabdrung Ngawang Namgyel, Amitayus, the great religious kings of Tibet, and the three cycles of deities (*Kagong Phursum*) which are also depicted three-dimensionally in the Memorial Chorten of Thimphu (see above, page 839).

The third temple, the largest, which has also been destroyed, had a large image of Padmasambhava and murals depicting him surrounded by his eight manifestations, as well as murals of the *Lama Gongdu* and *Vajrakila* cycles. Smaller shrines above this temple contain further images of Dorje Drolod, Amitayus and Kubera.

Orgyen Tsemo The summit of the ridge above Taktsang has three further temple complexes. Among them, **Orgyen Tsemo** with its amazing frescoes of Padmasmabhava and his followers, was a branch of Katok, built in 1408 and restored in 1958. **Ozergang** was constructed in 1646, and **Zangdok Pelri** in 1853. All the sites at Taktsang are visited by pilgrims from Bhutan and the Tibetan Buddhist world, although foreigners are currently only allowed to within 100 metres of the hermitage complex.

Drukgyel Dzong 16 kilometres north of Paro, at the end of the motorable road stands the **Drukgyel Dzong** ('fortress of the victorious Drukpas') built to commemorate victory over the Tibetans in 1644, and to protect the Paro valley from further invasions. The building was ruined by fire in 1951, and in 1985 a shingled roof was added to protect what remained of the building from further ruin. Situated on a hill, it stands against the snow peak of Mount Jomolhari (7,313 metres), protected by three towers and approached only from one direction, and gives the impression of shutting off the Paro valley. Its position ensured that no one could travel on the Paro-Tibet road without being seen. This has long been the most accessible route from Tibet into Bhutan, leading from Phari in the Dromo region across the Tremo La, and directly to Drugyel Dzong.

Tachogang In Southern Paro district, a few kilometres above Chuzom, and on the east
Lhakhang bank of the Paro River, is **Tachogang Lhakhang** – a celebrated temple constructed by Tangtong Gyelpo circa 1420 to commemorate one of his visionary experiences. The river confluence at **Chuzom**, which marks the southern extremity of Paro district, where the roads from Ha and Thimphu also converge, is indicated by three stupas – respectively in Nepalese, Tibetan, and Bhutanese styles.

Trekking in Northern Paro

1 Drugyel There is a demanding trek via Jomolhari Base Camp into Northern Thimphu
Dzong to upper district. It takes around seven days. Best season: late April, May, October. You
Thimphu get excellent views of the mountains and glaciers and pass gorges and waterfalls, cross rivers and see yaks in their pasture and alpine flowers,

rhododendrons and orchids according to the season.

From **Drukyel Dzong** in Paro the path rises steadily for some 12 kilometres up to the ruined **Soi Dzong** at the foot of the **Jomolhari** (7,313 metres), a truly dramatic sight. The base camp at Jomolhari, most sacred of mountains to the Bhutanese, is three days' trekking from Drugyel Dzong. Then the trail crosses a pass at 4,400 metres before descending into Thimphu district to the valley where the hilltop **Lingzhi Dzong** once guarded the frontier with Tibet. From there you have splendid views of the Jichu Drakye (6,974 metres) and Tseringkhang mountains. The path then continues through yak pastures to the Yele La pass (4,900 metres) before descending through the spectacular Wang-chu gorge, up to **Dodina** in the upper part of the Thimphu valley.

2 Paro to Ha via the Cheli La

From Paro, most of the early part of this trek is through dense forest. As you reach Cheli La, broad panoramas of the mountains around Jomolhari open out. Above the forest, the trekking is across yak pastures. There are two important passes, the Kale La and Sage La, both important burial areas. Towards the finish, you will descend into deciduous forest and re-enter the Paro Valley. Although comparatively short (under seven days), the variation in altitude and vegetation plus the rich flora and fauna and stunning views make it an exceptionally good trek in October-November and April.

3 Paro-Thimphu Trek (Druk Path)

Although most people drive from Paro to Thimphu, you can do a three-day easy trek along a path, instead of the road, going through a 3,900 metres pass. It gives the not-so-energetic a wonderful, relaxed insight into Bhutanese life. There are some fine ridge views of the mountains and pleasant stretches through lush forest. In April-May the rhododendrons are in bloom and are a spectacular sight. On the way, there are beautiful lakes and the famous monastery of **Phajoding** (3,058 metres) with its 18th century temples housing art works and paintings, which can also be visited from Thimphu on a day excursion but involves a three hours' climb.

Essentials

Sleeping

Eye of the Tiger cottages opposite Taktsang monastery are simple but very pleasant. *Gantey Resort*, refurbished and located in an old traditional manor opposite the dzong, is charming. *New Druk Hotel*, shaped like a dzong above the airport is very grand. BTCL *Olathang*, in a beautiful hillside setting overlooking valley, 3 kilometres from the village, pleasant rooms with bath in main building and in 14 cottages spread around the large grounds, restaurant, bar, shop. *Khyerchu Resorts*, opposite Khyerchu Lhakhang, on the bank of the river, has recently built cottages in a traditional style. While *Sonam Trophel*, in town, has very good food and modest accommodation.

Shopping

Chencho Handicrafts, on the main square, has a good selection and some unusual objects. There are also outlets for *Handicrafts Emporium* and *Druk Variety Handicrafts*. Another small souvenir shop is located at the airport.

Ha district ལྷ་བདེ / ཧད

Area: 1,707 sq km *This is the district named after the Had (or Lhade) River, locally pronounced as 'Ha', which converges with the Paro and Thimphu tributaries of the Wang-chu (Raidak) at Chuzom.*

The administrative capital is located in **Ha** (2,700 metres) – the only habitation in the district connected by a motorable road. The population is fairly isolated and, for climatic reasons, engaged for the most part in pastoral farming. According to a local legend, the valley was known as Had ('sudden') because two temples, one white and one black, are said to have spontaneously appeared in the valley below Mount Khyungdu (which separates this district from Tibet). The most important Buddhist establishments in Ha are the **Lhakhang Karpo**, linked with Padmasambhava, and the **Gyamdud** monastery, which has had associations with both the Barawa and Drukpa Kagyu schools. Formerly, there was an active trade with Tibet through the valley of the Amo-chu (Torsa), which enters West Bhutan from the Dromo (Chumbi) valley and forms the western boundary of Ha district. A short seven-day trekking route from Paro to Southeast Ha has already been described (see above).

Samtse district བསམ་རྩེ

Area: 1,582 sq km *This is the westernmost district of Bhutan, which shares its north and west borders with Sikkim, and its south frontier with West Bengal.*

The administrative capital is located at **Samtse**. The principal river of this district is the Di-chu (Jaldakha), which enters from Sikkim and flows into West Bengal. The towns of **Sibsu**, **Chengmari**, and **Samtse** which adjoin the Indian frontier have a large Lhotsampa (ie Nepalese) population, while the more remote village of **Dorokha** in the Amo valley borders on Ha, and is home to the Lhopu (Doya) people. Samtse district is known for its industries. The cement factory of Bhutan, the fruit processing plant and the distillery are all located here.

Chukha district ཆུ་ཁ

Area: 1,802 sq km *This somewhat sensitive border district provides Bhutan with its main land access to India in the south.*

Phuntsoling The administrative capital was, until the construction of the Chukha hydroelectric plant, located at **Chukha Dzong**, on the Wang-chu (Raidak) River, not far south of Chuzom, where its three main tributaries converge. Following the recent dam construction and the flooding of the Chukha valley, the capital has been moved south to **Phuntsoling** (*Bh* Phuentsholing), the largest town, on the Indian border, some 141 kilometres from Chuzom. Located three-four hours by road from Bagdogra Airport in West Bengal, and four and a half hours' drive from Chuzom, Phuntsoling is a typical frontier town, situated on the left bank of the Amo (Torsa) River, where Bhutanese, Nepalese, Bengali and Indian cultures meet head on. A traditionally painted gateway welcomes visitors to the Bhutanese frontier post. Commercially it is an important town with small-scale industries (dairy, soft drinks, matches). All imported goods to the capital Thimphu transit through Phuntsoling, so each morning trucks (and buses) roar through the streets. The town is not particularly attractive, but has an interesting mix of population and a definite tropical air. There is a newly constructed **Zangdokpelri** temple, modelled on the palace of Padmasambhava, with images of the latter's eight manifestations at ground level, Avalokiteshvara, on the mid-level, and Amitabha on the uppermost level. These three types of images are representative respectively of the three buddha-bodies.

Sleeping Phuntsoling is the usual night halt for travellers entering Bhutan by road from India. Welcomgroup *Druk*, T2426, and *Namgyel*, PO Box 99, T2293, are the best hotels with good restaurants. For simple accommodation and good Indian meals *Kunga* opposite *Druk* is fine. All are comfortable.

Kharbandi Monastery From Phuntsoling, nestling at the foot of the Himalaya, the spectacular 175 kilometres' drive to Thimphu and Paro via Chuzom reaches altitudes of 3,000 metres. Ascending steeply through teak jungle landscape, the first stop is at **Kharbandi Monastery** above the town at 400 metres, with fine views over the foothills and the Bengal plains. The main temple, constructed in 1967, contains images of Shakyamuni Buddha, Padmasambhava, and Zhabdrung Ngawang Namgyel, as well as paintings depicting the deeds of the Buddha. The complex is encircled by the eight stupas, which symbolize the important events of the Buddha's life. At Kharbandi there is also a police immigration checkpoint, and a technical college.

The road continues to rise through a series of switchback turns, as it leaves the Amo valley behind, and traverses the tropical jungle. At **Gedu** (2,200 metres) there is a truckers stop and a large plywood factory which has now closed. Then, entering the misty and humid Wang-chu valley via Taktichu, where leeches abound during the monsoon season, the countryside becomes sparsely populated. A bridge crosses the Wang-chu adjacent to the Chukha hydroelectric plant, after which the road then rises to **Bunakha**, where the Bhutan Tourism Corporation Ltd has a small restaurant, and the prosperous farming village of **Chapcha**. At Chapcha La pass (2,900 metres) the entire Wang-chu gorge is visible, snaking its way southwards to the Bengal plains. On the descent, the road continues to follow the river through a narrow gorge to Chuzom.

Punakha district སྤུ་ན་ཀ

The administrative capital is located at Punakha, where the Mo-chu and Pho-chu tributaries of the Puna Tsangchu (Sankosh) converge. Area: 974 sq km

Punakha town **Punakha town** is close enough to Thimphu to make a long day-trip feasible. A two hours' drive on the new road crosses the spectacular **Dochu La pass** (3,050 metres) with excellent views of the northern peaks early morning from October to March. The pass is 45 minutes' drive from the Simtokha Dzong turn-off to the south of Thimphu. During the ascent, you will pass through the police checkpoint at **Hongtso**, where a large 16th century temple, **Hongtso Lhakhang**, is located, and where the local populace includes many Bhutanese nationals of Tibetan origin. *Dochu La Café* at the pass serves refreshments. The long 65 kilometres descent to Lobeysa (1,300 metres) traverses both temperate and semi-tropical zones, and takes two and a half hours. The valley here is in a rainshadow area, lower than most midland valleys with a mild climate allowing rice, oranges and a variety of vegetables to be grown. At **Lobeysa**, where the roads to Punakha and Wangdu Phodrang diverge, there is the hill-top **Chime Temple** associated with Drukpa Kun-le, the renowned yogin or 'divine madman' of Bhutan, where infertile Bhutanese women will go on pilgrimage. two kilometres beyond Lobeysa on the Punakha road is the beautifully located *Zandopelri Hotel* opened in 1994. Punakha town (1,350 metres) is located some 10 kilometres further north.

The main site at Punakha is the **Punthang Dechen Phodrang Dzong**, which stands at the confluence of the Pho-chu (Father) and Mo-chu (Mother) tributaries. Built in 1637, the dzong served as the winter capital of Bhutan for 300 years, despite being damaged by fires in the 17th and 18th century, as well as in 1986, and by floods in 1897 and 1994. The present king has commissioned extensive restorations. Even now, it functions as the winter headquarters of the Je Khenpo (Head Monastic Preceptor of Bhutan), and, apart from its courtyard, it is open to foreign visitors only in summer when the monks reside at Thimphu. The original 17th century construction is said to have been predicted by Padmasambhava, who had frequented the site during the eighth century. Within the complex, the first courtyard contains administrative buildings (since the dzong functions as the capital of Punakha district). The second courtyard is occupied mostly by a recently constructed temple, dedicated to the deity Cakrasamvara. A third courtyard contains the large monastic assembly hall, which is still under renovation. The central tower, with its great assembly hall, were chosen as the location for the coronation of Bhutan's first king in 1907. Altogether, there are 21 temples, the most sacred perhaps being the **Machen Lhakhang**, where the body of the Zhabdrung (d 1651) is kept in a reliquary. The principal image is a self-originated Avalokiteshvara in the form known as Kharsapani, which the Zhabdrung himself had brought from Ralung, and which the Tibetan armies had unsuccessfully attempted to retrieve in the 17th century. An annual festival is held at Punakha to commemorate these events during the first month of the lunar calendar.

Gasa district དགའར་ས

Area: 4,409 sq km   *The northern frontier of Gasa is separated from the Khangmar county of Tibet by the formidable Himalayan snow range, which stretches from Mount Gyelpo Matsen (7,158 metres) to Mount Zongaphugang (7,060 metres) and Mount Kulha Kangri (7,554 metres). Local traders still gain access to Khangmar via the frontier passes of Yak La and Phiru La. Bhutan's highest mountain, Gangkar Punsum (7,540 metres) is also located in this district, making the northern reaches attractive to mountaineering expeditions and trekking groups.*

Trekking in Gasa district

1 Punakha to Gasa & Laya   The motorable road ceases 30 kilometres north of Punakha Dzong at Tashinthang in the Mo-chu valley, and from that point onwards, the trekking routes to the northern parts of Gasa district begin. It is possible to undertake an 11-day trek to Laya (3,850 metres), starting and ending in Punakha, with four full days in Laya. The first part of this route leads to **Gasa**, a once thriving market, also in the Mo-chu valley, where yak caravans would congregate. Today, with Tibetan trade being severely curtailed, its role has been considerably diminished. There is a dzong at Gasa, now given Dzongkhak (district) status, which directly administers the northern settlements of Laya and Lunana, and a renowned medicinal hotsprings. **Laya** (3,850 metres), the second highest village in Bhutan, is situated at the foot of Mount Matsang Gyelpo (7,158 metres), and near the source of the Mo-chu. The inhabitants of Laya still worship divinities, which may be related to the Bon pre-Buddhist religion; and guard their villages of painted wooden houses with wood images. Here, yak herders dressed in a very distinctive costume, live and tend their yaks; the women too are more reminiscent of nomadic Tibetan peoples with their long hair and plaited cane pointed hats. You will see herdsmen in blackened yak-hair tents or stone houses, prayer flags and thread crosses, which are offered to demons as ransoms. In the higher reaches there are large flocks of blue sheep, and the takin which is rare elsewhere in the Himalaya. Bears are relatively common, and the guides often make a lot of noise so as not to take them by surprise. Best season: spring and autumn. The monsoon is to be avoided owing to the overwhelming number of leeches between Punakha and Gasa. The Laya trek can be combined with the Jomolhari trek (see above, page 872), which makes a strenuous 15-day trek crossing several 4,000 metres passes into Paro.

One of the most difficult treks of all, this takes 18 days, and is for the very fit, experienced trekker as it crosses five passes over 5,000 metres. The trail goes first from Punakha to **Laya** (see above) in four days. Beyond Laya, there is a demanding three-day trek, traversing the **Gangla Karchung Pass** (5,100 metres), which is the first of the three steep passes over 5,000 metres offering superb views of the East Himalaya. Descending to **Woche** (3,850 metres) in the beautiful northern region of Lunana, near the source of the Pho-chu, you trek for two days through **Thega**, **Chozo Valley** with its dzong, and to the regional capital **Thanza** (4,050 metres). A further five days' trek to the south crosses **Rinchenzo La pass** (5,220 metres) to intersect with the motor road at **Nikarchu Bridge** where you can get transport back to Thimphu or Trongsar. The mountain views, particularly those of Mount Gangkar Punsum (7,239 metres), are spectacular and you pass lakes, glacial rivers, moraines, beautiful forests with Himalayan birds and flower-filled alpine meadows. Uncertain weather conditions add to the difficulty of this trek. Best season: August-September. Difficult as it is, some intrepid trekkers prefer to extend the Lunana trek to over 21 days, by combining it with the Jomolhari trek – altogether 356 kilometres, crossing eight high passes, sometimes known as the 'snowman trek'.

(margin note) **2 Punakha to Gasa, Laya & Lunana**

(margin, vertical) Bhutan

Wangdu district དབང་འདུས

The administrative capital is located at Wangdu Phodrang (Bh Wangduephodrang). The northern extremity of Wangdu district, which borders the Lhodrak county of Tibet, includes the headwaters of the Mangde-chu; but the greater part of the district comprises the mid-reaches of the Puna Tsang-chu (Sankosh) valley, along with those of its Dang-chu and Hang-chu tributaries. In the east of the district the Black Mountains form a watershed between the main rivers of West and East Bhutan.

(margin note) Area: 4,038 sq km

At Lobeysa to the south of Punakha, there is a southerly turn-off for **Wangdu Phodrang** (nine kilometres distant), which is sometimes referred to as the gateway to Central and East Bhutan. The large dzong, constructed 1638-83, stands impressively on a rocky outcrop, and strategically dominates the main roads which intersect below it: those to Punakha and Thimphu in the north, Tsirang in the south, and Trongsar in the east. It is said that the protector deity Mahakala appeared in a vision to Zhabdrung Ngawang Namgyel, exhorting

(margin note) **Wangdu Phodrang**

Bhutan

him to build a fortress on a rocky spur where ravens fly off in all four directions. Hence the name Wangdu Phodrang ('palace gathering all within its power'). The dzong, which is only open to foreign visitors during the annual Tsechu ceremony, contains the administrative centre for the whole district, as well as a monastic assembly hall containing large images of the Buddhas of the Three Times. The town at Wangdu is currently under construction. Local handicrafts include bamboo work, as well as stone and slate carving.

Sleeping In town, a small, spartan *Guest House*, with 6 clean rooms, some with bath, simple meals, camping on lawn, suitable overnight stop for trekkers. The *Dragon Nest Resort*, which is beautifully located along the river, has 17 rooms with attached bathroom. The lovely *Dechen Cottages* in Mendegang, are 15 kilometres before Wangdu, on the Thimphu road.

Eating The *Black Crane Restaurant* is recommended.

The Black Mountains From the crossroads at the bridge below Wangdu Phodrang, it is a 129 kilometres (three and a half hours' drive) to Trongsar in Central Bhutan, a 71 kilometres (two and a half hours' drive) to Thimphu, or a four hours' drive to Tsirang in the south. Taking the central road, you drive due east via **Chuzomsa** and **Tikke**, and ascend into the Black Mountains. The entire region of the **Black Mountains** is the preserve of nomadic yak-herders and shepherds; and there is a Dairy Research Station in the isolated valley of **Gogona**.

Ganteng Gonpa Seven kilometres after the small village of Nobding on the Wangdu-Trongsar road, there is a turn-off to the right which leads into the glacial **Phobjika valley** (3,000 metres). This truly spacious valley, unusual in Bhutan but reminiscent of many in Tibet, is the location of the beautiful **Ganteng Gonpa** (*Bh* Gantey Gonpa), the only monastery of the Nyingma school of Tibetan Buddhism on the west side of the Black Mountains. The complex was founded in 1613 by Pema Trinle, a grandson of the treasure-finder Pema Lingpa, and now has five temples within its central tower. Here the liturgies of Pema Lingpa's tradition are maintained by the monks and by the married Buddhist practitioners, whose families inhabit the large village which surrounds the monastery. The Phobjika valley is also the winter haunt of the amazing black-neck crane, which migrates here from Central Asia and can be seen circling above the fields from November-March. The higher pastures above the valley are ideal for yaks who subsist on the high-altitude dwarf bamboo which grows in abundance. For those wishing to avoid the motor road, there is an easy three to four days' trek from Phobjika valley, where you see the beautiful Ganteng monastery, down to **Wangdu Phodrang**, passing through small villages and splendid forests of giant junipers, daphne bushes, rhododendrons and magnolia. The rhododendron season (April) is highly recommended, since you can then see hundreds in bloom.

Sleeping *Thekchen Guesthouse* has basic ammenities.

Nikarchu Returning to the main road, the drive continues eastwards through rhododendron and magnolia forest for 14 kilometres to the watershed at **Pele La** pass (3,300 metres), which in clear weather offers a splendid view of Jomolhari to the northwest. On the far side of the pass, the road descends near the large village of Rukubji to the bridge at **Nikarchu**, from where the trekking route to Lunana can be reached (see above). Beyond Nikarchu, you pass out of Wangdu and into the Trongsar district of Central Bhutan.

The southern road from the bridge at Wangdu follows a newly constructed motor route into Tsirang.

Tsirang district རྩེ་རང་

The administrative capital of Tsirang is located at Damphu. This district, which Area: 639 sq km
lacks an external frontier, is now linked by a recently constructed motor road
which follows the course of the Puna Tsang-chu (Sankosh) with Wangdu
Phodrang in the north and Khalikhola on the Indian frontier. Its major villages:
Damphu, *Lamidangra, and Dagapela are in the heart of the orange and carda-*
mom growing part of the country, and the population is predominantly
Lhotsampa.

Bhutan

Takar district སྤུག་དགར་

The administrative capital is located at Takar (Bh Dagana) on the Takar-chu, a Area: 1,389 sq km
tributary of the Puna Tsang-chu, which rises east of Chuzom. Like Tsirang, this
district is also known for its orange and cardamom plantations, but the
motorable road, often destroyed by monsoon rains, has ensured its isolation.
During the 18th and 19th centuries, this district was the seat of a powerful
governor.

Central Bhutan

A trip to Central Bhutan allows you to discover diverse aspects of the country but be prepared for long drives and rustic comfort at the lodges. Allow about 10 days for a worthwhile trip. From June-September the roads are sometimes blocked by landslides. The districts comprised within Central Bhutan are those of Trongsar and Bumtang in the north, and those of Gelekphuk and Shemgang in the south.

Trongsar district སྒྲོང་གསར

Area: 1,807 sq km   *The administrative capital is located at Trongsar (Bh Trongsa). Bounded on the west by the Black Mountains, which form a watershed between West and East Bhutan, this district corresponds to the valley of the Mangde-chu, an important tributary of the Drangme-chu (Manas), rising below Mount Gangkar Punsum.*

Trongsar Dzong   The central motor road, constructed in 1985, links Wangdu with Trongsar. After the descent from Pele La pass to Nikarchu (see above), you enter into the district of Trongsar, and drive through a narrow gorge to **Chendebji Chorten**. Here, there are two stupas: the older in Nepalese style, which was constructed in 18th century by Lama Shida for geomantic purposes, and the more recent one in Bhutanese style, which dates from 1982. On leaving the gorge, the road then follows the Mangde-chu, and descends dramatically along the edge of a sheer precipice into **Trongsar**, which is visible some 20 kilometres below. At 2,200 metres, and 130 kilometres east of Wangdu Phodrang, **Trongsar Dzong** is the largest and most impressive dzong in Bhutan, standing on a spur above the deep Mangde gorge and dominated by a two-wing watchtower ('Ta Dzong'), from which all approaches could be monitored with ease. The original dzong was established by the Zhabdrung in 1647 on the site of a temple founded by his great-grandfather in 1543. Subsequently enlarged in 1652 and 1771, it has also been damaged by an earthquake (1897), and repaired in the present century. This huge, many-levelled fortress has a maze of courtyards and covered passages, and 23 temples, among which those dedicated to Maitreya, Yamantaka, Hevajra, and Kalacakra are most important. A stupa shrine stands on the site where the original 16th century temple once stood; and there is an active printing press, utilizing the traditional xylographic method. The monastic community of Trongsar moves in summer to **Kurje Monastery** in Bumtang.

During the 19th century, Trongsar was the seat of the most powerful governor of the country, commanding the whole of the central and eastern region. One of these governors (*Trongsar Ponlop*), Ugyen Wangchuck, became the first hereditary King of Bhutan in 1907, for which reason the dzong at Trongsar is revered as the ancestral home of Bhutan's royal family (tourists need a permit to visit).

The new village of Trongsar above the dzong has been under construction since 1982. The shopkeepers of this community, perched on the mountainside, are largely Bhutanese of Tibetan origin.

Sleeping   BTCL *Sherubling Lodge*, near the school, has 6 simple heated rooms and 6 cottages with bath, limited catering. *Yangkhyil* in town is simpler but great for excellent meals in its warm kitchen. The *Nidakarsum Hotel*, next to the Yangkhyil, and in the same style, is also pleasant. The newly built *Norling Hotel* is the only one in town offering rooms with attached bathrooms.

The road from Trongsar to Bumtang extends eastwards for 29 kilometres, as far as **Yuto La** pass (3,400 kilometres), which marks the border between Trongsar and Bumtang districts. En route you will have a stunning view of the Trongsar Dzong before entering the forested approach to the pass. — Yuto La

The southern road from Trongsar follows the Mangde-chu downstream before cutting westwards to Gelekphuk on the Indian frontier, some 237 kilometres distant. For the first 15 kilometres this road runs parallel to the Wangdu road, before turning southeast. **Kunga Rabten**, the winter palace of Bhutan's second king lies beside this road, 20 kilometres south of Trongsar. Farming villages are to be seen by the roadside but further south the gorge narrows. The road plunges down to 1,400 metres, passing through a wild uninhabited region. — Kunga Rabten

Bhutan

Shemgang district གཞལ་སྒང་

The administrative capital is located at Shemgang, some 107 kilometres south of Trongsar on a wind-exposed ridge above the Mangde-chu gorge. The district is characterized by its forested mountain slopes, where the Mangde-chu and Bumtang-chu tributaries of the Drangme-chu (Manas) cut deep gorges, interspersed occasionally with random rice growing areas. Most of Shemgang district may be considered as a botanical paradise, in that it contains carnivorous plants, rare species of orchid, and so forth. Descending from 1,900 metres in the north to 200 metres in the south, the land is covered by tropical forests, yielding most of Bhutan's bamboo and rattan produce, as well as bananas, mangoes, edible roots, and so forth. — Area: 2,116 sq km

The first temple to be constructed on the site of the recently reconstructed **Shemgang Dzong** dates from a foundation established by the Tibetan lama Drogon Shangkyeme in 1163. The whole of Shemgang and Mongar districts formerly belonged to the ancient region of **Khyeng**, where the inhabitants speak Khyeng-ka, a distinctive dialect of Bumtang-ka. At **Nabji** village near Shemgang an ancient pillar said to be commemorating an eighth century treaty between King Sendhaka and King Nawoche attests to the antiquity of this region. A number of the principalities or enclaves of Khyeng, which are nowadays incorporated within Shemgang district, such as **Buli** and **Nyakhar**, successfully maintained their autonomy until their absorption into the Bhutanese state during the 17th century. These sites, however, are fairly inaccessible in that they are not connected by motorable routes. After passing through Shemgang Dzong, the main road leaves the Mangde-chu valley to enter Sarpang district.

Sarpang district གསར་སྒང་

*The administrative capital is located at **Sarpang** on the Indian border, 237 kilometres from Trongsar. This district is one of the four which, between them, extend along the entire length of the southern border, and it encorporates within it* — Area: 2,288 sq km *important border towns, such as **Kalilkhola**, giving road access to Wangdu via the Puna Tsang-chu (San-kosh) valley; Sarpang, giving road access to Shemgang and Trongsar, and the trading centre of **Gelekphuk**. The landscape is similar to that of Shemgang district, but the population is largely Lhotsampa.*

Bumtang district བུམ་ཐང

Area: 2,714 sq km

*The administrative capital of Bumtang is located at Jakar. Bumtang (Bh Bumthang) is the name given to a complex of four sacred valleys which are often regarded as the religious or cultural heart of Bhutan. The district follows the course of the Bumtang-chu, from its sources around Lhedam near the Lhodrak Tibetan border and downstream towards its confluence with the Mangde-chu in Shemgang district. In its mid-reaches there are four rivers which converge to form the 'vase-shaped' bulge of Bumtang, namely: the Chamkhar-chu (the main river) which forms the **Chokhor** valley; the Chume-chu which forms the **Chu-me** valley; the Tang-chu forming the **Tang** valley; and the Ura-chu forming the **Ura** valley. All these valleys are wide and gently sloping, offering a sense of spaciousness, almost unequalled elsewhere in the country. Among them, Chokhor and Chu-me are agricultural, while Tang and Ura are largely pastoral valleys. Bhutan's highest mountain, Gangkar Punsum (7,540 metres) is also located on the border of this district with Wangdu. Tibet is reached through the Monla Karchung pass (currently closed). Though accessible by road, most of the interesting temples and beautiful monasteries are only accessible to trekkers. It is also a fantastic area for day-walks. With beautifully painted wooden house façades, it looks best in the autumn when the buckwheat paints the fields deep orange.*

Bumtang is the stronghold of the Nyingmapa school in Bhutan, chiefly on account of the activities of three important Nyingmapa lamas of the 14th and 15th century: Longchen Rabjampa, Dorje Lingpa, and Pema Lingpa – the last of whom was actually born in Bumtang. The construction of the motor road and the implementation of development projects through Swiss, Austrian, and Indian government aid have brought a new prosperity to this once isolated rural area. The following account describes the sights of Bumtang, following the course of the motor road in succession through the valleys of Chu-me, Chokhor, Tang and Ura.

Chu-me Valley

After crossing the **Yuto La** pass on the drive eastwards from Trongsar (see above), you enter the broad 18 kilometres long Chu-me valley (2,700 metres) at **Gyetsa**. The land is fertile, yielding crops of wheat, barley, potatoes, and the local staple buckwheat. To the left of the road you will see **Buli Lhakhang**, a shrine established by descendants of Dorje Lingpa in 15th century, and **Samtenling**, one of the monasteries founded by Longchen Rabjampa during his 10 years exile in Bumtang. Higher up the hillside is **Tharpaling**, also founded by Longchen Rabjampa in 1352. Its lower floor has images of Padmasambhava, Longchen Rabjampa, Trisong Detsen, and Jigme Lingpa; while the upper storey has images of Samantabhadra, Padmasambhava, and Longchen Rabjampa; as well as splendid paintings depicting Sukhavati paradise, and so forth. The communal hall of an adjacent school (built 1985) has paintings depicting the lineage of Longchen Rabjampa. Above Tharpaling is **Chodrak**, a monastery of the Drukpa Kagyu school, originally dating from the time of Lorepa (1187-1250) but renovated only in 18th century by Ngawang Trinle.

Continuing down the Chu-me valley, you pass on the right side of the road the summer palace of Bhutan's second king, **Domkhar Tashicholing**, and the hydroelectric power station at **Chorten Nyingpo Lhakhang**, a Drukpa Kagyu temple founded in 1587. Towards the lower end of the valley, the village of **Zug-ne** is famous for its reputedly seventh century geomantic temple (with a central image of Vairocana Buddha) and its woven woollen fabrics. The nearby **Trakar** (*Bh* Prakar) or 'white monkey' temple contains the embalmed remains of Lama Dawa Gyeltsen, the son of Pema Lingpa, whose incarnation lineage has played an important role in the Buddhist tradition of Bumtang and the Lhodrak region of Tibet to the north. At **Nyimalung Monastery** (b 1900) the monastic discipline and liturgies of the Nyingma tradition are particularly renowned. Reaching the lower extremity of Chu-me valley, the road crosses Kiki La pass (2,900 metres) to enter Chokhor valley.

Chokhor Valley

From **Kiki La** pass, the entire breadth of Chokhor valley is visible on a clear day. The short nine kilometres descent brings you to **Jakar Dzong** ('White Bird Fortress'), the administrative capital of the whole Bumtang district, altitude 2,800 metres. The village of Jakar which occupies the plains below the dzong is currently undergoing rapid urbanization (by Bhutanese standards), and there are many small shops, mostly owned by Bhutanese nationals of Tibetan origin. A bridge spanning the Chamkhar-chu carries the motor road eastward into Tang, Ura, and East Bhutan. Jakar Dzong was constructed by

Bumtang Valleys

Zhabdrung Ngawang Namgyel in 1646 on the site of an earlier 16th century Drukpa Kagyu monastery. Subsequent rebuilding was undertaken in 1683 and more recently in 1905. It is an elegant building, with a central tower (containing a Maitreya temple) separating the administrative and monastic courtyards. The monastic assembly hall has an image of the meditational deity Vajrakila, while a second temple contains images of the Drukpa Kagyu lineage holders.

On the left side of the road below the dzong is **Jakar Lhakhang**, a Nyingmapa temple founded by Dorje Lingpa in 1445, while four kilometres above the dzong to the northwest is **La-me Monastery**, a 19th century building which served as a royal residence and more recently as home to the Forest Institute, but which is today partially destroyed due to the excessive rotting of its wooden structure. Following the west bank of the Chamkhar-chu upstream, you pass by a Swiss dairy farm (where you can buy authentic swiss cheese, honey, and alcoholic fruit drinks), and a mechanical workshop. The **Wangdu Choling Palace** (built 1856) is renowned as the birthplace of the first king's father, and the gardens now contain a splendid tourist guesthouse in traditional design. Upstream from the palace and beyond the archery range is the Bumtang hospital, which was built with Swiss aid in 1988-89, and the **Chakhar** ('iron castle') residence of the eighth century king Sendhaka.

Jampa Lhakhang The most ancient of all the temples in Bumtang is probably the seventh century **Jampa Lhakhang** (permission needed), which like Kyerchu in the Paro valley, was a geomantic temple constructed by the Tibetan king Songtsen Gampo, this time on the 'left knee of the ogress'. It is said that when Padmasambhava taught Buddhism to King Sendhaka during the eighth century, he did so from the temple roof. The original temple contains a large image of Maitreya, flanked by the eight standing bodhisattvas, four on each side. Later 19th century shrines at Jampa Lhakhang include the **Kalacakra Temple**, the **Guru Lhakhang** (with images of Padmasambhava, Avalokiteshvara, and Amitayus), the **Sangye Lhakhang** (with images depicting the Seven Generations of Past Buddhas), and the **Chorten Lhakhang** (dedicated to the relics of a Karma Kagyu lama who passed away in 1940).

Kurje Lhakhang North of Jampa Lhakhang is the **Kurje Lhakhang** (permission needed), named after the site where Padmasambhava is said to have left the imprint of his body in rock. The site has three temples forming a grand complex reminiscent of Samye in Tibet, and is occupied in summertime by the monks of Trongsar Dzong, who hold their annual Tsechu ceremony here. The oldest temple dating from 1652 contains images (upstairs) of the Buddhas of the Three Times, and (downstairs) the cave containing the body imprint and images depicting the Eight Manifestations of Padmasambhava. An upstairs carving depicts the subjugation of the demon Shelging Karpo by Padmasambhava in the form of a garuda bird, which is said to have occurred at this site.

The second temple contains an enormous 10 metres image of Padmasambhava flanked by his eight manifestations, and the third was newly consecrated in 1990. In front of the complex are the **three funeral chortens** of the three past kings of Bhutan. The whole complex is enclosed by a wall of 108 stupas.

Thangbi Lhakhang, one and a half hours' walk above Kurje was founded by Zhamar IV of the Karma Kagyu school in 1470. It contains images of the Buddhas of the Three Times (downstairs) and of Jowo Rinpoche (upstairs), as well as a large shrine room dedicated to the protector deities.

Following the east bank of the Bumtang-chu upstream from Jakar Dzong, you drive past **Konchoksum Lhakhang**, where there is a celebrated bell with an eighth century inscription, linking it to the royal family of Tibet. The main image is Vairocana Buddha, flanked by Padmasambhava, and Avalokiteshvara, as well as later Nyingmapa masters such as Longchen Rabjampa and Pema Lingpa.

Further north is **Tamzhing Lhakhang**, which was founded in 1501 by Pema Lingpa and maintains the liturgical traditions and spiritual practices of Pema Lingpa at the present day. Long regarded as a branch monastery of **Lhalung**, the residence of the Peling Sungtrul incarnations in Lhodrak, this temple has been revitalized by an influx of Tibetan refugee monks from Lhalung in 1959. It contains (downstairs) images of Padmasambhava and his eight manifestations, and (upstairs) Amitayus. The paintings of Tamzhing are particularly renowned: especially those of the ground floor vestibule, which are among the oldest surviving paintings in Bhutan. The new temple of **Namkhe Nyinpo** above Jakar town has splendid paintings.

Tang Valley

After crossing the bridge at Jakar, the main road swerves southwards, following the east bank of the Bumtang-chu downstream for five kilometres, and then turns northeast as far as the sheep-breeding farm of **Dechen Pelrithang**, altitude 2,800 metres. At this point there is an unpaved turn-off on the left, which leads into the narrow gorge of the Tang valley. The land here is more suited to sheep farming and has been left fairly undeveloped. The most famous site in Tang is **Mebartsho** gorge, where Pema Lingpa is said not only to have discovered *terma* from its depths, but to have done so in public, holding an oil lamp in his hand which remained burning as he emerged from the waters with his treasure! Hence the name of the site Mabartsho ('Blazing Fire Lake'). Pilgrims can still be seen here placing small lighted lamps on the river.

In a recessed cliff, some one and a half hours' walk uphill from Mebartsho, you can visit **Kungzandra Monastery**, founded in 1488 by Pema Lingpa on a site formerly consecrated by Padmasambhava and his student Namkei Nyingpo in person. There are three temples: the **Wangkhang** dedicated to Avalokiteshvara; the **Ozerphuk** dedicated to Pema Lingpa's son Dawa Gyeltsen, who meditated in the grotto here; and the **Khandroma Lhakhang**, containing a gilded copper image of Pema Lingpa.

Driving upstream, you reach the **Rimochen Temple**, founded by Dorje Lingpa and named after the markings left on a large rock by Padmasambhava. The motorable road has its terminus at **Ugyen Choling**, a 19th century palace built on the site of an earlier hermitage, once sanctified by the presence of both Longchen Rabjampa and Dorje Lingpa. A four-hour walk upstream from this point brings you to **Thowadra Monastery** (3,400 metres), occupied since the late 18th century by the followers of Jigme Lingpa and Jigme Kundrol, who maintain the *Longchen Nyingthig* tradition. The site marks the entrance to **Khenpajong**, a "hidden and sacred land" consecrated by Padmasambhava to the east of Lhedam in North Bumtang and in Lhuntse district.

Ura Valley

Ura is the highest of Bumtang's four valleys, and the road climbs from Tang in a series of switchback bends through open countryside. The approach to Ura La pass (3,600 metres) offers a splendid view of Bhutan's highest peak, Mount Gangkar Punsum. **Ura** village (3,100 metres) consists of closely built shingled

Kuje Temple in
Bumtang, Bhutan

houses, where the community subsists on the basis of pastoral farming and the potato crop. The Ura Lhakhang, built in 1986 and dedicated to Padmasambhava, contains beautiful paintings of the Nyingma school and is worth visiting. The **Shingkar** monastery, founded by Longchen Rabjampa circa 1350, is 30 minutes' drive on an unpaved surface from the main road.

Trekking in Bumtang district

The four valleys of Bumtang give the visitor an opportunity to explore the remote countryside of Central Bhutan where life has remained virtually unchanged for centuries. You can watch people producing baskets, weaving on traditional looms or making hand-made paper from daphne bark. One easy five to six days' trek which remains below 3,500 metres, starts near **Kurje Lhakhang**, and follows the Chamkhar-chu upstream to the old temple of **Ngang Lhakhang**, before crossing a pass into the Tang valley at **Ugyen Choling**. This trek offers sufficient time for the visitor to see the most important sites of the Chokhor valley, which have already been described: Jampa Lhakhang, Kurje Lhakhang, and Tamzhing Lhakhang foremost among them. Note that most of the temples require a permit to be visited. Best season: April-May, late September to mid-November.

Sleeping **In Jakar**: the *Mountain Lodge*, the *UD Guesthouse*, the *Tshering Guesthouse*, and the *Village Lodge*, the last of which is recommended for its service and excellent pool. The lovely BTCL *Wangdu Choling Lodge*, near an old 19th century palace is full of charm with its painted bungalows and its large elaborately decorated dining room, simple meals (Continental and Bhutanese), handicrafts shop. *Swiss Guest House*, above the Swiss Farm at Karsunphe, recently reconstructed, has a cosy atmosphere. *Tamzhing Guesthouse*, near Tamzhing monastery, has 8 rooms, and a delightfully peaceful atmosphere. **In Ura**: the *Shingkar Village Guesthouse* has 6 simple rooms. **NB** Electricity supply is still erratic in Bumtang.

MONGAR DISTRICT **863**

East Bhutan

The best time for a trip east is April/May and October/November. The east is wonderful in winter as it is warmer than West Bhutan but there can be snow on the road from Bumtang to Mongar. The region is more densely populated (with the exception of the extreme northeast), broadly corresponding to the valleys of the Kuru-chu and Tawang-chu tributaries of the Drangme-chu (Manas).

Mongar district མོང་འགར་

The administrative capital of the district is located at Mongar in the valley of the Kuru-chu. In the eastern part of the district, where the people speak Tsangla (Sharchopkha dialect), the Drangme-chu flows through Damotse (Dametsi). The two rivers converge in the extreme south of the district, where the Khyeng-ka dialect is prevalent.

Area:1,947 sq km

After leaving Ura valley in Bumtang, the road ascends through conifer forest to the **Tumsing La** pass at 3,800 metres. From there in three hours you make a dramatic descent to **Namning** (only 700 metres) and a semi-tropical area; it is a spectacular drive, as the road in places is dug out of the precipitous cliffs. Village houses have roofs made of bamboo matting, and the staple crop is maize. After crossing the Kuru-chu at 650 metres, the road climbs again for 13 kilometres to reach the town of Mongar (1,700 metres), 141 kilometres from Ura. On the ascent there is a turn-off on the left for Lhuntse in Northeast Bhutan.

Mongar (1,600 metres) is a small, sleepy town built across the open hillside, with a lovely dzong, constructed in 19th century and rebuilt in 1953. As with other dzong, it combines both administrative and monastic functions, housing within it two temples. Prior to its construction, the main dzong of the district was situated to the west of the Kuri-chu river at the low-lying **Shongar Dzong** (now in ruins). The town has a number of shops and an excellent hospital.

The best accommodation in Mongar is to be found at the BTCL *Shongar Lodge* near the dzong. This simple guesthouse is basic, with electricity and water supply still erratic. Also in town, is the *Druk Kuendun Guesthouse*.

Sleeping

Try the *Samling Restaurant* in town.

Eating

From Mongar you can take a three-day side trip to **Lhuntse Dzong** (described below), or drive straight to **Tashigang**. The latter road reaches the eastern border of Mongar and Tashigang districts, over a 70 kilometres' drive. At first it ascends through forested terrain to Kori La pass (2,450 metres), and thereafter descending through **Yadi** village, it cuts a series of switchbacks in the hillside to reach the Tawang-chu (Manas), also known as the Gamri-chu. Following that river upstream, you could then drive 15 kilometres on a winding dirt-track road to **Dramitse Urgyen Choling**, the largest monastery of East Bhutan, which was founded in the late 16th century by a female descendant of Pema Lingpa known as Chodron Zangmo. The monastery has undergone various phases of restoration, and its central tower contains temples dedicated to

Dramitse Urgyen Choling

Bhutan

Padmasambhava and the Sisters of Longevity, the Tsering Chenga, who are important protectors. At Dramitse there are both monastic and lay communities of Buddhist practitioners.

The southern part of Mongar district, where the Kuru-chu and Drangme-chu rivers have their confluence, is isolated and as yet unconnected by motorable roads. It is a region where the Khyeng-ka dialect predominates.

Lhuntse district ལྷུན་རྩེ

Area: 2,888 sq km

The administrative capital is at Lhuntse, near the confluence of the Kuru-chu with its Khoma-chu tributary. This densely populated district, formerly called Kurto ('upper Kuru-chu valley') is inhabited by people speaking a dialect of Bumtang-ka. Its mountain villages are known for their fine weaving and the village women spend most of their days at the loom. The steep terrain is really suitable for exploring on foot.

The northeast of the district (out of bounds for foreigners) is occupied by the sacred "hidden land" of **Khenpajong**, and the northern border at **Ngortong Zampa** has easy access to the Lhodrak region of Tibet, in that the Kuru-chu which it spans flows directly through that part of southern Tibet into Bhutan. The meagre cross-border traffic is monitored from **Senge Dzong** in the mid-reaches of the Kuru-chu. Further northeast, Phode La pass (4,965 metres) separates Bhutan from the **Kharchu** hillside of Lhodrak in Tibet. The Kings of Bhutan originally come from Dungkar village in the north of Lhuntse district where a descendant of Pema Lingpa settled.

The motor road from the turn-off at Lingmitang below Mongar heads northwards into Lhuntse district, following the forested Kuru-chu gorge upstream, and on to **Lhuntse Dzong**, some 77 kilometres distant. The massive Lhuntse Dzong (*Altitude*: 1,700 metres) was constructed in 1654 on a site of a 16th century temple associated with the grandfather of Zhabdrung Ngawang Namgyel. The protector shrine is dedicated to Mahakala, and the main temples to Padmasambhava, Avalokiteshvara, and Aksobhya Buddha. The assembly hall which houses 100 monks contains images of the Buddhas of the Three Times.

Tashigang district བཀྲ་ཤིས་སྒང

Area: 2,283 sq km

The administrative capital of this most densely populated district of Bhutan is located at Tashigang (Bh Trashigang). The valleys which sustain such a large population are those of the Tawang-chu which enters East Bhutan from Tsona county of Tibet, and the Gamri-chu, rising above Sakteng on the border, which converge north of Tashigang Dzong to form the Drangme-chu (Manas). East of Tashigang are the high altitude valleys of Merak and Sakteng, inhabited by yak and sheep pastoralists who wear a distinctive costume. The eastern frontier passes of Nyingzang La and Ngonkha La lead directly to Tawang (disputed territory, now in Arunachal Pradesh), via the Bhutanese settlements of Radi and Sakteng.

From Mongar it is a quick three hours' journey to **Tashigang** (*altitude* 1,150 metres), the biggest and busiest town in East Bhutan and, after Thimphu, the second largest mountain town of the country. The town looks attractive with its painted houses amid flowering bougainvilleas, its tiny shops, and the 'square' and cafés which hum with activity at the end of the day. Tropical fruits and crops thrive; apple is pressed into juice to produce cider and brandy. The local *endi* silk is spun from silkworms bred on castor oil plants. The impregnable **Tashigang Dzong** which stands on a spur overlooking the Drangme-chu river 400 metres below, was built in 1659, and later enlarged and renovated on two occasions. The temples contained within it include the **Lama Lhakhang** (dedicated to the Eight Vidyadhara masters of Tantric Buddhism in ancient India), the **Guru Lhakhang** (dedicated to Padmasambhava's Eight Manifestations), the **Tsozhing Lhakhang** (dedicated to the Kagyu and Nyingma lineages), and the **Gonkhang** (dedicated to the protector Mahakala). With its single courtyard sharing both administrative and monastic functions, this dzong is unique in Bhutan.

Tashigang has the *Dudjom Guesthouse* and the BCTL run *Killing Guesthouse*. **Sleeping** *Puensum* on the main square is by far the best place to eat and relax. Next to it, is the excellent *Pema* bakery.

The road south from Tashigang to Samdrup Jongkhar district, newly built in 1963-65, covers 180 kilometres in about six hours, following ridges rather than valleys most of the way. En route you pass **Kanglung**, Bhutan's only university campus which was established in 1978; and **Khaling** where there is a school for the blind and a weaving centre. After **Wamrong** and **Trimshing** villages, you pass the **Riserbu** hospital, and the turn-off for Pema Gatsel district before reaching the district frontier at **Deothang** (870 metres), the last stop before the plains and one-time scene of a British defeat during the Anglo-Bhutanese war of 1865.

Tashi Yangtse district བཀྲ་ཤིས་ཡང་རྩེ

This newly created district occupies the valley of the Kulong-chu, a major tribu- Area: 1,438 sq km *tary of the Tawang-chu, which flows through the extreme northeast of the country to its confluence at Tashigang. In the extreme northeast of the district the Me La pass leads into the Tsona county of Tibet.*

From Tashigang, you can take a fascinating day-trip to **Chorten Kora** and **Tashi Yangtse** (*Bh* Trashi Yangtse), driving some 50 kilometres up the Kulong-chu valley. The drive takes about three hours. En route you will pass through **Gom Kora**, a meditation haunt of Padmasambhava, and then enter the Kulong valley at Doksum. The **Tashi Yangtse Dzong** (constructed 1656) is set in the lush gorge of the Kulong-chu at 1,850 metres. The dzong formerly commanded the trade route between Tashigang and Bumtang via Lhuntse before the advent of the motor road, and it is approached across the river by way of an old drawbridge covered with bamboo mats. Further north the gorge opens out to reveal the huge white stupa of **Chorten Kora**, fashioned in Nepalese style in 1782 to fulfil one of Padmasambhava's prophecies. It is now the site of the new district headquarters. In March, it is the scene of an important religious festival for the inhabitants of East Bhutan.

Pema Gatsel district པདྨ་དགའ་ཚལ

The administrative capital of this small district is located at Pema Gatsel (Bh Area: 518 sq km *Pemagatshel). Much of the land is occupied by the **Dungsam Wildlife Reserve** (180 square kilometres), which is named after an ancient kingdom once established in this region. The northern border of the district is separated from Mongar* *district by the Drangme-chu (Manas). The main town is approached via a turn-off south of Wamrong on the Tashigang-Samdrup Jongkar road. You will notice that many of the houses in this region are raised on stilts, reminiscent of many parts of Southeast Asia, and roofed with bamboo matting.*

Samdrup Jongkhar
district བསམ་འགྲུབ་ཇོང་མཁར

Area: 2,308 sq km *The administrative capital is located at Samdrup Jongkhar, 18 kilometres south of Deothang, and seven hours' drive from Tashigang. With a Lhotsampa, Indian and Drukpa population, **Samdrup Jongkhar** is the tropical gateway to Assam, and has grown into an important market town serving the mountain districts of East Bhutan. Two rivers, which rise further north, flow into Assam through this district: the Nyera Ama-chu through the border town of **Bangtar** and the Jomo-chu (Dhanasiri) through the border town of **Daifam**. From Samdrup Jongkhar, one can cross the border and go to Guwahati airport in Assam, a good four hours' drive (special permission needed).*

Sleeping   Samdrup Jongkhar has simple hotels, serving good food. The best is the *Jigten Hotel*.

Bhutan background

History

Archaeology Despite the lack of archaeological research, stone implements found in Bhutan suggest that the mid-mountain belt was inhabited by humans circa 2,000 BC. Bhutan's recorded history dates the establishment of the Buddhist geomantic temples of **Kyerchu** in the west (Paro district) and of **Jampa Lhakhang** in central (Bumtang district) to the reign of the Tibetan king Songtsen Gampo, who unified most of the Tibetan plateau during the seventh century, and constructed such temples in order to stabilize the border regions of his empire (see above, page 672). The indigenous inhabitants of Bhutan during that period seem to have been those whose descendants even now occupy much of Central and East Bhutan, the Sharchokpa or 'Easterners', who have affinity with the Monpa of Southeast Tibet and Arunachal Pradesh. The people of Tibetan descent, formerly known in Bhutan as the Ngalong (ie the 'earliest to rise up within the fold of Tibetan Buddhism'), appear to have settled there gradually, following the unification of Songtsen Gampo's Empire. During the eighth century, when Buddhism became the established religion of Tibet, Bhutan is believed to have been officially converted to the Tibetan form of Buddhism by the accomplished spiritual master Padmasambhava, at the invitation Sendhaka, the local king of the Bumtang region. Pilgrimage sites associated with Padmasambhava and his followers include **Taktsang** in Paro, **Kurje** in Bumtang, and **Monka Nering Senge Dzong** in Lhuntse.

Tibetan Buddhist missionary activity Following the disintegration of the Tibetan Empire in the ninth century, waves of settlers arrived from Tibet to occupy Bhutan, then known as Lhomon, 'Southern Mon'. Between the 11th and 15th century, the major Tibetan schools of Buddhism, notably the Nyingma, Sakya, and Kagyu, established monasteries and temples throughout the Bhutanese valleys, as cultural and economic ties with Tibet continued to have paramount importance. Among these, the renowned institutions of the **Nyingma** school included the various branches of the East Tibetan monastery of Katok, such as **Orgyan Tsemo** and **Pang Karpo** in Paro (founded by Katokpa V in 13th century), as well as **Chidzong** and **Baling** in Shar; the eight monasteries founded by Longchen Rabjampa (14th century) in Central Bhutan, during his sojourn in exile from Tibet; and the sites associated with Guru Chowang (13th century in Lhuntse); Dorjelingpa (14th century in Bumtang, Paro and Shar); the celebrated bridge-building engineer Tangtong Gyelpo (15th century in Paro), and, above all, Pema Lingpa (1450-1521) whose familial and incarnate lineages have continued down to the present day in Central and Eastern Bhutan and the Lhodrak region of Southern Tibet.

Monasteries of the **Sakya** school were also established in Bhutan at **Lhading** (*Bh* Hedi), north of Paro in the 13th century, and by Trinle Rabyang of the Ngor sub-school at **Chizhing** (*Bh* Pchishing) and elsewhere during the 15th century; while the Nenying tradition of the **Kadam** school had limited influence in West Bhutan during the 15th century.

Among all the diverse traditions of Tibetan Buddhism, the one which exerted the most influence on Bhutanese spiritual and secular life has been the Kagyu school, early branches of which were founded during the 11th-12th century at **Langmoling** in Tang (by Ngok Choku Dorje), at **Thangkhabe** (*Bh* Thangbi) in Chokhor (by the Karma Kagyu school), and at **Chelkha** in North Paro and **Donyon Dzong** in Thimphu (by Lhanangpa and his followers). In the 14th century, the Barawa sub-school was established at **Drangyekha** in Paro by Barawa Gyeltsen

Dzongs

These were originally built as monasteries/fortresses, strategically sited to defend the country from hostile Tibetan armies who sought to reintegrate Bhutan within Tibet. They became centres of religious as well as secular power. Traditionally they have also been the centres of artistic and intellectual life and their construction, ornamentation and maintenance have absorbed much of the nation's wealth. The high whitewashed walls are made of earth and stone (mud is trampled into wooden brick moulds, the labour being provided by the community). The wooden windows and balconies (built without nails) are richly ornamented. The interior walls are usually covered with murals depicting episodes in Buddhist legend.

The villagers congregate at the dzong for the major festivals and for seasonal agricultural feasts which provide them an opportunity to wear their finest clothes and for merrymaking after the religious ceremony. Tsechus, held on the 10th day of the month, are celebrated in different parts of the kingdom, through the year, to commemorate the deeds of Padmasambhava. In the non-religious festivals archery is a highly popular sport. The archers aim at targets at a distance of about 150m and every village has its own range. Religious Cham dances can be very colourful and spectacular, performed in special costumes and masks to the accompaniment of drums and cymbals. Mask makers can sometimes be seen at work during festivals. There dancers often enact a ritual purification of negativity and may conclude with the display of a prized tangka.

Pelzang. Among the many Kagyu sub-schools such as these, dominance in Bhutan was eventually achieved by the **Drukpa** from the 13th century onwards: Lorepa of the Lower Drukpa school founded **Chodrak** in Bumtang, and Chilkarwa of the Upper Drukpa school founded **Chikarkha** in Paro; while various monasteries representative of the powerful Middle Drukpa school were founded throughout West Bhutan by descendants of Phajo Drukgom Zhikpo. It was he who succeeded in forging a vital link between West Bhutan and the major Drukpa monastery of **Ralung** in Tibet (see above, page 253). During 15th and 16th century, King Peljor and a number of Drukpa hierarchs from Ralung in Tibet visited Bhutan and founded important Drukpa monasteries in Paro and Thimphu valleys.

Although Bhutan was throughout this period a significant region for Tibetan Buddhist missionary activity, the country clearly lacked political unity. Only Western Bhutan was dominated by Drukpa families. Then, during the 17th century **Zhabdrung Ngawang Namgyel** (1594-1651), the hierarch of Ralung monastery, which was the principal seat of the Drukpa school in Tibet, founded the Bhutanese unified state. When the Tsangpa ruler of Tibet disputed his incarnate status within the Drukpa school, he fled to the south, to find sanctuary in the ancestral Drukpa domains of West Bhutan. There, he constructed a series of fortified castles (dzong) on the Tibetan model; and successfully repelled five Tibetan and Mongolian attacks between 1616 and 1648. Internally, he defeated a grand coalition of hostile Buddhist schools, known as the 'five groups of lamas', and thus established the whole of West Bhutan under his rule. Central and East Bhutan were integrated within the new Bhutanese state after his death in 1656.

From 1616 until 1907, Bhutan was governed in accordance with the theocratic system introduced by Zhabdrung Ngawang Namgyel. The religious authority of the country was embodied in the person of the **Je Khenpo** ('Chief Monastic Preceptor' or 'Chief Abbot') and temporal authority in that of the **Desi** ('Temporal Ruler'), both of whom were subservient to the Zhabdrung and his subsequent incarnations.

Theocractic control

Three provinces (Dagana, Paro and Trongsar) were created, each under the direct control of a governor (*ponlop*); while the fortified castles which developed as centres of local administration and bastions of Buddhist learning, were governed by the *dzongpon*. This dual system and its legal code based on Buddhist principles endured until 1907 despite the inherent threat of decentralization frequently posed by powerful provincial governors and local officials during the hiatus following the death of the Zhabdrung and the accession to power of his recognized incarnation. The 18th and 19th century were characterized by internecine disputes instigated by the regents, governors, and dzongpon.

From earliest times until the mid-18th century, the inhabitants of Bhutan had remained firmly within the Tibetan cultural orbit, notwithstanding the aforementioned conflicts. The intractable and virtually impenetrable terrain of South Bhutan ensured that contact with the Indian sub-continent was minimal, with only the Maharaja of neighbouring Cooch Behar having diplomatic relations. This situation rapidly changed with the advent of the British East India Company who, through their quest for trading concessions, forced the Bhutanese to look southwards. Specifically, Warren Hastings sent a mission into the 'Land of the Thunder Dragon' in the 1770s, headed by George Bogle (who was also ordered to plant potatoes there!). In 1841 the **British** annexed the Duars plain and created the present boundary, agreeing to pay a small annual subsidy as long as the Bhutanese remained peaceful. However, Bhutanese raiders continued to make forays across the border, carrying off Indians as slaves. In 1863, the visit of a British representative who forced his way into Bhutan did not please the Bhutanese, and so he was not treated well. A war followed but the British failed to invade Bhutan. In 1865 the Treaty of Sinchula was ratified, ensuring that the Duars were regained by the British in exchange for monetary compensation to the Bhutanese.

By 1865, the fabric of the dual theocratic system had been worn down in consequence of this period of turmoil, leaving Central and East Bhutan in the power of the provincial governor of Trongsar, Jigme Namgyel. His son, Ugyen Wangchuck, who inherited the governership in 1881, inflicted a severe defeat on the governor of Paro at Thimphu, thereby forging a renewed sense of national unity in 1885. The governor then entered into an increasing co-operation with the British, acting as an intermediary between them and the Tibetans in 1904 at the time of the Younghusband expedition into Tibet. With British support, he was successfully elected as the hereditary monarch of Bhutan in 1907 and theocracy abolished *de facto*. Secular and religious rule was vested in his family; and the Zhabdrung's theocracy was abruptly and forcefully ended.

Twentieth Century In 1910, in return for an increase in its annual subsidy, Bhutan agreed to accept British guidance in its external affairs. Bhutan, however, did not receive help in building roads, expanding communications and developing the economy as did Sikkim which was then a British protectorate. The pace of development was therefore much slower.

Following the death of Ugyen Wangchuck in 1926, his son Jigme Wangchuck became the second king, reigning until his own death in 1952. During this period, a few western-style schools were established with British aid, and Bhutanese students were encouraged to study in India. Under a 1949 treaty between Bhutan and newly independent India, Bhutan entered a non-binding agreement to 'be guided by the advice' of India in its foreign affairs. It was, however, the third king Jigme Dorje Wangchuck who consciously altered the course of Bhutan's political isolation and began the process of modernization and economic development in the aftermath of the abortive uprising in Tibet against the Chinese occupation in 1959. He initiated a road-building programme, which gradually made the country more accessible to the outside world. Then, in 1971, shortly before his death, he successfully applied for

UN membership. The affection with which the third king is regarded in Bhutan is reflected in the grandeur of his impressive **Memorial Chorten**, subsequently erected in Thimphu. The fourth and present king, Jigme Senge Wangchuck, ascended the throne in 1972 at the age of 17. His policy has been to promote socio-economic development, while preserving the Buddhist heritage of Bhutan. Through his efforts, Bhutan has become a member of many international organizations, including the Nonaligned Movement, the South Asian Association for Regional Cooperation, the Asian Development Bank, the Colombo Plan, the World Bank, the International Monetary Fund, and the Universal Postal Union. In addition, Bhutan has diplomatic relations with India, Bangladesh, Nepal, Maldives, Kuwait, Switzerland, Norway, the European Union, Japan, Sri Lanka, and Thailand.

Prior to the 20th century the inhospitable terrain of South Bhutan remained uninhabited until small numbers of ethnic Nepalis began moving into the foothills. This modest migration continued throughout the first half of the 20th century, as Nepali forest labourers were brought in, later settling as tenant farmers and eventually acquiring Bhutanese nationality in 1958. However, with the recent opening up of the country and the endeavour to develop its infrastructure, large numbers of economic migrants followed in the wake of those early settlers, the majority of them ethnic Nepali. These latecomers were declared illegal immigrants in 1988. The Nepalis are mostly found in the five southern districts, where they outnumber the indigenous Bhutanese, but when employed as civil servants, they are posted all over the country. They are now estimated to comprise 30 per cent of the total national population.

Bhutan Background

Land and environment

Geology and landscape

Location Bhutan lies between 89° and 92° east and 27° and 28° north. The Indian states of Sikkim, West Bengal, Assam, and Arunachal Pradesh occupy the entire 605 kilometres length of its west, south, and east borders respectively, while the Dromo, Khangmar, Lhodrak and Tsona counties of Tibet lie to its north, forming a 470 kilometres border. In general, the elevation of the land ranges from more than 7,000 metres in the north to only 300 metres in the south.

Terrain In the north, separating the country from Tibet, lies a relatively narrow chain of glacial mountains belonging to the High Himalayan range, with several peaks over 7,000 metres. From west to east these peaks include: **Jomolhari** (7,313 metres), the most famous and picturesque; Jichu Drakye (6,974 metres); Matsen Gyelpo (*Bh* Masangang, 7,158 metres); Terigang (7,060 metres); Jejehangphu Gang (7,158 metres); Gangphu Gang (7,170 metres); Dzongaphu Gang (7,060 metres); and **Gangkar Punsum** (7,540 metres) which is the highest mountain entirely within the borders of Bhutan. Even higher and more imposing is the massive **Kulha Kangri** (7,554 metres), slightly to the northeast, on the border with Lhodrak. Ancient trade routes traverse these snow ranges through the high passes: Tremo La, Yak La, Phiru La, Monla Karchung La, and Phode La; while the slightly less daunting passes: Me La, Nyingzang La, and Ngonkha La connect East Bhutan with Tsona and Arunachal. In general, those peaks of the High Himalayan range form a watershed between the north and south flowing tributaries of the Brahmaputra River. All the rivers in Bhutan flow south. Yet among them there are three that originate north of the range in Tibet: the Amo-chu (Torsa), which enters West Bhutan from the Dromo (Chumbi) valley; the Kuru-chu, which enters Northeast Bhutan from Lhodrak; and the Tawang-chu (Gamri/Drangme), which enters East Bhutan from Tsona. In the far west, the Di-chu (Jaldakha) enters from Sikkim. All other tributaries have their sources within Bhutan. In the extreme northwest the alignment of the Tibet-Bhutan border has been repeatedly disputed by China.

The largest part of the country belongs to the middle Himalayan range with altitudes ranging from 1,100 to 4,000 metres. Here, the Black Mountains form a watershed between West and East Bhutan and are crossed via the **Pele La pass** (3,369 metres). The rivers of West Bhutan which flow to the west of that pass include the Di-chu (Jaldakha), the Amo (Torsa), the Wang-chu (Raidak) with its Ha (Lhade), Paro, and Thimphu tributaries, and the Puna Tsang-chu (Sankosh). Those flowing east of the pass, which converge to form the Drangme-chu (Manas), include the Trongsar (Tongsa/Mangde) and the Bumtang-chu of Central Bhutan, as well as the Kuru-chu, Kulong-chu, and Tawang-chu (Gamri) of East Bhutan. In the far southeast of the country, the Bada-chu and Dhanasiri-chu follow their distinct courses into Assam.

In the more densely populated south the border with India, which was established by the British in the 18th and 19th centuries, generally runs along the base of the abruptly rising Himalayan foothills (average altitude 300-1,600 metres). Here, the aforementioned rivers cut their way through to reach the Brahmaputra River lowlands of West Bengal and Assam, thereby forming the 18 'gates' of the **Duars** (*Hindi* – gates). All the motor roads from the south pass through the Duars. In the west the boundary with Sikkim was also established by the British and accepted by India; while the boundary to the east currently follows the de-facto Sino-Indian frontier.

The country is divided into 20 administrative districts or 'dzongkhak'; among which Samtse, Chukha, Gelekphuk, and Samdrup Jongkhar border India on the west and south. Those of Ha, Paro, Thimphu, Gasa, Wangdu, Bumtang, Lhuntse, Tashi Yangtse, and Tashigang border Tibet on the north and east. The central districts of Tagkar (Dagana), Tsirang, Punakha, Trongsar (Tongsa), Shemgang, Pema Gatsel and Mongar lack an external frontier. Motorable roads now link the southern border towns of Phuntsoling, Khalikhola, Sarpang, and Samdrup Jongkar with the capital and central parts of the country; and there is also a lateral paved road linking the districts of Ha, Paro, Thimphu, Wangdu, Trongsar, Bumtang, Mongar and Tashigang. Apart from the northeast roads to Lhuntse and Tashi Yangtse, the north of Bhutan is even now only accessible on ancient trekking and caravan trading routes. In all, the motorable roads cover 3,216 kilometres.

Climate

The monsoon begins in June and lasts until end of September when 85 per cent of the annual rainfall is received. The windward south-facing mountain slopes are the wettest areas. The climate within the mountains varies greatly according to sunshine, precipitation and wind conditions, yet it basically resembles the middle European climate.

In the **Duars Plain** and up to 1,500 metres, the climate is subtropical with high humidity and heavy rainfall (2,000-5,000 millimetres). The climate of the **mid-mountain belt** varies, such that low-lying parts of Punakha, Mongar, Tashigang, and Lhuntse have cool winters and hot summers, whereas the higher valleys of Ha, Paro, Thimphu, Trongsar, and Bumtang, ranging from 2,200-4,500 metres endure a temperate climate with cold, sometimes snowy, winters and somewhat cooler summers. The rainfall of these mid-mountain valleys averages 1,000-1,500 millimetres per year; and in the winter snowfall can close many passes. In **North Bhutan**, above 4,500 metres, an alpine/arctic climate prevails, with most areas permanently covered with snow and ice. Here the winters are severe and the summers generally cool.

The daily air mass exchange between highlands and lowlands often causes stormy winds which frequently prevent rainfall in the middle portions of cross valleys so that between 900 to 1,800 metres it is quite dry, requiring irrigation for farming, while higher up it is often wet.

Across the country, the minimum temperatures range from -10°C (Paro, Thimphu) to 15°C (Southern Foothills); and the max from 30°C (Paro, Thimphu) to 35°C (Southern Foothills). More specifically, in the mid-mountain belt which is visited by most tour groups, from mid-March to mid-June, the temperature range is 26°C-5°C; in the monsoon season from mid-June to late September the range is 24°C-15°C; and in winter from mid-November to mid-March, the days are dry, averaging 16-18°C, while the nights, early mornings, and evenings have freezing temperatures. Mountain vistas are best in the Autumn (October-mid November), and in the Spring.

Temperature

Bhutan Background

Flora and fauna

Vegetation The three vegetation and climatic zones found throughout the Himalayan countries are also apparent in Bhutan. In the south the wet Duars are covered in lush forest with bamboo, fern, hanging plants, and giant orchids amid the banyan, giant sal and teak trees. As you move higher into mountainous terrain, the tropical vegetation gives way to the deciduous and conifer forests of the temperate zone, and there is still a wide range of trees: poplar, ash, aspen, magnolia, oak, and beautiful rhododendron. Above 3,000 metres bamboo and conifer forests take over, alongside fir, larch, and cypress. At 4,000 metres birch, pine and rhododendron dominate and then give way to high alpine juniper, edelweiss, blue poppies, gentian, and other medicinal plants. Mosses and lichens can occasionally be found at the highest altitudes in North Bhutan, but it is only in Northeast Bhutan, bordering on Lhodrak, that the forest penetrates the otherwise bleak north side of the main Himalaya range.

Wildlife In South Bhutan the forests abound with monkeys, including the rare golden langur, as well as deer, buffalo, wild boar, bears, snakes, leopards, rhino, and even tigers. The mid-mountain belt is home to the red panda, wild boar, Himalayan black bear, pheasant, and hornbill; while remote valleys around Bumtang and Gangteng (Gantey) are the preferred winter destination of the black-necked crane. In North Bhutan, the high alpine valleys are frequented by yaks, tahr, the rare and protected *bharal* blue sheep, the snow leopard, and the takin which live above 4,000 metres. The **blue sheep** (*Pseudois nayaur*), rare elsewhere in the Himalaya, have thick sheep-like horns but goat-like legs with dark stripes on the flanks. They prefer plateaus for grazing and have a split lip which enables them to pull grass straight out of the ground rather than crop it. Takins (*Budorcas taxicolor*) are larger (over one metre at the shoulders), and short-legged. They have a shaggy dark brown coat with a lighter back; the snout is swollen and their thick horns splay out and then up and back. They live in small herds, often above the tree-line, and in spite of their stocky appearance are remarkably agile on steep slopes. The winter draws them down to bamboo and rhododendron forests, from which they emerge to graze in meadows, morning and evening.

There are also many species of birds and butterflies, fish, such as the celebrated masheer, and various reptiles. Wildlife parks cover much of the border regions. In the extreme north the **Jigme Dorje Wangchuck Sanctuary** occupies 7,813 square kilometres; and there are at least 11 others covering the mid-mountain belt and the south. Among the latter, the best known is the **Manas Wildlife Sanctuary** (463 square kilometres), which stretches across the border into Assam, and may be entered from the Indian side (closed at present). In Central Bhutan further wildlife reserves are being established in the Black Mountains and in Ura. At present, some 26 per cent of the land in Bhutan has been turned into natural conservation areas.

Bhutan Background

Culture

People

There are two main population groups in Bhutan: the **Drukpa** (approximately 67 per cent) of Tibetan and Monpa origin, and the **Lhotsampa** (approximately 30 per cent) of Nepalese origin. The remaining three per cent of the population comprise indigenous tribal groups, such as the Toktop, Doya, and Lepcha of Southwest Bhutan, and the Santal who migrated there from North Bihar. Among the two larger groups, the Drukpa include within their numbers the **Ngalong** of West Bhutan who speak the Tibetan dialect known as Dzongkha, now the official language of Bhutan; the '**drokpa**' nomads of North Bhutan; the Monpa of Wangdu Phodrang, Shemgang and Trongsar districts who speak an East Bodish language; the unrelated Monpa of Merak and Sakteng, who speak a language akin to Tibetan; and the most populous group, the **Sharchokpa** of East Bhutan, who speak a Tibeto-Burman language known as Tsangla, which has not yet been classified. The Nepali-speaking Lhotsampa of South Bhutan belong mainly to the high castes and to the Rai, Gurung and Limbu tribes, and because of their different language and religion they have not intermingled with the Drukpa.

Since 1959 immigration from Nepal has been banned and the Government wishes to avoid a repetition of what happened in Sikkim (where, in 1975 the King was overthrown by the majority Nepali-speaking population). The problem of the people of Nepalese origin who left Bhutan since 1991 for refugee camps in Southeast Nepal is the subject of talks between Nepal and Bhutan.

Bhutan has the lowest population density of any country in South Asia. Most people live along the south border and in the high valleys of the mid-mountain belt, particularly along the east-west trade route that passes through Thimphu and Punakha. In mountain regions the Drukpa are predominant, whilst the south is largely settled by Nepalis.

National language

Since the Drukpa share a common heritage of culture, language and religion with Tibet, the written language, here known as 'cho-ke', employs the classical Tibetan script. The colloquial form of Tibetan given national status in Bhutan is, as stated above, known as *Dzongkha*, the dialect of West Bhutan. The teaching of the national language is compulsory at all levels of education, although English is the medium of instruction. Primary education has been encouraged since the 1960s with the opening of state funded schools throughout the country.

Daily life

National dress   The people take pride in their clothing which, like the dress worn by the neighbouring Tibetans of Dromo, Khangmar, and Lhodrak, is influenced by the harshness of the Himalayan climate. The men wear a long *kho* (robe), hitched up to the knees with a sash, and long boots, while women wear an *onju* or *gyenja* (blouse), a *kira* (ankle-length robe, wrapped around from under the arm, held by silver brooches), a belt, and a *togo* (short jacket). Traditionally, special ceremonial scarves are worn – the king and the Je Khenpo (Chief Monastic Preceptor or Abbot) wear saffron yellow, the ministers orange, senior officials red and the ordinary subjects white, while the women wear red scarves with woven motifs.

Village houses with mud walls have a lower floor for animals; the upper floor for living is made of wood and bamboo lattices covered with mud plaster. Shuttered windows with a trefoil arch shape are colourfully painted. Roofs are covered with wooden shingles weighted down with stones. In North and Central Bhutan, house walls are made of stone and in the east, bamboo houses are constructed on stilts. Lighting was once provided by oil lamps, but now by kerosene or elecricity.

Crafts

Traditional handicrafts, expensively priced, are made largely for the indigenous market rather than the tourist trade. There is little mechanization, and no competition to encourage lower pricing. Different parts of the country are renowned for different products: bamboo baskets from Khyeng, brocade from Lhuntse, raw silk from East Bhutan, woodwork from Tashi Yangtse, metalwork from Thimphu, and yak-hair products from the nomadic North Bhutanese handloom woven fabrics are particularly renowned, each having a distinctive name depending on its unique combination of fibre, colour and pattern. Cotton, wool, silk, yak, and nettle fibres may be used to weave material in striped, banded or checked patterns. Gold and silver jewellery is made in the Tibetan style, often inset with coral, freshwater pearl, or *zi* (banded chalcedony/etched agate), and occasionally with turquoise. Wooden drinking bowls, inlaid with silver, and laquered bowls are prized among the woodwork of Tashi Yangtse in East Bhutan. Waterproof bamboo or rattan baskets, including the celebrated round picnic basket, are fashioned in interesting geometric designs in Khyeng; while strong light-weight paper is made from the bark of the Daphne and Edgeworthia shrubs.

Religion

Religion plays a crucial role in social affairs. The **Drukpa Kagyu** school of Tibetan Buddhism is the state religion but the **Nyingma** school is also well represented, particularly in central and east districts.

As stated above, there are unique political and military circumstances through which the Drukpa Kagyu, among all the various schools of Tibetan Buddhism, came to dominate the religious life of the country. This school was founded at **Druk** in Tibet by Tsangpa Gya-re Yeshe Dorje (1161-1211), whose foremost students formed its three main branches: the Middle Drukpa school at Ralung, the Upper Drukpa school in West Tibet and Ladakh, and the Lower Drukpa school at Uri and Karpo Cho-lung. Among these, the Middle Drukpa school first reached Bhutan during the 13th century through the missionary efforts of Drukgom Zhikpo and his descendants, who established strong links between West Bhutan and Ralung. In particular, Kunga Peljor founded a number of Middle Drukpa monasteries in West Bhutan during the 15th century; and it was to these that during the 17th century

Zhabdrung Ngawang Namgyel (1594-1651), the hierarch of Ralung monastery, fled to escape the persecution of the King of Tsang, thereby founding the Bhutanese state. In this way, the Drukpa Kagyu school gave its name to the newly emergent state of Bhutan.

There are around 6,000 monks in Bhutan, approximately half being subsidized under the authority of the Je Khenpo of the Drukpa Kagyu school; and the remainder subsisting on private patronage. Each of the larger dzong houses several hundred monks. By contrast, there are only about 250 nuns. In addition to monastic Buddhism, there are also a number of important reincarnating tulkus who are responsible for maintaining their own distinctive spiritual lineages, whether Bhutanese or Tibetan in origin; and approximately 15,000 respected lay practitioners, known as Ngakpa or Gomchen. Many Nyingma temples are privately owned, and passed on through familial lines of succession from one generation to the next. All those fully engaged in Buddhist practice, whether monastic or not, are highly respected by the people and by the government, for whom they provide spiritual guidance and support through their private meditations, communal prayers, ceremonial rituals, and religious festivals.

The laity, in turn, place great emphasis on the importance of making offerings at their household shrines, performing daily prayers, circumambulating stupas and temples, going on pilgrimage, and sponsoring religious ceremonies. As in other Buddhist countries, there is a universal understanding of the importance of the accumulation of merit for the spiritual well-being and development of each individual in this life and in subsequent lives after death. In South Bhutan, where the dominant population is Nepalese, religious ceremonies correspond to those of contemporary Hindu and Newar society in Nepal.

Religious festivals

These are important events throughout the Tibetan Buddhist world – commemorating the deeds of the Buddha, or those of the great masters of the past associated with one tradition or another. In Bhutan, in addition to the standard festivals associated with the Buddha's life, the most renowned of these are the **Tsechu** ('10th day') festivals commemorating the deeds of Padmasambhava, the eighth century master of the Nyingma school who is credited with the introduction of the most profound Buddhist teachings into Tibet and Bhutan. Each 10th day of the lunar calendar is said to commemorate a special event in the life of Padmasambhava; and some of these are dramatized in the context of a religious festival, which may last from three to five days (one of which usually but not invariably falls on the 10th day of the lunar month). The regional dzong and remote village communities tend to hold their distinct annual Tsechu festival, providing the local populace with a wonderful occasion to dress up, gather together, and enjoy themselves in a convivial light-hearted atmosphere. It is also an occasion for them to renew their faith and receive blessings by watching the sacred dances, or receiving 'empowerment' from an officiating lama. The dances, each aspect of which has symbolic meaning, are performed by trained monks and laymen wearing ornate costumes, and, in some cases, impressive masks. At Paro, Wangdu, Mongar and Tashigang, among other places, a large painted scroll known as a *Tongdrol* is exhibited for a few hours in the course of the Tsechu festival, enabling the people to throng forward to obtain its blessing on that auspicious day; since such painted scrolls are said to 'confer liberation by their sight alone' (*tongdrol*). For the 1999 festival calendar, see above page 833.

Religious dances (*cham*)

These may be generally classed according to three distinct themes: **morality plays; purificatory rites** which exorcise demonic forqces; and **triumphal celebrations of Buddhism**, glorifying the deeds of Padmasambhava, and so forth. Among these, the first type is exemplified by the lewd Dance of the Princes and Princesses (*pho-le mo-le*), in which dancers depict two princes who return from a foreign war to cut off the noses of their adulterous princesses; the Dance of the Stag and Hunting Dogs (*sha-ba sha-khyi*), in which the hermit saint Milarepa saves the life of a hunted stag and converts its pursuing hounds and hunter to Buddhism; and the Dance of the Judgement of the Dead (*raksha marcham*), derived from the *Tibetan Book of the Dead*, in which the executors of the rites of the Lord of Death dramatically pass judgement on two recently deceased individuals, one evil and the other virtuous.

The second type (purificatory dances of exorcism) is exemplified by the famous Black Hat dance (*shanag*) in which dancers wearing large wide-brimmed black hats, high boots, and silk brocade costumes, exorcise demonic forces from the dancing arena, in a parody of the assassination of the apostate ninth century Tibetan king Langdarma; the Dance of the Ging and Tsholing (*ging-dang tsholing*), in which two waves of terrifying deities in the entourage of Padmasambhava successively appear to take possession of the dancing arena; and the dance of the lords of the charnel ground (*durtro dakpo dagmo*), in which the eight great charnel grounds of ancient India are ritually guarded by two skeleton-clad dancers.

The third category is exemplified by the Drum Dance of Dramitse Monastery (*dramitse ngacham*), in which 12 animal-masked figures in Padmasambhava's entourage enact the victory of Buddhism; the Lute Dance (*dranyen cham*), in which the founding of the Drukpa Kagyu school is celebrated; and the elaborate Dance of Padmasambhava's Eight Manifestations (*gu-ru tsen-gye*). The accompanying orchestra beats out the rhythm of the dance as they play their long horns (*dungchen*), oboes (*gyaling*), drums (*nga*), cymbals (*silnyen/babchal*), shinbone trumpets (*kangling*), conch shells (*dung*), skull-drums (*damaru*), and bells (*drilbu*).

Secular festivals and dances

Non-religious festivals include the traditional new year (*losar*) festivals and the recently introduced commemoration days indicative of the modern nation state. The former include the official new year (*gyelpo losar*) held in February/March, the agricultural new year (*sonam losar*) held in November/December, and the Nepalese new year in April. The latter include National Day (commemorating the institution of the monarchy on 17 December 1907); the King's Birthday (11 November), and Coronation Day (2 June). Such secular festivals are occasions for merry-making and archery contests. Secular music and song vary, corresponding to the cultural divide between the Drukpa and Nepalese parts of the country. The instruments, rhythms, ballads, and working songs of the Drukpa reflect the folk and popular culture of Tibet, while those of the Lhotsampa are close to the music of Nepal.

Modern country and government

Statistics

Official Name   Druk-Yul
Capital   Thimphu
National Flag   Saffron and orange red, divided diagonally, with a white dragon in the centre
Official Language   Dzongkha
Key statistics   *Population*: 1995, 600,000; Urban 4%; Drukpas 67%; Nepalese origin 30%; others 3%. *Population density*: 12.76 per square kilometres. *Birth rate*: 3.9%. *Death rate*: 0.9%. *Life expectancy*: 65 years. *Literacy*: 47.5%, M 54%, F 40%. *GDP*: 540 USD. *Land use*: forested 72%, permanent pasture and agriculture 9%, snow/glacier 7.5%, scrub forest 8.1, other 11%. *Growth rate*: 3.1%. *Religion*: Buddhist 70%, Hindu 28%, other 2%.

Government

The king is the Chief of State. The cabinet (*lhengye zhungtsog*) is chaired by a minister who is Head of Government on an annual rotation basis. It comprises the Ministers of Foreign Affairs and Finance, the Chairman of the Planning Commission; the Minister of Home Affairs; the Chairmen of the Special Commission for Cultural Affairs and the Royal Civil Service Commission; the Ministers of Health & Education, Trade & Industry, and Agriculture; the Chairman of the National Environment Commission, along with the Vice-minister for Communications, as well as the Chief of the Royal Bhutan Army and Police. In 1953 King Jigme Dorje Wangchuck (1952-72) inaugurated a National Assembly, the *Tshogdu*, which meets biannually at Tashi Chodzong in Thimphu and has some representative power, in that 100 out of its 150 members are directly elected for a three-year term by a limited electorate, comprising village elders and heads of households. The remaining members of the National Assembly comprise 10 representing the monastic community and 40 royal appointees. The resolutions passed by the National Assembly are implemented by a nine-member Royal Advisory Council (*lodro'i tsogde*), which the king set up in 1965. There is no written constitution and no independent judiciary, although there is a high court of six judges presided over by the Chief Justice. A written legal code, established on modern lines, has been in existence since 1959 and any new laws have to be passed by the National Assembly. The judicial sector is nowadays undergoing major changes.

The modern reorganization of Bhutan's system of regional and local government has resulted in a more decentralized multi-tiered administration, at the heart of which is the division of the country into 20 districts (*dzongkhag*). Each district is headed by its own commissioner (*dzongdag*), who is appointed by the king and responsible to the Ministry of Home Affairs; while the districts themselves are subdivided into smaller blocks of hamlets or villages (*gewog*) under the authority of an elected village headman (*gup*). The State Monastic Community, which is represented in the National Assembly and on the Royal Advisory Council, has been subsidized by the government since 1968, and its vast land holdings have been gradually purchased by the government for redistribution among the peasantry. At its head is the Je Khenpo, head of the Drukpa Kagyu school in Bhutan.

After Bhutan joined the UN in 1971, the government sought to exercise an increasing autonomy in its foreign policy, despite the important role which newly independent India had inherited from the British in 1947 as an arbiter of Bhutanese foreign affairs, and the major source of foreign aid. Internally, too, although the present King Jigme Senge Wangchuck continues to wield considerable power, his reign has been marked by a great improvement in the country's infrastructure; in the development of roads, buildings, telecommunications, and an increasing decentralization of both administrative power and economic decision making. All is now geared towards the development of agriculture, private enterprise and environmental conservation. This does not mean, however, that social services are neglected, and a priority is also given to education and healthcare, which are both free of charge.

Recent developments

The early 1990s have been marked by major unrest in the neighbouring Indian state of Assam and other parts of North India. The response of the Bhutanese government was to strengthen its programme of self-reliance and to underline its commitment to maintaining traditional Bhutanese values. The king has toured extensively and renewed support for the wearing of national dress has come from many parts of the country, especially in the south, bordering India. Language posed a particular problem, as English was increasingly becoming the lingua franca of the educated. While promoting the use of Dzongkha, the king also took steps to encourage the Hindu population of the south to feel integrated with the Buddhist population, himself taking part in one of the major Hindu festivals.

The Bhutanese have long been wary of the comparatively recent historical trend of Nepali migration, which eventually led to the demise of the monarchy in neighbouring Sikkim, and the incorporation of that country within India. In 1990, a new census declared many people of Nepalese descent to be illegal immigrants. This sparked off anti-government propaganda by dissidents and terrorism, which led many Nepalis to leave the country. By the end of 1992, 70,000 Nepalis had gathered in the refugee camps of East Nepal. Dissidents formed the political organization BNDP. In September 1990 violent mass demonstrations were mounted and government offices ransacked in South Bhutan protesting against 'racism', the denial of democratic and human rights, and ethnic cleansing. The king threatened to abdicate but was persuaded to remain by the National Assembly. He then granted amnesty to hundreds of detainees and announced exemption of rural and labour tax in 1992 for all Lhotsampas, encouraging them not to leave the country. Schools, development projects and health services which had been suspended since 1990 because of the unrest, were ordered to reopen in 1993. Bilateral talks are now taking place between the Bhutanese and the Nepalese governments to solve the problem of the people in the camps.

The plea put forward is that without military and economic might, the very survival of the tiny country, the last bastion of Mahayana Buddhism, depends on Bhutan retaining its cultural identity.

A new problem has emerged since 1997 in which Bhutan is an unwilling player. The Bodo and ULFA (United Liberation Front of Assam) separatists who are seeking independence from the Indian state of Assam and have mounted a violent insurgency over the last 10 years, have taken refuge in the deep jungles of Southeast Bhutan. From this base they exact unjust demands from the local population and launch their attacks against the Indian army. Bhutan is now consulting with India on how to deal with this threat to its national security.

Bhutan has played an active part in the SAARC meetings, and has welcomed contacts with the outside world, increasing the annual tourist influx to 6,000.

Satellite dishes are tolerated but there is no national TV. Video rental shops flourish and they are uncensored.

Economy

In 1998, the per capita income was estimated at US$540, and the annual growth rate at 3.1 percent; although the inflation rate stands at 13 percent. As much as 80 percent of GDP was in the rural sector but this contributed less than two percent of tax revenue. Although these figures tend to place Bhutan among the least developed nations, the country is unlike others within that category, in that there is no famine, little malnutrition, good housing, a favourable ratio of population to cultivated land, with approximately 98 percent of the land being owned by the peasants who work it. Motorable roads, airline services and modern satellite communication systems now link Bhutan with the outside world, propelling the country rapidly away from its long-sought isolation.

Agriculture

Over 91 percent of the population depends on agriculture and livestock rearing, which together account for some 50 percent of GDP, despite the fact that only two percent of the land is arable. The most important areas of cultivation are in the Duars and the river valleys of Central Bhutan. The main crops are maize (output 40,000 tonnes), and rice (output 43,000 tonnes), cultivated on the valley floors and, wherever possible, on the terraced and irrigated slopes up to 2,400 metres. Between 2,400 metres and 2,900 metres, millet (7,000 tonnes), wheat (5,000 tonnes), buckwheat and barley (4,000 tonnes) are also grown. Hot pepper (output 7,000 tonnes) is the favoured vegetable in kitchen gardens all over the country. Apples (5,000 tonnes) and potatoes (33,000 tonnes) are particularly important cash crops for the mid-mountain belt, while at altitudes between 300 metres and 1,300 metres, oranges (62,000 tonnes) and sugarcane (12,000 tonnes) are abundant. Farming is at the subsistence level and in recent years rice has had to be imported. Cattle, pigs, horses, sheep, and goats contribute greatly to the economy; yaks are the main livestock over 3,500 metres.

The extensive forests, which cover 72 percent of the land, are scientifically managed, but nonetheless damaged by shifting cultivation in the east and also by ageing and blight. The Bhutanese government is very conservation oriented and is assisted in this task by various international organizations. A small dairy farm was started at Bumtang in Central Bhutan with Swiss help and produces excellent cheese.

The curtailment of trade with Tibet in 1959 encouraged economic dependence on India and smuggling. Even now trade with Tibet is minimal, and restricted to specific trade fairs in Lhodrak and Southern Tibet, at which Bhutanese delegations participate, and local cross-border smuggling. In these ways, grain and sugar are carried on yak trains into Tibet and watches, thermos flasks, crockery, and shoes from China are imported. By contrast, trade with India has contributed immensely to Bhutan's economic development, with road building, small cottage industries, fruit processing, and hydro-electric power plant construction expanding rapidly.

Industry and resources

Bhutan has no oil or natural gas. It is mining dolomite (output 50,000 tonnes) and limestone (100,000 tonnes) for export to India, along with marble and slate. It also mines 30,000 tonnes of coal a year. The main industries are hydro-electricity (output 344 MW), which accounts for 25 percent of government revenue, cement (output 36 million tonnes), calcium carbide and ferro-alloys, as well as distillery products (47,000 tonnes), but Bhutan is also producing veneer woods and plywood (three million tonnes), and high density polythene pipe. Its main exports, mostly to India but also to Bangladesh, are cement, timber, block boards, electricity, cardamom, processed food, fruit and alcoholic drinks. The main imports, 60 percent of which are obtained from India and the remainder through trade with Japan, EU, USA and so forth, are petroleum, fuel, machinery, fabrics, vehicles, and grain.

Development In 1961, the present king's father initiated a continuing series of five-year plans, which at the outset focused on the development of road construction and basic administrative infrastructures. The third and fourth of these plans focused on the economic exploitation of Bhutan's natural resources including forestry, agriculture, mining, and electricity. During the eighties and nineties, these plans have focused on administrative decentralization, privatization, health, education, and the strengthening of the environment and Bhutan's cultural heritage.

Tourism

This is deliberately kept on a small scale with only 6,000 tourists in 1998 with revenue from amounting to US$7.25 million. Although FIT tourism is permitted, this option proves to be extremely expensive, and the majority of visitors are advised to form or join a tour group (which may consist of as few as one or two people only). As late as the early 1960s the only way to Thimphu was either on foot or by pack animal. The building of roads began in 1960 on the issue of a royal decree. By 1964 the first all-weather road had been completed from Paro to the new capital Thimphu; and there are now some 3,216 kilometres of roads (paved and unpaved), linking India with Central Bhutan, and the central valleys with each other.

Since the Tourist Authority of Bhutan requires tourists to pay a fixed daily rate, currently in the region of US$165-200, depending on the season. This includes accommodation, food, transport, driver and local guide, only affluent tourists from Western countries, virtually all in tour groups, see this marvellous, peaceful country with its charming and friendly people. In general, prices vary according to the season and the group-size, with larger groups being offered greater discounts. Nonetheless, travel in Bhutan still proves to be more expensive than comparable travel in Tibet. Itineraries may be varied to take local festivals into account; but since 1988 most of the important monasteries, temples, and dzong have been denied access to foreign tourists. Permission to visit specific sites may exceptionally be obtained from the Secretary of the Special Commission for Cultural Affairs. Currently only a few sites of historic or cultural importance may be visited, and these are indicated in the course of the regional descriptions which follow.

Since the privatization of the Bhutan Tourism Corporation (BTC) in 1992, there are now 46 tour operators in Bhutan, of which the top five in descending order are Ethometho, Yangphel, BTCL, International Treks and Tours, and Bhutan Mandala Tours.. Visitors should be aware, however, that few agencies are able to handle large groups, and amongst them, the biggest are BTCL (Bhutan Tourism Corporation Limited) and Ethometho. Guides are trained by the Tourism Authority of Bhutan, and some have developed a specialized expertise in flora, fauna, Buddhism, and so forth. The construction of hotels in recent years implies that this exclusive destination will continue to open its doors gradually to an increasing number of Western and Japanese visitors, but also to Indian tourists who benefit from special conditions and fares, and do not have to pay the US dollar rate.

Philately Bhutan joined the Universal Postal Union only in 1969 but since then has made a speciality of exporting stamps, particularly novelty stamps (three-dimensional, circular, on silk and metal) and stamps depicting Buddhist imagery. These are now a significant source of foreign exchange, and it is possible to purchase Bhutanese stamps by mail order. For information, contact the Chief Controller of Stamps, Philatelic Bureau, GPO, Thimphu, Bhutan, F00975-223108.

An iconographic guide of Tibetan Buddhism

14

An iconographic guide of Tibetan Buddhism

It is impossible to visit Tibet without being overwhelmed by religious imagery. The sheer scale is breathtaking – the Potala Palace in Lhasa has 1,000 rooms, housing approximately 200,000 images! It will help both your understanding and enjoyment if you can recognize some of these images.

This guide contains the names of the deities or images most frequently depicted in the Buddhist temples and monasteries of Tibet. Illustrations of some of these are also appended. It is important to remember that, with the probable exception of images representing the ancient historic kings of Tibet, the others are not regarded as concrete or inherently existing beings in the Judeo-Christian or even in the Hindu sense. Rather, the deities are revered as pure expressions of buddha-mind, who are to be visualized in the course of meditation in their pure light forms: a coalescence of pure appearance and emptiness. Through such meditations, blessings are obtained from the mentors of the past; spiritual accomplishments are matured through the meditational deities, enlightened activities are engaged in through the agency of the dakinis, and spiritual development is safe-guarded by the protector deities. These therefore are the four main classes of image to be observed in Tibetan shrines. Among them, the images representing the spirit-ual teachers of the past are exemplified by Buddha Shakyamuni, Padmasambhava and Tsongkhapa; those representing the meditational deities by Vajrakumara, Cakrasamvara and Kalacakra; those representing dakinis or female agents of enlightened activity by Vajravarahi; and the protector deities by Mahakala, Shridevi, and so forth.

Temples: what to expect

Most temples have an entrance portico replete with murals depicting the Four Guardian Kings of the four directions and the Wheel of Rebirth (*bhavacakra*) on the outer wall. Within the main gate, there are often images of the gatekeepers Vajrapani (east) and Hayagriva (west), watching over the portals, while the murals of the inner wall nearest the gate depict the protector deities. The central hall, which is of variable size (depending on the number of columns), contains the rows of seats which are occupied by the monastic body during ritual ceremonies, with the thrones or elevated seats of the main lamas furthest from the gate. Proceeding clockwise around the hall, the side-walls may well depict scenes from the life of Buddha Shakyamuni, or other historical figures. Eventually you will reach the innermost wall (facing the gate and beyond the thrones), against which the rows of clay or guilded copper images, sacred scriptures, and reliquary stupas are positioned. These will vary according to the tradition which the temple or monastery represents, although images of the Buddhas of the Three Times are commonly depicted here. There may additionally be an inner sanctum containing the most precious images housed within the temple, with its own circumambulatory pathway. In front of the images, offerings will be arrayed, including water offering bowls, butter lamps and torma-offering cakes, while donations will be left by the faithful as a meritorious action.

The guide

Acala (*Tib* Miyowa)   one of the 10 wrathful kings (*dashakrodha*), forming a peripheral group of meditational deities in certain mandalas.

Akashagarbha (*Tib* Namkei Nyingpo)   one of the eight major bodhisattvas, yellow in colour, symbolizing the buddha's sense of smell and holding a sword which cuts through dissonant emotions. See **Icon 36**.

Aksobhya (*Tib* Mikyopa)   one of the five peaceful meditational buddhas forming the buddha-body of perfect resource (*sambhogakaya*), collectively known as the Buddhas of the Five Families. Aksobhya is blue in colour, symbolizing the purity of form and the mirror-like clarity of buddha-mind. He holds a vajra to symbolize that emptiness and compassion are without duality. See **Icon 4**.

Amitabha (*Tib* Opame)   one of the five peaceful meditational buddhas forming the buddha-body of perfect resource (*sambhogakaya*), collectively known as the Buddhas of the Five Families. Amitabha is red in colour, symbolizing the purity of perception and the discerning aspect of buddha-mind. He holds a lotus to symbolize the purification of attachment and the altruistic intention. See **Icon 6**.

Amitayus (*Tib* Tsepame)   a meditational deity with nine aspects, who is included among the Three Deities of Longevity, red in colour, and holding a vase full of the nectar of immortality. See **Icon 45**.

Amoghasiddhi (*Tib* Donyo Drupa)   one of the five peaceful meditational buddhas forming the buddha-body of perfect resource (*sambhogakaya*), collectively known as the Buddhas of the Five Families. Amoghasiddhi is green in colour, symbolizing the purity of habitual tendencies and the activity aspect of buddha-mind. He holds a sword to symbolize the cutting off of dissonant emotions through buddha-activity. See **Icon 7**.

Amritakundalin (*Tib* Dutsi Kyilwa)   one of the gatekeepers of the mandalas of meditational deities, dark-green in colour, symbolizing the inherent purity of sensory contact, and holding a crossed-vajra which subdues egotism.

Apchi   a doctrinal protectress of the Drigung Kagyu school, who assumes both peaceful and wrathful forms.

Atisha (*Tib* Jowoje)   a saintly Buddhist master from Bengal (982-1054), who introduced the Kadampa teachings into Tibet. See **Icon 93**.

Avalokiteshvara (*Tib* Chenrezik)   one of the eight major bodhisattvas and the patron deity of Tibet, white in colour, symbolizing the buddha's compassion and sense of taste, and holding a lotus untainted by flaws. There are various forms of this most popular bodhisattva: the 11-faced 1,000-armed form known as Mahakarunika (Tu-je Chenpo, Zhal Chu-chikpa, **Icon 42**), the four-armed form (Chenrezik Chak Zhipa, **Icon 39**), a two-armed form known as Kharsapani (**Icon 44**), the lion-riding form called Simhanada (**Icon 43**), the soothing form called Mind at Rest (Semnyi Ngalso), or Jowo Lokeshvara, and the standing form called Padmapani, the last of which is usually red in colour (**Icon 33**).

Begtse   a sword-wielding form of the protector deity **Mahakala**.

Bhairava (*Tib* Jikje)   a wrathful bull-headed meditational deity (in Buddhism), or a wrathful counterpart of Shiva (in Hinduism).

Bhaisajyaguru (*Tib* Sangye Menla)   the central buddha of medicine, otherwise called Vaiduryaprabharaja, who is blue in colour, holding a bowl containing the panacea myrobalan. See **Icon 12**.

Bodongpa Chokle Namgyel (1375-1451)   one of Tibet's most prolific writers, the author of approximately 100 treatises, a product of the Bodong E college, who established his own distinctive school of Buddhism in Tibet.

Brahma (*Tib* Tsangpa)   a four-faced protector deity associated with the world system of form (in Buddhism), the creator divinity (in Hinduism).

Buddha Shakyamuni (*Tib* Shakya Tupa)   the historical Buddha (sixth to fifth centuries BC), known prior to his attainment of buddhahood as Siddhartha or Gautama, who is also revered as the fourth of the thousand buddhas of this aeon. He is depicted in diverse forms, seated, standing, or reclining (at the point of his decease), and with diverse hand-gestures (symbolizing past merits, generosity, meditation, teaching, fearlessness and so forth). The Jowo form depicts him as a bodhisattva prior to his attainment of buddhahood, and the form Munindra depicts him as he appears among the devas. See **Icon 9**.

Buddhas of the Five Families (*Skt* Pancajina/*Tib* Gyelwa Riknga)   the five buddhas of the buddha-body of perfect resource (*sambhogakaya*; **Icons 3-7**). See listed separately **Aksobhya**, **Amitabha**, **Amoghasiddhi**, **Ratnasambhava**, and **Vairocana**.

Buddhas of the Three Times (*Tib* Dusum Sangye)   see listed separately the Buddha of the past **Dipamkara** (**Icon 8**), the Buddha of the present **Shakyamuni** (**Icon 9**), and the Buddha of the future **Maitreya** (**Icon 10**).

Buton Rinchendrub (1290-1364)   compiler of the Buddhist canon, and major scholar within the Zhalupa tradition of Tibetan Buddhism. See **Icon 109**.

Cakrasamvara (*Tib* Khorlo Demchok)   a four-faced 12-armed wrathful meditational deity, blue in colour, in union with his consort Vajravarahi, trampling upon Bhairava and Kali, and thus representing the Buddhist transmutation of the mundane Hindu divinity Shiva and his consort. See **Icon 54**.

Changkya Qutuqtu III Rolpei Dorje (1717-86)   a holder of high office in Manchu China, who was responsible for escorting Dalai Lama VII to Lhasa, and for the prolonged military campaigns against the Bonpo in Gyarong.

Chenrezi Semnyi Ngalso   see under **Avalokiteshvara**.

Cimara (*Tib* Tsimara)   wrathful protector deity of Samye Monastery, and foremost of the *tsen* class of doctrinal protectors, greenish red in colour.

Cintamani(cakra) Tara   see under **Tara**.

Dalai Lama (*Tib* Gyelwa Rinpoche)   revered as the human embodiment of Avalokiteshvara, the patron deity of Tibet who symbolizes compassion, the successive Dalai Lamas (see page 679) have, since the mid-17th century, assumed both spiritual and temporal authority in Tibet. Among them, the most significant have probably been Dalai Lama III Sonam Gyatso (1543-88; **Icon 116**), Dalai Lama V Ngawang Lobzang Gyatso (1617-82; **Icon 118**), Dalai Lama VI Tsangyang Gyatso (1683-1706; **Icon 120**), Dalai Lama VII Kalzang Gyatso (1708-57), Dalai Lama XIII Tupten Gyatso (1876-1933; **Icon 121**), and the present Dalai Lama XIV (b 1935; **Icon 122**).

Damsi a group of nine sibling demons who have violated their commitments and are said to endanger infant children.

Dashakrodha kings (*Tib* Trowo Chu)   a group of 10 peripheral meditational deities known as the 10 wrathful kings, comprising Usnisacakravartin, Prajnantaka, Yamantaka, Vighnantaka, Padmantaka, Mahabala, Takkiraja, Shumbharaja, Acala, and Niladanda.

Desi Sangye Gyatso (1677-1705)   an important regent of Tibet and author of seminal commentaries on medicine, astrology, religious history, and other subjects. See **Icon 119**.

Dharmaraja (*Tib* Chogyel)   see **Yama Dharmaraja**.

Dharmatala   one of two peripheral figures, sometimes classed alongside the group of **sixteen elders**. He is described as a layman (*upasaka*) who looked after the 16 elders during their visit to China.

Dipamkara Buddha (*Tib* Sangye Marmedze)   the third buddha of this aeon, also known as Kashyapa Buddha, who was the one immediately preceding Shakyamuni. See **Icon 8**.

Dolpopa Sherab Gyeltsen (1292-1361)   the most influential scholar of the Jonangpa school, who was a pre-eminent master of the tantras and an exponent of the *zhentong* philosophy. See **Icon 110**.

Dorje Drakden   a doctrinal protector in the retinue of Pehar, who possesses the medium of Nechung, the state oracle of Tibet.

Dorje Drolo   a wrathful tiger-riding form of Padmasambhava (**Icon 91**). See under **Eight Manifestations of Padmasambhava**.

Dorje Lekpa   a goat-riding doctrinal protector of the Dzogchen teachings, wearing a wide-brimmed hat, who was bound under an oath of allegiance to Buddhism by Padmasambhava in the Oyuk district of West Tibet.

Dorje Yudronma   a doctrinal protectress of the Menmo class, with whom the great Nyingmapa master Longchen Rabjampa is said to have had a particular affinity. See **Icon 62**.

Drigungpa Jikten Gonpo (1143-1217)   one of the foremost students of Phakmodrupa and founder of the Drigung Kagyu school, based at Drigung Til Monastery. See **Icon 101**.

Dromtonpa Gyelwei Jungne (1004-64)   the foremost Tibetan student of Atisha and founder of Reting Monastery. See **Icon 94**.

Drubpa Kabgye   the eight wrathful meditational deities of the Nyingma school, viz: Yamantaka, Hayagriva, Shriheruka, Vajramrita, Vajrakila, Matarah, Lokastotrapuja, and Vajramanrabhiru.

Drukchen   the title of the successive heads of the Drukpa Kagyu school, for an enumeration of whom, see page 254.

Dzogchen Pema Rigdzin (1625-97)   the founder of Dzogchen Monastery in Kham.

Eight Awareness-holders (*Skt* astavidyadhara/*Tib* rigdzin gye)   the eight Indian lineage-holders of the eight transmitted precepts of Mahayoga, who are said to have been contemporaries of Padmasambhava, namely: Manjushrimitra, Nagarjuna, Humkara, Vimalamitra, Prabhahasti, Dhanasamskrita, Rambuguhya-Devacandra, and Shantigarbha.

Eight Bodhisattvas (*Tib* nyese gye)   the eight major bodhisattvas, standing figures who are often depicted flanking images of Shakyamuni Buddha. See listed separately: **Manjushri (Icon 31), Vajrapani (Icon 32), Avalokiteshvara (Icon 33), Ksitigarbha (Icon 34), Nivaranaviskambhin (Icon 35), Akashagarbha (Icon 36), Maitreya (Icon 37),** and **Samantabhadra (Icon 38)**.

Eight Classes of Spirits (*Tib* lhade gye)   a series of lesser spirits or demons, who are to be appeased or coerced by means of ritual offerings.

Eight Deities of the Transmitted Precepts   see **Drubpa Kabgye**.

Eight Manifestations of Padmasambhava (*Tib* guru tsen gye)   the eight principal forms assumed by Padmakara at different phases of his career, namely: **Saroruhavajra** (birth; **Icon 84**), **Padma Gyelpo** (kingship; **Icon 85**), **Shakya Senge** (ordination; **Icon 86**), **Loden Chokse** (mastery of the teachings; **Icon 87**), **Padmasambhava** (establishment of Buddhism in Tibet; Icon 88), **Nyima Ozer** (subjugation of demons; **Icon 89**), **Senge Dradrok** (subjugation of non-Buddhists;

Icon 90), and **Dorje Drolo** (concealment of terma; **Icon 91**).

Eight Medicine Buddhas (*Tib* menla deshek gye)   the successive buddhas revered as the precursors of Buddhist medicine, viz: Sunamaparikirtana, Svaraghosaraja, Suvarnabhadravimala, Ashokottama, Dharmakirtisagaraghosa, Abhijnanaraja, Shakyaketu, and Bhaisajyaguru. For an illustration of the last of these, who is also the central medicine buddha, see **Icon 12**.

Eight Taras who Protect from Fear (*Tib* Dolma Jikpa Gye Kyobma)   a group of female divinities, who offer protection from eight specific types of fear, viz: Manasimhabhayatrana (pride and lions), Mohahastibhayatrana (delusion and elephants), Dvesagniprashamani (hatred and fire), Irsyasarpavisapaharani (envy and poisonous snakes), Kudristicoropadravanivarani (wrong view and thieves), Ghoramatsaryashrinkhalamocani (avarice and fetters), Ragaughavegavartashosani (attachment and rivers), and Samshayapishacabhayatrana (doubt and carnivorous demons). See also under **Tara**.

Eighty-four Mahasiddhas (*Tib* Drubtob Gyachu Gyezhi)   a group of 84 tantric masters of ancient India, for the life-stories of which, see J Robinson, *Buddhas Lions*.

Ekajati (*Tib* Ralchikma)   an important protectress of the Dzogchen teachings, characteristically depicted with a single hair-knot, a single eye and a single breast.

Five Founders of Sakya (*Tib* Gongma Nga)   the successors of Khon Konchok Gyelpo who founded Sakya in 1073, viz: Sachen Kunga Nyingpo (1092-1158; **Icon 104**), Sonam Tsemo (1142-82; **Icon 105**), Drakpa Gyeltsen (1147-1216; **Icon 106**), Sakya Pandita Kunga Gyeltsen (1182-1251; **Icon 107**), and Drogon Chogyel Phakpa (1235-80; **Icon 108**).

Four Guardian Kings (*Skt* Caturmaharajaika/*Tib* Gyelchen Zhi)   the guardian kings of the four directions, whose martial forms are frequently depicted on the walls of a temple portico, viz: Dhritarastra (east), Virudhaka (south), Virupaksa (west), and Vaishravana (north). **Icons 123-126**.

Gampopa (1079-1153)   the student of Milarepa and source of the four major and eight minor Kagyu schools. See **Icon 98**.

Ganesh (*Skt* Ganapati or Vinayaka/*Tib* Tsokdak)   the elephant-headed offspring of Shiva (in Hinduism), an obstacle-causing or obstacle-removing protector deity (in Buddhism).

Genyen   a group of 21 aboriginal divinities, most of whom are identified with snow peaks.

Gonpo Maning (*Skt* Mahapandaka Mahakala)   a spear-wielding two-armed form of the protector deity Mahakala. See **Icon 58**.

Guhyasamaja (*Tib* Sangwa Dupa)   a six-armed seated meditational deity, two forms of which are recognized: Aksobhyavajra (according to the Arya tradition) and Manjuvajra (according to the Buddhajnanapada tradition). The former is light-blue in colour, embraced by the consort Sparshavajra, and has three faces, symbolizing the transmutation of the three poisons: delusion, attachment, and hatred. See **Icon 51**.

Guru Chowang (1212-70)   a great treasure-finder of the Nyingma school.

Gyelpo Ku-nga   the five aspects of the important protector deity Pehar, known respectively as the kings of body, speech, mind, attributes, and activities. See **Icons 63-67**.

Hanuman   the monkey god of Hinduism.

Hayagriva (*Tib* Tamdrin)   a wrathful horse-headed meditational deity of the Nyingma school who is generally red in colour, symbolic of buddha-speech, and included among the **Drubpa Kabgye**. He also appears as a gatekeeper in certain mandalas, and, as the renowned tamer of the egotistical demon Rudra, is frequently positioned (along with Vajrapani) at the entrance of a temple.

Hevajra (*Tib* Kyedorje)   a wrathful counterpart of the meditational deity Aksobhya, deep-blue in colour, who is depicted in a dancing posture, with two, four, six, or 16 arms, and in union with the consort Nairatmya. See **Icon 56**.

Huashang   one of two peripheral figures, sometimes classed alongside the group of **sixteen elders**. He is described as a monk (*Ch* hoshang) who looked after the 16 elders during their visit to China.

Hundred Peaceful and Wrathful Deities (*Tib* Zhitro Lhatsok, Dampa Rikgya)   the assembly of the 42 peaceful deities and 58 wrathful deities, according to the *Guhyagarbha Tantra*, the basis for the visionary account of the *Tibetan Book of the Dead*.

Jambhala (*Tib* Dzambhala)   a protector deity of wealth, yellow in colour, frequently depicted holding a gemstone.

Jamchen Choje Shakya Yeshe   a student of Tsongkhapa, who founded Sera Monastery in 1419.

Jampa   see **Maitreya**.

Jamyang Choje Tashi Palden   a student of Tsongkhapa, who founded Drepung Monastery in 1416.

Je Yabsesum   the collective name given to Tsongkhapa (1357-1419) and his two foremost students, Gyeltsabje Darma Rinchen (1364-1431) and Khedrubje Gelek Pelzang (1385-1438), who were the first throne-holders of Ganden Monastery and thus the founders of the Gelukpa school. The last of these was also retrospectively recognized as Panchen Lama I. See **Icons 113-115**.

Jikme Lingpa (1730-98)   an important Nyingmapa yogin who revealed the highly influential teaching-cycle known as the *Innermost Spirituality of Longchenpa* (*Longchen Nyingtig*).

Jowo   see **Jowo Shakyamuni**.

Jowo Lokeshvara   see under **Avalokiteshvara**.

Jowo Shakyamuni   a form of Buddha Shakyamuni, as a bodhisattva, prior to his attainment of buddhahood.

Kalachakra (*Tib* Dukhor, Dukyi Khorlo) a wrathful meditational deity, blue in colour, with four faces and 12 upper arms and 24 lower arms, embraced by the consort Vishvamata, symbolizing the transmutation of the wheel of time. See **Icon 53**.

Kali in Hinduism, the female consort of Mahadeva, an aspect of Shiva.

Karmapa the oldest succession of incarnating lamas recognized in Tibet, embodying Avalokiteshvara's compassion and presiding over the Karma Kagyu school. For a listing of the 17 Karmapas from Karmapa I Dusum Khyenpa onwards, see page 137. See also **Icon 99**.

Katokpa the title assumed by the first 13 hierarchs of Katok Monastery in East Tibet, founded by Katokpa I Dampa Deshek in 1159.

Kharsapani see under **Avalokiteshvara**.

Krishna (*Tib* nagpo) one of the incarnations of Visnu (in Hinduism).

Ksitigarbha (*Tib* Sayi Nyingpo) one of the eight major bodhisattvas, white in colour, symbolizing the buddha's eyes, and holding a sprouting gemstone of pristine cognition. See **Icon 34**.

Kubera (*Tib* Tadak Kubera) a protector deity of wealth, known as the 'lord of horses', black in colour, brandishing a sword and holding a jewel-spitting mongoose.

Kurukulla (*Tib* Rikchema) a red coloured female meditational deity in dancing posture, holding a flowery bow and arrow, symbolizing her charisma to fascinate and overpower even hostile forces.

Lokeshvara (*Tib* Jikten Wangchuk) an abbreviation of **Avalokiteshvara**.

Longchen Rabjampa (1308-63) pre-eminent scholar, treasure-finder, and systematizer of the Nyingma tradition. See **Icon 111**.

Longdol Lama Ngawang Lobzang (1719-95) an erudite encyclopaedist, who was a student of Dalai Lama VII and teacher of Jamyang Zhepa II Konchok Jikme Wangpo.

Lords of the Three Enlightened Families (*Tib* Riksu Gonpo) the three main bodhisattvas associated with the early Mahayana transmissions, namely Manjughosa symbolizing discriminative awareness; Avalokiteshvara symbolizing compassion; and Vajrapani symbolizing power. See **Icons 39-41**.

Machen Pomra protector deity embodied in the snow peaks of the Amnye Machen range; one of the **Twelve Subterranean Goddesses**.

Mahakala (*Tib* Nagpo Chenpo) a class of supramundane protector deities, 75 aspects of which are recognized. Among these, the most widespread are Four-armed Mahakala (*Skt* Caturbhujamahakala; **Icon 57**); Six-armed Mahakala (*Skt* Sadbhujamahakala), Gonpo Maning (*Skt* Mahapandaka Mahakala; **Icon 58**), Tiger-riding Mahakala (*Tib* Gonpo Takzhon), Begtse, and Panjaranatha (*Tib* Gonpo Gur; **Icon 59**), the last of which is preferred among the Sakyapa.

Mahakarunika (*Tib* Tu-je Chenpo) see under **Avalokiteshvara**.

Mahottara Heruka (*Tib* Chemchok Heruka)   the wrathful counterpart of the primordial buddha Samantabhadra, is dark-brown, with three faces symbolizing the three approaches to liberation, six arms symbolizing the six perfections, and four legs symbolizing the four supports for miraculous ability, trampling upon Mahedeva and Umadevi.

Maitreya (*Tib* Jampa)   one of the eight major bodhisattvas (**Icon 37**) and the future buddha (**Icon 10**), whitish-yellow in colour, symbolizing the buddha's loving kindness and sight, and holding an orange bush which dispels the fever of dissonant emotions.

Manjughosa (*Tib* Jampeyang, Jamyang)   one of the eight major bodhisattvas (**Icon 31**) who is depicted upright, whitish-green in colour and holding a lily, which symbolizes the renunciation of dissonant emotions. In a more familiar seated posture, he is one of the lords of the three enlightened families (**Icon 40**), orange in colour, symbolizing the buddha's discriminative awareness and tongue, and holding a sword which cuts through obscurations and a book of discriminative awareness. Other important forms include Manjushri Vadisimha, Manjushri Kumarabhuta, White Manjushri, and the five aspects which appeared in the visions of Tsongkhapa.

Manjushri (*Tib* Jampel)   see **Manjughosa**.

Manjuvajra (*Tib* Jampei Dorje)   a form of the meditational deity Guhyasamaja, according to the tradition of Buddhajnanapada.

Marici (*Tib* Ozerchenma)   the red goddess of the dawn, who is propitiated for the removal of obstacles.

Marpa (1012-96)   Marpa Chokyi Wangchuk, the student of Naropa and first Tibetan exponent of the Karma Kagyu lineage, whose disciples included Milarepa. See **Icon 96**.

Matsyendranath   an aspect of Avalokiteshvara ('lord of fish') which is revered in Nepal, the white form known as Jamali being enshrined in Asan, and the red form, Bukham, in Patan.

Maudgalyayana (*Tib* Maudgal bu)   one of the two foremost students of Shakyamuni, who passed away before the Buddha's parinirvana. See **Icon 14**.

Milarepa (1040-1123/1052-1135)   the great yogin and ascetic poet of the Kagyu lineage, who was the student of Marpa and teacher of Gampopa. See **Icon 97**.

Nairatmya (*Tib* Dakmema)   female consort of the meditational deity Hevajra, symbolizing selflessness or emptiness.

Narayana (*Tib* Jukse)   one of the incarnations of the Hindu deity Visnu.

Ngok Lotsawa Lekpei Sherab   founder of the Kadampa monastery of Sangpu Neutok and a major student of the 11th century Bengali master Atisha.

Ngorchen Kunga Zangpo (b 1382)   who founded the monastery of Ngor Evam Chode in 1429, giving rise to the influential Ngorpa branch of the Sakya school.

Nivaranaviskambhin (*Tib* Dripa Namsel)   one of the eight major bodhisattvas, reddish-yellow in colour, symbolizing the buddha's ears, and holding a wheel of gems because he teaches the Buddhist doctrine. See **Icon 35**.

Nyangrel Nyima Ozer (1136-1204)   a major treasure-finder (*terton*) of the Nyingma school.

Nyatri Tsenpo   the first king of the Yarlung Dynasty. See **Icon 77**.

Nyenchen Tanglha   the protector deity embodying the mountain range of the same name, which forms a watershed between the Brahmaputra River and the Jangtang lakes. The main peak looms over Lake Namtso Chukmo.

Padmakara (*Tib* Pema Jungne)   the form assumed by Padmasambhava at the time when he and his consort Mandarava were burnt at the stake in Zahor, but miraculously transformed their pyre into a lake. See **Icon 81**.

Padmapani   see under **Avalokiteshvara**.

Padmasambhava   the form assumed by Padmasambhava (ie Guru Rinpoche) while establishing Buddhism in Tibet. See **Icon 88**.

Panchen Lama   the emanations of the Buddha Amitabha, ranking among Tibet's foremost incarnate successions. Among them, Panchen Lama IV Chokyi Gyeltsen (1567-1662; **Icon 117**) was an important teacher of Dalai Lama V.

Panjaranatha (*Tib* Gonpo Gur)   see under **Mahakala**.

Paramadya (*Tib* Palchok Dangpo)   a major meditational deity of the Yogatantra and Mahyoga class.

Parvati consort of the Hindu deity Shiva.

Pehar an important protector deity within the Nyingma and Geluk traditions. See also **Gyelpo Ku-nga**.

Pelpung Situ the incarnations of Tai Situpa, including Situ VIII Chokyi Jungne who, in 1727, founded the largest Karma Kagyu monastery at Pelpung within the kingdom of Derge. For a full enumeration of the Tai Situpas, see page 466.

Pema Totrengtsal   the form assumed by Padmasambhava while manifesting as the meditational deity Vajrakumara to subdue the demons of the Kathmandu valley at Yanglesho (Pharping).

Phadampa Sangye   the 11th-12th century South Indian yogin who propagated the Chodyul and Zhiche teachings in the highland region of Western Tibet.

Phakmodrupa Dorje Gyelpo (1110-70)   student of Gampopa and progenitor of the eight lesser branches of the Kagyu school, including the Drigungpa, Taklungpa and Drukpa branches. See **Icon 100**.

Phakpalha   the title of the principal incarnate lama of Chamdo Jampaling Monastery in Kham, which was founded between 1436-44 by Jangsem Sherab Zangpo.

Prajnaparamita (*Tib* Yum Chenmo)   the female meditational deity embodying the perfection of discriminative awareness, golden yellow in colour, and holding emblems such as the book, sword, lotus, vajra and rosary, which are indicative of supreme insight. See **Icon 48**.

Rahula (*Tib* Za)   an important protector deity within the Nyingma school, depicted as a dark brown or black multi-headed semi-human semi-serpentine figure. See **Icon 61**.

Ratnasambhava (*Tib* Rinchen Jungne)   one of the five peaceful meditational buddhas forming the buddha-body of perfect resource (*sambhogakaya*), collectively known as the Buddhas of the Five Families. Ratnasambhava is yellow in colour, symbolizing the purity of sensations or feelings and the equanimity or sameness of buddha-mind. He holds a gemstone to symbolize that his enlightened attributes are spontaneously present and that he fulfils the hopes of all beings. See **Icon 5**.

Ravana (*Tib* Dradrok-kyi bu)   the 10-headed ogre of Lanka, slain by Rama in the course of the Hindu epic *Ramayana*.

Rechungpa (1084-1161)   a yogin who, like Gampopa, was one of Milarepa's foremost students.

Remati (*Tib* Magzorma)   an aspect of the protectress Shridevi, who rides a mule and holds a sickle or a sandalwood club and a blood-filled skull. She is propitiated in order to overwhelm internal passions and outer disruptions due to warfare.

Remdawa   Zhonu Lodro (1349-1412) a great exponent of the Madhyamaka philosophy within the Sakya tradition, who became one of Tsongkhapa's most significant teachers.

Rigdzin Ngagi Wangpo (1580-1639)   the third successive emanation of Rikdzin Godemchen, founder of the Northern Treasures (Jangter) tradition of the Nyingma school. In 1632 he established the monastery of Dorje Drak in South Tibet.

Rinchen Zangpo (958-1055)   the great translator and contemporary of Atisha whose centre of activity was in Far-west Tibet and the adjacent areas of Spiti and Ladakh.

Sakya Pandita   see under **Five Founders of Sakya**.

Samantabhadra (*Tib* Kuntu Zangpo)   the male or subjective aspect of the primordial buddha-body of actual reality (*dharmakaya*), blue in colour, symbolizing the ground of buddha-mind or luminosity. See **Icon 1**.

Samantabhadra (bodhisattva) (*Tib* Jangsem Kuntu Zangpo)   one of the eight major bodhisattvas, reddish-green in colour, symbolizing the buddha's nose, and holding a corn-ear of gemstones because he fulfils the hopes of beings. See **Icon 38**.

Samantabhadri (*Tib* Kuntu Zangmo)   the female or objective aspect of the primordial buddha-body of actual reality (*dharmakaya*), blue in colour, symbolizing the ground of phenomenal appearances or emptiness. See **Icon 1**.

Iconographic Guide

Samayatara (*Tib* Damtsik Dolma)   a wrathful female meditational deity, consort of the Buddha Amoghasiddhi.

Sarvavid Vairocana (*Tib* Kunrik Nampar Nangze)   see under **Vairocana**.

Seven Generations of Past Buddhas (*Tib* Sangye Rabdun)   the seven buddhas of the immediate past, in sequence: Vipashyin (**Icon 11**), Shikhin, Vishvabhuk, Krakucchanda, Kanakamuni, Kashyapa, and Shakyamuni.

Shakyamuni   see **Buddha Shakyamuni**.

Shakyamuni Aksobhyavajra (*Tib* Shakya Tupa Mikyo Dorsem)   the aspect of Shakyamuni Buddha depicted in the Ramoche Jowo image, which was originally brought to Tibet from Nepal by Princess Bhrikuti in the seventh century.

Shakyashri (1127-1225)   the great Kashmiri scholar who visited Tibet in his later years, influencing all traditions.

Shantaraksita (*Tib* Zhiwei Tso/Khenpo Bodhisattva) a monastic preceptor of Zahor, who officiated at Nalanda Monastery prior to his arrival in Tibet at the invitation of King Trisong Detsen. He ordained the first seven trial monks in Tibet and was responsible for the construction of Samye Monastery, which he modelled on Odantapuri Monastery in Magadha. See **Icon 82**.

Shariputra (*Tib* Shari-bu)   one of the two foremost students of Shakyamuni, who passed away before the Buddha's parinirvana. See **Icon 13**.

Shiva (*Tib* Lha Wangchuk)   the Hindu divinity of destruction; a mundane protector deity in Buddhism.

Shridevi (*Tib* Palden Lhamo)   a major protectress and female counterpart of Mahakala, who has both peaceful and wrathful forms, the latter being a ferocious three-eyed form, dark-blue in colour, and riding a mule. Remati (see above) is included among her aspects. See **Icon 60**.

Simhanada (*Tib* Senge Ngaro)   see under **Avalokiteshvara**.

Simhavaktra (*Tib* Senge Dongma)   a lion-headed meditational deity, who is the female aspect of Padmasambhava, dark blue in colour and holding a vajra-chopper and skull cup, which symbolize that she dispels obstacles to enlightened activity.

Sitatapatra (*Tib* Dukar)   a female umbrella-wielding meditational deity, depicted with a thousand arms, who is propitiated in order to remove obstacles.

Six Ornaments (*Tib* Gyen Druk)   the six great Buddhist commentators of ancient India, viz: Nagarjuna and Aryadeva who developed the Madhyamaka philosophy; the brothers Asanga and Vasubandhu who developed the Yogacara, Cittamatra, and Vaibhasika philosophies; and Dignaga and Dharmakirti who developed a systematic Buddhist logic. See **Icons 69-74**.

Six Sages of the Six Realms (*Tib* Tupa Druk)   six buddha aspects said to appear respectively in the six realms of existence in order to teach the way to liberation from sufferings, respectively: Munindra (among the gods), Vemacitra (among the antigods), Shakyamuni (among humans), Simha (among animals), Jvalamukha (among tormented spirits), and Yama Dharmaraja (among the hells).

Six-armed Mahakala (*Tib* Gonpo Chak Drukpa)   see under **Mahakala**.

Sixteen Elders (*Tib* Neten Chudruk)   a group of elders (*sthavira*) and contemporaries of Shakyamuni Buddha, who were traditionally assigned to promote the Buddhist teachings in the world throughout time, and who have been particularly venerated in Chinese Buddhism, where they are known as arhats (*Ch* lohan). See Icons **15-30**.

Songtsen Gampo   the seventh century unifying king of Tibet who made Lhasa the capital of his newly emergent nation and espoused the Buddhist teachings, revered thereafter as an emanation of the compassionate bodhisattva Avalokiteshvara. See **Icon 79**.

Taklung Tangpa Tashipel (1142-1210)   a foremost student of Phakmodrupa Dorje Gyelpo, who founded the Taklung Kagyu sub-school and the monastery of the same name in 1178. See **Icon 102**.

Tangtong Gyelpo (1385-1464)   the Leonardo of Tibet, renowned as a mystic, revealer of treasure-doctrines, engineer, master bridge-builder, and the inventor of Tibetan opera. See **Icon 112**.

Tara (*Tib* Dolma)   a female meditational deity, who is identified with compassion and enlightened activity. There are aspects of Tara which specifically offer protection from worldly tragedies and fear of the elements (see above, **Eight Taras who Protect from Fear**), and an enumeration of 21 aspects of Tara is well-documented. Among these the most popular are Green Tara (*Tib* Doljang; **Icon 49**), who is mainly associated with protection, and White Tara (*Tib* Dolkar; **Icon 46**), who is associated with longevity. In addition, the form known as Cintamani (cakra) Tara is a meditational deity of the Unsurpassed Yogatantra class.

Terdak Lingpa (1646-1714)   a great treasure-finder who revitalized the Nyingmapa tradition and founded Mindroling Monastery in 1670.

Thirty-five Confession Buddhas (*Tib* ltung-bshags-kyi lha so-lnga)   a group of 35 buddhas associated with the specific practice of purifying non-virtuous habits, in which the names of each are invoked in turn (usually in conjunction with physical prostrations).

Thousand Buddhas of the Aeon (*Tib* Sangye Tongtsa)   the thousand buddhas of the present aeon, whose names are enumerated in the *Bhadrakalpikasutra*. Among these Shakyamuni Buddha was the fourth, and the next to appear in the world will be Maitreya.

Three Ancestral Religious Kings (*Tib* Chogyel Mepo Namsum)   the three foremost Buddhist kings of ancient Tibet, namely Songtsen Gampo who unified the country and espoused Buddhism in the seventh century (**Icon 79**), Trisong Detsen who established the spiritual practices and monastic ordinations of Buddhism in the eighth century (**Icon 83**), and Tri Ralpachen who sought to end Tibetan militarism and lavishly sponsored Buddhist activity in the ninth century (**Icon 92**).

Three Deities of Longevity (*Tib* Tselha Namsum)   see respectively **Amitayus** (**Icon 45**), **White Tara** (**Icon 46**), and **Vijaya** (**Icon 47**).

Iconographic Guide

Thubpa Gangchentso   see under **Vairocana**.

Thubwang (*Skt* Munindra)   see **Buddha Shakyamuni**.

Tiger-riding Mahakala (*Tib* Gonpo Takzhon)   see under **Mahakala**.

Tonmi Sambhota   the seventh century inventor of the Tibetan capital letter script (*uchen*). See **Icon 80**.

Trailokyavijaya (*Tib* Khamsum Namgyel)   a peripheral deity, sometimes assuming a peaceful guise alongside the eight standing bodhisattvas, and sometimes in a wrathful form alongside the Dashakrodha kings.

Tri Ralpachen   see under **Three Ancestral Religious Kings**.

Trisong Detsen   see under **Three Ancestral Religious Kings**.

Tsangpa Gya-re Yeshe Dorje (1161-1211)   the first Drukchen (head of the Drukpa Kagyu school). See **Icon 103**. For a full enumeration of the Drukchen emanations, see above, page .

Tsering Che-nga   five female protector deities associated with the snow peaks of the Everest Range, viz: Miyowa Zangma, Tingi Zhelzangma, Tashi Tseringma, Drozangma, and Drinzangma.

Tseringma   see under **Tsering Che-nga**.

Tsongkhapa (and his foremost students)   see **Je Yabsesum**.

Tuken Lobzang Chokyi Nyima (1737-1802)   the incarnation of Tuken Ngawang Choki Gyatso of Gonlung Jampaling Monastery in Amdo. In 1801 he wrote the *Crystal Mirror of Philosophical Systems*.

Twelve Subterranean Goddesses (*Tib* Tenma Chunyi)   a group of 12 protector goddesses of the earth, who are associated with specific mountain localities, such as Kongtsun Demo, the protectress of Kongpo; and Machen Pomra, the protectress of the Amnye Machen range.

Twelve Tenma   see **Twelve Subterranean Goddesses**.

Twenty-five Tibetan Disciples (*Tib* Jewang Nyernga)   the Tibetan disciples of Padmasambhava, including King Trisong Detsen, Yeshe Tsogyel, Vairotsana, Nubchen Sangye Yeshe, Nyak Jnanakumara, and so forth.

Twenty-one Taras (*Tib* Dolma Nyishu Tsachik)   see under **Tara**.

Two Gatekeepers (*Tib* gokyong nyi)   in most temples the gates are guarded on the inner side by large images of Hayagriva (west) and Vajrapani or Acala (east).

Two Supreme Ones (*Tib* Chok Nyi)   the ancient Indian Vinaya masters, Gunaprabha and Shakyaprabha, who are sometimes classed alongside the **Six Ornaments**. See **Icons 75-76**. Note that some traditions identify Nagarjuna and Asanga as the Two Supreme Ones and, instead, place the Vinaya masters among the Six Ornaments.

Ucchusmakrodha (*Tib* Trowo Metsek)   a wrathful aspect of the meditational deity Hayagriva, in which form the spirit of rampant egotism (Rudra) is tamed.

Usnisavijaya (*Tib* Tsuktor Namgyel)   a three-headed multi-armed wrathful deity, who is the first and foremost of the **Dashakrodha kings**.

Vairocana (*Tib* Nampar Nangze)   one of the five peaceful meditational buddhas forming the buddha-body of perfect resource (*sambhogakaya*), collectively known as the Buddhas of the Five Families. Vairocana is white in colour, symbolizing the purity of consciousness and the emptiness of buddha-mind. He holds a wheel to symbolize that his teachings cut through the net of dissonant emotions. See **Icon 3**. Among other aspects of Vairocana are the four-faced form Sarvavid Vairocana (*Tib* Kunrik Nampar Nangze; **Icon 50**) in which all the peripheral buddhas are embodied, and Muni Himamahasagara (*Tib* Thubpa Gangchentso), in and around whose body all world systems are said to evolve.

Vairotsana   one of the 25 disciples of Padmasambhava, revered as a major translator of Sanskrit texts and a lineage holder of the Dzogchen tradition.

Vaishravana (*Tib* Nam-mang To-se)   the guardian king of the northern direction, who, like Jambhala and Manibhadra, is associated with wealth, and wields a banner and a jewel-spitting mongoose in his hands.

Vajradhara (*Tib* Dorje Chang)   an aspect of the buddha-body of actual reality (*dharmakaya*), appearing in a luminous form complete with the insignia of the buddha-body of perfect resource (*sambhogakaya*). He is dark blue in colour, seated, holding a vajra and bell in his crossed hands. See **Icon 2**.

Vajrakila (*Tib* Dorje Phurba)   a wrathful meditational deity of the Nyingma and Sakya schools in particular, and one of the **Drubpa Kabgye**. He is depicted dark-blue in colour, with three faces, and six arms, and wielding a ritual dagger (*kila/phurba*) which cuts through obstacles to enlightened activity.

Vajrakumara (*Tib* Dorje Zhonu)   an aspect of the meditational deity Vajrakila. See **Icon 52**.

Vajrapani (*Tib* Chakna Dorje)   one of the eight major bodhisattvas and one of the lords of the three enlightened families, blue in colour, symbolizing the buddha's power and sense of hearing, and holding a vajra because he has subjugated sufferings. There are various forms of this bodhisattva, among which the standing peaceful form (**Icon 32**), and the two-armed wrathful form, raising a vajra in the right hand and a noose in the left (**Icon 41**) are most frequently depicted.

Vajrasattva (*Tib* Dorje Sempa)   an aspect of **Aksobhya (Icon 4)** who may appear in a blue form or a white form, holding a vajra in his right hand and a bell in the left, symbolizing purification and the indestructible reality of skilful means and emptiness.

Vajrasattva Yab-yum (*Tib* Dorsem Yabyum)   the meditational deity **Vajrasattva** in union with his female consort.

Vajravarahi (*Tib* Dorje Phagmo)   a female meditational deity who is the consort of Cakrasamvara, generally red in colour and with the emblem of the sow's head above her own. See **Icon 55**.

Iconographic Guide

Vajravidarana (*Tib* Dorje Namjom)   a peaceful meditational deity, seated and holding a crossed-vajra to the heart with the right hand and a bell in the left.

Vajrayogini (*Tib* Dorje Neljorma)   a female meditational deity, red in colour and with a semi-wrathful facial expression. There are several aspects, including the one known as Kecari, the practices of which are associated mainly with the Kagyu school.

Vijaya (*Tib* Namgyelma)   an eight-armed three-headed meditational deity, who is one of the **Three Deities of Longevity**, white in colour and holding a small buddha-image in her upper right hand. Statues of Vijaya are often inserted within Victory Stupas. See **Icon 47**.

Vimalamitra (*Tib* Drime Drakpa)   a Kashmiri master and contemporary of Padmasambhava who introduced his own transmission of Dzogchen in Tibet, and was responsible for disseminating the *Guhyagarbha Tantra*.

Virupa   one of the Eighty-four Mahasiddhas of ancient India who was a progenitor of the profound instructions set down in the *Path and Fruit* teachings of the Sakya school.

Visnu (*Tib* Khyabjuk)   the Hindu divinity of preservation; a mundane protector in Buddhism.

Yama Dharmaraja (*Tib* Shinje Chogyel)   a protector deity favoured by the Geluk school, dark blue in colour and bull-headed, and brandishing a club and a snare. He is identified with Yama, the 'lord of death'. See **Icon 68**.

Yamantaka (*Tib* Zhinje-zhed)   a wrathful meditational deity, with red, black and bull-headed aspects who functions as the opponent of the forces of death. Practices associated with Yamantaka are important in the Nyingma and Geluk schools.

Yamari (*Tib* Zhinje)   see **Yamantaka**.

Yangdak Heruka (*Skt* Shriheruka)   a wrathful meditational deity associated with buddha-mind, from the Nyingma cycle known as the **Drubpa Kabgye**.

Yeshe Tsogyel   one of the foremost disciples and female consorts of Padmasambhava, formerly the wife of King Trisong Detsen.

Yutok Yonten Gonpo (1127-1203)   renowned exponent of Tibetan medicine.

Zhamarpa   the title given to the successive emanations of Zhamarpa Tokden Drakpa Senge (1283-1349), a student of Karmapa III. The monastery of Yangpachen in Damzhung county later became their principal seat.

1 **Samantabdhara** with **Samantabhadri** (Tib. *Kunzang Yabyum*)

2 Vajradhara (Tib. *Dorje Chang*)

3 Buddhas of the Five Families: **Vairocana** (Tib. *Nampar Nangze*)

4 Buddhas of the Five Families: **Aksobhya-Vajrasattva** (Tib. *Mikyopa Dorje Sempa*)

5 Buddhas of the Five Families: **Ratnasambhava** (Tib. *Rinchen Jungne*)

6 Buddhas of the Five Families: **Amitabha** (Tib. *Opame*)

7 Buddhas of the Five Families: **Amoghasiddhi** (Tib. *Donyo Drupa*)

8 Buddhas of the Three Times: **Dipamkara** (Tib. *Marmedze*)

Iconographic Guide

Iconographic Guide

9 Buddhas of the Three Times: **Shakyamuni** (Tib. *Shakya Tupa*)

10 Buddhas of the Three Times: **Maitreya** (Tib. *Jampa*)

11 **Vipashyin** (Tib. *Namzik*), first of the Seven Generations of Past Buddhas (*Sangye Rabdun*)

12 **Bhaisajyaguru** (Tib. *Sangye Menla*), foremost of the Eight Medicine Buddhas (*Menla Deshek Gye*)

13 **Shariputra** (Tib. *Shari-bu*)

14 **Maudgalyayana** (Tib. Maudgal-bu)

15 Sixteen Elders: **Angaja** (Tib. *Yanlak Jung*)

16 Sixteen Elders: **Bakula** (Tib. *Bakula*)

17 Sixteen Elders: **Ajita** (Tib. *Mapampa*)

18 Sixteen Elders: **Rahula** (Tib. *Drachendzin*)

19 Sixteen Elders: **Vanavasin** (Tib. *Naknane*)

20 Sixteen Elders: **Cudapanthaka** (Tib. *Lamtrenten*)

21 Sixteen Elders: **Kalika** (Tib. *Duden*)

22 Sixteen Elders: **Bharadvaja** (Tib. *Bharadvadza*)

23 Sixteen Elders: **Vajriputra** (Tib. *Dorje Moyibu*)

24 Sixteen Elders: **Panthaka** (Tib. *Lamten*)

Iconographic Guide

Iconographic Guide

25 Sixteen Elders: **Bhadra** (Tib. *Zangpo*)

26 Sixteen Elders: **Nagasena** (Tib. *Luyide*)

27 Sixteen Elders: **Kanakavatsa** (Tib. *Serbe'u*)

28 Sixteen Elders: **Gopaka** (Tib. *Beche*)

29 Sixteen Elders: **Kanaka Bharadvaja**
(Tib. *Serchen*)

30 Sixteen Elders: **Abheda** (Tib. *Michedpa*)

31 Eight Bodhisattvas: **Manjushri**
(Tib. *Jampal*)

32 Eight Bodhisattvas: **Vajrapani**
(Tib. *Chakna Dorje*)

33 Eight Bodhisattvas: **Avalokiteshvara**
(Tib. *Chenrezik*)

34 Eight Bodhisattvas: **Ksitigarbha**
(Tib. *Sayi Nyingpo*)

35 Eight Bodhisattvas: **Nivaranaviskambhin**
(Tib. *Dripa Namsel*)

36 Eight Bodhisattvas: **Akashagarbha**
(Tib. *Namkei Nyingpo*)

37 Eight Bodhisattvas: **Maitreya**
(Tib. *Jampa*)

38 Eight Bodhisattvas: **Samantabhadra**
(Tib. *Kuntu Zangpo*)

39 Lords of the Three Enlightened Families:
Four-armed Avalokiteshvara
(Tib. *Chenrezik Chakzhipa*)

40 Lords of the Three Enlightened Families:
Manjughosa (Tib. *Jampeyang*)

Iconographic Guide

Iconographic Guide

41 Lords of the Three Enlightened Families: **Vajrapani** (Tib. *Chakna Dorje*)

42 Aspects of Avalokiteshvara: **Eleven-faced/ Thousand-armed Mahakarunika** (*Zhal Chuchikpa*)

43 Aspects of Avalokiteshvara: **Simhanada** (Tib. *Senge Ngaro*)

44 Aspects of Avalokiteshvara: **Kharsapani** (Tib. *Kharsapani*)

45 Three Deities of Longevity: **Amitayus** (Tib. *Tsepame*)

46 Three Deities of Longevity: **White Tara** (Tib. *Dolkar*)

47 Three Deities of Longevity: **Vijaya** (Tib. *Namgyelma*)

48 Meditational Deities: **Prajnaparamita** (Tib. *Yum Chenmo*)

49 Meditational Deities: **Green Tara**
(*Droljang*)

50 Meditational Deities: **Sarvavid Vairocana**
(Tib. *Kunrik Nampar Nangze*)

51 Meditational Deities: **Guhyasamaja**
(Tib. *Sangwa Dupa*)

52 Meditational Deities: **Vajrakumara**
(Tib. *Dorje Zhonu*)

53 Meditational Deities: **Kalacakra**
(Tib. *Dungkor*)

54 Meditational Deities: **Cakrasamvara**
(Tib. *Khorlo Dompa*)

55 Meditational Deities: **Vajravarahi**
(Tib. *Dorje Pamo*)

56 Meditational Deities: **Hevajra**
(Tib. *Kye Dorje*)

Iconographic Guide

Iconographic Guide

ༀ། །དཔལ་ལྡན་མགོན་པོ་ཕྱག་བཞི་པ། །

ༀ། །འཇིགས་བྱེད་ལས་མགོན་པོ་མ་ནིང་རིང་ནི། །

57 Protector Deities: **Four-armed Mahakala** (Tib. *Gonpo Chak Zhipa*)

58 Protector Deities: **Mahapandaka Mahakala** (Tib. *Gonpo Maning*)

59 Protector Deities: **Panjaranatha** (Tib. *Gonpo Gur*)

60 Protector Deities: **Shrivi** (Tib. *Palden Lhamo*)

ༀ། །ཁྱབ་འཇུག་ཆེན་རྒྱལ་པོ་རཱ་ཧུ་ལ། །

ༀ། །རྫུན་མ་རྡོ་རྗེ་གཡུ་ཡི་སྒྲོན་མ་མཆོག །

61 Protector Deities: **Rahula** (Tib. *Za*)

62 Protector Deities: **Dorje Yudronma**

63 Five Aspects of Pehar: **Kuyi Gyelpo**

64 Five Aspects of Pehar: **Sung-gi Gyelpo**

65 Five Aspects of Pehar: **Tukyi Gyelpo**

66 Five Aspects of Pehar: **Yonten-gyi Gyelpo**

67 Five Aspects of Pehar: **Trinle Gyelpo**

68 Dharmaraja (Tib. *Damchen Chogyel*)

69 Six Ornaments and Two Supreme Ones: **Nagarjuna** (Tib. *Phakpa Ludrub*)

70 Six Ornaments and Two Supreme Ones: **Aryadeva** (Tib. *Phakpa Lha*)

71 Six Ornaments and Two Supreme Ones: **Asanga** (Tib. *Thok-me*)

72 Six Ornaments and Two Supreme Ones: **Vasubandhu** (Tib. *Yiknyen*)

Iconographic Guide

73 Six Ornaments and Two Supreme Ones: **Dignaga** (Tib. *Choklang*)

74 Six Ornaments and Two Supreme Ones: **Dharmakirti** (*Chodrak*)

75 Six Ornaments and Two Supreme Ones: **Gunaprabha** (*Yonten-o*)

76 Six Ornaments and Two Supreme Ones: **Shakyapraha** (*Shakya-o*)

77 Three Early Tibetan Kings: **Nyatri Tsenpo**

78 Three Early Tibetan Kings: **Lhatotori Nyentsen**

79 Three Early Tibetan Kings: **Songtsen Gampo**

80 **Tonmi Sambhota**

81 Founders of the Nyingma School:
Padmakara (Tib. *Pema Jungne*)

82 Founders of the Nyingma School:
Shantaraksita (Tib. *Khenpo Bodhisattva/
Zhiwatso*)

83 Founders of the Nyingma School:
King Trisong Detsen

84 Eight Manifestations of Padmasambhava:
Saroruhavajra (*Tsokye Dorje Chang*)

85 Eight Manifestations of Padmasambhava:
Pema Gyelpo

86 Eight Manifestations of Padmasambhava:
Shakya Senge

87 Eight Manifestations of Padmasambhava:
Loden Chokse

88 Eight Manifestations of Padmasambhava:
Padmasambhava

Iconographic Guide

89 Eight Manifestations of Padmasambhava: **Nyima Ozer**

90 Eight Manifestations of Padmasambhava: **Senge Dradrok**

91 Eight Manifestations of Padmasambhava: **Dorje Drolo**

92 King Ralpachen

93 Founders of Kadampa School: **Atisha** (Tib. *Jowoje*)

94 Founders of Kadampa School: **Dromtonpa**

95 Founders of Kadampa School: **Ngok Lekpei Sherab**

96 Founders of Kagyu School: **Marpa**

ཨ་ གངས་ཅན་ལྗུང་ཀུན་གྱི་རྗེས་མི་ལ་རས། །

ཨ་ ཀྱེ་ལས་གཉགས་སྒམ་གུན་རནམ་མེད་སྒྲུན་ཡོ་པོ། །

97 Founders of Kagyu School: **Milarepa**

98 Founders of Kagyu School: **Gampopa**

ཨ། །ཪ་བདུན་རང་གུ་གཉྱས་གྲུན་ཅུན་ང་ས་པ། །

ཨ། །བདེ་གཤེགས་ཕག་མོ་གྲུ་པའི་རྣམ་འགྱུར་ཡང་མོ་ཉྱ། །

99 Founders of Kagyu School:
Karmapa I, Dusum Khyenpa

100 Founders of Kagyu School:
Phakmodrupa Dorje Gyelpo

ཨ། །འབྲི་ཁུང་ཇིག་གསུམ་མགོན་པོཉ་རྒྱལ་པའི་སྒྲུ་དང་། །

101 Founders of Kagyu School:
Drigungpa Jikten Gonpo

102 Founders of Kagyu School:
Taklung Tangpa Tashipel

ཨ།ག་ཚང་པ་རྒྱ་རས་ཡེ་ཤེས་རྡོ་རྗེ་ནི་མཆོག། །

ཨ། །ཀུན་དགའ་སྙིང་པོ་བཀྲ་ཤིས་རྒྱལ་འཕགས་པ། །

103 Founders of Kagyu School:
Tsangpa Gya-re Yeshe Dorje

104 Five Founders of Sakya: **Kunga Nyingpo**

Iconographic Guide

ཨ། ཁྱི་བློ་གྲོས་རྒྱལ་མཚན་བསོད་ནམས་རྩེ་མོ་ལ་སྐྱབས། །

105 Five Founders of Sakya: **Sonam Tsemo**

ༀ། ཁྱི་རྗེ་བཙུན་གྲགས་པ་རྒྱལ་མཚན་ལ།ཕྱག་འཚལ། །

106 Five Founders of Sakya: **Drakpa Gyeltsen**

ༀ། ཁྱི་རྗེ་བཙུན་ས་པཎ་ཆེན་པོ་ལ་ཕྱག་འཚལ། །

107 Five Founders of Sakya: **Sakya Pandita**

ༀ། ཁྱི་འགྲོ་མགོན་ཆོས་རྒྱལ་འཕགས་པ་ལ་སྐྱབས་སུ་མཆི། །

108 Five Founders of Sakya:
Drogon Chogyel Phakpa

ༀ། །བུ་སྟོན་རིན་ཆེན་གྲུབ་པ་ལ་ཕྱག་འཚལ་ལོ། །

109 **Buton Rinchen Drub**

ༀ། །ཀུན་མཁྱེན་དོལ་པོ་པར་རབ་ཏུ་གསོལ་བ་འདེབས། །

110 **Dolpopa Sherab Gyeltsen**

ༀ། །ཀློང་ཆེན་རབ་འབྱམས་ལ་གསོལ་བ་འདེབས། །

111 **Longchen Rabjampa**

ༀ། །ཐང་སྟོང་རྒྱལ་པོ་ལ་གསོལ་བ་འདེབས། །

112 **Tangtong Gyelpo**

ཨ། །གངས་རུན་བབན་རྗེ་རྩོགས་པ་འཚོང་བུ་ཀ། །

113 Founders of Gelukpa School:
Tsongkhapa

ཨ།།འདབ་སྐལ་ན་ཀྱེ་ཚ་དར་ཆེ་རན་ཆེན་ལ་བདགས་ཀ།

114 Founders of Gelukpa School:
Gyeltsab Darma Rinchen

ཨ།།མཁས་གྲུབ་རྗེ་དགེ་ལེགས་དཔལ་བམ་པ་དགོ་བ་སྐ།།

115 Founders of Gelukpa School:
Khedrubje Gelekpel

ཨ།།ཨན་ན་སྲྀད་མ་བསོད་ནམས་ན་མཚོ་ལ་འཚོ་ཅ།

116 Masters of the Gelukpa Tradition:
Dalai Lama III Sonam Gyatso

ཨ།།བཀ་བཀྱ་ཚ་ཆེམ་མཆོག་རྡོ་བཟང་ཆོས་ཀྱི་རྒྱན་ལ་བདགས་ཀ།།

117 Panchen Lama IV, Lobzang Chogyen

ཨ།།ཐམས་ཅད་མཁྱེན་པ་ངྀ་དབང་རྡོ་བཟང་རྒྱ་མཚོ་ལ་སྐ།།

118 Dalai Lama V, Ngawang Lobzang
Gyatso

ཨ། །ༀ་རེ་གསལ་མ་སྲྀད་ཚང་ལ་རྒྱ་མཚོ་ལ་བཀྲ་ཤྀས་ཀ།།

119 Desi Sangye Gyatso

ཨ།།ཚང་ར་ན་དགམས་ཚ་ཚངས་དབྱངས་རྒྱ་མཚོ་ལ་ཀ།།

120 Dalai Lama VI, Rigdzin Tsangyang
Gyatso

121 Dalai Lama XIII, Tubten Gyatso

122 Dalai Lama XIV, Tendzin Gyatso

123 Dhritarastra, Guardian King of the East

124 Virudhaka, Guardian King of the South

125 Virupaksa, Guardian King of the West

126 Vaishravana, Guardian King of the North

Footnotes

15

Footnotes

Glossary

A

abhidharma   A class of Buddhist literature pertaining to phenomenology, psychology, and cosmology

All-surpassing Realisation   (*thogal*) A meditative technique within the Esoteric Instructional Class of Atiyoga, the highest teachings of the Nyingma school, through which the buddha-body of form (*rupakaya*) is manifestly realized

amban   A Manchu ambassador of the imperial Qing dynasty

Anuttarayogatantra   The unsurpassed yogatantras, which focus on important tantric subject matters, such as 'inner radiance' and 'illusory body'

Anuyoga   The eighth of the nine vehicles of Buddhism according to the Nyingma school, in which the perfection stage of meditation (*sampannakrama*) is emphasized

apsara   Offering goddess, celestial nymph

argali   (*Ovis ammon Hodgsoni Blyth*) A type of wild sheep

Arpacana Mantra   The mantra of the bodhisattva Manjughosa (*Om Arapacana Dhih*), the recitation of which generates discriminative awareness (*prajna*) and intelligence

Atiyoga   The ninth of the nine vehicles of Buddhism according to the Nyingma school, in which the resultant three buddha-bodies (*trikaya*) are effortlessly perfected, and the generation and perfection stages of meditation are both effortlessly present

Avatamsakasutra   The title of the longest Mahayana sutra (excluding the Prajnaparamita literature)

B

bahal   A Newari temple

bangrim   The terraced steps of a stupa, symbolising the bodhisattva and buddha levels

beyul   A hidden land conducive to meditation and spiritua life, of which there are several in trhe Hiamlayan region, such as Pemako in SE Tibet, and Khenpajong in NE Bhutan

Bhadracaryapranid- hanaraja   The title of an important aspirational prayer which is part of the **Avatamsakasutra**

bharal   A species of blue sheep (Tib *nawa*; *Pseudois nayaur* Hodg)

bindu   The finial of a stupa, symbolising the buddha-body of actual reality (*dharmakaya*). The term also refers to the generative fluids of human physiology (according to Tibetan medicine and tantra), and to the seminal points of light appearing in the practice of **All- Surpassing Realisation**

bodhicitta   (Tib *jangchub sem*) The enlightened mind which altruistically acts in the interest of all beings, combining discriminative awareness with compassion

bodhicitta vow   The aspiration to attain full enlightenment or buddhahood for the benefit of all beings

bodhisattva   (Tib *Jangchub Sempa*) A spiritual trainee who has generated the altruistic mind of enlightenment (*bodhicitta*) and is on the path to full buddhahood, remaining in the world in order to eliminate the sufferings of others. Ten successive bodhisattva levels (*bhumi*) are recognized

Bodongpa   An adherent of the Bodong tradition, stemming from Bodong Chokle Namgyel

body of light   The rainbow body of great transformation, in which the impure material body is transformed into one of light, through the practice of the **All-Surpassing Realisation**

Bon   An ancient spiritual tradition, pre-dating the advent of Buddhism in Tibet, which is considered by scholars to be of Zoroastrian or Kashmiri Buddhist origin, but which has, over centuries, assimilated many aspects of indigenous Tibetan religion and Buddhism

border-taming temple   (Tib *Tadul Lhakhang*) A class of stabilising geomantic temples, reputedly constructed by King Songtsen Gampo in the border regions of Tibet

bumpa   The bulbous dome of a stupa

C

calm abiding   (Skt *shatipathana*, Tib *zhi-ne*) A state of mind characterized by the stabilisation of atten- tion on an internal object of observation, conjoined with the calming of external distractions to the mind

Caryatantra   The name of a class of tantra and the fifth of the nine vehicles according to the Nyingma school. Equal emphasis is placed on internal meditation and external rituals

caterpillar fungus   (*Cordiceps sinensis*) A medicinal plant used in the treatment of general debility and kidney disease

cave hermitage   (Tib *zimpuk/ grubpuk*) A remotely located mountain cave utilized as a hermitage for meditative retreats

chaitya   A chapel within a large temple, also used as a synonym for **stupa**

cham   Religious dance

chang   Barley ale or fortified wine (occasionally made of other grains)

charnel ground   A sky burial site, where human corpses are dismembered and compassionately fed to vultures

cho-ke   The name given in Bhutan to the classical Tibetan language, which is the medium of Buddhist literature, in contrast to the colloquial Dzongka language/dialect

Chod (yul)   A meditative rite ('Object of Cutting') in which the egotistical obscurations at the root of all delusions and sufferings are compassionately visualized as a feast-offering on behalf of unfortunate spirits or ghosts, often frequenting **charnel grounds**

chorten   See **stupa**

Chosi Nyiden   The name given to the combined spiritual and temporal form of government maintained in Tibet from 1641 to 1951, and in Bhutan until 1902

chu   river

chuba   Tibetan national dress, tied at the waist with a sash. For men it takes the form of a long-sleaved coat, and for women a long dress, with or without sleaves, which may be shaped or shapeless

chulen   The practice of subsisting upon nuitritious elixirs and vitamins extracted from herbs and minerals, undertaken for reasons of health or as a spiritual practice

D

dadar   An arrow employed in longevty empowerments, marriage and fertility rites, and during harvest festivals

Dasain   Principal Hindu festival dedicated to Durga, the consort of Shiva in her wrathful form, slaying the demon Mahisha, which is held in Nepal over a 10-day period in Sept-Oct

de'u   Enigmatic riddle of the Bon tradition

debri   Mural paintings, frescoes

desi   The title of the regents of the Dalai lamas (in Tibet) and of the Zhabdrungs (in Bhutan), who often wielded considerable political power, particularly during the minority years of the incarnation under their charge

dharma (Tib *cho*) The theory and practice of the Buddhist doctrine, including its texts and transmissions

discriminative awareness (Skt *prajna*/Tib *sherab*) The faculty of intelligence inherent within the minds of all beings, which enables them to examine the characterisrtics of things and events, thus making it possible to make judgements and deliberations

district-controlling temple (Tib *Runon Lhakhang*) a class of stabilising geomantic temples, reputedly constructed by King Songtsen Gampo in Central Tibet, forming an inner ring around the central Jokhang temple

dogar Tibetan opera

Drepung Zhoton the Yoghurt festival held at Drepung one day prior to the start of the operatic Yoghurt festival of Norbulingka

dri fermale of the yak (*Bos grunniens*)

Drigungpa An adherent of the Drigung sub-order of the Kagyu school of Tibetan Buddhism

drokpa nomad

drubchu A sacred spring, said to have been brought forth from the ground through the meditative prowess of one of Tibet's great Buddhist masters

drubkhang Meditation hermitage

Drubtab Gyatsa ('Hundred Means for Attainment') A cycle of short medittative practices contained in the Kangyur, which were translated into Tibetan by Bari Lotsawa

Drukpa Kagyupa An adherent of the Drukpa sub- order of the Kagyu school of Tibetan Buddhism, which predominates in Bhutan

drung story

dukhang The assembly hall of a large monastery, in which the monks affiliated to the various colleges will congregate

Durga puja See **Dasain**

Dzogchen Great Perfection, a synonym for **Atiyoga**

dzong County (administrative unit in Tibet), fortress, castle

dzongkha Colloquial language/dialect of Bhutan

dzongkhak District (administrative unit in Bhutan)

dzongpon District governor (in Bhutan)

E

eight attributes of pure water coolness, sweetness, lightness, softness, clearness, soothing quality, pleasantness and wholesomeness

eight auspicious symbols (Tib *tashi tagye*) umbrella, fish, conch, eternal knot, vase, wheel, and victory-banner, and flower

eight stupas symbolising the major events of the Buddha's life Eight styles of stupa reliquary, respectively symbolising the Buddha's birth, subjugation of Mara, enlightenment, teaching, descent from Tusita (after teaching his late mother), victory, revelation of miracles, and decease

empowerment (Skt *abhiseka*/Tib *wangkur*) A ritual performed by a Buddhist master, which is an essential prerequisite, empowering prospective trainees into the practice of tantra by activating the potential inherent in their mental continuum

emptiness (Skt *shunyata*/Tib *tongpanyi*) The absence of inherent existence and self-identity with respect to all phenomena, the ultimate reality underlying all phenomenal appearances

enlightened mind See **bodhicitta**

enlightenment stupa (Tib *jangchub chorten*) One of the eight types of stupa, this one symbolising the Buddha's enlightenment

eternal knot (Skt *srivatsa*/Tib *palbe'u*) One of the **eight auspicious symbols**, and one of the 32 major marks of a buddha's body, some- times rendered in English as 'heart-orb' since it is found at the heart of the Buddha

extensive lineage of conduct The transmission of Mahayana Buddhism which Asanga received in ancient India from Maitreya, and which emphasizes the elaborate conduct and development of the bodhisattva, in contrast to the 'profound lineage

Footnotes

of view', which Nagarjuna received from Manjughosa

extraneous emptiness (Tib *zhentong*) The view that buddha-attributes are extraneously empty of mundane impurities and dualities, but not intrinsically empty in a nihilistic sense

F

Father Class of Unsurpassed Yogatantras One of the three subdivisions of the Unsurpassed Yogatantras (Anuttarayogatantra), according to the later schools of Tibetan Buddhism, exemplified by tantra-texts, such as the *Guhyasamaja* and *Yamari*

four classes of tantra See respectively: **Kriyatantra**, **Caryatantra**, **Yogatantra** and **Anuttarayogatantra**

four harmonious brethren (Tib *tunpa punzhi*) An artistic motif symbolising fraternal unity and respect for seniority, in which a partridge, rabbit, monkey, and elephant assist each other to pluck fruits from a tree

G

gakhyil A gemstone emblem comprising two or three segments

Ganden Tripa Title given to the head of the Gelukpa school of Tibetan Buddhism

gandharva (Tib *driza*) Denizens of space or celestian musicians who subsist on odours

garuda A mythological bird normally depicted with an owl-like sharp beak, often holding a snake, and with large powerful wings. In Buddhism, it is the mount of Vajrapani, symbolising the transmutative power which purifies certain malevolent influences and pestilences

Gelukpa An indigenous school of Tibetan Buddhism, founded in the 14th century by Tsongkhapa, which, from the 17th century onwards, came to dominate the spiritual life of Tibet and Mongolia

generation stage of meditation (Skt *utpattikrama*/Tib *kye-rim*) The creative stage of meditation in which mundane forms, sounds, and thoughts are gradually meditated upon as natural expressions of deities, mantras, and buddha-mind

geshe (Skt *kalyanamitra*) Spiritual benefactor (of the Kadampa tradition), philosophical degree of a scholar-monk, a scholar-monk holding the geshe degree

gesture of calling the earth as a witness to past mer-its (*bhumisparshamudra*) The hand-gesture of the Buddha utilized during the subjugation of Mara through which he touches the ground, calling the goddess of the earth (Sthavira) to bear witness to his past merits

ghat Steps by the bank of a river, jetty

gomchen Experienced meditator

gongma Chinese emperor

Great Prayer Festival (Tib *Monlam Chenmo*) A festival held in Lhasa during the first month of the lunar calendar, instituted by Tsongkhapa in 1409

Great Seal (Skt *mahamudra*/Tib *chakya chenpo*) The realisation of emptiness as the ultimate nature of reality (according to the sutras), and the supreme accomplishment of buddhahood according to the tantras). The term also refers to the dynamic meditative techniques through which these goals are achieved

Greater Vehicle (Skt *Mahayana*/Tib *Tekpa Chenpo*) The system or vehicle of Buddhism prevailing in Tibet, Mongolia, China, Korea, and Japan, emphasising the attainment of complete liberation of all sentient beings from obscurations and sufferings (rather than the goal of the Lesser Vehicle which is more self-centred and lacks a full understanding of emptiness). The Greater Vehicle includes teachings based on both sutra-texts and tantra-texts

Gu-ge style The artistic style prevalent in Far-west Tibet (Ngari) and adjacent areas of NW India (Ladakh,

Spiti), exhibiting Kashmiri influence

gyaphib A Chinese-style pavilion roof

gyelpo losar Official Tibetan New Year, held at the beginning of the first month of the lunar calendar, which normally falls within February or early March

H

harmika The square section of a stupa, above the dome, on which eyes are sometimes depicted

I

incarnation (Tib *yangsi*) The human form taken by an incarnate lama (*tulku*) following his decease in a previous life

Indra Jatra A Hindu festival held in Nepal honour of the god of rain (Aug-Sept)

Industructible Vehicle (Skt *Vajrayana*/Tib *Dorje Tekpa*) The aspect of the **Greater Vehicle** emphasising the fruitional tantra teachings and meditative techniques concerning the unbroken mental continuum from ignorance to enlightenment. It includes the vehicles of **Kriyatantra**, **Caryatantra**, **Yogatantra**, **Anuttarayogatantra**, **Mahayoga**, **Anuyoga** and **Atiyoga**

Inner Tantra The three inner classes of tantra. See under **Mahayoga**, **Anuyoga** and **Atiyoga**

Innermost Spirituality of Vimalamitra (*Bima Nyingthig*) The title of a collection of esoteric instructions belonging to the **man-ngag-de** (esoteric instructional) class of **Atiyoga**, which were introduced to Tibet from India by Vimalamitra during the early 9th century, and later redacted by Longchen Rabjampa in the 14th century

J

Janai Purnima A Hindu festival held at the Kumbeshvara Temple in Patan, Kathmandu, in honour of Mahadeva, when high caste hindus renew their sacred threads

Jatakamala A stylized account of the Buddha's past lives as a bodhisattva, in Sanskrit verse, composed by Ashvaghosa, and translated into Tibetan

Je Khenpo Title of the chief monastic preceptor of the Drukpa Kagyu school in Bhutan

Jonangpa An adherent of the Jonang school of Tibetan Buddhism

K

kadam (-style) stupa A small rounded stupa, the design of which is said to have been introduced into Tibet by Atisha during the 11th century

Kadampa An adherent of the Kadam school of Tibetan Buddhism, founded by Atisha in the 11th century

Kagyupa An adherent of the Kagyu school of Tibetan Buddhism, founded in Tibet by Marpa during the 11th century

Kalaratri The eighth night of the Hindu festival of **Dasain** (Durga Puja) when animal sacrifices are made in Kathmandu's Taleju Temple

Kangyur An anthology of the translated scriptures of the sutras and tantras, the compilation of which is attributed to Buton Rinchendrub

Karma Gadri A school of art, which evolved in Kham, integrating Tibetan iconography with Chinese landscape themes and perspective

Karma Kagyu A sub-order of the Kagyu school, founded by Karmapa I during the 12th century

kashag The official name of the pre-1959 Tibetan cabinet

khatvanga A hand-emblem, held by Padmasambhava and several wrathful deities, comprising a staff skewered with a stack of three dry skulls and surmounted by an iron trident

kho/baku A woman's dress (in Bhutan)

Khyenri A school of painting associated with the 16th century master Jamyang Khyentse Wangchuk

kira The waistband or cumberband of

Footnotes

a Tibetan or Bhutanese **chuba**

Kriyatantra   The name of a class of tantra and the fourth of the nine vehicles according to the Nyingma school. Greater emphasis is placed on external rituals than on internal meditation

kumbum   A stupa containing many thousands of images, and often multiple chapels, sometimes known as 'Tashi Gomang' stupa

kunzang khorlo   (Skt *sarvatobhadra*) A type of geometric poetry in the shape of a wheel, the lines of which read in all directions

kyang   The Asiatic wild ass (*Equus hemionus* Pallas)

L

la   Mountain pass

la-do   A stone assuming the function of a life-supporting talisman (*la-ne*)

la-guk   A rite for summoning or drawing in the life-supporting energy or talisman of another

la-shing   A tree assuming the function of a life-supporting talisman (*la-ne*)

labrang   The residence of an incarnate lama within a monastery

lam   road

Lama Chodpa   A text on the practice of *guruyoga* ('union with the guru'), written by Panchen Lama IV

lama   Spiritual mentor (Skt *guru*)

Lamdre   A unique collection of meditative practices related to the meditational deity Hevajra, which are pre-eminent in the Sakya school, outlining the entire theory and practice of the **Greater Vehicle**

lamrim   (Skt *pathakrama*) The graduated path to enlightenment, and the texts expounding this path

Lato style   A localized and less cosmopolitan style of Tibetan panting, associated with sites in the highland region of W Tibet

latse   Top of a mountain pass, the cairn of prayer flags adorning a mountain pass

Lesser Vehicle   (Skt *Hinayana*/Tib *Tekmen*) The system or vehicle of Buddhism prevalent in Sri Lanka,

Thailand and Burma, emphasising the four truths and related teachings through which an individual seeks his own salvation, rather than the elimination of others' sufferings

lhakhang   Buddhist temple

lhamo   Female deity (Skt *devi*)

life-supporting talisman   (Tib *la-ne*) An object imbued with a sympathetic energy force, said to sustain the life of its owner

Ling Gesar   The legendary warrior king, who is the hero of Tibetan epic poetry

lingam   See **Shiva lingam**

losar   Tibetan New Year

lumo   Female naga-spirit (Skt *nagini*)

lung-gom   A set of meditative practices in which the vital energy (*lung*) of the body, including the respiratory cycle, is controlled and regulated

lungta   Tibetan mantras printed on cloth for use as prayer flags, which are activated by the power of the wind, or on paper as an offering to local mountain divinities, in which case they are tossed into the air on a mountain pass

M

Madhyamaka   The philosophical system of Mahayana Buddhism based on the Middle Way, which seeks to comprehend, either by means of syllogistic reasoning or by reductio ad absurdum, the emptiness or absence of inherent excistence with respect to all phenomena. A distinction is drawn between the ultimate truth, or emptiness, and the relative truth in which all appearances exist conventionally

Mahamudra   See **Great Seal**

Mahayoga   The name of a class of tantra and the seventh of the nine vehicles according to the Nyingma school, emphasising the generation stage of meditation (*utpattikrama*)

man-ngagde   (Skt *upadeshavarga*) The inner-most class of instructions according to **Atiyoga**

mandala   (Tib *kyilkhor*) A symbolic two or three dimensional representation of the palace of a given meditational deity, which is of crucial importance during the generation stage of meditation

mani (-stone) wall A wall adorned with stone tablets engraved with the mantras of the deity Avalokiteshvara, embodiment of compassion

Mani Kabum The title of an early Tibetan historical work, said to have been concealed as a terma-text by King Songtsen Gampo in the 7th century, and to have been rediscovered during the 12th century by three distinct treasure-finders (*terton*)

mani prayer-wheel (Tib *dungkhor*) A large prayer wheel containing mantras of the deity Avalokiteshvara, embodiment of compassion

mantra (Tib *ngak*) A means of protecting the mind from mundane influences through the recitation of incantations associated with various meditational deities, thereby transforming mundane speech into buddha-speech. Mantra also occurs as a synonym for tantra

mantra vows The various commitments maintained by those who have been empowered to practice the tantras

mantrin (Tib *ngakpa*) A practitioner of the mantras, who may live as a lay householder rather than a renunciate monk

-me The lower part of a valley

meditational deity (Skt *istadevata*/Tib *yidam*) A peaceful or wrathful manifestation of buddha-mind, which becomes the object of a meditator's attention, as he or she seeks to cultivate experientially specific buddha-attributes by merging inseperably with that deity

momo A Tibetan dumpling

monk (Skt *bhiksu*/Tib *gelong*) One who maintains the full range of monastic vows as designated in the Vinaya texts

Mother Class of Unsurpassed Yogatantras One of the three subdivisions of the Unsurpassed Yogatantras (Anuttarayogatantra), according to the later schools of Tibetan Buddhism, exemplified by tantra-texts, such as the *Cakrasamvara* and *Hevajra*

Mt Potalaka Abode of the deity Avalokiteshvara, said in some sources to be located in S India

mu A 'sky-cord' of light on which the ancient 'immortal' kings of Tibet were said to leave this world at the time of their succession

mumo A female mu spirit, said to cause dropsy

muntsam Meditation retreat in darkness

N

naga A powerful water spirit which may take the form of a serpent or semi-human form similar to a mermaid/man

Nagaraja King of naga spirits

Namchu Wangden A series of vertically stacked letters symbolising elemental power and buddha-attributes

Namgyel Chorten See **Victory Stupa**

nectar (Skt *amrita*/Tib *dutsi*) The ambrosia of the gods which grants immortality, metaphorically identified with the Buddhist teachings

New Translation Schools (Sarmapa) Those maintaining the Buddhsit teachings which were introduced into Tibet from India from the late 10th century onwards, and which are contrasted with th Nyingma school, representing the earlier dissemination of Buddhism. The New Translation Schools include those of the **Kadampa, Kagyupa, Sakyapa, Jonangpa and Zhalupa**

ngakpa See **mantrin**

nine (hierarchical) vehicles (Skt *navayana*/Tib *tekpa rimpa gu*) According to the Nyingma school of Tibetan Buddhism, these comprise the three vehicles of pious attendants (*shravaka*), hermit buddhas (*pratyekabuddha*) and bodhisattvas, which are all based on the sutras; as well as the six vehicles of Kriyatantra, Caryatantra, Yogatantra, Mahayoga, Anuyoga, and Atiyoga, which are all based on the tantras. Each of these is

entered separately in this glossary

Northern Treasures (Tib *jangter*) The terma tradition derived from Rigdzin Godemchen's 14th century discoveries in the Zangzang area of Northern Tibet

Nyang Chojung Taranatha's history of the Nyang-chu valley

nyenmo A plague-inducing demoness of the soil

Nyingma Gyudbum The anthology of the Collected Tantras of the Nyingmapa, most of which were translated into Tibetan during 8th-9th centuries and kept unrevised in their original format

Nyingma Kama The anthology of the oral teachings or transmitted precepts of the Nyingma school, accumulated over the centuries, and published most recently by the late Dudjom Rinpoche

Nyingmapa An adherent of the Nyingma school of Tibetan Buddhism, founded in Tibet by Shantaraksita, Padmasambhava, King Trisong Detsen, and Vimalamitra

nyung-ne A purificatory fast (*upavasa*)

offering mandala A symbolic representation of the entire universe, which is mentally offered to an object of refuge, such as the Buddha or one's spiritual mentor

onju/gyenja A woman's blouse (in Bhutan and Tibet)

Outer Tantra The three outer classes of tantra. See under **Kriyatantra, Caryatantra** and **Yogatantra**

pagoda A distinctive style of multi-storied tower, temple or stupa

Pala style Bengali style of Buddhist art

pandita Scholar, a Buddhist scholar of ancient India

Parinirvanasutra The sutra expounding the events surrounding the Buddha's decease

Path and Fruit See **Lamdre**

penma (*Potentilla fructicosa*) A type of twig used in the constuction of the corbels of certain Tibetan buildings for aesthetic reasons, and to provide a form of ventilation

perfection stage of meditation (Skt *sampannakrama*/Tib *dzog-rim*) The techniques for controlling the movement of vital energy (*vayu*) and **bindu** within the central channel of the body through which inner radiance (*prabhasvara*) and coemergent pristine cognition (*sahajajnana*) are realized. It is contrasted with the **generation stage of meditation**

Phakmodrupa The dynasty of Tibetan kings who ruled Tibet from Nedong during the 14th-15th centuries

phurba A ritual dagger, which is the hand-emblem of the meditational deity Vajrakila/Vajrakumara, penetrating the obscurations of mundane existence

pilgrim's circuit (Tib *khorlam*) A circumambulatory walkway around a shrine or temple, along which pilgrims will walk in a clockwise direction

place of attainment (Tib *drub-ne*) A sacred power-place where great spiritual masters of the past meditated and attained their realizations

Ponlop The title of a district governor in pre-1902 Bhutan

Prajnaparamita A class of Mahayana literature focussing on the bodhisattva paths which cultivate the 'perfection of discriminative awareness'

prayer flag A flag printed with sacred mantra syllables and prayers, the power of which is activated by the wind

prayer wheel A large fixed wheel (*dungkhor*) or small hand-held wheel (*tu-je chenpo*), containing sacred mantra-syllables or prayers, the power of which is activated by the spinning motion of the wheel

profound lineage of view The transmission of Mahayana Buddhism which Nagarjuna received in ancient India from Manjughosa, and which emphasizes the profound view of emptiness, in contrast to the 'extensive lineage of conduct', which Asanga received from Maitreya

protecter shrine   (*gonkhang*) A temple or chapel dedicated to the class of protector deities (Skt *dharmapala*/Tib *chokyong*)

puja   Offering ceremony

Q

qan   A Mongol chieftan or king

qutuqtu   The Mongol equivalent of **tulku** ('incarnate lama')

R

rainbow body   (*ja-lu*) The buddha-body of great transformation, in which the impure material body is transformed into one of light, through the practice of the **All-Surpassing Realisation**

Ranjana   (*lantsa*) The medieval Sanskrit script of Newari Buddhism from which the Tibetan capital letter script (*u-chen*) is said to have been derived

Ratnakuta   An important section of the Mahayana sutras, which, along with the prajnaparamita literature, largely represent the second promulgation of the Buddhist teachings

reliquary   (*dung-ten*) A stupa containing buddha-relics or the relics/embalmed remains of a great spiritual master

residential college/unit   (*khangtsang*) The residential quarters of a large monastic college, often inhabited by monks from one specific region of the country

Ringpungpa   The dynasty of Tibetan princes who usurped the power of the Phakmodrupa kings during the late 15th century and ruled much of Tibet from Rinpung in Tsang, until they themselves were usurped by the kings of Tsang, based in Zhigatse

ritual dagger   See **phurba**

rongpa   villager

runon   See **district controlling temple**

S

sacred outlook   (*dak-nang*) The pure vision through which all phenomenal appearances, including rocks and topographical features, may assume the forms of deities

Sakyapa   An adherent of theSakya school of Tibetan Buddhism, founded by Gayadhara, Drokmi, and Khon Konchok Gyelpo in the 11th century

sand mandala   A two- dimensional representation of the palace of a given meditational deity, made of finely ground coloured powders or sands

sangha   The Buddhist monastic community (Tib *gendun*)

self-arising (object/image)   (*rang-jung*) A naturally produced object or image, emerging of its own accord from stone, wood, and the like, in which great sanctity is placed

self-arising seed-syllable A   (*A rang-jung*) a 'naturally produced' seed-syllable A, indicative of **emptiness**

self-arising terma stone   (*rangjung terdo*) A 'naturally produced' stone, said to have been discovered as **terma**

serdung   A reliquary stupa made of gold

Seven Trial Monks   The first Tibetan monks ordained in the 8th century by Shantaraksita

sexagenary year cycle   (*rab-jung*) The cycle of 60 years on which Tibetan chronology is based (rather than centuries). This system was originally adopted in Tibet from the *Kalacakra Tantra*, and each year of the sixty years was later given a distinctive name combining one of the 12 animals and one of the five elements of the Chinese system

shakti   Energy or power inherent in the female consort of the Hindu deity Shiva

Shambhala   A mysterious hidden land, often identified with Central

Footnotes

Asia, where the *Kalackra Tantra* was disseminated, and from where, it is said, messianic kings will emerge during the next millenium to subdue tyrranical empires on earth

Shangpa Kagyu   A branch of the Kagyu school which originated from the Tibetan yogin Khyungpo Naljor of Shang rather than Marpa

shastra   A treatise or commentary elucidating points of scripture or science (Tib *ten-cho*)

shen   A type of Bonpo priest

shikhara   The curved spire of a Hindu temple

Shiva lingam   The Hindu deity Shiva embodied in a phallic emblem

sign of accomplishment   A sign or intimation of success in spiritual practice

six-syllable mantra   The mantra of the bodhisattva Avalokiteshvara (*Om Mani Padme Hum*), the syllables of which respectively generate compassion for the sufferings endured by gods, antigods, humans, animals, ghosts, and denizens of the hells

sky-burial site   (*dutro*) See **charnel ground**

sok-shing   The central pillar of a building or the wooden axis inside an image, which acts as a life-support

sonam losar   The agricultural new year, held 1 month prior to the official new year (in Bhutan and parts of Tibet)

stone footprint   The imprint of the foot of a great spiritual master of the past, left in stone as a sign of yogic prowess

stupa   (Tib *chorten*) The most well-known type of sacred monument in the Buddhist world, symbolising the buddha-body of reality (*dharmakaya*), and holding the relics of the Buddha or some great spiritual master. For illustrations of the eight types of stupa recognized in the Tibetan world

Sukhavati   The buddha-field of Amitabha, the meditational buddha of the west

supine ogress   An anthropomorphic description of the dangerous terrain

of the Tibetan landscape, which King Songtsen Gampo tamed by constructing a series of geomantic temples

sutra   (Tib *do*) The discourses of the Buddha, belonging to either the **Lesser Vehicle** or the **Greater Vehicle**, which were delivered by Shakyamuni Buddha, and which expound the causal path to enlightenment in a didactic manner, in contrast to the **tantras**

Sutra of the Auspicious Aeon   (*Bhadrakalpikasutra*) The title of a sutra enumerating the thousand budhas of this 'auspicious aeon', of whom Shakyamuni was the fourth and Maitreya will be the fifth

swastika (Tib *yungdrung*) A Buddhist symbol of good auspicies, included among the thirty-two excellent major marks of a buddha's body. The inverse swastika is also a Bon symbol

syllable A   The seed-syllable inherent in all syllables, which is indicative of **emptiness**

tadul   See **border taming temple**

talismanic object/place   (*la-ne*) See **life-supporting talisman**

tangka   Tibetan painted scroll

tangka wall   (*goku*) A large wall located within the grounds of a monastery, on which large applique tangkas are hung during specific festivals

Tangyur   An anthology of the translated scriptures of the Indian treatises on Buddhism and classical sciences, the compilation of which is attributed to Buton Rinchendrub

tantra   The continuum from ignorance to enlightenment

tantra-text   (Tib *gyud*) Canonical texts delivered by the buddhas, which emphasize the resultant approach to buddhahood, in contrast to the causal or didactic approach of the **sutras**

teaching gesture   (*dharmacakramudra*) The hand-gesture of the Buddha utilized during the teaching of the Buddhist doctrine

terma (Skt *nidhi*) The texts and sacred objects formerly concealed at geomantic power-places on the Tibetan landscape during the 7th-9th centuries, in the manner of a time capsule, which were later revealed in subsequent centuries by the trea-sure-finders (*terton*) appointed to dis-cover them. Other termas, known as gong-ter, are revealed directly from the nature of buddha-mind

thread-cross (Tib *do*) A wooden framed structure crossed with many layers of coloured threads, used as a device for trapping and exorcising evil forces or demons

three approaches to liberation (Tib *namtar gosum*) As expounded in the **Greater Vehicle**, these are: emptiness, aspirationlessness and signlessness

three buddha-bodies (*trikaya*) The buddha-body of actual reality (*dharmakaya*) or emptiness underly-ing all phenomena; the buddha-body of perfect resource (*sambhogakaya*) whose light-forms appear in medita-tion to advanced level bodhisattvas; and the buddha-body of emanation (*nirmanakaya*) which manifests materially in the world to guide living beings from suffering

three roots (Skt *trimula*/Tib *tsawa sum*) The spiritual mentor (*lama*) who confers blessing, the meditational deity (*yidam*) who con-fers spiritual accomplishments, and the dakini (*khandroma*) who embod-ies enlightened activity

three world systems (*tridhatu*) Those of desire, form and formlessness

three-dimensional palace (*vimana*) The celestial palace of a given meditational deity

thukpa soup, noodle soup

Tishri The title of imperial preceptor to the Mongol Yuan emperors

-to The upper reaches of a valley

togo jacket, shirt

tongdrol Liberation by sight, an object conferring liberation by sight

torana Stucco halo of an image, arched pediment above a gateway

torma (Skt *bali*) Ritual offering-cake

tratsang A college within a large monastery

treasure chest (Tib *terdrom*) Con-tainer in which terma are concealed and from which they are subse-quently discovered

treasure See **terma**

treasure-finder (Tib *terton*) The prophesied discoverer of a terma-text or terma-object

treasure-site (Tib *terka*) Locations in which terma are concealed and discovered

tsampa The staple Tibetan food con-sisting of ground and roasted barley flour, which is mixed with tea as a dough

tsatsa Mininiture votive terracotta image, sometimes inserted within a stupa

Tsechu The tenth day of the lunar month, associated with the activities of Padmasambhava, and on which feast-offering ceremonies are held. These may assume the form of grand religious dance performances, for which reason, in Bhutan, the term refers to **cham** festivals

tsewang Longevity **empowerment**

tshe-chu Water-of-life spring

tsuklakhang large temple (Skt *vihara*)

tulku Incarnate lama, emanation, bud-dha-body of emanation (*nirmanakaya*)

tummo The name of a yogic practice of the perfection stage of meditation in which an inner heat is generated within the body to burn away all obscurations and generate the coemergence of bliss and emptiness

Tusita A low-level paradise within the world-system of desire (*kamadhatu*) where the future buddha Maitreya is presently said to reside

Twelve Deeds of Shakyamuni The 12 principal sequential acts in the Buddha's life, viz: residence in Tusita paradise, conception, birth, study, marriage, renunciation, asceticism, reaching the point of enlightenment, vanquishing demonic obstacles, per-fect enlighten- ment, teaching and final nirvana at the time of death

Footnotes

U

Uchen   The Tibetan capital letter script

udumbara lotus   A hugh mythical lotus, said to blossom once every 500 years

V

vajra   (Tib *dorje*) The indestructible reality of buddhahood, a sceptre-like ritual object symbolizing this indestructible reality, or skillful means

vajra and bell   (*vajragantha*) A set of ritual implements, respectively symbolising skilful means and discriminative awareness

Vajra Guru mantra   The mantra of Pasmasambhava (*Om Ah Hum Vajra Guru Padma Siddhi Hum*)

vajradhatu   (Tib *dorje ying*) The indestructible expanse of reality

Vartula   The Indic script from which the cursive Tibetan U-me script is said to be derived

Victory/Vijaya Stupa   (Tib *namgyel chorten*) One of the eight types of stupa, this one symbolising the Buddha's victory over mundane influences

vihara   A large Buddhist temple

Vinaya   (Tib *dulwa*) The rules of Buddhist monastic discipline, the texts outlining these rules

W

wheel and deer emblem   A motif symbolizing the deer park at Rsipatana (Sarnath) where the Buddha gave his first teaching, turning the doctrinal wheel in a deer park

wheel of rebirth   (Skt *bhavacakra*/Tib *sidpei khorlo*) A motif depicting the sufferings of the various classes of sentient beings within cyclic existence and the causal processes which give rise to their rebirth

wind-horse   See **lungta**

Y

yaksa   A type of malevolent mountain spirit

yangdul lhakhang   The remote group of 'further taming' geomantic temples, reputedly constructed by King Songtsen Gampo, outside the line of the 'border-taming temples'

yantra   Yogic exercises (in Buddhism), a magical geometric diagram (in Hinduism)

Yogatantra   The name of a class of tantra and the sixth of the nine vehicles according to the Nyingma school. Greater emphasis is placed on internal meditation than upon external rituals

Yoghurt festival   See **Zhoton**

yogin   (Tib *neljorpa*) A male practitioner engaged in intensive meditative practices

yogini   (Tib *neljorma*) A female practitioner engaged in intensive meditative practices

Z

Zangdok Pelri style   A mode of temple construction symbolising the 3-storeyed palace of Padmasambhava

Zhalupa   An adherent of the Zhalu tradition, associated with Zhalu Monastery (founded 1040)

Zhidag   A type of local divinity

Zhije   The meditative technique of 'pacification' introduced to Tibet by Phadampa Sangye

Zhoton   The Yoghurt operatic festival, held at Norbulingka in Lhasa in Aug

zi   A species of etched agate or banded chalcedony, highly valued in Tibet

Zikpa Ngaden   Tsongkhapa's five vsions of diverse aspects of Manjushri

Footnotes

Footnotes

Footnotes

Footnotes

Footnotes

Shorts

Special interest pieces on and about Tibet

Index

Note: Coloured map references are given in italics. Thus 'Dingri *M2C1*' will be found on colour map 2 in grid C1

Maps

Footnotes

Will you help us?

We try as hard as we can to make each Footprint Handbook as up-to-date and accurate as possible but, of course, things always change. Many people write to us - with corrections, new information, or simply comments.

If you want to let us know about an experience or adventure - hair-raising or mundane, good or bad, exciting or boring or simply something rather special - we would be delighted to hear from you. Please give us as precise information as possible, quoting the edition number (you'll find it on the front cover) and page number of the Handbook you are using.

Your help will be greatly appreciated, especially by other travellers. In return we will send you details about our special guidebook offer.

Write to Elizabeth Taylor
Footprint Handbooks
6 Riverside Court
Lower Bristol Road
Bath
BA2 3DZ
England
or email info@footprint.cix.co.uk

Complete listing

Sales & distribution

Footprint Handbooks
6 Riverside Court
Lower Bristol Road
Bath BA2 3DZ
T 01225 469141
F 01225 469461
E Mail handbooks@
footprint.cix.co.uk

Australia
Peribo Pty
58 Beaumont Road
Mt Kuring-Gai
NSW 2080
T (02) 9457 0011
F (02) 9457 0022

Austria
Freytag-Berndt Artaria
Kohlmarkt 9
A-1010 Wien
T 01 533 2094
F 01 533 8685

Belgium
Craenen BVBA
Mechelsesteenweg 633
B-3020 Herent
T 016 23 90 90
F 016 23 97 11

Canada
Ulysses Travel Publications
4176 rue Saint-Denis
Montréal
Québec H2W 2M5
T (514) 843 9882
F (514) 843 9448

Caribbean
Kingston Publishers
10,LOJ Industrial Complex
7 Norman Road
Kingston CSO
Jamaica
T 001876 928 8898
F 001876 928 5719

**Europe – Central
& Eastern**
Michael Timperley
MTM
E Mail 100421.2070@
compuserve.com
T +852 2525 6264
F +852 2918 1034

**Europe – Germany,
Austria, Scandinavia,
Spain, Portugal**
Bill Bailey
16 Devon Square
Newton Abbott
Devon TQ12 2HR.UK
T 01626 331079
F 01626 331080

Denmark
Kilroy Travel
Skindergade 28
DK-1159 Copenhagen K
T 33 11 00 44
F 33 32 32 69

Nordisk Korthandel
Studiestraede 26-30 B
DK-1455 Copenhagen K
T 33 13 26 38
F 33 91 26 38

Scanvik Books
Esplanaden 8B
DK-1263 Copenhagen K
T 33 12 77 66
F 33 91 28 82

Finland
Akateeminen Kirjakauppa
Keskuskatu 1
FIN-00100 Helsinki
T 09 12141
F 09 121 4441

Suomalainen
Kirjakauppa
Koivuvaarankuja 2
01640 Vantaa 64
F 08 52 78 88

France
L'Astrolabe
46 rue de Provence
F-75009 Paris 9e
T 1 42 85 42 95
F 1 45 75 92 51

VILO Diffusion
25 rue Ginoux
F-75015 Paris
T 01 45 77 08 05
F 01 45 79 97 15

Germany
GeoCenter ILH
Schockenriedstrasse 44
D-70565 Stuttgart
T 0711 781 94610
F 0711 781 94654

Brettschneider
Fernreisebedarf
Feldkirchnerstrasse 2
D-85551 Heimstetten
T 089 990 20330
F 089 990 20331

Geobuch Gmbh
Rosental 6
D-80331 München
T 089 265030
F 089 263713

Gleumes
Hohenstaufenring 47-51
D-50674 Köln
T 0221 215650

Globetrotter Ausrustungen
Wiesendamm 1
D-22305 Hamburg
F 040 679 66183

Dr Götze
Bleichenbrücke 9
D-2000 Hamburg 1
T 040 3031 1009-0

Hugendubel Buchhandlung
Nymphenburgerstrasse 25
D-80335 München
T 089 238 9412
F 089 550 1853

Kiepert Buchhandlung
Hardenbergstrasse 4-5
D-10623 Berlin 12
T 030 311880

Greece
GC Eleftheroudakis
17 Panepistemiou
Athens 105 64
T 01 322 2255
F 01 323 9821

India
Roli Books
M-75 GK II Market
New Delhi 110048
T (011) 646 0886
F (011) 646 7185

Israel
Geographical Tours
8 Tverya Street
Tel Aviv 63144
T 03 528 4113
F 03 629 9905

Italy
Librimport
Via Biondelli 9
I-20141 Milano
T 02 8950 1422
F 02 8950 2811

Kenya
Novelty Wholesalers
PO Box 47407
Nairobi
T 2 743157 F 2 743157

Netherlands
Nilsson & Lamm bv
Postbus 195
Pampuslaan 212
N-1380 AD Weesp
T 0294 494949
F 0294 494455

Norway
Narvesen Distribusjon
Bertrand Narvesens Vei 2
Postboks 6219 Etterstad
N-0602 Oslo 6
T 22 57 32 00
F 22 68 24 65

Schibsteds Forlag A/S
Akersgata 32 - 5th Floor
Postboks 1178 Sentrum
N-0107 Oslo
T 22 86 30 00
F 22 42 54 92

Tanum
PO Box 1177 Sentrum
N-0107 Oslo 1
T 22 41 11 00
F 22 33 32 75

Pakistan
Pak-American Commercial
Zaib-un Nisa Street
Saddar
PO Box 7359
Karachi
T 21 566 0419
F 21 568 3611

South Africa
Faradawn CC
PO Box 1903
Saxonwold 2132
T 011 885 1787
F 011 885 1829

South America
Humphrys Roberts
Associates
Caixa Postal 801-0
Ag.Jardim da Gloria
06700-970 Cotia SP
Brazil
T 011 492 4496
F 011 492 6896

Southeast Asia
APA Publications
38 Joo Koon Road
Singapore 628990
T 865 1600
F 861 6438

Spain
Altaïr, Balmes 69
08007 Barcelona
T 93 3233062
F 93 4512559

Bookworld España
Pje Las Palmeras 25
29670 San Pedro
Alcántara, Málaga
T 95 278 6366
F 95 278 6452

Sweden
Hedengrens Bokhandel
PO Box 5509
S-11485 Stockholm
T 8 6115132

Kart Centrum
Vasagatan 16
S-11120 Stockholm
T 8 111699

Lantmateriet Kartbutiken
Kungsgatan 74
S-11122 Stockholm

Switzerland
Artou, 8 rue de Rive
CH-1204 Geneva
T 022 311 4544
F 022 781 3456

Office du Livre OLF SA
ZI 3, Corminboeuf
CH-1701 Fribourg
T 026 467 5111
F 026 467 5466

Schweizer Buchzentrum
Postfach
CH-4601 Olten
T 062 209 2525
F 062 209 2627

Travel Bookshop
Rindermarkt 20
Postfach 216
CH-8001 Zürich
T 01 252 3883
F 01 252 3832

USA
NTC/ Contemporary
4255 West Touhy Avenue
Lincolnwood
Illinois 60646-1975
T (847) 679 5500
F (847) 679 2494

Counties & regions of the Tibetan Plateau

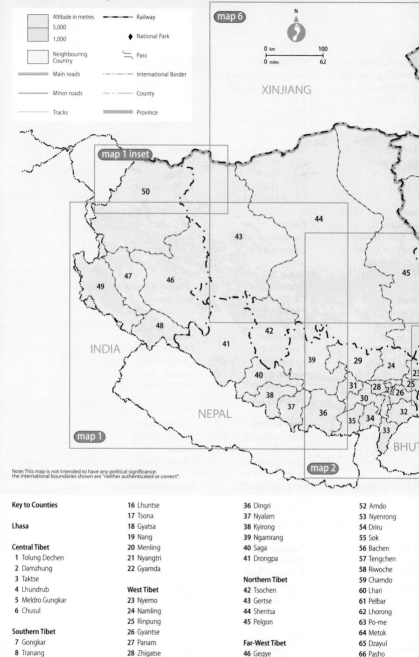

Altitude in metres
5,000
1,000

Neighbouring Country

Main roads

Minor roads

Tracks

Railway

National Park

Pass

International Border

County

Province

map 6

XINJIANG

N

0 km 100
0 miles 62

map 1 inset

50

44

43

45

47 46

49

48

42

41

39 29 24 23

40 31 28 27 26 25

38 30

37 36 35 34 32

33

INDIA

NEPAL

BHUTA

map 1

map 2

Note: This map is not intended to have any political significance:
the international boundaries shown are "neither authenticated or correct".

Key to Counties

Lhasa

Central Tibet
1 Tolung Dechen
2 Damzhung
3 Taktse
4 Lhundrub
5 Meldro Gungkar
6 Chusul

Southern Tibet
7 Gongkar
8 Tranang
9 Nedong/Tsetang
10 Chongye
11 Tso-me
12 Lhodrak
13 Nakartse
14 Zangri
15 Chusum

16 Lhuntse
17 Tsona
18 Gyatse
19 Nang
20 Menling
21 Nyangtri
22 Gyamda

West Tibet
23 Nyemo
24 Namling
25 Rinpung
26 Gyantse
27 Panam
28 Zhigatse
29 Zhetongmon
30 Sakya
31 Lhartse
32 Khangmar
33 Dromo
34 Gampa
35 Tingkye

36 Dingri
37 Nyalam
38 Kyirong
39 Ngamrang
40 Saga
41 Drongpa

Northern Tibet
42 Tsochen
43 Gertse
44 Shentsa
45 Pelgon

Far-West Tibet
46 Gegye
47 Senge Tsangpo
48 Purang
49 Tsamda
50 Rutok

East Tibet
51 Nakchu

52 Amdo
53 Nyenrong
54 Driru
55 Sok
56 Bachen
57 Tengchen
58 Riwoche
59 Chamdo
60 Lhari
61 Pelbar
62 Lhorong
63 Po-me
64 Metok
65 Dzayul
66 Pasho
67 Drayab
68 Dzogang
69 Markham
70 Dechen
71 Gyeltang
72 Balung
73 Mili

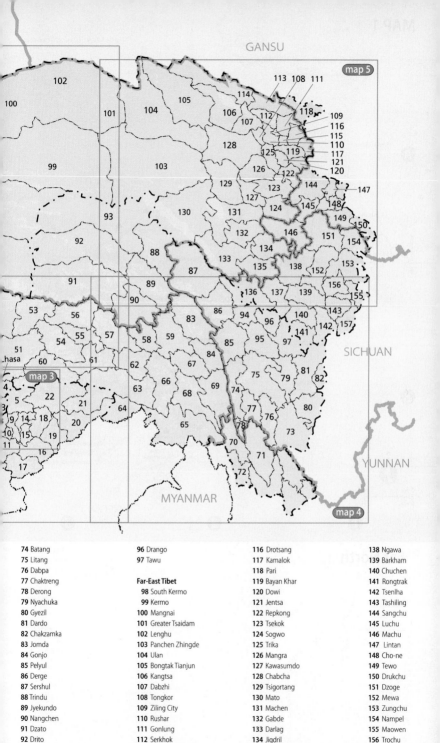

MAP 1

GANSU

map 5

map 3

SICHUAN

hasa

YUNNAN

MYANMAR

map 4

74 Batang
75 Litang
76 Dabpa
77 Chaktreng
78 Derong
79 Nyachuka
80 Gyezil
81 Dardo
82 Chakzamka
83 Jomda
84 Gonjo
85 Pelyul
86 Derge
87 Sershul
88 Trindu
89 Jyekundo
90 Nangchen
91 Dzato
92 Drito
93 Chumarleb
94 Kandze
95 Nyarong

96 Drango
97 Tawu

Far-East Tibet
98 South Kermo
99 Kermo
100 Mangnai
101 Greater Tsaidam
102 Lenghu
103 Panchen Zhingde
104 Ulan
105 Bongtak Tianjun
106 Kangtsa
107 Dabzhi
108 Tongkor
109 Ziling City
110 Rushar
111 Gonlung
112 Serkhok
113 Mongyon
114 Chilen
115 Tsongkha Khar

116 Drotsang
117 Kamalok
118 Pari
119 Bayan Khar
120 Dowi
121 Jentsa
122 Repkong
123 Tsekok
124 Sogwo
125 Trika
126 Mangra
127 Kawasumdo
128 Chabcha
129 Tsigortang
130 Mato
131 Machen
132 Gabde
133 Darlag
134 Jigdril
135 Padma
136 Serthal
137 Dzamtang

138 Ngawa
139 Barkham
140 Chuchen
141 Rongtrak
142 Tsenlha
143 Tashiling
144 Sangchu
145 Luchu
146 Machu
147 Lintan
148 Cho-ne
149 Tewo
150 Drukchu
151 Dzoge
152 Mewa
153 Zungchu
154 Nampel
155 Maowen
156 Trochu
157 Lungu

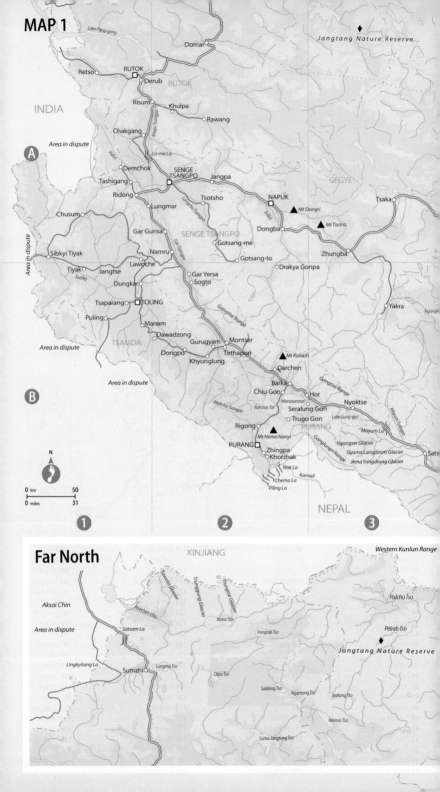

MAP 1

Lake Pang-gong

Domar

Jangtang Nature Reserve

Retso

RUTOK

Derub

RUTOK

INDIA

Risum

Khulpa

Rawang

Chakgang

La-me La

Area in dispute

A

Demchok

SENGE TSANGPO

Jangpa

GEGYE

Tashigang

Ridong

Tsotsho

NAPUK

Mt Dongri

Tsaka

Chusum

Lungmar

Mt Tsotra

Dongba

Gar Gunsa

SENGE TSANGPO

Sibkyi Tiyak

Namru

Gotsang-me

Zhungba

Area in dispute

Tiyak

Lawoche

Gotsang-to

Jangtse

Sutlej

Dungkar

Gar Yersa

Drakya Gonpa

Yakra

Sogto

Tsaparang

TOLING

Puling

Manam

Gangthe Range

Dawadzong

Gurugyam

Montser

Dongpo

Tirthapuri

Mt Kailash

TSAMDA

Khyunglung

Darchen

Area in dispute

Barka

Gangtise Range

B

Chiu Gon

Hor

Nyoktse

Manasarovar

Mabcha Tsangpo

Rakshas Tal

Seralung Gon

Lake Gung-gyu

Mayum Tsangpo

Rigong

Trugo Gon

PURANG

Mayum La

N

Mt Nemo Nanyi

Ngangser Glacier

PURANG

Zhingpa

Ganglungri Range

Gyama Langdzom Glacier

Khorzhak

Nak La

Karnali

Jema Yungdrung Glacier

Sats

0 km   50

Chema La

0 miles   31

Piling La

NEPAL

①   ②   ③

Far North

XINJIANG

Western Kunlun Range

Aksai Chin

Tawota Glacier

Trungung Glacier

Trungtse Glacier

Pulchu Tso

Area in dispute

Kitechen-chu

Kotra Tso

Pelrab Tso

Satsam La

Pangtak Tso

Jangtang Nature Reserve

Lingkyitang La

Orpa Tso

Lungma Tso

Sumzhi

Saldang Tso

Ngamong Tso

Jyakong Tso

Memar Tso

Luma Jangtong Tso

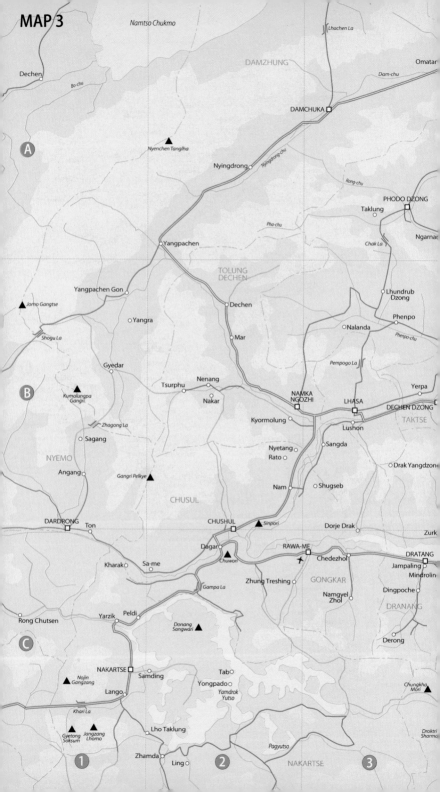

MAP 3

Namtso Chukmo

Dechen

Bo-chu

A

Nyenchen Tanglha

DAMZHUNG

Lhachen La

Omatar

Dam-chu

DAMCHUKA

Nyingdrong

Nyingdrong-chu

Rong-chu

PHODO DZONG

Taklung

Ngarnar

Yangpachen

Chak La

TOLUNG
DECHEN

Lhundrub
Dzong

Pha-chu

Yangpachen Gon

Dechen

Phenpo

Jomo Gangtse

Yangra

Mar

Nalanda

Phenpo-chu

Shogu La

Gyedar

Nenang

Pempogo La

Yerpa

B

Kumalungpa
Gangri

Tsurphu

Nakar

NAMKA
NGOZHI

LHASA

DECHEN DZONG

TAKTSE

Zhagong La

Kyormolung

Lushon

Sagang

Nyetang

Sangda

NYEMO

Rato

Angang

Gangri Pelkye

Nam

Shugseb

Drak Yangdzon

CHUSUL

DARDRONG

Ton

CHUSHUL

Sinpori

Dorje Drak

Zurk

Dagar

RAWA-ME

DRATANG

Chuwon

Chedezhol

Jampaling

Kharak

Sa-me

Zhung Treshing

GONGKAR

Mindrolin

Gampa La

Namgyel
Zhol

Dingpoche

DRANANG

Rong Chutsen

Yarzik

Peldi

Donang
Sangwari

Derong

C

NAKARTSE

Tab

Nojin
Gangzang

Samding

Yongpado

Chungkha
Mori

Lango

Yamdrok
Yutso

Khari La

Gyetong
Soksum

Jangzang
Lhomo

Lho Taklung

Droktri
Sharma

Zhamda

Ling

Pagyutso

NAKARTSE

1

2

3